U.S. MASTER™ D

Key De

MW01568163

Quick Tax Facts

MACRS RECOVERY PERIODS

FOR COMMON ASSETS (¶191)

	GDS	ADS
Tractor units for over-the-road use	3	4
Trailers and trailer-mounted containers	5	6
Automobiles, taxis, trucks (light general purpose)	5	5
Trucks (heavy general purpose)	5	6
Buses	5	9
Breeding cattle and dairy cattle (purchased)	5	7
Computers and peripheral equipment	5	5
Typewriters, calculators, copiers, accounting machines	5	6
Research and experimentation property	5	Class Life
Office furniture and fixtures (such as desks, files, safes, communications equipment, etc.)	7	10
Vessels, barges, tugs and similar water transportation equipment not used in marine construction	10	18
Single purpose agricultural or horticultural structure	10	15
Other farm buildings	20	25
Trees or vines bearing fruits or nuts placed in service after 1988	10	20
Retail motor fuel outlets	15	20
Service station building and land improvements used in marketing petroleum products	15	20
Land improvements (such as shrubbery, fences, roads, and bridges)	15	20
Residential rental property	27.5	40
Nonresidential real property placed in service before May 13, 1993	31.5	40
Nonresidential real property placed in service after May 12, 1993	39	40

- See Rev. Proc. 87-56 at ¶191 for comprehensive asset classifications.

MAXIMUM CODE SEC. 179

EXPENSE ALLOWANCE (¶300)

Tax Years Beginning in:	2007	2008	2009	2010
Maximum Deduction	$125,000	$250,000	$250,000	$134,000

LUXURY CAR DEPRECIATION CAPS

(¶200)

Placed in Service	Year 1	Year 2	Year 3	Year 4 and later
2004	2,960 *	4,800	2,850	1,675
2005	2,960	4,700	2,850	1,675
2006	2,960	4,800	2,850	1,775
2007	3,060	4,900	2,850	1,775
2008–2009	2,960 **	4,800	2,850	1,775

Trucks and vans use limits on back page.

*$10,610 if 50% bonus depreciation claimed or 30% rate elected in place of 50% rate.

**$10,960 if 50% bonus depreciation claimed.

CCH

Depreciation Caps

For Trucks/Vans Purchased in 2005 — 2009 (¶200)

Placed in Service	Year 1	Year 2	Year 3	Year 4 and later
2005–2006	$3,260	$5,200	$3,150	$1,875
2007	$3,260	$5,200	$3,050	$1,875
2008	$3,160 *	$5,100	$3,050	$1,875
2009	$3,060 **	$4,900	$2,950	$1,775

*$11,160 if 50% bonus depreciation claimed.
**$11,060 if 50% bonus depreciation claimed.

MACRS Depreciation Table

For Personal Business Property (¶180)

General Depreciation System (Half-Year Convention; 200 Percent DB Method)
(3, 5, 7, and 10-year property other than farm property)

Recovery Year	3-year	5-year	7-year	10-year
1	33.33	20.00	14.29	10.00
2	44.45	32.00	24.49	18.00
3	14.81	19.20	17.49	14.40
4	7.41	11.52	12.49	11.52
5		11.52	8.93	9.22
6		5.76	8.92	7.37
7			8.93	6.55
8			4.46	6.55
9				6.56
10				6.56
11				3.28

MACRS Depreciation Table

For Residential Rental Property (¶180)

Residential Rental Property (Recovery Period 27.5 Years; SL Method)

Recovery	Month Property Placed in Service					
Year	1	2	3	4	5	6
1	3.485	3.182	2.879	2.576	2.273	1.970
2-9	3.636	3.636	3.636	3.636	3.636	3.636
10	3.637	3.637	3.637	3.637	3.637	3.637
11	3.636	3.636	3.636	3.636	3.636	3.636
12	3.637	3.637	3.637	3.637	3.637	3.637
	7	8	9	10	11	12
1	1.667	1.364	1.061	0.758	0.455	0.152
2-9	3.636	3.636	3.636	3.636	3.636	3.636
10	3.636	3.636	3.636	3.636	3.636	3.636
11	3.637	3.637	3.637	3.637	3.637	3.637
12	3.636	3.636	3.636	3.636	3.636	3.636

- A complete set of MACRS depreciation tables are at ¶180.

Quick Tax Facts

CCH

2010 U.S. Master™ Depreciation Guide

CCH Editorial Staff Publication

Access the Latest New Depreciation Developments

A special webpage created by CCH for the *U.S. Master Depreciation Guide*® will keep you up-to-date with late-breaking tax legislative and administrative developments occurring after publication of the 2010 edition. Visit *CCHGroup.com/MasterDepreciationGuide* to find the information you'll need to keep *U.S. Master Depreciation Guide*® your first source for practical tax guidance.

CCH
a Wolters Kluwer business

ISBN 978-0-8080-2222-0

4025 W. Peterson Ave.
Chicago, IL 60646-6085
1 800 248 3248
www.CCHGroup.com

Printed in the United States of America

PREFACE

Old depreciation systems may not die—but they do eventually seem to fade away. The Modified Accelerated Cost Recovery System (MACRS), introduced by the Tax Reform Act of 1986 and applicable to most tangible depreciable property placed in service after 1986, now dominates a stage formerly shared with both the Accelerated Cost Recovery System (ACRS), introduced by the Economic Recovery Tax Act of 1981, and the Treasury Department's Asset Depreciation Range (ADR) System, which was given a statutory basis by the Revenue Act of 1971.

Both MACRS and ACRS bear a special relationship to the ADR class life guidelines in that, under either system, property is generally classified by reference to class lives. Rev. Proc. 87-56, as modified by Rev. Proc. 88-22, prescribes class lives (and sets forth recovery periods) for MACRS property (¶ 191). Optional tables set forth in Rev. Proc. 87-57 and included in this publication may, with certain exceptions, be used to compute MACRS deductions.

Special rules superimposed on both ACRS and MACRS for automobiles and other personal-use-type property placed in service or leased after June 18, 1984, modify cost recovery for some categories of property. They cap annual depreciation deductions for so-called luxury cars and slow the recovery of the cost of cars and other "listed" property unless such listed property is used more than 50 percent for business.

The *2010 U.S. Master™ Depreciation Guide* covers all of these rules, including:

- ☐ recent legislation and administrative guidance (see 2009 Highlights on next page);
- ☐ depreciation fundamentals at ¶ 3–¶ 76;
- ☐ Code Sec. 197 intangibles at ¶ 12–¶ 64;
- ☐ Change of accounting rules when depreciation has not been claimed or incorrectly computed ¶ 75;
- ☐ MACRS at ¶ 80–¶ 191;
- ☐ web site development costs at ¶ 125;
- ☐ bonus depreciation guidance at ¶ 127D–¶ 127I;
- ☐ passenger automobiles and other listed property at ¶ 200–¶ 214;
- ☐ car trade-ins at ¶ 214;
- ☐ audit guidelines for service stations at ¶ 110 and ¶ 125;
- ☐ cost segregation at ¶ 127–¶ 127C;
- ☐ ACRS at ¶ 220–¶ 290;
- ☐ the Code Sec. 179 expensing election at ¶ 300–¶ 304 and ¶ 487;
- ☐ the ADR system at ¶ 400–¶ 485;
- ☐ general (pre-1981) depreciation at ¶ 330–¶ 384; and
- ☐ planning for acquisitions and dispositions of depreciable property at ¶ 486–¶ 488.

Optional IRS tables for computing MACRS deductions accompany the discussions of appropriate classes of property, the alternative depreciation system, and the rules for recomputing allowances for purposes of the alternative minimum tax.

Selected regulations and proposed regulations are reproduced beginning at ¶ 510, and CCH-prepared depreciation decimal tables appear at ¶ 601–¶ 640.

Access the Latest New Depreciation Developments

A special webpage created by CCH for the *U.S. Master Depreciation Guide®* will keep you up-to-date with late-breaking tax legislative and administrative developments occurring after publication of the 2010 edition. Visit *CCHGroup.com/MasterDepreciationGuide* to find the information you'll need to keep *U.S. Master Depreciation Guide®* your first source for practical tax guidance.

2009 HIGHLIGHTS

Legislation—American Recovery and Reinvestment Act of 2009 (P.L. 111-5)

$250,000 section 179 allowance extended through 2009. The increased Code Sec. 179 expensing allowance provided for tax years beginning in 2008 is extended one additional year. Thus, for the years beginning in 2009, the Code Sec. 179 dollar limitation is $250,000 and the investment limitation is $800,000 (Code Sec. 179, as amended by P.L. 111-5). See ¶ 300

Bonus depreciation extended through 2009. The bonus depreciation deduction is extended one year to apply to property placed in service before January 1, 2010 (January 1, 2011, in the case of qualifying property with a longer production period and certain noncommercial aircraft) (Code Sec. 168(k), as amended by P.L. 111-5). See ¶ 127D.

Corporate election to forgo bonus depreciation and claim accelerated research or AMT credit. A corporation that makes the accelerated credit election in its first tax year ending after March 31, 2009, may also make an election to exclude extension property (Code Sec. 168(k)(4)(H)(i), as added by P.L. 111-5). Extension property is property that qualifies for bonus depreciation only by reason of the one-year extension of the bonus depreciation provision by P.L. 111-5 (i..e, the provision that makes bonus depreciation available to qualifying property placed in service in 2009 (in 2010 for property with a long production period and certain noncommercial aircraft)) (Code Sec. 168(k)(4)(H)(iii), as added by P.L. 111-5). Thus, if this election is made the corporation may claim bonus depreciation on the extension property and the extension property is not taken into account in determining the accelerated AMT and/or research credit. If the corporation does not make the election to exclude extension property, a separate bonus depreciation amount, maximum amount, and maximum increase amount are computed and applied to eligible qualified property which is extension property and to eligible qualified property which is not extension property.

A corporation that did not make the accelerated credit election for its first tax year ending after March 31, 2009 may make the election to apply the provision to its first tax year ending after December 31, 2008 and all subsequent tax years. The election only applies to eligible qualified property that is extension property (Code Sec. 168(k)(4)(H)(ii), as added by P.L. 111-5).

Property placed in service after March 31, 2008 is not eligible qualified property if it was subject to a binding contract in effect before April 1, 2008 (Code Sec. 168(k)(4)(D)(ii), as added by P.L. 111-5).

See ¶ 127D.

Legislation—Emergency Economic Stabilization Act of 2008 (P.L. 110-343)

Placed-in-service deadline for qualified leasehold improvements and restaurant property extended through 2009. The special 15-year recovery period that applies to qualified leasehold improvements (¶ 126) and restaurant property (¶ 110) is extended two years to apply to property placed in service on or before December 31,

2009 (Code Sec. 168(e)(3)(E)(iv) and (v), as amended by P.L. 110-343). An improvement to a restaurant will not longer need to be made to a building that is at least three years old provided that the improvement is placed in service in 2009. Bonus depreciation may not be claimed on restaurant property placed in service in 2009.

15-year recovery period for restaurant buildings in 2009. Restaurant buildings will also qualify for a 15-year recovery period if placed in service in 2009 (Code Sec. 168(e)(7), as amended by P.L. 110-343). Bonus depreciation may not be claimed on a 15-year restaurant building.

15-year recovery period for qualified retail improvement property in 2009. A qualified interior improvement to a building used for a retail business is depreciated under MACRS over 15 years using the straight-line method if the improvement is placed in service during the 2009 calendar year and the building is at least three years old when the improvement is placed in service (Code Sec. 168(e)(8), as added by P.L. 110-343). Bonus depreciation may not be claimed on qualified retail improvement property. See ¶ 126.

5-year recovery period for new farm machinery and equipment placed in service in 2009. New machinery or equipment (other than a grain bin, cotton ginning asset, fence or land improvement) used in a farming business and placed in service in 2009 is depreciated as MACRS 5-year property. Normally, a 4-year recovery period applies to such property (Code Sec. 168(e)(3)(B)(vii), as added by P.L. 110-343). See ¶ 118.

50 percent bonus depreciation and increased section 179 allowance for qualified disaster assistance property. A 50 percent additional depreciation allowance (bonus depreciation) is permitted for the tax year in which qualified disaster assistance property is placed in service. The provision applies to property placed in service after December 31, 2007, with respect to Presidentially declared disasters declared after such date and occurring before January 1, 2010. In general, qualified disaster assistance property is new real or personal property that replaces property that is damaged or destroyed in a Presidentially declared disaster area (Code Sec. 168(n), as added by P.L. 110-343). See ¶ 127H.

The Code Sec. 179 dollar limitation and investment limitation is increased by $100,000 and $600,000, respectively, for qualified disaster assistance property that is also section 179 property (Code Sec. 179(e), as added by P.L. 110-343). See ¶ 306B.

Qualified Indian reservation property depreciation recovery periods. The shortened modified accelerated cost recovery system (MACRS) recovery periods that apply to qualified Indian reservation property have been extended for two years through December 31, 2009. Thus, the shortened recovery periods will continue to apply to qualified Indian reservation property placed in service before January 1, 2010 (Code Sec. 168(j)(8), as amended by P.L. 110-343).

Motorsports entertainment complexes. The 7-year MACRS recovery period for motorsports entertainment complexes and related ancillary and support facilities is extended to property placed in service in 2008 and 2009 (Code Sec. 168(i)(15)(D), as amended by P.L. 110-343). See ¶ 106.

Bonus depreciation for cellulosic biofuel plant property. The 50 percent bonus depreciation provision for biomass ethanol plant property is expanded to apply to facilities that produce cellulosic biofuel in addition to cellulosic ethanol (Code Sec. 168(l), as amended by P.L. 110-343. See ¶ 127I.

10-year recovery period for smart electric meters and grid systems. A 10-year recovery period and 150-percent declining balance method is provided for any qualified smart electric meter and any qualified smart electric grid system, effective for property placed in service after October 3, 2008 (Code Sec. 168(e)(3)(D)(iii) and (iv), as added by P.L. 110-343). See ¶ 108.

Bonus depreciation for reuse and recycling property. A 50-percent bonus depreciation allowance may be claimed on the adjusted basis of qualified reuse and recycling property acquired and placed in service after August 31, 2008. Reuse and recycling property is machinery and equipment (not including buildings, real estate, rolling stock or equipment used to transport reuse and recyclable materials) that is used exclusively to collect, distribute, or recycle qualified reuse and recyclable materials. Machinery and equipment include appurtenances such as software necessary to operate the equipment. Qualified reuse and recyclable materials are scrap plastic, glass, textiles, rubber, packaging, and metal, as well as recovered fiber and electronic scrap (Code Sec. 168(m)(3), as added by the Emergency Economic Stabilization Act of 2008). See¶ 127J.

Environmental remediation costs. The election to deduct environmental remediation costs is extended for two years to cover qualifying expenditures paid or incurred before January 1, 2010 (Code Sec. 198(h), as amended by P.L. 110-343).

Mine safety equipment. The expensing election for qualified advanced mine safety equipment is extended one year to apply to new property placed in service before January 1, 2010 (Code Sec. 179E(g), as amended by P.L. 109-432).

Code Sec. 181 film and television production expensing election. The election to expense film and television productions is extended one year to apply to productions that commence on or before December 31, 2009. The requirement that the production cost no more than $15 million is eliminated, effective for productions that commence after December 31, 2007. Thus, effective for productions commencing after December 31, 2007 and on or before December 31, 2009, the first $15 million of production costs may be expensed (Code Sec. 181, as amended by P.L. 110-343).

Legislation—The Housing Assistance Act of 2008 (P.L. 110-289)

Corporate election to claim unused AMT and research credit by foregoing bonus depreciation. A corporation may elect to claim a limited amount of its unused credits for pre-2006 AMT tax liabilities and/or pre-2006 research expenditures by electing in its first taxable year ending after March 31, 2008 to forgo bonus depreciation on any qualifying bonus depreciation property placed in service any time after March 31, 2008 (Code Sec. 168(k)(4), as added by P.L. 110-289; Rev. Proc. 2008-65, I.R.B. 2008-44, October 10, 2008, providing regulatory type guidance). If the election is made the corporation must depreciate the property using the MACRS straight-line method. The credit is approximately equal to 20 percent of the bonus depreciation amount that could have been deducted but may not exceed the lesser of (1) 6 percent of the corporation's unused pre-2006 credit amounts or (2) $30 million. Since the credit is refundable, corporations benefiting most from the election are those with a net operating loss that would otherwise receive no immediate tax savings by claiming bonus depreciation. See ¶ 127D.

GO Zone bonus depreciation deadline for beginning construction eliminated. The December 31, 2008 deadline for beginning construction projects in the GO Zone in order to be eligible to receive the bonus depreciation deduction provided by Code Sec. 1400N(d) has been eliminated (Code Sec. 1400N(d)(3)(B), as amended by the Housing Assistance Act). See ¶ 127F.

Legislation—The Heartland, Habitat, Harvest, and Horticulture Act of 2008 (P.L. 110-246).

Race horses treated as three-year property beginning in 2009. The Heartland, Habitat, Harvest, and Horticulture Act of 2008 reduces the recovery period for race horses that are two years or younger when placed in service from seven years to three years, effective for horses placed in service after December 31, 2008 and before January 1, 2014 (Code Sec. 168(e)(3)(A)(i), as amended by P.L. 110-246). See ¶ 118.

Legislation—The Economic Stimulus Act of 2008 (P.L. 110-185)

50 percent bonus depreciation reinstated for 2008. The Economic Stimulus Act reinstates the 50 percent bonus depreciation allowance for one year (Code Sec. 168(k), as amended by P.L. 110-185). In general, the 50 percent bonus allowance will apply to qualifying property acquired after December 31, 2007 and before January 1, 2009 (January 1, 2010 for certain property with a long production period, including commercial and noncommercial aircraft). The new law does not make any changes to the types of property that qualify for bonus depreciation or to the rules relating to application of the provision. It simply reinstates the allowance for a one year period. This was accomplished by amending the existing bonus depreciation text (Code Sec. 168(k)) by changing the various acquisition and placed-in-service dates scattered throughout the provision (Code Sec. 168(k), as amended by P.L. 110-185). See ¶ 127D.

Luxury car depreciation cap increased by $8,000 if bonus depreciation claimed. The first-year depreciation cap on cars, trucks, and vans with a GVWR of 6000 pounds or less is increased by $8,000 if bonus depreciation is claimed (Code Sec. 168(k)(2)(F), as amended by P.L. 110-185). See ¶ 200.

Code Sec. 179 expense allowance increased to $250,000 in tax years beginning in 2008. The Code Sec. 179 maximum dollar limitation is temporarily increased to $250,000 for tax years beginning in 2008. The investment limitation is set at $800,000 (Code Sec. 179(b)(7), as added by P.L. 110-185). The 2009 dollar and investment limitations are $133,000 and $530,000, respectively (Rev. Proc. 2008-56). See ¶ 300.

Kansas Disaster Area bonus depreciation and increased section 179 expensing allowance. Taxpayers may claim an additional first-year depreciation allowance equal to 50 percent of the adjusted basis of qualified Recovery Assistance property acquired on or after May 5, 2007, and placed in service on or before December 31, 2008 in the Kansas disaster area (Act § 15345 of the Heartland, Habitat, Harvest and Horticulture Act of 2008, P.L. 110-246; Notice 2008-67, I.R.B. 2008-32, July 23, 2008, providing regulatory type guidance). See ¶ 127G.

The Code Sec. 179 dollar limit and investment limits are increased by $100,000 and $600,000, respectively, in the case of qualified section 179 Recovery Assistance property acquired on or after May 5, 2007, and placed in service before January 1, 2009 in the Kansas disaster area (Act Sec. 15345 of the Heartland, Habitat, Harvest, and Horticulture Act of 2008 (P.L. 110-246)). See ¶ 306A.

The Kansas disaster area consists of specified counties in a Presidentially declared disaster area that were affected by severe storms and tornados that began on May 4, 2007.

IRS Regulations and Administrative Guidance

Modifications to automatic change of accounting method procedure allow structural components to be treated as property unit. The automatic accounting method change procedure (Rev. Proc. 2008-52) is modified to allow a taxpayer to change to a unit of property that is permissible under applicable legal authority for determining when the taxpayer has disposed of a building and its structural components for depreciation purposes and for the determination of gain or loss. A similar change applies to tangible depreciable assets other than a building and structural components (Rev. Proc. 2009-39, I.R.B. 2009-38, August 27, 2009). See ¶ 162.

Election to claim AMT and research credits in lieu of bonus depreciation. The IRS has provided guidance on how and when a business makes the election to forego bonus depreciation on property placed in service after March 31, 2008 and before January 1, 2010 and, instead, take a special refundable credit of pre-2006 AMT and/or research credits. The guidance defines extension property, the time and manner for making the Code Sec. 168(k)(4)(H) elections, and the computation of the bonus depreciation amount used in determining the increased credits. Rev. Proc. 2008-65, I.R.B. 2008-44 and Rev. Proc. 2009-16, I.R.B. 2009-6 are modified (Rev. Proc. 2009-33, I.R.B. 2009-29). See ¶ 127D.

Short tax year ACRS depreciation - deemed asset acquisition election (Code Sec. 338). A consolidated group was entitled to one-month's depreciation for the short tax year that the target was considered a member of the consolidated group. No depreciation was allowed for the short tax year that closed upon the target's acquisition because the target's asset's were considered disposed of in that tax year and no ACRS deduction is allowed in the year of disposition of ACRS personal property (Brunswick Corporation, DC, 2009-1 USTC ¶ 51,131). See ¶ 307.

Assets used in converting corn to fuel grade ethanol. A proposed revenue ruling concludes that the appropriate depreciation classification of tangible assets used in converting corn to fuel grade ethanol is asset class 49.5, Waste Reduction and Resource Recovery Plants, of Rev. Proc. 87-56, 1987-2 C.B. 674, and not asset class 28.0, Manufacture of Chemicals and Allied Products, of Rev. Proc. 87-56 (Notice 2009-64, I.R.B. 2009-36).

2009 luxury car depreciation caps and lease inclusion tables. The depreciation caps for cars and trucks placed in service in 2009 are released. Lease inclusion tables for vehicles first least in 2009 are provided (Rev. Proc. 2009-24, I.R.B. 2009-17). See ¶ 200 and following.

2009 standard mileage rate. The standard mileage rate for 2009 is 55 cents per mile (Rev. Proc. 2008-72, I.R.B. 2008-50. See ¶ 217.

Updated Luxury Car Chart

The quick reference tables that list trucks, vans, and SUVs with a gross vehicle weight rating (GVWR) in excess of 6,000 pounds are updated to include 2010 models. A table of trucks in excess of 6,000 lbs GVWR and a cargo bed length of less than 6 feet which are subject to a section 179 expensing limit of $25,000 is also provided. See page 1053 in the Appendix. The IRS has indicated to CCH that the status of an SUV as a truck, which is eligible for exemption from the depreciation caps if its GVWR is in excess of 6,000 pounds, should be based on the classification of the SUV by the manufacturer pursuant to Department of Transportation rules. This means that an SUV built on a unibody (i.e., car chassis) may qualify as a truck and be exempt from the depreciation caps if it has a GVWR in excess of 6,000 pounds. See ¶ 208.

November 2009

TABLE OF CONTENTS

Paragraph

The Depreciation Story

Fundamentals

Paragraph

Modified ACRS (MACRS)

Depreciation Planning

Paragraph

Appendices of Selected Final, Temporary, and Proposed Regulations

The Depreciation Story

Historical Background

¶ 1

From 1913 to Now

Until 1934, taxpayers were given broad leeway to estimate useful lives of their depreciable assets. Then—to help finance public works launched during the Great Depression—the Treasury stiffened its stance and required taxpayers to prove that the lives they selected were appropriate (T.D. 4422). Revenue goals were achieved, but problems of proof saddled taxpayers with unrealistically long useful lives for many of their depreciable assets.

Bulletin F—1942

The Treasury's conservative policy was further implemented in 1942 by the issuance of Bulletin F, an item-by-item listing of useful lives. The issuance of Bulletin F may have been precipitated by the Revenue Act of 1942, under which, for the first time, gain recognized from the sale of depreciable business property qualified as capital gain. Slowing depreciation reduced the amount of deductions against ordinary income that, upon sale of an asset, would be recoverable from the taxpayer only as capital gain.

In the 1954 Code, Congress authorized the use of accelerated methods of depreciation, including the 200-percent declining-balance and sum of the years-digits methods. This accelerated cost recovery considerably encouraged a number of taxpayers to buy or build new plants and equipment.

Special guidelines—1962

In 1962, the pendulum swung almost all the way back to where it had been before 1934. The IRS abandoned Bulletin F and adopted special guidelines under Rev. Proc. 62-21, 1962-2 CB 418, for examination of depreciation deductions. These guidelines were issued to reduce taxpayer-agent controversy over individual asset lives and to liberalize depreciation rates. This was done by replacing Bulletin F's item-by-item listing with broad industry classes of assets. To be assured that a deduction would not be challenged on audit, it was necessary to show that retirement and replacement policies for a class of assets were consistent with the class life used for that category of assets. This could have been done:

(1) by the use of the complicated reserve ratio test, or

(2) on the basis of all the facts and circumstances.

The guideline lives for machinery and equipment averaged 30 percent to 40 percent less than those previously suggested.

This more relaxed view, however, did not come about until it was reasonably certain that Congress would pass, in the 1962 Revenue Act, a provision taxing gain on the sale of depreciable personal property as ordinary income to the extent of depreciation taken. This eased IRS concern that a more liberal depreciation policy would permit wholesale conversion of ordinary income into capital gain.

For the first three years under the 1962 guidelines, taxpayers did not have to meet the reserve ratio test. Further, a transitional rule was initially granted which provided a period equal to the class guideline life to move toward and eventually meet the reserve ratio test. In spite of the three-year moratorium and the transitional rule, difficulties arose.

To cope with these difficulties, the IRS issued Rev. Proc. 65-13, 1965-1 CB 759, in which it offered a new form of the reserve ratio test, the guideline form, to overcome deficiencies of the initial form of the test, the tabular form. The guideline form of the test permitted the computation of the reserve ratio standard to be tailored to individual circumstances. Also, additional transitional rules were introduced in an attempt to make it possible for many taxpayers, who would otherwise be unable to do so, to pass the reserve ratio test.

Class Life Asset Depreciation Range System (ADR)—1971

When, in 1971, the guideline transitional allowances began running out, many taxpayers were expected to fail to meet the reserve ratio test. Moreover, in the IRS, it was a widely held view that the test was impracticable and unworkable. It was in this atmosphere that the new Class Life Asset Depreciation Range System (ADR) came into being. This system provided class lives for broad classes of assets and a range from which a life could be selected for depreciation purposes. Originally, the Treasury approved Regulations (June 1971) for an ADR System covering only machinery and equipment and excluding buildings and land improvements. Later, the 1971 Revenue Act gave the ADR System legal authority, expanded it to include buildings and land improvements, and made some changes. The Treasury approved amendments to the ADR Regulations reflecting this Act.

Further, the Treasury prescribed a Class Life System (CLS) under which a taxpayer could choose a class life for the post-1970 depreciation of assets placed in service before 1971. This system had class lives only, no ranges. As under ADR, the reserve ratio test did not apply.

However, certain buildings and Sec. 1250 property were temporarily removed from the ADR system under a transitional rule that provided an election to exclude such property from the less favorable ADR system even if this system was used for non-Sec. 1250 property. In such case, useful lives could be determined under Rev. Proc. 62-21, above.

In 1974, buildings and other Sec. 1250 property were withdrawn from the application of the ADR system until such time as Sec. 1250 property was explicitly included in ADR classes prescribed by the Treasury (P.L. 93-625 (1974), Act Sec. 5; S. Rept. 93-1357, 1975-1 CB 517, 523).

Thus, although the Treasury is authorized to include buildings and Sec. 1250 property in the ADR system, it generally has not done so except to the extent that Sec. 1250 property is included within a specific business activity class (Rev. Proc. 77-3, 1977-1 CB 535).

This was the posture of the rules prior to the Accelerated Cost Recovery System (ACRS) introduced by the Economic Recovery Tax Act of 1981 and the Modified Accelerated Cost Recovery System (MACRS) introduced by the Tax Reform Act of 1986. It continues to be the posture of the rules for property placed in service before 1981 and for some post-1980 property not qualifying for either of these systems.

Accelerated Cost Recovery System (ACRS)—1981

Along with simplifying cost recovery, the Accelerated Cost Recovery System (ACRS), introduced by the Economic Recovery Tax Act of 1981, was designed to stimulate capital formation.

By 1984, legislative concern had shifted to controlling the size of the deficit and curbing real estate tax shelters and tax-motivated real estate transactions. With the Tax Reform Act of 1984, Congress slowed down cost recovery for real property (other than low-income housing) placed in service after March 15, 1984, by increasing the minimum recovery period to 18 (from 15) years. Moreover, for 18-year property, a mid-month convention was adopted so that property placed in service (or disposed of) in any particular month was regarded as placed in service (or disposed of) in the middle (rather than at the start) of that month.

For property placed in service after May 8, 1985, and not subject to transitional rules and that otherwise would have been 18-year property, P.L. 99-121 (1985) increased the recovery period to 19 years.

The 1984 Act also slowed depreciation for "luxury" automobiles by capping annual cost recovery and deliberalized depreciation rules for Code Sec. 280F "listed" property (cars, home computers, and certain other property that lends itself to personal use), unless such property was used more than 50 percent for business.

Modified Accelerated Cost Recovery System (MACRS)—1986

The Modified Accelerated Cost Recovery System (MACRS), the latest major chapter in the ongoing depreciation story, applies to most tangible depreciable property placed in service after 1986 and could be elected for comparable property placed in service before 1987 but after July 31, 1986.

Although sharing the statutory designation of Accelerated Cost Recovery System with its statutory predecessor (ACRS), MACRS is an entirely new system. Classes of property are revised, and methods and conventions are prescribed (rather than embodied in specified recovery percentages). Perhaps the most dramatic change introduced by MACRS is the limiting of cost recovery to straight-line depreciation over 27.5 years for residential rental property and to straight-line depreciation over 31.5 or 39 years for most other depreciable real property.

MACRS includes an alternative system under which depreciation is deducted under the straight-line method over generally longer periods than under regular MACRS. This system is mandatory for tangible property used predominantly outside the United States, certain property leased to tax-exempt entities, property financed with tax exempt bonds, and, subject to various requirements, property imported from a country that the President determines to be maintaining certain trade restrictions or engaging in certain trade practices. A system is also provided for computing depreciation for purposes of minimum tax.

Since ACRS liberalized the rules for recovering the cost of most tangible depreciable property, special rules were included to prevent transfers between related parties or transactions in which users stayed the same from "churning" pre-1981 property into recovery (ACRS) property. Similar rules are included under MACRS but are modified so as not to shield otherwise qualifying property from the largely less generous treatment accorded under MACRS than under ACRS.

Some chapters of the depreciation story bear a special relationship to the repealed regular investment credit. As originally introduced, ACRS was supplementary to a general 10-percent credit for the cost of most tangible personal property and other categories of property (exclusive of buildings and their components). For property placed in service after 1982, the double benefit was reduced, and, for property placed in service after 1985, it was completely eliminated (to some extent retroactively) by the repeal of the credit. Thus, simply comparing the MACRS rules to the prior ACRS rules does not fully reflect the impact of the Tax Reform Act of 1986 on overall cost recovery.

Three major revenue procedures provided further guidance for depreciating MACRS property. Rev. Proc. 87-56, 1987-2 CB 674, sets forth the class lives to be used for purposes of MACRS. Rev. Proc. 87-57, 1987-2 CB 687, provides optional tables for computing recovery allowances and explains the basic operation of MACRS. Rev. Proc. 89-15, 1989-1 CB 816, sets forth rules for short-year computations.

Despite the advent of these depreciation systems and class life tables, the depreciation Code provision ranks in the top 14 Code provisions causing disputes between taxpayers and the IRS, according to a 1993 study by the General Accounting Office.

Fundamentals

Depreciation

¶ 3

Depreciable Property

Depreciation is a reasonable allowance for the exhaustion, wear and tear, and obsolescence on certain types of property used in a trade or business or for the production of income (Code Sec. 167(a)). Depreciation is an accounting concept that treats an allocable part of the cost of certain limited-life assets as an expense (return of capital) in determining taxable income. This expense is also deducted (matched against income) over the number of years that the asset is expected to be used or a specified recovery period rather than deducted all in one year.

Amortization is similar to depreciation but generally refers to the periodic recovery of the cost of an intangible asset. Amortization and depreciation are both authorized by Code Sec. 167(a).

What is depreciable

Property is depreciable if it (1) is used for business or held for the production of income; (2) has a determinable useful life exceeding one year; and (3) wears out, decays, becomes obsolete, or loses value from natural causes.

Assets with useful lives that do not exceed one year may be currently deducted as expenses (rather than depreciated) for the year in which their costs are incurred.

Useful life is determined by reference to the useful life of the asset in the taxpayer's trade or business (the period over which it will be used by the taxpayer) and not by its physical condition. Under ACRS and MACRS, assets are generally assigned a recovery (depreciation) period which applies regardless of an asset's actual useful life in a taxpayer's business. However, if the actual useful life is one year or less, then the cost of the asset can be expensed. For example, industrial garments and dust control items (e.g., mops, towels, mats) which were leased to a variety of customers had a useful life to an industrial laundry corporation of one year or less and could be currently expensed (*Prudential Overall Supply*, TC Memo. 2002-103, Dec. 54,723(M)).

Depreciation generally should not be claimed on an asset that is acquired and disposed of in the same tax year. See ¶ 160.

The cost of certain depreciable assets may be expensed entirely in a single tax year under Code Sec. 179 at the election of a taxpayer (¶ 300). A de minimis expensing rule for relatively immaterial purchases may also allow a taxpayer to fully deduct the cost of otherwise depreciable assets. See ¶ 307.

For ACRS and MACRS property, statutorily prescribed recovery periods are the deemed useful life of property and a definite useful life, item (2) above, need not be proved if the property is a wasting asset, according to the Tax Court (*R.L. Simon*, 103 TC 247, Dec. 50,059, aff'd, CA-2, 1995-2 USTC ¶ 50,552 (Nonacq. 1996-2 CB 2); *B.P. Liddle*, 103 TC 285, Dec. 50,060, aff'd, CA-3, 1995-2 USTC ¶ 50,488). The Court of Appeals for the Eighth Circuit, citing the *Liddle* and *Simon* cases, has indicated that even imperceptible physical damage to or impact upon a particular item of property during its usage is sufficient to qualify a property for depreciation (*R. O'Shaughnessy*, CA-8, 2003-1 USTC ¶ 50,522).

Musical instruments. Accordingly, even though they had no known useful life, nineteenth-century violin bows that were tangible property, used by professional violinists in their trade or business, and subject to wear and tear qualified as five-year ACRS recovery property (*Simon*). A similar result was reached regarding a seventeenth-century bass viol under similar circumstances (*Liddle*). See also ¶ 220, ¶ 228 and ¶ 340. Under MACRS, a five-year recovery period applies to musical instruments used by professional musicians (Asset Class 57.0) (¶ 104).

The fact that the value of the bows as collectibles had appreciated was irrelevant because economic and statutory depreciation need not be coincident. Accounting for depreciation of assets is an annual offset to gross income by deductions that represent the exhaustion, wear and tear, or obsolescence of an income-producing asset. Accounting for changes in the value of depreciable property because of market conditions (such as inflation or scarcity) is reportable as gain or loss upon the sale of the depreciable asset.

Show cars. Show cars (exotic automobiles possessing state-of-the-art high technology) that would become obsolete over time were depreciable (*B. Selig*, 70 TCM 1125, Dec. 50,975(M)) even though a definite useful life could not be shown. The cars were not similar to antique cars placed in a museum which are nondepreciable because they do not deteriorate in a controlled environment (*Harrah's Club*, CtCls, 81-1 USTC ¶ 9677).

Artwork and decorative displays. Artwork which is displayed for business purposes normally does not suffer from wear or tear or obsolescence, and, therefore, is not depreciable under ACRS (*W.C. Clinger*, 60 TCM 598, Dec. 46,832(M); Prop. Reg. § 1.168-3(a) (ACRS); Rev. Rul. 68-232, 1968-1 CB 79 ((pre-ACRS) artwork has no determinable useful life and, therefore is nondepreciable)). These cases and rulings, however, deal with valuable (appreciating) pieces of art and were decided prior to the enactment of ACRS and MACRS when an asset had to have a reasonably estimatable useful life in order to depreciated. Logically, nonappreciating artwork, for which there is no incentive to protect from wear and tear, should be depreciable even if the wear and tear is essentially minuscule. Senate Report 95-1263, 1978-3 CB (Vol. 1) 315, 415, which accompanied the Revenue Act of 1978, states that tangible personal property for investment tax credit purposes includes small pictures of scenery, persons, and the like which are attached to walls or suspended from the ceiling. Note that tangible personal property was eligible for the investment credit only if it was depreciable. The Senate Report appears to have considered such "art" as a depreciable asset. The IRS Field Directive on the Planning and Examination of Cost Segregation Issues in the Restaurant Industry reproduced in the appendix of this guide specifically provides a 5-year recovery period for pictures and other decorative props but excludes appreciating artwork, such as a Persian rug that does not suffer wear and tear, from depreciation. The five-year recovery period applies because personal property used in a restaurant falls within Asset Class 57.0 ofRev. Proc. 87-56 relating to assets used in a retail trade or business.

Idle assets. Depreciation should be claimed on a business asset even when it is temporarily idle (not in use). Thus, the basis for gain or loss must be reduced by the depreciation allowable during a period of idleness, even though no depreciation was claimed (*P. Dougherty Co.*, CA-4, 47-1 USTC ¶ 9117; 159 F2d 269).

Unless an asset is permanently withdrawn from use in a business or income-producing activity through a sale, abandonment, retirement, or other disposition, it is considered temporarily idle and should be depreciated (*D.L. Hamby*, 56 TCM 783, CCH Dec. 45,204(M)). A taxpayer who has failed to claim depreciation on an idle asset should be able to file an application for a change in accounting method and deduct the unclaimed depreciation as a Code Sec. 481(a) adjustment. The application for a change in accounting method may be filed as late as three years after the tax year of the sale. See ¶ 75.

A building or other asset which is placed up for sale by a trade or business remains depreciable even though it is no longer actively used in the business so long as it has not been converted to personal use or otherwise retired or abandoned. Thus, a taxpayer that was discontinuing its poultry business was entitled to continue claiming depreciation deductions on poultry buildings which no longer housed poultry during the two-year period that the taxpayer was attempting to sell the building (*M.R. Lenington*, 25 TCM 1350, TC Memo. 1966-264, CCH Dec. 28,201(M)). A more common application of the principle likely involves unoccupied residential and commercial real estate which was formerly leased to tenants but is now held by the lessor for sale.

When depreciation begins and ends — placed in service requirement

Depreciation may not be claimed until the tax year that the property is placed in service for either the production of income or use in a trade or business. A similar rule applies to the Code Sec. 179 deduction and to various amortization deductions as well as the investment tax credit.

Property is considered placed in service when it is in a condition or state of readiness and available for a specially assigned function (Prop. Reg. § 1.168-2(l)(2) at ¶ 525; Reg.§ 1.167(a)-11(e)(1)(i); Field Service Advice Memorandum 199916040, date not given; republished to include previously redacted information on April 29, 2005). An asset can be considered placed in service prior to its actual use if it is in a state of readiness and availability for actual use and nothing within the taxpayer's control prevents its actual use. For example, an operational automobile was placed in service in the year purchased even though the taxpayer decided not to register and use the car until the following year when he returned from vacation (*M. Giles*, 50 TCM 1342, TC Memo. 1985-543, Dec.42,455(M)).

> ***Example (1):*** James Elm is a building contractor who specializes in constructing office buildings. He bought a truck last year that had to be modified to lift materials to second-story levels. The installation of the lifting equipment was completed and James accepted delivery of the modified truck on January 10 of this year. The truck was placed in service on January 10, the date it was ready and available to perform the function for which it was bought even though it was not actually used until after January 10. The placed-in-service date is not the date of first use (IRS Publication 946 (How to Depreciate Property)).

The definition of placed in service for purposes of the investment tax credit and depreciation are the same. The investment tax credit regulations set forth nonexclusive examples illustrating situations in which actual use is not required for an asset to be considered placed in service (Reg. § 1.46-3(d)).

- Parts are acquired and set aside during the tax year for use as replacements for a particular machine (or machines) in order to avoid operational time loss

- Operational farm equipment is acquired during the taxable year and it is not practicable to use such equipment for its specifically assigned function in the taxpayer's business of farming until the following year

- Equipment is acquired for a specifically assigned function and is operational but is undergoing testing to eliminate any defects

The ITC regulations further provide that fruit-bearing trees and vines are not placed in service until they have reached an income-producing stage and that materials and parts to be used in the construction of an item of equipment are not considered placed in service merely by reason of their acquisition.

The depreciation regulations additionally provide (Prop. Reg. § 1.168-2(l)(2); Reg.§ 1.167(a)(11)(e)(1)):

- In the case of a building which is intended to house machinery and equipment, readiness and availability is determined without regard to whether the housed machinery or equipment has been placed in service
- Where a building is essentially an item of machinery or equipment, or the use of the building is so closely related to the use of the machinery or equipment that it clearly can be expected to be replaced or retired when the property it initially houses is replaced or retired, the determination of readiness or availability of the building is made by taking into account the readiness and availability of such machinery or equipment

Factors outside of taxpayer's control preventing actual use. In some instances where depreciation has been allowed for property in a state of readiness but not yet placed into actual use, the taxpayer has done all that was in its power to make the property operational but due to circumstances outside of its control it is not possible to actually use the property. This rule is based on the operational farm equipment exception described above. Thus, if a farmer purchases an operational tractor in November but doesn't begin actual use until the next spring it is considered placed in service in November. The weather preventing actual and practicable use of the tractor is out of the farmer's control. In another case involving weather, barges were placed in service in December when they were ready for service even though they were frozen in the water and could not be actually used until the following May (*Sears Oil Co., Inc.*, CA-2, 66-1 USTC ¶ 9384, 359 F2d 191). Depreciation was allowable with respect to an air conditioner even though, because of weather conditions, the taxpayer did not actually use the air conditioner until the following year (*Schrader*, CA-6, 78-2 ustc ¶ 9824). A metal shredder was considered placed in service during the tax year of purchase even though it was not operational during that tax year because a power company was unable to install an overhead electrical connection to the plant due to litigation regarding an easement for the power lines. The installation of the electrical connection was not in the taxpayer's control (*SMC Corp.*, CA-6, 82-1 USTC ¶ 9309, 675 F2d 113). See, also , *Northern States Power*, CA-8, 98-2 USTC ¶ 50,671 and *Connecticut Yankee Atomic Power Company*, 97-2 USTC ¶ 50,693, 38 FedCl 721, discussed below.

If a taxpayer fails to take steps that are within its control to make a machine operational and capable of actual use, the asset cannot be considered placed in service until those steps are taken.

> ***Example (2):*** Donald Steep, a calendar-year taxpayer, bought a machine for his business in 2008. The machine was delivered in 2008. However, it was not installed and operational until 2009. It is considered placed in service in 2009 when Steep installed and made the machine operational and capable of actual use. If the machine had been ready and available for use (i.e., was operational) when it was delivered in 2008, it would be considered placed in service in 2008 even if it was not actually used until 2009 (IRS Publication 946, How to Depreciate Property).

Spare parts. The regulations allow depreciation of uninstalled spare parts of operating machinery that are necessary to avoid operational down time (Reg. § 1.46-3(d)). Nuclear fuel assemblies were considered placed in service in the year purchased, delivered, assembled, and tested because they were then ready and available for use. Installation was not necessary. The spare parts exception applied (*Northern States Power*, CA-8, 98-2 USTC ¶ 50,671; *Connecticut Yankee Atomic Power Company*, Ct. Cls. 97-2 USTC ¶ 50,693). In addition, the court relied on the exception which allows the depreciation of otherwise operational equipment which is not practicable to place in service. The Eighth Circuit specifically rejected the requirement that the circumstance preventing actual use (here, the shut down of the plant) must be outside of the taxpayer's control. It was sufficient that the shut down of the plant was not practicable.

Component parts and machinery used in single system. The upper reservoir component of a pumped storage hydroelectric plant was not placed in service until the entire plant was placed in service. The reservoir and physical plant operated as one integrated unit to produce electrical power (*Consumers Power*, 89 TC 710, Dec. 44,250). Telephone switching equipment and toll carriers were not considered placed in service even though capable of performing individual functions because wiring for the systems in which they were to operate had not been completed and employees had not been trained to use the equipment (*Siskiyou Communications*, 60 TCM. 475, Dec. 46,797(M)). See also *Hawaiian Indep. Refinery, Inc*, 83-1 USTC ¶ 9141, 697 F.2d 1063 (Fed. Cir.), cert. denied 464 U.S. 816 (1983) (two offsite components not considered separately from refinery in considering applicable construction date because all were designed as a single unit and together they functionally formed a single property).

Buildings placed in service in stages. The proposed ACRS regulations recognize that a building (for example, a high-rise) may be placed in service in stages. These regulations provide that each significant portion of a building should be separately depreciated as it is placed in service. Placed in service means made available for use in a finished condition, for example, as when a certificate of occupancy is issued. However, the same recovery period and depreciation method must be used to depreciate the entire building. For example, this rule, when applied to MACRS residential rental property, would mean that a taxpayer could not depreciate one portion of the building over a 27.5 year period and elect ADS (40-year depreciation period) for another portion of the building. The regulations explain the allocation of basis among the completed portions and provide examples (Proposed Reg. § 1.168-2(e)(3) and (5) at ¶ 525).

Equipment used in retail stores. Equipment located in new retail stores, which is to be used in connection with the trade or business conducted in those stores, is placed in service upon the opening of the stores (assuming the equipment is otherwise installed and ready for use). If the equipments is installed in an existing store that is being remodeled depreciation begins when the equipment is installed (*Piggly Wiggly Southern, Inc.*, 84 TC 739, Dec. 42,039, aff'd on another issue, CA-11, 86-2 USTC ¶ 9789). See "*Taxpayer must be engaged in trade or business*", below.

Leased buildings and leased equipment. Property which is held for leasing to others is considered placed in service when it is first held out for lease if it is otherwise ready for use (*W.R. Waddell*, 86 TC 848, Dec. 43,023 (electrocardiogram (ECG) terminals); *J.A. Helfand*, 47 TCM 1203, Dec. 41,030(M) (commercial real property); *M.H. Wood*, 61 TCM 2571, Dec. 47,334(M) (solar water-heating equipment)).

Example (3): On April 6, Sue Thorn bought a house to use as residential rental property. She made several repairs and had it ready for rent on July 5. At that time, she began to advertise it for rent in the local newspaper. The house is considered placed in service in July when it was ready and available for rent. She can begin to depreciate it in July (IRS Publication 946 (How to Depreciate Property).

Leased equipment which is returned after the termination or expiration of the lease may continue to be depreciated (even though it is generating no income) until it is permanently withdrawn from the leasing business, for example, by being sold or specifically identified as no longer available for leasing (IRS Letter Ruling

9811004, November 18, 1997). This can be viewed as an application of the "idle asset" rule which allows a taxpayer to claim depreciation on temporarily idle assets.

Motion pictures, books, recordings, patents. Motion picture rights, book manuscript rights, master recording rights, and patent rights are placed in service when the film, book, product or process is first released for exhibition, distribution and sale, or is used in a trade or business or for the production of income (Rev. Rul. 79-285, 1979-2 CB 91). However, patents are not placed in service before the issue date.

Taxpayer must be engaged in trade or business. The Tax Court has ruled that depreciation may start no sooner than the tax year that a taxpayer begins to engage in the trade or business in which the asset will be used (*Piggly Wiggly Southern, Inc.*, 84 TC 739, Dec. 42,039, aff'd on another issue, CA-11, 86-2 USTC 9789, 803 F2d 1572, holding that refrigeration units installed in the taxpayer's new grocery stores were not placed in service until the stores opened to the public and that refrigeration units installed in taxpayer's remodeled stores that had previously been open to the public were placed in service). One implication of this rule is that depreciation is not considered a start-up expense under Code Sec. 195 (IRS Letter Ruling 9235004, May 20, 1992). See, also, ¶ 132, "Application of short tax year rules to a new business."

Relationship of placed in service date to depreciation conventions. The date on which depreciation begins under a convention (¶ 86) or a particular method of depreciation does not determine the date on which the property is first placed in service (Reg. § 1.167(a)-11(e)(1)). Thus, the applicable convention specifies when the recovery period begins for depreciable property after it is determined when the property is first placed in service.

> ***Example (4):*** An existing calendar-year business purchased 5-year MACRS property that was in a state of readiness for a specially assigned function on August 1. The property was depreciated using the half-year convention. Although the property is considered placed in service on August 1, the recovery period for such property begins on July 1.

The depreciation of an asset ends when the asset is retired from service (by sale, exchange, abandonment, or destruction) (Reg. § 1.167(a)-10). Generally, depreciation for the year in which an asset is retires is computed by using the applicable depreciation convention (see ¶ 86 (MACRS), ¶ 160 (MACRS), ¶ 280 (ACRS), and ¶ 358 (pre-ACRS)).

Placed in service date incorrectly determined. See ¶ 75 for handling depreciation calculations if the placed-in-service date was incorrectly determined.

¶ 5

Tangible Property

Tangible property is divided into two basic types: real property (such as land, land improvements, buildings, and structural components of buildings); and personal property (such as business machinery and equipment, office furniture and fixtures, and appliances that are furnished to tenants).

See ¶ 116, ¶ 127, ¶ 127A, ¶ 127B, and ¶ 127C for a discussion of the definitions of buildings, structural components, and personal property.

Demolition of buildings or other property

The adjusted basis of a "structure" that is demolished and the cost of demolition (less any salvage) is capitalized and added to the basis of the land. The rule applies to the owner or lessee of the structure (Code Sec. 280B).

The term structure only includes a building and its structural components as defined in Reg. § 1.48-1(e) (Reg. § 1.280B-1). Thus, adjusted basis and demolition costs of a variety of otherwise inherently permanent structures that are not considered buildings, such as oil and gas storage tanks, blast furnaces, and coke ovens, may be claimed as a current loss under Code Sec. 165 if such structures are not purchased with the intention of demolishing them. See ¶ 162. Code Sec. 280B was designed to lay the thorny intent question to rest, at least in the case of buildings. In the case of the demolition or destruction of land improvements which are not buildings where the intent issue remains relevant, the case law under Code Sec. 165 and Reg. § 1.165-3, should be referred to. See, for example, *A.M. Wilson*, 41 TCM 381, TC Memo. 1980-514, CCH Dec. 37,407(M) (value of an orchard which the taxpayer intended to destroy at the time the land was acquired had to be capitalized).

If a building acquired with the intent to demolish is used for business or income-producing purposes for some time before it is demolished, a portion of the cost basis not to exceed the present value of the right to receive rentals during the period of its expected use may be allocated to the building and depreciated over that period (Reg. § 1.165-3(a)(2)(i)).

Special rules apply to the destruction or abandonment of leasehold improvements. See ¶ 126.

Rehabilitation v. demolition. A modification or rehabilitation of a building will not be considered a demolition if the following conditions are satisfied:

(1) 75 percent or more of the existing external walls of the building are retained in place as internal or external walls and

(2) 75 percent or more of the existing internal structural framework of the building is retained in place.

If the building is a certified historic structure, the modification must also be part of a certified rehabilitation.

If these conditions are met, the costs of the modifications are generally added to the basis of the building and recovered through depreciation unless the costs are properly accountable for under some other Code provision, for example, as deductible repairs (Rev. Proc. 95-27, 1995-1 CB 704). In certain cases, the modification of a historic structure or a building placed in service before 1936 may qualify for the rehabilitation credit under Code Sec. 47.

Environmental cleanup costs

Capitalized environmental cleanup costs concerning certain property are depreciable.

Depreciation was allowed for the costs of groundwater treatment facilities (wells, pipes, pumps, and other equipment used to extract, treat, and monitor contaminated groundwater) that were considered capital expenditures because these facilities have a useful life exceeding one year (Rev. Rul. 94-38, 1994-1 CB 35). However, other soil remediation and ongoing groundwater treatment expenditures to restore land to its original condition were ordinary and necessary business expenses rather than capital expenditures. Since land is not depreciable, amounts expended to restore land to its original condition were not capital expenditures under Code Sec. 263(a)(2). The cost of acquiring and installing underground storage tanks that were filled with waste material and then sealed, never to be used again, was currently deductible. Current deduction was also allowed for the cost of removing, cleaning, and disposing of the old tanks, as well as the ongoing cost of monitoring the new tanks (Rev. Rul. 98-25, 1998-1 CB 689). Amounts currently deductible under these rulings (including depreciation on groundwater treatment facilities) are required to be capitalized under Code Sec. 263A (Rev. Rul. 2004-18, 2004-1 CB 509, clarifying Rev. Rul. 94-38 and Rev. Rul. 98-25).

For the treatment of costs associated with the removal or replacement of underground storage tanks see, IRS Coordinated Issue Paper, entitled REPLACEMENT OF UNDERGROUND STORAGE TANKS AT RETAIL GASOLINE STATIONS, as revised July 10, 2002. Reproduced in full text at ¶ 145,500 of the CCH IRS POSITIONS REPORTER.

Expenditures incurred by a corporation to remove asbestos from its boiler house were nondeductible improvements to property that were depreciable as nonresidential real property (IRS Letter Ruling 9411002, November 19, 1993). The IRS has announced, however, that Letter Ruling 9411002 is under reconsideration in connection with a study project on environmental cleanup costs.

A taxpayer may elect to expense qualified environmental remediation expenditures paid or incurred in connection with the abatement or control of hazardous substances at a qualified contamination site if state certification is obtained (Code Sec. 198. The provision is effective for costs paid or incurred after August 5, 1997 and before January 1, 2010. Election procedures are provided in Rev. Proc. 98-47, 1998-2 CB 319.

Inventory and self-constructed assets

Inventory held for sale to customers is not depreciable. Depreciation on property used by a business to construct its own assets may not be currently deducted. Instead, such depreciation must be capitalized as part of the cost of the constructed assets and be deducted over the depreciation period for the constructed assets. Depreciation on assets used to manufacture a taxpayer's own inventory must be capitalized under the uniform capitalization rules (Code Sec. 263A(a)). In effect, depreciation expense is reflected in the computation of cost of goods sold and is recovered as items are sold.

A "primary purpose" test is applied to determine whether property which is held for sale or lease is considered inventory or depreciable property (*Latimer-Looney Chevrolet, Inc.,* 19 TC 120, CCH Dec. 19,280 (Acq.)).

Containers

Containers that are part of inventory are not depreciable. Some durable containers used to ship products may be depreciated if they have a life longer than one year, qualify as property used in a trade or business, and title to them does not pass to the buyer. Factors considered in determining whether a container may be depreciated include: (1) whether the sales contract, sales invoice, or acknowledgement of order indicates that title is retained; (2) whether the invoice treats the containers as separate items; and (3) whether the taxpayer's records properly state the basis in such (Rev. Rul. 75-34, 1995-1 CB 271). Trailer mounted containers, if depreciable, are MACRS 5-year property (Asset Class 00.27). Leased containers that were moved from trailers to cargo ships and vice versa were Asset Class 00.27 assets (IRS Letter Ruling 7939004, May 30, 1979).

See also ¶ 152.

Land and land improvements

Unimproved, raw land is not depreciable (Reg. § 1.167(a)-2).

If depreciable, land improvements are usually treated as 15-year property under MACRS. The following paragraphs discuss various types of land improvements. See ¶ 110 and ¶ 127C for additional discussion of land improvements.

Apartment complex. Sidewalks, concrete driveways, asphalt streets and concrete curbs, playground equipment, fencing, and landscaping constructed or installed in connection with an apartment complex were land improvements (IRS Letter Ruling 8848039, September 2, 1988). The ruling notes that certain portions of the costs may not qualify for depreciation because they might be considered land. For example, this might impact part of the costs of the streets and landscaping.

Playground equipment. Playground equipment treated as a land improvement included swing sets, climbers, slides, see-saws, merry-go-rounds, picnic tables, pipe-frame park benches, basketball backboards, football/soccer goal posts, flag staffs or poles, softball backstops, jogging trails, and stationary aerobic equipment.

The treatment of all types of playground equipment as a land improvement by Letter Ruling 8848039 is not particularly well explained by the ruling and is probably unwarranted. Land improvements must be inherently permanent (see ¶ 127C). Picnic tables, aerobic equipment, and benches for example, do not appear to meet this requirement unless, possibly, they are cemented into the ground. Note that an LMSB directive on cost segregation in the restaurant industry dated December 8, 2003 categorizes "playground equipment" under the "Restaurant Decor Accessories" entry as 5-year property and not as a land improvement. The context of the "playground equipment" entry, however, could be interpreted to refer to playground equipment located within a restaurant building. Definitionally, land improvements do not include property located within or attached to a building. The 5-year recovery period applies because this is the period assigned to property (other than land improvements) used in the restaurant business (Asset Class 57.0 of Rev. Proc. 87-56 at ¶ 191).

Golf courses. In general, a golf course consists of three types of components: the land, depreciable land improvements, and non-depreciable land improvements. Depreciable land improvements include bulkheads, cart paths, drainage systems, and irrigation systems.

IRS guidance allows land preparation costs related to land above subterranean drainage and irrigation systems to be depeciated as a land improvement over 15 years. Specifically, land preparation costs undertaken in the original construction or reconstruction of a golf course green, bunker, tee, fairway, or rough are depreciable to the extent attributable to the preparation of the area above a subterranean irrigation and/or sprinkler system or other depreciable asset. A taxpayer who purchases an existing golf course or constructs a new golf course may allocate a portion of the purchase or construction price to the value of such land preparation costs, as well as to the underlying irrigation and sprinkler systems, pursuant to the rules for cost segregation. Current owners may also conduct a cost segregation study to reclassify these assets as depreciable property. See ¶ 127.

Previously, it was unclear whether land preparation above a subterranean irrigation or sprinkler system was nondepreciable land or a depreciable land improvement. The IRS, however, ruled, with respect to golf course greens, in Rev. Rul. 2001-60, 2001-2 CB 587, that such costs are depreciable. As noted below, owners of golf courses are also applying the principles of Rev. Rul. 2001-60 to other types of golf course land improvements such as bunkers, tees, fairways, and roughs.

Rev. Rul. 2001-60 holds that the costs of land preparation undertaken in the original construction or reconstruction of traditional push-up or natural soil greens are inextricably associated with the land and, therefore, nondepreciable. This is the same position taken in Rev. Rul. 55-290, which is modified and superseded by Rev. Rul. 2001-60. Traditional greens are essentially landscaping that involves some reshaping or regrading of the land. The soil is pushed up or reshaped to form the green. A subsurface drainage system is not utilized (hoses and sprinklers, if any, are adjacent to the greens). See, also, *The Edinboro Company*, DC-Pa., 63-2 USTC ¶ 9759 (no depreciation on purchased golf course, including tees, greens, fairways, and traps); *Atlanta Athletic Club*, 61 TCM 2011, Dec. 47,195(M) (no depreciation or current deduction for golf course improvements required to host P.G.A. championship tournament); *University Country Club, Inc.*, 64 TC 460, Dec. 33,277 (no depreciation on golf course, grass, and driving range).

Significantly, Rev. Rul. 2001-60 allows depreciation on the portion of a "modern green" that is so closely associated with depreciable assets, such as a network of underground drainage tiles or pipes, that the land preparation will be retired, abandoned, or replaced contemporaneously with those depreciable assets. Specifically, depreciation may be claimed on the costs of land preparation above the drainage system, for example, a gravel and/or sand layer, rootzone layer, and turf grass. These costs of land preparation undertaken by a taxpayer in the original construction or reconstruction of modern greens may be capitalized and depreciated over the recovery period of the tiles, pipes, etc., with which the land is associated because the land preparation must be destroyed to replace the irrigation or sprinkler system. Drainage and sprinkler systems are land improvements (Asset Class 00.3) with a 15-year recovery period, according to the ruling; thus the associated land preparation costs are also 15-year property. General earthmoving, grading, and initial shaping of the area surrounding and underneath the modern green that occur before the construction are inextricably associated with the land and are nondepreciable, according to the ruling. Note that the cost of the land on which the modern green is built is not depreciable. The ruling limits depreciation to the cost of the land preparation *above* the drainage or sprinkler system.

The IRS has issued a "Field Directive on Depreciable Golf Course Land Improvements and the Impact of Rev. Rul. 2001-60" (February 7, 2002) which addresses the proper treatment of golf course land improvements other than greens in the light of the rationale of Rev. Rul. 2001-60. The Directive applies the principles of Rev. Rul. 2001-60 to bunkers, fees, fairways, and roughs.

The Field Directive provides that if a bunker contains depreciable assets such as a liner, and/or drain tiles or pipes the cost of improving the land above those items is depreciable.

If a tee contains underlying depreciable assets such as drain tiles or pipes, the cost of the land preparation above the underlying depreciable assets is also depreciable since the land preparation would have to be replaced if the drain tiles or pipes were replaced.

In the case of a fairway, a portion of the costs of final grading, preparation, seed (including any grow-out period costs), and sod are depreciable if the fairway has underlying depreciable irrigation and drainage pipes. The Directive provides the following example.

> ***Example (1):*** The removal of a 6-inch drainage pipe that carries runoff from a fairway would require a 12-inch wide ditch. Depreciation may be claimed on fairway land preparation costs attributable to 12 inches times the length of the pipe. Thus, if 30,000 feet of pipe are installed on a golf course, 30,000 square feet of land preparation costs are depreciable.
>
> If there are drainage or irrigation pipes underlying a rough, land preparation costs are subject to depreciation to the extent the land preparation above the pipes would be replaced if the pipes were replaced.

As in Rev. Rul. 55-290, the new ruling allows a current deduction for operating expenses for sod, seed, soil, and other sundry maintenance costs.

Appendix Section 6.04 of Rev. Proc. 2008-52 contains automatic change of accounting method consent procedures for persons seeking to conform to the holding of Rev. Proc. 2001-60. See ¶ 75. See, also, "IRS LMSB Industry Directive Issued on February 25, 2002: Audit Procedures for Golf Course Land Improvements –Change in Accounting Method, March 11, 2004," which provides general guidance to IRS personnel who review an application for an accounting method change.

In Chief Counsel Advice 200116043, February 13, 2001, which was issued prior to Rev. Proc. 2001-60, IRS auditors were advised to concentrate on "extreme" positions taken by taxpayers. These positions are cases in which a taxpayer:

(1) expensed, as an operating cost, reconstruction costs for greens, tees, and sand bunkers on an existing course;

(2) claimed depreciation on "push-up" or natural soil greens and tees;

(3) expensed or depreciated construction or reconstruction costs of fairways and roughs; and

(4) allocated golf course construction costs to residential building lots.

With the exception of fairways and roughs with irrigation or drainage pipes, these positions would still be considered extreme even after the issuance of Rev. Rul. 2001-60. However, the undepreciated cost of a depreciable golf course improvement may be deductible as an abandonment loss if the improvement is removed or replaced as part of a rennovation prior to being fully depreciated. An abandonment loss may also be available with respect to a nondepreciable improvement that is removed or replaced if adequate records can substantiate the adjusted basis of the removed or replaced property. For example, if a nondepreciable push-up green is leveled, then the cost or other basis of the push-up green may be deductible as an abandonment loss (whether or not it is replaced with a new green). See ¶ 162 for a discussion of abandonment and retirement losses.

Golf courses (other than miniature golf courses) are specifically excluded from Asset Class 79.0 of Rev. Proc. 87-56 (Recreation). Rev. Proc. 87-56 does not otherwise mention golf courses. Rev. Proc. 72-10, 1972-1 CB 721, which sets forth the depreciation periods under the ADR depreciation system, specifically indicates in the text of the description for Asset Class 00.3 (Land Improvements) that the cost of general grading of land, "as in the case of cemeteries and golf courses," is not a land improvement and is not depreciable under any other class. The Rev. Proc. 62-21 depreciation period guideline (see ¶ 1), in its definition of land improvements, excluded "land improvements which are a major asset of a business, such as cemeteries or golf courses."

Grading and land preparation costs. Raw (unimproved) land is not depreciable (Reg. § 1.167(a)-2). Land preparation costs, however, may be depreciable if they are directly associated with the construction of a depreciable building (Rev. Rul. 65-265. 1965-2 CB 52). Thus, in Rev. Rul. 65-265, costs attributable to excavation, grading, and removing soil necessary to the proper setting of buildings were added to the depreciable basis of the buildings in an industrial complex. The cost of general grading, not directly associated with the construction of the building, however, was added to the basis of the land. See, also, for example, *Eastwood Mall Inc.*, DC Oh., 95-1 USTC ¶ 50,236 (aff'd, CA-6, unpublished opinion, 59 F3d 170 (1995)), which concludes that the cost of clearing, grubbing, blasting, filling, and grading 100 acres of uneven land into an earthen plateau used for the construction of a shopping mall was not depreciable since these improvements were permanent and would not be reincurred if the mall building was rebuilt or replaced. The IRS did not dispute the depreciability of the cost of digging spaces and trenches for the mall building's foundations and utilities and the cost of installing utilities and sewers and paving roads and parking lots.

The cost of clearing, grubbing, cutting, filling, and rough and finish grading necessary to bring land to a suitable grade for the development of a mobile home part was nondepreciable and added to the basis of the land. However, the cost of excavation and backfilling required for the construction of laundry facilities and a storm sewer system that would be destroyed when those assets were replaced was included in the depreciable basis of those assets (Rev. Rul. 80-93, 1980-1 CB 50).

Costs incurred for fill dirt that is used to raise the level of a building construction site are inextricably associated with the land and, therefore, are not depreciable. Costs incurred for fill dirt used to set the foundation of a building are depreciable, as are earth-moving costs incurred for digging spaces and trenches for a building's foundations and utilities (IRS Letter Ruling 200043016, July 14, 2000).

The cost of backfilling a lake to create additional land on which to expand a taxpayer's steel mill facilities was nondepreciable (Rev. Rul. 77-270, 1977-2 CB 79).

The initial grading and clearing costs related to the costs of acquiring right-of-way easements for electrical transmission and distribution lines are depreciable even though these costs are not necessarily incurred again when the lines are replaced on the same easements (Rev. Rul. 72-403, 1972-2 CB 102). These costs are specifically excluded from the definition of a land improvement by Asset Class 00.3 and Asset Class 49.14 (see ¶ 191). These costs were previously depreciated under MACRS as 7-year property (property without an assigned class life). Effective for property placed in service after October 22, 2004, this property is treated as MACRS 20-year property (Code Sec. 168(e)(3)(F), as added by the 2004 Jobs Act). See ¶ 112.

The cost of boundary and mortgage surveys are included in the basis of the land. The cost of percolation tests and contamination studies may be included in the basis of a building if these tests would have to be reperformed if the building was destroyed and reconstructed. This test is applied without regard to whether a local ordinance required such a survey to be reperformed (IRS Letter Ruling 200043016, July 14, 2000).

Staking costs should be allocated between depreciable and nondepreciable assets. For example, staking relating to sidewalks may be added to the basis of the sidewalk and depreciated. Staking relating to nondepreciable landscaping is added to the basis of the land, along with the landscaping costs (IRS Letter Ruling 200043016, July 14, 2000).

Mobile home parks. The cost of clearing, grading, terracing, and landscaping was an integral part of the construction and development of a taxpayer's mobile home park and depreciable over the same period as the related pads, patios, and other depreciable improvements (*Trailmont Park Inc.*, 30 TCM 871, Dec. 30,950(M)). The court concluded that the improvements in question were not an inextricable part of the land alone but were directly related to and a necessary part of the construction of the depreciable assets necessary to the operation of the park. Furthermore, any other use of the land would require its reshaping as the land configuration was usable only to support a park. See, also, *R.W. Tunnel*, DC Del., 74-1 USTC 9122, for a case involving a mobile home park (cost of clearing and thinning woods into a configuration suitable only for a mobile park was depreciable where clearing and thinning actually reduced value of land for residential construction purposes; landscaping, including gravel streets, were depreciable since they would have to be destroyed to put the land to any other use; general grading costs, including filling of marshland, which increased the value of the land, were nondepreciable).

Other improvements to land that may be depreciable include sidewalks, roads, canals, drainage facilities, waterways, sewers, wharves, docks, bridges, fences, and radio and television towers. See ¶ 110.

Parking lots. Parking lots are considered land improvements. Note, for example, that parking lots are specifically mentioned as a type of land improvement in Rev. Proc. 87-56, Asset Class 80.0 (Theme and Amusement Parks). As to the depreciability of land preparation costs associated with a parking lot, see "*Roads,*" below. The IRS has ruled that an open-air parking structure is a building (39-year real property) and not a land improvement (Applicable Recovery Period Under Code Sec. 168(a) for Open-Air Parking Structures, Coordinated Issue Paper (LMSB4-0709-029) (Effective Date July 31, 2009). See ¶ 127C.

The cost of resurfacing or applying sealcoat on a parking lot is a current expense (*Toledo Home Federal Savings and Loan Assn.*, DC Ohio, 62-1 USTC ¶ 9366, 203 FSupp 491; *W.K. Coors*, 60 TC 368, Dec. 32,003 (Acq.)).

A parking lot located at a steam production plant was 20-year property (Asset Class 49.13) since land improvements related to assets used in the steam power production of electricity are specifically included in Asset Class 49.13. Although land improvements are described in an asset category (Asset Class 00.3) as 15-year property, Asset Class 49.13 specifically includes land improvements related to assets used in the steam power production of electricity. However, a parking lot located 100 miles from the plant at the corporate headquarters was 15-year property (Asset Class 00.3) because in the IRS's view it "is not related to the plant that produces the electricity" as required by Asset Class 49.13 (Rev. Rul. 2003-81, 2003-2 CB 126). Apparently, the types of assets used in activities conducted at the corporate headquarters, even though connected with the business of producing electricity, are not considered by the IRS "as used" in the production of electricity within the meaning of Asset Class 49.13.

Playground equipment. Playground equipment located on an apartment complex and treated as a land improvement included swing sets, climbers, slides, seesaws, merry-go-rounds, picnic tables, pipe-frame park benches, basketball backboards, football/soccer goal posts, flag staffs or poles, softball backstops, jogging trails, and stationary aerobic equipment (IRS Letter Ruling 8848039, September 2, 1988).

The treatment of all types of playground equipment as a land improvement by IRS Letter Ruling 8848039 is not particularly well explained by the ruling and is probably unwarranted. Land improvements must be inherently permanent (see ¶ 127C). Picnic tables, aerobic equipment, and benches for example, do not appear to meet this requirement unless, possibly, they are cemented into the ground. Note that an LMSB directive on cost segregation in the restaurant industry dated December 8, 2003 categorizes "playground equipment" under the "Restaurant Decor Accessories" entry as 5-year property and not as a land improvement. The context of the "playground equipment" entry, however, could be interpreted to refer to playground equipment located within a restaurant building. Definitionally, land improvements do not include property located within or attached to a building. The 5-year recovery period applies because this is the period assigned to property (other than land improvements) used in the restaurant business (Asset Class 57.0 of Rev. Proc. 87-56 at ¶ 191).

Roads. Rev. Rul. 65-265 concludes that the cost of excavating, grading, and removing soil directly connected to the construction of roadways located between industrial buildings in an industrial park was depreciable. However, the ruling was subsequently clarified to indicate that this holding was premised upon the peculiar circumstances which would require regrading of the roads if the buildings were reconstructed. According to the clarification, the costs of grading roadways may be depreciable where it can be established that the grading is associated with a depreciable asset and the grading will be retired, abandoned, or replaced contemporaneously with the asset (Rev. Rul. 68-193, 1968-1 CB 79, *clarifying* Rev. Rul. 65-265). See, also, Rev. Rul. 88-99, 1988-2 CB 33, which hold that the cost of constructing a logging road (roadbeds, surfacing, bridges, culverts) that would be abandoned after four years when timber was harvested is depreciable; however, if the road will not be abandoned the cost of constructing the roadbed is not depreciable since its useful life is indeterminable. The IRS affirms the position taken in Rev. Rul. 88-99 in an Industry Specialization Program (ISP) Coordinated Issue Paper (Logging Truck Roads, October 31, 1991). Similarly, the cost of roads and trails that led to improvements on a ranch were depreciable because they would be abandoned if the improvements were abandoned (*Rudolph Investment Corp.*, 31 TCM 573, Dec. 31,421(M)).

An IRS Field Service Advice (FSA) provides additional clarification on the IRS position with respect to the depreciability of road building costs (IRS Letter Ruling 200021013). The depreciability of road building costs, under this ruling, hinges largely upon establishing that the road will have a limited or determinable useful life. For example, if the road will be abandoned when a related asset will be abandoned (as in the *Rudolph* case, above), then depreciation of all the capitalized road building costs is allowable. Certain of the roads involved in the FSA connected ski resort buildings and structures (such as ski lifts, a ski lodge, parking lots, restaurants, and snow grooming equipment). The FSA concluded that the roads would not be abandoned because the structures would not be abandoned, but rather, would be rebuilt, if they were to deteriorate. Also, if certain structures were abandoned the roads would continue to be used to service other facilities. Moreover, abandonment due to the expiration of lease permits with respect to the federal land on which the resort was built was unlikely since the permits were renewable for an indefinite period.

It is worth noting that the roads in *Rudolph* also led to improvements (specifically, residences, barns, corrals, chutes, fences, and pasture) which arguably would be replaced upon deterioration rather than abandoned. The court, however, unlike the FSA, did not discuss the probability of abandonment, simply finding that the roads were depreciable because they would be abandoned if the related improvements were abandoned. The FSA states that *Rudolph* is factually distinguishable because the types of improvements in *Rudolph* are different from those involved in the FSA. Presumably, the *Rudolph* improvements, in the IRS view, were more likely to be abandoned or would be abandoned over time.

The FSA provides that the costs directly related to surfacing (e.g., graveling or paving) a road are depreciable even if the particular circumstances do not allow depreciation of the costs related to clearing land, grading, and construction of the roadbed. This is so because surfacing needs to be replaced over time (i.e., has a definite or limited useful life).

A road is considered a land improvement and, if depreciable, usually would be recovered over a 15-year period under MACRS. See ¶ 110.

The taxpayer in the FSA argued that the IRS's requirement that a road have a determinable or limited useful life in order to be depreciable was inappropriate in the context of ACRS and MACRS because these systems assign recovery periods without regard to an asset's actual useful life. The IRS, however, rejected this view, stating that ACRS and MACRS simply provide the rules for determining the amount of a depreciation deduction and not the rules for determining the more fundamental question of whether an asset is depreciable. These rules, according to the IRS, are governed by Code Sec. 167 and the regulations thereunder which require that an asset must have a determinable useful life in a taxpayer's trade or business. Although not discussed in the FSA, the Tax Court has ruled in two decisions (which were also affirmed at the appellate level) that musical instruments that appreciate in value and have no determinable useful life are depreciable so long as they are subject to wear and tear because they are actually being used. These decisions may provide a basis for challenging the position taken by the IRS in this FSA and similar earlier rulings which hinge upon establishing a determinable useful life. See ¶ 3.

Site utilities. Site utilities at a hotel/casino complex were structural components (¶ 127) and not land improvements. Site utilities included underground piping that connected water, sewer, and gas services to the building and overground and underground lines that connected electric service to the building. These items were used to distribute city furnished utility services to the building and were not directly associated with specific items of machinery and equipment (IRS Field Service Advice 200203009, October 3, 2001).

However, various components of an electrical distribution system (pine poles, aerial lines, transformers, meters, street lighting) and water distribution system (valves, fire hydrants, fittings, tapping sleeves, PVC water pipe, water meters) that were installed and maintained by the taxpayer in connection with an apartment complex were depreciable land improvements. These items were not classified as Rev. Proc. 87-56 Asset Class 49.14, Electric Utility Transmission and Distribution Plant, and Asset Class 49.3, Water Utilities, because those classifications only apply to taxpayers that sell electricity and water (IRS Letter Ruling 8848039, September 2, 1988).

Trees, shrubbery and other landscaping. The IRS officially maintains that trees and shrubbery may be depreciated only if they would be destroyed upon the replacement of a depreciable asset such as a building at the end of their useful life.

> ***Example (2):*** A taxpayer constructs a new commercial building and incurs costs for clearing, general grading, top soil, seeding, finish grading, and planting perennial shrubbery and trees. Some bushes and trees are planted next to the building and other bushes and trees are planted around the perimeter of a parking lot. The IRS allows the bushes and trees planted next to the building to be depreciated because they have a determinable useful life that is closely associated with the building. All other costs are added to the basis of the land and are not depreciable because they have no determinable life (Rev. Rul. 74-265, 1974-1 CB 56; GCM 35693 (February 26, 1974); IRS Publication 946, How to Depreciate Property).

It appears that the IRS position is that the costs of clearing and general and finish grading in the immediate vicinity of the building is not depreciable since these costs would not be reincurred if the building is destroyed and replaced.

Although Rev. Rul. 74-265 (a pre-MACRS ruling) provides that the cost of the trees and shrubbery are recovered over the life of the related building, under MACRS the cost of depreciable shrubbery and trees should be recovered over 15 years as a land improvement. Depreciable shrubbery is specifically included in Asset Class 00.3 (Land Improvements). Asset Class 00.3 provides a 15-year MACRS recovery period. Also noteworthy is IRS Publication 527 (Residential Rental Property) which contains a table which indicates that depreciable shrubbery is recovered over 15-years and IRS Letter Ruling 8848039 (September 2, 1988) which allows a 15-year recovery period for depreciable trees and shrubs planted next to residential rental property.

Several cases (to which the IRS has not acquiesced) have held that an asset may be depreciable under MACRS even if it has no determinable useful life. This could be the basis for arguing that landscaping not located next to a building is deductible. See ¶ 3.

Trees and bushes planted on a farm to serve as a windbreak to prevent soil erosion and to conserve moisture in the fields, thus increasing farm production and revenue, were nondepreciable (*G. Everson*, CA-9, 97-1 USTC ¶ 50,258). Note, however, that windbreaks may be currently deductible as soil and water conservation expenditures under Code Sec. 175.

Personal (nonbusiness) assets

Personal assets, such as a residence used by an individual or an automobile used only for personal purposes are not depreciable (Reg. § 1.167(a)-2)). If an asset is used partly for personal purposes and partly for business or investment purposes, only the portion of the asset used for business or investment purposes is depreciable.

Professional library

A professional library may be depreciated. A current business expense deduction is allowed for technical books, journals and business information services that have a useful life of one year or less.

Generally, books will fall within MACRS Asset Class 57.0 (¶ 190)—assets used in a wholesale or retail trade or in personal or professional services—and have a depreciation period of five years. For example, the IRS Market Segment Specialization Paper (MSSP) for attorneys indicates that permanent volumes used in a law library are 5-year property (Asset Class 57.0). Presumably, books used in connection with research and experimentation (as that term is used in Code Sec. 174, i.e., research and development costs in a laboratory or experimental sense) are also 5-year property (Item C of Rev. Proc. 87-56, relating to certain property for which recovery periods assigned; Code Sec. 168(e)(3)(B)(v); Code Sec. 168(i)(11)).

Property subject to a lease

Generally, for post-August 10, 1993, acquisitions of property subject to a lease, the purchaser must allocate the entire cost to the basis of the property. No portion of the cost may be allocated to the acquired leasehold interest (Code Sec. 167(c)(2); Reg. § 1.197-2(c)(8)).

> ***Example (3):*** A taxpayer purchases a shopping center that is under lease to tenants operating retail stores. The portion of the purchase price of the shopping center that is attributable to any favorable aspects of the leases is treated as part of the basis of the shopping center.

Leasehold acquistion costs

The cost of acquiring an interest as a lessee of tangible property is amortized over the term of the lease (Code Sec. 178 and Reg. § 1.162-11(a)).

A taxpayer may pay to acquire an existing lease from a *lessee.* In general, the amount paid to the lessee for the leasehold interest is also amortized over the term of the lease.

Leasehold acquisition costs are not amortizable under Code Sec. 197. See ¶ 52.

The term of the lease (i.e., amortization period) includes all renewal options and any other period that the lessor and lease purchaser expect the lease to be renewed if less than 75 percent of the cost is for the term of the lease remaining on the purchase date without regard to renewal options that the lease purchaser may exercise (Code Sec. 178; Reg. § 1.178-1(b)).

Example (4): A taxpayer enters into a lease for $10,000. The lease term is 20 years with two options to renew for periods of five years each. If at least $7,500 of the acquisition cost is allocable to the 20-year original term of the lease, then the taxpayer may amortize the $10,000 cost over a 20-year period whether or not the lease will be renewed.

Example (5): Same facts as *Example (4)*, except that $7,000 is allocable to the original term of the lease. Since less than 75% of the leasehold acquisition cost is allocable to the original term of the lease, the $10,000 acquisition cost is amortizable over 30 years (20-year original term plus 10-year renewal period). However, if the taxpayer can establish that it is more probable that the renewal options will not be exercised than that they will be exercised, the amortization period is limited to the 20-year original term of the lease.

An amortization period that does not include the period of a renewal option that is not expected to be exercised must be increased to include the renewal period in the tax year that a reasonable expectation that the renewal option will be exercised arises (Reg. § 1.178-3(b)).

In applying the 75-percent test, the lease cost is allocated between the original term and renewal periods based on the facts and circumstances. The allocation may, in certain circumstances, be based upon a present value computation (Reg. § 1.178-1(b)(5)).

Repairs or improvements

The cost of a repair is currently deductible. However, an improvement that increases the value of a property, makes it more useful, or lengthens its useful life is capitalized and depreciated. See ¶ 126.

¶ 10

Intangible Property

In deciding how to recover the cost of intangible property, a determination must first be made as to whether the intangible property qualifies for an amortization deduction under Code Sec. 197. This process involves two considerations: a particular intangible property must constitute a section 197 intangible, and the section 197 intangible must be an amortizable section 197 intangible.

If a Code Sec. 197 amortization deduction is allowed on an intangible, no other depreciation or amortization deduction may be claimed on such property (Code Sec. 197(b)). Depreciation-amortization treatment under Code Sec. 167 may apply (if other requirements are met) to an intangible that is not amortizable under Code Sec. 197.

See also the discussion on amortization at ¶ 70 and ¶ 320 through ¶ 326.

Capitalized costs

The capitalized costs of amortizable section 197 intangibles are ratably amortized over a 15-year period generally beginning with the month of acquisition regardless of their actual useful life (Code Sec. 197(a)). The section 197 amortization rules do not apply to intangible property for which a current business expense deduction may be claimed.

Amortizable basis

The amount amortized is the adjusted basis for purposes of determining gain (usually cost) of an amortizable section 197 intangible (Code Sec. 197(a)). See also ¶ 70.

Section 197 intangibles acquired pursuant to an asset acquisition to which Code Sec. 338 or Code Sec. 1060 applies should be treated as Class IV assets.

Consequently, the purchase price of section 197 intangibles so acquired is the amount by which the total purchase price (as reduced by the Class I Assets) exceeds the value of assets included in Class II and Class III (Reg. § 1.197-2(f)(4)(ii)).

Amortization deductions

Intangible property that is not amortizable under Code Sec. 197 is amortizable if an ascertainable limited life can be determined (Reg. § 1.167(a)-3) and the property has an ascertainable value.

Both MACRS and ACRS are inapplicable to intangible assets (Code Sec. 168(a)) (see ¶ 140 and ¶ 228).

Depreciation of intangible assets under certain accelerated depreciation methods (including the declining-balance and the sum of the years-digits methods) was not permitted under former Code Sec. 167(c) (before repeal by the Omnibus Budget Reconciliation Act of 1990 (P.L. 101-508) to eliminate deadwood but not to change the rule of law).

Intangible assets may be depreciated under any reasonable method (Code Sec. 167(a)). The straight-line method must be used absent a different acceptable method (Reg. § 1.167(b)-1(a)).

A method other than the straight-line method is appropriate provided that, considering the facts of the case, it results in a fair allocation of the basis of the asset to periods in which income is realized (*Citizens & Southern Corp.*, 91 TC 463, Dec. 45,036, aff'd per curiam, CA-11, 91-1 USTC ¶ 50,043; *IT&S of Iowa, Inc.*, 97 TC 496, Dec. 47,735; *Computing & Software, Inc.*, 64 TC 223, Dec. 33,197, (Acq.) 1976-2 CB 1; *Trustmark Corp.*, 67 TCM 2764, Dec. 49,813(M), TC Memo. 1994-184). (See also ¶ 28.)

Other permissible methods for depreciating certain intangible assets include the income forecast method (Rev. Rul. 60-358, 1960-2 CB 68, amplified by Rev. Rul. 64-273, 1964-2 CB 62) (see also ¶ 364) and the sliding-scale method (*Kiro, Inc.*, 51 TC 155, Dec. 29,205 (Acq., 1974-2 CB 3)). See ¶ 364.

¶ 12

Amortizable Section 197 Intangibles

A section 197 intangible is amortizable if it is acquired after August 10, 1993, and held in connection with a trade or business or in an activity engaged in for the production of income (Code Sec. 197(c)(1)). An irrevocable election allowed taxpayers to apply Code Sec. 197 to property acquired after July 25, 1991 (Temp. Reg. § 1.197-1T).

The standard for determining when an amortizable section 197 intangible is held in connection with the conduct of a trade or business is the standard under Code Sec. 162. This determination will depend on the facts of each case, in particular when the taxpayer began carrying on a trade or business within the meaning of Code Sec. 162 (CCA Letter Ruling 200137050, August 8, 2001).

Amortization period

Amortizable section 197 intangibles are amortized over 15 years beginning the later of the first day of the month of acquisition or, in the case of property held in connection with the conduct of a trade or business or an income-producing activity, the first day of the month in which the conduct of the trade or business or the activity begins (Reg. § 1.197-2(f)(1)). No amortization deduction is claimed in the month of disposition.

Assets treated as section 197 intangibles

The following assets are considered section 197 intangibles:

(1) goodwill (¶ 18);

(2) going concern value (¶ 20);

(3) workforce in place (¶ 22);

(4) information base (¶ 24);

(5) patent, copyright, formulas, process, design, pattern, know-how, format, or similar item (¶ 26);

(6) customer-based intangible (¶ 28);

(7) supplier-based intangible (¶ 30);

(8) government license or permit (¶ 32);

(9) covenant not to compete if part of the acquisition of a trade or business (¶ 34); and

(10) franchise, trademark, or trade-name (¶ 36).

Any right under a license, contract, or other arrangement for the use of property that would be a section 197 intangible is generally treated as a section 197 intangible. A term interest in a section 197 intangible is treated as a section 197 intangible (Reg. § 1.197-2(b)(11)). Royalty payments under a contract for the use of a section 197 intangible unconnected with the purchase of a trade or business are generally currently deductible (Reg. § 1.197-2(f)(3)(iii)).

Exclusions

The following assets are specifically excluded from the definition of a section 197 intangible and, therefore, are not amortizable under Code Sec. 197 under any circumstance:

(1) any interest in a corporation, partnership, trust, or estate (¶ 42);

(2) any interest under an existing futures contract, foreign currency contract, notional principal contract, or other similar financial contract (¶ 44);

(3) any interest in land (¶ 46);

(4) certain computer software (¶ 48);

(5) any interest under an existing lease of tangible property (¶ 52) or any existing indebtedness (¶ 54);

(6) sport franchises acquired on or before October 22, 2004 (¶ 56);

(7) mortgage servicing rights (¶ 58); and

(8) certain transaction costs incurred in connection with nonrecognition transactions (¶ 60 and ¶ 64).

Exclusion for certain separately acquired intangibles

Generally, a section 197 intangible does not have to be obtained in connection with the acquisition of a trade or business in order to qualify as an *amortizable* section 197 intangible. However, the following assets are not amortizable under Code Sec. 197 unless acquired as part of the acquisition of a trade or business or substantial portion thereof (Code Sec. 197(e)(4)):

(1) any interest in a film, sound recording, video tape, book, or similar property;

(2) any right to receive tangible property or services under a contract or granted by a government;

(3) an interest in a patent or copyright; and

(4) any right under a contract or granted by a government if the right has a fixed duration of less than 15 years, or is fixed as to amount and would be recoverable under a method similar to the unit-of-production method.

Although only certain section 197 intangibles need to be acquired in connection with the acquisition of a trade or business in order to be amortized under Code Sec. 197, all section 197 intangibles need to be used in connection with the conduct of a trade or business or an income-producing activity to be so amortized (Code Sec. 197(c)(1)).

See ¶ 50 for details regarding the exclusion for separately acquired intangibles.

Self-created intangibles

Generally, amortization under Code Sec. 197 is not allowed in the case of a section 197 intangible created by the taxpayer ("self-created intangibles"). Such intangibles, however, may be amortizable over 15 years under a separate safe-harbor provision described at ¶ 66. A self-created intangible, however, is amortizable under Code Sec. 197 if it is created in connection with a transaction or series of related transactions involving the acquisition of a trade or business (Code Sec. 197(c)(2); Reg. § 1.197-2(d)(2)).

A section 197 intangible is created by a taxpayer to the extent the taxpayer makes payments or otherwise incurs costs for its creation, production , development, or improvement. This also applies if the payment ect. is made to a third party to create the intangible for the taxpayer. For example, a taxpayer who pays a third party to develop a technological process that will be owned by the taxpayer may not treat the technological process as an amortizable section 197 intangible because it is self-created. However, a section 197 intangible is not self-created to the extent that it results from the entry into or renewal of a contract for the use of an existing section 197 intangible. For example, capitalized legal and professional fees incurred by a licensee in connection with the entry into or renewal of a contract for the use of know-how or similar property is not a self-created intangible (Reg. § 1.197-2(d)(2)).

Goodwill created through a taxpayer's own efforts in running a business is considered a self-created intangible (Field Service Advice Memorandum 200106006, October 17, 2000).

The exception from Code Sec. 197 treatment for self-created intangibles does not apply to:

(1) licenses, permits, or other rights granted by the government;

(2) a covenant not to compete entered into in connection with the acquisition of a business; and

(3) a franchise, trademark, or tradename (¶ 36).

A license, permit, or other right granted by the government that is not acquired in connection with the acquisition of a trade or business is amortizable over its duration if such duration is fixed for a period of less than 15 years. See ¶ 32.

A covenant not to compete is amortizable under Code Sec. 197 only if it is entered into in connection with the acquisition of a trade or business. Thus, the cost of covenants entered into by an existing employer with departing employees or officers are recovered over the term of the agreement as under pre-Code Sec. 197 law. See ¶ 34.

Loss disallowed on certain sales and dispositions

No loss is recognized when a taxpayer disposes of an amortizable section 197 intangible if the taxpayer (or a related person) retains other section 197 intangibles that were acquired in the same transaction or series of related transactions. The disallowed loss is allocated among the adjusted bases of the retained intangibles (Code Sec. 197(f)(1); Reg. § 1.197-2(g)(1)). This rule applies to abandoned and worthless amortizable section 197 intangibles.

Recapture

An amortizable section 197 intangible is treated as depreciable property for purposes of recapture (Code Sec. 197(f)(7); Reg.§ 1.197-2(g)(8)). A special recapture rule applies if more than one amortizable sec. 197 intangible is sold in the same transaction. See also *"Dispositions of amortizable section 197 intangibles"* at ¶ 160 for a discussion of the section 197 recapture rules.

Section 1231 asset

If used in a trade or business and held for more than one year, gain or loss on the disposition of an amortizable section 197 asset generally qualifies as section 1231 gain or loss. Nonamortizable or depreciable intangibles generally qualify as capital assets under Code Sec. 1221 (IRS Letter Ruling 200243002, July 16, 2002).

¶ 14

Anti-churning Rules for Section 197 Intangibles

Certain section 197 intangibles acquired in certain transactions do not qualify for an amortization deduction under Code Sec. 197 (Code Sec. 197(f)(9); Reg. § 1.197-2(d)(3)).

An amortization deduction is barred under anti-churning rules for a section 197 intangible that is goodwill, going-concern value, or that would not otherwise be depreciable or amortizable but for Code Sec. 197, if it is acquired after August 10, 1993, and the taxpayer:

(1) or a related person held or used the intangible at any time during the period beginning on July 25, 1991, and ending on August 10, 1993;

(2) acquired the intangible from a person who held it any time during the period beginning on July 25, 1991, and ending on August 10, 1993, and, as part of the transaction, the user of the intangible did not change; or

(3) grants the right to use the intangible to a person (or a person related to such person) who held or used the intangible at any time during the period beginning on July 25, 1991, and ending on August 10, 1993 (Code Sec. 197(f)(9)(A)).

Related persons

For purposes of the anti-churning rules, related persons include (a) relationships similar to those indicated at ¶ 266 but applying 20-percent stock and partnership ownership percentage tests and (b) persons engaged in trades or businesses under common control (Code Sec. 197(f)(9)(C)). Persons are treated as related if the requisite relationship exists immediately before or after the acquisition of the intangible.

Anti-abuse rule

No section 197 amortization deduction is allowed if a section 197 intangible is acquired in a transaction, one of the principal purposes of which is to avoid the requirement that the intangible be acquired after August 10, 1993, or to avoid the anti-churning rules (Code Sec. 197(f)(9)(F)).

Partnerships

In determining whether the anti-churning rules apply to an increase in the basis of partnership property under Code Sec. 732 (basis of distributed property other than money), 734 (optional adjustment to basis of undistributed partnership property), or 743 (optional adjustment to basis of partnership property), the determinations are made at the partner level. Each partner is treated as having owned or used the partner's proportionate share of the partnership property (Code Sec. 197(f)(9)(E); Reg. § 1.197-2(h)(12)(i)).

Example: The anti-churning rules do not apply to any increase in the basis of partnership property that occurs upon the acquisition of an interest in a partnership that made a Code Sec. 754 election to utilize the optional adjustment to the basis of partnership property if the person acquiring the partnership interest is not related to the person selling the partnership interest (Reg. § 1.197-2(k), *Example 14*).

Partial exception election

A partial exception to the anti-churning rules is provided if these rules would not apply to an acquired intangible but for the 20-percent stock and partnership ownership percentage tests and if the person from whom the intangible is acquired elects to (1) recognize gain on the disposition and (2) pay a tax on the gain that, when added to any other federal income tax imposed on the gain, equals the product of the gain times the highest income tax rate applicable to such person. In this case, the anti-churning rules apply to the acquired intangible only to the extent that the acquiror's adjusted basis in the intangible exceeds the recognized gain (Code Sec. 197(f)(9)(B); Reg. § 1.197-2(h)(9)).

Franchises, trademarks, and trade names

Deductible transferee payments made in connection with the transfer of a franchise, trademark, or trade name under Code Sec. 1253(d) are treated as an amortization deduction. Consequently, a franchise, trademark, or trade name for which such payments were made is not subject to the anti-churning rules (Code Sec. 197(f)(9)(A); Reg. § 1.197-2(h)(3)).

Transfer from decedent

Also, the anti-churning rules do not apply to intangibles acquired from a decedent (Code Sec. 197(f)(9)(D); Reg. § 1.197-2(h)(5)).

¶ 18

Goodwill

Section 197 treatment

Section 197 intangibles include goodwill, which is considered to be the value of a trade or business that is attributable to the expectancy of continued customer patronage, whether due to name or reputation of the trade or business or to any other factor (Code Sec. 197(f)(1); Reg. § 1.197-2(b)(1)). Goodwill is a section 197 intangible if it is acquired in connection with the acquisition of a trade or business or a substantial portion of a trade or business. Goodwill that is the result of the taxpayer's own efforts (self-created goodwill) is not amortizable under Code Sec. 197.

Goodwill and going concern value which are amortizable section 197 intangibles are not capital assets for purposes of Code Sec. 1221, but if used in a trade or business and held for more than one year, gain or loss upon their disposition generally qualifies as section 1231 gain or loss (IRS Letter Ruling 200243002, July 16, 2002).

Depreciation if section 197 does not apply

Goodwill which is not amortizable under section 197 is generally not depreciable because it has an indefinite useful life or, even if it is considered an asset that does waste, its useful life cannot be determined with reasonable accuracy (Reg. § 1.167(a)-3).

¶ 20

Going-Concern Value

Section 197 treatment

Section 197 intangibles include going-concern value, which is the additional value that attaches to property because it is an integral part of a going concern. It includes the value attributable to the ability of a trade or business to continue to operate and generate income without interruption in spite of a change in ownership (Code Sec. 197(d)(1); Reg. § 1.197-2(b)(2)).

Depreciation if section 197 does not apply

The depreciation rules applicable to going-concern value that is not amortizable under Code Sec. 197 are similar to the rules for goodwill (*Ithaca Industries, Inc.*, CA-4, 94-1 USTC ¶ 50,100, cert. denied taxpayer 10/3/94) (see ¶ 18). Thus, no depreciation is allowed on this asset unless it has an ascertainable value and a limited useful life that can be determined with reasonable accuracy.

¶ 22

Work Force in Place

Section 197 treatment

The composition of a work force (experience, education, or training), the terms and conditions of employment whether contractual or otherwise, and any other value placed on employees or their attributes are included within this category of section 197 intangibles (Code Sec. 197(d)(1)). Thus, this category pertains to the cost of acquiring an existing employment contract (or contracts) or a relationship with employees or consultants (including but not limited to a key employee contract or relationship) as part of the acquisition of a business (Reg. § 1.197-2(b)(3)).

Depreciation if section 197 does not apply

If this intangible asset is not amortizable under Code Sec 197, the following rules apply. Generally, no depreciation is allowed on this intangible asset unless it has an ascertainable value and a limited useful life that can be determined with reasonable accuracy.

The mass-asset rule is often used to prohibit depreciation of a work force in place if this asset constitutes a self-regenerating asset that may change but never waste. This rule treats the individual employees comprising a work force as a single asset and, even though the individual components of the asset may rise or fall over time or expire or be replaced, there are only minimal fluctuations and no measurable loss in the value of the whole.

For purposes of the mass-asset rule, the distinguishing feature of a true mass asset is its ability to self-regenerate (the asset's maintenance is not accompanied by significant efforts of the owner other than those already expended in the initial formation or purchase of the asset).

An amortization deduction was denied for an acquired work force that was not subject to any predetermined contractual or other limit because it lacked a limited useful life and was not an amortizable intangible asset. However, it was not the mass-asset rule that barred the deduction because this company's work force was preserved only through the company's substantial training and recruiting efforts and it was not a self-regenerating asset (*Ithaca Industries, Inc.*, CA-4, 94-1 USTC ¶ 50,100, cert. denied taxpayer 10/3/94).

For a detailed discussion of the amortization of assembled workforce under the pre-Code Sec. 197 rules, see IRS Industry Specialization Program (ISP) Coordinated Issue Paper, Amortization of Assembled Workforce, (as revised February 19, 1996 and reproduced in full text in the CCH IRS POSITIONS Reporter at ¶ 80,115).

¶ 24
Information Base

Section 197 treatment

Business books and records; operating systems; customer lists; subscription lists; insurance expirations; patient or client files; the intangible value attributable to technical manuals, training manuals or programs, data files, and accounting or inventory control systems; and lists of newspaper, magazine, radio or television advertisers are included in this category of section 197 intangibles (Code Sec. 197(d)(1); Reg. § 1.197-2(b)(4)).

Depreciation if section 197 does not apply

If these intangible assets are not amortizable under Code Sec. 197, a depreciation deduction is allowed provided that they have an ascertainable value and a limited useful life that can be determined with reasonable accuracy.

¶ 26
Patents, Copyrights, Formulas, Processes, Designs, Patterns, and Know-How

Section 197 treatment

Any patent, copyright, formula, process, design, pattern, know-how, format, or other similar item is included in this category of section 197 intangibles. It also includes package designs, computer software, and interests in films, sound recordings, video tapes, books or other similar property, except as otherwise provided (Code Sec. 197(d)(1); Reg. § 1.197-2(b)(5)).

Certain computer software is considered a section 197 intangible only if acquired in a transaction involving the acquisition of assets constituting a trade or business (see ¶ 12 and ¶ 48).

Unless acquired in connection with the acquisition of a business or a substantial portion thereof, an interest (such as a license) in a film, sound recording, video tape, book or similar property is not an amortizable section 197 intangible (Reg. § 1.197-2(c)(5)). Similarly, patents and copyrights not acquired in connection with the acquisition of a trade or business are not amortizable under Code Sec. 197 (Reg. § 1.197-2(c)(7)). See ¶ 50.

Depreciation if section 197 does not apply

Computer software. See ¶ 48.

Patents and copyrights. If an interest in a patent or copyright is not amortizable under Code Sec. 197 because it is separately acquired (¶ 50), the depreciation deduction for a tax year is equal to the amount of the purchase price paid during the tax year in situations where the purchase price is payable on an annual basis as either a fixed amount per use or a fixed percentage of the revenue derived from the use. Otherwise, the basis of the patent or copyright (or an interest therein) is depreciated ratably over its remaining useful life or under the income forecast method. If a patent or copyright becomes worthless in any year before its legal expiration, the adjusted basis may be deducted in that year (Reg. § 1.167(a)-6; Reg. § 1.167(a)-14(c)(4)).

Amortization on a patent or copyright that is not a section 197 intangible begins when it is placed in service (Reg. § 1.167(a)-14). A patent or copyright may be depreciated over its remaining useful life (Reg. § 1.167(a)-10(b)). Rev. Rul. 79-285 provides that rights to patents and master recordings are first placed in service when products or processes resulting from the these rights are first released for distribution and sale, or are used in the taxpayer's trade or business or for the production of income. The ruling states, however, that patents are not considered placed in service prior to the issue date. However, due to the law change described below, the ruling's reference to "issue date" should probably be changed to "application filing date."

The straight-line method may be used to depreciate the cost of a patent or copyright. For example, if a patent is acquired and placed in service by a calendar-year taxpayer on July 1 for $10,000 and its remaining useful life as of that date is 10 years, the straight-line deduction is $500 ($10,000 ÷ 10 × 6/12).

Prior to June 8, 1995, patents generally had a legal life of 17 years starting from the date the patent was issued. Patents granted on or after June 8, 1995, generally have a 20-year legal life measured from the date of the first filing of the patent application. Patents that were in force before June 8, 1995, or that result from an application filed before June 8, 1995, generally have a term that is the greater of (1) 20 years from the date the application was first filed or (2) 17 years from the date of grant (35 U.S.C. § 154).

For copyrighted material published before 1978, the U.S. copyright term was for 28 years, and copyrights could be renewed for a second term of 28 years.

For works created after 1977, the copyright term is for the life of the author plus 70 years. The copyright term for joint works created after 1977 is the life of the last surviving author plus 70 years. Where works made for hire are created after 1977, the copyright period is 95 years from the date of first publication or a term of 120 years from the year of creation, whichever expires first (17 USC §§ 302, 303, and 304).

There must be a sale of the capital asset (the patent) rather than a license agreement (right to use the product) in order for the transferee to qualify as the owner for depreciation purposes. A sale exists if there is a transfer of the exclusive right to make, use, and sell a particular product in the United States for the full term of a patent because none of the attributes of ownership is retained (*Magee-Hale Park-O-Meter Co.*, 15 TCM 254, Dec. 21,616(M), TC Memo. 1956-57). However, a transfer of the attributes of ownership is not precluded by a security provision designed to protect the transferor's right to receive compensation under the sale agreement (*Newton Insert Co.*, 61 TC 570, Dec. 32,439, aff'd per curiam, CA-9, 77-1 USTC ¶ 9132, 545 F2d 1259).

Package design costs. Prior to the issuance of the final *INDOPCO* intangibles capitalization regulations (Reg. § 1.263(a)-4 and Reg.§ 1.263(a)-5 as adopted by T.D. 9107, filed with the Federal Register on December 31, 2003), the cost of developing and designing product packages generally had to be capitalized. These regulations are generally effective for amounts paid or incurred on or after December 31, 2003.

Reg.§ 1.263(a)-4(b)(3)(v) of the final *INDOPCO* regulations provides that amounts paid to develop a package design are treated as amounts that do not create a separate and distinct intangible asset. Thus, these amounts are not required to be capitalized and may be currently deducted.

The cost of purchasing an existing package design cost, however, continues to be subject to capitalization but typically may be amortized under Code Sec. 197 over 15 years.

If a package design cost is not deductible under the *INDOPCO* regulations or amortizable under Code Sec. 197, three alternative methods of accounting for package design costs are provided—the capitalization method, the design-by-design capitalization and 60-month amortization method, and the pool-of-cost capitalization and 48-month amortization method (Rev. Proc. 97-35, 1997-2 CB 448, as modified by Rev. Proc. 98-39, 1998-1 CB 1320).

Under the capitalization method, a package design with an ascertainable useful life is amortized using the straight-line method over its useful life, beginning with the month in which the package design is placed in service. If the package design has no ascertainable useful life, no depreciation or amortization deduction is allowed (Reg. § 1.167(a)-3), and package design costs may be deducted only upon the disposition, abandonment, or modification of the package design (Reg. § 1.165-2(a); Rev. Rul. 89-23, 1989-1 CB 85).

Under the design-by-design capitalization method, the basis of each package design is capitalized and amortized using the straight-line method over a 60-month period, beginning with the month the design is treated as placed in service using a half-year convention. This method applies to both an intangible asset with no ascertainable useful life and an intangible asset with an ascertainable useful life substantially exceeding one year. If the package design is disposed of or abandoned within the amortization period, the remaining unamortized basis of the design may be deducted in the tax year of disposition or abandonment.

Under the pool-of-cost capitalization method, all package design costs incurred during a tax year are capitalized and amortized using the straight-line method over a 48-month period, beginning with the month the costs are treated as incurred using a half-year convention. This method applies to all package design costs, regardless of whether they have an ascertainable useful life that extends substantially beyond the end of the tax year in which the costs are incurred. However, no deduction is allowed for the unamortized cost of a design that is (a) never placed in service or (b) disposed of or abandoned within the amortization period.

Capitalized costs under either of these three methods are determined by applying the capitalization rules of Code Sec. 263 in the case of package design costs incurred in tax years beginning after December 31, 1993. The uniform capitalization rules of Code Sec. 263A apply to costs incurred in tax years beginning after December 31, 1986 and before January 1, 1994 (Rev. Proc. 98-39, 1998-1 CB 1320, modifying Rev. Proc. 97-35, 1997-2 CB 448).

These three methods do not apply to package design costs that qualify as Code Sec. 197 intangibles (generally, package designs acquired by purchase) (Rev. Proc. 98-39).

Automatic consent to change to one of these three procedures is provided in Rev. Proc. 2008-52 (Appendix Section 10.01). Rev. Proc. 2008-52 does not apply to a taxpayer who wants to change to the capitalization method for costs of developing or modifying any package design cost that has an ascertainable useful life.

The following IRS Coordinated Issue Papers provide useful background on the treatment of package design costs: IRS Coordinated Issue Paper (Package Design Costs, October 31, 1991) reproduced in the CCH IRS POSITIONS REPORTER at ¶ 110,505 (decoordinated effective September 28, 2007, due to modification by

Reg.§ 1.263(a)-4 on capitalization of intangibles) and ISP Settlement Guidelines for Package Design Costs (September 21, 1992) reproduced in the CCH IRS POSITIONS REPORTER at ¶ 180,355.

Graphic design costs. Expenditures relating to the graphic design of cigarette packaging materials (cartons, soft-packs, and crush-proof boxes) and cigarette papers, tips, and other components of the cigarette product were currently deductible business expenses (*RJR Nabisco Inc.*, 76 TCM 71, CCH Dec. 52,786(M); Nonacq. I.R.B. 1999-40). Note that this case involved the 1984 tax year. Rev. Rul. 89-23, which defines package design costs for purposes of Rev. Proc. 97-35, above, appears to treat the types of expenditures considered in *RJR* as package design costs. See, also, FSA 200147035, August 15, 2001, which rejects the *RJR* case.

¶ 28
Customer-Based Intangibles

Section 197 treatment

This category of section 197 intangibles encompasses the composition of market, market share, and any other value resulting from future provision of goods or services under relationships (contractual or otherwise) in the ordinary course of business with customers. It includes the portion of the purchase price of an acquired trade or business that is attributable to an existing customer base, circulation base, undeveloped market or market growth, insurance in force, the existence of a qualification to supply goods or services to a particular customer, mortgage servicing contracts, investment management contracts, or other relationships with customers that involve the future provision of goods or services (Code Sec. 197(d)(1) and (2); Reg. § 1.197-2(b)(6)).

For financial institutions, deposit base and similar items are also included in customer-based intangibles (Code Sec. 197(d)(2); Reg. § 1.197-2(b)(6)).

Depreciation if section 197 does not apply

For those assets in this group that are not amortizable under Code Sec. 197, a depreciation deduction is allowed using the straight-line method over their respective useful lives, provided that they have (1) ascertainable values and (2) limited useful lives that can be ascertained with reasonable accuracy.

Insurance expirations. Purchased insurance expirations that were considered a mass (single) asset with an ascertainable value separate from goodwill and a useful life of not more than ten years from the date of purchase were depreciable (*Richard S. Miller & Sons, Inc.*, CtCls, 76-2 USTC ¶ 9481, 537 F2d 446). The principal value of this asset is in the information about the customer and the indication of the most advantageous time to solicit a policy renewal.

The mass-asset rule is often used to prohibit depreciation of certain customer-based intangibles because they constitute self-regenerating assets that may change but never waste. See the discussion of the mass-asset rule at ¶ 22.

Bank core deposits. An acquired bank deposit base was depreciable because it had an ascertainable value and a limited useful life that could be measured with reasonable accuracy (*Citizens & Southern Corp.*, 91 TC 463, aff'd CA-11, 91-1 USTC ¶ 50,043, 919 F2d 1492; *Colorado National Bankshares, Inc.*, 60 TCM 771, Dec. 46,875(M), aff'd CA-10, 93-1 USTC ¶ 50,077).

A bank deposit base is a purchased intangible asset which represents the present value of the future stream of income to be derived from employing the purchased core deposits. The value of the deposit base is the ascertainable probability that inertia will cause depositors to leave their funds on deposit for predictable periods. Depreciation was allowed on the portion of the purchase price attributable to the present value of the difference between the ongoing cost of maintaining the core deposits and the cost of the market alternative for funding loans and other investments. The fact that new accounts were opened as old accounts closed did not make the original purchased deposit base self-regenerating.

Because of discounting and the fact that it was shown that bank core deposits decline more quickly in the years immediately following acquisition, accelerated depreciation was allowed for a particular year representing that portion of the present value of the income stream (or cost savings) determined as of the date of acquisition of bank core deposits which was attributable to the current year (*Citizens & Southern Corp.*, supra; *IT&S of Iowa, Inc.*, 97 TC 496, Dec. 47,735).

For a detailed discussion of the tax treatment of bank core deposits under the pre-Code Sec. 197 rules, see IRS Industry Specialization Program (ISP) Coordinated Issue Paper, Core Deposit Intangibles (October 31, 1991) reproduced in full text in the CCH IRS POSITIONS Reporter at ¶ 165,050.

Newspaper subscription list. A purchased newspaper subscription list was depreciable where it met the two tests indicated above (*Donrey Inc.*, CA-8, 87-1 USTC ¶ 9143, 809 F2d 534). The value of the list was the present value of the difference in advertising revenues generated by the subscription list compared to the revenues of an equivalent paper without a subscription list.

An acquired intangible asset denominated "paid subscribers" (at-will subscribers, each of whom had requested that the paper be delivered regularly to a specified address in return for payment of the subscription price rather than subscribers who had paid in advance) had substantial value above that of a mere list of customers. The asset met the two tests indicated above and was depreciable using the straight-line method over stipulated useful lives (*Newark Morning Ledger Co.*, SCt, 93-1 USTC ¶ 50,228). The asset constituted a finite set of identifiable subscriptions, each of which had a limited useful life that could be measured with reasonable accuracy and was not self-regenerating. The value of the intangible asset was the present value of the after-tax subscription revenues to be derived from the paid subscribers, less the cost of collection, plus the present value of the tax savings resulting from the depreciation of the asset.

(Although the useful life of the asset was limited, an evidentiary concession apparently saved the deduction from failing the test that the asset's useful life must be measurable with reasonable accuracy. That is, the useful life of the pre-sale goodwill attributable to the subscribers' subscription habits (faithfulness) was not shown to be coextensive with the predicted life of the subscriptions, which was based on the assumption that the total number of subscribers would remain stable.)

For a detailed discussion of the tax treatment of customer subscription lists under the pre-Code Sec. 197 rules, see IRS Industry Specialization Program (ISP) Coordinated Issue Paper, Customer Subscription Lists (October 31, 1991) reproduced in full text in the CCH IRS POSITIONS Reporter at ¶ 135,825.

Additional ISP papers

For a detailed discussion of the amortization of market based intangibles under the pre-Code Sec. 197 rules, see IRS Industry Specialization Program (ISP) Coordinated Issue Paper, Amortization of Market Based Intangibles (as revised February 19, 1996) and reproduced in the CCH IRS Positions Reporter at ¶ 80,125.

For a detailed discussion of the amortization of order backlog (unfilled customer orders or contracts at the time of acquisition of a business) under the pre-Code Sec. 197 rules, see IRS Industry Specialization Program (ISP) Coordinated

Issue Paper, Amortization of Order Backlog (as revised February 19, 1996) and reproduced in the CCH IRS POSITIONS Reporter at ¶ 80,135.

For a detailed discussion of the amortization of customer-based intangibles under the pre-Code Sec. 197 rules, see IRS Industry Specialization Program (ISP) Coordinated Issue Paper, Customer Based Intangibles (as revised February 19, 1996) and reproduced in the CCH IRS POSITIONS Reporter at ¶ 80,275.

¶ 30
Supplier-Based Intangibles

Section 197 treatment

Any value resulting from future acquisitions of goods or services under relationships (contractual or otherwise) in the ordinary course of business with suppliers of goods or services to be used or sold by the taxpayer constitutes supplier-based intangibles (Code Sec. 197(d)(3)). This value includes the portion of the purchase price of an acquired trade or business that is attributable to existing favorable relationships with persons that provide distribution services, such as favorable shelf or display space at a retail outlet, a favorable credit rating, or favorable supply contracts (Reg. § 1.197-2(b)(7)).

Depreciation if section 197 does not apply

If these intangibles are not amortizable under Code Sec. 197, they are depreciable provided that they have an ascertainable value and a limited useful life that can be determined with reasonable accuracy (*Ithaca Industries, Inc.*, 97 TC 253, Dec. 47,536, aff'd on another issue, CA-4, 94-1 USTC ¶ 50,100, cert. denied taxpayer 10/3/94).

¶ 32
License, Permit, or Other Right Granted by the Government

Section 197 treatment

Section 197 intangibles include licenses, permits, or other rights granted by the government. Liquor licenses, taxicab medallions, airport landing or takeoff rights, regulated airline routes, and television or radio broadcasting licenses are included in this category (Code Sec. 197(d)(1)(D); Reg. § 1.197-2(b)(8)).

Licenses, permits, or other rights granted by the government and which are not acquired in connection with the acquisition of a trade or business are not amortizable under Code Sec. 197 if they have a fixed duration of less than 15 years or are fixed in amount and would be recoverable under a method similar to the unit-of-production method. In effect, this rule allows taxpayers the advantage of recovering the cost over the shorter term of the license, permit, or right. See ¶ 50.

A right to receive tangible property or services that is granted by a government is not an amortizable section 197 intangible if the right is separately acquired (Reg. § 1.197-2(c)(6)). See ¶ 50.

In determining whether the license, permit, or other right granted by the government has a fixed duration of less than 15 years potential renewal periods are taken into account if based on all the facts and circumstances in existence at any time during the taxable year in which the right is acquired, the facts clearly indicate a reasonable expectancy of renewal (Reg.§ 1.167(a)-14(a)). For example, the IRS ruled that PCS licenses (personal communication system licenses issued to cell phone companies) issued by the FCC for a ten-year period were under the circumstances likely to be renewed and, therefore, were section 197 intangibles because they had a fixed duration in excess of 15 years (CCA Letter Ruling 200137050, August 8, 2001).

Costs paid or incurred for the renewal of any amortizable section 197 license, permit, or other right granted by a government are amortized over the 15-year period that begins in the month of renewal (Reg. § 1.197-2(f)(3)(B)(4)).

A government-granted right in an interest in land (Code Sec. 197(e)(2)) (see ¶ 46) or in an interest under a lease of tangible property (Code Sec. 167(c)(2)) (see ¶ 52) is excluded from this category.

Depreciation if section 197 does not apply

For these intangibles that are not amortizable under Code Sec. 197, the value of a particular intangible is depreciable over the term of the license, permit or right.

However, an amortization deduction was denied for the cost of a liquor license and a taxicab license that represented a renewal privilege extending the existence of each for an indeterminable period because these privileges lacked a limited useful life (*Morris Nachman et al.*, CA-5, 51-2 USTC ¶ 9483; *W.K. Co.*, 56 TC 434, Dec. 30,798, aff'd CA-7 (unpublished order 5/21/73)).

Similarly, the cost of liquor license which is renewable is not amortizable because its life cannot be estimated with reasonable certainty (Rev. Rul. 70-248, 1970-1 CB 172).

For emission allowances see, ¶ 50.

¶ 34

Covenants Not to Compete

Section 197 treatment

This category of section 197 intangibles includes a covenant not to compete that is entered into in connection with the acquisition of a trade or business or a substantial portion thereof. For this purpose, an interest in the trade or business of a corporation or a partnership may be acquired through the direct purchase of its assets or by purchasing stock or partnership interests (Code Sec. 197(d)(1)(E); Reg. § 1.197-2(b)(9)).

Amounts paid under a covenant not to compete after the tax year in which the covenant is executed are amortized ratably over the remaining amortization period applicable to the covenant as of the beginning of the month that the amount is paid or incurred.

Arrangements similar to covenants not to compete are also covered, such as excessive compensation or rental paid to a former owner of a business for continuing to perform services or for the use of property if they benefit the trade or business.

Any amount paid or incurred pursuant to an amortizable section 197 covenant not to compete must be capitalized (Code Sec. 197(f)(3)).

A special rule defers a loss upon the disposition or worthlessness of an amortizable covenant until the disposition or worthlessness of all trades or businesses acquired in connection with the covenant (Code Sec. 197(f)(1)(B); Reg. § 1.197-2(g)(1)(iii)).

Depreciation if section 197 does not apply

A covenant not to compete that is not amortizable under Code Sec. 197 generally has a specified term and is, therefore, depreciable using the straight-line method.

A covenant not to compete was amortizable over the life of the covenant rather than a shorter period for which the payments were to be made because there was no evidence that the covenant was only enforceable for the shorter period (*Warsaw Photographic Associates, Inc.*, 84 TC 21, Dec. 41,822).

No current-year write-off was permitted for the remaining amounts owed under a covenant not to compete upon the death of the covenantor because no loss was incurred (*ABCO Oil Corp.*, 58 TCM 1280, Dec. 46,343(M), TC Memo. 1990-40).

No portion of the premium that a target corporation paid to two stockholders to repurchase its stock in order to avert a hostile takeover attempt was amortizable. The stock repurchase agreement allocated all of the financial consideration to stock and none to the non-stock items, such as a standstill covenant not to acquire any of the company's stock for a specified period (*Lane Bryant, Inc.*, CA-FC, 94-2 USTC ¶ 50,481).

A covenant not to compete is not amortizable under Code Sec. 197 or the pre-Code Sec. 197 rules unless (1) the covenant is genuine, i.e., it has economic significance apart from the tax consequences, (2) the parties intended to attribute some value to the covenant at the time they executed their formal buy-sell agreement, and (3) the covenant has been properly valued. For a detailed discussion of these requirements, see IRS Industry Specialization Program (ISP) Coordinated Issue Paper, Covenants Not to Compete (as revised September 1, 1998, and reproduced in full text in the CCH IRS POSITIONS Reporter at ¶ 80,245).

Income received pursuant to a covenant not to compete is treated as ordinary income. Such income should not be subject to self-employment tax since that tax applies to income derived from a "trade or business carried on" by a taxpayer. However, if the payment is actually for services rendered to the payor, for example, consulting services, then the self-employment tax applies (unless the services are performed as an employee) (*F.W. Steffens,* CA-11, 83-1 USTC ¶ 9425).

Covenants not to compete with related parties. Code Sec. 267(a)(2) may operate to defer amortization deductions with respect to unpaid amounts for a covenant not to compete with a related taxpayer (Temp. Reg. § 1.267(a)-2T(b)).

¶ 36

Franchises, Trademarks or Trade Names

Section 197 treatment

Franchises, trademarks or trade names are section 197 intangibles (Code Sec. 197(d)(1); Reg. § 1.197-2(b)(10)). See ¶ 56 for sports franchises.

A franchise includes any agreement that provides one of the parties to the agreement the right to distribute, sell, or provide goods, services, or facilities within a specified area (Code Sec. 1253(b)(1)).

Any license, permit, or other right granted by a governmental unit that otherwise meets the definition of a franchise, such as an FCC broadcast license or cable television franchise, is treated as a franchise. Thus, these licenses do not qualify for any exception from the definition of a section 197 intangible under Code Sec. 197(e)(4) (Reg. § 1.197-2(b)(10)).

The renewal of a franchise, trademark, or trade name that is a section 197 intangible is treated as an acquisition of the franchise, trademark, or trade name for those costs incurred in connection with the renewal (Code Sec. 197(f)(4)).

Costs paid or incurred to renew a franchise, trademark, or trade name are amortized over the 15-year period that begins in the month of the renewal (Reg. § 1.197-2(f)(3)(B)(4)).

Certain contingent payments (amounts dependent on productivity, use, or disposition) that are paid or incurred during the tax year regarding the transfer of a franchise, trademark, or trade name are deductible by the transferee as a trade or business expense provided that they are incurred in the conduct of a trade or business (Code Sec. 1253(d)(1)(A)). This deduction is restricted to payments that are (a) contingent amounts paid as part of a series of amounts payable at least annually throughout the term of the transfer agreement and (b) substantially equal in amount or to be paid under a fixed formula (Code Sec. 1253(d)(1)(B)).

Contingent payments (deductible as a business expense within the above situation) are not charged to the capital account of the intangible, are excluded from the basis of the intangible asset acquired by the transferee, and do not qualify for amortization under Code Sec. 197 (Code Secs. 1253(d)(2) and 197(f)(4)(C)). All other amounts, whether fixed or contingent, that are paid on account of the transfer of a franchise, trademark, or trade name that are section 197 intangibles are chargeable to capital account and are ratably amortized over a 15-year period (Reg. § 1.197-2(g)(6)).

Depreciation if section 197 does not apply

The rule that specifically prohibited the allowance of depreciation deductions regarding trademark or trade name expenditures was repealed for expenditures paid or incurred after October 2, 1989 (except for certain binding contracts) (former Code Sec. 167(r)) before repeal by the Omnibus Budget Reconciliation Act of 1989 (P.L. 101-239). Thus, expenditures for the acquisition of a new trademark or trade name may be amortizable under the general principles applicable to intangible assets.

Similar rules apply to the purchase of an existing trademark, trade name, or franchise; however, Code Sec. 1253 may allow more favorable treatment for certain transfers.

Contingent payments. Regarding the amortization aspects of such provision, the treatment of contingent serial payments made for the transfer, sale, or other disposition of a franchise, trademark, or trade name by a transferee that do not qualify for a business expense deduction (Code Sec. 1253(d)(1)) because they are not payable at least annually for the entire term of the transfer agreement or are not substantially equal in amount depends on when the intangible was acquired.

For franchises, trademarks or trade names generally acquired after August 10, 1993, contingent payments that are not deductible as business expenses are treated as amounts chargeable to a capital account (Code Sec. 1253(d)(2)). Consequently, they are includible in section 197 intangible property and are amortized under the straight-line method over a 15-year period beginning with the month in which the intangible was acquired (Code Sec. 197(a)).

For franchises, trademarks or trade names generally acquired before August 11, 1993, contingent payments that are not deductible as business expenses are also treated as an amount chargeable to a capital account (Code Sec. 1253(d)(3)(A), before amendment by the Omnibus Budget Reconciliation Act of 1993 (P.L. 103-66)). There are two choices for recovering this capital.

(1) An election could be made to amortize this amount under the straight-line method over a 25-year period beginning with the tax year in which the transfer occurred (Code Sec. 1253(d)(3)(B), before amendment by the Omnibus Budget Reconciliation Act of 1993 (P.L. 103-66)).

(2) The amount may be amortized under the general principles applicable to intangible property, provided that the asset has an ascertainable limited

life which can be determined with reasonable accuracy and it has an ascertainable value (Reg. § 1.167(a)-3).

Noncontingent payments. Amounts not dependent upon productivity, use or disposition are noncontingent payments.

(A) The treatment of an initial fee paid by a transferee where the transferor retains no significant power, right, or continuing interest in the transferred intangible and the transfer is a sale or exchange qualifying for capital gain treatment depends on when the intangible was acquired.

(1) For franchises, trademarks and trade names generally acquired after August 10, 1993, an initial fee paid by a transferee in a sale or exchange of an intangible is an amount chargeable to a capital account (Code Sec. 1253(d)(2)). Consequently, it is includible in section 197 intangible property and is amortized under the straight-line method over a 15-year period beginning with the month in which the intangible was acquired (Code Sec. 197(a)).

(2) For these intangibles generally acquired before August 11, 1993, an initial fee paid by a transferee in a sale or exchange of an intangible is also an amount chargeable to a capital account (Code Sec. 1253(d)(3)(A), before amendment by the Omnibus Budget Reconciliation Act of 1993 (P.L. 103-66)). However, this capital may be recovered by an amortization deduction under the general principles applicable to intangible property provided that the asset has a limited useful life that can be determined with reasonable accuracy and it has an ascertainable value (Reg. § 1.167(a)-3).

(B) The treatment of an initial fee paid by a transferee where the transferor retains a significant power, right, or continuing interest in the transferred intangible and the transfer is considered a license depends on when the intangible was acquired.

(1) For these intangibles generally acquired after August 10, 1993, an initial fee paid by a transferee in a license of an intangible is an amount chargeable to a capital account (Code Sec. 1253(d)(2)). Consequently, it is includible in section 197 intangible property and is amortized under the straight-line method over a 15-year period beginning with the month in which the intangible was acquired (Code Sec. 197(a)).

(2) For these intangibles generally acquired before August 11, 1993, an initial fee paid by a transferee in a license of an intangible that the transferee treats as an amount chargeable to a capital account is subject to the following deduction rules (Code Sec. 1253(d), before amendment by the Omnibus Budget Reconciliation Act of 1993 (P.L. 103-66)).

The transferee may amortize a single lump-sum noncontingent payment which is made in discharge of an initial fee that does not exceed $100,000 under the straight-line method over the shorter of 10 consecutive tax years or the term of the agreement (Code Sec. 1253(d)(2)(A)(i), before amendment by the Omnibus Budget Reconciliation Act of 1993 (P.L. 103-66)).

For transfers generally after October 2, 1989, and before August 11, 1993, this amortization deduction is not allowed if the single lump-sum payment is in discharge of an initial fee that is larger than $100,000 (Code Sec. 1253(d)(2)(B), before amendment by the Omnibus Budget Reconciliation Act of 1993 (P.L. 103-66)). In this situation, there are two choices for recovering capital:

(1) An election could be made to amortize this amount under the straight-line method over a 25-year period beginning with the tax year in which the transfer occurred (Code Sec. 1253(d)(3)(B), before amendment by the Omnibus Budget Reconciliation Act of 1993 (P.L. 103-66)).

(2) The amount may be amortized under the general principles applicable to intangible property, provided that the asset has a limited useful life that can be determined with reasonable accuracy and an ascertainable value (Reg. § 1.167(a)-3).

¶ 40

Disqualified Intangibles

The categories of intangible property discussed at ¶ 42-60 are specifically excluded from the term section 197 intangibles (Code Sec. 197(e)). Thus, they do not qualify for the amortization deduction under Code Sec. 197. Accordingly, depreciation-amortization treatment under Code Sec. 167 may apply to these intangibles if they have a limited life that can be determined with reasonable accuracy and an ascertainable value.

¶ 42

Interests in a Corporation, Partnership, Trust, or Estate

The cost of acquiring these interests is not amortizable under Code Sec. 197 whether or not such interests are regularly traded on an established market (Code Sec. 197(e)(1)(A); Reg. § 1.197-2(c)(1)).

¶ 44

Interests Under Certain Financial Contracts

Interests excluded from section 197 intangibles include an existing futures contract, foreign currency contract, notional principal contract, interest rate swap, or other similar financial contracts (Code Sec. 197(e)(1)(B)).

An interest under a mortgage servicing contract, credit card servicing contract, or other contract to service indebtedness that was issued by another person, and any interest under an assumption reinsurance contract are not excluded from the definition of a section 197 intangible by reason of this exception (Reg. § 1.197-2(c)(2)).

¶ 46

Interests in Land

This exclusion from section 197 intangibles includes a fee interest, life estate, remainder, easement, mineral rights, timber rights, grazing rights, riparian rights, air rights, zoning variances, and any other similar rights, such as a farm allotment, quota for farm commodities, or crop acreage base (Code Sec. 197(e)(2); Reg. § 1.197-2(c)(2)).

However, an airport landing or takeoff right, regulated airline route, and a franchise to provide cable television services are not excluded from the definition of section 197 intangible by reason of this exception (Reg. § 1.197-2(c)(3)).

The cost of acquiring a license, permit, or other land improvement right, such as a building construction permit or use permit, is taken into account in the same manner as the underlying improvement (Reg. § 1.197-2(c)(3)).

Easements. Right-of-way easements for oil pipelines, electric transmission lines, etc., are depreciable using the straight-line method if a useful life can be established. See also ¶ 5 as to grading and land preparation costs with respect to an easement.

¶ 48
Computer Software

Depreciable computer software generally acquired after August 10, 1993, that is not an amortizable section 197 intangible is depreciated using the straight-line method over a three-year period beginning on the first day of the month that the software is placed in service. Salvage value is considered zero. No amortization is allowed in the month of disposition. In a short tax year the amortization deduction is based on the number of months in the tax year (Code Sec. 167(f); Reg. § 1.167(a)-14)).

The three-year amortization period also applies to separately acquired computer software whose costs are separately stated and required to be capitalized (Reg. § 1.167(a)-14; Rev. Proc. 2000-50).

Computer software whose cost is included, without being separately stated, in the cost of the hardware or other tangible property is treated as part of the cost of the hardware or other tangible property (Reg. § 1.167(a)-14(b); Rev. Proc. 2000-50). For example, software programs loaded onto a computer and included in the price of the computer without being separately stated, are depreciated as part of the cost of the computer, i.e., over five years under MACRS.

"Off-the-shelf" computer software is eligible for expensing under Code Sec. 179 if placed in service in a tax year beginning in 2003 through 2009. See ¶ 302.

Computer software is considered a section 197 intangible only if acquired in a transaction involving the acquisition of assets constituting a trade or business. However, computer software that is readily available for purchase by the general public, is subject to a nonexclusive license, and has not been substantially modified is not a section 197 intangible even if acquired in connection with the acquisition of a trade or business (Code Sec. 197(e)(3)). The publicly available exception is detailed in Reg. § 1.197-2(c)(4)(i) at ¶ 587).

Computer software defined. Computer software is defined broadly to include any program designed to cause a computer to perform a desired function. However, a database or similar item is not considered computer software unless it is in the public domain and is incidental to the operation of otherwise qualifying computer software (Code Sec. 197(e)(3)(B)).

Software includes computer programs of all classes (such as operating systems, executive systems, monitors, compilers, translators, assembly routines, utility programs, and application programs).

Refer to Reg. § 1.197-2(c)(4)(iv) at ¶ 587 and Rev. Proc. 2000-50 for additional details regarding the definition of computer software.

Developed software. Depreciable software programs developed by a taxpayer are treated in a manner similar to that of research and development expenses under Code Sec. 174 (Rev. Proc. 2000-50, superseding Rev. Proc. 69-21). They may be either (1) deducted as a current expense or (2) capitalized and amortized using the straight-line method over a period of three years beginning in the month the software is placed in service or over 60 months from the date of completion of development if a Code Sec. 174(b) election is made (Reg. § 1.167(a)-14(b)(1); Rev. Proc. 2000-50).

Rented software. Rental payments for leased software programs that are not subject to Code Sec. 197 may be deductible as a business expense over the term of the lease as provided in Reg. § 1.162-11 (Reg. § 1.167(a)-14(b)(2)). Code Sec. 197 applies to certain costs incurred with respect to leased software (that is, costs to acquire a section 197 intangible that is a limited interest in software).

Licensing transactions. Software costs are currently deductible if they are not chargeable to capital account under the Code Sec. 197 rules applicable to licensing transactions and are otherwise currently deductible. For this purpose, a payment described in Reg. § 1.162-11 is not currently deductible if, without regard to that regulation, the payment is properly chargeable to capital account (Reg. § 1.197-2(a)(3)). A proper and consistent practice of taking software costs into account under Reg. § 1.162-11 may, however, be continued if the costs are not subject to Code Sec. 197.

Enterprise software. A recent IRS letter ruling addresses in specific detail the proper tax treatment of various costs, including consulting costs, associated with a corporation's purchase, development, and implementation of Enterprise Resource Planning (ERP) software and related hardware (IRS Letter Ruling 200236028, June 4, 2002). ERP software is a shell that integrates different software modules for financial accounting, inventory control, production, sales and distribution, and human resources. Any taxpayer that has or intends to install ERP software (or any other major software) should carefully review this ruling.

The ruling concludes that:

(1) The cost of purchased ERP software (including sales tax) is amortized ratably over 36 months;

(2) Employee training and related costs (maintenance, troubleshooting, running reports) under the consulting contract during the training period are deductible as current expenses;

(3) Separately stated computer hardware costs are depreciated as 5-year MACRS property;

(4) The costs of writing machine readable code software (and an allocable portion of modeling and design of additional software) under the taxpayer's consulting contracts are treated as developed software and currently deductible in a manner similar to research and development expenditures pursuant to Rev. Proc. 2002-50. See "*Developed software*," above; and

(5) The costs of option selection and implementation of existing embedded ERP templates (and an allocable portion of the costs of modeling and design of additional software) under the taxpayer's consulting contracts are installation/modification costs that are amortized as part of the purchased ERP software over 36 months.

With respect to item five, treatment as developed software was predicated upon the fact that the taxpayer bore the risk of failure. Though not specifically stated in the ruling, if the consultant had guaranteed success, these costs would likely have been amortized over 36 months.

Useful life less than one year. Computer software with a useful life of less than one year is currently deductible as a business expense.

Y2K expenses. Costs incurred to convert or replace computer software to recognize dates beginning in the year 2000 (i.e., year 2000 costs) must be treated in accordance with the guidelines contained in Rev. Proc. 2000-50 (Rev. Proc. 97-50, as modified by Rev. Proc. 2000-50).

Pre-Code Sec. 197 rules. For depreciable computer software generally purchased before August 11, 1993, if the cost of the software is not separately stated but is included in the price of the computer hardware, the entire amount is treated as the cost of the hardware (tangible property) and is depreciable under MACRS over a five-year recovery period. If the cost of the purchased software (intangible property) is separately stated, the cost is amortized using the straight-line method over a period of five years (unless a shorter useful life is established) (Rev. Proc. 69-21, prior to being superseded by Rev. Proc. 2000-50).

The final regulations under Code Sec. 197 and 167(f) are generally effective for property acquired after January 25, 2000.

Case law. Purchased software may also involve the question of whether intangible computer program information is independent from the tangible medium used as a means of delivery. If it is independent, the software is intangible personal property (*Bank of Vermont*, DC Vt., 88-1 USTC ¶ 9169). If the medium is inherently connected to the existence of the computer program information itself, the software is tangible property (*Texas Instruments, Inc.*, CA-5, 77-1 USTC ¶ 9384, 551 F2d 576). Purchased computer program master source codes were inextricably connected with the medium (tapes and discs) because the investment could not be placed in a productive usable form without the tangible medium. The feasibility of receiving the data without the tapes and discs (via computer-to-computer telephone link and transfer of the data to tapes and discs by the taxpayer) was irrelevant (*Comshare Inc.*, CA-6, 94-2 USTC ¶ 50,318).

Change in accounting method. The IRS will grant automatic consent to change to a method of accounting for software costs that is described in Rev. Proc. 2000-50 (Rev. Proc. 2004-11, deleting and replacing Appendix Section 2B of Rev. Proc. 2002-9).

¶ 50

Separately Acquired Interests

The following interests and rights are not a section 197 intangible if they are not acquired in a transaction involving the acquisition of the assets of a trade or business or a substantial portion thereof (Code Sec. 197(e)(4)):

(1) an interest (such as a licensee) in a film, sound recording, video tape, book or similar property (including the right to broadcast or transmit a live event) (Reg. § 1.197-2(c)(5));

(2) a right to receive tangible property or services under a contract or granted by a governmental entity (Reg. § 1.197-2(c)(6));

(3) an interest in a patent or copyright (Reg. § 1.197-2(c)(7)); and

(4) a right received under a contract (or granted by a governmental entity) if the right has a fixed duration of less than 15 years *or* is fixed in amount and would be recoverable under a method similar to the unit-of-production method.

The item (4) exclusion does not apply to goodwill, going concern value, a covenant not to compete, a franchise, trademark, or tradename, a customer-based intangible, a customer-related information base, or any other similar item (Reg. § 1.197-2(c)(13)). With certain exceptions, these intangibles are amortizable under Code Sec. 197 even though separately acquired.

With respect to item (4), the basis of a right to an unspecified amount over a fixed duration of less than 15 years is amortized ratably over the period of the right. The basis of a right to a fixed amount is amortized for each tax year by multiplying the basis by a fraction. The numerator is the amount received during the tax year and the denominator is the total amount received or to be received (Reg. § 1.197-2(c)(2)).

The manner of recovering the cost of a right to receive tangible property or services described in item (2) is similar to the item (4) methodology (Reg. § 1.167(a)-14(c)(1)).

Only those costs incurred by a manufacturer in connection with acquisition of a manufacturing certificate (permit) issued by a government agency for a specific products which were required to be capitalized under Code Sec. 263(a) were amortizable under Code Sec. 197. Depending upon the development of additional facts and analysis, certain identified costs may be treated as pre-production costs of the product under Code Sec. 263A or, alternatively, allowable as a credit or deduction under Code Secs 41 and 174 (Field Service Advice Memorandum 200137023, June 13, 2001).

Emission allowances. The tax treatment of a sulfur dioxide emission allowance issued by the Environmental Protection Agency is detailed in Rev. Proc. 92-91, 1992-2 CB 503. The Committee Report for the Revenue Reconciliation Act of 1993 (P.L. 103-66) indicates that Code Sec. 197 is not intended "to disturb the result in Rev. Proc. 92-91." See footnote 144 of the report. As a result, it appears that such emission allowances do not need to be amortized under Code Sec. 197.

In general, Rev. Proc. 92-91 provides that emission allowances are not depreciable under any method, including the unit-of-production method, and that the cost of an allowance is recovered as sulfur dioxide is emitted. However, capitalization may be required in some instances and the cost of make-up allowances purchased at the end of the year are deducted under the taxpayer's method of accounting pursuant to Code Sec. 461.

¶ 52

Interests Under Existing Leases of Tangible Property

The acquisition of an interest as a lessor or a lessee under an existing lease or sublease of tangible real or personal property is excluded from the definition of a section 197 intangible (Code Sec. 197(e)(5); Reg. § 1.197-2(c)(8)). See also ¶ 5.

¶ 54

Interests Under Existing Indebtedness

Creditor or debtor interests in an indebtedness that is in existence on the date the interest is acquired, except for a deposit base and other similar items of a financial institution specified in Code Sec. 197(d)(2)(B), are not section 197 intangibles (Code Sec. 197(e)(5); Reg. § 1.197-2(c)(9)). Thus, the value of assuming an existing indebtedness with a below-market interest rate or the premium paid for acquiring a debt interest with an above-market interest rate is not amortizable under Code Sec. 197.

Additionally, mortgage servicing rights, to the extent that they are stripped coupons within the meaning of Code Sec. 1286, are not section 197 intangibles by reason of this exception. See also ¶ 58.

¶ 56

Sports Franchises

A franchise to engage in professional football, basketball, baseball, or any other professional sport, as well as any item acquired in connection with such a franchise, is not a section 197 intangible if it is acquired on or before October 22, 2004 (Code Sec. 197(e)(6), prior to being stricken by the American Jobs Creation Act of 2004 (P.L. 108-357); Reg. § 1.197-2(c)(10)).

The IRS has issued a comprehensive MSSP audit guide covering most tax issues involved in purchasing and operating a sports franchise (Market Segment Specialization Program (MSSP) Audit Technique Guide—Sports Franchises (8-99)). Among depreciation-related issued covered are depreciation of a sports stadium (including leasehold improvements) and amortization of player contracts and broadcasting rights.

¶ 58

Residential Mortgage Servicing Rights

The right to service indebtedness that is secured by residential property is not a section 197 intangible unless it is acquired in a transaction or series of related transactions involving the acquisition of the assets (other than the mortgage servicing rights) of a trade or business or of a substantial portion of a trade or business (Code Sec. 197(e)(7); Reg. § 1.197-2(c)(11)).

Depreciable residential mortgage servicing rights generally acquired after August 10, 1993, that are not section 197 intangibles may be depreciated under the straight-line method over a nine-year period under Code Sec. 167(f) (Reg. § 1.167(a)-14(d)). Such rights generally acquired before August 11, 1993, were depreciated over their useful lives (Reg. § 1.167(a)-3). See also ¶ 10.

However, a mortgage servicing right that is treated as a stripped coupon under Code Sec. 1286 is not depreciable (Rev. Rul. 91-46, 1991-2 CB 358).

¶ 60

Corporate Transaction Costs

Fees paid for professional services and other transactions incurred in a corporate organization or reorganization (Code Secs. 351-368) in which gain or loss is not recognized are not section 197 intangibles (Code Sec. 197(e)(8); Reg. § 1.197-2(c)(11)).

Corporate charters. Corporate charters generally are for indefinite periods and therefore are not depreciable. However, an election may be made to deduct the first $5,000 of organizational expenses (subject to a phase-out rule) and amortizing the remainder using the straight-line method over a 15-year period beginning with the month in which the corporation begins business (Code Sec. 248).

¶ 64

Certain Nonrecognition Transfers

In certain exchanges of section 197 intangibles, a transferee is treated as the transferor with respect to the portion of adjusted basis which does not exceed the adjusted basis of the transferor. This step-into-the-shoes rule applies to a section 197 intangible acquired:

(1) in any transaction between members of the same affiliated group during a tax year for which a consolidated return is filed, or

(2) in nonrecognition transactions under Code Secs. 332, 351, 361, 721, 731, 1031, or 1033 (Code Sec. 197(f)(2); Reg. § 1.197-2(g)(1)(C)).

Example: An individual amortized a section 197 intangible for five years, and the remaining unamortized basis of the asset is $300,000. In a like-kind exchange, the intangible and $100,000 are exchanged for another section 197 intangible. The adjusted basis of the acquired intangible is $400,000. Of such amount, $300,000 attributable to the basis of the old property is amortized over the remaining 10-year period attributable to the old property and $100,000 is amortized over a 15-year period.

¶ 66

15-Year Safe-Harbor for Self-Created Intangibles

Reg.§ 1.167(a)-3(b) provides a safe harbor that allows a taxpayer to amortize certain created intangibles that do not have readily ascertainable useful lives over a

15-year period using the straight-line method and no salvage value. For example, amounts paid to acquire memberships or privileges of indefinite duration, such as a trade association membership, are covered by this safe harbor. The provision applies to intangibles created on or after December 31, 2003 (Reg.§ 1.167(a)-3(b), as added by T.D. 9107). Change of accounting method procedures are described below.

Eligible intangibles are those not specifically excluded from the scope of the provision. The following intangibles, described in more detail below, are not eligible:

(1) Any intangible acquired from another person;

(2) Created financial interests;

(3) Any intangible that has a useful life that can be estimated with reasonable accuracy;

(4) Any intangible that has an amortization period or useful life that is specifically prescribed by the Code, regulations, or other published IRS guidance; or

(5) Any intangible for which an amortization period or useful life is specifically proscribed by the Code, regulations, or other published IRS guidance.

The safe-harbor also does not apply to any amount that is required to be capitalized by Reg.§ 1.263(a)-5. In general, these are amounts paid to facilitate an acquisition of a trade or business, a change in the capital structure of a business entity, and certain other transactions.

Intangibles acquired from another person. The safe-harbor provision does not apply to intangibles described in Reg.§ 1.263(a)-4(c) (Reg.§ 1.167(a)-3(b)(1)(i)). This regulation requires the capitalization of amounts paid to another party to acquire any intangible from that party in a purchase or similar transaction. The regulation lists numerous examples (i.e., a nonexclusive list) of intangibles within the scope of the provision. The following intangibles are specifically listed:

(1) An ownership interest in a corporation, partnership, trust, estate, limited liability company, or other entity;

(2) A debt instrument, deposit, stripped bond, stripped coupon, regular interest in a REMIC or FASIT, or any other intangible treated as debt for federal income tax purposes;

(3) A financial instrument, such as a notional principal contract, foreign currency contract, futures contract, a forward contract, an option, and any other financial derivative;

(4) An endowment contract, annuity contract, or insurance contract;

(5) A lease;

(6) A patent or copyright;

(7) A franchise, trademark or tradename;

(8) An assembled workforce;

(9) Goodwill or going concern value;

(10) A customer list;

(11) A servicing right;

(12) A customer-based intangible or supplier-based intangible;

(13) Computer software; and

(14) An agreement providing either party the right to use, possess or sell the first five types of intangibles described above (certain ownership interests through nonfunctional currency).

Note that many of these intangibles may be amortized over 15 years under Code Sec. 197.

Created financial interests. The 15-year safe harbor amortization provision does not apply to a created financial interest described in Reg.§ 1.263(a)-4(d)(2) (Reg.§ 1.167(a)-3(b)(1)(i)). The specified financial interests are:

(1) An ownership interest in a corporation, partnership, trust, estate, limited liability company, or other entity;

(2) A debt instrument, deposit, stripped bond, stripped coupon (including a servicing right treated for federal income tax purposes as a stripped coupon), regular interest in a REMIC or FASIT, or any other intangible treated as debt for federal income tax purposes;

(3) A financial instrument, such as a letter of credit, credit card agreement, notional principal contract, foreign currency contract, futures contract, forward contract, an option, and any other financial derivative;

(4) An endowment contract, annuity contract, or insurance contract that has or may have cash value;

(5) Non-functional currency; and

(6) An agreement that provides either party the right to use, possess or sell a financial interest described in items (1)-(5), above.

Intangibles with reasonably certain useful life. The safe harbor does not apply to created intangibles that have readily ascertainable useful lives on which amortization can be based. Taxpayers may amortize intangible assets with reasonably estimable useful lives in accordance with Reg.§ 1.167(a)-3(a). For example, prepaid expenses, contracts with a fixed duration, and certain contract terminations have readily ascertainable useful lives. Prepaid expenses are amortized over the period covered by the prepayment. Amounts paid to induce another to enter into a contract with a fixed duration are amortized over the duration of the contract. Amounts paid by a lessor to terminate a lease contract are amortized over the remaining term of the lease (*Peerless Weighing and Vending Machine Corp.*, 52 T.C. 850, Dec. 29,713).

Intangibles with assigned useful life. The safe-harbor provision does not apply to any intangible that has an amortization period or useful life that is specifically prescribed by the Code, regulations, or other published IRS guidance. For example, an expense may not be amortized under this provision if it is amortizable under Code Sec. 167(f)(1)(A) (prescribing a 36-month life for certain computer software); Code Sec. 171 (prescribing rules for determining the amortization period for bond premium); Code Sec. 178 (prescribing the amortization period for costs to acquire a lease); Reg. § Reg.§ 1.167(a)-14(d)(1) (prescribing a 108-month useful life for mortgage servicing rights); Code Sec. 197(prescribing a 15 year amortization period for amortizable section 197 intangibles); Code Sec. 195 (prescribing a 180 month amortization period for capitalized start-up expenses); Code Sec. 248 (prescribing a 180 month amortization period for capitalized organizational expenditures); or Code Sec. 709 (prescribing a 180 month amortization period for capitalized partnership organization and syndication fees).

Amounts paid to facilitate an acquisition of a trade or business, a change in the capital structure of a business entity, and certain other transactions. The 15-year safe harbor amortization provision does not apply to an amount that must be capitalized under Reg.§ 1.263(a)-5 (Reg.§ 1.167(a)-3(b)(2)). In general, Reg.§ 1.263(a)-5 requires a taxpayer to capitalize an amount paid to facilitate each of the following transactions:

(1) An acquisition of assets that constitute a trade or business (whether the taxpayer is the acquirer in the acquisition or the target of the acquisition);

(2) An acquisition by the taxpayer of an ownership interest in a business entity if, immediately after the acquisition, the taxpayer and the business entity are related within the meaning of Code Sec. 267(b) or Code Sec. 707(b);

(3) An acquisition of an ownership interest in the taxpayer (other than an acquisition by the taxpayer of an ownership interest in the taxpayer, whether by redemption or otherwise);

(4) A restructuring, recapitalization, or reorganization of the capital structure of a business entity;

(5) A transfer described in Code Sec. 351 and Code Sec. 721 (whether the taxpayer is the transferor or transferee);

(6) A formation or organization of a disregarded entity;

(7) An acquisition of capital;

(8) A stock issuance;

(9) A borrowing. A borrowing means any issuance of debt, including an issuance of debt in an acquisition of capital or recapitalization and a debt issued in a debt or debt exchange under Reg.§ 1.1001-1-3; and

(10) Writing an option.

25-year amortization period for certain intangibles related to benefits arising from the provision, production, or improvement of real property. A taxpayer must increase the 15-year safe-harbor amortization period to 25 years if the intangible asset is described in Reg.§ 1.263(a)-4(d)(8) (Reg.§ 1.167(a)-3(b)(1)(iv)).

Under Reg.§ 1.263(a)-4(d)(8), a taxpayer must capitalize amounts paid for real property if the taxpayer transfers ownership of the real property to another person (except to the extent the real property is sold for fair market value) and if the real property can reasonably be expected to produce significant economic benefits to the taxpayer after the transfer.

The regulation also requires a taxpayer to capitalize amounts paid to produce or improve real property owned by another (except to the extent the taxpayer is selling services at fair market value to produce or improve the real property) if the real property can reasonably be expected to produce significant economic benefits for the taxpayer.

For purposes of this regulation, real property includes property indefinitely affixed to real property such as roads, bridges, tunnels, pavements, wharves and docks, breakwaters and sea walls, elevators, power generation and transmission facilities, and pollution control facilities.

Example (1): A shipping company contributes a breakwater to a port authority to enable the authority to build a larger breakwater that will benefit the company by enabling it to unload its ships in bad weather. The adjusted basis of the breakwater at the time of contribution may be amortized over 25 years (Reg.§ 1.263(a)-4(d)(8), Example 1).

Example (2): A contribution of $100,000 to a city to structurally improve an existing bridge to enable the taxpayer's trucks to use the bridge is capitalized. The capitalized amount can be amortized over 25 years (Reg.§ 1.263(a)-4(d)(8), Example 2).

Impact fees and dedicated improvements contributed by developers are not amortizable under this safe-harbor provision (Reg.§ 1.263(a)-4(d)(8)(iv), and (v), Example 3).

How to compute the safe harbor amortization deduction. Amortization under this provision is determined by amortizing the basis of the intangible asset ratably over the 15 (or 25) year assigned useful life beginning on the first day of the month in which the intangible asset is placed in service by the taxpayer. No amortization deduction may be claimed in the month of disposition (Reg.§ 1.167(a)-3(b)(3)).

Changes in accounting method. In conjunction with the issuance of T.D. 9107, the IRS has issued three revenue procedures that taxpayers must use to obtain automatic consent to change to a method of accounting provided for in Reg.§ 1.167(a)-3(b).

The first revenue procedure applies to a taxpayer that makes the change in its first tax year ending on or after December 31, 2003 (Rev. Proc. 2004-23, 2004-1 CB 785, as modified by Rev. Proc. 2004-57, 2004-2 CB 498). The next revenue procedure applies to a taxpayer's second tax year ending on or after December 31, 2003 (Rev. Proc. 2005-9, 2005-1 CB 303, as modified by Rev. Proc. 2005-17, 2005-1 CB 797).

The third procedure applies to tax years ending on or after December 31, 2005 and for any earlier tax year that is after the taxpayer's second tax year ending on or after December 31, 2003 (Rev. Proc. 2006-12 , 2006-1 CB 310, superseding Rev. Proc. 2004-23, 2004-1 CB 785, and Rev. Proc. 2005-9, 2005-1 CB 303). This third procedure was modified to allow a taxpayer to utilize the advance consent procedures when seeking a change to a method of accounting provided in the final regulations in conjunction with a change for the same item to a method of accounting utilizing the 3 1/2 month rule authorized by Reg. § 1.461-4(d)(6)(ii) or the recurring item exception authorized by Reg. § 1.461-5 (Rev. Proc. 2006-37, 2006-2 CB 499, modifying Rev. Proc. 2006-12).

The IRS announced in the preamble to the related proposed regulations (REG-125638-01, 2003-1 C.B. 373) that it would not grant a request to change to a method of accounting provided for in T.D. 9107 for a tax year earlier than the effective date provided by the final regulations. These procedure contains special guidance for a taxpayer that made an unauthorized change in method of accounting.

¶ 67

15-year Safe-Harbor Amortization of Film Industry Creative Property Costs

The IRS has issued a safe-harbor method of accounting that allows taxpayers in the film industry to amortize creative property costs ratably over a 15-year period. The safe-harbor is effective for tax years ending *on or after* December 31, 2003 (Rev. Proc. 2004-36; Rev. Proc. 2008-52, Appendix Section 14.06).

The safe-harbor allows a taxpayer to amortize the cost of purchasing creative property, such as a film script or production rights to a book or play, in the tax year that the cost of the creative property is written off for financial accounting purpose in accordance with Statement of Position 00-2, as issued by the American Institute of Certified Public Accountants (AICPA) on June 12, 2000. Under these guidelines, a write-off is allowed if the property is not scheduled for production within three years of acquisition. (Only a small percentage of creative property is set for production within three years). If a taxpayer decides not to set the property for production at an earlier time, the write-off is allowed then.

Prior to issuance of this safe harbor, taxpayers were required (for tax purposes) to capitalize creative property costs and could not recover these costs through depreciation (e.g., under the income-forecast method) or amortization unless a film or similar property was actually produced.

In related guidance, the IRS ruled that a Code Sec. 165(a) loss for the capitalized costs of acquiring or developing a creative property may not be claimed unless the producer establishes an intention to abandon the property and an affirmative act of abandonment occurs, or there is an identifiable event that evidences a closed or completed transaction that establishes worthlessness (Rev. Rul. 2004-58, 2004-1 CB 1043). Since creative properties not set for production are generally retained indefinitely, Code Sec. 165(a) deductions are generally not available. Consequently, the safe-harbor method is of particular benefit to the film industry and should also encourage the acquisition of creative property from script writers, novelists, and playwrights.

Creative property costs defined. For purposes of the 15-year amortization safe harbor, creative property costs are costs to *acquire and develop* (for purposes of potential future film development, production, and exploitation):

(1) screenplays;

(2) scripts;

(3) story outlines;

(4) motion picture production rights to books and plays; and

(5) similar properties.

Costs that are written off under SOP 00-2 must be amortized under the safe-harbor ratably over 15 years beginning on the first day of the second half of the tax year in which the write-off occurs. All creative property costs that are written off in the same tax year for financial accounting purposes are aggregated and treated as a single asset for amortization purposes.

Once amortization with respect to a creative property cost begins, the taxpayer must continue amortizing the cost even if (1) the creative property is later set for production or (2) the creative property is disposed of in a sale, exchange, abandonment, or other disposition.

Upon a disposition, the basis of the creative property is considered zero. Thus, no loss is recognized upon the disposition and any gain is ordinary income.

However, if a taxpayer disposes of all of its creative property (e.g., through the sale of the taxpayer's entire trade or business), any gain attributable to the disposition of creative property costs that were amortized under the safe-harbor is ordinary income to the extent of the amortization allowed.

Additional costs paid or incurred after amortization begins. Additional costs may be paid or incurred with respect to a creative property in a tax year after amortization has begun with respect to the initial costs for that property. These additional costs are amortized over a 15-year period beginning on the first day of the second half of the tax year in which they are paid or incurred.

A taxpayer may set a creative property for production in a tax year after amortization of creative costs has begun (e.g., the taxpayer sets the property in production more than three years from the time of the first capitalization transaction). Creative costs paid or incurred after the property has been set for production must be capitalized and depreciated using an allowable depreciation method at the time the property is placed in service by the taxpayer. Costs for which amortization has begun are continued to be amortized over the remainder of the 15-year amortization period.

Procedures for changing to safe-harbor method. Taxpayers who wish to change to this safe-harbor method for amortizing qualifying creative property costs should follow the automatic consent procedures of Rev. Proc. 2008-52, Appendix Section 14.06.

Audit protection. Certain taxpayers may currently be using a method consistent with the safe-harbor method for a tax year that ends before December 31, 2003. The IRS will not challenge the use of such a consistent method in an audit. Similarly, if the issue is currently under examination, before an appeals office, or before the U.S. Tax Court for a tax year that ends before December 31, 2003, the issue will not be pursued by the IRS.

Losses for abandonment or worthlessness of creative property. In conjunction with issuance of the 15-year amortization safe-harbor, the IRS has issued a revenue ruling which holds that a taxpayer may not deduct the costs of acquiring and developing creative property as a loss under Code Sec. 165(a) unless the taxpayer (1) establishes an intention to abandon the property and there is an affirmative act of abandonment, or (2) there is an identifiable event or events that evidence a closed and completed transaction establishing worthlessness (Rev. Rul. 2004-58, 2004-1CB 1043).

The ruling effectively prevents a taxpayer from claiming a Code Sec. 165(a) loss deduction for most creative property costs because taxpayers typically retain rights to a creative property indefinitely even if a decision not to proceed to production has been made. The fact that a taxpayer writes off creative property costs under SOP 00-2 does not establish an abandonment loss or a loss for worthlessness.

The ruling described three fact situations:

In the first situation, a taxpayer purchases the exclusive rights to a script for the remainder of its copyright term. The taxpayer makes a decision not to set the script to production and writes the cost off for financial accounting purposes. The taxpayer, however, retains all rights to the script indefinitely. No Code Sec. 165(a) deduction may be claimed.

In the second situation, a taxpayer purchases limited exploitation rights to a screenplay. All rights in the screenplay expire after four years if it is not set into production. The screenplay is not set to production within four years. At the end of the third year the taxpayer may write the costs off for financial accounting purposes. However, a Code Sec. 165(a) deduction may not be claimed until the fourth year when all the rights tot he screenplay have expired.

In the third situation, a taxpayer purchases exclusive motion picture rights from the author of a novel. The fact that no other studio will purchase the rights from the taxpayer does not establish the worthlessness of those rights. So long as the taxpayer retains the rights, no Code Sec. 165(a) deduction may be claimed.

¶ 68

Research and Experimental Expenditures

Research and experimental expenditures paid or incurred in connection with a trade or business may be treated as not chargeable to a capital account and currently deducted as a research expense instead of depreciated (Code Sec. 174(a)(1); Reg. § 1.174-3(a)). Depreciation deductions on property used in connection with research or experimentation are research expenditures (Code Sec. 174(c); Reg. § 1.174-2(b)(1)).

An election may be made to defer and amortize research and experimental expenditures chargeable to a capital account regarding property that has no determinable useful life and, therefore, is not depreciable (Code Sec. 174(b); Reg. § 1.174-4(a)(2)). These deferred expenses are amortized using the straight-line method over five years, beginning with the month in which benefits are first realized. If during the amortization period the deferred expenses result in the development of depreciable property, the unrecovered expenditures must be depreciated beginning with the time the asset becomes depreciable in character (Reg. § 1.174-4(a)(4)).

Expenditures that are neither treated as a currently deductible research expense nor deferred and amortized under Code Sec. 174(b) must be charged to a capital account (Reg. § 1.174-1). Depreciation of such assets would depend on whether there is a determinable useful life.

¶ 70

Cost or Other Basis for Depreciation

For property depreciable under the Modified Accelerated Cost Recovery System, depreciation is computed using the table percentages on the unadjusted depreciable basis of the property (Reg. § 1.168(b)-1(a)(3); Reg. § 1.167(g)-1)). Unadjusted depreciable basis is the basis of property for purposes of Code Sec. 1011 (i.e., the basis of the property for purposes of determining gain or loss) without regard to any adjustments described in Code Sec. 1016(a)(2) and (3) (i.e., adjustments for depreciation and amortization previously claimed). This basis reflects the reduction in basis for the percentage of the taxpayer's use of property for the taxable year other than in the taxpayer's trade or business (or for the production of income), for any portion of the basis the taxpayer properly elects to treat as an expense under Code Sec. 179, Code Sec. 179C (relating to the election to expense certain refineries), or any similar provision, and for any adjustments to basis provided by other provisions of the Code and the regulations under the Code (other than Code Sec. 1016(a)(2) and (3)) (for example, a reduction in basis by the amount of the disabled access credit pursuant to Code Sec. 44(d)(7)). See below.

Adjusted depreciable basis is the unadjusted depreciable basis of the property less the adjustments described in Code Sec. 1016(a)(2) and (3) for depreciation. If the MACRS percentage tables are not used, depreciation is computed on the adjusted depreciable basis as of the close of the tax year.

The starting point for determining the unadjusted basis is typically the cost of the asset. Special rules apply if the asset was not acquired by purchase (e.g., the asset was acquired in an exchange, by inheritance, as a gift, or converted from personal to business use).

Cost may be increased by amounts such as sales tax (if not separately deducted as an itemized deduction), freight charges, installation costs, and testing costs. In the case of real property, cost may be increased by settlement costs such as legal and recording fees, abstract fees, survey charges, owner's title insurance, and amounts owed by the seller but paid for by the buyer, such as back taxes or interest, recording or mortgage fees, charges for improvements or repairs, and sales commissions. It may be necessary to allocate these items between land (not depreciable) and a building located on the land (depreciable).

In many cases a downward basis adjustment is required in the tax year that a deduction or credit is claimed with respect to the property (usually in the tax year that the property is placed in service or acquired). Thus, before computing depreciation, cost or other basis (as increased by items similar to those above) is adjusted downward for any applicable items described in Code Sec. 1016 (other than depreciation) including but not limited to the following:

(1) 100 percent of the rehabilitation investment credit, 50 percent of the business energy credit, and 50 percent of the reforestation investment credit (Code Secs. 50(c));

(2) 100 percent of the deduction for clean-fuel vehicles and clean-fuel vehicle refueling property (for property placed in service after June 30, 1993, and before 2006) (Code Secs. 179A(e)(6)(A) and 1016(a)(24));

(3) 100 percent of the credit for qualified electric vehicles (for property placed in service after June 30, 1993, and before 2007) (Code Secs. 30(d)(1) and 1016(a)(25));

(4) 100 percent of the railroad tax maintenance credit (Code Secs. 45G(e)(3) and Code Sec. 1016(a)(29));

(5) 100 percent of the deduction for complying with EPA sulfur regulations (Code Sec. 179B(c) and Code Sec. 1016(a)(28));

(6) 100 percent of the deduction for energy efficient commercial buildings (Code Sec. 179D(e) and Code Sec. 1016(a)(31));

(7) 100 percent of the energy efficient home credit (Code Sec. 45L(e) and 1016(a)(32));

(8) 100 percent of the credit for nonbusiness energy property (Code Secs. 25C(f) and Code Sec. 1016(a)(33));

(9) 100 percent of the credit for residential energy efficient property (Code Secs. 25D(f) and 1016(a)(34));

(10) 100 percent of the alternative motor vehicle credit which consists of four component credits (Code Sec. 30B(h)(4) and Code Sec. 1016(a)(35)):

(a) qualified fuel cell motor vehicle credit

(b) advanced lean burn technology motor vehicle credit

(c) qualified hybrid motor vehicle credit

(d) qualified alternative fuel motor vehicle credit

(11) 100 percent of the alternative fuel refueling property credit (Code Sec. 30C(e) and Code Sec. 1016(a)(36)); and

(12) 100 percent of the gas guzzler excise tax imposed by Code Sec. 4064 on certain automobiles (Code Sec. 1016(d)).

At this point, if property is not used 100 percent for production of income or business purposes, the basis on which depreciation is computed must be apportioned (Code Sec. 167(a); Reg. § 1.167(a)-5)).

The adjusted basis of the property before depreciation (including the bonus depreciation allowance, see ¶ 127D) must be reduced for any cost recovered under cost recovery provisions other than depreciation (Rev. Proc. 87-57, 1987-2 CB 687). Thus, no depreciation is allowed on the portion of basis for which the following are claimed:

(1) amortization (see ¶ 10);

(2) depletion;

(3) the Code Sec. 179 expense deduction (see ¶ 300);

(4) the Code Sec. 190 deduction for expenditures to remove architectural and transportation barriers to the handicapped and elderly (Code Sec. 190(a)(1));

(5) the enhanced oil recovery credit (Code Sec. 43(d)(1)); and

(6) the disabled access credit (Code Sec. 44(d)(7)).

The result is the unadjusted basis for depreciation purposes (the basis immediately before depreciation deductions).

The bonus depreciation allowance (¶ 127D) is computed on the adjusted basis. For example, if an item of property costs $100,000 and a taxpayer expensed $50,000 under Code Sec. 179, the first-year 50 percent bonus depreciation allowance is $25,000 (($100,000 - $25,000) × 50%). The regular MACRS depreciation deductions are computed on the remaining basis of $25,000 ($100,000 - $50,000 - $25,000).

Cars

The depreciable basis of a car is its cost reduced by any credits and deductions (other than depreciation) claimed. Cost includes sales taxes, destination charges, and dealer preparation. The cost is reduced by the clean-fuel vehicle deduction, the qualified electric vehicle credit, and the alternative motor vehicle credit for vehicles, including hybrid vehicles, placed in service after December 31, 2005 (Code Sec. 30B).

For purposes of computing depreciation, the basis of a vehicle that is subject to the gas guzzler tax because it belongs to a model type whose fuel economy rating is less than 22.5 miles per gallon or is not otherwise exempt (Code Sec. 4064) must be reduced by the amount of the tax (Code Sec. 1016(d)).

Like-kind exchanges

See ¶ 167.

Property converted from personal to business use

A special rule applies to property converted from personal to business or investment use, such as where a personal residence is converted into rental property (Reg. § 1.167(g)-1). In this case, the basis for depreciation is the lesser of the fair market value at the time of the conversion or the adjusted basis of the property at that time.

Gifts

If, at the time of a gift, the fair market value of the gifted property is equal to or exceeds the adjusted basis of the property in the hands of the donor, the donor's adjusted basis is used for purposes of computing depreciation, depletion, amortization and gain or loss. However, the donor's adjusted basis must be increased by the part of any gift tax paid with respect to the property that is attributable to the difference between the fair market value of the property and its adjusted basis (Code Sec. 1015(a), Code Sec. 1015(d)(1), and Code Sec. 1015(d)(6)). To determine this portion of the gift tax, the gift tax with respect to the property is multiplied by a fraction, the numerator of which is the difference between the fair market value of the property and its adjusted basis and the denominator of which is the value of the gift. The amount of gift tax deemed paid with respect to a gift is determined in accordance with the rules set forth in Code Sec. 1015(d)(2).

Example (1): Tom Kline deeds John Jones a building as a gift. The building has an adjusted basis of $110,000 and a fair market value of $200,000. Tom pays a $50,000 gift tax with respect to the property. The gift tax that is attributable to the net increase in value of the gift is $22,500 ($50,000 × ($90,000/$200,000)).

In the case of a gift made before 1977, the gift tax basis adjustment is equal to the gift tax paid with respect to the gift except that the gift tax adjustment may not increase the adjusted basis of the property above its fair market value at the time of the gift (Code Sec. 1015(a); Code Sec. 1015(d)(1)).

If the donor's adjusted basis exceeds the fair market value of the gift, the donee's basis for purposes of determining depreciation, depletion, or amortization is the donor's adjusted basis at the time of the gift. The basis for determining gain is also the donor's adjusted basis; however the property's basis for purposes of determining loss is its fair market value at the time of the gift (Code Sec. 1015(a)).

In the case of a gift made after 1976, it is not necessary to make an adjustment for any gift tax paid where the fair market value of the property is less than its adjusted basis since there is no net appreciation in the value of the gift (Code Sec. 1015(d)(6)). If the gift was made before 1977, the rules in the preceding paragraph apply to determine the adjustment to basis for the gift tax.

Special gift tax basis adjustment rules apply to property acquired by gift before September 2, 1958 (Code Sec. 1015(d)(1)(B)).

Real property received as a gift should be depreciated using MACRS. However, if personal property received as a gift was owned by the donor in 1986, MACRS only applies if the first-year MACRS deduction (using the half-year convention) is equal to or smaller than the first-year deduction that would apply under ACRS. Most of the time the MACRS deduction will be less since MACRS recovery periods are generally longer.

Inherited property

The depreciable basis of property acquired by bequest, devise, inheritance, or by the decedent's estate from a decedent is its stepped-up basis (Code Sec. 1014(b)). Real and personal property received by bequest, etc., should be depreciated using MACRS even if the decedent owned the property in 1986.

If an election is made to value property includible in a decedent's gross estate as of the alternate valuation date for estate tax purposes (Code Sec. 2032(a)), that value relates back to the date of the decedent's death and is the basis upon which depreciation subsequent to the date of death is computed for income tax purposes (Rev. Rul. 63-223, 1963-2 CB 100).

The stepped-up basis rule of Code Sec. 1014(b)generally applies to the partnership interest acquired from a deceased partner and not the partnership assets themselves. The basis of the assets would typically be stepped-up by making a timely Code Sec.754 election. This rule also applied in a husband-wife partnership where the partnership was deemed to continue following the death of the husband for purposes of winding up its affairs (*Estate of Ernest Skaggs*, 75 TC 191, CCH Dec. 37,379).

Allocation of purchase price when business or multiple assets purchased

Where depreciable and nondepreciable properties are bought for a single price, the purchase price must be allocated between these depreciable and nondepreciable assets on the basis of their fair market values so that depreciation on only the depreciable assets can be determined (Reg. § 1.167(a)-5).

If the fair market values of the properties are uncertain, costs may be allocated among them based on their assessed values for real estate tax purposes. While (assessment) valuation for real estate tax purposes may not furnish correct value, such drawback will not cause it to be rejected for purposes of determining the *relative* value of land and a building for the purpose of allocating cost basis (*2554-58 Creston Corp.*, 40 TC 932, Dec. 26,294). However, an allocation of cost may not be made solely according to assessed values when better evidence (such as an engineering report) exists to determine fair market value (IRS Letter Ruling 9110001, August 2, 1990).

Any transfer of a group of assets constituting a trade or business where the purchaser's basis is determined wholly by reference to the consideration paid for the assets is an applicable asset acquisition (Code Sec. 1060). In such case, the seller and the purchaser each must allocate the consideration among the assets transferred in the same manner as the amounts are allocated under the residual method (Code Sec. 338(b)(5)) relating to certain stock purchases treated as asset acquisitions (Code Sec. 1060(a)).

Regarding an acquisition of a combination of depreciable and nondepreciable assets for a lump sum in an applicable asset acquisition, the basis for depreciation of a depreciable asset cannot exceed the amount of consideration allocated to that asset under Code Sec. 1060 and Reg. § 1.1060-1 (Temp. Reg. § 1.167(a)-5T).

Other rules

Basis unknown. No depreciation is allowed if the taxpayer is unable to establish basis. General ledger entries ordinarily are not acceptable evidence of cost for depreciation purposes unless supported by book entries or reliable secondary evidence.

Liens and contingent liabilities. The basis of property was not reduced because it was subject to a lien or because only a part of the actual purchase price was paid (*B.B. Crane*, SCt, 47-1 USTC ¶ 9217, 331 US 1). No depreciation was allowed on that portion of basis which was attributable to contingent liabilities (costs that may never be incurred) (*W.R. Waddell*, 86 TC 848, Dec. 43,023, aff'd per curiam CA-9, 88-1 USTC ¶ 9192, 841 F2d 264).

Nonrecourse debt. In many tax shelter cases where the stated purchase price of an asset was grossly inflated over the asset's fair market value by purported nonrecourse debt, the nonrecourse debt was not considered a valid debt for income tax purposes and it was not includible in basis.

Whether a nonrecourse debt is a valid debt includible in basis depends on the validity of the repayment assumption. One approach for testing nonrecourse debt compares the fair market value of the property in relation to the stated purchase price and/or the principal amount of the indebtedness. A nonrecourse debt is treated as a valid debt only if the acquired property reasonably secures payment of the obligation. Another approach utilized in tax shelter cases involving nonrecourse debt where the principal was payable out of exploitation proceeds holds that an obligation, even if a recourse debt, will not be treated as a valid debt where payment, according to its terms, is too contingent. Under these circumstances, depreciable basis cannot exceed the fair market value of the property (*W.R. Waddell, supra; G.B. Lemmen*, 77 TC 1326, Dec. 38,510, (Acq.) 1983-2 CB 1).

Leased property. For the basis of tangible leased property, see ¶ 5.

Imputed interest. Imputed interest costs are includible in depreciable basis (IRS Letter Ruling 9101001, September 11, 1990).

Partnership basis adjustment. In the event that the basis of a partnership's recovery property is increased under Code Sec. 734(b) (relating to the optional adjustment to the basis of undistributed partnership property) or Code Sec. 743(b) (relating to the optional adjustment to the basis of partnership property) as a result of the distribution of property to a partner or the transfer of an interest in a partnership, the increased portion of the basis is taken into account as if it were newly purchased recovery property placed in service when the distribution or transfer occurs. No change is made for purposes of determining the depreciation allowance for the portion of the basis for which there is no increase (Reg. § 1.734-2(e)(1); Reg. § 1.743-1(j)(4)(i)).

If the basis of a partnership's recovery property is decreased under Code Sec. 734(b) or Code Sec. 743(b) as a result of the distribution of property to a partner or the transfer of a partnership interest, the decrease is taken into account over the remaining recovery period of the property (Reg. § 1.734-2(e)(2); Reg. § 1.743-1(j)(4)(ii)).

Example (2): Anne, who owns a 20% interest in the Anzac Partnership, sells her entire interest to Brian for $600,000. The Anzac Partnership's sole asset is a nonresidential building (including the land on which is stands) that was placed in service after

1986. Assume that the portion of the Code Sec. 743(b) basis adjustment allocable to the building increases the basis of the building with respect to Brian from $100,000 to $300,000 and that the portion of the basis adjustment allocable to the land increases the basis of the land is from $100,000 to $300,000. The amount of the basis adjustment allocable to the building ($200,000) is taken into account as if it were newly purchased property placed in service on the date that Anne sold her interest in Anzac. This portion of the basis has a new 39-year recovery period that begins on the date of sale. No change is made with respect to the calculation of depreciation allowances for the portion of the basis of the building (i.e., $100,000) not affected by the basis adjustment under Code Sec. 743.

See ¶ 127 for partnership tax planning opportunities involving cost segregation studies.

Assessments. An assessment for improvements or other items that increase the value of a property are added to the basis of the property and not deducted as a tax. Such improvements may include streets, sidewalks, water mains, sewers, and public parking facilities. The amount of such an assessment may be a depreciable asset, for example, the cost of an assessment for sidewalks paid for by a business taxpayer. Assessments for maintenance or repair or meeting interest charges on the improvements are currently deductible as a real property tax (Code Sec. 164(c)(1), Reg. § 1.164-4, Rev. Proc. 73-188).

Taxes. Any tax paid in connection with the acquisition of a property is included in the basis of the property. A tax paid in connection with the disposition of a property reduces the amount realized on the disposition (Code Sec. 164(a)).

Casualty losses and similar basis adjustments that occur during depreciation period. For the manner of computing depreciation if a mid-stream basis adjustment is required, see ¶ 179.

¶ 74

Who Is Entitled to the Depreciation Deduction?

The right to deduct depreciation is not predicated upon ownership of the legal title to property but upon capital investment in the property (*Gladding Dry Goods Co.*, 2 BTA 336, Dec. 642). The test is who bears the burden of exhaustion of the capital investment (*F. & R. Lazarus & Co.*, SCt, 39-2 USTC ¶ 9793, 308 US 252). Thus, a company had a capital investment in property and was entitled to depreciation because a transaction in which a bank held legal title to the property was a loan secured by the property involved rather than a sale and leaseback.

A farmer-stockholder in a nonprofit mutual corporation had no depreciable investment in a dam constructed for the corporation. Although he was assessed a pro-rata share of the cost of a loan obtained by the corporation to finance the dam, he was not personally liable on the debt and did not suffer the burden of exhaustion of the property (*R.L. Hunter*, 46 TC 477, Dec. 28,025).

Generally, the owner of the property makes the capital investment and claims the depreciation deduction. Factors considered in determining who has the benefits and burdens of ownership include: (1) whether legal title passes; (2) how the parties treat the transaction; (3) whether an equity was acquired in the property; (4) whether the contract creates a present obligation on the seller to execute and deliver a deed and a present obligation on the buyer to make payments; (5) whether the right of possession is vested in the buyer; (6) which party pays the property taxes; (7) which party bears the risk of loss or damage to the property; and (8) which party receives the profits from the operation and sale of the property (*Grodt and McKay Realty Inc.*, 77 TC 1221, Dec. 38,472). See, also, *E.R. Arevalo*, 124 TC 244, Dec. 56,026 (depreciation denied to taxpayer who invested in payphones and held legal title but did not receive benefits and burdens of ownership).

Lease or purchase

Whether a transaction is treated as a lease or as a purchase for tax purposes is important in determining who is entitled to a depreciation deduction. In determining whether a transaction is a lease or a purchase, judicially formulated standards consider whether the transaction (1) is genuinely a multiple party transaction, (2) has economic substance, (3) is compelled by business realities, and (4) is imbued with tax-independent considerations that are not shaped solely by tax-avoidance features.

For a nonleveraged lease or a real property lease transaction to be considered a lease under such rules, the lessee may not hold title to, or have an equity interest in, the property. The lessor must show that the transaction had a bona fide business purpose (the property was used for a business or other income-producing purpose) and that there is a reasonable expectation of profit from such transaction independent of tax benefits. In addition, the lessor must retain meaningful benefits and burdens of ownership that in turn consider whether (a) the lessee has an option to acquire the property at the end of the lease for a nominal amount, (b) the residual value of the property to the lessor is nominal, and (c) the lessor could force the lessee to purchase the property at the end of the lease.

For leveraged leases of equipment (property financed by a nonrecourse loan from a third party) the following criteria must be met in order for a transaction to be considered a lease for tax purposes: (1) the lessor must have at least a 20-percent at-risk investment in the property; (2) any lessee option to purchase the property at the end of the lease must be exercisable at fair market value; (3) the lessee must have no investment in the property; (4) the lessee must not loan money to the lessor (or guarantee a lessor loan) to enable the lessor to acquire such property; (5) the lessor must expect to receive a profit and a positive cash flow from the transaction exclusive of tax benefits; and (6) the fair market value of the property at the end of the lease term must equal at least 20 percent of the value when the lease was entered and the useful life of the property at the end of the lease must equal at least the longer of one year or 20 percent of the original useful life (Rev. Proc. 2001-28, 2001-1 CB 1156; Rev. Proc. 2001-29, 2001-1 CB 1160).

Where equipment or other depreciable property is leased with an option to buy, the lessor is allowed depreciation and the lessee deducts the rent paid. However, if the lease is in substance a sale of the property, the lessee is allowed to depreciate the leased property and may not deduct the payments as rent (Rev. Rul. 55-540, 1955-2 CB 39).

Factors implying that there was a sale rather than a lease include: (1) payments are specifically applicable to the purchase price if the option is exercised; (2) the lessee will acquire title upon payment of a stated amount of rentals; (3) the lessee is required to pay a substantial part of the purchase price in the early years of the asset's life; (4) the rental payments exceed a fair rental value; (5) the option purchase price is nominal compared with the expected value of the asset when the option is exercised; (6) some part of the payments is designated as interest; and (7) the lease may be renewed at nominal rentals over the useful life of the property.

Life tenant, trust and estate

The holder of a life estate that is not purchases from a related person who retains a remainder interest is allowed a depreciation deduction as if the life tenant were the absolute owner of the property (Code Sec. 167(d)). Thereafter, any remaining depreciation is allowed to the remainderman (Reg. § 1.167(h)-1(a)). However, as noted below under the discussion for term interests, if a taxpayer purchases a life estate and the remainderman is related to the taxpayer, the taxpayer may not claim depreciation or amortization deductions. This rule does not apply to interests acquired by gift, bequest, or inheritance.

In computing depreciation, a life tenant must use the prescribed recovery period of an asset rather than a shorter life expectancy of the life tenant (*M. Penn*, CA-8, 52-2 USTC ¶ 9504, 199 F2d 210, cert. denied, 344 US 927).

A trust or estate must compute a depreciation deduction on properties it holds in its capacity as a separate tax entity before the deduction is apportioned between the trust and its beneficiaries or the estate and the estate heirs, legatees, and devisees. A trust or estate is allowed a depreciation deduction only to the extent that it is not allowable to beneficiaries (Code Sec. 642(e)).

For property held in trust, the depreciation deduction is apportioned between the income beneficiaries and the trustee on the basis of the trust income allocable to each, unless the governing instrument (or local law) requires or permits the trustee to maintain a reserve for depreciation (Reg. § 1.167(h)-1(b)). In the latter case, the deduction is first allocated to the trustee to the extent that income is set aside for a depreciation reserve. Any part of the deduction exceeding the income set aside for the reserve is apportioned between the income beneficiaries and the trustee on the basis of the trust income allocable to each.

For an estate, the depreciation allowance is apportioned on the basis of the income of the estate allocable to the estate heirs, legatees and devisees (Reg. § 1.167(h)-1(c)).

Although a depreciation deduction is apportioned on the basis of the income of the trust or the income of the estate allocable to each of the parties (without regard to the depreciation deduction allocable to them), the amount of a depreciation deduction allocated to a beneficiary may exceed the amount of the latter's pro rata share of such income (Rev. Rul. 74-530, 1974-2 CB 188).

If an election is made to value property includible in a decedent's gross estate as of the alternate valuation date for estate tax purposes (Code Sec. 2032(a)), that value relates back to the date of the decedent's death and is the basis upon which depreciation subsequent to the date of death is computed for income tax purposes (Rev. Rul. 63-223, 1963-2 CB 100).

Term interests

A "term interest in property" means a life interest in property, an interest in property for a term of years, or an income interest in a trust (Code Secs. 167(e)(5)(A) and 1001(e)(2)).

The purchaser of a term interest in property held for business or investment is generally entitled to amortize the cost of the term interest over its stated term or depreciate the cost over the applicable depreciation period if the term interest relates to depreciable property such as a building. However amortization/depreciation may not be claimed if the holder of the remainder interest is a related person (Code Sec. 167(e)(1); *1220 Realty Corp.*, CA-6, 63-2 USTC ¶ 9703, 322 F2d 495). For this purpose, a related person is anyone bearing a relationship to the taxpayer that is described in Code Sec. 267(b) or (e) (Code Sec. 167(e)(5)(B)). The constructive ownership rules of Code Sec. 267(c) apply in determining whether persons are related.

If the remainderman is a related person, the purchaser is required to reduce the basis of the property by the amortization or depreciation deduction disallowed solely by the related-remainderman rule (Code Sec. 167(e)(3)(A)). The remainderman's basis in the property is increased by the disallowed deductions (Code Sec. 167(e)(3)(B)). No increase in the remainderman's basis is made for disallowed deductions attributable to periods during which the term interest is held by (1) an exempt organization or (2) a nonresident alien individual or foreign corporation if income from the term interest is not effectively connected with the conduct of a trade or business in the United States (Code Sec. 167(e)(4)).

The holder of a life or terminable interest acquired by gift, bequest, or inheritance is not subject to the rule barring a depreciation or amortization deduction where there is a related remainderman (Code Sec. 167(e)(2)(A)) (income from these term interests may not be reduced for shrinkage in the value of such interests due to a lapse of time (Code Sec. 273)).

The holder of dividend rights that were separated from any Code Sec. 305(e) stripped preferred stock is not subject to the restrictions on depreciation deductions imposed where there is a related remainderman if the rights were purchased after April 30, 1993 (Code Sec. 167(e)(2)(B)).

A depreciable interest may not be created where none previously existed. Thus, no amortization or depreciation deduction is allowed on a term interest created by a taxpayer who divides or splits a fee interest in nondepreciable business property into a retained term interest and a transferred remainder interest (even if the remainderman who acquires the remainder interest is unrelated to the taxpayer) (*Lomas Santa Fe, Inc.*, 74 TC 662, Dec. 37,052, aff'd CA-9, 82-2 USTC ¶ 9658, 693 F2d 71).

Where a taxpayer purchases a term interest in raw land and buildings and uses the property for business or investment purposes and the person holding the remainder interest is not related to the taxpayer, the taxpayer may amortize the cost of the term interest that is allocable to the land over the period of the term interest and depreciate the cost that is allocable to the buildings using the Modified Accelerated Cost Recovery System (MACRS) (IRS Letter Ruling 200852013, September 24, 2008).

Landlord and tenant

A landlord can depreciate property already on the premises when the property is leased and any improvements constructed by the landlord during the term of the lease. A tenant can deduct depreciation for permanent improvements made to the leased property by the tenant (Reg. § 1.167(a)-4). See also ¶ 126 and ¶ 258.

¶ 75

Incorrect Depreciation Claimed/Accounting Method Changes

The deduction for depreciation is an annual allowance. The depreciation deduction for the current tax year may not be increased by the amount of depreciation allowable but not claimed in a previous tax year or decreased by the amount of excess depreciation claimed in a prior tax year (Reg. § 1.167(a)-10(a)).

Basis reduction—computing taxable income and depreciation recapture. The basis of depreciable property for purposes of determining gain or loss is reduced by the amount of allowable depreciation if this is greater than the amount of depreciation actually claimed that resulted in a tax benefit (Code Sec. 1016(a)(2); Reg. § 1.1016-3). A depreciation deduction is considered to have resulted in a tax benefit if it was treated as part of an NOL and reduced taxes in an NOL carryback or carryforward year (Reg. § 1.1016-3(e)(2)).

Example (1): Assume that a taxpayer determines the following allowed and allowable amounts with respect to an asset:

Year	*Amount Allowed (which reduced taxes)*	*Amount Allowable*	*Greater of Allowed or Allowable*
1	$6,500	$6,000	$6,500
2	4,000	4,000	4,000
3	4,500	6,000	6,000
			$16,500

The taxpayer should reduce the basis of the asset by $16,500 (Reg. § 1.1016-3(h), *Example (1)*).

Proposed Reg. § 1.1016-3 explains how to compute allowable depreciation on ACRS assets (i.e., assets placed in service after 1980 and before 1987). In general, if no depreciation deduction was claimed, the regular (i.e., non-elective recovery periods and methods) are applied. If depreciation was claimed under a proper method for one or more years but not claimed in other years, allowable depreciation is computed using the method chosen by the taxpayer.

No MACRS regulations on this subject have been issued. However, Rev. Proc. 2008-52 (I.R.B. 2008-36), successor to Rev. Proc. 2002-9 (2002-1 CB 327), relating to automatic accounting method changes, provides that allowable depreciation is determined under the MACRS GDS (unless ADS is required or has been elected for a class of property (Appendix Section 6). Accordingly, if a taxpayer elected the GDS straight-line method or GDS 150-percent declining-balance method with respect to a class of property, allowable depreciation is computed using those elective methods for an item of property that falls within a property class to which the election applied. Otherwise, regular GDS method applies. See ¶ 84 for a discussion of GDS, ADS, etc.

> ***Example (2):*** A taxpayer makes an election to use the GDS 150% declining-balance method with respect to 5-year property placed in service in 2009. She later discovers that she failed to claim depreciation on an item of 5-year property placed in service in 2009. Assume ADS is not required for that property. Allowable depreciation should be computed using the 150% declining-balance method.

Rev. Proc. 2008-52, Appendix Section 6.01(6), also provides guidance on the definition of allowable depreciation under Code Sec. 167, ACRS, and Code Sec. 197. Under this guidance, allowable depreciation does not include depreciation that is limited by other provisions of the Code, such as the luxury car rules of Code Sec. 280F. Another possible example of depreciation that is limited by a Code provision is depreciation that may not be claimed by reason of the 2 percent adjusted gross income floor for certain miscellaneous itemized deductions (Code Sec. 67(a)).

The rule requiring basis reduction for unclaimed (allowable) depreciation applies for purposes of determining gain or loss. Note that when computing depreciation recapture, a taxpayer need not recapture as ordinary income unclaimed depreciation (Code Sec. 1245(a)(2)(B); Code Sec. 1250(b)(3)). See ¶ 488. Note also that unrecaptured section 1250 gain which is subject to a 25-percent capital gains rate (as opposed to the normally applicable 20-percent rate) does not include gain attributable to allowable depreciation. Only gain attributable to depreciation that was actually claimed and unrecaptured is subject to the 25-percent rate (Code Sec. 1(h)(7)(A)).

A taxpayer who used an impermissible method of accounting and sold or disposed of a depreciable asset on which insufficient or no depreciation was claimed may file a Form 3115 to claim the depreciation through a Code Sec. 481(a) adjustment on an amended return for the year of the sale or on an original return for the year of the sale (Rev. Proc. 2008-52, Appendix 6.17; Rev. Proc. 2007-16, I.R.B. 2007-4). This procedure is presumably unavailable if the incorrect depreciation was attributable to a math or posting error since math and posting errors are not considered methods of accounting. See ¶ 488, "*Computing gain or loss—depreciation allowed or allowable rule.*"

When is a depreciation accounting method adopted? A permissible method of accounting for depreciation or amortization is adopted after filing one return and cannot be changed on an amended return. If an impermissible method of accounting for depreciation is used, the impermissible method is adopted after filing two returns and cannot be changed on an amended return.

Certain depreciation changes do not relate to an accounting method and may only be made on an amended return. For example, the correction of a math or posting error may only be made on an amended return for open years. See discussion below for changes that are considered changes of accounting method and changes such as math and posting errors that are not.

Generally, if a taxpayer has adopted a method of accounting for depreciation, a change can only be made by obtaining IRS consent using the automatic (Rev. Proc. 2008-52, as modified by Rev. Proc. 2009-39) or advance consent (Rev. Proc. 92-27, as modified by Rev. Proc. 2009-39) procedures, as applicable. The IRS, however, will also allow a taxpayer who has only filed one return to *change from an impermissible method* using the appropriate change of accounting method procedure (automatic or advance consent, depending upon the type of change). This eliminates the need to file an amended return to make the change. This rule is generally effective for a Form 3115 filed for a tax year ending on or after December 30, 2003 (Rev. Proc. 2008-52, Appendix Section 6.01(b); Rev. Proc. 2007-16, I.R.B. 2007-4).

> ***Example:*** XYZ corporation misclassifies an item of 5 year property as 10 year property on its 2008 tax return. It discovers the error when preparing its 2009 tax return. XYZ has not adopted a method of accounting because it has not filed two incorrect returns. Generally, this error would be fixed by filing an amended return for 2008. However, pursuant to Rev. Proc. 2007-16, XYZ may choose to fix the error by applying the change of accounting method procedures and make a Code Sec. 481(a) adjustment on its 2009 tax return. It is not necessary to file an amended return for 2008.

A taxpayer who has consistently expensed costs that should be capitalized and depreciated (repairs, for example) has adopted an accounting method and must obtain permission to change that method.

Changes in depreciation that are and are not accounting method changes. Regulations describe in detail changes in depreciation that are considered changes in accounting method and changes that are not (Reg.§ 1.446-1(e)(2)(d); Reg.§ 1.167(e)-1).

With respect to a change in depreciation or amortization that is a change of accounting method under the regulations, the regulations apply to a change of accounting method made for a depreciable or amortizable asset placed in service in a tax year ending on or after December 30, 2003. With respect to a change in depreciation or amortization that is not a change in method of accounting, the regulations apply to a change made for assets placed in service in tax years ending on or after December 30, 2003 (Reg.§ 1.446-1(e)(4); Reg.§ 1.167(e)-1).

The regulations generally provide that a change in the depreciation method, period of recovery, or convention of a depreciable or amortizable asset is a change in method of accounting (Reg.§ 1.446-1(e)(2)(ii)(d)(2)(i)).

Other changes in accounting method include (Reg.§ 1.446-1(e)(2)(ii)(d)(2)):

(1) changing the treatment of an asset from depreciable to nondepreciable or vice versa (e.g., from an inventory item to a depreciable asset);

(2) changing a policy of expensing particular assets in the year of purchase to depreciating those assets or vice versa;

(3) changes to correct bonus depreciation and depreciation deductions affected by such a change;

(4) a change in the accounting for depreciable assets from single asset accounting to multiple asset accounting (pooling), or vice versa, or from one type of multiple asset accounting to a different type of multiple asset accounting; and

(5) a change in the method of identifying which mass assets accounted for in multiple asset accounts or pools have been disposed (e.g., from specific identification to a FIFO method).

The regulations resolve (in the IRS's favor) a conflict that has arisen between the courts regarding whether the reclassification of a misclassified MACRS asset is a change in accounting method (Reg.§ 1.446-1(e)(2)(ii)(d)(2)(i)).

By way of background, the Tenth Circuit first affirmed the long-standing IRS position that a taxpayer who misclassifies a MACRS asset and claims incorrect depreciation on two or more returns has adopted an accounting method (*S.M. Kurzet*, 2000-2 USTC ¶ 50,671) and, therefore, must take a Code Sec. 481(a) adjustment into account. The Fifth and Eighth Circuits, as well as the Tax Court, however, ruled that such a reclassification is not a change in accounting method by reason of Reg. § 1.446-1(e)(2)(ii)(*b*) (*Brookshire Brothers Holding, Inc.*, CA-5, 2003-1 USTC ¶ 50,214; *R. O'Shaughnessy*, CA-8, 2003-1 USTC ¶ 50,522; and *Green Forest Manufacturing Inc.*, 85 TCM 1020, T.C. Memo. 2003-75, CCH Dec. 55,083(M)). That regulation provides that a change in method of accounting does not include an adjustment in the useful life of a depreciable asset. Traditionally, if there is no accounting method change under this regulation, depreciation is corrected by adjustments in current and future years.

The new regulations move the useful life exception in Reg. § 1.446-1(e)(2)(ii)(*b*) to Reg. § 1.446-1(e)(2)(ii)(d))(3))(i) and clarify that it only applies to property depreciated under Code Sec. 167 (i.e., not to property depreciated under MACRS or ACRS). However, a change to or from a useful life (or a recovery or amortization period) that is specifically assigned (e.g., 36 months for software under Code Sec. 167(f)(1)) is a change in accounting method (Reg. § 1.446-1(e)(2)(ii)(d)(3))(i)).

The correction of a mathematical or posting error (e.g., an asset is omitted from a depreciation schedule or misclassified as the result of a data entry error) is not considered a change of accounting method and may only be corrected on an amended return for an open tax year (Reg. § 1.446-1(e)(2)(ii)(b)).

The correction of an internal inconsistency is also not considered the adoption of an accounting method. For example, an internal inconsistency exists if identical assets are not depreciated similarly (*H.E. Butt Grocery Store Co.*, DC Tex. 2000-2 USTC ¶ 50,649)

Other changes that are not considered a change in accounting method include:

(1) a change in use (¶ 169) that causes a change in recovery period or method;

(2) making a late depreciation or amortization election or revoking a timely made election (permission is generally obtained by submitting a request for a private letter ruling);

(3) a change in salvage value (unless a salvage value of zero is expressly required, as in the case of ACRS, MACRS, and Section 197 assets); and

(4) a change in the placed in service date of an asset.

See Reg. § 1.446-1(e)(2)(ii)(d)(3))(v) for rules explaining how to take into account depreciation adjustments required if a correction is made to the placed in service date.

Special rule for assets placed in service in tax years ending before December 30, 2003. For property placed in service in a tax year ending before December 30, 2003 (i.e., the effective date of the final regulations), the IRS will not assert that a change in computing depreciation under Code Sec. 167, 168, 197, 1400I, 1400L(c), or ACRS for depreciable or amortizable property that is treated as a capital asset is a change in accounting method under Code Sec. 446(e) (IRS Chief Counsel Notice CC-2004-007, January 28, 2004, as clarified by Chief Counsel Notice 2004-024, July 14, 2004).

This means, with respect to an asset placed in service in a tax year ending before December 30, 2003, for which an amended return may still be filed under the statute of limitations, a taxpayer may choose to file amended returns (for the year the asset was placed in service and subsequent affected years) or Form 3115 with the current tax year in order to correct the depreciation period. Since amended returns may only be filed for open tax years, this exception is now generally inapplicable and a change of accounting method will need to be made by filing a Form 3115 and taking a Code Sec. 481 adjustment for the year of the change.

In general, an amended return must be filed by the later of (1) three years from the date the original return which claimed the incorrect depreciation was filed or (2) two years from the date that the tax was paid for the year that the incorrect depreciation was claimed. For purposes of item (1), a return filed early is considered filed on the due date. A refund is limited to the amount of tax paid during the three-year period (plus any extension of time to file the original return) prior to filing the amended return.

The amended return option may be preferable if a taxpayer has claimed too little depreciation with respect to an asset placed in service in an open tax year. For example, interest may be payable on a tax overpayment reported on an amended return. Interest is not payable on a Code Sec. 481(a) adjustment. Also, a taxpayer may be in a lower tax bracket in an open tax year.

The following example is based on an example appearing in the Chief Counsel Notice:

> ***Example:*** A taxpayer conducts a cost segregation study in 2004 and reclassified building elements placed in service in 2001 as 5-year property. The taxpayer may file an amended return for 2001 (and affected subsequent years) or follow the change of accounting method procedures by filing Form 3115 and claiming a Code Sec. 481(a) adjustment.

This change in the IRS's litigating position does not apply to (1) an adjustment in useful life under Code Sec. 167 (other than MACRS, Code Sec. 1400I, Code Sec. 14000L, or ACRS) if the useful life is not specifically assigned by the Code, regulations, or other IRS guidance; (2) to any adjustment to correct an incorrect classification or characterization of depreciable property under the class life asset depreciation range system (CLADR property); (3) or to a change in computing depreciation or amortization due to a posting error, a mathematical error, a change in underlying facts (other than a change in the placed-in-service date), a change in use of property in the hands of the same taxpayer, the making of a late election, or a revocation of an election. Items (1)-(3) are not changes in accounting method.

The change in litigating position doe not apply to a change in the treatment of property from a non-capital asset (e.g., inventory, materials and supplies) to a capital, depreciable or amortizable asset (or vice versa), or to a change from expensing the cost of depreciable or amortizable property to capitalizing and depreciating or amortizing the cost (or vice versa). These changes are a change in method of accounting.

The IRS has clarified the application of Chief Counsel Notice CC-2004-007 in a subsequently issued Chief Counsel Notice—Chief Counsel Notice CC-2004-024, July 14, 2004. CC-2004-024 provides that:

(1) A Code Sec. 481(a) adjustment is not required or permitted to be claimed on an amended return filed pursuant to CC-2004-007;

(2) A taxpayer may not file amended returns for some years and a Form 3115 for other tax years with respect to the same asset;

(3) Amended returns may be filed to "unwind" a Form 3115 that was filed under the automatic or advance consent change of accounting method procedures before the issuance of Chief Counsel Notice CC-2204-007. The year for which the change was effective, however, must still be an open tax year.

The rule in item (2) would prevent a taxpayer who placed an asset in service in a closed year from filing amended returns for open tax years and filing a Form 3115 to claim a Code Sec. 481(a) adjustment with respect to the depreciation that should have been claimed in the closed tax years.

Automatic and advance consent accounting method change procedures. The IRS's most recently updated automatic consent procedures for taxpayers who have adopted an impermissible method of accounting for depreciation (or amortization) and have either claimed no allowable depreciation, less depreciation than allowable, or more depreciation than allowable is provided in Rev. Proc. 2008-52, I.R.B. 2008-36, which updates and supersedes Rev. Proc. 2002-9, 2002-1 CB 327. Generally, Form 3115 must be attached to the taxpayer's tax return for the year of change by the original due date (including extensions). A copy must also be filed with the National Office no later than when the original is filed with the taxpayer's return (see Section 6.02 (not the Appendix) of Rev. Proc. 2008-52; IRS Letter Ruling 200334026, May 14, 2003 (extension of time to file copy with National Office granted).

Taxpayers who qualify under the automatic procedure are permitted to change to a method of accounting under which the allowable amount of depreciation is claimed. The unclaimed depreciation from years prior to the year of change is taken into account as a net negative (taxpayer favorable) adjustment in the year of change, generally effective for tax years ending on or after December 31, 2001 (Section 5.04 (not the Appendix) of Rev. Proc. 2008-52; Rev. Proc. 2002-19, 2002-1 CB 696, modifying Rev. Proc. 2002-9). Taxpayers requesting changes for a tax year ending on or after December 31, 2001, and on or before April 30, 2002, could request application of the former four-year adjustment period. Certain taxpayers who had change of accounting method applications for a tax year ending before December 31, 2001, pending on March 14, 2002, were allowed to defer the year of change in order to take advantage of the new one-year adjustment period (Rev. Proc. 2002-54).

Prior to modification of Rev. Proc. 2002-9, the Code Sec. 481(a) adjustment period for positive and negative adjustments was four years unless the total adjustment was less than $25,000, in which case a taxpayer could elect to take the adjustment into account in the year of change. The four-year spread (or election for adjustments of less than $25,000) continues to apply to net positive adjustments (e.g., where too much depreciation was claimed).

In general, the automatic consent procedure applies to property which is owned by a taxpayer at the beginning of the year of change (see above, however, for a special rule that applies to disposed property) and for which depreciation is claimed under Code Secs. 56(a)(1) (AMT depreciation), 56(g)(4)(A) (AMT ACE depreciation), 167, 168 (ACRS and MACRS), 197 (15-year amortization), 1400I , 1400L(c) or under any type of additional first-year depreciation provision such as Code Sec. 168(k), New York Liberty Zone property, Gulf Opportunity Zone property, and Kansas Disaster Area property. The procedure does not apply to specified property, including intangible property amortized under Code Sec. 167 (except for property excluded from Code Sec. 197 by Code Sec. 167(f)) and property depreciated under the Asset Depreciation Range (ADR) system. The procedure does not apply if a taxpayer is seeking to change the useful life of an asset that is depreciated under Code Sec. 167 but does apply to a change in recovery period under ACRS or MACRS. However, the procedure does not apply if a taxpayer wants to reclassify section 1250 property to an asset class that does not explicitly include section 1250 property (Appendix Section 6.01(1)(c)(v) of Rev. Proc. 2008-52; Appendix Section 2.01(1)(d)(v) of Rev. Proc. 2002-9, as replaced by Rev. Proc. 2007-16). For example, automatic consent is not available with respect to an item of a building, such as a wall or acoustical ceiling tile that a taxpayer has treated as section 1250 property, but now wishes to treat as 5-year section 1250 property under Asset Class 57.0 (Distributive Trades and Services) because this asset class does not include section 1250 property.

This rule is in response to the *Walgreen Co.* case, in which a taxpayer unsuccessfully argued that certain types of Section 1250 property are includible in Asset Class 57.0 (relating to retail trades, see ¶ 104) and, therefore, depreciable as 5-year property (*Walgreen Co.*, 72 TCM 382, Dec. 51,503(M)). This rule does not prevent a taxpayer from using the automatic consent procedure to reclassify items that were incorrectly depreciated as Section 1250 (real) property as Section 1245 (personal) property. For example, a taxpayer may use the automatic consent procedure in connection with a cost segregation study that determines that certain items that were included in the basis of commercial or residential rental property should have been separately depreciated as personal property over a five- or seven-year period. However, a statement of law and facts supporting such a reclassification must be submitted (Rev. Proc. 2008-52, Appendix Section 6.01(3)(b)(vii)).

The automatic consent procedure applies to a taxpayer that wants to change to a unit of property that is permissible under applicable legal authority for determining when the taxpayer has disposed of a building (as defined in Reg.§ 1.48-1(e)(1)) and its structural components (as defined in Reg.§ 1.48-1(e)(2)) for depreciation purposes. Such a change owill affect the determination of gain or loss from the disposition of the building (including its structural components). See Sec. 2.10 of Rev. Proc. 2009-39, modifying Rev. Proc. 2008-52 by adding new Appendix Sec. 6.24. A similar rule allows a taxpayer that wants to change to a unit of property that is permissible under applicable legal authority for determining when the taxpayer has disposed of a section 1245 property or a depreciable land improvement for depreciation purposes. This change also will affect the determination of gain or loss from the disposition of the section 1245 property or the depreciable land improvement. See Sec. 2.11 of Rev. Proc. 2009-39, modifying Rev. Proc. 2008-52 by adding new Appendix Sec. 6.25. In either case, a taxpayer must provide specific legal authority supporting the taxpayer's proposed unit of property for determining when the property is disposed of. Other limitations apply. See, also, ¶ 162.

If the automatic consent procedures of Rev. Proc. 208-52 do not apply to a taxpayer's situation, then the Rev. Proc. 97-27 advance accounting method change guidelines should be followed. If the automatic consent procedures of Rev. Proc.

2008-52, as modified by Rev. Proc. 2009-39, apply to a taxpayer's situation, then the taxpayer may not use the advance consent procedures contained in Rev. Proc. 97-27, as modified by Rev. Proc. 2009-39. The reduction of the Code Sec. 481(a) adjustment period for net negative adjustments from four years to one year described above also applies to adjustments required under Rev. Proc. 97-27, as modified by Rev. Proc. 2009-39.

Permissible to permissible method under Code Sec. 167. Appendix Section 6.02 of Rev. Proc. 2008-52 (which correlates to Appendix Section 2.02 of Rev. Proc. 2002-9, as replaced by Rev. Proc. 2007-16) provides an automatic consent procedure for changing from a permissible depreciation method under Code Sec. 167 to another permissible method under Code Sec. 167. The procedure, for example, covers a change from the straight-line method to the sum-of-the-years digits method, the sinking fund method, the unit-of-production method, or the declining-balance method using any proper percentage of the straight-line method rate. If a change is made from one permissible method to another permissible method, there is no Code Sec. 481(a) adjustment and no change to the basis of an asset is made as the result of the change in accounting method (Reg. § 1.446-1(e)(2)(ii)(d)(5)(iii)).

Permissible to permissible method under Code Sec. 168 (MACRS). In order to change from one permissible method to another permissible method of depreciation under MACRS a taxpayer must file for permission using the advance consent procedures contained in Rev. Proc. 97-27, as modified by Rev. Proc. 2009-39. No Code Sec. 481(a) adjustment is made (Reg. § 1.446-1(e)(2)(ii)(d)(5)(iii)).

¶ 76

Reporting Depreciation and Amortization on Form 4562

Noncorporate taxpayers (including S corporations) are not required to file Form 4562, Depreciation and Amortization, for a current tax year unless any of the following deductions are claimed: a depreciation or amortization deduction on an asset placed in service in the current tax year; a Sec. 179 expense deduction (including a carryover from a previous year); a depreciation deduction on any vehicle or other listed property (regardless of when the listed property was placed in service); or a deduction based on the standard mileage rate (which reflects an allowance for depreciation expense) (Form 4562 is not required if this computation is made on Form 2106, Employee Business Expenses or Form 2106-EZ, Unreimbursed Employee Business Expenses). Noncorporate taxpayers exempt from filing Form 4562 enter their depreciation deduction directly on the appropriate line of their return.

A corporation (other than an S corporation) claiming depreciation or amortization on any asset, regardless of when placed in service, must file Form 4562.

A separate Form 4562 is required for each separate business or activity of a taxpayer. However, Part I, which is used to claim the Code Sec. 179 expense deduction, is completed in its entirety on only one form where multiple forms are filed.

A Form 4562 must be filed to claim an amortization deduction in the first year of an asset's amortization period. The first-year amortization deduction is reported in Part VI on line 42 (line reference to 2008 Form 4562). The amounts reported in Part VI are then transferred to the "Other Expenses" or "Other Deductions" line of the income tax return. A statement should be attached to the return in the first year of the amortization period. Required information includes the following: a description of the costs amortized, the date that the amortization period begins, the amortizable amount, the Code section under which amortization is claimed, the amortization period or percentage, and the amortization deduction for the year.

In a tax year after the first amortization deduction is reported on Form 4562, amortization deductions should be reported directly only on the "Other Expenses" or "Other Deductions" line of the income tax return *unless* the taxpayer is otherwise required to file Form 4562. If the taxpayer must file Form 4562, for example, because listed property is still in service or new property has been placed in service, then the amortization deduction for such year should also be reported on Part VI line 43 of Form 4562.

2007 Form 4562-FY. Following reinstatement of the Code Sec. 168(k) bonus depreciation allowance for property placed in service in 2008, the IRS released a special version of Form 4562 to be filed by taxpayers with a 2007-2008 fiscal year (IRS News Release IR-2008-22, February 21, 2008).

Modified ACRS (MACRS)

Modified Accelerated Cost Recovery System

¶ 80

Introduction

Notwithstanding some shared terminology, the Accelerated Cost Recovery System (ACRS) introduced by the Economic Recovery Tax Act of 1981 (ERTA) and the Modified Accelerated Cost Recovery System (modified ACRS, or MACRS) introduced by the Tax Reform Act of 1986 are intrinsically different systems for deducting the cost of tangible depreciable property.

ACRS (the discussion of which begins at ¶ 220) shuns the word "depreciation," providing instead a deduction "with respect to recovery property." MACRS abandons the concept of recovery property and prescribes its own methods for determining the depreciation deduction accorded under older rules that still apply to most nonrecovery property. MACRS, in contrast to ACRS, recognizes salvage value but assigns it a value of zero.

Although the two systems use some similar names to classify personal property, it should be noted that, pursuant to the applicable conventions (see ¶ 86), the cost of 3-year property, 5-year property, or 10-year property placed in service under MACRS generally must be recovered over one more tax year (four, six, or 11 years) as compared to the cost of similarly named classes of property placed in service under ACRS.

Distinctions

One seemingly basic distinction is that, in contrast to ACRS, under which the annual deduction is generally a designated percentage of unadjusted basis, MACRS may require appropriate basis adjustments to compute second- and subsequent-year deductions. Optional MACRS tables furnished by the IRS provide percentages that are applied to the unadjusted basis of property in a manner similar to statutory percentages provided to compute ACRS deductions.

Other differences include depreciation methods; conventions; property classifications; short tax year rules; and rules for computing depreciation of personal property in the year of disposition.

The following table compares deductions that would be allowed for an item of personal property costing $10,000 and classified as 5-year property under ACRS with an item costing the same, classified as 5-year property under MACRS, and subject to the half-year convention:

Year	*ACRS*	*MACRS*
1	$1,500	$2,000
2	2,200	3,200
3	2,100	1,920
4	2,100	1,152
5	2,100	1,152
6	...	576

(The computations disregard MACRS bonus depreciation.)

Rounding

In rounding applicable rates, a taxpayer may adopt any convention that is reasonable, consistent, and accurate to at least one-hundredth of one percent for recovery periods of less than 20 years and one-thousandth of one percent for longer recovery periods. No convention may be applied to recover more than 100 percent of the property's recoverable basis (Rev. Proc. 87-57, 1987-2 CB 687).

¶ 82

Transitional Rules

Although, generally, MACRS applies to all otherwise eligible property placed in service after 1986, prior contracts and/or construction may render some post-1986 property still subject to ACRS. Property so affected, referred to as transition property, may include (1) property with a class life in the 7-to-19-year range and placed in service before 1989, and (2) property with a longer class life and real property placed in service before 1991.

Since transition property is subject to ACRS, it is more fully discussed at ¶ 228. So-called anti-churning rules, which may also require that the cost of some property placed in service after 1986 be recovered under ACRS (or a pre-ACRS method), are discussed at ¶ 142.

An irrevocable election, on an asset-by-asset basis, was available to apply the MACRS rules to property other than transition property that was placed in service after July 31, 1986, and before January 1, 1987.

MACRS General Depreciation System (GDS)

¶ 84

Applicable Depreciation Methods

There are two depreciation systems under MACRS, the MACRS general depreciation system (GDS) (discussed below) and the MACRS alternative depreciation system (ADS) (see ¶ 150).

The cost of most tangible depreciable property generally placed in service after 1986 is recovered using (1) the applicable depreciation method, (2) the applicable recovery period (see ¶ 100 –¶ 126), and (3) the applicable convention (see ¶ 86).

Under GDS, applicable depreciation methods are prescribed for each class of property. Applicable depreciation methods include the 200-percent declining-balance method, the 150-percent declining-balance method (which may be elected), and the straight-line method (which may be elected).

Under ADS (which may be elected) the applicable depreciation method is the straight-line method.

A half-year convention (¶ 88) applies in the tax year personal property is acquired unless the mid-quarter convention applies because 40 percent or more of the aggregate bases of MACRS personal property was placed in service in the last quarter of the tax year (¶ 92). A mid-month convention applies to MACRS real property (¶ 90).

200-percent declining-balance method

The 200-percent declining-balance method is used to depreciate 3-year, 5-year, 7-year, and 10-year property (other than crop bearing trees or vines). The cost of trees or vines placed in service after 1988 are recovered using the straight-line method (Code Sec. 168(b)(3)(E)). A switch is made to the straight-line method in the first tax year that the straight-line method, when applied to the adjusted basis remaining at the beginning of the year, results in a larger deduction. The table percentages take this switch into account.

150-percent declining-balance method

The 150-percent declining-balance method is used to depreciate 15- and 20-year property; farm property that is 3-, 5-, 7-, 10-, 15-, or 20-year property (see below); and 3-, 5-, 7-, and 10-year property for which an election is made (see below). As in the case of the 200-percent declining-balance method, a switch is made to the straight-line method in the tax year that the straight-line method results in a greater deduction.

150-percent declining-balance method election

A taxpayer may make an irrevocable election to use the 150-percent declining-balance method to depreciate 3-, 5-, 7-, or 10-year property (other than fruit- or nut-bearing trees or vines), as well as 15-or 20-year property (Code Sec. 168(b)(2)(C); Code Sec. 168(b)(5)).

The election applies to all assets within a property class (including farm property within a property class) for which an election is made and which are placed in service during the tax year of the election. The election is made on Form 4562. No special election statement is attached to the return. See below for making the election on an amended return.

The applicable recovery period depends on the date that the property for which the election is made is placed in service. For property placed in service before January 1, 1999, the ADS recovery period for a property applies (¶ 150) (Code Sec. 168(c)(2), prior to being stricken by P.L. 105-206). For property placed in service after December 31, 1998, the regular recovery period for a property applies (¶ 100) (Code Sec. 168(c), as amended by P.L. 105-206). No alternative minimum tax depreciation adjustment is necessary with respect to a property for which this election is made since the applicable AMT depreciation method for 3-, 5-, 7-, 10-, 15-, and 20-year property is the 150-percent declining-balance method over the ADS recovery period (for property placed in service before 1999) or the regular recovery period (for property placed in service after 1998). See ¶ 170.

The effect of the election with respect to 15- and 20-year property placed in service before 1999 is to substitute the ADS recovery period for the regular 15- or 20-year recovery period. The 150-percent declining-balance method applies to such property whether or not the election is made. In the case of 15-and 20-year property placed in service after 1998, the election would have no impact since the regular 15- or 20-year tax recovery period will apply whether or not the election is made.

A half-year or mid-quarter convention (¶ 86) applies to property depreciated using the 150-percent declining-balance method.

Straight-line method

The straight-line method is mandatory for residential rental property (¶ 114), nonresidential real property (¶ 116), water utility property (¶ 113), railroad gradings and tunnel bores (¶ 120), certain fruit or nut bearing trees and vines (¶ 108), qualified 15-year leasehold improvement property (¶ 126), qualified 15-year restaurant property (¶ 110), and qualified 15-year retail improvement property (¶ 110). The straight-line method is applied over the GDS recovery periods (¶ 100 and following).

A mid-month convention applies to nonresidential real property, residential rental property, and railroad grading and tunnel bores. A half-year or mid-quarter convention applies to all other property depreciated using a straight-line method. See ¶ 86.

Straight-line election

For other property classes (i.e., 3-, 5-, 7-, 10-, 15-, and 20-year property), a taxpayer may elect the straight-line method over the GDS recovery periods. The election applies to all property within a class for which an election is made that is placed in service during the tax year. The election is irrevocable and is made on Form 4562 (Code Sec. 168(b)(3)(D); Code Sec. 168(b)(5)). No special election statement is attached to the return. See below for making the election on an amended return.

MACRS Alternative Depreciation System (ADS)

The straight-line method also applies to property depreciated using ADS. A taxpayer may make an irrevocable ADS election (Code Sec. 168(g)(7)). The ADS election differs from the straight-line election discussed above in that longer recovery periods are generally required under ADS. No special election statement is attached to the return. See below for making the election on an amended return.

Farm property

Farm business property (other than real property) placed in service after 1988 is depreciated under the 150-percent declining-balance method (instead of the 200-percent declining-balance method) unless an election was made to deduct preproduction expenditures, in which case the MACRS alternative depreciation system (ADS) must be used (Code Sec. 168(b)(2)(B); Code Sec. 263A(e)(2)). The

MACRS depreciation tables 14 through 18, at ¶ 180, that pertain to depreciation computations for the alternative minimum tax incorporate the 150-percent declining-balance method. Thus, depreciation for farm business property computed under the 150-percent declining-balance method may be determined under Table 14 if the half-year convention is used and under Tables 15 through 18 if the mid-quarter convention is used. An exception is provided for such property placed in service before July 1, 1989, if certain action (construction or binding contract) was taken on or before July 14, 1988 (Act Sec. 6028 of P.L. 100-647).

A farmer may make the straight-line and ADS elections described above.

See, also, ¶ 118 for rules relating to farmers.

Straight-line, 150 DB, and ADS election on amended return

Generally, these elections must be made by the due date of the return (including extensions) for the year that the property is placed in service. The election is made on Form 4562 by completing the form properly and applying the elected method. See IRS Publication 946 (How to Depreciate Property). If the election is not made on the original return, it can be made by filing an amended return within six months of the due date of the original return (excluding extensions). IRS Publication 946 says the following: "Attach the election to the amended return and write 'Filed pursuant to section 301.9100-2' on the election statement. File the amended return at the same address you filed the original return."

Alternative minimum tax

For rules explaining the allowable depreciation deduction for alternative minimum tax purposes see ¶ 170.

¶ 86

Applicable Convention

In computing MACRS deductions for the tax year in which property is placed in service and the year of disposition, averaging conventions are used to establish when the recovery (depreciation) period begins and ends. After depreciation for a full tax year is computed using the appropriate method, the appropriate averaging convention is applied to arrive at the amount of deductible depreciation. IRS depreciation tables incorporate the appropriate convention (except for the year of an early disposition (see ¶ 180)). The applicable convention is not elective, but rather one of three conventions (half-year (¶ 88), mid-month (¶ 90), and mid-quarter (¶ 92)) that applies to specified property (Code Sec. 168(d)).

These averaging conventions apply to depreciation computations whether made under the MACRS genreal depreciation system (GDS) (i.e., the regular MACRS method), the MACRS straight-line method, or the MACRS alternative depreciation system (ADS). The recovery period begins on the date specified under the applicable convention.

The same convention that is applied to depreciable property in the tax year in which it is placed in service must also be used in the tax year of disposition (Reg. § 1.168(d)-1(c)(1)).

No depreciation deduction is allowed for property placed in service and disposed of in the same tax year (Reg. § 1.168(d)-1(b)(3))..

See ¶ 160 for special rules that apply with respect to each convention in the year of a disposition.

See also ¶ 179 and ¶ 180 for sample calculations using the applicable conventions..

Special rules for applying averaging conventions in a short tax year are discussed at ¶ 132.

¶ 88

Half-Year Convention

The half-year convention applies to property other than residential rental property, nonresidential real property, and railroad grading and tunnel bores (Code Sec. 168(d)(1)). Under this convention, the recovery period begins or ends on the midpoint of the tax year (Code Sec. 168(d)(4)(A)). Thus, one-half of the depreciation for the first year of the recovery period is allowed in the tax year in which the property is first placed in service, regardless of the date the property is placed in service during the tax year.

If property is held for the entire recovery period, a half-year of depreciation is allowable in the tax year in which the recovery period ends.

Generally, a half-year of depreciation is allowed in the tax year of disposition if there is a disposition of property before the end of the recovery period (an "early disposition"). A half-year of depreciation is allowed on an asset subject to the half-year convention in the last year of its recovery period whether or not it is disposed of.

See ¶ 160 for special rules that apply with respect to the half-year convention in the year of a disposition.

Once it is determined that this convention applies, it applies to all depreciable property (other than residential rental property, nonresidential real property, and railroad grading and tunnel bores) placed in service during the tax year.

¶ 90

Mid-month Convention

The mid-month convention applies to residential rental property (including low-income housing), nonresidential real property, and railroad grading and tunnel bores (Code Sec. 168(d)(2)). Under this convention, the recovery period begins or ends on the midpoint of the month. The MACRS deduction is based on the number of months that the property was in service. Thus, one-half month of depreciation is allowed for the month that property is placed in service and for the month of disposition if there is a disposition of property before the end of the recovery period.

See ¶ 160 for special rules that apply with respect to the mid-month convention in the year of a disposition. See also ¶ 179 and ¶ 180.

¶ 92

Mid-quarter Convention

The mid-quarter convention applies to all MACRS property placed in service during a tax year (other than MACRS residential rental property, nonresidential real property, and railroad grading and tunnel bores) if more than 40 percent of the aggregate bases of such property is placed in service during the last three months of the tax year (Code Sec. 168(d)(3); Reg. § 1.168(d)-1(b)). Under this convention, the recovery periods for all MACRS property (other than MACRS residential rental property, nonresidential real property, and railroad grading and tunnel bores) placed in service, or disposed of, during any quarter of a tax year begin or end on the midpoint of that quarter.

A quarter is a period of three months. The first, second, third, and fourth quarters in a tax year begin on the first day of the first month, the first day of the fourth month, the first day of the seventh month, and the first day of the tenth month of the tax year, respectively.

In determining whether the mid-quarter convention is applicable, the aggregate basis of property placed in service in the last three months of the tax year must be computed regardless of the length of the tax year. Thus, if a short tax year consists of three months or less, the mid-quarter convention applies regardless of when depreciable property is placed in service during the tax year (see ¶ 132).

In applying the 40-percent test, the following rules are utilized:

(1) The depreciable basis of property not subject to MACRS is disregarded (Code Sec. 168(d)(3)(A)).

(2) Amounts expensed under Code Sec. 179 are disregarded (Reg. § 1.168(d)-1(b)(4); IRS Letter Ruling 9126014, March 29, 1991).

(3) The depreciable basis of MACRS nonresidential real property, residential rental property, and railroad grading and tunnel bores is disregarded (Code Sec. 168(d)(3)(b)(i)).

(4) The depreciable basis of MACRS listed property is included (unless otherwise disregarded, for example, because it is expensed under Code Sec. 179) (Reg. § 1.168(d)-1(b)(2)).

(5) MACRS property placed in service and disposed of within the same tax year is disregarded (Code Sec. 168(d)(3)(B)(ii)). However, if such property is subsequently reacquired and again placed in service during the same tax year, depreciable basis as of the later of the dates placed in service is included (Reg.§ 1.168(d)-1(b)(3)).

(6) The portion of the basis of MACRS property that is attributable to personal use is disregarded (Reg. § 1.168(d)-1(b)(4)).

The first-year 30-percent or 50-percent MACRS bonus depreciation allowance does not reduce depreciable basis for purposes of determining whether the mid-quarter convention applies. For other reductions, see ¶ 70.

By properly allocating the Code Sec. 179 deduction or timing purchases of depreciable property, a taxpayer may be able to trigger or avoid the mid-quarter convention. These and other mid-quarter convention planning opportunities are discussed at ¶ 486.

See ¶ 160 for special rules that apply with respect to the mid-quarter convention in the year of a disposition. See ¶ 179 and ¶ 180 for examples that illustrate the computation of depreciation using the mid-quarter convention.

The following examples illustrate whether or not the mid-quarter convention applies.

Example (1): In October, a calendar-year taxpayer purchases a truck and places it in service. There is no election to expense any part of the cost of the truck under Code Sec. 179, and this is the only asset placed in service during the tax year. The 40% test is satisfied and the mid-quarter convention applies because 100% of the depreciable basis of property placed in service during the tax year is placed in service during the last three months of the tax year. Two years later, in April (before the end of the asset's recovery period), the truck is sold. The mid-quarter convention must be used in determining the depreciation deduction for the truck in the year of disposition.

Example (2): During the current tax year, a calendar-year taxpayer purchased and placed in service the following items:

January: A light general purpose truck that cost $8,000;

August: An office desk that cost $5,000 and a safe that cost $1,000;

November: A computer that cost $3,000.

No amount was expensed under Code Sec. 179. In September, the truck and the desk are sold. Thus, the truck and desk were placed in service and disposed of in the same tax year. In determining whether the mid-quarter convention applies to depreciable property placed in service during the current tax year, the depreciable basis of the truck and the desk are not considered. For purposes of the 40% test, the amount of the aggregate bases of property placed in service during the current tax year is $4,000 ($1,000 safe + $3,000 computer). The depreciable basis of property placed in service during the last three months of the tax year is $3,000 (the computer), which exceeds $1,600 (40% of the $4,000 aggregate bases of property placed in service during the current tax year). Thus, the mid-quarter convention applies to the safe and the computer. No depreciation is allowed on the truck and desk because they were placed in service and disposed of in the same tax year.

Example (3): The facts are the same as in *Example (2)*, except that the truck is acquired in December for $7,000 and is not sold. The truck is considered placed in service in December and its basis is included in determining whether the mid-quarter convention applies. The amount of the aggregate bases of property placed in service during the current tax year is $11,000 ($1,000 safe + $3,000 computer + $7,000 truck). The depreciable basis of property placed in service during the last three months of the tax year is $10,000 ($3,000 computer + $7,000 truck), which exceeds $4,400 (40% of the $11,000 aggregate bases of property placed in service during the current tax year). Thus, the mid-quarter convention applies to the truck, safe, and computer.

Election for tax year that includes September 11, 2001

Taxpayers were permitted to elect to apply the half-year convention in a tax year that included September 11, 2001, in the third or fourth quarter to all property that would otherwise be subject to the mid-quarter convention (Notice 2001-70, 2001-2 CB 437; Notice 2001-74, 2001-2 CB 551).

Taxpayers who filed their return for the tax year that included September 11, 2001, in the third or fourth quarter without making the election (for example, because the election was announced after the return was filed) were required to seek permission to make the election on an amended return filed pursuant to Reg. § 301.9100-3. The IRS, however, issued Notice 2003-45 (I.R.B. 2003-29, 86), to relieve taxpayers of this administrative burden (IRS Letter Ruling 200352009, September 15, 2003). Under Notice 2003-45, taxpayers were permitted to file an amended return by December 31, 2003, to make the election.

The IRS intends to amend its regulations under Code Sec. 168 to incorporate this guidance. The relief applied whether or not a taxpayer was directly affected by the terrorist attacks.

Aggregate basis of property

For purposes of the 40-percent test, the aggregate basis of property is the sum of the depreciable bases of all items of depreciable property that are considered in applying this test (Reg. § 1.168(d)-1(b)(4)).

Like-kind exchanges and involuntary conversions

Special rules apply if a taxpayer acquires property in a like-kind exchange or involuntary conversion (Reg. § 1.168-6(f)). See ¶ 167.

Affiliated group

If a taxpayer is a member of an affiliated group under Code Sec. 1504, without regard to Code Sec. 1504(b), all the members of the group that are included on the consolidated return are treated as one taxpayer for purposes of applying the

40-percent test. Thus, the depreciable bases of all property placed in service by members of a consolidated group during a consolidated return year are considered (unless otherwise excluded) in applying the 40-percent test to determine whether the mid-quarter convention applies to property placed in service by members during the consolidated return year. The test is applied separately to the depreciable bases of property placed in service by any member of an affiliated group that is not included in a consolidated return for the tax year during which the property is placed in service (Reg. § 1.168(d)-1(b)(5)).

For a subsidiary created by a member of an affiliated group during the consolidated return year that is itself a member of the group, the depreciable bases of property placed in service by the subsidiary during the consolidated return year of formation is included with the depreciable bases of property placed in service in such year by other members in applying the 40-percent test. The newly formed subsidiary is treated as being in existence for the entire consolidated return year for purposes of applying the applicable convention to determine when the recovery period begins (Reg. § 1.168(d)-1(b)(5)).

The depreciable bases of property placed in service by a corporation that joins or leaves a consolidated group during the portion of the consolidated return year that it is a member of the group is included with the depreciable bases of property placed in service during the consolidated return year by other members in applying the 40-percent test. For such property, the corporation is treated as being a member of the consolidated group for the entire consolidated return year for purposes of applying the applicable convention to determine when the recovery period begins. However, the depreciable bases of property placed in service while the corporation is not a member of the group is not considered by the affiliated group (Reg. § 1.168(d)-1(b)(5)).

For depreciable property placed in service by a corporation in the tax year ending immediately before it joins a consolidated group or beginning immediately after it leaves a consolidated group, the applicable convention is applied to such property under the rules applicable to either a full tax year or a short tax year, as appropriate (Reg. § 1.168(d)-1(b)(5)).

For purposes of the 40-percent test, depreciable basis does not include adjustments resulting from transfers of property between members of the same affiliated group filing a consolidated return. Accordingly, such property is considered as placed in service on the date that it is placed in service by the transferor-member (or first transferor-member to place such property in service if there are multiple transfers between members). The depreciable basis of such property for purposes of the 40-percent test is the depreciable basis of the transferor-member (or the first transferor-member to place such property in service if there are multiple transfers between members) (Reg. § 1.168(d)-1(b)(5)).

Example (4): A new subsidiary is formed on August 1 of the current tax year by a member of a consolidated group that files a calendar-year consolidated return. The subsidiary places depreciable property in service on August 5. If the mid-quarter convention applies to property placed in service by the members of the consolidated group (including the newly formed subsidiary), the recovery period of the property placed in service by the subsidiary begins on the midpoint of the third quarter of the consolidated return year (August 15). If the half-year convention applies to such property, it begins on the midpoint of the consolidated return year (July 1).

Example (5): A calendar-year corporation joins a consolidated group on July 1 of the current tax year and is included in a calendar-year consolidated return. For purposes of the 40% test, the amount of the depreciable bases of property placed in service before the corporation joined the group is not considered, but the amount of the depreciable bases of property placed in service during the period July 1 through December 31 is included with the amount of the depreciable bases of property placed in service by other members of the group during the entire consolidated return year.

However, in applying the applicable convention to determine when the recovery period begins for depreciable property placed in service for the period July 1 to December 31, the new member is treated as a member of the consolidated group for the entire consolidated return year. Thus, if the half-year convention applies to depreciable property placed in service by the group (including the depreciable basis of property placed in service after June 30 by the new member), the recovery period of the property begins on the midpoint of the consolidated return year (July 1).

Example (6): A consolidated group files a calendar-year consolidated return. One member of the group purchases $50,000 of depreciable property and places it in service on January 5 of the current tax year. On December 1 of the current tax year, the property is transferred to another of the group for $75,000. For purposes of applying the 40% test to the group, the property is treated as placed in service on January 5, the date that the transferor placed the property in service, and the depreciable basis of the property is $50,000, the transferor's depreciable basis.

See, also, ¶ 132, for an additional discussion on the MACRS depreciation computation for short tax years of new subsidiaries.

Partnerships and S corporations

For property placed in service by a partnership or an S corporation, the 40-percent test is generally applied at the partnership or corporate level. However, such test is applied at the partner, shareholder, or other appropriate level if a partnership or an S corporation is formed or availed of for the principal purpose of either avoiding the application of the mid-quarter convention or having it apply where it otherwise would not apply (Reg. § 1.168(d)-1(b)(6)).

Certain nonrecognition transactions

Generally, the depreciable basis of transferred property in a nontaxable transfer under Code Sec. 332, 351, 361, 721, or 731 is not considered by the transferor in applying the 40-percent test if the property was placed in service in the year of transfer. Such property is deemed placed in service by the transferee on the date of transfer and must be considered by the transferee in applying the 40-percent test. These rules do not cover transfers between members of a consolidated group (Reg. § 1.168(d)-1(b)(7)).

However, the date that the transferor placed the property in service must be used in applying the applicable convention to determine when the recovery period for the transferred property begins. Thus, if the mid-quarter convention applies to property transferred in a nonrecognition transaction indicated above, the recovery period for the property begins on the midpoint of the quarter of the tax year that the transferor placed the property in service.

If the transferor placed the transferred property in service in a short tax year, the transferor is treated as having a 12-month tax year beginning on the first day of the short tax year for purposes of applying the applicable convention and allocating the depreciation deduction between the transferor and the transferee. The depreciation deduction is allocated based on the number of months in the transferor's tax year that each party held the property in service. The transferor would include the month that the property is placed in service and exclude the month in which the transfer occurs.

The balance of the depreciation deduction for the transferor's tax year in which the property was transferred is allocated to the transferee. For the remainder of the transferee's current tax year (if the transferee has a different tax year than the transferor) and for subsequent tax years, the depreciation deduction for the transferee is calculated by allocating to the transferee's tax year the depreciation attributable to each recovery year, or portion thereof, that falls within the transferee's tax year.

The transferor may use either the mid-quarter or the half-year convention in determining the depreciation deduction for the transferred property if the applicable convention is not determined by the time the income tax return for the year of transfer is filed because the transferee's tax year has not ended. However, the transferor must indicate such fact on the depreciation form. If the transferee determines that a different convention applies to the transferred property, the transferor should redetermine the depreciation deduction and file an amended return within the period of limitation (Reg. § 1.168(d)-1(b)(7)).

Example (7): During the current tax year, a calendar-year taxpayer purchases $100,000 of satellite equipment and $15,000 of computer equipment. The former is placed in service in January and the latter is placed in service in February. On October 1, the computer equipment is transferred to a calendar-year partnership in a nontaxable transaction under Code Sec. 721. During the current tax year, the partnership purchases 30 office desks for a total of $15,000 and places them in service in June.

In applying the 40% test, the computer equipment is treated as placed in service by the transferee-partnership on the date of transfer (October 1) because the equipment was transferred in a nontaxable transfer in the same tax year that it was placed in service by the transferor. The $15,000 depreciable basis of the computer equipment that is placed in service during the last three months of the transferee's tax year exceeds $12,000 (40% of the $30,000 aggregate depreciable bases of property placed in service by the transferee during the tax year ($15,000 desks + $15,000 computer equipment)). Thus, the transferee satisfies the 40% test and the mid-quarter convention applies to the property placed in service by the transferee (including the transferred property).

In applying the mid-quarter convention to the computer equipment, the recovery period of the equipment begins on the mid-point of the first quarter of the transferor's tax year (February 15). The depreciation deduction allowable for the transferor's tax year is $5,250 ($15,000 × 35%) (Table 2 at ¶ 180, first-year table percentage for five year property subject to mid-quarter convention and placed in service in first quarter).

The depreciation deduction is allocated between the transferor and the transferee based on the number of months that each held the property in service. For this purpose, the computer equipment is treated as in service for 11 months (Feb.-Dec.) during the transferor's tax year and the transferor held it for 8 of the 11 months (Feb.-Sep.). Thus, the transferor's depreciation deduction on the computer equipment is $3,818 (8⁄11 × $5,250). The balance of the depreciation deduction on the computer equipment for the transferor's tax year, $1,432 (3⁄11 × $5,250), is allocated to the transferee.

In the following tax year, the transferee's depreciation deduction on the computer equipment is $3,900 ($15,000 × 26%) (second-year table percentage).

This example is based on the example in Reg. § 1.168(d)-1(b)(7).

Classification and Recovery Period of Property

¶ 100

MACRS Property Classes and Recovery Periods

A "Quick-Reference" recovery-period chart is reproduced in the back of this book before the Index. This chart lists numerous types of assets and business activities, as well as the recovery period for these assets and the assets used in these business activities. If the particular asset or business activity is discussed in this book, a cross-reference is provided. Rev. Proc. 87-56, which provides a comprehensive table of depreciation periods is reproduced at ¶ 191.

Each item of property depreciated under MACRS is assigned to a property class which establishes the number of years over which the basis of an asset is recovered (the recovery period). A comprehensive IRS table of these property classes and depreciation periods (including ADS recovery periods) for MACRS property is contained in Rev. Proc. 87-56, which is reproduced at ¶ 191. The explanations at ¶ 190 and ¶ 191 explain how to determine the recovery period of a particular asset.

Recovery years are 12-month periods. The 12-month period begins on the date that the property is considered placed in service under the applicable convention. For example, if an automobile with a five-year recovery period is placed in service in the 2009 calendar tax year and the half-year convention applies, the recovery period begins on July 1, 2009, and ends on June 30, 2014. Depreciation will be claimed in each of six tax years (2009, 2010, 2011, 2012, 2013, and 2014) even though the recovery period is only five years.

The applicable recovery periods are not elective but are prescribed for each property class. The specific recovery period will depend upon whether the property is being depreciated under the general MACRS depreciation rules (GDS) or the alternative MACRS depreciation system (ADS).

The following are the property classes and GDS recovery periods (Code Sec. 168(c)):

Property Class	*Recovery Period*
3-year property	3-years (¶ 102)
5-year property	5-years (¶ 104)
7-year property	7-years (¶ 106)
10-year property	10-years (¶ 108)
15-year property	15-years (¶ 110)
20-year property	20-years (¶ 112)
Water utility property	25-years (¶ 113)
Residential rental property	27.5-years (¶ 114)
Nonresidential real property	39 or 31.5 years (¶ 116)
Railroad grading and tunnel bores	50-years (¶ 120)

Longer recovery periods generally apply if the alternative MACRS depreciation system (ADS) is used (¶ 150).

Shorter recovery periods may apply to property used on an Indian reservation (¶ 124).

Property is classified based upon the property's class life (if any) unless a different recovery class is assigned under Code Sec. 168(e)(2) (residential rental and nonresidential real property), Code Sec. 168(e)(3) (property assigned to a recovery class notwithstanding the class life of the property, if any), or Code Sec. 168(e)(4) (railroad grading and tunnel bores).

Class lives and recovery periods for MACRS purposes are set forth in Rev. Proc. 87-56, 1987-2 CB 674, and vary in some respects from the class lives set forth in Rev. Proc. 83-35, 1983-1 CB 745, which is still effective for property depreciated under ACRS or the Class Life Asset Depreciation Range (CLADR) System. Class lives and recovery periods as prescribed under Rev. Proc. 87-56 are set forth at ¶ 190.

¶ 102

3-Year Property

Three-year property is defined as property with a class life of four years or less (Code Sec. 168(e)(1)), but also includes certain property specifically designated as 3-year property by Code Sec. 168(e)(3). The 200-percent declining-balance method applies (¶ 84).

Three-year property includes (but is not limited to):

(1) Tractor units for use over the road (Asset Class 00.26).

Tractor units are not defined for depreciation purposes, but presumably the definition provided in Reg. § 145.4051-1(e)(1) for excise tax purposes would apply. In general, this regulation provides that a tractor is a highway vehicle primarily designed to tow a vehicle, such as a trailer or semitrailer, but which does not carry cargo on the same chassis as the engine. A vehicle equipped with air brakes and/or a towing package is presumed to be a tractor.

In contrast to a tractor unit, a truck (5-year property) is a highway vehicle primarily designed to transport its load on the same chassis as the engine even if it is also equipped to tow a vehicle, such as a trailer or semitrailer (Reg. § 145.4051-1(e)(2)).

Assets used in the commercial and contract carrying of freight by road, except transportation assets included in classes with prefix 00.2 are 5-year property (Asset Class 42.0).

(2) Breeding hogs (Asset Class 01.23).

(3) Any race horse over two years old when placed in service (Code Sec. 168(e)(3)(A)(i); (Asset Class 01.223)).

(4) Any horse other than a race horse which is more than 12 years old when placed in service (Code Sec. 168(e)(3)(A)(ii); Asset Classes 01.222 and 01.224)).

Horses not described in categories (3) and (4) are 7-year property (Asset Class 01.225). A race horse is generally considered placed in service when its training begins.

Race horses placed in service after December 31, 2008 and on or before January 1, 2014, are three-year property (Code Sec. 168(e)(3)(A)(i), as amended by P.L. 110-246). Under prior law, race horses that were two years or younger when placed in service were depreciated as 7-year MACRS property. A race horse is generally considered placed in service when its training begins. This is usually at the end of its yearling year, which is typically less than two years after birth. A race horse that has previously raced is generally considered placed in service when purchased from the prior owner.A horse's age is measured by reference to its actual birth date rather than the racing industry's treatment of January 1 of the year of birth as the birth date (Prop. Reg. § 1.168-3(c)(iii) (ACRS); Rev. Proc. 87-56, 1987-2 CB 674, as clarified and modified by Rev. Proc. 88-22, 1988-1 CB 785).

Reg. § 1.1231-2(c)(1) provides rules and examples for determining whether a horse is a race horse. Presumably, these guidelines may be used for depreciation classification purposes.

(5) Qualified rent-to-own property (Code Sec. 168(e)(3)(A)(iii)).

Qualified rent-to-own property is treated as 3-year property, effective for property placed in service after August 5, 1997 (Code Sec. 168(e)(3)(A)(iii)). A 4-year ADS period is assigned. In general, qualified rent-to-own property is property held by a rent-to-own dealer for purposes of being subject to a rent-to-own contract (Code Sec. 168(i)(14)). Previously, such property was classified as 5-year property (Asset Class 57.0, Distributive Trades and Services) (Rev. Rul. 95-52, 1995-2 CB 27; Rev. Proc. 95-38, 1995-2 CB 397). See, also, ¶ 364.

Computer software that is not amortizable under Code Sec. 197 is amortized over a 3-year period using the straight-line method beginning in the month it is placed in service (Code Sec. 167(f)(1); Reg. § 1.167(a)-14). See ¶ 48.

See ¶ 191 for a table of Asset Classes and recovery periods.

¶ 104

5-Year Property

Property with a class life of more than four but less than 10 years is generally classified as 5-year property (Code Sec. 168(e)(1)). In addition, certain property is specifically categorized as 5-year property even though the class life does not fall within this class life range (Code Sec. 168(e)(3)(B)). The 200-percent declining-balance method applies (¶ 84).

Five-year property includes (but is not limited to):

(1) cars and light general purpose trucks (Code Sec. 168(e)(3)(B)(i)) as well as heavy general purpose trucks (Asset Classes 00.22, 00.241, and 00.242 at ¶ 191);

A light general purpose truck includes trucks for use over the road with actual unloaded weight of less than 13,000 pounds. Heavy general purpose trucks are trucks for use over the road with actual unloaded weight of 13,000 pounds or greater. Heavy general purpose trucks include concrete ready mix trucks and ore trucks (see Asset Class definitions at ¶ 101). The distinction between light and heavy trucks, which are both 5-year property, is important if the MACRS alternative depreciation system (ADS) is used because a heavy truck has an ADS depreciation period of 6 years and a light truck has a 5-year ADS period.

A recreational vehicle (RV) or motor home is a light general purposes truck if its unloaded weight is less than 13,000 pounds. Otherwise an RV or motor home is a heavy general purpose truck (IRS Letter Ruling 8630022, April 25, 1986). This ruling was issued to an S corporation that owned and leased various types of RV vehicles pursuant to lease agreements. Note, also, that an RV or motor home would not be subject to the passenger automobile depreciation caps since it would be considered a truck with a (loaded) gross vehicle weight rating in excess of 6,000 pounds. See ¶ 208. As to eligibility of an RV or motor home for the Code Sec. 179 deduction, see the ¶ 302 discussion of "*Lodging facilities.*"

A truck is a highway vehicle primarily designed to transport its load on the same chassis as the engine even if it is also equipped to tow a vehicle, such as a trailer or semitrailer (Reg. § 145.4051-1(e)(2)).

The IRS in its market segmentation specialization program for the garden supplies industry classifies a dump truck as a heavy truck.

Indianapolis race cars are 7-year property (Asset Class 79.0, relating to property used for recreation or entertainment on payment of a fee for admission) and not 5-year property (Asset Class 00.22, automobiles) (CCA 200052019, September 27, 2000).

(2) taxis and buses (Asset Classes 00.22 and 00.23);

(3) airplanes not used in commercial or contract carrying of passengers or freight; all helicopters (Asset Class 00.21);

Commercial/contract airplanes are 7-year property (Asset Class 45.0).

The IRS, in response to a CCH inquiry, says that planes used in a pilot school are 5-year property.

(4) trailers and trailer-mounted containers (Asset Class 00.27) (see ¶ 5);

Tractor units that pull trailers are 3-year property (Asset Class 00.26). Tractor units are defined in Reg. § 145.4051-1(e)(i). See ¶ 102.

(5) computers and peripheral equipment (Code Sec. 168(i)(2)(B)) (Asset Class 00.12);

A computer is a programmable electronically activated device capable of accepting information, applying prescribed processes to the information, and supplying the results of these processes with or without human intervention. It usually consists of a central processing unit containing extensive storage, logic, arithmetic, and control capabilities (Code Sec. 168(i)(2)(B); Asset Class 00.12 description).

Peripheral equipment consists of auxiliary machines designed to be placed under the control of the computer. Examples include: card readers, card punches, magnetic tape feeds, high speed printers, optical character readers, tape cassettes, mass storage units, paper tape equipment, keypunches, data entry devices, teleprinters, terminals, tape drives, disc drives, disc files, disc packs, visual image projector tubes, card sorters, plotters, and collators (Assets Class 00.12 description).

Peripheral equipment does not include (1) typewriters, calculators, adding and accounting machines, copiers, duplicating equipment, and similar equipment or (2) equipment of a kind used primarily for amusement or entertainment of the user.

Computers and peripheral equipment are one of three types of qualified technological equipment (see below) which are assigned a five-year GDS recovery period by Code Sec. 168(e)(3)(B)(iv). Asset Class 00.12 is entitled “Information Systems” and consists entirely of computers and peripheral equipment.

In general, the definitions of computers and peripheral equipment contained in Code Sec. 168(i)(2) and Asset Class 00.12 are nearly identical. A five-year GDS and ADS recovery period applies in each case. One important difference, however, is that Asset Class 00.12 only applies to computers and peripheral equipment that are “used in administering normal business transactions and the maintenance of business records, their retrieval and analysis.” No such requirement exists under the Code Sec. 168(i)(2) definition.

Peripheral equipment does not include any equipment which is an integral part of other property which is not a computer (Code Sec. 168(i)(2)(B)(iv)). In this regard, Asset Class 00.12 states that peripheral equipment “does not include equipment that is an integral part of other capital equipment that is included in other classes of economic activity, i.e., computers used primarily for process or production control, switching, channeling, and automating distributive trades and services such as point of sale (POS) computer systems."

In Chief Counsel Advice 200229021 (April 12, 2002), the IRS ruled that assets relating to hydroelectric and nuclear power plants such as control and/or monitoring systems, nuclear simulator complex, radiation measurement and detection equipment, dispatch boards, supervisory control units, relays and meters, training simulator, and pilot wire protection were not computer or peripheral equipment under Asset Class 00.12 because the equipment was not used in administering normal business transactions and the maintenance of business records, their retrieval and analysis. In addition, these assets did not qualify under Asset Class 00.12 or Code Sec. 168(i)(2) because they are an integral part of property which is not a computer.

Computer software that is not a Code Sec. 197 intangible is generally amortized over 3 years beginning in the month it is placed in service. However, software that is part of the purchase price of a computer is depreciated over 5 years as part of the cost of the computer. Separately purchased off-the-shelf computer software is eligible for expensing under Code Sec. 179 if placed in service in a tax year that begins before 2010.

See ¶ 48 for details concerning the depreciation of computer software.

(6) data handling equipment other than computers, such as typewriters, calculators, adding and accounting machines, copiers, duplicating equipment, and similar equipment (Code Sec. 168(i)(2)(B)(iv); Asset Class 00.13);

(7) semi-conductor manufacturing equipment (Code Sec. 168(e)(3)(B)(ii));

This category includes printed wiring board and printed wiring assembly production equipment.

(8) computer-based telephone central office switching equipment (Code Sec. 168(e)(3)(B)(iii); Asset Class 48.121);

(9) qualified technological equipment, which is defined as computers and peripheral equipment (see above), high technology telephone station equipment installed on a customer's premises, and high technology medical equipment (Code Sec. 168(e)(3)(B)(iv));

These types of qualified technological equipment are defined in Code Sec. 168(i)(2).

Telephone station equipment (teletypewriters, telephones, booths, private exchanges, and comparable equipment described in Asset Class 48.13)) which is not considered qualified technological equipment is 7-year property.

(10) section 1245 property used in connection with research and experimentation as that term is defined for purposes of Code Sec. 174 (Code Sec. 168(e)(3)(B)(v); Code Sec. 168(i)(11));

Under ACRS (pre-1986) proposed regulations, research and experimentation property is defined as section 1245 property *predominantly* used in connection with research and experimentation (as described in Code Sec. 174 and Reg. § 1.174-2(a)). The property must be used (A) by its owner to conduct research and experimentation in its owner's trade or business, (B) by its owner to conduct research and experimentation for another person, (C) by a lessee to conduct research and experimentation in its trade or business, or (D) by the lessee to conduct research and experimentation for another person (Prop. Reg. § 1.168-3(c)(iii)). No MACRS regulations defining research and experimentation property have yet been issued. The ACRS and MACRS Code definitions ("section

1245 property used in connection with research and experimentation expenditures . . . " etc.), however, are identical.

See ¶ 168 for depreciation computation if a property's use changes to or from research and experimentation during its recovery period.

See ¶ 68 regarding capitalization and expensing of research and experimentation expenditures under Code Sec. 174.

(11) certain geothermal, solar, and wind energy property; and certain biomass property used by qualifying small power production facilities (Code Sec. 168(e)(3)(B)(vi); Reg. § 1.48-9);

(12) breeding cattle and dairy cattle (Asset Class 01.21) and breeding sheep and breeding goats (Asset Class 01.24);

Raised cattle usually have no depreciable basis because associated costs are currently deducted. See ¶ 118 for a discussion of farm property.

(13) assets used in construction by certain contractors, builders, and real estate subdividers and developers (Asset Class 15.0);

(14) logging machinery and equipment and road building equipment used by logging and sawmill operators and pulp manufacturers for their own account (Asset Class 24.1) (see Asset Classes 24.2 and 24.3 for sawmill equipment depreciation periods);

(15) assets used in the commercial and contract carrying of freight by road, except for transportation assets included in classes with the prefix 00.2 (Asset Class 42.0, Motor Transport—Freight);

(16) assets used in the urban and interurban commercial and contract carrying of passengers by road, except for transportation assets included in classes with the prefix 00.2 (Asset Class 41, Motor Transport—Passengers);

Transportation assets with prefix 00.2 generally include automobiles (5-year property), light and heavy trucks (5-year property), tractor units for use over-the road (three-year property), and trailers and trailer-mounted containers (five-year property);

(17) qualified New York Liberty Zone leasehold improvement property (see ¶ 124A);

(18) assets used in distributive trades and services, including assets used in wholesale and retail trade and personal and professional services and assets used in marketing petroleum and petroleum products (see below) (Asset Class 57.0).

(19) new farm machinery or equipment (other than a grain bin, cotton ginning asset, fence or land improvement) placed in service in 2009 (Code Sec. 168(e)(3)(B)(vii), as added by P.L. 110-343). See ¶ 118.

Personal and professional services/retail and wholesale trades

Asset Class 57.0 encompasses a large number of taxpayers. As in the case of any business activity class (business activity classes are described in Table B-2 of Rev. Proc. 87-56 at ¶ 191), recovery periods for specific assets described in Table B-1 take precedence even if the asset is used in the Asset Class 57.0 activity. For example, office furniture used by a lawyer is considered 7-year property because it is listed in Table B-1 (Asset Class 00.11). However, professional reference books (e.g., a professional library purchased by a lawyer) used in the same office are 5-year property (Asset Class 57.0) because books are not described in Table B-1. However, if a specific asset listed in Table B-1 is also specifically listed in the Table

B-2 business activity classification, then the recovery period for the business activity classification in Table B-2 governs. This situation, however, is rare and does not affect Asset Class 57.0 since no specific asset types are listed there. See ¶ 191 for additional discussion of these points.

Examples of personal and professional services are not specifically set forth in the description for MACRS Asset Class 57.0 contained in Rev. Proc. 87-56. However, Rev. Proc. 77-10 (1977-1 CB 548), which provided class lives for purposes of the ADR depreciation system, listed some examples of personal and professional services included within this classification. Rev. Proc. 77-10 specifically listed hotels and motels, laundry and dry cleaning establishments, beauty and barber shops, photographic studios and mortuaries as examples of personal service businesses. Examples of professional service businesses cited by Rev. Proc. 77-10 included services offered by doctors, dentists, lawyers, accountants, architects, engineers, and veterinarians. Assets used in the provision of repair and maintenance services, assets used in providing fire and burglary protection services are also included. Equipment or facilities used by a cemetery organization, news agency, teletype wire service, and frozen food lockers were included.

Rev. Proc. 77-10 also indicates that wholesale and retail trade includes activities of purchasing, assembling, storing, sorting, grading, and selling goods at the wholesale or retail level. Specific examples are restaurants, cafes, coin-operated dispensing machines, and the brokerage of scrap metal.

Activities involving the sale of merchandise, food and other items to the general public for personal or household consumption, and the rendering of services incidental to the sale of goods are considered retail activities rather than manufacturing (Rev. Rul. 81-66, 1981 CB 19).

A manufacturer stored food and meat products that it manufactured in distribution centers before selling the products to others. Citing Rev. Rul. 77-476 (see ¶ 190), the IRS held that the taxpayer was not engaged in a wholesale distributive trade or business (Asset Class 57.0). Instead, assets related to the distribution centers were classified as seven-year property (Asset Class 20.4, Manufacture of Other Food and Kindred Products). Test kitchens were also included in Asset Class 20.4 (Chief Counsel Advice 200137026, June 14, 2001).

Rev. Proc. 77-10 listed glassware, silverware, crockery, china, linens, napkins, tablecloths, towels, sheets, pillowcases used by a restaurant or hotel or motel as falling within the retail/wholesale and personal/professional service category. However, the IRS recently issued a procedure under which smallwares used by restaurants and bars can be deducted in the year of purchase. See ¶ 125.

Rental businesses. Taxpayers who rent consumer durables, other than pursuant to rent-to-own contracts, are engaged in an Asset Class 57.0 business activity, according to the IRS (Rev. Rul. 95-52, 1995-2 CB 27). Consumer durables rented pursuant to a rent-to-own contract were depreciated over five-years as Asset Class 57.0 property prior to enactment of Code Sec. 168(e)(3)(A)(iii), which now provides a three-year recovery period for such property. See ¶ 102.

Tuxedo rental is an Asset Class 57.0 activity.

The rental of furniture is generally considered an Asset Class 57.0 activity. However, if the furniture is used in an office, then the IRS may require that it be depreciated over seven years as office furniture. See "*Office furniture, fixtures, and equipment,*" below.

Generally, the IRS will determine the depreciation period of an asset by reference to the use to which the lessee puts the property unless a separate asset class has been established for the lessor's business activity. See ¶ 191, "*Leased property.*"

Residential rental property. The IRS has ruled that the rental of MACRS 27.5-year residential rental property is a Class 57.0 activity. As a result, appliances (e.g., stoves and refrigerators), furniture, carpets, blinds, and window treatments, etc., used in such property are 5-year property (five-year GDS recovery period and nine-year ADS recovery period). IRS Publication 527 (Residential Rental Property) and Form 4562 (Depreciation and Amortization) which have consistently categorized this property as 7-year property, have been corrected (Announcement 99-82, 1999-2 CB 244)).

Office furniture, fixtures, and equipment. According to guidelines contained in the IRS Internal Revenue Manual, a common issue in the retail industry is whether furniture, fixtures, and equipment is 7-year property (MACRS asset class 00.11 (Office furniture, fixtures, and equipment) (¶ 106) or 5-year property under MACRS Asset Class 57.0 (IRM Handbook No. 4.4.3, Sub-section 4.20.1 (4-30-1999)). The guidelines state: "The decision is based entirely on the asset's use rather than its inherent nature. If a table is used on the retail floor for display or for cutting material, then it is 5-year property under Class 57.0. That same table, however, in the store manager's office is not used directly in retailing and therefore becomes 7-year property under Class 00.11."

Norwest Corporation and Subsidiaries, 70 TCM 416, Dec. 50,834(M) involved the depreciation of furniture and fixtures used in a bank. The IRS conceded that furniture which was only suitable for use in a bank (property unique to banks) was 5-year property (Asset Class 57.0). However, the IRS argued, and the court agreed, that furniture and fixtures that were suitable for use in a variety of businesses were not removed from Asset Class 00.11 (7-year property) to Asset Class 57.0 merely because they were used by a bank. This decision and the audit guidelines can be reconciled on the grounds that the cutting/display table in the audit guideline example is not being used as office furniture.

In a subsequent case involving the same taxpayer, the Tax Court delved into the issue in more detail and established a priority rule. If an asset is described in both an asset category (Asset Classes 00.11 through 00.4) and an activity category (Asset Classes 01.1 through 80.0), the asset category classification will prevail (*Norwest Corporation and Subsidiaries*, 111 TC 105, Dec. 52,830). See ¶ 190 for details.

It appears that this priority rule is causing problems for taxpayers in the short-term furniture rental business. This business involves the temporary rental of furniture for business or residential use. Taxpayers in this service industry have apparently depreciated all such furniture over a five-year period as Asset Class 57.0 property without objection from the IRS. In the wake of the *Norwest* decision, however, it has been reported that IRS auditors are taking the position that when such furniture is rented for office use the priority rule applies and it should be depreciated as 7-year property (Asset Class 00.11). While the IRS position may be correct, it can result in unfortunate complications when the same furniture is rented multiple times for office use and residential use. In such case, the furniture is reclassified in the year in which its use changes and special depreciation calculations are required (Code Sec. 168(i)(5); Prop. Reg. § 1.168(i)-4 (explaining the rule in the context of ACRS)). See ¶ 169 for computational details. It may be necessary to enact legislation similar to that which applies to rent-to-own property (Code Sec. 168(e)(3)(A); Code Sec. 168(i)(14)) to eliminate this problem. See, for example, H.R. 1597 (introduced April 3, 2003, in the first session of the 108th Congress), which would retroactively classify office furniture held by a rental dealer for short-term rentals of no longer than 18 months as five-year property.

IRS Asset Class descriptions are provided at ¶ 191.

¶ 106

7-Year Property

Property with a class life of at least 10 but less than 16 years or without any class life (and not classified as residential rental property or nonresidential real property) is generally classified as 7-year property (Code Sec. 168(e)(3)(C)). The 200-percent declining-balance method applies (¶ 84).

Office furniture, fixtures, and equipment. This class includes desks, files, safes, overhead projectors, cell phones or cellular phones, fax machines, and communications equipment not used included in other property classes (Asset Class 00.11). Note that the heading for this asset class refers to "office" furniture and equipment. Thus, for example, furniture in a hotel or motel room presumably does not fit into this classification, but rather would be considered property used in the provision of personal services (Asset Class 57.0) and have a five-year depreciation period. However, furniture used in the manager's office in a hotel or motel would be considered Asset Class 00.11 property. See ¶ 104 for additional information on office furniture and equipment, including office equipment held for rental.

Railroad assets. Certain railroad asset are 7-year property. These include railroad machinery and equipment (Asset Class 40.1), roadway accounts (Asset Class 40.1) and railroad track (Asset Class 40.4), and railroad cars and locomotives, except those owned by railroad transportation companies (Asset Class 00.25). Other railroad assets are given longer recovery periods. See Asset Classes 40.1 through 40.54. Railroad grading and tunnel bores have a 50-year recovery period (see ¶ 120).

Subway cars were classified as personal property with no class life (IRS Letter Ruling 8711110, December 18, 1986). Under MACRS such property has a seven-year recovery period.

A Class II or Class III railroad may elect a safe-harbor procedure (the "track maintenance allowance method") for accounting for track structure expenditures (Rev. Proc. 2002-65, 2002-2 CB 700). Safe-harbor procedures that apply to a railroad that files (or is a member of a combined reporting group that files) a Railroad Annual Report R-1 ("Form R-1") with the Surface Transportation Board based on the same reporting period as the taxpayer's taxable year are provided in Rev. Proc. 2001-46, 2001-2 CB 263. A Class II or III railroad that is reclassified as a Class I railroad required to file a Form R-1 may be able to change to the safe-harbor procedure of Rev. Proc. 2001-46.

Air transport. Includes assets (except helicopters) used in commercial and contract carrying of passengers and freight by air. See Asset Class 45.0 for details. Other aircraft and helicopters are 5-year property (Asset Class 00.21). See ¶ 104. For the treatment of maintenance costs, see ¶ 125.

Livestock and horses. Certain livestock, breeding or work horses 12 years old or less when placed in service, and other horses (Asset Classes 01.1, 01.221, and 01.225) (see ¶ 191) are 7-year property. See ¶ 118.

Agricultural and horticultural structures. Single-purpose agricultural or horticultural structures generally placed in service before 1989 are also 7-year property, but they are classified as 10-year property if placed in service after 1988 unless subject to transitional rules. See ¶ 118.

Certain assets used in agricultural activities. Depreciable assets used in agricultural activities are 7-year property under Asset Class 01.1 of Rev. Proc. 87-56. This category includes machinery, equipment, grain bins, and fences (but no other land improvements) used in the production of crops, plants, vines, and trees; livestock; the operation of farm dairies, nurseries, greenhouses, sod farms, mushroom cellars, cranberry bogs, apiaries (i.e., bee keeping activities), and fur farms; and the performance of agriculture, animal husbandry, and horticultural services. However, any machinery or equipment (other than a grain bin, cotton ginning asset, fence, or land improvement), the original use of which begins with the taxpayer in 2009, and that is placed in service by the taxpayer in a farming business in 2009, has a recovery period of five years under GDS (Code Sec. 168(e)(3)(B)(vii), as added by the Emergency Economic Stabilization Act of 2008 (P.L. 110-343)). See ¶ 118.

Fishing vessels. A fishing vessel, does not have an assigned class life under MACRS and, therefore, is seven-year property (IRS Audit Technique Guide for the Alaskan Commercial Fishing Industry: Catcher Vessels: Part I (July 1995), (reproduced in full text in the IRS POSITIONS REPORTER at ¶ 200,645). The guide notes that fishing vessels are not considered water transportation equipment (10-year property described in Asset Class 00.28).

The ADS period for personal property with no class life is 12 years.

It is important to note that the IRS audit guide for the Alaskan Commercial Fishing Industry distinguishes between fishing vessels and fish processing and fish tendering vessels. According to a section covering depreciation in Part II of the guide, if the primary or exclusive activity of a vessel is processing fish or operating as a tender by transporting fish to a shore-based or floating processor, such vessel is an Asset Class 00.28 asset with a ten-year recovery period. This conclusion seems correct with respect to a tender vessel since its primary activity relates to the transportation of fish. However, a processing vessel arguably may be classified as 7-year property (Asset Class 20.4, Manufacture of Other Food and Kindred Products). The audit guide in fact indicates that a processing vessel falls within this class but concludes that it is removed by virtue of being described as a specific asset type in Asset Class 00.28. Apparently, the IRS considers a processing vessel (like a tendering vessel) to be engaged in a transportation activity. This was the position taken in IRS Letter Ruling 9502001 (June 30, 1994) which categorized a factory trawler which harvested and processed fish as an Asset Class 00.28 vessel even though the primary activity of the trawler was, according to the IRS, described in Asset Class 20.4.

The guide appears to take the position that catcher/harvester vessels that have the capacity only to "head and gut" and freeze fish are not primarily engaged in a processing or transportation activity and, therefore, qualify as 7-year property.

The depreciable basis of a vessel does not include the amount of funds withdrawn from a capital construction fund established under Sec. 607 of the Merchant Marine Act (MMA) to pay for the vessel (Code Sec. 7518). Thus, no depreciation deductions are allowed in determining regular tax liability or net income from self-employment if a fishing vessel is purchased entirely with withdrawn amounts (IRS Letter Ruling 200022007, February 15, 2000).

Gathering systems (oil and gas). The Energy Tax Incentives Act of 2005 (P.L. 109-59) classifies a natural gas gathering line as 7-year MACRS property with a 14 year alternative depreciation system (ADS) recovery period if:

(1) the original use commenced with the taxpayer after April 11, 2005;

(2) the property was placed in service after April 11, 2005; and

(3) the taxpayer or a related party did not enter into a binding contract for the construction of the pipeline on or before April 11, 2005 (or, in the case of self-constructed property, the taxpayer or a related party did not start construction on or before that date) (Code Sec. 168(e)(3)(C)(iv), as added by P.L. 109-59; Act Sec. 1326(e) of P.L. 109-59 (relating to effective date)).

No alternative minimum tax adjustment is required if the natural gas gathering line qualifies for the 7-year recovery period under this provision (Code Sec. 56(a)(1)(B), as amended by the Act).

A natural gas gathering line is defined to mean (1) the pipe, equipment, and appurtenances determined to be a gathering line by the Federal Energy Regulatory Commission (FERC) and (2) the pipe, equipment, and appurtenances used to deliver natural gas from the wellhead or a commonpoint to the point at which the gas first reaches a processing plant, an interconnection with a transmission pipeline for which a certificate as an interstate transmission pipeline has been issued by the FERC, an interconnection with an intrastate transmission pipeline, or a direct interconnection with a local distribution company, a gas storage facility, or an industrial consumer (Code Sec. 168(i)(17), as added by the Act).

The correct depreciation period for oil and gas pipeline gathering systems that do not qualify as MACRS property under the preceding rule (e.g., because placed in service before the effective date) is in dispute. The two possible classifications are: (1) Asset Class 13.2, which provides a 7-year recovery period for "assets used by petroleum and natural gas producers for drilling wells and the production of petroleum and natural gas, including gathering pipelines . . . " and (2) Asset Class 46.0, which provides a 15-year recovery period for "assets used in private, commercial, and contract carrying of petroleum, gas, and other products by means of pipes and conveyors."

The Tax Court has held that interconnected subterranean pipelines leading from wells to a processing plant and related compression facilities (gathering systems) were 15-year MACRS property (Asset Class 46.0—Pipeline Transportation) because the taxpayer was a nonproducer (*Duke Energy Natural Gas Corporation*, 109 TC 416, Dec. 52,395; similarly, *Clajon Gas Co., L.P.*, 119 TC 197, Dec. 54,919). However, the Tenth, Eighth, and Sixth Circuit Court of Appeals have classified such property as 7-year MACRS property.

The Court of Appeals for the Tenth Circuit reversed the Tax Court's decision in *Duke*, and ruled that the assets were 7-year MACRS property (Asset Class 13.2—Exploration for and Production of Petroleum and Natural Gas Deposits) because the pipelines were used for the benefit of the producer with whom the taxpayer contracted to transport the gas to production facilities (*Duke Energy Natural Gas Corporation*, CA-10, 99-1 USTC ¶ 50,449 (Nonacq., 1999-2 CB xvi)). In an action on decision (AOD 1999-017 (November 22, 1999)), the IRS Chief Counsel issued a recommendation of nonacquiescence to the Tenth Circuit's *Duke Energy* decision. Most recently, the Court of Appeals for the Eighth Circuit followed Tenth Circuit's reasoning and reversed the Tax Court's *Clajon* decision (*Clajon Gas Co. L.P.*, 2004-1 USTC ¶ 50,123). The Sixth Circuit has also determined that a natural gas pipeline gathering system owned by a nonproducing partnership engaged in the business of transporting natural gas to a processing plant was seven-year property (*Saginaw Bay Pipeline Co., et al.*, CA-6, 2003-2 USTC ¶ 50,592, rev'g DC Mich., 2001-2 USTC ¶ 50,642). In addition, a Wyoming district court has sided with the Tenth, Eighth, and Sixth Circuits (*J.D. True*, DC Wyo., 97-2 USTC ¶ 50,946).

An oil pipeline used by a utility to deliver fuel to a generating facility was not Asset Class 46.0 property. Asset Class 46.0 is not intended to cover private fuel systems (Rev. Rul. 77-476, 1977-2 CB 5).

Alaska natural gas pipeline. Alaska natural gas pipeline is 7-year MACRS property (Code Sec. 168(e)(3)(C)(iii), as added by the American Jobs Creation Act of 2004 (P.L. 108-357)). Alaska natural gas pipeline is qualifying pipeline property placed in service in Alaska after December 31, 2013 or which is treated as placed in service on January 1, 2014, if the taxpayer who places the property in service after December 31, 2004 and before January 1, 2014, elects such treatment. Qualifying property includes the pipe, trunk lines, related equipment, and appurtenances used to carry natural gas, but does not include any gas processing plant. (Code Sec. 168(i)(16), as added by the American Jobs Creation Act of 2004, effective for property placed into service after December 31, 2004). Election procedures are provided in Notice 2006-47.

Assets used in recreation businesses. Assets used in the provision of entertainment services for payment of a fee or admission charge are 7-year MACRS property with a 10-year ADS depreciation period (Asset Class 79.0). Examples include assets used in bowling alleys, billiard and pool halls, theaters, concert halls, and miniature golf courses. Specialized land improvements and structures such as golf courses, sports stadia, race tracks, and ski slopes are specifically excluded from this class. Buildings which house the assets used in providing the entertainment services are also excluded and treated as 39-year real property. See the description for Asset Class 80.0 at ¶ 191 and IRS Letter Ruling 200508015 which concludes that an outdoor music theatre was an Asset Class 79.0 activity and not a theme or amusement park (Asset Class 80.0 activity).

The IRS has ruled that slot machines and video terminals placed in casinos, bars, hotels, and restaurants pursuant to space leases (site owner leases space to machine owner in return for share of profits) are assets used in a recreation business. Similarly, slot machines, video lottery terminals, and supporting casino equipment, such as furniture and fixtures for slots, poker, roulette, blackjack, baccarat, bingo, and keno located within a taxpayer's casino/hotel are seven-year property. According to the IRS, this property does not qualify as five-year property as qualified technological equipment, an information system (Asset Class 00.12), or property used in a distributive trade or service (Asset Class 57.0) (Coordinated Issue Paper for the Gaming Industry, April 10, 2000; this Coordinated Issue Paper was updated in nearly identical form with an effective/reissue date of September 28, 2001).

Indianapolis racing cars are 7-year property (Asset Class 79.0). The race cars were not 3-year property (Asset Class 00.22, automobiles) (CCA 200052019, September 27, 2000).

For the classification of casino riverboats and barges, see ¶ 125.

Assets used in theme and amusement parks. These assets are also seven-year property but have an ADS period of 12.5 years (Asset Class 80.0 at ¶ 191). For example, VIP structures and smoking lounges, kiosks, and other structures from which concession sales at a theme or amusement park are made are Asset Class 80.0 assets (i.e., "appurtenances associated with a ride, attraction, amusement, or theme setting within the park", as described in Asset Class 80.0). A theme or amusement park is characterized by amusements, rides, or other attractions *permanently* situated on park land. See IRS Letter Ruling 200508015.

Motorsports entertainment complexes. The American Jobs Creation Act of 2004 (P.L. 108-357) categorizes "motorsports entertainment complexes" placed in service after October 22, 2004 and before January 1, 2010 as 7-year property (Code Sec. 168(e)(3)(C)(ii), as added by P.L. 108-357 and amended by P.L. 110-343).

A motorsports entertainment complex is defined as a racing track facility situated permanently on land and which hosts 1 or more racing events for automobiles, trucks, or motorcycles during the 36-month period following the first day of the month in which the facility is placed in service. The events must be open to the public for the price of admission. Specified ancillary and support facilities provided for the benefit of complex patrons are also treated as 7-year motorsports entertainment complex property if owned by the person who owns the complex (Code Sec. 168(i)(15), as added by P.L. 108-357).

Historically, auto race tracks were treated by the IRS the same as theme or amusement parks and were thus depreciated over a seven-year period (Asset Class 80.0). However, the IRS has recently started to challenge the seven-year period and begun to assign a depreciation period of 15 years or more. See, for example, Technical Advice Memorandum 200526019, March 10, 2005.

The new law provides that race track facilities placed into service after October 22, 2004 may not be treated as 7-year property under Asset Class 80.0 (Act Sec. 704(e)(2) of P.L. 108-357). This provision is not part of the Code and does not have an expiration date. Thus, unless the preceding January 1, 2010 expiration date is extended, it appears that motorsports entertainment complexes placed in service after 2007 may once again be subject to treatment as 15-year property.

No inference should be drawn from this provision regarding the proper treatment of property placed in service on or before October 22, 2003 (the date of enactment of P.L. 108-357) (Act Sec. 704(e)(3) of P.L. 108-357).

Property with no class life. Personal property and section 1245 real property with no class life is categorized as 7-year property. Personal property is given a 12-year ADS period. A 40-year ADS period applies to section 1245 real property with no class life (Code Sec. 168(e)(3)(C), (g)(2)(C), and (g)(3)(E)). The definitions of personal and section 1245 real property are discussed at ¶ 127C.

¶ 108

10-Year Property

Property with a class life of at least 16 but less than 20 years is classified as 10-year property (Code Sec. 168(e)(3)(D)). The 200-percent declining-balance method generally applies (¶ 84). 10-year property includes (but is not limited to):

(1) vessels (e.g., yachts), barges, tugs, and similar means of water transportation, but not used in marine construction or as a fishing vessel (Asset Class 00.28);

(2) single-purpose agricultural or horticultural structures generally placed in service after 1988 (Asset Class 01.4) (150-percent declining balance method generally applies; see below);

(3) fruit- or nut-bearing trees or vines placed in service after 1988 (straight-line method may apply; see below); and

(4) smart electric meters and smart electric grid systems (150-percent declining balance method applies, see below)

Vessels and barges

Fishing vessels have no assigned class life and are considered 7-year property. See ¶ 106. Vessels used in marine construction are 5-year property (Asset Class 15.0). Assets used in the contract or commercial carrying of freight or passengers by water, except for assets included in classes which begin with the prefix 00.2 (e.g., a vessel), including land improvements, are 15-year property (Asset Class 44.0).

The depreciable basis of a vessel does not include the amount of funds withdrawn from a capital construction fund established under Sec. 607 of the Merchant Marine Act (MMA) to pay for the vessel (Code Sec. 7518).

Salvage value must be estimated for ships, barges, and other vessels placed in service before 1981 and depreciated under the pre-ACRS rules (IRS Industry Specialization Program (ISP) Coordinated Issue Paper, I.R.C. Section 167 Salvage Value (October 7, 1996), reproduced in the CCH IRS POSITIONS REPORTER at ¶ 172,490).

The IRS has ruled in a Field Service Advice (FSA) (Field Service Advice Memorandum 199922033, March 3, 1999) that a three-story entertainment facility built on a barge which was no longer capable of water transportation, was nonresidential real property. A later FSA dealing with a similar facility concluded that additional factual development was needed. However, based on the facts presented, the FSA tended toward the conclusion that the barge was nonresidential real property (Field Service Advice Memorandum 199950004, August 30, 1999). See, also, ¶ 125 (*Gambling Boats and Barges*).

A vessel includes every description of watercraft or other artificial contrivance used, or capable of begins used, as a means of transportation on water (Code Sec. 7701(m)(1)(7); 1 USC section 3; ISP Coordinated Issue Paper: Shipping and Gaming Industries: Class Life of Floating Gaming Facilities, March 12, 2001; reproduced in CCH IRS Positions Reporter (IRPO) at ¶ 173,155).

A barge is a non-self propelled vessel (46 USC section 2101(2); ISP Coordinated Issue Paper cited above).

See, also, "*Leased property*" at ¶ 191.

Single purpose structures

Single-purpose agricultural or horticultural structures (item 2) include:

(1) enclosures or structures specifically designed, constructed, and used to house, raise, and feed a particular type of livestock (including poultry but not horses) and to house related equipment;

(2) greenhouses specifically designed, built, and used for commercial production of plants; and

(3) structures specifically designed, constructed, and used for commercial production of mushrooms.

5-, 7-, and 10-year farm property placed in service after 1988 is generally depreciated using the 150 percent declining balance method. See ¶ 118 for a detailed discussion of single-purpose agricultural or horticultural structures.

Trees and vines

Trees and vines described in item (3) must be depreciated under the straight-line method over the regular recovery period (10-years) unless ADS (straight-line method and 20-year recovery period) applies (Code Sec. 168(b)(3)(E)).

Under a transitional rule, the straight-line method and 10-year recovery period do not apply to property acquired pursuant to a written contract which was binding on July 14, 1988, and placed in service before January 1, 1990 (Act Sec. 6027(c)(2) of P.L. 100-647).

As explained in the Conference Committee Report for the Technical and Miscellaneous Revenue Act of 1988 (P.L. 100-647), the IRS treats fruit or nut bearing trees or vines placed in service before 1989 as a land improvement (Asset Class 00.3) with a MACRS recovery period of 15 years (20 years under ADS). Some taxpayers, however, have asserted that such property is personal property with no class life, and, therefore, is depreciable over seven years (12 years under ADS).

The placed-in-service date occurs and depreciation on an orchard, grove, or vineyard begins in the tax year that the trees or vines reach the income-producing stage (i.e., bear fruit, nuts, or grapes in commercially viable quantities) (Rev. Rul. 80-25, 1980-1 CB 65; Rev. Rul. 69-249, 1969-1 CB 31; Reg. § 1.46-3(d)(2)).

Such property also qualifies for the Code Sec. 179 expense allowance (IRS Market Segment Specialization Program (MSSP) Guide for Grain Farmers). If an orchard, grove, or vineyard is purchased prior to reaching the income-producing stage, the allowance should apparently be claimed in the tax year that the trees or vines reach the income-producing stage since Code Sec. 179(a) specifically provides that the deduction is claimed in the tax year that the acquired property is placed in service.

Smart electric meters and grid systems

A 10-year recovery period applies to qualified smart electric meters and qualified smart electric grid systems placed in service after October 3, 2008 (Code Sec. 168(e)(3)(D)(iii) and (iv), as added by the Emergency Economic Stabilization Act of 2008 (P.L. 110-343)). The 150-percent declining balance method is assigned as the applicable depreciation method (Code Sec. 168(b)(2)(C), as added by P.L. 110-343). Normally the 200-percent declining balance method is used to depreciate 10-year property.

But for this provision, property which qualifies as a smart electric meter or a smart electric grid system would generally be treated as property described in Asset Class 49.14 of Rev. Proc. 87-56 at ¶ 191. Such property is MACRS 20-year property with a 30 year alternative depreciation system (ADS) recovery period.

The 30-year alternative depreciation system (ADS) period continues to apply to qualified smart electric meters and grid systems.

A qualified smart electric meter is any time-based meter and related communication equipment placed in service by a taxpayer who is a supplier of electric energy or a provider of electric energy services, and which is capable of being used by the taxpayer as part of a system that:

(1) Measures and records electricity usage data on a time-differentiated basis in at least 24 separate time segments per day;

(2) Provides for the exchange of information between the supplier or provider and the customer's smart electric meter in support of time-based rates or other forms of demand response;

(3) Provides data to such supplier or provider so that the supplier or provider can provide energy usage information to customers electronically; and

(4) Provides net metering (Code Sec. 168(i)(18), as added by P.L. 110-343; Joint Committee on Taxation, Technical Explanation of H.R. 7060, the "Renewable Energy and Job Creation Tax Act of 2008" (JCX-75-08)).

No definition of net metering appears to be provided. However, previous versions of the provision have defined the term as the ability of the meter to provide a credit to the customer for providing electricity to the supplier or provider.

A qualified smart electric grid system is any smart grid property used as part of a system for electric distribution grid communications, monitoring, and management placed in service by a taxpayer who is a supplier of electric energy or a provider of electric energy services. Smart grid property includes electronics and related equipment that is capable of:

(1) Sensing, collecting, and monitoring data of or from all portions of a utility's electric distribution grid;

(2) Providing real-time, two-way communications to monitor to manage such grid; and

(3) Providing real-time analysis of an event prediction based upon collected data that can be used to improve electric distribution system reliability, quality, and performance (Code Sec. 168(i)(19), as added by P.L. 110-343).

Property that would otherwise have a class life of less than 10 years does not qualify as a qualified smart electric meter or a qualified smart electric grid system (Code Sec. 168(i)(18)(A)(ii) and (19)(A)(ii), as added by P.L. 110-343).

MACRS property with a class life of less than 16 years but 10 or more years is classified as seven-year property. If the class life is less than 10 years but more than 4 years it is classified as five-year property. Property with a class life of 4 years or less is considered three-year property (Code Sec. 168(e)(1)). The rule that property with a class life of less than 10 years does not qualify as a smart meter or smart electric grid system means that the new provision does not change the depreciation period of property that would otherwise qualify as 3-year or 5-year property. On the other hand, seven-year property is depreciated as 10-year property under this provision because seven-year property has a class life of 10 years or more but less then 16 years. It is unclear why Congress would want to apply a longer recovery period to seven-year property insofar as the provision is intended to provide an energy incentive. Nevertheless, as previously indicated, most property that qualifies as a smart electric meter or a smart electric grid is assigned a class life of 30 years, and therefore would be treated as MACRS 20-year property but for this new provision.

The unenrolled version of the bill (H.R. 1424) provided that property with a class life of less than *16* years did not qualify as a qualified smart electric meter or a qualified smart electric grid system. If the final version of the bill had been so enacted, then 7-year property that otherwise qualifies as a smart electric meter or a smart electric grid would have continued to be depreciated as MACRS seven-year property.

¶ 110

15-Year Property

Fifteen-year property includes property with a class life of at least 20 but less than 25 years (Code Sec. 168(e)(1)). Such property includes municipal wastewater plants, telephone distribution plant and comparable equipment, certain depreciable land improvements (such as sidewalks, roads, docks, bridges, fences, landscaping, and shrubbery), assets used in producing cement (but not cement products), water carrier assets not qualifying as 10-year property, pipelines, and service station buildings (Code Sec. 168(e)(3)(E)). Generally, 15-year property is depreciated using the 150 percent declining-balance method.

Fifteen-year property includes (but is not limited to):

(1) depreciable land improvements not specifically included in another asset class (Asset Class 00.3);

(2) qualified leasehold improvements to the interior portion of nonresidential real property that is at least three years old and which is placed in service by a lessor or lessee pursuant or under the terms of a lease after October 22, 2004 and before January 1, 2010 (Code Sec. 168(e)(3)(E)(iv), as added by P.L. 108-357 and amended by P.L. 110-343). See "Qualified leasehold improvements" at ¶ 126;

(3) qualified restaurant property placed in service after October 22, 2004 and before January 1, 2010 (Code Sec. 168(e)(3)(E)(v), as added by P.L. 108-357 and amended by P.L. 110-343). See below;

(4) qualified retail improvement property placed in service after December 31, 2008 and before January 1, 2010 (i.e., the 2009 calendar year) (Code Sec. 168(e)(3)(E)(ix), as added by P.L. 110-343). See "Qualified retail improvement property" at ¶ 126;

(5) municipal wastewater treatment plants (Code Sec. 168(e)(3)(E); Asset Class 50);

(6) telephone distribution plant and comparable equipment used for two-way exchange of voice and data communications (Code Sec. 168(e)(3)(E); (Asset Class 48.14);

(7) assets used in producing cement (but not cement products) (Asset Class 32.2);

(8) water transportation assets used in the commercial and contract carrying of freight and passengers by water if not included in an asset class with the prefix 00.2 (Asset Class 44.0);

(9) certain pipeline transportation assets (¶ 106) (Asset Class 46.0);

(10) qualifying retail motor fuel outlets (Code Sec. 168(e)(3)(E));

(11) section 1250 assets, including service station buildings, and depreciable land improvements (whether section 1245 or section 1250 property), used in marketing petroleum and petroleum products (Asset Class 57.1);

(12) car wash buildings and related land improvements (Asset Class 57.1);

According to the IRS, a car wash tunnel is included in Asset Class 57.1 even if gasoline or petroleum products are not sold at the location. A 15-year depreciation period applied to the entire car wash structure, including office space which was separated from the car wash frame by a wall (IRS Audit Technique Guide for the Car Wash Industry, reproduced in the CCH IRS POSITIONS REPORTER at ¶ 202,950).

(12) billboards (Asset Class 00.3 (Asset Class 57.1 if used in petroleum marketing) (see ¶ 127A, "*Signs*"));

(13) assets, including land improvements, used in electric utility nuclear power production (Asset Class 49.12);

The costs of constructing a spent nuclear fuel interim storage facility (SNFISF) to temporarily hold a utility's spent nuclear fuel were not currently deductible as business expenses (Code Sec. 162) or losses (Code Sec. 165). The SNFISF was depreciable over 15 years under Asset Class 49.12 (IRS Letter Ruling 9719007, January 17, 1997). The costs associated with the construction, operation, and decommissioning of an independent spent fuel storage installation (ISFSI) were, however, deductible as an abandonment loss (¶ 162) in the year paid or incurred where the related nuclear plant was abandoned and decommissioned (IRS Letter Ruling 200012082, December 22, 1999).

(14) Assets used in the commercial and contract carrying of freight and passengers by water except transportation assets included in classes with the prefix 00.2 (e.g., vessels) (Asset Class 44.0);

(15) Gas utility trunk pipelines and related storage facilities (Asset Class 49.24); and

(16) Initial clearing and grading land improvements pertaining to any gas utility property, effective for property placed into service after October 22, 2004 (Code Sec. 168(e)(3)(E)(vi), as added by the 2004 Jobs Act). The ADS period under the new provision is 20 years (Code Sec. 168(g)(3)(B), as amended by the American Jobs Creation Act of 2004 (P.L. 108-357)).

Initial clearing and grading costs are specifically excluded from Asset Class 49.24 (Gas Utility Trunk Pipelines and Related Storage) and Asset Class 00.3, relating to land improvements. Thus, according to the Conference Committee Report for the American Jobs Creation Act, they were depreciated as 7-year MACRS property (section 1245 real property for which no class life is provided).

(17) Natural gas distribution lines placed in service after April 11, 2005 and before before January 1, 2011 (Code Sec. 168(e)(3)(E)(viii), as added by the Energy Tax Incentives Act of 2005).

The original use of the distribution line must commence with the taxpayer after April 11, 2005. The taxpayer or a related party may not have entered into a binding contract for construction of the property on or before April 11, 2005, or, in the case of self-constructed property, started construction on or before April 11, 2005 (Act Sec. 1325(c) of the Energy Act). A 35-year ADS recovery period is assigned (Code Sec. 168(g)(3)(B), as amended by the Energy Act). Natural gas distribution lines which do not qualify for a 15-year recovery period under this provision are treated as MACRS 20-year property under Asset Class 49.21 (Gas Utility Distribution Facilities) of Rev. Proc. 87-56.

(18) Section 1245 property used in the transmission at 69 or more kilovolts of electricity for sale, if placed in service after April 11, 2005 (Code Sec. 168(e)(3)(E)(vii), as added by the Energy Tax Incentives Act of 2005).

The original use must begin with the taxpayer after April 11, 2005. The taxpayer or a related party may not have entered into a binding contract for the construction on or before April 11, 2005, or, in the case of self-constructed property, have started construction on or before April 11, 2005 (Act Sec.1309(c) of the Energy Act). A 30-year ADS period applies. Property that qualifies under this provision was previously treated as 20-year MACRS property under Asset Class 49.14 (Electric Utility Transmission and Distribution Plant) of Rev. Proc. 87-56.

Land improvements

Depreciable land improvements described in Asset Class 00.3 are 15-year property. Such land improvements include improvements made directly to or added to land, whether section 1245 or section 1250 (real) property. A structure is not a land improvement unless it is inherently permanent. See ¶ 127C. However, buildings and structural components as defined in Reg. § 1.48-1(e) do not qualify as land improvements. See ¶ 127 and ¶ 128.

Most land improvements are section 1250 property. Certain land improvements are section 1245 property because described in Code Sec. 1245(a)(3)(B) (e.g., tangible property used as an integral part of manufacturing, production, or extraction or of furnishing transportation, communications, electrical energy, gas, water, or sewage disposal services). See below.

Land improvements must qualify as a depreciable asset in order to be depreciated. See ¶ 5 for additional discussion of land improvements.

If a land improvement is section 1250 property an AMT adjustment is required unless the taxpayer elected ADS or the MACRS straight-line method or bonus depreciation was claimed. See ¶ 170. In addition, the section 1250 depreciation recapture rules apply. Under these rules, depreciation claimed in excess of straight-line depreciation is subject to recapture as ordinary if an asset is disposed of at a gain. See ¶ 160.

Examples of land improvements include:

(1) sidewalks;

(2) roads (¶ 5);

(3) canals;

(4) waterways;

(5) drainage facilities;

(6) sewers (but not municipal sewers);

(7) wharves and docks (however, see Asset Class 44.0, below);

(8) bridges;

(9) fences (nonagricultural);

(10) landscaping (¶ 5);

(11) shrubbery (¶ 5);

(12) radio and television transmitting towers; and

(13) parking lots (¶ 5).

Sidewalks, concrete driveways, asphalt streets and concrete curbs, playground equipment, fencing, and landscaping constructed or installed in connection with an apartment complex were land improvements (IRS Letter Ruling 8848039, September 2, 1988). The ruling notes that certain portions of the costs may not qualify for depreciation because they might be considered land. For example, this might impact part of the costs of the streets and landscaping. See ¶ 5 for determining portion of road and landscaping costs that are considered depreciable.

Playground equipment treated as a land improvement included swing sets, climbers, slides, see-saws, merry-go-rounds, picnic tables, pipe-frame park benches, basketball backboards, football/soccer goal posts, flag staffs or poles, softball backstops, jogging trails, and stationary aerobic equipment. See, also, ¶ 5 for additional discussion.

In the same ruling, various components of an electrical distribution system (pine poles, aerial lines, transformers, meters, street lighting) and water distribution system (valves, fire hydrants, fittings, tapping sleeves, PVC water pipe, water meters) that were installed by the taxpayer were also land improvements. These items were not classified as Asset Class 49.14, Electric Utility Transmission and Distribution Plant, and Asset Class 49.3, Water Utilities, because those classifications only apply to taxpayers that *sell* electricity and water.

Parking lots are considered land improvements. Note, for example, that parking lots are specifically mentioned as a type of land improvement in Rev. Proc. 87-56 Asset Class 80.0 (Theme and Amusement Parks) at ¶ 191. See ¶ 5. The IRS has recently ruled that open-air parking structures are buildings (39-year property) and not land improvements (Applicable Recovery Period Under Code Sec. 168(a) for Open-Air Parking Structures, Coordinated Issue Paper (LMSB4-0709-029) (Effective Date July 31, 2009)). See ¶ 127C.

Specialized land improvements or structures such as golf courses (¶ 5), sports stadiums, race tracks, ski slopes, and buildings which house assets used in entertainment services are specifically excluded from Asset Class 79.0 (Recreation) which has a seven-year recovery period.

It appears that a dam is generally considered a depreciable land improvement under MACRS with a 15-year recovery period under Asset Class 00.3 (Land Improvements) unless described in another asset class (e.g., dams are described in Asset Class 49.11 (Electric Utility Hydraulic Production Plant)). An earthen dam used by a farmer may qualify as a currently deductible soil and water conservation expenditure. In *R.L. Hunter*, 46 TC 477, Dec. 28,025, a dam was treated as a depreciable asset with a determinable useful life. See ¶ 118 for additional information concerning dams.

Land improvements included in another asset class

Land improvements specifically included in an asset class other than Asset Class 00.3 (Land Improvements) are not treated as 15-year property described in Asset Class 00.3. The following asset classes include specific references to the treatment of land improvements (land improvements are either included or excluded):

(1) Asset Class 01.1 (Agriculture) (agricultural fences but no other land improvements are 7-year property);

(2) Asset Class 26.1 (Manufacture of Pulp and Paper);

(3) Asset Class 28.0 (Manufacture of Chemicals and Allied Products);

(4) Asset Class 33.3 (Manufacture of Foundry Products);

(5) Asset Class 33.4 (Manufacture of Primary Steel Mill Products);

(6) Asset Class 37.32 (Ship and Boat Building Dry Docks and Land Improvements);

(7) Asset Class 40.2 (Railroad Structures and Similar Improvements);

(8) Asset Class 44.0 (Water Transportation);

(9) Asset Class 46.0 (Pipeline Transportation);

(10) Asset Class 48.14 (Telephone Distribution Plant);

(11) Asset Class 48.2 (Telegraph, Ocean Cable, and Satellite Communications);

(12) Asset Class 49.11 (Electric, Gas, Water and Steam, Utility Services; Electric Utility Hydraulic Production Plant);

(13) Asset Class 49.12 (Electric Utility Nuclear Production Plant);

(14) Asset Class 49.13 (Electric Utility Steam Production Plant);

(15) Asset Class 49.14 (Electric Utility Transmission and Distribution Plant);

(16) Asset Class 49.15 (Electric Utility Combustion Turbine Production Plant);

(17) Asset Class 49.223 (Substitute Natural Gas-Coal Gasification);

(18) Asset Class 49.24 (Gas Utility Trunk Pipeline and Related Storage Facilities);

(19) Asset Class 49.25 (Liquefied Natural Gas Plant);

(20) Asset Class 49.5 (Waste Reduction and Resource Recovery Plants);

(21) Asset Class 57.1 (Distributive Trades and Services-Billboard, Service Station Buildings, and Petroleum Marketing Land Improvements);

(22) Asset Class 79.0 (Recreation); and

(23) Asset Class 80.0 (Theme and Amusement Parks).

Property used in manufacturing, production, extraction, and certain other activities classified as section 1245 real property land improvements

Section 5.05 of Rev. Proc. 87-56 provides that Asset Class 00.3 land improvements include "other tangible property" described in Reg. § 1.48-1(d). This is property which is not tangible personal property (within the meaning of Code Sec. 1245(a)(3)(A)) (¶ 127C) and which is used as an integral part of manufacturing, production, or extraction, or as an integral part of furnishing transportation, communications, electrical energy, gas, water, or sewage disposal services, or which constitutes a research or storage facility used in connection with any of these activities. However, section 5.05 further provides that a structure that is essentially an item of machinery or equipment, or a structure that houses property used as an integral part of any of these activities if the use of the structure is so closely related to the use of such property that the structure clearly can be expected to be replaced when the property it initially houses is replaced, is included in the asset guideline class appropriate to the equipment to which it is related.

Tangible personal property is property other than (1) a building and a structural component of a building, (2) an improvement to land, or (3) a inherently permanent structure or a structural component of an inherently permanent structure. See ¶ 116.

Reg. § 1.48-1(d) defines other tangible property as tangible property (other than a building and its structural components) used as an integral part of manufacturing, production, or extraction, or as an integral part of furnishing transportation, communications, electrical energy, gas, water, or sewage disposal services by a person engaged in a trade or business of furnishing any such service, or which constitutes a research or storage facility used in connection with any of the foregoing activities. The regulation further define the terms "manufacturing, production, and extraction," "research and storage facilities," "integral part,", and gives examples of transportation and communication businesses.

"Other intangible property" described in the regulation is the same property described in Code Sec. 1245(a)(3). Thus, an item which is considered a land improvement under this rule is section 1245 real property for various purposes of the Code, including depreciation recapture and AMT calculations.

If an item of "other tangible property" is described in an asset class other than Asset Class 00.3 or "land improvements" are included in an asset class other than Asset Class 00.3 then the depreciation period of the item of other tangible property should be determined by reference to that other asset class. See "Land improvements included in another asset class," above.

See ¶ 127C for a discussion of other tangible property and property in the nature of machinery.

A permancy test was applied to determine whether petroleum storage tanks, which both the IRS and taxpayer agreed were section 1245(a)(3)(E) property, should be treated as a land improvement (*PDV America, Inc. and Subsidiaries v Commr*, Dec. 55,638(M), TC Memo. 2004-118). The court determined that the tanks were not permanent, based partly upon a history of past removals and relocations, and treated the tanks as five-year property under Asset Class 57.0 ("section 1245 assets used in marketing petroleum") rather than 15-year property under Asset

Class 57.1 ("land improvements, whether section 1245 property or section 1250 property...used in the marketing of petroleum").

The IRS has ruled that a structure which housed equipment in a waste-treatment production facility was essentially an item of machinery or equipment and, therefore, was not a land improvement (or a building or structure component). The structure instead was classified as 7-year property under Asset Class 49.5 (Waste Reduction and Resource Recovery Plants) (IRS Letter Ruling 200013038, December 27, 1999).

Real estate developers

The cost of improvements to subdivided real estate that is held for sale are not generally depreciable by a developer. Rather, these costs are capital expenditures, allocable to the basis of the developer in the subdivided lots (*W.C. & A.N. Miller Development Co.*, 81 TC 619, Dec. 40,486).

Streets, sewage, and utility systems built by a real estate developer were not depreciable as tangible property or amortizable as intangible property where the developer was required to dedicate the property to the city and the city was responsible for the cost of maintenance and reconstruction of the assets (IRS Letter Ruling 200017046, September 10, 1999). However, the transfer of the assets to the city in exchange for the proceeds of a bond sale was a disposition.

15-year qualified restaurant property

The American Jobs Creation Act of 2004 (P.L. 108-357) created a new category of 15-year property called "qualified restaurant property." This category applies to property placed in service after October 22, 2004 and before January 1, 2010 (Code Sec. 168(e)(3)(E)(v), as added by P.L. 108-357 and amended by the Economic Stabilization Act of 2008 (P.L. 110-343)). The straight-line method applies to such property (Code Sec. 168(b)(3)(H), as added by P.L. 108-357). If the MACRS alternative depreciation system (ADS) is elected or otherwise applies, the applicable MACRS recovery period is 39 years and the straight-line method applies (Code Sec. 168(g)(3)(B), as amended by P.L. 108-357). Whether or not ADS is elected, the applicable convention is the half-year convention, unless the mid-quarter convention applies.

The 15-year recovery period is not elective. However, a taxpayer could effectively elect out by making an ADS election. An ADS election, however, would apply to all types of MACRS 15-year property placed in service by the taxpayer during the tax year.

Qualified restaurant property defined for property placed in service after October 22, 2004 and before January 1, 2009. In the case of property placed in service after October 22, 2004 and before January 1, 2009, qualified restaurant property is any section 1250 property which is an improvement to a building if the improvement is placed in service more than three years after the date the building was first placed in service and more than 50 percent of the building's square footage is devoted to preparation of and seating for on-premises consumption of prepared meals (Code Sec. 168(e)(7), prior to amendment by P.L. 110-343).

The three-year period is measured from the date that the building was originally placed in service, whether or not it was originally placed in service by the taxpayer. For example, improvements to a restaurant building that is at least three years old at the time the taxpayer buys the building may qualify.

Qualified restaurant property defined for property placed in service after December 31, 2008 and before January 1, 2010. The 15-year recovery period for qualified restaurant property was scheduled to expire, effective for property placed in service after December 31, 2007, but was extended an additional two years by the Emergency Economic Act of 2008 (P.L. 110-343) (Code Sec. 168(e)(3)(E)(v), as amended by P.L. 110-343). Under the new law, restaurant improvements placed in service before January 1, 2010 continue to qualify as 15-year property. The same rules described above for restaurant improvements continue to apply with the significant exception that for property placed in service after December 31, 2008 and before January 1, 2010 (i.e., property placed in service during calendar year 2009), an improvement will qualify even if the improved restaurant building was not at least three years old when the improvement was made. The three-year requirement continues to apply to improvements placed in service in 2008 and earlier (Code Sec. 168(e)(7), as amended by P.L. 110-343, effective for property placed in service after December 31, 2008 (Division C, Act Sec. 305(b)(2), of P.L. 110-343 providing the effective date).

P.L. 110-343 also expands the definition of qualified restaurant property to include a building placed in service after December 31, 2008, and before January 1, 2010 (i.e., during the 2009 calendar year), if more than 50 percent of the building's square footage is devoted to preparation of, and seating for on-premises consumption of, prepared meals (Code Sec. 168(e)(7), as amended by P.L. 110-343). Such a building is depreciated similarly to an improvement to a restaurant building. Thus, the building is depreciated over 15 years (39 years under the MACRS alternative depreciation system (ADS)) using the straight-line method and the half-year or mid-quarter convention.

As amended, Code Sec. 168(e)(7), appears to apply the 15-year recovery period to a restaurant building whether it is new construction or an existing structure. The heading of Division C Act Sec. 505(b) of P.L. 110-343, which amended Code Sec. 168(e)(7), however, is entitled "Treatment to include new construction." In addition, an undesignated summary document prepared by the Joint Committee on Taxation makes a reference to "new restaurants" (Senate Finance Committee Summary Amendment to the Substitute Amendment to H.R.6049). Possibly, these references to new construction and new restaurants were intended to relate to elimination of the rule that an improvement previously only qualified for a 15-year recovery period if made to a restaurant that was at least three years old (i.e., improvements to new construction will now qualify for a 15-year recovery period if the improvement is made in 2009). The committee report for the provision (JCX-75-08) does not reflect the extension of the 15-year recovery period to restaurant buildings, and, therefore offers no insight into the issue.

Bonus depreciation. Effective for property placed in service after December 31, 2008, bonus depreciation under Code Sec. 168(k) may not be claimed on qualified restaurant property (Code Sec. 168(e)(7)(B), as amended by P.L. 110-343; Division C, Act Sec. 305(b)(2), of P.L. 110-343 providing the effective date). Thus, structural improvements placed in service in 2008 may be able to qualify for bonus depreciation. See ¶ 127D for discussion of bonus depreciation which was temporary reinstated by the Economic Stimulus Act for property acquired after December 31, 2007 and placed in service before January 1, 2009 (January 1, 2010 for property with a long production period).

Treatment of nonqualifying property. Prior to enactment of this provision, a section 1250 improvement to a restaurant building would be depreciated over 39 years beginning in the month that it was placed in service using the mid-month convention. The new law does not change the current rule that allows an improvement to a restaurant that is section 1245 property (personal property) to be depreciated as MACRS five-year property (Asset Class 57.0) under the MACRS cost segregation rules.

Chart of qualifying restaurant improvements. The IRS issued an "Industry Directive" which contains a detailed chart that categorizes various original restaurant components as section 1250 property (depreciable over 39 years) or section 1245 property (depreciable over five years under the cost segregation rules) (LMSB Directive on Cost Segregation in the Restaurant Industry reproduced as a Quick Reference Table in the appendix of this guide). Items listed in this chart as section 1250 property and placed in service after October 22, 2004 and before January 1, 2010, as an improvement can qualify for 15-year depreciation under the new law. Examples of such qualifying items include, electrical system components not dedicated to specific machinery or kitchen equipment, most interior and exterior lighting, elevators and escalators, fire protection systems, security systems, fireplaces, permanent floor coverings (other than carpeting), floors, most HVACs (heating ventilating and air conditioning units) unless dedicated solely to the kitchen, most plumbing unless dedicated to specific equipment, restroom accessories and partitions, walls, permanent wall coverings, and roofs.

The provision only applies to improvements to a building. Improvements that are not part of or attached to the restaurant building, for example, a detached sign supported on a concrete foundation, sidewalk, or depreciable landscaping, would generally constitute separately depreciable land improvements which also have a 15-year recovery period but may be depreciated using the 150-percent declining balance method. Other unattached improvements may qualify for a shorter recovery period if not considered a land improvement.

Relationship to qualified leasehold improvement property. A 15-year recovery period and straight-line depreciation method also apply to "qualified leasehold improvement property" placed in service after the October 22, 2004 and before January 1, 2010 (Code Sec. 168(e)(6), as amended by P.L. 110-343). Qualified leasehold improvement property is generally defined as section 1250 leasehold improvements made to commercial property by a lessor or lessee pursuant to a lease more than three years after the commercial property was placed in service. In certain circumstances, an improvement made by a lessor or lessee of a restaurant building could apparently qualify for a 15-year recovery period either as qualified leasehold improvement property or as qualified restaurant property. The provision for qualified restaurant property, however, is much broader in that it is not limited to leasehold improvements or by other restrictions that apply to qualified leasehold improvement property. See ¶ 126 for a discussion of qualified leasehold improvement property.

Coordination with Code Sec. 179 and depreciation recapture. The shortened depreciation period does not change the status of qualified restaurant property as section 1250 property. Since the Code Sec. 179 expense allowance only applies to section 1245 property (Code Sec. 179(d)(1)), qualified restaurant property may not be expensed.

Alternative minimum tax. No AMT depreciation adjustment is required for restaurant improvement property because the straight-line method applies. See ¶ 170.

Gasoline service stations and convenience stores

Section 1250 property, including service station buildings and land improvements, whether section 1245 property or section 1250 property, primarily used in the marketing of petroleum and petroleum products is treated as 15-year property under MACRS (Asset Class 57.1). Section 1245 property, not described above, which is primarily used for such a purpose is treated as five-year property under MACRS (Asset Class 57.0).

See ¶ 125 for service station equipment and canopy depreciation.

Effective for property placed in service after August 19, 1996, section 1250 property that qualifies as a "retail motor fuel outlet" is 15-year real property whether or not food or other convenience items are sold at the outlet (Code Sec. 168(e)(3)(E)(iii)). A 20-year ADS recovery period applies (Code Sec. 168(g)(3)(B)).

The definition of a retail motor fuels outlet is not provided in Code Sec. 168(e)(3)(E)(iii). The controlling committee report, however, provides a definition which is discussed at length in an IRS Coordinated Issue Paper for Petroleum and Retail Industries Convenience Stores, issued April 2, 1997. This paper modifies an earlier ISP paper, dated March 1, 1995, which outlines the treatment of convenience stores prior to enactment of Code Sec. 168(e)(3)(E)(iii).

The ISP paper, however, discusses the definition of a retail motor fuels outlet only in the context of a convenience store (C-store) even though the committee report and text of Code Sec. 168(e)(3)(E)(iii) apply the definition generally to "section 1250" property.

With respect to C-stores the ISP paper states:

> "A C-store contains none of the features typically associated with traditional service stations such as service bays, tiring changing and repair facilities, and car lifts. The C-store provides no services relating to the maintenance of automobiles and trucks and employs no mechanics or other personnel who specialize in caring for motor vehicles. The typical employee resembles an employee found in other consumer goods retail facilities. . . . Because a C-store does not provide the services offered by a traditional service station, we do not believe that a C-store building can be a 'service station building' within the meaning of Asset Class 57.1. However, the building can still be treated as 15-year property if it is primarily used in petroleum marketing or is a retail motor fuels outlet."

According to the ISP paper, a C-store will qualify as a retail motor fuels outlet (15-year property) if one or more of the following tests are met:

(1) more than 50 percent of the gross revenues generated by the C-store are derived from gasoline sales (the committee report and other IRS guidance, including IRS Publication 946, use the phrase "petroleum sales," so that oil sales would be also be included); or

(2) 50 percent or more of the floor space in the building (including restrooms, counters, and other areas allocable to traditional service station "services") are devoted to the petroleum marketing activity (the committee report and, other IRS guidance, including IRS Publication 946, use the phrase "petroleum marketing sales" in place of "the petroleum marketing activity"); or

(3) the C-store building is 1400 square feet or less.

The earlier ISP Paper, which was issued on March 1, 1995, provided a similar definition except that a convenience store had to satisfy *both* tests (1) *and* (2) or be 1400 square feet or less in order to qualify as Asset Class 57.1 property.

Definition of gross revenues and floor space. The background section of the April 2, 1997 ISP paper indicates that typically, only about 10 to 20 percent of a C-store's floor space is devoted to the marketing of petroleum products. "This includes facilities such as counters relating to the sale of gasoline dispensed from pump islands, as well as automobile supplies such as oil, anti-freeze, and window-washer fluid (which are marketed along with other consumer goods). The remainder of the

C-store floor space is devoted to office area, storage, restrooms, food preparation, walk-in cooler, general sales area, and, in some cases, seating for customers." Thus, the paper appears to take the position that in addition to the space devoted to the sale of oil and gasoline, space devoted to the sale of car-related products, such as anti-freeze, oil filters, wiper blades, etc., is attributable to a petroleum marketing activity for purposes of item (2) in the preceding definition.

However, the IRS takes a more restrictive view in Appendix 6.01 of Rev. Proc. 2008-52 which relates to accounting method changes. This procedure requires a taxpayer who is changing the classification of an item of section 1250 property placed in service after August 19, 1996, to a retail motor fuels outlet, to include the following statement with Form 3115:

> "For purposes of § 168(e)(3)(E)(iii) of the Internal Revenue Code, the taxpayer represents that (A) 50 percent or more of the gross revenue generated from the item of § 1250 property is from the sale of petroleum products (not including gross revenue from related services, such as the labor cost of oil changes and gross revenue from the sale of nonpetroleum products such as tires and oil filters), (B) 50 percent or more of the floor space in the item of property is devoted to the sale of petroleum products (not including floor space devoted to related services, such as oil changes and floor space devoted to nonpetroleum products such as tires and oil filters), or (C) the item of § 1250 property is 1,400 square feet or less."

Rev. Proc. 2008-52 supersedes Rev. Proc. 2002-9 which contains the identical requirement.

In response to a CCH query, a spokesperson from the examination division of the IRS confirmed that service bay areas are not treated as floor space devoted to a petroleum marketing activity because such space is used primarily to provide services and is not used primarily for the sale of petroleum products (oil and gas). (However, the Court of Appeals for the Eighth Circuit, has considered service bay and similar areas as floor space devoted to a petroleum marketing activity by applying a "traditional service station" standard. See discussion in "*Multiple Buildings*", below). With respect to the gross receipts test, the spokesperson indicated that only receipts from oil and gas sales are treated as receipts from a petroleum marketing activity.

The ISP paper indicates that gross revenue from petroleum sales should be compared to gross revenue from all other sources (e.g., food items, beverages, lottery, video rentals, etc.). Gross revenue includes all excise and sales taxes.

The IRS, however, has issued an audit technique guide for gas retailers under its market segment specialization program (MSSP Audit Technique Guide on Gas Retailers, March 23, 2003) which adds an arrow to the taxpayer's quiver. The guide now includes a description of the rules relating to qualification as a retail motor fuels outlet. The description of the gross receipts and floor space test treats floor space devoted to the sale of automotive related products and receipts from such products as floor space and gross receipts from petroleum products for purposes of the 50-percent tests.

> "The gross revenue attributable to the petroleum sales (motor fuel, lube oil, battery, tires, auto accessories and other traditional motor fuel retail outlet sales) should be compared to gross revenue from all other sources (for example, food items, beverages, lottery, video rentals, etc.). If the petroleum sales as reflected in (a) receipts or (b) floor

space utilization, are greater than the non-petroleum sales receipts or floor use, the building qualifies as 15-year property."

The test should be applied on an annual basis. If the test is met (or not met) in one tax year and not met (or met) in another tax year the property must generally be reclassified. In other words, the property has undergone a change in use described in Code Sec. 168(i)(5). See ¶ 168 for change in use rules. Rev. Proc. 97-10 (1997-1 CB 680), however, citing legislative history, indicates that there is no change in use if the failure to meet (or not meet) the test is only "temporary." According to the Coordinated Issue Paper, a failure to meet (or not meet) the test is temporary if caused by a temporary fluctuation in revenue. For example, a special promotion which is run for six months could cause a temporary fluctuation in revenue. According to the legislative history, if a property is placed in service near the end of the tax year and the use of the property is not representative of the subsequent use of the property, the test may be applied in the subsequent tax year.

A building may qualify as a retail motor fuels outlet (15-year property) whether or not the taxpayer-owner is the operator of the motor fuels business. Also, in applying the gross revenue tests, the owner of a building must aggregate the gross revenues of all businesses operated in the building (such as a restaurant or video arcade) whether or not such businesses are operated by the owner (Rev. Rul. 97-29, I.R.B. 1997-28, 4).

A taxpayer could elect to apply this provision to property placed in service before August 20, 1996 (Act Sec. 1120(c) of P.L. 104-188). The election, however, was required to be made by July 14, 1997 (Rev. Proc. 97-10 describes the election procedure).

Taxpayers who depreciated a building placed in service before August 20, 1996 over 15-years are treated as having made the election if the property qualifies as a retail motor fuels outlet under these guidelines.

The recovery period for a retail motor fuels outlet is 20 years under the MACRS alternative depreciation system (Code Sec. 168(g)(3)(B)).

The fact that a building is considered a convenience store (i.e., fails the test) will not affect the treatment of other assets used in the business as property used to market petroleum. For example, adjacent car wash buildings and associated land improvements used for the marketing of petroleum products such as pump islands and canopies are considered Asset Class 57.1 property eligible for a 15-year depreciation period. (Removable canopies may be considered 5-year property. See ¶ 125.) Tanks, pipelines, and pumps fall within Asset Class 57.0 and may be depreciated over five years.

Multiple buildings—revenues and floor space test applied. The Court of Appeals for the Eight Circuit has affirmed a district court's ruling that the revenue and floor spaced tests are applied on a building by building basis (*Iowa 80 Group, Inc. & Subsidiaries*, CA-8, 2003-2 USTC ¶ 50,703, aff'g DC Iowa, 2002-2 USTC ¶ 50,474). Thus, the classifications of a main building, diesel fuel center, truckomat (truck wash), and service (repair) center at a truck stop had to be determined by applying the gross revenue test and floor space tests separately to each structure. The taxpayer lost its argument that the buildings should be treated as a single retail motor fuel "*outlet.*" Apparently, the main building (presumably the most expensive) could only qualify for the 15-year recovery period if the revenue attributable to all of the buildings, including the main building, was aggregated.

The taxpayer's brief provides some additional details of interest. For example, the IRS applied the gross revenue test by taking into account the gross revenue earned by various lessees in the main building of the truck stop complex (e.g., a

Wendy's restaurant and Dairy Queen). This is in accord with Rev. Rul. 97-29. It should be noted that the IRS did not include the lease payments to the taxpayer/owner as part of the gross revenue from the building.

If fuel was paid for within the main building, then those revenues were counted toward the gross revenue test as it applied to the main building. However, revenue from fuel paid for outside of the main building in a diesel fuel center was apparently only taken into account in determining the classification of the diesel fuel center.

For procedural reasons, the district court did not consider floor space allocation issues. The Eighth Circuit remanded the case to the district court to rule on these issues. Upon remand, the district court concluded that the floor space test was not satisfied and this conclusion was affirmed by the Eighth Circuit (*Iowa 80 Group Inc. & Subsidiaries*, CA-8, 2005-1 USTC ¶ 50,343, aff'g DC Iowa, 2005-1 USTC ¶ 50,342). The appellate court applied a "traditional service station" test. Floor space on the second floor of the building attributed to the movie theater, arcade, showers, laundromat, and TV lounge were not features normally associated with a traditional service station and, therefore, were not considered devoted to petroleum marketing sales. However, citing the 1995 and 1997 Coordinated Issue Papers discussed above, it concluded that service bays, tire changing and repair facilities, and car lifts are part of a traditional service station.

AMT adjustment required. An AMT depreciation adjustment is required on Section 1250 property, such as a retail motor fuel outlet, which is not depreciated using the straight-line method for regular tax purposes unless the bonus depreciation deduction is claimed on the property. See ¶ 170.

¶ 112

20-Year Property

Property with a class life of 25 or more years is classified as 20-year property (Code Sec. 168(e)(1)).

Farm buildings. Farm buildings, such as barns and machine sheds, are 20-year MACRS property (Asset Class 01.3 of Rev. Proc. 87-56). See ¶ 118 for a discussion of farm property.

Municipal sewers. Municipal sewers placed in service before June 13, 1996 are 20-year property (Code Sec. 168(e)(3)(F), prior to being stricken by P.L. 104-188)). A 25-year recovery period now applies to municipal sewers. See ¶ 113.

Property used by utility to gather, treat, and distribute of water. Twenty-year property also includes property placed in service before June 13, 1996, which is used by a utility in the gathering, treatment, and commercial distribution of water. See ¶ 113 for the treatment of such property placed in service after June 12, 1996.

Assets used in the transmission and distribution of electricity. Assets that are used in the transmission and distribution of electricity *for sale* are included in Asset Class 49.14 of Rev. Proc. 87-56 and have an MACRS recovery period of 20 years and an ADS recovery period of 30 years (IRS Letter Ruling 8848039, September 2, 1988). However, assets used in the transmission and distribution of electricity at 69 or more kilovolts for sale are treated as 15-year property if placed in service after April 11, 2005 and certain other requirements are met. See ¶ 110.

Initial clearing and grading costs described in Rev. Rul. 72-403 are specifically excluded from Asset Class 49.14 and from Asset Class 00.3 relating to land improvements. Taxpayers have been depreciating these costs as MACRS 7-year property (section 1245 real property for which no class life is provided). The recovery period for the cost of the initial clearing and grading land improvements pertaining to any electric utility transmission and distribution plant has been increased from seven years to 20 years, effective for property placed in service after October 22, 2004 (Code Sec. 168(e)(3)(F), as added by the 2004 Jobs Act (P.L. 108-357)). The ADS period is 25 years (Code Sec. 168(g)(3)(B), as amended by P.L. 108-357).

Depreciation method and convention for 20-year property. MACRS twenty-year property is depreciated for regular tax purposes over a 20-year recovery period using the 150-percent declining balance method with a switch to the straight-line method in the tax year that maximizes the deduction. The half-year or mid-quarter convention apply.

¶ 113

Water Utility Property

The cost of water utility property is recovered over a period of 25 years using the straight-line method (Code Sec. 168(b)(3) and Code Sec. 168(c), as amended by the Small Business Job Protection Act of 1996 (P.L. 104-188)). See ¶ 112 for the treatment of water utility property placed in service before June 13, 1996.

Water utility property is defined as (1) property that is an integral part of the gathering, treatment, or commercial distribution of water, and that, would have a 20-year recovery period if the 25-year recovery period was not assigned to it, and (2) any municipal sewer (Code Sec. 168(e)(5), as added by the Small Business Job Protection Act of 1996 (P.L. 104-188), effective for property placed in service after June 12, 1996, other than property placed in service pursuant to a binding contract in effect before June 10, 1996, and at all times thereafter before the property is placed in service). Water utility property is described in Asset Classes 49.3 and 51 of Rev. Proc. 87-56 (reproduced at ¶ 190).

¶ 114

Residential Rental Property

Residential rental property is depreciated over a 27.5-year recovery period using the straight-line method and the mid-month convention.

Residential rental property includes buildings or structures for which 80 percent or more of the gross rental income is rental income from dwelling units (Code Sec. 168(e)(2)(A)). If any portion of the building or structure is occupied by the taxpayer, the gross rental income from the property includes the fair rental value of the unit occupied by the taxpayer.

A dwelling unit is a house or apartment used to provide living accommodations. A dwelling unit does not include a unit in a hotel, motel, or other establishment in which more than 50 percent of the units are used on a transient basis. Thus, if a motel, etc., rents more than 50 percent of its units on a transient basis, it cannot be classified as residential rental property regardless of the amount of gross rental income derived from its permanently rented units.

The definition of residential rental property prior to enactment of ACRS was similar to the current definition. Thus, although Reg. § 1.167(j)-3(b) was withdrawn by the IRS in 1993, it provides useful information concerning the manner in which residential rental property status is determined.

Mobile homes and manufactured homes that are residential rental property and elevators and escalators that are located in a residential rental property are also included in this class. The recovery period for this property is also 27.5 years. A mobile home or a manufactured home that is transportable, however, may be considered personal property. See ¶ 127C.

It is possible for a nursing home to qualify as a residential rental property (IRS Letter Ruling 8239121, June 30, 1982; IRS Letter Ruling 9825024, March 20, 1998; IRS Letter Ruling 8240067, July 7, 1982; IRS Letter Ruling 7848036, August 30, 1978).

Generally, a home office is depreciated as nonresidential real property. However, if the office is located in an apartment occupied by the owner of a residential rental property, the home office is depreciable as 27.5 year residential rental property (CCA Letter Ruling 200526002, May 9, 2005). For home office depreciation recapture rules, see ¶ 488.

Appliances used in residential rental property are 5-year property. See ¶ 104.

Example (1): In May, Jones pays $240,000 for real property of which $40,000 is allocable to land and $200,000 is allocable to a building consisting of a single store front and 6 similar upper-story apartments. Jones, a calendar-year taxpayer, moves into one of the apartments and, pursuant to existing leases, receives $400 per month for each of the other 5 apartments and $700 per month for the store. Since the gross rental income from the apartments is less than 80% of the gross rental income from the building, the building is not 27.5-year rental property and must be depreciated over a 39-year recovery period as nonresidential real property (¶ 116).

Example (2): The facts are the same as in *Example (1)*, except that each apartment rents for $500 per month. Since gross rental income from the apartments (counting $500 per month for the owner-occupied unit) totals 80% or more of the gross rental income from the building, the building is 27.5-year residential rental property. Assuming depreciation is allocated in proportion to rents, Jones's depreciation deduction is $3,931, which is computed as follows: $200,000 adjusted basis of the building × .03636 (straight-line method rate determined by dividing 1 by 27.5 years in the recovery period) × 7.5/12 (to reflect the mid-month convention and the number of months that the building is deemed placed in service during the year) = $4,545 depreciation if the building was used 100% for the production of income. Such amount, $4,545, is multiplied by 32/37 ($3,200/$3,700) = $3,931 in order to limit the claimed deduction to the portion of depreciation not allocable to personal use.

Example (3): The facts are the same as in *Example (1)*. Since the property does not qualify as 27.5-year residential property, it is 39-year nonresidential property. Before any adjustment for personal use, depreciation for the year that the property is placed in service is $3,205 ($200,000 adjusted basis × .02564 (the MACRS straight-line rate is 1 divided by 39 years in the recovery period)) × 7.5/12 (to reflect the mid-month convention and the number of months the building is deemed placed in service during the year). The actual deduction is $2,791 (27/31 × $3,205, reflecting the ratio of rents ($2,700 per month) to $2,700 + the monthly rental value ($400) of the owner-occupied apartment).

As the example indicates, the 11.5-year longer recovery period for nonresidential real property than for residential rental property reduces current depreciation deductions by about 29.5 percent.[1]

Personal residence converted to residential rental property. MACRS is used to depreciate a personal residence that is converted to rental property after 1986 regardless of the date that the personal residence was purchased (IRS Publication 946 (How To Depreciate Property), p. 8; Prop. Reg. § 1.168(i)-4(b) at ¶ 568).

Building placed in service in stages. Residential rental property, such as a highrise, may be placed in service in stages, as occupancy certificates are issued. If so, each completed stage may be separately depreciated. See ¶ 226.

---

[1] (1/27.5 – 1/39.0) / 1/27.5.

Allocate purchase price to land. When computing depreciation on residential rental property and nonresidential real property, keep in mind that the portion of the purchase price allocable to land is not included in the depreciable basis of the building (Reg. § 1.167(a)-2; Reg. § 1.168(a)-1).

¶ 116

Nonresidential Real Property

Nonresidential real property is tangible Code Sec. 1250 property with a class life of 27.5 years or more that is not residential rental property (Code Sec. 168(e)(2)(B)). This class also includes elevators and escalators that are part of a building which is nonresidential real property as well as other structural components. Typical examples of nonresidential real property are office buildings, shopping malls, and industrial buildings such as factories.

Generally, a home office is depreciated as nonresidential real property. However, if the office is located in an apartment occupied by the owner of a residential rental property, the home office is depreciable as 27.5 year residential rental property (CCA Letter Ruling 200526002, May 9, 2005). For home office depreciation recapture rules, see ¶ 488.

The cost of nonresidential real property is recovered under the straight-line method over a recovery period of 39 years for property generally placed in service after May 12, 1993.

For nonresidential real property generally placed in service before May 13, 1993, cost is recovered under the straight-line method over a recovery period of 31.5 years.

The mid-month convention must be used to compute depreciation on nonresidential real property.

Under a transitional rule, nonresidential real property placed in service before January 1, 1994, may be treated as 31.5-year property if the taxpayer or a qualified person (1) entered into a binding written contract to purchase or construct the property before May 13, 1993, or (2) construction began for these persons before such date (Omnibus Budget Reconciliation Act of 1993 (P.L. 103-66), Act Sec. 13151(b)(2)). A qualified person is a person who transfers his or her rights in such contract or property to the taxpayer before the property is placed in service.

Land is not depreciable. Accordingly, the depreciable basis of a commercial building does not include any cost allocable to the land.

If a commercial building is placed in service in stages, each completed stage may be separately depreciated. See ¶ 226.

Definition of section 1250 property and section 1245 property

Section 1250 property is defined as any real property (other than section 1245 property, as defined in Code Sec. 1245(a)(3)) which is or has been property of a character subject to the allowance for depreciation provided in Code Sec. 167 (Code Sec. 1250(c)).

Real property is defined by Reg. § 1.1250-1(e)(3) to mean any property which is not personal property within the meaning of Reg. § 1.1245-3(b). This regulation defines personal property by reference to the definition of tangible personal property within the meaning of investment tax regulation § 1.48-1(c).

In general, Reg. § 1.48-1(c) defines tangible personal property as any tangible property except:

(1) land;

(2) buildings and structural components of buildings (see ¶ 127); and

(3) land improvements (viz., inherently permanent structures (and their structural components) such as swimming pools, paved parking areas, wharves and docks, bridges, and fences (land improvements are generally assigned a 15-year depreciation period under MACRS (Asset Class 00.3) (see ¶ 110));

Tangible personal property includes all property (other than structural components) which is contained in or attached to a building. Thus, such property as production machinery, printing presses, transportation and office equipment, refrigerators, grocery counters, testing equipment, display racks and shelves, and neon and other signs, which is contained in or attached to a building constitutes tangible personal property (§ 1.48-1(c)).

All property which is in the nature of machinery (other than structural components of a building or other inherently permanent structure) is considered tangible personal property even though located outside a building. Thus, for example, a gasoline pump, hydraulic car lift, or automatic vending machine, although annexed to the ground, shall be considered tangible personal property (§ 1.48-1(c)).

Section 1250 property does not include property that it is described in Code Sec. 1245(a)(3). If an item of section 1245 real property is not assigned a class life in Rev. Proc. 87-56, then it is treated as section 1245 real property with no class life and is assigned a MACRS seven-year recovery period (40-year ADS recovery period) (Code Sec. 168(e)(3)(C); Code Sec. 168(g)(3)(E)). Note that any section property described in Code Sec. 1245(a)(3) which is not personal property is considered section 1245 real property. The section 1245 recapture rules apply to this property.

Code Sec. 1245(a)(3) covers the following depreciable property:

(1) personal property;

(2) tangible property (other than a building and its structural components) used as an integral part of manufacturing, production, or extraction or of furnishing transportation, communications, electrical energy, gas, water, or sewage disposal services; research facilities used in connection with any of these activities; facilities used in connection with any of these activities for the bulk storage of fungible commodities (including commodities in a liquid or gaseous state);

(3) real property (other than real property described in item (2)) to the extent that its adjusted basis reflects amortization deductions under Code Sec. 169 (relating to pollution control facilities), the expense allowance under Code Sec. 179, the expense allowance under Code Sec. 179A for qualified clean-fuel vehicle property (generally, certain storage and fuel dispensing facilities), the former amortization deduction for railroad grading and tunnel bores (Code Sec. 185); the former amortization deduction for child care facilities (Code Sec. 188); the deduction for expenditures to remove architectural and transportation barriers (Code Sec. 190); the deduction for qualified tertiary injectant expenses (Code Sec. 193); and the amortization deduction for reforestation expenditures (Code Sec. 194);

(4) single purpose agricultural and horticultural structures (10-year MACRS recovery period (¶ 108));

(5) a storage facility (not including a building or its structural components) used in connection with the distribution of petroleum or any primary product of petroleum; or

(6) any railroad grading or tunnel bore (MACRS assigns a 50-year recovery period (¶ 120)).

Section 5.05 of Rev. Proc. 87-56 provides that tangible property described in item (2) above (see Reg.§ 1.48-1(d)) is an Asset Class 00.3 land improvement with a 15 year recovery period. However, a structure that is essentially an item of machinery or equipment or a structure that houses property used as an integral part of an activity described in item (2), if the use of the structure is so closely related to the use of the property that the structure clearly can be expected to be replaced when the property it initially houses is replaced, is included in the asset guideline class appropriate to the equipment to which it is related.

See ¶ 127 and following for additional details regarding the definition of tangible personal property, section 1245 real property, land improvements, buildings, and structural components.

¶ 118

Farm Property

Machinery and equipment, grain bins, and fences used in agriculture are classified as 7-year MACRS property (Rev. Proc. 87-56, Asset Class 01.1). Agriculture is defined as the production of crops or plants, vines, and trees; livestock; the operation of farm dairies, nurseries, greenhouses, sod farms, mushroom cellars, cranberry bogs, apiaries (i.e., bee production activities), and fur farms; and the performance of agricultural, animal husbandry, and horticultural services (Asset Class 01.1). *However, any machinery or equipment (other than a grain bin, cotton ginning asset, fence, or land improvement), the original use of which begins with the taxpayer in 2009 (i.e., new property), and that is placed in service by the taxpayer in a farming business (as defined in Code Sec. 263A(e)(4) and discussed below) in 2009, has a recovery period of five years (i.e., is MACRS 5-year property) (Code Sec. 168(e)(3)(B)(vii), as added by the Emergency Economic Stabilization Act of 2008 (P.L. 110-343)). Such property has a recovery period of 10 years under ADS (Code Sec. 168(g)(3)(B), as amended by P.L. 110-343).*

The term machinery is not limited to a complex machine such as a farm tractor but may be something as simple as a lever ((*L. Trentadue*, 128 TC No. 8, Dec. 56,886), holding that vineyard trellising was 7-year property (Asset Class 01.1) and not a land improvement).

Farm buildings other than single purpose agricultural or horticultural structures are 20-year property (Asset Class 01.3). Single purpose agricultural or horticultural structures (defined in Code Sec. 168(i)(13)) placed in service after 1988 are 10-year property (Asset Class 01.4). A machine shed would fall into this category. Land improvements (other than machinery and equipment, grain bins, and fences) are 15-year property (Asset Class 00.3). See ¶ 110.

200-percent DB method prohibited

Three-, 5-, 7-, and 10-year property placed in service after 1988 and used in a "farming business" as defined in Code Sec. 263A(e)(4) may not be depreciated using the 200-percent DB method which is normally applicable to these property classes (the 150-percent DB method has always applied to 15-and 20-year property whether or not used in farming). Instead, farming property in these classes is depreciated using the 150-percent DB method (unless the ADS or straight-line method is required or elected) (Code Sec. 168(b)(2)(B)). As a result, Depreciation Tables 1-5 at ¶ 180 do not apply to such property. Instead, Tables 14-18 (the AMT tables because these tables incorporate the 150-percent DB method) are used in conjunction with the asset's regular (GDS) recovery period.

For purposes of Code Sec. 263A, the term farming business means the trade or business of farming which also includes (a) the trade or business of operating a nursery or sod farm and (b) the raising or harvesting of trees bearing fruit, nuts, or other crops, or ornamental trees. An evergreen tree is not an ornamental tree if it is more than 6 years old when it is severed from its roots (Code Sec. 263A(e)(4)). The UNICAP regulations define a farming business to mean a trade or business involving the cultivation of land or the raising or harvesting of any agricultural or horticultural commodity (Temp. Reg. § 1.263A-4T(a)(3)). Horticulture is defined by Webster's Ninth New Collegiate Dictionary as "the science and art of growing fruits, vegetables, flowers, or ornamental plants." IRS Publication 946 (How to Depreciate Property) also clarifies that a farming business includes the raising, shearing, feeding, caring for, training, and managing of animals.

Temp. Reg. § 1.448-1T(d)(2) indicates, in the context of accounting methods, that a farming business does not include the processing of commodities or products beyond those activities normally incident to growing, raising, or harvesting of such products. IRS Publication 225 (Farmer's Tax Guide) also applies this rule in defining a farming business for depreciation purposes.

For additional information see ¶ 84.

ADS mandatory if election made to deduct preproduction expenditures

A farmer that elected not to apply the uniform capitalization rules to any plant produced in the farming business must use ADS for all property used predominantly in the farming business that is placed in service in any year that the election is in effect (Code Sec. 263A(e)(2)).

Depreciation periods

The following chart, which is adapted from the IRS Audit Technique Guide for Grain Farmers (July 1995) (reproduced in the CCH IRS POSITIONS REPORTER at ¶ 205,500), shows the MACRS depreciation period for various types of common farm assets. *However, note that new machinery and equipment (Asset Class 01.1 of Rev. Proc. 87-56) placed in service by a taxpayer engaged in a farming business is considered 5-year property if placed in service in 2009, as explained above.*

Asset	*Asset Class (¶ 191)*	*MACRS GDS*	*MACRS ADS*
Airplane	00.21	5	6
Auto	00.22	5	5
Calculators	00.13	5	6
Cattle (Dairy or Breeding)	01.21	5	7
Communications Equipment	00.11	7 ***	10
Computer and Peripheral Equipment	00.12	5	5
Copiers	00.13	5	6
Cotton Ginning Assets	01.11	7	12
Farm Buildings (General Purpose)	01.3	20	25
Farm Equipment and Machinery	01.1	7 ****	10
Fences (Agricultural)	01.1	7	10
Goats (Breeding or Milk)	01.24	5	5
Grain Bin	01.1	7	10
Greenhouse	01.4	10 *	15
Helicopter	00.21	5	6
Hogs (Breeding)	01.23	3	3
Horses (Nonrace, < 12 yrs.)	01.221	7	10
Horses (Nonrace, 12 yrs. and older)	01.222	3	10

Asset	*Asset Class (¶ 191)*	*MACRS GDS*	*MACRS ADS*
Logging Equipment	24.1	5	6
Machinery	01.1	7 ****	10
Mobile homes on permanent foundations (Farm tenants)	00.3	15	20
Office equipment	00.11	7	10
Office fixtures and furniture	00.11	7	10
Orchards (Code Sec. 168(e)(3)(D))	—	10 **	20
Paved feedlots	00.3	15	20
Property with no class life (personal)	—	7	12
Property with no class life (real)	—	7	40
Pumps and irrigation equipment	01.1	7***	10
Sheep (breeding)	01.24	5	5
Single purpose agricultural or horticultural structure	01.4	10 *	15
Solar property (Code Sec. 168(e)(3)(B)(vi))	—	5	12
Tile (drainage), water wells	00.3	15	20
Tractor units (over-the-road)	00.26	3	4
Trailer for use over-the-road	00.27	5	6
Trees/vines (Code Sec. 168(e)(3)(D))	—	10 **	20
Truck (heavy duty, general purpose)	00.242	5	6
Truck (light, < 13,000 lbs.)	00.241	5	5
Underground pipe and well	00.3	15	20
Vineyard (Code Sec. 168(e)(3)(D))	—	10 **	20
Water wells	00.3	15	20
Wind energy property (Code Sec. 168(e)(3)(B)(vi))	—	5	12

* 7 years if placed in service before 1989.
** 15 years if placed in service before 1989.
*** Not including communications equipment listed in other Asset Classes.
**** 5 years if new machinery or equipment placed in service in 2009.

Livestock

Breeding and dairy cattle are five-year property (Asset Class 01.21). Sheep and goats used for breeding are 5-year property (Asset Class 01.24). Breeding hogs are 3-year property (Asset Class 01.23).

Immature livestock acquired for draft, dairy, or breeding purposes is eligible for depreciation in the tax year it reaches maturity, i.e., when it reaches the age when it can be worked, milked, or bred. The basis for depreciation is the initial cost for the immature livestock plus freight and other costs related to the acquisition (IRS Market Segment Specialization Program Guide (MSSP) for Livestock (May 11, 2000); IRS Publication 225 (Farmer's Tax Guide); Reg. § 1.46-3(d)(2)(ii)).

The expenses of raising animals are currently deductible; therefore, raised animals have no depreciable basis.

Depreciable livestock (horses, cattle, hogs, sheep, goats, and mink and other furbearing animals) qualify for the Code Sec. 179 expense allowance (Reg. § 1.1245-3(a)(4); IRS Publication 225 (Farmer's Tax Guide)).

The Farmer's Tax Guide did not discuss the eligibility of depreciable livestock for the bonus depreciation allowance. Most commentators, however, believe that depreciable livestock that is purchased for breeding should qualify provided that the livestock was not previously bred. If the livestock was previously bred, the original use requirement for bonus depreciation (¶ 127D) would be violated. See, also, "*Horses*," below.

Horses

The depreciation period for a horse depends upon its age and use. A breeding or work horse that is 12 years old or less at the time that it is placed into service is 7-year property; if more than 12 years old it is 3-year property (Asset Classes 01.221 and 01.222). A horse that is more than 12 years old when placed in service and is not a race horse, breeding horse, or work horse is 3-year property (Asset Class 01.224). A race horse that is more than two years old when placed in service is 3-year property (Asset Class 01.223). Any horse not described above is 7-year property (Asset Class 01.225).

Effective for race horses placed in service after December 31, 2008 and before January 1, 2014, all race horses are treated as three-year property (Code Sec. 168(e)(3)(A)(i), as amended by P.L. 110-246). Under prior law, race horses that were two years or younger when placed in service were depreciated as 7-year MACRS property. A race horse is generally considered placed in service when its training begins. This is usually at the end of its yearling year, which is typically less than two years after birth. A race horse that has previously raced is generally considered placed in service when purchased from the prior owner. A horse's age is measured by reference to its actual birth date rather than the racing industry's treatment of January 1 of the year of birth as the birth date (Prop. Reg. § 1.168-3(c)(iii) (ACRS); Rev. Proc. 87-56, 1987-2 CB 674, as clarified and modified by Rev. Proc. 88-22, 1988-1 CB 785).

Reg. § 1.1231-2(c)(1) provides rules and examples for determining whether a horse is a race horse. Presumably, these guidelines may be used for depreciation classification purposes.

Geldings cannot be placed in service in a breeding operation except in working or "teasing" applications (IRS Market Segment Specialization Guide (MSSP) for Livestock (May 11, 2000)).

A retired race horse purchased for breeding purposes does not qualify for bonus depreciation (Temp. Reg. § 1.168(k)-1T(b)(3)(v), *Example 3*). The example involves a race horse acquired by the racer on April 1, 2000 and then purchased by the taxpayer on October 1, 2003. The example simply says that the original use requirement is not satisfied. Under the original use requirement (as in effect at the time the regulations were issued), the original use must commence with the *taxpayer* after September 10, 2001. Since original use is defined as the first use to which the property is put whether or not that use commences with the taxpayer (see ¶ 127D for a discussion of the original use requirement), this example should not be read to mean that if the racer had acquired the horse after September 10, 2001, the original use requirement would have been satisfied. The original use requirement would not have been satisfied because the original use commenced with the racer and not the taxpayer. See Another point worth noting is that the horse was a depreciable asset in the hands of the racer. If the horse was raised and held as nondepreciable inventory by the seller and sold to the taxpayer after September 10, 2001, then it seems that the original use requirement would be satisfied. This situation would be analogous to the sale of a new vehicle after September 10, 2001 from a car dealership's inventory.

Ratites (ostrich, emu, rhea)

An IRS Market Segment Specialization Guide (MSSP) for Livestock (May 11, 2000) provides guidance concerning the tax treatment of persons engaged in the business of raising ostrich, emu, and rhea. These birds are members of the ratite family of birds. According to the guide, the birds are not considered livestock for purposes of Code Sec. 1231, and, therefore, are not considered section 1231 property for purposes of determining gain or loss upon their sale. However, it is the IRS position that ratites are livestock for other purposes of the Code.

Ratites are considered personal property with no class life and, therefore, by default have a seven-year depreciation period (12 years under ADS). Fences, rearing pens, incubators and hatchers are also 7-year property. A hatchery building may qualify as a single-purpose agricultural structure (10-year property). However, old barns, sheds, and the like which have been merely converted to hatchery facilities do not qualify.

Ratites purchased for breeding "probably" qualify for the Code Sec. 179 expense allowance, according to the MSSP which cites IRS Letter Ruling 8817003, holding that rare birds purchased for breeding purposes qualify for expensing under Code Sec. 179. However, ratites purchased for breeding may not be expensed until they are placed in service (presumably the year that they are capable of breeding, which is the rule applicable to livestock purchased for breeding).

The issue of the applicability of Code Sec. 195 (which allows five-year amortization of start-up costs beginning in the month a trade or business begins) to new ratite producers who were not previously in the business of farming is unsettled, according to the MSSP. Some authorities feel that a taxpayer is not yet engaged in the animal breeding business until the animals are placed in service as breeding stock. Thus, if a taxpayer acquires ratite chicks to be raised for breeding, farm expenses are capitalized until the animals are ready for breeding.

Alternative livestock

The MSSP notes that taxpayers may raise miniature donkeys, miniature horses, llamas (including vicuna, guanaco, alpaca), deer, elk, reindeer, bison, miniature pigs, sport sheep, lemurs, big cats, wallabies, wallaroos, monkeys, parrots, alligators, and munchkin cats. If depreciable, these animals are 7-year property (12-year ADS period). Animals purchased for resale are not depreciable. Breeding animals qualify for the Code Sec. 179 expense allowance in the year that they are placed in service for breeding purposes (i.e., are capable of breeding).

Dogs

A farmer may use dogs to herd cattle, sheep, pigs, etc. If such a dog is purchased (and, therefore, has a basis), it should be depreciable. It appears such an animal is property without a class life and, therefore, has a seven-year recovery period.

Irrigation systems and water wells

IRS Publication 225 (Farmer's Tax Guide) states that farmers may depreciate irrigation systems and wells composed of masonry, concrete, tile, metal, or wood. The costs of moving dirt to make irrigation systems and water wells composed of these materials is also depreciable. The publication further provides that irrigation systems and waterwells are depreciable over 15 years as a land improvement. However, the IRS Audit Technique Guide for Grain Farmers listed "pumps and irrigation" systems as 7-year property. This Guide may be referring to above ground systems.

A drip irrigation system installed primarily underground in connection with a vineyard was a 15-year land improvement, according to the Tax Court (*L. Trentadue*, 128 TC No. 8, Dec. 56,886). If the system had been primarily installed above the ground the court indicated that it would likely be considered personal property depreciable over 7 years (Asset Class 01.1). The court further indicated that if the issue had been presented it would have allowed certain above ground portions of the irrigation system such as tubing, emmiters, and the like to be separately depreciated as personal property. The court also concluded that a well was a 15-year land improvement.

Dams, ponds, and terraces

IRS Publication 225 further provides that, in general, earthen damns, ponds, and terraces are not depreciable unless the structures have a determinable useful life. See, however, ¶ 3, which discusses recent decisions that negate the determinable useful life requirement in the context of ACRS and MACRS. Note that the publication provides that expenditures for such assets may be deductible as soil and water conservation expenditures under Code Sec. 175. For additional information concerning dams, see "Land improvements" at ¶ 110.

Vineyards

A trellising system was agricultural machinery with a 7-year recovery period (Asset Class 01.1). The components of the trellises could be moved and reused, the trellises were not designed to remain permanently in place, and the trellising posts were not set in concrete and could easily be removed from the ground (*L. Trentadue*, 128 TC No. 8, Dec. 56,886). The taxpayer used vertical shoot positioning (VSP) and T-trellis design systems.

A drip irrigation system was a 15-year land improvement. If the system had been primarily installed above the ground the court indicated that it would likely be considered personal property depreciable over 7 years (Asset Class 01.1). Certain above-ground portions of the drip irrigation system could likely have been depreciated separately as personal property. A well was classified as a land improvement (*L. Trentadue*, 128 TC No. 8, Dec. 56,886).

Single purpose agricultural or horticultural structure

A single purpose agricultural or horticultural structure as defined in Code Sec. 168(i)(13) is considered section 1245 property and, therefore, qualifies for the Code Sec. 179 expense allowance (Code Sec. 1245(a)(3)(D)). The definition is borrowed from former Code Sec. 48(p). Such structures are 10-year property for purposes of MACRS (Asset Class 01.4) if placed in service after 1988. The ADS period is 15 years.

The detailed requirements for qualification are set forth in Reg. § 1.48-10.

In general, to qualify, a structure must either be a single purpose livestock structure or a single purpose horticultural structure.

Specific design and use tests—single purpose livestock structure. A single purpose livestock structure is defined as any enclosure or structure specifically designed and constructed exclusively to:

(1) house, raise, and feed a particular type of livestock (including poultry but not horses) and, at the taxpayer's option, their produce (e.g., milk and eggs held for sale); and

(2) house the equipment (including any replacements) necessary for the housing, raising, and feeding of livestock (or poultry) and their produce (Reg. § 1.48-10(b)).

The term "housing, raising, and feeding" includes the full range of livestock breeding and raising activities, including ancillary post-production activities.

The structure must be used exclusively for these purposes. The livestock structure may be used for storing feed or machinery (related to these purposes), but more than strictly incidental use for storing feed or machinery will disqualify the structure. The structure may not be used for processing or marketing. If more than one-third of a structure's total usable volume is devoted to storage (feed, for example), a rebuttable presumption arises that the storage function is not incidental. The feed stored must be for use by the type of livestock for which the structure was constructed (Reg. § 1.48-10(e)(1)).

The livestock structure must also house the equipment necessary to house, raise, and feed the livestock. For example, a structure with no equipment and used only to house feeder cattle while they are fed hay is not a qualifying livestock structure (Reg. § 1.48-10(b)(4)). The equipment must be an integral part of the structure (i.e., physically attached to or part of the structure). Examples are equipment that contains the livestock, provides them with food and water, or controls temperature, lighting, or humidity. Equipment, such as loading chutes, necessary to conduct ancillary post-production activities may be housed in the structure.

The structure must be designed, constructed, and used with respect to one particular type (species) of livestock. For example, a structure designed as a single purpose hog-raising facility will not qualify if it is used to raise dairy cows. A structure used to house more than one type of livestock also fails the exclusive use test. A structure which originally qualified as a single-purpose livestock structure is disqualified if it is placed in service and later modified to accommodate a different species of livestock (e.g., a hog-raising facility is placed in service and later modified to raise chickens) (Reg. § 1.48-10(b)(3)).

A structure used solely to house the produce of livestock or equipment is not a qualifying structure. For example, a structure used solely for storing milk will not qualify. Eggs held for hatching and newborn livestock are considered livestock and not the produce of livestock.

A dairy facility will qualify if it is used for activities consisting of the (1) production of milk or (2) of the production of milk and the housing, raising, or feeding of dairy cattle. In addition the facility must be used to house equipment (including replacements) necessary for these activities (Reg. § 1.48-10(b)(2)).

Single purpose horticultural structure. A single purpose horticultural structure is a:

(1) greenhouse specifically designed and constructed for the commercial production of plants (including plant products such as flowers, vegetables, or fruits); or

(2) a structure specifically designed and constructed for the commercial production of mushrooms (Reg. § 1.48-10(c)).

The structure must be used exclusively for these purposes.

A single purpose horticultural structure may, but is not required to, house equipment necessary to carry out the commercial production of plants or mushrooms.

The commercial production of plants and mushrooms includes ancillary post-production activities.

Work space. An enclosure or structure which contains work space may be treated as a single purpose agricultural or horticultural structure only if the work space is used for:

(1) the stocking, caring for, or collecting of livestock, plants, or mushrooms (as the case may be) or their produce;

(2) the maintenance of the structure; or

(3) the maintenance or replacement of the equipment or stock enclosed or housed therein (Reg. § 1.48-10(f)).

An agricultural or horticultural structure that contains an area to process or market the product is an impermissible use. For example, if a taxpayer sets up a sales counter within a greenhouse, the greenhouse will not qualify as a horticultural structure (Reg. § 1.48-10(j), *Example (2)*).

Ancillary post-production activities. Such activities include gathering, sorting, and loading livestock, plants, and mushrooms, and packing unprocessed plants, mushrooms, and the live offspring and unprocessed produce of the livestock. Ancillary post-production activities do not include processing activities, such as slaughtering or packing meat, or marketing activities (Reg. § 1.48-10(f)).

Specifically designed and constructed requirement. A structure is considered specifically designed and constructed for a qualifying purpose if it is not economic to design and construct the structure for the intended qualifying purpose and then use the structure for a different purpose (Reg. § 1.48-10(d)).

Types of greenhouses. The IRS has issued a market segment specialization guide for the garden supplies industry (February 1, 2000). The guide lists five common types of greenhouses which are all depreciable over a ten year period. These include:

(1) Detached A-frame truss greenhouse—This is a separate structure (as opposed to a lean-to next to a building) made from aluminum, iron, steel, or wood and covered with glass or plastic.

(2) Ridge and furrow A-frame truss greenhouse range—This is several A-frames side by side with no interior walls, same structure and coverings as above.

(3) Quonset style greenhouse—This is made from pipe arches and covered with plastic (looks like army barracks).

(4) Lath or shadehouse—Simply a roof made of fencing or fabric to provide shade on plants (no walls). Some garden centers set these up in parking lots.

(5) Brick cold frame or hotbed—This is made of concrete blocks or wood, covered with glass or plastic. Generally, low to the ground. A hotbed structure has heat on the floor.

Demolition of greenhouse. The cost of demolishing and preparing the land for a new greenhouse is added to the basis of the new greenhouse.

Depreciation method for operators of a greenhouse. Generally, the operation of a greenhouse is considered a farming business. As such the 150-percent declining balance method is required in lieu of the 200-percent declining balance method unless the straight-line method is elected. See ¶ 84.

The uniform capitalization rules (Code Sec. 263A) do not generally apply to greenhouse operators because taxpayers not required to be on the accrual method are excepted if the plants being produced have a pre-productive period of two years or less. However, if the greenhouse grows plants with a pre-productive period of more than two years, it can elect to avoid the UNICAP rules. If the election is made, the taxpayer must use the MACRS alternative depreciation system (ADS).

¶ 120

Railroad Grading and Tunnel Bores

Railroad grading and tunnel bores are included in a specially assigned recovery class with a 50-year recovery period. The MACRS straight-line method and the mid-month convention must be used to compute depreciation on this property (Code Sec. 168(c)(1)).

Railroad grading and tunnel bores include all improvements resulting from excavations (including tunneling), construction of embankments, clearings, diversions of roads and streams, sodding of slopes, and similar work necessary to provide, construct, reconstruct, alter, protect, improve, replace, or restore a roadbed or right-of-way for railroad track (Code Sec. 168(e)(4)).

See ¶ 106 for the depreciation period of other types of railroad assets.

¶ 124

Qualified Indian Reservation Property

For qualified Indian reservation property that is placed in service after 1993 and before January 1, 2010, special MACRS recovery periods are provided that result in faster writeoffs (Code Sec. 168(j), as amended by the Economic Stabilization Act of 2008 (P.L. 110-343) to extend the provision two years). These recovery periods are in lieu of the generally applicable recovery periods provided in Code Sec. 168(c). No AMT depreciation adjustment is required if these recovery periods are used.

Property Class	*Recovery Period*
3-year property	2 years
5-year property	3 years
7-year property	4 years
10-year property	6 years
15-year property	9 years
20-year property	12 years
Nonresidential real property	22 years

The IRS has not issued separate Indian reservation property depreciation tables. However, existing IRS tables can be used for 5-year Indian reservation property with a three-year recovery period, 15-year Indian reservation property with a nine-year recovery period, and 20-year Indian reservation property with a 12-year recovery period. For example, the existing half-year and mid-quarter convention tables for 3-year property with a three-year recovery period may be used to compute depreciation on 5-year Indian reservation property with a three-year recovery period.

CCH has prepared *Unofficial Tables* for 3-year Indian reservation property with a two-year recovery period, 7-year Indian reservation property with a four-year recovery period, 10-year Indian reservation property with a six-year recovery period, and nonresidential real Indian reservation property with a 22-year recovery period.

The location of IRS tables (where applicable) and unofficial CCH tables can be found in the Index to MACRS Percentage Tables at ¶ 180.

Qualified Indian reservation property includes 3-, 5-, 7-, 10-, 15-, 20-year property and nonresidential real property that is:

(1) used predominantly in the active conduct of a trade or business within an Indian reservation;

(2) not used or located outside an Indian reservation on a regular basis;

(3) not acquired (directly or indirectly) from a related person (as defined in Code Sec. 465(b)(3)(C)); and

(4) not used for certain gaming purposes (Code Sec. 168(j)(4)(A)).

Indian reservation defined. The term Indian reservation is defined in section 3(d) of the Indian Financing Act of 1974 (25 U.S.C. 1452(d)) and section 4(10) of the Indian Child Welfare Act of 1978 (25 U.S.C. 1903(10)). For purposes of section 3(d) of the Indian Financing Act of 1974, the term Indian reservation includes *former* Indian reservations. The definition of a *former* Indian reservation contained in section 3(d), as it pertains to the State of Oklahoma, was modified by the Taxpayer Relief Act of 1997 (P.L. 105-34) to include only lands that are both within a jurisdictional area of an Oklahoma Indian tribe and eligible for trust land status under 25 CFR Part 151 (Code Sec. 168(j) (6)). The modified definition is generally effective for property placed in service after December 31, 1993. However, it does not apply to MACRS 10-year, 7-year, 5-year, or 3-year property with a recovery period of 6 years or less under Code Sec. 168(j) if a taxpayer claimed depreciation on the property using the applicable Code Sec. 168(j) recovery period in the year it was placed in service on an original return filed before March 18, 1997 (Act Sec. 1604(c)(2) of P.L. 105-34). For a specific description of the localities in Oklahoma that are considered former Indian reservations, see Notice 98-45, I.R.B. 1998-35, 7.

Predominant and regular use tests: mobile assets. The IRS has issued an internal technical assistance memorandum (Letter Ruling 199947026) which considers the predominant and regular use tests (items (1) and (2), above) in the context of mobile assets. Mobile assets include rolling stock, trucks, cars, airplanes, buses, and mobile heavy equipment, such as oil and gas drilling equipment, cranes, and gain combines.

For purposes of the requirement that the asset be used predominantly within an Indian reservation, the memorandum concludes that the asset must be used more than 50 percent of the time during the tax year in the active conduct of a trade or business within an Indian reservation. The standard does not necessarily require that the asset be used or physically located within the reservation more than 50 percent of the time. The ruling states in this regard:

> "... our view is that the standard requires a connection between the trade or business operated within an Indian reservation and the use of the property in carrying on that trade or business. For example, a car that is used in the trade or business of providing taxi service only within an Indian reservation and is also used for personal purposes, must be used more than 50 percent of the time during the taxable year in that taxi service to satisfy the requirement of section 168(j)(4)(A)(i). Further, for example, we believe that in those instances where a corporate taxpayer's headquarters are located off an Indian reservation but the taxpayer operates a manufacturing plant within the Indian reservation, the standard of section 168(j)(4)(A)(i) is satisfied."

With respect to the requirement that an asset may not be used or located outside an Indian reservation on a *regular* basis, the IRS concluded that this means that the asset may "not be used or located outside the Indian reservation on more than an occasional or incidental basis during the tax year."

The determination of whether these two tests are satisfied, according to the ruling, is made in light of all of the facts and circumstances and is made on an asset-by-asset basis.

Change in use. The technical advice memorandum discussed above also notes that if a mobile asset (or other Indian reservation property) meets the definition of qualified Indian reservation property in one tax year but does not meet the definition in a later tax year while it continues to be held by the same person, then a change in use has occurred and Code Sec. 168(i)(5) applies in determining depreciation in the year that the change in use occurs.

Real property rental. The rental of real property located within a reservation is treated as the active conduct of a trade or business within an Indian reservation. The classification of property as real or personal is based on federal income tax law and not local (state law) (IRS Letter Ruling 200601020, September 19, 2005).

ADS. Qualified property does not include any property that must be depreciated using the MACRS alternative depreciation system (ADS). The determination of whether property is qualified is made without regard to the election to use ADS (¶ 150) and after applying the special rules for listed property not used predominantly in a qualified business (¶ 206) (Code Sec. 168(j)(4)(B); IRS Publication 946, How to Depreciate Property.

Qualified infrastructure property. Qualified infrastructure property located outside an Indian reservation may be eligible for faster writeoffs provided that the purpose of such property is to connect with qualified infrastructure property located within the reservation. Qualified infrastructure property is property that is depreciable under MACRS, benefits the tribal infrastructure, is available to the general public, and is placed in service in connection with the taxpayer's active conduct of a trade or business within the reservation. Such property includes, but is not limited to, roads, power lines, water systems, railroad spurs, and communication facilities.

¶ 124A

New York Liberty Zone Leasehold Improvement Property

Qualified New York Liberty Zone leasehold improvements to nonresidential real property that are placed in service after September 10, 2001, and before January 1, 2007, are classified as 5-year MACRS property unless an election out is made. The straight-line method must be used to depreciate this property. A nine-year ADS period applies (Code Sec. 1400L(c)(1), as added by the Job Creation and Worker Assistance Act of 2002 (P.L. 107-147)). The election out was retroactively provided by the Working Families Tax Relief Act of 2004 (P.L. 108-311). See below for details.

Because P.L. 107-147 was enacted after many taxpayers filed their 2000 or 2001 returns it is possible that qualifying New York Liberty Zone improvements were not properly classified and depreciated on those returns. The IRS has issued guidance (Rev. Proc. 2003-50) that allows a taxpayer to file an amended 2000 or 2001 return by December 31, 2003, to correct the problem or to file a Form 3115 with their 2003 return and claim a Code Sec. 481(a) adjustment.

Liberty Zone leasehold improvements that are eligible for a five-year recovery period are *not* also eligible for the 30- or 50-percent first-year bonus depreciation allowance under Code Sec. 168(k) or the 30-percent allowance under Code Sec. 1400L(b) (Code Sec. 168(k)(2)(C)(ii); Code Sec. 1400L(b)(2)(C)(iii)). See ¶ 127D and ¶ 127E for discussion of bonus depreciation.

Definition of qualifying property

The term "qualified New York Liberty Zone leasehold improvement property" means qualified leasehold improvement property as defined under new Code Sec. 168(k)(3) (see ¶ 127D) if:

(1) the building is located in the New York Liberty Zone;

(2) the qualifying improvement is placed in service after September 10, 2001, and before January 1, 2007; and

(3) no binding written contract for such improvement was in effect before September 11, 2001 (Code Sec. 1400L(c)(2)).

Qualified leasehold improvement property generally consists of interior improvements to nonresidential real estate. The term is defined in Code Sec. 168(k)(3) (see ¶ 127D). In general, qualified leasehold improvement property must satisfy the following requirements:

(1) the improvement must be to the interior portion of a building that is nonresidential real property;

(2) the improvement must be made under or pursuant to a lease by a lessee, sublessee, or lessor, or pursuant to a commitment to enter into a lease;

(3) the lessor and lessee may not be related persons;

(4) the portion of the building that is improved must be exclusively tenant-occupied (by a lessee or sublessee); and

(5) the improvement must be placed in service more than three years after the date that the building was first placed in service (Code Sec. 168(k)(3)).

Leasehold improvements to residential rental property, such as apartment buildings, are not considered qualified leasehold improvements. Exterior leasehold improvements to nonresidential real property, such as the addition of a roof, are also excluded from the definition.

The following improvements are specifically excluded from the definition of qualified leasehold improvement property:

(1) improvements that enlarge the building;

(2) elevators and escalators;

(3) any structural component benefiting a common area; and

(4) improvements to the internal structural framework of the building (Code Sec. 168(k)(3)(B)).

Improvements that do not qualify as New York Liberty Zone leasehold improvements may still be eligible for the 30-percent first-year bonus depreciation allowance under Code Sec. 168(k) or Code Sec. 1400L(b), according to the Joint Committee Explanation.

Location of New York Liberty Zone

The New York Liberty Zone is the area located on or south of Canal Street, East Broadway (east of its intersection with Canal Street), or Grand Street (east of its intersection with East Broadway) in the Borough of Manhattan in New York City (Code Sec. 1400L(h)).

Straight-line method applies

The MACRS straight-line method (and half-year or mid-quarter convention) must be used to depreciate qualified Liberty Zone leasehold improvement property (Code Sec. 1400L(c)(3)). Ordinarily, 5-year property is depreciated using a 200-percent declining-balance method switching to straight line in the year a larger deduction results.

ADS recovery period

A nine-year recovery period is assigned to qualified leasehold improvement property for purposes of the MACRS alternative depreciation system (ADS) under Code Sec. 168(g) (Code Sec. 1400L(c)(4)).

Alternative minimum tax

No depreciation adjustment will be required on qualified Liberty Zone leasehold improvements for alternative minimum tax (AMT) purposes because the straight-line method is used for regular tax purposes. AMT depreciation will be computed in the same manner as regular tax depreciation (i.e., five-year recovery period and straight-line method).

Code Sec. 179 expense deduction

The Code Sec. 179 expense allowance (¶ 300) may only be claimed on tangible Sec. 1245 property as defined in Code Sec. 1245 (a)(3). See ¶ 116. Thus, a qualified leasehold improvement should not qualify for the Code Sec. 179 expense allowance if it is a structural component (real property). The fact that the depreciation period for such an improvement is shortened by the new provision from 39 years (the depreciation period for structural components of nonresidential real property) to five years does not change an improvement's status as section 1250 real property.

Qualified leasehold improvement property status under Code Sec. 168(k)(3) or Code Sec. 1400L(c) can only apply to section 1250 property (Reg. § 1.168(k)-1(c)(1)). Elements of a building that are personal property (section 1245 property), as opposed to structural components (section 1250 property), may be depreciated under cost segregation principles over shortened recovery periods and may qualify for bonus depreciation and the Code Sec. 179 expense allowance.

Election out of New York Liberty Zone leasehold improvement property provision

A taxpayer may elect out of the New York Liberty Zone leasehold improvement property provision (Code Sec. 1400L(c)(5), as added by the Working Families Tax Relief Act of 2004 (P.L. 108-311); Rev. Proc. 2005-43). The election out may be made retroactively to apply to Liberty Zone leasehold improvement property placed in service after September 10, 2001. The election procedures are explained in Rev. Proc. 2005-43. An election out may only be revoked with IRS consent.

Recovery period if election out made. If an election out is made and the Liberty Zone leasehold improvement property was placed in service after October 22, 2004 and before January 1, 2006, the property is depreciated using a 15-year recovery period (9 years under ADS), the straight-line method, and the half-year or mid-quarter convention. In other words, it is depreciated as if it were 15-year qualified leasehold improvement property under Code Sec. 168(e)(3)(E)(iv) and (e)(6). See ¶ 126. If the Liberty Zone leasehold improvement property would not qualify for the 15-year recovery period because it was not placed in service after October 22, 2004 and before January 1, 2006, then it is depreciated as MACRS 39-year nonresidential real property (i.e., in the same manner as any other structural component) (Rev. Proc. 2005-43, Section 2.04; IRS Publication 946).

Bonus depreciation. Rev. Proc. 2005-43 states that no bonus depreciation may be claimed if the election out is made even if the 15-year recovery period applies (Rev. Proc. 2005-43, Sec. 2.04). In other words, it appears to be the IRS position that an election out does not transform the New York Liberty Zone leasehold improvement property into leasehold improvement property described in Code Sec. 168(k)(3) which does qualify for bonus depreciation if placed in service after September 10, 2001 and before January 1, 2005. The Committee Reports and Joint

Committee Blue Book explanation for this provision do not mention bonus depreciation.

Election procedures. An election out applies to all Liberty Zone leasehold improvement property placed in service during the tax year of the election. In general, the election must be made by the due date (including extensions) of the return for the tax year the improvements were placed in service in the manner prescribed in the instructions for Form 4562 (Depreciation and Amortization). However, an automatic 6-month extension from the due date of the return (excluding extensions) is available if the requirements of Reg. § 301.9100-2(c) and (d) are satisfied. Additional extensions may be requested under the rules in Reg.§ 301.9100-3. These procedure applies to any 2003 or 2004 return filed after June 29, 2005, except that additional extensions may be requested under Reg.§ 301.9100-3 if the deadlines described below for returns filed on or before June 29, 2004 are not met.

Special election procedures for 2000, 2001, 2002, 2003, and 2004 returns filed on or before June 29, 2004. A taxpayer who did not make an election out on a return filed on or before June 29, 2004 for the 2000 through 2004 tax years may make the election out by filing amended returns for the placed in service year and subsequent affected years before expiration of the limitations period for filing any of the amended return(s). In no event may an amended return be filed after June 29, 2007.

Alternatively, Form 3115 (Application for Change in Accounting Method) may be filed with the return for the tax year that includes June 29, 2005 or with the return for the first tax year that follows the tax year that includes June 29, 2005. A Code Sec. 481(a) adjustment for the excess depreciation claimed by using a 5-year recovery period would taken into account if this option is used.

Deemed election out. A taxpayer will be treated as having made an election out if the taxpayer failed to depreciate qualified Liberty Zone Leasehold improvement property placed in service during the 2000, 2001, 2002, 2003, or 2004 tax year using a 5-year recovery period and instead treated the property as 39-year nonresidential real property or 15-year qualified leasehold improvement property, as applicable.

¶ 125

Miscellaneous Property

Aircraft maintenance costs

Costs incurred by an airline to perform work on its aircraft airframe as part of a "heavy maintenance" visit generally are deductible as ordinary and necessary business expenses. However, costs incurred in conjunction with a heavy maintenance visit must be capitalized to the extent they materially add to the value of, substantially prolong the useful life of, or adapt the airframe to a new or different use. In addition, costs incurred as part of a plan of rehabilitation, modernization, or improvement must be capitalized and depreciated (Rev. Rul. 2001-4, I.R.B. 2001-3, 295, modified by Notice 2001-23, I.R.B. 2001-12, 911; Rev. Proc. 2002-9 (Appendix Section 1A.03)).

See, also, "*Engines*" and "*Rotable spare parts,*" below.

Art and décor

See ¶ 3 for depreciation of art, artwork, pictures, interior décor, and antiques.

Bed and breakfasts

Generally, the depreciable portion of a personal residence operated as a bed and breakfast is considered 39-year nonresidential real property because bed and breakfast rooms are rented on a transient basis, thus disqualifying the property as residential rental property. See ¶ 114 for the definition of residential rental property. According to an IRS audit guide, a frequent mistake of bed and breakfast owners is the deduction of depreciation for "common" areas (i.e., space used by the taxpayer's family and guests, such as the kitchen, living room dining, room, and den). Pursuant to Code Sec. 280A, depreciation may only be claimed for areas of the home (e.g., bedrooms) used exclusively for business purposes (IRS Audit Guide: Bed and Breakfasts: Market Segment Specialization Program (MSSP) (5-93), reproduced in the CCH IRS POSITIONS REPORTER at ¶ 202,101).

The IRS audit guide states that some taxpayers erroneously claim a current expense deduction for the entire cost of items such as kitchen cookware, appliances, tableware, linens, furniture, carpeting, and garden equipment. These costs should be capitalized (unless current expensing is allowed under Code Sec. 179) and depreciated. The guide does not indicate the proper depreciation period but presumably a bed and breakfast, like a hotel, is an Asset Class 57.0 business activity (relating to the provision of personal services) (see ¶ 104) and a five-year recovery period applies.

Only the cost of items directly related to rooms related to business may be deducted. For example, the cost of antiques placed in common areas may not be depreciated. The depreciable basis of an antique includes shipping and other acquisition costs, according to the guide.

Expenses incurred to repair or restore portions of a bed and breakfast used as a taxpayer's personal residence or portions that are considered common areas not used exclusively for business purposes, such as expenses to restore the exterior of a home, are not currently deductible. Also, expenses incurred in maintaining common exterior areas, such as expenses for yard work or landscaping are also not deductible (IRS Letter Ruling 8732002, April 2, 1987).

The audit guide notes that if a bed and breakfast contains a large number of rental rooms (for example, 20 rooms) it is more like a hotel or motel business and the deductibility of expenses is generally governed by Code Sec. 162 rather than Code Sec. 280A (which deals with personal residences used for business purposes).

Breast implants of exotic dancer

An exotic dancer (a.k.a., "Chesty Love") was allowed to depreciate the cost of breast implants. Each implant weighed about 10 pounds and the court concluded that the dancer derived no personal benefit due to their large and cumbersome size (*Cynthia Hess*, Tax Court Summary Opinion). Presumably, the implants were treated as MACRS 5-year property (Asset Class 57.0, property used in the provision of personal or professional services).

Cellular telephone property

The IRS has provided MACRS recovery periods for various types of property used by cellular telephone companies in IRS Letter Ruling 9825003 (January 30, 1998). A useful reference is a study prepared by Ernst & Young LLP, "Federal Tax Depreciation of Cellular Assets: The Need for Clarification on Cellular Equipment" (November 10, 1999), which was submitted to the IRS and made available as an "incoming treasury letter."

Engines

The cost of maintenance performed on tugboat engines every three to four years was currently deductible. The cost of the maintenance relative to the value of the tugboat was insubstantial and consisted primarily of labor costs. The maintenance did not amount to a complete overhaul, the cost of which is capitalized because it prolongs the life of the property. Here, the maintenance simply kept the boats running in ordinary operating condition (*Ingram Industries Inc.,* TC Memo. 2000-323, 80 TCM 532, CCH Dec. 54,088(M)). In *FedEx Corporation* (DC Tenn., 2003-2 USTC ¶ 50,697, aff'd CA-6 (unpublished opinion), 2005-1 USTC ¶ 50,186), expenses for overhauling aircraft engines were treated as deductible repairs. The aircraft and engine were considered a single unit of property in determining whether the expenses significantly added to the value of the property or prolonged its useful life. See, also, "*Rotable spare parts,*" below.

Forklifts and bobcats

No specific depreciation period is provided for a forklift or a bobcat in Rev. Proc. 87-56 (¶ 191). The applicable depreciation period will generally depend upon the business activity in which the taxpayer is engaged. For example, the IRS classified these assets when used by a nursery as 7-year property because a nursery is considered a farming business (Asset Class 01.1 at ¶ 191) (IRS market segment specialization program audit guide for the garden supplies industry). Similarly, a chipper used by a nursery is 7-year property. However, if the chipper were used by a professional tree trimmer, it would presumably be classified as 5-year property (Asset Class 57.0, relating to assets used in the provision of personal or professional services).

Gambling boats and barges

A casino riverboat that is in operating condition and coast-guard certified is 10-year property with an 18-year ADS period (Asset Class 00.28, Vessels, Barges, Tugs and Similar Water Transportation Equipment). If such a boat were to lose its certification or otherwise fail to be ready and available as an asset described in Asset Class 00.28 for any tax year, it would be subject to the change of use rules described in Code Sec. 168(i)(5) (ISP Coordinated Issue Paper: Shipping and Gaming Industries: Class Life of Floating Gaming Facilities, March 12, 2001; reproduced in CCH IRS Positions Reporter (IRPO) at ¶ 173,155).

Generally, a casino which is built on a barge (a vessel which is not self-propelled) is permanently moored and not ready and available for operation as water transportation equipment. Thus, it does not fall within Asset Class 00.28. The issue then becomes whether the casino is considered nonresidential real property (39-year recovery period) or is an asset described in Asset Class 79.0 (Recreation) with a 10-year recovery period. The fact that a gaming facility is permanently moored does not necessarily mean that it is an inherently permanent structure (i.e., a building) for depreciation purposes. The *Whiteco* case factors (see ¶ 127C) are applied to make this determination. For example, a multi-story barge that is permanently moored in a river canal which was dug, enclosed, and isolated from the river is 39-year real property. If upon application of the Whiteco factors, a particular gaming facility is determined to be impermanent then it falls within Asset Class 79.0 (ISP Coordinated Issue Paper referenced above).

Slot machines and other gambling devices are seven-year property. See ¶ 106.

Gasoline service stations

The IRS has released a revised Market Segment Specialization Program (MSSP) Audit Guide for gas retailers (issued October 3, 2001). The guide now covers many depreciation issues.

Asset Class 57.0 (5-year property) includes section 1245 property used in marketing petroleum and petroleum products.

Asset Class 57.1 (15-year property) includes (1) section 1250 assets, including service station buildings and (2) depreciable land improvements, whether section 1245 property or section 1250 property, used in the marketing of petroleum and petroleum products, but does not include any facilities related to petroleum and natural gas trunk pipelines. Car wash buildings and related land improvements are included in Asset Class 57.0. All other land improvements, buildings, and structural components are excluded.

A canopy falls within Asset Class 57.1 with a 15-year depreciation period unless it qualifies under the *Whiteco* test (see ¶ 127C) as personal property because it is a nonpermanent structure. In *JFM, Inc.* (67 TCM 3020, CCH Dec. 49,871(M), TC Memo. 1994-239)), canopies bolted down onto four to six special concrete footings were personal property (Asset Class 57.0) with a five-year recovery period. Some of the canopies in question had in fact been moved and reused. The audit guide notes that "the absence of a plan to move a modular structure is not critical, that is, indefinite installation does not taint the personal property characterization."

The IRS selected the recovery period for the depreciation of gasoline pump canopies as an issue for the 2002 Industry Resolution (IIR) program (IRS News Release IR-2002-89, July 10, 2002). In response, the IRS issued Rev. Rul. 2003-54 (I.R.B. 2003-23) in May of 2003. The IRS and taxpayers agree that a canopy which is considered a permanent structure is depreciated over 15 years as a land improvement and that a removable canopy is 5-year personal property (Asset Class 57.0). The area of contention is the standard for determining whether a canopy is personal property or a land improvement. In the vast majority of cases, IRS auditors were taking the position that canopies are land improvements, according to the National Association of Convenience Stores (http://www.cstorecentral.com).

Rev. Rul. 2003-54 describes a typical standalone gasoline pump canopy in use by about 90 percent of service stations. The canopy can be removed cost effectively within a short period of time. The ruling concludes, on the basis of the *Whiteco* factors (¶ 127), that the canopy is tangible personal property and depreciable over five years (Asset Class 57.0). However, the supporting concrete footings are inherently permanent structures and depreciable over 15 years (Asset Class 57.1). Rev. Rul. 2003-54 indicates that taxpayers who have been claiming depreciation deductions in any other manner for two or more tax years may receive automatic consent to change their accounting method pursuant to Appendix 6.06 of Rev. Proc. 2008-52 (see ¶ 75). If a taxpayer has been treating its gasoline canopies and footings in accordance with this ruling, the IRS will not raise the issue in an audit. If the issue is a matter under consideration in examination, in appeals, or before the Tax Court with respect to a tax year that ends before May 8, 2003, it will not be pursued further by the IRS.

Modular (i.e., movable) service station buildings (e.g., a kiosk) and modular car wash buildings will generally qualify as five-year personal property because they are nonpermanent structures. Otherwise a service station building or car wash building that is a permanent structure is 15-year property. A building in which nonpetroleum products are sold (e.g., a convenience store) is considered 39-year nonresidential real property unless it qualifies as a "retail motor fuels outlet" in which case a 15-year recovery period applies. See ¶ 110.

Underground storage tanks, gasoline pumps, hydraulic car lifts, other mechanical equipment, piping, shelves, counters, refrigerators, neon and other signs (contained in or attached to a building), and vending machines are five-year property (Asset Class 57.0).

A parking lot is 15-year property (Asset Class 57.1).

Gym equipment

Gymnasium equipment purchased by a taxpayer engaged in a health club or similar business is presumably 5-year property on the grounds that the taxpayer is providing professional or personal services to the persons who pay to use the equipment (Asset Class 57.0) (see ¶ 104). The depreciation period for equipment purchased by a company for the use of its employees is based on the business activity of the company (assuming the activity is described in Rev. Proc. 87-56). For example, in a Chief Counsel Advice, the IRS ruled that unspecified equipment in a company's "wellness center" was seven-year property where the company was engaged in a farming business (Asset Class 01.1) or a food and meat manufacturing business (Asset Class 20.4) (Chief Counsel Advice 200137026). If the company's business activity is not described, then the equipment would have no class life and be treated as seven-year property (see ¶ 106).

Impact fees

The IRS has ruled that impact fees incurred by real property developers in connection with the construction of a new residential rental building are indirect costs that, pursuant to Code Secs. 263(a) and 263A, should be capitalized and added to the basis of the buildings constructed. (Impact fees are one-time charges imposed by a state or local government to finance specific capital improvements, generally located offsite (e.g., schools, police, and fire buildings).) If the residential buildings are depreciable the impact fees may be recovered through depreciation deductions when they are placed in service. Such fees may also be included in the eligible basis of the buildings for purposes of computing the low income housing credit (Rev. Rul. 2002-9).

This ruling appears to be an IRS "about face." For example, in Technical Advice Memorandum 200043016 (July 14, 2000) local impact fees collected to pay for a variety of capital improvements could not be added to the basis of the constructed property and depreciated. The IRS concluded that the taxpayer merely acquired a business benefit (an intangible asset) with no determinable useful life. TAM 200043016, in fact, was subsequently modified to conform to Rev. Rul. 2002-9 (see TAM 200227009, March 11, 2002).

Taxpayers may use the automatic change of accounting method procedures of Appendix 6.04 of Rev. Proc. 2008-52 (¶ 75).

ISO 9000 costs

Costs incurred by a taxpayer to obtain, maintain, or renew IS0 9000 certification are deductible as ordinary and necessary business expenses, except to the extent that they result in the creation or acquisition of an asset having a useful life substantially beyond the tax year (e.g., a quality manual) (Rev. Rul. 2000-4, 2000-1 CB 331; Appendix Section 3.02 of Rev. Proc. 2008-52.

Painting and remodeling

The cost of painting the interior or exterior of an existing building is normally considered a deductible repair. However, if the painting is part of a remodeling project, then the costs of the project are capitalized and depreciated under the so-called "rehabilitation doctrine" (*J.M. Jones*, 57-1 USTC ¶ 9517; IRS Pub. 587, Depreciating Your Home). For example, if a rental room is repainted, the cost of repainting is a currently deductible rental expense. If the room is extensively remodeled, the remodeling costs, including the painting costs, are depreciated as 27.5-year residential rental property beginning in the month that the remodeling is completed. However, costs attributable to personal property elements of a residential rental remodeling effort could be depreciated under the cost segregation rules as five-year personal property (Asset Class 57.0). See ¶ 127 and following.

Proposed regulations provide that repairs that are made at the same time as an improvement, but that do not directly benefit or are not incurred by reason of the improvement, are not required to be capitalized. When these new proposed regulations are finalized, the judicially-created plan of rehabilitation doctrine will be obsolete, particularly with regard to the assertion that the doctrine transforms otherwise deductible repair costs into capital improvement costs solely because the repairs are performed at the same time as an improvement, or are pursuant to a maintenance plan, even though the repairs do not improve the property. However, Code Sec. 263A continues to require a taxpayer to capitalize otherwise deductible repair costs if the taxpayer improves a unit of property and the otherwise deductible repair costs directly benefit or are incurred by reason of the improvement to the property (NPRM-REG-168745-03 published in the Federal Register on March 10, 2008; Proposed Reg.§ 1.263(a)-3).

Restaurants and taverns—smallwares

Taxpayers engaged in the business of operating a restaurant or tavern to claim a current deduction for smallwares in the year of purchase (Rev. Proc. 2002-12). Previously, a five-year recovery period applied (Asset Class 57.0). This current deduction treatment does not apply to smallwares purchased by a start-up business. The treatment of these smallwares is governed by Code Sec. 195. Under Code Sec. 195, a taxpayer may elect to deduct the first $5,000 of its start-up expenditures. The remaining expenditures are amortized over fifteen years beginning in the month in which an active trade or business begins. The $5,000 current deduction, however, is reduced one dollar for each dollar that total start-up expenditures exceed $50,000. Note that Code Sec. 195 does not apply to a taxpayer who is currently operating one or more restaurants and is opening a new restaurant.

Smallwares include (1) glassware and paper or plastic cups; (2) flatware (silverware) and plastic utensils; (3) dinnerware (dishes) and paper or plastic plates; (4) pots and pans; (5) table top items; (6) bar supplies; (7) food preparation utensils and tools; (8) storage supplies; (9) service items; and (10) small appliances costing no more than $500 each. Refer to Rev. Proc. 2002-12 for specific examples of these items.

The operation of a restaurant includes cafeterias, special food services, such as food service contractors, caterers, and mobile food services. The operation of a restaurant or tavern may also include food or beverage services at grocery stores, hotels and motels, amusement parks, theaters, casinos, country clubs, and similar social or recreational facilities.

Smallwares purchased and stored at a warehouse or facility other than the restaurant where the smallwares will be used are not currently deductible until they are received by the restaurant or facility where they will be used and are available for use.

Automatic change in accounting method procedures are provided in Section 6 of Rev. Proc. 2002-12 and Appendix Section 3.03 of Rev. Proc. 2008-52. A taxpayer must change its accounting method under these procedures in order to take advantage of the rule provided in Rev. Proc. 2002-12. The Code Sec. 481(a) adjustment (i.e., the cost of existing smallware less depreciation claimed) will be deducted in a single tax year.

Improvements to a restaurant placed in service after October 22, 2004, and before January 1, 2010, may qualify as 15-year MACRS property if specified requirements are satisfied. A restaurant building placed in service in 2009 may also be able to qualify as 15-year MACRS property. See ¶ 110.

Roof

The IRS has maintained, as well as most courts, that the replacement of all of the shingles or asphalt on a roof is a capital expenditure. The replacement of a portion of a leaking roof, however, is usually regarded as a currently deductible repair expense.

Recently issued proposed regulations, however, would allow taxpayers to deduct the cost of repairing or replacing a roof provided that the replacement roof is of approximately the same quality of as the roof that is repaired or replaced. These are not reliance regs (i.e., cannot be used as authority for taking a position until finalized). The test applied is whether there is a betterment within the meaning of the proposals. For example, the replacement of wood shingles with 50-year asphalt shingles after a storm is a betterment and the costs are capitalized (Proposed Reg.§ 1.263(a)-3(f)(3), Example (9)). Replacement with the same wood shingles or comparable asphalt shinges is currently deductible (Proposed Reg.§ 1.263(a)-3(f)(3), Examples (7) and (8)). Under the proposed regulations, expenditures that ameliorate a material defect that exists prior to the acquisition of property are generally capitalized. Thus, a defective roof that is replaced after acquistion of a property may need to be capitalized under the proposals. See Proposed Reg.§ 1.263(a)-3(f)(3), Example (5). Although these proposed regulations may not be relied upon until published as final regulations, they illustrate the trend in IRS thinking and the likely future rule.

With respect to case law, in *Badger Pipeline Company*, 74 TCM 856, Dec. 52,292(M), the Tax Court indicated that it would treat the replacement of a few slate roof tiles as a repair, but the replacement of all of the roof tiles as a capital expenditure. In *Pierce Estates*, 16 TC 1020, Dec. 18,270, the Tax Court treated the cost of replacing a corrugated metal roof as a capital expenditure but the cost of patching leaks on an asphalt roof as currently deductible repairs. In *Oberman Manufacturing Co.*, 47 TC 471, Dec. 28,334, however, the cost of removing and replacing the entire perlite and asphalt and gravel covering on a roof (as well as replacing an expansion joint) was held to be a deductible repair. The court indicated that the work merely kept the building in operating condition and did not increase the useful life or the value of the building.

The *Oberman* decision was cited in a Tax Court small case summary opinion (these opinions are not reviewable and may not be cited as authority), which held that replacement of all of the "top layers" of the roof of a one-story residential rental house with fiberglass sheets and hot asphalt was a deductible repair (*N. Campbell*, T.C. Summary Opinion 2002-117). A subsequent Tax Court small case summary opinion, again citing *Oberman*, also allowed the current deduction of roof replacement costs (*T.J. Northen Jr.* and *S. Cox*, T.C. Summary Opinion 2003-113). The case involved a 26,000 square foot commercial building. The roof leaked in one location. Nevertheless, the roofing company removed all tar and gravel down to the plywood, replaced twenty-eight sheets of dry rotted plywood, and sprayed with a primer and a polyurethane foam coating before applying new tar and gravel. An air conditioning unit also had to be removed and reattached to repair the roof. The Court reasoned that the work was done to prevent leakage, keep the property in operating condition and did not prolong the life of the property, increase its value, or make it adaptable to another use.

A taxpayer may elect to have a case tried under the small tax case procedures if the deduction involves $50,000 or less (Code Sec. 7463). If the deficiency exceeds this amount, the taxpayer may obtain jurisdiction by conceding the excess. There is no appeal from a small tax case decision.

In *D.W. Stark* (77 TCM 1181, CCH Dec. 53,202(M)), "roofing material was removed down to the wooden structure of the building," a new roof drain was added, and a new roof was reapplied. These expenditures had to be capitalized. The *Oberman* decision was distinguished. The facts are unclear but in *Stark* perhaps the plywood covering on which a roof is placed may have been removed. Stark appears to be the only roofing case in which *Oberman* is cited by another court (other than the summary decisions mentioned above).

Another case that held that the cost of a new roof had to be capitalized is *C.E. Drozda*, T.C. Memo. 1984-19, CCH Dec. 40,926(M). This case, however, does not offer any particular insight into its reasoning.

In *Vanalco, Inc.*, 78 TCM 251, Dec. 53,493(M), the replacement of 10 percent of the roofing material and underlying decking on an industrial building to stop leaks was considered a deductible expense. The court ruled that there was no plan to replace the entire roof even though a substantial portion of the roof had been previously replaced in earlier tax years.

In *G.H. Hable*, 48 TCM 1079, Dec. 41,481(M), the IRS unsuccessfully argued that the replacement of barn shingles blown off during a storm was a capital expenditure (similarly, *G.W. Pontel*, 42 TCM 113, Dec. 37,988(M)).

The depreciation of a roof is computed as explained at ¶ 126. For additional cases holding that the cost of a new roof is not deductible, see annotations at CCH Standard Federal Tax Reporter ¶ 8630.60 and following and ¶ 13,709.567.

When a roof is replaced, gain or loss is not recognized. The costs associated with the construction of the original roof remain part of the depreciable basis of the building. If the roof replaced in not the original roof, but separately depreciated, the IRS contends that a taxpayer should continue to depreciate the replaced roof. See ¶ 162.

Rotable spare parts

The IRS has announced that it will allow taxpayers to treat rotable spare parts as depreciable capital assets in situations substantially similar to those of the *Hewlett-Packard* and *Honeywell* cases (Rev. Rul. 2003-37). In the *Hewlett-Packard* case, a computer maintenance business was conducted by the seller of the computers pursuant to standardized maintenance agreements (*Hewlett-Packard*, CA-FC, 96-1 USTC ¶ 50,046). Malfunctioning computer parts were replaced with spare parts from a rotable pool. The IRS contended that each exchange of parts was a sale of inventory. The Appellate Court ruled that the parts were a depreciable capital asset. The Tax Court and the Eighth Circuit ruled similarly in *Honeywell* (*Honeywell Inc. and Subsidiaries*, 64 TCM 437, CCH Dec. 48,412(M), aff'd, CA-8 (unpublished opinion), 27 F3d 577).

The IRS has provided a safe harbor method of accounting to treat rotable spare parts as depreciable assets, rather than as inventory, in accordance with Rev. Rul. 2003-37, generally effective for tax years ending on or after December 31, 2006. Taxpayers can obtain automatic consent to adopt the new safe harbor if they account for their rotable spare parts in accordance with specific provisions in Rev. Proc. 2007-48 (Rev. Proc. 2007-48, I.R.B. 2007-29; Rev. Proc. 2008-52, Appendix Section 10.06).

The safe harbor may be used by a taxpayer that has gross sales (less returns) of rotable spare parts from the taxpayer's maintenance operation that do not exceed

10 percent of the taxpayer's total gross revenues (less returns) from its maintenance operation for the taxable year. In addition, the taxpayer must:

(1) repair customer-owned (or customer-leased) equipment under warranty or maintenance agreements that are provided to the customer for either no charge or a predetermined fee that does not change during the term of the agreement (regardless of the taxpayer's costs to comply with the agreement);

(2) be obligated under the warranty or maintenance agreements to repair the customer's equipment (including all parts and labor related to the repair) for either no charge or a nominal service fee that is unrelated to the actual cost of parts and labor provided;

(3) maintain a pool or pools of spare parts that are used primarily in the taxpayer's maintenance operation of repairing customer-owned (or customer-leased) equipment under warranty or maintenance agreements, exchange the spare parts for defective parts in the customer-owned (or customer-leased) equipment, and generally repairs and reuse the defective parts in its pool of spare parts; and

(4) have a depreciable interest in the rotable spare parts and has placed in service the rotable spare parts after 1986.

A taxpayer using the safe harbor method of accounting for rotable spare parts must:

(1) capitalize the cost of the rotable spare parts under Code Sec. 263(a) and depreciate these parts using MACRS ;

(2) establish one or more pools for the rotable spare parts;

(3) identify the disposed rotable spare parts; and

(4) determine a depreciable basis of the rotable spare parts.

Rev. Proc. 2007-48 explains how the parts are to be depreciated under MACRS and the manner in which the pools are established, the disposed parts are identified, and the basis of the parts determined.

A taxpayer that is not eligible to use the safe harbor method may request to change its method of accounting for treating rotable spare parts by filing a Form 3115 with the Commissioner in accordance with the requirements of Reg. § 1.446-1(e)(3)(i) and the advance consent procedures of Rev. Proc. 97-27.

The IRS previously took the position that rotable spare parts maintained by a manufacturer to service *customer-owned* computer and data processing equipment are nondepreciable inventory. However, rotable spare parts held exclusively to service equipment *leased* to customers could be treated as depreciable capital assets. Rotable spare parts held both for servicing customer-owned equipment and leased equipment, according to the prior IRS position, were properly treated as inventory (IRS Industry Specialization Program (ISP) Coordinated Issue Paper, "Rotable" Spare Parts (as revised on July 31, 1992) and reproduced in the CCH IRS POSITIONS REPORTER at ¶ 100,575).

Rotable spare parts are parts that are removed from machines and replaced with new or repaired parts. The removed parts are usually repaired and placed in a spare parts pool, that may also include new parts, for future use on other machines.

Airplane engines which were removed every six months, overhauled, and placed in a spare parts pool for use on other planes when their engines were overhauled were treated as separately depreciable assets (GCM 36728, May 14, 1976).

Proposed regulations (which may not be relied upon until finalized) provide that rotable or temporary spare parts treated as materials and supplies will be considered used or consumed in the tax year in which the taxpayer disposes of the parts. This rule prevents taxpayers from prematurely deducting the cost of a unit of property by systematically replacing components with rotable spare parts. The IRS anticipates that taxpayers with rotable or temporary spare parts that are not discarded after their original use generally will prefer to capitalize their costs and treat those parts as depreciable assets. The proposed regulations provide for an election to capitalize these costs (Proposed Reg.§ 1.162-3; Proposed Reg.§ 1.263(a)-3(e)(3)).

Many taxpayers currently treat rotable spare parts as capital expenditures depreciable over the life of the unit of property in which the rotables are used. See Rev. Rul. 69-200, 1969-1 CB 60. Under these proposed regulations, taxpayers may elect to treat an amount paid for a material and supply as a capital expenditure. In general, the election is made separately for each material and supply and is revocable only with IRS consent. The election is made by capitalizing the cost of the material and supply in the year the cost is incurred and beginning depreciation of the item in the year it is placed in service.

Tires and tubes

The IRS has issued Rev. Proc. 2002-27 which provides a method (the "original tire capitalization method") for accounting for the cost of original and replacement truck tires. Under the original tire capitalization method, a taxpayer:

(1) capitalizes the cost of the original tires of a qualifying vehicle (whether purchased separately or equipped on the vehicle when purchased) using the same depreciation method, recovery period, and convention applicable to the vehicle on which the tires are first installed and

(2) treats the original tires as disposed of when the vehicle is disposed of.

Thus, the cost of original tires must be depreciated over the depreciation period of the vehicle even if they have been disposed of. Furthermore, no current expense deduction can be claimed for original tires even if they wear out in one year or less.

Although original tires that wear out in one year or less cannot be expensed, the cost of all replacement tires may be claimed as a current deduction regardless of their useful life.

If elected, the original tire capitalization method applies to all original and replacement tires mounted on all of a taxpayer's light general purpose trucks (Asset Class 00.241 (5-year property)), heavy general purpose trucks (Asset Class 00.242 (5-year property)), tractor units for use over-the-road (Asset Class 00.26 (3-year property)), trailers (Asset Class 00.27 (5-year property)), and converter dollies (converter gears) (a converter dolly is an accessory used to convert a semitrailer to a full trailer (Reg. § 48.4061-(b)(2)). The procedures contained in Rev. Proc. 2002-27, therefore, do not apply to tires used on buses (Asset Class 00.23) or automobiles and taxis (Asset Class 00.22).

Rev. Proc. 2002-27 is generally effective for tax years ending on or after December 31, 2001. The ruling contains detailed guidance on automatic change of accounting method procedures. See, also, Appendix 6.05 of Rev. Proc. 2008-52.

A taxpayer that does not choose to use the original tire capitalization method on its qualifying vehicles must account for the cost of its original and replacement tires in accordance with the case law and rulings cited by the IRS in section 2.03 of the ruling. This precedent allows the cost of truck tires and tubes which are consumed within one year to be claimed as a current deduction. The depreciation period for other original and replacement truck tires, however, is determined by reference to the business activity of the taxpayer and not the depreciation period of the vehicle. The truck tires are considered an asset entirely separate from the vehicle to which they are attached. See, for example, IRS Field Service Advice 200122002, January 30, 2001.

In many instances if the original tire capitalization method is not used, the truck tires will be treated as 5-year property under Asset Class 42.0 (Motor Transport-Freight, relating to assets (other than vehicles) used in the commercial and contract carrying of freight by road). Classification by reference to business activity rather than truck type may be disadvantageous in the case of tractor units for use over-the-road since these trucks are treated as 3-year property under MACRS (Asset Class 00.26).

Rev. Proc. 2002-27 is clearly disadvantageous to a taxpayer that consumes all of its tires (original and replacement) within one year since no expense deduction can be claimed on the original tires. In most other situations, Rev. Proc. 2002-27 seems preferable as it allows the cost of all replacement tires to be deducted in full.

Retreads. Following the release of Rev. Proc. 2002-27, the IRS clarified that a taxpayer who does not elect the OTC method should capitalize and depreciate the cost of retreaded tires as separate assets whether the retreaded tires are used as the original set of tires or as replacements. The cost may be deducted as a repair if the tire is consumed in less than one year (Chief Counsel Advice 200252091, October 31, 2002; clarified by Chief Counsel Advice 200307087, February 19, 2003).

The ruling further clarifies that a taxpayer who has elected the OTC method should treat retreaded tires that are acquired as the first set of tires on newly-acquired vehicles as "original tires" that are depreciated as part of the cost of the vehicle.

Retreads that are received in exchange for original or replacement tires should be considered "replacement tires" whose cost may be claimed as a current deduction. The ruling notes that a retread company may return the taxpayer's original tires or replace them with different tires. The conclusions reached by the ruling do not appear to depend on whether or not the taxpayer receives its original tires from the retreader.

Certain taxpayers who use their cars for business purposes may either elect the standard mileage rate or use the actual expense method (¶ 217). No depreciation deduction is claimed if the standard mileage rate is used. It appears that most taxpayers who decide not to use the standard mileage rate recover the cost of the original equipment tires through depreciation deductions on the vehicle and then deduct the cost of replacement tires in full (IRS Publication 463; Form 2106 instructions). This treatment is consistent with the original tire capitalization method.

Tools, shop equipment, laboratory equipment

The IRS has ruled that tools, shop equipment, and laboratory equipment, such as lathes, bandsaws, hydraulic presses used by a utility involved in the generating, transmitting, and distributing of electricity were used in furtherance of its business activity and, therefore, includible in the business activity class of Rev. Proc. 87-56 in which they were primarily used. The tools were used in the following property class business activities: Asset Class 49.13, Electric Utility Steam Production Plant; Asset Class 49.14, Electric Utility Transmission and Distribution Plant, and Asset Class

49.21, Gas Utility Distribution Facilities (CCA Letter Ruling 200246006, August 5, 2002). It is useful to note that the fact that these Asset Classes list specific types of assets did not preclude the inclusion of the tools etc., within the asset classification so long as the tools were used in the furtherance of the business activity described by the Asset Class. Thus, in general, it appears that a taxpayer should include tools etc. in the asset class for their business activity as described in Rev. Proc. 87-56. Tools with a useful life of less than one year, however, are currently deductible.

Web site development costs

The tax treatment of the costs of developing and maintaining a web site has not been officially addressed by the IRS. Although some taxpayers have been deducting the entire cost of creating a web site as an "advertising" expense, it seems clear that such a wholesale treatment is not acceptable to the IRS. Some of the cost of creating or purchasing a web site, however, may be currently deductible as a software development cost. Rev. Proc. 2000-50 and Rev. Proc. 69-21 (prior to being superseded by Rev. Proc. 2000-50) allow taxpayers to currently deduct software development costs in the same manner as a research and development expenditure under Code Sec. 174.

One important change to Rev. Proc. 69-21 made by Rev. Proc. 2000-50 should be noted. Rev. Proc. 2000-50 now states that, "[t]his revenue procedure does not apply . . . to costs that a taxpayer has treated as a research and experimentation expenditure under § 174." This change clarifies that amounts that a taxpayer deducts under the authority of Rev. Proc. 2000-50 are considered deducted by virtue of Code Sec. 162 and do not necessarily qualify as research and experimental expenditures under Code Sec. 174. Some taxpayers have interpreted Rev. Proc. 69-21 as meaning that all software expenditures qualify as research and experimental expenditures under Code Sec. 174 and are deductible under that section. The distinction is important for taxpayers who want to claim the research and development credit since only expenditures that are deductible under Code Sec. 174 can qualify for the credit. Also, for a start-up business, Code Sec. 195 requires the capitalization of ordinary and necessary business expenses incurred during the start-up period; this requirement, however, does not apply to amounts for which a deduction is allowable Code Sec. 174. Thus, software development costs cannot qualify for current deduction by a start-up company unless they also qualify for deduction under Code Sec. 174.

It should be noted that when an independent contractor is paid to develop software, software development costs are deductible under Code Sec. 174 only if the purchaser is at risk that the project will fail (Reg. § 1.174-2(b)(2)).

The following material regarding the tax treatment of web site development costs appeared in the Spring 2000, *ISP Digest Data Processing*. This is an unofficial publication of the IRS's Data Processing ISP (Industry Specialization Program). It does not represent the IRS's official position (no official position has been taken as of press time). In addition, a related outline, is also reproduced below. Both items were drafted by Robert L. Rible, in his capacity as the Technical Advisor for the Data Processing Industry, within the Pre-filing and Technical Guidance Office of the Large and Mid-Size Business Division (Washington D.C.).

In short, the discussion strictly construes the types of expenses that qualify for a current deduction as software development or as a currently deductible advertising cost. It takes the position that a web site should primarily be viewed as an item of software amortizable over three years when placed in service. The creation of web site pages with a software tool would not be considered software development that is currently deductible as a software development cost. Software development costs that are eligible for current deduction under Rev. Proc. 2000-50 would relate to the cost of writing source code (i.e., programming) that enables a computer to perform a desired function. In most cases, according to the outline, direct HTML coding of a web page would not qualify as software development. Currently deductible advertising expenses would be limited to costs that relate to material that is changed or updated on a regular basis. Permanent elements of a cite which do not qualify as currently deductible software development expenditures would generally be amortized over three years by including such costs in the basis of the web site and treating the web site as if it were a software asset.

Arguably, the treatment of a web site as amortizable three-year software seems favorable to the taxpayer in that costs capitalized into a web site would likely not otherwise be recoverable because a web site does not usually have a determinable useful life.

Web Site Design Costs (Text from Spring 2000, ISP Digest Data Processing)

Another issue arising in the area of software programs is the treatment of web site design costs. In fact, during the last filing season there were a number of questions about this topic from the Taxpayer Service Division, as taxpayers were curious about how these costs should be treated. First, the same issue about who bears the economic risk for the work being done is present. If the taxpayer does not bear the risk, he is clearly getting purchased software, and it should be treated as the asset it is. For a good discussion of the "at risk" issue, see FSA 199930016 [Field Service Advice—CCH.], issued on September [April—CCH.]27, 1999. But if he does bear the risk, then the same old question arises: does the work of designing the web site constitute software development? Frequently, the process of making this design involves the use of purchased software, such as Adobe PageMill 3.0™, Microsoft FrontPage 2000™, or Macromedia's Dreamweaver 2™. Such software packages contain templates that enables one to configure the web page in any way that the designer wants. As with the ERP and CRM software [references are to discussion of Enterprise Resource Planning and Customer Relationship Management Software that appear earlier in the *Digest*—CCH.], using templates is not software development. So if the taxpayer or his outside consultant is designing the web site using such software, it can be maintained that he is getting an asset with a useful life beyond the first taxable year.

One argument that some taxpayers may want to use is that the cost of the web site design is deductible as an advertising expense. Advertising expenses usually get to be expensed currently, as per Reg. § 1.162(a). But the Service has argued—in the context of package design costs—that such "design costs more closely resemble nonrecurring promotional or advertising expenditures that result in benefits to the taxpayer which extend beyond the year in which the expenditures are incurred; such expenditures are a capital investment and are not currently deductible" (Rev. Rul. 89-23, 1989-1 CB 85). And more recently the Service has argued that, "Only in the unusual circumstance where advertising is directed toward obtaining future benefits significantly beyond those traditionally associated with ordinary product advertising or with institutional goodwill advertising, must the costs of that advertising be capitalized" (Rev. Rul. 92-80, I.R.B. 1992-39). In a recent court case, *RJR Nabisco Inc., et al., v. Commis-*

> *sioner*, TC Memo. 1998-252, the government lost its argument that such package design costs should be capitalized. But a nonacquiescence on this case was issued on October 4, 1999 (AOD/CC 1999-012), in which it is stated that, "The Service has expressly determined that package design costs are essentially different from deductible advertising costs." The situation involving a web site design is very similar to the package design issue in the food and beverage industry. See the coordinated issue paper in this industry for a complete discussion of the issue. Even though there is an advertising aspect to both package designs and web site designs, it can be argued that the costs of making these designs are capital expenditures under § 263.
>
> A relevant court case is *Alabama Coca-Cola Bottling Co. v. Commissioner*, TC Memo. 1969-123. The taxpayer argued that billboards, signs and scoreboards were a current advertising expense. But the court concluded that they were assets with a life of more than one year, insofar as the structure of the items remained from year to year, even though their contents may change many times during a year. In the case of a web site, there are going to be periodic changes to them, because of changes in products sold, changes in personnel, changing financial conditions, etc. The changes that are made on a monthly or other regular basis are clearly ordinary advertising expenses, but the basic web site design that may endure over a longer period of time can easily be seen to be an asset. Again, as a form of purchased software, this asset should be given a three year life under § 167(f). Some companies are spending hundreds of thousands of dollars on these web site designs, so its is an issue of some materiality. [end of IRS text—CCH]

The IRS outline below indicates that even the creation of a web page using HTML coding (as opposed to purchased software such as Microsoft FrontPage™) is probably not software development for purposes of Rev. Proc. 2000-50 and its predecessor, Rev. Proc. 69-21. However, in fact, many taxpayers have been deducting the cost of directly coded HTML graphics related to the look and feel of a web site such as borders, color, fonts, frames, background, toolbars, menubars, banners, logos, buttons, hyperlinks, and blank forms for ordering products or obtaining user information as a software development cost.

Full Text IRS Outline

- Most companies now have web sites on the internet. They contain information about a company's products, personnel, services, and even its financials.
- These web sites are frequently designed using purchased software, such a Adobe PageMill 3.0™, Microsoft FrontPage 2000™, or Macromedia's Dreamweaver 2™.
- Such software packages contain templates that enable one to design the web page in any way that the designer wants. Sometimes HTML code is directly integrated into the design project.
- In addition, sometimes HTML (hypertext markup language) code is used to create a web page. HTML is very simple code, and is not a classical programming language, such as COBOL, FORTRAN, or C++ etc.

• One common definition of an HTML document is that it is "simply a plain-text document that has HTML tags embedded in it."

• The definition of software contained in sections 167(f) and 197(e)(3)(B) of the Internal Revenue Code is that it is a "program designed to cause a computer to perform a desired function." Such programs are dynamic and can be used over and over again in various and different ways at various times.

• A web page is more of a fixed, static document that is just there. The internet browser on the computer and the software on the server computer feeding the system are what cause the computer to perform various functions.

• **Legally, a number of points can be made:**

• If the taxpayer does not bear the economic risk for the work being done to create the web site, but is getting something from an outside contractor which is guaranteed to work, at a set dollar amount, it can be argued that he is buying an asset, not just paying for a service. See *FSA 199930016*, September [April—CCH.] 27, 1999, for a good discussion of the risk issue in relation to software projects.

• Even if he does bear the economic risk for the work done, it can still be questioned as to whether what he is paying for is software development or not. Using templates and even writing in HTML code may not constitute "software development." No source code is being written using a classical programming language. "Software" as the IRC defines it is not being created ("a program that causes a computer to perform a desired function").

• If such work does not constitute software development, it cannot be expensed under the provisions of Rev. Proc. 69-21 [now superseded by Rev. Proc. 2000-50—CCH.], which permits all true software development to be expensed, even if the work does not constitute actual research and development.

• To consider web site design similar to research and development under section 174 is stretching the human imagination beyond its normal limits.

• Insofar as an asset with a life beyond one year is being acquired, the cost of creating it should be capitalized and amortized.

• Because a web site is similar to software and is used in conjunction with software (the browser and the server's software), these costs of development should be amortized over 36 months under section 167(f), beginning with the day that it is placed on the world-wide web.

• Some may argue that web site design costs should be deducted as advertising expenses under section 162-1(a) of the Income Tax Regulations.

• But a web site may be considered analogous to a billboard. See *Alabama Coca-Cola Bottling Co. v. Comm.*, T.C. Memo. 1969-123. In this case the court decided that billboards were assets with a life beyond one taxable year, even though the contents may change periodically. The cost of the billboard structure itself could not be deducted as a current advertising expense. A web site can be considered a similar asset, in that the basic web site design may endure from year to year, even though the contents on the web site may change weekly, monthly, or annually. [End of text of IRS outline—CCH]

Impact of Code Sec. 195. Code Sec. 195 requires taxpayers who create a web site for the purpose of entering a new trade or business to capitalize the costs of creating a web site that are paid or incurred before the day active conduct of the trade or business begins. The rule, however, only applies to costs that would otherwise be deductible in the year paid or incurred. An election may be made to amortize these costs over a five-year period (or a longer period selected by the taxpayer) beginning in the month that the active trade or business begins (Code Sec. 195(b) prior to amendment by the American Jobs Creation Act of 2004 (P.L. 108-357)). See below for rules that apply under P.L. 108-357.

Thus, for example, otherwise deductible consulting fees may be considered an amortizable start-up cost under Code Sec. 195 in the case of a taxpayer that is starting an on-line business (as opposed to an existing taxpayer that is expanding its current business to include an internet site).

Importantly, any costs that are deductible under Code Sec. 174 (e.g., software development costs), are not considered start-up costs and may be currently deducted (Code Sec. 195(c)).

The IRS has ruled that depreciation deductions are not Code Sec. 195 start-up costs because an asset is not considered placed in service until a trade or business activity begins (IRS Letter Ruling 9235004, May 20, 1992). Consequently, depreciation on hardware and software purchased by a start-up internet company cannot begin until the business activity commences (presumably when the web site is up and running).

Effective for amounts paid or incurred after October 22, 2004, taxpayers may elect to deduct up to $5,000 of start-up expenditures in the tax year in which their trade or business begins (Code Sec. 195(b), as amended by P.L. 108-357). The $5,000 amount must be reduced (but not below zero) by the amount by which the start-up expenditures exceed $50,000. The remainder of any start-up expenditures, those that are not deductible in the year in which the trade or business begins, must be ratably amortized over the 180-month period (15 years) beginning with the month in which the active trade or business begins. A similar rule applies to corporations and partnerships (Code Sec. 248(a) and Code Sec. 709(b), as amended by P.L.108-357).

Financial accounting. The Emerging Issues Task Force of the Financial Accounting Standards Board (FASB) reached a consensus on Issue No. 00-2, Accounting for Web Site Development Costs, at a March 16, 2000, meeting.

Additional information on e-commerce issues

Http://www.cob.sjsu.edu/facstaff/nellen_a/e-links.html is a web site that contains articles and links relating to e-commerce tax issues, including web site development costs. Click on the link entitled "Federal Domestic Tax Issues of E-Commerce."

Zoning variance

The costs of obtaining zoning variations were added to the depreciable basis of buildings constructed by a developer where the variations related to the buildings themselves. However, the cost of obtaining zoning changes that related to the use of the land were added to the basis of the land (*Maguire/Thomas Partners Fifth & Grand, Ltd., Depreciation*, 89 TCM 799, Dec. 55,935(M)).

¶ 126
Additions and Improvements

Additions or improvements made to property, including improvements by a lessee or lessor to leased property, are treated as separate property items for MACRS depreciation purposes (Code Sec. 168(i)(6)). In general, depreciation on additions or improvements is computed in the same way as depreciation would be computed on the property added to or improved if such property had been placed in service at the same time as the addition or improvement. However, a 15-year recovery period applies to qualified restaurant property (¶ 110) and qualified leasehold improvement property (see discussion below) placed into service after October 22, 2004 and before January 1, 2010 and to qualified retail improvement property placed in service after December 31, 2008 and before January 1, 2010 (see discussion below).

Depreciation on an addition or improvement begins in the tax year that it is placed into service; however depreciation cannot begin before the tax year that the property to which the addition or improvement is made is placed into service (Code Sec. 168(i)(6)(B)).

> ***Example:*** In January of the current tax year, the deck of a residential rental house that is depreciated under the ACRS rules is replaced and placed in service. The deck must be depreciated under the MACRS rules and is considered 27.5-year residential rental property because the house would be 27.5-year residential rental property if it had been placed in service in January of the current tax year.

See ¶ 125 for a discussion of the treatment of roofs.

The additions and improvements covered by this rule include those that are in the nature of structural components which are considered section 1250 (real) property—for example, walls and partitions or certain wiring and plumbing. See ¶ 127 which discusses the difference between structural components and personal property which may be depreciated without reference to the depreciation period of the building.

In the case of an improvement to listed property, such as a car (see ¶ 206-¶ 214), an improvement that must be capitalized is treated as new depreciable property and must be depreciated under the same method and recovery period as the listed property that is improved.

Depreciating retired structural component

The retirement of a structural component of real property is not a disposition in the view of the IRS whether the component is ACRS or MACRS property (Prop. Reg. § 1.168-2(l)(1); IRS Field Service Advice 200001005, September 10, 1999). Thus, a taxpayer (other than a lessor or lessee as explained below) who abandons or destroys a structural component does not claim a gain or loss but, rather, continues to depreciate the component. See ¶ 162 for details.

Recovery of leasehold improvements in general

The cost of a leasehold improvement is recovered under MACRS without regard to the length of the lease (Code Sec. 168(i)(8)(A)). If upon termination of the lease, an improvement made and depreciated by the lessee is not retained by the lessee, the lessee may compute gain or loss on the improvement by reference to the remaining adjusted basis of the improvement (see the Joint Committee Blue Book for the 1986 Tax Reform Act, p. 108).

The lessee claims depreciation deductions for improvements made by the lessee even if the terms of the lease provide that legal title belongs to the lessor at the moment the improvements are made. Legal title is not necessary to claim depreciation deductions (*M.A. McGrath*, T.C. Memo. 2002-231, Dec. 54,873(M)).

Pursuant to Code Sec. 109, a lessor's gross income does not include the value of improvements made by a lessee on a lessor's property that become the lessor's property upon the termination or forfeiture of the lease. However, this rule does not apply to the extent that the improvements represent the liquidation of lease rentals. Nor does it apply with respect to improvements representing rental income during the period of the lease (Reg. § 1.109-1).

If a lessee makes a capital expenditure in lieu of rent, the lessee may claim a current deduction for rent. The lessor is treated as receiving rent (taxable income) in the amount of the expenditures for the improvements and then using the rent to make the improvements. Thus, the lessor reports rent income and claims depreciation deductions on the improvements. In order for this nonstatutory exception to apply, the lessor and lessee must clearly intend that some or all of the lessee's capital expenditures are rent (*M.A. McGrath*, T.C. Memo. 2002-231, Dec. 54,873(M)).

The IRS has contended that a lessor must continue to depreciate an improvement made by the lessor that is a structural component of a building even if the improvement is retired at the end of the lease term. (See ¶ 162 for background information.) The 1996 Small Business Job Protection Act (P.L. 104-188), however, added Code Sec. 168(i)(8)(B), which provides that a lessor who disposes of a leasehold improvement (made by the lessor for the lessee) may take the adjusted basis of the improvement into account for purposes of determining gain or loss if the improvement is irrevocably disposed of or abandoned by the lessor at the termination of the lease. This provision applies to improvements disposed of or abandoned after June 12, 1996 (Code Sec. 168(i)(8)(B)). Thus, for example, if the leasehold improvement is abandoned, the lessor may claim an ordinary loss in the amount of the improvement's remaining adjusted basis.

The Conference Committee Report for P.L. 104-188 clarifies that the provision does not apply to the extent that Code Sec. 280B applies to the demolition of a structure, a portion of which may include leasehold improvements. Code Sec. 280B requires the capitalization to the land of amounts expended by an owner or lessee for the demolition of a structure as well as losses sustained on account of such demolition. See ¶ 5.

An abandonment loss claimed by a lessor with respect to a leasehold improvement is reported on Form 4797, Part II, line 10 along with ordinary gains and losses from other Section 1231 assets (IRS Publication 225).

15-year qualified leasehold improvement property

The American Jobs Creation Act of 2004 (P.L. 108-357) created a new category of 15-year MACRS property referred to as "qualified leasehold improvement property" (Code Sec. 168(e)(3)(E)(iv), as added by P.L. 108-357 and amended by P.L. 110-343). In general, qualified leasehold improvement property is an improvement made by a lessor or lessee pursuant to or under a lease to the interior portion of nonresidential real property after October 22, 2004 and before January 1, 2010. See below.

Assuming that a leasehold improvement is not qualified leasehold improvement property, it is depreciated over the same depreciation period that would apply to the improved property if the improved property were placed in service at the same time as the improvement (Code Sec. 168(i)(6)). Thus, if a structural improvement is made in 2008 to a commercial building placed in service in 1979, the improvement is depreciated over 39 years since the building would be MACRS nonresidential real property (¶ 116) if placed in service in 2008.

Some typical examples of leasehold improvements include interior walls, partitions, flooring, lighting, plumbing, and other fixtures. If a leasehold improvement is section 1245 property as explained at ¶ 127 it is depreciable over a shorter recovery period (usually 5- or 7-years).

"Qualified leasehold improvement property" placed in service after October 22, 2004 and before January 1, 2010, is 15-year MACRS property with a 15-year recovery period (Code Sec. 168(e)(3)(E)(iv), as added by P.L. 108-357 and amended by P.L. 110-343). As explained below, the improvements must be made to the interior portion of nonresidential real property. The applicable depreciation method is the MACRS straight-line method (Code Sec. 168(b)(3)(G), as added by P.L. 108-357). If the MACRS alternative depreciation system (ADS) is elected or otherwise applies, the recovery period is 39 years and the recovery method is the straight-line method (Code Sec. 168(g)(3)(B), as amended by P.L. 108-357). Whether or not ADS is elected, the applicable convention is the half-year convention unless the mid-quarter convention applies.

This provision is not elective. If the requirements for qualification are met, then the improvement must be depreciated over 15 years using the straight-line method. A taxpayer, however, could effectively avoid the provision by electing ADS and depreciating the improvements over 39 years. However, the ADS election would also apply to any other MACRS 15-year property that the taxpayer happened to place in service in the same tax year (Code Sec. 168(g)(7)).

Qualified leasehold improvement property is defined the same way as the term is defined in Code Sec. 168(k)(3) for purposes of the bonus depreciation deduction. The IRS has issued bonus depreciation regulations which provide guidance concerning the definition of qualified leasehold improvement property under Code Sec. 168(k)(3) (Reg.§ 1.168(k)-1(c)). These regulations should apply equally to the definition for purposes of the new 15-year recovery period. See ¶ 127D for a discussion of bonus depreciation, including the definition of qualified leasehold improvement property.

Under the bonus depreciation provision, qualified leasehold improvement property is any improvement to an interior portion of nonresidential real property if the following requirements are satisfied:

(1) the improvement is made under or pursuant to a lease by the lessee, any sublessee, or the lessor (a commitment to enter into a lease is treated as a lease for this purpose);

(2) the lease is not between related persons;

(3) the building (or portion that the improvement is made to) is occupied exclusively by the lessee or sublessee;

(4) the improvement is section 1250 property (i.e., a structural component); and

(5) the improvement is placed into service more than 3 years after the date that the building was first placed into service (Code Sec. 168(k)(3); Reg.§ 1.168(k)-1(c)).

Improvements to residential rental property do not qualify. The building must be nonresidential real property (section 1250 property with a class life of 27.5 years or greater that is not residential rental property (Code Sec. 168(e)(2)(B)), such as an office building, retail store, or industrial building.

A commitment to enter into a lease is treated as a lease, with the parties to the commitment treated as the lessor and lessee (Reg. § 1.168(k)-1(c)(3)(vi)).

The lease may not be between related persons. Members of an affiliated group (as defined in Code Sec. 1504) are related persons. Persons with a relationship described in Code Sec. 267(b)are related persons. However, the phrase "80 percent or more" is substituted in each place that the phrase "more than 50 percent" appears (Reg.§ 1.168(k)-1(c)(3)(vi)).

A leasehold improvement which is section 1245 property may be separately depreciated over a shorter recovery period (usually 5 or 7 years depending upon the business activity in which the improvement is primarily used) under the MACRS cost segregation rules. Examples of section 1245 leasehold improvements include removable carpeting and removable partitions. Qualified section 1250 leasehold improvements to nonresidential real property would normally be considered structural components depreciable over 39 years in the absence of this new provision.

Expenditures for the following are not qualified leasehold improvement property:

(1) the enlargement (as defined in Reg.§ 1.48-12(c)(10)) of the building;

(2) elevators and escalators;

(3) structural components (as defined in Reg.§ 1.48-1(e)(2)) that benefit a common area; and

(4) internal structural framework (as defined in Reg.§ 1.48-12(b)(3)(i)(D)).

The term "common area" generally refers to areas used by different lessees of a building, such as stairways, hallways, lobbies, common seating areas, interior and exterior pedestrian walkways and pedestrian bridges, loading docks and areas, and rest rooms (Reg.§ 1.168(k)-1(c)(3)(ii)).

Limitations on subsequent owners with respect to improvements placed in service by original lessor. An improvement made and depreciated by the lessor when the improvement is placed in service can be qualified leasehold improvement property only so long as the improvement is held by the lessor (Code Sec. 168(e)(6)(A), as added by P.L. 108-357).

This limitation prevents a subsequent purchaser of a building from using the 15-year depreciation period on leasehold improvements placed in service by the prior lessor-owner.

This limitation, however, is not triggered if the leasehold improvement is acquired from the original lessor by reason of the lessor's death Code Sec. 168(e)(6)(B)(i), as added by P.L. 108-357) or in any of the following types of transactions that qualify for nonrecognition treatment:

(1) transactions to which Code Sec. 381(a) applies (relating to corporate acquisitions in transactions involving the liquidation of subsidiaries or certain qualified reorganizations) (Code Sec. 168(e)(6)(B)(ii), as added by P.L. 108-357);

(2) a mere change in the form of conducting the trade or business so long as the property is retained in the trade or business as qualified leasehold improvement property and the taxpayer retains a substantial interest in the trade or business (Code Sec. 168(e)(6)(B)(iii), as added by P.L. 108-357);

(3) a like-kind exchange (Code Sec. 1031), involuntary conversion (Code Sec. 1033), or the sale of real estate which is reacquired in partial or full satisfaction of debt on the property (Code Sec. 1038) to the extent that the basis in the acquired leasehold improvement property is a carryover basis (Code Sec. 168(e)(6)(B)(iv), as added by P.L. 108-357); and

(4) a transaction described in Code Sec. 332 (complete liquidation of a subsidiary), Code Sec. 351 (transfers to controlled corporations), Code Sec. 361 (exchanges of property solely for corporate stock in a reorganization), Code Sec. 721 (contributions of property in exchange for a partnership interest), and Code Sec. 731 (distributions of property by partnerships to partners) to the extent that the basis of the leasehold improvement property in the hands of the taxpayer is determined by reference to its basis in the hands of the transferor or distributor (Code Sec. 168(e)(6)(B)(v), as added by P.L. 108-357).

The acquisition of property by a taxpayer from a transferee or acquiring corporation in a Code Sec. 332, 351, 361, 721, or 731 transaction described above also does not cease to be leasehold improvement property to the extent that the basis of the property in the hands of the taxpayer is determined by reference to its basis in the hands of the transferor or distributor (Code Sec. 168(e)(6)(B)(v), as added by P.L. 108-357).

15-year qualified retail improvement property

The Emergency Economic Stabilization Act of 2008 (P.L. 110-343) created a new category of MACRS property—"qualified retail improvement property"—effective for property placed in service after December 31, 2008 and before January 1, 2010 (i.e., property placed in service during the 2009 calendar year) (Code Sec. 168(e)(3)(E)(ix) and Code Sec. 168(e)(9), as added by the Emergency Economic Stabilization Act of 2008 (P.L. 110-343)). This property is treated as MACRS 15-year property and, accordingly, has a 15-year recovery period. A 39-year MACRS alternative depreciation system (ADS) recovery period applies if ADS is elected or required. The straight-line method must be used to depreciate qualified retail improvement property (Code Sec. 168(b)(3)(I)), as added by P.L. 110-343). The half-year convention applies unless the mid-quarter convention is applicable because the taxpayer placed more than 40 percent of the total basis of its depreciable property (other than residential rental and nonresidential real property) in service in the last quarter of its tax year.

But for this provision, qualified retail improvement property would be treated as nonresidential real property and depreciated over 39 years using the mid-month convention.

Although a 15-year recovery period applies, qualified retail improvement property does not lose its status as section 1250 property. Therefore, it does not qualify for the Code Sec. 179 expense allowance, which is limited to section 1245 property (Code Sec. 179(d)(1)). In addition, it remains subject to the Code Sec. 1250 recapture rules. Consequently, no depreciation recapture is required upon a disposition since the straight-line method is used. Except for property with a long production period, bonus depreciation under Code Sec. 168(k) is not available for property placed in service after December 31, 2008.

This provision is not elective. However, if a taxpayer elects to depreciate all types of 15-year MACRS property that it places in service during the tax year using the MACRS alternative depreciation system (ADS), it may depreciate its qualified retail improvement property using the straight-line method, a 39-year recovery period, and the half-year or mid-quarter convention. In effect, the ADS election operates as an election out of the provision.

Qualified retail improvement property defined. The following requirements must be met in order to meet the definition of a qualified retail improvement (Code Sec. 168(e)(8)(A) and (E), as added by P.L. 110-343):

- the property must be an improvement to an interior portion of a building that is nonresidential real property;
- the interior portion of the building must be open to the general public and used in the retail trade or business of selling tangible personal property to the general public;
- the improvement must be placed in service more than three years after the building was first placed in service; and
- the improvement must be placed in service after December 31, 2008, and before January 1, 2010 (i.e., it must be placed in service during the 2009 calendar year).

The following improvements are specifically disqualified from the definition of qualified retail improvement property (Code Sec. 168(e)(8)(D), as added by P.L. 110-343):

- elevators and escalators
- internal structural framework of a building
- structural components that benefit a common area
- improvements relating to the enlargement of a building

These types of improvements are also excluded from the definition of a qualified leasehold improvement which is eligible for a 15-year recovery period as discussed above (Code Sec. 168(k)(3)(B)). Thus, the definition of these terms provided in Reg. § 1.168(k)-1(c)(3) for purposes of the qualified leasehold improvement provision should apply equally to qualified retail improvement property.

Internal structural framework. Internal structural framework is defined to include all load-bearing internal walls and any other internal structural supports, including the columns, girders, beams, trusses, spandrels, and all other members that are essential to the stability of the building (Reg. § 1.48-12(b)(3)(i)(d)(iii); Reg. § 1.168(k)-1(c)(3)(v)).

Common area. A common area means any portion of a building that is equally available to all users of the building on the same basis for uses that are incidental to the primary use of the building. For example, stairways, hallways, lobbies, common seating areas, interior and exterior pedestrian walkways and pedestrian bridges, loading docks and areas, and rest rooms generally are treated as common areas if they are used by different lessees of a building (Reg. § 1.168(k)-1(c)(3)(ii)).

Enlargement. A building is enlarged to the extent that the total volume of the building is increased. An increase in floor space resulting from interior remodelling is not considered an enlargement. The total volume of a building is generally equal to the product of the floor area of the base of the building and the height from the underside of the lowest floor (including the basement) to the average height of the finished roof (as it exists or existed). For this purpose, floor area is measured from the exterior faces of external walls (other than shared walls that are external walls) and from the centerline of shared walls that are external walls (Reg. § 1.168(k)-1(c)(3)(iv); Reg. § 1.48-12(c)(10)).

Presumably, qualified retail improvement property must be section 1250 property (i.e., a structural component) even though this requirements is not specifically stated. Improvements to retail property that are section 1245 property should, therefore, continue to be eligible for a shortened recovery period under the cost segregation rules. Note that the definition in Code Sec. 168(k)(3) of a qualified leasehold improvement also does not specifically limit that provision to section 1250 property. Reg. § 1.168(k)-1(c), however, does impose this requirement.

Bonus depreciation denied. The 50-percent bonus depreciation deduction allowed by Code Sec. 168(k) may not be claimed on qualified retail improvement property (Code Sec. 168(e)(8)(D), as added by P.L. 110-343).

Improvement must be made by owner. Qualified retail improvement property retains its status only so long as the improvement is held by the owner that made the improvement (Code Sec. 168(e)(8)(B), as added by P.L. 110-343). For exceptions relating to acquisitions in certain nonrecognition transactions or by reason of the death of the original owner, see the above discussion of this rule as it applies to 15-year leasehold improvement property.

> ***Example:*** John Johnston owns a retail established and places a qualified retail improvement in service in 2009. Johnson sells the building with the improvement to Fred Jackson in 2010. Jackson may not separately depreciate the improvement as 15-year qualified retail improvement property.

ADS recovery period. The MACRS alternative depreciation system (ADS) recovery period for qualified retail improvement property is 39 years if ADS is elected or required (Code Sec. 168(g)(3)(b), as amended by P.L. 110-343). The half-year or mid-quarter convention applies even if ADS is used to depreciate the property over 39 years.

Alternative minimum tax. The straight-line depreciation deduction claimed on qualified retail improvement property is allowed in full for alternative minimum tax (AMT) purposes (Code Sec. 56(a)(1)(A)).

Qualified lessee construction allowance

A lessee of retail space who sells tangible personal property or services to the general public may exclude from income cash or rent reductions received from a lessor if the cash or reductions are used to construct or improve "qualified long-term real property," which reverts to the lessor at the termination of a lease with a term of 15-years or less. Such property is depreciable by the lessor as nonresidential real property. The lessor may claim gain or loss on the improvement in accordance with Code Sec. 168(i)(8)(B), as described above, if the improvement is disposed of or abandoned at the termination of the lease (Code Sec. 110, as added by the Taxpayer Relief Act of 1997 (P.L. 105-34), effective for leases entered into after August 5, 1997; Reg. § 1.110-1; Rev. Proc. 2009-39, modifying Rev. Proc. 2008-52, by adding Appendix Section 6.23, relating to accounting method changes).

The exclusion only applies to the extent that the construction allowance is used to construct or improve "qualified long-term real property." Qualified long-term real property is defined as nonresidential real property which is part of, or otherwise present at, the retail space and which reverts to the lessor at the termination of the lease (Code Sec. 110(c)(1)). Qualified long-term real property does not include personal property or any other property that qualifies as section 1245 property under Code Sec. 1245(a)(3) (Reg. § 1.110-1(b)(2)(i)). See ¶ 116 for a discussion of section 1245(a)(3) property.

The lease agreement must provide that the construction allowance is for the purpose of constructing or improving qualified long-term real property. The agreement does not need to provide that the entire construction allowance must be devoted to this purpose. However, exclusion only applies to the portion of the construction allowance that is spent on qualified long-term real property (Rev. Rul. 2001-20, I.R.B. 2001-18, 1143).

¶ 127

Cost Segregation: Distinguishing Structural and Personal Property Components of Buildings

The IRS has issued a 100 plus page Audit Techniques Guide (ATG) developed to assist IRS examiners in their review of cost segregation studies (Audit Technique Guide for Cost Segregation, revision date December 2007). The guide explains why cost segregation studies are performed, how such studies are prepared and what to look for when reviewing these studies. Although it is not an official IRS pronouncement and may not be cited as authority, specialists who prepare these studies, as well as practitioners who hire such specialists for their clients, will undoubtedly want to review this IRS guidance. The guidance includes property classification lists (section 1245 personal property vs. section 1250 structural components) and supporting authority for the classifications. Three separate classification lists are provided for the gambling, restaurant , and retail business industries. These lists were initially released in the form of IRS Field Directives.

The Field Directive pertaining to the restaurant industry is reproduced in as a Quick Reference Table in the appendix of this book.

The Cost Segregation Audit Guide is available on the IRS website at http://www.irs.gov.

Although component depreciation is not allowed under MACRS or ACRS, the Tax Court has ruled that items in a building that qualify as tangible personal property under the former investment tax credit (ITC) rules (as defined in Reg. § 1.48-1(c)) may be separately depreciated under MACRS and ACRS as personal property (*Hospital Corp. of America*, 109 TC 21, Dec. 52,163).

If a building component is not personal property under the former ITC rules, then it is considered a structural component. In the case of new construction, a building's structural components are part of the basis of the building and not depreciated separately. If a structural component is added to an existing building then it is depreciated separately using the same method and period that would apply to the building if the building were placed in service at the same time as the structural component (i.e., as 27.5-year residential rental property or 39-year nonresidential real property under MACRS). See ¶ 126.

Under the pre-ACRS (pre-1981) rules, taxpayers could generally depreciate structural components separately based on the useful life of the component. Personal property status was primarily important for purposes of qualifying for the investment tax credit.

Structural components of a building are specifically excluded from the definition of tangible personal property by the investment tax credit regulations.

Reg. § 1.48-1(e)(2) (which was adopted in 1964 by T.D. 6731) provides:

> "The term 'structural components' includes such parts of a building as walls, partitions, floors, and ceilings, as well as any permanent coverings therefor such as paneling or tiling; windows and doors; all components (whether in, on, or adjacent to the building) of a central air conditioning or heating system, including motors, compressors, pipes and ducts; plumbing and plumbing fixtures, such as sinks and bath-

tubs; electric wiring and lighting fixtures; chimneys; stairs, escalators, and elevators, including all components thereof; sprinkler systems; fire escapes; and other components relating to the operation or maintenance of a building. However, the term 'structural components' does not include machinery the sole justification for the installation of which is the fact that such machinery is required to meet temperature or humidity requirements which are essential for the operation of other machinery or the processing of materials or foodstuffs . . . ."

It is important to note an item is not a structural component (section 1250 property) even if it is listed unless the item relates to the operation or maintenance of the building. For example, plumbing or electrical wiring that services a machine that is not related to the operation or maintenance of a building is also considered unrelated to the operation and maintenance of the building and, therefore, is considered personal property.

The regulations do not define the term "operation and maintenance." Instead, examples of items that are generally considered related to the operation and maintenance of a building are listed. See Reg. § 1.48-1(e)(2), above. The regulations also list items that are "accessory to a taxpayer's business" and, therefore, not considered related to the building's operation and maintenance. See Reg. § 1.48-1(c), discussed below. When the operation and maintenance issue is in doubt, the manner of attachment and the likelihood of removal are decisive factors in determining whether the asset relates to the operation and maintenance of the building. The Courts generally apply the *Whiteco* permanency test described below in making this decision.

In Rev. Rul. 75-178, 1975 CB 9, the IRS ruled that the classification of property should be based "on the manner of attachment to the land or the structure and how permanently the property is designed to remain in place." In Rev. Rul. 75-178, the IRS reversed its prior position (Rev. Rul. 69-14, 1969-1 CB 26) that movable partitions were the functional equivalent of walls and, therefore, were structural components. It is clearly not the intent of Rev. Rul. 75-178 to replace the operation and maintenance standard set forth in the regulations. For example, a hinged door, even though much more easily removable than the partitions described in Rev. Rul. 69-14, is still considered by the IRS as a structural component because it relates to the operation and maintenance of the building.

The Tax Court in *Whiteco Industries* (65 TC 664, CCH Dec. 33,594) (¶ 127C) lists five factors that should be taken into account in applying the permanency test in the context of determining whether a *structure* should be considered *personal property or a building* (see ¶ 127C). These factors, however, are often used by courts in determining whether property which is attached to a building is a structural component. The factors are:

(1) Is the property capable of being moved, and has it in fact been moved?

(2) Is the property designed or constructed to remain permanently in place?

(3) Are there circumstances which tend to show the expected or intended length of affixation, i.e., are there circumstances which show the property may or will have to be moved?

(4) How substantial a job is removal of the property and how time-consuming is it? Is it readily movable?

(5) How much damage will the property sustain upon its removal?

(6) What is the manner of affixation of the property to the land?

The manner in which the permanency test is applied varies among courts, with the result that many decisions are conflicting and cannot be reconciled. Many decisions, for example, place little weight on the fact that an item of property can be readily removed, causing little or no damage to either the removed item or the structure to which it is attached. Instead, greater significance is placed on the fact that the property is intended to remain in place permanently. For this reason, doors, windows, tiling, and paneling, although readily removable, are considered structured components.

The characterization of property as personal under local law does not control its characterization as personal property for depreciation and investment credit purposes (Reg. § 1.48-1(c)).

With respect to the definition of tangible personal property, Reg. § 1.48-1(c) provides:

> "The term tangible personal property means any tangible property except land and improvements thereto, such as buildings or other inherently permanent structures (including items which are structural components of such buildings or structures). Thus, buildings, swimming pools, paved parking areas, wharves and docks, bridges, and fences are not tangible personal property. Tangible personal property includes all property (other than structural components) which is contained in or attached to a building. Thus, such property as production machinery, printing presses, transportation and office equipment, refrigerators, grocery counters, testing equipment, display racks and shelves, and neon and other signs, which is contained in or attached to a building constitutes tangible personal property for purposes of the credit allowed by section 38. Further, all property which is in the nature of machinery (other than structural components of a building or other inherently permanent structure) shall be considered tangible personal property even though located outside of a building. Thus, for example, a gasoline pump, hydraulic car lift, or automatic vending machine, although annexed to the ground, shall be considered tangible personal property."

The above regulation incorporates Congressional intent to treat property that relates to a taxpayer's specific business rather than being adaptable to most commercial uses as personal property even though contained in or attached to a building. A Senate Finance Committee Report provides that assets "accessory to the operation of a business such as machinery, printing presses, transportation or office equipment, refrigerators, individual air conditioning units, grocery counters, testing equipment, display racks, and shelves etc.," generally constitute tangible personal property even though treated as fixtures under local law (S. Rept. No. 1881, 87th Cong., 2d Sess. (1962), 1962-3 C.B. 707, 722). The regulation above qualifies the rule by providing that structural components of a building (i.e., components relating to the operation and maintenance of the building) do not qualify.

Senate Report 95-1263, 1978-3 CB (Vol. 1) 315, 415, which accompanied the Revenue Act of 1978, states that tangible personal property includes special lighting (including lighting to illuminate the exterior or a building or store, but not lighting to illuminate parking areas), false balconies, and other exterior ornamentation that have no more than an incidental relationship to the operation or maintenance of a building, and identity symbols that identify or relate to a particular retail establishment or restaurant such as special material attached to the exterior or interior of a building or store and signs (other than billboards). The Report further states that personal property includes floor coverings which are not an integral part of the floor itself, such as floor tile generally installed in a manner to be readily removed (that is not cemented, mudded, or otherwise permanently affixed to the building floor but, instead, has adhesives applied which are designed to ease its removal), carpeting, wall panel inserts such as those designed to contain condiments or to serve as a framing for pictures of the products of a retail establishment, beverage bars, ornamental fixtures (such as coat-of-arms), artifacts (if depreciable), booths for seating, movable and removable partitions, and large and small pictures of scenery, persons, and the like which are attached to walls or suspended from the ceiling.

Applying these investment tax credit standards, the court in the *Hospital Corp.* case treated as depreciable personal property electrical systems and wiring allocable to hospital equipment (based on electrical load), telephone and communications wiring and equipment, removable carpeting attached with a latex adhesive, vinyl wall and floor coverings, folding wall partitions, plumbing connections for equipment, kitchen water piping, kitchen steam lines, kitchen hoods and exhaust systems, special plumbing for x-ray machines, and patient handrails. Lights, bathroom accessories, acoustical ceilings, and boilers (where the amount of use for operating equipment was not shown) were structural components.

The depreciation period for the property categorized as personal property was five years under MACRS as it fell within Asset Class 57.0, relating to assets used in wholesale and retail trade or personal and professional services. The taxpayer was a hospital which provided personal and professional services. See ¶ 104 for a discussion of Asset Class 57.0. See ¶ 127B for rules in determining the depreciation period of personal property components of a building.

Note that personal property with no class life and for which no recovery period is assigned is treated as 7-year property under MACRS.

The IRS has issued an internal legal memorandum (IRS Letter Ruling 199921045, April 1, 1999) which sets forth the response that examiners should take to the Tax Court's decision. The memorandum does not dispute the holding of the court but aptly notes that "the determination of whether an asset is a structural component or tangible personal property is a facts and circumstances assessment . . . no bright line test exists."

Subsequent to the issuance of this memorandum the IRS acquiesced to the Tax Court's finding that the ITC rules applied in determining whether an item is personal property or a structural component but nonacquiesced with respect to the Tax Court's application of these rules to the items in question (I.R.B. 1995-35, 314, as corrected by Announcement 99-116, I.R.B. 1999-52, 763).

Cost segregation studies. The memorandum notes that a taxpayer bears the burden of determining the depreciable basis of equipment or assets that are considered personal property and sets forth standards for cost segregation studies. Additionally it states that an "accurate cost segregation study may not be based on non-contemporaneous records, reconstructed data, or taxpayer's estimates or assumptions that have no supporting records." In other words, taxpayers who are constructing buildings and plan to take advantage of this exception to component depreciation will need to maintain accurate records (including presumably architectural and engineering reports) that establish the items that constitute personal property and that properly allocate costs to these depreciable items. The memorandum also notes, with respect to buildings that are already in service, that a change in depreciation method (including a change in depreciation periods) is a change in method of accounting and requires IRS consent. The automatic consent procedures of Rev. Proc. 2008-52 (I.R.B. 2002-13) will apply. See ¶ 75. Note that Rev. Proc. 2008-52 specifically requires a taxpayer to attach a statement of the facts and law supporting the reclassification of assets from Sec. 1250 property to Sec. 1245 property (Appendix Section 6.01(3)(b)(vii)).

The *Boddie-Noel Enterprises, Inc.* case (CA-FC, 96-2 USTC ¶ 50,627) illustrates the importance of an adequately documented cost segregation study. Failure to meet cost substantiation requirements led to the denial of most ITC claims with respect to various elements of remodeled and newly constructed *Hardee's* restaurant buildings.

Scores of firms, often working with engineering and architectural consultants, specialize in the provision of cost segregation studies. (Use the search term "cost segregation" on any internet search engine and count the hits!) It is not unusual for these firms to classify 20 to 40 percent of the cost of new construction as personal property with a five- or seven-year recovery period and land improvements with a 15-year recovery period. Depending upon the size of the construction project, the federal tax savings can easily pay for the cost of the study. In addition, there are usually state and local tax benefits associated with the reclassification of real property as personal property. Many firms will make an initial determination as to whether a cost segregation study is warranted at no cost.

Cost segregation studies are typically conducted in connection with new construction projects; however, they are also available with respect to acquisitions of existing structures and can be used to justify depreciation reclassifications in the case of previously purchased structures.

Tax benefits of cost segregation. Classification of building components as personal property will save federal taxes and increase cash flow by accelerating depreciation deductions that reduce income taxes during the early years of a buildings recovery period. The tax savings are further enhanced if the personal property components also qualify for bonus depreciation under Code Sec. 168(k). See below.

If a cost segregation study is conducted on an existing building, the unclaimed depreciation on personal property components that were previously classified as real property can be deducted as a Code Sec. 481(a) adjustment in the year change. The automatic change of accounting rules of Rev. Proc. 2008-52, described in detail at ¶ 75, apply. Note that Appendix Section 6.01(3)(b)(vii) of Rev. Proc. 2008-52 requires that a statement of the law and facts supporting the reclassification of each property item from real property to personal property must be attached to Form 3115.

If a cost segregation study is performed on a building that was placed in service in a tax year that ended before December 30, 2003 (e.g., a 2002 tax year of a calendar-year taxpayer), the IRS will allow a taxpayer to file amended returns to claim the benefits of the cost segregation study (Chief Counsel Advice CC 2004-007, January 28, 2004). This option may make sense if the building was placed in service in a tax year for which the limitations period for filing an amended return has not expired. One possible benefit is that interest is payable by the IRS on a refund. No interest is payable on a negative (favorable) Code Sec. 481(a) adjustment. See ¶ 75.

Cost segregation may also result in the reduction of state and local real property taxes by reducing building costs allocable to real property. In addition, nearly half of all states provide sales and use tax exemptions for tangible personal property used in a manufacturing process or for research and development. A cost segregation study will identify such qualifying personal property. Note, however, that these tax savings will depend upon the classification of the property as real or personal by applying applicable state law.

Personal property components of a commercial building can qualify for the Code Sec. 179 expense allowance (¶ 300). The maximum deductible amount (dollar limitation) under Code Sec. 179 is $250,000 in a tax year beginning in 2008 and 2009. The applicable dollar limit is reduced by one dollar for each dollar of qualifying expenditures in excess of $800,000 in 2008 and 2009 (investment limitation). See ¶ 302. This generous investment limitation means that a taxpayer may expense up to $250,000 of the personal property elements of a commercial building placed in service in a tax year that begins in 2008 or 2009 provided the total dollar value of the personal property elements in the building (and any other qualifying property placed in service during the yearr) do not exceed $800,000. For tax years beginning in 2010, the dollar and investment limitations are $134,000 and $530,000 (as adjusted for inflation). For tax years beginning in 2011, the dollar and investment limitations are scheduled to return to $25,000 and $200,000, respectively. In the Gulf Opportunity Zone the dollar and investment limitations are increased by an additional $100,000 and $600,000 respectively, for property placed in service before January 1, 2008 (January 1, 2009 in certain devastated parishes and counties in the Gulf Opportunity Zone). See ¶ 306. A similar increase applies to qualified section 179 Recovery Assistance Property acquired on or after May 5, 2007 and placed in service in the Kansas disaster area before January 1, 2009 (see ¶ 306A) and to disaster assistance property placed in service in a presidentially declared disaster area after December 31, 2007 with respect to disasters declared after that date and occuring before January 1, 2010 (see ¶ 306B).

Note that personal property components of a residential rental property *generally* do not qualify for the Code Sec. 179 allowance because property used in the provision of lodging is excluded from the definition of section 179 property.

If a taxpayer changes its accounting method to reclassify building components as separately depreciable personal property, any Code Sec. 481(a) adjustment taken into account for regular tax purposes needs to be recomputed for AMT purposes. Thus, it is possible that the reclassification of components as personal property can trigger an AMT liability.

Depreciation recapture (¶ 160) does not apply to MACRS real property since it is depreciated using the straight-line method. Recapture does apply, however, to MACRS personal property. Under the Code Sec. 1245 recapture rules, the depreciation claimed on personal property components of a building is taxed as ordinary income to the extent of gain allocable from the sale of the building to the personal property (assuming the personal property has not been retired or replaced prior to the sale of the building). The remaining gain, if any, is treated as section 1231 gain. Thus, a taxpayer who uses cost segregation will lose the benefit of the capital gains tax rates on an amount of gain equal to the depreciation claimed on the components of the building that are classified as section 1245 property. The negative impact is mitigated the longer that a building is held before it is sold or if gain on the building will deferred in a section 1031 like-kind exchange.

Cost segregation studies are a useful tax savings technique for a partnership and its partners. For example, assume that a partnership that owns a commercial building conducts a cost segregation study six years after its formation and the acquisition of the building. A large section 481(a) depreciation adjustment may be obtained and the basis of short lived assets is reduced to zero (assuming a five-year recovery period for the personal property components). Further, if a new partner later purchases a partnership interest in that partnership, the new partner benefits from the study if a section 754 election is made because the new partner's 743 adjustment is allocated among all of the assets, including the short-lived assets with a zero basis. Sometimes a cost segregation study is conducted in conjunction with the sale of a partnership interest solely in order to maximize the tax savings for the new partner. As an extreme example, suppose a partnership owns a residential rental property and the property is fully depreciated. Although a cost segregation study would not benefit existing partners because the property is fully depreciated, a new partner with a section 743 adjustment in hand could benefit from the study by being able to allocate the adjustment among the assets identified in the study, including the short-lived assets. Thus, much of the adjustment could be recovered through depreciation deductions over five years (again, assuming a five-year recovery period). However, as a result of the reclassification, the original partners may eventually be disadvantaged by the requirement of ordinary income depreciation recapture on the building components that are reclassified as personal property.

Land improvements and personal property elements of a building may qualify for 50 percent MACRS bonus depreciation under Code Sec. 168(k) if acquired after 2007 and placed in service before 2010. Bonus depreciation, however, does not apply to property acquired pursuant to a binding contract entered into before 2008 or to property if construction began before that date (¶ 127D). Thus, if a building is acquired in 2008 pursuant to a contract entered into before 2008 the personal property elements would not qualify for bonus depreciation. If construction of a building begins before 2008, it is arguable that personal property elements of the building which are acquired and installed after 2007 should qualify for bonus depreciation since they are treated (i.e., depreciable) as property that is separate from the building. Presumably, however, the personal property elements of a constructed building are not considered placed in service any earlier than the building itself is placed in service.

New residential rental and non residential real property (including personal property components of the building) acquired in the Gulf Opportunity Zone after August 28, 2005 and placed in service before January 1, 2009 (January 1, 2011 in some cases) may be eligible for a 50 percent bonus depreciation deduction. The bonus deduction claimed on the portion of the building that is real property is treated as accelerated depreciation for purposes of the section 1250 recapture rules. See ¶ 127F. A similar rule applies to the Kansas Disaster Area (¶ 127G). Bonus depreciation is also allowed on residential rental and nonresidential real property (as well as personal property) that replaces property that is damaged or destroyed by a federally declared disaster that occurs before January 1, 2010 and is declared after 2008. See ¶ 127H.

¶ 127A

Cost Segregation: Specific Examples of Structural Components and Personal Property Components of a Building

The IRS has issued a cost segregation audit guide which categorizes an extensive list of building elements as either section 1245 personal property or section 1250 structural components. See ¶ 127.

As explained at ¶ 127, components of a building which qualify as personal property under the former investment tax credit rules can be depreciated as personal property rather than real property. Following are examples of particular building components and whether they are treated as personal property or structural components (real property).

For examples of costs that may be separately depreciable as land improvements see ¶ 5. Land improvements are generally depreciable over 15 years using the 150-percent declining-balance method. See ¶ 110.

Air conditioning. See "*HVAC and air conditioning units,*" below.

Air filtration systems. Mechanical devices contained in a manufacturing facility such as blowers, blower housings, dust collectors, exhaust equipment, and air washers used to remove fumes, smoke, dust, and heat, as well as air make-up units used to replace air and heat, were related to the operation of the building as a whole and, thus, were structural components. However, air handling equipment and safety equipment (fire curtains, detection equipment, and explosion hatches) necessary to and used directly with a single machine or process such as paint spraying or welding or which protects a particular area against a hazard created by a single machine or process is tangible personal property (Rev. Rul. 75-78, 1975-1 CB 8).

Carpeting. Wall-to-wall carpeting installed in guest rooms, office space, bar areas and dining rooms was personal property and not a structural component. The carpeting was attached to the floor by hooking it to wood strips that were nailed to the perimeter of the walls (Rev. Rul. 67-349, 1967-2 CB 48). Similarly, with respect to carpeting attached to a floor with an adhesive where the carpeting could be removed and cleaned without damage (IRS Letter Ruling 7847028, August 23, 1978). In the *Hospital Corp. of America* case (109 TC 21, Dec. 52,163) carpeting attached with a latex adhesive was considered removable and, therefore, was personal property.

The controlling Senate Finance Committee Report for the 1978 Revenue Act states that easily removable floor coverings should be considered an item of personal property. Interestingly, the Report could be read to provide a blanket rule that all carpeting is personal property (S. Rep. 95-1263, 1978-3 CB 415) Specifically, the report states: ". . . floor coverings which are not an integral part of the floor itself such as floor tile generally installed in a manner to be readily removed (that is not cemented, mudded, or otherwise permanently affixed to the building floor but, instead, has adhesives applied which are designed to ease its removal), carpeting, . . . are considered tangible personal property."

The *Hospital Corp. of America* case (109 TC 21, Dec. 52,163) cites the Committee Report, which in the taxpayer's view represented a per se rule that carpeting is personal property, but analyzed the treatment of the carpeting using the ease of removability standard.

The LMSB Directive on Cost Segregation in the Restaurant Industry (see the Quick Reference Tables of this book) indicates that for purposes of the restaurant industry all carpeting is treated as not permanently attached and not intended to be permanent. It does not appear that the IRS intends this rule to apply to all industries, as its Cost Segregation Audit Techniques Guide (which was issued after the LMSB) indicates that carpeting may or may not be section 1245 property depending upon the specific facts and circumstances. The audit guide, however, does list carpeting as section 1245 property (citing the Hospital Corporation case as authority) in a table which categorizes building components as section 1245 or section 1250 property.

Ceilings: suspended, acoustical, decorative. Suspended acoustical ceilings are, in the IRS view, structural components (IRS Policy Position Paper, ACRS and ITC Suspended Acoustical Ceilings, October 31, 1991, reproduced in CCH IRS Positions Reporter at ¶ 160,045). See, also, ISP Settlement Guidelines for ACRS and Investment Credit for Suspended Ceilings reproduced in the CCH IRS Positions Reporter at ¶ 181,385. Note that the Tax Court, in *Hospital Corp. of America* (109 TC 21, Dec.

52,163), also ruled that acoustical ceilings are nondepreciable structural components. In *Boddie-Noel Enterprises, Inc.*, (CA-FC, 96-2 USTC ¶ 50,627) suspended ceilings were structural components. The Tax Court held similarly in *Metro National Corporation* (52 TCM 1440, TC Memo. 1987-38, Dec. 43,649(M)) even though the court conceded that the acoustical tiles could be readily removed and replaced. The court in *Metro* also ruled that the fluorescent lighting (prefabricated fixtures in light metal housings) installed as part of the ceiling was a structural component.

Decorative ceilings in a hotel/casino complex were sufficiently integrated into the overall design of the buildings to be considered structural components even though they were capable of being moved (IRS Field Service Advice 200203009, October 3, 2001). The ceilings consisted of ornamental polished gold and copper panels suspended from the finished ceiling or glued to soffits or lowered drywall ceilings systems. Suspension grids were hung by hanger wires from hooks or eyes set in the floor above or bottom of the roof, and attached to walls with nails or screws. Components, including lighting fixtures and air conditioning registers were placed on the grid. The ceilings hid plumbing, wiring, sprinkler systems and air conditioning ducts. By serving as a channel for the return air, the ceilings also operated as a component of the heating and air conditioning system.

In the *Hospital Corp. of America* case (109 TC 21, Dec. 52,163) acoustical ceilings were structural components. In IRS Letter Ruling 8102012 (September 29, 1980) suspended ceilings which included panels that could be removed and replaced, were structural components.

Doors. Reg. § 1.48-1(e)(2) provides that doors (related to the operation and maintenance of a building) are structural components. The Courts have generally deferred to the regulation's classification. The fact that a door is easily removable should not on its own accord result in personal property classification—otherwise almost all doors would qualify as personal property. Doors generally are intended to remain permanently in place and are considered related to the operation of maintenance of the building.

Hotel room doors and a keycard locking system were structural components (IRS Letter Ruling 199924044, March 24, 1999 (released as a Written Technical Assistance document); IRS Field Service Advice 200203009, October 3, 2001).

An Eliason (brand name) lightweight double-action door with a window installed to prevent accidents in a heavily trafficked area between a serving line and kitchen was tangible personal property (*Morrison Incorporated*, 51 TCM 748, TC Memo. 1986-129, Dec. 42,963(M)). The decision is best supported on the basis of the specialized business needs exception described above and on the grounds that the door did not relate to the operation and maintenance of the building. The court stated that doors constitute a structural component only if they are a permanent part of the cafeteria building, so that their removal would affect the essential structure of the building.

In *La Petite Academy* (DC Mo., 95-1 USTC ¶ 50,193, aff'd CA-8 (unpublished opinion), 96-1 USTC ¶ 50,020), however, a district court found that a kitchen pass-through door, bypass doors used between classrooms, and a Dutch door that separated an entrance/reception area from children's classroom areas were structural components even though they were specially designed. The taxpayer made several "specialized business needs" arguments but the court concluded that the doors related to the operation and maintenance of the building.

Forty foot folding doors on an aircraft hanger were structural components. The doors related to the operation of the hanger by providing protection from the elements and vandalism (*J. McManus*, CA-7, 88-2 USTC ¶ 9623, 863 F2d 491).

Bank vault doors and bank record doors were not structural components but qualified as "equipment" under Reg. § 1.48-1(e) which was accessorial to the conduct of the banking business (Rev. Rul. 65-79, 1965-1 CB 26).

Energy maintenance system. An energy maintenance system installed in a building by a service provider to control all energy using systems (e.g., heating, cooling, lighting) was a structural component even though many of the components of the system could be easily removed (IRS Letter Ruling 8501009, September 28, 1984). The system was considered a component of a central air conditioning or heating system within the meaning of Reg. § 1.48-1(e)(2) which is definitionally a structural component regardless of ease of removability.

Electrical distribution systems. Certain property may service dual purposes. For example, electrical distribution systems may provide for the general power needs of a building (i.e., relate to the operation and maintenance of the building) and also provide power for specialized equipment that is not a structural component. The IRS now allows a percentage allocation of the cost in such instances.

The IRS initially opposed percentage allocations but lost several key court decisions.

The Seventh Circuit Court of Appeals ruled that 95 percent of the electrical load that was processed by a permanent electrical distribution system contained within a separate room in a corn milling factory was used to power specialized machinery that was accessory to the taxpayer's business (*Illinois Cereal Mills, Inc.*, CA-7, 86-1 USTC ¶ 9371). Therefore, 95 percent of the cost of system, which consisted of circuit breakers, transformers, power panels, switchboards, motor control centers, and associated wiring qualified for the ITC. The remaining five percent of the cost was attributable to electricity used to meet the building's general needs and, therefore, related to the building's operation and maintenance. A similar allocation between electricity for machinery and general use was made by the Tax Court with respect to an electrical distribution system in *Scott Paper Company* (74 TC 137, Dec. 36,920 (1980)).

Later, the Eleventh Circuit affirmed another Tax Court decision which held that the portion (percentage) of the primarily electrical system that was allocable to electrical power used by a cafeteria's food preparation equipment and appliances was personal property (*Morrison, Inc.*, CA-11, 90-1 USTC ¶ 50,034, 891 F2d 857, aff'g, 51 TCM 748, Dec. 42,963(M), TC Memo. 1986-129).

In *A.C. Monk & Co.* (CA-4, 82-2 USTC ¶ 9551), however, the Fourth Circuit ruled that a percentage allocation was improper. It looked at each individual component of a distribution system and determined whether that component was generally adaptable to uses other than the machinery to which it was designed to serve. "An electrical system providing power to machinery is a structural component if the system can feasibly be adapted to uses other than the specific machine it was designed to serve."

However, in a revised Action on Decision relating to the *Illinois Cereal Mills, Inc.*, case, the IRS decided that it will no longer challenge the functional (i.e., percentage) approach set forth in the *Scott Paper Company* case (Action on Decision, File No.: AOD/CC-1991-019, October 22, 1991).

An IRS Industry Specialization Program (ISP) Coordinated Issue Paper (reproduced in the CCH IRS POSITIONS REPORTER at ¶ 160,705) adopted the approach taken by the *A.C. Monk & Co.*, case with respect to mechanical service systems (electrical and plumbing) embedded or embodied within walls. However, this issue paper, which was decoordinated on March 3, 1992, appears to have been written before the AOD which authorizes the functional allocation approach.

In the *L.A. Duaine* case (49 TCM 588, TC Memo. 1985-39, Dec. 41,845(M)), the Tax Court ruled that electrical outlets and conduits providing localized power sources for specialized restaurant equipment was personal property. Similarly, with respect to kitchen equipment hookups of a hotel/casino complex (IRS Field Service Advice 200203009, October 3, 2001). It did not matter that the electrical kitchen components were of a standard design rather than specially designed. However, electrical outlets located in guest rooms and bathrooms that were not specifically associated with particular items of hotel equipment were structural components.

Exterior ornamentation. False balconies and other exterior ornamentation that has no more than an incidental relationship to the operation and maintenance of a building may qualify as personal property. However, a mansard roof system installed on a day care center was a structural component (*La Petite Academy*, DC Mo., 95-1 USTC ¶ 50,193, aff'd, CA-8 (unpublished opinion), 96-1 USTC ¶ 50,020). The mansard roof related to the operation and maintenance of the building because it protected various building components from water, snow, wind, and moisture damage.

Decorative facades placed around the entire exterior of a hotel/casino complex were structural components (IRS Field Service Advice 200203009, October 3, 2001). The facades consisted of a synthetic plaster, or stucco, that was cemented or bolted on in the form of a panel to the frames of the exterior walls of the buildings. They were not readily removable, designed to withstand an 85 mph wind load, and provided a barrier to the outside elements. Their removal would expose other building elements to degradation. The facades were designed and constructed with the expectation that they would remain in place indefinitely.

Fire detection and security protection systems. Fire protection systems are generally considered related to the operation and maintenance of a building and, accordingly, do not qualify as personal property. However, detachable smoke detectors and fire extinguishers are personal property.

Fire sprinklers and fire escapes are specifically categorized as structural components by Reg. § 1.48-1(e)(2), assuming they relate to the operation and maintenance of the building.

An automatic fire protection system which had a variety of components, each of which could be mechanically removed, was a structural component because it was designed to remain in place permanently and also because it was an integral part of the operation of the building. The system was viewed as including all component parts. Therefore, the computer which controlled the system was a structural component even though freestanding and transportable (Rev. Rul. 77-362, 1977-2 CB 8; G.C.M. 37070, March 30, 1977). Similarly, with respect to a fire detection system and security (burglary) detection system installed in the building of a service provider's customer even though the components of the systems, with the exception of wiring, were easily removed or detached from walls, ceilings, and other locations when a protection contract was terminated (IRS Letter Ruling 8501009, September 28, 1984). In spite of this private letter ruling, most cost segregation specialists treat security systems (e.g., cameras and other detachable or removable components) as personal property. Security systems are not considered related to the operation or maintenance of a building.

In *La Petite* (DC Mo., 95-1 USTC ¶ 50,193, aff'd, CA-8 (unpublished opinion), 96-1 USTC ¶ 50,020), the court ruled that a fire protection system consisting of horns, an alarm control panel, magnetic holder/closers on kitchen doors, emergency lighting fixtures, heat and smoke detectors, and exit light fixtures were structural components relating to the operation and maintenance of the building.

A fire protection system related to a single item of machinery or equipment, however, is personal property (Rev. Rul. 75-78, 1975-1 CB 8).

Floors and foundations, concrete. A concrete floor is generally a structural component. The Tax Court held that modifications to the slab behind restaurant counters in the form of a raised perimeter on which storage shelves were placed and sloped drainage basins were not personal property (*L.A. Duaine*, 49 TCM 588, TC Memo. 1985-39, Dec. 41,845(M)).

A 38-inch reinforced-concrete floor designed to withstand the weight of 50 to 2,000 ton stamping presses was considered personal property because it was considered a part of the machinery or equipment. Similarly, with respect to press rails and girders that supported the presses (Rev. Rul. 79-183, 1979-1 CB 44).

Floors, raised. A raised floor was a structural component. The floor was constructed when the building was constructed and stood about two feet above an unfinished floor. The space was used to facilitate the installation of wiring, plumbing, and ventilation for computers and other equipment. Removal of the raised floor would necessitate a major renovation of the interior of the building (IRS Field Service Advice 200110001, September 13, 2000, rev'g, upon reconsideration, IRS Field Service Advice 200033002, April 17, 2000). In contrast, a raised floor described in Rev. Rul. 74-391 (1974-2 CB 9) was personal property. There, the raised floor was installed over an existing floor. Its removal would have returned the building to its original condition and would not have necessitated extensive renovation.

Generators, emergency power. A casino's emergency power system which consisted of two emergency standby generators with associated fuel tanks, feeder lines, alternator and controls, and battery powered lighting for critical operations was personal property (Field Service Advice Memorandum 200203009, October 3, 2001). Apparently, the personal property classification applied because the systems operated the building's "emergency/safety features" and building equipment that was personal property. The IRS considered the systems as "accessory" to the conduct of the business and unrelated to the building's operation. However, the ruling takes the position that if a percentage of the power generators' output is attributable to building operations, then that percentage of the generators' cost is depreciable as a structural component.

In the *Hospital Corporation of America* case (109 TC 21, Dec. 52,163), the parties stipulated that emergency power generators were accessory to the conduct of the hospital's business and, therefore, were personal property.

Handrails. The IRS considers handrails and banisters as safety features related to the operation and maintenance of a building and, therefore, classifies these devices as structural components (IRS Letter Ruling 6612301720A, December 30, 1966). The Tax Court in the *Hospital Corp. of America* case (109 TC 21, Dec. 52,163), apparently agreed with this characterization but determined that handrails placed in corridors to assist hospital patients served a specialized business need and, therefore, constituted personal property.

HVAC and air conditioning units. All components (whether in, on, or adjacent to a building) of a central air-conditioning or heating system including motors, compressors, pipes and ducts are treated as structural components unless the sole justification for the installation is to meet the temperature or humidity requirements essential for the operation of other machinery or the processing of foodstuffs (Reg. § 1.48-1(e)(2)). For example, special air conditioning units which cool rooms dedicated to computer equipment should qualify for separate depreciation as personal property.

The sole justification test is narrowly construed. Air conditioning units installed by a grocery store did not satisfy the sole justification test even if the sole purpose of their installation was to protect foodstuffs from spoilage caused by high humidity because the store was not engaged in the processing of foodstuffs within the meaning of the regulation (*Circle K Corporation*, 43 TCM 1524, TC Memo. 1982-298, Dec. 39,058(M)).

The IRS maintains that HVAC units (heating, ventilating, and air conditioning systems) located in retail grocery stores or supermarkets that provide a comfortable temperature for customers as well meeting the temperature and humidity requirements of open front freezers are structural components of the building since they fail to meet the "sole justification" test of the regulations (IRS Policy Position Paper, Heating, Ventilating, and Air Conditioning (HVAC) Systems ITC, October 31, 1991, reproduced in CCH IRS POSITIONS REPORTER at ¶ 160,255). The IRS will not follow a Tax Court's contrary decision, which found that the test was satisfied where the HVACs had to be installed in order to maintain a building temperature that would allow the store's open front frozen food display cases to operate properly (*Piggly Wiggly Southern, Inc.*, 84 TC 739, Dec. 42,039, aff'd CA-11, 86-2 USTC ¶ 9789). In the *Boddie-Noel Enterprises* case (CA-FC, 96-2 USTC ¶ 50,627, no portion of the cost of a HVAC unit in a restaurant was eligible for the ITC. The taxpayer argued that the unit met the sole justification test with respect to cooling provided in the kitchen area but the court ruled that one of the primary purposes was to provide a comfortable working area for employees.

The term "central air conditioning or heating system" is not restricted to mean a system that cools or heats an entire building. The term also includes any air conditioning or heating or combination system which consists of two or more units, having accessory ducts, connections and other equipment necessary to make the equipment functional, regardless of where located or the manner of attachment (Rev. Rul. 67-359, 1967-2 CB 9).

Window air conditioning units and portable plug-in heaters are personal property (Rev. Rul. 75-77, 1975-1 CB 7). However, they do not qualify for the Code Sec. 179 expense allowance (Code Sec. 179(d)(1)).

Keycard locking system. A keycard door locking system installed to replace key locks on hotel doors was classified as a structural component depreciable over 39 years as nonresidential real property because the locking system was an integral part of a structural component (viz., the door) (IRS Letter Ruling 199924044, March 24, 1999 (released as a Written Technical Assistance document); IRS Field Service Advice 200203009, October 3, 2001).

Lighting, interior and exterior. Lighting fixtures relating to the operation and maintenance of a building are structural components (Reg. § 1.48-1(e)(2)). Security lighting mounted flush with a building's soffit, grow lights for plants mounted in the interior ceiling, and exterior pedestal lights mounted to a building's foundation to highlight landscaped areas and shrubbery or aid in the growth of plants were personal property since they only "incidentally" related to the operation of the building (*Metro National Corporation*, 52 TCM 1440, TC Memo. 1987-38, Dec. 43,649(M)).

The *Metro* decision relied on Senate Committee Report language which explains that personal property includes "special lighting (including lighting to illuminate the exterior of a building or store, but not lighting to illuminate parking areas), false balconies, and other exterior ornamentation that have no more than an incidental relationship to the operation and maintenance of a building . . . " (S. Rep. No. 95-1263 (1978), 1978-3 CB 315, 415).

With respect to the exterior security lighting, the Metro court provided as an additional reason for personal property classification, its belief that the lighting was "accessory to a business" since its purpose was to prevent unauthorized departures by psychiatric patients who resided in the building and reassure area residents with respect to security.

The court in *Metro*, however, also ruled that the fluorescent lighting (prefabricated fixtures in light metal housings) installed as part of an acoustical tile ceiling was a structural component.

If lighting serves both a decorative purpose and a function related to the operation and maintenance of the building it has been classified as a structural component. For example, in La Petite Academy, above, lighting which washed the exterior walls during the night time hours, thus making the building highly visible to passersby and, thereby providing passive advertising, was a structural component because the lighting was also used to "directly" light the walkways around the building. Lighting relating to building accessibility was, in the court's view, related to its operation and maintenance (*La Petite Academy*, DC Mo., 95-1 USTC ¶ 50,193, aff'd, CA-8 (unpublished opinion), 96-1 USTC ¶ 50,020).

In *L.A. Duaine* (49 TCM 588, TC Memo. 1985-39, Dec. 41,845(M)), interior and exterior ornamental lighting fixtures at a Taco Bell restaurant which provided the only artificial illumination in the customer eating area and along the walkways to the building related to the operation and maintenance of the building (i.e., were structural components).

Emergency lighting in a cafeteria that was required by state law and would enable customers to finish their meals in the event of a power outage was personal property (*Morrison Incorporated*, 51 TCM 748, Dec. 42,963(M) (1986)). The court characterized the emergency lighting as "special lighting" that was "accessory" to the taxpayer's business and, therefore, excepted from the general rule of the regulation which it deemed to apply to the cafeteria's "basic lighting." The lighting was also easily removable. The lighting consisted of ceiling and wall mounted fixtures, batteries, and connections to the electrical system that charged the batteries.

The court also ruled that chandeliers, decor wall lights, and dimmers were "special lighting," accessory to the cafeteria business, readily removable, and unrelated to the operation and maintenance of the building. The lighting was not a major source of lighting in the cafeteria (15-watt bulbs were used) and merely incorporated the taxpayer's decorative motif and complimented the interior design of the cafeteria.

In *Consolidated Freightways* (CA-9, 83-1 USTC ¶ 9420, 708 F2d 1385), the Ninth Circuit ruled that lighting fixtures were an integral part (structural component) of loading docks. The lighting was designed as a permanent feature and its removal would detract significantly from the usefulness of the dock's operations.

In an IRS Field Service Advice (IRS Field Service Advice 200203009, October 3, 2001), basic illumination in a hotel/casino complex was provided by recessed lighting (a structural component). However, decorative lighting fixtures, including chandeliers, wall sconces, track spot lighting, torch lighting, and wall wash fixtures were "special lighting" that was only incidental to the operation or maintenance of the building.

Molding, millwork, trim, finish carpentry, paneling. Detailed crown moldings for ceilings, ornate wall paneling systems, and lattice work for walls and ceilings which were manufactured for a hotel/casino complex were personal property (IRS Field Service Advice 200203009, October 3, 2001). This millwork easily removable and not integrated into the design or construction of the building in any way. Although its removal would affect the appearance of the buildings, it would not affect their operation in any way.

In the *Morrison* case (CA-11, 90-1 USTC ¶ 50,034, 891 F2d 857, aff'g, 51 TCM 748, TC Memo. 1986-129, Dec. 42,963(M)), lattice millwork and decor window treatments were personal property. These items served a decorative purpose and could be removed at little cost without permanently damaging the walls or ceilings.

Partitions and walls. In determining whether a partition is a structural component the courts generally focus on the issue of movability. The controlling Senate Finance Committee Report to the 1978 Revenue Act states that "movable and removable" partitions are personal property (S. Rep. No. 95-1263 (1978), 1978-3 CB 315, 415).

Movable partitions installed in an office building were personal property (*Minot Federal Savings & Loan Assn.*, CA-8, 71-1 USTC ¶ 9131, 435 F2d 1368). The partitions did not bear any structural load. They were installed by fastening a channel to the floor and ceiling, putting the partitions in and fastening them. They could be moved from floor to floor or building to building and stored when not in use.

A movable partition system consisting of ceiling height and glazed rail height partitions used to divide floor space into offices, rooms, and work areas was personal property (*King Radio Corporation, Inc.*, CA-10, 73-2 USTC ¶ 9766, 486 F2d 1091). These partitions were also fastened to floor and ceiling channels. The court ruled that Rev. Rul. 69-14 (1969-1 CB 26) incorrectly treated movable partitions as structural components.

In light of the preceding decisions, the IRS revoked its position with respect to movable partitions (Rev. Rul. 75-178, 1975-1 CB 9, revoking Rev. Rul. 69-14, 1969-2 CB 26).

However, "storefront partitions" which separated office space from an atrium were structural components even though the partitions could be rearranged. If the partitions were removed or eliminated, the offices of the tenant doctors and dentists on all three floors would open onto the atrium without any way of closing or otherwise securing the offices. Without the storefront partitions the building could not reasonably operate for its intended purpose as an office space rental property. There was an intention that the partitions remain permanently in place (although reconfigurations were possible) (*Metro National Corporation*, 52 TCM 1440, TC Memo. 1987-38, Dec. 43,649(M)).

A steel partition which separated two abutting metal aircraft hangers (i.e., in effect serving as the back wall of each hanger) was a structural component. Although removable, it added to the strength of the structure and, thus, related to the operation of the building (*J. McManus*, CA-7, 88-2 USTC ¶ 9623, 863 F2d 491).

Wall paneling, including gypsum board or dry wall, is normally considered a structural component. Alliance wall panels (a wall panel with a porcelain enamel surface laminated to gypsum board) used by a day care center in place of regular wall panels to take advantage of its qualities as a writing and magnetic surface were structural components because they could not be readily removed (*La Petite Academy*, DC Mo., 95-1 USTC ¶ 50,193, aff'd, CA-8 (unpublished opinion), 96-1 USTC ¶ 50,020).

Walls (ceiling height dry wall nailed or screwed on a frame of 2 × 4 studs) installed in shopping centers to meet the requirements of tenants were structural components. The walls were destroyed and not reusable when removed (*Dixie Manor, Inc.*, DC Ky., 79-2 USTC ¶ 9469, aff'd, per curiam, CA-6, 81-1 USTC ¶ 9332).

Windows. Windows are generally categorized as structural components Reg. § 1.48-1(e)(2). However, window treatments are personal property.

A walk-up teller's window and drive-up teller's window installed in a bank building and a drive-up teller's booth, however, were specialized equipment accessorial to the conduct of the banking business and unrelated to the operation of the structures as buildings (Rev. Rul. 65-79, 1965-1 CB 26). Thus, these windows qualified as personal property.

Plumbing and wiring. Plumbing and wiring that relates to the operation and maintenance of a building is a structural component (Reg. § 1.48-1(e)(2)). Permanently installed plumbing that serviced a cafeteria's kitchen equipment and machinery did not relate to the operation and maintenance of the cafeteria building and, therefore, was personal property (*Morrison Incorporated*, 51 TCM 748, Dec. 42,963(M) (1986)).

Plumbing and wiring may relate to the general operation and maintenance of a building and also service specialized equipment. In this case, a percentage allocation of cost should be made. See "*Electrical Distribution Systems*," above. If plumbing or wiring only services specialty equipment or machinery, then the entire cost may be treated as personal property.

A sewage disposal system, including tanks and motors located some distance from a shopping center and connected to the building only with pipes, was a structural component of the building because it related to its operation and maintenance. The unit, although capable of being removed, was inherently permanent since it was installed underground (*C.C. Everhart*, 61 TC 328, Dec. 32,241 (1973)).

Restrooms. Restroom accessories have generally been considered structural components on the grounds that they relate to the operation of the building. Vanity cabinets, counters, paper towel dispensers, electrical hand dryers, cup dispensers, purse shelves, toilet tissue holders, stainless steel soap dispensers and holders, sanitary napkin dispensers, waste receptacles, coat hooks, grab bars for the handicapped, and framed mirrors with shelves and ashtrays in employee and customer cafeteria restrooms were structural components (*Morrison Incorporated*, 51 TCM 748, Dec. 42,963(M) (1986)). Similarly, in *La Petite Academy* (DC Mo., 95-1 USTC ¶ 50,193, aff'd, CA-8 (unpublished opinion), 96-1 USTC ¶ 50,020), the court based its decision on the absence of intent to remove the accessories, rather than the actual ease of removability or relationship to the operation of the building.

The *Hospital Corp. of America* case (109 TC 21, Dec. 52,163) also characterized bathroom accessories for bathrooms located in patient rooms as structural components, rejecting the argument that patient bathrooms were provided as a specialized business need.

Although easily removable, toilet partitions were structural components (*Metro National Corporation*, 52 TCM 1440, TC Memo. 1987-38, Dec. 43,649(M)). The Court focused on the fact that the partitions were not likely to be removed and related to the operation and maintenance of the building (the court noted that movability "is not the sole test").

Plumbing and plumbing fixtures, related to the operation and maintenance of a building, such as toilets, sinks, and bathtubs, are structural components (Reg. § 1.48-1(e)(2)).

Security systems. See "*Fire protection and security systems,*" above.

Septic systems. A septic system attached to a commercial building was classified as section 1250 real property depreciable over 15 years (the depreciation period of the building under ACRS) (*J. Miller,* TC Memo. 1989-66, 56 TCM 1242, Dec. 45,485(M)). See, also, "*Plumbing and wiring,*" above, and "*Site utilities,*" below.

Signs, poles, pylons, and billboards. Signs and lettering attached to the outside of a building to identify or advertise a business are personal property. Neon signs contained in or attached to a building are personal property (Reg. § 1.48-1(c)).

Whether billboards are an inherently permanent structure and, therefore, considered a land improvement with a 15-year recovery property (Asset Class 00.3.) or section 1245 personal property, which is depreciable over a shorter period, generally depends upon application of the *Whiteco* tests dealing with the determination of permanancy. The Whiteco case (Whiteco Industries, 65 T.C. 664, CCH Dec. 33,594), in fact, involved the classification of outdoor signs and concluded that a sign face, stringers, poles, and lights were personal property.

In Rev. Rul. 80-151, billboards erected on wooden support poles were personal property. Billboards erected on welded steel frames were not pesonal property (i.e. were pemanent land improvements). In an earlier private ruling, the IRS similarly concluded that billboards that are erected on land and that are inherently permanent structures and not personal property. Inherently permanent billboards that were attached to the walls or roofs of buildings and that advertised products and services unrelated to the business activity carried on within the building were also section 1250 property (IRS Letter Ruling 6606309980A, June 30, 1966). In IRS Letter Ruling 200041027, July 10, 2000, both wooden and steel billboards were considered permanently affixed (i..e, land improvements).

If a billboard is used in connection with the marketing of petroleum or petroleum products, e.g., a sign at a service station, it falls within Asset Class 57.1 of Rev. Proc. 87-56 whether the billboard is section 1245 property or section 1250 property. These billboards have a 15-year depreciation period under Asset Class 57.1. Thus, in this situation, the issue of permanancy and their classification as a land improvement is not relevent.

According to the IRS cost segregation guide for the restaurant industry, reproduced in the appendix, light poles for parking areas and other poles poured in concrete footings or bolt-mounted for signage, flags, etc. are land improvements depreciable over 15 years. See "*Pole and pylons*" in the appendix's chart. This categorical classification as a land improvement appears incorrect. Land improvements are by definition permanent structures. In certain cases a pole, etc., may be easily removed and reused (in some cases even if imbedded in concrete) and, thus, considered section 1245 personal property. The IRS apparently misconstrued the meaning of Asset Class 00.3 which says that a land improvement is 15 year property "whether or not the land improvement is section 1250 property or section 1245 property." The reference to section 1245 property in Asset Class 00.3 can only refer to section 1245 property described in Code Sec. 1245(a)(3)(B), which relates to permanent structures used as an integral part of manufacturing, production, or extraction or of furnishing transportation, communications, electrical energy, gas, water, or sewage disposal services (integral use property). Although section 1245 property also includes section 1245 personal property described in Code Sec. 1245(a)(3)(A) such personal property is by definition nonpermanent. Since a land improvement must be permanent it cannot include section 1245 personal property but may include permanently installed section 1245 integral use property. See section 5.05 of Rev. Proc. 87-56 which specifically provides that integral use property is included in Asset Class 00.3. See 110 for additional discussion of land improvements.

The audit guide further provides that the sign face of a pylon sign is personal property (although the poles and pylons are not). The treatment of the sign face as personal property seems logical since it is likely very easily removed from the pole or pylon. The same logic could also apply to an electronic billboard or electronic sign that changes message or ad displays. The treatment of the mounting mechanism should depend upon the particular circumstances. Generally, a concrete foundation into which a pole or pylon is set, however, should be considered a permanent land improvement since it isn't intended to be removed and reused.

A *large* outdoor pylon sign which advertised a 3,000 room hotel/casino complex and was not attached to a building was a land improvement (15-year property, Asset Class 00.3) (IRS Field Service Advice 200203009, October 3, 2001). The taxpayer argued that the sign was personal property under the "sole justification" test. The IRS, however, *assumed* that under the *Whiteco* tests the sign was an inherently permanent structure and, therefore, excluded from the definition of personal property under Reg. § 1.48-1(c). Replaceable equipment and circuitry within the sign, however, could qualify as personal property. The IRS cited Rev. Rul. 69-170, 1969-1 CB 28) which held scoreboards and message boards, mounted on steel poles and attached to concrete foundations with steel bolts, were separate from a stadium structure and depreciable as land improvements. Replaceable equipment and circuitry within the sign could qualify as personal property. The IRS did not actually apply the Whiteco tests. This ruling seems at odds with the conclusion in the audit guide. The ruling however was issued before the audit guide was developed and released. The size of the sign may also be a consideration. The audit guide relates to signs used by restaurants which are typically much smaller than the casino sign at issue.

See, also, *Standard Oil Company (Indiana)*, 77 TC 349, CCH Dec. 38,141 (1981) and cases cited therein, which held that service station signs were personal property but imbedded poles and concrete foundations were land imrpovements.

Note that Code Sec. 1033(g) allows a taxpayer to elect to treat permanently affixed billboards ("outdoor advertising displays") as real property for purposes of Chapter 1 of the Code (e.g., Code Secs. 1031 and 1033). The election cannot be made with respect to any billboard for which the taxpayer has claimed a Code Sec. 179 expense deduction. The term outdoor advertising display includes "highway billboards affixed to the ground with wood or metal poles, pipes, or beams, with or without concrete footings." Thus, it appears that the permanently affixed standard for purposes of Code Sec. 1033(g) is not as stringent as the standard applied by the IRS in determining whether a billboard is personal or real property for investment tax credit or depreciation purposes. See Reg. § 1.1033(g)-1 for details.

Site utilities. Site utilities at a hotel/casino complex were structural components and not land improvements. Site utilities included underground piping that connected water, sewer, and gas services to the building and overground and underground lines that connected electric service to the building. These items were used to distribute city furnished utility services to the building and were not directly associated with specific items of machinery and equipment (IRS Field Service Advice 200203009, October 3, 2001).

However, various components of an electrical distribution system (pine poles, aerial lines, transformers, meters, street lighting) and water distribution system (valves, fire hydrants, fittings, tapping sleeves, PVC water pipe, water meters) that were installed and maintained by the taxpayer in connection with an apartment complex were depreciable land improvements. These items were not classified as Rev. Proc. 87-56 Asset Class 49.14, Electric Utility Transmission and Distribution Plant, and Asset Class 49.3, Water Utilities, because those classifications only apply to taxpayers that sell electricity and water (IRS Letter Ruling 8848039, September 2, 1988).

Wall and floor coverings. Pursuant to Reg. § 1.48-1(e)(2), "permanent" coverings for walls, floors, and ceilings that are structural components are also considered structural components.

In *Hospital Corp. of America* (109 TC 21, Dec. 52,163), strippable vinyl wall coverings were personal property because the wall coverings were not considered permanent. The IRS has taken the position that such coverings are a permanent, integral part of the wall and, as such, are structural components (unless attached to a movable partition). See, for example, IRS Letter Ruling 8404007 (September 28, 1983) in which the IRS ruled that strippable, fabric-backed, vinyl-coated wall coverings used in a hotel were structural components. However, in IRS Field Service Advice 200203009 (October 3, 2001), the IRS held that strippable wall paper and vinyl wall coverings used in a hotel/casino complex were personal property. The wall coverings were installed using strippable adhesive and could be removed easily for repair work and renovation projects without damaging the walls. The ruling approves the conclusion of the *Hospital Corporation of America* case.

Permanently glued wall and floor tiling used in the kitchen and work areas of a Taco Bell restaurant was a structural component even though it was apparently selected for "special use" considerations such as ease of cleaning and was not of a decorative nature suitable for general business purposes (*L.A. Duaine,* 49 TCM 588, TC Memo. 1985-39, Dec. 41,845(M)).

See, also, "*Carpeting,*" above.

Water heaters and related equipment. A water heater that services an entire building is a plumbing fixture and, therefore is considered a structural component.

A thermal recovery system that preheats water before its enters a water heater is, likewise, considered a structural component (*La Petite Academy,* DC Mo., 95-1 USTC ¶ 50,193, aff'd, CA-8 (unpublished opinion), 96-1 USTC ¶ 50,020).

Water softener. Water softeners have been classified as structural components (Rev. Rul. 83-146, 1983-2 CB 17).

For additional building components see the IRS Audit Technique Guide for Cost Segregation at http://www.irs.gov and also the restaurant building cost segregation table reproduced as a Quick Reference Table in the appendix of this guide.

¶ 127B

Cost Segregation: Determining Depreciation Period of Personal Property Components of a Building

Once an item is identified as a separately depreciable personal property building component (see ¶ 127A for examples) it must be assigned to the proper MACRS property class. MACRS property classes include 3-year, 5-year, 7-year, 10-year, 15-year, and 20-year property and residential rental and nonresidential real property. The 200-percent declining-balance method is generally used to depreciate 3-, 5-, 7-, and 10-year property; the 150-percent declining-balance method applies to 15- and 20-year property; and the straight-line method applies to residential rental and nonresidential real property and structural components.

The property class and recovery period for most property is prescribed by the IRS in a table contained in Rev. Proc. 87-56, (1987-2 CB 674) (reproduced at ¶ 191). The first part of the table lists a few types of depreciable assets that are used by most businesses (e.g., cars, computers, furniture). The second part of the table lists specific business assets used in particular activities.

If a particular asset is not listed in the first part of the table, then its property class and recovery period are determined by reference to the business activity in which the assets are primarily used. The property class for building components identified as personal property will usually depend upon the business activity of the taxpayer as identified in Rev. Proc. 87-56. If the business activity of the taxpayer is not listed in that revenue procedure or the asse's listed for the particular business activity would not include personal propety elements of a building, then the property is treated as 7-year MACRS property. This is the default classification for personal property with no class life (Code Sec. 168(e)(3)(C)).

Many taxpayers will be conducting a business activity described in Asset Class 57.0 of Rev. Proc. 87-56. Asset Class 57.0 applies to "Distributive Trades and Services" and prescribes a 5-year recovery period. It includes assets used in wholesale and retail trade, and personal and professional services.

Wholesale and retail trade includes (but is not limited to) purchasing, assembling, storing, sorting, grading, and selling goods at the wholesale or retail level. Restaurants and cafes are included in this category (Rev. Proc. 77-10, 1977-1 CB 548).

Examples of personal service activities include: hotels and motels, laundry and dry cleaning establishments, beauty and barber shops, photographic studios and mortuaries (Rev. Proc. 77-10). The IRS ruled that owners of residential rental property are considered engaged in a personal service activity (Announcement 99-82, 1999-2 CB 244).

All of the personal property components of the hospital building in the Hospital Corporation of America case (¶ 127) were classified as five-year property because the hospital was considered an asset used in the provision of professional services. The IRS has also ruled that personal property used in connection with residential rental property is five-year Asset Class 57.0 property (Announcement 99-62, 199-2 CB 244).

See ¶ 190 for a detailed discussion of property classification rules.

For examples of particular types of separately depreciable personal property building components, see ¶ 127A.

For examples of particular types of separately depreciable land improvements, see ¶ 5 and ¶ 110. Land improvements are generally depreciated over 15 years using the 150-percent declining-balance method regardless of the taxpayer's business activity. See ¶ 110.

¶ 127C

Cost Segregation: Determining Whether a Structure is Personal or Real Property

Often it may be unclear whether a particular structure is nonresidential real property (¶ 116) depreciable over 39 years, a land improvement depreciable over 15 years, or some other type of real or personal property depreciable over a shorter period under MACRS. See ¶ 127 for the distinction between personal property and a structural component of a building.

Code Sec. 168(e)(2)(B) defines nonresidential real property as section 1250 property that is neither residential rental property nor property with a class life of less than 27.5 years. Nonresidential real property may only include a building as that term is specially defined below under the appearance and function tests. Thus, if a particular structure is not section 1250 property or is identified in Rev. Proc. 87-56 (¶ 101) as having a class life of less than 27.5 years it is not nonresidential real property. For example, Asset Class 80.0 (Theme and Amusement Parks)) provides that certain buildings have a class life of 10 years and are depreciable over 7 years. These buildings are not 39-year nonresidential real property although they retain their status as section 1250 property.

All section 1250 property is considered real property. Section 1250 property consists of any property that is not section 1245 property. Section 1245 property includes personal property and certain types of real property described in Code Sec. 1245(a)(3). See ¶ 116.

The rules are set forth in the Code as follows.

Code Sec. 168(i)(12) defines section 1250 property by reference to the definition in Code Sec. 1250(c).

Code Sec. 1250(c) provides that section 1250 property is any real property (other than real property which is treated as section 1245 property because it is described in Code Sec. 1245(a)(3)) that is or has been property of a character subject to the allowance for depreciation. See ¶ 116.

Reg. § 1.1245-3(b) defines personal property by reference to Reg. § 1.48-1 (relating to the investment tax credit). Under this regulation personal property includes any tangible property other than land and improvements thereto, such as buildings or other inherently permanent structures, including structural components of such buildings and permanent structures (Reg. § 1.48-1(c)). Thus, buildings and their structural components are treated as section 1250 real property. Other "inherently permanent structures" and their components which are improvements to land are also section 1250 property unless described in Code Sec. 1245(a)(3) (i.e., the property is section 1245 real property as explained below).

In determining whether a structure is a building, the definition of a building, as contained in the investment tax credit regulations is applied (Reg. § 1.1245-3(c)(2); Reg. § 1.48-1). Thus, the multitude of cases and rulings which have addressed this issue in the context of eligibility for the former investment tax credit remain relevant for determining the proper depreciation treatment. Subscribers to the CCH STANDARD FEDERAL TAX REPORTER may wish to refer to the annotations at ¶ 4580.21 and following for a summary of these decisions.

In determining whether a structure is a building, the courts have developed two tests derived from the ITC regulations: (1) the inherent permanency test and (2) the appearance and function test. A structure is not considered a building by most courts if it fails either test. On the other hand, a structure will be considered a building if it satisfies both tests unless the structure is essentially an item of machinery or equipment or houses property used as an integral part of an activity specified in former Code Sec. 48(a)(1)(B)(i) if the use of the structure is so closely related to the use of such property that the structure can be expected to be replaced when the property it initially houses is replaced. Included among the activities specified in former Code Sec. 48(a)(1)(B)(i) are manufacturing, production, and extraction. See below for a discussion of these two exceptions.

Permanency test

With respect to the permanency test, Reg. § 1.48-1(c) provides, in part, that:

"For purposes of this section, the term 'tangible personal property' means any tangible property except land and improvements thereto, such as buildings or other inherently permanent structures (including items, which are structural components of such buildings or structures)."

Based on the preceding regulation, most courts will rule that a structure cannot be considered a building unless it is "inherently permanent." Thus, in general, if a structure can be readily disassembled and moved to a new location, it will be considered personal property and not a building (real property).

In applying the permanency test, the courts frequently consider the following factors which were developed by the Tax Court in the *Whiteco Industries* case (65 TC 664, CCH Dec. 33,594):

(1) Is the property capable of being moved, and has it in fact been moved?

(2) Is the property designed or constructed to remain permanently in place?

(3) Are there circumstances that tend to show the expected or intended length of affixation, i.e., are there circumstances that show that property may or will have to be moved?

(4) How substantial a job is removal of the property and how time-consuming is it? Is it readily movable?

(5) How much damage will the property sustain upon its removal?

(6) What is the manner of affixation of the property to the land?

For example, a small metal shed for storing tools which can be disassembled and reassembled at another location should be considered personal property under the permanency test.

The storage shed example, however, is a simple case, easily resolved in a taxpayer's favor. The application of the rule to larger and more expensive structures, which are necessarily more permanent in nature, is more difficult and will be subject to closer IRS scrutiny.

For example, it is less clear whether self-storage units are depreciable as buildings or personal property without a class life (i.e., seven-year property). The answer will depend on the application of the five factors above. Factor (3) would generally work against personal property classification since the typical operator of a self-storage business does not ever intend to remove or relocate the units. Such intent could exist, however, if the owner will disassemble and sell or relocate the units at a new location if the business does not operate profitably. The commentary which appears at the following web site takes the position that certain mini-storage units are 7-year property: http://www.mdbarnsflorida.com (click on "Important Tax Advantages"). See, however, IRS Letter Ruling 8248003 (September 28, 1981) in which the IRS ruled that a mini-warehouse structure (and its garage style doors) used for self-service storage warehousing was not personal property. Interestingly, this IRS letter ruling does not discuss the Whiteco factors and, in light of subsequent case law, such as *Fox Photo*, below, a taxpayer is now in a stronger position to argue for personal property classification.

One leading case, which was resolved in the taxpayer's favor, involved prefabricated "one-hour photo labs" erected on mall parking lots. The labs were 24 feet wide, 28 feet long, and 12 feet high. Although the labs had all of the appearances of a building and were attached to a concrete foundation, they were designed to be moved from one location to another if necessary by transporting one-half of the structure at a time on a flat-bed truck. Some structures were in fact removed over a two-day to three-day period and the cost of removal and relocation was less than the cost of a new replacement. The concrete foundation, however, was determined to be an inherently permanent structure, and, therefore, was not personal property (*Fox Photo Inc.*, 60 TCM 85, CCH Dec. 46,709(M)).

A smaller photo-processing "hut" which could be loaded on a trailer along with its attached concrete base in less than an hour without disassembly has also been classified as personal property (*Film N' Photos*, 37 TCM 709, CCH Dec. 35,125(M)).

In contrast, a specially designed warehouse for storing bulk merchandise (500' × 190' and 57' high) was considered permanent even though the taxpayer produced evidence that a similar structure had been disassembled, moved approximately 350 feet, and reassembled over a period of 3 months by a different taxpayer involved in the book printing business (*L.L. Bean*, CA-1, 98-1 USTC ¶ 50,454). This case illustrates that even though a building or structure *can be* moved such is not necessarily conclusive evidence that it is not inherently permanent. As the court in *Bean* notes, the fact that the London Bridge was disassembled and moved from England to the United States does not negate the inherent permanency of that structure. In determining that the warehouse was inherently permanent the court focused on the improbability and expense of relocation. The warehouse was specifically designed as an addition to the taxpayer's distribution center, the foundation was specially designed to meet the requirements of forklifts and weight loads and could only be replaced at considerable expense, the material and method of construction indicated the permanent nature of the structure, and substantial time and effort would be required to remove and re-erect the structure.

In *J. McManus,* DC, 87-2 USTC ¶ 9618, an airplane hanger, which was 34 feet wide and 200 feet long, was considered inherently permanent even though it could be disassembled by a four-person crew in about seven days and reassembled in a shorter period. The court indicated that even if the hanger was not an inherently permanent structure it would still be considered a building because it satisfied the appearance and function test.

Examples of nonpermanent structures:

Mobile homes set on concrete blocks and capable at all times of being moved from their sites on their own wheels (*J.H. Moore,* 58 TC 1045, Dec. 31,554, aff'd *per curiam*, CA-5, 74-1 USTC ¶ 9146).

Trailers used as offices if not affixed to the land or designed to remain permanently in place (Rev. Rul. 77-8, 1977-1 CB 3).

Steel petroleum storage tanks varying in size from 7,000 to 194,000 barrels (*PDV America, Inc*, 87 TCM 1330, TC Memo. 2004-118, Dec. 55,638(M)). See ¶ 110 for discussion of appropriate recovery period of tanks.

Appearance and function test

The appearance and function test is based on Reg. § 1.48-1(e), which provides:

> "The term 'building' generally means any structure or edifice enclosing a space within its walls, and usually covered by a roof, the purpose of which is, for example, to provide shelter or housing, or to provide working, office, parking, display, or sales space. The term includes, for example, structures such as apartment houses, factory and office buildings, warehouses, barns, garages, railway or bus stations, and stores. Such term includes any such structure constructed by, or for, a lessee even if such structure must be removed, or ownership of such structure reverts to the lessor, at the termination of the lease. Such term

does not include (i) a structure which is essentially an item of machinery or equipment, or (ii) a structure which houses property used as an integral part of an activity specified in section 48(a)(1)(B)(i) [relating to property used as an integral part of manufacturing, production, or extraction or furnishing transportation, communications, electrical energy, gas, water, or sewage disposal services (see below)—CCH.]if the use of the structure is so closely related to the use of such property that the structure clearly can be expected to be replaced when the property it initially houses is replaced. Factors which indicate that a structure is closely related to the use of the property it houses include the fact that the structure is specially designed to provide for the stress and other demands of such property and the fact that the structure could not be economically used for other purposes. Thus, the term 'building' does not include such structures as oil and gas storage tanks, grain storage bins, silos, fractionating towers, blast furnaces, basic oxygen furnaces, coke ovens, brick kilns, and coal tipples."

The appearance test relates to whether the structure looks like a building and generally only requires that the structure enclose a space within its walls and usually be covered by a roof.

The second part of the test requires that the building function as a building. In applying the function test, the courts have primarily focused on whether the structure provides working space for employees that is more than merely incidental to the primary function of the structure. Both the quantity and qualify of human activity inside of the structure may be considered in this regard.

For example, in *Munford Inc.*, CA-11, 88-2 USTC ¶ 9432, a 35,000 square foot refrigerated structure that was designed primarily to maintain sub-zero temperatures to prevent the spoilage of frozen foods prior to shipment to grocery stores was held not to be a building. Although employees routinely moved goods into and out of the structure, this activity was held to be incidental to the specialized purpose of the structure. Moreover, the activities of the employees were limited in both scope and duration due to the cold temperature of the structure. Similar holdings have applied to other refrigeration and specialized storage buildings (*Catron*, 50 TC 306, Dec. 28,960 (Acq. 1972-2 CB 1)) (refrigerated area of a large Quonset-like structure used for cold storage of apples); *Merchants Refrigerating Co.*, 60 TC 856, CCH Dec. 32,120, Acq. 1974-2 CB 3 (large freezer room used for the storage of frozen foods); *Central Citrus Co.*, 58 TC 365, CCH Dec. 31,403 (atmospherically controlled "sweet rooms" used to ripen fruit).

In *L.L. Bean, Inc.*, above, a specially designed warehouse for housing bulk merchandise in floor-to-ceiling storage racks that supported the frame and roof satisfied the function test because human activity was essential, rather than merely incidental, to the function of the facility. Moreover, the ITC regulations and legislative history specifically list a warehouse as an example of a building. The fact that the *Bean* facility was uniquely designed only enhanced its function as a warehouse; it did negate is classification as a warehouse.

In *G.G. Hart*, 78 TCM 114, Dec. 53,462(M), a tobacco barn was determined to be a building rather than section 1245 property described in Code Sec. 1245(a)(3)(B) (property other than a building used as an integral part of the manufacturing or production of tobacco). Although employees transported tobacco from the fields and hung the tobacco on racks over a six week period, this activity was only ancillary to the function of the structure as a curing facility and did not constitute the provision of working space. However, the use of the barn on a full time basis to prepare the tobacco for sale by stripping, grading, bailing, and boxing constituted the provision of working space that was more than incidental to the function of the structure as a curing facility. As a result the structure was a building (rather than section 1245 property) and did not qualify for the Code Sec. 179 expense allowance. Since the barn was classified as a building it could not be depreciated as a land improvement (Asset Class 00.3) over 15 years. (Buildings and structural components are specifically excluded from the definition of land improvements (see ¶ 110).) Instead, it was classified as a farm building (Asset Class 01.3) depreciable over 20 years (see ¶ 118).

In contrast to the *Hart* case, a tobacco shed in *Brown & Williamson Tobacco Corp.*, DC-Ky., 73-1 USTC ¶ 9317, was not considered a building where employees only placed and removed tobacco from storage racks.

Open-air parking structures. The IRS has ruled that an open-air parking structure is a building and that taxpayer who maintain that such a parking lot is a land improvement are likely subject to the twenty percent-accuracy penalty (Code Sec. 6662(b)(1)) (Applicable Recovery Period Under Code Sec. 168(a) for Open-Air Parking Structures, Coordinated Issue Paper (LMSB4-0709-029) (Effective Date July 31, 2009). The function test is met because Reg.§ 1.48-1(e) specifically provides that the provision of parking space is a building function. The appearance test is satisfied because the structure has a roof and encloses a space within its walls. It is not necessary that all walls extend to the ceiling. Furthermore, the structure provides shelter from the elements and has many components that commonly present in other types of buildings such as walls, floors, elevators, stairs, sprinkler systems, fire escapes, and electric wiring and lighting fixtures.

Other examples of buildings

The following structures have been classified as buildings:

Prefabricated structures used to store onions. 100 foot by 100 foot pre-fabricated shed used to store onions and which contained no specialized equipment was a building in the nature of a warehouse or garage (*G. Tamura*, CA-9, 84-2 USTC ¶ 9545, 734 F2d 470).

Truck loading docks. Truck loading docks that provided working space, had the appearance of a building, and were adaptable to other uses were buildings (*Consolidated Freightways*, CA-9, 83-1 USTC ¶ 9420, 708 F2d 1385). Similarly, *Yellow Freight System Inc.*, CA-8, 76-2 USTC ¶ 9478, 538 F2d 790; Rev. Rul. 71-203, 1971-1 CB 7.

Property in the nature of machinery is personal property

Property which is in the nature of machinery (other than structural components of a building or other inherently permanent structure) is considered tangible personal property even though located outside of a building (Reg. § 1.48-1(c)). The regulations, cite, by way of example, gasoline pumps, hydraulic car lifts, and automatic vending machines.

The regulations further provide that a structure which is essentially an item of machinery or equipment is not considered a building or structural component (Reg. § 1.48-1(e)). Although the IRS has taken the position that a structure which is in the nature of machinery is not personal property if that structure is inherently permanent (*B.R. Roberts*, 60 TC 861, CCH Dec. 32,121) it subsequently conceded that an inherently permanent structure in the nature of machinery may qualify as personal property (*J.B. Weirick*, 62 TC 446, CCH Dec. 32,668; *Munford*, 87 TC 463, Dec. 43,283). A structure which is essentially an item of machinery is depreciated as part of the machinery (i.e., over the same period as the machinery).

In *Weirick*, the Tax Court held that line towers whose sole function was to support cable pulley mechanisms and cables at a ski resort were so closely related to the function of the pulley mechanisms (machinery) that the towers were also considered part of the machinery even though the towers were permanently affixed to the land.

A specially engineered structure which supported an overhead crane was essentially a part of the crane and qualified as personal property. Any function it may have served as a building component was strictly incidental to its function as an essential part of the crane (Rev. Rul. 79-183, 1979-1 CB 44).

In dealing with structures housing certain industrial processes, the Tax Court stated that the machinery exception only applies if the structure is part of the industrial process (*Illinois Cereal Mills, Inc.*, 46 TCM 1001, CCH Dec. 40,342(M), aff'd CA-7, 86-1 USTC ¶ 9371).

In *Munford* (above), although the components of the 35,000 square foot refrigeration structure used to store frozen foods prior to shipment to grocery stores chains was property in the nature of machinery, the structural elements (foundation, walls, floor, roofing, supports, vapor barrier, insulation, and electrical components) were not in the nature of machinery because they were not so closely associated with the refrigeration system as to comprise an integral, single asset. In *Weirick* it was as cheap to replace the line towers and pulley mechanisms as a single unit as it was to replace the pulley mechanisms separately. In *Munford*, the refrigeration components would normally be replaced separately from the structural elements. The structural elements, according to the court, also served a function independent of the refrigeration machinery, such as keeping out humidity, reducing temperature migration, and providing an enclosed, protected space in which the frozen foods could be stored.

The regulations provide an exception from the definition of a *building* for a structure which is "essentially an item of machinery or equipment" (Reg. § 1.48-1(e)(1)(i)) (reproduced above). This exception, which encompasses equipment as well as machinery, is arguably broader than the Reg. § 1.48-1(c) exception discussed above. In *Munford*, the court noted that property may be considered an "item of machinery or equipment" for purposes of the exclusion from the definition of a building without necessarily constituting "property which is in the nature of machinery" within the meaning of Reg. § 1.48-1(c).

Certain real property described in Code Sec. 1245(a)(3)

In addition to personal property, Code Sec. 1245 property includes other tangible property (other than a building or its structural components):

(1) used as an integral part of manufacturing, production, or extraction or as an integral part of furnishing transportation, communications, electrical energy, gas, water, or sewage disposal services;

(2) that is a research facility used in connection with any activity described in item (1); or

(3) that is a facility used in connection with any activity described in item (1) for the bulk storage of fungible commodities (including commodities in a liquid or gaseous state) (Code Sec. 1245(a)(3)(B); Reg. § 1.1245-3(c); Reg.§ 1.48-1(d)).

This property cannot be considered nonresidential real property because it is specifically excluded from the definition of section 1250 property (see above).

The investment tax credit regulations detail the types of property that qualify under this exception (Reg. § 1.48-1(d)(2)). This property was described in former Code Sec. 48(a)(1)(B) as qualifying for the investment tax credit (ITC). The ITC rules apply for purposes of Code Sec. 1245.

With respect to item (1), the ITC regulations provide that certain structures housing property used for those activities are not considered buildings. See above.

Code Sec. 1245(a)(3) property also includes single purpose agricultural and horticultural structures, storage facilities used in connection with the distribution of petroleum, and railroad gradings and tunnel bores. These items, however, are assigned specific asset classes and recovery periods under MACRS and Rev. Proc. 87-56.

Property described in items (1) through (3), above, is generally classified by Sec. 5.05 of Rev. Proc. 87-56 as a land improvement (Asset Class 00.3) for purposes of MACRS. The MACRS depreciation period is, therefore, 15 years unless the improvement in question is specifically included in another property class described in Rev. Proc. 87-56. However, Sec. 5.05 provides that a structure that is essentially an item of machinery or equipment or a structure that houses property used as an integral part of an activity specified in former section 48(a)(1)(B)(i) of the Code (i.e., property used as an integral part of manufacturing, production, or extraction or of furnishing transportation, communications, electrical energy, gas, water, or sewage disposal services) if the use of the structure is so closely related to the use of the property that the structure clearly can be expected to be replaced when the property it initially houses is replaced, is included in the asset guideline class appropriate to the equipment to which it is related. Thus, such property would generally have a shorter recovery period than 15 years. See, also, ¶ 110.

MACRS Bonus Depreciation

¶ 127D

First-Year Additional Depreciation Allowance

Organization of explanation

This bonus depreciation discussion is organized as follows:

Computation of bonus deduction when basis increases or decreases after property placed in service

Property converted from personal use to business use or from business use to personal use

Change in depreciable use after placed in service year

Coordination with Code Sec. 47 rehabilitation credit

Coordination with Code Sec. 514 relating to debt-financed property

Election to claim 30-percent bonus depreciation in place of 50-percent bonus depreciation

Election out of bonus depreciation

Election to claim accelerated AMT and research credits in lieu of bonus depreciation

Special rules for 2000 and 2001 returns that included September 11, 2001

Economic Stimulus and Recovery Acts reinstate bonus depreciation for 2008 and 2009

The 50 percent bonus depreciation allowance provided for by Code Sec. 168(k) was generally last available for qualifying property placed in service before January 1, 2005 (before January 1, 2006 for property with a long production period). The Economic Stimulus Act of 2008 (P.L. 110-185) reinstated Code Sec. 168(k) bonus depreciation at the 50 percent rate for property acquired after December 31, 2007 and placed in service before January 1, 2009 (before January 1, 2010 for property with a long production period). The Economic Recovery and Stabilization Act of 2009 (P.L. 111-5) extends the provision one additional year. Thus, 50 percent bonus depreciation now applies to property acquired after December 31, 2007 and placed in service before January 1, 2010 (before January 1, 2011 for property with a long production period). Unlike the Code Sec. 179 expense allowance, there is no limit on the amount of bonus depreciation that may be claimed.

All of the operative rules described below for pre-Stimulus Act bonus depreciation are retained with two exceptions. First, the first-year depreciation cap on vehicles on which bonus depreciation is claimed is increased by $8,000. The pre-Stimulus Act rules generally provided for a $7,650 bump-up if bonus depreciation was claimed at a 50 percent rate (Code Sec. 168(k)(2)(F), as amended by P.L. 110-185). Second, the extended placed-in-service deadline for property with a longer production period (January 1, 2011 under the current rules) no longer applies to property that has a production period exceeding two years. Instead, the production period must exceed one year and the cost must exceed $1 million (Code Sec. 168(k)(2)(B)(i)(IV), as amended by P.L. 110-185). See "*Property with longer production periods eligible for extended placed-in-service date,*" below. All other operative rules are simply applied by reference to the new acquisition and placed-in-service deadlines.

The bonus depreciation regulations (i.e., Reg.§ 1.168(k)) apply to the reinstated bonus depreciation under Code Sec. 168(k), as amended by the Stimulus Act (Section 5.01 of Rev. Proc. 2008-54).

A corporation may elect for its first tax year ending after March 31, 2008 to claim a limited amount of its unused credits for pre-2006 AMT tax liabilities and/or pre-2006 research expenditures (Code Sec. 168(k)(4)). If the election is made the corporation may not claim the bonus depreciation deduction on property acquired after March 31, 2008 and must depreciate the bonus depreciation property using the MACRS straight-line method. However, a corporation may make a second election that allows it to claim bonus depreciation on property that is eligible for bonus depreciation solely because of the one year extension for property placed in service in 2009 ("extension property"). The credit is approximately equal to 20 percent of the bonus depreciation that could have been deducted but may not exceed the lesser of six percent of the corporation's unused pre-2006 credit amounts or $30 million. This limitation is applied separately for property that is not extension property and property that is extension property. See "Election to claim accelerated alternative minimum tax credit and research credit in lieu of bonus depreciation," below.

Overview

Prior to the Stimulus Act, qualifying property had to be placed in service before January 1, 2005 or in the case of certain property with a long production period, before January 1, 2006 (an additional one-year extension to January 1, 2007 was available if a taxpayer was unable to meet the January 1, 2006 deadline because of Hurricane Katrina, Rita, or Wilma (Act Sec. 105 of the Gulf Opportunity Zone Act of 2005, P.L. 109-35; IRS Announcement 2006-29, I.R.B. 2006-19)). Qualifying New York Liberty Zone property had to be placed in service before January 1, 2007. See ¶ 127E. Qualifying Gulf Opportunity Zone property must be placed in service after August 27, 2005 and before January 1, 2008 (extended deadlines apply to qualifying residential rental and nonresidential real property). See ¶ 127F.

Final bonus depreciation regulations adopted by T.D. 9283 (8/31/06) generally apply to property acquired by a taxpayer after September 10, 2001. These regulations deal with the bonus deduction formerly allowed under Code Sec. 168(k) and the New York Liberty Zone bonus allowance. However, the rules are equally applicable to bonus depreciation under the Stimulus Act, as well as Gulf Opportunity Zone bonus depreciation (Section 5.01 of Rev. Proc. 2008-54).

A taxpayer that seeks a change in method of accounting to comply with the final regulations for either: (1) the taxpayer's last tax year ending before October 18, 2006, if the taxpayer timely files (including extensions) its Federal income tax return after October 18, 2006, for that last tax year; or (2) the taxpayer's first tax year ending on or after October 18, 2006 should follow the procedures in Rev. Proc. 2006-43, I.R.B. 2006-4. For subsequent tax years, the automatic change in method of accounting procedures in Rev. Proc. 2002-9 (now superseded by Rev. Proc. 2008-52), or the advance consent change in method of accounting procedures in Rev. Proc. 97-27, 1997-1 C.B. 680 (as modified and amplified by Rev. Proc. 2002-19, and amplified, clarified, and modified by Rev. Proc. 2002-54) (or its successor) apply.

This paragraph ¶ 127D discusses the bonus depreciation provision of Code Sec. 168(k) both before and after the Stimulus and Recovery Acts. Other bonus depreciation provisions include:

- The New York Liberty Zone bonus depreciation provision (Code Sec. 1400L(b)) is discussed at ¶ 127E.
- The Gulf Opportunity Zone bonus depreciation provision (Code Sec. 1400N(d)) at ¶ 127F.
- The Kansas Disaster Area bonus depreciation provision at ¶ 127G for certain Kansas counties affected by storms in May of 2007.
- Bonus depreciation for replacement property purchased in connection with a Presidentially declared disaster (Code Sec. 168(n)) at ¶ 127H.
- Bonus depreciation for cellulosic biofuel plant property at ¶ 127I.

Under Code Sec. 168(k), bonus depreciation applies to new: (1) MACRS property with a recovery period of 20 years or less, (2) computer software as defined in, and depreciated under Code Sec. 167(f)(1) (off-the-shelf-software), (3) water utility property as defined in Code Sec. 168(e)(5) and depreciated under MACRS, and (4) qualified leasehold improvement property (as defined below) depreciated under MACRS.

With the limited exception of computer software that is depreciable under Code Sec. 167(f)(1), the additional allowance only applies to property that is depreciated using MACRS (Code Sec. 168(k)(2)(A)(i)(I), as added by P.L. 107-147; Reg. § 1.168(k)-1(b)(2)). For example, intangibles amortized over 15 years under Code Sec. 197 do not qualify for the bonus allowance. Property described in Code Sec. 168(f) which is specifically excluded from MACRS does not qualify (e.g., property depreciated under a method not expressed in a term of years, films and video tape, sound recordings, and property subject to the anti-churning rules).

The regular MACRS recovery period (i.e., the general depreciation system (GDS) recovery period) and not the ADS recovery period is used to determine if MACRS property has a 20-year or less recovery period even if ADS is elected (Reg. § 1.168(k)-1(b)(2)(i)(A)).

Under the current rules, bonus depreciation is applied at a 50 percent rate, with no election to use a 30 percent rate in place of the 50 percent rate. The Jobs and Growth Tax Relief Reconciliation Act of 2003 (P.L. 108-27) increased the pre-Stimulus Act bonus depreciation rate from 30 percent to 50 percent (Code Sec. 168(k)(4), as added by P.L. 108-27). The rate that applied depended upon the acquisition date of the qualifying property.

In general, the 30-percent rate applied to property acquired after September 10, 2001, and before May 6, 2003. The 50-percent rate applied to property acquired after May 5, 2003, and before January 1, 2005. No 30 or 50 percent bonus depreciation could be claimed on qualifying property unless it was placed in service before January 1, 2005. The placed in service date was January 1, 2006, for certain property with a long production period. See, "*Acquisition and placed-in-service dates,*" below, for a complete discussion of the acquisition and placed in service date requirements, including binding contract rules.

The additional allowance is equal to the applicable percentage of the "unadjusted depreciable basis" of the qualified property (Reg. § 1.168(k)-1(d)(1)). Unadjusted depreciable basis is the adjusted basis of the property for determining gain or loss reduced by any amount expensed under Code Sec. 179, and any adjustments to basis provided by the Code and regulations, other than depreciation deductions (Reg.§ 1.168(k)-1(a)(2)(iii)). Typically the unadjusted depreciable basis will be the cost of the property (adjusted downward to reflect any personal use) reduced by any amount expensed under Code Sec. 179. The regular MACRS deductions are computed after reducing the unadjusted depreciable basis by the additional first-year allowance.

The bonus deduction is claimed in the tax year that the qualifying property is placed in service (not the year of acquisition or the signing of an acquisition contract). The full 50 percent rate must be claimed (unless an election out is made).

The following examples illustrate the computation of the 50-percent bonus deprecation allowance.

> ***Example (1):*** Joseph Short purchases $100,000 of new machinery that is MACRS 5-year property. The half-year convention applies and no amount is expensed under Code Sec. 179. The property is purchased on June 1, 2009, and, therefore, qualifies for the 50% bonus depreciation rate under the current rules. The 2009 bonus depreciation

deduction is $50,000 ($100,000 cost × 50%). The depreciation table percentages for 5-year property (Table 1, below) are applied to a depreciable basis of $50,000 ($100,000 – $50,000).

Recovery Year			*Deduction*
2009	bonus depreciation		$50,000
2009	$50,000 ×	20% =	$10,000
2010	$50,000 ×	32% =	$16,000
2011	$50,000 ×	19.20% =	$9,600
2012	$50,000 ×	11.52% =	$5,760
2013	$50,000 ×	11.52% =	$5,760
2014	$50,000 ×	5.76% =	$2,880
			$100,000

The additional allowance is subject to the general rules regarding whether an item is deductible under Code Sec. 162 or subject to capitalization under Code Sec. 263 or Code Sec. 263A (Code Sec. 168(k)).

How bonus depreciation affects rate of recovery

The following three depreciation tables may be used to compare the effect of claiming bonus depreciation on the rate of recovery over the applicable recovery period, assuming that the half-year convention applies. Table 1 is the official IRS table, which contains table percentages that do not reflect the bonus depreciation deduction. These table percentages are applied to the cost of an asset after reduction by any section 179 expense allowance and bonus depreciation. Table 2 shows recovery percentages that apply when 30-percent bonus depreciation is claimed. Table 2 percentages are applied to the cost of the property less any amount deducted under section 179. Table 3 shows the percentages that apply when 50-percent bonus depreciation is claimed. These percentages are also applied to the cost of the property less any amount expensed under section 179. The first recovery year percentages in Tables 2 and 3 were increased (relative to the Table 1 percentages) to reflect the applicable bonus depreciation rate. The Table 2 and Table 3 percentages for subsequent recovery years were reduced (relative to the Table 1 percentages) to reflect the required reduction in basis by the bonus depreciation amount. The IRS will not be issuing revised tables similar to Table 2 and Table 3. This is because the bonus depreciation allowance must be calculated and reported separately on Form 4562. Tables 2 and 3 should not be used to prepare tax returns. They simply show the effect of claiming bonus depreciation on the rate of depreciation over the recovery period.

The following is the official IRS table used for computing MACRS deductions on 3-, 5-, 7-, 10-, 15-, and 20-year MACRS property when the half-year convention applies.

TABLE 1
General Depreciation System
Applicable Depreciation Method: 200- or 150-Percent
Declining Balance Switching to Straight Line
Applicable Recovery Periods: 3, 5, 7, 10, 15, 20 years
Applicable Convention: Half-Year

If the Recovery Year is:	and the Recovery Period is: 3-year	5-year	7-year	10-year	15-year	20-year
	the Depreciation Rate is:					
1	33.33	20.00	14.29	10.00	5.00	3.750
2	44.45	32.00	24.49	18.00	9.50	7.219
3	14.81	19.20	17.49	14.40	8.55	6.677
4	7.41	11.52	12.49	11.52	7.70	6.177
5		11.52	8.93	9.22	6.93	5.713
6		5.76	8.92	7.37	6.23	5.285
7			8.93	6.55	5.90	4.888
8			4.46	6.55	5.90	4.522
9				6.56	5.91	4.462
10				6.55	5.90	4.461
11				3.28	5.91	4.462
12					5.90	4.461
13					5.91	4.462
14					5.90	4.461
15					5.91	4.462
16					2.95	4.461
17						4.462
18						4.461
19						4.462
20						4.461
21						2.231

Caution: The following is an unofficial CCH prepared depreciation table that has adjusted percentages that reflect the 30-percent bonus depreciation deduction.

UNOFFICIAL CCH TABLE INCORPORATING 30-PERCENT BONUS DEPRECIATION

TABLE 2
General Depreciation System
Applicable Depreciation Method: 200- or 150-Percent
Declining Balance Switching to Straight Line
Applicable Recovery Periods: 3, 5, 7, 10, 15, 20 years
Applicable Convention: Half-Year

If the Recovery Year is:	and the Recovery Period is: 3-year	5-year	7-year	10-year	15-year	20-year
	the Depreciation Rate is:					
1	53.331	44.00	40.003	37.00	33.50	32.625
2	31.115	22.40	17.143	12.60	6.65	5.0533
3	10.367	13.44	12.243	10.08	5.985	4.6739

If the Recovery Year is:	3-year	5-year	7-year	10-year	15-year	20-year
			the Depreciation Rate is:			
4	5.187	8.064	8.743	8.064	5.39	4.3239
5		8.064	6.251	6.454	4.851	3.9991
6		4.032	6.244	5.159	4.361	3.6995
7			6.251	4.585	4.13	3.4216
8			3.122	4.585	4.13	3.1654
9				4.592	4.137	3.1234
10				4.585	4.13	3.1227
11				2.296	4.137	3.1234
12					4.13	3.1227
13					4.137	3.1234
14					4.13	3.1227
15					4.137	3.1234
16					2.065	3.1227
17						3.1234
18						3.1227
19						3.1234
20						3.1227
21						1.5617

Caution: The following is an unofficial CCH prepared depreciation table that has adjusted percentages that reflect the 50-percent bonus depreciation deduction.

UNOFFICIAL CCH DEPRECIATION TABLE INCORPORATING 50-PERCENT BONUS DEPRECIATION

TABLE 3
General Depreciation System
Applicable Depreciation Method: 200- or 150-Percent Declining Balance Switching to Straight Line
Applicable Recovery Periods: 3, 5, 7, 10, 15, 20 years
Applicable Convention: Half-Year

If the Recovery Year is:	3-year	5-year	7-year	10-year	15-year	20-year
			the Depreciation Rate is:			
1	66.665	60.00	57.145	55.00	52.50	51.875
2	22.225	16.00	12.245	9.00	4.750	3.6095
3	7.405	9.60	8.745	7.20	4.275	3.3385
4	3.705	5.76	6.245	5.76	3.850	3.0885
5		5.76	4.465	4.61	3.465	2.8565
6		2.88	4.460	3.685	3.115	2.6425
7			4.465	3.275	2.950	2.444
8			2.23	3.275	2.950	2.261
9				3.28	2.955	2.231
10				3.275	2.950	2.2305
11				1.640	2.955	2.231
12					2.950	2.2305
13					2.955	2.231

If the Recovery Year is:	3-year	5-year	7-year	10-year	15-year	20-year
			the Depreciation Rate is:			
14					2.950	2.2305
15					2.955	2.231
16					1.475	2.2305
17						2.231
18						2.2305
19						2.231
20						2.2305
21						1.1155

Example (2): Three-year property costing $100,000 and subject to the half-year convention is purchased on May 1, 2003. The taxpayer claimed 30% bonus depreciation. The combined first-year depreciation deduction and 30% bonus depreciation allowance is $53,331 ($100,000 × 53.331%). The second-year depreciation deduction is $31,115 ($100,000 × 31.115%). The third-year depreciation deduction is $10,367 ($100,000 × 10.367%). The fourth-year deduction is $5,187 ($100,000 × 5.187%). Table 2 is used.

Example (3): Three-year property costing $100,000 and subject to the half-year convention is purchased on May 7, 2009. The taxpayer claims the 50% bonus depreciation deduction. The combined first-year depreciation deduction and 50% bonus depreciation allowance is $66,665 ($100,000 × 66.665%). The second-year depreciation deduction is $22,225 ($100,000 × 22.225%). The third-year depreciation deduction is $7,405 ($100,000 × 7.405%). The fourth-year deduction is $3,705 ($100,000 × 3.705%). Table 3 is used.

Coordination with Code Sec. 179

The Code Sec. 179 expense allowance is claimed prior to the additional depreciation allowance (Reg. § 1.168(k)-1(d)).

Example (4): An item of 5-year property placed in service in December 2009 costs $100,000. The taxpayer expenses $20,000 of the cost under Code Sec. 179. The taxpayer's bonus depreciation is $40,000 ($80,000 × 50%). The depreciable basis after reduction by the Code Sec. 179 expense allowance and bonus depreciation is $40,000 ($100,000 – $20,000 – $40,000).

This required order of allocation will reduce the size of the bonus depreciation claimed on an asset with respect to which a Code Sec. 179 expense allowance is claimed. If bonus depreciation could be calculated prior to reduction by any amount expensed under Code Sec. 179, the bonus depreciation would have been $50,000 ($100,000 × 50%) rather than $40,000.

Taxpayers should continue to expense assets with the longest recovery (depreciation) period in order to accelerate the recovery of their costs. For example, given the choice of expensing the cost of 20-year property or 3-year property, the Code Sec. 179 expense allowance should be allocated to the 20-year property since the full cost of the 3-year property will be recovered in three years.

Property located in the New York Liberty Zone

The bonus depreciation provision discussed in this paragraph (¶ 127D) is authorized by Code Sec. 168(k). However, Code Sec. 1400L(b) contained a very similar but separate 30-percent bonus depreciation provision for qualified New York Liberty Zone property. The 50-percent rate did not apply to bonus depreciation claimed under the authority of Code Sec. 1400L(b) (Code Sec. 1400L(b)(1)(A) and Code Sec. 1400L(b)(2)(C)).

The New York Liberty Zone is an area in New York City directly affected by the September 11, 2001, terrorist attack.

Bonus depreciation on most property placed in service in the New York Liberty Zone before January 1, 2005 was claimed under the authority of Code Sec. 168(k). Thus, the 50-percent rate applied if such property was acquired after May 5, 2003, and placed in service before January 1, 2005. Bonus depreciation was generally claimed under the authority of Code Sec. 1400L(b) if the property was used (used property did not qualify for bonus depreciation under Code Sec. 168(k) but could qualify under Code Sec. 1400L(b)) or if it was placed in service after December 31, 2004, and on or before December 31, 2006 (Code Sec. 1400L(b) provides a placed-in-service date for New York Liberty Zone property that was two years longer for property placed in service outside the zone). Certain repaired or replaced real property was also eligible for bonus depreciation under Code Sec. 1400L(b) but not under Code Sec. 168(k).

See ¶ 127E for a discussion of the 30 percent additional depreciation allowance for New York Liberty Zone property.

Qualified New York Liberty Zone leasehold improvement property did not qualify for bonus depreciation (Code Sec. 168(k)(2)(C)(ii) and Code Sec. 1400L(b)(2)(C)(iii), as added by P.L. 107-147). However, this property does qualify for a reduced recovery period of five years. See ¶ 124A.

50 percent bonus depreciation is generally available under the Stimulus and Recovery Acts for property acquired after December 31, 2007 and placed in service before January 1, 2010 (before January 1, 2011 for certain property with a long production period). The Stimulus Act does not reinstate any special rules for New York Liberty Zone property. Thus, property located in that Zone will qualify for bonus depreciation on the same basis as property located outside of the Zone.

Bonus Depreciation for property in the Gulf Opportunity Zone, Kansas Disaster Area, or Federally Declared Disaster Area

A 50 percent bonus depreciation deduction may be claimed on qualifying property acquired on or after August 28, 2005 and placed in service in the Gulf Opportunity Zone before January 1, 2008 (before January 1, 2009 (before January 1, 2011 in certain cases) if the qualifying property is new residential rental or nonresidential real property) (Code Sec. 1400N(d), as added by the Gulf Opportunity Zone Act of 2005 (P.L. 109-135). See ¶ 127F.

A 50 percent bonus depreciation deduction is allowed on qualified Recovery Assistance property acquired on or after May 5, 2007, and placed in service on or before December 31, 2008 in the Kansas disaster area (Act § 15345 of the Heartland, Habitat, Harvest and Horticulture Act of 2008, P.L. 110-246; Notice 2008-67, I.R.B. 2008-32, July 23, 2008, providing regulatory type guidance). The placed in service deadline is extended to December 31, 2009 in the case of real property. See ¶ 127G.

An 50 percent additional depreciation allowance (bonus depreciation) is permitted for the tax year in which qualified disaster assistance property is placed in service. The provision applies to property placed in service after December 31, 2007, with respect to Presidentially declared disasters declared after such date and occurring before January 1, 2010. In general, qualified disaster assistance property is new real or personal property that replaces property that is damaged or destroyed in a Presidentially declared disaster area (Code Sec. 168(n), as added by the Emergency Economic Stabilization Act of 2008 (P.L. 110-343)). See ¶ 127H.

Alternative minimum tax

The regular tax bonus deprecation allowance may generally be claimed in full for alternative minimum tax purposes (Code Sec. 168(k)(2)(G)). However, if the unadjusted depreciable basis of the bonus depreciation property is different for AMT purposes than for regular tax purposes, the bonus deduction is the applicable percentage (50 percent under the Stimulus and Recovery Acts) of the AMT unadjusted depreciable basis (Reg.§ 1.168(k)-1(d)(1)(iii)). In addition, the regular tax MACRS deductions on bonus depreciation property may be claimed in full for AMT purposes, except that AMT MACRS deductions are computed on the property's AMT unadjusted depreciable basis as reduced by the AMT bonus allowance if the AMT unadjusted depreciable basis is different than the regular tax unadjusted depreciable basis (Reg.§ 1.168(k)-1(d)(2)(ii)). Thus, an election out of bonus depreciation could trigger an AMT tax liability.

Short tax year

The full bonus depreciation deduction may be claimed in a short tax year. However, as explained below, special rules apply to bonus depreciation property acquired by a partnership in the tax year that it is technically terminated under Code Sec. 708(b)(1)(B) or by an entity in a tax year that it engages in a step-in the shoes transaction described in Code Sec. 168(i)(7) (Reg.§ 1.168(k)-1(d)(1)(i)).

Earnings and profits

The bonus allowance is not allowable for purposes of computing a corporation's earnings and profits (Reg.§ 1.168(k)-1(f)(7)).

Section 1245 and section 1250 depreciation recapture

Since bonus depreciation is treated as a depreciation deduction, the entire deduction is potentially subject to recapture as ordinary income under Code Sec. 1245 when section 1245 property is sold at a gain. The Code Sec. 1250 recapture rules apply if the bonus allowance is claimed on section 1250 property even if the property is depreciated using the straight-line method under MACRS (e.g., qualified leasehold improvement property, and certain residential rental and nonresidential real property located in the New York Liberty Zone (¶ 127E), Gulf Opportunity GO Zone (¶ 127F), Kansas Disaster Area (¶ 127G), or a Federally Declared Disaster Area (¶ 127H). For purposes of recapture under section 1250, bonus depreciation is considered an accelerated depreciation method (Reg. § 1.168(k)-1(f)(3)). For example, the difference between the bonus deduction plus regular depreciation claimed on section 1250 qualified leasehold improvement property (see below) and the straight-line depreciation that would have been claimed on the property up to the time of disposition computed as if bonus depreciation had not been claimed is subject to recapture as ordinary income to the extent of gain realized on the disposition of the section 1250 property. See ¶ 488 for a discussion of the recapture rules under Code Secs. 1245 and 1250.

Except for listed property (¶ 208), such as a car or pick-up truck, no recapture of the bonus depreciation deduction claimed under Code Sec. 168(k) is required upon a decline of business use to 50 percent of less. See "Mandatory ADS property does not qualify for bonus depreciation," below.

Increase in first-year luxury car depreciation caps

Assuming that the election out of bonus depreciation is not made, the first-year Code Sec. 280F depreciation cap for passenger automobiles that qualify for bonus depreciation is increased by $8,000 for vehicles placed in service in 2008 and 2009 (Code Sec. 168(k)(2)(F), as amended by the Economic Stimulus Act of 2008 (P.L.

110-185) and the American Recovery and Reinvestment Act of 2009 (P.L. 111-5). Under the pre-Stimulus Act rules the increase was $4,600 if the 30-percent rate applied and by $7,650 if the 50-percent rate applied. (Code Sec. 168(k)(2)(E)(i), as added by P.L. 107-147 and Code Sec. 168(k)(4)(D); Reg. § 1.168(k)-1(f)(8)).

Because the increased cap applies only to a passenger automobile that is qualified property, a vehicle must be acquired after December 31, 2007 and before January 1, 2010 to qualify for the $8,000 increase. Under the pre-Stimulus rules the vehicle must be acquired after September 10, 2001, and placed in service before January 1, 2005, in order to obtain the benefit of the applicable $4,600 or $7,650 increase. Also, bonus depreciation must be claimed on the vehicle—the increase is not available if the election out is made. See the definition of qualified property, above. If a taxpayer elects out of the 50-percent rate in favor of the 30-percent rate, the applicable increase is $7,650.

The depreciation bump-up amounts are tripled for electric vehicles but only under the pre-Stimulus Act rules.

The bump-up amounts are not reduced in a short tax year. The Code Sec. 179 allowance may be applied against the bump-up amount (Preamble to T.D. 9283, filed with the Federal Register on August 28, 2006).

See ¶ 200 and following for a complete discussion of the depreciation cap rules.

Like-kind exchanges and involuntary conversions

The entire adjusted basis of property received in a like-kind exchange or acquired in an involuntary conversion may qualify for bonus depreciation. See ¶ 167.

Effective date

The bonus depreciation provision as originally enacted (Code Sec. 168(k)) generally applies to property placed in service after September 10, 2001, in tax years ending after that date (Act Sec. 101(b) of the Job Creation and Worker Assistance Act of 2002 (P.L. 107-147)). The final regulations generally apply to 30 percent bonus depreciation property, including New York Liberty Zone property, acquired after September 10, 2001 and to 50 percent bonus depreciation property acquired after May 5, 2003 (Reg. § 1.168(k)-1(g)). The changes made by the Stimulus Act apply to property placed in service after December 31, 2007, in tax years ending after that date (Act § 102(d) of P.L. 110-185).

Acquisition and placed-in-service dates

Under the current rules, property cannot qualify for the special allowance unless each of the following three requirements is met (Code Sec. 168(k)(2), as amended by the Economic Stimulus Act of 2008 (P.L. 110-185)):

(1) The original use of the property must commence with the taxpayer after December 31, 2007;

(2) The taxpayer must either acquire the property after December 31, 2007, or acquire the property pursuant to a written binding contract that was entered into after December 31, 2007, and before January 1, 2010; and

(3) The taxpayer must place the property in service before January 1, 2010. However, as explained below, certain property considered to have a longer production period only needs to be placed in service before January 1, 2011.

Under the pre-Stimulus Act rules property did not qualify for the special allowance unless each of the following three requirements were met (Code Sec. 168(k)(2), as added by P.L. 107-147 and prior to amendment by P.L. 110-185):

(1) The original use of the property must commence with the taxpayer after September 10, 2001 (after May 5, 2003, in order for the 50-percent rate to apply);

(2) The taxpayer must either acquire the property after September 10, 2001 (after May 5, 2003, in order for the 50-percent rate to apply), or acquire the property pursuant to a written binding contract that was entered into after September 10, 2001 (after May 5, 2003, in order for the 50-percent rate to apply), and before January 1, 2005; and

(3) The taxpayer must place the property in service before January 1, 2005. However, as explained below, certain property considered to have a longer production period only needs to be placed in service before January 1, 2006 (before January 1, 2007 under a limited exception for taxpayers affected by Hurricane Katrina, Rita, or Wilma).

The bonus depreciation regulations do not provide a definition of acquisition. However, the investment tax credit regulations provide that property is deemed acquired when reduced to physical possession or control (Reg. § 1.48-2(b)(6)). A similar definition is provided in the Code Sec. 167 depreciation regulations (Reg. § 1.167(c)-1(a)(2)).

Original use requirement

The original use requirement prevents used property from qualifying for bonus depreciation. Original use means the first use to which the property is put, whether or not that use corresponds to the use of the property by the taxpayer (Reg. § 1.168(k)-1(b)(3)). Original use begins when new property is first placed in service, whether for personal or business purposes (Preamble to T.D. 9283, filed with the Federal Register on August 28, 2006).

The Joint Committee on Taxation Explanation to P.L. 107-147 indicates that the factors used in determining whether property qualified as new section 38 property for purposes of the investment tax credit apply in determining whether the property is original use property. These factors are contained in Reg. § 1.48-2. The bonus depreciation regulations, however, contain no specific reference to the ITC regulations.

Additional capital expenditures incurred by a taxpayer to recondition or rebuild property that is acquired or owned by the taxpayer satisfy the original use requirement. However, the cost of reconditioned or rebuilt property does not satisfy the requirement. Property, whether acquired or self-constructed, which contains used parts will not be treated as reconditioned or rebuilt if the cost of the used parts is not more than 20 percent of the total cost of the property (Reg.§ 1.168(k)-1(b)(3)(i)). The question of whether property is reconditioned or rebuilt property is a question of fact. The preceding 20-percent rule is a safe-harbor. See, also, Rev. Rul. 68-111.

Example (5): Al Stevens, a taxpayer, purchases a used machine after September 10, 2009, for $50,000. Stevens then pays $20,000 to recondition the machine in 2009. No part of the $50,000 cost qualifies for additional depreciation because it is attributable to used property and is more than 20 percent of the total $70,000 cost. However, the $20,000 expenditure (whether it is added to the basis of the machine or capitalized and treated as a separate asset) will qualify.

Property that is converted from personal use to business use by the same taxpayer is considered as originally used by the taxpayer. However, if the taxpayer acquires property that was used for personal purposes by another person and the taxpayer then places that property in service for business purposes, the taxpayer is not considered the original user (Reg.§ 1.168(k)-1(b)(3)(ii)).

> ***Example (6):*** Tom Jacobs, a taxpayer, purchases a new machine on January 1, 2009 for personal use. He converts it to business use in June 2009. The machine may qualify for bonus depreciation. If the machine had been acquired before January 1, 2008 for personal use and then converted in 2009 for business use, it would not qualify for bonus depreciation because it was acquired before January 1, 2008.

Demonstration assets, such as a demonstrator vehicle held in inventory by an automobile dealer, may be considered as originally used by the purchaser (Reg.§ 1.168(k)-1(b)(3)(v), *Example 2*). The original use requirement was not violated where a manufacturer's use of a plane for purposes other than demonstration was less than two percent of the estimated flight time over the aircraft's useful life, and the manufacturer continued to hold it for sale during times it loaned it out or used it as a demonstrator (IRS Letter Ruling 200502004 September 30, 2004).

A horse that is acquired for racing by one person and then acquired by the taxpayer for breeding purposes does not qualify for bonus depreciation. The taxpayer is not considered the original user (Reg.§ 1.168(k)-1(b)(3)(v), *Example 3*).

The example involves a race horse acquired by the racer on April 1, 2000 and then purchased by the taxpayer on October 1, 2003. The example simply says that the original use requirement is not satisfied. Under the original use requirement, the original use must commence with the *taxpayer* after September 10, 2001. Since original use is defined as the first use to which the property is put whether or not that use commences with the taxpayer (see above), it does appear that this example should not be interpreted to mean that if the racer had acquired the horse after September 10, 2001, the original use requirement would have been satisfied. The original use requirement would not have been satisfied because the original use first commenced with the racer and not the taxpayer. Another point worth noting is that the horse was a depreciable asset in the hands of the racer. If the horse was raised and held as nondepreciable inventory by the seller and sold to the taxpayer after September 10, 2001, then arguably the original use requirement would be satisfied. This situation would be analogous to the sale of a new vehicle after September 10, 2001 from a car dealership's inventory.

Special original use and placed in service date rules apply to sale-leasebacks and sales of fractional interests. See below.

Placed-in-service date requirement

In order to qualify for bonus depreciation at the 50 percent rate under the current rules, the qualifying property must be placed in service before January 1, 2010 (before January 1, 2011 if an extended placed-in-service date applies).

In order to qualify for bonus depreciation under the pre-Stimulus Act rules, at either the 30-percent or 50-percent rate, the property had to be placed in service before January 1, 2005 (before January 1, 2006 if the extended placed-in-service date applied).

The placed-in-service date requirement is separate from the acquisition date requirement discussed above. The date of acquisition of a property is not necessarily the date it is placed in service. A property is considered placed in service for depreciation purposes when it is ready and available for use.

The extended placed-in-service dates apply to certain property with a longer production period and commercial and noncommercial aircraft. See below.

Property placed in service and disposed of in the same tax year does not qualify for bonus depreciation (Reg. § 1.168(k)-1(f)(1)). This is consistent with the rule which denies a depreciation deduction on property placed in service and disposed of in the same tax year (Reg. § 1.168(d)-1(b)(3)).

Special rules, described below, apply for purposes of determining when property involved in a sale-leaseback or syndication transaction is considered placed in service.

Property with longer production periods eligible for extended placed-in-service date

Under the current rules, the extended January 1, 2011 placed-in-service date applies to property that:

(1) has a recovery period of at least 10 years or is transportation property;

(2) is subject to the uniform capitalization rules (Code Sec. 263A); and

(3) has a production period exceeding one year and a cost exceeding $1 million (Code Sec. 168(k)(2)(B), as amended by the Economic Stimulus Act of 2008 (P.L. 110-185)).

Under the pre-Stimulus Act rules, the January 1, 2006, placed-in-service date applies to property that:

(1) has a recovery period of at least 10 years or is transportation property;

(2) is subject to the uniform capitalization rules (Code Sec. 263A); and

(3) has a production period exceeding two years, or a production period exceeding one year and a cost exceeding $1 million (Code Sec. 168(k)(2)(B), prior to amendment by the Economic Stimulus Act of 2008 (P.L. 110-185)).

In one of the few changes to the pre-Stimulus Act bonus depreciation rules, item (3) was been amended to eliminate the option that a property with a production period exceeding two years (regardless of cost) may qualify for an extended placed-in-service date (January 1, 2011 under the current rules). Under the current rules, the property must have a production period exceeding one year and a cost exceeding $1 million (Code Sec. 168(k)(2)(B)(i)(iv), as amended by the Stimulus Act).

Transportation property is defined as tangible personal property used in the trade or business of transporting persons or property, for example, a passenger aircraft (Code Sec. 168(k)(2)(B)(iii)).

A technical correction in the Working Families Tax Relief Act of 2004 (P.L. 108-311) clarified that requirement (2), above, is satisfied, regardless of the reason that the property is subject to the UNICAP.

Under the pre-Stimulus Act rules, the 30 percent rate applies to long production property acquired after September 10, 2001 and before May 6, 2003 or acquired pursuant to a binding contract entered into during that period. The 50 percent rate applies to long production property acquired after May 5, 2003 and before January 1, 2005 or acquired pursuant to a binding contract entered into during that period. In either case, the property must be placed in service before January 1, 2006 (Code Sec. 168(k)(2)(A) and (k)(4)(b)(ii) Code Sec. 168(k)(4)(b)(ii), as amended by P.L. 109-135). For purposes of this rule keep in mind that it is possible to place a property in service after its acquisition date. See ¶ 3.

Under the current rules, the bonus allowance is only claimed with respect to the adjusted basis of a property attributable to pre-January 1, 2010 manufacture, construction, or production even though the extended January 1, 2011 placed-in-service date applies (Code Sec. 168(k)(2)(B)(ii), as amended by P.L. 110-185 and P.L. 111-5).

Under the pre-Stimulus Act rules, although an extended January 1, 2006, placed-in-service date applied to property with longer production periods, the additional depreciation allowance applied only to the adjusted basis of the property attributable to manufacture, construction, or production before January 1, 2005 (Code Sec. 168(k)(2)(B)(ii), prior to amendment by the Economic Stimulus Act of 2008 (P.L. 110-185); Reg. § 1.168(k)-1(d)(1)(ii)).

The Joint Committee on Taxation Explanation to P.L. 107-147 indicates that it is intended that rules similar to Code Sec. 46(d)(3) (relating the former investment tax credit) as in effect prior to the Tax Reform Act of 1986 (P.L. 99-514) will apply for purposes of determining the amount of progress expenditures.

Noncommercial aircraft eligible for extended placed-in-service date

A separate provision extends the placed-in-service date for noncommercial aircraft to January 1, 2011 under the current rules and to January 1, 2006 under the pre-Stimulus Act rules.

Under the current rules, an aircraft that is *not* used in the trade or business of transporting persons or property (other than for agricultural or fire fighting purposes) will qualify for an extended January 1, 2011, placed-in-service date if the following requirements are met:

(1) the original use of the aircraft commences with the taxpayer after December 31, 2007;

(2) either:

(a) the aircraft was acquired by the taxpayer after December 31, 2007, and before January 1, 2010, and no written binding contract for the acquisition was in effect before January 1, 2008, or

(b) the aircraft was acquired pursuant to a written binding contract entered into after December 31, 2007, and before January 1, 2010;

(3) the aircraft is purchased and the purchaser, at the time of the contract for purchase, has made a nonrefundable deposit of the lesser of 10 percent of the cost or $100,000; and

(4) the aircraft has an estimated production period exceeding four months and a cost exceeding $200,000 (Code Sec. 168(k)(2)(A)(iv), as amended by the Economic Stimulus Act of 2008 (P.L. 110-185) and the American Recovery and Reinvestment Act of 2009 (P.L. 111-5); Code Sec. 168(k)(2)(C), as added by the American Jobs Creation Act of 2004 (P.L. 108-357).

With respect to the nonrefundable deposits requirement above, Section 5.02 of Rev. Proc. 2008-54 provides that the nonrefundable deposit requirement is satisfied if the purchaser, at the time of the purchase contract, has made a nonrefundable deposit of at least the lesser of 10 percent of the cost of the aircraft or $100,000.

Under the pre-Stimulus Act rules, the placed-in-service date for noncommercial aircraft was extended to January 1, 2006. An aircraft that is *not* used in the trade or business of transporting persons or property (other than for agricultural or firefighting purposes) qualified for the extended January 1, 2006, placed-in-service date if the following requirements were met:

(1) the original use of the aircraft commences with the taxpayer after September 10, 2001;

(2) either:

(a) the aircraft was acquired by the taxpayer after September 10, 2001, and before January 1, 2005, and no written binding contract for the acquisition was in effect before September 11, 2001, or

(b) the aircraft was acquired pursuant to a written binding contract entered into after September 10, 2001, and before January 1, 2005;

(3) the aircraft is purchased and at the time of the contract for purchase the purchaser made a nonrefundable deposit at least equal to 10 percent of the cost or $100,000; and

(4) the aircraft has an estimated production period exceeding four months and a cost exceeding $200,000 (Code Sec. 168(k)(2)(A)(iv), prior to amendment by the Economic Stimulus Act of 2008 (P.L. 110-185); Code Sec. 168(k)(2)(C), as added by the American Jobs Creation Act of 2004).

The restriction contained in Code Sec. 168(k)(2)(B)(ii) and described above which limits the basis of property eligible for the bonus depreciation deduction to pre-January 1, 2010 progress expenditures (pre-January 1, 2005, progress expenditures under the pre-Stimulus Act rules) does not apply to aircraft described in this provision (Code Sec. 168(k)(2)(B)(iv), as added by the 2004 Jobs Act).

For purposes of requirement (3), the term "purchase" is intended to have the same meaning as used in Code Sec. 179(d)(2) (H.R. Conf. Rep. No. 108-755). See ¶ 302.

Example (7): ABC corporation enters into a binding contract to purchase a corporate jet on January 1, 2008. The purchase price is $2,000,000. A $100,000 nonrefundable deposit is made. Production begins on February 1, 2008. Assuming that the production period for the aircraft exceeds four months, the entire cost should qualify for 50-percent bonus depreciation if production is completed before January 1, 2011 and the aircraft is placed in service before January 1, 2011.

Under the pre-Stimulus Act rules, the 30 percent rate applied to a noncommercial aircraft acquired after September 10, 2001 and before May 6, 2003 or acquired pursuant to a binding contract entered into during that period. The 50 percent rate applied if the aircraft was acquired after May 5, 2003 and before January 1, 2005 or acquired pursuant to a binding contract entered into during that period. In either case, the aircraft had to be placed in service before January 1, 2006 (Code Sec. 168(k)(2)(A) and (k)(4)(b)(ii), as amended by P.L. 109-135). Note that it is possible to place a property in service after its acquisition date. See ¶ 3.

January 1, 2006 placed in service date extended to January 1, 2007 if delay caused by hurricane

The January 1, 2006 extended placed-in-service date for property with longer production periods and noncommercial aircraft under the pre-Stimulus Act rules was extended another additional year to January 1, 2007 if the inability to place the property in service before January 1, 2006 was caused by Hurricane Katrina, Rita, or Wilma (Act Sec. 105 of the Gulf Opportunity Zone Act of 2005 (P.L. 109-135) (note: this is a noncode provision). A taxpayer could not qualify for the extension unless (1) the property was to be placed in service in the Gulf Opportunity Zone, the Rita GO Zone, or the Wilma GO Zone (as defined in Code Sec. 1400M) by a taxpayer affected by Hurricane Katrina, Rita, or Wilma, or (2) the property was manufactured in one of these Zones by a person affected by Hurricane Katrina, Rita, or Wilma (Act Sec. 105 of the Gulf Zone Act). A taxpayer took advantage of this provision by writing "Extension under Announcement 2006-29" across the top of its Form 4562, Depreciation and Amortization, for the placed-in-service year of the property (Announcement 2006-29, I.R.B. 2006-19). Supporting documentation did not need to be attached but must be maintained.

The provision did not modify the rule which prohibited a taxpayer from claiming the bonus depreciation deduction on post-December 31, 2004 progress expenditures. (As noted above, however, post-2004 progress expenditures may be taken into account in the case of a noncommercial aircraft). Thus, even if the January 1, 2006 placed-in-service date was extended for a particular property to January 1, 2007, the bonus deduction could be reduced or eliminated if the property was damaged or destroyed in the Gulf Zone and was being remanufactured or repaired. However, in some cases it was possible to qualify for the 50-percent additional first-year depreciation allowance specially enacted for property placed in service in the Gulf Opportunity Zone before January 1, 2007. The additional allowance, however, did not apply to property if a written binding contract for its acquisition was in effect before August 29, 2005 or, in the case of self-constructed property, manufacture, construction, or production began before August 29, 2005. See ¶ 127F.

Mandatory ADS property does not qualify for bonus depreciation

Property which pursuant to any Code provision or regulation must be depreciated using the MACRS alternative depreciation system (ADS) in the year that it is placed in service does not qualify for bonus depreciation. However, property that a taxpayer elects to depreciate using ADS is not disqualified (Code Sec. 168(k)(2)(D); Reg. § 1.168(k)-1(b)(2)(ii)(A)(2) and (B)(*1*)).

The following property must be depreciated using ADS and, therefore, does not qualify for bonus depreciation:

(1) tangible property used predominantly outside of the United States during the tax year;

(2) tax-exempt use property;

(3) tax-exempt bond-financed property; and

(4) property imported from a foreign country for which an Executive Order is in effect because the country maintains trade restrictions or engages in other discriminatory acts (Code Sec. 168(g)(1)).

If a property described in (1) through (4) changes use in a tax year after it is placed in service, the bonus deduction may not be claimed in the year the use changes. For example the bonus deduction may not be claimed on property placed in service outside of the United States in the tax year of acquisition and moved into the United States in a later tax year. Conversely, the bonus deduction is not disallowed or recaptured if property becomes ineligible for the bonus allowance in a tax year after it was placed in service because it is described in items (1) through (4). For example, the bonus deduction claimed on property placed in service in the U.S. in the tax year of acquisition is not disallowed or recaptured if the property is later moved outside of the U.S. in a later tax year (Reg. § 1.168(k)-1(f)(6)(iv)).

Listed property. If a listed property (¶ 208), such as a car, must be depreciated using ADS (¶ 150) in the year that it is placed in service because it is not predominantly used in a qualified business use, then bonus depreciation may not be claimed (Code Sec. 168(k)(2)(D)(i)(II); Reg. § 1.168(k)-1(b)(2)(ii)(A)(2)). Because the additional depreciation allowance is treated as depreciation, it is subject to recapture under the listed property rules if business use falls to 50 percent or less in a tax year after it is placed in service but within the applicable ADS recovery period that applies to the property (Code Sec. 168(k)(2)(F)(ii), as added by P.L. 107-147).

As defined in Code Sec. 280F(d)(4), listed property includes any passenger automobile, any other property used as a means of transportation, any property of a type generally used for purposes of entertainment, recreation, or amusement, any computer or peripheral equipment, any cellular telephone (or similar telecommunications equipment), and certain other property specified in regulations. See ¶ 208.

Farmers. Farmers who elect under Code Sec. 263A(d)(3) not to have the uniform capitalization rules apply, are required to depreciate farm property placed in service during any tax year that the election is in effect using ADS. Such farm property does not qualify for bonus depreciation. The prohibition applies even if the election was made by a person related to the taxpayer (Reg. § 1.168(k)-1(b)(2)(ii)(A)(2)).

Self-constructed property

Property that is manufactured, constructed, or produced by a taxpayer for the taxpayer's own use may qualify for bonus depreciation. if the taxpayer begins manufacturing, constructing, or producing the property after December 31, 2007, and before January 1, 2010 and places the property in service before January 1, 2010 (January 1, 2011 if the extended placed-in-service date applies) (Code Sec. 168(k)(2)(E)(i), as amended by the Economic Stimulus Act of 2008 (P.L. 110-185)).

Under the pre-Stimulus Act rules, property that was manufactured, constructed, or produced by a taxpayer for the taxpayer's own use could qualify for bonus depreciation if the taxpayer began manufacturing, constructing, or producing the property after September 10, 2001, and before January 1, 2005 and placed the property in service before January 1, 2005 (January 1, 2006 if the extended placed-in-service date applied (Code Sec. 168(k)(2)(E)(i), as added by P.L. 107-147 and amended by P.L. 108-27). The 50-percent rate applied if the manufacture, construction, or production began after May 5, 2003 and before January 1, 2005 (Code Sec. 168(k)(4)(C)).

Property that is manufactured, constructed, or produced for a taxpayer by another person under a written binding contract that is entered into prior to the manufacture, construction, or production of the property is considered to be manufactured, constructed, or produced by the taxpayer (Reg. § 1.168(k)-1(b)(4)(iii)(A)).

> ***Example (8):*** A utility begins construction of an electric generation power plant on September 1, 2001, and completed construction on May 1, 2004. No portion of the costs qualify for bonus depreciation because construction began before September 11, 2001 (Reg. § 1.168(k)-1(b)(4)(v), *Example 4*). If the construction had begun after September 10, 2001, and before May 6, 2003, all costs would qualify for bonus depreciation at the 30% rate if the project is completed before January 1, 2005 (Reg. § 1.168(k)-1(b)(4)(v), *Example 5*).
>
> The 50-percent rate would apply if construction began after May 6, 2003.

Manufacture, production, or construction begins when physical work of a significant nature begins. This is a facts and circumstances test. Physical work does not include preliminary activities such as planning or designing, securing financing, exploring, or researching. Physical work of a significant nature will not be considered to begin before the taxpayer pays or incurs more than 10 percent of the total cost of the property (excluding the cost of any land and preliminary activities) (Reg. § 1.168(k)-1(b)(iii)(B)). The preamble to T.D. 9091 rephrases the rule by stating that physical work of a significant nature has begun when the taxpayer incurs or pays more than 10 percent of the total cost of the property (excluding land and preliminary activities). The 10-percent test is a safe harbor. In applying this safe harbor, when another party manufactures, constructs, or produces property for the taxpayer, the safe harbor test must be met by the taxpayer.

Components of self-constructed property. Under the current rules, a component of a larger self-constructed property will not qualify for bonus depreciation if (1) a binding contract to acquire the component was in effect before January 1, 2008, or (2) manufacture, construction, or production of the component began before January 1, 2008 (Reg. § 1.168(k)-1(b)(4)(iii)(C)(1); Reg. § 1.168(k)-1(b)(4)(iii)(C)(2)).

If construction of the larger self-constructed property begins before January 1, 2008, then the larger self-constructed property and any acquired or self-constructed components do not qualify for bonus depreciation (Reg. § 1.168(k)-1(b)(4)(iii)(C)(1), fourth sentence; Reg. § 1.168(k)-1(b)(4)(iii)(C)(2), fourth sentence).

The larger self-constructed property may qualify for bonus depreciation if its manufacture, construction, or production begins after December 31, 2007, and before January 1, 2010, even though a pre-January 1, 2008, binding contract is in effect for a component of the self-constructed property (Reg. § 1.168(k)-1(b)(4)(iii)(C)(1), second sentence; Reg. § 1.168(k)-1(b)(4)(iii)(C)(2), second sentence). Individual components described in the immediately preceding paragraph which are ineligible for bonus depreciation, however, are not included in the basis of the larger self-constructed property for purposes of determining the bonus deduction (Reg. § 1.168(k)-1(b)(4)(iii)(C)(1), third sentence; Reg. § 1.168(k)-1(b)(4)(iii)(C)(2), third sentence).

If the manufacture, construction, or production of the larger self-constructed property begins on or after January 1, 2008, components for the larger self-constructed property which are acquired after December 31, 2007, and before January 1, 2010, may qualify for bonus depreciation assuming that no pre-January 1, 2008, binding contract was in effect with respect to the components. Self-constructed components will also qualify if construction begins during this period (Reg. § 1.168(k)-1(b)(4)(iii)(C)(1), last sentence; Reg. § 1.168(k)-1(b)(4)(iii)(C)(2), last sentence).

Under the pre-Stimulus Act rules, a component of a larger self-constructed property did not qualify for bonus depreciation if (1) a binding contract to acquire the component was in effect before September 11, 2001, or (2) manufacture, construction, or production of the component began before September 11, 2001. The 50-percent rate did not apply if a binding contract to acquire the component was in effect after September 10, 2001, and before May 6, 2003, or manufacture, construction, or production of the component began after September 10, 2001, and before May 6, 2003 (Reg. § 1.168(k)-1(b)(4)(iii)(C)(1); Reg. § 1.168(k)-1(b)(4)(iii)(C)(2)).

If construction of the larger self-constructed property began before September 11, 2001, then the larger self-constructed property and any acquired or self-constructed components did not qualify for bonus depreciation. If construction of the larger self-constructed property began after September 10, 2001, and before May 6, 2003, the acquired or self-constructed components and the larger self-constructed property did not qualify for bonus depreciation at the 50-percent rate (Reg. § 1.168(k)-1(b)(4)(iii)(C)(1), fourth sentence; Reg. § 1.168(k)-1(b)(4)(iii)(C)(2), fourth sentence).

The larger self-constructed property may qualify for bonus depreciation if its manufacture, construction, or production began after September 10, 2001, (30-percent rate) or after May 5, 2003 (50-percent rate), and before January 1, 2005, even though a pre-September 11, 2001, binding contract is in effect for a component of the self-constructed property (Reg. § 1.168(k)-1(b)(4)(iii)(C)(1), second sentence; Reg. § 1.168(k)-1(b)(4)(iii)(C)(2), second sentence). Individual components described in the immediately preceding paragraph which are ineligible for bonus depreciation, however, are not included in the basis of the larger self-constructed property for purposes of determining the bonus deduction (Reg. § 1.168(k)-1(b)(4)(iii)(C)(1), third sentence; Reg. § 1.168(k)-1(b)(4)(iii)(C)(2), third sentence).

> ***Example (9):*** A utility begins self-construction of an electric generation power plant on November 1, 2001. On August 1, 2001, the utility had entered into a binding contract for the construction of a new turbine which is a component part of the power plant. The cost of the turbine does not qualify for bonus depreciation because the binding contract was in effect prior to September 11, 2001. However, the new plant qualifies for bonus depreciation at the 30% rate since construction began after September 10, 2001, and before May 6, 2003. The basis of the new plant for purposes of computing bonus depreciation does not include the cost of the turbine (Reg. § 1.168(k)-1(b)(4)(v), *Example 6*). If construction of the plant had begun on August 1, 2001, and the binding contract for construction of the new turbine had been entered on November, 1 2001, the cost of the turbine still does not qualify for bonus depreciation because construction of the plant began before September 11, 2001 (Reg. § 1.168(k)-1(b)(4)(v), *Example 7*).

If the manufacture, construction, or production of the larger self-constructed property begins on or after January 1, 2005, components for the larger self-constructed property which are acquired after September 10, 2001, and before January 1, 2005, may qualify for bonus depreciation assuming that no pre-September 10, 2001, binding contract was in effect with respect to the components. Self-constructed components will also qualify if construction begins during this period (Reg. § 1.168(k)-1(b)(4)(iii)(C)(1), last sentence; Reg. § 1.168(k)-1(b)(4)(iii)(C)(2), last sentence).

Acquisition of property manufactured, constructed, or produced for related party. Property manufactured, constructed, or produced by a party related to a taxpayer does not qualify for bonus depreciation if the manufacture, construction, or production of the property by the related party begins before January 1, 2008 (before September 11, 2001 under the pre-Stimulus Act rules) (Code Sec. 168(k)(2)(E)(iv)). Such property does not qualify for bonus depreciation under the pre-Stimulus Act rules at the 50-percent rate if manufacture, construction, or production of the property by the related party began after September 10, 2001, and before May 6, 2003 (Reg. § 1.168(k)-1(b)(4)(iv)).

For this purpose, persons are related if they have a relationship specified in Code Sec. 267(b) or Code Sec. 707(b) and the regulations thereunder.

> ***Example (10):*** Related begins construction of an electric generation power plant on January 1, 2001. On May 10, 2003, prior to completion, Related sells the plant to taxpayer, for $10 million. Assuming that taxpayer and Related are related parties, taxpayer may not claim bonus depreciation on the $10 million cost. If the two parties are unrelated, the taxpayer could claim bonus depreciation on the $10 million cost at the 50% rate (Code Sec. 168(k)(2)(E)(iv); Reg. § 1.168(k)-1(b)(4)(v), *Example 10*).

For further information, see below, "*Binding contracts defined*".

Qualified leasehold improvement property

Under the current rules, bonus depreciation may be claimed on qualified leasehold improvement property acquired after December 31, 2007 and placed in service before January 1, 2010 (before January 1, 2011 if the extended placed-in-service date for property with a longer production period, discussed above, applies).

Under the pre-Stimulus Act rules, the additional depreciation allowance may be claimed on qualified leasehold improvement property acquired after September 10, 2001 and placed in service before January 1, 2005 (January 1, 2006, if the placed-in-service date exception for property with a longer production period, discussed above, applies).

Qualified leasehold improvement property is any section 1250 property which is an improvement to an interior portion of a building that is nonresidential real property (as defined in Code Sec. 168(e)(2)(B)) and which is made under or pursuant to a lease (as defined in Code Sec. 168(h)(7)) by the lessee, sublessee, or lessor. The improvement must be placed in service more than three years after the date the building was first placed in service by any person. In addition, the interior of the building must be occupied exclusively by the lessee or sublessee. The lease may not be between related persons (Code Sec. 168(k)(3), as added by P.L. 107-147; Reg. § 1.168(k)-1(c)(1)).

Leasehold improvements which are section 1245 (personal property) may qualify for bonus depreciation without regard to this provision for qualifying leasehold improvements that are section 1250 property.

Expenditures for (1) the enlargement (as defined in Reg. § 1.48-12(c)(10)) of a building (as defined in Reg. § 1.48-1(e)(1)), (2) any elevator or escalator (as defined in Reg. § 1.48-1(m)(2)), (3) any structural component (as defined in Reg. § 1.48-1(e)(2)) that benefits a common area, or (4) the internal structural framework (as defined in Reg. § 1.48-12(b)(3)(i)(D)(iii)) of a building are not considered qualified leasehold improvement property (Reg. § 1.168(k)-1(c)(2) and (3)).

The term "common area" generally refers to areas used by different lessees of a building, such as stairways, hallways, lobbies, common seating areas, interior and exterior pedestrian walkways and pedestrian bridges, loading docks and areas, and rest rooms (Reg. § 1.168(k)-1(c)(3)).

A commitment to enter into a lease is treated as a lease, with the parties to the commitment treated as the lessor and lessee (Reg. § 1.168(k)-1(c)(3)(vi)).

The lease may not be between related persons. Members of an affiliated group (as defined in Code Sec. 1504) are related persons. Persons with a relationship described in Code Sec. 267(b) are related persons. However, the phrase "80 percent or more" is substituted in each place that the phrase "more than 50 percent" appears (Reg. § 1.168(k)-1(c)(3)(vi)).

Qualified leasehold improvement property placed in service after October 22, 2004 (date of enactment of the American Jobs Creation Act of 2004) and before January 1, 2010 may be depreciable under MACRS over 15-years using the straight-line method. See ¶ 126.

Computer software

The additional depreciation allowance applies to computer software which is depreciable under Code Sec. 167(f) over three years using the straight-line method (Code Sec. 168(k)(2)(A)(i)(II)). In general, computer software is depreciable under Code Sec. 167(f) if it is not amortizable under Code Sec. 197 because it is either off-the-shelf computer software as defined in Code Sec. 197(e)(3)(A)(i) or is not acquired as part of the acquisition of a trade or business (Code Sec. 197(e)(3)). It should also be noted that eligible taxpayers may expense, under Code Sec. 179, off-the-shelf computer software placed in service in a tax year beginning after 2002 and before 2011. See ¶ 302.

Pollution control facilities

The bonus depreciation allowance may be claimed on a pollution control facility even if a taxpayer elects to amortize the facility under Code Sec. 169 (Reg. § 1.168(k)-1(f)(4)). The amortizable basis of the facility is reduced by the allowed or allowable bonus deduction (Reg. § 1.169-3). It appears that a taxpayer must make an election out of bonus depreciation if the taxpayer does not want to claim bonus depreciation on a pollution control facility whether or not amortization is elected.

Binding contracts defined

Property acquired pursuant to a binding contract in effect prior to January 1, 2008 does not qualify for bonus depreciation. Property acquired pursuant to a binding contract in effect after December 31, 2007 and before January 1, 2010 may qualify for bonus depreciation if the property is placed in service before January 1, 2010 (before January 1, 2011, for certain property with a long production period) (Code Sec. 168(k)(2)(A)(iii) as amended by the Economic Stimulus Acts of 2008 (P.L. 110-185) and the Economic Recovery and Reinvestment Tax Act of 2009 (P.L. 111-5)).

Under the pre-Stimulus Act rules, property which was acquired pursuant to a written binding contract that was in effect before September 11, 2001, could not qualify for bonus depreciation. Property acquired pursuant to a written binding contract entered into after September 10, 2001, and before May 6, 2003, could qualify for the 30-percent rate if the property was placed in service before January 1, 2005 (January 1, 2006, for certain longer-production property). Property acquired pursuant to a written binding contract entered into after May 5, 2003, could qualify for the 50-percent rate if the property was placed in service before January 1, 2005 (January 1, 2006, for certain longer-production property) (Code Sec. 168(k)(2)(A)(iii) and (k)(4)).

The regulations provide fairly detailed guidance on the definition of a binding contract (Reg. § 1.168(k)-1(b)(4)(ii)). In some situations a taxpayer will want to show that a binding contract existed, while in other situations (e.g., pre-January 1, 2008, agreements) nonbinding status will want to be demonstrated.

In general, a contract is binding if it is enforceable under state law against the taxpayer (e.g., the purchaser) or a predecessor and does not limit damages to a specified amount, for example, by use of a liquidated damages provision. A contract is not treated as limiting damages to a specified amount, however, if the contract limits damages to an amount that is at least equal to five percent of the total contract price. A contract may be considered binding even if local law limits a seller's damages to the difference between the contract price of an asset and its fair market value and, as a result, there will be little or no damages (Reg. § 1.168(k)-1(b)(4)(ii)(A)).

A contract may be binding even if it is subject to a condition, provided that the condition is not within the control of either of the parties or a predecessor. The fact that insubstantial terms remain to be negotiated does not prevent a contract that otherwise imposes significant obligations on a taxpayer from being considered binding. Binding contract status is not negated by the fact that the parties may make insubstantial changes to terms or conditions or that any term is to be determined by a standard beyond the control of either party (Reg. § 1.168(k)-1(b)(4)(ii)(B)).

An option to acquire or sell property is not a binding contract (Reg. § 1.168(k)-1(b)(4)(ii)(C)).

A supply agreement is not a binding contract if the amount and design specifications of the property to be purchased have not been specified (Reg. § 1.168(k)-1(b)(4)(ii)(D); Reg. § 1.168(k)-1(b)(4)(v), *Examples 1, 2, and 3*). Agreed pricing terms are not relevant in determining whether a supply agreement is a binding contract (Preamble to T.D. 9283, filed with the Federal Register on August 28, 2006).

A binding contract to acquire one or more components of a larger property is not considered a binding contract to acquire the larger property (Reg. § 1.168(k)-1(b)(4)(ii)(E)).

Binding contracts in effect with respect to original user or related party—disqualified transaction rule. The disqualified transaction rule provides that property does not qualify for bonus depreciation if the user of the property as of the date on which the property was originally placed in service, or a related party to the user, acquired, or had a written binding contract in effect for the acquisition of the property at any time before January 1, 2008 (before September 11, 2001 under the pre-Stimulus Act rules). In addition, property manufactured, constructed, or produced for the taxpayer or a related party does not qualify for bonus depreciation if the manufacture, construction, or production of the property for the taxpayer or a related party began at any time before January 1, 2008 (before September 11, 2001 under the pre-Stimulus Act rules). Under the pre-Stimulus Act rules, if such a binding contract is first effective after May 5, 2003, the 50-percent bonus depreciation rate for property acquired after May 5, 2003, did not apply. For purposes of these rules, persons are related if they have a relationship specified in Code Sec. 267(b) or Code Sec. 707(b) (Reg. § 1.168(k)-1(b)(4)(iv)(A)).

Reg. § 1.168(k)-1(b)(4)(v) contains a number of examples illustrating the application of the disqualified transaction rule.

Property will not qualify for the bonus depreciation deduction if any of the following persons have a written binding contract in effect for the acquisition of the property at any time on or before December 31, 2007 (September 10, 2001 under the pre-Stimulus Act rules):

(1) the user of the property on the date that the property was originally placed in service;

(2) a person related to a user of the property on the date that the property was originally placed in service; or

(3) a person related to the taxpayer (Code Sec. 168(k)(2)(E)(iv)(I)).

Likewise, property will not qualify for the bonus depreciation deduction if its manufacture, construction, or production began at any time on or before December 31, 2007 (September 10, 2001 under the pre-Stimulus Act rules), and the property was manufactured, constructed, or produced for:

(1) the user;

(2) a person related to a user of the property on the date that the property was originally placed in service; or

(3) a person related to the taxpayer (Code Sec. 168(k)(2)(E)(iv)(II), as added by P.L. 108-311).

As in the case of the regulations, the related party rules of Code Sec. 267(b) and Code Sec. 707(b) are used to determine if two persons are related (Code Sec. 168(k)(2)(E)(iv)(I), as added by P.L. 108-311).

Example (11): T.J. Johnson and Partnership ABC are related parties. Johnson enters into a pre-January 1, 2008, contract to purchase production machinery. Prior to placing the property in service, Johnson sells its rights to the machine to ABC. ABC may not claim the bonus depreciation deduction because Johnson had a binding contract for the purchase of the machine in effect before January 1, 2008, and Johnson is related to DEF.

Example (12): Assume that Corp. ABC and Corp DEF are related parties. Corp. ABC began construction on production machinery on December 1, 2007. If Corp. ABC sells rights to the property to DEF prior to using the property and placing it in service, DEF may not claim the bonus depreciation deduction because construction began before January 1, 2008, and ABC and DEF are related parties.

Example (13): ABC Corp. has a binding contract to purchase production equipment that is in effect before January 1, 2008. ABC sells the property to DEF and leases the property back within 3 months of placing the property in service. DEF may not claim the bonus depreciation deduction pursuant to the sale-leaseback rule (Code Sec. 168(k)(2)(D)(ii)) because ABC, the user of the property, had a binding contract for its acquisition in effect prior to January 1, 2008.

New York Liberty Zone. Property placed in service in the New York Liberty Zone before January 1, 2007 could qualify for a 30 percent bonus depreciation allowance under Code Sec. 1400L(b) if the property did not qualify for bonus depreciation under the more general provision of Code Sec. 168(k). Code Sec. 1400L(b)(2)(D) provides that rules similar to those contained in Code Sec. 168(k)(2)(E) apply to Liberty Zone property. By virtue of this cross reference, the related party rule discussed above also applied to Liberty Zone property. Regulations under Code Sec. 1400L also incorporate the Code Sec. 168(k) disqualified transaction regulations by cross reference (Reg. § 1.1400L(b)-1(c)(5)). See ¶ 127E for a discussion of the New York Liberty Zone bonus allowance.

Sale-leasebacks and syndication transactions

A limited exception to the original use requirement applies to sale-leasebacks. The rule applies to new property that is originally placed in service after December 31, 2007 (after September 10, 2001, under the pre-Stimulus Act rules), by a person who sells it to the taxpayer and then leases it from the taxpayer within three months after the date that the property was originally placed in service. In this situation, the property is treated as originally placed in service by the taxpayer-lessor and the placed-in-service date is deemed to occur no earlier than the date that the property is used by the lessee under the leaseback (Code Sec. 168(k)(2)(E)(ii); Reg. § 1.168(k)-1(b)(3)(iii)(A); Reg. § 1.168(k)-1(b)(5)(ii)(A); Reg. § 1.168(k)-1(b)(4)(v), *Example 11*).

If the property was originally placed in service after May 5, 2003 and before January 1, 2005, then the 50-percent bonus depreciation rate applied under this rule (Code Sec. 168(k)(4)(C), as added by P.L. 108-27; Reg. § 1.168(k)-1(b)(3)(iii)(A); Reg. § 1.168(k)-1(b)(5)(ii)(A)).

Syndication transactions. A similar rule applies to syndication transactions (Code Sec. 168(k)(2)(E)(iii); Reg. § 1.168(k)-1(b)(3)(iii)(B); Reg. § 1.168(k)-1(b)(5)(ii)(B)).

Under the pre-Stimulus Act rules, if:

(1) a lessor of property originally places new property in service after September 10, 2001 (or is considered to have originally placed it in service after September 10, 2001 by operation of the sale-leaseback rule described above);

(2) the property is sold by the lessor (or any subsequent purchaser) within three months after the lessor originally places the property in service *(or, in the case of multiple units of property subject to the same lease, within three months after the date the final unit is placed in service, so long as the period*

between the time the first unit is placed in service and the time the last unit is placed in service does not exceed 12 months); and

(3) the user of the property after the last sale during the three-month period remains the same as when the property was originally placed in service by the lessor;

then the property is treated as originally placed in service not earlier than the date of the last sale within the three-month period and the purchaser of the property in the last sale during the three-month period is considered the original user of the property (Reg. § 1.168(k)-1(b)(3)(iii)(B); Reg. § 1.168(k)-1(b)(5)(ii)(B)).

A similar rule applies under the Stimulus Act rules except that December 31, 2007 replaces September 10, 2001 in item (1), above.

If a sale-leaseback transaction described above is followed by a syndication transaction that satisfies the requirements in the immediately preceding paragraph, then the original user and placed-in-service date is determined in accordance with the rule for syndication transactions (Reg. § 1.168(k)-1(b)(3)(iii)(C); Reg. § 1.168(k)-1(b)(5)(ii)(C)).

Example (14): ABC Manufacturing Corporation purchases a new cargo container on January 1, 2009. It sells the cargo container to SYND corporation and leases it back from SYND on March 1, 2009. If there are no further transactions, SYND is considered to have originally placed the container in service on March 1, 2009, and may claim bonus depreciation. However, if SYND resells the container to an investor within three months after March 1, 2009, and ABC continues to use the container, the investor is considered to have originally placed the container in service on the date of purchase from SYND and may claim the bonus depreciation deduction.

Example (15): Assume the same facts above, except that the first investor sells the container to a second investor within three months after March 1, 2009. Assuming that ABC continues to use the container, the second investor is entitled to claim the bonus depreciation deduction.

Bonus depreciation is available to investors if a syndicator is the original purchaser of the equipment, leases the equipment, and then sells the equipment subject to the lease to investors.

Example (16): SYND corporation purchases a new cargo vessel on January 1, 2009, from a ship manufacturer and leases it on the same date to GHI corporation. If SYND sells the vessel to one or more investors before April 1, 2009, and GHI is still the lessee, the investors may claim the bonus depreciation deduction. However, if any investor resells its interest in the vessel before April 1, 2009, and GHI continues to lease the vessel, then the subsequent purchaser is entitled to the bonus depreciation deduction.

Special rule for multiple unit leases in syndicated transactions. Code Sec. 168(k)(2)(E)(iii) was amended by including the italicized language relating to multiple unit leases in requirement (2), above (Reg. § 1.168(k)-1(b)(3)(iii)(B)).

Example (17): SYN Inc. is the syndicator of a leasing transaction involving 100 cargo containers which are to be leased to ABC. The first container is purchased by SYN and leased to ABC on November 1, 2008. The last container is purchased within the required one-year period and leased to ABC on June 10, 2009. A person who purchases interests in the containers from SYN (or a subsequent purchaser from SYN) within 3 months after June 10, 2009, is treated as having originally placed the containers in service on the date of purchase and may be able to claim the bonus depreciation deduction.

The multiple unit provision only applies to property sold after June 4, 2004. Accordingly, interests in property purchased from a lessor on or before June 4,

2004, did not qualify for bonus depreciation under this provision under the pre-Stimulus rules (Reg. § 1.168(k)-1(g)(5)).

Fractional interests. If in the ordinary course of its business a person sells fractional interests in 30-percent or 50-percent bonus depreciation property to unrelated third parties, each first fractional owner (i.e., each first unrelated third party purchaser) of the property is considered as the original user of its proportionate share of the property. Furthermore, if the person engaged in the business of selling fractional interests uses the property before all of the fractional interests are sold and the property continues to be held primarily for sale, the original use of any fractional interest sold to an unrelated third party subsequent to the fractional interest seller's use, begins with the first unrelated purchaser of that interest (Reg. § 1.168(k)-1(b)(3)(iv)).

> ***Example (18):*** Fractional Seller Inc. holds out for sale 10 equal fractional interests in an aircraft. It sells five of the shares to A on January 1, 2003, and the remaining five shares to B on January 1, 2004. A and B are unrelated to Fractional Seller Inc. A may claim bonus depreciation at the 30% rate and B may claim bonus depreciation at the 50% rate under the pre-Stimulus rules (Reg. § 1.168(k)-1(b)(3)(v), *Example 4*).

Technical termination of partnership

If a partnership is technically terminated under Code Sec. 708(b)(1)(B) (sale or exchange of 50 percent of more of partnership interests in 12-months), bonus depreciation property placed in service during the tax year of termination by the terminated partnership is treated as originally placed in service by the new partnership on the date that the property is contributed by the terminated partnership to the new partnership (Reg. § 1.168(k)-1(b)(5)(iii)).

The new partnership claims the bonus deduction for the qualified bonus depreciation property placed in service during the tax year of the termination by the terminating partnership. The new partnership claims the deduction in the new partnership's tax year in which the property was contributed. However, if the new partnership disposes of the property in the same tax year that it received the property, no bonus depreciation deduction is allowed to the terminating or new partnership (Reg. § 1.168(k)-1(f)(1)(ii)).

> ***Example (19):*** Partnership AB purchases qualifying bonus depreciation property on February 1, 2009. The partnership is technically terminated as a result of the sale of partnership interests on March 1, 2009. New partnership AB may claim bonus depreciation (Reg. § 1.168(k)-1(f)(1)(iv), *Example 1*).
>
> The applicable rate (30 or 50 percent) under the pre-Stimulus Act rules is presumably determined by reference to the date of acquisition by the terminated partnership.

If a technical termination occurred in a tax year that ended on or before September 8, 2003, the IRS will allow any reasonable method of determining the additional first year depreciation deduction that is consistently applied by all parties to the transaction (Reg. § 1.168(k)-1(g)(2)).

Code Sec. 754 election

If bonus depreciation property is placed in service by a partnership in a tax year that it terminates under Code Sec. 708(b)(1)(B), any increase in basis of the property due to a Code Sec. 754 election is eligible for bonus depreciation (Reg. § 1.168(k)-1(f)(9)). This is the only situation in which a basis increase attributable to a section 754 election is eligible for bonus depreciation (Preamble to T.D. 9282, filed with the Federal Register on August 29, 2006).

Certain step-in-the-shoes transactions.

There is a special placed in service rule for Code Sec. 168(i)(7) step-in-the shoes transactions. Eligible property that is transferred in a Code Sec. 168(i)(7) transaction in the same tax year it is placed in service by the transferor is treated as originally placed in service on the date placed in service by the transferor. A Code Sec. 168(i)(7) transaction is a complete subsidiary liquidation (Code Sec. 332), transfer to a controlled corporation (Code Sec. 351), a nonrecognition reorganization (Code Sec. 361), a contribution to a partnership (Code Sec. 721), or a distribution by a partnership to a partner (Code Sec. 731) (Reg. § 1.168(k)-1(b)(5)(iv)).

The bonus deduction is allocated between the transferor and the transferee based on the number of months that each party held the property in service during the transferor's tax year in accordance with the rules described in Reg. § 1.168(d)-1(b)(7)(ii). Under these rules, the transferor is treated as holding the property during the month of acquisition while the transferee takes the month of the transfer into account. No bonus deduction is allowed to either the transferor or the transferee if the property is disposed of by the transferee (other than in another Code Sec. 168(i)(7) transaction) in the same tax year that the transferee received the property from the transferor (Reg. § 1.168(k)-1(f)(1)(iii)).

Example (20): Partnership AB, a calendar-year partnership, purchased and placed qualifying bonus depreciation property in service on February 1, 2009, for $6,000. It transfers the property to Partnership CD in a Code Sec. 721 transaction on June 10, 2009. The $3,000 bonus deduction ($6,000 × 50%) is allocated between the two partnerships on the basis of the number of months in AB's tax year that each partnership is deemed to have held the property in service. AB is considered to have held the property for 4 months (February, March, April, and May). CD is considered to have held the property for 7 months (June through December). As a result AB may deduct $1,091 ($3,000 × 4/11) and CD may deduct $1,909 ($3,000 × 7/11) (Reg. § 1.168(k)-1(f)(1)(iv), *Example 2*).

If a section 168(i)(7) transaction occurred in a tax year that ended on or before September 8, 2003, the IRS will allow any reasonable method of determining the additional first year depreciation deduction that is consistently applied by all parties to the transaction (Reg. § 1.168(k)-1(g)(2)).

Computation of bonus deduction when basis increases or decreases after property placed in service

The basis of property which qualifies for bonus depreciation may be subject to and upward or downward adjustment after the property has been placed in service. Such an adjustment could be caused, for example, by a contingent purchase price or a discharge of indebtedness.

If the basis of the property is redetermined on or before the last date that the property could have been placed in service and still qualify for the bonus deduction, then the bonus depreciation deduction must be redetermined. Under the current rules the last placed-in-service date is December 31, 2009 unless the extended December 31, 2010 deadline applies. Under the pre-Stimulus rules, the last placed-in-service date is December 31, 2004 (December 31, 2005, for certain property with a long production period and certain noncommercial aircraft) for bonus depreciation under Code Sec. 168(k) and December 31, 2005, for New York Liberty Zone property for which bonus depreciation is claimed under Code Sec. 1400L (see ¶ 127E). If the basis adjustment occurs after these dates, the bonus deduction is not redetermined (Reg. § 1.168(k)-1(f)(2)).

The regulations also explain how to compute the regular MACRS deductions on the increased or decreased basis.

Increase in basis. If there is an increase in basis, the taxpayer claims a bonus deduction on the increased basis in the tax year that the increase occurs. The taxpayer uses the same rate that applied to the underlying property (Reg. § 1.168(k)-1(f)(2)(i)).

The amount allowable as a depreciation deduction for the increase in basis is determined by first reducing the increase in basis by the bonus deduction allowed on the increased basis. The remaining increase in basis is depreciated over the recovery period that remains as of the beginning of the tax year in which the increase in basis occurred. The same depreciation method and convention that applies to the underlying property is used (Reg. § 1.168(k)-1(f)(2)(i)(A)). There is a different rule for computer software. An increase in the basis of computer software is depreciated ratably over the remainder of the 36-month period as of the beginning of the first day of the month in which the increase in basis occurs (Reg. § 1.168(k)-1(f)(2)(i)(B)). See Reg. § 1.168(k)-1(f)(2)(iv), *Example 1*, for an example illustrating computations when basis is increased.

Decrease in basis. If the basis of bonus depreciation property decreases in a tax year after it is placed in service, the taxpayer must include in income the excess amount of additional first year depreciation previously claimed. The excess amount is the decrease in basis times 30 percent or 50 percent (as appropriate). The taxpayer uses the same rate that applied to the underlying property. If the taxpayer did not previously claim the allowable amount of additional first year depreciation, the excess amount can be based on the amount actually claimed by the taxpayer. The actual amount can be used only if the taxpayer establishes the amount by adequate records or other sufficient evidence (Reg. § 1.168(k)-1(f)(2)(ii)).

To determine the amount includible in income for excess depreciation claimed (other than additional the first year allowance), the decrease in basis is first adjusted by the excess additional first year allowance. Then, the remaining amount of decrease in basis is included in income over the recovery period for that property remaining as of the beginning of the tax year that the decrease in basis occurs. The same depreciation method and convention that applies to the underlying property is used (Reg. § 1.168(k)-1(f)(2)(ii)(A)). There is a different rule for computer software. The computer software amount is included in income over the remainder of the 36-month period as of the beginning of the first day of the month in which the decrease in basis occurs (Reg. § 1.168(k)-1(f)(2)(ii)(B)).

See Reg. § 1.168(k)-1(f)(2)(iv), *Example 2*, for an example illustrating computations when basis is decreased.

Property converted from personal use to business use or from business use to personal use

The bonus deduction is not allowed if a taxpayer converts business or production of income property to personal use in the same tax year that it is placed in service for business use (Reg. § 1.168(k)-1(f)(6)(ii)). Property may qualify for bonus deprecation, however, if it is converted from personal use to business or production of income use in the same tax year that it was acquired or in a later tax year) (Reg. § 1.168(k)-1(f)(6)(iii)).

Property which is converted from personal use to business use by the same taxpayer will satisfy the original use requirement, assuming that the personal use was the first use of the property (i.e., the property was new when acquired by the taxpayer for personal use) (Reg. § 1.168(k)-1(b)(3)(ii)). The acquisition date for purposes of determining whether the 30-percent or 50-percent rate applies is determined by reference to the date the property was acquired for personal use. To qualify the personal use property must be converted to business use before January 1, 2010 (January 1, 2005 under the pre-Stimulus Act rules) (Reg. § 1.168(k)-1(f)(6)(iii)).

The basis for computing the bonus deduction on personal property converted to business use is the lesser of the fair market value at the time of conversion or the adjusted basis at the time of conversion (Reg. § 1.167(g)(1)) reduced by any amount expensed under Code Sec. 179.

Change in depreciable use after placed in service year

The use of a property may change and as a consequence, depreciation on the property may have to be computed using ADS or the use of ADS may be discontinued. For example, property used by a taxpayer in the United States may be moved abroad or vice versa, requiring the use or discontinuance of ADS.

The bonus depreciation regulations provide that if a property does not qualify for bonus depreciation in the year that it is placed in service (for example, because it is used abroad and ADS applies) bonus depreciation is not allowed in a subsequent year if a change in use occurs. Conversely, if a property qualified for bonus depreciation in the year it was placed in service but would not qualify in a later tax year because of a change in use, the bonus deduction is not recaptured (Reg. § 1.168(k)-1(g)(6)(iv)). This rule applies to any change in use described in Code Sec. 168(i)(5) and the regulations thereunder. The IRS has issued change in use regulations (Reg.§ 1.168(i)-(4) at ¶ 568).

Coordination with Code Sec. 47 rehabilitation credit

A taxpayer may claim bonus depreciation on qualified rehabilitation expenditures (as defined in Code Sec. 47(c)(2)) that qualify for bonus deduction. However, assuming no election out of bonus depreciation is made, the rehabilitation credit may only be claimed on the cost (or other applicable basis) of the rehabilitation expenditures less the amount claimed or allowable as bonus depreciation. The credit however only applies if the taxpayer depreciates the remaining basis of the rehabilitation expenditures using an MACRS straight-line method (Reg. § 1.168(k)-1(f)(10)).

Coordination with Code Sec. 514 relating to debt-financed property

The bonus depreciation deduction may not be claimed under Code Sec. 514(a)(3) on depreciable debt-financed property for purposes of determining the amount of unrelated business taxable income (Reg. § 1.168(k)-1(f)(11)).

Election to claim 30-percent bonus depreciation in place of 50-percent bonus depreciation

Under the pre-Stimulus Act rules a taxpayer could elect to claim bonus depreciation at the 30-percent rate on one or more classes of property placed in service during a tax year that would otherwise have qualified for the 50-percent rate. The election was made on a property-class by property-class basis (Code Sec. 168(k)(4)(E); Reg. § 1.168(k)-1(e)(1)(ii)). See, "*Election out of bonus depreciation,*" immediately below for further details.

If this election was made for 5-year property, the first-year "luxury car" depreciation cap is the cap that applies for cars for which the 50-percent rate is claimed (¶ 200).

Under the current rules there is no election to claim 30 percent bonus depreciation in place of the 50 percent rate.

Election out of bonus depreciation

Bonus depreciation must be claimed unless a taxpayer makes an election out. Once made, an election out cannot be revoked without IRS consent.

Taxpayers must make the election in the manner described in the instructions for Form 4562, *Depreciation and Amortization* (Reg. § 1.168(k)-1(e)(3)(ii)).

An election out (which includes an election to claim 30-percent bonus depreciation in place of 50-percent bonus depreciation under the pre-Stimulus Act rules) must be made by the due date (including extensions) of the return for the tax year in which the bonus depreciation property is placed in service (Reg. § 1.168(k)-1(e)(3)(i)). A taxpayer who files a timely return without making an election out can make the election by filing an amended return within 6 months of the due date of the return (excluding extensions). Write "Filed pursuant to section 301.9100-2" on the amended return (2008 Form 4562 instructions). A taxpayer who made an election out may also revoke that election without IRS consent by filing an amended return within six months (excluding extensions) of the due date of the return on which the election out was made if the taxpayer's original return was timely filed. If this rule does not apply, revocation is available only with IRS consent obtained by filing a letter ruling request (Reg. § 1.168(k)-1(e)(7)).

Under the pre-Stimulus Act rules, a taxpayer with 50 percent bonus depreciation property only needed to make one election to elect not to deduct both the 30-percent and the 50-percent additional first year depreciation for 50-percent bonus depreciation property.

If a taxpayer fails to make an election out, depreciation deductions on the qualifying property must be computed as if the bonus deduction had been claimed on the return, whether or not the bonus allowance was in fact claimed. A taxpayer cannot make an election out by filing a request to change accounting method (Reg. § 1.168(k)-1(e)(5)).

Special rules applied to a 2000 or 2001 return that includes September 11, 2001 (Rev. Proc. 2002-33; Reg. § 1.168(k)-1(e)(4)). These rules included a deemed election out for taxpayers who failed to make a formal election out. See below.

The election not to deduct the additional first-year depreciation for any class of property placed in service during the tax year is made separately by each person owning qualified property (for example, for each member of a consolidated group by the parent of the consolidated group, by the partnership, or by the S corporation) (Reg. § 1.168(k)-1(e)(3)(ii)).

The election out is made at the property class level. The election applies to all property in the class or classes for which the election out is made that is placed in service for the tax year of the election (Code Sec. 168(k)(2)(C)(iii), as added by P.L. 107-147; Reg. § 1.168(k)-1(e)(1)).

Property class refers to the 3-, 5-, 7-, 10-, 15-, 20-year asset classifications described in Code Sec. 168(e). However, water utility property as defined in Code Sec. 168(e)(5), computer software as defined in Code Sec. 167(f)(1), and qualified leasehold improvement property as defined in Code Sec. 168(k)(3) are treated as separate property classes (Reg. § 1.168(k)-1(e)(2)). Thus, for example, a taxpayer may make the election out for all 3-year property placed in service in the tax year. The election out cannot be made for some, but not all, 3-year property placed in service during the tax year. Similarly, the election out may be made for all qualifying software placed in service during a tax year or for all water utility property placed in service during a tax year.

The Jobs and Growth Tax Relief Reconciliation Act of 2003 (P.L. 108-27), which increased the bonus depreciation rate from 30 percent to 50 percent, contains a special rule that applies if a taxpayer places property in service during the tax year and some of the property qualified for the 30-percent rate while other property qualified for the 50-percent rate. In this situation, the election out of bonus depreciation was made separately for each class of property that qualifies for the 30-percent rate and for each class of property that qualifies for the 50-percent rate (Code Sec. 168(k)(2)(D)(iii); Reg. § 1.168(k)-1(e)(1)).

Example (21): A calendar-year taxpayer places 10 machines in service in 2003 before May 6, 2003, and 5 cars in service in 2003 after May 5, 2003. The machines and cars are five-year property (same MACRS property class). The taxpayer may (1) claim bonus depreciation on the machines (30% rate applies) and bonus depreciation on the cars (a 50% rate applies unless a 30% rate is elected); (2) elect not to claim bonus depreciation on the machines and elect not to claim bonus depreciation on the cars; (3) claim bonus depreciation on the cars (at the 50% rate unless a 30% rate is elected) and elect not to claim bonus depreciation on the machines; or (4) claim bonus depreciation on the machines (30% rate applies) and elect not to claim bonus depreciation on the cars.

Generally, no AMT adjustment is required on property on which bonus depreciation is claimed. Consequently the election out may trigger an AMT adjustment if the property would otherwise be subject to an adjustment (Reg. § 1.168(k)-1(e)(6)). The adjustment is generally required if an election out is made with respect to 3-, 5-, 7-, or 10-year property which is depreciated using the 200-percent declining-balance method. See ¶ 170 for a discussion of the AMT adjustment on MACRS property. The IRS has allowed a taxpayer to revoke a bonus depreciation election out in reliance on a CPA's advice where the election caused an AMT liability (IRS Letter Ruling 200626038, March 3, 2006).

Election to claim accelerated alternative minimum tax credit and research credit in lieu of bonus depreciation

A corporation may elect for its first tax year ending after March 31, 2008 to claim a portion of its unused alternative minimum tax and research credits that are attributable to tax years beginning before January 1, 2006 instead of taking the 50 percent Code Sec. 168(k) bonus depreciation deduction on any "eligible qualified property" (Code Sec. 168(k)(4), as added by the Housing Assistance Tax Act of 2008 (P.L. 110-289) and amended by the American Recovery and Reinvestment Tax Act of 2009 (P.L. 111-5); Joint Committee on Taxation, Technical Explanation of the Housing Assistance Tax Act of 2008, JCX-63-08, July 23, 2008; Rev. Proc. 2009-33, I.R.B. 2009-29, Rev. Proc. 2009-16, I.R.B. 2009-6, as modified by Rev. Proc. 2009-33, and Rev. Proc. 2008-65, I.R.B. 2008-44, as modified by Rev. Proc. 2009-33).

Eligible qualified property (defined more fully below) is generally property that is acquired after March 31, 2008, is not subject to a pre-April 1, 2008 binding acquisition contract, and is eligible for the Code Sec. 168(k) bonus depreciation allowance (Code Sec. 168(k)(4)(D), as added by P.L. 110-289 and amended by the Economic Recovery and Reinvestment Tax Act of 2009 (P.L. 111-5); Rev. Proc. 2009-33, I.R.B. 2009-29, Section 3.01). An electing corporation must use the straight-line method to depreciate any eligible qualified property on which bonus depreciation may not be claimed because of making the election (Code Sec. 168(k)(4)(A)(ii)), as added by P.L. 110-289). The Code only requires the use of the straight-line method. Thus, it appears that a corporation could elect to use the MACRS alternative depreciation system (ADS) since ADS uses the straight-line method. If no ADS election is made with respect to a property class, the property is depreciated using the straight-line method over the regular recovery period.

A corporation that made the election for its first tax year ending after March 31, 2008 may also make a separate election (supplemental election) not to have the Code Sec. 168(k)(4) election apply to "extension property" (Code Sec. 168(k)(4)(H)(i)(I), as added by P.L. 111-5). Extension property is generally defined as property which is eligible qualified property solely by reason of the one-year extension of the bonus depreciation provision by the Economic Recovery and Reinvestment Tax Act of 2009 (P.L. 111-5) (Code Sec. 168(k)(4)(H)(iii), as added by P.L. 111-5). Thus, extension property generally consists of property acquired after March 31, 2008 and placed in service after December 31, 2008 and before January 1, 2010 (before January 1, 2011 in the case of property with a longer production period and certain noncommercial aircraft) (Code Sec. 168(k)(4)(H)(ii), as added by P.L. 111-5; Rev. Proc. 2009-33, I.R.B. 2009-29, Section 3.01).

A corporation that did not make the election for its first tax year ending after March 31, 2008, may elect to apply the provision in its first tax year ending after December 31, 2008, and each subsequent tax year (Code Sec. 168(k)(4)(H)(i), as added by P.L. 111-5). The election will only apply to eligible qualified property that is extension property (Code Sec. 168(k)(4)(H)(ii), as added by P.L. 111-5).

The amount of the unused research and AMT credits attributable to tax years beginning before 2006 that may be claimed as an accelerated credit is limited to the "bonus depreciation amount" computed for the tax year. For any tax year, the bonus depreciation amount is 20 percent of the difference between (1) the aggregate bonus depreciation and regular depreciation that would be allowed on eligible qualified property placed in service during the tax year if bonus depreciation was claimed and (2) the aggregate depreciation that would be allowed on the eligible qualified property placed in service during the tax year if no bonus depreciation was claimed (Code Sec. 168(k)(4)(C)(i), as added by P.L. 110-289). However, the bonus depreciation amount may not exceed the "maximum increase amount." The maximum increase amount is the lesser of (1) 6 percent of the sum of the corporation's unused alternative minimum tax and research credits that are attributable to tax years beginning before January 1, 2006 or (2) $30 million (Code Sec. 168(k)(4)(C)(iii), as added by P.L. 110-289). This computation of the bonus depreciation amount and limitations are discussed more fully below.

If a corporation that made an election for its first tax year ending after March 31, 2008 does not make the supplemental election not to have the provision apply to extension property, then a separate bonus depreciation amount, maximum amount, and maximum increase amount is computed and applied to eligible qualified property which is extension property and to eligible qualified property which is not extension property (Code Sec. 168(k)(4)(H)(i)(II), as added by P.L. 111-5).

The amount of an accelerated credit is refundable (Code Sec. 168(k)(4)(F), as added by P.L. 110-289). Thus, a corporation may receive a payment for the credit amount even though it has no tax liability for the tax year the accelerated credit is claimed.

The election (including any allocation of the bonus depreciation amount between pre-2006 research and AMT credits) is revocable only with IRS consent (Code Sec. 168(k)(4)(G), as added by P.L. 110-289; Rev. Proc. 2008-65, Section 4.06).

Eligible qualified property defined. Eligible qualified property is defined the same as "qualified property" is in Code Sec. 168(k)(2) except that "March 31, 2008" is substituted for "December 31, 2007" wherever it appears in Code Sec.

168(k)(2)(A) and Code Sec. 168(k)(2)(E)(i) and (ii) and "April 1, 2008" is substituted for "January 1, 2008" in Code Sec. 168(k)(2)(A)(iii)(I)) (Code Sec. 168(k)(4)(D), as added by P.L. 110-289 and amended by P.L. 111-5).

Thus, in general, eligible qualified property is property that is eligible for bonus depreciation under Code Sec. 168(k) except that it must be acquired after March 31, 2008 (rather than after December 31, 2007) and placed in service before January 1, 2010 (before January 1, 2011 in the case of property with a long production period and certain noncommercial aircraft), and no binding acquisition contract may be in effect before April 1, 2008 (rather than before January 1, 2008). Original use of the property must commence with the taxpayer after March 31, 2008 (rather than after December 31, 2007); Code Sec. 168(k)(4)(D)(i); Rev. Proc. 2008-65, Section 3.02, as modified by Rev. Proc. 2009-33, Section 7.01).

In the case of a taxpayer manufacturing, constructing, or producing property for the taxpayer's own use, the property may qualify as eligible qualified property only if the taxpayer began manufacturing, constructing, or producing the property after March 31, 2008 and before January 1, 2010 (Code Sec. 168(k)(2)(E)(i); Code Sec. 168(k)(4)(D)(i); Rev. Proc. 2008-65, Section 3.02(3)).

In the case of eligible qualified property with a long production period, only adjusted basis attributable to manufacture, construction, or production after March 31, 2008 and before January 1, 2010 is taken into account in computing the bonus depreciation amount for purposes of this provision (Code Sec. 168(k)(4)(D)(iii)).

If new property is originally placed in service by a person after March 31, 2008, and is sold to a taxpayer and leased back to the person by the taxpayer within three months after the date the property was originally placed in service by the person, the taxpayer-lessor is considered the original user of the property and, for purposes of the January 1, 2010 and January 1, 2011 deadlines (Code Sec. 168(k)(2)(A)(iv)), the property is treated as originally placed in service by the taxpayer-lessor not earlier than the date on which the property is used by the lessee under the leaseback (Rev. Proc. 2008-65, Section 3.02(4)).

Eligible qualified property does not include property that is subject to the regular election under Code Sec. 168(k)(2)(D)(iii) not to claim bonus depreciation (Rev. Proc. 2008-65, Section 4.04).

See Rev. Proc. 2009-33, I.R.B. 2009-29, Section 3.01 and Rev. Proc. 2008-65, I.R.B. 2008-65, Section 3 for the definition of eligible qualified property. Note that certain dates in the definition of eligible qualified property contained in Section 3 of Rev. Proc. 2008-65 do not reflect the one-year extension of the bonus depreciation provision since that procedure was issued prior to enactment of the extension.

Example (22): QPEX Corporation has a calendar tax year. It acquires bonus depreciation property on February 1, 2008 and places it in service on December 31, 2008. This property is not eligible qualified property because it was not acquired after March 31, 2008. QPEX may claim bonus depreciation on this property even if it makes the accelerated credit election.

Example (23): APEX Corporation has a fiscal year that ends on April 30, 2008 and makes the accelerated credit election for its first tax year ending after March 31, 2008 (i.e., it fiscal tax year ending on April 30, 2008). APEX may not claim bonus depreciation on property acquired after March 31, 2008 and placed in service before January 1, 2010 (before January 1, 2011 for certain property with a longer production period and certain noncommercial aircraft). This property is eligible qualified property. Furthermore, APEX must use the MACRS straight-line method to compute depreciation on this eligible qualified property for regular and alternative minimum tax purposes. Note, however, that APEX may make a supplemental election to exclude "extension property" that is eligible qualified property (i.e., generally, bonus deprecation property placed in service in 2009) from the accelerated credit election.

Example (24): APEX Corporation has a 2007-2008 fiscal year that ends on April 30, 2008 and makes the accelerated credit election for its first tax year ending after March 31, 2008. APEX may claim bonus depreciation on bonus depreciation property acquired on or after January 1, 2008 and on or before March 31, 2008 if it places the property in service before January 1, 2010 (before January 1, 2011 in the case of long-production property and certain noncommercial aircraft). Bonus depreciation is claimed in the tax year in which the property is placed in service. It may not claim bonus depreciation on bonus depreciation property acquired after March 31, 2008 and placed in service on or before April 30, 2008 in its 2007-2008 fiscal year. It also may not claim bonus depreciation on bonus depreciation property acquired after March 31, 2008 and placed in service before January 1, 2009 in its 2008-2009 fiscal year. Any bonus depreciation property placed in service after December 31, 2008 and which qualifies for bonus depreciation solely on account of the one-year extension of the bonus depreciation provision by the Economic Recovery and Reinvestment Tax Act of 2009 (P.L. 111-5) is also subject to the election (i.e., no bonus depreciation may be claimed) *unless* APEX makes the election to exclude eligible qualified property that is extension property (i.e., makes the supplemental election described above not to apply the provision to *extension property*). In general, eligible qualified property is extension property if the property is acquired after March 31, 2008 and placed in service after December 31, 2008 and before January 1, 2010 (before January 1, 2011 in the case of property with a longer production period and certain noncommercial aircraft). Having made the accelerated credit election, APEX must use the straight-line method to compute depreciation on its eligible qualified property (i.e., the property which is excluded from bonus depreciation by reason of the election) for both regular and alternative minimum tax purposes.

Written binding contract. Property acquired pursuant to a written binding contract entered into on or before March 31, 2008 is not eligible qualified property (Joint Committee on Taxation, Technical Explanation of the Housing Assistance Tax Act of 2008, JCX-63-08, July 23, 2008). This rule is provided in a retroactive technical correction (Code Sec. 168(k)(4)(D)(ii), as added by P.L. 111-5). An exception described below applies to passenger aircraft.

Example 25: APEX, a calendar tax year corporation, acquires and places property in service in June 2008. The property was acquired pursuant to a binding contract entered into on February 15, 2008. APEX makes the accelerated credit election for its first tax year ending after March 31, 2008. The property is not eligible qualified property because it was subject to a binding contract in effect on or prior to March 31, 2008. APEX may claim bonus depreciation on the property. If the binding contract had been in effect before January 1, 2008 the property is not eligible for bonus depreciation whether or not APEX makes the accelerated credit election. Property subject to a binding contract entered into before January 1, 2008 is not eligible for bonus depreciation.

Special rule for passenger aircraft. The requirement that a binding contract may not be in effect prior to April 1, 2008 (Code Sec. 168(k)(2)(A)(iii)(I) as modified by Code Sec. 168(k)(4)(D)(ii)) does not apply to a passenger aircraft for purposes of determining whether the aircraft is eligible qualified property or for purposes of determining the bonus depreciation amount (Code Sec. 168(k)(4)(G)(iii), as added by P.L. 110-289; Joint Committee on Taxation, Technical Explanation of the Housing Assistance Tax Act of 2008, JCX-63-08, July 23, 2008; Rev. Proc. 2008-65, Section 3.03 and Section 5.02(4)). Thus, a passenger aircraft may be eligible qualified property if:

(1) it is acquired after March 31, 2008 and before January 1, 2010 and is placed in service before January 1, 2010 (before January 1, 2011 if the requirements described for transportation property or noncommercial aircraft are satisfied) or

(2) it is acquired pursuant to a written binding contract entered into after March 31, 2008 and before January 1, 2010 and it is placed in service before January 1, 2010 (before January 1, 2011 if the requirements described for transportation property or noncommercial aircraft are satisfied).

Thus, a passenger aircraft that is subject to a pre-April 1, 2008 contract or apparently even a pre-January 1, 2008 contract can be considered eligible qualified property for purposes of the Code Sec. 168(k)(4) election assuming all other requirements listed in Code Sec. 168(k)(2) for qualifying for the regular bonus depreciation deduction are satisfied. Further, the aircraft is taken into account in computing the bonus depreciation amount for the tax year that it is placed in service.

Note that a passenger aircraft may be able to qualify as property with a long production period (i.e. "transportation property") under Code Sec. 168(k)(2)(B) or as a noncommercial aircraft described in Code Sec. 168(k)(2)(C). Such an aircraft only needs to be placed in service before January 1, 2011 rather than before January 1, 2010 in order to qualify for bonus depreciation. However, only pre-January 1, 2010 progress expenditures qualify for bonus depreciation if the aircraft is considered property with a long production period (Code Sec. 168(k)(2)(B)(ii)). This limitation does not apply to noncommercial aircraft described in Code Sec. 168(k)(2)(C). Only bonus depreciation attributable to post March 31, 2008 and pre-January 1, 2010 progress expenditures may be taken into account in computing the bonus depreciation amount if a passenger aircraft is considered long production property (Code Sec. 168(k)(4)(D)(iii), as added by P.L. 110-289 and amended by P.L. 111-5; Sec. 5.02(5) of Rev. Proc. 2008-65 , as modified by Section 7.02 of Rev. Proc. 2009-33 by replacing January 1, 2009 with January 1, 2010 to reflect the one year extension of bonus depreciation provision by P.L. 111-5 after issuance of Rev. Proc. 2008-65). The Code does not provide a definition of the term passenger aircraft. Thus, a passenger aircraft may qualify as either long production property or a Code Sec. 168(k)(2)(C) noncommercial aircraft (or neither) depending upon the specific circumstances.

Definition of eligible qualified property that is not extension property. Eligible qualified property is not extension property if (1) it is acquired by the taxpayer after March 31, 2008, and placed in service by the taxpayer before January 1, 2009 or (2) it is long production period property (described in Code Sec. 168(k)(2)(B)) or a noncommercial aircraft (described in Code Sec. 168(k)(2)(C)), acquired after March 31, 2008, and placed in service by the taxpayer before January 1, 2010 (Rev. Proc. 2009-33, I.R.B. 2009-29, Section 3.02).

Definition of eligible qualified property that is extension property. Eligible qualified property is extension property if it (1) is acquired by the taxpayer after March 31, 2008, is placed in service by the taxpayer after December 31, 2008, and before January 1, 2010 (i.e., is placed in service in 2009), and is not a long production period property or noncommercial aircraft described in item (2) immediately above or (2) is long production period property (described in Code Sec. 168(k)(2)(B)) or a noncommercial aircraft (described in Code Sec. 168(k)(2)(C)), acquired after March 31, 2008, and placed in service by the taxpayer after December 31, 2009, and before January 1, 2011 (Code Sec. 168(k)(4)(H)(iii); Rev. Proc. 2009-33, I.R.B. 2009-29, Section 3.03). Note that bonus depreciation may be claimed on long production property placed in service in 2010 but the bonus depreciation deduction and bonus depreciation amount if a Code Sec. 168(k)(4) election is made is computed without regard to 2010 progress expenditures. This limitation does not apply to 2010 progress expenditures of a noncommercial aircraft described in Code Sec. 168(k)(2)(C).

Straight-line method must be used to depreciate eligible qualified property to which election applies. All eligible qualified property for which no bonus depreciation is allowed on account of a Code Sec. 168(k)(4) election must be depreciated for regular and AMT purposes using the straight-line method (Code Sec. 168(k)(4)(A)(ii), as added by P.L. 110-289).

The MACRS depreciation periods and conventions applicable to eligible qualified property are not affected if an accelerated credit election is made. For example, if a car with a five-year recovery period would be depreciated using the 200 percent declining balance method and half-year convention without regard to the election, it will be depreciated over a five-year recovery period using the straight-line method and half-year convention for regular (and AMT) tax purposes if it is subject to an accelerated credit election (Section 5.02(3) of Rev. Proc. 2008-65).

Effect of Code Sec. 168(k)(4) election on alternative minimum tax depreciation computation. No AMT depreciation adjustment is required on any MACRS property depreciated using the straight-line method (Code Sec. 56(a)(1)(A)(ii), last sentence). Thus, the election does not create any item of tax preference or adjustment related to the depreciation deduction claimed on eligible qualified property. Regular tax and AMT tax depreciation will be computed the same way. Note that in some cases an AMT adjustment would be required if the election was not made. Thus, the election may actually eliminate AMT depreciation adjustments that are otherwise required.

Computation of Bonus Depreciation Amount

The amount of the unused research and AMT credits attributable to tax years beginning before 2006 that may be claimed as an accelerated credit is limited to the "bonus depreciation amount" computed for the tax year. For any tax year, the bonus depreciation amount is 20 percent of the difference between (1) the aggregate bonus depreciation and regular depreciation that would be allowed on eligible qualified property placed in service during the tax year if bonus depreciation was claimed and (2) the aggregate depreciation that would be allowed on the eligible qualified property placed in service during the tax year if no bonus depreciation was claimed (Code Sec. 168(k)(4)(C)(i), as added by P.L. 110-289).

It is important to note that for purposes of computing the bonus depreciation amount any MACRS elections that apply are ignored. Specifically, the MACRS 150 percent declining balance method election (Code Sec. 168(b)(2)(C)), MACRS straight-line election (Code Sec. 168(b)(3)(D)), and alternative depreciation system (ADS) election (Code Sec. 168(g)(7)) are not taken into account. The computation of the bonus depreciation amount is also made without regard to the requirement that eligible qualified property must be depreciated for regular tax purposes using the straight-line method if the corporation makes the accelerated credit election (Code Sec. 168(k)(4)(C)(i), last sentence, as added by P.L. 110-289).

The bonus depreciation amount for any tax year may not exceed the "maximum amount." The maximum amount is equal to (1) the lesser of (a) 6 percent of the sum of the corporation's unused alternative minimum tax and research credits that are attributable to tax years beginning before January 1, 2006 or (b) $30 million reduced (but not below zero) by (2) the sum of the bonus depreciation amounts for all preceding tax years. (Code Sec. 168(k)(4)(C)(ii) and (iii), as added by P.L. 110-289).

If a corporation that made an election for its first tax year ending after March 31, 2008, does not make the supplemental election not to have the provision apply to extension property, then a separate bonus depreciation amount, maximum amount, and maximum increase amount is computed and applied to eligible qualified property which is not extension property and to eligible qualified property which is extension property (Code Sec. 168(k)(4)(H)(i)(II), as added by P.L. 111-5). If this supplemental election is made, then a bonus depreciation amount is only computed for eligible qualified property that is not extension property. Finally, a corporation that did not make the Code Sec. 168(k)(4) election for its first tax year ending after March 31, 2008, may make an election that only applies to extension property (Code Sec. 168(k)(4)(H)(ii)). Such a corporation will only compute a bonus depreciation amount for extension property.

Section 5 of Rev. Proc. 2008-65, as modified by Section 7.02 of Rev. Proc. 2009-33, explains how to compute the bonus depreciation amount, maximum amount, and maximum increase amount for eligible qualified property that is not extension property. Note that Rev. Proc. 2008-65 was issued prior to extension of the bonus depreciation provision through 2009 and, therefore, is drafted with reference to acquisition and placed in service deadlines that would only apply to eligible qualified property that is not extension property. For purposes of computing the bonus depreciation amount, maximum amount, and maximum increase amount on extension property, the IRS has indicated that Section 5 of Rev. Proc. 2008-65 (as modified by Section 7.02 of Rev. Proc. 2009-33) also applies except that (1) the bonus depreciation amount for extension property is only calculated with regard to eligible qualified property that is extension property and (2) the maximum amount is equal to the maximum increase amount reduced by the sum of the extension property bonus depreciation amounts for all preceding years (Section 5.02 of Rev. Proc. 2009-33). The separate calculation of bonus depreciation amounts for eligible qualified property that is not extension property and eligible qualified property that is extension property means that a corporation that does not make an election to exclude extension property may claim a maximum $30 million of refundable credits with respect to property that extension property and a maximum $30 million of refundable credits with respect to property that is not extension property (i.e., a potential total of $60 million in credits is available).

Example 26: ZPEX is a calendar year corporation. It places one item of eligible qualified property costing $100,000 in service on June 1, 2008 and makes the accelerated credit election for its first tax year ending after March 31, 2008. The property is 7-year MACRS property and the half-year convention and 200 percent declining balance method apply. Aggregate depreciation taking into account bonus depreciation is equal to the $57,145 sum of the $50,000 bonus depreciation that could have been claimed ($100,000 × 50%) and the $7,145 regular first-year MACRS deduction ($50,000 basis remaining after reduction by bonus allowance × 14.29% first-year table percentage for 7-year property subject to the 200 percent declining balance method). Aggregate depreciation claiming no bonus depreciation is $14,290 ($100,000 × 14.29% first-year table percentage). The bonus depreciation amount is $8,571 (($57,145 – $14,290) × 20%), assuming this amount is less than 6% of ZPEX's unused pre-2006 AMT and research credits.

ZPEX must use the MACRS straight-line depreciation method and half-year convention to compute its regular tax depreciation deductions (and AMT deductions) over the asset's 7-year recovery period because it made the accelerated credit election. The allowable 2008 depreciation deduction is $7,140 ($100,000 × 7.14% first year straight-line table percentage for 7-year property subject to the half-year convention).

By making the accelerated credit election, ZPEX's first-year depreciation deduction is reduced from $57,145 to $7,140. However, it may claim a refundable accelerated research or AMT credit in the amount of $8,571. Note that the $50,005 ($57,145 - $7,140) depreciation reduction is not "lost." It will be deducted over the remaining recovery period of the asset using the straight-line depreciation method.

Unless ZPEX makes the supplemental election not to apply the Code Sec. 168(k)(4) election to extension property, ZPEX will compute a separate bonus amount, maximum amount, and maximum increase amount for extension property that is acquired after March 31, 2008 and placed in service during 2009, or during 2010 for property that qualifies for an extended placed in service deadline.

Effect of section 179 deduction on computation of bonus depreciation amount. As in the case of the regular tax bonus depreciation calculation, the bonus depreciation amount is computed on the basis of an asset that remains after reduction by any amount expensed under Code Sec. 179. For example, if a calendar year corporation purchases one asset in May 2009 which cost $250,000 and expenses the entire cost of the asset under Code Sec. 179, there would be no 2009 bonus depreciation amount with respect to that asset to generate an accelerated research or AMT credit.

Property with a long production period. If eligible qualified property qualifies for the extended January 1, 2011 placed-in-service deadline (Code Sec. 168(k)(2)(A)(iv)) for property with a long production period (Code Sec. 168(k)(2)(B)) and is placed in service in 2010, only the adjusted basis of the property which is attributable to manufacture, construction, or production after March 31, 2009 and before January 1, 2010 is taken into account in determining the bonus depreciation amount (Code Sec. 168(k)(4)(D)(iii), as added by P.L. 110-289 and amended by P.L. 111-5; Sec. 5.02(5) of Rev. Proc. 2008-65, as modified by Section 7.02 of Rev. Proc. 2009-33 by replacing January 1, 2009 with January 1, 2010 to reflect the one year extension of bonus depreciation provision by P.L. 111-5 after issuance of Rev. Proc. 2008-65).

If a taxpayer begins construction after March 31, 2008 on long production property that is eligible qualified property and places the property in service in 2009, the property is not extension property. This is because the property would have qualified for bonus depreciation in the absence of the one-year extension by reason of the previously applicable January 1, 2010 placed-in-service deadline for property with a long production period. On the other hand, if such long production property is placed in service in 2010, it is extension property because it qualifies for bonus depreciation by reason of the one-year bonus depreciation extension which also extended the placed-in-service deadline for property with a long production period from January 1, 2010 to January 1, 2011 (Rev. Proc. 2009-33, Section 5.04, Example 1). However, as noted above, progress expenditures incurred in 2010 are not eligible for bonus depreciation and are not taken into taken into account in computing the bonus depreciation amount for extension property that is property with a long production period. Progress expenditures of eligible qualified property that is long-production period property incurred after March 31, 2008 and prior to January 1, 2010, however, are taken into account in computing the bonus depreciation amount.

Limitation on bonus depreciation amount. The bonus depreciation amount for any tax year may not exceed the "maximum increase amount" reduced (but not below zero) by the sum of the bonus depreciation amounts for all preceding tax years (Code Sec. 168(k)(4)(C)(ii), as added by P.L. 110-289). The bonus depreciation amount, as limited by this rule, is referred to as the "maximum amount" (Code Sec. 168(k)(4)(C)(ii); Rev. Proc. 2008-65, Section 5.03).

The maximum increase amount is the lesser of:

(1) $30 million, or

(2) 6 percent of the sum of the "business credit increase amount" (i.e., unused research credits from tax years beginning before 2006) and the "AMT credit increase amount" (i.e., unused AMT credits from tax years beginning before 2006) (Code Sec. 168(k)(4)(C)(ii) and (iii), as added by P.L. 110-289).

If the maximum increase amount is less than the otherwise applicable bonus depreciation amount the tax benefit of the accelerated credit election may be substantially diminished.

> ***Example 27:*** Assume that ZPEX corporation from Example 26 has $24,000 of unused AMT credit from its pre-2006 tax years and no unused research credits from that period. Its maximum increase amount for 2008 is $1,440 ($24,000 × 6%). Since this is less than its $8,571 bonus depreciation amount as computed in *Example 26*, ZPEX's bonus depreciation amount is limited to $1,440. If the election is made it may claim a $1,440 AMT credit in 2008 but would still need to defer a $50,005 depreciation deduction.

As previously noted, separate bonus depreciation amounts, maximum increase amounts, and maximum amounts are computed for qualified eligible property that is not extension property and eligible qualified property that is extension property if a corporation makes the Code Sec. 168(k)(4) election for its first tax year ending after March 31, 2008 and does not make the supplemental election not to apply the provision to extension property.

> ***Example 28:*** Omar Inc., a calendar tax year corporation, has $300 million in unused pre-2006 research and AMT credits. Its bonus depreciation amount for non-extension property placed in service after March 31, 2008 and before January 1, 2009 is $4 million. It may claim $4 million of refundable credits attributable to non-extension property for its 2008 tax year because $4 million is less than the $18 million maximum increase amount (the lesser of (a) $30 million or (b) $18 million (6% × $300 million)). Assume that Omar completes construction of property with a long production period in 2009 that also qualifies as non-extension property. The bonus depreciation amount on this property is computed as $8 million. The maximum increase amount is $18 million (the lesser of (a) $30 million or (b) $18 million (6% × $300 million)). The maximum amount is $14 million ($18 million reduced by the $4 million bonus depreciation amount for 2008 attributable to non-extension property). Since $8 million is less than $14 million Omar may claim $8 million in refundable credits attributable to non-extension property in its 2009 tax year. Assume further that Omar also places extension property in service in 2009 and the bonus depreciation amount for this property is $6 million. The maximum increase amount is $18 million (the lesser of (a) $30 million or (b) $18 million (6% × $300 million)). The maximum amount is also $18 million since there was no bonus depreciation amount claimed in 2008 with respect to *extension* property. Since $6 million is less than $18 million, Omar may claim $6 million in refundable credits attributable to extension property for its 2009 tax year.

Generally, the accelerated credit election will provide the greatest tax benefit to a corporation if: (1) it has a bonus depreciation amount that is not limited by the maximum increase amount and (2) it derives no immediate tax benefit from its bonus depreciation deductions because its taxable income without regard to those deductions is zero or less. In any event, a taxpayer should run a present value analysis taking into account expected tax bracket rates over the recovery period of assets affected by an election to determine whether or not it should be made.

Business credit increase amount. For purposes of determining the "maximum increase amount," the business credit increase amount is the portion of the general business credit (determined without regard to the Code Sec. 38(c) limitation based on tax liability for the corporation's first tax year ending after March 31, 2008, which is allocable to business credit carryforwards to the tax year which are from tax years beginning before January 1, 2006 and are properly allocable to the research credit determined under Code Sec. 41(a) (Code Sec. 168(k)(4)(E)(iii), as added by P.L. 110-289; Rev. Proc. 2008-65, Section 5.05). A business credit carryforward allocable to the research credit that was from a tax year beginning before January 1, 2006, but has expired before the first tax year ending after March 31,

2008, is not taken into account in determining the business credit increase amount (Rev. Proc. 2008-65, Section 5.05).

AMT credit increase amount. The AMT credit increase amount is equal to the portion of the minimum tax credit for the corporation's first tax year ending after March 31, 2008, determined by taking into account only the adjusted net minimum tax for tax years beginning before January 1, 2006. For purposes of this computation, credits are treated as allowed on a first-in, first-out basis (Code Sec. 168(k)(4)(E)(iv), as added by P.L. 110-289; Rev. Proc. 2008-65, Section 5.06, as modified by Rev. Proc. 2009-33, Section 7.03).

The actual reference in Code Sec. 168(k)(4)(E)(iv) to "adjusted minimum tax" was intended to be a reference to "adjusted *net* minimum tax." as defined in Code Sec. 53(d)(1)(B). The term "adjusted minimum tax" does not appear in the Code. See Rev. Proc. 2008-65, Section 5.06, as modified by Rev. Proc. 2009-33, section 7.03.

Allocation of bonus depreciation amount. A corporation, subject to the limitations below, may specify the portion, if any, of the bonus depreciation amount for the tax year that is allocated to the general business credit limitation and the AMT credit limitation (Rev. Proc. 2008-65, Section 6.01; Rev. Proc. 2009-16, Section. 4.01; Rev. Proc. 2009-33, Section 4.01). As explained above, if the Code Sec. 168(k)(4) election applies to both non-extension property (generally, eligible qualified property acquired after March 31, 2008 and before January 1, 2009) and extension property (generally, eligible qualified property acquired after March 31, 2008 and placed in service in 2009 and thereafter), separate bonus depreciation amounts are computed for each category.

To obtain an accelerated tax credit for an unused research credit, a corporation increases the general business tax credit limitation contained in Code Sec. 38(c) by the bonus depreciation amount for the tax year (Code Sec. 168(k)(4)(B)(i), as added by P.L. 110-289).

The bonus depreciation amount allocated to each type of credit is limited to the amount of the pre-2006 credit.

Thus, the allocation of the bonus depreciation amount to the Code Sec. 38(c) limit may not exceed the excess of:

(1) the "business credit increase amount" (generally, the taxpayer's pre-2006 research credit carryforwards), over

(2) the bonus depreciation amount allocated to the limitation for all preceding tax years (Code Sec. 168(k)(4)(E)(ii), as added by P.L. 110-289).

The amount of the pre-2006 research credit carryforwards is determined by applying the rules of Code Sec. 38(d).

The allocation of the bonus depreciation amount to the Code Sec. 53(c) tax liability limitation for the AMT tax credit may not exceed the excess of:

(1) the "AMT credit increase amount," (generally, the taxpayer's pre-2006 AMT credit carryforwards), over

(2) the bonus depreciation amount allocated to such limitation for all preceding tax years (Code Sec. 168(k)(4)(E)(ii), as added by P.L. 110-289).

In calculating the AMT credit increase amount, credits are treated as allowed on a first-in first-out basis (Code Sec. 168(k)(4)(E)(iv), as added by P.L. 110-289).

See Section 4.02 of Rev. Proc. 2009-16 and Section 5.03(2) of Rev. Proc. 2009-33 for special rules relating to the allocation of the group bonus depreciation amount among members of a controlled group.

Special rules for corporate partners. If a corporation that makes an accelerated credit election is also a partner, its distributive share of partnership items is determined as if the partnership did not claim bonus depreciation on any eligible qualified property that is subject to the election and as if it used the straight-line method to calculate depreciation on the property (Code Sec. 168(k)(4)(G), as added by P.L. 110-289; Joint Committee on Taxation, Technical Explanation of the Housing Assistance Tax Act of 2008, JCX-63-08, July 23, 2008; Rev. Proc. 2009-16, Section 5; Rev. Proc. 2008-65, Section 5.02(2)).

An electing corporate partner is required to notify the partnership if it is making the election for its first tax year ending after March 31, 2008. Notification is required on or before the due date (including extensions) of the electing corporate partner's federal income tax return for its first tax year ending after March 31, 2008. If the electing corporate partner makes the election by filing an amended return (as described below) it must notify the partnership on or before the date it files an amended return containing the election. If the electing corporate partner's first tax year ending after March 31, 2008 ends before December 31, 2008 and the corporate partner made the election on a timely filed original return and received a credit on such return, the electing corporate partner must notify the partnership on or before March 11, 2009 (Rev. Proc. 2009-16, Section 5.01(2)).

If a corporate partner makes the election, the partnership must provide the electing corporate partner with sufficient information to determine its distributive share of partnership items with respect to any eligible qualified property placed in service by the partnership during the tax year. This information must be provided in the time and manner required by Code Sec. 6031(b) and Temporary Reg.§1.6031(b)-1T(a)(3)(ii) and (b). If the partnership has filed its federal tax return for its first tax year ending after March 31, 2008, on or before February 9, 2009, and did not provide the electing corporate partner with sufficient information, the partnership must provide such information to the electing corporate partner by the later of May 11, 2009, or 90 calendar days after receiving the corporate partner's notification (Rev. Proc. 2009-15, Section 5.01(2)).

If a corporation is making the supplemental election to not apply the Code Sec. 168(k)(4) election to extension property it must provide written notification to any partnership in which it is a partner that it is making the election not to apply Code Sec. 168(k)(4) to extension property. This notification must be made on or before the due date (including extensions) of the corporation's federal income tax return for its first tax year ending after December 31, 2008. If the corporation makes a late election not to apply Code Sec. 168(k)(4) to extension property, the notification to the partnership must be made no later than the date the taxpayer files its federal income tax return containing the late election (Rev. Proc. 2009-33, Section 4.02(2)(b)).

If a corporation did not make the Code Sec. 168(k)(4) election for its first tax year ending after March 31, 2009 and is making the election for extension property placed in service in its first tax year ending after December 31, 2008, it must provide written notification to the partnership on or before the due date (including extensions) of its federal income tax return for its first tax year ending after December 31, 2008. If its makes a late extension property election, the notification to the partnership must be made no later than the date the corporation files its federal income tax return containing the late election (Rev. Proc. 2009-33, Section 6.02(2)(a)(iv)). The same rule applies to S corporations (Rev. Proc. 2009-33, Section 6.02(2)(b)(iv)). The partnership is required to provide the corporation with information necessary to make the required computation (Section 6.05(4) of Rev. Proc. 2009-33).

Controlled corporations. All corporations that make up a controlled group treated as a single employer for purposes of the work opportunity tax credit (under Code Sec. 52(a)) are treated as one taxpayer for purposes of the accelerated credit election for the first tax year ending after March 31, 2008. If the election is made by any member of the group, the entire group is treated as having made it (Code Sec. 168(k)(4)(C)(iv), as added by P.L. 110-289). For example, if the common parent of an affiliated group of corporations filing a consolidated return makes the accelerated credit election for one member of the affiliated group, then all members of the affiliated group are treated as one taxpayer for purposes of Code Sec. 168(k)(4) and as having made the election (Rev. Proc. 2008-65, Section 4.02). The same rules apply with respect to the election not to apply Code Sec. 168(k)(4) to extension property (Rev. Proc. 2009-33).

See Section 4.02 of Rev. Proc. 2009-16 for special rules relating to the allocation of the group bonus depreciation amount for eligible qualified property that is not extension property among members of a controlled group. If a supplemental election is not made to exclude extension property, a separate computation of the controlled group's bonus depreciation amount for extension property is required using the rules described in Section 4.02 of Rev. Proc. 2009-16 (Rev. Proc. 2009-33, Section 5.02).

A controlled group's bonus depreciation amount for extension property (the group extension property bonus depreciation amount) is computed in the same manner as the group bonus depreciation amount for non-extension property (as described in section 4.02(2) or 4.02(3)(b)(ii) of Rev. Proc. 2009-16, as applicable, but taking into account only extension property) (Rev. Proc. 2009-33, Section 5.02(2)).

For rules concerning the allocation of the group bonus depreciation amount for extension property amount members of a controlled group see Sec. 5.03(2) of Rev. Proc. 2009-33.

S corporations and S shareholders. An S corporation may make the accelerated credit election for its first tax year ending after March 31, 2008. However, any business or AMT credit limitation increases that result from the election are applied at the corporate level and not at the shareholder level.

If the election is made, an S corporation may not claim business credits or AMT credits in excess of its built in gains tax liability (Code Sec. 1374(a)) for the tax year. Any credits allowed as a result of the increase in the business or AMT credit limitations, which may be used only as an additional credit against the Code Sec. 1374(a) tax, are not refundable to the S corporation (Rev. Proc. 2009-16, Section 6).

Similar rules apply if the S corporation did not make an election for its first tax year ending after March 31, 2008 but makes an extension property election for its first tax year ending after December 31, 2008 (Rev. Proc. 2009-33, Section 6.05(3)).

Election procedures - in general

The IRS has provided procedures for the three types of elections allowed under Code Sec. 168(k)(4):

(1) The election to apply Code Sec. 168(k)(4) to all eligible qualified property placed in service in a corporation's first tax year ending after March 31, 2008 and all subsequent tax years (Code Sec. 168(k)(4)(A); Rev. Proc. 2009-16, Section 3, as modified by Rev. Proc. 2009-33, Section 8).

(2) The election not to apply Code Sec. 168(k)(4) to extension property placed in service after December 31, 2009 (this election is only available if the

corporation made the preceding election to apply Code Sec. 168(k)(4) to its first tax year ending after March 31, 2008 and all subsequent tax years) (Code Sec. 168(k)(4)(H)(i), as added by P.L. 111-5; Rev. Proc. 2009-33, Section 4).

(3) The election to apply Code Sec. 168(k)(4) to extension property placed in service after December 31, 2009 (this election is only available if the corporation did *not* make the election to apply Code Sec. 168(k)(4) to its first tax year ending after March 31, 2008 and all subsequent tax years) (Code Sec. 168(k)(4)(H)(i), as added by P.L. 111-5; Rev. Proc. 2009-33, Section 6).

Election procedures for first tax year ending after March 31, 2008

A corporate taxpayer must generally make the election for its first tax year ending after March 31, 2008 by the due date (including extensions) of the federal income tax return for the taxpayer's first tax year ending after March 31, 2008 (whether or not bonus depreciation property is placed in service in that tax year). However, special rules apply:

(1) if the corporation's first tax year ending after March 31, 2008 ends on or after December 31, 2008;

(2) if the corporation's first tax year ending after March 31, 2008 ends before December 31, 2008 and the corporation has not filed its original tax return for such tax year on or before March 11, 2009;

(3) if the corporation's first tax year ending after March 31, 2008 ends before December 31, 2008 and the corporation has filed its original tax return for such tax year on or before March 11, 2009;

(4) to controlled groups.

Limited relief described below for late elections is available.

Election procedures - corporation's first tax year ending after March 31, 2008 ends on or after December 31, 2008. If eligible qualified property was placed in service in a C corporation's first tax year ending on or after December 31, 2008, a C corporation makes the accelerated credit election for its first tax year ending after March 31, 2008 by (1) claiming the refundable credit on line 32g of 2008 Form 1120; (2) filing Form 3800 and/or Form 8827 to compute the credit as explained in the instructions; (3) filing 2008 Form 4562, indicating that the C corporation used the straight-line method and did not claim bonus depreciation on eligible qualified property; and (4) if the C corporation is a partner in a partnership, by notifying the partnership in accordance with Section 5.02 of Rev. Proc. 2009-16 (Rev. Proc. 2009-16, Section 3.04(3)).

An S corporation that places eligible qualified property in service in its first tax year ending on or after December 31, 2008, makes the accelerated credit election for its first tax year ending after March 31, 2008 by (1) making the appropriate adjustments to Line 22b of 2008 Form 1120S to reflect the results described in section 6.02 of Rev. Proc. 2009-16; (2) attaching an election statement to the Form 1120S and a statement showing the business credit and AMT credit limitations; and (3) filing 2008 Form 4562 indicating that the S corporation computed depreciation on eligible qualified property using the straight-line method and did not claim bonus depreciation on such property; and (4) if the S corporation is a partner in a partnership, notifying the partnership in accordance with Section 5.02 of Rev. Proc. 2009-16 (Rev. Proc. 2009-16, Section 3.04(2)).

If no eligible qualified property was placed in service in a C or S corporation's first tax year ending after March 31, 2008, an election statement for the first tax year ending after March 31, 2008 is made by attaching an election statement to the corporation's timely filed original tax return indicating that the corporation is making the Code Sec. 168(k)(4) election (Rev. Proc. 2009-16, Section 3.04(3)).

Election procedures - corporation's first tax year ending after March 31, 2008 ends before December 31, 2008 and the corporation has not filed its original tax return for such tax year on or before March 11, 2009. In this case, the corporation may make the election for its first tax year ending after March 31, 2008 either (1) by claiming Stimulus Act bonus depreciation on eligible qualified property on its timely filed return or (2) by filing a timely return that includes a 2007 Form 4562 that indicates that the corporation used the straight-line method and did not claim Stimulus bonus depreciation for all eligible qualified property. The accelerated credit is not claimed on the original return if the second option is used (Rev. Proc. 2009-16, Section 3.02(1)(a)(i)).

Except as provided in Section 3.03 of Rev. Proc. 2009-16, as modified by Section 8.02 of Rev. Proc. 2009-33, the corporation must file an amended return for the first tax year that ends after March 31, 2008 on or before the due date (without regard to extensions) of the return for the succeeding tax year (in the manner described in Section 3.02(2) of Rev. Proc. 2009-16).

If the corporation is a partner in a partnership, it must notifying the partnership in accordance with Section 5.02 of Rev. Proc. 2009-16 (Rev. Proc. 2009-16, Section 3.02(1)(a)(iii)).

If the corporation did not place eligible qualified property in service in its first tax year ending after March 31, 2008, it should attach an election statement to its timely-filed original return (Rev. Proc. 2009-16, Section 3.03(2)).

Election procedures - corporation's first tax year ending after March 31, 2008 ends before December 31, 2008 and the corporation has filed its original tax return for such tax year on or before March 11, 2009. The corporation must file an amended return for its first tax year ending after March 31, 2008 on or before the due date (without regard to extensions) of the return for the succeeding tax year (in the manner described in Section 3.02(2) of Rev. Proc. 2009-16) and, if the corporation is a partner in a partnership, notify the partnership in accordance with Section 5.02 of the procedure (Rev. Proc. 2009-16, Section 3.02(1)(b)).

If the corporation made the Code Sec. 168(k)(4) election on its timely filed original federal income tax return for its first tax year ending after March 31, 2008 and receives an accelerated credit on the return then an amended return is not filed. However, if the corporation is a partner in a partnership, it must also notify the partnership in accordance with Section 5.02 of Rev. Proc. 2009-16 (Rev. Proc. 2009-16, Section 3.03(1)).

If the corporation has not placed any eligible qualified property in service in its first tax year ending after March 31, 2008, and the corporation wishes to make the accelerated credit election and has not attached a statement making the election to its original return, the election statement should be attached to the amended return. If the corporation is a partner in a partnership, it must also notify the partnership in accordance with Section 5.02 of Rev. Proc. 2009-16 (Rev. Proc. 2009-16, Section 3.03(2)).

Election procedure - amended return. If an amended return is filed by a corporation that is not an S corporation for its first tax year ending after March 31, 2008 under either of the two election procedures described above for corporation's with a tax year ending before December 31, 2008: (1) the refundable credit is claimed on Line 5g of Form 1120X; (2) appropriate adjustments are made on lines 2, 3, and 4 of Form 1120X to reflect the depreciation adjustments that require the corporation to compute depreciation on eligible qualified property using the straight-line method without claiming the bonus depreciation deduction; and (3) indicate in Part II of the amended return that the corporation is making the Code Sec. 168(k)(4) election (Rev. Proc. 2009-16, Section 3.02(2)(a)).

An S corporation should (1) make adjustments described in Section 6.02 of Rev. Proc. 2009-16 on Line 22 of its Form 1120S; (2) make the appropriate depreciation adjustments; and (3) attach a statement to the amended Form 1120S indicating that it is making the Code Sec. 168(k)(4) election and a statement showing the calculation of the increases to the AMT and research credit limitations (Rev. Proc. 2009-16, Section 3.02(2)(b)).

If a corporation is required to file an amended return for its first tax year ending after December 31, 2008 and its succeeding tax year is a short tax year, special due dates for the amended return apply (Rev. Proc. 2008-19, Section 3.03(3), as added by Rev. Proc. 2009-33, Section 8.02).

Election procedure - controlled groups. See Section 3.05 of Rev. Proc. 2009-16 for rules regarding: (1) the determination of controlled group members; (2) time and manner of making the Code Sec. 168(k)(4) election for the first tax year ending after March 31, 2008; and (3) the effect of the Code Sec. 168(k)(4) election for members entering or leaving a controlled group.

Election procedures - limited relief for late elections. An automatic extension of 6 months from the due date of the federal tax return (excluding extensions) for the corporation's first tax year ending after March 31, 2008, is granted to make the Code Sec. 168(k)(4) election, provided the corporation timely filed its federal tax return for its first tax year ending after March 31, 2008, and the corporation satisfies the requirements in Reg.§301.9100-2(c) and Reg.§301.9100-2(d). Otherwise a corporation will need to obtain permission pursuant Reg. §301.9100-3 by establishing to the satisfaction of the IRS that it acted reasonably and in good faith, and that the grant of relief will not prejudice the interests of the Government (Rev. Proc. 2009-16, Section 3.06).

Election not to apply Code Sec. 168(k)(4) to extension property

The election not to apply Code Sec. 168(k)(4) to extension property placed in service in its first tax year ending after December 31, 2008 and in any subsequent tax year (Code Sec. 168(k)(4)(H)(i), as added by P.L. 111-5) must generally be made by the due date (including extensions) of the corporation's federal income tax return for its first tax year ending after December 31, 2008 (Rev. Proc. 2009-33, Section 4). A late election may be made by a corporation that filed such income tax return without making the election. See below.

An election statement is attached to the return indicating that the corporation is electing not to apply Code Sec. 168(k)(4) to extension property.

A corporation that is a partner must notify the partnership that it is making the election on or before the due date (including extensions) of its federal income tax return for its first tax year ending after December 31, 2008 (or by the date it files its federal income tax returning containing a late election).

Controlled groups. If all members of a controlled group are members of an affiliated group of corporations that file a consolidated return, the common parent makes the election not to apply Code Sec. 168(k)(4) to extension property on behalf of all members of the consolidated group on or before the due date (including extensions) of the consolidated return for the first tax year ending after December 31, 2008. Special rules apply if a separate federal income tax return is filed some or all members of a controlled group. See Section 4.03 of Rev. Proc. 2009-33.

Election procedures - limited relief for late elections. An automatic extension of 6 months from the due date of the federal tax return (excluding extensions) for the corporation's first tax year ending after December 31, 2008, is granted to make the election to exclude extension property, provided the corporation timely filed its federal tax return for its first tax year ending after December 31, 2008, and the corporation satisfies the requirements in Reg.§ 301.9100-2(c) and Reg.§ 301.9100-2(d). Otherwise a corporation will need to obtain permission pursuant Reg. § 301.9100-3 by establishing to the satisfaction of the IRS that it acted reasonably and in good faith, and that the grant of relief will not prejudice the interests of the Government (Rev. Proc. 2009-33, Section 4.04).

Extension property election

A corporation that did not make the Code Sec. 168(k)(4) election for its first tax year ending after March 31, 2008 may make an election to apply the Code Sec. 168(k)(4) election solely to extension property (Code Sec. 168(k)(4)(H)(ii)). Election procedures are provided in section 6 of Rev. Proc. 2009-33. The extension property election applies to all extension property placed in service in the taxpayer's first tax year ending after December 31, 2008 and in all subsequent tax years. The election must be made for the first tax year ending after December 31, 2008 even if the corporation does not place any extension property in service in that tax year.

Time for making extension election. Generally, the extension election must be made by the due date (including extensions) of the federal income tax return for the corporation's first tax year ending after December 31, 2008 (Section 6.02(1) of Rev. Proc. 2009-33). A late election is possible, as explained below.

C corporations. See Section 6.02(2)(a) of Rev. Proc. 2009-33 for manner in which C corporation that has placed extension property in service in its first tax year ending after December 31, 2008 makes the extension election. See Section 6.03 of Rev. Proc. 2009-33 if extension property was not placed in service in the first tax year ending after December 31, 2008.

S corporations. See Section 6.02(2)(b) of Rev. Proc. 2009-33 for manner in which an S corporation that has placed extension property in service in its first tax year ending after December 31, 2008 makes the extension election. See Section 6.03 of Rev. Proc. 2009-33 if extension property was not placed in service in the first tax year ending after December 31, 2008.

Controlled groups. See Section 6.04(1) of Rev. Proc. 2009-33 for rules regarding the determination of controlled group members for purposes of the extension election and the manner in which the extension election is made. See Section 6.04(2) of Rev. Proc. 2009-33 for the timing and manner in which controlled groups make the extension election.

Late extension property elections. An automatic extension of 6 months from the due date of the federal tax return (excluding extensions) for the corporation's first tax year ending after December 31, 2008, is granted to make the election to exclude extension property, provided the corporation timely filed its federal tax return for its first tax year ending after December 31, 2008, and the corporation satisfies the requirements in Reg. § 301.9100-2(c) and Reg.§ 301.9100-2(d). Otherwise a corporation will need to obtain permission pursuant Reg. § 301.9100-3 by establishing to the satisfaction of the IRS that it acted reasonably and in good faith, and that the grant of relief will not prejudice the interests of the Government (Section 6.06 of Rev. Proc. 2009-33).

Special rules for 2000 and 2001 returns that included September 11, 2001

Some taxpayers who filed their 2000/2001 or 2001/2002 fiscal-year return or 2001 calendar-year return failed to claim bonus depreciation on qualified property placed in service after September 10, 2001, because the bonus provision was enacted after their return was filed. (The provision was signed into law on March 9, 2002.) In response, the IRS first issued Rev. Proc. 2002-33, which provided taxpayers who filed a 2000 or 2001 return *before June 1, 2002*, without claiming bonus depreciation on qualifying property (including New York Liberty Zone property) an opportunity to claim the allowance (1) on an amended return filed on or before the due date (excluding extensions) of their federal tax return for the next succeeding tax year or (2) by filing a Form 3115, Application for Change in Accounting Method, with a timely filed return for the next succeeding tax year pursuant to the automatic change in accounting procedures of Rev. Proc. 2002-9, as modified by Rev. Proc. 2002-19. Under the procedure, a taxpayer who files a return before June 1, 2002, without claiming bonus depreciation on qualifying property (and without making a formal election out) and who fails to file an amended return or a Form 3115 is considered to have made a deemed election out of bonus depreciation.

The IRS subsequently issued Rev. Proc. 2003-50, which modifies and amplifies Rev. Proc. 2002-33 in a number of ways, including:

(1) the elimination of the requirement that the 2000 or 2001 return must have been filed before June 1, 2002, in order to obtain relief and the provision of additional time to file an amended return or a Form 3115 in order to claim the 30-percent bonus depreciation deduction; and

(2) allowing taxpayers who elected to expense property under Code Sec. 179 on the return for the tax year that included September 11, 2001, to change the selection of the property expensed. Rev. Proc. 2002-33 did not include this option. This option, however, was required to be exercised on an amended return filed by December 31, 2003.

These revised procedures apply to taxpayers that *timely* filed their 2000 or 2001 return for a tax year that includes September 11, 2001.

After December 31, 2003, a qualifying taxpayer will need to file Form 3115 in order to take advantage of the time extension to make the election. See option (3) (b), below. However, this post-2003 option is only available if the taxpayer's tax return for the first tax year succeeding the tax year that included September 11, 2001 (e.g., the 2002 return for a calendar-year taxpayer), was filed on or before July 21, 2003. Thus, if a calendar-year individual obtained a four-month extension to file his 2002 return, the option is not available if that return was filed after July 21, 2003.

Taxpayers who timely filed a 2000 or 2001 return for a tax year that includes September 11, 2001, and failed to claim the bonus depreciation allowance on a class of qualifying property (and who did not make a formal election not to claim the bonus depreciation deduction) are provided additional time to make the election (Rev. Proc. 2003-50, modifying and amplifying Rev. Proc. 2002-33).

Pursuant to Rev. Proc. 2003-50, a taxpayer may claim the bonus allowance for the 2000 or 2001 tax year that included September 11, 2001:

(1) by filing an amended return for the tax year that included September 11, 2001 (and any affected subsequent tax year), on or before December 31, 2003, and including the statement "Filed pursuant to Rev. Proc. 2003-50" at the top of the amended return;

(2) by filing Form 3115, Application for Change in Accounting Method, with the return for the first tax year succeeding the tax year that included

September 11, 2001, if this return has not been filed on or before July 21, 2003, and the taxpayer owns the property as of the first day of this tax year; or

(3) if the taxpayer's tax return for the first tax year succeeding the tax year that included September 11, 2001, was filed on or before July 21, 2003, by (a) filing an amended return on or before December 31, 2003, for the first tax year succeeding the tax year that included September 11, 2001, attaching a Form 3115 to the return, and including the statement "Filed Pursuant to Rev. Proc. 2003-50" at the top of the amended federal tax return; or (b) filing a Form 3115 with the taxpayer's timely filed federal tax return for the second tax year succeeding the tax year that included September 11, 2001, and ending on or before July 31, 2004, if the taxpayer owns the property as of the first day of this tax year.

Example (29): An individual timely filed his 2001 calendar-year return on August 10, 2002, without claiming bonus depreciation on qualifying property that was placed in service in October and November of 2001. No formal election out of bonus depreciation was made. He also filed his 2002 return on April 15, 2003. He still owns the property. This individual may claim bonus depreciation:

(1) On an amended 2001 return filed by December 31, 2003 (option (1), above).

The 2002 return is an "affected return" for purposes of option (1), above, since the bonus deduction claimed on the amended 2001 return will affect the depreciation computations on the previously filed 2002 return. Specifically, 2002 depreciation will need to be recomputed on the cost of the assets as reduced by the bonus deduction. Thus, pursuant to the terms of option (1), above, the 2002 return will also need to be amended by December 31, 2003.

(2) By filing an amended 2002 return by December 31, 2003, and attaching Form 3115 to this return (option 3(a), above).

The bonus depreciation deduction that was not claimed in 2001 is claimed as a Code Sec. 481(a) adjustment on the 2002 return. The adjustment for unclaimed bonus depreciation, however, would be reduced to reflect the fact that the regular first-year depreciation deductions were not computed on the cost (or other basis) of the assets after reduction by the bonus allowance. Depreciation deductions on the 2002 amended return would also need to be recomputed by reducing their cost by the bonus depreciation. Note that Code Sec. 481(a) adjustments may be claimed in a single tax year as explained in Rev. Proc. 2002-19.

(3) By filing a Form 3115 with the taxpayer's timely filed return for 2003 (option 3(b), above).

In this situation, the Code Sec. 481(a) adjustment is claimed on the 2003 return and should be equal to the unclaimed bonus depreciation for 2001 reduced by the excess depreciation claimed in 2001 and 2002 by virtue of the fact that 2001 and 2002 depreciation was not computed on cost reduced by bonus depreciation.

Formal and deemed elections out of 30-percent bonus depreciation for the return that includes September 11, 2001. If a taxpayer has not made a valid formal (i.e., written) election out of bonus depreciation on the return for the tax year that includes September 11, 2001, a deemed election out is considered made if:

(1) the return for the year that includes September 11, 2001, was timely filed;

(2) the 30-percent allowance was not claimed on qualifying property for which a depreciation deduction was claimed; and

(3) an amended return or a Form 3115 is not filed to claim the 30-percent allowance pursuant to the three options discussed above (Rev. Proc. 2002-33; Reg. § 1.168(k)-1(e)(4))..

¶ 127E

Bonus Depreciation for New York Liberty Zone Property

"Qualified New York Liberty Zone property" is eligible for an additional 30-percent first-year depreciation allowance (Code Sec. 1400L(b)(1)(A), as added by the Job Creation and Worker Assistance Act of 2002 (P.L. 107-147); Reg.§ 1.1400L(b)-1 at ¶ 599).

Bonus depreciation under the Liberty Zone provision (Code Sec. 1400L(b)) may not be claimed on property that qualified for the 30-percent or 50-percent additional first-year depreciation allowance that is provided by Code Sec. 168(k) (the "Code Sec. 168(k) allowance") and described at ¶ 127D (Code Sec. 1400L(b)(2)(C)(i)). Property that qualified for bonus depreciation under Code Sec. 168(k) is specifically excluded from the definition of "qualified New York Liberty Zone property" even if the property is located in the New York Liberty Zone.

Most property located in the New York Liberty Zone qualified for bonus depreciation under Code Sec. 168(k) rather than Code Sec. 1400L(b). However, qualification for New York Liberty Zone bonus depreciation is more liberal in some respects and, therefore, will cover certain property that is not eligible for bonus depreciation under Code Sec. 168(k). Most importantly, property placed in service after December 31, 2004 and before January 1, 2007 may qualify for New York Liberty Zone bonus depreciation (Code Sec. 1400L(b)(2)(A)(v)). Property generally only qualified for bonus depreciation under Code Sec. 168(k) if placed in service before January 1, 2005. Also, unlike regular bonus depreciation under Code Sec. 168(k), New York Liberty Zone bonus depreciation is available for residential rental or nonresidential real property that replaces certain destroyed or condemned real property and which is placed in service before January 1, 2010 (Code Sec. 1400L(b)(2)(A)(i)(II)) and for used property so long as the taxpayer was the first person to use the property in the New York Liberty Zone (Code Sec. 1400L(b)(2)(A)(iii)).

Although the bonus depreciation rate was increased from 30 percent to 50 percent for property that qualifies for bonus depreciation under Code Sec. 168(k), the 30-percent rate for property placed in service in the New York Liberty Zone that only qualifies for bonus depreciation under Code Sec. 1400L(b) (e.g., used property, certain real property, and property placed in service after December 31, 2004, and before January 1, 2007) was not increased.

Qualifying property must be acquired by purchase, as defined in Code Sec. 179(d) (see below) after September 10, 2001, and placed in service by the taxpayer on or before the "termination date," which is December 31, 2006 (December 31, 2009, in the case of qualifying residential rental and nonresidential real property).

Final regulations and change in accounting method

Final bonus depreciation regulations adopted by T.D. 9283 (8/31/06) generally apply to qualified New York Liberty Zone property acquired by a taxpayer after September 10, 2001 (Reg.§ 1.1400L(b)-1(g)).

A taxpayer that seeks a change in method of accounting to comply with the final regulations for either: (1) the taxpayer's last tax year ending before October 18, 2006, if the taxpayer timely files (including extensions) its Federal income tax return after October 18, 2006, for that last tax year; or (2) the taxpayer's first tax year ending on or after October 18, 2006 should follow the procedures in Rev. Proc. 2006-43, I.R.B. 2006-4. For subsequent tax years, the automatic change in method of accounting procedures in Rev. Proc. 2002-9 (or its successor Rev. Proc. 2008-52), if applicable, or the advance consent change in method of accounting procedures in

Rev. Proc. 97-27, 1997-1 C.B. 680 (as modified and amplified by Rev. Proc. 2002-19, and amplified, clarified, and modified by Rev. Proc. 2002-54) (or its successor) apply.

Location of New York Liberty Zone

The New York Liberty Zone is the area located on or south of Canal Street, East Broadway (east of its intersection with Canal Street), or Grand Street (east of its intersection with East Broadway) in the Borough of Manhattan in New York City (Code Sec. 1400L(h); Reg. § 1.1400L(b)-1(b)).

Basis for computing additional allowance

The basis for computing bonus depreciation on New York Liberty Zone property is determined in the same manner as for the bonus deduction under Code Sec. 168(k) (Reg. § 1.1400L(b)-1(d)). Thus, the 30-percent rate is generally applied to cost as reduced by any amount expensed under Code Sec. 179. See ¶ 127D.

Code Sec. 179 expense allowance increased by $35,000

The otherwise allowable Code Sec. 179 deduction is increased by an additional $35,000 for qualifying Liberty Zone property placed in service before January 1, 2007. See ¶ 305.

Election out

A taxpayer may elect out of the provision. Rules similar to those that apply under Code Sec. 168(k) apply under Code Sec. 1400L(b) (Code Sec. 1400L(b)(2)(C)(iv); Reg. § 1.1400L(b)-1(d)(3); Rev. Proc. 2002-33, as modified and amplified by Rev. Proc. 2003-50). Thus, the election out is made at the property class level. See ¶ 127D.

The final regulations, which apply retroactively, make it clear that if a taxpayer elects out of bonus depreciation under Code Sec. 168(k) with respect to a class of property, the taxpayer may claim bonus depreciation on Liberty Zone property that falls within the same class. See Rev. Proc. 2006-43, I.R.B. 2006-4, for change in accounting method procedures that a taxpayer must follow in order to claim bonus depreciation on New York Liberty Zone property which did not qualify under the temporary regulations.

Types of qualifying New York Liberty Zone property

The following types of property can qualify for the additional Liberty Zone depreciation allowance:

(1) property that is depreciable under MACRS and has a recovery period of 20 years or less;

(2) computer software which is depreciable under Code Sec. 167(f)(1)(B) using the straight-line method over 36 months;

(3) water utility property; and

(4) nonresidential real property or residential rental property that rehabilitates real property damaged, or replaces real property destroyed or condemned, as a result of the September 11, 2001, terrorist attack (Code Sec. 1400L(b)(2)(A)(i)).

The first three types of property are eligible for the Code Sec. 168(k) allowance described at ¶ 127D.

Additional requirements

The following additional requirements must also be met in order for property to qualify for the Code Sec. 1400L(b) bonus depreciation allowance:

(1) substantially all (80% or more) of the use of the property must be in the New York Liberty Zone (Code Sec. 1400L(b)(2)(A)(ii); Reg.§ 1.1400L(b)-1(c)(3)).

(2) the property must be used in the active conduct of a trade or business by the taxpayer in the Liberty Zone (Code Sec. 1400L(b)(2)(A)(ii));

(3) the original use of the property in the Liberty Zone must commence with the taxpayer after September 10, 2001 (Code Sec. 1400L(b)(2)(A)(iii));

(4) the property must be acquired by purchase, as defined in Code Sec. 179(d)(2) (see below) after September 10, 2001 (Code Sec. 1400L(b)(2)(A)(iv)); and

(5) the property must be placed in service by the taxpayer on or before the "termination date," which is December 31, 2006 (December 31, 2009, in the case of nonresidential real property and residential rental property) (see below for further qualification requirements for eligible real property) (Code Sec. 1400L(b)(2)(A)(v); Reg.§ 1.1400L(b)-1(c)(6)).

Property will not qualify if a binding written contract for the acquisition of the property was in effect before September 11, 2001 (Code Sec. 1400L(b)(2)(A)(iv)).

Property can qualify for the Code Sec. 168(k) allowance (¶ 127D) only if it is placed in service on or before December 31, 2004 (December 31, 2005, for certain property with a longer production period).

Except for listed property, an active conduct of a trade or business use requirement does not apply to the Code Sec. 168(k) allowance. Depreciable investment property may qualify for bonus depreciation under Code Sec. 168(k), but does not qualify for the Liberty Zone bonus depreciation allowance.

Substantially all requirement. The 80 percent test must be satisfied in the year the asset is placed in service. If business use in the Zone falls below 80 percent in a later tax year no recapture of the bonus deduction is required. However, if the asset is a listed property, such as a car, the bonus deduction and any amount expensed under section 179 is subject to recapture under the listed property rules in the year of the asset's assigned MACRS ADS recovery period that business use drops to 50 percent or less. See ¶ 206.

Related party use and binding contracts

Property will not qualify for the Liberty Zone bonus depreciation deduction if any of the following persons had a written binding contract in effect for the acquisition of the property at any time on or before September 10, 2001: (1) the user of the property on the date that the property was originally placed in service; (2) a person related to the user of the property on the date that the property was originally placed in service; or (3) a person related to the taxpayer. Likewise, property will not qualify for the bonus depreciation if its manufacture, construction, or production began at any time on or before September 10, 2001, and the property was manufactured, constructed, or produced for the user or the related parties listed above (Code Sec. 1400L(b)(2)(D), as amended by the Working Families Tax Relief Act of 2004 (P.L. 108-311) and Code Sec. 168(k)(2)(D)(iv), as amended by P.L. 108-311; Reg. § 1.1400L(b)-1(c)(5)).

Acquired by purchase requirement

Property is considered acquired by purchase if it meets the requirements prescribed by Code Sec. 179(d) and Reg. § 1.179-4(c) (Code Sec. 1400L(2)(A)(iv); Reg.§ 1.1400L(b)-1(c)(5)). Code Sec. 179(d)(2) defines "purchase" as any acquisition of property *except* property: (1) acquired from a person whose relationship to the taxpayer would bar recognition of a loss in any transaction between them under Code Sec. 267 or Code Sec. 707(b); (2) acquired from another member of a controlled group (substituting a more-than-50-percent ownership test for the at-least-80-percent ownership test in Code Sec. 1563(a)(1)); (3) the adjusted basis of which is determined in whole or in part by reference to the adjusted basis of the property in the hands of the person from whom the property was acquired (i.e., a substituted basis); or (4) acquired from a decedent with a fair-market value (stepped-up) basis.

The Code Sec. 168(k) allowance does not have an acquisition by purchase requirement.

Original use requirement and used property

Used property may qualify as long as it was not previously used in the Liberty Zone (Reg. § 1.1400L(b)-1(c)(4)). The original use of the property in the Liberty Zone must begin with the taxpayer after September 10, 2001. Additional capital expenditures incurred to recondition or rebuild property for which the original use in the Liberty Zone began with the taxpayer will also satisfy the original use requirement (Reg. § 1.1400L(b)-1(c)(4); Joint Committee on Taxation, *Technical Explanation of the "Job Creation and Worker Assistance Act of 2002"* (JCX-12-02), March 6, 2002).

Used property does not qualify for the Code Sec. 168(k) bonus allowance.

All other original use rules described in Reg. § 1.168(k)-1(b)(3) and applicable under Code Sec. 168(k) apply to Liberty Zone property. See "*Original use requirement*" at ¶ 127D.

Sale-leasebacks, syndication transactions, and fractional interests

The special rules for sale-leasebacks, syndication transactions, and sales of fractional interests that apply under Code Sec. 168(k) (¶ 127D) also apply to New York Liberty Zone Property (Code Sec. 1400L(b)(2)(D); Reg.§ 1.1400L(b)-1(c)(4) and (6)).

Self-constructed property

Property manufactured, constructed, or produced by a taxpayer for the taxpayer's own use is treated as acquired after September 10, 2001, if the taxpayer began manufacturing, constructing, or producing the property after September 10, 2001 (Code Sec. 1400L(b)(2)(D) and Code Sec. 168(k)(2)(D)(i); Reg. § 1.1400L(b)-1(c)(5)). Property that is manufactured, constructed, or produced for the taxpayer by another person under a contract that is entered into prior to the manufacture, construction, or production of the property is considered manufactured, constructed, or produced by the taxpayer (Reg. § 1.1400L(b)-1(c)(5); Reg. § 1.168(k)-1(b)(4)(iii); Joint Committee on Taxation, *Technical Explanation of the "Job Creation and Worker Assistance Act of 2002"* (JCX-12-02), March 6, 2002).

Eligible real property

Eligible real property is nonresidential real property or residential rental property that rehabilitates real property damaged, or replaces real property destroyed or condemned, as a result of the September 11, 2001, terrorist attack (Reg.§ 1.1400L(b)-1(c)(2)).

Property is treated as replacing real property destroyed or condemned if, as part of an integrated plan, the property replaces real property which is included in a continuous area which includes real property destroyed or condemned (Code Sec. 1400L(b)(2)(B); Reg.§ 1.1400L(b)-1(c)(2)).

Real property destroyed or condemned only includes circumstances in which an entire building or structure was destroyed or condemned as a result of the terrorist attacks. Otherwise, the property is considered damaged real property. If structural components of a building (for example, walls, floors, or plumbing fixtures) are damaged or destroyed and the building is not destroyed or condemned, then only costs related to replacing the damaged or destroyed components qualify for the additional allowance (Reg. § 1.1400L-1(c)(2)(B); Joint Committee on Taxation, Technical Explanation of the "Job Creation and Worker Assistance Act of 2002" (JCX-12-02), March 6, 2002).

The *replaced temporary regulations* defined real property as a building or its structural components, or other tangible real property except: (1) property described in Code Sec. 1245(a)(3)(B) (relating to depreciable property used as an integral part of a specified activity or as a specified facility); (2) property described in section Code Sec. 1245(a)(3)(D) (relating to a single purpose agricultural or horticultural structure); and (3) property described in Code Sec. 1245(a)(3)(E) (relating to storage facility used in connection with the distribution of petroleum or any primary product of petroleum). Under the definition contained in the former temporary regulations, nonresidential real property or residential rental property that rehabilitates or replaces any of the excluded properties that were damaged, destroyed, or condemned did not qualify for bonus depreciation. These exclusions to the definition of real property were retroactively eliminated in the final regulations. See Rev. Proc. 2006-43, I.R.B. 2006-45 for change in accounting procedures to claim bonus depreciation on property that now qualifies under the final regulations.

Rehabilitation credit. The final regulations provide that if qualified rehabilitation expenditures are qualified property under Code Sec. 168(k), 50-percent bonus depreciation property, or Liberty Zone property, a taxpayer may claim the additional first year depreciation deduction for the unadjusted depreciable basis of the qualified rehabilitation expenditures and may claim the rehabilitation credit (provided the requirements of Code Sec. 47 are met) for the remaining basis of the qualified rehabilitation expenditures (unadjusted depreciable basis less the additional first year depreciation deduction allowed or allowable, whichever is greater) provided the taxpayer depreciates the remaining adjusted depreciable basis of such expenditures using the straight line method. The taxpayer may also claim the rehabilitation credit for the portion of the basis of the qualified rehabilitated building that is attributable to the qualified rehabilitation expenditures if the taxpayer elects not to deduct the additional first year depreciation for the class of property that includes the qualified rehabilitated expenditures (Reg. § 1.1400L(b)-1(f)(9); Reg. § 1.1400L(b)-1(g)(6)).

Mandatory ADS property disqualified

Property which must be depreciated under the MACRS alternative depreciation system (ADS) does not qualify for the Code Sec. 1400L(b) allowance or the Code Sec. 168(k) allowance (Code Sec. 1400L(b)(2)(C)(ii); Reg. § 1.1400L(b)-1(c)(2)(ii)(C)). Property for which ADS is elected does qualify, assuming all other requirements are satisfied. The same rule applies to bonus depreciation under Code Sec. 168(k). See ¶ 127D.

Leasehold improvement property

"Qualified New York Liberty Zone leasehold improvement property" does not qualify for the Code Sec. 1400L(b) allowance or the Code Sec. 168(k) allowance (Code Sec. 1400L(b)(2)(C)(iii); Reg. § 1.1400L(b)-1(c)(2)(ii)(E). This property, however, may be depreciated using the straight-line method over five years. See ¶ 124A.

Alternative minimum tax

The Code Sec. 1400L(b) allowance may be claimed against alternative minimum tax in the tax year that the qualifying property is placed in service. No AMT adjustment is made. Also, no AMT adjustment is required for the regular MACRS allowances claimed on qualifying property if no election out is made (Code Sec. 1400L(b)(2)(E); Reg.§ 1.1400L(b)-1(d)). The same rule applies to property for which the Code Sec. 168(k) allowance is claimed (Code Sec. 168(k)(2)(F)). If the bonus depreciation deduction is claimed, no AMT adjustments are required on any of the regular MACRS depreciation deductions computed during the recovery period of the Liberty Zone property. See ¶ 127D.

¶ 127F

Bonus Depreciation for Gulf Opportunity Zone Property

Taxpayers may claim an additional first-year depreciation allowance equal to 50 percent of the adjusted basis of qualified Gulf Opportunity Zone (GO Zone) property acquired on or after August 28, 2005, and placed in service on or before December 31, 2007 (Code Sec. 1400N(d), as added by the Gulf Opportunity Zone Act of 2005 (P.L. 109-135); Notice 2006-77, as modified by Notice 2007-36 providing extensive regulatory type guidance). The place- in-service deadline is December 31, 2008 for nonresidential real property and residential rental property. However, if such real property is located in a country or parish within the GO Zone where more than 60 percent of the housing units were destroyed by hurricanes that occurred during 2005, the deadline is December 31, 2010, as explained below.

The GO Zone bonus allowance must be claimed unless an election out is made (Code Sec. 1400N(d)(2)(A)(iv)). Election procedures and a special deemed election out are described below. The deduction is subject to the general rules regarding whether an item is deductible under Code Sec. 162 or subject to the capitalization rules under Code Sec. 263 or Code Sec. 263A (Joint Committee on Taxation, Technical Explanation of the Gulf Opportunity Zone Act of 2005 (JCX-88-05)).

Generally, the GO Zone bonus deduction is equal to 50 percent of the cost of the property after reduction by any amount expensed under Code Sec. 179. MACRS depreciation deductions are then computed on the cost as reduced by the expensed amount and the bonus deduction. This is the same computational rule that applied under the Code Sec. 168(k) bonus depreciation provision described at ¶ 127D.

> ***Example (1):*** A taxpayer purchases $1,000 of qualifying Gulf Opportunity Zone property and places it in service in 2006. If the taxpayer claims a $200 Code Sec. 179 expense allowance on the property, the additional allowance is equal to $400 (($1,000 - $200) × 50%). The regular first-year MACRS depreciation deduction, assuming the property is 5-year MACRS property and the half-year convention applies, is $80 (($1,000 - $200 - $400) × 20% first year MACRS table percentage for 5-year property subject to half-year convention).

Sec. 179 expense allowance increased. The Code Sec. 179 allowance may be claimed on Gulf Opportunity Zone property that is also qualifying section 179 property. The new law increases the section 179 dollar limitation on section 179 Gulf Opportunity Zone property placed in service on or before December 31, 2007 by an additional $100,000 and the investment limitation by an additional $600,000 (Code Sec. 1400N(e), as added by the Gulf Zone Act). The placed-in-service deadline is extended one year if the section 179 property is located in a county or parish within the GO-Zone where more than 60 percent of the housing units were destroyed by hurricanes during 2005. See ¶ 306.

Qualifying Property

The GO Zone bonus allowance is claimed on "qualified Gulf Opportunity Zone property." Subject to the exceptions described below, qualified Gulf Opportunity Zone property is property:

(1) that is described in Code Sec. 168(k)(2)(A)(i) (i.e., property of a type that would qualify for bonus depreciation under Code Sec. 168(k)) or is new nonresidential real property or residential rental property;

(2) substantially all (80 percent or more) of the use of the property is in the Gulf Opportunity Zone (i.e., the GO Zone) and is in the active conduct of a trade or business by the taxpayer in the GO Zone;

(3) the original use of the property in the GO Zone commences with the taxpayer on or after August 28, 2005;

(4) the property is acquired by the taxpayer by purchase (within the meaning of Code Sec. 179(d) (see ¶ 302)) on or after August 28, 2005 and no written binding contract for the acquisition was in effect before August 28, 2005; and

(5) the property is placed in service by the taxpayer on or before December 31, 2007 (December 31, 2008 or December 31, 2010, as explained below, in the case of residential rental property or nonresidential real property).

Property described in Code Sec. 168(k)(2)(A)(i). In general, this is property with an MACRS recovery period of 20 years or less, computer software that is amortizable over 3 years under Code Sec. 167(f) (see ¶ 48), MACRS 25-year water utility property (see ¶ 113), and qualified leasehold improvement property as defined for purposes of the Code Sec. 168(k) bonus allowance (see "*Qualified leasehold improvement property*" at ¶ 127D).

Gulf Opportunity Zone defined. In general, the Gulf Opportunity Zone is the area of the Gulf Coast that was declared a disaster area by President Bush as a result of Hurricane Katrina and for which individual or public assistance is authorized (Code Sec. 1400M(1)). See IRS Publication 4492 (January 2006) for a list of counties located in Alabama, Louisiana, and Mississippi that are within the GO zone.

Residential rental and nonresidential real property.

Unlike the Code Sec. 168(k) bonus depreciation allowance (¶ 127D), the Gulf Zone bonus allowance may be claimed on residential rental and nonresidential real property. The property must be new because the original use within the zone must commence with the taxpayer. However, if used property located in the Zone is purchased and rehabilitated (e.g., first story water damage repaired), the cost of rehabilitation may qualify for the allowance. In addition, as explained under the *Original Use* discussion below, the cost of the damaged building may also qualify if its cost is not more than 20 percent of the total value of the property after it is rehabilitated.

The Gulf Zone bonus deduction is treated as an accelerated depreciation deduction for purposes of the section 1250 recapture rules. This treatment is also prescribed when the Code Sec. 168(k) bonus deduction (¶ 127D) is claimed on section 1250 property (Reg.§ 1.168(k)-1(f)(3)).

Rehabilitations to residential rental or nonresidential real property that is not MACRS property (for example, because placed in service before 1986 by the taxpayer) qualify for the bonus deduction because the cost of rehabilitation is treated as MACRS residential rental or nonresidential real property regardless of the depreciation method used to depreciate the rehabilitated building. As discussed below, however, no bonus deduction is allowed for nonresidential real property or rehabilitations to nonresidential real property located in a renewal community if an election is made to claim a current expense or amortization deduction under Code Sec. 1400I on the cost of new nonresidential real property placed in service by the taxpayer in a renewal community.

Generally, residential rental or nonresidential real property must be placed in service on or before December 31, 2008 in order to qualify for the GO-Zone bonus allowance. However, this deadline is extended to December 31, 2010 in the case of "specified Gulf Opportunity Zone extension property." Specified Gulf Opportunity Zone extension property is property located in a county or parish within the GO-Zone where more than 60 percent of the housing units were destroyed by any hurricanes during 2005 (Code Sec. 1400N(d)(6), as added by the Tax Relief and Health Care Act of 2006 (P.L. 109-432)). These are the Louisiana parishes of Calcasieu, Cameron, Orleans, Plaquemines, St. Bernard, St. Tammany, and Washington, and the Mississippi counties of Hancock, Harrison, Jackson, Pearl River, and Stone (Notice 2007-36). *Although the placed-in-service deadline is extended two years through December 31, 2010, only progress expenditures incurred through December 31, 2009 will qualify for the deduction.*

Personal property located in or on a building within one of these qualifying counties or parishes will qualify for the bonus allowance as specified Gulf Opportunity Zone extension property if the personal property is placed in service within 90 days after the building is placed in service, provided that the building is placed in service by the December 31, 2010 placed-in-service deadline. The progress expenditure rule does not apply to personal property. Thus, for example, if a building is placed in service on December 31, 2010, furniture and computers placed in service within the building within 90 days after December 31 qualify for the bonus allowance.

Note also that the 90 day rule appears to apply to personal property components of a building located within a qualifying county or parish that are identified in a cost segregation (¶ 127) study. If a building is not located within a qualifying county or parish, then personal property components identified in a cost segregation study appear to be subject to the unextended December 31, 2007 placed-in-service deadline for personal property while the structural components of the building are eligible for the unextended December 31, 2008 placed-in-service deadline for real property.

Active trade or business requirement

As noted below, Gulf Zone bonus depreciation may not be claimed unless substantially all (80 percent or more) of the use of the property in the Gulf Zone is in the active conduct of a trade or business. The following question and answer from the IRS web site (Headliner 149, February 24, 2006 at http://www.irs.gov/businesses/small/article/0,,id=154787,00.html) considers the active conduct of a trade or business requirement in the context of a residential rental property. Notice 2006-77 discussed below provides additional guidance.

Q: Regarding rental property – three scenarios:

(1) *A taxpayer operates multiple rental units. In November 2005, he acquires a new apartment house under construction and places it in service in February 2006. Does he qualify for the 50% bonus depreciation?*

(2) *A taxpayer had no rental property as of August 29, 2005. In December he acquires seven new houses (never previously placed in service) in the GO Zone, which he rents to displaced Katrina victims. Does he qualify for the 50% bonus depreciation?*

(3) *A taxpayer had no rental property as of August 29, 2005. In December, he acquires one new house (never previously placed in service) in the GO Zone, which he rents to a displaced business associate. Does he qualify for the 50% bonus depreciation? Is he engaged in an active trade or business?*

A: Like the Liberty Zone bonus, the GO Zone bonus applies to nonresidential real property and residential rental property. One of the requirements to be GO Zone property is that the property is in the active conduct of a trade or business by the taxpayer in the GO Zone. This requirement is similar to the one in the Liberty Zone bonus. The Liberty Zone bonus regulations do not define "active conduct."

With respect to rental real estate, the hurdle to get over is this active conduct requirement. There are two components to satisfy –

(1) *Trade or business – has the same meaning as in Code Sec. 162and the regulations thereunder.*

(2) *Active conduct – where Congress intended to treat all real estate rental as a active conduct in a trade or business, Congress provided such a provision (e.g., see Code Sec. 168(j)(5)). Because Code Sec. 1400N(d)does not contain a provision similar to that in Code Sec. 168(j)(5), it appears that some real estate rentals may not be in the active conduct of a trade or business for purposes of Code Sec. 1400N(d). Neither the statute nor the legislative history provides guidance on what standard to consider for "active conduct." Other Code sections have a standard. For example, there is the material participation standard in section 469 and the meaningful participation standard in Reg.§ 1.179-2(c)(6)(ii). Future guidance may be provided on what standard to apply for "active conduct."*

Guidance on the active trade or business requirement was provided by the IRS in Notice 2006-77. A taxpayer generally is considered to actively conduct a trade or business if the taxpayer meaningfully participates in the management or operations of the trade or business. A partner, member, or shareholder of a partnership, limited liability company, or S corporation, respectively, is considered to actively conduct a trade or business of the partnership, limited liability company, or S corporation if the partnership, limited liability company, or S corporation meaningfully participates (through the activities performed by itself, or by others on behalf of the partnership, limited liability company, or S corporation, respectively) in the management or operations of the trade or business. Similar rules apply to other pass-thru entities such as trusts or estates (Notice 2006-77).

Note that even if the active conduct standard that applies for purposes of the deduction is satisfied, the passive activity rules of Code Sec. 469 could operate to prevent the deduction if the Code Sec. 469 material participation standard is not satisfied by the partner or LLC member.

A triple-net lease in which the lessee is responsible for all of the costs relating to the building (for example, paying all taxes, insurance, and maintenance expenses) in addition to paying rent does not satisfy the material participation standard (Notice 2006-77, Sec. 3.02(3)(d), Example (4)).

Substantially all requirement

Substantially all of the use of the property (80 percent or more) must be in the GO Zone and in the active conduct of a trade or business by the taxpayer in the GO Zone. Thus, if more than 20 percent of the use of the property is either outside the counties and parishes designated as being part of the GO Zone or is not in the active conduct of a trade or business by the taxpayer in the GO Zone, then the property is not GO Zone property and is not eligible for the GO Zone additional first year depreciation deduction (Code Sec. 1400N(d)(2)(A); Notice 2006-77). This requirement is the same as the requirement in section Code Sec. 1400L(b)(2)(A)(ii) for the New York Liberty Zone bonus depreciation. Reg. § 1.1400L(b)-1(c)(3) defines "substantially all" as meaning 80 percent or more.

If the substantially all requirement is not satisfied in a tax year after the property is placed in service, the GO Zone bonus depreciation deduction must be recaptured as explained below.

Many vessels have a base of operations in the GO Zone but are used predominantly outside of the GO Zone. Apparently, taxpayers who purchase replacement vessels or repair damaged vessels will not qualify for the bonus allowance since 80 percent or more of the use is not within the GO-Zone.

Original use requirement

Generally, only new property qualifies for the additional bonus allowance. However, used property may also qualify if it has not been previously used for personal or business purposes within the Gulf Opportunity Zone by any person (i.e., its first use in the Zone must commence with the taxpayer). As explained below, additional capital expenditures incurred to recondition or rebuild property that is currently located in the GO Zone will qualify for the bonus deduction (Notice 2007-36, clarifying, modifying, and amplifying Section 2.02(3) of Notice 2006-77).

The original use rules for Code Sec. 168(k) bonus depreciation relating to sale-leasebacks, syndications, fractional interests, and certain other transactions also apply to Go Zone bonus depreciation (Section 5 of Notice 2007-36. See below.

Original use—rehabilitations of personal or real property. The cost of rehabilitations to real or personal business property located in the GO Zone meet the original use requirement. However, the materials and components used in the rehabilitation cannot previously have been used in the GO-Zone as this would violate the original use requirement. Also, as discussed below, no deduction is allowed for nonresidential real property or rehabilitations to nonresidential real property if a deduction for qualified revitalization buildings and rehabilitation expenditures is claimed under Code Sec. 1400I.

Generally, no portion of the cost of an existing building located in the GO-Zone can qualify for the GO-Zone bonus allowance because its original use in the GO-Zone is not by the taxpayer. An important exception, however, can apply to a substantially damaged building. Recent IRS guidance provides that the cost of a damaged building qualifies for bonus depreciation if it is not more than 20 percent of the total cost of the property taking into account the rehabilitations. This rule also applies to personal property—for example, used machinery and equipment originally located in the GO Zone that is rebuilt or reconditioned. This rule applies whether the property is acquired or self-constructed (Section 5 of Notice 2007-36, clarifying, modifying, and amplifying Section 2.02(3) of Notice 2006-77).

Example (2): John's rental unit is damaged in Hurricane Katrina. The cost of any rehabilitations made by John that are capitalized meet the original use requirement. John may claim the bonus deduction on the cost of the rehabilitations when he places them into service assuming all other requirements for claiming the bonus deduction are satisfied.

Example (3): John's rental unit is badly damaged in Hurricane Katrina. John spends $4 million rehabilitating or improving the building and then sells it to Sam for $5 million before placing the building back in service. $1 million of the cost is attributed to the building and $4 million to the rehabilitation expenditures. Sam may claim bonus depreciation on the $1 million cost (as well as the $4 million cost of the rehabilitation expenditures), assuming all other requirements for the deduction are met since only 20 percent of the total amount expended by Sam ($5 million × 20 percent = $1 million) is attributable to the damaged building (the "used part"). In effect, the $1 million cost of the building is considered new property (Example 4 of Section 5 of Notice 2007-36). Presumably, if Sam had purchased the damaged building from John for $1 million and spent at least $4 million on capitalized rehabilitations, the $1 million cost of the building (as well as the $4 million rehabilitation expenditures) would qualify for bonus depreciation since the 20 percent rule applies to property that is self-constructed by a taxpayer as well as property that is acquired by a taxpayer.

The following Question & Answer relating to the original use requirement is from the IRS web site (Headliner Volume 149 at http://www.irs.gov/businesses/small/article/0,,id=154787,00.html.

Q: A business's building is severely damaged by the storm. Can it claim the additional 50% depreciation in the following circumstances?

(1) *Business spends $450,000 restoring the building it operated in before the storm and an additional $600,000 expanding it.*

(2) *Business buys another pre-existing building in New Orleans for $1 million and spends another $450,000 adapting this building to its needs.*

A: These two questions deal with the original use requirement, which is one of the five requirements for satisfying the definition of GO Zone property. The original use rule for GO Zone property is similar to the original use rule for Liberty Zone property. See Temporary Reg.§ 1.168(k)-1T(b)(3) (now a final regulation, Reg.§ 1.168(k)-1(b)(3)—CCH) and Temporary Reg.§ 1.1400L(b)-1T(c)(4) (now a final regulation, Reg.§ 1.1400L(b)-1(c)(4)—CCH). (For these two questions, we have assumed the building is not rental property.)

(1) *Yes, assuming the improvements comprising the $1,050,000 are GO Zone property (e.g., the improvements are new components or are used components that are used for the first time in the GO Zone).*

(2) *No for the $1 million cost of the building because it does not satisfy the original use requirement. Yes for the $450,000 of additional capital expenditures to rebuild or recondition the building, assuming the improvements comprising the $450,000 are GO Zone property (e.g., the improvements are new components or are used components that are used for the first time in the GO Zone).*

Excluded property not qualifying for GO Zone bonus depreciation

The following property is not considered qualified Gulf Opportunity Zone property even if the preceding requirements are satisfied:

(1) property which must be depreciated under the MACRS alternative depreciation system;

(2) tax-exempt bond-financed property;

(3) qualified revitalization buildings with respect to which a deduction for revitalization expenditures is claimed under Code Sec. 1400I; and

(4) property used in connection with a private or commercial golf course, a country club, a massage parlor, a hot tub facility, a suntan facility, a liquor store, or a gambling or animal or racing property (Code Sec. 1400N(p)).

If specified Gulf Opportunity Zone extension property also qualifies for bonus depreciation under Code Sec. 168(k) (¶ 127D), the bonus depreciation is only claimed under the rules of Code Sec. 168(k) (Code Sec. 1400N(d)(6)(E)). The only property that could qualify under both provisions is new personal property acquired after 2007 and placed in service before 2010 in or on a building placed in service in a specified portion of the GO Zone (Section 6.01(2)(b) of Rev. Proc. 2008-54). See *Residential Rental and Nonresidential Real Property*, above.

Mandatory ADS property. Any property that must be depreciated using the MACRS alternative depreciation system (ADS), except by reason of an election to use ADS, does not qualify for the GO Zone bonus depreciation allowance. Thus, the GO Zone bonus depreciation allowance does not apply to tangible property used predominantly outside of the U.S., tax-exempt use property, tax-exempt bond financed property, and listed property, such as a car, not used more than 50 percent for business purposes. See "*Mandatory ADS property does not qualify for bonus depreciation*" at ¶ 127D for additional information.

Tax-exempt bond-financed property. If any portion of a property is financed with the proceeds of an obligation that pays interest that is exempt from tax under Code Sec. 103, no portion of the property qualifies for GO Zone bonus depreciation. Note that a new law provision of the Gulf Opportunity Zone Act authorizes the issuance of tax-exempt private activity bonds to finance the construction and rehabilitation of residential rental and nonresidential real property in the Gulf Opportunity Zone (Code Sec. 1400N(a)). Property financed to any extent under this provision will not qualify for the Gulf Zone bonus depreciation allowance.

Qualified revitalization buildings. Code Sec. 1400I allows a taxpayer to claim a current expense or amortization deduction on the cost of new nonresidential real property placed in service by the taxpayer in a renewal community (as defined in Code Sec. 1400E). The current expense or amortization deduction is also available for the cost of rehabilitating used nonresidential real property that is acquired by a taxpayer and placed in service in a renewal community. The current expense deduction is 50 percent of the qualified revitalization expenditures (i.e., 50 percent of the cost of a new building or 50 percent of the sum of the cost of rehabilitating an existing building plus a specified percentage of the cost of acquiring the existing building for rehabilitation). Alternatively, all expenditures that would be deductible without regard to the 50 percent limit may be amortized over a 120-month period. If a taxpayer elects to claim a current expense or amortization deduction, the GO Zone bonus allowance may not be claimed on the qualified revitalization building and, presumably, any rehabilitation expenditures.

The government has designated 40 renewal communities. These communities are listed at http://www.hud.gov/offices/cpd/economicdevelopment/programs/rc/index.cfm.

Golf courses etc. (prohibited activities). The deduction may not be claimed for any property used in connection with any private or commercial golf course, massage parlor, hot tub facility, suntan facility, or any store the principal business of which is the sale of alcoholic beverages for consumption off premises or any gambling or animal racing property (Code Sec. 1400N(p); Notice 2006-77).

If real property is used for both a prohibited activity and an non-prohibited activity, the portion of the real property (determined by square footage) that is not dedicated to the prohibited activity is eligible for the bonus deduction (assuming all other requirements are met).

A taxpayer's trade or business activity that has less than 10 percent of its total gross receipts derived from massages, tanning services, or a hot tub facility is not treated as, respectively, a massage parlor, a suntan facility, or a hot tub facility. For example, no portion of a physical therapy office or a beauty/day spa salon is treated as prohibited property if the taxpayer's gross receipts derived from massages, suntanning, and hot tub facilities are less than 10 percent of total gross receipts. Only gross receipts from the taxpayer's trade or business activity that includes the massages, tanning services, or hot tub facility are taken into account. If a taxpayer is a member of a consolidated group, only the gross receipts of the taxpayer (and not the consolidated group) are taken into account. Also, if the taxpayer is a partnership, S corporation, or other pass-thru entity, only the gross receipts of the pass-thru entity (and not the owners of the pass-thru entity) are taken into account (Notice 2006-77). Gross receipts are specially defined in Notice 2006-77. This exception does not apply to gambling and animal racing property.

Gambling and animal racing property. Gambling or racing property is any equipment, furniture, software, or other property used directly in connection with gambling, the racing of animals, or the on-site viewing of such racing, and the portion of any real property (determined by square footage) which is dedicated to gambling, animal racing, or the on-site viewing of such racing. The exclusion for real property does not apply if the dedicated portion is less than 100 square feet (Code Sec. 1400N(p), as added by the Gulf Zone Act). For example, no apportionment is required under this 100-square-foot de minimis rule in the case of a retail store that sells lottery tickets in a less than 100 square foot area (Notice 2006-77).

Hotels, restaurants, parking lots and other nongaming property that is attached to a gaming facility is eligible for the GO Zone additional first year depreciation deduction (assuming all other requirements under are met). For example, the GO Zone additional first year depreciation deduction for a building that is used as both a casino and a hotel is determined without regard to the portion of the building's unadjusted depreciable basis that bears the same percentage to the total unadjusted depreciable basis as the percentage of square footage dedicated to gambling (that is, the casino floor) bears to the total square footage of the building (Notice 2006-77).

Other exclusions. Property placed in service and disposed of during the same tax year does not qualify. However, rules similar to the rules in Reg.§ 1.168(k)-1(f)(1)(ii) and (iii) (technical termination of a partnership under Code Sec. 708(b)(1)(B) or transactions described in Code Sec. 168(i)(7)) apply. Property converted from business or income-producing use to personal use in the same taxable year in which the property is placed in service by a taxpayer does not qualify. If depreciable property is not GO Zone property in the tax year in which the property is placed in service by the taxpayer, the GO Zone additional first year depreciation deduction is not allowable for the property even if a change in use of the property subsequent to the placed-in-service year of the property results in the property being GO Zone property. See Reg.§ 1.168(k)-1(f)(6)(iv)(B) (Notice 2006-77).

If specified Gulf Opportunity Zone extension property also qualifies for bonus depreciation under Code Sec. 168(k) (¶ 127D), the bonus depreciation is only claimed under the rules of Code Sec. 168(k) (Code Sec. 1400N(d)(6)(E)). The only property that could qualify under both provisions is new personal property acquired after 2007 and placed in service before 2010 in or on a building placed in service in a specified portion of the GO Zone (Section 6.01(2)(b) of Rev. Proc. 2008-54). See *Residential Rental and Nonresidential Real Property*, above.

First-year depreciation caps on passenger automobiles not increased

The provision does not increase the first-year depreciation caps on passenger automobiles for which the additional depreciation allowance is claimed. A $7,650 bump-up was allowed if 50-percent bonus depreciation was claimed under Code Sec. 168(k) (Code Sec. 168(k)(2)(F)). Although new Code Sec. 1400N(d) incorporates certain rules contained in Code Sec. 168(k) by cross-reference (see, for example, Code Sec. 1400N(d)(3) and (4)), no cross reference incorporation to Code Sec. 168(k)(2)(F) is provided. It seems likely that the failure to increase in the first-year cap was intentional given that Congress did not provide for a bump-up in the cap for vehicles located in the New York Liberty Zone when it enacted the New York Liberty Zone bonus depreciation provision contained in Code Sec. 1400L(b). See "*Vehicles in the New York Liberty Zone* "at ¶ 200.

Self-construction property, sale-leasebacks, syndication transactions, and related parties

Rules similar to those contained under the Code Sec. 168(k) bonus depreciation provision for self-constructed property in Code Sec. 168(k)(2)(E)(i), sale leasebacks in Code Sec. 168(k)(2)(E)(ii)), syndication transactions in Code Sec. 168(k)(2)(E)(iii), and limitations related to users and related parties in Code Sec. 168(k)(2)(E)(iv) apply to qualified Gulf Opportunity Zone property by substituting August 27, 2005 for December 31, 2007 each place it appears and in the case of the self-constructed property rule without regard to the requirement contained in Code Sec. 168(k)(2)(E)(i) that manufacture, construction, or production must begin before January 1, 2009 (Code Sec. 1400N(d)(3), as added by the Gulf Opportunity Zone Act and amended by the Housing Assistance Act of 2008 (P.L. 110-289)).

Thus, under the self-constructed property rule as it applies to GO Zone property that is manufactured, constructed, or produced by a taxpayer for its own use qualifies for the additional allowance if the taxpayer begins the manufacture, construction, or production after August 27, 2005, and the property is placed in service before January 1, 2008 (January 1, 2009 in the case of residential rental and nonresidential real property (January 1, 2011 in the case of such property located in a specified county) (Code Sec. 1400N(d)(3), as added by the Gulf Opportunity Zone Act and amended by the Housing Assistance Act (P.L. 110-289), Code Sec. 168(k)(2)(E)(i); Reg. § 1.168(k)-1(b)(4)(iii)). Prior to amendment by P.L. 110-289, manufacture, construction, or production had to start after August 27, 2005 and before January 1, 2008 (Code Sec. 1400N(d)(3), prior to amendment by P.L. 110-289). The amended law now allows a taxpayer to claim GO-Zone bonus depreciation on real property if manufacture, construction, or production starts after August 27, 2005 and the property is placed in service before January 1, 2009 (January 1, 2011 if the property is placed in service in a specified county but only pre-January 1, 2010 progress expenditures qualify). Property manufactured, constructed, or produced for a taxpayer by another person under a contract entered into before the manufacture, construction, or production of the property is considered to be manufactured, constructed, or produced by the taxpayer.

The limitation related to users and related parties will prevent property from qualifying for the additional allowance if the user of the property as of the date on which the property was originally placed in service, or a related party to the user, acquired, or had a written binding contract in effect for the acquisition of the property at any time on or before August 27, 2005. In addition, property manufactured, constructed, or produced for the taxpayer or a related party does not qualify for the additional allowance if the manufacture, construction, or production of the property for the taxpayer or a related party began at any time on or before August 27, 2005. Persons are related if thcy have a relationship specified in Code Sec. 267(b) or Code Sec. 707(b) (Code Sec. 1400N(d)(3), as added by the Gulf Opportunity Zone Act; Code Sec. 168(k)(2)(E)(iv); Reg. § 1.168(k)-1(b)(4)(iv)(A)).

For additional information see ¶ 127D, "*Self-constructed property*", "*Sale-leasebacks*", "*Syndication transactions* " under "*Sale-leasebacks*", and "*Binding contracts in effect with respect to original user or related party—disqualified transaction rule*" under "*Binding contracts defined*".

Recapture upon decline in business use

The GO Zone bonus depreciation deduction may not be claimed unless substantially all (80 percent or more) of the property's use is in the taxpayer's trade or business in the GO Zone. Recapture rules similar to those that apply to property expensed under Code Sec. 179 apply if the qualified Gulf Opportunity Zone property ceases to be qualified Gulf Opportunity Zone property. Thus, if such property is used less than 80 percent in a trade or business activity within the GO-Zone during any year of the MACRS recovery period that applies for regular tax purposes, the benefit of the deduction will be recaptured (Code Sec. 1400N(d)(5), as added by the Gulf Zone Act; Notice 2008-25).

The recaptured benefit derived from claiming the GO Zone additional first-year depreciation deduction for the property is equal to the excess of the total depreciation claimed (including the GO Zone additional first year depreciation deduction) for the property for the tax years before the recapture year over the total depreciation that would have been allowable for the tax years before the recapture year had the GO Zone additional first year depreciation deduction not been claimed (regardless of whether such excess reduced the taxpayer's tax liability). The amount recaptured is treated as ordinary income for the recapture year. For the recapture year and subsequent tax years, the taxpayer's depreciation deductions are determined as if no GO Zone additional first year depreciation deduction was claimed with respect to the property. If, subsequent to the recapture year, a change in the use of the property results in the property again being GO Zone property, then the GO Zone additional first year depreciation deduction is not allowable for the property (Notice 2008-25).

Example (4): Five-year MACRS property costing $1,000 is placed in service in the Gulf Zone in 2006. A $500 bonus deduction is claimed. Regular depreciation is $100 (($1,000 − $500) × 20% regular first year table depreciation percentage). In 2007 business use in the Gulf Zone drops to 70 percent. Recapture in 2007 is the $400 difference between the depreciation, including bonus depreciation, claimed in 2006 ($600) and the depreciation that would have been allowed in 2006 without claiming the bonus deduction ($1,000 × 20% = $200). The 2007 depreciation deduction is $224 ($1,000 × 70% business use × 32% second-year table percentage).

Notice 2008-25 also contains example recapture calculations, including calculations for property that is relinquished in a like-kind exchange or as a result of an involuntary conversion. In the case of like-kind exchanges and involuntary conversions, if the replacement property is GO Zone property in the hands of the taxpayer, then there is no requirement to recapture. If the replacement property is not GO Zone property in the hands of the taxpayer and the property is not substantially used in the GO Zone or in the active conduct of a trade or business by the taxpayer in the GO Zone, then the taxpayer must recapture and adjust the basis accordingly. If the replacement property is not GO Zone property in the hands of the taxpayer but is substantially used in the GO Zone and in the active conduct of a trade or business by the taxpayer in the GO Zone, then there is no recapture requirement.

Coordination with section 179 recapture rules and listed property recapture rules. As noted above, the section 179 allowance ($125,000 in 2007 and $250,000 in 2008 and 2009) is increased by an additional $100,000 for qualifying section 179 Gulf Opportunity Zone property placed in service before January 1, 2008 (January 1, 2009 in certain counties and parishes). This additional increase is subject to recapture if the property ceases to be qualified GO Zone property because its business use in the GO Zone drops below 80 percent (Code Sec. 1400N(e)(4)). The entire section 179 deduction claimed on Gulf Zone property (e.g., the basic allowance of $125,000 in 2007 and the $100,000 increase for GO Zone property) is subject to recapture under the existing section 179 recapture rules (¶ 300) if combined business use within and outside of the Zone falls to 50 percent or less. Thus, if business use of Gulf Zone property within the Zone is below 80 percent and above 50 percent, the bonus deduction is subject to recapture and any section 179 expense claimed that is attributable to the $100,000 increase for GO Zone property is subject to recapture. However, if Gulf Zone bonus depreciation and the section 179 deduction is claimed on a listed property, as defined at ¶ 208 and business use falls to 50 percent or less during the alternative depreciation system (ADS) recovery period, the bonus deduction is subject to recapture and the listed property recapture rules (¶ 210) apply to determine the recaptured section 179 deduction amount. The recapture guidance provided in Notice 2008-25 does not explain how to coordinate the Gulf Zone bonus depreciation recapture rules with the section 179 recapture rules for listed and nonlisted property.

Example (5): Assume the same facts as in *Example (4)* except that a $100 section 179 expense allowance was also claimed. No portion of the allowance is attributable to the extra section 179 allowance for GO Zone property. The section 179 expense is not recaptured because business use is above 50 percent. 2006 bonus depreciation is $450 (($1,000 − $100) × 50%). Regular depreciation is $90 (($1,000 − $100 − $450) × 20%). Bonus recapture in 2007 is the $360 difference between the depreciation, including the section 179 expense allowance and bonus depreciation, claimed in 2006 ($100 + $450 + $90 = $640) and the depreciation (including section 179 allowance) that would have been allowed in 2006 without claiming the bonus deduction ($100 + (($1,000 − $100) × 20%)) = $280). The 2007 depreciation deduction is $202 (($1,000 − $100) × 70% business use × 32% second-year table percentage). Without using the table percentages 2007 depreciation is also calculated as $202 (($1,000 − $100 − $450 − $90 + $360) × 70% business use percentage × 40% DB rate for five-year property).

The recapture rule for Gulf Opportunity Zone bonus depreciation set forth in Notice 2008-25 is similar to the rule that applies under the listed property recapture rules (viz., recapture is the difference between total depreciation claimed in recovery years prior to the recapture year (including the section 179 expense allowance and bonus allowance) and the depreciation that would have been claimed if the section 179 allowance and bonus allowance had not been claimed. Note, however, that under the listed property recapture rules recapture of both the bonus deduction and section 179 deduction should be determined by using the alternative depreciation system (ADS). Furthermore, ADS must be used to compute depreciation throughout the remaining ADS recovery period of the asset beginning in the recapture year determined as if ADS had been used from the year that asset was placed in service and no bonus or section 179 deduction was ever claimed.

Example (6): Assume the same facts as *Example (5)* except that the asset is a 5-year MACRS listed property (which also has a 5-year alternative depreciation system (ADS) recovery period) and that business use drops to 40 percent in 2007. Now the listed property recapture rule (¶ 210) applies because the property is a listed property and business use dropped to 50 percent or below during the asset's ADS recovery period. Under the listed property recapture rules, recapture is the $540 difference between the total depreciation/bonus/section 179 expense claimed in 2006 ($640) and the depreciation that would have been allowed in 2006 under the MACRS alternative depreciation system (ADS) without claiming the section 179 allowance and bonus depreciation ($1,000 × 10% first-year ADS table percentage = $100). 2007 depreciation is $80 ($1,000 × 40% business use percentage × 20% second-year ADS table percentage for property with a 5-year ADS period). Without using table percentages, 2007 depreciation is also $80 ($1,000 – $100 – $450 – $90 + $540 × 40% business use × 22.22% ADS SL rate (1/ 4.5 remaining years in recovery period = 22.22%).

The manner of computing MACRS deductions without table percentages is explained at ¶ 179.

Alternative minimum tax

The 50-percent GO Zone bonus deduction may be claimed in full for alternative minimum tax purposes. The MACRS depreciation deductions computed for regular tax purposes on the adjusted basis of the qualified Gulf Opportunity Zone property that remains after reduction by the 50-percent allowance may also be claimed in full for AMT purposes (Code Sec. 1400N(d)(4), as added by Gulf Opportunity Zone Act). The AMT rules for qualified Gulf Opportunity Zone property are similar to those that apply under Code Sec. 168(k)(2)(G) of the Code Sec. 168(k) bonus depreciation provision. The related regulations issued under the Code Sec. 168(k) bonus depreciation provision are in Reg. § 1.168(k)-1(d)(1)(iii) and Reg. § 1.168(k)-1(d)(2)(ii). Note that an election out of GO-Zone bonus depreciation could trigger an AMT liability since depreciation deductions claimed on 3-, 5-, 7-, and 10-year MACRS property will generate an AMT depreciation adjustment if such property is depreciated using the 200 percent declining balance method, as is generally the case. See, also, "*Alternative minimum tax*" at ¶ 127D.

Election out of GO Zone bonus depreciation

The GO Zone bonus depreciation allowance must be claimed unless a taxpayer makes an election out. Revocation of an election out may only be made with IRS permission. An election out must be made separately for each class of property (Code Sec. 1400N(d)(2)(B)(iv)). Thus, for example, a taxpayer may elect out for all five-year MACRS property placed in service during the tax year. A separate election out would need to be made for other MACRS property classes. The election out only applies to property within an elected class that is placed in service during the tax year of the election

In the case of the MACRS residential rental and MACRS nonresidential real property classes, the election out also applies to all real property in the same property class (i.e., to all property in the residential rental class and to all property in the nonresidential real property class). For example, if a taxpayer places several MACRS nonresidential real property buildings in service during the tax year, the election out, if made, would apply to all of the buildings.

See Form 4562 instructions for election procedures.

The election is made by each person owning GO Zone property (for example, for each member of a consolidated group by the common parent of the group, by the partnership, or by the S corporation) (Notice 2006-77).

In general, the election is made by the due date (including extensions) of the federal income tax return for the tax year in which the GO Zone property is placed in service by the taxpayer. The election must be made in the manner prescribed on Form 4562, Depreciation and Amortization, and its instructions (Notice 2006-77). The election out requires the attachment of a statement to the taxpayer's timely filed return (including extensions) indicating the class of property for which the taxpayer is making the election and that, for such class of property, the taxpayer is electing not to claim the GO Zone additional first year depreciation deduction.

An election not to deduct the GO Zone additional first-year depreciation allowance is revocable only with the prior written consent of the Commissioner (Notice 2006-77, Sec. 4.04). Although a taxpayer may revoke an election to claim bonus depreciation under Code Sec. 168(k) (¶ 127D) (Reg. § 1.168(k)-1(e)(7)) or in the Kansas disaster area (127G) (Sec. 4.01 of Notice 2008-67) within 6 months after the original due date (excluding extensions) of the timely filed return on which the election was made, it does not appear that this option is available for the GO Zone bonus depreciation election (Section 4(04) of Notice 2006-77; Instructions to Form 4562).

If an election out is not made, depreciation is computed on the basis that remains taking into account the allowable GO-Zone allowance even if the allowance was not claimed (Notice 2006-77, Sec. 4.05).

Deemed election out rule for 2004 or 2005 federal income tax return filed before September 13, 2006. A taxpayer that files its 2004 or 2005 federal income tax return before September 13, 2006, is treated as having made a valid election out for a class of property that is GO Zone property placed in service by the taxpayer on or after August 28, 2005, during the taxpayer's 2004 or 2005 taxable year, if the taxpayer:

(1) on that return, did not claim the GO Zone additional first year depreciation deduction for that class of property but did claim depreciation; and

(2) does not file an amended federal tax return for the taxpayer's 2004 or 2005 taxable year on or before February 14, 2007, or a Form 3115, Application for Change in Accounting Method, with the taxpayer's federal tax return for the taxpayer's next succeeding taxable year, to claim the GO Zone additional first year depreciation deduction for that class of property (Notice 2006-77, Sec. 4.03(2)(b)).

Form 3115 is filed in accordance with the automatic change of accounting method procedures provided in Rev. Proc. 2002-9 (see 75) except that the scope limitations in section 4.02 of Rev. Proc. 2002-9 do not apply. A Code Sec. 481(a) adjustment is also required.

¶ 127G

Bonus Depreciation for Qualified Recovery Assistance Property Located in Kansas Disaster Area

Taxpayers may claim an additional first-year depreciation allowance equal to 50 percent of the adjusted basis of qualified Recovery Assistance property acquired on or after May 5, 2007, and placed in service on or before December 31, 2008 in the Kansas disaster area (Act § 15345 of the Heartland, Habitat, Harvest and Horticulture Act of 2008, P.L. 110-246 (May 5, 2008), applying Code Sec. 1400N(d); Notice 2008-67, I.R.B. 2008-32, July 23, 2008, providing regulatory type guidance). The placed-in-service deadline is December 31, 2009 in the case of nonresidential real property and residential rental property that is qualified Recovery Assistance property (Act § 15345 of P.L. 110-246, applying Code Sec. 1400N(d)).

Section 3 of Notice 2008-67 explains how to claim the deduction for tax years that include May 5, 2007 in situations where the return that includes that date has not been filed or has been filed without claiming the deduction.

The Kansas disaster area bonus allowance for qualifying Recovery Assistance property must be claimed unless an election out is made (Act § 15345 P.L. 110-246, applying Code Sec. 1400N(d)(2)(A)(iv)). See below for discussion of the election out rules. The deduction is subject to the general rules regarding whether an item is deductible under Code Sec. 162 or subject to the capitalization rules under Code Sec. 263 or Code Sec. 263A.

Generally, the Kansas disaster area bonus deduction is equal to 50 percent of the cost of the property after reduction of the cost by any amount expensed under Code Sec. 179. MACRS depreciation deductions are then computed on the cost as reduced by the expensed amount and the bonus deduction (Section 3.01 of Notice 2008-67). This is the same computational rule that applied under the Code Sec. 168(k) bonus depreciation provision described at ¶ 127D.

Example 1: A taxpayer purchases $1,000 of qualifying Recovery Assistance property and places it in service in the Kansas Disaster area in 2008. If the taxpayer claims a $200 Code Sec. 179 expense allowance on the property, the additional allowance is equal to $400 (($1,000 - $200) × 50%). The regular first-year MACRS depreciation deduction, assuming the property is 5-year MACRS property and the half-year convention applies, is $80 (($1,000 - $200 - $400) × 20% first year MACRS table percentage for 5-year property subject to half-year convention).

Relationship to Stimulus Act bonus depreciation. The Economic Stimulus Act of 2008 (P.L. 110-185) reinstated the Code Sec. 168(k) 50 percent bonus depreciation allowance effective for property acquired after December 31, 2007 that is not subject to a pre-January 1, 2008 binding contract allowed and which is placed in service before January 1, 2010. See ¶ 127D. No bonus deduction may be claimed under the Kansas disaster area bonus depreciation provision if a bonus depreciation deduction is also allowed for the property under Code Sec. 168(k) as reinstated by the Stimulus Act (Section 2.03(1) of Notice 2008-67; Section 6.02(2)(b) of Rev. Proc. 2008-54). In effect, this means that the bonus allowance for property located in the Kansas disaster area and acquired after December 31, 2007 and placed in service on or before December 31, 2009 will only apply to 27.5 year residential rental and 39-year nonresidential real property. (Real property (other than qualified leasehold improvement property as defined in Code Sec. 168(k)(3)), does not qualify for bonus depreciation under Code Sec. 168(k) but does qualify under the Heartland, Habitat, Harvest and Horticulture Act if the property is placed in service in the Kansas disaster area).

Sec. 179 expense allowance increased. The Code Sec. 179 allowance may be claimed on qualifying Recovery Assistance property that is also section 179 property. The new law increases the section 179 dollar limitation on section 179 Recovery Assistance property by an additional $100,000 and the investment limitation by an additional $600,000 (Act § 15345 of P.L. 110-246 , applying Code Sec. 1400N(e)). See ¶ 306A for a discussion of the increased Code Sec. 179 allowance.

Qualified recovery assistance property defined

The Kansas disaster area bonus allowance may only be claimed on "qualified Recovery Assistance property." The IRS refers to such property as RA property. Subject to the exceptions described below, qualified Recovery Assistance property is property (Act § 15345 of P.L. 110-246 , applying Code Sec. 1400N(d)(2); Section 2.01 of Notice 2008-67):

(1) that is described in Code Sec. 168(k)(2)(A)(i) (i.e., property of a type that would qualify for bonus depreciation under Code Sec. 168(k)) or is new nonresidential real property or residential rental property;

(2) substantially all of the use of the property (80 percent or more) is in the Kansas disaster area and is in the active conduct of a trade or business by the taxpayer in the Kansas disaster area;

(3) the original use of the property in the Kansas disaster area commences with the taxpayer on or after May 5, 2007;

(4) the property is acquired by the taxpayer by purchase (within the meaning of Code Sec. 179(d) (see ¶ 302)) on or after May 5, 2007, but only if no written binding contract for the acquisition was in effect before May 5, 2007; and

(5) the property is placed in service by the taxpayer on or before December 31, 2008 (December 31, 2009, in the case of new residential rental property or nonresidential real property).

Kansas disaster area defined. The Kansas disaster area is an area with respect to which a major disaster has been declared by the President under section 401 of the Robert T. Stafford Disaster Relief and Emergency Assistance Act (FEMA-1699-DR, as in effect on the date of the enactment) by reason of severe storms and tornados beginning on May 4, 2007, and determined by the President to warrant individual or individual and public assistance from the Federal Government under such Act with respect to damages attributable to such storms and tornados (Act § 15345 of P.L. 110-246. The Kansas disaster area is comprised of the following counties: Barton, Clay, Cloud, Comanche, Dickinson, Edwards, Ellsworth, Kiowa, Leavenworth, Lyon, McPherson, Osage, Osborne, Ottawa, Phillips, Pottawatomie, Pratt, Reno, Rice, Riley, Saline, Shawnee, Smith, and Stafford (Notice 2008-67).

Property described in Code Sec. 168(k)(2)(A)(i). In general, this is property with an MACRS recovery period of 20 years or less, computer software that is amortizable over 3 years under Code Sec. 167(f) (¶ 48), MACRS 25-year water utility property, and qualified leasehold improvement property as defined for purposes of the Code Sec. 168(k) bonus allowance. See ¶ 127D.

Residential rental and nonresidential real property and personal property components thereof. Unlike the Code Sec. 168(k) bonus depreciation allowance (¶ 127D), the Kansas disaster area bonus allowance may be claimed on MACRS residential rental and MACRS nonresidential real property (acquired on or after May 5, 2007 and placed in service on or before December 31, 2009).

The original use requirement (see below) prevents used nonresidential real property or used residential rental property from qualifying for the bonus deduction unless damaged property is purchased by a taxpayer and rehabilitation costs account for 80 percent or more of the total cost of the property (i.e., capitalized rehabilitation expenditures account for at least 80 percent of the sum of the cost of the damaged property and the amount spent on rehabilitations and improvements that are capitalized). The original use requirement requires that the original use of the materials used for repair or improvement in the Kansas disaster area must begin with the taxpayer. Thus, used material brought into the Kansas disaster area by the taxpayer may qualify but used material previously used in a personal or business activity by someone else within the Kansas disaster area does not.

Personal property components of a building identified in a cost segregation study are subject to the December 31, 2009 placed-in-service deadline for personal property under Code Sec. 168(k) if acquired after December 31, 2007 (¶ 127D) while the structural components of a building are subject to the December 31, 2009 placed-in-service deadline for real property that is qualified recovery assistance property. See "Excluded property not qualifying for Kansas disaster area bonus depreciation," below. Personal property components acquired on or after May 5, 2007 and before January 1, 2008 may qualify for bonus depreciation as qualified recovery assistance property if placed in service before January 1, 2009.

Example 2: A new commercial building is placed in service by a taxpayer in the Kansas disaster area on June 1, 2009. A cost segregation study indicates that 20 percent of the building's adjusted basis is attributable to personal property elements that are

MACRS five-year property. 80 percent of the building's adjusted basis will qualify for the 50-percent bonus depreciation deduction as recovery assistance property. The personal property elements may separately qualify for 50% bonus depreciation under Code Sec. 168(k) if they were acquired on or after January 1, 2008. If they were acquired on or after May 5, 2007 and before January 1, 2008, they will not qualify for bonus depreciation since they were placed in service after the December 31, 2008 deadline for personal property under the Kansas disaster area rules.

If real or personal property received in a like-kind exchange (replacement property) is qualified Recovery Assistance property then the carryover and noncarryover portions of the replacement property's basis should qualify for the Kansas disaster area bonus depreciation deduction. The issue has not been specifically addressed by the IRS in any of its guidance but this rule applied under the original bonus depreciation provision (Code Sec. 168(k)) and should apply to Kansas disaster area bonus depreciation (Reg. § 1.168(k)-1(f)(5)). See ¶ 127D. In general, replacement *real* property is qualified Recovery Assistance property if acquisition and the original use of the property in the Kansas disaster area begins with the taxpayer on or after May 5, 2007 and the property is placed in service on or before December 31, 2009. Thus, in the case of real property, the transaction must be structured so that the replacement property is newly constructed real property that was not previously placed in service for personal or business purposes by any other person prior to the exchange (i.e., original use must begin with the taxpayer). Note that property acquired pursuant to a binding contract that was in effect prior to May 7, 2007 does not qualify for Kansas disaster area bonus depreciation.

Substantially all requirement. Substantially all (80 percent or more) of the use of the property must be in the Kansas disaster area and in the active conduct of a trade or business by the taxpayer in the Kansas disaster area (Act § 15345 of P.L. 110-246 applying Code Sec. 1400N(d)(2)(A); Section 2.02(2) of Notice 2008-67 applying Section 3 of Notice 2006-77). This requirement is the same as the requirement in Code Sec. 1400L(b)(2)(A)(ii) for the New York Liberty Zone bonus depreciation. Reg. § 1.1400L(b)-1(c)(3) also defines "substantially all" as meaning 80 percent or more.

Original use requirement. The original use of the property in the Kansas disaster area must commence with the taxpayer on or after May 5, 2007 (Act § 15345 of P.L. 110-246 applying Code Sec. 1400N(d)(2)(A); Section 2.02(3) of Notice 2008-67 applying Section 5 of Notice 2007-36). Generally, this means that only new property qualifies for the additional allowance. However, used property may also qualify provided that it has not been previously used within the Kansas disaster area (i.e., its first use in the disaster area (whether for personal or business purposes) commences with the taxpayer). Additional capital expenditures to recondition or rebuild damaged real or personal property located in the Kansas disaster area may qualify for bonus depreciation (Section 2.02(3) of Notice 2008-67 applying Section 5 of Notice 2007-36.

The original use rules for Code Sec. 168(k) bonus depreciation relating to sale-leasebacks, syndications, fractional interests, and certain other transactions also apply to Kansas disaster area bonus depreciation (Section 2.02(3) of Notice 2008-67 applying Section 5 of Notice 2007-36. See ¶ 127F).

The cost of purchasing damaged property already located in the Kansas disaster area does not qualify for bonus depreciation because of the original use requirement. However, if the property is substantially rehabilitated by the seller after being taken out of service so that the original use is considered to begin with the purchasing taxpayer the entire cost of the property may qualify for bonus depreciation. Substantial rehabilitation means that at least 80 percent of the total capitalized cost of the property as rehabilitated, improved, or repaired is attributable to rehabilitation expenditures (Section 2.02(3) of Notice 2008-67, applying Section 5 of Notice 2007-36).

> ***Example 3:*** Zefron owns damaged real estate located in the Kansas disaster area. He then spends $4 million to rehabilitate the property. Following rehabilitation and prior to placing it into service he sells the property in 2009 to Homer for $5 million. At the time of sale, the fair market value of the improvements is $4 million. Homer may claim bonus depreciation on the entire cost of the property since at least 80 percent of its cost is attributable to qualifying rehabilitation expenditures ($5 million × 80% = $4 million) (Examples 3 and 4 in Section 5 of Notice 2007-36, as applied by Section 2.02(3) of Notice 2008-67).

If in the preceding example Homer had purchased the damaged property from Zefron for $1 million and then made $4 million of rehabilitation expenditures himself, the entire rehabilitated cost of the building ($5 million) would presumably be eligible for bonus depreciation. Section 5 of Notice 2007-36 provides that the substantial rehabilitation rule applies to self-constructed property as well as acquired property.

For additional discussion of the original use requirement as it relates to buildings see the related discussion for GO Zone bonus depreciation at ¶ 127F.

Active trade or business requirement. The property must be used 80 percent or more by the taxpayer in the active conduct of a trade or business within the Kansas disaster area in the tax year the property is placed in service (Section 2.02(2) of Notice 2008-67, applying Section 3 of Notice 2006-77). If this requirement is not satisfied in a later tax year during the property's regular MACRS recovery period, the bonus allowance is subject to recapture. See below.

The term "trade or business" has the same meaning as in Code Sec. 162 and the regulations thereunder. Thus, property held merely for the production of income or used in an activity not engaged in for profit (as described in Code Sec. 183) does not qualify for the Kansas disaster area additional first year depreciation deduction. The determination of whether a trade or business is actively conducted by the taxpayer is based on all of the facts and circumstances. The test is generally satisfied if the taxpayer meaningfully participates in the management or operations of the trade or business. A partner, member, or shareholder of a partnership, limited liability company, or S corporation, respectively, is considered to actively conduct a trade or business of the partnership, limited liability company, or S corporation if the partnership, limited liability company, or S corporation meaningfully participates (through the activities performed by itself, or by others on behalf of the partnership, limited liability company, or S corporation, respectively) in the management or operations of the trade or business. Similar rules apply to other pass-thru entities such as trusts or estates (Section 2.02(2) of Notice 2008-67, applying Section 3 of Notice 2006-77).

A triple-net lease in which the lessee is responsible for all of the costs relating to the building (for example, paying all taxes, insurance, and maintenance expenses) in addition to paying rent does not satisfy the material participation standard (Notice 2006-77, § 3.02(3)(d), Example (4), as applied by Sec. 2.02(2) of Notice 2008-67).

The active trade or business requirement is applied on a property-by-property basis (Section 2.02(2) of Notice 2008-67, applying Section 3 of Notice 2006-77).

The passive loss rules (Code Sec. 469 and at-risk rules (Code Sec. 465) are separately applied and could result in disallowance of an otherwise deductible Kansas disaster area bonus allowance. The deduction may also be disallowed by the Code Sec. 704(d) limitation on a partner's distributive share of partnership loss to the adjusted basis of the partner's interest in the partnership at the end of the partnership year in which the loss occurred (Section 2.06 of Notice 2008-67).

For further discussion of the active trade or business requirement in the context of residential rental property, see the discussion of IRS Headliner 149 at ¶ 127F.

Excluded property not qualifying for Kansas disaster area bonus depreciation

The following property is not considered qualified Recovery Assistance property in any circumstance (Act § 15345 of P.L. 110-246 applying Code Sec. 1400N(d)(2)(B); Code Sec. 1400N(p); Section 2.03 of Notice 2008-67):

(1) property which must be depreciated under the MACRS alternative depreciation system;

(2) tax-exempt bond-financed property;

(3) qualified revitalization buildings with respect to which a deduction for revitalization expenditures is claimed under Code Sec. 1400I; and

Mandatory ADS property. Any property that must be depreciated using the MACRS alternative depreciation system (ADS), except by reason of an election to use ADS, does not qualify for the Kansas disaster area bonus depreciation allowance. Thus, the additional depreciation allowance does not apply to tangible property used predominantly outside of the U.S., tax-exempt use property, tax-exempt bond financed property, and listed property, such as a car, not used more than 50 percent for business purposes. See "*Mandatory ADS exception*" at ¶ 127D for additional information.

Tax-exempt bond-financed property. If any portion of a property is financed with the proceeds of an obligation that pays interest that is exempt from tax under Code Sec. 103, no portion of the property qualifies for Kansas disaster area bonus depreciation.

Qualified revitalization buildings. Code Sec. 1400I allows a taxpayer to claim a current expense or amortization deduction for the cost of new nonresidential real property placed in service by the taxpayer in a renewal community (as defined in Code Sec. 1400E). The current expense or amortization deduction is also available for the cost of rehabilitating used nonresidential real property that is acquired by a taxpayer and placed in service in a renewal community. The current expense deduction is 50 percent of the qualified revitalization expenditures (i.e., 50 percent of the cost of a new building or 50 percent of the sum of the cost of rehabilitating an existing building plus a specified percentage of the cost of acquiring the existing building for rehabilitation). Alternatively, all expenditures that would be deductible without regard to the 50 percent limit may be amortized over a 120-month period. If a taxpayer elects to claim a current expense or amortization deduction, the Kansas disaster area bonus allowance may not be claimed on the qualified revitalization building and, presumably, any rehabilitation expenditures.

The IRS has designated 40 renewal communities. These communities are listed at http://www.hud.gov/offices/cpd/economicdevelopment/programs/rc/index.cfm.

Prohibited activities property. The *Gulf Zone bonus depreciation deduction* may not be claimed for any property used in connection with any private or commercial golf course, massage parlor, hot tub facility, suntan facility, or any store the principal business of which is the sale of alcoholic beverages for consumption off premises or any gambling or animal racing property (Act § 15345 of P.L. 110-246 applying Code Sec. 1400N(p); Notice 2006-77).

It appears that prohibited activities property may qualify for the Kansas disaster area bonus deduction. Act § 15345 of P.L. 110-246 did not specifically apply Code Sec. 1400N(p) to Kansas Recovery Assistance property and Notice 2008-67 does not specifically disqualify such property. IRS Publication 943 also does not specifically disqualify such property.

For additional discussion of prohibited activities property for GO-Zone bonus depreciation purposes, see ¶ 127F.

Other exclusions. Property placed in service and disposed of during the same tax year does not qualify. However, rules similar to the rules in Reg. § 1.168(k)-1(f)(1)(ii) and (iii) (technical termination of a partnership under Code Sec. 708(b)(1)(B) or transactions described in Code Sec. 168(i)(7)) apply. Property converted from business or income-producing use to personal use in the same taxable year in which the property is placed in service by a taxpayer does not qualify. If depreciable property is not qualified Recovery Assistance property in the tax year in which the property is placed in service by the taxpayer, the Kansas disaster area additional first year depreciation deduction is not allowable for the property even if a change in use of the property subsequent to the placed-in-service year of the property results in the property being qualified Recovery Assistance property (Reg. § 1.168(k)-1(f)(6)(iv)(B); Section 2.03 and 2.05 of Notice 2008-67).

Kansas disaster area bonus depreciation does not result in increased first-year luxury auto depreciation caps

A taxpayer who claims the Kansas disaster area bonus depreciation allowance on a passenger automobile is not allowed to increase the first-year depreciation caps (¶ 200). An $8,000 bump-up is allowed if 50-percent bonus depreciation is claimed under Stimulus Act bonus depreciation (Code Sec. 168(k)) for property acquired after December 31, 2007 and placed in service before January 1, 2009.

Bonus depreciation, MACRS depreciation allowances, and the section 179 allowance may not be claimed by a taxpayer that elects out of MACRS by electing the standard mileage rate.

Self-constructed property, sale-leasebacks, syndication transactions, and related parties

Rules similar to those contained under the Code Sec. 168(k) bonus depreciation provision (¶ 127D) for self-constructed property in Code Sec. 168(k)(2)(E)(i), sale leasebacks in Code Sec. 168(k)(2)(E)(ii)), syndication transactions in Code Sec. 168(k)(2)(E)(iii), and limitations related to users and related parties in Code Sec. 168(k)(2)(E)(iv) apply to qualified Recovery Assistance property by substituting May 4, 2007 for December 31, 2007 (Act § 15345 of P.L. 110-246 applying Code Sec. 1400N(d)(3), as amended by the Economic Stimulus Act of 2008, P.L. 110-185; Section 2.02(4) of Notice 2008-67).

Under the self-constructed property rule, Recovery Assistance property that is manufactured, constructed, or produced by a taxpayer for its own use qualifies for the additional allowance if the taxpayer begins the manufacture, construction, or production after May 4, 2007, and before January 1, 2009, and the property is placed in service before January 1, 2009 (January 1, 2010 in the case of residential rental and nonresidential real property) (Act § 15345 of P.L. 110-246 applying Code Sec. 1400N(d)(3), as amended by the Economic Stimulus Act of 2008, P.L. 110-185; Code Sec. 168(k)(2)(E)(i) as amended by the Economic Stimulus Act of 2008, P.L. 110-185, Act § 103(a) (February 13, 2008); Reg. § 1.168(k)-1(b)(4)(iii)). Property manufactured, constructed, or produced for a taxpayer by another person under a contract entered into before the manufacture, construction, or production of the property is considered to be manufactured, constructed, or produced by the taxpayer.

Act § 3082(b)(1) of the Housing Assistance Act of 2008 (P.L. 110-289) amended Code Sec. 1400N(d)(3)(B) (dealing with GO Zone bonus depreciation) to eliminate the requirement that the manufacture, construction, or production must begin before January 1, 2008. To make it clear that this change was also intended to apply to the Kansas disaster area it would have been necessary for Congress to make a conforming change to Act § 15345 of the Heartland, Habitat, Harvest, and Horticulture Act (P.L. 110-246). Nothing in the Housing Act's legislative history indicates that this change was also intended to apply to property located in the Kansas disaster area. (Note that the change would only have a possible effect on residential rental and nonresidential real property in the Kansas disaster area that is subject to a January 1, 2010 placed-in-service deadline). If it was the intent of Congress to eliminate this construction start deadline for real property located in the Kansas disaster it may be necessary to enact a technical correction. With the enactment of such a technical correction, a taxpayer who places real property in service before January 1, 2010 in the Kansas disaster area could qualify for bonus depreciation even though construction started after December 31, 2008. See ¶ 127F for a discussion of the elimination of the requirement that construction must begin before January 1, 2009 in the case of GO Zone property.

The limitation related to users and related parties will prevent property from qualifying for the additional allowance if the user of the property as of the date on which the property was originally placed in service, or a related party to the user, acquired, or had a written binding contract in effect for the acquisition of the property at any time on or before May 4, 2007. In addition, property manufactured, constructed, or produced for the taxpayer or a related party does not qualify for the additional allowance if the manufacture, construction, or production of the property for the taxpayer or a related party began at any time on or before May 4, 2007. Persons are related if they have a relationship specified in Code Sec. 267(b) or Code Sec. 707(b) (Act § 15345 of P.L. 110-246 applying Code Sec. 1400N(d)(3), as amended by the Economic Stimulus Act of 2008, P.L. 110-185, Act § 103(c)(9) (February 13, 2008); Code Sec. 168(k)(2)(E)(iv) as amended by the Economic Stimulus Act of 2008, P.L. 110-185, Act § 103(a) (February 13, 2008); Reg. § 1.168(k)-1(b)(4)(iv)(A)).

Recapture of Kansas disaster area bonus depreciation upon decline in business use

The Kansas disaster area bonus depreciation deduction may not be claimed unless the property is used substantially in the taxpayer's trade or business in the Kansas disaster area (i.e., 80 percent or more). Recapture rules similar to those that apply to property expensed under Code Sec. 179 apply if the qualified Recovery Assistance property ceases to be qualified Recovery Assistance property. Thus, if such property is used less than 80 percent in a trade or business during any year of its recovery period, the benefit of the deduction will be recaptured (Act § 15345 of P.L. 110-246 applying Code Sec. 1400N(d)(5); Section 2.07 of Notice 2008-67, applying recapture rules for GO-Zone property contained in Section 3 of Notice 2008-25 in a similar manner to Recovery Assistance property). Note that if a property is not used predominantly (more than 50 percent) for business in the tax year it is placed in service then it cannot qualify for expensing under Code Sec. 179.

The benefit derived from claiming the Kansas disaster area additional first-year depreciation deduction for the property is equal to the excess of the total depreciation claimed (including the Kansas disaster area additional first year depreciation deduction) for the property for the tax years before the recapture year over the total depreciation that would have been allowable for the tax years before the recapture year as a deduction under Code Sec. 167(f)(1) or Code Sec. 168, as applicable, had the Kansas disaster area additional first year depreciation deduction not been claimed (regardless of whether such excess reduced the taxpayer's tax liability). The amount recaptured is treated as ordinary income for the recapture year. For the recapture year and subsequent tax years, the taxpayer's depreciation deductions are determined as if no Kansas disaster area additional first year depreciation deduction was claimed with respect to the property (Notice 2008-25). Notice 2008-25 contains example recapture calculations, including calculations related to property that is relinquished in a like-kind exchange or as a result of an involuntary conversion.

See ¶ 127F for discussion of GO Zone property recapture rules which apply in a similar manner to Recovery Assistance property.

Kansas disaster area bonus depreciation: alternative minimum tax implications

The 50-percent Kansas disaster bonus deduction for qualified Recovery Assistance property may be claimed in full for alternative minimum tax purposes. The MACRS depreciation deductions computed for regular tax purposes on the adjusted basis of the qualified Recovery Assistance property that remains after reduction by the 50-percent allowance may also be claimed in full for AMT purposes (Act § 15345 of P.L. 110-246 applying Code Sec. 1400N(d)(4); Section 4.01 of Notice 2008-67). If the election out is made, then any AMT adjustment otherwise required on regular depreciation deductions remains in effect. The AMT rules for qualified Recovery Assistance property are similar to those that apply under Code Sec. 168(k)(2)(G) of the Code Sec. 168(k) bonus depreciation provision. The related regulations issued under the Code Sec. 168(k) bonus depreciation provision are in Reg. § 1.168(k)-1(d)(1)(iii) and (2)(ii).

Election out of Kansas disaster area bonus depreciation

The Kansas disaster area bonus depreciation allowance must be claimed unless a taxpayer makes an election out.[28] An election out must be made separately for each class of property. Thus, for example, a taxpayer may elect out for all five-year MACRS property placed in service during the tax year. A separate election out would need to be made for other MACRS property classes. The election out only applies to property within an elected class that is placed in service during the tax year of the election.

In the case of the MACRS residential rental and MACRS nonresidential real property classes, the election out also applies to all real property in the same property class (i.e., to all property in the residential rental class and to all property in the nonresidential real property class). For example, if a taxpayer places several MACRS nonresidential real property buildings in service during the tax year, the election out, if made, would apply to all of the buildings.

The election out is made by each person owning Recovery Assistance property (for example, for each member of a consolidated group by the common parent of the group, by the partnership, or by the S corporation) (Section 4.01 of Notice 2008-67).

In general, the election is made by the due date (including extensions) of the federal income tax return for the tax year in which the Recovery Assistance

---

[28] Act § 15345 of P.L. 110-246 applying Code Sec. 1400N(d)(2)(B)(iv); Section 4 of Notice 2008-67).

property is placed in service by the taxpayer. The election must be made in the manner prescribed on Form 4562, Depreciation and Amortization, and its instructions (Section 4.03(1) of Notice 2008-67). The election out requires the attachment of a statement to the taxpayer's timely filed return (including extensions) indicating the class of property for which the taxpayer is making the election and that, for such class of property, the taxpayer is electing not to claim the additional first year depreciation deduction for recovery assistance property.

An election not to deduct the Kansas disaster area additional first-year depreciation allowance is revocable only with the prior written consent of the Commissioner unless the revocation is made within six months after the due date of the original return (excluding extensions) (Section 4.01 of Notice 2008-67; Reg. § 1.168(k)-1(e)(7)).

If an election out is not made, depreciation is computed on the basis that remains taking into account the allowable Kansas disaster area allowance even if the allowance was not claimed (Section 4.01 of Notice 2008-67; Reg.§ 1.168(k)-1(e)(5).

Special rules for returns that include May 5, 2007. Taxpayers that file a return on or after August 11, 2008 for a tax year that includes May 5, 2007 should following the election out procedures contained in the Form 4562 instructions. Special rules apply to returns filed before August 12 for a tax year which include May 5, 2007, including a deemed election out (Section 4 of Notice 2008-67).

¶ 127H

Bonus Depreciation for Qualified Disaster Assistance Property

An additional depreciation allowance (bonus depreciation) is permitted for the tax year in which qualified disaster assistance property is placed in service (Code Sec. 168(n), as added by the Emergency Economic Stabilization Act of 2008 (P.L. 110-343)). The provision applies to property placed in service after December 31, 2007, with respect to federally (i.e., Presidentially) declared disasters declared after such date and occurring before January 1, 2010.

As explained below disaster assistance property is property (including real property) that rehabilitates or replaces property that is destroyed or damaged as the result of a Presidentially declared disaster.

The additional first-year depreciation deduction is equal to 50 percent of the adjusted basis of the qualified disaster assistance property. The adjusted basis of the property is reduced by the amount of the additional deduction before computing the amount otherwise allowable as a depreciation deduction for the tax year in which the property is placed in service and for any subsequent tax year (Code Sec. 168(n)(1), as added by P.L. 110-343).

Since the bonus allowance is computed on the property's adjusted basis, the basis of the property is first reduced by any Code Sec. 179 allowance claimed. For a special provision that increases the Code Sec. 179 allowance on disaster assistance property (Code Sec. 179(e), as added by P.L. 110-343), see ¶ 306B.

This provision is not elective. However, a taxpayer can make an election out on a property class by property class basis (Code Sec. 168(n)(2)(B)(v)).

Qualified disaster assistance property defined

Qualified disaster assistance property must meet all of the following tests:

- The property must be described in Code Sec. 168(k)(2)(A)(i) (i.e., MACRS recovery property with an recovery period of 20 years or less, computer software that is depreciable over three years, water utility property, or qualified leasehold improvement property) or be nonresidential real property or residential rental property.

- Substantially all (80 percent or more) of the use of the property must be in a disaster area with respect to a federally declared disaster occurring before January 1, 2010, and in the active conduct of the taxpayer's trade or business in that disaster area.

- The property must rehabilitate property damaged, or replace property destroyed or condemned, as a result of the disaster. Property is treated as replacing property destroyed or condemned if, as part of an integrated plan, it replaces property that is included in a continuous area that includes real property destroyed or condemned. The property must also be similar in nature to, and located in the same county as, the property being rehabilitated or replaced.

- The original use of the property in the disaster area must commence with an eligible taxpayer on or after the applicable disaster date.

- The property must be acquired by the eligible taxpayer by purchase on or after the applicable disaster date, but only if no written binding contract for the acquisition was in effect before that date. A purchase is defined by reference to the definition in Code Sec. 179(d) (¶ 302); therefore, it cannot be a transaction between related parties or members of the same controlled group, and the transferee's basis in the property cannot be determined by reference to the transferor's basis.

- The property must be placed in service by the eligible taxpayer on or before the date that is the last day of the third calendar year following the applicable disaster date (or the fourth calendar year in the case of nonresidential real property and residential rental property) (Code Sec. 168(n)(2)(A), as added by P.L. 110-343).

Used property that is acquired outside of the disaster area may qualify, as long as its first original use in the disaster area is by an eligible taxpayer.

Federally declared disaster defined. An eligible taxpayer is a taxpayer who has suffered an economic loss attributable to a federally declared disaster (Code Sec. 168(n)(3)(D), as added by P.L. 110-343). A federally declared disaster is any disaster subsequently determined by the President of the United States to warrant assistance by the federal government under the Robert T. Stafford Disaster Relief and Emergency Assistance Act (see 42 U.S.C. § 5121 et seq.) (Code Sec. 168(n)(3)(B), as added by P.L. 110-343). The disaster area is the area determined to warrant disaster assistance (Code Sec. 168(n)(3)(C), as added by P.L. 110-343). The applicable disaster date is the date the federally declared disaster occurs (Code Sec. 168(n)(3)(A), as added P.L. 110-343).

Exceptions. Qualified disaster assistance property does not include:

- any property that is eligible for bonus depreciation under Code Sec. 168(k) (¶ 127D) (without regard to any election under Code Sec. 168(k)(4) to forgo bonus depreciation in favor of an accelerated research or AMT credit), cellulosic biomass ethanol plant property (Code Sec. 168(l)), and qualified refuse and recycling property (Code Sec. 168(m));

- property that qualifies for bonus depreciation under the special rules for the Gulf Opportunity (GO) Zone (¶ 127F) (Code Sec. 1400N(d));

- any property used in connection with any private or commercial golf course, country club, massage parlor, hot tub facility, or suntan facility; any store whose principal business is the sale of alcoholic beverages for consumption off premises; or any gambling or animal racing property (i.e., property described in Code Sec. 1400N(p)(3));

• property that must be depreciated under the MACRS alternative depreciation system (ADS) (not including property for which an ADS election is made);

• property financed by tax-exempt bonds;

• qualified revitalization buildings for which the taxpayer has elected the Code Sec. 1400I commercial revitalization deduction; and

• if the taxpayer elects out of this bonus depreciation with respect to any class of property for any tax year, all property in that class placed in service during that tax year (Code Sec. 168(n)(2)(B), as added by P.L. 110-343).

Special rules

Bonus depreciation for qualified disaster assistance property applies to the taxpayer's self-constructed property if the taxpayer begins manufacturing, constructing, or producing the property after the applicable disaster date. Sale-leaseback property that a taxpayer places in service after the applicable disaster date, and then sells and leases back within three months, is treated as originally placed in service no earlier than the date on which the property is used under the taxpayer's leaseback. If property is originally placed in service after the applicable disaster date by a lessor, then is sold by the lessor or any subsequent purchaser within three months after being placed in service, and the user of the property after the last sale during that three-month period remains the same as when the property was originally placed in service, the property is treated as originally placed in service no earlier than the date of the last sale. Finally, property is not qualified disaster assistance property if the user or a related party has a pre-2008 contract to acquire or produce it (Code Sec. 168(n)(2)(B), as added by P.L. 110-343; see Code Sec. 168(k)(2)(E)).

AMT

As with regular Code Sec. 168(k) bonus depreciation (127D), the additional depreciation allowance for qualified disaster assistance property may be claimed for alternative minimum tax purposes in the tax year that qualifying property is placed in service. No AMT adjustment is required. Furthermore, no AMT adjustment is required on any regular depreciation deductions claimed on the property over its entire recovery period (Code Sec. 168(n)(2)(D), as added by P.L. 110-343; see Code Sec. 168(k)(2)(G) and Reg. § 1.168(k)-1(d)).

Recapture

The tax benefits of the bonus depreciation deduction must be recaptured as ordinary income in a tax year in which the qualified disaster assistance property ceases to be qualified disaster assistance property by applying rules similar to those contained in Code Sec. 179(d)(10) (Code Sec. 168(n)(2)(B), as added by P.L. 110-343). Thus, recapture is required if the property is removed from the disaster area or business use in the disaster area falls below 80 percent.

The 50-percent GO Zone bonus depreciation allowance (Code Sec. 1400N(d)) is also required to be recaptured by applying rules similar to those applicable to section 179 property. Under guidance issued by the IRS in Notice 2006-77, I.R.B. 2006-40, the benefit derived from claiming the GO Zone additional first year depreciation deduction for the property is equal to the excess of the total depreciation claimed (including the GO Zone additional first year depreciation deduction) for the property for the tax years before the recapture year over the total depreciation that would have been allowable for the tax years before the recapture year had the GO Zone additional first year depreciation deduction not been claimed. The amount recaptured is treated as ordinary income for the recapture year. For the recapture year and subsequent tax years, the taxpayer's depreciation deductions are determined as if no GO Zone additional first year depreciation deduction was claimed with respect to the property. See ¶ 127F.

Effective date

The provision applies to property placed in service after December 31, 2007, with respect to disasters declared after such date and occurring before January 1, 2010 (Division C, Act Sec. 710(b) of (P.L. 110-343)).

¶ 127I

Bonus Depreciation for Cellulosic Biofuel Plant Property

A 50-percent additional depreciation allowance may be claimed on the adjusted basis of qualified cellulosic biomass ethanol plant property (QCBEPP) acquired and placed in service after December 20, 2006. Effective for property placed in service after October 3, 2008, this provision is expanded to apply to qualified cellulosic biofuel plant property (Code Sec. 168(l), as added by the Tax Relief and Health Care Act (P.L. 110-343) and amended by the Emergency Economic Stabilization Act of 2008 (P.L. 110-343)).

Regular MACRS depreciation deductions are computed on the adjusted basis of the property after reduction by the 50 percent allowance (Code Sec. 168(l)(1)(B), as added by P.L. 109-432).

No AMT adjustment required

The deduction is claimed in full for purposes of determining alternative minimum tax liability. In addition, all MACRS depreciation deductions claimed on the QCBEPP and QCBPP are allowed in full in computing AMT (i.e., no depreciation adjustment is required) (Code Sec. 168(l)(6), as added by P.L. 109-432).

These are the same rules that apply to property on which the 30- or 50-percent bonus depreciation deduction under Code Sec. 168(k) is claimed. The bonus deduction and regular MACRS deductions on bonus depreciation property are allowed in full under the AMT (Code Sec. 168(k)(2)(G)). See ¶ 127D.

Qualified cellulosic biomass ethanol plant property (QCBEPP) defined

Effective for property placed in service before October 4, 2008, the Code Sec. 168(l) deduction applied to qualified cellulosic biomass ethanol plant property. To qualify as QCBEPP:

(1) the property must be depreciable and used in the United States solely to produce cellulosic biomass ethanol;

(2) the taxpayer must acquire the property by purchase (with the meaning of Code Sec. 179(d)) after December 20, 2006, the date of enactment of P.L. 109-432;

(3) no written binding contract for the purchase of the property may be in effect on or before December 20, 2006;

(4) the original use of the property must commence with the taxpayer after December 20, 2006 (see below for special rules relating to sale-leasebacks and syndicated leasing transactions);

(5) the property must be placed in service by the taxpayer before January 1, 2013 (Code Sec. 168(l)(2), prior to amendment by P.L. 110-343).

Cellulosic biomass ethanol means ethanol produced by enzymatic hydrolysis of any lignocellulosic or hemicellulosic matter that is available on a renewable or recurring basis (Code Sec. 168(l)(3), prior to amendment by P.L. 110-343).

Lignocellulosic or hemicellulosic matter that is available on a renewable or recurring basis includes (but is not limited to) bagasse (from sugar cane), corn stalks, and switchgrass (Joint Committee on Taxation, Technical Explanation of the Tax Relief and Health Care Act of 2006 (P.L. 109-432) (JCX-50-06)).

Since original use of the property must commence with the taxpayer, only new property may qualify as QCBEPP.

An acquisition of property is considered made by purchase within the meaning of Code Sec. 179(d) unless the property (1) is acquired from a person whose relationship to the taxpayer bars recognition of a loss in any transaction between them under Code Sec. 267 or Code Sec. 707(b); (2) is acquired in a transfer between members of a controlled group of corporations (substituting 50 percent for the 80 percent that would otherwise apply with respect to stock ownership requirements); (3) has a substituted basis (in whole or in part); or (4) has a stepped-up basis determined under Code Sec. 1014(a) relating to inherited property (Code Sec. 179(d)(2); Reg.§ 1.179-4(c)).

Qualified cellulosic biofuel plant property (QCBPP) defined

Effective for property placed in service after October 3, 2008, the Code Sec. 168(l) bonus deduction applies to qualified cellulosic biofuel plant property. The term cellulosic biofuel means any liquid fuel which is produced from any lignocellulosic or hemicellulosic matter that is available on a renewable or recurring basis (Code Sec. 168(l)(3), as amended by the Emergency Economic Stabilization Act of 2008 (P.L. 110-343)).

Cellulosic biofuel plant property must meet the following requirements:

(1) the property must be depreciable and used in the United States solely to produce cellulosic biomass;

(2) the taxpayer must acquire the property by purchase (within the meaning of Code Sec. 179(d)) after December 20, 2006, the date of enactment of P.L. 109-432;

(3) no written binding contract for the purchase of the property may be in effect on or before December 20, 2006;

(4) the original use of the property must commence with the taxpayer after December 20, 2006 (see below for special rules relating to sale-leasebacks and syndicated leasing transactions);

(5) the property must be placed in service by the taxpayer before January 1, 2013 (Code Sec. 168(l)(2), as added by P.L. 109-432 and amended by P.L. 110-343)).

Property manufactured, constructed, or produced by or for a taxpayer

Property manufactured, constructed, or produced by the taxpayer for the taxpayer's own use may qualify for the Code Sec. 168(l) bonus deduction if the taxpayer begins the manufacture, construction, or production of the property after December 20, 2006, and the property is placed in service before January 1, 2013. Property manufactured, constructed, or produced for the taxpayer by another person under a contract that is entered into prior to the manufacture, construction, or production of the property is considered manufactured, constructed, or produced by the taxpayer (Code Sec. 168(l)(5), as added by P.L. 109-432).

Sale-leasebacks

A limited exception to the original use requirement applies to sale-leasebacks. The rule applies to property originally placed in service after December 20, 2006, by a person who sells it to the taxpayer and then leases it from the taxpayer within three months after the date that the property was originally placed in service. In this situation, the property is treated as originally placed in service by the taxpayer (rather than the seller) and the placed-in-service date is deemed to occur no earlier than the date that the property is used under the leaseback (Code Sec. 168(l)(5), as added by P.L. 109-432).

Syndication transactions

The ultimate purchaser in a syndicated leasing transaction may be able to qualify for the 50-percent deduction. If property is originally placed in service by a lessor after December 20, 2006, and is sold by the lessor or any later purchaser within three months after the date the property was originally placed in service by the lessor, and the user of the property does not change during this three-month period, then the purchaser of the property in the last sale is considered to be the original user of the property and the property is treated as originally placed in service not earlier than the date of the last sale by the purchaser of the property in the last sale (Code Sec. 168(l)(5), as added by P.L. 109-432).

Limitation on certain users and related parties

Property does not qualify for the Code Sec. 168(l) deduction if the user of the property (as of the date on which the property is originally placed in service) or a person related (within the meaning of Code Sec. 267(b) or Code Sec. 707(b)) to such user or to the taxpayer had a written binding contract in effect for the acquisition of the property at any time on or before December 20, 2006, or in the case of property manufactured, constructed, or produced for such user's or person's own use, the manufacture, construction, or production of the property began at any time on or before December 20, 2006 (Code Sec. 168(l)(5), as added by P.L. 109-432).

The rules relating to manufactured, constructed, or produced property, sale leasebacks, syndication transactions, and limitations on certain users and related parties are borrowed directly from Code Sec. 168(k)(2)(E) except that the date of enactment of P.L. 109-432 is substituted for September 10, 2001 (the effective date of the Code Sec. 168(k) bonus depreciation provision) and the January 1, 2013 termination date of the QCBEPP provision is substituted for the January 1, 2005 (the termination date of the bonus depreciation provision). Thus, taxpayers should be able to rely on the related regulations issued under Code Sec. 168(k) for additional guidance. See ¶ 127D.

Tax-exempt bond-financed property excluded

Property financed with tax-exempt bonds cannot qualify as Code Sec. 168(l) property and, therefore, does not qualify for the additional deduction (Code Sec. 168(l)(4)(B), as added by P.L. 109-432).

Mandatory ADS property excluded

Property required to be depreciated under the MACRS alternative depreciation system (ADS) does not qualify as Code Sec. 168(l) property. The deduction is not denied if a taxpayer merely elects to depreciate the Code Sec. 168(l) property using ADS (Code Sec. 168(l)(4)(A), as added by P.L. 109-432). See ¶ 127D.

Election out

A taxpayer may elect not to claim the deduction with respect to any class of property for any tax year. The election out applies to all property in the class for which the election out is made and which is placed in service during the tax year.

Code Sec. 168(l) property placed in service during a tax year may consist of various MACRS property classes, e.g., 5-year property, 7-year property, 10-year property, etc. The election out is made at the property class level. A taxpayer may make an election out for some or all of the property classes (Code Sec. 168(l)(4)(C), as added by P.L. 109-432).

Recapture when property loses qualifying status

Recapture of the deduction is required in a tax year in which QCBEPP or QCBPP ceases to be QCBEPP or QCBBP. The recapture amount is computed in a similar manner to the recapture of the Code Section 179 deduction when section 179 property ceases to be used more than 50 percent in the active conduct of a taxpayer's trade or business during any year of the section 179 property's MACRS recovery period (Code Sec. 168(l)(7), as added by P.L. 109-432).

The 50-percent GO Zone bonus depreciation allowance (Code Sec. 1400N(d)) is also required to be recaptured by applying rules similar to those applicable to section 179 property. Under guidance issued by the IRS in Notice 2006-77, I.R.B. 2006-40, the benefit derived from claiming the GO Zone additional first year depreciation deduction for the property is equal to the excess of the total depreciation claimed (including the GO Zone additional first year depreciation deduction) for the property for the tax years before the recapture year over the total depreciation that would have been allowable for the tax years before the recapture year had the GO Zone additional first year depreciation deduction not been claimed. The amount recaptured is treated as ordinary income for the recapture year. For the recapture year and subsequent tax years, the taxpayer's depreciation deductions are determined as if no GO Zone additional first year depreciation deduction was claimed with respect to the property. See ¶ 127F.

Coordination with Code Sec. 179C election to expense refineries

The 50-percent deduction for QCBEPP or QCBPP does not apply to property with respect to which the taxpayer claims the 50-percent deduction allowed by Code Sec. 179C for qualified refinery property.

The potential for a duplicative deduction exists because qualified refinery property can include a facility that processes biomass via gas into a liquid fuel.

Effective date

The provision applies to property placed in service after December 20, 2006 in tax years ending after December 20, 2006 (Act Sec. 209(b) of the Tax Relief and Health Care Act of 2006 (P.L. 109-432)).

¶ 127J

Bonus Depreciation for Qualified Reuse and Recycling Property

A 50-percent additional depreciation allowance (bonus depreciation) may be claimed on the adjusted basis of *qualified reuse and recycling property* acquired and placed in service after August 31, 2008. The additional depreciation is claimed in the tax year the property is placed in service. The original use of the property must begin with the taxpayer after August 31, 2008 (i.e., the property must be new) (Code Sec. 168(m), as added by the Emergency Economic Stabilization Act of 2008 (P.L. 110-343)). Regular MACRS depreciation deductions are computed on the adjusted basis of the property beginning in the tax year the property is placed in service after reduction by the 50-percent allowance (Code Sec. 168(m)(1)(B), as added by P.L. 110-343).

Since this bonus depreciation deduction is computed on the adjusted basis of the property, it is computed after the original basis is reduced by any Code Sec. 179 allowance that is claimed. This is the same rule that applies when computing the bonus depreciation allowance under Code Sec. 168(k).

No AMT adjustment required

The bonus deduction is claimed in full for purposes of determining alternative minimum tax liability. In addition, all MACRS depreciation deductions claimed on the qualified reuse and recycling property are allowed in full in computing AMT (i.e., no depreciation adjustment is required) (Code Sec. 168(m)(2)(D), as added by P.L. 110-343).

Qualified reuse and recycling property defined

"Qualified reuse and recycling property" is reuse and recycling property that meets certain conditions. "Reuse and recycling property" is machinery and equipment (not including buildings, real estate, rolling stock or equipment used to transport reuse and recyclable materials) that is used exclusively to collect, distribute, or recycle qualified reuse and recyclable materials. Machinery and equipment include appurtenances such as software necessary to operate the equipment. "Qualified reuse and recyclable materials" are scrap plastic, glass, textiles, rubber, packaging, and metal, as well as recovered fiber and electronic scrap (Code Sec. 168(m)(3), as added by P.L. 110-343).

The term "recycle" or "recycling" means the process by which worn or superfluous materials are processed into materials for use in manufacturing consumer and commercial products, including packaging (Code Sec. 168(m)(3)(C), as added by P.L. 110-343).

"Electronic scrap" includes cathode ray tubes, flat panel screens or similar video display devices with screen sizes greater than 4 inches when measured diagonally, as well as central processing units (Code Sec. 168(m)(2)(A)(ii), as added by P.L. 110-343).

The original use of "qualified reuse and recycling property," must begin with the taxpayer after August 31, 2008. In addition, the property must either be acquired by purchase by the taxpayer after August 31, 2008 (but only if there is not written binding contract for the acquisition in effect before September 1, 2008), or acquired by the taxpayer pursuant to a written binding contract entered into after August 31, 2008 (Code Sec. 168(m)(2)(A), as added by P.L. 110-343).

"Purchase" for this purpose has the meaning given to such term in Code Sec. 179(d)(2), which defines the term as any acquisition of property, but excludes acquisitions from related parties, transfers of property from a decedent in which the acquiror takes a stepped-up basis in the property under Code Sec. 1014(a), or transfers in which the acquiror takes a substituted basis in the property, such as like-kind exchanges qualifying under Code Sec. 1031. In addition, property acquired by purchase will only be considered qualified reuse and recycling property if no written, binding contract for the acquisition was in effect before September 1, 2008 (Code Sec. 168(m)(2)(A)(i), as added by P.L. 110-343).

The requirement of an acquisition by purchase is not imposed on acquisitions pursuant to a written binding contract entered into after August 31, 2008 (Code Sec. 168(m)(2)(A)(iv), as added by the Emergency Economic Stabilization Act of 2008). Presumably, it was not the intent of Congress to eliminate the purchase requirement simply because the reuse or recycling property was acquired pursuant to a contract entered into after August 31, 2008. For example, as enacted, it appears that a taxpayer could enter into a post-August 31, 2008 contract for an acquisition from a related person and qualify for the deduction even though such an acquisition is not considered a purchase under Code Sec. 179(d)(2). A technical correction may be required.

Qualified reuse and recycling property must have a *useful life* of at least five years (Code Sec. 168(m)(2)(A)(ii), as added by P.L. 110-343). The term useful life is not defined. It appears in the context of this provision to refer to actual economic useful life to the taxpayer rather than the length of the assigned MACRS recovery period. The only MACRS recovery period which is less than five years is three years (i.e., three-year property). MACRS 3-year property does not include any type of property that would be considered qualified reuse or recycling property. Similar considerations prevent the term from being defined by reference to an asset's class life as set forth in Rev. Proc. 87-56, 1987-2 CB 674.

Self-constructed property

The special depreciation allowance may be claimed on qualified reuse and recycling property the taxpayer manufactures, constructs, or produces for its own use, if the taxpayer begins manufacturing, constructing, or producing the property after August 31, 2008 (Code Sec. 168(m)(2)(C), as added by P.L. 110-343).

Exceptions

A taxpayer cannot "double dip" and claim the special qualified reuse and recycling property depreciation allowance for any property for which it may claim bonus depreciation under Code Sec. 168(k). Thus, if bonus depreciation is available under either this new provision or Code Sec. 168(k) it must be claimed under Code Sec. 168(k). In addition, a taxpayer cannot take the special depreciation allowance on property which it is required to depreciate under the MACRS alternative depreciation system (ADS). However, if a taxpayer is not required to depreciate property under ADS, but elects to do so under Code Sec. 168(g)(7), the taxpayer may still claim the special depreciation allowance (Code Sec. 168(m)(2)(B), as added by P.L. 110-343).

Election out

A taxpayer may elect not to claim the deduction with respect to any MACRS assigned class of property for any tax year. The election out applies to all qualified reuse and recycling property in the particular MACRS property class (e.g., 5-, 7-, 10-, or 15-year property) for which the election out is made and which is placed in service during the tax year for which the election is made (Code Sec. 168(m)(2)(B)(iii), as added by P.L. 110-343).

MACRS General Asset Accounts

¶ 128

General Asset Accounts

An election may be made to group certain assets into one or more general asset accounts (GAAs) so that the assets in any particular GAA are depreciated under MACRS as a single asset (Code Sec. 168(i)(4)). The election is generally irrevocable and is binding for the year in which the election is made and for subsequent tax years in computing taxable income (Reg. § 1.168(i)-1(k)(1)). The election must be made on a timely filed return (including extensions) for the tax year in which the assets included in the GAA are placed in service (Reg. § § 1.168(i)-1(k)(2) and (3)).

Each person who owns an asset included in a general asset account must make the election. Thus, the election must be made by each member of a consolidated group, at the partnership level (not by each partner), or at the S corporation level (not by each shareholder) (Reg. § 1.168(i)-1(k)(1)).

For dispositions from a GAA, see ¶ 129.

The rules for MACRS general asset accounts are provided in Reg. § 1.168(i)-1. This regulation generally applies to property placed in service in tax years ending on or after October 11, 1994. For property subject to MACRS and placed in service after 1986, in tax years ending before October 11, 1994, the IRS will allow any reasonable method that is consistently applied to the taxpayer's general asset accounts (Reg. § 1.168(i)-1(l)). The IRS allowed taxpayers to make an election on Form 3115, filed no later than December 20, 1997, to elect to apply the conditions of Reg. § 1.169(i)-1 to property placed in service after 1986 in tax years ending before October 11, 1994 if no general asset account election had been previously made for such property (Rev. Proc. 97-30, 1997-1 CB 680).

Basis terminology

For purposes of the GAA rules, the term "unadjusted depreciable basis" (UDB) is the basis of an asset under Code Sec. 1011 before depreciation, amortization, or depletion deductions (without regard to adjustments under Code Sec. 1016(a)(2) and (3)) (Reg. § 1.168(i)-1(b)(1)).

The sum of the unadjusted depreciable bases of all assets included in the GAA is the "unadjusted depreciable basis of the general asset account" (UDB/GAA) (Reg. § 1.168(i)-1(b)(2)).

The term "adjusted depreciable basis of the general asset account" (ADB/GAA) is the unadjusted depreciable basis of the GAA less prior depreciation, amortization, and depletion basis adjustments (the adjustments to basis provided in Code Sec. 1016(a)(2) and (3)) (Reg. § 1.168(i)-1)(b)(3)).

The term "expensed cost" includes any allowable credit or deduction that is treated as a depreciation or amortization deduction under Code Sec. 1245 (such as the credit for qualified electric vehicles (Code Sec. 30); the Code Sec. 179 expense deduction; the deductions for clean-fuel vehicles and certain refueling property (Code Sec. 179A); and deductions for expenditures to remove architectural and transportation barriers to the handicapped and elderly (Code Sec. 190)) (Reg. § 1.168(i)-1(b)(4)).

Eligible property

Unlike the ACRS mass asset account rules (see Prop. Reg. § 1.168-2(h) and also ¶ 282), MACRS GAA treatment is not limited to mass assets. Assets that are subject to the MACRS general depreciation system or alternative depreciation system may be accounted for in one or more GAAs (Reg. § 1.168(i)-1(c)(1)).

However, an asset may be included in a GAA only to the extent of its unadjusted depreciable basis (as defined above). In essence, items that are not includible in depreciable basis are also excluded from unadjusted depreciable basis for assets in a GAA.

Assets that are eligible to be grouped into a single GAA may be divided into more than one GAA. However, each GAA must include only assets that are placed in service in the same tax year and have the same asset class (as set forth in Rev. Proc. 87-56 at ¶ 191), depreciation method, recovery period, and convention (Reg. § 1.168(i)-1(c)(2)). Assets without an asset class but which have the rest of the preceding characteristics in common may be grouped in a single GAA.

Note that the regulations provide that only assets in the same *Asset Class* as set forth in Rev. Proc. 87-56 may be placed in the same general asset account. Assets without an Asset Class may be included in their own account only if they share all of the other required characteristics. Since Rev. Proc. 87-56 provides an Asset Class for virtually every item of depreciable property, this rule appears to be of very limited application. The most significant exception would likely apply to personal property with no Class Life. Such property, is not assigned a specific Asset Class in Rev. Proc. 87-56 (it is listed at the end as item A along with certain other types of property with no Asset Class) and is assigned a seven-year recovery period. See ¶ 106.

Assets subject to the mid-quarter convention may only be grouped into a GAA with assets that are placed in service in the same quarter of the tax year.

Assets subject to the mid-month convention may only be grouped into a GAA with assets that are placed in service in the same month of the tax year.

Luxury cars subject to the Code Sec. 280F limitation on depreciation deductions must be grouped into a separate GAA. The luxury car caps are applied by multiplying the applicable cap by the number of automobiles in the account (Reg. § 1.168(i)-1(d)(2)).

An asset used both for personal and business (or for the production of income) purposes in the tax year in which the asset is first placed in service is ineligible for inclusion in a GAA (Reg. § 1.168(i)-1(c)(1)). An asset included in a GAA in a previous tax year becomes ineligible for such treatment and must be removed from the GAA as of the beginning of the tax year in which it is converted to personal use (Reg. § 1.168(i)-1(h)). For adjustments to the GAA (see ¶ 166).

If the basis of an asset in a GAA is increased because of the recapture of any allowable credit or deduction, GAA treatment for the asset terminates and the asset must be removed from the GAA as of the beginning of the tax year in which the recapture event occurs (Reg. § 1.168(i)-1(g)). This rule applies, for example, to assets for which there are basis adjustments because of the recapture of the credit for qualified electric vehicles (Code Sec. 30(d)(2)), investment credit (Code Sec. 50(c)(2)), Sec. 179 expense deduction (Code Sec. 179(d)(10)), and the deductions for clean-fuel vehicles and refueling property (Code Sec. 179A(e)(4)). For adjustments to the GAA (see ¶ 166).

Assets generating foreign source income may be included in a GAA if there is no substantial distortion of income (Reg. § 1.168(i)-1(c)(ii)). These assets are also subject to special rules specified in Reg. § 1.168(i)-1(f).

Depreciation computation

Depreciation deductions are determined for each GAA by using the applicable depreciation method, recovery period, and convention for the assets in the account as if the account is a single asset. Each GAA should have its own allowance for depreciation account to record the depreciation allowances (Reg. § 1.168(i)-1(d)(1)).

Depreciation limitation on luxury cars

For a GAA set up for luxury automobiles, the Code Sec. 280F limitation on depreciation is generally the applicable maximum cap multiplied by the number of automobiles remaining in the account at the beginning of the tax year. The latter is the number of automobiles originally in the account less those automobiles disposed of during the year or prior years that were removed from the account because they involved qualifying dispositions, certain nonrecognition transfers, abusive transfers, assets subject to recapture, or conversion to personal use (Reg. § 1.168(i)-1(d)(2)).

¶ 129

General Asset Account Dispositions

A disposition of an asset in a GAA (see ¶ 128) occurs when ownership of the asset is transferred or when the asset is permanently withdrawn from use in a business or in the production of income. A disposition includes a sale, exchange, retirement, physical abandonment, destruction of an asset or a transfer to a supplies or scrap account. However, the retirement of a structural component of real property is not considered a disposition (Reg. § 1.168(i)-1(e)(1)).

Any reasonable method consistently applied to a GAA may be used in determining the unadjusted depreciable basis of a disposed or converted asset (Reg. § 1.168(i)-1(i)).

The recognition and character of prior dispositions are unaffected by adjustments to a GAA that are required in certain situations for a current asset disposition (Reg. § 1.168(i)-1(j)).

The depreciation treatment for dispositions for a GAA depends on the situation and whether specified treatment is optional or mandatory. There are five situations: (1) a disposition of an asset that is not the disposition of all of the assets, or the last asset, in a GAA; (2) a disposition of all of the assets, or the last asset, in a GAA; (3) a qualifying disposition; (4) transfers involving a transferee in certain nonrecognition transfers under Code Sec. 168(i)(7); and (5) abusive transactions.

Situation (1) (General disposition rule)

For a disposition of an asset that is not the disposition of all of the assets, or the last asset, in a GAA, the unadjusted depreciable basis of the GAA and the amount in its related allowance for depreciation account are not reduced.

For purposes of determining gain or loss on the disposition, the asset is treated as having an adjusted basis of zero immediately before the disposition. Therefore, no loss is realized upon a disposition.

Any amount realized on a disposition is recognized as ordinary income up to the following amount: the sum of (a) the unadjusted depreciable basis of the GAA and (b) any expensed cost (as defined at ¶ 128) for assets in the account less (c) any amounts previously recognized as ordinary income upon the disposition of other assets in the account. The recognition and character of any amount realized above this limit is determined under other applicable Code provisions (excluding the recapture provisions of Code Secs. 1245 and 1250 or provisions of the Code that treat gain on a disposition as subject to those provisions).

In determining the basis of an asset acquired in certain nonrecognition transactions such as like-kind exchanges and involuntary conversions (but not the nonrecognition transactions subject to Code Sec. 168(i)(7)(B)), the amount of ordinary income recognized upon the disposition of an asset from a GAA is treated as the amount of gain recognized on the disposition (Reg. § 1.168(i)-1(e)(2)).

Example (1): A calendar-year corporation maintains one GAA for 10 machines that cost a total of $10,000 and are placed in service in year one. Of the 10 machines, one machine costs $8,200 and nine machines cost a total of $1,800. For this GAA, the 200% declining-balance depreciation method, a five-year recovery period, and the half-year convention are used. No Code Sec. 179 allowance or bonus-depreciation allowance was claimed for any of the machines. As of the beginning of year two, the balance in the allowance for depreciation account is $2,000 [(($10,000 – $0) × .40)/2].

In February of year two, the machine that cost $8,200 is sold to an unrelated party for $9,000. This machine is treated as having an adjusted basis of zero. On the corporation's tax return for year two, the entire $9,000 amount realized is recognized as ordinary income because such amount does not exceed the ordinary income treatment limitation: the unadjusted depreciable basis of the GAA ($10,000) plus any expensed cost for assets in the account ($0) less amounts previously recognized as ordinary income ($0).

The unadjusted depreciable basis and the allowance for depreciation account are not reduced upon the disposition of the machine. Thus, the depreciation allowance for year two is $3,200 (($10,000 – $2,000) × .40).

In June of year three, the corporation sells seven machines to an unrelated party for a total of $1,100. These machines are treated as having an adjusted basis of zero.

On the corporation's return for year three, of the $1,100 amount realized, only $1,000 is recognized as ordinary income (the unadjusted depreciable basis of $10,000 plus the expensed cost of $0, less the amount of $9,000 previously recognized as ordinary income). The recognition and character of the $100 amount realized above the ordinary income treatment limitation ($1,100 – $1,000) are determined under other applicable Code provisions (such as Code Sec. 1231) (but not the Code Sec. 1245 recapture provision).

The unadjusted depreciable basis and the allowance for depreciation account are not reduced upon the disposition of the machines. Thus, the depreciation deduction for year three is $1,920 (($10,000 – $5,200) × .40) (Reg. § 1.168(i)-1(e)).

Situation (2) (Empty account rule)

If there is a disposition of all of the assets, or the last asset, in a GAA, there is a choice of either applying the rules in Situation (1), above, or treating the GAA as terminated. The latter choice is made by reporting the gain, loss, or other deduction on a timely filed (including extensions) return for the tax year in which the disposition occurs.

If the GAA is treated as terminated, gain or loss for the GAA is determined under Code Sec. 1001(a) by considering the adjusted basis of the GAA at the time of disposition, which is its unadjusted depreciable basis less the depreciation allowed or allowable.

The recognition and character of the gain or loss are determined under other applicable Code provisions. To prevent double recapture, gain subject to recapture is limited to depreciation deductions (including any expensed cost or the additional depreciation allowed or allowable for the GAA) reduced by amounts previously recognized as ordinary income on other dispositions from the GAA (Reg. § 1.168(i)-1(e)(3)(ii)).

Example (2): A calendar-year corporation maintains a GAA for 1,000 calculators that cost a total of $60,000 and are placed in service in year one. For this GAA, the 200% declining-balance method, a five-year recovery period, and the half-year convention are used. No Code Sec. 179 allowance or bonus-depreciation allowance was claimed for any of the assets. In year two, 200 of the calculators are sold to an unrelated party for a total of $10,000, which was recognized as ordinary income.

In March of year three, the remaining calculators in the GAA are sold to an unrelated party for $35,000. A decision is made to terminate the GAA and determine gain or loss for the account.

On the date of disposition, there is $36,960 of depreciation for the GAA. Consequently, the adjusted depreciable basis of the account is $23,040 (unadjusted depreciable basis of $60,000 less $36,960 depreciation). The corporation recognizes a gain of $11,960 on the disposition (amount realized of $35,000 less the adjusted depreciable basis of $23,040).

The entire gain of $11,960 is subject to recapture as ordinary income under Code Sec. 1245 ($36,960 of depreciation plus $0 expensed cost for assets in the account minus the $10,000 amount previously recognized as ordinary income on other dispositions = $26,960 maximum recapture amount) (Reg. § 1.168-1(e)(3)(ii)).

Situation (3) (Qualifying disposition rule)

If there is a qualifying disposition of an asset in a GAA, there is a choice of either applying the rules in Situation (1), above, or terminating the GAA treatment for the asset disposed of as of the beginning of the tax year in which the qualifying disposition occurs. The latter choice is made by reporting the gain, loss, or other deduction on a timely filed (including extensions) return for the tax year in which the disposition occurs.

A qualifying disposition is a disposition that does not involve all the assets, or the last asset, remaining in a GAA and is:

(A) the direct result of a casualty or theft;

(B) a charitable contribution for which a charitable deduction is allowed;

(C) a direct result of a cessation, termination, or disposition of a business, manufacturing, or other income producing process, operation, facility, plant, or other unit (other than by transfer to a supplies or scrap account); or

(D) certain nonrecognition transactions such as like-kind exchanges and involuntary conversions (but not the nonrecognition transactions subject to Code Sec. 168(i)(7) involving corporations or partnerships (Reg. § 1.168(i)-1(e)(3)(iii)).

For a qualifying disposition, the amount of gain or loss for the asset disposed of is determined by comparing the amount realized to the adjusted basis of the asset at the time of disposition. In essence, depreciation is calculated outside of the GAA on the asset disposed of for the year of disposition. Also, the recapture rules apply to the asset disposed of.

For this purpose, the adjusted basis at the time of disposition is the unadjusted depreciable basis of the asset less the depreciation allowed or allowable for the asset, computed by using the depreciation method, recovery period, and convention applicable to the GAA in which the asset was included.

The recognition and character of the gain, loss, or deduction are determined under other applicable Code provisions. To prevent double recapture, gain subject to recapture is limited to the lesser of:

(A) depreciation deductions, including any expensed cost (or additional depreciation) allowed or allowable for the asset disposed of, or

(B) the excess of the original unadjusted depreciable basis of the GAA (plus the expensed cost for any Sec. 1245 property originally included in the GAA) over amounts previously recaptured as ordinary income or recognized upon earlier disposition as ordinary income under Situation (1) (Reg. § 1.168(i)-1(e)(3)(iii)).

Under this choice, the asset disposed of is removed from the GAA as of the first day of the tax year in which the qualifying disposition occurs. The unadjusted depreciable basis of the GAA is reduced by the unadjusted depreciable basis of the asset as of the first day of the tax year in which the disposition occurs. The allowance for depreciation account related to the GAA is reduced by the depreciation on the asset as of the end of the tax year before the year of disposition, which is computed by using the depreciation method, recovery period, and convention applicable to the GAA in which the asset was included.

For purposes of determining the amount of gain realized on subsequent dispositions that is subject to ordinary income treatment under the generally applicable GAA rules (i.e. Situation (1)), any expensed cost regarding the asset presently disposed of is disregarded.

Example (3): A calendar-year corporation maintains one GAA for 12 machines that each cost $15,000, for a total of $180,000 and are placed in service in year one. Nine of the machines representing a cost of $135,000 are used in plant A and three machines representing a cost of $45,000 are used in plant B. This GAA uses the 200% declining-balance depreciation method, a five-year recovery period, and the half-year convention. No Code Sec. 179 allowance or bonus-depreciation allowance was claimed for these machines.

As of the beginning of year three, the allowance for depreciation account related to this GAA has a balance of $93,600. In May of year three, the corporation sells plant B to an unrelated party. The sale proceeds allocable to each of the three machines is $5,000. Because this transaction is a qualifying disposition from a GAA, the corporation chooses to apply the qualified disposition method for determining any gain, loss or deduction.

As of the end of year two, the depreciation on the three machines disposed of is $23,400. On the corporation's return for year three, the depreciation allowance for the GAA is computed as follows. As of the beginning of year three, the unadjusted depreciable basis of the GAA is reduced from $180,000 to $135,000 ($180,000 less the basis of $45,000 for the three machines). The related allowance for depreciation account is decreased from $93,600 to $70,200 ($93,600 less the $23,400 depreciation balance for the three machines) as of the end of year two. Consequently, the depreciation deduction for the GAA for year three is $25,920 (($135,000 = $70,200) × 40%).

On the corporation's return for year three, gain or loss for each of the three machines is determined as follows. In year three, the depreciation allowed on each machine disposed of is $1,440 [(($15,000 = $7,000) × 40%)/2]. The adjusted basis of each machine for purposes of determining gain or loss is $5,760 (the adjusted depreciable basis of $7,200 removed from the GAA less the depreciation deduction of $1,440 for year three). Accordingly, a loss for each machine of $760 ($5,000 sales proceeds = $5,760 adjusted basis) is recognized in year three, which is subject to Code Sec. 1231 treatment (Reg. § 1.168(i)-1(e)(3)(iii)(D)).

Situation (4) (Transferee's substituted basis nonrecognition transfer rule)

For an asset in a GAA that is transferred in certain nonrecognition transactions specified in Code Sec. 168(i)(7)(B), in which the transferee is treated as the transferor for purposes of computing subsequent depreciation, it is mandatory that the transferor remove the transferred asset from the GAA as of the first day of the tax year in which the transaction occurs.

The unadjusted depreciable basis of the GAA is reduced by the unadjusted depreciable basis of the asset as of the first day of the tax year in which the disposition occurs. The allowance for depreciation account related to the GAA is reduced by the depreciation on the asset as of the end of the tax year before the year of transfer, which is computed by using the depreciation method, recovery period, and convention applicable to the GAA in which the asset was included.

For purposes of determining the amount of gain realized on subsequent dispositions that is subject to ordinary income treatment under the generally applicable (i.e. Situation (1)) GAA rules, any expensed cost regarding the asset presently transferred is disregarded.

The transferee is bound by the transferor's GAA election regarding the transferred asset to the extent of the transferor's adjusted basis in such asset. If all of the assets, or the last asset, in a GAA are transferred, the transferee's basis in the assets or asset transferred is the adjusted depreciable basis of the GAA as of the beginning of the transferor's tax year in which the transaction occurs less depreciation allocable to the transferor for the year of transfer (Reg. § 1.168(i)-1(e)(3)(iv)).

Situation (5) (Abusive transaction rule)

If an asset in a GAA is disposed of in certain abusive transactions, GAA treatment for the asset automatically terminates as of the first day of the tax year in which the disposition occurs. Gain, loss, depreciation, recapture, and other adjustments must be determined in the manner provided under Situation (3), above.

Abusive transactions are transactions (other than nonrecognition transactions described in Code Sec. 168(i)(7)(B)) for which a principal purpose is to achieve a tax benefit or result not otherwise available absent a GAA election.

Abusive transactions include a transaction made with a principal purpose of shifting income or deductions among taxpayers in a manner not otherwise possible absent a GAA election in order to take advantage of differing effective tax rates among taxpayers. They also include a GAA election made with a principal purpose of disposing of an asset in a GAA in order to utilize an expiring net operating loss or credit (Reg. § 1.168(i)-1(e)(3)(v)).

¶ 130

Mass Asset Accounting or Pooling Alternative

A taxpayer is permitted to account for certain assets in multiple asset accounts or pools. The MACRS regulations do not provide specific guidance on this subject. However, regulations dealing with change in accounting methods limit multiple asset accounting or pooling to "mass assets." The term mass assets is defined as a mass or group of individual items that are not necessarily homogeneous, each of which is minor in value relative to the total value of the mass or group, numerous in quantity, usually accounted for only on a total dollar or quantity basis, with respect to which separate identification is impracticable, and placed in service in the same tax year (Reg.§ 1.446-1(e)(2)(ii)(d)(2)(vii)).

The regulations provide that a change from the *specific identification method* of identifying assets which are disposed of to a *first-in, first-out method* under which mass assets disposed of in a tax year are deemed to be from the pool with the earliest placed-in service year is a change from one permissible accounting method to another permissible accounting method (Reg.§ 1.446-1(e)(2)(iii), Example 13).

Pooling of mass assets is also be permissible for assets that are amortized or depreciable under methods other than MACRS.

MACRS Short Tax Years

¶ 132

Applicable Convention Refinements

MACRS deductions are determined on a tax-year basis. In contrast, the applicable recovery period of an asset consists of recovery (12-month) years without regard to the underlying tax year. Because of the applicable conventions, the recovery year of an asset generally does not coincide with the tax year. Depreciation attributable to a recovery year is consequently allocated to the tax years that include the recovery year.

The discussions in this ¶ 132 and ¶ 134 provide rules for determining MACRS deductions that apply in the following situations:

(1) property is placed in service in a short tax year;

(2) a short tax year occurs during the recovery period of property; or

(3) a disposition of property occurs before the end of the recovery period (see also ¶ 160).

If any of the above situations exist, refinements are made to the use of the applicable conventions and the MACRS depreciation tables (¶ 180) may not be used.

Detailed guidance regarding MACRS depreciation computations for short tax years is provided by the IRS in Rev. Proc. 89-15, 1989-1 CB 816.

Application of short tax year rules to a new business

In some situations involving individuals who begin a new trade or business it may be unclear whether a short tax year exists. Rev. Proc. 89-15 does not specifically address this issue. All short tax year examples in that revenue procedure deal with corporations. Nor are there any relevant short tax year MACRS regulations. However, short tax year rules are included among the ACRS regulations issued by the IRS. See ACRS Proposed Reg. § 1.168-2(f)(2) at ¶ 525. Although, proposed regulations are not required to be followed by a taxpayer, it should not be inappropriate to do so in the absence of any other specific guidance. However, as noted below, the proposed regulations will cause an individual who begins a sole-proprietorship and has not been engaged in another trade or business activity during the year to have a short tax year. An employee is not considered a trade or business for this purpose. Some fixed asset software programs take an aggressive position, and do not apply the short tax year rules in a situation where an individual begins a sole proprietorship (Example 2, below) or takes his or her first job (Example 4, below) since there is no separate legal entity involved other than an individual taxpayer whose tax year is a complete calendar year.

Under the ACRS proposed regulations, the tax year of a person placing depreciable property in service does not include any month before the month in which the person begins engaging in *any* trade or business or holding depreciable property for the production of income. In applying this rule, an employee is not considered engaged in a trade or business by virtue of employment, except that the tax year includes any month during which a person is engaged in trade or business as an employee regarding depreciable property used for purposes of employment.

Example (1): An individual has a calendar tax year and was engaged in a trade of business since the beginning of the year. He starts a new sole proprietorship business (and acquires new depreciable property for use in the new business) at some point during the year. There is no short tax year for the depreciable property acquired for use in the new business because the tax year of the individual includes all months in which he was engaged in business. However, if the new business was formed as a separate legal entity, such as a partnership, C corporation, or S corporation, the new business (assuming that it adopts a calendar year) would have a short tax year.

Example (2): An individual, who was an employee since the beginning of the year and has a calendar tax year, purchases a car in July for use in the performance of her employment. The car was not placed in service in a short tax year because it was used in her trade or business as an employee and her tax year includes all months that she was an employee.

In June of the following calendar tax year, the individual purchases a truck for use in a new sole proprietorship business. She holds no other depreciable property for the production of income in such calendar year. In determining when a tax year begins for property not used in the trade or business of employment, the truck is considered placed in service in a short tax year because an employee is not considered engaged in a trade or business by virtue of employment.

Example (3): An individual has a calendar tax year and was actively engaged in a sole proprietorship trade or business since the beginning of the year. In July, he agrees to work for a corporation and purchases a new truck for use in the performance of his employment for the corporation. The truck is not placed in service in a short tax year because the tax year of the individual placing the truck in service includes all months during which he was engaged in a trade or business.

Example (4): An individual has a calendar tax year and graduates from college. In July, he begins work for a business and buys a car for use in his employment for the business. He holds no other depreciable property for the production of income in such year. The car is considered placed in service in a short tax year because the individual did not begin his trade or business of being an employee until July and he was not engaged in any other trade or business and did not hold other depreciable property for the production of income for the period before he became an employee.

Example (5): A corporation with a calendar tax year was engaged in one business from the beginning of the year and buys a restaurant business (and new depreciable property for use in the new business) in July. The corporation does not have a short tax year for the new depreciable property used in the new business because the tax year of the corporation placing the property in service includes all months during which it is engaged in a trade or business.

The IRS has applied pre-ACRS short tax year regulations (Reg.§ 1.167(a)-11(c)(2)(iv)) which are similar to the proposed ACRS regulations to ACRS property, noting that it was appropriate to do so since neither final nor temporary regulations had been issued under ACRS. Arguably, these pre-ACRS regulations could also be applied to MACRS property for the same reason. See, Technical Advice Memorandum 8935002 (May 12, 1989) and *R.A. McKnight,* 58 TCM 1390, CCH Dec. 46,374(M) in which the short tax year rules did not apply to an individual who began a business during the year but was also engaged for the entire year in the separate trade or business of being a corporate director. (The position of corporate director was not considered an employee for purposes of the short tax year rules).

Application of short tax year rules to new subsidiary filing consolidated return

A existing corporation may join a consolidated group or a consolidated group may form new corporation which joins the consolidated group. The following discussion considers how the MACRS rules for short tax years applies when the subsidiary files a consolidated return with the affiliated group. See, also, ¶ 92.

New corporation formed by consolidated group. MACRS regulations provide that all members of a consolidated group are treated as a single taxpayer for purposes of determining whether the mid-quarter or half-year convention applies to personal property placed in service by members of the consolidated group. If the group forms a new subsidiary, the subsidiary is treated as in existence for the entire tax year for this purpose (Reg. § 1.168(d)-1(b)(5)(i) and (ii)). An example in the regulation, illustrates that an asset purchased by a new subsidiary may be considered placed in service by the subsidiary before it is actually organized.

Example (6): Assume a member of a consolidated group that files its return on a calendar-year basis forms a subsidiary on August 1. The subsidiary places depreciable property in service on August 5. If the mid-quarter convention applies to property placed in service by the members of the consolidated group (including the newly-formed subsidiary), the property placed in service by the subsidiary on August 5 is deemed placed in service on the mid-point of the third quarter of the consolidated return year (i.e., August 15). If the half-year convention applies, the property is deemed placed in service on the mid-point of the consolidated return year (i.e., July 1) (Reg. § 1.168(d)-1(b)(5)(iii), Example).

A strict reading of the regulation provides that the subsidiary is treated as in existence for the entire tax year only for purposes of determining the applicable convention. However, insofar as the example shows the depreciation period for the subsidiary's assets as potentially starting on July 1, which is before the new subsidiary's August 1 through December 31 short tax year begins, it seems to contemplate that the subsidiary may compute and claim depreciation for a full tax year. In fact, this is the conclusion reached by the IRS in Technical Advice Memorandum 9235004, May 20, 1992 and IRS Letter Ruling 199944006, July 20, 1999). See, also, the preamble to the proposed version of the regulations, which indicates that the rule was adopted for purposes of simplification even though a short tax year computation for such property would result in a more accurate reflection of the depreciation that should be claimed (PS-54-89, December 31, 1990).

In contrast, under the ACRS (pre-MACRS) method, a short tax-year computation was required on assets acquired by a new subsidiary while a member of the consolidated group during a short tax year (*Hamilton Industries Inc.*, 97 TC 120 (1991), CCH Dec. 47,501)

Example (7): Hamilton Inc. is incorporated on May 12, 1982, as a subsidiary of Mayline. Mayline has a fiscal year ending on June 30. Hamilton commenced business on June 28, 1982 when it acquired depreciable assets. It has a short tax year (for depreciation purposes) running from June 28, 1982, to June 30, 1982. ACRS depreciation was allowed for 1/12 of a full tax year under the ACRS rules for calculating depreciation for a short tax year of one month or less.

IRS Technical Advice Memorandum 8424009 (March 19, 1984) reached similar results, holding that a subsidiary that was formed in December 1980, acquired assets in March 1981, and filed as a member of the consolidated group with a tax year ending in May 1981, was required to compute depreciation using the ACRS short tax year rules based on a short tax year that began in March 1981 when the assets were placed in service.

Existing corporation acquired by consolidated group. The MACRS regulations also deal with an existing target that joins a consolidated group on a day other than the first day of the consolidated group's tax year. The regulations provides that the target is treated as a member of the consolidated group for the entire year for purposes of determining the applicable convention with respect to property placed in service for the part of the tax year that the target is a member of the consolidated group (Reg. § 1.168(d)-1(b)(6)(vi)).

Example (8): A calendar-year corporation (target) joins a calendar-year consolidated group on July 1. For purposes of determining whether the half-year or mid-month convention applies to property placed in service by all members of the consolidated group, including the target while it is a member of the consolidated group, the consolidated group only takes into account property placed in service by the target after July 1 and before January 1 (Reg.§ 1.168(d)-1(b)(5)(viii), Example)).

Presumably, the target then computes depreciation on assets placed in service after June 30 and before January 1 using the applicable convention as if the target's tax year was a full tax year even though these assets were placed in service in a short tax year that runs from July 1 through December 31.

In the case of property placed in service or already in service in the target's tax year that ends immediately before joining the consolidated group, the regulations provide that depreciation is computed under the full tax year rules or short tax year rules, as applicable (Reg.§ 1.168(d)-1(b)(6)(vii)). Thus, in the preceding example, it appears that two short tax year computations are required on assets placed in service by the subsidiary before July 1: first, for the short-tax year that ended upon the acquisition of the target (January 1 through June 30) and, second, for the short tax year that the target is a member of the consolidated group (July 1 through December 31).

This rule is accord with the manner in which ACRS deductions would have been computed.

See, for example, *J. Cooke Inc.*, DC Va., 96-2 USTC 50,483, aff'd, CA-4, per curiam, unpublished opinion, 97-2 USTC 50,511, in which ACRS depreciation on a corporation's existing assets were computed using the short-tax year rules after it became a member of a consolidated group.

Example (9): On December 28, 1984, Cooke Inc., a calendar year corporation, acquires the common stock of another corporation which owns 350 horses. A consolidated return is filed. Based on the date of the transaction, the acquired subsidiary had a 1984 tax year beginning on December 29 and ending on December 31. Because of this short tax year, the acquired corporation was entitled to deduct only one-twelfth of the 1984 depreciation.

See, also, Technical Advice Memorandum 8424009 (March 19, 1984), in which ACRS short tax year computations were required on assets owned by a target prior to becoming a subsidiary for the short tax year that ended before it became a member of the consolidated group and for the short tax year that it was a member of the group.

Effect of deemed asset acquisition election. An IRS Field Service Advice considers depreciation computations on ACRS personal property when a deemed asset acquistion election (Code Sec. 338(g)) is made for a target that becomes a member of a consolidated group (Field Service Advice Memorandum 1993-0504-3, May 4, 1993).

In general, when a deemed asset election is made, a target is treated as selling all of its assets at the close of the acquisition date and as a new corporation that purchases all of its assets as of the beginning of the day after the acquisition date (Code Sec. 338(a)). The target's existing tax year ends at the close of the acquisition date and a new tax year begins on the day after the acquisition date (Reg. § 1.338-1(a)). A new depreciation period applies for the new tax year.

The FSA concludes that the consolidated group is entitled to one-month's depreciation for the short tax year that the target was considered a member of the consolidated group. No depreciation was allowed for the short tax year that closed upon the target's acquisition because the target's asset's were considered disposed of in that tax year and no ACRS deduction is allowed in the year of disposition of ACRS personal property. Note, however, that under MACRS depreciation is allowed in the tax year that personal property is disposed of by applying the applicable convention.

A similar result dealing with ACRS and a section 338 election was also reached in *Brunswick Corporation*, DC, 2009-1 USTC ¶ 51,131.

Effect of conventions on short tax year computations

How a short tax year affects MACRS computations depends on the nature of the property and the applicable convention. For property subject to the mid-month convention (residential rental property, nonresidential real property, and railroad grading and tunnel bores), allowances are determined without regard to short tax years.

The mid-month convention is applied without regard to the tax year (Code Sec. 168(d)(4)(B)) unlike the half-year and mid-quarter conventions which are applied to the tax year (Code Sec. 168(d)(4)(A) and (C)). Accordingly, consideration of the tax year is necessary in establishing when the recovery period begins and ends under the latter two conventions.

Half-year convention

Under the half-year convention, the recovery period of property placed in service or disposed of in a short tax year begins or ends on the midpoint of the short tax year, which always falls on either the first day or the midpoint of a month.

(1) For a short tax year that begins on the first day of a month or ends on the last day of a month, the length of the tax year is measured in months. The midpoint of the short tax year is determined by dividing the number of months in the tax year by two.

If such short tax year includes part of a month, that entire month is included in the number of months in the tax year. However, if there are successive short tax years, with one tax year ending and the following tax year beginning in the same calendar month, then the first short tax year does not include the month in which the first short tax year terminates.

> ***Example (10):*** Property subject to MACRS and the half-year convention is acquired in a short tax year that begins on June 20 and ends on December 31. Because the tax year ends on the last day of a month, the short tax year is measured in months. The short tax year consists of seven months (including the month of June) and the midpoint of the short tax year is seven divided by two, or 3.5 months. Thus, the recovery period of this property begins in the middle of September for purposes of allocating depreciation for the first recovery year to the short tax year.

> ***Example (11):*** A taxpayer has successive short tax years. The first short tax year begins on June 1 and ends on October 15. The second short tax year begins on October 16 and ends on May 31. Because the first short tax year begins on the first day of a month, the short tax year is measured in months. The first short tax year consists of four months (excluding the month of October) and the midpoint of such short tax year is four divided by two, or two months. The recovery period of property subject to MACRS and the half-year convention that is acquired in the first short tax year begins on August 1. The second short tax year consists of eight months (including the month of October) and the midpoint of such short tax year is eight divided by two, or four months. The recovery period of property subject to MACRS and the half-year convention that is acquired in the second short tax year begins on February 1.

Rev. Proc. 89-15 does not specifically address a situation in which the first short tax year consists of a period of less than a month and is followed by another short tax year. The guidelines if literally applied appear to require that the month in which the first short tax year occurs be taken into account in the following short tax year. In effect, this eliminates a depreciation deduction in the first short tax year since there are no longer any months in that year. For example, if a taxpayer has a short tax year beginning January 1, 2009 and ending January 25, 2009, and that short tax year is following by a short tax year beginning January 25, 2009 and ending December 31, 2009, January is pushed into the second short tax. The second short tax year consists of 12 full months (i.e., is in this situation converted to a full tax year for depreciation purposes) and 6 full months of depreciation is claimed taking into account the half-year convention (i.e., the asset is treated as placed in service on July 1, 2009). Note that the bonus depreciation allowance and Code Sec. 179 expense allowance are claimed without regard to the length of the short tax year (Reg.§ 1.168(k)-1(d)(1)(i); Reg. § 1.179-1(c)(1)). Thus, it would appear, that even if the entire regular depreciation deduction for the first short tax year is effectively pushed into the second short tax year, the section 179 allowance and bonus deduction should nevertheless be claimed in the first short tax year.

(2) For a short tax year that neither begins on the first day of a month nor ends on the last day of a month, the length of the tax year is measured in days. The midpoint of the short tax year is determined by dividing the number of days in the tax year by two. If the result is a day other than the first day or the midpoint of a month, the midpoint of the short tax year is shifted to the nearest preceding first day or midpoint of a month.

Example (12): Property subject to MACRS and the half-year convention is disposed of in a short tax year that begins on March 6 and ends on July 19. Because the short tax year neither begins on the first day of a month nor ends on the last day of a month, the short tax year is measured in days. The short tax year consists of 136 days and the midpoint is 136 divided by 2, or 68 days (March 6 through May 12). However, since the arithmetical midpoint result is a day other than the first day or the midpoint of a month, the midpoint of the short tax year is shifted to May 1, the nearest preceding first day of a month. Thus, the recovery period of such property ends on May 1.

Mid-quarter convention

See ¶ 92 for details of mid-quarter convention relief if the third or fourth quarter of a short tax year includes September 11, 2001.

Under the mid-quarter convention, property is deemed placed in service or disposed of on the midpoint of the quarter, which always falls on either the first day or the midpoint of a month, in the short tax year that it is placed in service or disposed of. A short tax year is divided into four quarters and then the midpoint of each quarter is determined.

In determining the applicability of the mid-quarter convention, the aggregate basis of property placed in service in the last three months of the tax year must be computed regardless of the length of the tax year. If a short tax year consists of three months or less, the mid-quarter convention applies regardless of when the depreciable property is placed in service during the tax year.

(1) For a short tax year that consists of four or eight full calendar months, the length of each quarter is measured in whole months.

Example (13): Taxpayer has a short tax year from March 1 through June 30. Property subject to MACRS is acquired as follows: $1,000 in March and $4,000 in June. Because the short tax year consists of four full calendar months, the length of each quarter is measured in whole months. Each quarter consists of one month (a four month short tax year divided by four), and this result is divided by two to determine the midpoint of each quarter (the middle of the month, in this case). Because 80% ($4,000 divided by $5,000) of the aggregate bases of property placed in service in the short tax year was placed in service in the last three months of the short tax year, the mid-quarter convention applies. Thus, for MACRS purposes, the recovery period of $1,000 of property begins in the middle of March, and the recovery period of $4,000 of property begins in the middle of June.

(2) For a short tax year that consists of anything other than four or eight full calendar months, the length of the short tax year and each quarter are measured in days. The midpoint of each quarter is determined by dividing the number of days in

the short tax year by four, and then by dividing the result by two. If the arithmetical midpoint of a quarter is a day other than the first day or midpoint of a month, the midpoint of the quarter is shifted to the nearest preceding first day or midpoint of the month.

Example (14): Under the mid-quarter convention, the MACRS midpoints of quarters in a short tax year that begins on March 1 and ends on July 20 (144 days) are determined as follows: The number of days in the short tax year (144) is divided by 4 to find the length of each quarter (36 days). The number of days in each quarter (36) is divided by two to find the midpoint of each quarter (18 days).

Quarter	*Arithmetical Midpoint*	*MACRS Midpoint of Quarter*
Mar. 1-Apr. 5	Mar. 18	Middle of March
Apr. 6-May 11	Apr. 23	Middle of April
May 12-Jun. 16	May 29	Middle of May
Jun. 17-Jul. 22	July 4	July 1

Mid-month convention

This convention is applied without regard to the tax year. The recovery period of property subject to the mid-month convention begins or ends on the midpoint of the calendar month in which the property is placed in service or disposed.

Code Sec. 179 expense allowance and bonus depreciation

The Code Sec. 179 expense allowance (¶ 300) is computed without regard to the length of the tax year (Reg. § 1.179-1(c)(1)). The first-year bonus-depreciation allowance (¶ 127D) is likewise claimed in full without regard to the length of the tax year (Reg.§ 1.168(k)-1T(d); IRS Publication 946).

¶ 134

Tax Year Refinements

After considering the applicable convention refinements indicated at ¶ 132, certain tax year refinements are made depending on the situation in determining MACRS deductions.

Detailed guidance regarding MACRS depreciation computations for short tax years is provided by the IRS in Rev. Proc. 89-15, 1989-1 CB 816.

First tax year in the recovery period

Depreciation for the first recovery year in the recovery period is computed by multiplying the taxpayer's basis in the property by the applicable depreciation rate. The depreciation allowance allocable to the first tax year that includes a portion of the first recovery year is derived by multiplying the depreciation for the first recovery year by a fraction, the numerator of which is the number of months (including fractions of months) the property is deemed to be in service during the tax year under the applicable convention and the denominator of which is 12.

Subsequent tax years in the recovery period

The correlation of depreciation allowances between recovery years and tax years after the first tax year in the recovery period may be made under either the allocation method or the simplified method. The correlation manner adopted must be consistently used until the tax year that a switch to the MACRS straight-line method is required because it produces a larger depreciation allowance. Depreciation allowances for short tax years that are computed for alternative minimum tax purposes under Code Sec. 56 must also be determined in a manner consistent with these rules.

Usually, the allocation method and the simplified method result in the same depreciation allowances. However, if after the first tax year, but before the switch to the straight-line method, there is a short tax year or a disposition of property, then the depreciation allowance for that year under the simplified method is less than under the allocation method.

(1) Allocation method. The depreciation attributable to each recovery year, or portion thereof, that falls within a tax year, whether the tax year is a 12-month year or a short tax year, is allocated to such tax year. For each recovery year included, the depreciation attributable to such recovery year is multiplied by a fraction, the numerator of which is the number of months (including fractions of months) of the recovery year that falls within the tax year and the denominator of which is 12.

If there is a disposition of property before the end of the recovery period, the applicable convention determines the date of disposition.

For the sake of simplification, it is assumed in the following examples that the taxpayer does not expense any amount under Code Sec. 179 and bonus depreciation is not claimed. As noted at ¶ 132, the expense allowance and bonus depreciation are claimed in full without regard to the length of the tax year. Regular depreciation deductions on the cost of an asset, after reduction by any amounts expensed and/or claimed as bonus depreciation, are affected by a short tax year, as illustrated in these examples.

Example (1): Initial short tax year

A calendar-year corporation began business on March 15. During its first tax year, the corporation placed in service tangible personal property consisting of $100 of 5-year property subject to MACRS depreciation. Assume that there are no other short tax years during the recovery period, the half-year convention is the applicable convention for such property, and the corporation made no elections under Code Sec. 168.

The applicable recovery period, applicable depreciation method, depreciation for the first tax year in the recovery period, depreciation for subsequent tax years in the recovery period, and the tax year of the switch to the straight-line method for such property are determined as follows:

Because the short tax year ends on the last day of the month, the length of the tax year is measured in months. The short tax year consists of 10 months (including March) and, under the half-year convention, the five-year recovery period of this property begins on the midpoint of the short tax year (10 months divided by 2 equals 5 months) (August 1). Thus, the corporation is entitled to 5 months of depreciation for the first recovery year in its first tax year.

The applicable depreciation method for 5-year property is the 200% declining-balance method, with a switch to the straight-line method for the first tax year in which the latter method produces a larger depreciation allowance. The applicable depreciation rate for the property is 40% (200% divided by 5, the number of years in the recovery period).

In the second tax year depreciation is computed on $100 for 7 months ($7/12$) since only 5 months ($5/12$) depreciation was claimed on that amount in the first (short) tax year. Depreciation is computed on $60 for the remaining 5 months ($5/12$) in the second tax year. The $60 figure is the $100 cost reduced by the $16.67 depreciation claimed in the first tax year and $23.33 claimed on the $100 for the first 7 months of the second tax year ($.40 \times \$100 \times 7/12 = \$23.33$; $\$100 - \$16.67 - \$23.33 = \$60$). Similar methodology is used for succeeding tax years in the recovery period.

Tax Yr.	*Method*		*Depreciation*
1	DB	($.40 \times \$100 \times 5/12$) . . . . =	$16.67
2	DB	($.40 \times \$100 \times 7/12$) + ($.40 \times \$60 \times 5/12$) . . . . =	33.33
3	DB	($.40 \times \$60 \times 7/12$) + ($.40 \times \$36 \times 5/12$) . . . . =	20.00
4	DB	($.40 \times \$36 \times 7/12$) + ($.40 \times \$21.60 \times 5/12$) . . . . =	12.00

Tax Yr.	Method		Depreciation
5	SL*	(1/(1 + 7/12) × $18 × 12/12) . . . . =	11.37
6	SL*	(1 × $6.63 × 12/12) . . . . =	6.63
		Total	$100.00

* **Note:** For the fifth tax year, a larger MACRS depreciation allowance is obtained by switching to the straight-line method because the allowance determined under the declining-balance method would be only $7.20 ((.40 × $21.60 × 7/12) + (.40 × $12.96 × 5/12)). Also, the rate under the straight-line method is determined at the beginning of a tax year and is applied to the unrecovered basis. For comparison purposes, depreciation under the straight-line method is computed as follows in determining the tax year of changeover to the straight-line method. The entire adjusted basis is recovered in the sixth tax year under the straight-line method since the remaining recovery period—7 months—is less than one year. See ¶ 179.

Tax Yr.	Adjusted Basis	×	Straight-Line Rate	×	Short Yr. Adjustment	=	Depreciation
1	$100.00		1/5		5/12		$8.33
2	83.33		1/(4 + 7/12)		12/12		18.18
3	50.00		1/(3 + 7/12)		12/12		13.95
4	30.00		1/(2 + 7/12)		12/12		11.61
5	18.00		1/(1 + 7/12)		12/12		11.37
6	6.63		1		12/12		6.63

Note that the figures in the adjusted basis column are determined by subtracting the total depreciation claimed in all earlier tax years under the 200% declining-balance method or straight-line method. For example, the $83.33 adjusted basis for tax year 2 is equal to the original cost ($100) reduced by the depreciation claimed in year 1 under the 200% declining-balance method ($16.67).

Example (2): Subsequent short tax years

A calendar-year corporation began business on May 1 of its first short tax year (May 1 through December 31). On that date, the corporation placed in service 5-year MACRS property acquired for $100. The property is depreciated under the declining-balance method using a half-year convention and the depreciation allowance for recovery years is correlated with tax years under the allocation method. In its second tax year, there is also a second short tax year (January 1 through June 30) because the corporation is acquired by a fiscal-year corporation with a June 30 year end and the corporations file a consolidated return. Depreciation for the first tax year in the recovery period, subsequent tax years, and the year of changeover to the straight-line method for such property is determined as follows:

Because the first short tax year ends on the last day of the month, the length of the tax year is measured in months. The short tax year consists of eight months, and under the half-year convention the five-year recovery period of this property begins at the midpoint of the short tax year (8 divided by 2 equals 4 months) (September 1). Thus, the corporation is entitled to four months of depreciation for the first recovery year in its first tax year.

The applicable depreciation method for 5-year property is the 200% declining-balance method, with a switch to the straight-line method for the first tax year in which the latter produces a larger depreciation allowance. The applicable depreciation rate for the property is 40% (200% divided by 5, the number of years in the recovery period).

The second tax year is also a short tax year consisting of six months and includes six months of depreciation for the first recovery year. The remaining two months of depreciation for the first recovery year and ten months of depreciation for the second recovery year are claimed in the third year.

Tax Yr.	Method		Depreciation
1	DB	(.40 × $100 × 4/12) . . . . =	$13.33
2	DB	(.40 × $100 × 6/12) . . . . =	20.00

Tax Yr.	*Method*		*Depreciation*
3	DB	(.40 × \$100 × 2/12) + (.40 × \$60 × 10/12) .... =	26.67
4	DB	(.40 × \$60 × 2/12) + (.40 × \$36 × 10/12) ..... =	16.00
5	SL*	(1/(2 + 2/12) × \$24 × 12/12) .... =	11.08
6	SL	(1/(1 + 2/12) × \$12.92 × 12/12) .... =	11.07
7	SL	(1 × \$1.85 × 12/12) .... =	1.85
		Total	\$100.00

* **Note:** For the fifth year, a larger MACRS depreciation allowance is obtained by switching to the straight-line method because the allowance determined under the declining-balance method would be \$9.60 ((.40 × \$36 × 2/12) + (.40 × \$21.60 × 10/12)). Also, the rate under the straight-line method is determined at the beginning of a tax year and is applied to the unrecovered basis. For comparison purposes, depreciation under the straight-line method is computed as follows in determining the tax year in which to change to the straight-line method.

Tax Yr.	*Adjusted Basis*	×	*Straight-Line Rate*	×	*Short Yr. Adjustment*	=	*Depreciation*
1	\$100.00		1/5		4/12		\$6.67
2	86.67		1/(4 + 8/12)		6/12		9.29
3	66.67		1/(4 + 2/12)		12/12		16.00
4	40.00		1/(3 + 2/12)		12/12		12.63
5	24.00		1/(2 + 2/12)		12/12		11.08
6	12.92		1/(1 + 2/12)		12/12		11.07
7	1.85		1		12/12		1.85

Example (3): Disposition before end of recovery period

Assume the same facts as in Example (1), above, except that there is a disposition of property on December 28 of the second tax year. The depreciation allowance for the second tax year must reflect the premature end of the recovery period. Because the half-year convention applies to such property, the recovery period of the property ends on the midpoint (July 1) of the second tax year. Thus, six months of depreciation for the first recovery year is allowed in the second tax year (five months of depreciation for the first recovery year was allowed in the first short tax year). The depreciation allowance for the second tax year is \$20 (.40 × \$100 × 6/12).

(2) Simplified method. (a) The unrecovered basis of property at the beginning of the tax year is multiplied by the applicable depreciation rate.

(b) If the tax year is a short tax year, the product in (a) is multiplied by a fraction, the numerator of which is the number of months (including fractions of months) in the tax year and the denominator of which is 12, in order to determine the depreciation allowance for the tax year.

(c) If there is a disposition of property in the tax year, the product in (a) is multiplied by a fraction, the numerator of which is the number of months the property is deemed in service under the applicable convention during the tax year and the denominator of which is 12 in order to determine the depreciation allowance for the tax year.

Example (4): Initial short tax year

Assume the same facts as in Example (1), above. Under the simplified method, the depreciation allowance for the *first* tax year in the recovery period is calculated in the same manner as under the allocation method in Example (1).

Depreciation allowances for subsequent tax years are calculated under the declining balance method by applying the applicable depreciation rate (40%) to the unrecovered basis of the property as of the beginning of the tax year. This calculation is made instead of allocating a portion of the depreciation attributable to the recovery years that fall within a tax year. Assuming the same facts as in Example (1), above, depreciation allowances under the simplified method are determined as follows:

Tax Yr.	Method			Depreciation
1	DB	(.40 × $100 × 5/12)	=	$16.67
2	DB	(.40 × $83.33 × 12/12)	=	33.33
3	DB	(.40 × $50.00 × 12/12)	=	20.00
4	DB	(.40 × $30.00 × 12/12)	=	12.00
5	SL*	(1/(1 + 7/12) × $18.00 × 12/12)	=	11.37
6	SL	(1 × $6.63 × 12/12)	=	6.63
		Total		$100.00

* **Note:** For the fifth tax year, a larger MACRS depreciation allowance is obtained by switching to the straight-line method because the allowance determined under the declining balance method would be $7.20 (.40 × $18). For comparison purposes, depreciation under the straight-line method is computed as indicated in Example (1), above, in determining the tax year of switch to the straight-line method.

Example (5): Subsequent short tax year

Assume the same facts as in Example (2), above, except that the simplified method is used. Under the simplified method, the depreciation allowance for the first tax year in the recovery period is calculated in the same manner as under the allocation method in Example (2), above.

Because the second tax year is also a short tax year, the depreciation allowance for such tax year is calculated by multiplying the unrecovered basis of the property at the beginning of such tax year by the applicable depreciation rate, and then multiplying the product by a fraction, the numerator of which is the number of months in the tax year and the denominator of which is 12.

Tax Yr.	Method			Depreciation
1	DB	(.40 × $100 × 4/12)	=	$13.33
2	DB	(.40 × $86.67 × 6/12)	=	17.33
3	DB	(.40 × $69.34 × 12/12)	=	27.74
4	DB	(.40 × $41.60 × 12/12)	=	16.64
5	SL*	(1/(2 + 2/12) × $24.96 × 12/12)	=	11.52
6	SL	(1/(1 + 2/12) × $13.44 × 12/12)	=	11.52
7	SL	(1 × $1.92 × 12/12)	=	1.92

* **Note:** For the fifth tax year, a larger MACRS depreciation allowance is obtained by switching to the straight-line method because the allowance determined under the declining-balance method would be $9.98 (.40 × $24.96 × 12/12). For comparison purposes, depreciation under the straight-line method is computed as follows in determining the tax year of switch to the straight-line method.

Tax Yr.	Adjusted Basis	×	Straight-Line Rate	×	Short Yr. Adjustment	=	Depreciation
1	$100.00		1/5		4/12		$6.67
2	86.67		1/(4 + 8/12)		6/12		9.29
3	69.34		1/(4 + 2/12)		12/12		16.64
4	41.60		1/(3 + 2/12)		12/12		13.14
5	24.96		1/(2 + 2/12)		12/12		11.52
6	13.44		1/(1 + 2/12)		12/12		11.52
7	1.92		1		12/12		1.92

Example (6): Disposition before end of recovery period

Assume the same facts as in Example (1) above, except that there is a disposition of property on December 28 of the second tax year and the simplified method is used. The depreciation allowance for the second tax year must reflect the premature end of the recovery period. Because the half-year convention applies to such property, the recovery period of the property ends on the midpoint (July 1) of the second tax year. The depreciation allowance for the second tax year is $16.67 (the unrecovered basis of the property at the beginning of the second tax year ($83.33) times the applicable rate (40%), and then multiplying the product by 6/12).

Excluded Property

¶ 140

Property Ineligible for MACRS

Most depreciable tangible property (see ¶ 3 and ¶ 5) placed in service after 1986 that is not otherwise excluded property must be depreciated under the MACRS rules. MACRS may be used to claim deductions on both new and used property. It does not apply to inventory, stock in trade, works of art that lack an ascertainable useful life (¶ 3), or land (as distinguished from the structures on it). However, apart from these rules of general application, various special rules exclude property from MACRS.

Certain categories of property are specifically excluded from eligibility for MACRS, even if they are placed in service after 1986 (Code Sec. 168(f)). These categories include:

(1) property for which an election was made to use a depreciation method not expressed in a term of years, such as the unit-of-production method (¶ 360), machine-hours method (¶ 360), operating-days method, or the income-forecast method (¶ 364). For this purpose, the retirement-replacement-betterment method or similar method is not considered a method that is not expressed in a term of years;

(2) public utility property, unless a normalization method of accounting is used;

(3) motion picture films, videotapes, and videocassette movies (Rev. Rul. 89-62, 1989-1 CB 78);

(4) sound recordings, such as discs, tapes, or other phonorecordings in which musical or other sounds are embodied; and

(5) intangible assets (see ¶ 10).

Because of the similarity and the largely identical language of the exclusionary rules under MACRS and those under ACRS, the following discussion focuses on the distinctions between the relevant MACRS rules and the ACRS rules discussed at ¶ 260–¶ 268.

Methods not expressed in a term of years

As under ACRS (see ¶ 260), a taxpayer may make an election out of MACRS by properly depreciating property under the unit-of-production method or any method not expressed in a term of years (see above and ¶ 364) in the first tax year that the property is placed in service *and* attaching the required statement to its return (Code Sec. 168(f)(1)). Recovering the cost of a car through the IRS prescribed standard mileage allowance or a mileage-based method is regarded as such an election (see ¶ 217).

The election is made by reporting the depreciation on line 15 of Form 4562 and attaching the election statement as described in the instructions for line 15 (viz., an attached sheet with a description of the property, its basis, and the depreciation method selected). The election must be made by the return due date (including extensions) for the tax year the property is placed in service or by filing an amended return within six months of the return due date (excluding extensions). The amended return election requires that the statement be attached to the amended return and "Filed pursuant to section 301.9100-2" written on it (IRS Publication 946 (How to Depreciate Property); Temporary Reg. § 301.9100-7T).

The election is not considered made if the required statement is not attached to the return (*New Gaming Systems, Inc.*, 82 TCM 794, Dec. 54,520(M)).

Prop. Reg. § 1.168-4(b) (¶ 535) provides, with respect to the similar ACRS (pre-1987) election, that the method elected must be a recognized method prior to 1981 within the particular industry for the type of property in question. The regulation also indicates that the election is made on an asset-by-asset basis and does not automatically apply to all property in the same recovery class placed in service in the same tax year.

The election out of MACRS election is irrevocable (Temporary Reg. § 301.9100-7T(i)). However, the election out of ACRS (Code Sec. 168(e)(2), prior to amendment by the 1986 Tax Reform Act) was revocable with IRS consent, although consent was granted only in extraordinary circumstances (Proposed Reg. § 1.168-5(e)(1)(iv) and Proposed Reg. § 1.168-5(e)(9).

Films and recordings

Motion picture films, video tapes, and sound recordings are expressly excluded from MACRS (Code Sec. 168(f)(3) and (4)). The exclusion for sound recordings extends to discs, tapes, or other phonorecordings resulting from the fixation of a series of sounds. Such assets are depreciable under the income forecast method or another method that would provide a reasonable allowance under Code Sec. 167(a). See ¶ 364.

Video cassettes

Video cassettes such as those purchased by video stores for rental to the general public fall in the category of "motion picture film, video tape, or sound recording." The cost less salvage value of video cassettes that have a useful life over one year may be depreciated under either the straight-line method over the useful life of the video cassettes in the particular taxpayer's business or the income forecast method (see ¶ 364) (Rev. Rul. 89-62, 1989-1 CB 78). Use of the latter method requires asset-by-asset income projections, and video cassettes may not be grouped except under a single title.

Eligible taxpayers who are able to show that particular video-cassettes do not have a useful life in excess of a single year are entitled to deduct the cost of such video cassettes as a current business expense. Such circumstances may arise, for instance, where a video rental store buys 60 videotapes of a new movie and claims a write-off for 12 tapes over a three-year period and a business expense deduction for the balance of the tapes in a single year as viewer interest wanes.

Public utility property

Property predominantly used to furnish or sell electricity, water, sewage disposal services, gas or steam (through a local distribution system), telephone services, or other communication services if furnished or sold by Comsat qualify for MACRS (as they did for ACRS), but only if accounting is normalized (Code Sec. 168(f)(2)). Normalization is discussed at ¶ 262.

Assets used in the production, transmission, and distribution of electricity, gas, steam, or water for sale including related land improvements are described in Asset Classes 49.11 through 49.4 of Rev. Proc. 87-56 at ¶ 191. The depreciation period will depend upon the applicable Asset Class.

The IRS has ruled on the proper classification of four assets used by a steam production plant that produces electricity for sale (Asset Class 49.13, 20-year property) (Rev. Rul. 2003-81, I.R.B. 2003-30). In making the classifications, the IRS applied the general rule that the depreciation period for an asset described in an "asset" category (Asset Classes 00.11 through 00.4) is applicable even if the asset is used in a "business" category (Asset Classes 01.1 and following) unless the asset is specifically described in the business category. See ¶ 190. Thus, a bookcase used to store training manuals and operation protocols in the plant supervisor's office is seven-year property because it is described in an asset category (Asset Class 00.11 relating to office furniture). A work bench used to repair plant machinery and equipment is 20-year property since it is not described in an asset category (Asset Class 49.13).

A parking lot located at the production plant is 20-year property (Asset Class 49.13) since land improvements related to assets used in the steam power production of electricity are specifically included in Asset Class 49.13. Although land improvements are described in an asset category (Asset Class 00.3) as 15-year property, Asset Class 49.13 specifically includes land improvements used in the steam power production of electricity. However, a parking lot located 100 miles from the plant at the corporate headquarters is 15-year property (Asset Class 00.3) because in the IRS's view it "is not related to the plant that produces the electricity" as required by Asset Class 49.13. Apparently, the types of activities conducted at the corporate headquarters, even though connected with the business of producing electricity, are not considered by the IRS "as used" in the production of electricity within the meaning of Asset Class 49.13.

The ruling indicates that the utility's non-tax categorizations such as FERC account practices are not controlling for purposes of federal depreciation classification.

The ruling also states the following under the heading "Audit Protection":

> "A utility taxpayer, which owns a steam production plant and engages in the production of electricity for sale, may continue to use its present method of treating the cost of depreciable property described in an asset category (asset classes 00.11 through 00.4) or a specific utility services activity class (asset classes 49.11 through 49.4) that was placed in service during any taxable year ending on or before June 27, 2003 if use of such method results in a longer recovery period than would be required by this revenue ruling."

Note that the audit "protection" only applies in situations where the taxpayer would be entitled to claim more depreciation if it changed its accounting method to comply with the ruling.

¶ 142

Anti-churning Rules

Since ACRS is generally more favorable than older depreciation rules, the provisions that ushered it in were accompanied by special rules designed to prevent the "churning" of pre-1981 assets into recovery property without any significant change in either its ownership or use (see ¶ 264). Similar rules, adopted largely by reference, prevent the churning of pre-1981 assets into MACRS property (Code Sec. 168(f)(5)). With exceptions for (1) residential rental property, (2) nonresidential real property, and (3) any property for which the ACRS allowance for the first full taxable year in which the property is placed in service would be more generous[1] than the corresponding MACRS deduction (assuming the half-year convention), similarly borrowed rules prevent the conversion of recovery property into property

[1] A TAMRA amendment clarifies Congress's intention to compare first-year deductions irrespective of whether or not *full* taxable years are involved.

that is depreciable under MACRS. Thus, under exception (3), a car (3-year property under ACRS but 5-year property under MACRS) purchased from a related taxpayer after 1986 would not be depreciable under ACRS if the related taxpayer owned the car in 1986.

Care must be exercised in comparing first-year percentages because classes of MACRS property are not identical to similarly named classes of ACRS property. Thus, under the following chart, the anti-churning rules would not prevent office furniture, 5-year property under ACRS, from becoming 7-year property under MACRS:

	MACRS	*ACRS*
3-year	33.33%	25%
5-year	20%	15%
7-year	14.29%	. . .
10-year	10%	8%

Example (1): In June of 1986, Smith's brother buys a car. In June of 1989, Smith purchases the car from his brother for use in a business. The car is depreciable under MACRS (for which, under the half-year convention, first-year depreciation would be 20%) rather than under ACRS (for which first-year depreciation would be 25%) even though Smith's brother (a related party) owned it in 1986.

Subject to this more-generous test, personal property acquired after 1986 (after July 31, 1986, if MACRS was elected under transitional rules) is excluded from MACRS under the anti-churning rules if:

(1) it was owned or used by the taxpayer or a related party during 1986;

(2) it was acquired from a person owning it during 1986, and, as part of the transaction, the user of the property stays the same;

(3) it is leased to a person who owned or used it during 1986 (or a person related to such person); or

(4) the property was not MACRS property in the hands of the transferor due to the application of rules (1) or (3), and the user of the property does not change.

Example (2): In 1989, Higgins purchases a computer from his sister, who had placed it in service in June of 1986. Since the computer was 5-year property under both ACRS and MACRS, first-year depreciation would be more generous under MACRS (20%, assuming the half-year convention) than under ACRS (15%). Higgins must use ACRS.

In general, real property, other than residential rental property or nonresidential real property, acquired after 1986 (after July 31, 1986 if MACRS was elected under transitional rules) is excluded from MACRS under the anti-churning rules if:

(1) the taxpayer or a party related to the taxpayer owned it in 1986, or

(2) the property is leased back to a party (or a person related to such party) who owned it during 1986.

The anti-churning rule also applies to real property (other than residential rental property and nonresidential real property) acquired after 1986 in a nontaxable exchange described in Code Sec. 1031, 1033, 1038 or 1039 for property that the taxpayer or a related person owned during 1986, but only to the extent of the substituted basis of the property received.

If, under the anti-churning rules, MACRS is precluded, the taxpayer must use ACRS (unless it is also precluded) or some other appropriate method.

Personal property and real property (including residential rental property and nonresidential real property) acquired after 1980 which is subject to the ACRS anti-churning rules described at ¶ 264 because of ownership, use, etc., in 1980 may not be depreciated under MACRS (Code Sec. 168(f)(5)(A)(i)).

The MACRS anti-churning rules do not apply to property transferred by reason of (a) the death of a taxpayer, or (b) the acquisition of more than 90 percent of a partnership interest by parties unrelated to the selling partner (Code Sec. 168(f)(5)(A) referring to former Code Sec. 168(e)(4)(H) and (D), respectively (before repeal by the Tax Reform Act of 1986 (P.L. 99-514)).

¶ 144

Nonrecognition Transactions

The basis of property received by a transferee in certain nonrecognition transactions must be depreciated by the transferee as if the transfer did not take place to the extent of the transferor's adjusted basis immediately before the transfer. These transactions include distributions in complete liquidation of a subsidiary (under Code Sec. 332), transfers to controlled corporations (under Code Sec. 351), exchanges of property solely for corporate stock in a reorganization (under Code Sec. 361), contributions of property in exchange for a partnership interest (under Code Sec. 721), and partnership distributions of property (under Code Sec. 731). This "step-in-the-shoes" rule extends to members of an affiliated group filing a consolidated return, but it does not apply in the case of a partnership termination where 50 percent or more of the interest in partnership capital and profits is sold or exchanged within a 12-month period (Code Sec. 168(i)(7)).

Except for regulations relating to application of the mid-quarter convention (Reg.§ 1.168(d)-1(b)(7) at ¶ 560), the IRS has not issued MACRS regulations that cover this rule. However, ACRS Prop. Reg. § 1.168-5(b) (relating to pre-1987 Code Sec. 168(f)(10)) at ¶ 540 illustrates the application of a generally similar rule as it applies in the context of ACRS property transfers. The principles there should be equally applicable to MACRS property.

The IRS has issued regulations explaining the allocation of the bonus depreciation deduction in these step-in-the-shoes transactions (Reg. § 1.168(k)-1(f)). See ¶ 127D.

For like-kind exchanges (Code Sec. 1031) and involuntary conversions (Code Sec. 1033), see ¶ 167.

¶ 145

Property Reacquired by a Taxpayer

Code Sec. 168(i)(7)(C) states: "Under regulations, property which is disposed of and then reacquired by the taxpayer shall be treated for purposes of computing the deduction allowable under subsection (a) [the MACRS deduction—CCH.] as if such property had not been disposed of."

No regulations relating to this rule have been issued under MACRS.

A similar rule was provided under ACRS (Code Sec. 168(f)(10)(C), prior to 1987). This rule is explained in ACRS Prop. Reg. § 1.168-5(c) at ¶ 540.

MACRS Alternative Depreciation System

¶ 150

MACRS Alternative Depreciation System (ADS)

Under the MACRS alternative depreciation system (ADS), the applicable depreciation method for all property is the straight-line method (Code Sec. 168(g)(2)(A)). The deduction is computed by applying the straight-line method (without regard to salvage value), the applicable convention, and the applicable prescribed (generally longer) recovery period for the respective class of property.

ADS *must* be used for:

(1) tangible property used predominantly outside the United States (¶ 152);

(2) tax-exempt use property leased to a tax-exempt entity (¶ 152);

(3) tax-exempt bond-financed property (¶ 152);

(4) property imported from a foreign country for which an Executive Order is in effect because the country maintains trade restrictions or engages in other discriminatory acts (¶ 152); and

(5) listed property, such as a car or truck, used 50 percent or less in a qualified business use (¶ 210).

Property which must be depreciated using ADS does not qualify for any of the various bonus depreciation deductions (¶ 127D through ¶ 127J). Property for which ADS is elected (see below), however, may qualify.

Farmers

Certain farmers who elect to deduct preproductive period costs of certain plants (not apply the uniform capitalization rules) for the first tax year during which such property is produced must depreciate all property used predominantly in any of their farming businesses that is placed in service during any year that the election is in effect under the MACRS alternative depreciation system (Code Sec. 263A(e)(2); Notice 87-76, 1987-2 CB 384). See also ¶ 84 and ¶ 160.

Other uses

The alternative depreciation system is used for purposes of computing the earnings and profits of foreign or domestic corporations (Code Sec. 312(k)(3)).

In computing depreciation for alternative minimum tax purposes on property placed in service before 1999, the alternative depreciation system must be used on certain property. See ¶ 170.

The allowable depreciation deductions for luxury cars (¶ 200) and other listed property (¶ 208) used 50 percent or less in business are also determined under the alternative depreciation system (Code Sec. 280F(b)(1)). See ¶ 206.

ADS election

Instead of using the MACRS general depreciation system (GDS), taxpayers may irrevocably elect to apply the alternative depreciation system to any class of property for any tax year (Code Sec. 168(g)(7)). If elected, the alternative depreciation system applies to all property in the MACRS class placed in service during the tax year. However, for residential rental property and nonresidential real property, the election may be made on a property-by-property basis.

This ADS election differs from the MACRS straight-line election (¶ 84) in that the ADS usually requires longer straight-line recovery periods.

¶ 152

MACRS Alternative Depreciation System Property

A brief description of the categories of property for which the use of the MACRS alternative depreciation system (ADS) is mandatory (see ¶ 150) is provided below. Note that bonus depreciation may not be claimed on *mandatory* ADS property.

Foreign-use property

Generally, this category includes property physically located outside the United States more than half of the taxable year or more than half of the year considering only that part beginning on the day on which the property is placed in service (Reg. § 1.48-1(g)(1)). It does not include property owned by a U.S. corporation or a U.S. citizen and predominantly used in a U.S. possession (by such corporation or citizen or a corporation created under the laws of the possession) unless such corporation or citizen is entitled to shelter income under various Code provisions relating to U.S. possessions. Other exclusions include: communications satellites; any satellite or spacecraft launched from within the United States; certain aircraft, railroad rolling stock, vessels, motor vehicles, and containers used in transportation to and from the United States; submarine telephone cables, offshore drilling equipment, and certain other resource exploration property used in international waters (Code Sec. 168(g)(4)).

Change in use. Special rules apply when property formerly used in the U.S. is used predominantly outside the U.S. or when property formerly used predominantly outside of the U.S. is moved into the U.S. These rules are described at ¶ 169.

Cargo containers used predominantly outside of the U.S. Code Sec. 168(g)(4)(E), as amended by P.L. 101-508, provides that ADS does not apply to containers of a United States person which are used in the transportation of property to *and* from the United States. The IRS has interpreted the exception, as in effect prior to amendment by P.L. 101-508, to apply to containers used substantially in the *direct* transportation of property to *or* from the United States (Rev. Rul. 90-9, 1990-1 CB 46). Prior to P.L. 101-508, the exception was not specifically stated in Code Sec. 168, but rather, based on a cross reference to a similar definition contained in former Code Sec. 48(a)(2)(B)(v) (relating to the investment tax credit).

In Rev. Rul. 90-9, the IRS also ruled that a taxpayer must depreciate cargo containers using ADS (and may not claim the investment credit) if the taxpayer cannot document that its containers were used substantially in the direct transportation of property to *or* from the United States during the tax year. Documentation is required on a container-by-container basis for each year of the depreciation recovery period and investment tax credit recapture period. However, fall-back positions based on valid statistical sampling are acceptable. See, also, IRS Letter Ruling 9045001 (May 3, 1990) upon which the position of Rev. Rul. 90-9 is based. An irrevocable election is provided by Rev. Proc. 90-10, 1990-1 CB 467, to United States owners of qualifying intermodal cargo containers to treat 50 percent of containers placed in service during the election year as meeting the exception for direct transportation to or from the United States. If this election is made it is not necessary to maintain records that trace the usage of the containers as required by Rev. Rul. 90-9. The retroactive application of Rev. Rul. 90-9 and Rev. Proc. 90-10 was upheld in *Norfolk Southern Corp.*, CA-4, 98-1 USTC ¶ 50,273, 140 F3d 240.

An undated FSA (Field Service Advice) provides significant guidance with respect to the application of Rev. Rul. 90-9 and Rev. Proc. 90-10, including the use of statistical analysis to establish the use of intermodal containers (FSA 9999-9999-273; 99 ARD 210-12 (cite for location in CCH Advance Release Documents)).

See, also, ¶ 5.

Maquiladora. Tangible property transferred by a U.S. entity to a maquiladora located in Latin America and used predominantly outside of the U.S. during the tax year in an assembly process must be depreciated under ADS unless one of the preceding exclusions apply. If the transferred property was being depreciated under an accelerated method of accounting while located in the U.S. the switch to the straight-line method under ADS in the first year the property is used outside of the U.S. is not considered a change in accounting method for which a Code Sec. 481 adjustment is required (ISP Coordinated Issue Paper on the Maquiladora Industry, issued July 23, 1997).

The IRS has issued settlement guidelines confirming that a U.S. entity is required to use the MACRS ADS depreciation system in the year tangible property is transferred to a maquiladora if the property is located more than 50 percent during the tax year of transfer on the maquiladora (Appeals Industry Specialization Program Settlement Guidelines Industry: Maquiladora Issue: Section 168(g), April 8, 2005). The ADS deduction is determined by applying the MACRS change in use regulations (Reg.§ 1.168(i)-4(d) reproduced at ¶ 568 and discussed at ¶ 168 and ¶ 169).

However, the guidelines provides that if the property is transferred across the U.S. border in the tax year that the taxpayer places the property in service, the appropriate depreciation method for the first tax year is based on the primary use of the property for that tax year. In other words, the property will either be depreciated using ADS for the entire year or the MACRS general depreciation system for the entire year. The primary use of the property may be determined in any reasonable manner that is consistently applied to the taxpayer's property. See Reg.§ 1.168(i)-4(e).

The guidelines also discuss the application of the change in accounting method rules and provide that the failure to switch to the ADS method in the tax year required will trigger the change in accounting method rules (¶ 75) if the entity files two or more consecutive tax returns before switching to the ADS method.

Regulations. There are currently no MACRS regulations dealing with foreign-use property. However, ACRS has a rule which modifies the otherwise applicable recovery period for foreign-use property and this rule is discussed in Prop. Reg. § 1.168-2(g) at ¶ 525. Issues relating to the definition of foreign-use property contained in this regulation should also apply to MACRS property.

Tax-exempt use property

Tax-exempt use property leased to a tax-exempt entity must be depreciated using ADS. The recovery period of tax-exempt use property subject to a lease may in no event be less than 125 percent of the lease term (Code Sec. 168(g)(3)(A)).

Tax-exempt use property includes (Code Sec. 168(h)(1)):

(1) tangible property other than nonresidential real property leased to a tax-exempt entity; and

(2) that part of nonresidential real property leased to a tax-exempt entity under a disqualified lease if the portion of the property so leased is more than 35 percent of the property.

Generally effective for leases entered into after March 12, 2004, the American Jobs Creation Act of 2004 expands the definition of tax-exempt use property to include the following intangible property if it is leased to a tax-exempt entity and would otherwise be considered tax-exempt use property under Code Sec. 168(h):

(1) computer software, as described in Code Sec. 167(f)(1)(B) and otherwise amortizable over 36 months (¶ 48) Code Sec. 167(f)(1)(C), as added by the 2004 Jobs Act);

(2) the following separately acquired interests and rights which are specifically excluded by Code Sec. 197(e)(4) from the definition of a section 197 intangible:

(a) patent or copyright interests, as described in Code Sec. 197(e)(4)(C) (¶ 26),

(b) a right held under a contract or granted by a governmental unit to receive tangible property or services, as described in Code Sec. 197(e)(4)(B) (¶ 32), and

(c) a right held under a contract or granted by a governmental unit that has a fixed duration of less than 15 years, or that is fixed as to amount and recoverable under a method similar to the unit-of-production method, as described in Code Sec. 197(e)(4)(D) (¶ 50) (Code Sec. 167(f)(2), as amended by the 2004 Jobs Act); and

(3) Code Sec. 197 intangibles (¶ 12) (Code Sec. 197(f)(10), as added by the 2004 Jobs Act).

Any grant of a right to use property to a tax-exempt entity is a disqualified lease if:

(1) any part of the property was financed with a tax-exempt obligation of a state or a political subdivision of a state, and the entity participated in the financing;

(2) it is coupled with an option to purchase involving the tax-exempt entity;

(3) its term exceeds 20 years; or

(4) it is a leaseback of property used by the entity more than three months before the lease.

A tax-exempt entity is defined as (Code Sec. 168(h)(2)):

(1) the United States, any State or political subdivision, any possession of the United States, or any agency or instrumentality of the preceding;

(2) any organization (other than a Code Sec. 521 farmer's cooperative) exempt from U.S. income tax; and

(3) any foreign person or entity unless more than half of the gross income derived from the use is taxable or passed through to a U.S. shareholder under Code Sec. 951 rules relating to controlled foreign corporations (Code Sec. 168(h)(2)).

For leases entered into after October 3, 2004, the definition of tax-exempt entity for purposes of Code Sec. 168 is expanded to include Indian tribal governments (Code Sec. 168(h)(2)(A), as amended by the 2004 Jobs Act).

Any portion of property that is predominantly used in an unrelated trade or business from which the income is taxable under Code Sec. 511 is not tax-exempt use property or treated as property leased under a disqualified lease (Code Sec. 168(h)(1)(D)). Nor shall property be treated as tax-exempt use property merely because it is subject to a lease of less than three years and less than the greater of one year or 30 percent of the property's present class life (Code Sec. 168(h)(1)(C)). Subject to exceptions (such as where the property itself has been financed under tax-exempt obligations or a sale and leaseback are involved), qualified technological equipment leased to a tax-exempt entity for a term of no more than five years is not tax-exempt use property (Code Sec. 168(h)(3)). Generally effective for leases entered into after March 12, 2004, a renewal period (up to 24 months) under a lessee's option to renew at a fair market value rent is not treated as extending the term of the lease for such property (Code Sec. 168(h)(3)(A), as amended by the 2004 Jobs Act).

The tax-exempt use character of property leased to a partnership is determined at the partner level (Code Sec. 168(h)(5)). Thus, for purposes of the applicable rules, property leased to a partnership is treated as leased to the partners in proportions based on partnership rules for determining distributive shares of deductions and other items.

A special rule applies to like-kind exchanges after April 19, 1995, between related parties that are designed to circumvent the tax-exempt use property rules. Property received by a taxpayer from a related party in a like-kind exchange for tax-exempt use property that is made to avoid the application of the MACRS ADS must be depreciated by the taxpayer using the same method, convention, and the remaining recovery period as that of the transferred tax-exempt use property (Reg. § 1.168(h)-1).

This rule applies only to the portion of the taxpayer's basis in the tainted property that does not exceed the taxpayer's basis in the transferred tax-exempt use property or is not subject to the nonrecognition transaction rules provided in Code Sec. 168(i)(7) (see ¶ 144). For purposes of this rule, parties are deemed related if they bear a relationship specified in Code Sec. 267(b) or 707(b)(1).

The term of a lease includes options to renew (Code Sec. 168 (i)(3)(A)(i)). In determining the length of a lease term for leases executed after April 19, 1995, an additional period of time during which a tax-exempt lessee may not continue to be the lessee is included in the lease term if the lessee or a related party retains financial responsibility (Reg. § 1.168(i)-2). For this purpose, parties are deemed related if they bear a relationship specified in Code Sec. 168(h)(4).

Tax-exempt bond-financed property

This category generally includes any property placed in service after 1986 to the extent it is financed, directly or indirectly, by bonds (issued after March 1, 1986) on which income is exempt from tax under Code Sec. 103(a) (Code Sec. 168(g)(5)). The extent to which property is deemed financed by the proceeds of such bonds is determined on the basis of the order in which property is placed in service. Qualified residential projects—projects at all times meeting a median-income test for occupants—are excluded from the definition of tax-exempt bond-financed property. For purposes of this exception, the issuer must elect, at the time of the issuance of the bonds, which of two tests applies. Under one of the tests, at least 20 percent of the residential units must be occupied by individuals whose income is no more than half of the area median gross income. Under the alternate test, 40 percent is substituted for 20 percent, and 60 percent is substituted for 50 percent.

Transitional rules shield tax-exempt bond-financed facilities from the alternative depreciation system if certain action was taken before March 2, 1986.

Imported property

This category includes only property manufactured or produced in a foreign country and subject to an Executive Order (Code Sec. 168(g)(6)). The President may issue such an order pursuant to a determination that:

(1) such country maintains variable import fees or other burdensome nontariff trade restrictions inconsistent with trade agreements; or

(2) unjustifiably restricts U.S. commerce by, among other things, engaging in discriminatory acts or tolerating cartels. To be considered "imported," property must (1) be completed outside the United States, its possessions, and Puerto Rico or (2) less than 50 percent of its basis must be attributable to value added within the United States, its possessions, or Puerto Rico.

¶ 156

MACRS Alternative Depreciation System Recovery Periods

This paragraph describes the applicable recovery periods under the MACRS alternative depreciation system (ADS). Recovery periods are 12-month periods that begin on the date the property is deemed placed in service under the applicable convention. These ADS recovery periods are reflected in detail in Rev. Proc. 87-56 at ¶ 191.

The following recovery periods generally apply for purposes of ADS (Code Sec. 168(g)(2) and Code Sec. 168(g)(3)):

In the case of	*ADS Recovery Period*
Qualified technological equipment	5 years
Automobile or light general purpose truck	5 years
Personal property with no class life	12 years
Sec. 1245 property which is real property with no class life	40 years
Nonresidential real and residential rental property	40 years
Railroad grading and tunnel bores	50 years
Water utility property	50 years
All other property	The class life

Municipal sewers placed in service before June 13, 1996 were assigned a class life of 50 years for ADS purposes.

The term "qualified technological equipment" includes computers and peripheral equipment, high technology medical equipment, and certain high-technology telephone station equipment. See Code Sec. 168(i)(2).

Subject to a binding contracts exception, the 50-year ADS recovery period for water utility property generally applies to property placed in service after June 12, 1996 (Code Sec. 168(g)(2)(C)(iv), as amended by the Small Business Job Protection Act of 1996 (P.L. 104-188)). Water utility property is defined at ¶ 113.

Some property is assigned a special class life solely for ADS purposes (Code Sec. 168(g)(3)). This specially assigned class life is treated as the appropriate ADS recovery period. The following chart lists selected property with a specially assigned class life:

Property	*ADS Class life/ADS Recovery period (in years)*
(1) Rent-to-own property	4
(2) Semi-conductor manufacturing equipment	5
(3) Computer-based telephone central office switching equipment	9.5

Property	ADS Class life/ADS Recovery period (in years)
(4) Railroad track	10
(5) Single-purpose agricultural and horticultural structures	15
(6) Any tree or vine bearing fruit or nuts	20
(7) Retail motor fuels outlets	20
(8) Telephone distribution plant and comparable equipment	24
(9) Municipal wastewater treatment plants	24
(10) Qualified 15-year restaurant property, 15-year leasehold improvement property, and 15-year retail improvement property	39

Tax-exempt use property subject to a lease. For tax-exempt use property subject to a lease, the ADS recovery period is the longer of the asset's class life or 125 percent of the lease term (Code Sec. 168(g)(3)(A)).

The ADS recovery periods for MACRS property can be found in Rev. Proc. 87-56, which is reproduced at ¶ 191.

Dispositions of MACRS Property

¶ 160

Early Disposition Deduction; Recapture

A disposition is the permanent withdrawal of property from use in a trade or business or in the production of income. A withdrawal may be made by sale, exchange, involuntary conversion, retirement, abandonment, or destruction. The adjusted basis of abandoned property is deductible as a loss. See ¶ 162.

A disposition of property before the end of its recovery period is referred to as an early disposition. A MACRS deduction is usually allowed in the year of disposition of personal or real property unless the asset is disposed of in the same tax year that it was placed in service. See "Property acquired and disposed of in the same tax year," below.

Conventions

The same applicable convention that applied in the year that property was placed in service must also be used in the year of disposition.

For residential rental and nonresidential real property, the mid-month convention (¶ 90) must be used. Under the mid-month convention, property disposed of anytime during a month is treated as disposed of in the middle of that month. Thus, the month of disposition is treated as one-half month of use for purposes of prorating the depreciation calculated for a full tax year.

For property subject to the half-year convention (¶ 88), the deduction for the year of an early disposition is one-half the depreciation determined for the full tax year. However, as explained below, if property subject to the half-year convention is disposed of in the last year of the asset's recovery period the depreciation deduction is the same as if the asset had not been sold.

For property subject to the mid-quarter convention (¶ 92), depreciation determined for the full tax year is multiplied by the following percentages for the quarter of the tax year in which the disposition occurred: first quarter, 12.5 percent; second quarter, 37.5 percent; third quarter, 62.5 percent; and fourth quarter, 87.5 percent. However, if property subject to the mid-quarter convention is disposed of in the last year of the asset's recovery period, a special rules applies. See "Disposition in last year of recovery period," below.

Short tax year

For a disposition of property in a short tax year, the unrecovered basis of property is multiplied by the depreciation rate and then by a fraction the numerator of which is the number of months the property is considered in service and the denominator of which is 12. An allocation method may also be used. See ¶ 134.

Property acquired and disposed of in same tax year

If MACRS property subject to the half-year or mid-quarter convention (i.e., section 1245 property) is acquired and disposed of in the same tax year no MACRS deduction is allowed (IRS Publication 946 (How To Depreciation Property); Reg. § 1.168(d)-1(b)(3)). This rule is effective for property placed in service in tax years ending after January 30, 1991 (Reg.§ 1.168(d)-1(d)(1)). For earlier tax years it was permissible (though not required) to claim a depreciation deduction on property subject to the mid-quarter convention and placed in service and disposed of in the same tax year. However, in the case of property subject to the half-year convention, it appears no deduction could be claimed because under the half-year convention the property would be treated as acquired and disposed of on the same date. See the preamble to T.D. 8444 for additional details.

It appears that taxpayers were permitted to claim depreciation deductions on MACRS residential rental and nonresidential real property placed in service and disposed of in the same tax year if the acquisition and disposition occurred in a tax year ending on or before June 17, 2004 (Reg.§ 1.168(i)-4(c) stating the rule and Reg.§ 1.168(i)-4(g) providing the effective date). Although these regulations deal with changes in use of MACRS property (see ¶ 168), they specifically state that "No depreciation deduction is allowable for MACRS property placed in service and disposed of in the same taxable year." The rule is not limited to personal property. Compare Reg.§ 1.168(d)-1(b)(3) and Reg.§ 1.168(d)-1((d) which state the rule in the context of a discussion of the half-year and mid-quarter convention for personal property. Logically, the rule for real property should have been provided in MACRS regulations dealing with the application of the mid-month convention, rather than changes in use, but the IRS has not yet issued regulations dealing with the mid-month convention. Interestingly, however, since after the issuance of T.D. 8444, IRS Publication 946 has stated, without distinguishing between personal and real property, that depreciation may not be claimed on an asset placed in service and disposed of during the same tax year. Possibly, the writers of the Publication are interpreting the rule in Reg.§ 1.168(d)-1(b)(3) and Reg.§ 1.168(d)-1((d) to apply to real as well as personal property. Note that a long-standing depreciation recapture rule provides that all depreciation claimed on real property held for less than one year is subject to recapture as ordinary income (Code Sec. 1250(b)(1)). Thus, even if a taxpayer claims MACRS depreciation on real property sold and disposed of in the same tax year, the benefit of the deduction would be recaptured in the same tax year.

The cost of property acquired and disposed of in the same tax year is not taken into account in determining whether the mid-quarter convention applies to other property placed in service during that tax year (Code Sec. 168(d)(3)(B)(ii)

No depreciation deduction is allowed if a property is purchased for business use and converted to personal use in the same tax year (Reg.§ 1.168(i)-4(c)).

Disposition in last year of recovery period

It appears that the disposition of property subject to the half-year convention at any time in the tax year in which the last recovery year ends is not an early disposition that would result in claiming only one-half of the depreciation otherwise allowed for that tax year.

Example (1): MACRS 3-year property is placed in service in 2008 by a calendar-year taxpayer. The property cost $1,000. Bonus depreciation (¶ 127D) is $500 ($1,000 × 50%). Depreciable basis to which the regular table percentages are applied is $500 ($1,000 − $500). Under the half-year convention the recovery period begins on the midpoint of 2008 and ends on the midpoint of 2011. If the property is sold at any time during the 2011 tax year the half-year convention treats the property as if it was disposed of on the midpoint of 2011 (Code Sec. 168(d)(4)(A)). As a consequence there is no early disposition and the year 2011 depreciation deduction is not reduced. The deduction is equal to $37.05 ($500 × 7.41% (4th year recovery percentage from Table 1 at ¶ 180)).

However, if property subject to the mid-quarter convention is disposed of in the tax year in which the recovery period ends, an early disposition may occur.

Example (2): MACRS 3-year property is placed in service in December 2009 (fourth quarter) by a calendar-year taxpayer. The property cost $2,000. Bonus depreciation (¶ 127D) is $1,000 ($2,000 × 50%). Depreciable basis to which the regular table percentages are applied is $1,000 ($2,000 − $1,000). (The full amount of bonus depreciation is allowed even if the mid-quarter convention applies). Under the mid-quarter convention the recovery period begins on the mid-point of November 2009 and ends on the mid-point of November 2012. If the property is sold in 2012 prior to the beginning of the fourth quarter, then it is considered sold prior to the end of the recovery period and an early disposition has taken place. For example, if the property is sold in the second quarter on June 10, 2012, the property is considered sold on the midpoint of May and only 4 ½ months depreciation (January through mid-May) may be claimed for the 2012 tax year. The fourth-year table depreciation percentage for 3-year property placed in service in the fourth quarter under the mid-quarter convention (10.19% (Table 5 at ¶ 180)) may not be used because it reflects depreciation for 10½ months (January through the mid-point of November) rather than 4½ months. Instead, depreciation for the 4½ month period may be determined by using the last-year table percentage to determine depreciation for the 10½ month period ($1,000 × 10.19% = $101.90) and claiming 42.86% (4.5 ÷ 10.5) of that amount or $43.67 ($101.90 × 42.86% = $43.67) to reflect depreciation for the 5½ month period that the property is considered placed in service in the year of disposition under the mid-quarter convention. Alternatively, depreciation could be determined for one month ($101.90 ÷ 10.5 = $9.705) and this amount multiplied by 4.5 ($9.705 × 4.5 = $43.67).

Depreciation recapture rules

If section 1245 property is disposed of at a gain during the tax year, a specified amount (the "recapture amount") to the extent of recognized gain is treated as ordinary income. This recapture amount is recognized notwithstanding any other Code provision. Recapture only applies to depreciation allowed or allowable for periods after December 31, 1961 (Code Sec. 1245; Reg. § 1.1245-1(a)(1)). See ¶ 488, "*Keep records to reduce depreciation recapture—allowed or allowable rule*," for a rule that will usually limit recapture to depreciation actually claimed.

In the case of a sale, exchange, or involuntary conversion, the recapture amount is equal to the lower of:

(1) the recomputed basis of the property, or

(2) the amount realized

reduced by the adjusted basis of the property (Code Sec. 1245(a)(1); Reg. § 1.1245-1(b)).

The recomputed basis is the property's adjusted basis plus previously allowed or allowable depreciation or amortization (including the Code Sec. 179 expense deduction, the Code Sec. 190 deduction for expenditures to remove architectural and transportation barriers to the handicapped and elderly, the Code Sec. 193 deduction for tertiary injectants, and, for property generally acquired before August 11, 1993 (see ¶ 10 and ¶ 36), deductions under Code Sec. 1253(d)(2) and (3) (before amendment by the Omnibus Budget Reconciliation Act of 1993 (P.L. 103-66)) regarding fixed sum amounts paid on the transfer of a franchise, trademark or trade name) reflected in the adjusted basis (Code Sec. 1245(a)(2)).

Example (3): A depreciable machine is sold for $100. Its adjusted basis is $20. It cost $30 and $10 of depreciation has been claimed. The recapture amount is $10. This is the excess of the lesser of (1) $80 (the amount realized) or (2) $30 (the recomputed basis ($20 adjusted basis + $10 depreciation claimed) over $20 (the adjusted basis).

As can be seen in the preceding example, the rule for sales, exchanges, and involuntary conversions in effect provides that depreciation is recaptured to the extent of the lesser of the (1) depreciation claimed or the (2) gain recognized.

In the case of a disposition other than a sale, exchange, or involuntary conversion, the recapture amount is equal to the lower of:

(1) the recomputed basis of the property, or

(2) the fair market value of the property on the date of disposition

reduced by the adjusted basis of the property (Code Sec. 1245(a)(1); Reg. § 1.1245-1(c)).

Example (4): A corporation distributes section 1245 property to its shareholders as a dividend. The property has a $2,000 adjusted basis, a recomputed basis of $3,300, and a fmv of $3,100. $1,100 ($3,100 - $2,000) is recognized by the corporation as ordinary income even though Code Sec. 311(a) would otherwise preclude recognition of gain to the corporation.

The recapture amount recognized by a transferor in a transaction to which Code Sec. 332, 351, 361, 721, or 731 applies may not exceed the amount of gain recognized by the transferor (Code Sec. 1245(b)(3)).

Example (5): A taxpayer transfers depreciated property to a controlled corporation in exchange for stock (no boot received) in a transaction to which Code Sec. 351 applies. No gain or loss is recognized. Accordingly, no amount is recaptured.

The IRS and certain courts have ruled that the transfer of property by the owner of a wholly-owned corporation to that corporation is governed by Code Sec. 351 even though no stock is received (*S. Lessenger*, CA-2, 89-1 USTC ¶ 9254; Rev. Rul. 64-155, 1964-1 CB 138). Thus, if no gain is recognized (because no boot is received), there should be no depreciation recapture.

Depreciable real property, other than real property that is Code Sec. 1245 property (see ¶ 127C), is subject to depreciation recapture under Code Sec. 1250. Gain on the sale or other disposition of Code Sec. 1250 property is treated as ordinary income rather than capital gain to the extent of the excess of post-1969 depreciation allowances over the depreciation that would have been available under the straight-line method. However, if Code Sec. 1250 property is held for one year or less, all depreciation (and not just the excess over straight-line depreciation) is recaptured (Code Sec. 1250(b)(1)). Special phaseout rules reduce recapture for certain property. Certain amounts are excluded in determining the amount of additional depreciation taken before the disposition of Code Sec. 1250 property (Code Sec. 1250(b)).

For a disposal of recapture property in an installment sale, any recapture income (ordinary income under Code Sec. 1245 or 1250) is recognized in the year of disposition, and any gain in excess of the recapture income is reported under the installment method (Code Sec. 453(i)). See ¶ 488.

The reduction of the capital gains rates for individuals, estates, and trusts by the 1997 Taxpayer Relief Act (P.L. 105-34) does not affect the amount of depreciation on section 1250 property which is subject to recapture as ordinary income. However, gain to the extent of any unrecaptured depreciation on section 1250 property, is subject to the 25-percent capital gains rate if the gain is treated as capital gain under Code Sec. 1231. Gain in excess of unrecaptured section 1250 depreciation would be eligible for the lower 15-percent capital gains rate. See, also, ¶ 488.

Sales or exchanges with related parties. Any gain from the sale or exchange of depreciable property with certain related persons may be recaptured as ordinary income if the property is depreciable in the hands of the related transferee (Code Sec. 1239). This rule is not limited to MACRS property. See ¶ 488.

Depreciation subject to recapture

Gain on the disposition of section 1245 property (¶ 116) is treated as ordinary income to the extent of previously allowed MACRS deductions. If property from a general asset account is disposed of, the full amount of proceeds realized on the disposition is treated as ordinary income.

An expense deduction for property for which a Code Sec. 179 expense election was made is treated as depreciation for recapture purposes (Code Sec. 1245(a)). Note that the Code Sec. 179 expense allowance may only be claimed on Section 1245 property. Thus, the entire amount expensed (not simply the amount expensed in excess of straight-line depreciation) is potentially subject to recapture. For the recapture of a Code Sec. 179 expense deduction where business use fails to exceed 50 percent, see ¶ 210 and ¶ 300.

Bonus depreciation (¶ 127D), including bonus depreciation claimed on New York Liberty Zone property (¶ 127E), Gulf Opportunity Zone property (¶ 127F), Kansas Disaster Area property (¶ 127G) and Disaster Assistance property (¶ 127H) is also subject to recapture. If bonus depreciation is claimed on section 1250 property, it is treated as an accelerated depreciation deduction and is subject to recapture to the extent that it exceeds the straight-line depreciation that would have been allowed (Reg. § 1.168(k)-1(f)(3)).

The amount of the investment credit downward basis adjustment is treated as a depreciation deduction for recapture purposes (Code Sec. 50(c)(4)).

Land improvements are generally section 1250 property; however in some instances a land improvement may be section 1245 property. See ¶ 110. 15-year qualified leasehold improvement property (¶ 126), 15-year restaurant property (¶ 110), and 15-year qualified retail improvement property (¶ 110) retain their status as section 1250 property even though they are temporarily assigned a 15-year MACRS recovery period. 15-year retail motor fuel outlets (¶ 110) are also section 1250 property.

MACRS residential rental property and nonresidential real property placed in service after 1986 must be depreciated under the straight-line MACRS method. Therefore, recapture of depreciation on such section 1250 property is not required, since no depreciation in excess of straight-line depreciation could have been claimed. However, as noted above, and also explained at ¶ 488, depreciation claimed on section 1250 property that is not recaptured as ordinary income may be subject to a 25 percent tax rate as section 1250 unrecaptured gain. Thus, in the case of MACRS real property, all depreciation claimed is potentially subject to tax at a 25 percent rate if the recognized gain is at least equal to the amount of depreciation claimed.

As noted above, gain on the sale or other disposition of depreciable realty subject to Code Sec. 1250 recapture is treated as ordinary income to the extent of the excess of depreciation claimed over straight-line depreciation and any remaining gain is treated as long-term capital gain under Code Sec. 1231. For corporations (but not S corporations), the amount treated as ordinary income on the sale or other disposition of Code Sec. 1250 property is increased by 20 percent of the additional amount that would be treated as ordinary income if the property were subject to recapture under the rules of Code Sec. 1245 property (Code Sec. 291(a)(1)). This rule does not apply to Code Sec. 1250 property that is part of a certified pollution control facility for which a rapid amortization election is made.

See ¶ 488 for depreciation recapture planning issues.

See ¶ 280 and ¶ 488 for ACRS recapture.

Recapture of the Code Sec. 179A deduction

Code Sec. 179A allows taxpayers to claim a current deduction for a specified amount of the cost of qualified clean-fuel vehicle property and qualified clean-fuel vehicle refueling property placed in service after June 30, 1993 and before January 1, 2006.

Separate recapture rules apply to each type of property. In computing the recapture amount, the deduction is only taken into account to the extent the taxpayer received a tax benefit (Reg. § 1.179A-1(d)). The recapture amount is added to the basis of the property.

Clean-fuel vehicle property is subject to recapture if, within three full years of the date the related vehicle is placed in service, the vehicle: (1) is modified so that it no longer runs on clean-burning fuel; (2) is used in a manner described in Code Sec. 50(b) (relating to predominant use outside the U.S., use by a tax-exempt organization, and use by governmental units or foreign persons or entities); or (3) otherwise ceases to meet the definitional requirements for qualified clean-fuel property (Reg. § 1.179A-1(b)(1)).

Refueling property is subject to recapture if, at any time before the end of the property's MACRS recovery period, the property: (1) ceases to meet the definitional requirements for qualified clean-fuel refueling property; (2) is not used at least 50 percent in the taxpayer's trade or business during the tax year; or (3) is used in a manner described in Code Sec. 50(b) (Reg. § 1.179A-1(b)(2)(i)).

Recapture also applies if a taxpayer sells clean fuel vehicle property or clean fuel vehicle refueling property knowing that the vehicle or property will be used in a manner that will trigger recapture. Otherwise a sale or disposition is not a recapture event.

In the case of clean-fuel vehicle property, 100 percent of the deduction that resulted in a tax benefit is recaptured if the date of the recapture event is within the first full year after the date that the vehicle was placed in service. The recapture percentage is 66⅔ percent if the recapture event occurs during the second full year of service and 33⅓ percent if the recapture event occurs during the third full year of service (Reg. § 1.179A-1(d)(1)).

The recapture amount in the case of refueling property is the amount of the allowable deduction that resulted in a tax benefit multiplied by the ratio of the remaining recovery period of the property to the total recovery period (Reg. § 1.179A-1(d)(2)).

A deduction claimed under Code Sec. 179A is treated as a depreciation deduction for purposes of the Code Sec. 1245 recapture rules if the underlying property is depreciable (Reg. § 1.179A-1(f)).

Credit for qualified electric vehicles

The credit for qualified electric vehicles (Code Sec. 30) is subject to recapture. Recapture is required if a vehicle is modified within three full years from the date it is placed in service so that it no longer is powered primarily by electricity or is used in a manner described in Code Sec. 50(b), as outlined above. Recapture is not triggered by a sale or other disposition unless a taxpayer sells the vehicle knowing that the purchaser intends to modify or use the vehicle in a way that would trigger recapture (Reg. § 1.30-1(b)(2)).

The recapture percentage is 100 percent if the date of the recapture event falls within the first full year after the date the vehicle is placed in service, 66⅔ percent if the recapture event falls within the second full year of service, and 33⅓ percent if the recapture event falls within the third full year of service (Reg. § 1.30-1(b)(5)).

The recaptured amount is added to the basis of the vehicle. The credit is treated as a depreciation deduction for Code Sec. 1245 recapture purposes if the vehicle is depreciable (Reg. § 1.30-1(b)(6) and (7)).

Recapture of preproductive period plant cost deduction

If certain farmers elect under Code Sec. 263A(d) (3) to deduct preproductive period costs of certain plants instead of capitalizing them (see ¶ 150), the plants produced are treated as Code Sec. 1245 property (Code Sec. 263A(e) (1)). Accordingly, any gain realized upon disposition is recaptured as ordinary income to the extent that the total amount of the deductions which, but for the election, would have been required to be capitalized. In calculating the amount of gain that is recaptured, either the farm-price or unit-livestock method is used in determining the deductions that would otherwise have been capitalized (Temp. Reg. § 1.263A-4T(c) (6) (vi)).

Dispositions of amortizable Sec. 197 intangibles

An amortizable Sec. 197 intangible is treated as depreciable property for purposes of recapture (Code Sec. 197(f) (7)). Amortization deductions under Code Sec. 197 are recaptured as ordinary income under Code Sec. 1245 to the extent of gain upon the disposition of an amortizable Sec. 197 intangible.

If Sec. 197 intangibles are transferred in certain nonrecognition transfers, the transferee is treated as the transferor to the extent of the transferor's basis for purposes of determining subsequent Sec. 197 amortization deductions.

No loss is recognized upon the disposition (or worthlessness) of an amortizable Sec. 197 intangible acquired in a transaction if other amortizable Sec. 197 intangibles acquired in the transaction (or in a series of related transactions) are retained. Instead, the adjusted bases of the retained amortizable Sec. 197 intangibles are increased by the amount of the unrecognized loss.

A loss may be recognized on the disposition of a separately acquired Sec. 197 intangible.

A covenant not to compete may not be treated as disposed of or worthless prior to the disposition or determination of worthlessness of the entire interest in the trade or business for which the covenant not to compete was created.

Effective for dispositions after August 8, 2005, if more than one amortizable section 197 intangible is disposed of in a transaction or series of related transactions, all of the section 197 intangibles are treated as a single section 197 intangible for purposes of the depreciation recapture rules (Code Sec. 1245(b) (8), as added by the Energy Tax Incentives Act of 2005 (P.L. 109-58)).

This rule does not apply to any section 197 intangible with an adjusted basis in excess of its fair market value (i.e., an intangible that will generate a loss deduction).

Example: A taxpayer acquires two section 197 intangibles for $45,000. Asset A is assigned a cost basis of $15,000 and Asset B is assigned a cost basis of $30,000. The annual section 197 amortization deduction for Asset A is $1,000 ($15,000/15) and $3,000 for Asset B ($45,000/15). Assume the assets are sold three years later for $45,000. At the time of the sale the adjusted basis of Asset A is $12,000 ($15,000 - $3,000) and the adjusted basis of Asset B is $21,000 ($30,000 - $9,000). The total recapture potential is $12,000 ($3,000 + $9,000). Under prior law, the actual amount recaptured will depend upon how the $45,000 sales price is allocated between the two assets. For example, if $12,000 is allocated to Asset A and $33,000 is allocated to Asset B, no gain or loss is recognized on Asset A and $12,000 gain is recognized on Asset B. Only $9,000 of the gain is recaptured as ordinary income and the remaining $3,000 gain is section 1231 gain. Under the new law, $12,000 gain is recognized but all of that gain is recaptured as ordinary income.

¶ 162

Gain or Loss on Sales, Exchanges, Abandonment, Retirement, Obsolescence, and Other Dispositions

Proposed ACRS regulations summarize some general rules which apply for purposes of determining gain or loss on the disposition of ACRS recovery property that is not contained in a mass asset account (Prop. Reg. § 1.168-6 at ¶ 545). It is appropriate for taxpayers to apply these rules to MACRS property. Although proposed regulations are not binding on a taxpayer or the IRS, the Service will generally not challenge a taxpayer's reliance on a proposed regulation if the taxpayer's situation fits within the strict confines of that proposed regulation (IRS Field Service Advice 199937022, June 17, 1999, discussed below).

The term disposition is defined by ACRS Prop. Reg. § 1.168-2(l)(1) at ¶ 525 to mean the permanent withdrawal of property from use in the taxpayer's trade or business or use for the production of income. Dispositions include sales, exchanges, retirements, abandonments, or destruction. Transfers by gift or by reason of death are not dispositions.

In the case of a sale or exchange, recognized gain or loss is determined by applying the controlling Code provision (Prop. Reg. § 1.168-6(a)(1)).

If an asset is physically abandoned, a taxpayer may deduct a loss (the loss is ordinary since there is no sale or exchange of a capital asset) in the amount of the adjusted basis in the year of abandonment. The taxpayer must intend to discard the asset irrevocably, by not intending to use the asset again, nor intending to retrieve it for sale, exchange or other disposition (Prop. Reg. § 1.168-6(a)(2)). The loss deduction for an abandonment of nondepreciable property is authorized by Reg. § 1.165-2, as discussed below.

An abandonment loss is claimed as an ordinary loss on line 10 Part II of Form 4797 (IRS Publication 225 (2009 returns)).

Gain is not recognized if a taxpayer disposes of an asset other than by sale, exchange, or physical abandonment (for example, where the asset is transferred to a supplies or scrap account). Loss is recognized to the extent that the adjusted basis exceeds the fair market value at the time of the disposition. The transfer of an asset to a supplies or scrap account falls within this rule (Prop. Reg. § 1.168-6(a)(3)). Again, the loss is an ordinary loss.

The conversion of a depreciable asset to personal use is not a disposition that triggers a loss (Prop. Reg. § 1.168-6(a)(3)).

The IRS has ruled that a corporation that placed a manufacturing facility which it had closed down in an account labeled "Assets Held for Sale" could not deduct a retirement loss in the year the facility was placed in the account because the taxpayer intended and, in fact, accomplished a sale in a later tax year (Field Service Advice 199937022, June 17, 1999). The FSA, citing *B.R. Kittredge*, CA-2, 37-1 USTC ¶ 9165, indicates that the asset was still considered in business use although it was withdrawn from active use in the business.

Retirement of structural components. The ACRS regulations provide that the retirement (whether ordinary or abnormal) of a structural component of real property is not a disposition (Prop. Reg. § 1.168-2(l)(1)). By way of example, the regulations provide that if the roof on 15-year ACRS property is replaced, no gain or loss is recognized with respect to the replaced roof (Prop. Reg. § 1.168-6)).

The regulations clearly cover the treatment of an original roof the cost of which is part of a building's basis. However, if a replacement roof were itself replaced at some later date, a taxpayer should be able to stop depreciating the replaced roof and recognize loss (equal to the undepreciated basis) since the replaced roof is considered a separate depreciable asset. On the other hand, the replacement of the original roof should not cause the recognition of loss because the original roof is depreciated as part of the overall cost of the building rather than as a separate asset with its own depreciable basis. Nevertheless, it appears that the IRS takes the position (based on Prop. Reg. § 1.168-2(l)(1)) that the retirement of a structural component does not trigger gain or loss even if the retired component was separately depreciated. In a Field Service Advice, the IRS states: "The abandonment or retirement of a structural component of a building generally does not constitute a disposition. Accordingly, no loss deduction is allowed on the retirement of such property. The taxpayer continues to recovery the cost of such property through ACRS or MACRS deductions" (IRS Field Service Advice 200001005, September 10, 1999; see also, Field Service Advice 200141026, July 11, 2001).

This issue has also arisen in the context of improvements made by a lessor and abandoned or destroyed upon the termination of the lease. The 1996 Small Business Job Protection Act (P.L. 104-188) made an amendment to Code Sec. 168(i)(8)(B) to specifically provide that a lessor may claim an ordinary loss deduction upon the abandonment or irrevocable disposition of an improvement which is made by the lessor for the lessee. The lessor is not required to continue depreciating the abandonment or retirement of the improvement. Lessees who abandon improvements may also claim an ordinary loss deduction. The present law section of the related conference report provides additional background. See ¶ 126.

Additions and improvements added after 1986 are treated as MACRS property. Thus, a new roof or other new addition/improvement/structural component would be treated as 39-year nonresidential real property (assuming the building is commercial property) and separately depreciated as such (see ¶ 126).

The IRS recently modified the automatic change of accounting revenue procedure (Rev. Proc. 2008-52) to allow a taxpayer that wants to change to a unit of property that is permissible under applicable legal authority for determining when the taxpayer has disposed of a building (as defined in Reg.§ 1.48-1(e)(1)) and its structural components (as defined in Reg.§ 1.48-1(e)(2)) for depreciation purposes. This change also will affect the determination of gain or loss from the disposition of the building (including its structural components). See Sec. 2.10 of Rev. Proc. 2009-39, modifying Rev. Proc. 2008-52 by adding new Appendix Sec. 6.24. A similar rule allows a taxpayer that wants to change to a unit of property that is permissible under applicable legal authority for determining when the taxpayer has disposed of a section 1245 property or a depreciable land improvement for depreciation purposes. This change also will affect the determination of gain or loss from the disposition of the section 1245 property or the depreciable land improvement. See Sec. 2.11 of Rev. Proc. 2009-39, modifying Rev. Proc. 2008-52 by adding new Appendix Sec. 6.25. In either case, a taxpayer must provide specific legal authority supporting the taxpayer's proposed unit of property for determining when the property is disposed of. Other limitations apply.

Pre-ACRS rules

The proposed ACRS regulations dealing with abandonments and retirements are essentially the same as regulations that apply to pre-ACRS property that is not in a multiple item account under the general depreciation rules. A multiple property account is one in which several items have been combined with a single rate of depreciation assigned to the entire account. (ADR has its own set of rules). Thus, these pre-ACRS regulations and the related case law are useful in understanding situations in which an asset will be considered abandoned or retired.

See ¶ 380 for rules regarding retirements of pre-ACRS property from item accounts and ¶ 382 for rules regarding retirements of pre-ACRS property from multiple-asset accounts.

Although the proposed ACRS regulations do not define the term "retirement" it is defined in Reg. § 1.167(a)-8(a) which provides:

> ". . . the term 'retirement' means the permanent withdrawal of depreciable property from use in the trade or business or in the production of income. The withdrawal may be made in several ways. For example, the withdrawal may be made by selling or exchanging the asset, or by actual abandonment. In addition, the asset may be withdrawn from such productive use without disposition as, for example, by being placed in a supplies or scrap account."

If an asset is permanently retired but is not disposed of or physically abandoned (as for example, when the asset is transferred to a supplies or scrap account) gain is not recognized. Loss is recognized to the extent of the adjusted basis of the asset over the greater of estimated salvage value or fair market value if the retirement is abnormal, the retirement is a normal retirement from a single asset account, or in the case of certain retirements from multiple asset accounts (Reg. § 1.167(a)-8(a)(3)).

The IRS has ruled that transfers of dismantled assets to a supplies account are considered retirements (Rev. Rul. 80-311, 1980-2 CB 5; IRS Letter Ruling 8646008, August 5, 1986).

As in the case of the proposed ACRS regulations, a physical abandonment requires an irrevocable intent to discard the asset so that it will neither be used again by the taxpayer nor retrieved for sale, exchange, or other disposition. The mere nonuse of property is not a physical abandonment (*Hillcone Steamship Company*, 22 TCM 1096, CCH Dec. 26,265(M)).

The regulations provide that retirements may be "normal" or "abnormal." Reg. § 1.167(a)-8(b) states:

> "In general, a retirement shall be considered a normal retirement unless the taxpayer can show that the withdrawal of the asset was due to a cause not contemplated in setting the applicable depreciation rate. For example, a retirement is considered normal if made within the range of years taken into consideration in fixing the depreciation rate and if the asset has reached a condition at which, in the normal course of events, the taxpayer customarily retires similar assets from use in his business. On the other hand, a retirement may be abnormal if the asset is withdrawn at an earlier time or under other circumstances, as, for example, when the asset has been damaged by casualty or has lost its usefulness suddenly as the result of extraordinary obsolescence."

Obsolescence is defined in Reg. § 1.167(a)-9. In general, that regulation allows a taxpayer to redetermine the useful life of an asset for purposes of computing depreciation if the useful life has been shortened by obsolescence greater than that assumed in determining the useful life. This aspect of the regulation is of no relevance under ACRS and MACRS since the depreciation period is statutorily set irrespective of the actual useful life of an asset to a taxpayer. However, if the usefulness of depreciable property is suddenly terminated as the result of obsolescence, then the taxpayer may be entitled to a loss deduction for extraordinary obsolescence if the asset is permanently withdrawn from use in the trade or business. Such a retirement is considered an abnormal retirement, as discussed in the paragraph above.

Extraordinary obsolescence occurred where a city refused to grant a health permit due to the discovery by the purchasing taxpayer of a building's structural defects and the permit was necessary to operate the building as a restaurant/bar (*De Cou*, 103 TC 80, CCH Dec. 49,998). The building was boarded up (i.e., permanently withdrawn from business) and subsequently demolished because it was more expensive to repair the building than replace it. Although the structural defects occurred over the course of several years (before the taxpayer purchased the building), the building's usefulness to the taxpayer suddenly and unexpectedly terminated upon the discovery of the defects and the subsequent suspension of the building's health permit. The taxpayer was entitled to an ordinary loss deduction equal to the building's adjusted basis (fair market and salvage value were zero, so no reduction was made to adjusted basis).

A loss sustained before a building's demolition (as a result, for example, of a building's abnormal retirement because of a casualty or extraordinary obsolescence), is not disallowed under Code Sec. 280B, which requires capitalization of losses sustained on account of the demolition of a structure (IRS Notice 90-21, 1990-1 CB 332; *De Cou*, above). However, the actual costs of demolition would be capitalized under Code Sec. 280B. See ¶ 5.

In contrast to *De Cou*, where the loss deduction was claimed in the same year that the structural defects were discovered, the health permit withdrawn, and the building retired, a loss deduction was denied where the loss was claimed in a tax year after the discovery of asbestos in a building allegedly caused a sudden and unexpected termination of its usefulness (*L. Gates*, DC Pa., 98-1 USTC 50,353, aff'd CA-3 (unpublished opinion), 98-2 USTC ¶ 50,814). Furthermore, in a footnote citing Code Sec. 1016, the court indicated that the taxpayer may not be allowed to include the unclaimed loss in the basis of the land when the building is demolished.

A threat of condemnation in which compensation would be given for damage cannot give rise to an obsolescence deduction (*Keller Street Development Company*, CA-9, 63-2 UTSC ¶ 9734).

A bank which vacated a building in which it operated computers and then sold the building in a later tax year was not entitled to an abandonment loss or an extraordinary obsolescence loss (measured by the difference between its fair market value and adjusted basis) in the tax year the building was vacated. Instead, depreciation deductions should have been claimed during that period it was unoccupied (Field Service Advice Memorandum 200141026, July 11, 2001). There was no abandonment because the taxpayer did not irrevocably discard the building in a manner that prevented it from selling the building. The ruling recognized that based on the particular circumstances the bank could argue that it withdrew the building as a result of new developments in the banking industry which rendered it economically worthless thereby resulting in an obsolescence deduction. However, the ruling concludes that the closing of the building was not unusual or unexpected in the industry.

There appear to be no cases which directly consider whether an item of property which is abandoned or retired prior to being placed in service (for depreciation purposes) can be considered depreciable property for purposes of Reg. § 1.167(a)-8. However, in the *Keller* case, an obsolescence deduction was allowed for specialized brewery machinery that had never been used and had become worthless due to a change in market conditions. It is unclear whether the machinery was considered placed in service.

Abandonments of nondepreciable property

The preceding discussion relates to abandonments of depreciable property. Abandonment losses for nondepreciable property are authorized under Reg. § 1.165-2. Although the regulation heading refers to "obsolescence of nondepreciable property," the term obsolescence is best construed to mean "abandonment." In other words, retirements of nondepreciable property which are not abandonments may not be deducted under Reg. § 1.165-2. The abandonment rule of Reg. § 1.165-2 for nondepreciable property differs somewhat from that provided in Reg. § 1.167-8 in that the abandonment must arise "from the sudden termination of the usefulness" of the asset. This distinction, however, appears to be generally disregarded by the case law (*Coors Porcelain Co.*, 52 TC 682, CCH Dec. 29,680, aff'd, CA-10, 70-2 USTC ¶ 9539).

Abandonments and cancellation of debt

Generally, ordinary income is realized if a debt for which a taxpayer is personally liable and secured by the abandoned property is canceled. Exceptions apply if the cancellation is intended as a gift, the debt is qualified farm debt (see IRS Pub. 225, *Farmer's Tax Guide*), the debt is qualified real property business debt (see IRS Pub. 334, *Tax Guide for Small Business* (chapter 5)), or the taxpayer is insolvent or bankrupt (see IRS Pub. 908, *Bankruptcy Tax Guide*) (Code Sec. 61; Code Sec. 108).

Abandonments of leasehold improvements

A lessor may claim an ordinary loss deduction with respect to improvements that the lessor abandons. A similar rule applies to lessee's who abandon an improvement. See ¶ 126.

Retirement in connection with installation or replacement

If the retirement or removal of a depreciable asset, such a telephone pole by a utility company, occurs in connection with the installation or production of a replacement asset, the costs incurred in removing the retired asset are not required to be capitalized under Code Sec. 263 or the uniform capitalization rules of Code Sec. 263A (Rev. Rul. 2000-7; Rev. Proc. 2008-52 (Appendix Section 10.03, relating to automatic change of accounting method)). The removal costs are allocated to the retired assets. The ruling does not apply to the removal of a component of a depreciable asset, the costs of which are either deductible or capitalizable based on whether the replacement of the component constitutes a repair or an improvement.

Demolitions

See ¶ 5.

Like-Kind Exchanges and Involuntary Conversions

¶ 167

Depreciation of Basis

This discussion of the depreciation computation of MACRS property received in a like-kind exchange or involuntary conversion is organized as follows.

Background and effective date of final regulations

Election out of final regulations

Replacement property and relinquished property must generally be MACRS property

Land is still not depreciable

Final regulations in general

Section 179 allowance and bonus depreciation

Luxury car rules (cross reference to ¶ 214)

Effect of like-kind exchange or involuntary conversion in determining whether the mid-quarter convention applies

Disposition of replacement property during same tax year relinquished property acquired

General Principles of Computation

How to make the MACRS depreciation computations on property received in a like-kind exchange or in an involuntary conversion

Depreciation computation on exchanged basis if recovery period and depreciation method of relinquished and replacement property are both the same

Depreciation computation on exchanged basis if recovery period and/or depreciation method are different

Applicable convention

Depreciation Deductions in Year of Disposition and Year of Replacement

Deduction on relinquished property in year of disposition

Deduction on replacement property in year of acquisition

Deferred-like-kind exchange transactions

Exchanges of multiple properties

Deduction on replacement property in year of exchange

Involuntary conversions: replacement property placed in service before disposition of relinquished property

Computations With Optional Depreciation Tables

Depreciation on relinquished property in year of disposition using tables.

Depreciation on excess basis using tables

Depreciation on exchanged basis using tables

Transaction coefficient when using tables

Background and effective date of final regulations. Final regulations explain how to depreciate MACRS property acquired in a like-kind exchange Code Sec. 1031 or an involuntary conversion under Code Sec. 1033 provided that the relinquished or converted property was also depreciated under MACRS or the taxpayer made a valid election to exclude the relinquished property from MACRS pursuant to Code Sec. 168(f)(1) (relating to property depreciated under the unit-of-production method or any method of depreciation not expressed in a term of years (other than the retirement-replacement-betterment method or similar method) (T.D. 9314, filed in the Federal Register on February 27, 2007). The final regulations are generally effective for a like-kind exchange or an involuntary conversion for which the time of disposition and time of replacement both occur after February 27, 2004. However, if the relinquished property was excluded from MACRS under Code Sec. 168(f)(1), a special effective date applies (Reg. § 1.168(i)-6(k)).

Taxpayers may apply the final regulations (or prior guidance) to pre-effective date exchanges. Taxpayers who filed returns on or before February 27, 2004 may change their accounting method to comply with the final regulations or earlier guidance (e.g., Notice 2000-4 (2001-1 CB 313)) by following the automatic consent procedures of Rev. Proc. 2002-9 (Reg. § 1.168(i)-6(k)(2)(i) and Reg. § 1.168(i)-6(k)(2)(ii)). Note that Rev. Proc. 2002-9 has been superseded by Rev. Proc. 2008-52.

The final regulations adopt temporary regulations (T.D. 9115, filed with the Federal Register on March 1, 2004) with a few minor clarifications. The temporary regulations were also generally effective for like-kind exchanges and involuntary conversions in which the time of disposition and the time of replacement both occur after February 27, 2004 (Temporary Reg. § 1.168(i)-6T(k)(1)).

The IRS first issued guidance in Notice 2000-4 (2000-1 CB 313). This notice generally provided that MACRS replacement property received in a Code Sec. 1031 like-kind exchange or a Code Sec. 1033 involuntary conversion is depreciated over the remaining recovery period of, and using the same depreciation method and convention as, the relinquished MACRS property. Any excess of the basis in the replacement MACRS property over the adjusted basis of the relinquished MACRS property is depreciated as newly purchased MACRS property. The Notice applied to replacement MACRS property placed in service after January 3, 2000 if the time of disposition of the relinquished property or the time of replacement occur on or before February 27, 2004 (i.e., effective date of the temporary regulations which replaced the Notice).

For property placed in service before January 3, 2000, some taxpayers depreciated replacement property in a manner consistent with the Notice by applying the methodology of ACRS Proposed Reg. § 1.168-5(f). This regulation provides rules for ACRS property received in a like-kind exchange or involuntary conversion as a replacement for ACRS property relinquished in a like-kind exchange or involuntarily converted. Other taxpayers depreciated the entire basis of replacement property as new MACRS property.

Notice 2000-4 provided that for acquired MACRS property placed in service before January 3, 2000 (in an exchange or involuntary conversion in which the relinquished property is depreciated under MACRS), the IRS will allow a taxpayer to continue to use a bifurcated basis methodology that is consistent with the Notice and the Proposed ACRS regulations or to treat the entire basis of the acquired property as new MACRS property. Taxpayer who treated the entire basis of acquired property as newly purchased MACRS property were allowed to change their accounting methods in their first or second taxable year ending after January 3, 2000 to comport with the bifurcated methodology prescribed by Notice 2000-4.

Election out of final regulations. A taxpayer may elect as provided in the instructions to Form 4562 (Depreciation and Amortization) not to apply the final regulations to a post-effective date exchange or conversion. The election is made separately for each like-kind exchange or involuntary conversion by the due date (including extensions) of the taxpayer's return for the year of replacement. See Reg. § 1.168(i)-6(j) for election details. In general, this election should be considered if the recovery period of the replacement property is shorter than the remaining recovery period of the relinquished property or the depreciation method of the replacement property is more accelerated than the depreciation method of the relinquished property. The election is revocable only in extraordinary circumstances.

If the election is made, the sum of the exchanged basis and excess basis (if any) is treated as property placed in service at the time of replacement and the adjusted depreciable basis of the relinquished MACRS property is treated as disposed of at the time of disposition. The election not to apply the regulations does not affect the application of the depreciation recapture rules of Code Secs. 1245 and 1250 (Reg. § 1.168(i)-6(i)(1)).

Replacement and relinquished property must generally be MACRS property. The final regulations, Notice 2000-4, and the temporary regulations only apply if the replacement property received by a taxpayer is depreciated by the taxpayer using MACRS (the method used by any prior owner of the replacement property is irrelevant). Subject to the exception below, the relinquished property must also have been depreciated by the taxpayer using MACRS. For example, if a taxpayer exchanges a building that is depreciated under MACRS for a building that another person is depreciating under ACRS or a pre-ACRS method, the final regulations apply to the taxpayer (unless an election out is made) because the building given up by the taxpayer was depreciated using MACRS and the replacement building received by the taxpayer will be depreciated under MACRS (Reg. § 1.168(i)-6(c)(2)). However, the regulations would not apply to the person who relinquished the ACRS building since the building that person gave up was not depreciated under ACRS. See in this regard, IRS Letter Ruling 8929047, April 25, 1989, which concludes that the proposed ACRS regulations do not apply to the exchange of ACRS property for MACRS property. Therefore, the *entire basis* of an airplane received by a taxpayer in a post-1986 transaction for an airplane being depreciated by the taxpayer under ACRS had to be depreciated as new MACRS property.

The final regulations allow a taxpayer to elect to treat relinquished property which was excluded from MACRS by reason of an election under Code Sec. 168(f)(1) (relating to unit-of-production property and certain other methods not expressed in a term of years) as MACRS property (Reg. § 1.168(i)-6(i)(2)). This option was not provided in the temporary regulations. The election, however, applies to like-kind exchanges and involuntary conversions occurring on, after, or before February 26, 2007. A taxpayer who filed a return without making the election may make the change by filing for a change of accounting method pursuant to the automatic consent procedures of Rev. Proc. 2002-9 (Reg. § 1.168(i)-6(k)(3)). If this election is made the sum of the "exchanged basis" (carryover basis) and "excess basis" (any additional cash paid for replacement property) is treated as MACRS property placed in service at the time of the replacement.

Land is still not depreciable. Neither Notice 2000-4 nor the temporary and final regulations should be interpreted to allow a taxpayer to depreciate land received in a like-kind exchange or involuntary conversion (Preamble to T.D. 9115).

Final regulations in general. The regulations mainly focus on the computation of the depreciation deductions on the depreciable exchanged basis (carryover basis attributable to business/investment use) of the property received in a like-kind exchange or involuntary conversion. The excess basis is typically the amount of any additional cash or boot paid for the property received. The excess basis is simply depreciated as if it were new property separately acquired and placed in service in the year of replacement (Reg. § 1.168(i)-6(d)(1)).

Section 179 allowance and bonus depreciation. Although the Code Sec. 179 allowance may be claimed on the excess basis of the replacement property (assuming all other requirements are met), it may not be claimed on the exchanged basis of the replacement property even if nondepreciable property (e.g., land) is replaced with depreciable property (Reg. § 1.168(i)-6(g)). The bonus depreciation deduction (assuming all other requirements are met) may be claimed on the both the exchanged and excess basis (Reg. § 1.168(k)-1(f)(5)). See ¶ 127D.

Luxury car rules. See ¶ 214 for a discussion of the application of these regulations to the luxury car depreciation caps under Code Sec. 280F when a car or other vehicle is involved in a trade-in in that is treated as a like-kind exchange.

Effect of like-kind exchange or involuntary conversion in determining whether the mid-quarter convention applies. In determining whether the mid-quarter convention applies to the excess basis (noncarryover/boot basis) of the replacement property (and to other property placed in service during the tax year the replacement property is placed in service), the excess basis of replacement property is always taken into account in the quarter that the replacement property is placed in service (Reg. § 1.168(i)-6(f)(2)). The exchanged (carryover) basis of the replacement property is not taken into account in determining whether the mid-quarter convention applies to the excess basis and to any other property placed in service during the tax year (Reg. § 1.168(i)-6(f)(1)(iii)). However, special rules apply if, in the same tax year (1) property is acquired (but not in a like-kind exchange or involuntary conversion) and (2) disposed of in a like-kind exchange or involuntary conversion (Reg. § 1.168(i)-6(f)(1)(i) and Reg. § 1.168(i)-6(f)(1)(ii)). See *"Applicable convention,"* below.

If depreciable property is acquired for nondepreciable property in a like-kind exchange or involuntary conversion, both the exchanged basis and excess basis of the replacement property is taken into account in the year of replacement in determining whether the mid-quarter convention applies (Reg. § 1.168(i)-6(f)(3)).

The exchanged (carryover basis) of the replacement property is generally depreciated using the convention that applies to the relinquished property. However, if the mid-month convention applies to either the relinquished or replacement property, the exchanged basis is depreciated using the mid-month convention.

Disposition of replacement property during same tax year relinquished property acquired. If replacement property is disposed of in the same tax year that the relinquished property was placed in service, no MACRS deduction may be claimed on either property (Reg. § 1.168(i)-6(d)).

General Principles of Computation

How to make the MACRS depreciation computations on property received in a like-kind exchange or in an involuntary conversion. The manner in which depreciation computations are computed on the exchanged (carryover) basis of property received in a like-kind exchange or involuntary conversion will depend upon whether the recovery period and depreciation method of the replacement property are the same or different than the recovery period and depreciation method of the relinquished property.

Depreciation computation on exchanged basis if recovery period and depreciation method of relinquished and replacement property are both the same. In most like-kind exchanges and involuntary conversions the replacement property will have the same depreciation period and depreciation method as the relinquished property because both items of property are identical and have the same MACRS recovery period. For example, a commercial building will replace a commercial building (39-year recovery period and straight-line method), a residential rental property will replace a residential rental property (27.5 year recovery period and straight-line method), or similar types of personal property will be exchanged, such as an airplane for an airplane (seven-year recovery period and 200 percent declining-balance method).

If both the recovery period and depreciation method of the replacement property are the same as the recovery period and depreciation method of the relinquished property, the depreciable exchanged basis of the replacement property is depreciated over the remaining recovery period of the relinquished property using the same method and convention that applied to the relinquished property. Depreciation allowances for the depreciable exchanged basis are determined by multiplying the depreciable exchanged basis by the applicable depreciation rate for each year (Reg. § 1.168(i)-6(c)(3)(ii)).

Example (1): Building A is acquired in March 2006 for $100,000 and relinquished in a deferred exchange in March 2009. It is replaced by Building B in May 2009. Building A and B are 39-year real property depreciated using the straight-line method. Thus, the depreciation period (39 years) and depreciation method (straight-line method) and convention (mid-month) for the buildings are the same.

Total depreciation claimed through May 2009 on Building A is $7,692 computed as follows:

	Year	Deduction	
	2006	$2,030	($100,000/39 × 9.5 months/12 months)
	2007	2,564	($100,000/39)
	2008	2,564	($100,000/39)
	2009	534	($100,000/39 × 2.5 months/12 months)
Total		7,692	

Beginning in May 2009, the depreciable exchanged basis of Building B is depreciated over the remaining recovery period of Building A. The remaining recovery period of Building A is 36 years immediately after the disposition (39 – 9.5/12 – 1 – 1 – 2.5/12). The depreciable exchanged basis is $92,308 ($100,000 – $7,692). Depreciation is computed as follows:

	Year	Deduction	
	2009	$1,602	($92,308/36 × 7.5 months/12 months)
	2010-2045	2,564	($92,308/36)
	2046	962	($92,308/36 × 4.5 months/12 months)
Total		$92,308	

Assume that $50,000 cash was also paid for Building B. The excess basis of Building B is $50,000 and this amount is depreciated over 39-years beginning in May 2009 using the mid-month convention.

See, also, Reg. § 1.168(i)-6(c)(6), Example 1.

Depreciation computation on exchanged basis if recovery period and/or depreciation method are different. The following rules apply if the recovery period of the replacement property is different than the recovery period of the relinquished property or the depreciation method of the replacement property is different than the depreciation method of the relinquished property or both the method and period are different (Reg. § 1.168(i)-6(c)(3)(iii) and Reg. § 1.168(i)-6(c)(4)).

If the recovery period for the replacement property is the same as the recovery period for the relinquished property, the depreciation allowances for the depreciable exchanged basis of the replacement property beginning in the year of replacement are determined using the recovery period of the relinquished property (Reg. § 1.168(i)-6(c)(3)(iii)).

If the recovery period prescribed for the replacement property is longer than the recovery period prescribed for the relinquished property, the depreciable exchanged basis of the replacement property is depreciated over the remaining recovery period of the replacement property (Reg. § 1.168(i)-6(c)(4)(i)).

If the recovery period prescribed for the replacement property is shorter than the recovery period prescribed for the relinquished property, the depreciable exchanged basis of the replacement property is depreciated over the remaining recovery period of the relinquished MACRS property (Reg. § 1.168(i)-6(c)(4)(ii)).

If the depreciation method for the replacement property is the same as the depreciation method for the relinquished property at the time of disposition, the depreciation allowances for the depreciable exchanged basis of the replacement property are determined using the depreciation method that applies to the relinquished property (Reg. § 1.168(i)-6(c)(3)(iii)).

If the depreciation method for the replacement property is less accelerated than the depreciation method for the relinquished property at the time of disposition, the depreciable exchanged basis is depreciated using the less accelerated depreciation method (Reg. § 1.168(i)-6(c)(4)(iii)(A)).

If the depreciation method for the replacement property is more accelerated than the depreciation method that applies to the relinquished property at the time of disposition, the depreciation allowances for the depreciable exchanged basis of the replacement property are determined using the method that applies to the relinquished property (Reg. § 1.168(i)-6(c)(4)(iv)(A)).

When comparing depreciation methods, in the case of the relinquished property, the method taken into consideration is the method that applies in the year of disposition. The method that applies to the replacement property is the method that would apply in the year of disposition of the relinquished property if the replacement property had been placed in service at the same time as the relinquished property (Reg. § 1.168(i)-6(c)(3)(i)).

Example (2): An item of seven-year property that was depreciated using the 200 percent declining balance method is exchanged for an item of 15-year property that is depreciable using the 150 percent declining balance method, and in the year of disposition the seven-year property is depreciated using the straight-line method because of the required switch from the 200 percent declining balance method to the straight-line method in the year that the straight-line method produces a larger deduction. The depreciation method of the seven-year property is considered to be the straight-line method and not the 200 percent declining balance method. Thus, the 15-year property will be depreciated using the straight-line method over the recovery period that would remain if it had been placed in service at the same time as the seven-year property.

Example (3): In the year of disposition, the 200 percent declining balance method applies to relinquished property and the 150 percent declining balance method would apply to the replacement property if it had been placed in service at the same time as the relinquished property. The switch to the straight-line method from either of the declining balance methods has not occurred. The 150 percent declining balance method applies to determine the applicable depreciation rate until the required switch to the straight-line method (i.e., in the tax year that the rate for the straight-line method produces a larger deduction than the rate for the 150 percent declining balance method) (Reg. § 1.168(i)-6(c)(4)(iii)(B)).

Example (4): Assume that in the year of disposition in the preceding example, the straight-line depreciation method would apply to the replacement property if it had been placed in service at the same time as the relinquished property. In this situation, the depreciable exchanged basis is depreciated using a rate based on the straight-line method (Reg. § 1.168(i)-6(c)(4)(iii)(B)).

For purposes of determining whether the depreciation method or recovery period of the replacement property is the same or different than the depreciation method or recovery period of the relinquished property, any straight-line, 150% declining balance, or MACRS alternative depreciation system (ADS) election made with respect to the relinquished property is taken into account (Reg. § 1.168(i)-6(c)(3)(i)).

Applicable convention. The convention for depreciating the exchanged (carryover) basis of property received in a like-kind exchange or involuntary conversion is determined under the following rules if the recovery period or depreciation method of the exchanged assets differ.

The exchanged basis (carryover basis) is depreciated using the mid-month convention if either the replacement or relinquished property is subject to the mid-month convention (i.e., the replacement or relinquished property is MACRS residential rental property or MACRS nonresidential real property) (Reg. § 1.168(i)-6(c)(4)(v)(A)). In each of the examples below the mid-convention applies because either the exchanged or relinquished property is subject to the mid-month convention. Each example illustrates how to determined the length of the remaining recovery period over which the exchanged basis is depreciated by taking into account the applicable convention. Note that in each case the remaining recovery period is determined by reference to the recovery period of the property with the longest recovery period.

Example (5): 27.5-year residential rental property placed in service in March 2007 is exchanged for 39-year real property in September 2010. Depreciation deductions on the exchanged basis of the 39-year real property are computed under the mid-month convention over the portion of the 39-year recovery period that would remain under the mid-month convention if the 39-year property had been placed in service in mid-March 2007 and disposed of in mid-September 2010.

Example (6): 20-year property subject to the mid-quarter convention is exchanged for 39-year real property in June 2011. The 20-year real property was placed in service in March 2008. Under the mid-quarter convention, the 20-year property is considered placed in service on the mid-point of February 2008 and disposed of on the mid-point of May 2011. The exchanged basis of the 39-year real property is depreciated using the mid-month convention over the portion of the 39-year recovery period that would remain under the mid-month convention if it had been placed in service in mid-February 2008 and disposed of in mid-May 2011.

Example (7): 20-year property subject to the half-year convention was placed in service in March 2008 and exchanged for 27.5-year real property on February 10, 2014. The exchanged basis of the 27.5-year real property is depreciated using the mid-month convention over the portion of the 27.5 year recovery period that would remain under the mid-month convention if it had been placed in service on July 1, 2008 (deemed placed-in-service date of 20-year property under half-year convention) and disposed of on July 1, 2014 (deemed disposition date of 20-year property under half-year convention) (viz. 21.5 years—27.5 years less 6 years depreciation that would have been claimed from mid-July 2008 through mid-July 2014 under the mid-month convention) (Reg. § 1.168(i)-6(c)(6), Example (2)).

Example (8): 39-year real property placed in service in March 2008 is exchanged for 15 year property subject to the half year convention on June 3, 2012. The exchanged basis of the 15-year property is depreciated using the mid-month convention over the remaining recovery period of the building (Reg. § 1.168(i)-6(c)(6), Example (3)). However, note that in this situation an election out of the regulations should be considered so that the exchanged basis could be depreciated over 15 years.

In the all the examples above the straight-line method will be used to determined the applicable depreciation rate. In any like-kind exchange in which real property (or any other property depreciated under the straight-line method) is involved, the straight-line method will apply. Note, however, that the straight-line method will also apply if the relinquished property is being depreciated in the year of disposition using the straight-line method due to the required switch from a declining balance method to the straight-line method in the year that the straight-line method produces a larger deduction. Similarly, the straight-line method will apply if the straight-line method would have applied to the replacement property in the year of disposition of the relinquished property if it had been placed in service at the same time as the relinquished property.

The exchanged (carryover) basis of the replacement property is depreciated using the same convention that applied to the relinquished property if neither the replacement property nor the relinquished property is subject to the mid-month convention (i.e., is not real property) and the relinquished property was not acquired and disposed of in the same tax year (Reg. § 1.168(i)-6(c)(4)(v)(B)).

Example (9): 5-year property subject to the half-year convention is placed in service in March 2008 and exchanged for 7-year property in April 2010. The depreciable exchanged basis of the replacement property is depreciated using the half-year convention applicable to the relinquished property over the recovery period of the replacement property that would remain if it had been placed in service in 2008 since the recovery period of the replacement property is longer than the recovery period of the relinquished property. The remaining recovery period is 5 years (7 – 1/2 year depreciation in 2008 – 1 year depreciation in 2009 – 1/2 year depreciation in 2010).

Example (10): Assume the same facts as in Example 9 except that 7-year property subject to the half-year convention was placed in service in March 2008 and exchanged for 5-year property in 2010. The depreciable exchanged basis of the 5-year replacement property is depreciated using the half-year convention applicable to the relinquished property. The depreciable exchanged basis is depreciated over the remaining recovery period of the 7-year property since the recovery period of the relinquished property (7 years) is longer than the recovery period of the replacement property (5 years). The remaining recovery period is 5 years (7 – 1/2 year depreciation in 2008 – 1 year depreciation in 2009 – 1/2 year depreciation in 2010).

Example (11): 3-year property subject to the mid-quarter convention is placed in service in January 2008. It is exchanged for 10-year property in December 2010. The mid-quarter convention applies to the depreciable exchanged basis. The depreciable exchanged basis is depreciated over the recovery period of the replacement property that would remain under the mid-quarter convention if it had been placed in service in the first-quarter of 2008 and disposed of in the fourth quarter of 2010. The remaining recovery period is 8 years (10 – 10.5/12 year depreciation claimed in 2008 under mid-quarter convention – 1 year depreciation in 2009 and – 1.5 year depreciation claimed in 2010 under the mid-quarter convention) (Reg. § 1.168(i)-6(c)(6), Example (4)).

In determining whether the mid-quarter convention applies to the excess basis (noncarryover/boot basis) of the replacement property (and to other property placed in service during the tax year the replacement property is placed in service), the excess basis of replacement property is always taken into account in the quarter that the replacement property is placed in service (Reg. § 1.168(i)-6(f)(2)).

In determining under the 40 percent test whether the mid-quarter convention applies to property placed in service during a tax year in which replacement property is received, the exchanged basis of the property received is ignored if the relinquished property was acquired in an earlier tax year than the tax year in which the relinquished property is disposed of and the replacement property is received (i.e., acquisition of relinquished property occurs in one tax year and disposition of relinquished property and replacement of relinquished property occur in a later tax year(s)) (Reg. § 1.168(i)-6(f)(1)(iii)). However, if the replacement property is received in a tax year subsequent to the tax year that the relinquishment of property was acquired and disposed (i.e., acquisition and disposition of relinquished property occur in same tax year and replacement of relinquished property occurs in a later tax year), the exchanged basis of the replacement property (determined without any adjustments for depreciation deductions during the taxable year) is taken into account in the year of replacement in the quarter the replacement MACRS property was placed in service by the acquiring taxpayer (Reg. § 1.168(i)-6(f)(1)(ii)). If the relinquished property is disposed of and the replacement property is received in the same tax year that the relinquished property was acquired (i.e., acquisition, disposition, and replacement occur in same tax year), the exchanged basis of the replacement property (determined without any adjustments for depreciation deductions during the taxable year) is taken into account in the year of replacement in the quarter the relinquished MACRS property was placed in service by the acquiring taxpayer (Reg. § 1.168(i)-6(f)(1)(i)).

If depreciable property is acquired for nondepreciable property in a like-kind exchange or involuntary conversion, both the exchanged basis and excess basis of the replacement property is taken into account in the year of replacement in determining whether the mid-quarter convention applies (Reg. § 1.168(i)-6(f)(3)).

Depreciation Deductions in Year of Disposition and Year of Replacement

The following rules apply in determining the depreciation deduction on relinquished and acquired (replacement) property in the year of disposition and year of replacement.

Deduction on relinquished property in year of disposition. Generally, the depreciation allowance on relinquished property in the year of disposition is computed by multiplying the allowable depreciation deduction for the property for the full year by a fraction, the numerator of which is the number of months the property is deemed to be placed in service during the year of disposition (taking into account the applicable convention of the relinquished property), and the denominator of which is 12 (Reg. § 1.168(i)-6(c)(5)(i)(A)). See, for example, *Example (12)*, below.

However, if the remaining recovery period of the relinquished property as of the beginning of the tax year of disposition expires before the date of disposition the taxpayer may claim the remaining undepreciated basis of the relinquished property as a depreciation deduction in the year of disposition. In this case, no portion of the basis of the replacement property is treated as an exchanged basis (Reg. § 1.168(i)-6(c)(5)(i)(B); Reg. § 1.168(i)-6(c)(6), Example 5). This rule was not contained in the temporary regulations.

No depreciation deduction may be claimed on relinquished property that is placed in service and disposed of by a taxpayer or involuntarily converted in the same tax year. No depreciation deduction may be claimed by a taxpayer on relinquished or replacement property if the replacement property is disposed of by the taxpayer in the same tax year that the relinquished property was placed in service (Reg. § 1.168(i)-6(c)(5); Reg. § 1.168(i)-6(c)(6), Example 6).

Deduction on replacement property in year of acquisition. The date that the replacement property is treated as placed in service by a taxpayer is determined by reference to the convention that applies to the replacement property under the like-kind exchange rules (Reg. § 1.168(i)-6(c)(5)(ii)(A)). See "Applicable convention for exchanged basis," above.

The remaining recovery period of the replacement property at the time of replacement is the excess of the recovery period for the replacement property as determined under the like-kind exchange rules that remains after reduction by the period of time that the replacement property would have been in service if it had been placed in service when the relinquished property was placed in service and removed from service at the time of disposition of the relinquished property. This period of time is determined by using the convention that applied to the relinquished MACRS property for purposes of determining its deemed acquisition and disposition dates. The length of time the replacement MACRS property would have been in service is determined by using these dates and the convention that applies to the replacement MACRS property (Reg. § 1.168(i)-6(c)(5)(ii)(A)). See Examples (5) through (11), above for examples showing how to determine remaining recovery period of replacement property at time of replacement.

The depreciation allowance in the tax year of replacement for the depreciable exchanged basis of the replacement property is computed as follows:

(1) determine the depreciation rate as of the beginning of the tax year of the replacement by taking into account the remaining recovery period of the replacement property as of the beginning of the tax year of replacement and depreciation method prescribed for the depreciable exchanged basis of the replacement property;

(2) add the depreciation deduction claimed on the relinquished property in the year of the disposition to the depreciable exchanged basis; and

(3) the depreciable exchanged basis as increased is multiplied by the depreciation rate and the product is multiplied by a fraction, the numerator of which is the number of months that the replacement property is deemed to be in service in the year of replacement under the convention applicable to the exchanged basis and the denominator of which is 12 (Reg. § 1.168(i)-6(c)(5)(ii)(B)).

It is important to note that for purposes of computing the depreciation rate (item (1)), the rate is determined by taking into account the recovery period of the replacement property that would remain *as of the beginning of the year* of disposition of the relinquished property. For this purpose, the replacement property is deemed to have been originally placed in service under the convention applicable to the exchanged basis but at the time the relinquished MACRS property was deemed to be placed in service under the convention that applied to the relinquished property when it was placed in service (Reg. § 1.168(i)-6(c)(5)(v)).

Example (12): A parking lot with a 15 year recovery period and depreciated using the half-year convention and 150 percent declining balance method is placed in service on January 1, 2006. On April 1, 2009, the lot is exchanged for 39-year residential rental property for which the straight-line method and mid-month convention is prescribed. The exchanged basis will be depreciated using mid-month convention (the mid-month convention applies if either the replacement property or relinquished property is depreciated using the mid-month convention) and the straight-line method (since the straight-line method is less accelerated than the 150 percent declining balance method).

For purposes of determining the applicable depreciation rate under the straight-line method in the year of replacement, the building's remaining depreciation period *as of the beginning of 2009* is 36 years and 6.5 months. This is determined by assuming that the building is placed in service on the date that the parking lot was placed in service under the half-year convention. Under the half-year convention the parking lot was placed in service on July 1, 2006. If the building was placed in service on July 1, 2006, then under the mid-month convention (which applies to the building) 5 1/2 month's depreciation would have been claimed in 2006 (1/2 month in July and 5 months in August through December) and an additional 2 year's depreciation would have been claimed in 2007 and 2008. Thus, as of January 1, 2009, the remaining recovery period is 36 years and 6.5 months (39 - 5.5/12 - 2) or 36.541 years. 6.5 month is equivalent to .541 years (6.5/12 = .541).

The straight-line depreciation rate for 2009 is therefore .027737 (1/36.541). This rate is applied to the exchanged basis (carryover basis) of the building increased by the amount of depreciation claimed on the parking lot in 2009. The rate for 2010 is .02814 (1/35.541). This amount is applied to the unrecovered basis at the beginning of 2010 (i.e., the basis to which the 2010 rate applied reduced by the amount of depreciation claimed in 2010) (Reg. § 1.168(i)-6(c)(6), Example 8).

Example (13): A bridge (15-year property) subject to the half-year convention and 150 percent declining balance method is placed in service in January 2002 at a cost of $1,000,000,000. It is exchanged for a residential rental building (subject to the mid-month convention) in January 2008. Since the recovery period of the residential rental building is longer than the recovery period of the bridge and the straight-line method is less accelerated than the 150 percent declining balance method, the building is depreciated using the straight-line method over the amount of its 27.5 year recovery period that would remain if it had been placed at the same time as the bridge (taking into account the convention that applies to the bridge in the year of acquisition and disposition). Since the half-year convention applied to the bridge, the remaining recovery period of the building is determined as if it had been placed in service on July 1, 2002 and disposed of on July 1, 2008. 5 1/2 months depreciation would have been claimed on the building in 2002 (1/2 month in July and a full month in each month of August through December) and 6 1/2 months depreciation would have been claimed on the building in 2008 (one full month for in each month of January through June and 1/2 month in July). One full year would have been claimed in 2003, 2004, 2005, 2006, and 2007. Thus, the remaining recovery period at the time of replacement is 21.5 years (27.5 - 5.5/12 (2002) - 5 (2003 - 2007) - 6.5/12 (2008)). The remaining recovery period at the beginning of the tax year of replacement is 20.9583 years (21.5 - 6.5/12).

The applicable straight-line rate for the year of replacement is .0477 (1/20.9583). Assuming that the undepreciated basis of the bridge after its disposition in the trade is $626,400, the exchanged basis is also $626,400. In determining the depreciation deduction on the exchanged basis of the building in the year of replacement, the exchanged basis is increased by the depreciation claimed on the bridge in the year of disposition. Assume that the depreciation deduction on the bridge in 2008 taking into account the half-year convention was $29,500 ($1,000,000 × 5.9% table percentage × 50% to reflect half-year convention). The depreciation rate is therefore applied to $655,900 ($626,400 + $29,500). Thus, the depreciation deduction for 2008 on the replacement property, taking into account the period that the replacement property was in service in 2008 by applying the mid-month convention (i.e., from the midpoint of July 2008) is $14,340 ($655,900 × .0477 × 5.5/12). The depreciation rate for 2009 is .0501 (1/19.9583). The 2009 depreciation deduction is $32,142 ($655,900 - $14,340 × .0501) (Reg. § 1.168(i)-6(c)(6), Example 2).

Example (14):

Asset	Method	Conv.	Rec. Per.	Acquired	Exchanged
Office Building	S/L	MM	39	1-1-99	1-15-2008
Transmitting Tower	150%DB	HY	15	1-15-2008	

A taxpayer places an office building (39-year real property depreciated using the straight-line method and mid-month convention) in service in January 2000. On January 1, 2008, the real property is exchanged for a transmitting tower (15-year property subject to 150% DB method). Since the depreciation period for the real property (39 years) is longer than the depreciation period for the tower (15-years), the depreciable exchanged basis of the tower is depreciated over the remaining recovery period of the building as of the January 1, 2008 date of the exchange. The mid-month convention applies to the tower since the mid-month convention applies if either the relinquished or replacement property is subject to the mid-month convention. Under the mid-month convention the office building has been in service 8 years up to the time of disposition taking into account the mid-month convention (mid-January 2000 through mid-January 2008) and 31 years remain in the recovery period (39 – 8). The straight-line method and mid-month convention apply to compute the deductions on the depreciable exchanged basis of the tower.

The office building cost $100,000 and $20,406 of depreciation was claimed through 2007. The 2008 deduction on the office building is $107 ($100,000 × 1/39) (this represents a full year's deduction) × 1/2 (number of months deemed in service under the mid-month convention in 2008)/12). The depreciable exchanged basis of the tower after the exchange is $79,487 ($100,000 – $20,406 – $107). The 2008 deduction for the tower is $2,457 ($79,487 × .03226 × 11.5/12). 11.5 is the number of months that the tower is in service in 2008 taking into account the mid-month convention.

The straight-line depreciation rate for the tower in the year of acquisition is based on the recovery period that would remain as of the beginning of the tax year of disposition (not the recovery period that remains as of the time of disposition) (Reg. § 1.168(i)-6(c)(5)(ii)(B)(1)). The remaining recovery period is 31.0417 years (39 – 7.9583 years depreciation claimed as of January 1, 2008 ((11.5 months (2000) + 7 years (2001 - 2007) = 7.9583). The straight-line rate for the year of replacement is .0322 (1/31.0417). This rate is applied to $79,684 (the depreciable exchanged basis of the office building ($79,487) increased by the depreciation claimed on the building in the year of disposition ($107)) (Reg. § 1.168(i)-6(c)(5)(ii)(B)(2)). The depreciation deduction on the tower in 2008 is therefore $2,459 ($79,684 × .0322 × 11.5/12). 11.5 is the number of months the tower was in service under the mid-month convention.

In 2009 and each full recovery year during the remaining recovery period, the depreciation deduction on the exchanged basis of the tower is equal to $2,566 ($79,684 × .0322) (Reg. § 1.168(i)-6(c)(6), Example 3).

Note that in the preceding example, the taxpayer could maximize deductions on the tower by simply electing out of the regulations. If an election out is made, the tower could be depreciated over 15 years using the half-year convention and 150% DB method rather than over the 31 years that remain in the building's recovery period using the straight line method.

Example (15): A tool, costing $60,000, is exchanged for equipment.

Asset	Method	Conv.	Rec. Per.	Acquired	Exchanged
Tool	S/L (elective)	MQ	3	2-1-2006	6-15-2008
Equipment	200 DB	HY	7	6-15-2008	

Since the recovery period of the equipment (7 years) is longer than the recovery period of the tool (3) years, the equipment is depreciated as if it had originally been placed in service on 2-15-2006 (date tools were placed in service under mid-quarter convention) using a 7-year recovery period. Also since the recovery method of the equipment (200% DB method) is more accelerated than the recovery method of the tool (S/L) at the time of replacement (2008), the exchanged basis of the equipment is depreciated using the S/L method. Since the mid-quarter convention was used to depreciate the tools (relinquished property) and the replacement property is not real property, the mid-quarter convention is used to depreciate the exchanged basis (Reg. § 1.168(i)-6(c)(4)(v)(B)).

If the equipment had originally been placed in service on 2-15-2006 it would also be considered placed in service on the same date under the mid-quarter convention and its remaining recovery period at the time of the exchange would be 4.75 years (7 - .875 years (or 10.5/12 months) (2006) - 1 year (2007) - .375 years (or 4.5/12 months) (2008) = 4.75 years).

Depreciation on the tools, assuming they cost $60,000, through 2007 is computed as follows:

Year	Deduction	
2006	$17,500	($60,000 × 1/3 × 10.5/12)
2007	20,000	($60,000 × 1/3)

The depreciation allowance on the tools in 2008 is computed by multiplying the allowable depreciation deduction for the tools for 2008 without regard to the exchange by a fraction, the numerator of which is the number of months the tools are deemed to be placed in service during 2008 (taking into account the mid-quarter convention and the disposition), and the denominator of which is 12 (Reg. § 1.168(i)-6(c)(5)(i)).

The regular depreciation deduction for the tools in 2008 without regard to the exchange is computed as follows:

2008	$7,500	($60,000 × 1/3 × 4.5/12)

4.5 is the number of months that the tools are considered to be in service in 2008 if disposed of in June under the mid-quarter convention (January 1 — May 15 = 4.5 months).

The remaining recovery period of the depreciable exchanged basis (i.e., the equipment) as of the beginning of 2007 is determined by assuming (a) the equipment has a 7-year recovery period, (b) the mid-quarter convention applies, and (c) that the equipment was placed in service in the first-quarter of 2006. The remaining recovery period as of the beginning of 2008 is, therefore, deemed to be 5.125 years (7 - .875 years (or 10.5/12 months) (2006) - 1 year (2007) = 5.125 years).

The depreciation rate, which is determined by reference to the remaining recovery period as of the beginning of the tax year (Reg. § 1.168(i)-6(c)(5)(ii)(B)) is, therefore, 0.1951 (1/5.125). The exchanged basis is $15,000 ($60,000 cost of tools - $17,500 (2006 depreciation) - $20,000 (2007 depreciation) - $7,500 (2008 depreciation prior to exchange). The exchanged basis is increased by $7,500 to $22,500 (Reg. § 1.168(i)-6(c)(5)(ii)(B)). The deduction on the replacement equipment in the replacement year is, therefore, $2,744 ($22,500 × 19.51% × 7.5/12). 7.5 is the number of months that the equipment is deemed in service under the mid-quarter convention if acquired in June, 2008 (i.e., May 15 through December 31) (Reg. § 1.168(i)-6(c)(6), Example 4).

Example (16): The facts are the same as in Example above except that the exchange takes place in June 2009. Under these facts, the remaining recovery period of the tool at the beginning of 2009 is 1.5 months and, as a result, is less than the 5-month period between the beginning of 2009 (year of disposition) and June 2009 (time of disposition). As a result, the 2009 depreciation allowance for the tools is $2,500 ($2,500 adjusted depreciable basis at the beginning of 2009 ($60,000 original basis minus $17,500 depreciation deduction for 2006 minus $20,000 depreciation deduction for 2007 minus $20,000 depreciation deduction for 2008)). Because the exchanged basis of the equipment is $0.00 no depreciation is allowable for the equipment (Reg. § 1.168(i)-6(c)(5)(i)(B); Reg. § 1.168(i)-6(c)(6), Example 5).

Deferred like-kind exchanges transactions. No depreciation may be claimed on relinquished MACRS property during the period between the disposition of the relinquished property and acquisition of the replacement property in a deferred exchange (except to the extent that depreciation is allowed under the applicable convention). The regulations reserve the issue of whether an exchange accommodation titleholder (or other intermediary) may claim depreciation (Reg. § 1.168(i)-6(c)(5)(iv)).

Exchanges of multiple properties. The determination of the basis of property acquired in a like-kind exchange involving multiple properties is described in Reg. § 1.1031(j)-1 and the determination of the basis of multiple properties acquired as a result of an involuntary conversion is described in Reg. § 1.1033(b)-1. Once basis in property is determined or allocated is so determined, these depreciation regulations apply to compute the depreciation allowable with respect to such basis (T.D. 9314, preamble).

Involuntary conversions: replacement property placed in service before disposition of relinquished property. A taxpayer who places replacement property from an involuntary conversion in service before disposing of the involuntarily converted property (see Code Sec. 1033(a)(2)(B), relating to acquisitions under threat of condemnation) should compute depreciation on the unadjusted depreciation basis of the replacement property without regard to the special rules under these regulations. However, at the time the relinquished property is disposed of the taxpayer should determine the exchanged and excess basis of the replacement property and begin to compute depreciation in accordance with the regulations. Furthermore, in the tax year that the relinquished property is disposed, the excess of the depreciation deductions allowable on the unadjusted depreciable basis of the replacement property over the depreciation deductions that would have been allowable on the depreciable excess basis of the replacement property from the date that the replacement property was placed in service (under the applicable convention) to the time of disposition of the relinquished property is recaptured (i.e., included in taxable income). Special rules apply if bonus depreciation is claimed on the replacement property (Reg. § 1.168(I)-6(d)(4)).

Computations Using the Optional Depreciation Tables

A taxpayer may use the optional depreciation tables to compute depreciation on the replacement property, whether or not the tables were used on the relinquished property (Reg. § 1.168(i)-6(e)(1)).

Depreciation on relinquished property in year of disposition using tables. Using the optional tables, the depreciation deduction on the relinquished property in the year of disposition is determined by multiplying the cost of the property (as reduced by any amount expensed under section 179 and as bonus depreciation) by the appropriate table percentage. The product is then adjusted to take into account the applicable convention (Reg. § 1.168(i)-6(e)(2)(i)).

> ***Example (18):*** 7-year property purchased in 2005 for $100,000 and subject to the half-year convention is involuntarily converted or exchanged in 2009. No amount was expensed or claimed as bonus depreciation. The 2009 deduction is $4,465 ($100,000 × .0893 (fifth year table percentage expressed as a decimal) × 6/12 to reflect the half-year convention.

Depreciation on excess basis using tables. Any excess basis in the replacement property (e.g., additional cash paid for the replacement property in a trade-in) is treated as property placed in service at the time of the replacement. The excess basis is depreciated using the applicable table for the property (Reg. § 1.168(i)-6(e)(3)). The excess basis may be eligible for the Code Sec. 179 expense allowance and bonus depreciation. See "*Section 179 allowance and bonus depreciation,*" above.

Depreciation on exchanged basis using tables. The depreciation allowances for the depreciable exchanged basis are determined by applying table percentages from the table that corresponds to the recovery period, depreciation method, and convention of the replacement property that is determined under the rules that apply when the tables are not used (Reg. § 1.168(i)-6(e)(2)(ii)(A)).

The following steps apply in determining the depreciation deduction for the exchanged basis during each year of its remaining recovery period:

(1) Determine the appropriate depreciation table;

(2) Determine the appropriate recovery year from the table;

(3) The applicable table percentage (expressed as a decimal) for that year is multiplied by a transaction coefficient;

(4) The applicable depreciation rate for the year, as determined in (3), is applied to the depreciable exchanged basis.

The appropriate recovery year for the year of replacement is always the same recovery year that applied to the relinquished property in the year of its disposition (Reg. § 1.168(i)-6(e)(2)(ii)(B)(1)).

In the year of replacement, the depreciation deduction on the depreciable exchanged basis is adjusted to reflect the applicable convention (i.e., multiplied by a fraction, the numerator of which is the number of months (or partial months) the replacement property is deemed to be in service under the applicable convention and the denominator of which is 12) (Reg. § 1.168(i)-6(e)(2)(ii)(B)(2)).

If the replacement property has unrecovered depreciable basis after the final recovery year (this might occur in a deferred exchange), the unrecovered basis is claimed as a depreciation deduction in the tax year that corresponds to the final recovery year (Reg. § 1.168(i)-6(e)(2)(iii)).

Transaction coefficient when using tables. The transaction coefficient is equal to the following formula:

1/(1-x)

x is equal to the sum of the annual depreciation rates from the appropriate depreciation table (item 1) expressed as a decimal for the tax years beginning with the placed-in-service year of the relinquished property through the tax year immediately prior to the year of disposition.

The transaction coefficient is not recomputed each year.

Example (19): 5-year property placed in service in 2007 is exchanged for 7-year property in 2009. Assume that the appropriate table for computing depreciation on the depreciable exchanged basis of the replacement property is the table that applies to 7-year property using the half-year convention and 200% DB method. The sum of the recovery percentages expressed as a decimal for the first two recovery years prior to the exchange in the third recovery year is .3878 (.1429 + .2449). The transaction coefficient is 1.6335 (1/(1 - .3878)).

Example (20): 5-year property costing $10,000 is placed in service in 2009. The half-year convention and 200% DB method apply to the 5-year property. Table 1 for 5-year property is used to compute deductions. The property is exchanged in 2010 for 7-year property

Since the replacement property has a longer recovery period (7 years vs. 5 years) and the same depreciation method applies in the disposition year to both the 5-year year property (200% DB method) and to the 7-year property if it had been placed in service in 2009 (200% DB method), the appropriate depreciation table for depreciating the exchanged basis of the replacement property is the table that applies to 7-year property, subject to the 200% DB method and the half-year convention (Table 1 for 7-year property at ¶ 180). The half-year convention applies because the 5-year property was depreciated using the half-year convention and the replacement property is not real property subject to the mid-month convention.

The depreciable exchanged basis of the 7-year property is $3,840 ($10,000 – $2,000 depreciation claimed on the 5-year property in 2009 ($10,000 × 20%) – $3,200 claimed in 2010 ($10,000 × 32%), and – $960 claimed in 2011 ($10,000 × 19.2% × 6/12 to reflect half-year convention)).

The depreciation deduction on the depreciable exchanged basis in 2011 is determined by reference to the third-year table percentage (17.49% or .1749) since this is the recovery that would apply to the replacement property in 2011 if it had been placed in service in 2009.

The transaction coefficient is 1.6335 (1/(1 – (.1429 + .2449)).

The depreciation rate for 2011 is, therefore, .2857 (.1749 × 1.6335).

The depreciation deduction on the exchanged basis in 2011 is $549 ($3,840 × .2857 × 6/12 (to reflect half-year convention)).

The depreciation rate for 2012 is .2040 (.1249 (year 4 table rate) × 1.6335).

The depreciation deduction on the exchanged basis in 2009 is $783 ($3,840 × .2040). (Reg. § 1.168(i)-6(e)(4), Example 1).

Example (21): 5-year property costing $100,000 is placed in service in 2006. This property is subject to the half year convention and is depreciated using the 200DB method. The table percentage from Table 1 ¶ 164.01 for five-year property is used.

In 2010 (the fifth recovery year) the 5-year property is involuntarily converted.

In 2012, the 5-year property is replaced with 7-year property that would have been depreciated using the 200% DB method and half-year convention if placed in service in 2006.

Depreciation claimed on the 5-year property through 2010 amounted to $88,480 ($100,000 - $20,000 ($100,000 x .20) - $32,000 ($100,000 x .32) - $19,200 ($100,000 x .1920) - $11,520 ($100,000 x .1152) - $5,760 ($100,000 x .1152 x 6/12).

The adjusted depreciable basis of the 5-year property at the time of replacement was $11,520 ($100,000 - $88,480).

The appropriate depreciation table for the 7-year property is based on the depreciation method that was being used to compute depreciation on the 5-year property in the year of its disposition. Referring to Table 1 at ¶ 180and the depreciation percentages for 5-year property, it can be seen that in the fifth recovery year a switch was made from the 200DB method to the straight-line method when the (straight-line) rate became 11.52%. (Note that the DB rate and straight-line rate were identical in the fourth recovery year, therefore, the switch was actually considered made under IRS guidelines in the fifth recovery year). Since the 5-year property was being depreciated using the straight-line rate at the time of its disposition in its fifth recovery year, the 7-year replacement property must be depreciated using the straight-line method. The appropriate table, therefore, is the straight-line table for 7-year property subject to the half-year convention. These percentages are located in Table 8 at ¶ 180. This table would presumably not have been used if the disposition had occurred in the fourth recovery year when the DB and SL rates were identical.

For purposes of computing depreciation deductions on the exchanged basis the transaction coefficient, as determined by reference to this table, is 2.00 (1/(1 -.0714 - .1429 - .1429 - .1428) = 2.00).

The depreciation deduction on the exchanged basis for 2012 is determined by reference to the fifth-year table percentage (14.29% or .1429) and taking into account the half-year convention. The 2012 deduction is $1,646 ($11,520 depreciable exchanged basis after the involuntary conversion x .1429 x 2.00 x 6/12).

The depreciation deduction for 2013 (the sixth recovery year) is $3,290 ($11,520 x .1428 x 2.00)).

The depreciation deduction for 2014 (the seventh recovery year) is $3,292 ($11,520 x .1429 x 2.00)).

In the last recovery year (the eighth recovery year), the depreciation deduction is $1,645 ($11,520 x .0714 x 2.00)). However, since $1,645 is less than the unrecovered basis of $3,292 ($11,520 - $1,646 - $3,290 - $3,292), the entire unrecovered basis is deducted. (Reg. § 1.168(i)-6(e)(4), Example (2)).

Example (22): A computer is purchased in 2007 for $5,000 and destroyed (involuntarily converted) in a fire in 2009. The computer was depreciated using the 200DB method and half-year convention (Table 1 (at ¶ 164.01) percentages for five-year property). The computer was replaced in 2009.

The depreciation claimed in 2007 through 2009 on the destroyed computer amounted to $3,080 ($5,000 – $1,000 ($5,000 × .20) – $3,200 ($5,000 × .32) – $480 ($5,000 × .1920 × 6/12)).

The exchanged basis of the replacement computer acquired in 2006 is $1,920 ($5,000 – $3,080).

The replacement computer will be depreciated using the same depreciation method, recovery period, and convention as the destroyed computer. The applicable table for computing depreciation deductions on the exchanged basis is the same table that applies to the destroyed computer.

The transaction coefficient is 2.08 (1/1 – .20 – .32).

The depreciation rate for computing depreciation on the exchanged basis in 2009 is .40 (.192 × 2.08). The 2009 deduction, taking into account the half-year convention, is $384 ($1,920 × .40 × 6/12).

Depreciation for 2010 and 2011 is $460 ($1,920 × .1152 × 2.08 each year.

Depreciation for 2012 (the last recovery year) is $230 ($1,920 × .0576 × 2.08). However, since the unrecovered basis of $616 ($1,920 – $384 – $460 – $460) is greater than $230, the entire unrecovered basis is claimed as a deduction (Reg. § 1.168(i)-6(e)(4), Example (3)).

Change in Use

¶ 168

MACRS Property Converted to Personal Use or Business Use

Special rules contained in IRS regulations may apply to determine MACRS depreciation when a taxpayer changes the use to which property is put (Reg.§ 1.168(i)-4, as added by T.D. 9132).

Changes in use covered by the rules include a conversion of personal use property to business or income-producing use property and vice versa. Most significantly, a change in use includes a change in the taxpayer's use of MACRS property that causes the property to have a different recovery period, depreciation method, or both (¶ 169). For example, a change in use occurs if a taxpayer switches the business activity in which a property is used, causing it to have a new recovery period.

Effective date of change in use regulations. The change in use regulations generally apply to a change in use of MACRS property that occurs in a tax year ending on or after June 17, 2004. For a change in use of MACRS property after December 31, 1986, in a tax year ending before June 17, 2004, the IRS will allow any reasonable method that is consistently applied. A taxpayer may also choose, on a property-by-property basis, to apply the regulations to MACRS property placed in service before June 17, 2004 (Reg.§ 1.168(i)-4(g), preamble to T.D. 9132).

Changing accounting methods to conform to regulations. A change to conform to the regulations due to a change in use of MACRS property in a tax year ending on or after December 30, 2003 is a change in method of accounting if the taxpayer has adopted a method of accounting (for example, by filing two or more returns using the nonconforming method). The automatic consent procedures of Rev. Proc. 2008-52 apply (see ¶ 75). The regulations provide that taxpayer may (i.e., is not required to) treat a change to conform to the regulations due a change in use after December 31, 1986, in a tax year ending before December 30, 2003 as a change in method of accounting. Thus, an amended return may be filed for an open tax year in this situation. Procedures for obtaining consent to change accounting methods to conform to the regulations are provided in Reg.§ 1.168(i)-4(g)(2).

Personal Property Converted to Business or Income-Producing Use

Personal-use property converted to business or income-producing use is treated as placed in service by the taxpayer on the date of the conversion. This type of conversion includes property that was previously used by the taxpayer for personal purposes, including real property (other than land) that is acquired before 1987 and converted from personal use to business or income-producing use after 1986, and depreciable property that was previously used by a tax-exempt entity before it changed to a taxable entity (Reg.§ 1.168(i)-4(b)).

Upon a conversion to business or income-producing use, the depreciation allowance for the tax year of change and any subsequent tax year is determined as though the property was placed in service by the taxpayer on the date on which the conversion occurs. Thus, the taxpayer may choose any applicable depreciation method, recovery period, and convention for the property in the year of change, consistent with any depreciation election made by the taxpayer for that year. The depreciable basis of the property for the year of change is the lesser of its fair market value or its adjusted depreciable basis (as defined in Reg.§ 1.168(b)-1(a)(4)), as applicable, at the time of the conversion to business or income-producing use.

Example (1): Anne Elyse, a calendar-year taxpayer, purchases a house in 1985 that she occupies as her principal residence. In February 2009, Ms. Elyse ceases to occupy the house and converts it to residential rental property. At the time of the conversion to residential rental property, the house's fair market value (excluding land) is $130,000 and the adjusted depreciable basis attributable to the house (excluding land) is $150,000. Ms. Elyse is considered to have placed in service residential rental property in February 2009 with a depreciable basis of $130,000. Ms. Elyse depreciates the residential rental property under the general depreciation system by using the straight-line method, a 27.5-year recovery period, and the mid-month convention. Thus, the depreciation allowance for the house for 2009 is $4,137, after taking into account the mid-month convention (($130,000 adjusted depreciable basis multiplied by the applicable depreciation rate of 3.636% (1/27 .5)) multiplied by the mid-month convention fraction of 10.5/12).

Property converted from personal to business or income-producing use may qualify for bonus depreciation if the property was acquired after September 10, 2001 and converted to business or income-producing use before January 1, 2005 (Reg. § 1.168(k)-1(f)(6)(iii)). Similarly, property acquired after December 31, 2007 and converted to business or income-producing use before January 1, 2010 may also qualify for bonus depreciation.

However, it appears that property converted from personal use to business use should not qualify for expensing under Code Sec. 179 because it was not acquired for use in the active conduct of a taxpayer's trade or business as required by Code Sec. 179(d)(1).

MACRS Property Converted to Personal Use

A conversion of MACRS property from business or income-producing use to personal use is treated as a disposition of the property. Depreciation for the year of change is computed by taking into account the applicable convention. Existing IRS guidance (Rev. Rul. 69-487, 1969-2 C.B. 165) indicates that no gain, loss, or depreciation recapture is recognized upon the conversion (Reg. § 1.168(i)-4(c)).

The depreciation allowance for MACRS property for the year of change is determined by first multiplying the adjusted depreciable basis of the property (as defined in Reg.§ 1.168(b)-1(a)(4)) as of the first day of the year of change by the applicable depreciation rate for that tax year. This amount is then multiplied by a fraction, the numerator of which is the number of months (including fractions of months) the property is deemed in service during the year of change (taking into account the applicable convention) and the denominator of which is 12. No depreciation deduction is allowable for MACRS property placed in service and disposed of in the same tax year. See ¶ 160. Upon the conversion to personal use, no gain, loss, or depreciation recapture is recognized. However, the recapture provisions apply to any disposition of the converted property by the taxpayer at a later date (Reg.§ 1.168(i)-4(c)).

Example (2): Seven-year property is placed in service in 2009 and used 100% for business. In 2010, the property is converted to personal use. The half-year convention applied in 2009. Assume that the property cost $100,000 and no amount was expensed under Code Sec. 179. 2009 depreciation was $14,286 ($100,000 × 1/7 × 2 × 6/12 to reflect half-year convention). In 2010, the taxpayer is also entitled to one-half year's depreciation or $12,245 ($85,714 × 1/7 × 2 × 6/12 to reflect half-year convention that applies during the year of the deemed disposition).

If an amount has been expensed under Code Sec. 179, and a property which is not listed property is converted to personal use before the end of its recovery period, the Code Sec. 179 expense deduction (but not any bonus deduction) is subject to recapture under Code Sec. 179(d)(10) because business use has declined to 50 percent or less. See ¶ 300 for a discussion of this recapture rule.

If the property converted to personal use is a listed property (such as an automobile) the difference between the depreciation claimed (including any amount expensed under Code Sec. 179 or claimed as bonus depreciation) and the amount that would have been claimed using the alternative depreciation system is recaptured pursuant to Code Sec. 280F(b)(2) because business use has declined to 50 percent or less (Reg.§ 1.168(i)-4(c)). See ¶ 210.

¶ 169

Changes in MACRS Property Use Resulting in Different Recovery Period or Method

MACRS regulations provide the rules for determining the annual MACRS depreciation allowances if a change in use of a property results in a different recovery period, depreciation method, or both. Generally, the rules differ depending upon whether the use changes in the tax year in which the property is placed in service or after the tax year the property is placed in service (Reg.§ 1.168(i)-4(d)).

A change in computing the depreciation allowance *in the tax year the use of the property changes* to comply with the change in use regulations is not a change in accounting method under Code Sec. 446(e) (Reg.§ 1.168(i)-4(f)). If a taxpayer does not apply the regulations in the tax year that the change in use occurs and has filed two or more returns, then it may be necessary to obtain consent to change accounting methods. See, "*Effective date of change in use regulations,*" at ¶ 168 above.

If MACRS property is depreciated using the depreciation tables before the change in use, the taxpayer may continue to depreciate the property using the tables after the change in use. However, the taxpayer is not required to do so. A taxpayer who did not use the tables may only switch to the tables if the change in use results in a shorter recovery period or more accelerated depreciation method.

MACRS Property Changes Use in Same Tax Year Placed in Service. If the use of MACRS property changes during its placed-in-service year, the depreciation allowance is simply determined by reference to the primary use of the property during that tax year. However, in determining whether MACRS property is used within or outside the United States during the placed-in-service year, the predominant use, instead of the primary use, of the MACRS property governs. Further, in determining whether MACRS property is tax-exempt use property or imported property covered by an Executive order during the placed-in-service year, the use of the property at the end of the placed-in-service year governs. If property is so categorized at year-end, the ADS system would apply; otherwise the GDS system would apply. Moreover, MACRS property is tax-exempt bond financed property during the placed-in-service year if a tax-exempt bond for the MACRS property is issued during that year. Depreciation on MACRS property that changes to tax-exempt bond financed property in the placed-in-service year is also determined under the ADS system (Reg.§ 1.168(i)-4(e)).

MACRS Property Changes Use in Tax Year After Placed in Service. The regulations provide computation rules for MACRS property if a taxpayer changes the use of property after the property's placed-in-service year but the property continues to be MACRS property in the hands of the taxpayer. The rules apply if the property continues to be MACRS property owned by the same taxpayer and, as a result of the change in use, has a different recovery period, a different depreciation method, or both. For example, this rule applies to MACRS property that:

(1) Begins or ceases to be used predominantly outside the United States;

(2) Results in a change in the property class of the property (eg., 3-year property converted to 5-year property) due to a change in the use of the property; or

(3) Begins or ceases to be tax-exempt use property (Reg. § 1.168(i)-4(d)).

In general, the regulations provide that a change in the use of MACRS property occurs when the primary use of the MACRS property in the tax year is different from its primary use in the immediately preceding tax year. If a change in the use of MACRS property has occurred, the depreciation allowance for the MACRS property for the year of change is determined as though the change in the use of the MACRS property occurred on the first day of the year of change (Reg.§ 1.168(i)-4(d)(2)).

Computation if change in use results in shorter recovery period or more accelerated depreciation method. If a change in the use of MACRS property results in a *shorter* recovery period and/or a *more accelerated* depreciation method (for example, MACRS property ceases to be used predominantly outside the United States), the adjusted depreciable basis of the property (as defined in Reg.§ 1.168(b)-1(a)(4)) as of the beginning of the year of change is depreciated over the shorter recovery period and/or by the more accelerated depreciation method beginning with the year of change as though the MACRS property was first placed in service in the year of change. Under certain circumstances, this rule may adversely affect taxpayers (Reg.§ 1.168(i)-4(d)(3)).

For example, if a change in the use of MACRS property would result in a shorter recovery period, a taxpayer must depreciate that MACRS property over the new shorter recovery period even if the remaining portion of the original longer recovery period is less than the new shorter recovery period. To avoid this adverse effect, the regulations allow a taxpayer to elect to continue to depreciate the MACRS property for which the new recovery period is shorter or a more accelerated method is allowed as though the change in use had not occurred. The election is made by computing depreciation on Form 4562 as if the change in use had not occurred.

Example (1): A taxpayer changes the use of 20-year property subject to the 150% DB method to a use which results in its conversion to 5-year property subject to the 200% DB method. Assume that the change in use occurs during the 18th year of the 20-year recovery period. If no election out of the regulations is made, the taxpayer will recover the remaining basis of the property by depreciating it as though it were five-year property placed in service in the year of the change in use. If an election out is made, the basis is recovered over the 2 remaining recovery years in the 20-year recovery period.

Assuming that the election out is not made, the depreciation allowances for the MACRS property for any 12-month taxable year beginning with the year of change are determined by multiplying the adjusted depreciable basis of the MACRS property as of the first day of each tax year by the applicable depreciation rate for each tax year. In determining the applicable depreciation rate for the year of change and subsequent tax years, the taxpayer may choose any applicable depreciation method and recovery period for the MACRS property in the year of change, consistent with any MACRS depreciation election made by the taxpayer for that year. If there is a change in the use of MACRS property, the applicable convention that applies to the MACRS property is the same as the convention that applied before the change in the use of the MACRS property. However, the depreciation allowance for the year of change for the MACRS property is determined without applying the applicable convention, unless the MACRS property is disposed of during the year of change. Special rules apply to the computation of the depreciation allowance under the optional depreciation tables as explained below. If the year of change or any subsequent tax year is less than 12 months, the depreciation allowance must be adjusted for a short taxable year (Reg.§ 1.168(i)-4(d)(3)).

MACRS property which has a shorter or longer recovery period or a more or less accelerated depreciation method as a result of a change in use in a tax year after it was placed in service is not eligible in the year of change for (1) the election to depreciate under the unit-of-production method or any method of depreciation not expressed in a term of years, (2) the Code Sec. 179 expensing election or (3) the additional first-year depreciation deduction (bonus depreciation) (there is no affect, however, on previously claimed bonus depreciation). For purposes of determining whether the mid-quarter convention would apply to other MACRS property placed in service during the year of change, the basis of the MACRS property which changes use in a tax year after it was placed in service is not taken into account in applying the 40 percent mid-quarter convention test (Reg.§ 1.168(i)-4(d)(3)(i)(C); Reg.§ 1.168(i)-4(d)(4)(i)).

Example (2): ABC Corp., a calendar-year corporation, places $100,000 of 7-year property in service in 2004. The property is subject to the half-year convention and depreciated using the 200% DB method. Depreciation claimed through 2008 amounted to $77,689. In 2009, the primary business use of the property changes, and, as a result, it is reclassified as 5-year property. As of January 1, 2009, the adjusted depreciable basis is $22,311 ($100,000 - $77,689). ABC may (1) elect to continue depreciating the property as 7-year property or (2) depreciate the property as 5-year property placed in service in 2009. 2009 depreciation, assuming option (2) is chosen, is $8,924 ($22,311 × 40% (1/5 × 2)). Note that although 2009 is considered the first-year of the five-year recovery period, no adjustment is made for the half-year convention.

Computation if change in use results in longer recovery period or slower depreciation method. If a change in the use of MACRS property (in a tax year after it has been placed in service) would result in a *longer* recovery period and/or *slower depreciation* method (for example, MACRS property begins to be used predominantly outside the United States), the adjusted depreciable basis of the property is depreciated over the longer recovery period and/or by the slower depreciation method beginning with the year of change as though the taxpayer originally placed the MACRS property in service with the longer recovery period and/or slower depreciation method. Accordingly, the adjusted depreciable basis of the MACRS property as of the beginning of the year of change is depreciated over the remaining portion of the new, longer recovery period as of the beginning of the year of change (Reg.§ 1.168(i)-4(d)(4)).

The depreciation allowances for the MACRS property for any 12-month taxable year beginning with the year of change are determined by multiplying the adjusted depreciable basis of the MACRS property as of the first day of each tax year by the applicable depreciation rate for each taxable year. The applicable convention that applies to the MACRS property is the same as the convention that applied before the change in the use of the MACRS property. If the year of change or any subsequent tax year is less than 12 months, the depreciation allowance is adjusted for a short tax year (Reg.§ 1.168(i)-4(d)(4)).

If a change in use results in a longer recovery period and/or a slower depreciation method, a taxpayer may choose to use the depreciation tables in the tax year of a change in use and the following years in the remaining recovery period only if the table percentages were used prior to the change-in-use year (Reg.§ 1.168(i)-4(d)(5)(i)). See below.

Assuming that the optional tables are not used, the following rules apply for purposes of determining the applicable depreciation rate (which is based on the applicable method and recovery period) for the year of change and any subsequent tax years:

The applicable depreciation method in the year of change or a subsequent tax year is the method that would have applied in the year of change or the subsequent tax year if the taxpayer had used the longer recovery period and/or the slower depreciation method in the placed in service year of the property. For example, if the 200 percent or 150 percent declining balance method would have applied in the placed-in-service year but the method would have switched to the straight line method in the year of change (or any prior tax year) the applicable depreciation method in the year of change is the straight-line method (Reg.§ 1.168(i)-4(d)(4)(ii)(A)).

The applicable recovery period is either (Reg.§ 1.168(i)-4(d)(4)(ii)(B)):

(1) The longer recovery period resulting from the change in the use if the applicable depreciation method is the 200- or 150-percent declining balance method (as determined above) unless the recovery period did not change as a result of the change in the use, in which case the applicable recovery period is the same recovery period that applied before the change in the use; or

(2) The number of years remaining as of the beginning of each tax year (taking into account the applicable convention) had the taxpayer used the longer recovery period in the placed-in-service year of the property if the applicable depreciation method is the straight line method (as determined above) unless the recovery period did not change as a result of the change in the use, in which case the applicable recovery period is the number of years remaining as of the beginning of each taxable year (taking into account the applicable convention) based on the recovery period that applied before the change in the use.

Example (3): International Corp. places $100,000 of property in service in 2007. The property has a five-year recovery period, is subject to the half-year convention, and the 200% declining-balance method applies. In 2009, the property is moved outside of the U.S. As a result of this change in use, ADS is required. Assume the ADS recovery period is nine years. The ADS system uses the straight-line method. Assume further that International Corp. claimed a total of $52,000 of depreciation in 2007 and 2008 and that the adjusted depreciable basis of the property is, therefore, $48,000 ($100,000 – $52,000) at the beginning of 2009. 2009 depreciation is computed on $48,000 as if the property had originally been placed in service outside of the U.S. in 2007. If the property had been placed in service outside of the U.S. in 2007, the remaining recovery period at the beginning of 2009 would have been 7.5 years (9 years less 1/2 year depreciation in 2007 (half-year convention applied) and 1 year depreciation in 2008). The straight-line rate for 2009 is 1/7.5 or 13.33%. 2009 depreciation is $6,398 ($48,000 × 13.33%). Depreciation for 2010 is $6,398 ($41,602 adjusted depreciable basis × 15.38% (1/6.5 years remaining in the recovery period) (Reg.§ 1.168(i)-4(d)(6)).

Computing MACRS Deductions Upon Change in Use With Optional Depreciation Tables. A taxpayer who used a depreciation table to compute depreciation prior to the change-in-use year may use a depreciation table in the change-in-use year and later years in the applicable recovery period. A taxpayer who previously used the table percentages is not required to continue using table percentages. If the taxpayer did not use table percentages before the change in use, table percentages may only be used (beginning in the year of change) if the change in use results in a shorter recovery period and/or a more accelerated depreciation method (Reg. § 1.168(i)-5(i)).

Computation using tables when change in use results in shorter recovery period and/or more accelerated depreciation method. Assuming that the change in use results in a shorter recovery period and/or a more accelerated depreciation method, a taxpayer has the option of using the table percentages whether or not the table percentages were being used before the change in use. The depreciation allowances using table percentages are determined by multiplying the adjusted depreciable basis of the asset as of the beginning of the tax year of the change by the first-year table percentage. The second year table percentage is applied in the following tax year and so on until the end of the new shorter recovery period. The appropriate percentage table is based on the depreciation system, depreciation method, and recovery period applicable to the MACRS property in the year of change, as discussed above. Note that the applicable convention is the same convention that applied to the property before the change in use (Reg. § 1.168(i)-5(ii)(A)).

> ***Example (4):*** Assume the same facts as in Example 2. Since the change in use results in a shorter recovery period, ABC Corporation may compute the deductions in the change of use and subsequent years using the optional table percentages. This choice is available whether or not the property was originally depreciated using the tables. Assuming the tables will be used, the appropriate table is the table that applies to 5-year property subject to the half-year convention. The 2009 deduction using this table is $4,462 ($22,311 × 20% (first-year table percentage for 5-year property subject to half-year convention). Note that the first-year table percentage (20%) reflects the half-year convention.

Taxpayers should be aware that using the table percentages when the change in use results in a shorter recovery period or more accelerated depreciation method will result in less depreciation in the year of change in use because the applicable convention is factored into the first-year depreciation table percentage. If the table percentages are not used, the convention is not taken into account in the year of change, and a full year of depreciation may be claimed without regard to the convention, as illustrated in Example 2, above.

Computation using tables when change in use results in longer recovery period and/or less accelerated depreciation method. If a change in use results in a longer recovery period and/or less accelerated depreciation method, the table percentages may be used in the year of change and subsequent tax years only if the table percentages were already being used. If the table percentages were being used, however, it is not necessary to continue using table percentages (Reg.§ 1.168(i)-5(i)). The applicable table is the one that corresponds to the depreciation method, recovery period, and convention that would have applied to the MACRS property in the placed-in-service year if the property had been originally placed in service by the taxpayer with the longer recovery period and/or slower depreciation method (Reg.§ 1.168(i)-5(ii)(B)(1)).

> ***Example (5):*** Five-year property subject to the half-year convention is placed in service in 2007 and depreciated using the 200% DB method. The table percentages for 5-year property in Table 1 were used. In 2009, the property is converted to farm use. Farm property must be depreciated using the 150% DB method. No change to the recovery period, however, is required. As a result, in computing depreciation in 2009, Table 14 percentages for 5-year property are used if use of a table is chosen. Note that Table 14 reflects the 150% DB method and the half-year convention.

Once the appropriate table is determined, the taxpayer locates the table rate (percentage) that would have applied in the year of change if the table had been used when the property was originally placed in service. Thus, in the preceding example, the third-year percentage (17.85% or .1785) is used since the first-year percentage (15.00%) would have applied in 2006, the second-year percentage

(25.50%) would have applied in 2007, and the third-year percentage (17.85%) in 2008.

Next, the applicable table depreciation rate (expressed as a decimal percentage) is multiplied by a transaction coefficient.

The transaction coefficient is equal to 1/(1 – x) where x is equal to the sum of the annual depreciation rates from the appropriate table from the year the property was originally placed in service through the year immediately prior to the year of change. For example, the transaction coefficient for the preceding example is 1.68 [1/(1 – (.15 + .2550))]. The depreciation rate for the third recovery year expressed as a decimal (.1785) is then multiplied by the transaction coefficient (1.68) (.1785 × 1.68 = .30). The product of the annual depreciation rate and the transaction coefficient is then multiplied by the adjusted depreciable basis of the asset.

> ***Example (6):*** Assume the same facts as in Example 3, above, except that International Corp. used the depreciation tables in 2007 and 2008. This gives International the option of electing to use depreciation tables in 2007. If this election is made, the applicable table is the ADS table for property with a 9-year recovery period subject to the half-year convention since the half-year convention applied in 2007 when the property was originally placed in service (Table 8 at ¶ 180). The third year table percentage for property with a 9-year ADS recovery period from Table 8 is 11.11. The adjusted depreciable basis is multiplied by this percentage and the product is then multiplied by the transactional coefficient [1/1 – (.0556 + .1111), which equals 1.200]. .0556 is the first-year percentage from Table 8 expressed as a decimal and .1111 is the second-year percentage from Table 8 expressed as a decimal. The 2009 depreciation allowance using the optional table is, therefore, $6,399) [$48,000 × (.1111 (third-year table percentage expressed as a decimal) × 1.200)].

In computing depreciation deductions during all years of the remaining depreciation period, the transaction coefficient and unadjusted depreciable basis do not change.

> ***Example (7):*** 2009 depreciation in the preceding example is also $6,399 [$48,000 × (.1111 (fourth-year table percentage) × 1.200)].

¶ 169A

Increased Business Use After Recovery Period

Depreciation on MACRS property that is used only partially for business or investment purposes does not necessarily end upon expiration of an asset's recovery period. Additional depreciation may be claimed if the percentage of business or investment use in a tax year after the recovery period ends exceeds the average percentage of business or investment use during the recovery period (Code Sec. 168(i)(5); ACRS Prop. Reg. § 1.168-2(j)(2)).

No MACRS regulations have been issued detailing the computational rules. However, a similar rule applied under ACRS (Code Sec. 168(f)(13) (pre-1986)) and was explained in ACRS Prop. Reg. § 1.168-2(j)(2).

Under Prop. Reg. § 1.168-2(j)(2), a taxpayer determines the average percentage of business/investment use during the recovery period. In the first post-recovery period year that the percentage of business/investment use is greater than the average percentage of business/investment use, a depreciation allowance is claimed as if the property were placed in service at the beginning of that year. The deduction is computed by multiplying the original cost as reduced by prior depreciation (or the fair market value at the beginning of the tax year if this is less than cost reduced by prior depreciation) by the first-year recovery percentage. This amount is then multiplied by the percentage by which business/investment use for that year increased over the average business/investment use during the prior recovery period. The same procedure is followed for each subsequent year in the "second" recovery period. For any year in the "second" recovery period that business/investment use does not exceed the average business/investment use for the first recovery period, no deduction is allowed. The total depreciation that a taxpayer may claim may not exceed the original cost of the property. If the original cost is not recovered during the "second" recovery period, then the process may be applied to a "third" recovery period. The average business/investment use, however, would be redetermined by taking into account all of the years in the first and second recovery periods.

Example (1): A calendar-year taxpayer places an item of 5-year MACRS property costing $1,000 in service in 2004. The half-year convention applies. Assume that business use during each year of the recovery period (2004-2009) is 50% and that deductions were claimed as follows:

Year	*Calculation*	*Deduction*
2004	$1,000 × 20% × 50%	$100.00
2005	$1,000 × 32% × 50%	160.00
2006	$1,000 × 19.20% × 50%	96.00
2007	$1,000 × 11.52% × 50%	57.60
2008	$1,000 × 11.52% × 50%	57.60
2009	$1,000 × 5.76% × 50%	28.80
	Total	$500.00

Assume that business use is 60% in 2010, 40% in 2011, 60% in 2012, 70% in 2013, 60% in 2014, and 20% in 2015. Assume further that at the beginning of 2010, the fair market value of the machine is greater than the remaining $500 undepreciated basis ($1,000 – $500 depreciation = $500). Average business/investment use during the first recovery period was 50%. For each year in the second recovery period that business/investment use exceeds this percentage, the taxpayer may claim an additional depreciation deduction. The depreciation deductions in the second recovery period are computed as follows:

Year	*Calculation*	*Deduction*
2010	$500 × 20% × 10%	$10.00
2011		00.00
2012	$500 × 19.20% × 10%	9.20
2013	$500 × 11.52% × 20%	11.52
2014	$500 × 5.76% × 10%	2.88
2015		00.00
	Total	$33.60

This cycle would be repeated beginning in 2016 because the taxpayer has not recovered the total cost ($1,000) of the property. If the fair market value of the property in the beginning of 2016 is less than the undepreciated basis ($1,000 – $500 – 33.60 = $466.40), then the recovery percentages are applied against the fair market value.

See, also, *Example (2)* in ACRS Prop. Reg. § 1.168-2(j)(7).

Alternative Minimum Tax

¶ 170

Computing AMT Depreciation

MACRS property

In computing alternative minimum taxable income (AMTI) for alternative minimum tax (AMT) purposes, certain adjustments may have to be made to MACRS deductions claimed for regular tax purposes.

No adjustment is ever necessary if regular tax depreciation is computed using the MACRS alternative depreciation system (ADS).

Effective for property placed in service after December 31, 1998, an AMT adjustment for property depreciated under MACRS will only apply to MACRS 3-, 5-, 7-, and 10-year section 1245 property depreciated using the 200-percent declining-balance method or section 1250 MACRS recovery property regardless of recovery period depreciated using a method other than the straight-line method (Code Sec. 56(a)(1)(A), as amended by the Taxpayer Relief Act of 1997 (P.L. 105-34)). As explained below, however, no AMT adjustment is required on any property for which the bonus depreciation deduction is claimed.

Section 1250 property. MACRS residential rental property and MACRS nonresidential real property (two types of section 1250 property) are always depreciated using the straight-line method. Therefore, no AMT adjustment is ever required for such property if placed in service after December 31, 1998. 15-year restaurant improvement property (¶ 110), 15-year qualified leasehold improvement property (¶ 126), and 15-year qualified retail improvement property (¶ 126) are also section 1250 property. No AMT adjustment is required, however, because this property is also depreciated under MACRS using the straight-line method. On the other hand, an adjustment is required for section 1250 property depreciated using the 150 percent declining balance method, such as 15-year retail motor fuel establishments (¶ 110) and 15-year section 1250 land improvements (¶ 110).

Property depreciated using certain special methods. No adjustment is required for property that is depreciated under a method such as the unit-of-production method or any other method that is not expressed in terms of years; certain public utility property; films and video tapes; and sound recordings (Code Sec. 56(a)(1)(B)).

Indian reservation property. The regular tax depreciation deduction claimed on Indian reservation property placed in service after 1993 and before 2010 is allowed for AMT purposes (Code Sec. 168(j)(3)). See ¶ 124 for special recovery periods that apply in computing MACRS depreciation on Indian reservation property.

AMT gain or loss. The basis of a property for determining AMT gain or loss is reduced by AMT depreciation and not regular tax depreciation. See ¶ 486.

Code Sec. 179 deduction allowed in full. The Code Sec. 179 expense deduction is allowed in full for AMT purposes.

Bonus depreciation. Any bonus depreciation allowance claimed for regular tax purposes is allowed in full for alternative minimum tax purposes. Furthermore, no AMT depreciation adjustment is required on the regular tax MACRS depreciation deductions calculated on property for which bonus depreciation is claimed (i.e., the regular tax MACRS depreciation deductions are claimed in full in computing AMT (Code Sec. 168(k)(2)). Thus, no AMT adjustment is required on MACRS 3-, 5-, 7-, and 10-year property even if depreciated for regular tax purposes using the 200-percent declining-balance method (or section 1250 property depreciated using a method other than the straight-line method) provided that the bonus allowance is claimed. This rule for bonus depreciation property is subject to an exception. Specifically, if the depreciable basis of the qualifying bonus depreciation property for AMT purposes is different than the regular tax depreciable basis (i.e., the basis of the property is affected by another type of AMT adjustment in the year it is placed in service), the AMT bonus allowance is computed on the AMT basis (Reg.§ 1.168(k)-1(d)(1)(iii)), and the AMT depreciation deductions (computed using the MACRS method, recovery period, and convention used for regular tax purposes) are computed on the AMT basis as reduced by the amount of bonus depreciation allowed for AMT purposes (Reg.§ 1.168(k)-1(d)(2)(ii)).

When a taxpayer makes an election out of bonus depreciation, an AMT adjustment is only required if the property would otherwise have been subject to an AMT adjustment. In general, bonus depreciation may be claimed on new MACRS property with a recovery period of 20 years or less which is acquired after (a) September 10, 2001, and placed in service before January 1, 2005 or (b) acquired after December 31, 2007 and placed in service before January 1, 2010. See ¶ 127D.

These AMT rules for bonus depreciation claimed under Code Sec. 168(k) apply equally to bonus depreciation that is claimed on New York Liberty Zone property (¶ 127E), Gulf Opportunity Zone property (¶ 127F), Kansas Disaster Area property (¶ 127G), and Presidentially Declared Disaster Area property (¶ 127H).

Reporting AMT adjustment on Form 4626 or Form 6251. The MACRS depreciation "adjustment" is the difference between regular tax depreciation and AMT depreciation. To compute alternative minimum taxable income on Form 4626 (corporations) or Form 6251 (individuals), regular taxable income is increased by any positive depreciation adjustment (where regular tax MACRS depreciation exceeds AMT depreciation) and reduced by any negative adjustment (where AMT depreciation exceeds regular tax MACRS depreciation). After combining all positive and negative adjustments, the total net adjustment for post-1986 (MACRS) depreciation is entered on the appropriate line of the alternative minimum tax form (Form 6251 in the case of individuals and Form 4626 for corporations).

AMT adjustments for MACRS property placed in service before 1999

(1) For residential rental property and nonresidential real property placed in service before January 1, 1999, the allowable MACRS AMT deduction is computed under the alternative depreciation system (ADS) (i.e., straight-line method and 40-year recovery period). The AMT depreciation adjustment for MACRS residential and nonresidential real property, however, is repealed effective for property placed in service after December 31, 1998. The AMT deduction on other types of section 1250 property which is not depreciated using the straight-line method for regular tax purposes is computed using ADS if the property was placed in service before 1999 and the straight-line method and regular recovery period if the property was placed in service after 1998.

Example (1): A taxpayer places a 27.5-year residential rental building in service in May of 1998. The depreciable basis of the property is $100,000. MACRS depreciation for regular tax purposes in 2009 is $3,636 ($100,000 × 3.636%). ADS depreciation is $2,500 ($100,000 × 2.5%). The $1,136 difference is an AMT adjustment. If the building had been placed in service after 1998, regular tax and AMT depreciation would have been computed the same way and no AMT adjustment would have been required.

(2) For tangible personal property placed in service before January 1, 1999, and depreciated under the elective MACRS straight-line method for regular tax purposes, the MACRS deduction is recomputed under the alternative depreciation system (ADS) (i.e., by using the straight-line method over the ADS recovery period

for the property). No AMT depreciation adjustment is made for tangible personal property depreciated for regular tax purposes using the elective MACRS straight-line method effective for property placed in service after December 31, 1998.

Example (2): A taxpayer places a barge (10-year property) in service for business purposes on January 3, 1998. The barge cost $100,000. The taxpayer elects the straight-line MACRS method. Under this method, a 10-year recovery period applies. MACRS elective straight-line regular tax depreciation for 2008 is $10,000 ($100,000 × 5.00% (last year percentage from Table 8 at ¶ 180)). Under the MACRS alternative depreciation system (ADS), a 18-year recovery period applies. Allowable AMT depreciation for 2008 is $5,560 ($100,000 × 5.56% (Table 8 at ¶ 180)). The 2008 AMT depreciation adjustment is ($560) ($5000 – $5,560) (a negative or favorable AMT adjustment). If the furniture had been placed in service after 1998 and either the MACRS straight-line method or ADS method had been elected for regular tax purposes, regular tax and AMT depreciation would have been computed the same way and no AMT adjustment would have been required.

(3) For tangible personal property placed in service before January 1, 1999, and depreciated using the nonelective MACRS 150-percent declining-balance method or 200-percent declining-balance method for regular tax purposes, the MACRS AMT deduction is computed by using the 150-percent declining-balance method over the ADS recovery period. Effective for property placed in service after December 31, 1998, no AMT adjustment is made for tangible personal property depreciated under MACRS for regular tax purposes using the 150-percent declining-balance method. AMT depreciation on tangible personal property depreciated under MACRS for regular tax purposes using the 200-percent declining-balance method will be computed using the 150-percent declining-balance method and the depreciation period used by the taxpayer for regular tax purposes (rather than the applicable ADS depreciation period). Note that under MACRS, the 200-percent declining-balance method applies to 3-, 5-, 7-, and 10-year property that is not farming property and for which the 150-percent declining-balance method, MACRS straight-line method, or ADS method have not been elected. The 150-percent declining-balance method applies to 15- and 20-year property.

Example (3): Ten-year MACRS property costing $1,000 is placed in service in 2009. No bonus deduction is claimed. 2009 regular tax depreciation using the 200% declining-balance method, 10-year recovery period, and half-year convention is $100 ($1,000 × 10%) (Table 1 at ¶ 180). 2009 AMT depreciation using the 150% declining-balance method, 10-year recovery period, and half-year convention is $75 ($1,000 × 7.50%) (Table 14 at ¶ 180 (first-year recovery percentage for property with a 10-year recovery period). The AMT depreciation adjustment is $25 ($100 – $75).

Example (4): Assume the same facts as in *Example (3)*, except that the ten-year property was placed in service in 1998. In this case, AMT depreciation would be computed using the 150% declining-balance method and the *ADS recovery period* rather than the regular tax recovery period. Assume that the ADS recovery period is 15 years. The 2009 regular tax depreciation is $0 since the asset is fully depreciated. AMT depreciation for 2009 would be $59 ($1,000 × 5.91%) (Table 14 at ¶ 180 (twelfth year percentage for property with 15-year ADS recovery period)). The 2009 AMT adjustment is ($59) ($0 – $59) (a negative (favorable) adjustment on Form 6251 or Form 4626).

A taxpayer may avoid AMT depreciation adjustments on 3-, 5-, 7-, and 10-year section 1245 property placed in service after 1998 by electing to depreciate such property for regular tax purposes using the 150-percent declining-balance method. If this election is made, the depreciation deductions allowed for regular tax purposes will also be allowed for AMT purposes. (It is not necessary to make this election to avoid an AMT adjustment if the taxpayer claims bonus depreciation.) For property placed in service before 1999, the recovery period under this election for both regular and AMT depreciation is the applicable alternative depreciation system (ADS) recovery period for the property. If this election is made for property placed in service after calendar-year 1998, the standard recovery period (i.e., 3, 5, 7, or 10 years) applies for regular income tax and AMT purposes. The 150-percent declining-balance election is described in more detail at ¶ 84.

The following charts show how AMT tax depreciation is computed when regular tax depreciation is computed as shown.

MACRS PROPERTY FOR WHICH BONUS DEPRECIATION CLAIMED

If bonus depreciation is claimed on MACRS property, then regular tax depreciation and AMT depreciation is computed in the same manner. Further, the bonus depreciation allowance is also claimed in full for AMT purposes. See the preceding discussion.

MACRS PROPERTY PLACED IN SERVICE AFTER 1998

MACRS Regular Tax Depreciation Method (¶ 84)	*MACRS AMT Tax Depreciation Method*
200-percent declining-balance method (*3-*, *5-*, *7-*, *10-*year property which is not section 1250 real property)	Use 150-percent declining-balance method and regular tax depreciation period
150-percent declining-balance method (*15-*, *20-*year property which is not section 1250 real property)	No adjustment required, compute AMT and regular tax depreciation the same way
150-percent declining-balance method election (*3-*, *5-*, *7-*, *10*, *15*, *20-*year property which is not section 1250 property)	No adjustment required, compute AMT and regular tax depreciation the same way
Straight-line (*27.5-*year residential and *31.5-* or *39-*year nonresidential real property)	No adjustment required, compute AMT and regular tax depreciation the same way
Straight-line election (*3-*, *5-*, *7-*, *10-*, *15-*, *20-*year property)	No adjustment required, compute AMT and regular tax depreciation the same way
MACRS ADS method (elective or nonelective)	No adjustment required, compute AMT and regular tax depreciation the same way on real and personal property
Section 1250 Property if straight-line method not used	Compute AMT depreciation using straight-line method and regular tax depreciation period

MACRS PROPERTY PLACED IN SERVICE AFTER 1986 AND BEFORE 1999

MACRS Regular Tax Depreciation Method (¶ 84)	*MACRS AMT Tax Depreciation Method*
200-percent declining-balance method (*3-*, *5-*, *7-*, *10-*year property which is not section 1250 property)	Use 150-percent declining-balance method and ADS recovery period
150-percent declining-balance method (*15-*, *20-*year property which is not section 1250 property)	Use 150-percent declining-balance method and ADS recovery period
150-percent declining-balance method election (*3-*, *5-*, *7-*, *10*, *15*, *20-*year property which is not section 1250 property)	No adjustment required, compute AMT and regular tax depreciation the same way

MACRS Regular Tax Depreciation Method (¶ 84)	*MACRS AMT Tax Depreciation Method*
Straight-line (*27.5*-year residential real property and *31.5*- or *39*-year nonresidential real property)	Use ADS (recovery period 40 years)
Section 1250 property not depreciated using straight-line method	Use straight-line method and ADS recovery period
Straight-line election (*3-*, *5-*, *7-*, *10-*, *15-*, *20-*year property)	Use ADS
MACRS ADS method (elective or nonelective)	No adjustment required, compute AMT and regular tax depreciation the same way on real and personal property

In applying these rules, the same convention must be used in computing the MACRS deduction for AMT purposes that is used for computing such deduction for regular tax purposes.

The above rules are also used to refigure depreciation for AMT purposes that is capitalized to inventory under the uniform capitalization rules of Code Sec. 263A.

Pre-MACRS property

The following items pertaining to depreciation constitute tax preference items that must be added to regular taxable income in computing AMTI. These preferences are measured in an item-by-item manner that ignores negative balances (where AMT depreciation exceeds the depreciation for regular tax purposes on an item of property). In other words, the adjustment is computed separately for each item of property and only positive (unfavorable) adjustments are taken into account.

(1) The excess of accelerated depreciation on nonrecovery (pre-ACRS/MACRS) real property over straight-line depreciation.

(2) For noncorporate taxpayers and personal holding companies only, the excess of accelerated depreciation on leased nonrecovery (pre-ACRS/MACRS) personal property over straight-line depreciation.

(3) The excess of the ACRS deduction for 15-, 18-, or 19-year property (whichever applies) or low-income housing over the straight-line deduction that is available if salvage value is not included and a 15-, 18-, or 19-year recovery period (whichever applies) for real property or a 15-year recovery period for low-income housing is used. There is no tax preference if the actual recovery period used for regular tax purposes is longer than 15, 18, or 19 years (whichever applies).

(4) For noncorporate taxpayers and personal holding companies only, the excess of the ACRS deduction for leased recovery property (excluding 15-, 18-, or 19-year real property and low-income housing) over the straight-line depreciation deduction that is available if a half-year convention is used, salvage value is not included, and the following recovery periods are used:

In the case of:	*The recovery period is:*
3-year property	5 years
5-year property	8 years
10-year property	15 years
15-year public utility property	22 years

However, there is no tax preference if the actual recovery period used for regular tax purposes is longer than that listed above.

Depreciation claimed as employee business expense or other type of miscellaneous itemized deduction

It is not necessary to make a depreciation adjustment for AMT purposes if the depreciation is claimed on Schedule A as a miscellaneous itemized deduction subject to the 2% of adjusted gross income (AGI) floor. This is because the entire deduction on Schedule A for miscellaneous itemized deductions is disallowed for AMT purposes. See, also, the discussion of the allowed or allowable rules at ¶ 75.

¶ 172

Corporate Adjusted Current Earnings Adjustment

C corporations must adjust AMTI for adjusted current earnings (ACE). The ACE adjustment is reported on line 4(e) of Form 4626 (Alternative Minimum Tax - Corporations) and computed on a worksheet contained in the instructions for Form 4626.

ACE means the pre-adjustment AMTI reduced or increased by required adjustments, including an adjustment for ACE depreciation (Code Sec. 56(g)(4)); "pre-adjustment AMTI" means AMTI determined without the ACE adjustment and without the alternative tax net operating loss deduction.

Pre-adjustment AMTI is increased by 75 percent of any excess ACE over pre-adjustment AMTI and is decreased by 75 percent of any excess pre-adjustment AMTI over ACE. The decrease for any tax year is limited to the excess of the aggregate increases in AMTI for prior tax years over the aggregate decreases in AMTI for such prior years (Code Sec. 56(g)).

For purposes of computing ACE, the ACE depreciation expense is subtracted from the depreciation deductions already included in the pre-adjustment AMTI (the depreciation deduction claimed for regular tax purposes as modified by the AMT depreciation adjustments and the AMT accelerated depreciation tax preference items). The difference (which may represent a positive or negative amount) is the ACE depreciation adjustment component that is includible in ACE. The amount of allowable ACE depreciation depends mainly upon the method used and the date that an asset was placed in service.

(1) For property generally placed in service after 1993, depreciation for ACE purposes is determined in the same manner as for determining AMTI (¶ 170) (Code Sec. 56(g)(4), as amended by the Omnibus Budget Reconciliation Act of 1993 (P.L. 103-66)). Thus, the ACE depreciation component is in effect eliminated because there is no difference (between the depreciation deduction included in pre-adjustment AMTI and the depreciation deduction computed for ACE purposes) includible in ACE. See line 2(b)(1) worksheet instructions.

The bonus depreciation deduction is not allowed when computing earnings and profits (Reg. § 1.168(k)-1(f)(7)). Generally, no deduction is allowed when computing ACE for items that are not deductible when computing earnings and profits. Such amounts are entered on line 4 of the ACE worksheet. However, it does not appear that bonus depreciation should be entered on line 4 because this rule only applies to deduction items that are permanently disallowed (see instructions to line 4). The bonus deduction is not permanently disallowed for earnings and profits purposes; it is deferred insofar as the disallowed bonus deduction will be recovered over the earnings and profits depreciation period for the asset. See ¶ 310 for rules regarding earnings and profits.

(2) For property placed in service before 1994 in a tax year that begins after 1989, ACE depreciation is computed under the alternative MACRS depreciation

system (ADS) using the straight-line method over the ADS recovery period. The ACE depreciation adjustment must continue to be determined in this manner for property subject to this adjustment.

(3) For MACRS property placed in service in a tax year beginning before 1990, ACE depreciation is computed on the adjusted basis of the property for AMTI purposes as of the close of the last tax year beginning before 1990 using the straight-line method over the remainder of the ADS recovery period. The same convention that applies for regular tax purposes must be used to determine the remaining ADS recovery period.

> ***Example (1):*** A calendar-year corporation purchased and placed in service on August 1, 1987, a telephone distribution plant. This was the only depreciable property placed in service during 1987. Thus, the half-year convention is the applicable convention. The adjusted basis of the property at the close of December 31, 1989, for AMTI purposes is $2,150,000. The alternate MACRS recovery period that would have applied to such property is 24 years (from July 1, 1987, through June 30, 2011). Thus, the recovery period for ACE purposes begins on January 1, 1990, and ends on June 30, 2011. For ACE purposes, the depreciation deduction determined under the straight-line method over each of the remaining years of the 21½-year ACE recovery period is $100,000.

(4) For ACRS recovery property placed in service in a tax year beginning before 1990, ACE depreciation is computed on the adjusted basis of the property for regular tax purposes as of the close of the last tax year beginning before 1990 using the straight-line method over the remainder of the ADS recovery period had such recovery period originally applied. The same convention that applies for regular tax purposes must be used to determine the remaining ADS recovery period, except that the mid-quarter convention does not apply.

> ***Example (2):*** A calendar-year corporation purchased and placed in service on December 1, 1986, a telephone distribution plant. The applicable convention that would have applied to such property without regard to the mid-quarter convention is the half-year convention. The adjusted basis of the property on January 1, 1990, for regular tax purposes is $1,025,000. The alternative MACRS recovery period for such property is 24 years (from July 1, 1986, through June 30, 2010). Thus, the ACE recovery period begins on January 1, 1990, and ends on June 30, 2010. For ACE purposes, the depreciation deductions under the straight-line method over each of the remaining 20½ years of the ACE recovery period is $50,000.

(5) For property depreciated under a method of depreciation not expressed in a term of years, certain public utility property, films and video tapes, and sound recordings, ACE depreciation is determined by treating the depreciation allowed for regular tax purposes as the amount allowed under the alternative depreciation system without regard to when such property was placed in service.

(6) For pre-1981 property and property not subject to ACRS or MACRS because of the anti-churning rules, ACE depreciation is determined in the same manner as for regular tax purposes.

Basis in subsequent years for ACE computations is derived from the use of the ACE depreciation method.

The ACE adjustment for AMT purposes does not apply to S corporations, regulated investment companies, real estate investment trusts, or real estate mortgage investment conduits.

MACRS Depreciation Calculations and Tables

¶ 179

Computing MACRS Deductions Without Optional Tables

The MACRS deduction is computed without the optional percentage tables (¶ 180) by first determining the rate of depreciation (dividing the number one by the recovery period). This basic rate is multiplied by the declining-balance factor allowed for the class of property being depreciated (1.5 or 2 for the 150-percent or 200-percent declining-balance method, respectively, whichever is applicable). In general, the 200-percent DB method applies to 3-, 5-, 7-, and 10-year property unless the 150-percent DB method, ADS, or the straight-line method is applies or is elected. The 150-percent DB method applies to 15- and 20-year property unless ADS or the straight-line method is elected. See ¶ 84.

The computation of MACRS deductions without the use of tables is discussed in detail by the IRS in Rev. Proc. 87-57, 1987-2 CB 687.

The adjusted depreciable basis of the property is multiplied by the declining-balance rate and the applicable convention is applied in computing depreciation for the first tax year. (This discussion assumes that tax years are 12 months in duration; for short tax years, see ¶ 132.) The depreciation claimed in the first tax year is subtracted from the adjusted depreciable basis before applying the declining-balance rate in determining the depreciation deduction for the second tax year.

The depreciation rate (in percentage terms) may also be determined by dividing the specified declining-balance percentage (150 percent or 200 percent) by the applicable recovery period.

A depreciation rate based on the straight-line method is used beginning in the tax year in which the depreciation deduction is greater than the depreciation deduction that would result using the 150-percent or 200-percent declining-balance method (whichever is applicable for the property).

Under the MACRS straight-line method, a new applicable depreciation rate is determined for each tax year in the applicable recovery period. For any tax year, the applicable depreciation rate (in percentage terms) is determined by dividing one by the length of the applicable recovery period remaining as of the beginning of such tax year. The rate is applied to the unrecovered basis of such property in conjunction with the appropriate convention. If, as of the beginning of any tax year, the remaining recovery period is less than one year, the applicable depreciation rate under the straight-line method for that year is 100 percent.

The adjusted depreciable basis is the cost or other basis reduced by any Code Sec. 179 expense allowance (¶ 300) and first-year bonus depreciation (¶ 127D), including bonus depreciation claimed on New York Liberty Zone property (¶ 127E), Gulf Opportunity Zone property (¶ 127F), Kansas Disaster Area property (¶ 127G), and Disaster Assistance Property (¶ 127H) (Reg. § 1.168(k)-1(a)(2)). When computing bonus depreciation, the cost or other basis is first reduced by the section 179 allowance. For example, if an item of new machinery costs $2,000 and the taxpayer expenses $500 under Code Sec. 179, the cost is first reduced to $1,500. Bonus depreciation is then computed ($1,500 × 50% = $750). The cost is then reduced by the bonus depreciation to $750 ($1,500 – $750) and the regular MACRS depreciation deductions are computed with reference to this amount (the adjusted depreciable basis). See ¶ 127D for additional examples.

Example using 200-percent DB method and half-year convention

Example (1): An item of 7-year property is purchased for $10,000 and placed in service in the current tax year. No Code Sec. 179 expense allowance or bonus depreciation is claimed. The adjusted depreciable basis of the property is $10,000. The basic rate is 1 divided by 7, or 14.285%. The 200% declining-balance method rate of 28.57% is determined by multiplying 14.285% by 2. The adjusted depreciable basis of the property ($10,000) is multiplied by 28.57% to obtain $2,857, which is then divided by 2 (for the half-year convention) to arrive at the MACRS deduction of $1,429 for the first tax year.

For the second tax year, depreciation is computed by subtracting $1,429 from $10,000 to determine the $8,571 remaining adjusted depreciable basis of the property. This amount ($8,571) is multiplied by 28.57% to determine the MACRS deduction of $2,449.

For the third tax year, a similar procedure is used to determine the MACRS deduction of $1,749 ($8,571 – $2,449 = $6,122 × 28.57%).

For the fourth tax year, the MACRS deduction is $1,249 ($6,122 – $1,749 = $4,373 × 28.57%).

For the fifth tax year, the MACRS deduction is $893 ($4,373 – $1,249 = $3,124 × 28.57%).

For the sixth tax year, depreciation under the 200% declining-balance method would be $637 ($3,124 – $893 = $2,231 × 28.57%). However, a larger MACRS deduction is obtained by switching to the straight-line method ($3,124 – $893 = $2,231 × 40% (the straight-line rate is 1 divided by the 2.5 years remaining in the recovery period at the beginning of the tax year) = $892).

For the seventh tax year, depreciation is computed under the same method as in the sixth year and is $893 ($2,231 – $892 = $1,339 × 66.67% (the straight-line rate is 1 divided by 1.5 years remaining in the recovery period at the beginning of the tax year)).

For the eighth tax year, the MACRS deduction is the remaining basis of the property ($1,339 – $893 = $446). The straight-line rate for such year is 100% because the remaining recovery period at the beginning of the tax year (one-half year) is less than one year ($446 × 1.00 = $446).

Example using 150-percent DB method and half-year convention

Example (2): Depreciation on 5-year property purchased by a calendar-year taxpayer in January of the current tax year at a cost of $15,000 is computed under the elective MACRS 150% declining-balance method over a 5-year recovery period using the half-year convention. A $5,000 Code Sec. 179 expense allowance is claimed. No bonus depreciation is claimed. The adjusted depreciable basis of the property is $10,000 ($15,000 – $5,000).

Depreciation computed without the use of the IRS tables is determined as follows: the declining-balance depreciation rate is determined and compared with the straight-line rate. A switch is made to the straight-line rate in the year depreciation equals or exceeds that determined under the declining-balance method. The applicable rate is applied to the unrecovered basis. The 150% declining-balance depreciation rate is 30% (1 ÷ 5 (recovery period) × 1.5). The straight-line rate (which changes each year) is 1 divided by the length of the applicable recovery period remaining as of the beginning of each tax year (after considering the applicable convention for purposes of determining how much of the applicable recovery period remains as of the beginning of the year). The switch to the straight-line method is made in year 4 since this is the first year that the straight-line rate is greater than the 150% DB rate. For year 4, the straight-line rate is 40% (1 ÷ 2.5). For year 5, the straight-line rate is 66.67% (1 ÷ 1.5). For year 6, the straight-line rate is 100% because the remaining recovery period is less than one year.

Yr.	Method	Rate		Unrecovered Depreciable Basis		Depreciation
1	DB	30%	×	$10,000 × 30% (half-yr. conv.)	=	$1,500
2	DB	30%	×	(10,000 – 1,500) = $8,500	=	2,550
3	DB	30%	×	(8,500 – 2,550) = 5,950	=	1,785
4	SL	40%	×	(5,950 – 1,785) = 4,165	=	1,666
5	SL	66.67%	×	(4,165 – 1,666) = 2,499	=	1,666
6	SL	100%	×	(2,499 – 1,666) = 833	=	833
				Total		$10,000

Example using straight-line method and half-year convention

Example (3): Five-year property is placed in service in March of the current tax year at a cost of $100. No Code Sec. 179 expense allowance or bonus depreciation is claimed. An election is made to depreciate the property under the MACRS straight-line method over a five-year recovery period using the half-year convention. The depreciation deduction for the first tax year is $10 ($100 × 20% (the straight-line rate is 1 ÷ 5) × ½ (to reflect the half-year convention)).

For the second tax year, depreciation is computed by subtracting $10 from $100 to arrive at the $90 remaining adjusted depreciable basis of the property. Such amount ($90) is multiplied by 22.22% (the straight-line rate is 1/4.5 (the remaining recovery period at the beginning of the second tax year)) to determine the MACRS deduction of $20.

For the third tax year, the MACRS deduction is $20 (($90 – $20) × 28.57% (the straight-line rate is 1/3.5)).

For the fourth tax year, the MACRS deduction is $20 (($70 – $20) × 40% (the straight-line rate is 1/2.5)).

For the fifth tax year, the MACRS deduction is $20 (($50 – $20) × 66.67% (the straight-line rate is 1/1.5)).

For the sixth tax year, the MACRS deduction is $10, the remaining unrecovered adjusted depreciable basis of the property ($30 – $20 = $10). The straight-line rate for such tax year is 100% because the remaining recovery period at the beginning of the tax year (one-half year) is less than one year ($10 × 100% = $10).

Computation using mid-quarter convention

The MACRS deduction for the first tax year for property subject to the mid-quarter convention (¶ 92) is computed by first determining the depreciation deduction for the full tax year and then multiplying it by the following percentages for the quarter of the tax year that the property is placed in service:

Quarter of acquisition

First quarter	87.5%
Second quarter	62.5%
Third quarter	37.5%
Fourth quarter	12.5%

The MACRS mid-quarter depreciation tables (see Tables 2, 3, 4, and 5 at ¶ 180) incorporate these percentages in the first year depreciation percentage. Thus, these percentages only need to be used if a taxpayer computes depreciation without the table percentages in the year the property is placed into service.

If property subject to the mid-quarter convention is disposed of prior to the end of its recovery period, then the property is considered disposed of at the midpoint of the quarter of the disposition. To compute the allowable depreciation deduction, multiply the depreciation deduction for a full year by the percentage from the table below for the quarter that the property is disposed in. These table percentages, however, should not be used if the property is disposed of in the tax year in which the recovery period ends. See ¶ 160.

Quarter of disposition

First quarter	12.5%
Second quarter	37.5%
Third quarter	62.5%
Fourth quarter	87.5%

Example (4): A calendar-year taxpayer made the following purchases during the tax year: a $4,000 machine that is placed in service in January; $1,000 of office furniture that is placed in service in September; and a $5,000 computer that is placed in service in October. No Code Sec. 179 deduction or bonus depreciation is claimed. The total of the bases of all property placed in service is $10,000. Because the basis of the computer ($5,000), which was placed in service during the last 3 months of the tax year, exceeds 40% of the total bases of all property ($10,000) placed in service during the tax year, the mid-quarter convention must be used for all 3 items. The machine and office furniture are 7-year property and the computer is 5-year property under MACRS.

Depreciation for the machine and furniture is computed by dividing 1 by 7 resulting in a rate of 14.285%. Since the 7-year property is depreciated using the 200% declining-balance method, 14.285% is multiplied by 2 to arrive at the declining-balance rate, 28.57%. The depreciable basis of the machine ($4,000) is multiplied by 28.57% to compute the depreciation, $1,143, for a full year. Since the machine was placed in service in the first quarter of the tax year, $1,143 is multiplied by 87.5% (the mid-quarter percentage for the first quarter) to arrive at the MACRS deduction of $1,000 for the machine for the tax year.

Depreciation for the furniture is determined by multiplying the basis of the furniture ($1,000) by 28.57% to arrive at the depreciation, $286, for the full year. Because the furniture was placed in service in the third quarter of the tax year, $286 is multiplied by 37.5% to arrive at the MACRS deduction of $107 for the furniture for the tax year.

Depreciation for the computer is computed by dividing 1 by 5 resulting in a rate of 20%. Because 5-year property is depreciated using the 200% declining-balance method, 20% is multiplied by 2 to arrive at the declining-balance rate of 40%. The depreciable basis of the computer ($5,000) is multiplied by 40%, resulting in depreciation of $2,000 for a full year. Because the computer was placed in service in the fourth quarter of the tax year, $2,000 is multiplied by 12.5% (mid-quarter percentage for the fourth quarter) to arrive at the MACRS deduction of $250 for the computer for the tax year.

In determining whether the mid-quarter convention applies, the cost of the property is reduced by any Code Sec. 179 expense deduction claimed but not by any bonus depreciation claimed (see ¶ 92). Also, the amount of Code Sec. 179 expense allowance (¶ 300) or bonus depreciation deduction (¶ 127D) to which a taxpayer is entitled is not affected by the mid-quarter convention. For example, if a taxpayer places a machine costing $350,000 in service in December 2009 and the mid-quarter convention applies, the taxpayer may expense $250,000 (the 2009 limit) under Code Sec. 179.

Computing MACRS depreciation when there is a basis adjustment such as a casualty loss during recovery period

When the basis of a depreciable property is affected by a casualty loss, the taxpayer must stop using the MACRS depreciation table percentages in the year of the casualty loss (Rev. Proc. 87-57, Section 8.02). The basis of the property, as reduced by any deductible the casualty loss and increased by any repair expenses, is multiplied by the applicable depreciation rate for the tax year of the casualty. The entire basis of the property is recovered over the remaining depreciation period.

Example (5): A taxpayer purchased 7-year property in 2008 for $100,000. Assume that no bonus depreciation or Code Sec. 179 expense allowance was claimed. The first-year deduction, asssuming that the half year convention applies, is $14,290 ($100,000 x 14.29% first-year table percentage). In 2009, the property is damaged in a hurricane. The deductible casualty loss was $10,000. $15,000 was spent to repair the property. The adjusted basis of the property at the end of 2009 is $90,710 ($100,000 - $14,290 - $10,000 + $15,000).

The applicable 200 percent declining balance rate for 7-year property is 1/7 x 2 or 28.57%. The 2009 deduction is $26,201 ($90,710 x 28.57%).

Depreciation is computed over the remaining recovery period by applying the 200 percent declining balance rate to the basis that remains as of the beginning of each tax year during the remaining recovery period. As explained above, a switch is made to the straight-line percentage in the year that it produces a larger deduction than the 200 percent declining balance method.

Yr.	*Method*	*Rate*		*Unrecovered Depreciable Basis*		*Depreciation*
2008	DB	14.29%	×	$100,000	=	$14,290
2009	DB	28.57%	×	$90,710	=	$25,916
2010	DB	28.57%	×	$64,794	=	$18,512
2011	DB	28.57%	×	$46,282	=	$13,223
2012	DB	28.57%	×	$33,059	=	$9,445
2013	SL	40%	×	$23,614 = 833	=	9,446
2014	SL	66.67%	×	$14,168	=	$9,446
2015	SL	100%	×	$4,722	=	$4,722
				Total		$105,000

The total depreciation deductions are equal to the original cost ($100,000) less the deducted casualty loss ($10,000) plus the repair costs ($15,000).

When an addition or improvement is made to a property it is depreciated separately over the MACRS recovery period that applies to the property to which the addition or improvement is made. However, in the case of a casualty, the capitalized repair costs are included in the depreciable basis of the damaged property and recovered over the remaining recovery period of the damaged property. See IRS Publication 946 (Depreciation and Amortization).

If MACRS residential rental property or nonresidential real property is damaged in a casualty, a taxpayer should decrease the basis of the property as of the beginning of the tax year of the casualty by the amount of any casualty loss and increase the basis by any repair costs incurred during the tax year. The straight-line table percentages may not be used. Instead divide 1 by the number of years that remain in the recovery period and apply this percentage to the remaining basis as of the beginning of the tax year.

Example (6): An MACRS residential rental property (27.5-year recovery period) is placed in service in 2008 in March by a calendar year taxpayer. The building cost $100,000. The first year deduction using the applicable table percentage was $2,879 ($100,000 × 2.879%). If the taxpayer deducts a $20,000 casualty loss in 2009 and spends $5,000 in repair costs during 2009, the basis of the property as of the end of 2009 is $85,000 ($100,000 - $20,000 + $5,000). Under the mid-month convention 9.5 months depreciation were claimed in 2008 (mid-month of March through December). This is the equivalent of .79 years (9.5 months/12 months). The remaining recovery period as of the beginning of 2009 is 26.71 years (27.5 – .79). The applicable straight-line rate for 2009 is 3.744% (1/26.71). The depreciation deduction for 2009 is $3,182 ($85,000 × 3.744 %). The applicable straight-line rate for 2010 3.890% (1/25.71). Assuming no additional repair expenses are paid in 2010, the deduction for 2010 is $3,183 ($85,000 – $3,182) × 3.890%)).

The preceding computation rules also apply when there are other types of basis adjustments (other than for casualty loss deductions) to an MACRS property in a tax year after it is placed into service. For example, basis may be reduced or increased due to changes in a contingent sales price or forgiveness of debt (Proposed Reg.§ 1.168-2(d)(3) at ¶ 525).

¶ 180

Computing MACRS Deductions With Tables

MACRS depreciation tables contain the annual depreciation percentage rates that are applied to the adjusted depreciable basis of a depreciable asset in each year of its recovery (depreciation) period. Adjusted depreciable basis is generally equal to cost less the Code Sec. 179 allowance (¶ 300) and any amount claimed as a bonus depreciation deduction (¶ 127D and following)). Bonus depreciation is 50% of cost after reduction by any amount expensed under Code Sec. 179 Reg.§ 1.168(k)-1(a)(2). The regular MACRS depreciation deductions are then computed on the adjusted depreciable basis (cost as reduced by the section 179 expense allowance and bonus depreciation).

The depreciation tables generally may be used to compute depreciation instead of the statutorily prescribed method and convention over the applicable recovery period. The tables incorporate the appropriate convention and a switch from the declining-balance method to the straight-line method in the year that the latter provides a depreciation allowance equal to, or larger than, the former. (Note: The Code provides for a switch to the straight-line method for the first year for which it will yield a larger allowance). The tables may be used for any item of property (that otherwise qualifies for MACRS) placed in service in a tax year (Rev. Proc. 87-57, 1987-2 CB 687, as amplified and clarified by Rev. Proc. 89-15, 1989-1 CB 816).

Exceptions

If a table is used to compute the annual depreciation allowance for any item of property, it must be used throughout the entire recovery period of such property. However, a taxpayer may not continue to use a table if there are any adjustments to the basis of the property for reasons other than (1) depreciation allowances (such as a reduction for a casualty loss), or (2) an addition or improvement to such property that is subject to depreciation as a separate item of property.

If the basis of property is reduced as a result of a casualty to the property or some other mid-stream basis adjustment, the tables may no longer be used and depreciation for the year of adjustment and the remainder of the recovery period is computed on the amount of adjusted basis of the property at the *end* of the tax year of adjustment and the remaining recovery period. See ¶ 179 for an example of the computation.

The MACRS depreciation tables may not be used to depreciate property in a short tax year or thereafter. See ¶ 132 and ¶ 134 for short tax year computations. The depreciation table percentages are also inapplicable if an asset is disposed of before the end of its recovery (depreciation) period. See ¶ 160. However, the examples below illustrate how to make adjust the table percentage result in the year of an early disposition.

Application

The appropriate table depends on the depreciation system (general MACRS (GDS) or alternative MACRS (ADS)), and the applicable method, convention and recovery period. The tables list the percentage depreciation rates to be applied to the unadjusted basis of property in each tax year.

Tables 1 through 13 may be used for any property placed in service during a tax year. Tables 14 through 18 must be used for the alternative minimum tax computation or if a taxpayer has elected the MACRS 150-percent declining-balance method for regular tax depreciation calculations.

For three-, five-, seven-, and ten-year farm business property generally placed in service after 1988, the 200-percent declining-balance method is not available. The 150-percent declining-balance method with a switch to the straight-line method must be used. Consequently, for such property, Tables 1-5 may not be used. Instead, Tables 14-18, which incorporate the 150-percent declining-balance method and the appropriate convention, may be used.

Examples of calculations using MACRS percentage tables

The following examples illustrate how to use the depreciation tables to calculate MACRS deductions.

Example (1): An item of 5-year property costing $21,000 is placed in service in August 2009. If the taxpayer claims a $1,000 section 179 expense allowance, MACRS bonus depreciation is equal to $10,000 (($21,000 – $1,000) × 50%) and the basis, prior to the computation of the regular MACRS depreciation allowances is reduced to $10,000 ($21,000 – $1,000 – $10,000). Assume the half-year convention applies and GDS (200% DB) is chosen. The Table 1 percentages for 5-year property are applied to the $10,000 adjusted depreciable basis as follows:

Year	*Calculation*		*Deduction*
2009	$10,000 × 20%		$ 2,000
2010	$10,000 × 32%		3,200
2011	$10,000 × 19.20%		1,920
2012	$10,000 × 11.52%		1,152
2013	$10,000 × 11.52%		1,152
2014	$10,000 × 5.76%		576
		Total	$10,000

Example (2): Suppose that the 5-year property in *Example (1)* was sold in 2009. Technically, the tables may not be used to compute the deduction since the year 3 percentage for 2009 (19.20%) does not reflect the half-year convention (which allows one-half of a full year's depreciation in the year of disposition). However, this problem can be circumvented by using the year 3 table percentage but only claiming one-half of the deduction so computed ($10,000 × 19.20% × 50% = $960).

Example (3): Nonresidential real property is placed in service in March of 2009 by a calendar-year taxpayer. The cost of the building (excluding land) is $100,000. The taxpayer chooses to compute depreciation using the GDS percentages based on the straight-line method and 39-year recovery period. Accordingly, the Table 7A percentages are used. The column 3 percentages apply because the building was placed in service in the third month (March) of the tax year.

Year	*Calculation*		*Deduction*
2009	$100,000 × 2.033%		$ 2,033
2010 - 2047	$100,000 × 2.564%		2,564
2048	$100,000 × 0.535%		535
		Total	$100,000

Example (4): Assume the same facts as *Example (3)* except that the building was sold in December 2012. The property was in service for 11.5 months during the 2012 calendar tax year (January 1 through Mid-December). Note that the mid-month convention applies to real property; therefore, the building was considered sold in mid-December and one-half month's depreciation is allowed for that month. Depreciation for 2012 is computed as follows: $100,000 × 2.564% (column 3 percentage for property placed in service in March) × 11.5/12 (to reflect 11.5 months of a full year's deduction) = $2,457.

Example (5): An item of construction equipment costing $10,000 is placed in service in December 2009 by a calendar year taxpayer. This is the only depreciable property placed in service during 2009. The equipment is five-year property with a MACRS alternative depreciation system (ADS) recovery period of 6 years (Asset Class 15.0 at ¶ 191). The Taxpayer elects ADS, does not expense any amount under Code Sec. 179, and elects out of first-year bonus depreciation. The midquarter convention applies since more than 40% of the bases of all personal property was placed in service in the last quarter of the tax year (¶ 92). Depreciation should be calculated using the 6-year column from Table 12 (ADS mid-quarter convention table for property placed in service in the fourth quarter). The calculations are as follows:

Year	*Calculation*	*Deduction*
2009	$10,000 × 2.08%	$ 208
2010	$10,000 × 16.67%	1,667
2011	$10,000 × 16.67%	1,667
2012	$10,000 × 16.67%	1,667
2013	$10,000 × 16.66%	1,666
2014	$10,000 × 16.67%	1,667
2015	$10,000 × 14.58%	1,458
	Total	$10,000

Example (6): Assume the same facts as in *Example (5)* except that the machinery is sold in January of 2011. Under the mid-quarter convention the property is treated as sold on the mid-point of the first quarter (i.e., mid-February) and one and one-half months of a full year's depreciation may be deducted. Depreciation for 2011 is, therefore, $208 ($10,000 × 16.67% × 1.5/12 (to reflect one and one-half months depreciation)).

Disposition in last year of recovery period

For rules regarding the computation of depreciation on an item of personal property disposed of in the last year of its recovery period see ¶ 160.

Partial business use computation

If a depreciable asset is only used partially for business/investment purposes, the cost of the asset is multiplied by the business/investment use percentage. Any amount expensed under Code Sec. 179 is then subtracted from this amount.

Example (7): A new machine costing $100,000 is purchased on January 17, 2009. The machine is 5-year property and is used 80% for business in 2009. The taxpayer elects to expense $20,000 of the cost.

Regular first-year depreciation using the first-year table percentage (20%) is $12,000 computed as follows:

(($100,000 × 80%) – $20,000) × 20% = $12,000

Electronic depreciation calculator

An interactive calculator for computing MACRS deductions and creating depreciation schedules is available on CCH IntelliConnect.under the Practice Tools node of the browse tree.

→Caution: Tables 1-5 may not be used for three-, five-, seven-, or ten-year farm business property. Instead, Tables 14-18 may be used, depending on the appropriate depreciation convention.←

INDEX TO MACRS PERCENTAGE TABLES

MACRS INDIAN RESERVATION PROPERTY TABLES (see ¶ 124)

Recovery Period	*Method*	*Convention*	*Table*	*Page*
22 years	S/L	Mid-month	22	467

→Caution: Table 1, below, may not be used for three-, five-, seven-, or ten-year farm business property generally placed in service after 1988. Table 14, below, incorporates the 150-percent declining-balance method and a half-year convention that may be used for such property.←

TABLE 1
General Depreciation System
Applicable Depreciation Method: 200- or 150-Percent
Declining Balance Switching to Straight Line
Applicable Recovery Periods: 3, 5, 7, 10, 15, 20 years
Applicable Convention: Half-Year

If the Recovery Year is:	and the Recovery Period is:					
	3-year	5-year	7-year	10-year	15-year	20-year
	the Depreciation Rate is:					
1	33.33	20.00	14.29	10.00	5.00	3.750
2	44.45	32.00	24.49	18.00	9.50	7.219
3	14.81	19.20	17.49	14.40	8.55	6.677
4	7.41	11.52	12.49	11.52	7.70	6.177
5		11.52	8.93	9.22	6.93	5.713
6		5.76	8.92	7.37	6.23	5.285
7			8.93	6.55	5.90	4.888
8			4.46	6.55	5.90	4.522
9				6.56	5.91	4.462
10				6.55	5.90	4.461
11				3.28	5.91	4.462
12					5.90	4.461
13					5.91	4.462
14					5.90	4.461
15					5.91	4.462
16					2.95	4.461
17						4.462
18						4.461
19						4.462
20						4.461
21						2.231

→Caution: Table 2, below, may not be used for three-, five-, seven-, or ten-year farm business property generally placed in service after 1988. Table 15, below, incorporates the 150-percent declining-balance method and the mid-quarter convention that may be used for such property.←

TABLE 2
General Depreciation System
Applicable Depreciation Method: 200- or 150-Percent Declining Balance Switching to Straight Line
Applicable Recovery Periods: 3, 5, 7, 10, 15, 20 years
Applicable Convention: Mid-quarter (property placed in service in first quarter)

If the Recovery Year is:	and the Recovery Period is:					
	3-year	5-year	7-year	10-year	15-year	20-year
	the Depreciation Rate is:					
1	58.33	35.00	25.00	17.50	8.75	6.563
2	27.78	26.00	21.43	16.50	9.13	7.000
3	12.35	15.60	15.31	13.20	8.21	6.482
4	1.54	11.01	10.93	10.56	7.39	5.996
5		11.01	8.75	8.45	6.65	5.546
6		1.38	8.74	6.76	5.99	5.130
7			8.75	6.55	5.90	4.746
8			1.09	6.55	5.91	4.459
9				6.56	5.90	4.459
10				6.55	5.91	4.459
11				0.82	5.90	4.459
12					5.91	4.460
13					5.90	4.459
14					5.91	4.460
15					5.90	4.459
16					0.74	4.460
17						4.459
18						4.460
19						4.459
20						4.460
21						0.557

→Caution: Table 3, below, may not be used for three-, five-, seven-, or ten-year farm business property generally placed in service after 1988. Table 16, below, incorporates the 150-percent declining-balance method and the mid-quarter convention that may be used for such property.←

TABLE 3
General Depreciation System
Applicable Depreciation Method: 200- or 150-Percent
Declining Balance Switching to Straight Line
Applicable Recovery Periods: 3, 5, 7, 10, 15, 20 years
Applicable Convention: Mid-quarter (property placed in
service in second quarter)

If the Recovery Year is:	and the Recovery Period is:					
	3-year	5-year	7-year	10-year	15-year	20-year
	the Depreciation Rate is:					
1	41.67	25.00	17.85	12.50	6.25	4.688
2	38.89	30.00	23.47	17.50	9.38	7.148
3	14.14	18.00	16.76	14.00	8.44	6.612
4	5.30	11.37	11.97	11.20	7.59	6.116
5		11.37	8.87	8.96	6.83	5.658
6		4.26	8.87	7.17	6.15	5.233
7			8.87	6.55	5.91	4.841
8			3.33	6.55	5.90	4.478
9				6.56	5.91	4.463
10				6.55	5.90	4.463
11				2.46	5.91	4.463
12					5.90	4.463
13					5.91	4.463
14					5.90	4.463
15					5.91	4.462
16					2.21	4.463
17						4.462
18						4.463
19						4.462
20						4.463
21						1.673

→*Caution: Table 4, below, may not be used for three-, five-, seven-, or ten-year farm business property generally placed in service after 1988. Table 17, below, incorporates the 150-percent declining-balance method and the mid-quarter convention that may be used for such property.*←

TABLE 4
General Depreciation System
Applicable Depreciation Method: 200-or 150-Percent
Declining Balance Switching to Straight Line
Applicable Recovery Periods: 3, 5, 7, 10, 15, 20 years
Applicable Convention: Mid-quarter (property placed in
service in third quarter)

If the Recovery Year is:	and the Recovery Period is:					
	3-year	5-year	7-year	10-year	15-year	20-year
	the Depreciation Rate is:					
1	25.00	15.00	10.71	7.50	3.75	2.813
2	50.00	34.00	25.51	18.50	9.63	7.289
3	16.67	20.40	18.22	14.80	8.66	6.742
4	8.33	12.24	13.02	11.84	7.80	6.237
5		11.30	9.30	9.47	7.02	5.769
6		7.06	8.85	7.58	6.31	5.336
7			8.86	6.55	5.90	4.936
8			5.53	6.55	5.90	4.566
9				6.56	5.91	4.460
10				6.55	5.90	4.460
11				4.10	5.91	4.460
12					5.90	4.460
13					5.91	4.461
14					5.90	4.460
15					5.91	4.461
16					3.69	4.460
17						4.461
18						4.460
19						4.461
20						4.460
21						2.788

→Caution: Table 5, below, may not be used for three-, five-, seven-, or ten-year farm business property generally placed in service after 1988. Table 18, below, incorporates the 150-percent declining-balance method and the mid-quarter convention that may be used for such property.←

TABLE 5
General Depreciation System
Applicable Depreciation Method: 200- or 150-Percent
Declining Balance Switching to Straight Line
Applicable Recovery Periods: 3, 5, 7, 10, 15, 20 years
Applicable Convention: Mid-quarter (property placed in
service in fourth quarter)

If the Recovery Year is:	and the Recovery Period is:					
	3-year	5-year	7-year	10-year	15-year	20-year
	the Depreciation Rate is:					
1	8.33	5.00	3.57	2.50	1.25	0.938
2	61.11	38.00	27.55	19.50	9.88	7.430
3	20.37	22.80	19.68	15.60	8.89	6.872
4	10.19	13.68	14.06	12.48	8.00	6.357
5		10.94	10.04	9.98	7.20	5.880
6		9.58	8.73	7.99	6.48	5.439
7			8.73	6.55	5.90	5.031
8			7.64	6.55	5.90	4.654
9				6.56	5.90	4.458
10				6.55	5.91	4.458
11				5.74	5.90	4.458
12					5.91	4.458
13					5.90	4.458
14					5.91	4.458
15					5.90	4.458
16					5.17	4.458
17						4.458
18						4.459
19						4.458
20						4.459
21						3.901

TABLE 6
General Depreciation
System—Residential Rental Property
Applicable Depreciation Method: Straight Line
Applicable Recovery Period: 27.5 years
Applicable Convention: Mid-month

If the Recovery Year is:	and the Month in the First Recovery Year the Property is Placed in Service is:											
	1	2	3	4	5	6	7	8	9	10	11	12
	the Depreciation Rate is:											
1	3.485	3.182	2.879	2.576	2.273	1.970	1.667	1.364	1.061	0.758	0.455	0.152
2	3.636	3.636	3.636	3.636	3.636	3.636	3.636	3.636	3.636	3.636	3.636	3.636
3	3.636	3.636	3.636	3.636	3.636	3.636	3.636	3.636	3.636	3.636	3.636	3.636
4	3.636	3.636	3.636	3.636	3.636	3.636	3.636	3.636	3.636	3.636	3.636	3.636
5	3.636	3.636	3.636	3.636	3.636	3.636	3.636	3.636	3.636	3.636	3.636	3.636
6	3.636	3.636	3.636	3.636	3.636	3.636	3.636	3.636	3.636	3.636	3.636	3.636
7	3.636	3.636	3.636	3.636	3.636	3.636	3.636	3.636	3.636	3.636	3.636	3.636
8	3.636	3.636	3.636	3.636	3.636	3.636	3.636	3.636	3.636	3.636	3.636	3.636
9	3.636	3.636	3.636	3.636	3.636	3.636	3.636	3.636	3.636	3.636	3.636	3.636
10	3.637	3.637	3.637	3.637	3.637	3.637	3.636	3.636	3.636	3.636	3.636	3.636
11	3.636	3.636	3.636	3.636	3.636	3.636	3.637	3.637	3.637	3.637	3.637	3.637
12	3.637	3.637	3.637	3.637	3.637	3.637	3.636	3.636	3.636	3.636	3.636	3.636
13	3.636	3.636	3.636	3.636	3.636	3.636	3.637	3.637	3.637	3.637	3.637	3.637
14	3.637	3.637	3.637	3.637	3.637	3.637	3.636	3.636	3.636	3.636	3.636	3.636
15	3.636	3.636	3.636	3.636	3.636	3.636	3.637	3.637	3.637	3.637	3.637	3.637
16	3.637	3.637	3.637	3.637	3.637	3.637	3.636	3.636	3.636	3.636	3.636	3.636
17	3.636	3.636	3.636	3.636	3.636	3.636	3.637	3.637	3.637	3.637	3.637	3.637
18	3.637	3.637	3.637	3.637	3.637	3.637	3.636	3.636	3.636	3.636	3.636	3.636
19	3.636	3.636	3.636	3.636	3.636	3.636	3.637	3.637	3.637	3.637	3.637	3.637
20	3.637	3.637	3.637	3.637	3.637	3.637	3.636	3.636	3.636	3.636	3.636	3.636
21	3.636	3.636	3.636	3.636	3.636	3.636	3.637	3.637	3.637	3.637	3.637	3.637

If the Recovery Year is:	and the Month in the First Recovery Year the Property is Placed in Service is:											
	1	2	3	4	5	6	7	8	9	10	11	12
	the Depreciation Rate is:											
22	3.637	3.637	3.637	3.637	3.637	3.637	3.636	3.636	3.636	3.636	3.636	3.636
23	3.636	3.636	3.636	3.636	3.636	3.636	3.637	3.637	3.637	3.637	3.637	3.637
24	3.637	3.637	3.637	3.637	3.637	3.637	3.636	3.636	3.636	3.636	3.636	3.636
25	3.636	3.636	3.636	3.636	3.636	3.636	3.637	3.637	3.637	3.637	3.637	3.637
26	3.637	3.637	3.637	3.637	3.637	3.637	3.636	3.636	3.636	3.636	3.636	3.636
27	3.636	3.636	3.636	3.636	3.636	3.636	3.637	3.637	3.637	3.637	3.637	3.637
28	1.970	2.273	2.576	2.879	3.182	3.485	3.636	3.636	3.636	3.636	3.636	3.636
29	0.000	0.000	0.000	0.000	0.000	0.000	0.152	0.455	0.758	1.061	1.364	1.667

TABLE 7
General Depreciation
System—Nonresidential Real Property
Placed in Service before May 13, 1993
Applicable Depreciation Method: Straight Line
Applicable Recovery Period: 31.5 years
Applicable Convention: Mid-month

If the Recovery Year is:	and the Month in the First Recovery Year the Property is Placed in Service is:											
	1	2	3	4	5	6	7	8	9	10	11	12
	the Depreciation Rate is:											
1	3.042	2.778	2.513	2.249	1.984	1.720	1.455	1.190	0.926	0.661	0.397	0.132
2	3.175	3.175	3.175	3.175	3.175	3.175	3.175	3.175	3.175	3.175	3.175	3.175
3	3.175	3.175	3.175	3.175	3.175	3.175	3.175	3.175	3.175	3.175	3.175	3.175
4	3.175	3.175	3.175	3.175	3.175	3.175	3.175	3.175	3.175	3.175	3.175	3.175
5	3.175	3.175	3.175	3.175	3.175	3.175	3.175	3.175	3.175	3.175	3.175	3.175
6	3.175	3.175	3.175	3.175	3.175	3.175	3.175	3.175	3.175	3.175	3.175	3.175
7	3.175	3.175	3.175	3.175	3.175	3.175	3.175	3.175	3.175	3.175	3.175	3.175
8	3.175	3.174	3.175	3.174	3.175	3.174	3.175	3.175	3.175	3.175	3.175	3.175
9	3.174	3.175	3.174	3.175	3.174	3.175	3.174	3.175	3.174	3.175	3.174	3.175
10	3.175	3.174	3.175	3.174	3.175	3.174	3.175	3.174	3.175	3.174	3.175	3.174
11	3.174	3.175	3.174	3.175	3.174	3.175	3.174	3.175	3.174	3.175	3.174	3.175
12	3.175	3.174	3.175	3.174	3.175	3.174	3.175	3.174	3.175	3.174	3.175	3.174
13	3.174	3.175	3.174	3.175	3.174	3.175	3.174	3.175	3.174	3.175	3.174	3.175
14	3.175	3.174	3.175	3.174	3.175	3.174	3.175	3.174	3.175	3.174	3.175	3.174
15	3.174	3.175	3.174	3.175	3.174	3.175	3.174	3.175	3.174	3.175	3.174	3.175
16	3.175	3.174	3.175	3.174	3.175	3.174	3.175	3.174	3.175	3.174	3.175	3.174
17	3.174	3.175	3.174	3.175	3.174	3.175	3.174	3.175	3.174	3.175	3.174	3.175
18	3.175	3.174	3.175	3.174	3.175	3.174	3.175	3.174	3.175	3.174	3.175	3.174
19	3.174	3.175	3.174	3.175	3.174	3.175	3.174	3.175	3.174	3.175	3.174	3.175
20	3.175	3.174	3.175	3.174	3.175	3.174	3.175	3.174	3.175	3.174	3.175	3.174

If the Recovery Year is:	and the Month in the First Recovery Year the Property is Placed in Service is:											
	1	2	3	4	5	6	7	8	9	10	11	12
	the Depreciation Rate is:											
21	3.174	3.175	3.174	3.175	3.174	3.175	3.174	3.175	3.174	3.175	3.174	3.175
22	3.175	3.174	3.175	3.174	3.175	3.174	3.175	3.174	3.175	3.174	3.175	3.174
23	3.174	3.175	3.174	3.175	3.174	3.175	3.174	3.175	3.174	3.175	3.174	3.175
24	3.175	3.174	3.175	3.174	3.175	3.174	3.175	3.174	3.175	3.174	3.175	3.174
25	3.174	3.175	3.174	3.175	3.174	3.175	3.174	3.175	3.174	3.175	3.174	3.175
26	3.175	3.174	3.175	3.174	3.175	3.174	3.175	3.174	3.175	3.174	3.175	3.174
27	3.174	3.175	3.174	3.175	3.174	3.175	3.174	3.175	3.174	3.175	3.174	3.175
28	3.175	3.174	3.175	3.174	3.175	3.174	3.175	3.174	3.175	3.174	3.175	3.174
29	3.174	3.175	3.174	3.175	3.174	3.175	3.174	3.175	3.174	3.175	3.174	3.175
30	3.175	3.174	3.175	3.174	3.175	3.174	3.175	3.174	3.175	3.174	3.175	3.174
31	3.174	3.175	3.174	3.175	3.174	3.175	3.174	3.175	3.174	3.175	3.174	3.175
32	1.720	1.984	2.249	2.513	2.778	3.042	3.175	3.174	3.175	3.174	3.175	3.174
33	0.000	0.000	0.000	0.000	0.000	0.000	0.132	0.397	0.661	0.926	1.190	1.455

TABLE 7A
General Depreciation
System—Nonresidential Real Property
Placed in Service after May 12, 1993
Applicable Depreciation Method: Straight Line
Applicable Recovery Period: 39 years
Applicable Convention: Mid-month

If the Recovery Year is:	and the Month in the First Recovery Year the Property is Placed in Service is:											
	1	2	3	4	5	6	7	8	9	10	11	12
	the Depreciation Rate is:											
1	2.461	2.247	2.033	1.819	1.605	1.391	1.177	0.963	0.749	0.535	0.321	0.107
2 - 39	2.564	2.564	2.564	2.564	2.564	2.564	2.564	2.564	2.564	2.564	2.564	2.564
40	0.107	0.321	0.535	0.749	0.963	1.177	1.391	1.605	1.819	2.033	2.247	2.461

[IRS Pub. 946]

TABLE 8
General and Alternative Depreciation Systems
Applicable Depreciation Method: Straight Line
Applicable Recovery Periods: 2.5 — 50 years
Applicable Convention: Half-year

If the Recovery Year is:	and the Recovery Period is: 2.5	3.0	3.5	4.0	4.5	5.0	5.5	6.0	6.5	7.0	7.5	8.0	8.5	9.0	9.5
	the Depreciation Rate is:														
1	20.00	16.67	14.29	12.50	11.11	10.00	9.09	8.33	7.69	7.14	6.67	6.25	5.88	5.56	5.26
2	40.00	33.33	28.57	25.00	22.22	20.00	18.18	16.67	15.39	14.29	13.33	12.50	11.77	11.11	10.53
3	40.00	33.33	28.57	25.00	22.22	20.00	18.18	16.67	15.38	14.29	13.33	12.50	11.76	11.11	10.53
4		16.67	28.57	25.00	22.23	20.00	18.18	16.67	15.39	14.28	13.33	12.50	11.77	11.11	10.53
5				12.50	22.22	20.00	18.19	16.66	15.38	14.29	13.34	12.50	11.76	11.11	10.52
6						10.00	18.18	16.67	15.39	14.28	13.33	12.50	11.77	11.11	10.53
7								8.33	15.38	14.29	13.34	12.50	11.76	11.11	10.52
8										7.14	13.33	12.50	11.77	11.11	10.53
9												6.25	11.76	11.11	10.52
10														5.56	10.53

If the Recovery Year is:	and the Recovery Period is: 10.0	10.5	11.0	11.5	12.0	12.5	13.0	13.5	14.0	14.5	15.0	15.5	16.0	16.5	17.0
	the Depreciation Rate is:														
1	5.00	4.76	4.55	4.35	4.17	4.00	3.85	3.70	3.57	3.45	3.33	3.23	3.13	3.03	2.94
2	10.00	9.52	9.09	8.70	8.33	8.00	7.69	7.41	7.14	6.90	6.67	6.45	6.25	6.06	5.88
3	10.00	9.52	9.09	8.70	8.33	8.00	7.69	7.41	7.14	6.90	6.67	6.45	6.25	6.06	5.88
4	10.00	9.53	9.09	8.69	8.33	8.00	7.69	7.41	7.14	6.90	6.67	6.45	6.25	6.06	5.88
5	10.00	9.52	9.09	8.70	8.33	8.00	7.69	7.41	7.14	6.90	6.67	6.45	6.25	6.06	5.88
6	10.00	9.53	9.09	8.69	8.33	8.00	7.69	7.41	7.14	6.89	6.67	6.45	6.25	6.06	5.88
7	10.00	9.52	9.09	8.70	8.34	8.00	7.69	7.41	7.14	6.90	6.67	6.45	6.25	6.06	5.88
8	10.00	9.53	9.09	8.69	8.33	8.00	7.69	7.41	7.15	6.89	6.66	6.45	6.25	6.06	5.88

If the Recovery Year is:	and the Recovery Period is: 10.0	10.5	11.0	11.5	12.0	12.5	13.0	13.5	14.0	14.5	15.0	15.5	16.0	16.5	17.0
	the Depreciation Rate is:														
9	10.00	9.52	9.09	8.70	8.34	8.00	7.69	7.41	7.14	6.90	6.67	6.45	6.25	6.06	5.88
10	10.00	9.53	9.09	8.69	8.33	8.00	7.70	7.40	7.15	6.89	6.66	6.45	6.25	6.06	5.88
11	5.00	9.52	9.09	8.70	8.34	8.00	7.69	7.41	7.14	6.90	6.67	6.45	6.25	6.06	5.89
12			4.55	8.69	8.33	8.00	7.70	7.40	7.15	6.89	6.66	6.45	6.25	6.06	5.88
13					4.17	8.00	7.69	7.41	7.14	6.90	6.67	6.45	6.25	6.06	5.89
14							3.85	7.40	7.15	6.89	6.66	6.46	6.25	6.06	5.88
15									3.57	6.90	6.67	6.45	6.25	6.06	5.89
16											3.33	6.46	6.25	6.06	5.88
17													3.12	6.07	5.89
18															2.94

If the Recovery Year is:	and the Recovery Period is: 17.5	18.0	18.5	19.0	19.5	20.0	20.5	21.0	21.5	22.0	22.5	23.0	23.5	24.0	24.5
	the Depreciation Rate is:														
1	2.86	2.78	2.70	2.63	2.56	2.500	2.439	2.381	2.326	2.273	2.222	2.174	2.128	2.083	2.041
2	5.71	5.56	5.41	5.26	5.13	5.000	4.878	4.762	4.651	4.545	4.444	4.348	4.255	4.167	4.082
3	5.71	5.56	5.41	5.26	5.13	5.000	4.878	4.762	4.651	4.545	4.444	4.348	4.255	4.167	4.082
4	5.71	5.55	5.41	5.26	5.13	5.000	4.878	4.762	4.651	4.545	4.445	4.348	4.255	4.167	4.082
5	5.72	5.56	5.40	5.26	5.13	5.000	4.878	4.762	4.651	4.546	4.444	4.348	4.255	4.167	4.082
6	5.71	5.55	5.41	5.26	5.13	5.000	4.878	4.762	4.651	4.545	4.445	4.348	4.255	4.167	4.082
7	5.72	5.56	5.40	5.26	5.13	5.000	4.878	4.762	4.651	4.546	4.444	4.348	4.255	4.167	4.082
8	5.71	5.55	5.41	5.26	5.13	5.000	4.878	4.762	4.651	4.545	4.445	4.348	4.255	4.167	4.082
9	5.72	5.56	5.40	5.27	5.13	5.000	4.878	4.762	4.651	4.546	4.444	4.348	4.255	4.167	4.081
10	5.71	5.55	5.41	5.26	5.13	5.000	4.878	4.762	4.651	4.545	4.445	4.348	4.255	4.167	4.082
11	5.72	5.56	5.40	5.27	5.13	5.000	4.878	4.762	4.651	4.546	4.444	4.348	4.256	4.166	4.081
12	5.71	5.55	5.41	5.26	5.13	5.000	4.878	4.762	4.651	4.545	4.445	4.348	4.255	4.167	4.082

If the Recovery Year is:	and the Recovery Period is: 17.5	18.0	18.5	19.0	19.5	20.0	20.5	21.0	21.5	22.0	22.5	23.0	23.5	24.0	24.5
	the Depreciation Rate is:														
13	5.72	5.56	5.40	5.27	5.13	5.000	4.878	4.762	4.651	4.546	4.444	4.348	4.256	4.166	4.081
14	5.71	5.55	5.41	5.26	5.13	5.000	4.878	4.762	4.651	4.545	4.445	4.348	4.255	4.167	4.082
15	5.72	5.56	5.40	5.27	5.13	5.000	4.878	4.762	4.651	4.546	4.444	4.348	4.256	4.166	4.081
16	5.71	5.55	5.41	5.26	5.12	5.000	4.878	4.762	4.651	4.545	4.445	4.348	4.255	4.167	4.082
17	5.72	5.56	5.40	5.27	5.13	5.000	4.878	4.762	4.652	4.546	4.444	4.347	4.256	4.166	4.081
18	5.71	5.55	5.41	5.26	5.12	5.000	4.878	4.762	4.651	4.545	4.445	4.348	4.255	4.167	4.082
19		2.78	5.40	5.27	5.13	5.000	4.878	4.761	4.652	4.546	4.444	4.347	4.256	4.166	4.081
20				2.63	5.12	5.000	4.879	4.762	4.651	4.545	4.445	4.348	4.255	4.167	4.082
21						2.500	4.878	4.761	4.652	4.546	4.444	4.347	4.256	4.166	4.081
22								2.381	4.651	4.545	4.445	4.348	4.255	4.167	4.082
23										2.273	4.444	4.347	4.256	4.166	4.081
24												2.174	4.255	4.167	4.082
25														2.083	4.081

If the Recovery Year is:	and the Recovery Period is: 25.0	25.5	26.0	26.5	27.0	27.5	28.0	28.5	29.0	29.5	30.0	30.5	31.0	31.5	32.0
	the Depreciation Rate is:														
1	2.000	1.961	1.923	1.887	1.852	1.818	1.786	1.754	1.724	1.695	1.667	1.639	1.613	1.587	1.563
2	4.000	3.922	3.846	3.774	3.704	3.636	3.571	3.509	3.448	3.390	3.333	3.279	3.226	3.175	3.125
3	4.000	3.922	3.846	3.774	3.704	3.636	3.571	3.509	3.448	3.390	3.333	3.279	3.226	3.175	3.125
4	4.000	3.922	3.846	3.774	3.704	3.636	3.571	3.509	3.448	3.390	3.333	3.279	3.226	3.175	3.125
5	4.000	3.922	3.846	3.774	3.704	3.636	3.571	3.509	3.448	3.390	3.333	3.279	3.226	3.175	3.125
6	4.000	3.921	3.846	3.774	3.704	3.636	3.571	3.509	3.448	3.390	3.333	3.279	3.226	3.175	3.125
7	4.000	3.922	3.846	3.773	3.704	3.636	3.572	3.509	3.448	3.390	3.333	3.279	3.226	3.175	3.125

If the Recovery Year is:	25.0	25.5	26.0	26.5	27.0	27.5	28.0	28.5	29.0	29.5	30.0	30.5	31.0	31.5	32.0
	the Depreciation Rate is:														
8	4.000	3.921	3.846	3.774	3.704	3.636	3.571	3.509	3.448	3.390	3.333	3.279	3.226	3.175	3.125
9	4.000	3.922	3.846	3.773	3.704	3.637	3.572	3.509	3.448	3.390	3.333	3.279	3.226	3.175	3.125
10	4.000	3.921	3.846	3.774	3.704	3.636	3.571	3.509	3.448	3.390	3.333	3.279	3.226	3.174	3.125
11	4.000	3.922	3.846	3.773	3.704	3.637	3.572	3.509	3.448	3.390	3.333	3.279	3.226	3.175	3.125
12	4.000	3.921	3.846	3.774	3.704	3.636	3.571	3.509	3.448	3.390	3.333	3.279	3.226	3.174	3.125
13	4.000	3.922	3.846	3.773	3.703	3.637	3.572	3.509	3.448	3.390	3.334	3.279	3.226	3.175	3.125
14	4.000	3.921	3.846	3.773	3.704	3.636	3.571	3.509	3.448	3.390	3.333	3.279	3.226	3.174	3.125
15	4.000	3.922	3.846	3.774	3.703	3.637	3.572	3.509	3.449	3.390	3.334	3.278	3.226	3.175	3.125
16	4.000	3.921	3.846	3.773	3.704	3.636	3.571	3.509	3.448	3.390	3.333	3.279	3.226	3.174	3.125
17	4.000	3.922	3.846	3.774	3.703	3.637	3.572	3.509	3.449	3.390	3.334	3.278	3.226	3.175	3.125
18	4.000	3.921	3.846	3.773	3.704	3.636	3.571	3.508	3.448	3.390	3.333	3.279	3.226	3.174	3.125
19	4.000	3.922	3.846	3.774	3.703	3.637	3.572	3.509	3.449	3.390	3.334	3.278	3.226	3.175	3.125
20	4.000	3.921	3.847	3.773	3.704	3.636	3.571	3.508	3.448	3.390	3.333	3.279	3.226	3.174	3.125
21	4.000	3.922	3.846	3.774	3.703	3.637	3.572	3.509	3.449	3.389	3.334	3.278	3.225	3.175	3.125
22	4.000	3.921	3.847	3.773	3.704	3.636	3.571	3.508	3.448	3.390	3.333	3.279	3.226	3.174	3.125
23	4.000	3.922	3.846	3.774	3.703	3.637	3.572	3.509	3.449	3.389	3.334	3.278	3.225	3.175	3.125
24	4.000	3.921	3.847	3.773	3.704	3.636	3.571	3.508	3.448	3.390	3.333	3.279	3.226	3.174	3.125
25	4.000	3.922	3.846	3.774	3.703	3.637	3.572	3.509	3.449	3.389	3.334	3.278	3.225	3.175	3.125
26	2.000	3.921	3.847	3.773	3.704	3.636	3.571	3.508	3.448	3.390	3.333	3.279	3.226	3.174	3.125
27			1.923	3.774	3.703	3.637	3.572	3.509	3.449	3.389	3.334	3.278	3.225	3.175	3.125
28					1.852	3.636	3.571	3.508	3.448	3.390	3.333	3.279	3.226	3.174	3.125
29							1.786	3.509	3.449	3.389	3.334	3.278	3.225	3.175	3.125
30									1.724	3.390	3.333	3.279	3.226	3.174	3.125
31											1.667	3.278	3.225	3.175	3.125
32													1.613	3.174	3.125
33															1.562

If the Recovery Year is:	and the Recovery Period is:														
	32.5	33.0	33.5	34.0	34.5	35.0	35.5	36.0	36.5	37.0	37.5	38.0	38.5	39.0	39.5
	the Depreciation Rate is:														
1	1.538	1.515	1.493	1.471	1.449	1.429	1.408	1.389	1.370	1.351	1.333	1.316	1.299	1.282	1.266
2	3.077	3.030	2.985	2.941	2.899	2.857	2.817	2.778	2.740	2.703	2.667	2.632	2.597	2.564	2.532
3	3.077	3.030	2.985	2.941	2.899	2.857	2.817	2.778	2.740	2.703	2.667	2.632	2.597	2.564	2.532
4	3.077	3.030	2.985	2.941	2.899	2.857	2.817	2.778	2.740	2.703	2.667	2.632	2.597	2.564	2.532
5	3.077	3.030	2.985	2.941	2.899	2.857	2.817	2.778	2.740	2.703	2.667	2.632	2.597	2.564	2.532
6	3.077	3.030	2.985	2.941	2.899	2.857	2.817	2.778	2.740	2.703	2.667	2.632	2.597	2.564	2.532
7	3.077	3.030	2.985	2.941	2.898	2.857	2.817	2.778	2.740	2.703	2.667	2.632	2.597	2.564	2.532
8	3.077	3.030	2.985	2.941	2.899	2.857	2.817	2.778	2.740	2.703	2.667	2.631	2.597	2.564	2.532
9	3.077	3.030	2.985	2.941	2.898	2.857	2.817	2.778	2.740	2.703	2.667	2.632	2.597	2.564	2.532
10	3.077	3.030	2.985	2.941	2.899	2.857	2.817	2.778	2.740	2.703	2.667	2.631	2.598	2.564	2.532
11	3.077	3.030	2.985	2.941	2.898	2.857	2.817	2.778	2.740	2.703	2.667	2.632	2.597	2.564	2.532
12	3.077	3.030	2.985	2.941	2.899	2.857	2.817	2.778	2.740	2.703	2.667	2.631	2.598	2.564	2.532
13	3.077	3.030	2.985	2.941	2.898	2.857	2.817	2.778	2.740	2.703	2.667	2.632	2.597	2.564	2.532
14	3.077	3.030	2.985	2.941	2.899	2.857	2.817	2.778	2.740	2.703	2.667	2.631	2.598	2.564	2.531
15	3.077	3.031	2.985	2.941	2.898	2.857	2.817	2.778	2.740	2.703	2.666	2.632	2.597	2.564	2.532
16	3.077	3.030	2.985	2.941	2.899	2.857	2.817	2.778	2.740	2.703	2.667	2.631	2.598	2.564	2.531
17	3.077	3.031	2.985	2.941	2.898	2.857	2.817	2.778	2.740	2.703	2.666	2.632	2.597	2.564	2.532
18	3.077	3.030	2.985	2.941	2.899	2.857	2.817	2.778	2.740	2.702	2.667	2.631	2.598	2.564	2.531
19	3.077	3.031	2.985	2.941	2.898	2.857	2.817	2.778	2.739	2.703	2.666	2.632	2.597	2.564	2.532
20	3.077	3.030	2.985	2.941	2.898	2.857	2.817	2.778	2.740	2.702	2.667	2.631	2.598	2.564	2.531
21	3.077	3.031	2.985	2.941	2.899	2.857	2.817	2.778	2.739	2.703	2.666	2.632	2.597	2.564	2.532
22	3.077	3.030	2.985	2.941	2.898	2.857	2.817	2.777	2.740	2.702	2.667	2.631	2.598	2.564	2.531
23	3.077	3.031	2.985	2.941	2.899	2.857	2.817	2.778	2.739	2.703	2.666	2.632	2.597	2.564	2.532
24	3.077	3.030	2.985	2.941	2.898	2.857	2.817	2.777	2.740	2.702	2.667	2.631	2.598	2.564	2.531

If the Recovery Year is:	32.5	33.0	33.5	34.0	34.5	35.0	35.5	36.0	36.5	37.0	37.5	38.0	38.5	39.0	39.5
	the Depreciation Rate is:														
25	3.077	3.031	2.985	2.942	2.899	2.857	2.817	2.778	2.739	2.703	2.666	2.632	2.597	2.564	2.532
26	3.077	3.030	2.985	2.941	2.898	2.857	2.817	2.777	2.740	2.702	2.667	2.631	2.598	2.564	2.531
27	3.077	3.031	2.985	2.942	2.899	2.857	2.817	2.778	2.739	2.703	2.666	2.632	2.597	2.564	2.532
28	3.077	3.030	2.985	2.941	2.898	2.858	2.817	2.777	2.740	2.702	2.667	2.631	2.598	2.564	2.531
29	3.077	3.031	2.985	2.942	2.899	2.857	2.817	2.778	2.739	2.703	2.666	2.632	2.597	2.564	2.532
30	3.077	3.030	2.985	2.941	2.898	2.858	2.817	2.777	2.740	2.702	2.667	2.631	2.598	2.564	2.531
31	3.076	3.031	2.986	2.942	2.899	2.857	2.817	2.778	2.739	2.703	2.666	2.632	2.597	2.564	2.532
32	3.077	3.030	2.985	2.941	2.898	2.858	2.816	2.777	2.740	2.702	2.667	2.631	2.598	2.564	2.531
33	3.076	3.031	2.986	2.942	2.899	2.857	2.817	2.778	2.739	2.703	2.666	2.632	2.597	2.565	2.532
34		1.515	2.985	2.941	2.898	2.858	2.816	2.777	2.740	2.702	2.667	2.631	2.598	2.564	2.531
35				1.471	2.899	2.857	2.817	2.778	2.739	2.703	2.666	2.632	2.597	2.565	2.532
36						1.429	2.816	2.777	2.740	2.702	2.667	2.631	2.598	2.564	2.531
37								1.389	2.739	2.703	2.666	2.632	2.597	2.565	2.532
38										1.351	2.667	2.631	2.598	2.564	2.531
39												1.316	2.597	2.565	2.532
40														1.282	2.531

and the Recovery Period is:

If the Recovery Year is:	40.0	40.5	41.0	41.5	42.0	42.5	43.0	43.5	44.0	44.5	45.0	45.5	46.0	46.5	47.0
	the Depreciation Rate is:														
1	1.250	1.235	1.220	1.205	1.190	1.176	1.163	1.149	1.136	1.124	1.111	1.099	1.087	1.075	1.064
2	2.500	2.469	2.439	2.410	2.381	2.353	2.326	2.299	2.273	2.247	2.222	2.198	2.174	2.151	2.128
3	2.500	2.469	2.439	2.410	2.381	2.353	2.326	2.299	2.273	2.247	2.222	2.198	2.174	2.151	2.128
4	2.500	2.469	2.439	2.410	2.381	2.353	2.326	2.299	2.273	2.247	2.222	2.198	2.174	2.151	2.128
5	2.500	2.469	2.439	2.410	2.381	2.353	2.326	2.299	2.273	2.247	2.222	2.198	2.174	2.151	2.128

If the Recovery Year is:	40.0	40.5	41.0	41.5	42.0	42.5	43.0	43.5	44.0	44.5	45.0	45.5	46.0	46.5	47.0
	the Depreciation Rate is:														
6	2.500	2.469	2.439	2.410	2.381	2.353	2.326	2.299	2.273	2.247	2.222	2.198	2.174	2.151	2.128
7	2.500	2.469	2.439	2.410	2.381	2.353	2.326	2.299	2.273	2.247	2.222	2.198	2.174	2.150	2.128
8	2.500	2.469	2.439	2.410	2.381	2.353	2.326	2.299	2.273	2.247	2.222	2.198	2.174	2.151	2.128
9	2.500	2.469	2.439	2.410	2.381	2.353	2.325	2.299	2.273	2.247	2.222	2.198	2.174	2.150	2.128
10	2.500	2.469	2.439	2.410	2.381	2.353	2.326	2.299	2.273	2.247	2.222	2.198	2.174	2.151	2.128
11	2.500	2.469	2.439	2.410	2.381	2.353	2.325	2.299	2.273	2.247	2.222	2.198	2.174	2.150	2.128
12	2.500	2.469	2.439	2.410	2.381	2.353	2.326	2.299	2.273	2.247	2.222	2.198	2.174	2.151	2.128
13	2.500	2.469	2.439	2.410	2.381	2.353	2.325	2.299	2.273	2.247	2.222	2.198	2.174	2.150	2.128
14	2.500	2.469	2.439	2.409	2.381	2.353	2.326	2.299	2.273	2.247	2.222	2.198	2.174	2.151	2.128
15	2.500	2.469	2.439	2.410	2.381	2.353	2.325	2.299	2.273	2.247	2.222	2.198	2.174	2.150	2.128
16	2.500	2.469	2.439	2.409	2.381	2.353	2.326	2.299	2.273	2.247	2.222	2.198	2.174	2.151	2.128
17	2.500	2.469	2.439	2.410	2.381	2.353	2.325	2.299	2.273	2.247	2.222	2.198	2.174	2.150	2.127
18	2.500	2.469	2.439	2.409	2.381	2.353	2.326	2.299	2.273	2.247	2.222	2.198	2.174	2.151	2.128
19	2.500	2.469	2.439	2.410	2.381	2.353	2.325	2.299	2.273	2.247	2.222	2.198	2.174	2.150	2.127
20	2.500	2.469	2.439	2.409	2.381	2.353	2.326	2.299	2.273	2.247	2.222	2.198	2.174	2.151	2.128
21	2.500	2.469	2.439	2.410	2.381	2.353	2.325	2.299	2.273	2.247	2.222	2.198	2.174	2.150	2.127
22	2.500	2.469	2.439	2.409	2.381	2.353	2.326	2.299	2.273	2.247	2.222	2.198	2.174	2.151	2.128
23	2.500	2.469	2.439	2.410	2.381	2.353	2.325	2.299	2.272	2.247	2.222	2.198	2.174	2.150	2.127
24	2.500	2.469	2.439	2.409	2.381	2.353	2.326	2.299	2.273	2.247	2.222	2.198	2.174	2.151	2.128
25	2.500	2.469	2.439	2.410	2.381	2.353	2.325	2.299	2.272	2.247	2.222	2.198	2.174	2.150	2.127
26	2.500	2.469	2.439	2.409	2.381	2.353	2.326	2.299	2.273	2.247	2.222	2.198	2.174	2.151	2.128
27	2.500	2.469	2.439	2.410	2.381	2.353	2.325	2.299	2.272	2.247	2.223	2.198	2.174	2.150	2.127
28	2.500	2.469	2.439	2.409	2.381	2.353	2.326	2.299	2.273	2.247	2.222	2.198	2.174	2.151	2.128
29	2.500	2.469	2.439	2.410	2.381	2.353	2.325	2.299	2.272	2.247	2.223	2.198	2.174	2.150	2.127
30	2.500	2.469	2.439	2.409	2.381	2.353	2.326	2.299	2.273	2.248	2.222	2.197	2.174	2.151	2.128
31	2.500	2.469	2.439	2.410	2.381	2.353	2.325	2.299	2.272	2.247	2.223	2.198	2.174	2.150	2.127
32	2.500	2.470	2.439	2.409	2.381	2.353	2.326	2.299	2.273	2.248	2.222	2.197	2.174	2.151	2.128

If the Recovery Year is:	40.0	40.5	41.0	41.5	42.0	42.5	43.0	43.5	44.0	44.5	45.0	45.5	46.0	46.5	47.0
			the Depreciation Rate is:												
33	2.500	2.469	2.439	2.410	2.381	2.353	2.325	2.298	2.272	2.247	2.223	2.198	2.174	2.150	2.127
34	2.500	2.470	2.439	2.409	2.381	2.353	2.326	2.299	2.273	2.248	2.222	2.197	2.174	2.151	2.128
35	2.500	2.469	2.439	2.410	2.381	2.353	2.325	2.298	2.272	2.247	2.223	2.198	2.174	2.150	2.127
36	2.500	2.470	2.139	2.409	2.381	2.353	2.326	2.299	2.273	2.248	2.222	2.197	2.174	2.151	2.128
37	2.500	2.469	2.439	2.410	2.381	2.353	2.325	2.298	2.272	2.247	2.223	2.198	2.174	2.150	2.127
38	2.500	2.470	2.439	2.409	2.381	2.353	2.326	2.299	2.273	2.248	2.222	2.197	2.174	2.151	2.128
39	2.500	2.469	2.439	2.410	2.381	2.353	2.325	2.298	2.272	2.247	2.223	2.198	2.174	2.150	2.127
40	2.500	2.470	2.439	2.409	2.381	2.353	2.326	2.299	2.273	2.248	2.222	2.197	2.173	2.151	2.128
41	1.250	2.469	2.439	2.410	2.380	2.352	2.325	2.298	2.272	2.247	2.223	2.198	2.174	2.150	2.127
42			1.220	2.409	2.381	2.353	2.326	2.299	2.273	2.248	2.222	2.197	2.173	2.151	2.128
43					1.190	2.352	2.325	2.298	2.272	2.247	2.223	2.198	2.174	2.150	2.127
44							1.163	2.299	2.273	2.248	2.222	2.197	2.173	2.151	2.128
45									1.136	2.247	2.223	2.198	2.174	2.150	2.127
46											1.111	2.197	2.173	2.151	2.128
47													1.087	2.150	2.127
48															1.064

and the Recovery Period is:

If the Recovery Year is:	47.5	48.0	48.5	49.0	49.5	50.0
			the Depreciation Rate is:			
1	1.053	1.042	1.031	1.020	1.010	1.000
2	2.105	2.083	2.062	2.041	2.020	2.000
3	2.105	2.083	2.062	2.041	2.020	2.000
4	2.105	2.083	2.062	2.041	2.020	2.000
5	2.105	2.083	2.062	2.041	2.020	2.000

If the Recovery Year is:	47.5	48.0	48.5	49.0	49.5	50.0
			the Depreciation Rate is:			
6	2.105	2.083	2.062	2.041	2.020	2.000
7	2.105	2.083	2.062	2.041	2.020	2.000
8	2.105	2.083	2.062	2.041	2.020	2.000
9	2.105	2.083	2.062	2.041	2.020	2.000
10	2.105	2.083	2.062	2.041	2.020	2.000
11	2.105	2.083	2.062	2.041	2.020	2.000
12	2.105	2.083	2.062	2.041	2.020	2.000
13	2.105	2.083	2.062	2.041	2.020	2.000
14	2.105	2.083	2.062	2.041	2.020	2.000
15	2.105	2.083	2.062	2.041	2.020	2.000
16	2.105	2.083	2.062	2.041	2.020	2.000
17	2.105	2.083	2.062	2.041	2.020	2.000
18	2.105	2.083	2.062	2.041	2.020	2.000
19	2.105	2.084	2.062	2.041	2.020	2.000
20	2.105	2.083	2.062	2.041	2.020	2.000
21	2.105	2.084	2.062	2.041	2.020	2.000
22	2.105	2.083	2.062	2.041	2.020	2.000
23	2.105	2.084	2.062	2.041	2.020	2.000
24	2.105	2.083	2.062	2.041	2.020	2.000
25	2.105	2.084	2.062	2.041	2.020	2.000
26	2.106	2.083	2.062	2.041	2.020	2.000
27	2.105	2.084	2.062	2.041	2.020	2.000
28	2.106	2.083	2.062	2.041	2.020	2.000
29	2.105	2.084	2.062	2.041	2.020	2.000
30	2.106	2.083	2.062	2.041	2.020	2.000
31	2.105	2.084	2.062	2.041	2.021	2.000
32	2.106	2.083	2.062	2.041	2.020	2.000

If the Recovery Year is:	47.5	48.0	48.5	49.0	49.5	50.0
	the Depreciation Rate is:					
33	2.105	2.084	2.062	2.041	2.021	2.000
34	2.106	2.083	2.062	2.040	2.020	2.000
35	2.105	2.084	2.062	2.041	2.021	2.000
36	2.106	2.083	2.062	2.040	2.020	2.000
37	2.105	2.084	2.061	2.041	2.021	2.000
38	2.106	2.083	2.062	2.040	2.020	2.000
39	2.105	2.084	2.061	2.041	2.021	2.000
40	2.106	2.083	2.062	2.040	2.020	2.000
41	2.105	2.084	2.061	2.041	2.021	2.000
42	2.106	2.083	2.062	2.040	2.020	2.000
43	2.105	2.084	2.061	2.041	2.021	2.000
44	2.106	2.083	2.062	2.040	2.020	2.000
45	2.105	2.084	2.061	2.041	2.021	2.000
46	2.106	2.083	2.062	2.040	2.020	2.000
47	2.105	2.084	2.061	2.041	2.021	2.000
48	2.106	2.083	2.062	2.040	2.020	2.000
49		1.042	2.061	2.041	2.021	2.000
50				1.020	2.020	2.000
51						1.000

TABLE 9
General and Alternative Depreciation Systems
Applicable Depreciation Method: Straight Line
Applicable Recovery Periods: 2.5 — 50 years
Applicable Convention: Mid-quarter (properly placed in service in first quarter)

If the Recovery Year is:	and the Recovery Period is:														
	2.5	3.0	3.5	4.0	4.5	5.0	5.5	6.0	6.5	7.0	7.5	8.0	8.5	9.0	9.5
	the Depreciation Rate is:														
1	35.00	29.17	25.00	21.88	19.44	17.50	15.91	14.58	13.46	12.50	11.67	10.94	10.29	9.72	9.21
2	40.00	33.33	28.57	25.00	22.22	20.00	18.18	16.67	15.38	14.29	13.33	12.50	11.77	11.11	10.53
3	25.00	33.33	28.57	25.00	22.22	20.00	18.18	16.67	15.39	14.28	13.33	12.50	11.76	11.11	10.53
4		4.17	17.86	25.00	22.23	20.00	18.18	16.67	15.38	14.29	13.33	12.50	11.77	11.11	10.53
5				3.12	13.89	20.00	18.18	16.66	15.39	14.28	13.34	12.50	11.76	11.11	10.52
6						2.50	11.37	16.67	15.38	14.29	13.33	12.50	11.77	11.11	10.53
7								2.08	9.62	14.28	13.34	12.50	11.76	11.11	10.52
8										1.79	8.33	12.50	11.77	11.12	10.53
9												1.56	7.35	11.11	10.52
10														1.39	6.58

If the Recovery Year is:	and the Recovery Period is:														
	10.0	10.5	11.0	11.5	12.0	12.5	13.0	13.5	14.0	14.5	15.0	15.5	16.0	16.5	17.0
	the Depreciation Rate is:														
1	8.75	8.33	7.95	7.61	7.29	7.00	6.73	6.48	6.25	6.03	5.83	5.65	5.47	5.30	5.15
2	10.00	9.52	9.09	8.70	8.33	8.00	7.69	7.41	7.14	6.90	6.67	6.45	6.25	6.06	5.88
3	10.00	9.52	9.09	8.70	8.33	8.00	7.69	7.41	7.14	6.90	6.67	6.45	6.25	6.06	5.88

If the Recovery Year is:	10.0	10.5	11.0	11.5	12.0	12.5	13.0	13.5	14.0	14.5	15.0	15.5	16.0	16.5	17.0
			the Depreciation Rate is:												
4	10.00	9.53	9.09	8.69	8.33	8.00	7.69	7.41	7.14	6.90	6.67	6.45	6.25	6.06	5.88
5	10.00	9.52	9.09	8.70	8.33	8.00	7.69	7.41	7.14	6.90	6.67	6.45	6.25	6.06	5.88
6	10.00	9.53	9.09	8.69	8.34	8.00	7.69	7.41	7.14	6.90	6.67	6.45	6.25	6.06	5.88
7	10.00	9.52	9.09	8.70	8.33	8.00	7.69	7.41	7.14	6.90	6.67	6.45	6.25	6.06	5.88
8	10.00	9.53	9.09	8.69	8.34	8.00	7.69	7.41	7.15	6.89	6.66	6.45	6.25	6.06	5.88
9	10.00	9.52	9.09	8.70	8.33	8.00	7.70	7.40	7.14	6.90	6.67	6.45	6.25	6.06	5.88
10	10.00	9.53	9.10	8.69	8.34	8.00	7.69	7.41	7.15	6.89	6.66	6.45	6.25	6.06	5.88
11	1.25	5.95	9.09	8.70	8.33	8.00	7.70	7.40	7.14	6.90	6.67	6.45	6.25	6.06	5.88
12			1.14	5.43	8.34	8.00	7.69	7.41	7.15	6.89	6.66	6.45	6.25	6.06	5.89
13					1.04	5.00	7.70	7.40	7.14	6.90	6.67	6.46	6.25	6.06	5.88
14							0.96	4.63	7.15	6.89	6.66	6.45	6.25	6.06	5.89
15									0.89	4.31	6.67	6.46	6.25	6.06	5.88
16											0.83	4.03	6.25	6.07	5.89
17													0.78	3.79	5.88
18															0.74

			and the Recovery Period is:												
If the Recovery Year is:	17.5	18.0	18.5	19.0	19.5	20.0	20.5	21.0	21.5	22.0	22.5	23.0	23.5	24.0	24.5
			the Depreciation Rate is:												
1	5.00	4.86	4.73	4.61	4.49	4.375	4.268	4.167	4.070	3.977	3.889	3.804	3.723	3.646	3.571
2	5.71	5.56	5.41	5.26	5.13	5.000	4.878	4.762	4.651	4.545	4.444	4.348	4.255	4.167	4.082
3	5.71	5.56	5.41	5.26	5.13	5.000	4.878	4.762	4.651	4.545	4.444	4.348	4.255	4.167	4.082
4	5.71	5.56	5.40	5.26	5.13	5.000	4.878	4.762	4.651	4.546	4.444	4.348	4.255	4.167	4.082
5	5.72	5.55	5.41	5.26	5.13	5.000	4.878	4.762	4.651	4.545	4.445	4.348	4.255	4.167	4.082
6	5.71	5.56	5.40	5.26	5.13	5.000	4.878	4.762	4.651	4.546	4.444	4.348	4.255	4.167	4.082
7	5.72	5.55	5.41	5.26	5.13	5.000	4.878	4.762	4.651	4.545	4.445	4.348	4.255	4.167	4.082
8	5.71	5.56	5.40	5.26	5.13	5.000	4.878	4.762	4.651	4.546	4.444	4.348	4.255	4.167	4.082

If the Recovery Year is:	and the Recovery Period is: 17.5	18.0	18.5	19.0	19.5	20.0	20.5	21.0	21.5	22.0	22.5	23.0	23.5	24.0	24.5
	the Depreciation Rate is:														
9	5.72	5.55	5.41	5.26	5.13	5.000	4.878	4.762	4.651	4.545	4.445	4.348	4.255	4.167	4.082
10	5.71	5.56	5.40	5.27	5.13	5.000	4.878	4.762	4.651	4.546	4.444	4.348	4.256	4.166	4.081
11	5.72	5.55	5.41	5.26	5.13	5.000	4.878	4.762	4.651	4.545	4.445	4.348	4.255	4.167	4.082
12	5.71	5.56	5.40	5.27	5.13	5.000	4.878	4.762	4.651	4.546	4.444	4.348	4.256	4.166	4.081
13	5.72	5.55	5.41	5.26	5.13	5.000	4.878	4.762	4.651	4.545	4.445	4.348	4.255	4.167	4.082
14	5.71	5.56	5.40	5.27	5.12	5.000	4.878	4.762	4.651	4.546	4.444	4.348	4.256	4.166	4.081
15	5.72	5.55	5.41	5.26	5.13	5.000	4.878	4.762	4.651	4.545	4.445	4.348	4.255	4.167	4.082
16	5.71	5.56	5.40	5.27	5.12	5.000	4.878	4.762	4.651	4.546	4.444	4.348	4.256	4.166	4.081
17	5.72	5.55	5.41	5.26	5.13	5.000	4.878	4.762	4.652	4.545	4.445	4.348	4.255	4.167	4.082
18	3.57	5.56	5.40	5.27	5.12	5.000	4.878	4.761	4.651	4.546	4.444	4.347	4.256	4.166	4.081
19		0.69	3.38	5.26	5.13	5.000	4.878	4.762	4.652	4.545	4.445	4.348	4.255	4.167	4.082
20				0.66	3.20	5.000	4.879	4.761	4.651	4.546	4.444	4.347	4.256	4.166	4.081
21						0.625	3.049	4.762	4.652	4.545	4.445	4.348	4.255	4.167	4.082
22								0.595	2.907	4.546	4.444	4.347	4.256	4.166	4.081
23										0.568	2.778	4.348	4.255	4.167	4.082
24												0.543	2.660	4.166	4.081
25														0.521	2.551

If the Recovery Year is:	and the Recovery Period is: 25.0	25.5	26.0	26.5	27.0	27.5	28.0	28.5	29.0	29.5	30.0	30.5	31.0	31.5	32.0
	the Depreciation Rate is:														
1	3.500	3.431	3.365	3.302	3.241	3.182	3.125	3.070	3.017	2.966	2.917	2.869	2.823	2.778	2.734
2	4.000	3.922	3.846	3.774	3.704	3.636	3.571	3.509	3.448	3.390	3.333	3.279	3.226	3.175	3.125
3	4.000	3.922	3.846	3.774	3.704	3.636	3.571	3.509	3.448	3.390	3.333	3.279	3.226	3.175	3.125
4	4.000	3.922	3.846	3.774	3.704	3.636	3.571	3.509	3.448	3.390	3.333	3.279	3.226	3.175	3.125
5	4.000	3.922	3.846	3.774	3.704	3.636	3.571	3.509	3.448	3.390	3.333	3.279	3.226	3.175	3.125

If the Recovery Year is:	and the Recovery Period is: 25.0	25.5	26.0	26.5	27.0	27.5	28.0	28.5	29.0	29.5	30.0	30.5	31.0	31.5	32.0
	the Depreciation Rate is:														
6	4.000	3.922	3.846	3.774	3.704	3.636	3.572	3.509	3.448	3.390	3.333	3.279	3.226	3.175	3.125
7	4.000	3.921	3.846	3.773	3.704	3.636	3.571	3.509	3.448	3.390	3.333	3.279	3.226	3.175	3.125
8	4.000	3.922	3.846	3.774	3.704	3.636	3.572	3.509	3.448	3.390	3.333	3.279	3.226	3.174	3.125
9	4.000	3.921	3.846	3.773	3.704	3.636	3.571	3.509	3.448	3.390	3.333	3.279	3.226	3.175	3.125
10	4.000	3.922	3.846	3.774	3.704	3.637	3.572	3.509	3.448	3.390	3.333	3.279	3.226	3.174	3.125
11	4.000	3.921	3.846	3.773	3.704	3.636	3.571	3.509	3.448	3.390	3.333	3.279	3.226	3.175	3.125
12	4.000	3.922	3.846	3.774	3.704	3.637	3.572	3.509	3.448	3.390	3.333	3.279	3.226	3.174	3.125
13	4.000	3.921	3.846	3.773	3.703	3.636	3.571	3.509	3.448	3.390	3.334	3.278	3.226	3.175	3.125
14	4.000	3.922	3.846	3.774	3.704	3.637	3.572	3.509	3.448	3.390	3.333	3.279	3.226	3.174	3.125
15	4.000	3.921	3.846	3.773	3.703	3.636	3.571	3.509	3.449	3.390	3.334	3.278	3.226	3.175	3.125
16	4.000	3.922	3.846	3.774	3.704	3.637	3.572	3.509	3.448	3.390	3.333	3.279	3.226	3.174	3.125
17	4.000	3.921	3.846	3.773	3.703	3.636	3.571	3.509	3.449	3.390	3.334	3.278	3.226	3.175	3.125
18	4.000	3.922	3.846	3.774	3.704	3.637	3.572	3.508	3.448	3.390	3.333	3.279	3.226	3.174	3.125
19	4.000	3.921	3.847	3.773	3.703	3.636	3.571	3.509	3.449	3.390	3.334	3.278	3.226	3.175	3.125
20	4.000	3.922	3.846	3.774	3.704	3.637	3.572	3.508	3.448	3.390	3.333	3.279	3.225	3.174	3.125
21	4.000	3.921	3.847	3.773	3.703	3.636	3.571	3.509	3.449	3.390	3.334	3.278	3.226	3.175	3.125
22	4.000	3.922	3.846	3.774	3.704	3.637	3.572	3.508	3.448	3.389	3.333	3.279	3.225	3.174	3.125
23	4.000	3.921	3.847	3.773	3.703	3.636	3.571	3.509	3.449	3.390	3.334	3.278	3.226	3.175	3.125
24	4.000	3.922	3.846	3.774	3.704	3.637	3.572	3.508	3.448	3.389	3.333	3.279	3.225	3.174	3.125
25	4.000	3.921	3.847	3.773	3.703	3.636	3.571	3.509	3.449	3.390	3.334	3.278	3.226	3.175	3.125
26	0.500	2.451	3.846	3.774	3.704	3.637	3.572	3.508	3.448	3.389	3.333	3.279	3.225	3.174	3.125
27			0.481	2.358	3.703	3.636	3.571	3.509	3.449	3.390	3.334	3.278	3.226	3.175	3.125
28					0.463	2.273	3.572	3.508	3.448	3.389	3.333	3.279	3.225	3.174	3.125
29							0.446	2.193	3.449	3.390	3.334	3.278	3.226	3.175	3.125
30									0.431	2.118	3.333	3.279	3.225	3.174	3.125
31											0.417	2.049	3.226	3.175	3.125

If the Recovery Year is:	and the Recovery Period is: 25.0	25.5	26.0	26.5	27.0	27.5	28.0	28.5	29.0	29.5	30.0	30.5	31.0	31.5	32.0
	the Depreciation Rate is:														
32													0.403	1.984	3.125
33															0.391

If the Recovery Year is:	and the Recovery Period is: 32.5	33.0	33.5	34.0	34.5	35.0	35.5	36.0	36.5	37.0	37.5	38.0	38.5	39.0	39.5
	the Depreciation Rate is:														
1	2.692	2.652	2.612	2.574	2.536	2.500	2.465	2.431	2.397	2.365	2.333	2.303	2.273	2.244	2.215
2	3.077	3.030	2.985	2.941	2.899	2.857	2.817	2.778	2.740	2.703	2.667	2.632	2.597	2.564	2.532
3	3.077	3.030	2.985	2.941	2.899	2.857	2.817	2.778	2.740	2.703	2.667	2.632	2.597	2.564	2.532
4	3.077	3.030	2.985	2.941	2.899	2.857	2.817	2.778	2.740	2.703	2.667	2.632	2.597	2.564	2.532
5	3.077	3.030	2.985	2.941	2.899	2.857	2.817	2.778	2.740	2.703	2.667	2.632	2.597	2.564	2.532
6	3.077	3.030	2.985	2.941	2.898	2.857	2.817	2.778	2.740	2.703	2.667	2.632	2.597	2.564	2.532
7	3.077	3.030	2.985	2.941	2.899	2.857	2.817	2.778	2.740	2.703	2.667	2.632	2.597	2.564	2.532
8	3.077	3.030	2.985	2.941	2.898	2.857	2.817	2.778	2.740	2.703	2.667	2.631	2.597	2.564	2.532
9	3.077	3.030	2.985	2.941	2.899	2.857	2.817	2.778	2.740	2.703	2.667	2.632	2.597	2.564	2.532
10	3.077	3.030	2.985	2.941	2.898	2.857	2.817	2.778	2.740	2.703	2.667	2.631	2.598	2.564	2.532
11	3.077	3.030	2.985	2.941	2.899	2.857	2.817	2.778	2.740	2.703	2.667	2.632	2.597	2.564	2.532
12	3.077	3.030	2.985	2.941	2.898	2.857	2.817	2.778	2.740	2.703	2.667	2.631	2.598	2.564	2.532
13	3.077	3.030	2.985	2.941	2.899	2.857	2.817	2.778	2.740	2.703	2.667	2.632	2.597	2.564	2.532
14	3.077	3.030	2.985	2.941	2.898	2.857	2.817	2.778	2.740	2.703	2.667	2.631	2.598	2.564	2.531
15	3.077	3.030	2.985	2.941	2.899	2.857	2.817	2.778	2.740	2.703	2.666	2.632	2.597	2.564	2.532
16	3.077	3.031	2.985	2.941	2.898	2.857	2.817	2.778	2.740	2.703	2.667	2.631	2.598	2.564	2.531
17	3.077	3.030	2.985	2.941	2.899	2.857	2.817	2.778	2.740	2.702	2.666	2.632	2.597	2.564	2.532
18	3.077	3.031	2.985	2.941	2.898	2.857	2.817	2.778	2.740	2.703	2.667	2.631	2.598	2.564	2.531
19	3.077	3.030	2.985	2.941	2.899	2.857	2.817	2.778	2.739	2.702	2.666	2.632	2.597	2.564	2.532
20	3.077	3.031	2.985	2.941	2.898	2.857	2.817	2.778	2.740	2.703	2.667	2.631	2.598	2.564	2.531

If the Recovery Year is:	and the Recovery Period is: 32.5	33.0	33.5	34.0	34.5	35.0	35.5	36.0	36.5	37.0	37.5	38.0	38.5	39.0	39.5
	the Depreciation Rate is:														
21	3.077	3.030	2.985	2.941	2.899	2.857	2.817	2.777	2.739	2.702	2.666	2.632	2.597	2.564	2.532
22	3.077	3.031	2.985	2.941	2.898	2.857	2.817	2.778	2.740	2.703	2.667	2.631	2.598	2.564	2.531
23	3.077	3.030	2.985	2.941	2.899	2.857	2.817	2.777	2.739	2.702	2.666	2.632	2.597	2.564	2.532
24	3.077	3.031	2.985	2.941	2.898	2.857	2.817	2.778	2.740	2.703	2.667	2.631	2.598	2.564	2.531
25	3.077	3.030	2.985	2.942	2.899	2.857	2.817	2.777	2.739	2.702	2.666	2.632	2.597	2.564	2.532
26	3.077	3.031	2.985	2.941	2.898	2.857	2.817	2.778	2.740	2.703	2.667	2.631	2.598	2.564	2.531
27	3.077	3.030	2.985	2.942	2.899	2.858	2.817	2.777	2.739	2.702	2.666	2.632	2.597	2.564	2.532
28	3.077	3.031	2.985	2.941	2.898	2.857	2.817	2.778	2.740	2.703	2.667	2.631	2.598	2.564	2.531
29	3.077	3.030	2.985	2.942	2.899	2.858	2.817	2.777	2.739	2.702	2.666	2.632	2.597	2.564	2.532
30	3.076	3.031	2.986	2.941	2.898	2.857	2.816	2.778	2.740	2.703	2.667	2.631	2.598	2.564	2.531
31	3.077	3.030	2.985	2.942	2.899	2.858	2.817	2.777	2.739	2.702	2.666	2.632	2.597	2.564	2.532
32	3.076	3.031	2.986	2.941	2.898	2.857	2.816	2.778	2.740	2.703	2.667	2.631	2.598	2.564	2.531
33	1.923	3.030	2.985	2.942	2.899	2.858	2.817	2.777	2.739	2.702	2.666	2.632	2.597	2.564	2.532
34		0.379	1.866	2.941	2.898	2.857	2.816	2.778	2.740	2.703	2.667	2.631	2.598	2.565	2.531
35				0.368	1.812	2.858	2.817	2.777	2.739	2.702	2.666	2.632	2.597	2.564	2.532
36						0.357	1.760	2.778	2.740	2.703	2.667	2.631	2.598	2.565	2.531
37								0.347	1.712	2.702	2.666	2.632	2.597	2.564	2.532
38										0.338	1.667	2.631	2.598	2.565	2.531
39												0.329	1.623	2.564	2.532
40														0.321	1.582

If the Recovery Year is:	and the Recovery Period is: 40.0	40.5	41.0	41.5	42.0	42.5	43.0	43.5	44.0	44.5	45.0	45.5	46.0	46.5	47.0
	the Depreciation Rate is:														
1	2.188	2.160	2.134	2.108	2.083	2.059	2.035	2.011	1.989	1.966	1.944	1.923	1.902	1.882	1.862
2	2.500	2.469	2.439	2.410	2.381	2.353	2.326	2.299	2.273	2.247	2.222	2.198	2.174	2.151	2.128

If the Recovery Year is:	and the Recovery Period is: 40.0	40.5	41.0	41.5	42.0	42.5	43.0	43.5	44.0	44.5	45.0	45.5	46.0	46.5	47.0
	the Depreciation Rate is:														
3	2.500	2.469	2.439	2.410	2.381	2.353	2.326	2.299	2.273	2.247	2.222	2.198	2.174	2.151	2.128
4	2.500	2.469	2.439	2.410	2.381	2.353	2.326	2.299	2.273	2.247	2.222	2.198	2.174	2.151	2.128
5	2.500	2.469	2.439	2.410	2.381	2.353	2.326	2.299	2.273	2.247	2.222	2.198	2.174	2.150	2.128
6	2.500	2.469	2.439	2.410	2.381	2.353	2.326	2.299	2.273	2.247	2.222	2.198	2.174	2.151	2.128
7	2.500	2.469	2.439	2.410	2.381	2.353	2.326	2.299	2.273	2.247	2.222	2.198	2.174	2.150	2.128
8	2.500	2.469	2.439	2.410	2.381	2.353	2.326	2.299	2.273	2.247	2.222	2.198	2.174	2.151	2.128
9	2.500	2.469	2.439	2.410	2.381	2.353	2.325	2.299	2.273	2.247	2.222	2.198	2.174	2.150	2.128
10	2.500	2.469	2.439	2.410	2.381	2.353	2.326	2.299	2.273	2.247	2.222	2.198	2.174	2.151	2.128
11	2.500	2.469	2.439	2.410	2.381	2.353	2.325	2.299	2.273	2.247	2.222	2.198	2.174	2.150	2.128
12	2.500	2.469	2.439	2.410	2.381	2.353	2.326	2.299	2.273	2.247	2.222	2.198	2.174	2.151	2.128
13	2.500	2.469	2.439	2.410	2.381	2.353	2.325	2.299	2.273	2.247	2.222	2.198	2.174	2.150	2.128
14	2.500	2.469	2.439	2.410	2.381	2.353	2.326	2.299	2.273	2.247	2.222	2.198	2.174	2.151	2.128
15	2.500	2.469	2.439	2.409	2.381	2.353	2.325	2.299	2.273	2.247	2.222	2.198	2.174	2.150	2.128
16	2.500	2.469	2.439	2.410	2.381	2.353	2.326	2.299	2.273	2.247	2.222	2.198	2.174	2.151	2.128
17	2.500	2.469	2.439	2.409	2.381	2.353	2.325	2.299	2.273	2.247	2.222	2.198	2.174	2.150	2.127
18	2.500	2.469	2.439	2.410	2.381	2.353	2.326	2.299	2.273	2.247	2.222	2.198	2.174	2.151	2.128
19	2.500	2.469	2.439	2.409	2.381	2.353	2.325	2.299	2.273	2.247	2.222	2.198	2.174	2.150	2.127
20	2.500	2.469	2.439	2.410	2.381	2.353	2.326	2.299	2.273	2.247	2.222	2.198	2.174	2.151	2.128
21	2.500	2.469	2.439	2.409	2.381	2.353	2.325	2.299	2.272	2.247	2.222	2.198	2.174	2.150	2.127
22	2.500	2.469	2.439	2.410	2.381	2.353	2.326	2.299	2.273	2.247	2.222	2.198	2.174	2.151	2.128
23	2.500	2.469	2.439	2.409	2.381	2.353	2.325	2.299	2.272	2.247	2.222	2.198	2.174	2.150	2.127
24	2.500	2.469	2.439	2.410	2.381	2.353	2.326	2.299	2.273	2.247	2.222	2.198	2.174	2.151	2.128
25	2.500	2.469	2.439	2.409	2.381	2.353	2.325	2.299	2.272	2.247	2.222	2.198	2.174	2.150	2.127
26	2.500	2.469	2.439	2.410	2.381	2.353	2.326	2.299	2.273	2.247	2.223	2.198	2.174	2.151	2.128
27	2.500	2.469	2.439	2.409	2.381	2.353	2.325	2.299	2.272	2.247	2.222	2.198	2.174	2.150	2.127
28	2.500	2.469	2.439	2.410	2.381	2.353	2.326	2.299	2.273	2.247	2.223	2.198	2.174	2.151	2.128

If the Recovery Year is:	40.0	40.5	41.0	41.5	42.0	42.5	43.0	43.5	44.0	44.5	45.0	45.5	46.0	46.5	47.0
	and the Recovery Period is: the Depreciation Rate is:														
29	2.500	2.469	2.439	2.409	2.381	2.353	2.325	2.299	2.272	2.248	2.222	2.198	2.174	2.150	2.127
30	2.500	2.470	2.439	2.410	2.381	2.353	2.326	2.299	2.273	2.247	2.223	2.197	2.174	2.151	2.128
31	2.500	2.469	2.439	2.409	2.381	2.353	2.325	2.299	2.272	2.248	2.222	2.198	2.174	2.150	2.127
32	2.500	2.470	2.439	2.410	2.381	2.353	2.326	2.299	2.273	2.247	2.223	2.197	2.174	2.151	2.128
33	2.500	2.469	2.439	2.409	2.381	2.353	2.325	2.298	2.272	2.248	2.222	2.198	2.174	2.150	2.127
34	2.500	2.470	2.439	2.410	2.381	2.353	2.326	2.299	2.273	2.247	2.223	2.197	2.174	2.151	2.128
35	2.500	2.469	2.439	2.409	2.381	2.353	2.325	2.298	2.272	2.248	2.222	2.198	2.174	2.150	2.127
36	2.500	2.470	2.439	2.410	2.381	2.353	2.326	2.299	2.273	2.247	2.223	2.197	2.174	2.151	2.128
37	2.500	2.469	2.439	2.409	2.381	2.353	2.325	2.298	2.272	2.248	2.222	2.198	2.174	2.150	2.127
38	2.500	2.470	2.439	2.410	2.381	2.353	2.326	2.299	2.273	2.247	2.223	2.197	2.174	2.151	2.128
39	2.500	2.469	2.439	2.409	2.381	2.352	2.325	2.298	2.272	2.248	2.222	2.198	2.174	2.150	2.127
40	2.500	2.470	2.440	2.410	2.380	2.353	2.326	2.299	2.273	2.247	2.223	2.197	2.173	2.151	2.128
41	0.312	1.543	2.439	2.409	2.381	2.352	2.325	2.298	2.272	2.248	2.222	2.198	2.174	2.150	2.127
42			0.305	1.506	2.380	2.353	2.326	2.299	2.273	2.247	2.223	2.197	2.173	2.151	2.128
43					0.298	1.470	2.325	2.298	2.272	2.248	2.222	2.198	2.174	2.150	2.127
44							0.291	1.437	2.273	2.247	2.223	2.197	2.173	2.151	2.128
45									0.284	1.405	2.222	2.198	2.174	2.150	2.127
46											0.278	1.373	2.173	2.151	2.128
47													0.272	1.344	2.127
48															0.266

If the Recovery Year is:	47.5	48.0	48.5	49.0	49.5	50.0
	and the Recovery Period is: the Depreciation Rate is:					
1	1.842	1.823	1.804	1.786	1.768	1.750
2	2.105	2.083	2.062	2.041	2.020	2.000

If the Recovery Year is:	and the Recovery Period is: 47.5	48.0	48.5	49.0	49.5	50.0
	the Depreciation Rate is:					
3	2.105	2.083	2.062	2.041	2.020	2.000
4	2.105	2.083	2.062	2.041	2.020	2.000
5	2.105	2.083	2.062	2.041	2.020	2.000
6	2.105	2.083	2.062	2.041	2.020	2.000
7	2.105	2.083	2.062	2.041	2.020	2.000
8	2.105	2.083	2.062	2.041	2.020	2.000
9	2.105	2.083	2.062	2.041	2.020	2.000
10	2.105	2.083	2.062	2.041	2.020	2.000
11	2.105	2.083	2.062	2.041	2.020	2.000
12	2.105	2.083	2.062	2.041	2.020	2.000
13	2.105	2.083	2.062	2.041	2.020	2.000
14	2.105	2.083	2.062	2.041	2.020	2.000
15	2.105	2.083	2.062	2.041	2.020	2.000
16	2.105	2.083	2.062	2.041	2.020	2.000
17	2.105	2.083	2.062	2.041	2.020	2.000
18	2.105	2.084	2.062	2.041	2.020	2.000
19	2.105	2.083	2.062	2.041	2.020	2.000
20	2.105	2.084	2.062	2.041	2.020	2.000
21	2.105	2.083	2.062	2.041	2.020	2.000
22	2.105	2.084	2.062	2.041	2.020	2.000
23	2.105	2.083	2.062	2.041	2.020	2.000
24	2.106	2.084	2.062	2.041	2.020	2.000
25	2.105	2.083	2.062	2.041	2.020	2.000
26	2.106	2.084	2.062	2.041	2.020	2.000
27	2.105	2.083	2.062	2.041	2.020	2.000
28	2.106	2.084	2.062	2.041	2.020	2.000

If the Recovery Year is:	and the Recovery Period is: 47.5	48.0	48.5	49.0	49.5	50.0
	the Depreciation Rate is:					
29	2.105	2.083	2.062	2.041	2.020	2.000
30	2.106	2.084	2.062	2.041	2.020	2.000
31	2.105	2.083	2.062	2.041	2.020	2.000
32	2.106	2.084	2.062	2.040	2.021	2.000
33	2.105	2.083	2.062	2.041	2.020	2.000
34	2.106	2.084	2.062	2.040	2.021	2.000
35	2.105	2.083	2.062	2.041	2.020	2.000
36	2.106	2.084	2.062	2.040	2.021	2.000
37	2.105	2.083	2.061	2.041	2.020	2.000
38	2.106	2.084	2.062	2.040	2.021	2.000
39	2.105	2.083	2.061	2.041	2.020	2.000
40	2.106	2.084	2.062	2.040	2.021	2.000
41	2.105	2.083	2.061	2.041	2.020	2.000
42	2.106	2.084	2.062	2.040	2.021	2.000
43	2.105	2.083	2.061	2.041	2.020	2.000
44	2.106	2.084	2.062	2.040	2.021	2.000
45	2.105	2.083	2.061	2.041	2.020	2.000
46	2.106	2.084	2.062	2.040	2.021	2.000
47	2.105	2.083	2.061	2.041	2.020	2.000
48	1.316	2.084	2.062	2.040	2.021	2.000
49		0.260	1.288	2.041	2.020	2.000
50				0.255	1.263	2.000
51						0.250

TABLE 10
General and Alternative Depreciation Systems
Applicable Depreciation Method: Straight Line
Applicable Recovery Periods: 2.5 — 50 years
Applicable Convention: Mid-quarter (property placed in service in second quarter)

and the Recovery Period is:

If the Recovery Year is:	2.5	3.0	3.5	4.0	4.5	5.0	5.5	6.0	6.5	7.0	7.5	8.0	8.5	9.0	9.5
			the Depreciation Rate is:												
1	25.00	20.83	17.86	15.63	13.89	12.50	11.36	10.42	9.62	8.93	8.33	7.81	7.35	6.94	6.58
2	40.00	33.33	28.57	25.00	22.22	20.00	18.18	16.67	15.38	14.29	13.33	12.50	11.77	11.11	10.53
3	35.00	33.34	28.57	25.00	22.22	20.00	18.18	16.67	15.38	14.28	13.33	12.50	11.76	11.11	10.53
4		12.50	25.00	25.00	22.22	20.00	18.18	16.66	15.39	14.29	13.34	12.50	11.77	11.11	10.53
5				9.37	19.45	20.00	18.19	16.67	15.38	14.28	13.33	12.50	11.76	11.11	10.52
6						7.50	15.91	16.66	15.39	14.29	13.34	12.50	11.77	11.11	10.53
7								6.25	13.46	14.28	13.33	12.50	11.76	11.11	10.52
8										5.36	11.67	12.50	11.77	11.12	10.53
9												4.69	10.29	11.11	10.52
10														4.17	9.21

and the Recovery Period is:

If the Recovery Year is:	10.0	10.5	11.0	11.5	12.0	12.5	13.0	13.5	14.0	14.5	15.0	15.5	16.0	16.5	17.0
			the Depreciation Rate is:												
1	6.25	5.95	5.68	5.43	5.21	5.00	4.81	4.63	4.46	4.31	4.17	4.03	3.91	3.79	3.68
2	10.00	9.52	9.09	8.70	8.33	8.00	7.69	7.41	7.14	6.90	6.67	6.45	6.25	6.06	5.88
3	10.00	9.52	9.09	8.70	8.33	8.00	7.69	7.41	7.14	6.90	6.67	6.45	6.25	6.06	5.88
4	10.00	9.53	9.09	8.70	8.33	8.00	7.69	7.41	7.14	6.90	6.67	6.45	6.25	6.06	5.88
5	10.00	9.52	9.09	8.69	8.33	8.00	7.69	7.41	7.14	6.90	6.67	6.45	6.25	6.06	5.88
6	10.00	9.53	9.09	8.70	8.33	8.00	7.69	7.41	7.14	6.90	6.67	6.45	6.25	6.06	5.88

If the Recovery Year is:	10.0	10.5	11.0	11.5	12.0	12.5	13.0	13.5	14.0	14.5	15.0	15.5	16.0	16.5	17.0
	the Depreciation Rate is:														
7	10.00	9.52	9.09	8.69	8.34	8.00	7.69	7.41	7.15	6.89	6.66	6.45	6.25	6.06	5.88
8	10.00	9.53	9.09	8.70	8.33	8.00	7.69	7.41	7.14	6.90	6.67	6.45	6.25	6.06	5.88
9	10.00	9.52	9.09	8.69	8.34	8.00	7.69	7.40	7.15	6.89	6.66	6.45	6.25	6.06	5.88
10	10.00	9.53	9.09	8.70	8.33	8.00	7.70	7.41	7.14	6.90	6.67	6.45	6.25	6.06	5.88
11	3.75	8.33	9.10	8.69	8.34	8.00	7.69	7.40	7.15	6.89	6.66	6.45	6.25	6.06	5.88
12			3.41	7.61	8.33	8.00	7.70	7.41	7.14	6.90	6.67	6.46	6.25	6.06	5.89
13					3.13	7.00	7.69	7.40	7.15	6.89	6.66	6.45	6.25	6.06	5.88
14							2.89	6.48	7.14	6.90	6.67	6.46	6.25	6.06	5.89
15									2.68	6.03	6.66	6.45	6.25	6.06	5.88
16											2.50	5.65	6.25	6.06	5.89
17													2.34	5.31	5.88
18															2.21

and the Recovery Period is:

If the Recovery Year is:	17.5	18.0	18.5	19.0	19.5	20.0	20.5	21.0	21.5	22.0	22.5	23.0	23.5	24.0	24.5
	the Depreciation Rate is:														
1	3.57	3.47	3.38	3.29	3.21	3.125	3.049	2.976	2.907	2.841	2.778	2.717	2.660	2.604	2.551
2	5.71	5.56	5.41	5.26	5.13	5.000	4.878	4.762	4.651	4.545	4.444	4.348	4.255	4.167	4.082
3	5.71	5.56	5.41	5.26	5.13	5.000	4.878	4.762	4.651	4.545	4.444	4.348	4.255	4.167	4.082
4	5.71	5.56	5.40	5.26	5.13	5.000	4.878	4.762	4.651	4.545	4.444	4.348	4.255	4.167	4.082
5	5.72	5.55	5.41	5.26	5.13	5.000	4.878	4.762	4.651	4.546	4.445	4.348	4.255	4.167	4.082
6	5.71	5.56	5.40	5.26	5.13	5.000	4.878	4.762	4.651	4.545	4.444	4.348	4.255	4.167	4.082
7	5.72	5.55	5.41	5.26	5.13	5.000	4.878	4.762	4.651	4.546	4.445	4.348	4.255	4.167	4.082
8	5.71	5.56	5.40	5.26	5.13	5.000	4.878	4.762	4.651	4.545	4.444	4.348	4.255	4.167	4.082
9	5.72	5.55	5.41	5.27	5.13	5.000	4.878	4.762	4.651	4.546	4.445	4.348	4.255	4.167	4.081
10	5.71	5.56	5.40	5.26	5.13	5.000	4.878	4.762	4.651	4.545	4.444	4.348	4.255	4.167	4.082

If the Recovery Year is:	17.5	18.0	18.5	19.0	19.5	20.0	20.5	21.0	21.5	22.0	22.5	23.0	23.5	24.0	24.5
			the Depreciation Rate is:												
11	5.72	5.55	5.41	5.27	5.13	5.000	4.878	4.762	4.651	4.546	4.445	4.348	4.255	4.166	4.081
12	5.71	5.56	5.40	5.26	5.13	5.000	4.878	4.762	4.651	4.545	4.444	4.348	4.256	4.167	4.082
13	5.72	5.55	5.41	5.27	5.13	5.000	4.878	4.762	4.651	4.546	4.445	4.348	4.255	4.166	4.081
14	5.71	5.56	5.40	5.26	5.12	5.000	4.878	4.762	4.651	4.545	4.444	4.348	4.256	4.167	4.082
15	5.72	5.55	5.41	5.27	5.13	5.000	4.878	4.762	4.651	4.546	4.445	4.348	4.255	4.166	4.081
16	5.71	5.56	5.40	5.26	5.12	5.000	4.878	4.762	4.651	4.545	4.444	4.348	4.256	4.167	4.082
17	5.72	5.55	5.41	5.27	5.13	5.000	4.878	4.762	4.652	4.546	4.445	4.348	4.255	4.166	4.081
18	5.00	5.56	5.40	5.26	5.12	5.000	4.878	4.762	4.651	4.545	4.444	4.347	4.256	4.167	4.082
19		2.08	4.73	5.27	5.13	5.000	4.878	4.761	4.652	4.546	4.445	4.348	4.255	4.166	4.081
20				1.97	4.48	5.000	4.878	4.762	4.651	4.545	4.444	4.347	4.256	4.167	4.082
21						1.875	4.269	4.761	4.652	4.546	4.445	4.348	4.255	4.166	4.081
22								1.786	4.070	4.545	4.444	4.347	4.256	4.167	4.082
23										1.705	3.889	4.348	4.255	4.166	4.081
24												1.630	3.724	4.167	4.082
25														1.562	3.571

and the Recovery Period is:

If the Recovery Year is:	25.0	25.5	26.0	26.5	27.0	27.5	28.0	28.5	29.0	29.5	30.0	30.5	31.0	31.5	32.0
			the Depreciation Rate is:												
1	2.500	2.451	2.404	2.358	2.315	2.273	2.232	2.193	2.155	2.119	2.083	2.049	2.016	1.984	1.953
2	4.000	3.922	3.846	3.774	3.704	3.636	3.571	3.509	3.448	3.390	3.333	3.279	3.226	3.175	3.125
3	4.000	3.922	3.846	3.774	3.704	3.636	3.571	3.509	3.448	3.390	3.333	3.279	3.226	3.175	3.125
4	4.000	3.922	3.846	3.774	3.704	3.636	3.571	3.509	3.448	3.390	3.333	3.279	3.226	3.175	3.125
5	4.000	3.922	3.846	3.774	3.704	3.636	3.571	3.509	3.448	3.390	3.333	3.279	3.226	3.175	3.125
6	4.000	3.921	3.846	3.774	3.704	3.636	3.572	3.509	3.448	3.390	3.333	3.279	3.226	3.175	3.125
7	4.000	3.922	3.846	3.774	3.704	3.636	3.571	3.509	3.448	3.390	3.333	3.279	3.226	3.175	3.125

If the Recovery Year is:	25.0	25.5	26.0	26.5	27.0	27.5	28.0	28.5	29.0	29.5	30.0	30.5	31.0	31.5	32.0
			the Depreciation Rate is:												
8	4.000	3.921	3.846	3.773	3.704	3.636	3.572	3.509	3.448	3.390	3.333	3.279	3.226	3.175	3.125
9	4.000	3.922	3.846	3.774	3.704	3.636	3.571	3.509	3.448	3.390	3.333	3.279	3.226	3.174	3.125
10	4.000	3.921	3.846	3.773	3.704	3.637	3.572	3.509	3.448	3.390	3.333	3.279	3.226	3.175	3.125
11	4.000	3.922	3.846	3.774	3.704	3.636	3.571	3.509	3.448	3.390	3.333	3.279	3.226	3.174	3.125
12	4.000	3.921	3.846	3.773	3.704	3.637	3.572	3.509	3.448	3.390	3.334	3.279	3.226	3.175	3.125
13	4.000	3.922	3.846	3.774	3.703	3.636	3.571	3.509	3.448	3.390	3.333	3.279	3.226	3.174	3.125
14	4.000	3.921	3.846	3.773	3.704	3.637	3.572	3.509	3.448	3.390	3.334	3.278	3.226	3.175	3.125
15	4.000	3.922	3.846	3.774	3.703	3.636	3.571	3.509	3.449	3.390	3.333	3.279	3.226	3.174	3.125
16	4.000	3.921	3.846	3.773	3.704	3.637	3.572	3.509	3.448	3.390	3.334	3.278	3.226	3.175	3.125
17	4.000	3.922	3.846	3.774	3.703	3.636	3.571	3.509	3.449	3.390	3.333	3.279	3.226	3.174	3.125
18	4.000	3.921	3.846	3.773	3.704	3.637	3.572	3.508	3.448	3.390	3.334	3.278	3.226	3.175	3.125
19	4.000	3.922	3.846	3.774	3.703	3.636	3.571	3.509	3.449	3.390	3.333	3.279	3.226	3.174	3.125
20	4.000	3.921	3.847	3.773	3.704	3.637	3.572	3.508	3.448	3.390	3.334	3.278	3.226	3.175	3.125
21	4.000	3.922	3.846	3.774	3.703	3.636	3.571	3.509	3.449	3.389	3.333	3.279	3.225	3.174	3.125
22	4.000	3.921	3.847	3.773	3.704	3.637	3.572	3.508	3.448	3.390	3.334	3.278	3.226	3.175	3.125
23	4.000	3.922	3.846	3.774	3.703	3.636	3.571	3.509	3.449	3.389	3.333	3.279	3.225	3.174	3.125
24	4.000	3.921	3.847	3.773	3.704	3.637	3.572	3.508	3.448	3.390	3.334	3.278	3.226	3.175	3.125
25	4.000	3.922	3.846	3.774	3.703	3.636	3.571	3.509	3.449	3.389	3.333	3.279	3.225	3.174	3.125
26	1.500	3.431	3.847	3.773	3.704	3.637	3.572	3.508	3.448	3.390	3.334	3.278	3.226	3.175	3.125
27			1.442	3.302	3.703	3.636	3.571	3.509	3.449	3.389	3.333	3.279	3.225	3.174	3.125
28					1.389	3.182	3.572	3.508	3.448	3.390	3.334	3.278	3.226	3.175	3.125
29							1.339	3.070	3.449	3.389	3.333	3.279	3.225	3.174	3.125
30									1.293	2.966	3.334	3.278	3.226	3.175	3.125
31											1.250	2.869	3.225	3.174	3.125
32													1.210	2.778	3.125
33															1.172

and the Recovery Period is:

If the Recovery Year is:	32.5	33.0	33.5	34.0	34.5	35.0	35.5	36.0	36.5	37.0	37.5	38.0	38.5	39.0	39.5
			the Depreciation Rate is:												
1	1.923	1.894	1.866	1.838	1.812	1.786	1.761	1.736	1.712	1.689	1.667	1.645	1.623	1.603	1.582
2	3.077	3.030	2.985	2.941	2.899	2.857	2.817	2.778	2.740	2.703	2.667	2.632	2.597	2.564	2.532
3	3.077	3.030	2.985	2.941	2.899	2.857	2.817	2.778	2.740	2.703	2.667	2.632	2.597	2.564	2.532
4	3.077	3.030	2.985	2.941	2.899	2.857	2.817	2.778	2.740	2.703	2.667	2.632	2.597	2.564	2.532
5	3.077	3.030	2.985	2.941	2.898	2.857	2.817	2.778	2.740	2.703	2.667	2.632	2.597	2.564	2.532
6	3.077	3.030	2.985	2.941	2.899	2.857	2.817	2.778	2.740	2.703	2.667	2.632	2.597	2.564	2.532
7	3.077	3.030	2.985	2.941	2.898	2.857	2.817	2.778	2.740	2.703	2.667	2.632	2.597	2.564	2.532
8	3.077	3.030	2.985	2.941	2.899	2.857	2.817	2.778	2.740	2.703	2.667	2.631	2.597	2.564	2.532
9	3.077	3.030	2.985	2.941	2.898	2.857	2.817	2.778	2.740	2.703	2.667	2.632	2.598	2.564	2.532
10	3.077	3.030	2.985	2.941	2.899	2.857	2.817	2.778	2.740	2.703	2.667	2.631	2.597	2.564	2.532
11	3.077	3.030	2.985	2.941	2.898	2.857	2.817	2.778	2.740	2.703	2.667	2.632	2.598	2.564	2.532
12	3.077	3.030	2.985	2.941	2.899	2.857	2.817	2.778	2.740	2.703	2.667	2.631	2.597	2.564	2.532
13	3.077	3.030	2.985	2.941	2.898	2.857	2.817	2.778	2.740	2.703	2.667	2.632	2.598	2.564	2.532
14	3.077	3.030	2.985	2.941	2.899	2.857	2.817	2.778	2.740	2.703	2.666	2.631	2.597	2.564	2.531
15	3.077	3.031	2.985	2.941	2.898	2.857	2.817	2.778	2.740	2.703	2.667	2.632	2.598	2.564	2.532
16	3.077	3.030	2.985	2.941	2.899	2.857	2.817	2.778	2.740	2.703	2.666	2.631	2.597	2.564	2.531
17	3.077	3.031	2.985	2.941	2.898	2.857	2.817	2.778	2.740	2.703	2.667	2.632	2.598	2.564	2.532
18	3.077	3.030	2.985	2.941	2.899	2.857	2.817	2.778	2.740	2.702	2.666	2.631	2.597	2.564	2.531
19	3.077	3.031	2.985	2.941	2.898	2.857	2.817	2.778	2.739	2.703	2.667	2.632	2.598	2.564	2.532
20	3.077	3.030	2.985	2.941	2.899	2.857	2.817	2.778	2.740	2.702	2.666	2.631	2.597	2.564	2.531
21	3.077	3.031	2.985	2.941	2.898	2.857	2.817	2.778	2.739	2.703	2.667	2.632	2.598	2.564	2.532
22	3.077	3.030	2.985	2.941	2.899	2.857	2.817	2.777	2.740	2.702	2.666	2.631	2.597	2.564	2.531
23	3.077	3.031	2.985	2.941	2.898	2.857	2.817	2.778	2.739	2.703	2.667	2.632	2.598	2.564	2.532
24	3.077	3.030	2.985	2.942	2.899	2.857	2.817	2.777	2.740	2.702	2.666	2.631	2.597	2.564	2.531
25	3.077	3.031	2.985	2.941	2.898	2.857	2.817	2.778	2.739	2.703	2.667	2.632	2.598	2.564	2.532

If the Recovery Year is:	32.5	33.0	33.5	34.0	34.5	35.0	35.5	36.0	36.5	37.0	37.5	38.0	38.5	39.0	39.5
			the Depreciation Rate is:												
26	3.077	3.030	2.985	2.942	2.899	2.857	2.817	2.777	2.740	2.702	2.666	2.631	2.597	2.564	2.531
27	3.077	3.031	2.985	2.941	2.898	2.857	2.817	2.778	2.739	2.703	2.667	2.632	2.598	2.564	2.532
28	3.077	3.030	2.985	2.942	2.899	2.858	2.817	2.777	2.740	2.702	2.666	2.631	2.597	2.564	2.531
29	3.077	3.031	2.985	2.941	2.898	2.857	2.817	2.778	2.739	2.703	2.667	2.632	2.598	2.564	2.532
30	3.076	3.030	2.985	2.942	2.899	2.858	2.816	2.777	2.740	2.702	2.666	2.631	2.597	2.564	2.531
31	3.077	3.031	2.986	2.941	2.898	2.857	2.817	2.778	2.739	2.703	2.667	2.632	2.598	2.564	2.532
32	3.076	3.030	2.985	2.942	2.899	2.858	2.816	2.777	2.740	2.702	2.666	2.631	2.597	2.564	2.531
33	2.692	3.031	2.986	2.941	2.898	2.857	2.817	2.778	2.739	2.703	2.667	2.632	2.598	2.564	2.532
34		1.136	2.612	2.942	2.899	2.858	2.816	2.777	2.740	2.702	2.666	2.631	2.597	2.565	2.531
35				1.103	2.536	2.857	2.817	2.778	2.739	2.703	2.667	2.632	2.598	2.564	2.532
36						1.072	2.464	2.777	2.740	2.702	2.666	2.631	2.597	2.565	2.531
37								1.042	2.397	2.703	2.667	2.632	2.598	2.564	2.532
38										1.013	2.333	2.631	2.597	2.565	2.531
39												0.987	2.273	2.564	2.532
40														0.962	2.215

and the Recovery Period is:

If the Recovery Year is:	40.0	40.5	41.0	41.5	42.0	42.5	43.0	43.5	44.0	44.5	45.0	45.5	46.0	46.5	47.0
			the Depreciation Rate is:												
1	1.563	1.543	1.524	1.506	1.488	1.471	1.453	1.437	1.420	1.404	1.389	1.374	1.359	1.344	1.330
2	2.500	2.469	2.439	2.410	2.381	2.353	2.326	2.299	2.273	2.247	2.222	2.198	2.174	2.151	2.128
3	2.500	2.469	2.439	2.410	2.381	2.353	2.326	2.299	2.273	2.247	2.222	2.198	2.174	2.151	2.128
4	2.500	2.469	2.439	2.410	2.381	2.353	2.326	2.299	2.273	2.247	2.222	2.198	2.174	2.151	2.128
5	2.500	2.469	2.439	2.410	2.381	2.353	2.326	2.299	2.273	2.247	2.222	2.198	2.174	2.151	2.128
6	2.500	2.469	2.439	2.410	2.381	2.353	2.326	2.299	2.273	2.247	2.222	2.198	2.174	2.150	2.128
7	2.500	2.469	2.439	2.410	2.381	2.353	2.326	2.299	2.273	2.247	2.222	2.198	2.174	2.151	2.128

If the Recovery Year is:	40.0	40.5	41.0	41.5	42.0	42.5	43.0	43.5	44.0	44.5	45.0	45.5	46.0	46.5	47.0
			the Depreciation Rate is:												
8	2.500	2.469	2.439	2.410	2.381	2.353	2.326	2.299	2.273	2.247	2.222	2.198	2.174	2.150	2.128
9	2.500	2.469	2.439	2.410	2.381	2.353	2.326	2.299	2.273	2.247	2.222	2.198	2.174	2.151	2.128
10	2.500	2.469	2.439	2.410	2.381	2.353	2.325	2.299	2.273	2.247	2.222	2.198	2.174	2.150	2.128
11	2.500	2.469	2.439	2.410	2.381	2.353	2.326	2.299	2.273	2.247	2.222	2.198	2.174	2.151	2.128
12	2.500	2.469	2.439	2.410	2.381	2.353	2.325	2.299	2.273	2.247	2.222	2.198	2.174	2.150	2.128
13	2.500	2.469	2.439	2.410	2.381	2.353	2.326	2.299	2.273	2.247	2.222	2.198	2.174	2.151	2.128
14	2.500	2.469	2.439	2.409	2.381	2.353	2.325	2.299	2.273	2.247	2.222	2.198	2.174	2.150	2.128
15	2.500	2.469	2.439	2.410	2.381	2.353	2.326	2.299	2.273	2.247	2.222	2.198	2.174	2.151	2.128
16	2.500	2.469	2.439	2.409	2.381	2.353	2.325	2.299	2.273	2.247	2.222	2.198	2.174	2.150	2.128
17	2.500	2.469	2.439	2.410	2.381	2.353	2.326	2.299	2.273	2.247	2.222	2.198	2.174	2.151	2.127
18	2.500	2.469	2.439	2.409	2.381	2.353	2.325	2.299	2.273	2.247	2.222	2.198	2.174	2.150	2.128
19	2.500	2.469	2.439	2.410	2.381	2.353	2.326	2.299	2.273	2.247	2.222	2.198	2.174	2.151	2.127
20	2.500	2.469	2.439	2.409	2.381	2.353	2.325	2.299	2.273	2.247	2.222	2.198	2.174	2.150	2.128
21	2.500	2.469	2.439	2.410	2.381	2.353	2.326	2.299	2.273	2.247	2.222	2.198	2.174	2.151	2.127
22	2.500	2.469	2.439	2.409	2.381	2.353	2.325	2.299	2.273	2.247	2.222	2.198	2.174	2.150	2.128
23	2.500	2.469	2.439	2.410	2.381	2.353	2.326	2.299	2.272	2.247	2.222	2.198	2.174	2.151	2.127
24	2.500	2.469	2.439	2.409	2.381	2.353	2.325	2.299	2.273	2.247	2.222	2.198	2.174	2.150	2.128
25	2.500	2.469	2.439	2.410	2.381	2.353	2.326	2.299	2.272	2.247	2.222	2.198	2.174	2.151	2.127
26	2.500	2.469	2.439	2.409	2.381	2.353	2.325	2.299	2.273	2.247	2.222	2.198	2.174	2.150	2.128
27	2.500	2.469	2.439	2.410	2.381	2.353	2.326	2.299	2.272	2.247	2.223	2.198	2.174	2.151	2.127
28	2.500	2.469	2.439	2.409	2.381	2.353	2.325	2.299	2.273	2.247	2.222	2.198	2.174	2.150	2.128
29	2.500	2.469	2.439	2.410	2.381	2.353	2.326	2.299	2.272	2.248	2.223	2.197	2.174	2.151	2.127
30	2.500	2.469	2.439	2.409	2.381	2.353	2.325	2.299	2.273	2.247	2.222	2.198	2.174	2.150	2.128
31	2.500	2.470	2.439	2.410	2.381	2.353	2.326	2.299	2.272	2.248	2.223	2.197	2.174	2.151	2.127
32	2.500	2.469	2.439	2.409	2.381	2.353	2.325	2.298	2.273	2.247	2.222	2.198	2.174	2.150	2.128
33	2.500	2.470	2.439	2.410	2.381	2.353	2.326	2.299	2.272	2.248	2.223	2.197	2.174	2.151	2.127
34	2.500	2.469	2.439	2.409	2.381	2.353	2.325	2.298	2.273	2.247	2.222	2.198	2.174	2.150	2.128

If the Recovery Year is:	40.0	40.5	41.0	41.5	42.0	42.5	43.0	43.5	44.0	44.5	45.0	45.5	46.0	46.5	47.0
	the Depreciation Rate is:														
35	2.500	2.470	2.439	2.410	2.381	2.353	2.326	2.299	2.272	2.248	2.223	2.197	2.174	2.151	2.127
36	2.500	2.469	2.439	2.409	2.381	2.353	2.325	2.298	2.273	2.247	2.222	2.198	2.174	2.150	2.128
37	2.500	2.470	2.439	2.410	2.381	2.353	2.326	2.299	2.272	2.248	2.223	2.197	2.174	2.151	2.127
38	2.500	2.469	2.439	2.409	2.381	2.353	2.325	2.298	2.273	2.247	2.222	2.198	2.174	2.150	2.128
39	2.500	2.470	2.439	2.410	2.381	2.352	2.326	2.299	2.272	2.248	2.223	2.197	2.173	2.151	2.127
40	2.500	2.469	2.440	2.409	2.380	2.353	2.325	2.298	2.273	2.247	2.222	2.198	2.174	2.150	2.128
41	0.937	2.161	2.439	2.410	2.381	2.352	2.326	2.299	2.272	2.248	2.223	2.197	2.173	2.151	2.127
42			0.915	2.108	2.380	2.353	2.325	2.298	2.273	2.247	2.222	2.198	2.174	2.150	2.128
43					0.893	2.058	2.326	2.299	2.272	2.248	2.223	2.197	2.173	2.151	2.127
44							0.872	2.011	2.273	2.247	2.222	2.198	2.174	2.150	2.128
45									0.852	1.967	2.223	2.197	2.173	2.151	2.127
46											0.833	1.923	2.174	2.150	2.128
47													0.815	1.882	2.127
48															0.798

and the Recovery Period is:

If the Recovery Year is:	47.5	48.0	48.5	49.0	49.5	50.0
	the Depreciation Rate is:					
1	1.316	1.302	1.289	1.276	1.263	1.250
2	2.105	2.083	2.062	2.041	2.020	2.000
3	2.105	2.083	2.062	2.041	2.020	2.000
4	2.105	2.083	2.062	2.041	2.020	2.000
5	2.105	2.083	2.062	2.041	2.020	2.000
6	2.105	2.083	2.062	2.041	2.020	2.000
7	2.105	2.083	2.062	2.041	2.020	2.000
8	2.105	2.083	2.062	2.041	2.020	2.000
9	2.105	2.083	2.062	2.041	2.020	2.000

If the Recovery Year is:	and the Recovery Period is: 47.5	48.0	48.5	49.0	49.5	50.0
	the Depreciation Rate is:					
10	2.105	2.083	2.062	2.041	2.020	2.000
11	2.105	2.083	2.062	2.041	2.020	2.000
12	2.105	2.083	2.062	2.041	2.020	2.000
13	2.105	2.083	2.062	2.041	2.020	2.000
14	2.105	2.083	2.062	2.041	2.020	2.000
15	2.105	2.083	2.062	2.041	2.020	2.000
16	2.105	2.083	2.062	2.041	2.020	2.000
17	2.105	2.083	2.062	2.041	2.020	2.000
18	2.105	2.084	2.062	2.041	2.020	2.000
19	2.105	2.083	2.062	2.041	2.020	2.000
20	2.105	2.084	2.062	2.041	2.020	2.000
21	2.105	2.083	2.062	2.041	2.020	2.000
22	2.105	2.084	2.062	2.041	2.020	2.000
23	2.105	2.083	2.062	2.041	2.020	2.000
24	2.105	2.084	2.062	2.041	2.020	2.000
25	2.106	2.083	2.062	2.041	2.020	2.000
26	2.105	2.084	2.062	2.041	2.020	2.000
27	2.106	2.083	2.062	2.041	2.020	2.000
28	2.105	2.084	2.062	2.041	2.020	2.000
29	2.106	2.083	2.062	2.041	2.020	2.000
30	2.105	2.084	2.062	2.041	2.020	2.000
31	2.106	2.083	2.062	2.041	2.020	2.000
32	2.105	2.084	2.062	2.040	2.021	2.000
33	2.106	2.083	2.062	2.041	2.020	2.000
34	2.105	2.084	2.062	2.040	2.021	2.000
35	2.106	2.083	2.062	2.041	2.020	2.000

If the Recovery Year is:	and the Recovery Period is: 47.5	48.0	48.5	49.0	49.5	50.0
	the Depreciation Rate is:					
36	2.105	2.084	2.061	2.040	2.021	2.000
37	2.106	2.083	2.062	2.041	2.020	2.000
38	2.105	2.084	2.061	2.040	2.021	2.000
39	2.106	2.083	2.062	2.041	2.020	2.000
40	2.105	2.084	2.061	2.040	2.021	2.000
41	2.106	2.083	2.062	2.041	2.020	2.000
42	2.105	2.084	2.061	2.040	2.021	2.000
43	2.106	2.083	2.062	2.041	2.020	2.000
44	2.105	2.084	2.061	2.040	2.021	2.000
45	2.106	2.083	2.062	2.041	2.020	2.000
46	2.105	2.084	2.061	2.040	2.021	2.000
47	2.106	2.083	2.062	2.041	2.020	2.000
48	1.842	2.084	2.061	2.040	2.021	2.000
49		0.781	1.804	2.041	2.020	2.000
50				0.765	1.768	2.000
51						0.750

TABLE 11
General and Alternative Depreciation Systems
Applicable Depreciation Method: Straight Line
Applicable Recovery Periods: 2.5 — 50 years
Applicable Convention: Mid-quarter (property placed in service in third quarter)

If the Recovery Year is:	and the Recovery Period is: 2.5	3.0	3.5	4.0	4.5	5.0	5.5	6.0	6.5	7.0	7.5	8.0	8.5	9.0	9.5
	the Depreciation Rate is:														
1	15.00	12.50	10.71	9.38	8.33	7.50	6.82	6.25	5.77	5.36	5.00	4.69	4.41	4.17	3.95
2	40.00	33.33	28.57	25.00	22.22	20.00	18.18	16.67	15.38	14.29	13.33	12.50	11.76	11.11	10.53
3	40.00	33.34	28.57	25.00	22.22	20.00	18.18	16.67	15.39	14.28	13.33	12.50	11.77	11.11	10.53
4	5.00	20.83	28.58	25.00	22.23	20.00	18.18	16.66	15.38	14.29	13.33	12.50	11.76	11.11	10.52
5			3.57	15.62	22.22	20.00	18.18	16.67	15.39	14.28	13.34	12.50	11.77	11.11	10.53
6					2.78	12.50	18.19	16.66	15.38	14.29	13.33	12.50	11.76	11.11	10.52
7							2.27	10.42	15.39	14.28	13.34	12.50	11.77	11.11	10.53
8									1.92	8.93	13.33	12.50	11.76	11.11	10.52
9											1.67	7.81	11.77	11.11	10.53
10													1.47	6.95	10.52
11															1.32

If the Recovery Year is:	and the Recovery Period is: 10.0	10.5	11.0	11.5	12.0	12.5	13.0	13.5	14.0	14.5	15.0	15.5	16.0	16.5	17.0
	the Depreciation Rate is:														
1	3.75	3.57	3.41	3.26	3.13	3.00	2.88	2.78	2.68	2.59	2.50	2.42	2.34	2.27	2.21
2	10.00	9.52	9.09	8.70	8.33	8.00	7.69	7.41	7.14	6.90	6.67	6.45	6.25	6.06	5.88
3	10.00	9.52	9.09	8.70	8.33	8.00	7.69	7.41	7.14	6.90	6.67	6.45	6.25	6.06	5.88
4	10.00	9.52	9.09	8.69	8.33	8.00	7.69	7.41	7.14	6.90	6.67	6.45	6.25	6.06	5.88
5	10.00	9.53	9.09	8.70	8.33	8.00	7.69	7.41	7.14	6.90	6.67	6.45	6.25	6.06	5.88
6	10.00	9.52	9.09	8.69	8.33	8.00	7.69	7.41	7.14	6.89	6.67	6.45	6.25	6.06	5.88

If the Recovery Year is:	and the Recovery Period is: 10.0	10.5	11.0	11.5	12.0	12.5	13.0	13.5	14.0	14.5	15.0	15.5	16.0	16.5	17.0
	the Depreciation Rate is:														
7	10.00	9.53	9.09	8.70	8.34	8.00	7.69	7.41	7.14	6.90	6.66	6.45	6.25	6.06	5.88
8	10.00	9.52	9.09	8.69	8.33	8.00	7.70	7.40	7.14	6.89	6.67	6.45	6.25	6.06	5.88
9	10.00	9.53	9.09	8.70	8.34	8.00	7.69	7.41	7.15	6.90	6.66	6.45	6.25	6.06	5.88
10	10.00	9.52	9.09	8.69	8.33	8.00	7.70	7.40	7.14	6.89	6.67	6.45	6.25	6.06	5.88
11	6.25	9.53	9.10	8.70	8.34	8.00	7.69	7.41	7.15	6.90	6.66	6.45	6.25	6.06	5.88
12		1.19	5.68	8.69	8.33	8.00	7.70	7.40	7.14	6.89	6.67	6.45	6.25	6.06	5.89
13				1.09	5.21	8.00	7.69	7.41	7.15	6.90	6.66	6.46	6.25	6.06	5.88
14						1.00	4.81	7.40	7.14	6.89	6.67	6.45	6.25	6.06	5.89
15								0.93	4.47	6.90	6.66	6.46	6.25	6.06	5.88
16										0.86	4.17	6.45	6.25	6.07	5.89
17												0.81	3.91	6.06	5.88
18														0.76	3.68

If the Recovery Year is:	and the Recovery Period is: 17.5	18.0	18.5	19.0	19.5	20.0	20.5	21.0	21.5	22.0	22.5	23.0	23.5	24.0	24.5
	the Depreciation Rate is:														
1	2.14	2.08	2.03	1.97	1.92	1.875	1.829	1.786	1.744	1.705	1.667	1.630	1.596	1.563	1.531
2	5.71	5.56	5.41	5.26	5.13	5.000	4.878	4.762	4.651	4.545	4.444	4.348	4.255	4.167	4.082
3	5.71	5.56	5.40	5.26	5.13	5.000	4.878	4.762	4.651	4.545	4.444	4.348	4.255	4.167	4.082
4	5.72	5.56	5.41	5.26	5.13	5.000	4.878	4.762	4.651	4.545	4.444	4.348	4.255	4.167	4.082
5	5.71	5.55	5.40	5.26	5.13	5.000	4.878	4.762	4.651	4.546	4.444	4.348	4.255	4.167	4.082
6	5.72	5.56	5.41	5.26	5.13	5.000	4.878	4.762	4.651	4.545	4.445	4.348	4.255	4.167	4.082
7	5.71	5.55	5.40	5.26	5.13	5.000	4.878	4.762	4.651	4.546	4.444	4.348	4.255	4.167	4.082
8	5.72	5.56	5.41	5.26	5.13	5.000	4.878	4.762	4.651	4.545	4.445	4.348	4.255	4.167	4.081
9	5.71	5.55	5.40	5.27	5.13	5.000	4.878	4.762	4.651	4.546	4.444	4.348	4.255	4.166	4.082
10	5.72	5.56	5.41	5.26	5.13	5.000	4.878	4.762	4.651	4.545	4.445	4.348	4.255	4.167	4.081

If the Recovery Year is:	and the Recovery Period is: 17.5	18.0	18.5	19.0	19.5	20.0	20.5	21.0	21.5	22.0	22.5	23.0	23.5	24.0	24.5
	the Depreciation Rate is:														
11	5.71	5.55	5.40	5.27	5.13	5.000	4.878	4.762	4.651	4.546	4.444	4.348	4.256	4.166	4.082
12	5.72	5.56	5.41	5.26	5.13	5.000	4.878	4.762	4.651	4.545	4.445	4.348	4.255	4.167	4.081
13	5.71	5.55	5.40	5.27	5.13	5.000	4.878	4.762	4.651	4.546	4.444	4.348	4.256	4.166	4.082
14	5.72	5.56	5.41	5.26	5.13	5.000	4.878	4.762	4.651	4.545	4.445	4.348	4.255	4.167	4.081
15	5.71	5.55	5.40	5.27	5.12	5.000	4.878	4.762	4.651	4.546	4.444	4.348	4.256	4.166	4.082
16	5.72	5.56	5.41	5.26	5.13	5.000	4.878	4.762	4.652	4.545	4.445	4.348	4.255	4.167	4.081
17	5.71	5.55	5.40	5.27	5.12	5.000	4.878	4.762	4.651	4.546	4.444	4.348	4.256	4.166	4.082
18	5.72	5.56	5.41	5.26	5.13	5.000	4.878	4.762	4.652	4.545	4.445	4.347	4.255	4.167	4.081
19	0.71	3.47	5.40	5.27	5.12	5.000	4.878	4.761	4.651	4.546	4.444	4.348	4.256	4.166	4.082
20			0.68	3.29	5.13	5.000	4.879	4.762	4.652	4.545	4.445	4.347	4.255	4.167	4.081
21					0.64	3.125	4.878	4.761	4.651	4.546	4.444	4.348	4.256	4.166	4.082
22							0.610	2.976	4.652	4.545	4.445	4.347	4.255	4.167	4.081
23									0.581	2.841	4.444	4.348	4.256	4.166	4.082
24											0.556	2.717	4.255	4.167	4.081
25													0.532	2.604	4.082
26															0.510

If the Recovery Year is:	and the Recovery Period is: 25.0	25.5	26.0	26.5	27.0	27.5	28.0	28.5	29.0	29.5	30.0	30.5	31.0	31.5	32.0
	the Depreciation Rate is:														
1	1.500	1.471	1.442	1.415	1.389	1.364	1.339	1.316	1.293	1.271	1.250	1.230	1.210	1.190	1.172
2	4.000	3.922	3.846	3.774	3.704	3.636	3.571	3.509	3.448	3.390	3.333	3.279	3.226	3.175	3.125
3	4.000	3.922	3.846	3.774	3.704	3.636	3.571	3.509	3.448	3.390	3.333	3.279	3.226	3.175	3.125
4	4.000	3.922	3.846	3.774	3.704	3.636	3.571	3.509	3.448	3.390	3.333	3.279	3.226	3.175	3.125
5	4.000	3.921	3.846	3.774	3.704	3.636	3.571	3.509	3.448	3.390	3.333	3.279	3.226	3.175	3.125
6	4.000	3.922	3.846	3.774	3.704	3.636	3.572	3.509	3.448	3.390	3.333	3.279	3.226	3.175	3.125

If the Recovery Year is:	and the Recovery Period is: 25.0	25.5	26.0	26.5	27.0	27.5	28.0	28.5	29.0	29.5	30.0	30.5	31.0	31.5	32.0
	the Depreciation Rate is:														
7	4.000	3.921	3.846	3.773	3.704	3.636	3.571	3.509	3.448	3.390	3.333	3.279	3.226	3.175	3.125
8	4.000	3.922	3.846	3.774	3.704	3.636	3.572	3.509	3.448	3.390	3.333	3.279	3.226	3.175	3.125
9	4.000	3.921	3.846	3.773	3.704	3.636	3.571	3.509	3.448	3.390	3.333	3.279	3.226	3.175	3.125
10	4.000	3.922	3.846	3.774	3.704	3.636	3.572	3.509	3.448	3.390	3.333	3.279	3.226	3.174	3.125
11	4.000	3.921	3.846	3.773	3.704	3.637	3.571	3.509	3.448	3.390	3.333	3.279	3.226	3.175	3.125
12	4.000	3.922	3.846	3.774	3.704	3.636	3.572	3.509	3.448	3.390	3.334	3.279	3.226	3.174	3.125
13	4.000	3.921	3.846	3.773	3.703	3.637	3.571	3.509	3.448	3.390	3.333	3.278	3.226	3.175	3.125
14	4.000	3.922	3.846	3.774	3.704	3.636	3.572	3.509	3.448	3.390	3.334	3.279	3.226	3.174	3.125
15	4.000	3.921	3.846	3.773	3.703	3.637	3.571	3.509	3.449	3.390	3.333	3.278	3.226	3.175	3.125
16	4.000	3.922	3.846	3.774	3.704	3.636	3.572	3.509	3.448	3.390	3.334	3.279	3.226	3.174	3.125
17	4.000	3.921	3.846	3.773	3.703	3.637	3.571	3.508	3.449	3.390	3.333	3.279	3.226	3.175	3.125
18	4.000	3.922	3.846	3.774	3.704	3.636	3.572	3.509	3.448	3.390	3.334	3.279	3.226	3.174	3.125
19	4.000	3.921	3.846	3.773	3.703	3.637	3.571	3.508	3.449	3.390	3.333	3.279	3.226	3.175	3.125
20	4.000	3.922	3.847	3.774	3.704	3.636	3.572	3.509	3.448	3.390	3.334	3.279	3.226	3.174	3.125
21	4.000	3.921	3.846	3.773	3.703	3.637	3.571	3.508	3.449	3.390	3.333	3.278	3.225	3.175	3.125
22	4.000	3.922	3.847	3.774	3.704	3.636	3.572	3.509	3.448	3.389	3.334	3.279	3.226	3.174	3.125
23	4.000	3.921	3.846	3.773	3.703	3.637	3.571	3.508	3.449	3.390	3.333	3.278	3.225	3.175	3.125
24	4.000	3.922	3.847	3.774	3.704	3.636	3.572	3.509	3.448	3.389	3.334	3.279	3.226	3.174	3.125
25	4.000	3.921	3.846	3.773	3.703	3.637	3.571	3.508	3.449	3.390	3.333	3.278	3.225	3.175	3.125
26	2.500	3.922	3.847	3.774	3.704	3.636	3.572	3.509	3.448	3.389	3.334	3.279	3.226	3.174	3.125
27		0.490	2.404	3.773	3.703	3.637	3.571	3.508	3.449	3.390	3.333	3.278	3.225	3.175	3.125
28				0.472	2.315	3.636	3.572	3.509	3.448	3.389	3.334	3.279	3.226	3.174	3.125
29						0.455	2.232	3.508	3.449	3.390	3.333	3.278	3.225	3.175	3.125
30								0.439	2.155	3.389	3.334	3.279	3.226	3.174	3.125
31										0.424	2.083	3.278	3.225	3.175	3.125

If the Recovery Year is:	and the Recovery Period is: 25.0	25.5	26.0	26.5	27.0	27.5	28.0	28.5	29.0	29.5	30.0	30.5	31.0	31.5	32.0
	the Depreciation Rate is:														
32												0.410	2.016	3.174	3.125
33														0.397	1.953

If the Recovery Year is:	and the Recovery Period is: 32.5	33.0	33.5	34.0	34.5	35.0	35.5	36.0	36.5	37.0	37.5	38.0	38.5	39.0	39.5
	the Depreciation Rate is:														
1	1.154	1.136	1.119	1.103	1.087	1.071	1.056	1.042	1.027	1.014	1.000	0.987	0.974	0.962	0.949
2	3.077	3.030	2.985	2.941	2.899	2.857	2.817	2.778	2.740	2.703	2.667	2.632	2.597	2.564	2.532
3	3.077	3.030	2.985	2.941	2.899	2.857	2.817	2.778	2.740	2.703	2.667	2.632	2.597	2.564	2.532
4	3.077	3.030	2.985	2.941	2.899	2.857	2.817	2.778	2.740	2.703	2.667	2.632	2.597	2.564	2.532
5	3.077	3.030	2.985	2.941	2.899	2.857	2.817	2.778	2.740	2.703	2.667	2.632	2.597	2.564	2.532
6	3.077	3.030	2.985	2.941	2.898	2.857	2.817	2.778	2.740	2.703	2.667	2.632	2.597	2.564	2.532
7	3.077	3.030	2.985	2.941	2.899	2.857	2.817	2.778	2.740	2.703	2.667	2.632	2.597	2.564	2.532
8	3.077	3.030	2.985	2.941	2.898	2.857	2.817	2.778	2.740	2.703	2.667	2.631	2.597	2.564	2.532
9	3.077	3.030	2.985	2.941	2.899	2.857	2.817	2.778	2.740	2.703	2.667	2.632	2.597	2.564	2.532
10	3.077	3.030	2.985	2.941	2.898	2.857	2.817	2.778	2.740	2.703	2.667	2.631	2.598	2.564	2.532
11	3.077	3.030	2.985	2.941	2.899	2.857	2.817	2.778	2.740	2.703	2.667	2.632	2.597	2.564	2.532
12	3.077	3.030	2.985	2.941	2.898	2.857	2.817	2.778	2.740	2.703	2.667	2.631	2.598	2.564	2.532
13	3.077	3.030	2.985	2.941	2.899	2.857	2.817	2.778	2.740	2.703	2.667	2.632	2.597	2.564	2.532
14	3.077	3.030	2.985	2.941	2.898	2.857	2.817	2.778	2.740	2.703	2.667	2.631	2.598	2.564	2.532
15	3.077	3.031	2.985	2.941	2.899	2.857	2.817	2.778	2.740	2.703	2.666	2.632	2.597	2.564	2.531
16	3.077	3.030	2.985	2.941	2.898	2.857	2.817	2.778	2.740	2.702	2.667	2.631	2.598	2.564	2.532
17	3.077	3.031	2.985	2.941	2.899	2.857	2.817	2.778	2.740	2.703	2.666	2.632	2.597	2.564	2.531
18	3.077	3.030	2.985	2.941	2.898	2.857	2.817	2.778	2.740	2.702	2.667	2.631	2.598	2.564	2.532
19	3.077	3.031	2.985	2.941	2.899	2.857	2.817	2.778	2.740	2.703	2.666	2.632	2.597	2.564	2.531
20	3.077	3.030	2.985	2.941	2.898	2.857	2.817	2.778	2.739	2.702	2.667	2.631	2.598	2.564	2.532

If the Recovery Year is:	32.5	33.0	33.5	34.0	34.5	35.0	35.5	36.0	36.5	37.0	37.5	38.0	38.5	39.0	39.5
	and the Recovery Period is:														
	the Depreciation Rate is:														
21	3.077	3.031	2.985	2.941	2.899	2.857	2.817	2.778	2.740	2.703	2.666	2.632	2.597	2.564	2.531
22	3.077	3.030	2.985	2.941	2.898	2.857	2.817	2.777	2.739	2.702	2.667	2.631	2.598	2.564	2.532
23	3.077	3.031	2.985	2.941	2.899	2.857	2.817	2.778	2.740	2.703	2.666	2.632	2.597	2.564	2.531
24	3.077	3.030	2.985	2.942	2.898	2.857	2.817	2.777	2.739	2.702	2.667	2.631	2.598	2.564	2.532
25	3.077	3.031	2.985	2.941	2.899	2.857	2.817	2.778	2.740	2.703	2.666	2.632	2.597	2.564	2.531
26	3.077	3.030	2.985	2.942	2.898	2.858	2.817	2.777	2.739	2.702	2.667	2.631	2.598	2.564	2.532
27	3.077	3.031	2.985	2.941	2.899	2.857	2.817	2.778	2.740	2.703	2.666	2.632	2.597	2.564	2.531
28	3.077	3.030	2.985	2.942	2.898	2.858	2.817	2.777	2.739	2.702	2.667	2.631	2.598	2.564	2.532
29	3.076	3.031	2.985	2.941	2.899	2.857	2.817	2.778	2.740	2.703	2.666	2.632	2.597	2.564	2.531
30	3.077	3.030	2.986	2.942	2.898	2.858	2.817	2.777	2.739	2.702	2.667	2.631	2.598	2.564	2.532
31	3.076	3.031	2.985	2.941	2.899	2.857	2.816	2.778	2.740	2.703	2.666	2.632	2.597	2.564	2.531
32	3.077	3.030	2.986	2.942	2.898	2.858	2.817	2.777	2.739	2.702	2.667	2.631	2.598	2.564	2.532
33	3.076	3.031	2.985	2.941	2.899	2.857	2.816	2.778	2.740	2.703	2.666	2.632	2.597	2.564	2.531
34	0.385	1.894	2.986	2.942	2.898	2.858	2.817	2.777	2.739	2.702	2.667	2.631	2.598	2.565	2.532
35			0.373	1.838	2.899	2.857	2.816	2.778	2.740	2.703	2.666	2.632	2.597	2.564	2.531
36					0.362	1.786	2.817	2.777	2.739	2.702	2.667	2.631	2.598	2.565	2.532
37							0.352	1.736	2.740	2.703	2.666	2.632	2.597	2.564	2.531
38									0.342	1.689	2.667	2.631	2.598	2.565	2.532
39											0.333	1.645	2.597	2.564	2.531
40													0.325	1.603	2.532
41															0.316

If the Recovery Year is:	and the Recovery Period is: 40.0	40.5	41.0	41.5	42.0	42.5	43.0	43.5	44.0	44.5	45.0	45.5	46.0	46.5	47.0
	the Depreciation Rate is:														
1	0.938	0.926	0.915	0.904	0.893	0.882	0.872	0.862	0.852	0.843	0.833	0.824	0.815	0.806	0.798
2	2.500	2.469	2.439	2.410	2.381	2.353	2.326	2.299	2.273	2.247	2.222	2.198	2.174	2.151	2.128
3	2.500	2.469	2.439	2.410	2.381	2.353	2.326	2.299	2.273	2.247	2.222	2.198	2.174	2.151	2.128
4	2.500	2.469	2.439	2.410	2.381	2.353	2.326	2.299	2.273	2.247	2.222	2.198	2.174	2.151	2.128
5	2.500	2.469	2.439	2.410	2.381	2.353	2.326	2.299	2.273	2.247	2.222	2.198	2.174	2.151	2.128
6	2.500	2.469	2.439	2.410	2.381	2.353	2.326	2.299	2.273	2.247	2.222	2.198	2.174	2.151	2.128
7	2.500	2.469	2.439	2.410	2.381	2.353	2.326	2.299	2.273	2.247	2.222	2.198	2.174	2.150	2.128
8	2.500	2.469	2.439	2.410	2.381	2.353	2.326	2.299	2.273	2.247	2.222	2.198	2.174	2.151	2.128
9	2.500	2.469	2.439	2.410	2.381	2.353	2.326	2.299	2.273	2.247	2.222	2.198	2.174	2.150	2.128
10	2.500	2.469	2.439	2.410	2.381	2.353	2.325	2.299	2.273	2.247	2.222	2.198	2.174	2.151	2.128
11	2.500	2.469	2.439	2.410	2.381	2.353	2.326	2.299	2.273	2.247	2.222	2.198	2.174	2.150	2.128
12	2.500	2.469	2.439	2.410	2.381	2.353	2.325	2.299	2.273	2.247	2.222	2.198	2.174	2.151	2.128
13	2.500	2.469	2.439	2.409	2.381	2.353	2.326	2.299	2.273	2.247	2.222	2.198	2.174	2.150	2.128
14	2.500	2.469	2.439	2.410	2.381	2.353	2.325	2.299	2.273	2.247	2.222	2.198	2.174	2.151	2.128
15	2.500	2.469	2.439	2.409	2.381	2.353	2.326	2.299	2.273	2.247	2.222	2.198	2.174	2.150	2.128
16	2.500	2.469	2.439	2.410	2.381	2.353	2.325	2.299	2.273	2.247	2.222	2.198	2.174	2.151	2.128
17	2.500	2.469	2.439	2.409	2.381	2.353	2.326	2.299	2.273	2.247	2.222	2.198	2.174	2.150	2.127
18	2.500	2.469	2.439	2.410	2.381	2.353	2.325	2.299	2.273	2.247	2.222	2.198	2.174	2.151	2.128
19	2.500	2.469	2.439	2.409	2.381	2.353	2.326	2.299	2.273	2.247	2.222	2.198	2.174	2.150	2.127
20	2.500	2.469	2.439	2.410	2.381	2.353	2.325	2.299	2.273	2.247	2.222	2.198	2.174	2.151	2.128
21	2.500	2.469	2.439	2.409	2.381	2.353	2.326	2.299	2.273	2.247	2.222	2.198	2.174	2.150	2.127
22	2.500	2.469	2.439	2.410	2.381	2.353	2.325	2.299	2.273	2.247	2.222	2.198	2.174	2.151	2.128
23	2.500	2.469	2.439	2.409	2.381	2.353	2.326	2.299	2.272	2.247	2.222	2.198	2.174	2.150	2.127
24	2.500	2.469	2.439	2.410	2.381	2.353	2.325	2.299	2.273	2.247	2.222	2.198	2.174	2.151	2.128
25	2.500	2.469	2.439	2.409	2.381	2.353	2.326	2.299	2.272	2.247	2.222	2.198	2.174	2.150	2.127
26	2.500	2.469	2.439	2.410	2.381	2.353	2.325	2.299	2.273	2.247	2.222	2.198	2.174	2.151	2.128

If the Recovery Year is:	and the Recovery Period is: 40.0	40.5	41.0	41.5	42.0	42.5	43.0	43.5	44.0	44.5	45.0	45.5	46.0	46.5	47.0
	the Depreciation Rate is:														
27	2.500	2.469	2.439	2.409	2.381	2.353	2.326	2.299	2.272	2.247	2.223	2.198	2.174	2.150	2.127
28	2.500	2.469	2.439	2.410	2.381	2.353	2.325	2.299	2.273	2.247	2.222	2.198	2.174	2.151	2.128
29	2.500	2.469	2.439	2.409	2.381	2.353	2.326	2.299	2.272	2.247	2.223	2.198	2.174	2.150	2.127
30	2.500	2.469	2.439	2.410	2.381	2.353	2.325	2.299	2.273	2.248	2.222	2.197	2.174	2.151	2.128
31	2.500	2.469	2.439	2.409	2.381	2.353	2.326	2.299	2.272	2.247	2.223	2.198	2.174	2.150	2.127
32	2.500	2.470	2.439	2.410	2.381	2.353	2.325	2.299	2.273	2.248	2.222	2.197	2.174	2.151	2.128
33	2.500	2.469	2.439	2.409	2.381	2.353	2.326	2.298	2.272	2.247	2.223	2.198	2.174	2.150	2.127
34	2.500	2.470	2.439	2.410	2.381	2.353	2.325	2.299	2.273	2.248	2.222	2.197	2.174	2.151	2.128
35	2.500	2.469	2.439	2.409	2.381	2.353	2.326	2.298	2.272	2.247	2.223	2.198	2.174	2.150	2.127
36	2.500	2.470	2.439	2.410	2.381	2.353	2.325	2.299	2.273	2.248	2.222	2.197	2.174	2.151	2.128
37	2.500	2.469	2.439	2.409	2.381	2.353	2.326	2.298	2.272	2.247	2.223	2.198	2.174	2.150	2.127
38	2.500	2.470	2.439	2.410	2.381	2.353	2.325	2.299	2.273	2.248	2.222	2.197	2.174	2.151	2.128
39	2.500	2.469	2.439	2.409	2.381	2.353	2.326	2.298	2.272	2.247	2.223	2.198	2.174	2.150	2.127
40	2.500	2.470	2.439	2.410	2.380	2.352	2.325	2.299	2.273	2.248	2.222	2.197	2.174	2.151	2.128
41	1.562	2.469	2.439	2.409	2.381	2.353	2.326	2.298	2.272	2.247	2.223	2.198	2.173	2.150	2.127
42		0.309	1.525	2.410	2.380	2.352	2.325	2.299	2.273	2.248	2.222	2.197	2.174	2.151	2.128
43				0.301	1.488	2.353	2.326	2.298	2.272	2.247	2.223	2.198	2.173	2.150	2.127
44						0.294	1.453	2.299	2.273	2.248	2.222	2.197	2.174	2.151	2.128
45								0.287	1.420	2.247	2.223	2.198	2.173	2.150	2.127
46										0.281	1.389	2.197	2.174	2.151	2.128
47												0.275	1.358	2.150	2.127
48														0.269	1.330

If the Recovery Year is:	and the Recovery Period is: 47.5	48.0	48.5	49.0	49.5	50.0
	the Depreciation Rate is:					
1	0.789	0.781	0.773	0.765	0.758	0.750
2	2.105	2.083	2.062	2.041	2.020	2.000
3	2.105	2.083	2.062	2.041	2.020	2.000
4	2.105	2.083	2.062	2.041	2.020	2.000
5	2.105	2.083	2.062	2.041	2.020	2.000
6	2.105	2.083	2.062	2.041	2.020	2.000
7	2.105	2.083	2.062	2.041	2.020	2.000
8	2.105	2.083	2.062	2.041	2.020	2.000
9	2.105	2.083	2.062	2.041	2.020	2.000
10	2.105	2.083	2.062	2.041	2.020	2.000
11	2.105	2.083	2.062	2.041	2.020	2.000
12	2.105	2.083	2.062	2.041	2.020	2.000
13	2.105	2.083	2.062	2.041	2.020	2.000
14	2.105	2.083	2.062	2.041	2.020	2.000
15	2.105	2.083	2.062	2.041	2.020	2.000
16	2.105	2.083	2.062	2.041	2.020	2.000
17	2.105	2.083	2.062	2.041	2.020	2.000
18	2.105	2.084	2.062	2.041	2.020	2.000
19	2.105	2.083	2.062	2.041	2.020	2.000
20	2.105	2.084	2.062	2.041	2.020	2.000
21	2.105	2.083	2.062	2.041	2.020	2.000
22	2.105	2.084	2.062	2.041	2.020	2.000
23	2.105	2.083	2.062	2.041	2.020	2.000
24	2.106	2.084	2.062	2.041	2.020	2.000
25	2.105	2.083	2.062	2.041	2.020	2.000
26	2.106	2.084	2.062	2.041	2.020	2.000

If the Recovery Year is:	and the Recovery Period is: 47.5	48.0	48.5	49.0	49.5	50.0
	the Depreciation Rate is:					
27	2.105	2.083	2.062	2.041	2.020	2.000
28	2.106	2.084	2.062	2.041	2.020	2.000
29	2.105	2.083	2.062	2.041	2.020	2.000
30	2.106	2.084	2.062	2.041	2.020	2.000
31	2.105	2.083	2.062	2.041	2.020	2.000
32	2.106	2.084	2.062	2.041	2.020	2.000
33	2.105	2.083	2.062	2.041	2.021	2.000
34	2.106	2.084	2.062	2.040	2.020	2.000
35	2.105	2.083	2.062	2.041	2.021	2.000
36	2.106	2.084	2.062	2.040	2.020	2.000
37	2.105	2.083	2.061	2.041	2.021	2.000
38	2.106	2.084	2.062	2.040	2.020	2.000
39	2.105	2.083	2.061	2.041	2.021	2.000
40	2.106	2.084	2.062	2.040	2.020	2.000
41	2.105	2.083	2.061	2.041	2.021	2.000
42	2.106	2.084	2.062	2.040	2.020	2.000
43	2.105	2.083	2.061	2.041	2.021	2.000
44	2.106	2.084	2.062	2.040	2.020	2.000
45	2.105	2.083	2.061	2.041	2.021	2.000
46	2.106	2.084	2.062	2.040	2.020	2.000
47	2.105	2.083	2.061	2.041	2.021	2.000
48	2.106	2.084	2.062	2.040	2.020	2.000
49	0.263	1.302	2.061	2.041	2.021	2.000
50			0.258	1.275	2.020	2.000
51					0.253	1.250

TABLE 12
General and Alternative Depreciation Systems
Applicable Depreciation Method: Straight Line
Applicable Recovery Periods: 2.5 — 50 years
Applicable Convention: Mid-quarter (property placed in service in fourth quarter)

If the Recovery Year is:	and the Recovery Period is: 2.5	3.0	3.5	4.0	4.5	5.0	5.5	6.0	6.5	7.0	7.5	8.0	8.5	9.0	9.5
	the Depreciation Rate is:														
1	5.00	4.17	3.57	3.13	2.78	2.50	2.27	2.08	1.92	1.79	1.67	1.56	1.47	1.39	1.32
2	40.00	33.33	28.57	25.00	22.22	20.00	18.18	16.67	15.39	14.29	13.33	12.50	11.76	11.11	10.53
3	40.00	33.33	28.57	25.00	22.22	20.00	18.18	16.67	15.38	14.28	13.33	12.50	11.77	11.11	10.53
4	15.00	29.17	28.57	25.00	22.22	20.00	18.18	16.67	15.39	14.29	13.33	12.50	11.76	11.11	10.52
5			10.72	21.87	22.23	20.00	18.19	16.66	15.38	14.28	13.33	12.50	11.77	11.11	10.53
6					8.33	17.50	18.18	16.67	15.39	14.29	13.34	12.50	11.76	11.11	10.52
7							6.82	14.58	15.38	14.28	13.33	12.50	11.77	11.11	10.53
8									5.77	12.50	13.34	12.50	11.76	11.11	10.52
9											5.00	10.94	11.77	11.11	10.53
10													4.41	9.73	10.52
11															3.95

If the Recovery Year is:	and the Recovery Period is: 10.0	10.5	11.0	11.5	12.0	12.5	13.0	13.5	14.0	14.5	15.0	15.5	16.0	16.5	17.0
	the Depreciation Rate is:														
1	1.25	1.19	1.14	1.09	1.04	1.00	0.96	0.93	0.89	0.86	0.83	0.81	0.78	0.76	0.74
2	10.00	9.52	9.09	8.70	8.33	8.00	7.69	7.41	7.14	6.90	6.67	6.45	6.25	6.06	5.88
3	10.00	9.52	9.09	8.69	8.33	8.00	7.69	7.41	7.14	6.90	6.67	6.45	6.25	6.06	5.88
4	10.00	9.52	9.09	8.70	8.33	8.00	7.69	7.41	7.14	6.90	6.67	6.45	6.25	6.06	5.88
5	10.00	9.53	9.09	8.69	8.33	8.00	7.69	7.41	7.14	6.90	6.67	6.45	6.25	6.06	5.88

If the Recovery Year is:	and the Recovery Period is: 10.0	10.5	11.0	11.5	12.0	12.5	13.0	13.5	14.0	14.5	15.0	15.5	16.0	16.5	17.0
	the Depreciation Rate is:														
6	10.00	9.52	9.09	8.70	8.34	8.00	7.69	7.41	7.14	6.90	6.67	6.45	6.25	6.06	5.88
7	10.00	9.53	9.09	8.69	8.33	8.00	7.69	7.41	7.14	6.89	6.67	6.45	6.25	6.06	5.88
8	10.00	9.52	9.09	8.70	8.34	8.00	7.69	7.40	7.15	6.90	6.66	6.45	6.25	6.06	5.88
9	10.00	9.53	9.09	8.69	8.33	8.00	7.70	7.41	7.14	6.89	6.67	6.45	6.25	6.06	5.88
10	10.00	9.52	9.09	8.70	8.34	8.00	7.69	7.40	7.15	6.90	6.66	6.45	6.25	6.06	5.88
11	8.75	9.53	9.09	8.69	8.33	8.00	7.70	7.41	7.14	6.89	6.67	6.45	6.25	6.06	5.88
12		3.57	7.96	8.70	8.34	8.00	7.69	7.40	7.15	6.90	6.66	6.45	6.25	6.06	5.89
13				3.26	7.29	8.00	7.70	7.41	7.14	6.89	6.67	6.45	6.25	6.06	5.88
14						3.00	6.73	7.40	7.15	6.90	6.66	6.46	6.25	6.06	5.89
15								2.78	6.25	6.89	6.67	6.45	6.25	6.06	5.88
16										2.59	5.83	6.46	6.25	6.06	5.89
17												2.42	5.47	6.07	5.88
18														2.27	5.15

If the Recovery Year is:	and the Recovery Period is: 17.5	18.0	18.5	19.0	19.5	20.0	20.5	21.0	21.5	22.0	22.5	23.0	23.5	24.0	24.5
	the Depreciation Rate is:														
1	0.71	0.69	0.68	0.66	0.64	0.625	0.610	0.595	0.581	0.568	0.556	0.543	0.532	0.521	0.510
2	5.71	5.56	5.41	5.26	5.13	5.000	4.878	4.762	4.651	4.545	4.444	4.348	4.255	4.167	4.082
3	5.71	5.56	5.40	5.26	5.13	5.000	4.878	4.762	4.651	4.545	4.444	4.348	4.255	4.167	4.082
4	5.72	5.56	5.41	5.26	5.13	5.000	4.878	4.762	4.651	4.546	4.444	4.348	4.255	4.167	4.082
5	5.71	5.55	5.40	5.26	5.13	5.000	4.878	4.762	4.651	4.545	4.444	4.348	4.255	4.167	4.082
6	5.72	5.56	5.41	5.26	5.13	5.000	4.878	4.762	4.651	4.546	4.445	4.348	4.255	4.167	4.082
7	5.71	5.55	5.40	5.26	5.13	5.000	4.878	4.762	4.651	4.545	4.444	4.348	4.255	4.167	4.082
8	5.72	5.56	5.41	5.26	5.13	5.000	4.878	4.762	4.651	4.546	4.445	4.348	4.255	4.167	4.082
9	5.71	5.55	5.40	5.26	5.13	5.000	4.878	4.762	4.651	4.545	4.444	4.348	4.255	4.167	4.081

If the Recovery Year is:	and the Recovery Period is: 17.5	18.0	18.5	19.0	19.5	20.0	20.5	21.0	21.5	22.0	22.5	23.0	23.5	24.0	24.5
	the Depreciation Rate is:														
10	5.72	5.56	5.41	5.27	5.13	5.000	4.878	4.762	4.651	4.546	4.445	4.348	4.255	4.166	4.082
11	5.71	5.55	5.40	5.26	5.13	5.000	4.878	4.762	4.651	4.545	4.444	4.348	4.256	4.167	4.081
12	5.72	5.56	5.41	5.27	5.13	5.000	4.878	4.762	4.651	4.546	4.445	4.348	4.255	4.166	4.082
13	5.71	5.55	5.40	5.26	5.13	5.000	4.878	4.762	4.651	4.545	4.444	4.348	4.256	4.167	4.081
14	5.72	5.56	5.41	5.27	5.13	5.000	4.878	4.762	4.651	4.546	4.445	4.348	4.255	4.166	4.082
15	5.71	5.55	5.40	5.26	5.12	5.000	4.878	4.762	4.651	4.545	4.444	4.348	4.256	4.167	4.081
16	5.72	5.56	5.41	5.27	5.13	5.000	4.878	4.762	4.652	4.546	4.445	4.348	4.255	4.166	4.082
17	5.71	5.55	5.40	5.26	5.12	5.000	4.878	4.762	4.651	4.545	4.444	4.348	4.256	4.167	4.081
18	5.72	5.56	5.41	5.27	5.13	5.000	4.878	4.762	4.652	4.546	4.445	4.347	4.255	4.166	4.082
19	2.14	4.86	5.40	5.26	5.12	5.000	4.878	4.762	4.651	4.545	4.444	4.348	4.256	4.167	4.081
20			2.03	4.61	5.13	5.000	4.878	4.761	4.652	4.546	4.445	4.347	4.255	4.166	4.082
21					1.92	4.375	4.879	4.762	4.651	4.545	4.444	4.348	4.256	4.167	4.081
22							1.829	4.166	4.652	4.546	4.445	4.347	4.255	4.166	4.082
23									1.744	3.977	4.444	4.348	4.256	4.167	4.081
24											1.667	3.804	4.255	4.166	4.082
25													1.596	3.646	4.081
26															1.531

If the Recovery Year is:	and the Recovery Period is: 25.0	25.5	26.0	26.5	27.0	27.5	28.0	28.5	29.0	29.5	30.0	30.5	31.0	31.5	32.0
	the Depreciation Rate is:														
1	0.500	0.490	0.481	0.472	0.463	0.455	0.446	0.439	0.431	0.424	0.417	0.410	0.403	0.397	0.391
2	4.000	3.922	3.846	3.774	3.704	3.636	3.571	3.509	3.448	3.390	3.333	3.279	3.226	3.175	3.125
3	4.000	3.922	3.846	3.774	3.704	3.636	3.571	3.509	3.448	3.390	3.333	3.279	3.226	3.175	3.125
4	4.000	3.922	3.846	3.774	3.704	3.636	3.571	3.509	3.448	3.390	3.333	3.279	3.226	3.175	3.125
5	4.000	3.922	3.846	3.774	3.704	3.636	3.571	3.509	3.448	3.390	3.333	3.279	3.226	3.175	3.125

If the Recovery Year is:	and the Recovery Period is: 25.0	25.5	26.0	26.5	27.0	27.5	28.0	28.5	29.0	29.5	30.0	30.5	31.0	31.5	32.0
	the Depreciation Rate is:														
6	4.000	3.921	3.846	3.773	3.704	3.636	3.572	3.509	3.448	3.390	3.333	3.279	3.226	3.175	3.125
7	4.000	3.922	3.846	3.774	3.704	3.636	3.571	3.509	3.448	3.390	3.333	3.279	3.226	3.175	3.125
8	4.000	3.921	3.846	3.773	3.704	3.636	3.572	3.509	3.448	3.390	3.333	3.279	3.226	3.175	3.125
9	4.000	3.922	3.846	3.774	3.704	3.636	3.571	3.509	3.448	3.390	3.333	3.279	3.226	3.174	3.125
10	4.000	3.921	3.846	3.773	3.704	3.636	3.572	3.509	3.448	3.390	3.333	3.279	3.226	3.175	3.125
11	4.000	3.922	3.846	3.774	3.704	3.637	3.571	3.509	3.448	3.390	3.333	3.279	3.226	3.174	3.125
12	4.000	3.921	3.846	3.773	3.704	3.636	3.572	3.509	3.448	3.390	3.333	3.279	3.226	3.175	3.125
13	4.000	3.922	3.846	3.774	3.703	3.637	3.571	3.509	3.448	3.390	3.334	3.279	3.226	3.174	3.125
14	4.000	3.921	3.846	3.773	3.704	3.636	3.572	3.509	3.448	3.390	3.333	3.278	3.226	3.175	3.125
15	4.000	3.922	3.846	3.774	3.703	3.637	3.571	3.509	3.449	3.390	3.334	3.279	3.226	3.174	3.125
16	4.000	3.921	3.846	3.773	3.704	3.636	3.572	3.509	3.448	3.390	3.333	3.278	3.226	3.175	3.125
17	4.000	3.922	3.846	3.774	3.703	3.637	3.571	3.508	3.449	3.390	3.334	3.279	3.226	3.174	3.125
18	4.000	3.921	3.846	3.773	3.704	3.636	3.572	3.509	3.448	3.390	3.333	3.278	3.226	3.175	3.125
19	4.000	3.922	3.846	3.774	3.703	3.637	3.571	3.508	3.449	3.390	3.334	3.279	3.226	3.174	3.125
20	4.000	3.921	3.846	3.773	3.704	3.636	3.572	3.509	3.448	3.390	3.333	3.278	3.226	3.175	3.125
21	4.000	3.922	3.847	3.774	3.703	3.637	3.571	3.508	3.449	3.389	3.334	3.279	3.226	3.174	3.125
22	4.000	3.921	3.846	3.773	3.704	3.636	3.572	3.509	3.448	3.390	3.333	3.278	3.225	3.175	3.125
23	4.000	3.922	3.847	3.774	3.703	3.637	3.571	3.508	3.449	3.389	3.334	3.279	3.226	3.174	3.125
24	4.000	3.921	3.846	3.773	3.704	3.636	3.572	3.509	3.448	3.390	3.333	3.278	3.225	3.175	3.125
25	4.000	3.922	3.847	3.774	3.703	3.637	3.571	3.508	3.449	3.389	3.334	3.279	3.226	3.174	3.125
26	3.500	3.921	3.846	3.773	3.704	3.636	3.572	3.509	3.448	3.390	3.333	3.278	3.225	3.175	3.125
27		1.471	3.366	3.774	3.703	3.637	3.571	3.508	3.449	3.389	3.334	3.279	3.226	3.174	3.125
28				1.415	3.241	3.636	3.572	3.509	3.448	3.390	3.333	3.278	3.225	3.175	3.125
29						1.364	3.125	3.508	3.449	3.389	3.334	3.279	3.226	3.174	3.125
30								1.316	3.017	3.390	3.333	3.278	3.225	3.175	3.125
31										1.271	2.917	3.279	3.226	3.174	3.125

If the Recovery Year is:	and the Recovery Period is: 25.0	25.5	26.0	26.5	27.0	27.5	28.0	28.5	29.0	29.5	30.0	30.5	31.0	31.5	32.0
	the Depreciation Rate is:														
32												1.229	2.822	3.175	3.125
33														1.190	2.734

If the Recovery Year is:	and the Recovery Period is: 32.5	33.0	33.5	34.0	34.5	35.0	35.5	36.0	36.5	37.0	37.5	38.0	38.5	39.0	39.5
	the Depreciation Rate is:														
1	0.385	0.379	0.373	0.368	0.362	0.357	0.352	0.347	0.342	0.338	0.333	0.329	0.325	0.321	0.316
2	3.077	3.030	2.985	2.941	2.899	2.857	2.817	2.778	2.740	2.703	2.667	2.632	2.597	2.564	2.532
3	3.077	3.030	2.985	2.941	2.899	2.857	2.817	2.778	2.740	2.703	2.667	2.632	2.597	2.564	2.532
4	3.077	3.030	2.985	2.941	2.899	2.857	2.817	2.778	2.740	2.703	2.667	2.632	2.597	2.564	2.532
5	3.077	3.030	2.985	2.941	2.899	2.857	2.817	2.778	2.740	2.703	2.667	2.632	2.597	2.564	2.532
6	3.077	3.030	2.985	2.941	2.899	2.857	2.817	2.778	2.740	2.703	2.667	2.632	2.597	2.564	2.532
7	3.077	3.030	2.985	2.941	2.898	2.857	2.817	2.778	2.740	2.703	2.667	2.632	2.597	2.564	2.532
8	3.077	3.030	2.985	2.941	2.899	2.857	2.817	2.778	2.740	2.703	2.667	2.631	2.597	2.564	2.532
9	3.077	3.030	2.985	2.941	2.898	2.857	2.817	2.778	2.740	2.703	2.667	2.632	2.597	2.564	2.532
10	3.077	3.030	2.985	2.941	2.899	2.857	2.817	2.778	2.740	2.703	2.667	2.631	2.597	2.564	2.532
11	3.077	3.030	2.985	2.941	2.898	2.857	2.817	2.778	2.740	2.703	2.667	2.632	2.598	2.564	2.532
12	3.077	3.030	2.985	2.941	2.899	2.857	2.817	2.778	2.740	2.703	2.667	2.631	2.597	2.564	2.532
13	3.077	3.030	2.985	2.941	2.898	2.857	2.817	2.778	2.740	2.703	2.667	2.632	2.598	2.564	2.532
14	3.077	3.030	2.985	2.941	2.899	2.857	2.817	2.778	2.740	2.703	2.667	2.631	2.597	2.564	2.532
15	3.077	3.030	2.985	2.941	2.898	2.857	2.817	2.778	2.740	2.703	2.667	2.632	2.598	2.564	2.531
16	3.077	3.031	2.985	2.941	2.899	2.857	2.817	2.778	2.740	2.703	2.666	2.631	2.597	2.564	2.532
17	3.077	3.030	2.985	2.941	2.898	2.857	2.817	2.778	2.740	2.702	2.667	2.632	2.598	2.564	2.531
18	3.077	3.031	2.985	2.941	2.899	2.857	2.817	2.778	2.740	2.703	2.666	2.631	2.597	2.564	2.532
19	3.077	3.030	2.985	2.941	2.898	2.857	2.817	2.778	2.740	2.702	2.667	2.632	2.598	2.564	2.531
20	3.077	3.031	2.985	2.941	2.899	2.857	2.817	2.778	2.739	2.703	2.666	2.631	2.597	2.564	2.532

If the Recovery Year is:	and the Recovery Period is: 32.5	33.0	33.5	34.0	34.5	35.0	35.5	36.0	36.5	37.0	37.5	38.0	38.5	39.0	39.5
	the Depreciation Rate is:														
21	3.077	3.030	2.985	2.941	2.898	2.857	2.817	2.778	2.740	2.702	2.667	2.632	2.598	2.564	2.531
22	3.077	3.031	2.985	2.941	2.899	2.857	2.817	2.778	2.739	2.703	2.666	2.631	2.597	2.564	2.532
23	3.077	3.030	2.985	2.941	2.898	2.857	2.817	2.777	2.740	2.702	2.667	2.632	2.598	2.564	2.531
24	3.077	3.031	2.985	2.941	2.899	2.857	2.817	2.778	2.739	2.703	2.666	2.631	2.597	2.564	2.532
25	3.077	3.030	2.985	2.942	2.898	2.857	2.817	2.777	2.740	2.702	2.667	2.632	2.598	2.564	2.531
26	3.077	3.031	2.985	2.941	2.899	2.857	2.817	2.778	2.739	2.703	2.666	2.631	2.597	2.564	2.532
27	3.077	3.030	2.985	2.942	2.898	2.858	2.817	2.777	2.740	2.702	2.667	2.632	2.598	2.564	2.531
28	3.077	3.031	2.985	2.941	2.899	2.857	2.817	2.778	2.739	2.703	2.666	2.631	2.597	2.564	2.532
29	3.076	3.030	2.985	2.942	2.898	2.858	2.817	2.777	2.740	2.702	2.667	2.632	2.598	2.564	2.531
30	3.077	3.031	2.985	2.941	2.899	2.857	2.817	2.778	2.739	2.703	2.666	2.631	2.597	2.564	2.532
31	3.076	3.030	2.986	2.942	2.898	2.858	2.816	2.777	2.740	2.702	2.667	2.632	2.598	2.564	2.531
32	3.077	3.031	2.985	2.941	2.899	2.857	2.817	2.778	2.739	2.703	2.666	2.631	2.597	2.564	2.532
33	3.076	3.030	2.986	2.942	2.898	2.858	2.816	2.777	2.740	2.702	2.667	2.632	2.598	2.564	2.531
34	1.154	2.652	2.985	2.941	2.899	2.857	2.817	2.778	2.739	2.703	2.666	2.631	2.597	2.565	2.532
35			1.120	2.574	2.898	2.858	2.816	2.777	2.740	2.702	2.667	2.632	2.598	2.564	2.531
36					1.087	2.500	2.817	2.778	2.739	2.703	2.666	2.631	2.597	2.565	2.532
37							1.056	2.430	2.740	2.702	2.667	2.632	2.598	2.564	2.531
38									1.027	2.365	2.666	2.631	2.597	2.565	2.532
39											1.000	2.303	2.598	2.564	2.531
40													0.974	2.244	2.532
41															0.949

If the Recovery Year is:	and the Recovery Period is: 40.0	40.5	41.0	41.5	42.0	42.5	43.0	43.5	44.0	44.5	45.0	45.5	46.0	46.5	47.0
	the Depreciation Rate is:														
1	0.313	0.309	0.305	0.301	0.298	0.294	0.291	0.287	0.284	0.281	0.278	0.275	0.272	0.269	0.266
2	2.500	2.469	2.439	2.410	2.381	2.353	2.326	2.299	2.273	2.247	2.222	2.198	2.174	2.151	2.128
3	2.500	2.469	2.439	2.410	2.381	2.353	2.326	2.299	2.273	2.247	2.222	2.198	2.174	2.151	2.128
4	2.500	2.469	2.439	2.410	2.381	2.353	2.326	2.299	2.273	2.247	2.222	2.198	2.174	2.151	2.128
5	2.500	2.469	2.439	2.410	2.381	2.353	2.326	2.299	2.273	2.247	2.222	2.198	2.174	2.151	2.128
6	2.500	2.469	2.439	2.410	2.381	2.353	2.326	2.299	2.273	2.247	2.222	2.198	2.174	2.150	2.128
7	2.500	2.469	2.439	2.410	2.381	2.353	2.326	2.299	2.273	2.247	2.222	2.198	2.174	2.151	2.128
8	2.500	2.469	2.439	2.410	2.381	2.353	2.326	2.299	2.273	2.247	2.222	2.198	2.174	2.150	2.128
9	2.500	2.469	2.439	2.410	2.381	2.353	2.325	2.299	2.273	2.247	2.222	2.198	2.174	2.151	2.128
10	2.500	2.469	2.439	2.410	2.381	2.353	2.326	2.299	2.273	2.247	2.222	2.198	2.174	2.150	2.128
11	2.500	2.469	2.439	2.410	2.381	2.353	2.325	2.299	2.273	2.247	2.222	2.198	2.174	2.151	2.128
12	2.500	2.469	2.439	2.410	2.381	2.353	2.326	2.299	2.273	2.247	2.222	2.198	2.174	2.150	2.128
13	2.500	2.469	2.439	2.410	2.381	2.353	2.325	2.299	2.273	2.247	2.222	2.198	2.174	2.151	2.128
14	2.500	2.469	2.439	2.409	2.381	2.353	2.326	2.299	2.273	2.247	2.222	2.198	2.174	2.150	2.128
15	2.500	2.469	2.439	2.410	2.381	2.353	2.325	2.299	2.273	2.247	2.222	2.198	2.174	2.151	2.128
16	2.500	2.469	2.439	2.409	2.381	2.353	2.326	2.299	2.273	2.247	2.222	2.198	2.174	2.150	2.128
17	2.500	2.469	2.439	2.410	2.381	2.353	2.325	2.299	2.273	2.247	2.222	2.198	2.174	2.151	2.127
18	2.500	2.469	2.439	2.409	2.381	2.353	2.326	2.299	2.273	2.247	2.222	2.198	2.174	2.150	2.128
19	2.500	2.469	2.439	2.410	2.381	2.353	2.325	2.299	2.273	2.247	2.222	2.198	2.174	2.151	2.127
20	2.500	2.469	2.439	2.409	2.381	2.353	2.326	2.299	2.273	2.247	2.222	2.198	2.174	2.150	2.128
21	2.500	2.469	2.439	2.410	2.381	2.353	2.325	2.299	2.273	2.247	2.222	2.198	2.174	2.151	2.127
22	2.500	2.469	2.439	2.409	2.381	2.353	2.326	2.299	2.273	2.247	2.222	2.198	2.174	2.150	2.128
23	2.500	2.469	2.439	2.410	2.381	2.353	2.325	2.299	2.272	2.247	2.222	2.198	2.174	2.151	2.127
24	2.500	2.469	2.439	2.409	2.381	2.353	2.326	2.299	2.273	2.247	2.222	2.198	2.174	2.150	2.128
25	2.500	2.469	2.439	2.410	2.381	2.353	2.325	2.299	2.272	2.247	2.222	2.198	2.174	2.151	2.127
26	2.500	2.469	2.439	2.409	2.381	2.353	2.326	2.299	2.273	2.247	2.222	2.198	2.174	2.150	2.128

If the Recovery Year is:	and the Recovery Period is: 40.0	40.5	41.0	41.5	42.0	42.5	43.0	43.5	44.0	44.5	45.0	45.5	46.0	46.5	47.0
	the Depreciation Rate is:														
27	2.500	2.469	2.439	2.410	2.381	2.353	2.325	2.299	2.272	2.247	2.222	2.198	2.174	2.151	2.127
28	2.500	2.469	2.439	2.409	2.381	2.353	2.326	2.299	2.273	2.247	2.223	2.198	2.174	2.150	2.128
29	2.500	2.469	2.439	2.410	2.381	2.353	2.325	2.299	2.272	2.247	2.222	2.197	2.174	2.151	2.127
30	2.500	2.469	2.439	2.409	2.381	2.353	2.326	2.299	2.273	2.248	2.223	2.198	2.174	2.150	2.128
31	2.500	2.469	2.439	2.410	2.381	2.353	2.325	2.299	2.272	2.247	2.222	2.197	2.174	2.151	2.127
32	2.500	2.469	2.439	2.409	2.381	2.353	2.326	2.299	2.273	2.248	2.223	2.198	2.174	2.150	2.128
33	2.500	2.470	2.439	2.410	2.381	2.353	2.325	2.299	2.272	2.247	2.222	2.197	2.174	2.151	2.127
34	2.500	2.469	2.439	2.409	2.381	2.353	2.326	2.298	2.273	2.248	2.223	2.198	2.174	2.150	2.128
35	2.500	2.470	2.439	2.410	2.381	2.353	2.325	2.299	2.272	2.247	2.222	2.197	2.174	2.151	2.127
36	2.500	2.469	2.439	2.409	2.381	2.353	2.326	2.298	2.273	2.248	2.223	2.198	2.174	2.150	2.128
37	2.500	2.470	2.439	2.410	2.381	2.353	2.325	2.299	2.272	2.247	2.222	2.197	2.174	2.151	2.127
38	2.500	2.469	2.439	2.409	2.381	2.353	2.326	2.298	2.273	2.248	2.223	2.198	2.174	2.150	2.128
39	2.500	2.470	2.439	2.410	2.381	2.353	2.325	2.299	2.272	2.247	2.222	2.197	2.174	2.151	2.127
40	2.500	2.469	2.439	2.409	2.380	2.352	2.326	2.298	2.273	2.248	2.223	2.198	2.173	2.150	2.128
41	2.187	2.470	2.439	2.410	2.381	2.353	2.325	2.299	2.272	2.247	2.222	2.197	2.174	2.151	2.127
42		0.926	2.135	2.409	2.380	2.352	2.326	2.298	2.273	2.248	2.223	2.198	2.173	2.150	2.128
43				0.904	2.083	2.353	2.325	2.299	2.272	2.247	2.222	2.197	2.174	2.151	2.127
44						0.882	2.035	2.298	2.273	2.248	2.223	2.198	2.173	2.150	2.128
45								0.862	1.988	2.247	2.222	2.197	2.174	2.151	2.127
46										0.843	1.945	2.198	2.173	2.150	2.128
47												0.824	1.902	2.151	2.127
48														0.806	1.862

If the Recovery Year is:	and the Recovery Period is: 47.5	48.0	48.5	49.0	49.5	50.0
	the Depreciation Rate is:					
1	0.263	0.260	0.258	0.255	0.253	0.250
2	2.105	2.083	2.062	2.041	2.020	2.000
3	2.105	2.083	2.062	2.041	2.020	2.000
4	2.105	2.083	2.062	2.041	2.020	2.000
5	2.105	2.083	2.062	2.041	2.020	2.000
6	2.105	2.083	2.062	2.041	2.020	2.000
7	2.105	2.083	2.062	2.041	2.020	2.000
8	2.105	2.083	2.062	2.041	2.020	2.000
9	2.105	2.083	2.062	2.041	2.020	2.000
10	2.105	2.083	2.062	2.041	2.020	2.000
11	2.105	2.083	2.062	2.041	2.020	2.000
12	2.105	2.083	2.062	2.041	2.020	2.000
13	2.105	2.083	2.062	2.041	2.020	2.000
14	2.105	2.083	2.062	2.041	2.020	2.000
15	2.105	2.083	2.062	2.041	2.020	2.000
16	2.105	2.083	2.062	2.041	2.020	2.000
17	2.105	2.083	2.062	2.041	2.020	2.000
18	2.105	2.084	2.062	2.041	2.020	2.000
19	2.105	2.083	2.062	2.041	2.020	2.000
20	2.105	2.084	2.062	2.041	2.020	2.000
21	2.105	2.083	2.062	2.041	2.020	2.000
22	2.105	2.084	2.062	2.041	2.020	2.000
23	2.105	2.083	2.062	2.041	2.020	2.000
24	2.105	2.084	2.062	2.041	2.020	2.000
25	2.106	2.083	2.062	2.041	2.020	2.000
26	2.105	2.084	2.062	2.041	2.020	2.000

If the Recovery Year is:	and the Recovery Period is: 47.5	48.0	48.5	49.0	49.5	50.0
	the Depreciation Rate is:					
27	2.106	2.083	2.062	2.041	2.020	2.000
28	2.105	2.084	2.062	2.041	2.020	2.000
29	2.106	2.083	2.062	2.041	2.020	2.000
30	2.105	2.084	2.062	2.041	2.020	2.000
31	2.106	2.083	2.062	2.041	2.020	2.000
32	2.105	2.084	2.062	2.041	2.020	2.000
33	2.106	2.083	2.062	2.041	2.021	2.000
34	2.105	2.084	2.062	2.040	2.020	2.000
35	2.106	2.083	2.062	2.041	2.021	2.000
36	2.105	2.084	2.061	2.040	2.020	2.000
37	2.106	2.083	2.062	2.041	2.021	2.000
38	2.105	2.084	2.061	2.040	2.020	2.000
39	2.106	2.083	2.062	2.041	2.021	2.000
40	2.105	2.084	2.061	2.040	2.020	2.000
41	2.106	2.083	2.062	2.041	2.021	2.000
42	2.105	2.084	2.061	2.040	2.020	2.000
43	2.106	2.083	2.062	2.041	2.021	2.000
44	2.105	2.084	2.061	2.040	2.020	2.000
45	2.106	2.083	2.062	2.041	2.021	2.000
46	2.105	2.084	2.061	2.040	2.020	2.000
47	2.106	2.083	2.062	2.041	2.021	2.000
48	2.105	2.084	2.061	2.040	2.020	2.000
49	0.790	1.823	2.062	2.041	2.021	2.000
50			0.773	1.785	2.020	2.000
51					0.758	1.750

TABLE 13
Alternative Depreciation System
Applicable Depreciation Method: Straight Line
Applicable Recovery Period: 40 years
Applicable Convention: Mid-month

If the Recovery Year is:	and the Month in the First Recovery Year the Property is Placed in Service is:											
	1	2	3	4	5	6	7	8	9	10	11	12
	the Depreciation Rate is:											
1	2.396	2.188	1.979	1.771	1.563	1.354	1.146	0.938	0.729	0.521	0.313	0.104
2 - 40	2.500	2.500	2.500	2.500	2.500	2.500	2.500	2.500	2.500	2.500	2.500	2.500
41	0.104	0.312	0.521	0.729	0.937	1.146	1.354	1.562	1.771	1.979	2.187	2.396

TABLE 14
Alternative Minimum Tax (see section 7 of this revenue procedure)
Applicable Depreciation Method: 150-Percent Declining Balance Switching to Straight Line
Applicable Recovery Periods: 2.5 — 50 years
Applicable Convention: Half-year

If the Recovery Year is:	and the Recovery Period is: 2.5	3.0	3.5	4.0	4.5	5.0	5.5	6.0	6.5	7.0	7.5	8.0	8.5	9.0	9.5
	the Depreciation Rate is:														
1	30.00	25.00	21.43	18.75	16.67	15.00	13.64	12.50	11.54	10.71	10.00	9.38	8.82	8.33	7.89
2	42.00	37.50	33.67	30.47	27.78	25.50	23.55	21.88	20.41	19.13	18.00	16.99	16.09	15.28	14.54
3	28.00	25.00	22.45	20.31	18.52	17.85	17.13	16.41	15.70	15.03	14.40	13.81	13.25	12.73	12.25
4		12.50	22.45	20.31	18.52	16.66	15.23	14.06	13.09	12.25	11.52	11.22	10.91	10.61	10.31
5				10.16	18.51	16.66	15.23	14.06	13.09	12.25	11.52	10.80	10.19	9.65	9.17
6						8.33	15.22	14.06	13.09	12.25	11.52	10.80	10.19	9.64	9.17
7								7.03	13.08	12.25	11.52	10.80	10.18	9.65	9.17
8										6.13	11.52	10.80	10.19	9.64	9.17
9												5.40	10.18	9.65	9.17
10														4.82	9.16

If the Recovery Year is:	and the Recovery Period is: 10.0	10.5	11.0	11.5	12.0	12.5	13.0	13.5	14.0	14.5	15.0	15.5	16.0	16.5	17.0
	the Depreciation Rate is:														
1	7.50	7.14	6.82	6.52	6.25	6.00	5.77	5.56	5.36	5.17	5.00	4.84	4.69	4.55	4.41
2	13.88	13.27	12.71	12.19	11.72	11.28	10.87	10.49	10.14	9.81	9.50	9.21	8.94	8.68	8.43
3	11.79	11.37	10.97	10.60	10.25	9.93	9.62	9.33	9.05	8.80	8.55	8.32	8.10	7.89	7.69
4	10.02	9.75	9.48	9.22	8.97	8.73	8.51	8.29	8.08	7.88	7.70	7.51	7.34	7.17	7.01
5	8.74	8.35	8.18	8.02	7.85	7.69	7.53	7.37	7.22	7.07	6.93	6.79	6.65	6.52	6.39
6	8.74	8.35	7.98	7.64	7.33	7.05	6.79	6.55	6.44	6.34	6.23	6.13	6.03	5.93	5.83

If the Recovery Year is:	and the Recovery Period is: 10.0	10.5	11.0	11.5	12.0	12.5	13.0	13.5	14.0	14.5	15.0	15.5	16.0	16.5	17.0
	the Depreciation Rate is:														
7	8.74	8.35	7.97	7.64	7.33	7.05	6.79	6.55	6.32	6.10	5.90	5.72	5.55	5.39	5.32
8	8.74	8.35	7.98	7.63	7.33	7.05	6.79	6.55	6.32	6.10	5.90	5.72	5.55	5.39	5.23
9	8.74	8.36	7.97	7.64	7.33	7.04	6.79	6.55	6.32	6.10	5.91	5.72	5.55	5.39	5.23
10	8.74	8.35	7.98	7.63	7.33	7.05	6.79	6.55	6.32	6.11	5.90	5.72	5.55	5.39	5.23
11	4.37	8.36	7.97	7.64	7.32	7.04	6.79	6.55	6.32	6.10	5.91	5.72	5.55	5.39	5.23
12			3.99	7.63	7.33	7.05	6.78	6.55	6.32	6.11	5.90	5.72	5.55	5.39	5.23
13					3.66	7.04	6.79	6.56	6.32	6.10	5.91	5.72	5.54	5.38	5.23
14							3.39	6.55	6.31	6.11	5.90	5.72	5.55	5.39	5.23
15									3.16	6.10	5.91	5.72	5.54	5.38	5.23
16											2.95	5.72	5.55	5.39	5.23
17													2.77	5.38	5.23
18															2.62

If the Recovery Year is:	and the Recovery Period is: 17.5	18.0	18.5	19.0	19.5	20.0	20.5	21.0	21.5	22.0	22.5	23.0	23.5	24.0	24.5
	the Depreciation Rate is:														
1	4.29	4.17	4.05	3.95	3.85	3.750	3.659	3.571	3.488	3.409	3.333	3.261	3.191	3.125	3.061
2	8.20	7.99	7.78	7.58	7.40	7.219	7.049	6.888	6.733	6.586	6.444	6.309	6.179	6.055	5.935
3	7.50	7.32	7.15	6.98	6.83	6.677	6.534	6.396	6.264	6.137	6.015	5.898	5.785	5.676	5.572
4	6.86	6.71	6.57	6.43	6.30	6.177	6.055	5.939	5.827	5.718	5.614	5.513	5.416	5.322	5.231
5	6.27	6.15	6.04	5.93	5.82	5.713	5.612	5.515	5.420	5.328	5.240	5.153	5.070	4.989	4.910
6	5.73	5.64	5.55	5.46	5.37	5.285	5.202	5.121	5.042	4.965	4.890	4.817	4.746	4.677	4.610
7	5.24	5.17	5.10	5.03	4.96	4.888	4.821	4.755	4.690	4.627	4.564	4.503	4.443	4.385	4.327
8	5.08	4.94	4.81	4.69	4.57	4.522	4.468	4.415	4.363	4.311	4.260	4.210	4.160	4.111	4.062
9	5.08	4.94	4.81	4.69	4.58	4.462	4.354	4.252	4.155	4.063	3.976	3.935	3.894	3.854	3.814
10	5.08	4.94	4.81	4.69	4.57	4.461	4.354	4.252	4.155	4.063	3.976	3.890	3.808	3.729	3.655

If the Recovery Year is:	and the Recovery Period is: 17.5	18.0	18.5	19.0	19.5	20.0	20.5	21.0	21.5	22.0	22.5	23.0	23.5	24.0	24.5
	the Depreciation Rate is:														
11	5.08	4.94	4.81	4.69	4.58	4.462	4.354	4.252	4.155	4.063	3.976	3.890	3.808	3.729	3.655
12	5.08	4.95	4.81	4.69	4.57	4.461	4.354	4.252	4.155	4.063	3.976	3.890	3.808	3.729	3.655
13	5.09	4.94	4.82	4.69	4.58	4.462	4.354	4.252	4.155	4.064	3.976	3.890	3.808	3.730	3.655
14	5.08	4.95	4.81	4.69	4.57	4.461	4.354	4.252	4.155	4.063	3.976	3.890	3.808	3.729	3.655
15	5.09	4.94	4.82	4.69	4.58	4.462	4.354	4.252	4.155	4.064	3.976	3.890	3.808	3.730	3.655
16	5.08	4.95	4.81	4.69	4.57	4.461	4.354	4.252	4.155	4.063	3.976	3.890	3.808	3.729	3.655
17	5.09	4.94	4.82	4.69	4.58	4.462	4.354	4.252	4.155	4.064	3.976	3.889	3.808	3.730	3.655
18	5.08	4.95	4.81	4.70	4.57	4.461	4.354	4.252	4.156	4.063	3.976	3.890	3.807	3.729	3.655
19		2.47	4.82	4.69	4.58	4.462	4.353	4.251	4.155	4.064	3.976	3.889	3.808	3.730	3.655
20				2.35	4.57	4.461	4.354	4.252	4.156	4.063	3.976	3.890	3.807	3.729	3.655
21						2.231	4.353	4.251	4.155	4.064	3.976	3.889	3.808	3.730	3.655
22								2.126	4.156	4.063	3.976	3.890	3.807	3.729	3.655
23										2.032	3.976	3.889	3.808	3.730	3.654
24												1.945	3.807	3.729	3.655
25														1.865	3.654

If the Recovery Year is:	and the Recovery Period is: 25.0	25.5	26.0	26.5	27.0	27.5	28.0	28.5	29.0	29.5	30.0	30.5	31.0	31.5	32.0
	the Depreciation Rate is:														
1	3.000	2.941	2.885	2.830	2.778	2.727	2.679	2.632	2.586	2.542	2.500	2.459	2.419	2.381	2.344
2	5.820	5.709	5.603	5.500	5.401	5.306	5.214	5.125	5.039	4.955	4.875	4.797	4.722	4.649	4.578
3	5.471	5.374	5.280	5.189	5.101	5.016	4.934	4.855	4.778	4.704	4.631	4.561	4.493	4.427	4.363
4	5.143	5.057	4.975	4.895	4.818	4.743	4.670	4.599	4.531	4.464	4.400	4.337	4.276	4.216	4.159
5	4.834	4.760	4.688	4.618	4.550	4.484	4.420	4.357	4.297	4.237	4.180	4.124	4.069	4.016	3.964
6	4.544	4.480	4.417	4.357	4.297	4.239	4.183	4.128	4.074	4.022	3.971	3.921	3.872	3.824	3.778
7	4.271	4.216	4.163	4.110	4.059	4.008	3.959	3.911	3.864	3.817	3.772	3.728	3.685	3.642	3.601

If the Recovery Year is:	and the Recovery Period is: 25.0	25.5	26.0	26.5	27.0	27.5	28.0	28.5	29.0	29.5	30.0	30.5	31.0	31.5	32.0
	the Depreciation Rate is:														
8	4.015	3.968	3.922	3.877	3.833	3.790	3.747	3.705	3.664	3.623	3.584	3.545	3.506	3.469	3.432
9	3.774	3.735	3.696	3.658	3.620	3.583	3.546	3.510	3.474	3.439	3.404	3.370	3.337	3.304	3.271
10	3.584	3.515	3.483	3.451	3.419	3.387	3.356	3.325	3.294	3.264	3.234	3.204	3.175	3.146	3.118
11	3.583	3.515	3.448	3.383	3.321	3.262	3.205	3.150	3.124	3.098	3.072	3.047	3.022	2.996	2.971
12	3.584	3.515	3.448	3.383	3.321	3.262	3.205	3.150	3.096	3.044	2.994	2.945	2.899	2.854	2.832
13	3.583	3.515	3.448	3.383	3.321	3.262	3.205	3.150	3.096	3.044	2.994	2.945	2.899	2.854	2.809
14	3.584	3.515	3.448	3.383	3.321	3.262	3.205	3.150	3.096	3.044	2.994	2.945	2.899	2.854	2.809
15	3.583	3.515	3.448	3.383	3.321	3.262	3.205	3.150	3.096	3.044	2.994	2.945	2.899	2.854	2.809
16	3.584	3.515	3.448	3.383	3.322	3.262	3.205	3.150	3.096	3.044	2.994	2.945	2.899	2.854	2.809
17	3.583	3.515	3.448	3.383	3.321	3.262	3.205	3.150	3.096	3.044	2.994	2.945	2.899	2.854	2.809
18	3.584	3.516	3.448	3.383	3.322	3.262	3.205	3.150	3.096	3.044	2.994	2.946	2.899	2.854	2.809
19	3.583	3.515	3.448	3.383	3.321	3.262	3.205	3.150	3.096	3.044	2.994	2.945	2.899	2.854	2.809
20	3.584	3.516	3.447	3.384	3.322	3.262	3.205	3.150	3.096	3.044	2.993	2.946	2.899	2.854	2.809
21	3.583	3.515	3.448	3.383	3.321	3.262	3.205	3.150	3.096	3.044	2.994	2.945	2.899	2.854	2.809
22	3.584	3.516	3.447	3.384	3.322	3.262	3.205	3.150	3.096	3.044	2.993	2.946	2.898	2.854	2.809
23	3.583	3.515	3.448	3.383	3.321	3.262	3.205	3.150	3.096	3.044	2.994	2.945	2.899	2.854	2.809
24	3.584	3.516	3.447	3.384	3.322	3.262	3.205	3.151	3.096	3.044	2.993	2.946	2.898	2.854	2.809
25	3.583	3.515	3.448	3.383	3.321	3.262	3.205	3.150	3.096	3.044	2.994	2.945	2.899	2.854	2.810
26	1.792	3.516	3.447	3.384	3.322	3.262	3.205	3.151	3.096	3.044	2.993	2.946	2.898	2.853	2.809
27			1.724	3.383	3.321	3.262	3.205	3.150	3.096	3.044	2.994	2.945	2.899	2.854	2.810
28					1.661	3.263	3.205	3.151	3.096	3.044	2.993	2.946	2.898	2.853	2.809
29							1.602	3.150	3.095	3.044	2.994	2.945	2.899	2.854	2.810
30									1.548	3.043	2.993	2.946	2.898	2.853	2.809
31											1.497	2.945	2.899	2.854	2.810
32													1.449	2.853	2.809
33															1.405

If the Recovery Year is:	and the Recovery Period is: 32.5	33.0	33.5	34.0	34.5	35.0	35.5	36.0	36.5	37.0	37.5	38.0	38.5	39.0	39.5
	the Depreciation Rate is:														
1	2.308	2.273	2.239	2.206	2.174	2.143	2.113	2.083	2.055	2.027	2.000	1.974	1.948	1.923	1.899
2	4.509	4.442	4.377	4.314	4.253	4.194	4.136	4.080	4.025	3.972	3.920	3.869	3.820	3.772	3.725
3	4.301	4.240	4.181	4.124	4.068	4.014	3.961	3.910	3.860	3.811	3.763	3.717	3.671	3.627	3.584
4	4.102	4.048	3.994	3.942	3.892	3.842	3.794	3.747	3.701	3.656	3.613	3.570	3.528	3.488	3.448
5	3.913	3.864	3.815	3.768	3.722	3.677	3.634	3.591	3.549	3.508	3.468	3.429	3.391	3.353	3.317
6	3.732	3.688	3.645	3.602	3.560	3.520	3.480	3.441	3.403	3.366	3.329	3.294	3.259	3.225	3.191
7	3.560	3.520	3.481	3.443	3.406	3.369	3.333	3.298	3.263	3.229	3.196	3.164	3.132	3.100	3.070
8	3.396	3.360	3.325	3.291	3.258	3.225	3.192	3.160	3.129	3.099	3.068	3.039	3.010	2.981	2.953
9	3.239	3.208	3.177	3.146	3.116	3.086	3.057	3.029	3.001	2.973	2.946	2.919	2.893	2.867	2.841
10	3.090	3.062	3.034	3.007	2.980	2.954	2.928	2.903	2.877	2.852	2.828	2.804	2.780	2.756	2.733
11	2.947	2.923	2.898	2.875	2.851	2.828	2.804	2.782	2.759	2.737	2.715	2.693	2.671	2.650	2.629
12	2.811	2.790	2.769	2.748	2.727	2.706	2.686	2.666	2.646	2.626	2.606	2.587	2.567	2.548	2.529
13	2.766	2.725	2.685	2.646	2.608	2.590	2.572	2.555	2.537	2.519	2.502	2.485	2.467	2.450	2.433
14	2.766	2.725	2.685	2.646	2.608	2.571	2.535	2.500	2.466	2.434	2.402	2.386	2.371	2.356	2.341
15	2.766	2.725	2.685	2.646	2.608	2.571	2.535	2.500	2.466	2.434	2.402	2.370	2.340	2.310	2.281
16	2.766	2.725	2.685	2.646	2.608	2.571	2.535	2.500	2.466	2.434	2.402	2.370	2.340	2.310	2.281
17	2.766	2.725	2.685	2.646	2.608	2.571	2.535	2.500	2.467	2.434	2.402	2.370	2.340	2.310	2.281
18	2.766	2.725	2.685	2.646	2.609	2.571	2.535	2.500	2.466	2.434	2.402	2.370	2.340	2.310	2.281
19	2.766	2.725	2.685	2.646	2.608	2.571	2.535	2.500	2.467	2.434	2.402	2.370	2.340	2.310	2.281
20	2.766	2.725	2.685	2.646	2.609	2.571	2.535	2.500	2.466	2.434	2.402	2.370	2.340	2.310	2.281
21	2.766	2.725	2.685	2.646	2.608	2.571	2.535	2.500	2.467	2.434	2.402	2.370	2.340	2.310	2.281
22	2.767	2.725	2.685	2.646	2.609	2.571	2.535	2.500	2.466	2.434	2.402	2.370	2.340	2.310	2.281
23	2.766	2.725	2.685	2.646	2.608	2.571	2.535	2.500	2.467	2.433	2.402	2.370	2.340	2.310	2.281
24	2.767	2.724	2.685	2.646	2.609	2.571	2.535	2.500	2.466	2.434	2.402	2.370	2.340	2.310	2.281
25	2.766	2.725	2.684	2.646	2.608	2.571	2.535	2.500	2.467	2.433	2.402	2.370	2.339	2.310	2.281
26	2.767	2.724	2.685	2.646	2.609	2.571	2.535	2.500	2.466	2.434	2.402	2.370	2.340	2.310	2.281

If the Recovery Year is:	and the Recovery Period is: 32.5	33.0	33.5	34.0	34.5	35.0	35.5	36.0	36.5	37.0	37.5	38.0	38.5	39.0	39.5
	the Depreciation Rate is:														
27	2.766	2.725	2.684	2.646	2.608	2.571	2.536	2.500	2.467	2.433	2.402	2.370	2.339	2.310	2.281
28	2.767	2.724	2.685	2.646	2.609	2.572	2.535	2.501	2.466	2.434	2.402	2.370	2.340	2.310	2.281
29	2.766	2.725	2.684	2.646	2.608	2.571	2.536	2.500	2.467	2.433	2.402	2.370	2.339	2.310	2.281
30	2.767	2.724	2.685	2.646	2.609	2.572	2.535	2.501	2.466	2.434	2.402	2.371	2.340	2.310	2.281
31	2.766	2.725	2.684	2.646	2.608	2.571	2.536	2.500	2.467	2.433	2.401	2.370	2.339	2.310	2.281
32	2.767	2.724	2.685	2.646	2.609	2.572	2.535	2.501	2.466	2.434	2.402	2.371	2.340	2.310	2.281
33	2.766	2.725	2.684	2.646	2.608	2.571	2.536	2.500	2.467	2.433	2.404	2.370	2.339	2.310	2.281
34		1.362	2.685	2.645	2.609	2.572	2.535	2.501	2.466	2.434	2.402	2.371	2.340	2.310	2.281
35				1.323	2.608	2.571	2.536	2.500	2.467	2.433	2.401	2.370	2.339	2.310	2.281
36						1.286	2.535	2.501	2.466	2.434	2.402	2.371	2.340	2.310	2.281
37								1.250	2.467	2.433	2.401	2.370	2.339	2.310	2.281
38										1.217	2.402	2.371	2.340	2.310	2.281
39												1.185	2.339	2.309	2.282
40														1.155	2.281

If the Recovery Year is:	and the Recovery Period is: 40.0	40.5	41.0	41.5	42.0	42.5	43.0	43.5	44.0	44.5	45.0	45.5	46.0	46.5	47.0
	the Depreciation Rate is:														
1	1.875	1.852	1.829	1.807	1.786	1.765	1.744	1.724	1.705	1.685	1.667	1.648	1.630	1.613	1.596
2	3.680	3.635	3.592	3.549	3.508	3.467	3.428	3.389	3.351	3.314	3.278	3.242	3.208	3.174	3.141
3	3.542	3.500	3.460	3.421	3.382	3.345	3.308	3.272	3.237	3.202	3.169	3.135	3.103	3.071	3.040
4	3.409	3.371	3.334	3.297	3.262	3.227	3.193	3.159	3.126	3.094	3.063	3.032	3.002	2.972	2.943
5	3.281	3.246	3.212	3.178	3.145	3.113	3.081	3.050	3.020	2.990	2.961	2.932	2.904	2.876	2.849
6	3.158	3.126	3.094	3.063	3.033	3.003	2.974	2.945	2.917	2.889	2.862	2.836	2.809	2.784	2.758
7	3.040	3.010	2.981	2.952	2.924	2.897	2.870	2.843	2.817	2.792	2.767	2.742	2.718	2.694	2.670
8	2.926	2.899	2.872	2.846	2.820	2.795	2.770	2.745	2.721	2.698	2.674	2.652	2.629	2.607	2.585

If the Recovery Year is:	and the Recovery Period is: 40.0	40.5	41.0	41.5	42.0	42.5	43.0	43.5	44.0	44.5	45.0	45.5	46.0	46.5	47.0
	the Depreciation Rate is:														
9	2.816	2.791	2.767	2.743	2.719	2.696	2.673	2.651	2.629	2.607	2.585	2.564	2.543	2.523	2.503
10	2.710	2.688	2.666	2.644	2.622	2.601	2.580	2.559	2.539	2.519	2.499	2.480	2.460	2.441	2.423
11	2.609	2.588	2.568	2.548	2.529	2.509	2.490	2.471	2.452	2.434	2.416	2.398	2.380	2.363	2.345
12	2.511	2.492	2.474	2.456	2.438	2.421	2.403	2.386	2.369	2.352	2.335	2.319	2.303	2.287	2.271
13	2.417	2.400	2.384	2.367	2.351	2.335	2.319	2.304	2.288	2.273	2.257	2.242	2.228	2.213	2.198
14	2.326	2.311	2.296	2.282	2.267	2.253	2.238	2.224	2.210	2.196	2.182	2.169	2.155	2.141	2.128
15	2.253	2.226	2.212	2.199	2.186	2.173	2.160	2.148	2.135	2.122	2.110	2.097	2.085	2.072	2.060
16	2.253	2.226	2.198	2.172	2.146	2.121	2.097	2.073	2.062	2.051	2.039	2.028	2.017	2.005	1.994
17	2.253	2.226	2.198	2.172	2.146	2.121	2.097	2.073	2.050	2.027	2.005	1.983	1.962	1.941	1.931
18	2.253	2.226	2.198	2.172	2.147	2.121	2.097	2.073	2.050	2.027	2.005	1.983	1.961	1.941	1.920
19	2.253	2.226	2.199	2.172	2.146	2.121	2.097	2.073	2.050	2.027	2.005	1.983	1.962	1.941	1.920
20	2.253	2.226	2.198	2.172	2.147	2.121	2.097	2.074	2.050	2.027	2.005	1.983	1.961	1.941	1.920
21	2.253	2.225	2.199	2.172	2.146	2.122	2.097	2.073	2.050	2.027	2.005	1.983	1.962	1.941	1.920
22	2.253	2.226	2.198	2.172	2.147	2.121	2.097	2.074	2.050	2.027	2.005	1.983	1.961	1.941	1.920
23	2.253	2.225	2.199	2.172	2.146	2.122	2.097	2.073	2.050	2.027	2.005	1.983	1.962	1.941	1.920
24	2.253	2.226	2.198	2.172	2.147	2.121	2.097	2.074	2.050	2.027	2.004	1.983	1.961	1.941	1.920
25	2.253	2.225	2.199	2.172	2.146	2.122	2.097	2.074	2.050	2.027	2.005	1.983	1.962	1.941	1.920
26	2.253	2.226	2.198	2.172	2.147	2.121	2.097	2.073	2.050	2.027	2.004	1.983	1.961	1.941	1.920
27	2.253	2.225	2.199	2.172	2.146	2.122	2.097	2.074	2.050	2.027	2.005	1.983	1.962	1.941	1.920
28	2.253	2.226	2.198	2.172	2.147	2.121	2.097	2.073	2.050	2.027	2.004	1.983	1.961	1.941	1.920
29	2.253	2.225	2.199	2.172	2.146	2.122	2.097	2.074	2.050	2.027	2.005	1.983	1.962	1.941	1.920
30	2.253	2.226	2.198	2.172	2.147	2.121	2.097	2.073	2.050	2.027	2.004	1.983	1.961	1.941	1.920
31	2.253	2.225	2.199	2.172	2.146	2.122	2.097	2.074	2.050	2.027	2.005	1.983	1.962	1.941	1.920
32	2.253	2.225	2.198	2.172	2.147	2.121	2.097	2.073	2.050	2.027	2.004	1.983	1.961	1.941	1.920
33	2.252	2.226	2.199	2.172	2.146	2.122	2.097	2.074	2.050	2.027	2.005	1.983	1.962	1.941	1.920
34	2.253	2.225	2.198	2.172	2.147	2.121	2.097	2.073	2.050	2.027	2.004	1.983	1.961	1.940	1.920

If the Recovery Year is:	and the Recovery Period is: 40.0	40.5	41.0	41.5	42.0	42.5	43.0	43.5	44.0	44.5	45.0	45.5	46.0	46.5	47.0
	the Depreciation Rate is:														
35	2.252	2.226	2.199	2.173	2.146	2.122	2.097	2.074	2.050	2.027	2.005	1.983	1.962	1.941	1.920
36	2.253	2.225	2.198	2.172	2.147	2.121	2.098	2.073	2.050	2.027	2.004	1.982	1.961	1.940	1.920
37	2.252	2.226	2.199	2.173	2.146	2.122	2.097	2.074	2.050	2.027	2.005	1.983	1.962	1.941	1.920
38	2.253	2.225	2.198	2.172	2.147	2.121	2.098	2.073	2.050	2.027	2.004	1.982	1.961	1.940	1.920
39	2.252	2.226	2.199	2.173	2.146	2.122	2.097	2.074	2.050	2.027	2.005	1.983	1.962	1.941	1.921
40	2.253	2.225	2.198	2.172	2.147	2.121	2.098	2.073	2.049	2.027	2.004	1.982	1.961	1.940	1.920
41	1.126	2.226	2.199	2.173	2.146	2.122	2.097	2.074	2.050	2.027	2.005	1.983	1.962	1.941	1.921
42			1.099	2.172	2.147	2.121	2.098	2.073	2.049	2.027	2.004	1.982	1.961	1.940	1.920
43					1.073	2.122	2.097	2.074	2.050	2.027	2.005	1.983	1.962	1.941	1.921
44							1.049	2.073	2.049	2.027	2.004	1.982	1.961	1.940	1.920
45									1.025	2.026	2.005	1.983	1.962	1.941	1.921
46											1.002	1.982	1.961	1.940	1.920
47													0.981	1.941	1.921
48															0.960

If the Recovery Year is:	and the Recovery Period is: 47.5	48.0	48.5	49.0	49.5	50.0
	the Depreciation Rate is:					
1	1.579	1.563	1.546	1.531	1.515	1.500
2	3.108	3.076	3.045	3.014	2.984	2.955
3	3.010	2.980	2.951	2.922	2.894	2.866
4	2.915	2.887	2.860	2.833	2.806	2.780
5	2.823	2.797	2.771	2.746	2.721	2.697
6	2.734	2.709	2.685	2.662	2.639	2.616
7	2.647	2.625	2.602	2.580	2.559	2.538
8	2.564	2.543	2.522	2.501	2.481	2.461

If the Recovery Year is:	and the Recovery Period is: 47.5	48.0	48.5	49.0	49.5	50.0
	the Depreciation Rate is:					
9	2.483	2.463	2.444	2.425	2.406	2.388
10	2.404	2.386	2.368	2.351	2.333	2.316
11	2.328	2.312	2.295	2.279	2.262	2.246
12	2.255	2.239	2.224	2.209	2.194	2.179
13	2.184	2.169	2.155	2.141	2.127	2.114
14	2.115	2.102	2.089	2.076	2.063	2.050
15	2.048	2.036	2.024	2.012	2.000	1.989
16	1.983	1.972	1.961	1.951	1.940	1.929
17	1.921	1.911	1.901	1.891	1.881	1.871
18	1.900	1.880	1.861	1.842	1.824	1.815
19	1.900	1.880	1.861	1.842	1.824	1.806
20	1.900	1.880	1.861	1.842	1.824	1.806
21	1.900	1.880	1.861	1.842	1.824	1.806
22	1.900	1.880	1.861	1.842	1.824	1.806
23	1.900	1.880	1.861	1.842	1.824	1.806
24	1.900	1.880	1.861	1.842	1.824	1.806
25	1.900	1.880	1.861	1.842	1.824	1.806
26	1.900	1.880	1.861	1.842	1.824	1.806
27	1.900	1.880	1.861	1.842	1.824	1.806
28	1.900	1.880	1.861	1.842	1.824	1.806
29	1.900	1.880	1.861	1.843	1.824	1.806
30	1.900	1.881	1.861	1.842	1.824	1.806
31	1.900	1.880	1.861	1.843	1.824	1.806
32	1.900	1.881	1.861	1.842	1.824	1.806
33	1.900	1.880	1.861	1.843	1.824	1.806
34	1.900	1.881	1.861	1.842	1.824	1.806

If the Recovery Year is:	and the Recovery Period is: 47.5	48.0	48.5	49.0	49.5	50.0
	the Depreciation Rate is:					
35	1.900	1.880	1.861	1.843	1.824	1.806
36	1.900	1.881	1.861	1.842	1.824	1.806
37	1.900	1.880	1.861	1.843	1.824	1.806
38	1.900	1.881	1.861	1.842	1.824	1.806
39	1.900	1.880	1.861	1.843	1.824	1.806
40	1.900	1.881	1.862	1.842	1.824	1.806
41	1.900	1.880	1.861	1.843	1.824	1.806
42	1.900	1.881	1.862	1.842	1.824	1.805
43	1.900	1.880	1.861	1.843	1.824	1.806
44	1.900	1.881	1.862	1.842	1.824	1.805
45	1.900	1.880	1.861	1.843	1.825	1.806
46	1.900	1.881	1.862	1.842	1.824	1.805
47	1.900	1.880	1.861	1.843	1.825	1.806
48	1.899	1.881	1.862	1.842	1.824	1.805
49		0.940	1.861	1.843	1.825	1.806
50				0.921	1.824	1.805
51						0.903

TABLE 15
Alternative Minimum Tax (see section 7 of this revenue procedure)
Applicable Depreciation Method: 150-Percent Declining Balance Switching to Straight Line
Applicable Recovery Periods: 2.5 — 50 years
Applicable Convention: Mid-quarter (property placed in service in first quarter)

If the Recovery Year is:	and the Recovery Period is: 2.5	3.0	3.5	4.0	4.5	5.0	5.5	6.0	6.5	7.0	7.5	8.0	8.5	9.0	9.5
	the Depreciation Rate is:														
1	52.50	43.75	37.50	32.81	29.17	26.25	23.86	21.88	20.19	18.75	17.50	16.41	15.44	14.58	13.82
2	29.23	28.13	26.79	25.20	23.61	22.13	20.77	19.53	18.42	17.41	16.50	15.67	14.92	14.24	13.61
3	18.27	25.00	21.98	19.76	17.99	16.52	15.27	14.65	14.17	13.68	13.20	12.74	12.29	11.86	11.46
4		3.12	13.73	19.76	17.99	16.52	15.28	14.06	13.03	12.16	11.42	10.77	10.20	9.89	9.65
5				2.47	11.24	16.52	15.27	14.06	13.02	12.16	11.42	10.77	10.19	9.64	9.15
6						2.06	9.55	14.06	13.03	12.16	11.41	10.76	10.20	9.65	9.15
7								1.76	8.14	12.16	11.42	10.77	10.19	9.64	9.15
8										1.52	7.13	10.76	10.20	9.65	9.15
9												1.35	6.37	9.64	9.14
10														1.21	5.72

If the Recovery Year is:	and the Recovery Period is: 10.0	10.5	11.0	11.5	12.0	12.5	13.0	13.5	14.0	14.5	15.0	15.5	16.0	16.5	17.0
	the Depreciation Rate is:														
1	13.13	12.50	11.93	11.41	10.94	10.50	10.10	9.72	9.38	9.05	8.75	8.47	8.20	7.95	7.72
2	13.03	12.50	12.01	11.56	11.13	10.74	10.37	10.03	9.71	9.41	9.13	8.86	8.61	8.37	8.14
3	11.08	10.71	10.37	10.05	9.74	9.45	9.18	8.92	8.67	8.44	8.21	8.00	7.80	7.61	7.42
4	9.41	9.18	8.96	8.74	8.52	8.32	8.12	7.93	7.74	7.56	7.39	7.23	7.07	6.92	6.77
5	8.71	8.32	7.96	7.64	7.46	7.32	7.18	7.04	6.91	6.78	6.65	6.53	6.41	6.29	6.17
6	8.71	8.32	7.96	7.64	7.33	7.04	6.78	6.53	6.31	6.10	5.99	5.89	5.80	5.71	5.63

If the Recovery Year is:	and the Recovery Period is: 10.0	10.5	11.0	11.5	12.0	12.5	13.0	13.5	14.0	14.5	15.0	15.5	16.0	16.5	17.0
	the Depreciation Rate is:														
7	8.71	8.32	7.96	7.64	7.33	7.04	6.77	6.54	6.31	6.11	5.90	5.72	5.54	5.38	5.23
8	8.71	8.32	7.96	7.64	7.33	7.04	6.78	6.53	6.31	6.10	5.91	5.72	5.54	5.38	5.23
9	8.71	8.32	7.96	7.64	7.33	7.04	6.77	6.54	6.31	6.11	5.90	5.72	5.54	5.38	5.23
10	8.71	8.31	7.97	7.63	7.32	7.04	6.78	6.53	6.31	6.10	5.91	5.71	5.54	5.38	5.23
11	1.09	5.20	7.96	7.64	7.33	7.04	6.77	6.54	6.31	6.11	5.90	5.72	5.54	5.38	5.23
12			1.00	4.77	7.32	7.03	6.78	6.53	6.31	6.10	5.91	5.71	5.54	5.38	5.22
13					0.92	4.40	6.77	6.54	6.32	6.11	5.90	5.72	5.54	5.38	5.23
14							0.85	4.08	6.31	6.10	5.91	5.71	5.55	5.38	5.22
15									0.79	3.82	5.90	5.72	5.54	5.38	5.23
16											0.74	3.57	5.55	5.37	5.22
17													0.69	3.36	5.23
18															0.65

If the Recovery Year is:	and the Recovery Period is: 17.5	18.0	18.5	19.0	19.5	20.0	20.5	21.0	21.5	22.0	22.5	23.0	23.5	24.0	24.5
	the Depreciation Rate is:														
1	7.50	7.29	7.09	6.91	6.73	6.563	6.402	6.250	6.105	5.966	5.833	5.707	5.585	5.469	5.357
2	7.93	7.73	7.53	7.35	7.17	7.008	6.849	6.696	6.551	6.411	6.278	6.150	6.026	5.908	5.794
3	7.25	7.08	6.92	6.77	6.62	6.482	6.347	6.218	6.094	5.974	5.859	5.748	5.642	5.539	5.440
4	6.63	6.49	6.36	6.23	6.11	5.996	5.883	5.774	5.669	5.567	5.469	5.374	5.282	5.193	5.107
5	6.06	5.95	5.85	5.74	5.64	5.546	5.453	5.362	5.273	5.187	5.104	5.023	4.945	4.868	4.794
6	5.54	5.45	5.37	5.29	5.21	5.130	5.054	4.979	4.905	4.834	4.764	4.696	4.629	4.564	4.500
7	5.08	5.00	4.94	4.87	4.81	4.746	4.684	4.623	4.563	4.504	4.446	4.389	4.333	4.279	4.225
8	5.08	4.94	4.81	4.69	4.57	4.459	4.354	4.293	4.245	4.197	4.150	4.103	4.057	4.011	3.966
9	5.08	4.95	4.81	4.69	4.57	4.459	4.354	4.252	4.154	4.061	3.972	3.888	3.808	3.761	3.723
10	5.08	4.94	4.81	4.69	4.57	4.459	4.354	4.252	4.154	4.061	3.972	3.888	3.808	3.729	3.654

If the Recovery Year is:	and the Recovery Period is: 17.5	18.0	18.5	19.0	19.5	20.0	20.5	21.0	21.5	22.0	22.5	23.0	23.5	24.0	24.5
	the Depreciation Rate is:														
11	5.08	4.95	4.81	4.69	4.57	4.459	4.354	4.252	4.154	4.061	3.973	3.888	3.808	3.729	3.654
12	5.09	4.94	4.81	4.69	4.57	4.460	4.354	4.252	4.154	4.061	3.972	3.888	3.808	3.730	3.654
13	5.08	4.95	4.81	4.69	4.57	4.459	4.355	4.252	4.154	4.061	3.973	3.888	3.808	3.729	3.654
14	5.09	4.94	4.81	4.69	4.57	4.460	4.354	4.252	4.154	4.061	3.972	3.888	3.808	3.730	3.654
15	5.08	4.95	4.82	4.68	4.57	4.459	4.355	4.252	4.154	4.061	3.973	3.888	3.808	3.729	3.654
16	5.09	4.94	4.81	4.69	4.57	4.460	4.354	4.252	4.154	4.061	3.972	3.888	3.808	3.730	3.654
17	5.08	4.95	4.82	4.68	4.57	4.459	4.355	4.252	4.153	4.061	3.973	3.889	3.808	3.729	3.654
18	3.18	4.94	4.81	4.69	4.58	4.460	4.354	4.251	4.154	4.061	3.972	3.888	3.808	3.730	3.654
19		0.62	3.01	4.68	4.57	4.459	4.355	4.252	4.153	4.061	3.973	3.889	3.808	3.729	3.654
20				0.59	2.86	4.460	4.354	4.251	4.154	4.060	3.972	3.888	3.808	3.730	3.654
21						0.557	2.722	4.252	4.153	4.061	3.973	3.889	3.808	3.729	3.654
22								0.531	2.596	4.060	3.972	3.888	3.808	3.730	3.654
23										0.508	2.483	3.889	3.809	3.729	3.654
24												0.486	2.380	3.730	3.654
25														0.466	2.284

If the Recovery Year is:	and the Recovery Period is: 25.0	25.5	26.0	26.5	27.0	27.5	28.0	28.5	29.0	29.5	30.0	30.5	31.0	31.5	32.0
	the Depreciation Rate is:														
1	5.250	5.147	5.048	4.953	4.861	4.773	4.688	4.605	4.526	4.449	4.375	4.303	4.234	4.167	4.102
2	5.685	5.580	5.478	5.380	5.286	5.194	5.106	5.021	4.938	4.859	4.781	4.706	4.634	4.563	4.495
3	5.344	5.251	5.162	5.075	4.992	4.911	4.832	4.757	4.683	4.611	4.542	4.475	4.410	4.346	4.285
4	5.023	4.942	4.864	4.788	4.714	4.643	4.574	4.506	4.441	4.377	4.315	4.255	4.196	4.139	4.084
5	4.722	4.652	4.584	4.517	4.453	4.390	4.329	4.269	4.211	4.154	4.099	4.046	3.993	3.942	3.892
6	4.439	4.378	4.319	4.262	4.205	4.150	4.097	4.044	3.993	3.943	3.894	3.847	3.800	3.754	3.710
7	4.172	4.121	4.070	4.020	3.972	3.924	3.877	3.831	3.787	3.743	3.700	3.657	3.616	3.576	3.536

If the Recovery Year is:	and the Recovery Period is: 25.0	25.5	26.0	26.5	27.0	27.5	28.0	28.5	29.0	29.5	30.0	30.5	31.0	31.5	32.0
	the Depreciation Rate is:														
8	3.922	3.878	3.834	3.793	3.751	3.710	3.669	3.630	3.591	3.552	3.515	3.478	3.441	3.405	3.370
9	3.687	3.650	3.615	3.578	3.543	3.508	3.473	3.439	3.405	3.372	3.339	3.307	3.275	3.243	3.212
10	3.582	3.513	3.447	3.383	3.346	3.316	3.287	3.258	3.229	3.200	3.172	3.144	3.116	3.089	3.062
11	3.582	3.513	3.447	3.384	3.321	3.261	3.204	3.148	3.095	3.044	3.013	2.989	2.965	2.942	2.918
12	3.582	3.513	3.447	3.383	3.321	3.261	3.204	3.148	3.095	3.044	2.994	2.945	2.898	2.853	2.809
13	3.582	3.513	3.447	3.384	3.321	3.261	3.204	3.149	3.095	3.044	2.994	2.945	2.898	2.853	2.809
14	3.582	3.513	3.447	3.383	3.321	3.261	3.204	3.148	3.095	3.044	2.994	2.945	2.898	2.853	2.809
15	3.582	3.513	3.447	3.384	3.321	3.261	3.204	3.149	3.095	3.044	2.994	2.945	2.898	2.852	2.809
16	3.582	3.513	3.447	3.383	3.321	3.261	3.204	3.148	3.095	3.044	2.994	2.945	2.898	2.853	2.809
17	3.582	3.513	3.447	3.384	3.321	3.262	3.204	3.149	3.095	3.044	2.994	2.945	2.898	2.852	2.809
18	3.582	3.513	3.447	3.383	3.321	3.261	3.204	3.148	3.095	3.044	2.994	2.945	2.898	2.853	2.809
19	3.581	3.513	3.447	3.384	3.322	3.262	3.204	3.149	3.095	3.044	2.994	2.945	2.898	2.852	2.809
20	3.582	3.513	3.446	3.383	3.321	3.261	3.204	3.148	3.095	3.044	2.994	2.945	2.898	2.853	2.809
21	3.581	3.513	3.447	3.384	3.322	3.262	3.203	3.149	3.095	3.044	2.993	2.945	2.898	2.852	2.808
22	3.582	3.512	3.446	3.383	3.321	3.261	3.204	3.148	3.096	3.044	2.994	2.945	2.898	2.853	2.809
23	3.581	3.513	3.447	3.384	3.322	3.262	3.203	3.149	3.095	3.044	2.993	2.945	2.898	2.852	2.808
24	3.582	3.512	3.446	3.383	3.321	3.261	3.204	3.148	3.096	3.044	2.994	2.945	2.898	2.853	2.809
25	3.581	3.513	3.447	3.384	3.322	3.262	3.203	3.149	3.095	3.044	2.993	2.945	2.898	2.852	2.808
26	0.448	2.195	3.446	3.383	3.321	3.261	3.204	3.148	3.096	3.044	2.994	2.945	2.898	2.853	2.809
27			0.431	2.115	3.322	3.262	3.203	3.149	3.095	3.044	2.993	2.944	2.898	2.852	2.808
28					0.415	2.038	3.204	3.148	3.096	3.045	2.994	2.945	2.897	2.853	2.809
29							0.400	1.968	3.095	3.044	2.993	2.944	2.898	2.852	2.808
30									0.387	1.903	2.994	2.945	2.897	2.853	2.809
31											0.374	1.840	2.898	2.852	2.808
32													0.362	1.783	2.809
33															0.351

If the Recovery Year is:	and the Recovery Period is: 32.5	33.0	33.5	34.0	34.5	35.0	35.5	36.0	36.5	37.0	37.5	38.0	38.5	39.0	39.5
	the Depreciation Rate is:														
1	4.038	3.977	3.918	3.860	3.804	3.750	3.697	3.646	3.596	3.547	3.500	3.454	3.409	3.365	3.323
2	4.429	4.365	4.302	4.241	4.182	4.125	4.069	4.015	3.962	3.910	3.860	3.811	3.763	3.717	3.671
3	4.225	4.166	4.110	4.054	4.001	3.948	3.897	3.847	3.799	3.752	3.706	3.661	3.617	3.574	3.532
4	4.030	3.977	3.926	3.876	3.827	3.779	3.733	3.687	3.643	3.600	3.557	3.516	3.476	3.436	3.398
5	3.844	3.796	3.750	3.705	3.660	3.617	3.575	3.534	3.493	3.454	3.415	3.377	3.340	3.304	3.269
6	3.666	3.624	3.582	3.541	3.501	3.462	3.424	3.386	3.350	3.314	3.278	3.244	3.210	3.177	3.145
7	3.497	3.459	3.421	3.385	3.349	3.314	3.279	3.245	3.212	3.179	3.147	3.116	3.085	3.055	3.025
8	3.336	3.302	3.268	3.235	3.203	3.172	3.141	3.110	3.080	3.050	3.021	2.993	2.965	2.937	2.910
9	3.182	3.152	3.122	3.093	3.064	3.036	3.008	2.980	2.953	2.927	2.901	2.875	2.849	2.824	2.800
10	3.035	3.008	2.982	2.956	2.931	2.906	2.881	2.856	2.832	2.808	2.785	2.761	2.738	2.716	2.693
11	2.895	2.872	2.849	2.826	2.803	2.781	2.759	2.737	2.716	2.694	2.673	2.652	2.632	2.611	2.591
12	2.766	2.741	2.721	2.701	2.682	2.662	2.642	2.623	2.604	2.585	2.566	2.548	2.529	2.511	2.493
13	2.766	2.725	2.684	2.645	2.607	2.571	2.535	2.514	2.497	2.480	2.464	2.447	2.431	2.414	2.398
14	2.766	2.725	2.684	2.645	2.607	2.571	2.535	2.500	2.466	2.433	2.401	2.370	2.340	2.322	2.307
15	2.766	2.725	2.684	2.645	2.607	2.571	2.535	2.500	2.466	2.433	2.401	2.370	2.340	2.310	2.281
16	2.766	2.725	2.684	2.645	2.607	2.571	2.535	2.500	2.466	2.433	2.401	2.370	2.340	2.310	2.281
17	2.766	2.725	2.684	2.645	2.608	2.571	2.535	2.500	2.466	2.433	2.401	2.370	2.340	2.310	2.281
18	2.767	2.725	2.684	2.645	2.607	2.571	2.535	2.500	2.466	2.433	2.401	2.370	2.340	2.310	2.281
19	2.766	2.725	2.684	2.645	2.608	2.571	2.535	2.500	2.466	2.433	2.401	2.370	2.340	2.310	2.281
20	2.767	2.725	2.685	2.645	2.607	2.571	2.535	2.500	2.466	2.433	2.401	2.370	2.340	2.310	2.281
21	2.766	2.725	2.684	2.645	2.608	2.571	2.535	2.500	2.466	2.433	2.401	2.370	2.340	2.310	2.281
22	2.767	2.725	2.685	2.645	2.607	2.571	2.535	2.500	2.466	2.433	2.401	2.370	2.340	2.310	2.281
23	2.766	2.725	2.684	2.646	2.608	2.571	2.535	2.501	2.466	2.433	2.401	2.370	2.340	2.310	2.281
24	2.767	2.725	2.685	2.645	2.607	2.570	2.535	2.500	2.466	2.433	2.401	2.370	2.340	2.310	2.281
25	2.766	2.724	2.684	2.646	2.608	2.571	2.535	2.501	2.466	2.433	2.401	2.370	2.340	2.310	2.281
26	2.767	2.725	2.685	2.645	2.607	2.570	2.536	2.500	2.466	2.433	2.401	2.370	2.340	2.310	2.281

If the Recovery Year is:	and the Recovery Period is: 32.5	33.0	33.5	34.0	34.5	35.0	35.5	36.0	36.5	37.0	37.5	38.0	38.5	39.0	39.5
	the Depreciation Rate is:														
27	2.766	2.724	2.684	2.646	2.608	2.571	2.535	2.501	2.466	2.433	2.401	2.370	2.339	2.310	2.281
28	2.767	2.725	2.685	2.645	2.607	2.570	2.536	2.500	2.466	2.433	2.401	2.370	2.340	2.310	2.281
29	2.766	2.724	2.684	2.646	2.608	2.571	2.535	2.501	2.466	2.433	2.401	2.370	2.339	2.310	2.281
30	2.767	2.725	2.685	2.645	2.607	2.570	2.536	2.500	2.466	2.433	2.401	2.370	2.340	2.310	2.280
31	2.766	2.724	2.684	2.646	2.608	2.571	2.535	2.501	2.467	2.434	2.401	2.370	2.339	2.310	2.281
32	2.767	2.725	2.685	2.645	2.607	2.570	2.536	2.500	2.466	2.433	2.401	2.370	2.340	2.310	2.280
33	1.729	2.724	2.684	2.646	2.608	2.571	2.535	2.501	2.467	2.434	2.401	2.370	2.339	2.310	2.281
34		0.341	1.678	2.645	2.607	2.570	2.536	2.500	2.466	2.433	2.402	2.370	2.340	2.310	2.280
35				0.331	1.630	2.571	2.535	2.501	2.467	2.434	2.401	2.370	2.339	2.310	2.281
36						0.321	1.585	2.500	2.466	2.433	2.402	2.370	2.340	2.310	2.280
37								0.313	1.542	2.434	2.401	2.369	2.339	2.309	2.281
38										0.304	1.501	2.370	2.340	2.310	2.280
39												0.296	1.462	2.309	2.281
40														0.289	1.425

If the Recovery Year is:	and the Recovery Period is: 40.0	40.5	41.0	41.5	42.0	42.5	43.0	43.5	44.0	44.5	45.0	45.5	46.0	46.5	47.0
	the Depreciation Rate is:														
1	3.281	3.241	3.201	3.163	3.125	3.088	3.052	3.017	2.983	2.949	2.917	2.885	2.853	2.823	2.793
2	3.627	3.584	3.541	3.500	3.460	3.420	3.382	3.344	3.307	3.271	3.236	3.202	3.168	3.135	3.102
3	3.491	3.451	3.412	3.374	3.336	3.300	3.264	3.229	3.195	3.161	3.128	3.096	3.065	3.034	3.003
4	3.360	3.323	3.287	3.252	3.217	3.183	3.150	3.118	3.086	3.055	3.024	2.994	2.965	2.936	2.908
5	3.234	3.200	3.167	3.134	3.102	3.071	3.040	3.010	2.981	2.952	2.923	2.895	2.868	2.841	2.815
6	3.113	3.082	3.051	3.021	2.991	2.963	2.934	2.906	2.879	2.852	2.826	2.800	2.774	2.749	2.725
7	2.996	2.967	2.939	2.912	2.885	2.858	2.832	2.806	2.781	2.756	2.732	2.708	2.684	2.661	2.638
8	2.884	2.857	2.832	2.806	2.782	2.757	2.733	2.709	2.686	2.663	2.640	2.618	2.596	2.575	2.554

If the Recovery Year is:	and the Recovery Period is: 40.0	40.5	41.0	41.5	42.0	42.5	43.0	43.5	44.0	44.5	45.0	45.5	46.0	46.5	47.0
	the Depreciation Rate is:														
9	2.776	2.752	2.728	2.705	2.682	2.660	2.638	2.616	2.594	2.573	2.552	2.532	2.512	2.492	2.472
10	2.671	2.650	2.628	2.607	2.586	2.566	2.546	2.526	2.506	2.487	2.467	2.448	2.430	2.411	2.393
11	2.571	2.552	2.532	2.513	2.494	2.475	2.457	2.439	2.421	2.403	2.385	2.368	2.351	2.334	2.317
12	2.475	2.457	2.440	2.422	2.405	2.388	2.371	2.354	2.338	2.322	2.306	2.290	2.274	2.258	2.243
13	2.382	2.366	2.350	2.335	2.319	2.304	2.288	2.273	2.258	2.243	2.229	2.214	2.200	2.186	2.171
14	2.293	2.278	2.264	2.250	2.236	2.222	2.209	2.195	2.181	2.168	2.154	2.141	2.128	2.115	2.102
15	2.252	2.225	2.198	2.172	2.156	2.144	2.132	2.119	2.107	2.095	2.083	2.071	2.059	2.047	2.035
16	2.252	2.225	2.198	2.172	2.147	2.121	2.097	2.073	2.050	2.027	2.013	2.002	1.992	1.981	1.970
17	2.253	2.225	2.198	2.172	2.146	2.121	2.097	2.073	2.050	2.027	2.005	1.983	1.961	1.940	1.920
18	2.252	2.225	2.198	2.172	2.147	2.121	2.097	2.073	2.050	2.027	2.005	1.983	1.961	1.940	1.920
19	2.253	2.225	2.198	2.172	2.146	2.121	2.097	2.073	2.050	2.027	2.005	1.983	1.961	1.940	1.920
20	2.252	2.225	2.198	2.172	2.147	2.121	2.097	2.073	2.050	2.027	2.005	1.983	1.961	1.940	1.920
21	2.253	2.225	2.198	2.172	2.146	2.121	2.097	2.073	2.050	2.027	2.005	1.983	1.961	1.940	1.920
22	2.252	2.225	2.198	2.172	2.147	2.121	2.097	2.073	2.050	2.027	2.005	1.983	1.961	1.940	1.920
23	2.253	2.225	2.198	2.172	2.146	2.121	2.097	2.073	2.050	2.027	2.005	1.983	1.961	1.940	1.920
24	2.252	2.225	2.198	2.172	2.147	2.121	2.097	2.073	2.050	2.027	2.005	1.983	1.961	1.940	1.920
25	2.253	2.225	2.198	2.172	2.146	2.121	2.097	2.073	2.050	2.027	2.004	1.983	1.961	1.940	1.920
26	2.252	2.225	2.198	2.172	2.147	2.121	2.097	2.073	2.050	2.027	2.005	1.982	1.961	1.940	1.920
27	2.253	2.225	2.198	2.172	2.146	2.122	2.097	2.073	2.049	2.027	2.004	1.983	1.961	1.940	1.920
28	2.252	2.225	2.199	2.172	2.147	2.121	2.097	2.073	2.050	2.027	2.005	1.982	1.961	1.940	1.920
29	2.253	2.225	2.198	2.172	2.146	2.122	2.097	2.073	2.049	2.027	2.004	1.983	1.961	1.941	1.920
30	2.252	2.225	2.199	2.172	2.147	2.121	2.097	2.073	2.050	2.027	2.005	1.982	1.961	1.940	1.920
31	2.253	2.225	2.198	2.172	2.146	2.122	2.097	2.073	2.049	2.027	2.004	1.983	1.961	1.941	1.920
32	2.252	2.225	2.199	2.172	2.147	2.121	2.096	2.073	2.050	2.027	2.005	1.982	1.961	1.940	1.920
33	2.253	2.225	2.198	2.172	2.146	2.122	2.097	2.073	2.049	2.027	2.004	1.983	1.961	1.941	1.920
34	2.252	2.225	2.199	2.173	2.147	2.121	2.096	2.073	2.050	2.027	2.005	1.982	1.961	1.940	1.920

If the Recovery Year is:	and the Recovery Period is: 40.0	40.5	41.0	41.5	42.0	42.5	43.0	43.5	44.0	44.5	45.0	45.5	46.0	46.5	47.0
	the Depreciation Rate is:														
35	2.253	2.225	2.198	2.172	2.146	2.122	2.097	2.073	2.049	2.027	2.004	1.983	1.961	1.941	1.920
36	2.252	2.225	2.199	2.173	2.147	2.121	2.096	2.073	2.050	2.027	2.005	1.982	1.962	1.940	1.920
37	2.253	2.225	2.198	2.172	2.146	2.122	2.097	2.073	2.049	2.027	2.004	1.983	1.961	1.941	1.920
38	2.252	2.225	2.199	2.173	2.147	2.121	2.096	2.073	2.050	2.027	2.005	1.982	1.962	1.940	1.920
39	2.253	2.225	2.198	2.172	2.146	2.122	2.097	2.073	2.049	2.027	2.004	1.983	1.961	1.941	1.920
40	2.252	2.225	2.199	2.173	2.147	2.121	2.096	2.073	2.050	2.027	2.005	1.982	1.962	1.940	1.920
41	0.282	1.390	2.198	2.172	2.146	2.122	2.097	2.073	2.049	2.027	2.004	1.983	1.961	1.941	1.920
42			0.275	1.358	2.147	2.121	2.096	2.073	2.050	2.027	2.005	1.982	1.962	1.940	1.920
43					0.268	1.326	2.097	2.073	2.049	2.027	2.004	1.983	1.961	1.941	1.920
44							0.262	1.295	2.050	2.027	2.005	1.982	1.962	1.940	1.920
45									0.256	1.267	2.004	1.983	1.961	1.941	1.920
46											0.251	1.239	1.962	1.940	1.920
47													0.245	1.213	1.919
48															0.240

If the Recovery Year is:	and the Recovery Period is: 47.5	48.0	48.5	49.0	49.5	50.0
	the Depreciation Rate is:					
1	2.763	2.734	2.706	2.679	2.652	2.625
2	3.071	3.040	3.009	2.979	2.950	2.921
3	2.974	2.945	2.916	2.888	2.861	2.834
4	2.880	2.853	2.826	2.800	2.774	2.749
5	2.789	2.763	2.738	2.714	2.690	2.666
6	2.701	2.677	2.654	2.631	2.608	2.586
7	2.615	2.593	2.572	2.550	2.529	2.509
8	2.533	2.512	2.492	2.472	2.453	2.433

If the Recovery Year is:	and the Recovery Period is: 47.5	48.0	48.5	49.0	49.5	50.0
	the Depreciation Rate is:					
9	2.453	2.434	2.415	2.397	2.378	2.360
10	2.375	2.358	2.340	2.323	2.306	2.290
11	2.300	2.284	2.268	2.252	2.236	2.221
12	2.228	2.213	2.198	2.183	2.169	2.154
13	2.157	2.144	2.130	2.116	2.103	2.090
14	2.089	2.077	2.064	2.052	2.039	2.027
15	2.023	2.012	2.000	1.989	1.977	1.966
16	1.959	1.949	1.938	1.928	1.917	1.907
17	1.900	1.888	1.878	1.869	1.859	1.850
18	1.900	1.880	1.861	1.842	1.824	1.806
19	1.900	1.880	1.861	1.842	1.824	1.806
20	1.900	1.880	1.861	1.842	1.824	1.806
21	1.900	1.880	1.861	1.842	1.824	1.806
22	1.900	1.880	1.861	1.842	1.824	1.806
23	1.900	1.880	1.861	1.842	1.824	1.806
24	1.900	1.880	1.861	1.842	1.824	1.806
25	1.900	1.880	1.861	1.842	1.824	1.806
26	1.900	1.880	1.861	1.842	1.824	1.806
27	1.900	1.880	1.861	1.842	1.824	1.806
28	1.900	1.880	1.861	1.842	1.824	1.805
29	1.900	1.880	1.861	1.842	1.824	1.806
30	1.900	1.880	1.861	1.842	1.824	1.805
31	1.900	1.880	1.861	1.842	1.824	1.806
32	1.900	1.881	1.861	1.842	1.824	1.805
33	1.900	1.880	1.861	1.842	1.823	1.806
34	1.900	1.881	1.861	1.842	1.824	1.805

If the Recovery Year is:	and the Recovery Period is: 47.5	48.0	48.5	49.0	49.5	50.0
	the Depreciation Rate is:					
35	1.900	1.880	1.861	1.842	1.823	1.806
36	1.900	1.881	1.861	1.842	1.824	1.805
37	1.900	1.880	1.861	1.842	1.823	1.806
38	1.900	1.881	1.861	1.842	1.824	1.805
39	1.900	1.880	1.861	1.842	1.823	1.806
40	1.900	1.881	1.861	1.842	1.824	1.805
41	1.900	1.880	1.861	1.842	1.823	1.806
42	1.900	1.881	1.861	1.842	1.824	1.805
43	1.900	1.880	1.861	1.843	1.823	1.806
44	1.901	1.881	1.861	1.842	1.824	1.805
45	1.900	1.880	1.861	1.843	1.823	1.806
46	1.901	1.881	1.862	1.842	1.824	1.805
47	1.900	1.880	1.861	1.843	1.823	1.806
48	1.188	1.881	1.862	1.842	1.824	1.805
49		0.235	1.163	1.843	1.823	1.806
50				0.230	1.140	1.805
51						0.226

TABLE 16
Alternative Minimum Tax (see section 7 of this revenue procedure)
Applicable Depreciation Method: 150-Percent Declining Balance Switching to Straight Line
Applicable Recovery Periods: 2.5 — 50 years
Applicable Convention: Mid-quarter (property placed in service in second quarter

If the Recovery Year is:	and the Recovery Period is: 2.5	3.0	3.5	4.0	4.5	5.0	5.5	6.0	6.5	7.0	7.5	8.0	8.5	9.0	9.5
	the Depreciation Rate is:														
1	37.50	31.25	26.79	23.44	20.83	18.75	17.05	15.63	14.42	13.39	12.50	11.72	11.03	10.42	9.87
2	37.50	34.38	31.38	28.71	26.39	24.38	22.62	21.09	19.75	18.56	17.50	16.55	15.70	14.93	14.23
3	25.00	25.00	22.31	20.15	18.36	17.06	16.45	15.82	15.19	14.58	14.00	13.45	12.93	12.44	11.98
4		9.37	19.52	20.15	18.36	16.76	15.26	14.06	13.07	12.22	11.49	10.93	10.65	10.37	10.09
5				7.55	16.06	16.76	15.26	14.06	13.07	12.22	11.49	10.82	10.19	9.64	9.16
6						6.29	13.36	14.07	13.07	12.22	11.49	10.82	10.19	9.65	9.16
7								5.27	11.43	12.23	11.48	10.83	10.19	9.64	9.16
8										4.58	10.05	10.82	10.20	9.65	9.17
9												4.06	8.92	9.64	9.16
10														3.62	8.02

If the Recovery Year is:	and the Recovery Period is: 10.0	10.5	11.0	11.5	12.0	12.5	13.0	13.5	14.0	14.5	15.0	15.5	16.0	16.5	17.0
	the Depreciation Rate is:														
1	9.38	8.93	8.52	8.15	7.81	7.50	7.21	6.94	6.70	6.47	6.25	6.05	5.86	5.68	5.51
2	13.59	13.01	12.47	11.98	11.52	11.10	10.71	10.34	10.00	9.68	9.38	9.09	8.83	8.57	8.34
3	11.55	11.15	10.77	10.42	10.08	9.77	9.47	9.19	8.92	8.67	8.44	8.21	8.00	7.80	7.60
4	9.82	9.56	9.31	9.06	8.82	8.60	8.38	8.17	7.97	7.78	7.59	7.42	7.25	7.09	6.93
5	8.73	8.34	8.04	7.88	7.72	7.56	7.41	7.26	7.12	6.97	6.83	6.70	6.57	6.44	6.32
6	8.73	8.34	7.98	7.64	7.33	7.04	6.78	6.55	6.35	6.25	6.15	6.05	5.95	5.86	5.76

If the Recovery Year is:	and the Recovery Period is: 10.0	10.5	11.0	11.5	12.0	12.5	13.0	13.5	14.0	14.5	15.0	15.5	16.0	16.5	17.0
	the Depreciation Rate is:														
7	8.73	8.34	7.98	7.64	7.33	7.04	6.79	6.55	6.32	6.10	5.91	5.72	5.55	5.38	5.25
8	8.73	8.34	7.98	7.64	7.33	7.05	6.78	6.55	6.32	6.11	5.90	5.72	5.55	5.39	5.23
9	8.73	8.34	7.99	7.64	7.33	7.04	6.79	6.54	6.32	6.10	5.91	5.72	5.55	5.38	5.23
10	8.73	8.35	7.98	7.63	7.33	7.05	6.78	6.55	6.32	6.11	5.90	5.72	5.54	5.39	5.23
11	3.28	7.30	7.99	7.64	7.33	7.04	6.79	6.54	6.32	6.10	5.91	5.72	5.55	5.38	5.23
12			2.99	6.68	7.32	7.05	6.78	6.55	6.32	6.11	5.90	5.72	5.54	5.39	5.23
13					2.75	6.16	6.79	6.54	6.32	6.10	5.91	5.72	5.55	5.38	5.24
14							2.54	5.73	6.33	6.11	5.90	5.72	5.54	5.39	5.23
15									2.37	5.34	5.91	5.72	5.55	5.38	5.24
16											2.21	5.00	5.54	5.39	5.23
17													2.08	4.71	5.24
18															1.96

If the Recovery Year is:	and the Recovery Period is: 17.5	18.0	18.5	19.0	19.5	20.0	20.5	21.0	21.5	22.0	22.5	23.0	23.5	24.0	24.5
	the Depreciation Rate is:														
1	5.36	5.21	5.07	4.93	4.81	4.688	4.573	4.464	4.360	4.261	4.167	4.076	3.989	3.906	3.827
2	8.11	7.90	7.70	7.51	7.32	7.148	6.982	6.824	6.673	6.528	6.389	6.256	6.128	6.006	5.888
3	7.42	7.24	7.07	6.91	6.76	6.612	6.472	6.337	6.207	6.083	5.963	5.848	5.737	5.631	5.528
4	6.78	6.64	6.50	6.37	6.24	6.116	5.998	5.884	5.774	5.668	5.565	5.467	5.371	5.279	5.189
5	6.20	6.08	5.97	5.86	5.76	5.658	5.559	5.464	5.371	5.281	5.194	5.110	5.028	4.949	4.872
6	5.67	5.58	5.49	5.40	5.32	5.233	5.152	5.073	4.996	4.921	4.848	4.777	4.707	4.639	4.573
7	5.18	5.11	5.04	4.98	4.91	4.841	4.775	4.711	4.648	4.586	4.525	4.465	4.407	4.349	4.293
8	5.08	4.94	4.81	4.69	4.57	4.478	4.426	4.375	4.324	4.273	4.223	4.174	4.126	4.078	4.030
9	5.08	4.94	4.81	4.69	4.57	4.463	4.354	4.252	4.155	4.063	3.975	3.902	3.862	3.823	3.784
10	5.08	4.95	4.81	4.69	4.57	4.463	4.354	4.252	4.155	4.063	3.975	3.890	3.808	3.729	3.655

If the Recovery Year is:	and the Recovery Period is: 17.5	18.0	18.5	19.0	19.5	20.0	20.5	21.0	21.5	22.0	22.5	23.0	23.5	24.0	24.5
	the Depreciation Rate is:														
11	5.08	4.94	4.81	4.69	4.57	4.463	4.354	4.252	4.155	4.062	3.975	3.890	3.808	3.729	3.655
12	5.09	4.95	4.82	4.69	4.57	4.463	4.355	4.252	4.155	4.063	3.975	3.891	3.808	3.729	3.654
13	5.08	4.94	4.81	4.69	4.58	4.463	4.354	4.252	4.155	4.062	3.975	3.890	3.808	3.730	3.655
14	5.09	4.95	4.82	4.69	4.57	4.463	4.355	4.252	4.155	4.063	3.975	3.891	3.808	3.729	3.654
15	5.08	4.94	4.81	4.69	4.58	4.462	4.354	4.252	4.155	4.062	3.975	3.890	3.808	3.730	3.655
16	5.09	4.95	4.82	4.69	4.57	4.463	4.355	4.252	4.154	4.063	3.975	3.891	3.808	3.729	3.654
17	5.08	4.94	4.81	4.69	4.58	4.462	4.354	4.252	4.155	4.062	3.975	3.890	3.808	3.730	3.655
18	4.45	4.95	4.82	4.69	4.57	4.463	4.355	4.251	4.154	4.063	3.975	3.891	3.808	3.729	3.654
19		1.85	4.21	4.69	4.58	4.462	4.354	4.252	4.155	4.062	3.975	3.890	3.808	3.730	3.655
20				1.76	4.00	4.463	4.355	4.251	4.154	4.063	3.974	3.891	3.808	3.729	3.654
21						1.673	3.810	4.252	4.155	4.062	3.975	3.890	3.808	3.730	3.655
22								1.594	3.635	4.063	3.974	3.891	3.808	3.729	3.654
23										1.523	3.478	3.890	3.809	3.730	3.655
24												1.459	3.332	3.729	3.654
25														1.399	3.198

If the Recovery Year is:	and the Recovery Period is: 25.0	25.5	26.0	26.5	27.0	27.5	28.0	28.5	29.0	29.5	30.0	30.5	31.0	31.5	32.0
	the Depreciation Rate is:														
1	3.750	3.676	3.606	3.538	3.472	3.409	3.348	3.289	3.233	3.178	3.125	3.074	3.024	2.976	2.930
2	5.775	5.666	5.561	5.460	5.363	5.269	5.178	5.090	5.005	4.923	4.844	4.767	4.692	4.620	4.550
3	5.429	5.333	5.240	5.151	5.065	4.981	4.900	4.822	4.746	4.673	4.602	4.532	4.465	4.400	4.337
4	5.103	5.019	4.938	4.859	4.783	4.710	4.638	4.568	4.501	4.435	4.371	4.310	4.249	4.191	4.134
5	4.797	4.724	4.653	4.584	4.518	4.453	4.389	4.328	4.268	4.210	4.153	4.098	4.044	3.991	3.940
6	4.509	4.446	4.385	4.325	4.267	4.210	4.154	4.100	4.047	3.996	3.945	3.896	3.848	3.801	3.755
7	4.238	4.184	4.132	4.080	4.030	3.980	3.932	3.884	3.838	3.792	3.748	3.704	3.662	3.620	3.579

If the Recovery Year is:	25.0	25.5	26.0	26.5	27.0	27.5	28.0	28.5	29.0	29.5	30.0	30.5	31.0	31.5	32.0
	and the Recovery Period is:														
	the Depreciation Rate is:														
8	3.984	3.938	3.893	3.849	3.806	3.763	3.721	3.680	3.639	3.600	3.561	3.522	3.485	3.448	3.411
9	3.745	3.707	3.669	3.631	3.594	3.558	3.522	3.486	3.451	3.417	3.383	3.349	3.316	3.283	3.251
10	3.583	3.514	3.457	3.426	3.395	3.364	3.333	3.303	3.273	3.243	3.213	3.184	3.156	3.127	3.099
11	3.583	3.515	3.448	3.384	3.321	3.262	3.205	3.150	3.103	3.078	3.053	3.028	3.003	2.978	2.954
12	3.583	3.514	3.448	3.383	3.321	3.262	3.205	3.150	3.096	3.044	2.994	2.945	2.898	2.853	2.815
13	3.583	3.515	3.448	3.384	3.321	3.262	3.205	3.150	3.096	3.044	2.994	2.945	2.898	2.853	2.810
14	3.583	3.514	3.448	3.383	3.321	3.262	3.205	3.150	3.096	3.044	2.994	2.945	2.899	2.853	2.810
15	3.583	3.515	3.448	3.384	3.321	3.262	3.205	3.150	3.096	3.044	2.994	2.945	2.898	2.853	2.810
16	3.583	3.514	3.448	3.383	3.321	3.262	3.204	3.150	3.096	3.044	2.994	2.945	2.899	2.854	2.809
17	3.583	3.515	3.448	3.384	3.321	3.262	3.205	3.150	3.097	3.044	2.994	2.945	2.898	2.853	2.810
18	3.583	3.514	3.449	3.383	3.321	3.262	3.204	3.149	3.096	3.044	2.993	2.945	2.899	2.854	2.809
19	3.583	3.515	3.448	3.384	3.321	3.261	3.205	3.150	3.097	3.044	2.994	2.945	2.898	2.853	2.810
20	3.583	3.514	3.449	3.383	3.322	3.262	3.204	3.149	3.096	3.044	2.993	2.945	2.899	2.854	2.809
21	3.583	3.515	3.448	3.384	3.321	3.261	3.205	3.150	3.097	3.044	2.994	2.945	2.898	2.853	2.810
22	3.583	3.514	3.449	3.383	3.322	3.262	3.204	3.149	3.096	3.044	2.993	2.945	2.899	2.854	2.809
23	3.583	3.515	3.448	3.384	3.321	3.261	3.205	3.150	3.097	3.044	2.994	2.945	2.898	2.853	2.810
24	3.582	3.514	3.449	3.383	3.322	3.262	3.204	3.149	3.096	3.044	2.993	2.946	2.899	2.854	2.809
25	3.583	3.515	3.448	3.384	3.321	3.261	3.205	3.150	3.097	3.044	2.994	2.945	2.898	2.853	2.810
26	1.343	3.075	3.449	3.383	3.322	3.262	3.204	3.149	3.096	3.044	2.993	2.946	2.899	2.854	2.809
27			1.293	2.961	3.321	3.261	3.205	3.150	3.097	3.044	2.994	2.945	2.898	2.853	2.810
28					1.246	2.854	3.204	3.149	3.096	3.044	2.993	2.946	2.899	2.854	2.809
29							1.202	2.756	3.097	3.044	2.994	2.945	2.898	2.853	2.810
30									1.161	2.663	2.993	2.946	2.899	2.854	2.809
31											1.123	2.577	2.898	2.853	2.810
32													1.087	2.497	2.809
33															1.054

If the Recovery Year is:	and the Recovery Period is: 32.5	33.0	33.5	34.0	34.5	35.0	35.5	36.0	36.5	37.0	37.5	38.0	38.5	39.0	39.5
			the Depreciation Rate is:												
1	2.885	2.841	2.799	2.757	2.717	2.679	2.641	2.604	2.568	2.534	2.500	2.467	2.435	2.404	2.373
2	4.482	4.416	4.352	4.290	4.230	4.171	4.114	4.058	4.004	3.951	3.900	3.850	3.801	3.754	3.707
3	4.275	4.216	4.157	4.101	4.046	3.992	3.940	3.889	3.840	3.791	3.744	3.698	3.653	3.609	3.567
4	4.078	4.024	3.971	3.920	3.870	3.821	3.773	3.727	3.682	3.637	3.594	3.552	3.511	3.471	3.431
5	3.890	3.841	3.793	3.747	3.702	3.657	3.614	3.572	3.530	3.490	3.450	3.412	3.374	3.337	3.301
6	3.710	3.666	3.624	3.582	3.541	3.501	3.461	3.423	3.385	3.349	3.312	3.277	3.243	3.209	3.175
7	3.539	3.500	3.461	3.424	3.387	3.351	3.315	3.280	3.246	3.213	3.180	3.148	3.116	3.085	3.055
8	3.376	3.341	3.306	3.273	3.239	3.207	3.175	3.144	3.113	3.083	3.053	3.024	2.995	2.967	2.939
9	3.220	3.189	3.158	3.128	3.099	3.069	3.041	3.013	2.985	2.958	2.931	2.904	2.878	2.852	2.827
10	3.071	3.044	3.017	2.990	2.964	2.938	2.912	2.887	2.862	2.838	2.813	2.790	2.766	2.743	2.720
11	2.930	2.906	2.882	2.858	2.835	2.812	2.789	2.767	2.745	2.723	2.701	2.679	2.658	2.637	2.617
12	2.794	2.773	2.753	2.732	2.712	2.692	2.671	2.651	2.632	2.612	2.593	2.574	2.555	2.536	2.517
13	2.766	2.725	2.685	2.646	2.608	2.576	2.559	2.541	2.524	2.506	2.489	2.472	2.455	2.438	2.422
14	2.766	2.725	2.685	2.646	2.608	2.571	2.535	2.500	2.466	2.433	2.402	2.374	2.359	2.345	2.330
15	2.767	2.725	2.685	2.646	2.608	2.571	2.535	2.500	2.466	2.433	2.402	2.370	2.340	2.310	2.281
16	2.766	2.725	2.685	2.646	2.608	2.571	2.535	2.500	2.466	2.433	2.402	2.370	2.340	2.310	2.281
17	2.767	2.725	2.685	2.646	2.608	2.571	2.535	2.500	2.466	2.433	2.402	2.370	2.340	2.310	2.281
18	2.766	2.725	2.685	2.646	2.608	2.571	2.535	2.500	2.466	2.434	2.402	2.370	2.340	2.310	2.281
19	2.767	2.725	2.685	2.646	2.608	2.571	2.535	2.500	2.466	2.433	2.402	2.371	2.340	2.310	2.281
20	2.766	2.725	2.685	2.646	2.608	2.571	2.535	2.500	2.466	2.434	2.401	2.370	2.340	2.310	2.281
21	2.767	2.725	2.684	2.646	2.608	2.572	2.535	2.500	2.466	2.433	2.402	2.371	2.340	2.310	2.281
22	2.766	2.725	2.685	2.646	2.608	2.571	2.535	2.500	2.467	2.434	2.401	2.370	2.340	2.310	2.281
23	2.767	2.725	2.684	2.645	2.608	2.572	2.535	2.500	2.466	2.433	2.402	2.371	2.340	2.310	2.281
24	2.766	2.725	2.685	2.646	2.608	2.571	2.536	2.500	2.467	2.434	2.401	2.370	2.340	2.310	2.281
25	2.767	2.725	2.684	2.645	2.608	2.572	2.535	2.501	2.466	2.433	2.402	2.371	2.340	2.310	2.281

If the Recovery Year is:	32.5	33.0	33.5	34.0	34.5	35.0	35.5	36.0	36.5	37.0	37.5	38.0	38.5	39.0	39.5
			the Depreciation Rate is:												
26	2.766	2.725	2.685	2.646	2.608	2.571	2.536	2.500	2.467	2.434	2.401	2.370	2.340	2.310	2.281
27	2.767	2.724	2.684	2.645	2.608	2.572	2.535	2.501	2.466	2.433	2.402	2.371	2.339	2.310	2.281
28	2.766	2.725	2.685	2.646	2.608	2.571	2.536	2.500	2.467	2.434	2.401	2.370	2.340	2.310	2.281
29	2.767	2.724	2.684	2.645	2.608	2.572	2.535	2.501	2.466	2.433	2.402	2.371	2.339	2.310	2.281
30	2.766	2.725	2.685	2.646	2.608	2.571	2.536	2.500	2.467	2.434	2.401	2.370	2.340	2.310	2.281
31	2.767	2.724	2.684	2.645	2.608	2.572	2.535	2.501	2.466	2.433	2.402	2.371	2.339	2.310	2.281
32	2.766	2.725	2.685	2.646	2.608	2.571	2.536	2.500	2.467	2.434	2.401	2.370	2.340	2.310	2.281
33	2.421	2.724	2.684	2.645	2.608	2.572	2.535	2.501	2.466	2.433	2.402	2.371	2.339	2.310	2.281
34		1.022	2.349	2.646	2.608	2.571	2.536	2.500	2.467	2.434	2.401	2.370	2.340	2.309	2.281
35				0.992	2.282	2.572	2.535	2.501	2.466	2.433	2.402	2.371	2.339	2.310	2.281
36						0.964	2.219	2.500	2.467	2.434	2.401	2.370	2.340	2.309	2.281
37								0.938	2.158	2.433	2.402	2.371	2.339	2.310	2.281
38										0.913	2.101	2.370	2.340	2.309	2.280
39												0.889	2.047	2.310	2.281
40														0.866	1.995

and the Recovery Period is:

If the Recovery Year is:	40.0	40.5	41.0	41.5	42.0	42.5	43.0	43.5	44.0	44.5	45.0	45.5	46.0	46.5	47.0
			the Depreciation Rate is:												
1	2.344	2.315	2.287	2.259	2.232	2.206	2.180	2.155	2.131	2.107	2.083	2.060	2.038	2.016	1.995
2	3.662	3.618	3.575	3.533	3.492	3.452	3.412	3.374	3.336	3.300	3.264	3.229	3.194	3.161	3.128
3	3.525	3.484	3.444	3.405	3.367	3.330	3.293	3.258	3.223	3.189	3.155	3.122	3.090	3.059	3.028
4	3.393	3.555	3.318	3.282	3.247	3.212	3.178	3.145	3.113	3.081	3.050	3.019	2.990	2.960	2.931
5	3.265	3.231	3.197	3.163	3.131	3.099	3.068	3.037	3.007	2.977	2.948	2.920	2.892	2.865	2.838
6	3.143	3.111	3.080	3.049	3.019	2.989	2.961	2.932	2.904	2.877	2.850	2.824	2.798	2.772	2.747
7	3.025	2.996	2.967	2.939	2.911	2.884	2.857	2.831	2.805	2.780	2.755	2.731	2.706	2.683	2.660

If the Recovery Year is:	40.0	40.5	41.0	41.5	42.0	42.5	43.0	43.5	44.0	44.5	45.0	45.5	46.0	46.5	47.0
			the Depreciation Rate is:												
8	2.912	2.885	2.858	2.833	2.807	2.782	2.758	2.733	2.710	2.686	2.663	2.640	2.618	2.596	2.575
9	2.802	2.778	2.754	2.730	2.707	2.684	2.661	2.639	2.617	2.596	2.574	2.553	2.533	2.513	2.492
10	2.697	2.675	2.653	2.632	2.610	2.589	2.569	2.548	2.528	2.508	2.489	2.469	2.450	2.431	2.413
11	2.596	2.576	2.556	2.536	2.517	2.498	2.479	2.460	2.442	2.424	2.406	2.388	2.370	2.353	2.336
12	2.499	2.481	2.463	2.445	2.427	2.410	2.392	2.375	2.359	2.342	2.325	2.309	2.293	2.277	2.261
13	2.405	2.389	2.372	2.356	2.340	2.325	2.309	2.294	2.278	2.263	2.248	2.233	2.218	2.204	2.189
14	2.315	2.300	2.286	2.271	2.257	2.243	2.228	2.214	2.200	2.187	2.173	2.159	2.146	2.133	2.119
15	2.253	2.225	2.202	2.189	2.176	2.163	2.151	2.138	2.125	2.113	2.101	2.088	2.076	2.064	2.052
16	2.253	2.225	2.199	2.172	2.146	2.121	2.097	2.073	2.053	2.042	2.031	2.019	2.008	1.997	1.986
17	2.253	2.225	2.199	2.172	2.147	2.121	2.097	2.073	2.050	2.027	2.005	1.983	1.961	1.941	1.923
18	2.253	2.225	2.199	2.172	2.146	2.121	2.097	2.073	2.050	2.027	2.005	1.983	1.961	1.941	1.920
19	2.253	2.225	2.199	2.172	2.147	2.121	2.097	2.073	2.050	2.027	2.005	1.983	1.962	1.941	1.920
20	2.253	2.225	2.199	2.172	2.146	2.121	2.097	2.073	2.050	2.027	2.005	1.983	1.961	1.941	1.920
21	2.253	2.225	2.199	2.172	2.147	2.121	2.097	2.073	2.050	2.027	2.005	1.983	1.962	1.941	1.920
22	2.253	2.225	2.198	2.172	2.146	2.122	2.097	2.073	2.050	2.027	2.005	1.983	1.961	1.941	1.920
23	2.253	2.225	2.199	2.172	2.147	2.121	2.097	2.073	2.050	2.027	2.004	1.983	1.962	1.941	1.920
24	2.253	2.226	2.198	2.172	2.146	2.122	2.097	2.073	2.050	2.027	2.005	1.983	1.961	1.940	1.920
25	2.253	2.225	2.199	2.172	2.147	2.121	2.097	2.073	2.050	2.027	2.004	1.983	1.962	1.941	1.920
26	2.253	2.226	2.198	2.172	2.146	2.122	2.097	2.073	2.050	2.027	2.005	1.983	1.961	1.940	1.920
27	2.253	2.225	2.199	2.172	2.147	2.121	2.097	2.074	2.050	2.027	2.004	1.983	1.962	1.941	1.920
28	2.253	2.226	2.198	2.172	2.146	2.122	2.097	2.073	2.050	2.027	2.005	1.983	1.961	1.940	1.920
29	2.253	2.225	2.199	2.172	2.147	2.121	2.097	2.074	2.050	2.027	2.004	1.983	1.962	1.941	1.920
30	2.252	2.226	2.198	2.172	2.146	2.122	2.097	2.073	2.050	2.027	2.005	1.983	1.961	1.940	1.920
31	2.253	2.225	2.199	2.172	2.147	2.121	2.097	2.074	2.050	2.027	2.004	1.983	1.962	1.941	1.920
32	2.252	2.226	2.198	2.173	2.146	2.122	2.097	2.073	2.050	2.027	2.005	1.983	1.961	1.940	1.920
33	2.253	2.225	2.199	2.172	2.147	2.121	2.097	2.074	2.050	2.027	2.004	1.983	1.962	1.941	1.920
34	2.252	2.226	2.198	2.173	2.146	2.122	2.097	2.073	2.050	2.027	2.005	1.983	1.961	1.940	1.920

If the Recovery Year is:	40.0	40.5	41.0	41.5	42.0	42.5	43.0	43.5	44.0	44.5	45.0	45.5	46.0	46.5	47.0
	the Depreciation Rate is:														
35	2.253	2.225	2.199	2.172	2.147	2.121	2.097	2.074	2.050	2.027	2.004	1.983	1.962	1.941	1.921
36	2.252	2.226	2.198	2.173	2.146	2.122	2.097	2.073	2.050	2.027	2.005	1.983	1.961	1.940	1.920
37	2.253	2.225	2.199	2.172	2.147	2.121	2.097	2.074	2.050	2.027	2.004	1.982	1.962	1.941	1.921
38	2.252	2.226	2.198	2.173	2.146	2.122	2.097	2.073	2.050	2.027	2.005	1.983	1.961	1.940	1.920
39	2.253	2.225	2.199	2.172	2.147	2.121	2.097	2.074	2.050	2.027	2.004	1.982	1.962	1.941	1.921
40	2.252	2.226	2.198	2.173	2.146	2.122	2.097	2.073	2.050	2.027	2.005	1.983	1.961	1.940	1.920
41	0.845	1.947	2.199	2.172	2.147	2.121	2.097	2.074	2.050	2.027	2.004	1.982	1.962	1.941	1.921
42			0.824	1.901	2.146	2.122	2.098	2.073	2.050	2.027	2.005	1.983	1.961	1.940	1.920
43					0.805	1.856	2.097	2.074	2.050	2.026	2.004	1.982	1.962	1.941	1.921
44							0.787	1.814	2.050	2.027	2.005	1.983	1.961	1.940	1.920
45									0.769	1.773	2.004	1.982	1.962	1.941	1.921
46											0.752	1.735	1.961	1.940	1.920
47													0.736	1.698	1.921
48															0.720

and the Recovery Period is:

If the Recovery Year is:	47.5	48.0	48.5	49.0	49.5	50.0
	the Depreciation Rate is:					
1	1.974	1.953	1.933	1.913	1.894	1.875
2	3.096	3.064	3.033	3.003	2.973	2.944
3	2.998	2.968	2.939	2.911	2.883	2.855
4	2.903	2.875	2.848	2.822	2.795	2.770
5	2.811	2.786	2.760	2.735	2.711	2.687
6	2.723	2.699	2.675	2.652	2.629	2.606
7	2.637	2.614	2.592	2.570	2.549	2.528
8	2.553	2.533	2.512	2.492	2.472	2.452

If the Recovery Year is:	47.5	48.0	48.5	49.0	49.5	50.0
	the Depreciation Rate is:					
9	2.473	2.453	2.434	2.415	2.397	2.378
10	2.395	2.377	2.359	2.341	2.324	2.307
11	2.319	2.302	2.286	2.270	2.254	2.238
12	2.246	2.230	2.215	2.200	2.185	2.171
13	2.175	2.161	2.147	2.133	2.119	2.106
14	2.106	2.093	2.080	2.068	2.055	2.042
15	2.040	2.028	2.016	2.004	1.993	1.981
16	1.975	1.964	1.954	1.943	1.932	1.922
17	1.913	1.903	1.893	1.884	1.874	1.864
18	1.900	1.880	1.861	1.842	1.824	1.808
19	1.900	1.880	1.861	1.842	1.824	1.806
20	1.900	1.880	1.861	1.842	1.824	1.806
21	1.900	1.880	1.861	1.842	1.824	1.806
22	1.900	1.880	1.861	1.842	1.824	1.806
23	1.900	1.880	1.861	1.842	1.824	1.806
24	1.900	1.880	1.861	1.842	1.824	1.806
25	1.900	1.880	1.861	1.842	1.824	1.806
26	1.900	1.881	1.861	1.842	1.824	1.806
27	1.900	1.880	1.861	1.842	1.824	1.806
28	1.900	1.881	1.861	1.842	1.824	1.806
29	1.900	1.880	1.861	1.842	1.824	1.806
30	1.900	1.881	1.861	1.842	1.824	1.806
31	1.900	1.880	1.861	1.842	1.824	1.806
32	1.900	1.881	1.861	1.843	1.824	1.806
33	1.900	1.880	1.861	1.842	1.824	1.806
34	1.900	1.881	1.861	1.843	1.824	1.806
35	1.900	1.880	1.861	1.842	1.824	1.806

If the Recovery Year is:	47.5	48.0	48.5	49.0	49.5	50.0
			the Depreciation Rate is:			
36	1.900	1.881	1.861	1.843	1.824	1.806
37	1.900	1.880	1.861	1.842	1.824	1.806
38	1.900	1.881	1.861	1.843	1.824	1.806
39	1.900	1.880	1.861	1.842	1.824	1.806
40	1.900	1.881	1.861	1.843	1.824	1.806
41	1.900	1.880	1.862	1.842	1.824	1.806
42	1.900	1.881	1.861	1.843	1.824	1.806
43	1.900	1.880	1.862	1.842	1.824	1.806
44	1.900	1.881	1.861	1.843	1.824	1.806
45	1.900	1.880	1.862	1.842	1.823	1.805
46	1.900	1.881	1.861	1.843	1.824	1.806
47	1.900	1.880	1.862	1.842	1.823	1.805
48	1.663	1.881	1.861	1.843	1.824	1.806
49		0.705	1.629	1.842	1.823	1.805
50				0.691	1.596	1.806
51						0.677

TABLE 17
Alternative Minimum Tax (see section 7 of this revenue procedure)
Applicable Depreciation Method: 150-Percent Declining Balance Switching to Straight Line
Applicable Recovery Periods: 2.5 — 50 years
Applicable Convention: Mid-quarter (property placed in service in third quarter)

and the Recovery Period is:

If the Recovery Year is:	2.5	3.0	3.5	4.0	4.5	5.0	5.5	6.0	6.5	7.0	7.5	8.0	8.5	9.0	9.5
			the Depreciation Rate is:												
1	22.50	18.75	16.07	14.06	12.50	11.25	10.23	9.38	8.65	8.04	7.50	7.03	6.62	6.25	5.92
2	46.50	40.63	35.97	32.23	29.17	26.63	24.48	22.66	21.08	19.71	18.50	17.43	16.48	15.63	14.85
3	27.56	25.00	22.57	20.46	19.44	18.64	17.81	16.99	16.22	15.48	14.80	14.16	13.57	13.02	12.51
4	3.44	15.62	22.57	20.46	18.30	16.56	15.19	14.06	13.10	12.27	11.84	11.51	11.18	10.85	10.53
5			2.82	12.79	18.30	16.57	15.20	14.06	13.10	12.28	11.48	10.78	10.18	9.64	9.17
6					2.29	10.35	15.19	14.06	13.11	12.27	11.48	10.78	10.17	9.65	9.17
7							1.90	8.79	13.10	12.28	11.48	10.78	10.18	9.64	9.18
8									1.64	7.67	11.48	10.79	10.17	9.65	9.17
9											1.44	6.74	10.18	9.64	9.18
10													1.27	6.03	9.17
11															1.15

and the Recovery Period is:

If the Recovery Year is:	10.0	10.5	11.0	11.5	12.0	12.5	13.0	13.5	14.0	14.5	15.0	15.5	16.0	16.5	17.0
			the Depreciation Rate is:												
1	5.63	5.36	5.11	4.89	4.69	4.50	4.33	4.17	4.02	3.88	3.75	3.63	3.52	3.41	3.31
2	14.16	13.52	12.94	12.41	11.91	11.46	11.04	10.65	10.28	9.94	9.63	9.33	9.05	8.78	8.53
3	12.03	11.59	11.18	10.79	10.43	10.08	9.77	9.46	9.18	8.92	8.66	8.42	8.20	7.98	7.78

If the Recovery Year is:	10.0	10.5	11.0	11.5	12.0	12.5	13.0	13.5	14.0	14.5	15.0	15.5	16.0	16.5	17.0
	the Depreciation Rate is:														
4	10.23	9.93	9.65	9.38	9.12	8.88	8.64	8.41	8.20	7.99	7.80	7.61	7.43	7.26	7.09
5	8.75	8.51	8.33	8.16	7.98	7.81	7.64	7.48	7.32	7.17	7.02	6.87	6.73	6.60	6.47
6	8.75	8.34	7.97	7.63	7.33	7.05	6.79	6.65	6.54	6.42	6.31	6.21	6.10	6.00	5.90
7	8.75	8.34	7.97	7.63	7.33	7.05	6.79	6.55	6.31	6.10	5.90	5.72	5.55	5.45	5.38
8	8.74	8.34	7.97	7.63	7.33	7.05	6.79	6.54	6.31	6.10	5.90	5.72	5.55	5.38	5.23
9	8.75	8.34	7.97	7.63	7.33	7.05	6.79	6.55	6.32	6.10	5.91	5.72	5.55	5.39	5.23
10	8.74	8.34	7.97	7.63	7.32	7.05	6.79	6.54	6.31	6.10	5.90	5.72	5.55	5.38	5.23
11	5.47	8.35	7.96	7.63	7.33	7.05	6.79	6.55	6.32	6.10	5.91	5.72	5.55	5.39	5.23
12		1.04	4.98	7.64	7.32	7.04	6.80	6.54	6.31	6.10	5.90	5.72	5.55	5.38	5.23
13				0.95	4.58	7.05	6.79	6.55	6.32	6.11	5.91	5.72	5.55	5.39	5.22
14						0.88	4.25	6.54	6.31	6.10	5.90	5.72	5.55	5.38	5.23
15								0.82	3.95	6.11	5.91	5.73	5.55	5.39	5.22
16										0.76	3.69	5.72	5.55	5.38	5.23
17												0.72	3.47	5.39	5.22
18														0.67	3.27

and the Recovery Period is:

If the Recovery Year is:	17.5	18.0	18.5	19.0	19.5	20.0	20.5	21.0	21.5	22.0	22.5	23.0	23.5	24.0	24.5
	the Depreciation Rate is:														
1	3.21	3.13	3.04	2.96	2.88	2.813	2.744	2.679	2.616	2.557	2.500	2.446	2.394	2.344	2.296
2	8.30	8.07	7.86	7.66	7.47	7.289	7.116	6.952	6.794	6.644	6.500	6.362	6.230	6.104	5.982
3	7.58	7.40	7.22	7.06	6.90	6.742	6.596	6.455	6.320	6.191	6.067	5.947	5.833	5.722	5.616
4	6.94	6.78	6.64	6.50	6.37	6.237	6.113	5.994	5.879	5.769	5.662	5.559	5.460	5.364	5.272
5	6.34	6.22	6.10	5.99	5.88	5.769	5.666	5.566	5.469	5.375	5.285	5.197	5.112	5.029	4.949
6	5.80	5.70	5.61	5.51	5.42	5.336	5.251	5.168	5.088	5.009	4.932	4.858	4.785	4.715	4.646
7	5.30	5.23	5.15	5.08	5.01	4.936	4.867	4.799	4.733	4.667	4.604	4.541	4.480	4.420	4.362

If the Recovery Year is:	17.5	18.0	18.5	19.0	19.5	20.0	20.5	21.0	21.5	22.0	22.5	23.0	23.5	24.0	24.5
	the Depreciation Rate is:														
8	5.08	4.94	4.81	4.69	4.62	4.566	4.511	4.456	4.402	4.349	4.297	4.245	4.194	4.144	4.095
9	5.08	4.94	4.82	4.69	4.57	4.460	4.353	4.252	4.156	4.064	4.010	3.968	3.926	3.885	3.844
10	5.08	4.94	4.81	4.69	4.57	4.460	4.353	4.252	4.156	4.064	3.975	3.889	3.807	3.729	3.655
11	5.08	4.94	4.82	4.69	4.57	4.460	4.353	4.252	4.156	4.064	3.975	3.889	3.807	3.730	3.655
12	5.08	4.95	4.81	4.69	4.57	4.460	4.353	4.252	4.156	4.064	3.975	3.889	3.807	3.729	3.655
13	5.08	4.94	4.82	4.69	4.57	4.461	4.353	4.252	4.156	4.064	3.975	3.889	3.807	3.730	3.655
14	5.08	4.95	4.81	4.69	4.58	4.460	4.353	4.252	4.156	4.064	3.975	3.889	3.807	3.729	3.655
15	5.08	4.94	4.82	4.70	4.57	4.461	4.353	4.252	4.155	4.064	3.975	3.889	3.808	3.730	3.655
16	5.08	4.95	4.81	4.69	4.58	4.460	4.353	4.252	4.156	4.064	3.975	3.889	3.807	3.729	3.655
17	5.09	4.94	4.82	4.70	4.57	4.461	4.354	4.252	4.155	4.064	3.974	3.889	3.808	3.730	3.655
18	5.08	4.95	4.81	4.69	4.58	4.460	4.353	4.251	4.156	4.065	3.975	3.889	3.807	3.729	3.655
19	0.64	3.09	4.82	4.70	4.57	4.461	4.354	4.252	4.155	4.064	3.974	3.889	3.808	3.730	3.655
20			0.60	2.93	4.58	4.460	4.353	4.251	4.156	4.065	3.975	3.889	3.807	3.729	3.655
21					0.57	2.788	4.354	4.252	4.155	4.064	3.974	3.889	3.808	3.730	3.655
22							0.544	2.657	4.156	4.065	3.975	3.889	3.807	3.729	3.655
23									0.519	2.540	3.974	3.889	3.808	3.730	3.655
24											0.497	2.431	3.807	3.729	3.656
25													0.476	2.331	3.655
26															0.457

and the Recovery Period is:

If the Recovery Year is:	25.0	25.5	26.0	26.5	27.0	27.5	28.0	28.5	29.0	29.5	30.0	30.5	31.0	31.5	32.0
	the Depreciation Rate is:														
1	2.250	2.206	2.163	2.123	2.083	2.045	2.009	1.974	1.940	1.907	1.875	1.844	1.815	1.786	1.758
2	5.865	5.753	5.644	5.540	5.440	5.343	5.250	5.159	5.072	4.988	4.906	4.827	4.751	4.677	4.605
3	5.513	5.414	5.319	5.227	5.138	5.052	4.968	4.888	4.810	4.734	4.661	4.590	4.521	4.454	4.389
4	5.182	5.096	5.012	4.931	4.852	4.776	4.702	4.630	4.561	4.493	4.428	4.364	4.302	4.242	4.184

If the Recovery Year is:	and the Recovery Period is: 25.0	25.5	26.0	26.5	27.0	27.5	28.0	28.5	29.0	29.5	30.0	30.5	31.0	31.5	32.0
	the Depreciation Rate is:														
5	4.871	4.796	4.723	4.652	4.583	4.515	4.450	4.387	4.325	4.265	4.207	4.150	4.094	4.040	3.987
6	4.579	4.514	4.450	4.388	4.328	4.269	4.212	4.156	4.101	4.048	3.996	3.945	3.896	3.848	3.800
7	4.304	4.248	4.194	4.140	4.088	4.036	3.986	3.937	3.889	3.842	3.796	3.751	3.707	3.664	3.622
8	4.046	3.998	3.952	3.906	3.860	3.816	3.773	3.730	3.688	3.647	3.607	3.567	3.528	3.490	3.453
9	3.803	3.763	3.724	3.685	3.646	3.608	3.571	3.534	3.497	3.461	3.426	3.392	3.357	3.324	3.291
10	3.584	3.542	3.509	3.476	3.443	3.411	3.379	3.348	3.316	3.286	3.255	3.225	3.195	3.165	3.136
11	3.584	3.514	3.447	3.383	3.321	3.262	3.205	3.171	3.145	3.118	3.092	3.066	3.040	3.015	2.989
12	3.584	3.514	3.447	3.383	3.321	3.262	3.205	3.150	3.096	3.044	2.994	2.946	2.899	2.871	2.849
13	3.584	3.514	3.447	3.383	3.321	3.262	3.205	3.150	3.096	3.044	2.994	2.946	2.899	2.853	2.809
14	3.584	3.515	3.447	3.383	3.321	3.262	3.205	3.150	3.096	3.044	2.994	2.945	2.899	2.853	2.809
15	3.584	3.514	3.447	3.383	3.321	3.262	3.205	3.149	3.096	3.044	2.994	2.946	2.899	2.853	2.809
16	3.584	3.515	3.447	3.383	3.322	3.262	3.206	3.150	3.096	3.044	2.994	2.945	2.899	2.853	2.809
17	3.584	3.514	3.447	3.383	3.321	3.262	3.205	3.149	3.095	3.044	2.994	2.946	2.899	2.853	2.809
18	3.584	3.515	3.447	3.383	3.322	3.262	3.206	3.150	3.096	3.044	2.994	2.945	2.899	2.853	2.809
19	3.584	3.514	3.447	3.383	3.321	3.263	3.205	3.149	3.095	3.044	2.994	2.946	2.899	2.854	2.809
20	3.584	3.515	3.447	3.383	3.322	3.262	3.206	3.150	3.096	3.044	2.993	2.945	2.899	2.853	2.809
21	3.585	3.514	3.448	3.383	3.321	3.263	3.205	3.149	3.095	3.043	2.994	2.946	2.899	2.854	2.809
22	3.584	3.515	3.447	3.383	3.322	3.262	3.206	3.150	3.096	3.044	2.993	2.945	2.899	2.853	2.809
23	3.585	3.514	3.448	3.383	3.321	3.263	3.205	3.149	3.095	3.043	2.994	2.946	2.899	2.854	2.809
24	3.584	3.515	3.447	3.383	3.322	3.262	3.206	3.150	3.096	3.044	2.993	2.945	2.899	2.853	2.809
25	3.585	3.514	3.448	3.382	3.321	3.263	3.205	3.149	3.095	3.043	2.994	2.946	2.899	2.854	2.809
26	2.240	3.515	3.447	3.383	3.322	3.262	3.206	3.150	3.096	3.044	2.993	2.945	2.899	2.853	2.809
27		0.439	2.155	3.382	3.321	3.263	3.205	3.149	3.095	3.043	2.994	2.946	2.899	2.854	2.809
28				0.423	2.076	3.262	3.206	3.150	3.096	3.044	2.993	2.945	2.899	2.853	2.809
29						0.408	2.003	3.149	3.095	3.043	2.994	2.946	2.900	2.854	2.809
30								0.394	1.935	3.044	2.993	2.945	2.899	2.853	2.809

If the Recovery Year is:	and the Recovery Period is: 25.0	25.5	26.0	26.5	27.0	27.5	28.0	28.5	29.0	29.5	30.0	30.5	31.0	31.5	32.0
	the Depreciation Rate is:														
31										0.380	1.871	2.946	2.900	2.854	2.810
32												0.368	1.812	2.853	2.809
33														0.357	1.756

If the Recovery Year is:	and the Recovery Period is: 32.5	33.0	33.5	34.0	34.5	35.0	35.5	36.0	36.5	37.0	37.5	38.0	38.5	39.0	39.5
	the Depreciation Rate is:														
1	1.731	1.705	1.679	1.654	1.630	1.607	1.585	1.563	1.541	1.520	1.500	1.480	1.461	1.442	1.424
2	4.535	4.468	4.402	4.339	4.277	4.217	4.158	4.102	4.046	3.992	3.940	3.889	3.839	3.791	3.743
3	4.326	4.265	4.205	4.147	4.091	4.036	3.983	3.931	3.880	3.831	3.782	3.735	3.690	3.645	3.601
4	4.127	4.071	4.017	3.964	3.913	3.863	3.814	3.767	3.721	3.675	3.631	3.588	3.546	3.505	3.465
5	3.936	3.886	3.837	3.790	3.743	3.698	3.653	3.610	3.568	3.526	3.486	3.446	3.408	3.370	3.333
6	3.754	3.709	3.665	3.622	3.580	3.539	3.499	3.459	3.421	3.383	3.346	3.310	3.275	3.240	3.206
7	3.581	3.541	3.501	3.463	3.425	3.387	3.351	3.315	3.280	3.246	3.213	3.180	3.147	3.116	3.085
8	3.416	3.380	3.345	3.310	3.276	3.242	3.209	3.177	3.146	3.115	3.084	3.054	3.025	2.996	2.967
9	3.258	3.226	3.195	3.164	3.133	3.103	3.074	3.045	3.016	2.988	2.961	2.934	2.907	2.881	2.855
10	3.108	3.080	3.052	3.024	2.997	2.970	2.944	2.918	2.892	2.867	2.842	2.818	2.794	2.770	2.746
11	2.964	2.940	2.915	2.891	2.867	2.843	2.820	2.796	2.774	2.751	2.729	2.707	2.685	2.663	2.642
12	2.828	2.806	2.784	2.763	2.742	2.721	2.700	2.680	2.660	2.639	2.619	2.600	2.580	2.561	2.542
13	2.766	2.725	2.685	2.646	2.623	2.605	2.586	2.568	2.550	2.532	2.515	2.497	2.480	2.462	2.445
14	2.766	2.725	2.685	2.646	2.608	2.571	2.535	2.500	2.467	2.434	2.414	2.399	2.383	2.368	2.352
15	2.766	2.725	2.685	2.646	2.608	2.571	2.535	2.500	2.467	2.434	2.402	2.370	2.340	2.310	2.281
16	2.766	2.725	2.685	2.646	2.608	2.571	2.535	2.500	2.466	2.434	2.402	2.370	2.339	2.310	2.281
17	2.766	2.725	2.685	2.646	2.608	2.571	2.535	2.500	2.467	2.434	2.402	2.370	2.340	2.310	2.281
18	2.766	2.725	2.685	2.646	2.608	2.571	2.535	2.500	2.466	2.434	2.402	2.370	2.339	2.310	2.281
19	2.766	2.725	2.685	2.646	2.608	2.571	2.535	2.500	2.467	2.434	2.401	2.370	2.340	2.310	2.281

If the Recovery Year is:	and the Recovery Period is: 32.5	33.0	33.5	34.0	34.5	35.0	35.5	36.0	36.5	37.0	37.5	38.0	38.5	39.0	39.5
	the Depreciation Rate is:														
20	2.766	2.725	2.685	2.646	2.608	2.571	2.535	2.500	2.466	2.434	2.402	2.370	2.339	2.310	2.281
21	2.766	2.725	2.685	2.646	2.608	2.571	2.535	2.500	2.467	2.434	2.401	2.370	2.340	2.310	2.281
22	2.766	2.725	2.685	2.646	2.608	2.571	2.535	2.500	2.466	2.434	2.402	2.370	2.339	2.310	2.281
23	2.766	2.725	2.685	2.646	2.608	2.571	2.535	2.500	2.467	2.434	2.401	2.370	2.340	2.310	2.281
24	2.766	2.725	2.685	2.646	2.608	2.571	2.535	2.500	2.466	2.434	2.402	2.370	2.339	2.310	2.281
25	2.766	2.724	2.685	2.646	2.608	2.571	2.535	2.501	2.467	2.434	2.401	2.370	2.340	2.310	2.281
26	2.767	2.725	2.685	2.646	2.608	2.571	2.535	2.500	2.466	2.434	2.402	2.370	2.339	2.310	2.281
27	2.766	2.724	2.685	2.646	2.608	2.571	2.535	2.501	2.467	2.434	2.401	2.370	2.340	2.310	2.281
28	2.767	2.725	2.685	2.646	2.608	2.571	2.535	2.500	2.466	2.434	2.402	2.370	2.339	2.310	2.281
29	2.766	2.724	2.685	2.646	2.608	2.571	2.535	2.501	2.467	2.434	2.401	2.370	2.340	2.310	2.281
30	2.767	2.725	2.684	2.647	2.608	2.571	2.535	2.500	2.466	2.434	2.402	2.370	2.339	2.310	2.281
31	2.766	2.724	2.685	2.646	2.608	2.571	2.535	2.501	2.467	2.434	2.401	2.370	2.340	2.310	2.281
32	2.767	2.725	2.684	2.647	2.608	2.571	2.535	2.500	2.466	2.434	2.402	2.370	2.339	2.310	2.281
33	2.766	2.724	2.685	2.646	2.608	2.571	2.536	2.501	2.467	2.434	2.401	2.370	2.340	2.310	2.281
34	0.346	1.703	2.684	2.647	2.608	2.571	2.535	2.500	2.466	2.434	2.402	2.370	2.339	2.309	2.281
35			0.336	1.654	2.609	2.571	2.536	2.501	2.467	2.433	2.401	2.370	2.340	2.310	2.281
36					0.326	1.607	2.535	2.500	2.466	2.434	2.402	2.370	2.339	2.309	2.282
37							0.317	1.563	2.467	2.433	2.401	2.371	2.340	2.310	2.281
38									0.308	1.521	2.402	2.370	2.339	2.309	2.282
39											0.300	1.482	2.340	2.310	2.281
40													0.292	1.443	2.282
41															0.285

If the Recovery Year is:	and the Recovery Period is: 40.0	40.5	41.0	41.5	42.0	42.5	43.0	43.5	44.0	44.5	45.0	45.5	46.0	46.5	47.0
	the Depreciation Rate is:														
1	1.406	1.389	1.372	1.355	1.339	1.324	1.308	1.293	1.278	1.264	1.250	1.236	1.223	1.210	1.197
2	3.697	3.652	3.608	3.565	3.524	3.483	3.443	3.404	3.366	3.328	3.292	3.256	3.221	3.187	3.153
3	3.559	3.517	3.476	3.437	3.398	3.360	3.323	3.286	3.251	3.216	3.182	3.149	3.116	3.084	3.053
4	3.425	3.387	3.349	3.312	3.276	3.241	3.207	3.173	3.140	3.108	3.076	3.045	3.014	2.984	2.955
5	3.297	3.261	3.227	3.193	3.159	3.127	3.095	3.064	3.033	3.003	2.973	2.944	2.916	2.888	2.861
6	3.173	3.141	3.109	3.077	3.047	3.016	2.987	2.958	2.929	2.902	2.874	2.847	2.821	2.795	2.770
7	3.054	3.024	2.995	2.966	2.938	2.910	2.883	2.856	2.830	2.804	2.778	2.754	2.729	2.705	2.681
8	2.940	2.912	2.885	2.859	2.833	2.807	2.782	2.757	2.733	2.709	2.686	2.663	2.640	2.618	2.596
9	2.829	2.804	2.780	2.756	2.732	2.708	2.685	2.662	2.640	2.618	2.596	2.575	2.554	2.533	2.513
10	2.723	2.700	2.678	2.656	2.634	2.613	2.591	2.571	2.550	2.530	2.510	2.490	2.471	2.451	2.433
11	2.621	2.600	2.580	2.560	2.540	2.520	2.501	2.482	2.463	2.444	2.426	2.408	2.390	2.372	2.355
12	2.523	2.504	2.486	2.467	2.449	2.431	2.414	2.396	2.379	2.362	2.345	2.329	2.312	2.296	2.280
13	2.428	2.411	2.395	2.378	2.362	2.346	2.330	2.314	2.298	2.282	2.267	2.252	2.237	2.222	2.207
14	2.337	2.322	2.307	2.292	2.277	2.263	2.248	2.234	2.220	2.206	2.192	2.178	2.164	2.150	2.137
15	2.253	2.236	2.223	2.209	2.196	2.183	2.170	2.157	2.144	2.131	2.118	2.106	2.093	2.081	2.068
16	2.253	2.225	2.198	2.172	2.146	2.122	2.097	2.083	2.071	2.059	2.048	2.036	2.025	2.014	2.002
17	2.253	2.225	2.198	2.172	2.146	2.122	2.097	2.073	2.050	2.027	2.005	1.983	1.962	1.949	1.938
18	2.253	2.225	2.198	2.172	2.146	2.121	2.097	2.073	2.050	2.027	2.005	1.983	1.962	1.941	1.920
19	2.253	2.226	2.198	2.172	2.147	2.122	2.097	2.073	2.050	2.027	2.005	1.983	1.962	1.941	1.920
20	2.253	2.225	2.198	2.172	2.146	2.121	2.097	2.073	2.050	2.027	2.005	1.983	1.962	1.941	1.920
21	2.253	2.226	2.198	2.172	2.147	2.122	2.097	2.073	2.050	2.027	2.005	1.983	1.962	1.941	1.920
22	2.253	2.225	2.198	2.172	2.146	2.121	2.097	2.073	2.050	2.027	2.005	1.983	1.962	1.941	1.920
23	2.253	2.226	2.198	2.172	2.147	2.122	2.097	2.073	2.050	2.027	2.005	1.983	1.962	1.941	1.920
24	2.253	2.225	2.198	2.172	2.146	2.121	2.097	2.073	2.050	2.027	2.005	1.983	1.961	1.941	1.920
25	2.253	2.226	2.198	2.172	2.147	2.122	2.097	2.073	2.050	2.027	2.004	1.983	1.962	1.940	1.920
26	2.253	2.225	2.198	2.172	2.146	2.121	2.097	2.073	2.050	2.027	2.005	1.983	1.961	1.941	1.920

If the Recovery Year is:	40.0	40.5	41.0	41.5	42.0	42.5	43.0	43.5	44.0	44.5	45.0	45.5	46.0	46.5	47.0
	and the Recovery Period is:														
	the Depreciation Rate is:														
27	2.253	2.226	2.199	2.172	2.147	2.122	2.097	2.073	2.050	2.027	2.004	1.983	1.962	1.940	1.920
28	2.253	2.225	2.198	2.172	2.146	2.121	2.097	2.073	2.050	2.027	2.005	1.983	1.961	1.941	1.920
29	2.253	2.226	2.199	2.172	2.147	2.122	2.097	2.073	2.050	2.027	2.004	1.983	1.962	1.940	1.920
30	2.253	2.225	2.198	2.172	2.146	2.121	2.097	2.073	2.050	2.027	2.005	1.983	1.961	1.941	1.920
31	2.253	2.226	2.199	2.172	2.147	2.122	2.097	2.073	2.050	2.027	2.004	1.983	1.962	1.940	1.920
32	2.253	2.225	2.198	2.172	2.146	2.121	2.098	2.074	2.050	2.027	2.005	1.983	1.961	1.941	1.920
33	2.253	2.226	2.199	2.172	2.147	2.122	2.097	2.073	2.050	2.027	2.004	1.983	1.962	1.940	1.920
34	2.253	2.225	2.198	2.172	2.146	2.121	2.098	2.074	2.049	2.027	2.005	1.983	1.961	1.941	1.920
35	2.253	2.226	2.199	2.172	2.147	2.122	2.097	2.073	2.050	2.027	2.004	1.983	1.962	1.940	1.920
36	2.253	2.225	2.198	2.172	2.146	2.121	2.098	2.074	2.049	2.027	2.005	1.982	1.961	1.941	1.920
37	2.253	2.226	2.199	2.172	2.147	2.122	2.097	2.073	2.050	2.027	2.004	1.983	1.962	1.940	1.920
38	2.254	2.225	2.198	2.172	2.146	2.121	2.098	2.074	2.049	2.027	2.005	1.982	1.961	1.941	1.920
39	2.253	2.226	2.199	2.173	2.147	2.122	2.097	2.073	2.050	2.027	2.004	1.983	1.962	1.940	1.920
40	2.254	2.225	2.198	2.172	2.146	2.121	2.098	2.074	2.049	2.027	2.005	1.982	1.961	1.941	1.920
41	1.408	2.226	2.199	2.173	2.147	2.122	2.097	2.073	2.050	2.027	2.004	1.983	1.962	1.940	1.920
42		0.278	1.374	2.172	2.146	2.121	2.098	2.074	2.049	2.026	2.005	1.982	1.961	1.941	1.920
43				0.272	1.342	2.122	2.097	2.073	2.050	2.027	2.004	1.983	1.962	1.940	1.920
44						0.265	1.311	2.074	2.049	2.026	2.005	1.982	1.961	1.941	1.920
45								0.259	1.281	2.027	2.004	1.983	1.962	1.940	1.920
46										0.253	1.253	1.982	1.961	1.941	1.920
47												0.248	1.226	1.940	1.921
48														0.243	1.200

If the Recovery Year is:	and the Recovery Period is: 47.5	48.0	48.5	49.0	49.5	50.0
	the Depreciation Rate is:					
1	1.184	1.172	1.160	1.148	1.136	1.125
2	3.121	3.088	3.057	3.026	2.996	2.966
3	3.022	2.992	2.962	2.933	2.905	2.877
4	2.927	2.898	2.871	2.844	2.817	2.791
5	2.834	2.808	2.782	2.757	2.732	2.707
6	2.745	2.720	2.696	2.672	2.649	2.626
7	2.658	2.635	2.613	2.590	2.569	2.547
8	2.574	2.553	2.532	2.511	2.491	2.471
9	2.493	2.473	2.453	2.434	2.415	2.397
10	2.414	2.396	2.378	2.360	2.342	2.325
11	2.338	2.321	2.304	2.288	2.271	2.255
12	2.264	2.248	2.233	2.217	2.202	2.187
13	2.192	2.178	2.164	2.150	2.136	2.122
14	2.123	2.110	2.097	2.084	2.071	2.058
15	2.056	2.044	2.032	2.020	2.008	1.996
16	1.991	1.980	1.969	1.958	1.947	1.937
17	1.928	1.918	1.908	1.898	1.888	1.878
18	1.900	1.880	1.861	1.842	1.831	1.822
19	1.900	1.880	1.861	1.842	1.824	1.806
20	1.900	1.880	1.861	1.842	1.824	1.806
21	1.900	1.880	1.861	1.842	1.824	1.806
22	1.900	1.880	1.861	1.843	1.824	1.806
23	1.900	1.880	1.861	1.842	1.824	1.806
24	1.900	1.880	1.861	1.843	1.824	1.806
25	1.900	1.880	1.861	1.842	1.824	1.806
26	1.900	1.880	1.861	1.843	1.824	1.806

If the Recovery Year is:	and the Recovery Period is: 47.5	48.0	48.5	49.0	49.5	50.0
	the Depreciation Rate is:					
27	1.900	1.880	1.861	1.842	1.824	1.806
28	1.900	1.881	1.861	1.843	1.824	1.806
29	1.900	1.880	1.861	1.842	1.824	1.806
30	1.900	1.881	1.861	1.843	1.824	1.806
31	1.900	1.880	1.861	1.842	1.824	1.806
32	1.900	1.881	1.861	1.843	1.824	1.806
33	1.900	1.880	1.861	1.842	1.824	1.806
34	1.900	1.881	1.861	1.843	1.824	1.806
35	1.900	1.880	1.861	1.842	1.824	1.806
36	1.900	1.881	1.861	1.843	1.824	1.806
37	1.900	1.880	1.861	1.842	1.824	1.805
38	1.900	1.881	1.861	1.843	1.824	1.806
39	1.900	1.880	1.861	1.842	1.824	1.805
40	1.900	1.881	1.861	1.843	1.824	1.806
41	1.900	1.880	1.861	1.842	1.824	1.805
42	1.900	1.881	1.862	1.843	1.824	1.806
43	1.900	1.880	1.861	1.842	1.824	1.805
44	1.900	1.881	1.862	1.843	1.824	1.806
45	1.900	1.880	1.861	1.842	1.824	1.805
46	1.900	1.881	1.862	1.843	1.824	1.806
47	1.899	1.880	1.861	1.842	1.824	1.805
48	1.900	1.881	1.862	1.843	1.823	1.806
49	0.237	1.175	1.861	1.842	1.824	1.805
50			0.233	1.152	1.823	1.806
51					0.228	1.128

TABLE 18
Alternative Minimum Tax (see section 7 of this revenue procedure)
Applicable Depreciation Method: 150-Percent Declining Balance Switching to Straight Line
Applicable Recovery Periods: 2.5-50 years
Applicable Convention: Mid-quarter (property placed in service in fourth quarter)

If the Recovery Year is:	and the Recovery Period is:														
	2.5	3.0	3.5	4.0	4.5	5.0	5.5	6.0	6.5	7.0	7.5	8.0	8.5	9.0	9.5
	the Depreciation Rate is:														
1	7.50	6.25	5.36	4.69	4.17	3.75	3.41	3.13	2.88	2.68	2.50	2.34	2.21	2.08	1.97
2	55.50	46.88	40.56	35.74	31.94	28.88	26.34	24.22	22.41	20.85	19.50	18.31	17.26	16.32	15.48
3	26.91	25.00	23.18	22.34	21.30	20.21	19.16	18.16	17.24	16.39	15.60	14.88	14.21	13.60	13.03
4	10.09	21.87	22.47	19.86	17.93	16.40	15.14	14.06	13.26	12.87	12.48	12.09	11.70	11.33	10.98
5			8.43	17.37	17.93	16.41	15.14	14.06	13.10	12.18	11.41	10.74	10.16	9.65	9.24
6					6.73	14.35	15.13	14.06	13.10	12.18	11.41	10.75	10.16	9.65	9.17
7							5.68	12.31	13.10	12.19	11.41	10.74	10.16	9.64	9.17
8									4.91	10.66	11.41	10.75	10.16	9.65	9.17
9											4.28	9.40	10.17	9.64	9.17
10													3.81	8.44	9.18
11															3.44

If the Recovery Year is:	and the Recovery Period is:														
	10.0	10.5	11.0	11.5	12.0	12.5	13.0	13.5	14.0	14.5	15.0	15.5	16.0	16.5	17.0
	the Depreciation Rate is:														
1	1.88	1.79	1.70	1.63	1.56	1.50	1.44	1.39	1.34	1.29	1.25	1.21	1.17	1.14	1.10
2	14.72	14.03	13.40	12.83	12.31	11.82	11.37	10.96	10.57	10.21	9.88	9.56	9.27	8.99	8.73
3	12.51	12.03	11.58	11.16	10.77	10.40	10.06	9.74	9.44	9.16	8.89	8.64	8.40	8.17	7.96
4	10.63	10.31	10.00	9.70	9.42	9.15	8.90	8.66	8.43	8.21	8.00	7.80	7.61	7.43	7.25
5	9.04	8.83	8.63	8.44	8.24	8.06	7.87	7.69	7.52	7.36	7.20	7.04	6.90	6.75	6.61

If the Recovery Year is:	and the Recovery Period is: 10.0	10.5	11.0	11.5	12.0	12.5	13.0	13.5	14.0	14.5	15.0	15.5	16.0	16.5	17.0
	the Depreciation Rate is:														
6	8.72	8.32	7.95	7.63	7.33	7.09	6.96	6.84	6.72	6.60	6.48	6.36	6.25	6.14	6.03
7	8.72	8.31	7.96	7.63	7.33	7.05	6.78	6.53	6.31	6.10	5.90	5.75	5.66	5.58	5.50
8	8.72	8.32	7.95	7.62	7.33	7.05	6.78	6.53	6.31	6.10	5.90	5.72	5.54	5.38	5.22
9	8.72	8.31	7.96	7.63	7.33	7.05	6.78	6.53	6.31	6.10	5.90	5.72	5.54	5.38	5.23
10	8.71	8.32	7.95	7.62	7.32	7.05	6.78	6.54	6.31	6.10	5.91	5.72	5.54	5.38	5.22
11	7.63	8.31	7.96	7.63	7.33	7.05	6.78	6.53	6.31	6.10	5.90	5.72	5.54	5.38	5.23
12		3.12	6.96	7.62	7.32	7.04	6.78	6.54	6.30	6.10	5.91	5.72	5.55	5.38	5.22
13				2.86	6.41	7.05	6.78	6.53	6.31	6.09	5.90	5.72	5.54	5.38	5.23
14						2.64	5.94	6.54	6.30	6.10	5.91	5.72	5.55	5.38	5.22
15								2.45	5.52	6.09	5.90	5.73	5.54	5.37	5.23
16										2.29	5.17	5.72	5.55	5.38	5.22
17												2.15	4.85	5.37	5.23
18														2.02	4.57

If the Recovery Year is:	and the Recovery Period is: 17.5	18.0	18.5	19.0	19.5	20.0	20.5	21.0	21.5	22.0	22.5	23.0	23.5	24.0	24.5
	the Depreciation Rate is:														
1	1.07	1.04	1.01	0.99	0.96	0.938	0.915	0.893	0.872	0.852	0.833	0.815	0.798	0.781	0.765
2	8.48	8.25	8.03	7.82	7.62	7.430	7.250	7.079	6.916	6.760	6.611	6.469	6.332	6.201	6.076
3	7.75	7.56	7.38	7.20	7.03	6.872	6.720	6.573	6.433	6.299	6.170	6.047	5.928	5.814	5.704
4	7.09	6.93	6.78	6.63	6.49	6.357	6.228	6.104	5.985	5.870	5.759	5.652	5.549	5.450	5.354
5	6.48	6.35	6.23	6.11	5.99	5.880	5.772	5.668	5.567	5.469	5.375	5.284	5.195	5.110	5.027
6	5.93	5.82	5.72	5.63	5.53	5.439	5.350	5.263	5.179	5.097	5.017	4.939	4.864	4.790	4.719
7	5.42	5.34	5.26	5.18	5.11	5.031	4.958	4.887	4.817	4.749	4.682	4.617	4.553	4.491	4.430
8	5.08	4.94	4.83	4.77	4.71	4.654	4.596	4.538	4.481	4.425	4.370	4.316	4.263	4.210	4.159
9	5.08	4.94	4.81	4.69	4.57	4.458	4.352	4.252	4.169	4.124	4.079	4.034	3.991	3.947	3.904

If the Recovery Year is:	and the Recovery Period is: 17.5	18.0	18.5	19.0	19.5	20.0	20.5	21.0	21.5	22.0	22.5	23.0	23.5	24.0	24.5
	the Depreciation Rate is:														
10	5.08	4.94	4.81	4.69	4.57	4.458	4.352	4.252	4.156	4.062	3.972	3.888	3.807	3.730	3.665
11	5.08	4.95	4.81	4.69	4.57	4.458	4.352	4.252	4.156	4.062	3.972	3.887	3.807	3.729	3.655
12	5.08	4.94	4.82	4.69	4.57	4.458	4.352	4.252	4.156	4.062	3.973	3.888	3.807	3.730	3.655
13	5.08	4.95	4.81	4.69	4.57	4.458	4.352	4.252	4.155	4.062	3.972	3.887	3.807	3.729	3.655
14	5.08	4.94	4.82	4.69	4.57	4.458	4.352	4.252	4.156	4.061	3.973	3.888	3.807	3.730	3.655
15	5.08	4.95	4.81	4.69	4.57	4.458	4.352	4.252	4.155	4.062	3.972	3.887	3.806	3.729	3.655
16	5.08	4.94	4.82	4.69	4.57	4.458	4.352	4.252	4.156	4.061	3.973	3.888	3.807	3.730	3.655
17	5.08	4.95	4.81	4.68	4.57	4.458	4.353	4.252	4.155	4.062	3.972	3.887	3.806	3.729	3.655
18	5.08	4.94	4.82	4.69	4.57	4.459	4.352	4.252	4.156	4.061	3.973	3.888	3.807	3.730	3.655
19	1.90	4.33	4.81	4.68	4.57	4.458	4.353	4.252	4.155	4.062	3.972	3.887	3.806	3.729	3.655
20			1.81	4.10	4.57	4.459	4.352	4.251	4.156	4.061	3.973	3.888	3.807	3.730	3.655
21					1.72	3.901	4.353	4.252	4.155	4.062	3.972	3.887	3.806	3.729	3.655
22							1.632	3.720	4.156	4.061	3.973	3.888	3.807	3.730	3.655
23									1.558	3.554	3.972	3.887	3.806	3.729	3.655
24											1.490	3.402	3.807	3.730	3.656
25													1.427	3.263	3.655
26															1.371

If the Recovery Year is:	and the Recovery Period is: 25.0	25.5	26.0	26.5	27.0	27.5	28.0	28.5	29.0	29.5	30.0	30.5	31.0	31.5	32.0
	the Depreciation Rate is:														
1	0.750	0.735	0.721	0.708	0.694	0.682	0.670	0.658	0.647	0.636	0.625	0.615	0.605	0.595	0.586
2	5.955	5.839	5.728	5.620	5.517	5.417	5.321	5.229	5.139	5.052	4.969	4.888	4.809	4.734	4.660
3	5.598	5.496	5.397	5.302	5.211	5.122	5.036	4.953	4.873	4.796	4.720	4.647	4.577	4.508	4.442
4	5.262	5.172	5.086	5.002	4.921	4.842	4.766	4.693	4.621	4.552	4.484	4.419	4.355	4.293	4.233
5	4.946	4.868	4.792	4.719	4.648	4.578	4.511	4.446	4.382	4.320	4.260	4.202	4.145	4.089	4.035

If the Recovery Year is:	and the Recovery Period is: 25.0	25.5	26.0	26.5	27.0	27.5	28.0	28.5	29.0	29.5	30.0	30.5	31.0	31.5	32.0
	the Depreciation Rate is:														
6	4.649	4.582	4.516	4.452	4.389	4.329	4.269	4.212	4.155	4.101	4.047	3.995	3.944	3.894	3.846
7	4.370	4.312	4.255	4.200	4.146	4.093	4.041	3.990	3.940	3.892	3.845	3.798	3.753	3.709	3.666
8	4.108	4.059	4.010	3.962	3.915	3.869	3.824	3.780	3.737	3.694	3.653	3.612	3.572	3.532	3.494
9	3.862	3.820	3.779	3.738	3.698	3.658	3.619	3.581	3.543	3.506	3.470	3.434	3.399	3.364	3.330
10	3.630	3.595	3.561	3.526	3.492	3.459	3.426	3.393	3.360	3.328	3.296	3.265	3.234	3.204	3.174
11	3.582	3.513	3.446	3.383	3.321	3.270	3.242	3.214	3.186	3.159	3.132	3.105	3.078	3.051	3.025
12	3.582	3.513	3.446	3.382	3.321	3.262	3.204	3.148	3.095	3.043	2.994	2.952	2.929	2.906	2.883
13	3.582	3.513	3.446	3.383	3.321	3.262	3.204	3.148	3.095	3.043	2.994	2.945	2.898	2.853	2.808
14	3.582	3.513	3.446	3.382	3.321	3.262	3.204	3.148	3.095	3.043	2.994	2.945	2.898	2.853	2.808
15	3.582	3.513	3.446	3.383	3.321	3.262	3.204	3.148	3.095	3.043	2.994	2.945	2.898	2.853	2.808
16	3.583	3.513	3.446	3.382	3.321	3.262	3.204	3.148	3.095	3.043	2.994	2.946	2.898	2.852	2.809
17	3.582	3.513	3.446	3.383	3.322	3.262	3.204	3.148	3.095	3.043	2.994	2.945	2.898	2.853	2.808
18	3.583	3.513	3.446	3.382	3.321	3.262	3.204	3.149	3.095	3.043	2.994	2.946	2.898	2.852	2.809
19	3.582	3.513	3.446	3.383	3.322	3.262	3.204	3.148	3.095	3.043	2.993	2.945	2.898	2.853	2.808
20	3.583	3.513	3.446	3.382	3.321	3.262	3.204	3.149	3.095	3.044	2.994	2.946	2.898	2.852	2.809
21	3.582	3.512	3.447	3.383	3.322	3.262	3.204	3.148	3.095	3.043	2.993	2.945	2.898	2.853	2.808
22	3.583	3.513	3.446	3.382	3.321	3.263	3.204	3.149	3.095	3.044	2.994	2.946	2.898	2.852	2.809
23	3.582	3.512	3.447	3.383	3.322	3.262	3.205	3.148	3.095	3.043	2.993	2.945	2.898	2.853	2.808
24	3.583	3.513	3.446	3.382	3.321	3.263	3.204	3.149	3.095	3.044	2.994	2.946	2.898	2.852	2.809
25	3.582	3.512	3.447	3.383	3.322	3.262	3.205	3.148	3.095	3.043	2.993	2.945	2.898	2.853	2.808
26	3.135	3.513	3.446	3.382	3.321	3.263	3.204	3.149	3.095	3.044	2.994	2.946	2.898	2.852	2.809
27		1.317	3.016	3.383	3.322	3.262	3.205	3.148	3.095	3.043	2.993	2.945	2.898	2.853	2.808
28				1.268	2.906	3.263	3.204	3.149	3.095	3.044	2.994	2.946	2.898	2.852	2.809
29						1.223	2.804	3.148	3.094	3.043	2.993	2.945	2.899	2.853	2.808
30								1.181	2.708	3.044	2.994	2.946	2.898	2.852	2.809
31										1.141	2.619	2.945	2.899	2.853	2.808

If the Recovery Year is:	and the Recovery Period is: 25.0	25.5	26.0	26.5	27.0	27.5	28.0	28.5	29.0	29.5	30.0	30.5	31.0	31.5	32.0
	the Depreciation Rate is:														
32												1.105	2.536	2.852	2.809
33														1.070	2.457

If the Recovery Year is:	and the Recovery Period is: 32.5	33.0	33.5	34.0	34.5	35.0	35.5	36.0	36.5	37.0	37.5	38.0	38.5	39.0	39.5
	the Depreciation Rate is:														
1	0.577	0.568	0.560	0.551	0.543	0.536	0.528	0.521	0.514	0.507	0.500	0.493	0.487	0.481	0.475
2	4.589	4.520	4.453	4.387	4.324	4.263	4.203	4.145	4.088	4.034	3.980	3.928	3.877	3.828	3.779
3	4.377	4.314	4.253	4.194	4.136	4.080	4.025	3.972	3.920	3.870	3.821	3.773	3.726	3.680	3.636
4	4.175	4.118	4.063	4.009	3.956	3.905	3.855	3.807	3.759	3.713	3.668	3.624	3.581	3.539	3.498
5	3.982	3.931	3.881	3.832	3.784	3.738	3.692	3.648	3.605	3.563	3.521	3.481	3.441	3.403	3.365
6	3.798	3.752	3.707	3.663	3.620	3.578	3.536	3.496	3.457	3.418	3.380	3.343	3.307	3.272	3.237
7	3.623	3.582	3.541	3.501	3.462	3.424	3.387	3.350	3.315	3.280	3.245	3.212	3.178	3.146	3.114
8	3.456	3.419	3.382	3.347	3.312	3.278	3.244	3.211	3.178	3.147	3.115	3.085	3.055	3.025	2.996
9	3.296	3.263	3.231	3.199	3.168	3.137	3.107	3.077	3.048	3.019	2.991	2.963	2.936	2.909	2.882
10	3.144	3.115	3.086	3.058	3.030	3.003	2.976	2.949	2.923	2.897	2.871	2.846	2.821	2.797	2.773
11	2.999	2.974	2.948	2.923	2.898	2.874	2.850	2.826	2.802	2.779	2.756	2.734	2.711	2.689	2.668
12	2.861	2.838	2.816	2.794	2.772	2.751	2.729	2.708	2.687	2.666	2.646	2.626	2.606	2.586	2.566
13	2.766	2.725	2.690	2.671	2.652	2.633	2.614	2.595	2.577	2.558	2.540	2.522	2.504	2.486	2.469
14	2.766	2.725	2.685	2.646	2.608	2.570	2.535	2.500	2.471	2.455	2.439	2.423	2.407	2.391	2.375
15	2.766	2.725	2.685	2.646	2.607	2.571	2.535	2.500	2.467	2.433	2.401	2.370	2.339	2.310	2.285
16	2.766	2.725	2.685	2.645	2.608	2.570	2.535	2.500	2.467	2.433	2.401	2.370	2.339	2.310	2.281
17	2.766	2.725	2.685	2.646	2.607	2.571	2.535	2.500	2.467	2.433	2.401	2.370	2.339	2.310	2.281
18	2.766	2.725	2.685	2.645	2.608	2.570	2.535	2.500	2.467	2.433	2.401	2.370	2.339	2.310	2.281
19	2.766	2.725	2.685	2.646	2.607	2.571	2.535	2.500	2.466	2.433	2.401	2.370	2.340	2.310	2.281
20	2.766	2.725	2.685	2.645	2.608	2.570	2.535	2.500	2.467	2.433	2.401	2.370	2.339	2.310	2.281

If the Recovery Year is:	and the Recovery Period is: 32.5	33.0	33.5	34.0	34.5	35.0	35.5	36.0	36.5	37.0	37.5	38.0	38.5	39.0	39.5
	the Depreciation Rate is:														
21	2.766	2.725	2.685	2.646	2.607	2.571	2.535	2.500	2.466	2.433	2.401	2.370	2.340	2.310	2.281
22	2.766	2.725	2.685	2.645	2.608	2.570	2.535	2.500	2.467	2.433	2.401	2.370	2.339	2.310	2.281
23	2.766	2.725	2.685	2.646	2.607	2.571	2.535	2.501	2.466	2.433	2.401	2.370	2.340	2.310	2.281
24	2.766	2.725	2.685	2.645	2.608	2.570	2.535	2.500	2.467	2.433	2.401	2.370	2.339	2.310	2.281
25	2.766	2.725	2.685	2.646	2.607	2.571	2.535	2.501	2.466	2.433	2.401	2.370	2.340	2.310	2.281
26	2.766	2.725	2.685	2.645	2.608	2.570	2.535	2.500	2.467	2.433	2.401	2.370	2.339	2.310	2.281
27	2.766	2.725	2.685	2.646	2.607	2.571	2.535	2.501	2.466	2.434	2.401	2.369	2.340	2.310	2.281
28	2.766	2.725	2.685	2.645	2.608	2.570	2.535	2.500	2.467	2.433	2.401	2.370	2.339	2.310	2.281
29	2.766	2.724	2.685	2.646	2.607	2.571	2.535	2.501	2.466	2.434	2.401	2.369	2.340	2.310	2.281
30	2.766	2.725	2.684	2.645	2.608	2.570	2.535	2.500	2.467	2.433	2.401	2.370	2.339	2.310	2.281
31	2.766	2.724	2.685	2.646	2.607	2.571	2.535	2.501	2.466	2.434	2.401	2.369	2.340	2.310	2.281
32	2.766	2.725	2.684	2.645	2.608	2.570	2.535	2.500	2.467	2.433	2.401	2.370	2.339	2.310	2.281
33	2.766	2.724	2.685	2.646	2.607	2.571	2.535	2.501	2.466	2.434	2.401	2.369	2.340	2.310	2.281
34	1.037	2.384	2.684	2.645	2.608	2.570	2.535	2.500	2.467	2.433	2.401	2.370	2.339	2.310	2.281
35			1.007	2.315	2.607	2.571	2.534	2.501	2.466	2.434	2.402	2.369	2.340	2.309	2.281
36					0.978	2.249	2.535	2.500	2.467	2.433	2.401	2.370	2.339	2.310	2.281
37							0.950	2.188	2.466	2.434	2.402	2.369	2.340	2.309	2.281
38									0.925	2.129	2.401	2.370	2.339	2.310	2.281
39											0.901	2.073	2.340	2.309	2.282
40													0.877	2.021	2.281
41															0.856

If the Recovery Year is:	and the Recovery Period is: 40.0	40.5	41.0	41.5	42.0	42.5	43.0	43.5	44.0	44.5	45.0	45.5	46.0	46.5	47.0
	the Depreciation Rate is:														
1	0.469	0.463	0.457	0.452	0.446	0.441	0.436	0.431	0.426	0.421	0.417	0.412	0.408	0.403	0.399
2	3.732	3.687	3.642	3.598	3.556	3.514	3.473	3.433	3.395	3.357	3.319	3.283	3.248	3.213	3.179
3	3.592	3.550	3.509	3.468	3.429	3.390	3.352	3.315	3.279	3.243	3.209	3.175	3.142	3.109	3.077
4	3.458	3.419	3.380	3.343	3.306	3.270	3.235	3.201	3.167	3.134	3.102	3.070	3.039	3.009	2.979
5	3.328	3.292	3.257	3.222	3.188	3.155	3.122	3.090	3.059	3.028	2.998	2.969	2.940	2.912	2.884
6	3.203	3.170	3.137	3.105	3.074	3.043	3.013	2.984	2.955	2.926	2.898	2.871	2.844	2.818	2.792
7	3.083	3.053	3.023	2.993	2.964	2.936	2.908	2.881	2.854	2.828	2.802	2.776	2.751	2.727	2.703
8	2.968	2.939	2.912	2.885	2.858	2.832	2.807	2.782	2.757	2.732	2.708	2.685	2.662	2.639	2.617
9	2.856	2.831	2.805	2.781	2.756	2.732	2.709	2.686	2.663	2.640	2.618	2.596	2.575	2.554	2.533
10	2.749	2.726	2.703	2.680	2.658	2.636	2.614	2.593	2.572	2.551	2.531	2.511	2.491	2.471	2.452
11	2.646	2.625	2.604	2.583	2.563	2.543	2.523	2.504	2.484	2.465	2.447	2.428	2.410	2.392	2.374
12	2.547	2.528	2.509	2.490	2.472	2.453	2.435	2.417	2.400	2.382	2.365	2.348	2.331	2.315	2.298
13	2.451	2.434	2.417	2.400	2.383	2.367	2.350	2.334	2.318	2.302	2.286	2.271	2.255	2.240	2.225
14	2.359	2.344	2.328	2.313	2.298	2.283	2.268	2.253	2.239	2.224	2.210	2.196	2.182	2.168	2.154
15	2.271	2.257	2.243	2.230	2.216	2.203	2.189	2.176	2.162	2.149	2.136	2.123	2.110	2.098	2.085
16	2.253	2.225	2.198	2.172	2.146	2.125	2.113	2.101	2.089	2.077	2.065	2.053	2.042	2.030	2.019
17	2.253	2.225	2.198	2.172	2.146	2.122	2.097	2.073	2.050	2.027	2.005	1.986	1.975	1.965	1.954
18	2.253	2.225	2.198	2.172	2.147	2.122	2.097	2.073	2.050	2.027	2.005	1.983	1.961	1.940	1.920
19	2.253	2.225	2.198	2.172	2.146	2.121	2.097	2.073	2.050	2.027	2.005	1.983	1.961	1.940	1.920
20	2.253	2.225	2.198	2.172	2.147	2.122	2.097	2.073	2.050	2.027	2.005	1.983	1.961	1.940	1.920
21	2.253	2.225	2.198	2.172	2.146	2.121	2.097	2.073	2.049	2.027	2.005	1.983	1.961	1.940	1.920
22	2.253	2.225	2.198	2.172	2.147	2.122	2.097	2.073	2.050	2.027	2.005	1.983	1.961	1.940	1.920
23	2.253	2.225	2.198	2.172	2.146	2.121	2.097	2.073	2.049	2.027	2.005	1.983	1.961	1.940	1.920
24	2.253	2.225	2.198	2.172	2.147	2.122	2.097	2.073	2.050	2.027	2.005	1.983	1.961	1.940	1.920
25	2.253	2.225	2.198	2.172	2.146	2.121	2.097	2.073	2.049	2.027	2.005	1.983	1.961	1.940	1.920
26	2.252	2.225	2.198	2.172	2.147	2.122	2.097	2.073	2.050	2.027	2.005	1.983	1.961	1.940	1.920

If the Recovery Year is:	and the Recovery Period is:														
	40.0	40.5	41.0	41.5	42.0	42.5	43.0	43.5	44.0	44.5	45.0	45.5	46.0	46.5	47.0
	the Depreciation Rate is:														
27	2.253	2.225	2.198	2.172	2.146	2.121	2.097	2.073	2.049	2.027	2.004	1.983	1.961	1.940	1.920
28	2.252	2.225	2.198	2.172	2.147	2.122	2.097	2.073	2.050	2.027	2.005	1.983	1.962	1.940	1.920
29	2.253	2.225	2.198	2.172	2.146	2.121	2.097	2.073	2.049	2.027	2.004	1.983	1.961	1.940	1.920
30	2.252	2.225	2.198	2.172	2.147	2.122	2.097	2.073	2.050	2.027	2.005	1.983	1.962	1.941	1.920
31	2.253	2.225	2.198	2.172	2.146	2.121	2.097	2.073	2.049	2.027	2.004	1.983	1.961	1.940	1.920
32	2.252	2.225	2.198	2.172	2.147	2.122	2.097	2.073	2.050	2.027	2.005	1.983	1.962	1.941	1.920
33	2.253	2.225	2.198	2.172	2.146	2.121	2.097	2.073	2.049	2.027	2.004	1.983	1.961	1.940	1.920
34	2.252	2.225	2.198	2.172	2.147	2.122	2.097	2.073	2.050	2.027	2.005	1.983	1.962	1.941	1.920
35	2.253	2.225	2.198	2.172	2.146	2.121	2.097	2.073	2.049	2.027	2.004	1.983	1.961	1.940	1.920
36	2.252	2.225	2.198	2.172	2.147	2.122	2.097	2.073	2.050	2.027	2.005	1.983	1.962	1.941	1.920
37	2.253	2.225	2.198	2.172	2.146	2.121	2.097	2.073	2.049	2.027	2.004	1.983	1.961	1.940	1.920
38	2.252	2.224	2.199	2.172	2.147	2.122	2.097	2.073	2.050	2.027	2.005	1.983	1.962	1.941	1.920
39	2.253	2.225	2.198	2.172	2.146	2.121	2.097	2.073	2.049	2.027	2.004	1.983	1.961	1.940	1.920
40	2.252	2.224	2.199	2.172	2.147	2.122	2.097	2.073	2.050	2.027	2.005	1.983	1.962	1.941	1.920
41	1.971	2.225	2.198	2.171	2.146	2.121	2.097	2.072	2.049	2.027	2.004	1.982	1.961	1.940	1.919
42		0.834	1.924	2.172	2.147	2.122	2.097	2.073	2.050	2.027	2.005	1.983	1.962	1.941	1.920
43				0.814	1.878	2.121	2.097	2.072	2.049	2.026	2.004	1.982	1.961	1.940	1.919
44						0.796	1.834	2.073	2.050	2.027	2.005	1.983	1.962	1.941	1.920
45								0.777	1.793	2.026	2.004	1.982	1.961	1.940	1.919
46										0.760	1.754	1.983	1.962	1.941	1.920
47												0.743	1.716	1.940	1.919
48														0.728	1.680

If the Recovery Year is:	and the Recovery Period is: 47.5	48.0	48.5	49.0	49.5	50.0
	the Depreciation Rate is:					
1	0.395	0.391	0.387	0.383	0.379	0.375
2	3.145	3.113	3.081	3.050	3.019	2.989
3	3.046	3.016	2.986	2.956	2.927	2.899
4	2.950	2.921	2.893	2.866	2.839	2.812
5	2.857	2.830	2.804	2.778	2.753	2.728
6	2.767	2.742	2.717	2.693	2.669	2.646
7	2.679	2.656	2.633	2.610	2.588	2.567
8	2.595	2.573	2.552	2.531	2.510	2.490
9	2.513	2.492	2.473	2.453	2.434	2.415
10	2.433	2.415	2.396	2.378	2.360	2.342
11	2.356	2.339	2.322	2.305	2.289	2.272
12	2.282	2.266	2.250	2.235	2.219	2.204
13	2.210	2.195	2.181	2.166	2.152	2.138
14	2.140	2.127	2.113	2.100	2.087	2.074
15	2.073	2.060	2.048	2.036	2.023	2.011
16	2.007	1.996	1.984	1.973	1.962	1.951
17	1.944	1.933	1.923	1.913	1.903	1.893
18	1.900	1.880	1.864	1.854	1.845	1.836
19	1.900	1.880	1.861	1.842	1.824	1.806
20	1.900	1.880	1.861	1.842	1.824	1.806
21	1.900	1.880	1.861	1.842	1.824	1.806
22	1.900	1.880	1.861	1.842	1.824	1.806
23	1.900	1.880	1.861	1.842	1.824	1.806
24	1.900	1.880	1.861	1.842	1.824	1.805
25	1.900	1.880	1.861	1.842	1.824	1.806
26	1.900	1.880	1.861	1.842	1.824	1.805

If the Recovery Year is:	and the Recovery Period is: 47.5	48.0	48.5	49.0	49.5	50.0
	the Depreciation Rate is:					
27	1.900	1.880	1.861	1.842	1.824	1.806
28	1.900	1.880	1.861	1.842	1.824	1.805
29	1.900	1.880	1.861	1.842	1.824	1.806
30	1.900	1.881	1.861	1.842	1.824	1.805
31	1.900	1.880	1.861	1.842	1.824	1.806
32	1.900	1.881	1.861	1.842	1.823	1.805
33	1.900	1.880	1.861	1.842	1.824	1.806
34	1.900	1.881	1.861	1.842	1.823	1.805
35	1.900	1.880	1.861	1.842	1.824	1.806
36	1.900	1.881	1.861	1.842	1.823	1.805
37	1.900	1.880	1.861	1.842	1.824	1.806
38	1.900	1.881	1.861	1.842	1.823	1.805
39	1.900	1.880	1.861	1.843	1.824	1.806
40	1.900	1.881	1.861	1.842	1.823	1.805
41	1.899	1.880	1.861	1.843	1.824	1.806
42	1.900	1.881	1.861	1.842	1.823	1.805
43	1.899	1.880	1.862	1.843	1.824	1.806
44	1.900	1.881	1.861	1.842	1.823	1.805
45	1.899	1.880	1.862	1.843	1.824	1.806
46	1.900	1.881	1.861	1.842	1.823	1.805
47	1.899	1.880	1.862	1.843	1.824	1.806
48	1.900	1.881	1.861	1.842	1.823	1.805
49	0.712	1.645	1.862	1.843	1.824	1.806
50			0.698	1.612	1.823	1.805
51					0.684	1.580

TABLE 19
Unofficial (CCH-prepared)
Indian Reservation Property
3-year property
2-year recovery period
200-percent declining-balance method
Half-year and mid-quarter conventions

Recovery year	Half-year convention	Midquarter Convention (use percentages in column for quarter that property was placed in service)			
		Q-1	Q-2	Q-3	Q-4
1	50	87.5	62.5	37.5	12.5
2	50	12.5	37.5	62.5	87.5

TABLE 20
Unofficial (CCH-prepared)
Indian Reservation Property
7-year property
4-year recovery period
200-percent declining-balance method
Half-year and mid-quarter conventions

Recovery year	Half-year convention	Midquarter Convention (use percentages in column for quarter that property was placed in service)			
		Q-1	Q-2	Q-3	Q-4
1	25	43.75	31.25	18.75	6.25
2	37.5	28.13	34.37	40.63	46.87
3	18.75	14.06	17.19	20.31	23.44
4	12.5	12.5	12.5	12.5	12.5
5	6.25	1.56	4.69	7.81	10.94

TABLE 21
Unofficial (CCH-prepared)
Indian Reservation Property
10-year property
6-year recovery period
200-percent declining-balance method
Half-year and mid-quarter conventions

Recovery year	Half-year convention	Midquarter Convention (use percentages in column for quarter that property was placed in service)			
		Q-1	Q-2	Q-3	Q-4
1	16.67	29.17	20.83	12.5	4.17
2	27.78	23.61	26.39	29.17	31.94
3	18.52	15.74	17.59	19.44	21.3
4	12.35	10.49	11.73	12.96	14.2
5	9.87	9.88	9.88	9.88	9.87
6	9.87	9.88	9.88	9.88	9.88
7	4.94	1.23	3.70	6.17	8.64

TABLE 22
Unofficial (CCH-prepared)
Indian Reservation Property
Nonresidential Real Property
22-year recovery period
Straight-line method and mid-month convention

If the Recovery Year is:	And the Month in the First Recovery Year the Property is Placed in Service is:											
	1	2	3	4	5	6	7	8	9	10	11	12
	the Depreciation Rate is:											
1	4.356	3.977	3.598	3.22	2.841	2.462	2.083	1.705	1.326	0.947	0.568	0.189
2	4.545	4.545	4.545	4.545	4.545	4.545	4.545	4.545	4.545	4.545	4.545	4.545
3	4.545	4.545	4.545	4.545	4.545	4.545	4.545	4.545	4.545	4.545	4.545	4.545
4	4.546	4.546	4.546	4.545	4.545	4.546	4.546	4.545	4.545	4.546	4.546	4.546
5	4.545	4.545	4.545	4.546	4.546	4.545	4.545	4.546	4.546	4.545	4.545	4.545
6	4.546	4.546	4.546	4.545	4.545	4.546	4.546	4.545	4.545	4.546	4.546	4.546
7	4.545	4.545	4.545	4.546	4.546	4.545	4.545	4.546	4.546	4.545	4.545	4.545
8	4.546	4.546	4.546	4.545	4.545	4.546	4.546	4.545	4.545	4.546	4.546	4.546
9	4.545	4.545	4.545	4.546	4.546	4.545	4.545	4.546	4.546	4.545	4.545	4.545
10	4.546	4.546	4.546	4.545	4.545	4.546	4.546	4.545	4.545	4.546	4.546	4.546
11	4.545	4.545	4.545	4.546	4.546	4.545	4.545	4.546	4.546	4.545	4.545	4.545
12	4.546	4.546	4.546	4.545	4.545	4.546	4.546	4.545	4.545	4.546	4.546	4.546
13	4.545	4.545	4.545	4.546	4.546	4.545	4.545	4.546	4.546	4.545	4.545	4.545
14	4.546	4.546	4.546	4.545	4.545	4.546	4.546	4.545	4.545	4.546	4.546	4.546
15	4.545	4.545	4.545	4.546	4.546	4.545	4.545	4.546	4.546	4.545	4.545	4.545
16	4.546	4.546	4.546	4.545	4.545	4.546	4.546	4.545	4.545	4.546	4.546	4.546
17	4.545	4.545	4.545	4.546	4.546	4.545	4.545	4.546	4.546	4.545	4.545	4.545
18	4.546	4.546	4.546	4.545	4.545	4.546	4.546	4.545	4.545	4.546	4.546	4.546
19	4.545	4.545	4.545	4.546	4.546	4.545	4.545	4.546	4.546	4.545	4.545	4.545
20	4.546	4.546	4.546	4.545	4.545	4.546	4.546	4.545	4.545	4.546	4.546	4.546
21	4.545	4.545	4.545	4.546	4.546	4.545	4.545	4.546	4.546	4.545	4.545	4.545

If the Recovery Year is:	And the Month in the First Recovery Year the Property is Placed in Service is:											
	1	2	3	4	5	6	7	8	9	10	11	12
	the Depreciation Rate is:											
22	4.546	4.546	4.546	4.545	4.545	4.546	4.546	4.545	4.545	4.546	4.546	4.546
23	0.189	0.568	0.947	1.326	1.705	2.083	2.462	2.841	3.220	3.598	3.977	4.356

MACRS Recovery Periods

¶ 190

How to Determine an MACRS Asset's Depreciation Period

For MACRS property, the class lives and recovery periods for various assets are prescribed by an IRS table in Rev. Proc. 87-56, 1987-2 CB 674 (as clarified and modified by Rev. Proc. 88-22, 1988-1 CB 785). The table is reproduced at ¶ 191. A similar table is reproduced in IRS Publication 946 (Depreciation and Amortization).

See, also, ¶ 100 through ¶ 127C for discussion of specific MACRS property recovery periods and types of property falling within each recovery period. A Quick Reference Table in the Appendix also provides a list of recovery periods for various types of assets and includes cross references to related explanation discussions in this guide. The discussion in this paragraph explains how to use the IRS Rev. Proc. 87-56 table to determine the applicable recovery period.

The recovery period of a property is generally determined by its class life (Code Sec. 168(e)(1)). The class life of an item of property is the class life as of January 1, 1986, which is usually derived from the asset guideline period (midpoint class life) for the asset guideline class in which the property was classified under Rev. Proc. 83-35, which relates to the Asset Depreciation Range System.

Some property is assigned a MACRS general depreciation system (GDS) and/or alternative depreciation system (ADS) recovery period without regard to the class life provided for such property in Rev. Proc. 83-35. The assigned recovery period for such property is incorporated into the table (Code Sec. 168(e); Code Sec. 168(g)(2)).

Certain property with no class life for which recovery periods are assigned is described in items A-E following Asset Class 80.0 in the table. Personal property with no class life and Section 1245 real property with no class life is assigned a seven-year GDS recovery period and a 12-year and 40-year ADS recovery period, respectively (item A).

The first section of the table (Asset Classes 00.1100.4 (Table B-1)) covers specific depreciable assets used in all business activities and the second section (Asset Classes 01.180.0 (Table B-2)) generally lists specific types of assets used in particular business activities, e.g., production machinery and equipment for specified industries.

For each asset class, the table provides the class life of the property, the GDS recovery period (which also corresponds to the MACRS property class for the property), and the recovery period under the MACRS alternative depreciation system (ADS) for such property.

It is important to keep in mind when using Table B-2 that the classification of an asset is not based on the taxpayer's business activity but rather upon whether the particular asset is specifically described or considered used in furtherance of the particular activity described. Thus, it is necessary to determine the specific function and use of the asset in the taxpayer's business.

Although a particular asset class may include a list of assets included in the class, that list is not necessarily exclusive. Assets used in furtherance of the particular business activity described by the asset class may be included in that asset class. (CCA Letter Ruling 200246006, August 15, 2002). See the discussion under "*Tools*" at 125.

In another example, the IRS ruled that a parking lot located at a steam production plant was a "related land improvement" within the meaning of Asset Class 49.13 and, therefore, had to be depreciated over the 20 year recovery period prescribed for that asset class (Rev. Rul. 2003-81, I.R.B. 2003-30). The wording of Asset Class 49.13 requires that the land improvement be related to assets used in the steam power production of electricity. According to the IRS, the parking lot was related to the plant that produced electricity. On the other hand, although a parking lot located at the company's office building 100 miles away was used in connection with the taxpayer's business activity of producing electricity, it is was not considered related to assets that produced electricity as required by Asset Class 49.13. The office parking lot was, therefore, depreciable over 15-years as a land improvement described in Table B-1 Asset Class 00.3 entitled "Land Improvements." See *Parking lots* at 5. Presumably, if a cost segregation study were conducted on the office building, the personal property components would generally be classified as property without an assigned class life and would be depreciable over 7-years. On the other hand, if personal or professional services, or retail or wholesale services, are provided from a building, the personal property elements of the building would presumably be classified as 5-year property under Asset Class 57.0 because the building would be considered a necessary asset directly used in the provision of these services. For example, all the personal property elements of the hospital building in the Hospital Corporation of America case (127) were classified as 5-year property under Asset Class 57.0 because the building was considered an asset used to provide professional services.

Residential rental property and nonresidential real property

Residential rental property and nonresidential real property are depreciated over the respectively prescribed 27.5- or 39-year recovery period even if such property is used within an activity described in an asset class in Rev. Proc. 87-56 (Rev. Proc. 87-56, Section 5.02). However, in some cases buildings are specifically stated as includible within an asset class (e.g., certain buildings are included in Asset Class 80.0 relating to Theme and Amusement Parks) and would be depreciable over the period prescribed in the asset class.

Assets described in more than one asset class

If a specific asset, such as a land improvement, is listed in an Asset Class that appears in both the first section of the table (Asset classes 00.11 through 00.4 (Table B-1)) and the Asset Class that applies to the taxpayer's business activity in the second part of the table (Asset Classes 01.1 and following (Table B-2)) the depreciation period is determined by reference to the Asset Class in the second part of the table. Except for land improvements, very few assets are specifically described in both sections of the table. The rules are explained more fully at 191 but the following examples serve as good illustrations.

Example (1): An accountant buys a desk for business use. The desk is specifically described in Table B-1 under Asset Class 00.11, Office Furniture, Fixtures, and Equipment. The accountant now needs to refer to the second part of the table (Table B-1) to determine whether desks are specifically listed in her business activity. Her business activity falls within Asset Class 57.0 which covers taxpayers who provide personal and professional services. Desks, however, are not specifically described in Asset Class 57.0. Consequently, the depreciation period is determined by reference to Asset Class 00.11. Under Asset Class 00.11 the desk is treated as 7-year property.

Example (2): An accountant buys permanent hard covered reference books for his professional library. Books are not listed in the first part of the table (Table B-1) as a type of asset used in all business activities and are also not specifically listed in Asset Class 57.0 (the asset class for the accountant's business activity). In this instance, the depreciation period is determined by reference to Asset Class 57.0 and the books are, therefore, treated as 5-year property. If the taxpayer was not an accountant and was engaged in a another business activity that was not described in the second part of the table, the books would have been treated as personal property without a class life and, by default, would have been treated as 7-year property.

A fishing trawler was a specific asset classified in the first part of the Rev. Proc. 87-56 table as a vessel (Asset Class 00.28) and had a ten-year recovery period. This asset class controlled the depreciation period even though the trawler was used in a business activity described in Asset class 20.4 (Manufacture of Other Food and Kindred Products) because vessels are not specifically described in Asset Class 20.4 (IRS Letter Ruling 9502001, Jun. 30, 1994).

Taxpayer with multiple business activities

The ADR regulations provide that property is included in the asset guideline for the activity in which the property is primarily used. Property is classified according to the primary use even though the activity in which the property is primarily used is insubstantial in relation to all the taxpayer's activities (Reg. 1.167(a)-11(b)(4)(iii)(b)). In IRS Letter Ruling 9101003, September 25, 1990, the IRS states that this rule may be applied for MACRS purposes.

A limitation on the application of this rule is illustrated in Rev. Rul. 77-476 (1977-2 CB 5). In Rev. Rul. 77-476, a public utility owned a 50-mile pipeline through which it transported oil for use at its generating facility. The ruling holds that the pipeline is not Asset Class 46.0 property (relating to pipeline transportation) but is Asset Class 49.13 property (relating to electric utility steam production plants). Asset Class 46.0 was inapplicable because the utility did not have a separate business activity of transporting oil or other goods by pipeline.

In Chief Counsel Advice 200137026, the IRS states: "Where a taxpayer is engaged in more than one industrial or commercial activity, the cost of assets used in each activity are to be separated and depreciation deductions calculated separately for each activity. If an item of property is used in two industrial or commercial activities that correspond to two activities, depreciation deductions for the item are calculated based on the activity in which the item is primarily used. If two identical items (for example, two forklifts) are primarily used in each of two separate industrial or commercial activities of a taxpayer, depreciation deductions for each item are computed based on the activity in which the item is primarily used" (Chief Counsel Advice 200137026, June 14, 2001; IRS Letter Ruling 200203009, October 3, 2001).

If a particular asset is used in two activities, the cost of the asset is not allocated between the two activities. The total cost of the asset is classified according to the activity in which the asset is primarily used. This determination may be made in any reasonable manner (IRS Letter Ruling 200203009, October 3, 2001, relating to assets used in both casino and hotel operations). For example, in Rev. Proc. 97-10 (1997-1 C.B. 628), either a gross receipts test or a square foot test was used to determine whether a building is primarily used as a retail motor fuels outlet.

Leased property

Regulations, which were issued in the context of the Asset Depreciation Range System (ADR), provide that in the case of a lessor of property, unless there is an asset guideline class in effect for lessors of such property, the asset guideline class for the property shall be determined as if the property were owned by the lessee (Reg. 1.167(a)-11(e)(3)(iii)). *A.J. Hauptli, Jr.*, CA-10, 90-1 USTC 50,259, interpreted this rule to mean that where the lessee subleases the asset, the sublessee is the relevant reference point. Under the principal of this regulation, the depreciation period for MACRS property that is leased is also determined by reference to the lessee unless a separate asset class is in effect for the lessor.

The classification of vessels leased to a taxpayer's subsidiary which time charted the vessels for use in offshore oil drilling activities was determined by reference to the subsidiary's use, rather than the time charterer's use, where the time charter was considered a service contract and not a sublease (FSA 200232012, April 26, 2002). In an earlier ruling involving the same taxpayer, if a time charter is considered a sublease, the classification of the vessels is determined by reference to the use to which the time-charter puts the vessel. Vessels chartered during the tax year to multiple time charterers engaged in different business activities were classified in accordance with the business activity in which they were primarily used during the tax year (FSA 200221016, February 13, 2002). See "*Taxpayer with multiple business activities*" at 190.

Example: ABC corporation is in the business of leasing gas cylinders. It leases 1,000 cylinders to a manufacturer of grain and grain mill products (Asset Class 20.1 in Rev. Proc. 87-56). The cylinders are treated as 10-year property under Asset Class 20.1 because the leasing of gas cylinders is not an activity described in Rev. Proc. 87-56.

Under the ADR regulations, if an asset class is based upon the type of property, as distinguished from the activity in which it is used, for example trucks or railroad cars, the property is classified without regard to the activity of the lessee (Reg. 1.167(a)-11(e)(3)(iii)). See, also, "*Assets falling within more than one asset class*" at 190.

See, also, 5 under "*Inventory*" for leased property issues.

Other federal laws

A federal law other than the federal income tax law may not be used in determining the asset class in which a particular property falls unless it is specifically indicated in Code Sec. 168 or Rev. Proc. 87-56 (IRS Letter Ruling 9502001, Jun. 30, 1994).

Full Text Classification Guidelines from IRS Cost Segregation Audit Guide

The following text from the IRS Cost Segregation Audit Guide provides basic principles for determining the proper Rev. Proc. 87-56 Asset Class (i.e., recovery period) for MACRS assets.

Introduction

Chapter 6.3 - Depreciation Overview

In order to compute depreciation using proper class lives and recovery periods, assets must be assigned to the proper asset classes. Cost segregation studies generally produce listings or groups of assets, based on asset classes under ACRS (Accelerated Cost Recovery System) or MACRS (Modified Accelerated Cost Recovery System). This chapter provides a summary of the applicable authorities and available guidelines for classifying property into its appropriate class.

HISTORICAL BACKGROUND - A BRIEF RECAP

1. **Pre-ACRS MACRS Depreciation Methods - Prior to 1981**

Prior to the enactment of ACRS in 1981, depreciation deductions were generally calculated by applying the appropriate depreciation method to the basis, useful life, and salvage value of the asset. Taxpayers were permitted to use component depreciation, whereby assets were segregated into separate components with different useful lives, which were depreciated separately. Alternatively, taxpayers could elect to use the Asset Depreciation Range (ADR) system for computing depreciation deductions. Property was generally classified as either 1245 or 1250 property, based on the rules governing Investment Tax Credit (ITC), pursuant to Code 48 and the regulations thereunder.

2. **ACRS MACRS Depreciation Methods - Post-1980**

Following the enactment of the ACRS depreciation system in 1981, component depreciation was specifically prohibited. The Service position has been that this prohibition continued under the MACRS depreciation system, enacted in 1986. Generally, ACRS is effective for property placed in use between 1981 and 1986, and MACRS is effective for property placed in use after 1986.

3. **Hospital Corporation of America, Inc. v. Commissioner, 109 T.C. 21 (1997) ("HCA")**

In HCA, the Tax Court concluded that the taxpayer was permitted to apply ITC principles to classify property as either 1245 property or 1250 property for purposes of determining asset classes and recovery periods under ACRS and MACRS. In effect, the HCA decision has reinstated a form of component depreciation.

4. **Action on Decision (AOD) Number CC-1999-008**

In Action on Decision (AOD) Number CC-1999-008, the Service acquiesced to the application of ITC principles in the HCA case. However, the Service did not acquiesce to the particular results in this case (i.e., the Service did not agree with the classification of specific assets as qualifying 1245 property).

5. **Use of Cost Segregation Studies to Compute Depreciation Deductions**

Based on these developments, the use of cost segregation studies by taxpayers to accelerate depreciation deductions is expected to increase. The assignment of assets to the appropriate asset class is critical in determining the proper recovery period and, accordingly, the amount of depreciation.

GUIDELINES FOR THE CLASSIFICATION OF ASSETS - MACRS

1. **MACRS Rules - IRC 168**

Code 168(e) specifies the classification of property for purposes of computing the cost recovery allowance provided by MACRS. Property is classified according to class life as determined in Revenue Procedure 87-56, 1987-2 C.B. 674, unless statutorily classified otherwise in 168. There are no other exceptions. (Refer to the more detailed discussion of Rev. Proc. 87-56on page 6.3-3, Item 4).

2. **Asset Guideline Class**

Code 168(i)(1)establishes the class life for assets, as defined in Code 167(m) which, in turn, refers to Regulations 1.167(a)-11 for rules regarding the classification of property under the class life system.Reg. 1.167(a)-11(b)(4)(iii)(b) states that the selection of the appropriate asset guideline class is based on the business activity in which the asset is primarily used.

3. **General Depreciation System (GDS) and Alternative Depreciation System (ADS)**

Under MACRS, taxpayers must generally use the General Depreciation System (GDS), unless specifically required by law to use the Alternative Depreciation System (ADS), or unless the taxpayer elects to use ADS. (Refer to IRC 167 and 168, as well as IRS Publication 946, How to Depreciate Property, for additional details and explanations.)

A. GDS (General Depreciation System)

The GDS system contains nine property classes, based on the recovery period of an asset (3, 5, 7, 10, 15, 20, 25, 27.5, or 39 years). The taxpayer may generally utilize the 200 declining balance method, 150 declining balance method, or straight-line method for computing depreciation for most GDS property. However, 27.5-year property (residential rental property) and 39-year property (non-residential real property) must be depreciated using straight-line depreciation.

A. ADS (Alternative Depreciation System)

The ADS system must be used for the following property:

Listed property used 50 or less for business;

Tangible property used predominantly outside the U.S. during the year;

Tax-Exempt use property;

Tax-Exempt bond financed property; and

Property used predominantly in a farming business and placed in service in any tax year during which an election has been made not to apply the uniform capitalization rules to certain farming costs.

The use of ADS may also be elected for any property eligible for depreciation under GDS. The recovery periods under ADS are generally longer than the recovery periods under GDS, and straight-line methods must be used.

1. Revenue Procedure 87-56, 1987-2 C.B. 674

Revenue Procedure 87-56contains the "Table Of Class Lives And Recovery Periods," which is reproduced as "Table B" in IRS Publication 946, "How to Depreciate Property." This table provides guidance as to the classification of assets and for the determination of the proper recovery period.

2. IRS Publication 946, "How to Depreciate Property"

Publication 946 explains how to compute depreciation deductions. Appendix B in the publication reproduces the "Table Of Class Lives And Recovery Periods" from Rev. Proc. 87-56, which provides guidance for classifying an asset according to the business activity in which the asset is primarily used.

The publication divides the table into two sections (Tables B-1 and B-2). Both tables must be consulted in determining the correct recovery period for specific assets. Table B-1, Specific Depreciable Assets Used In All Business Activities, Except As Noted, generally lists assets used in all business activities. Table B-2, Depreciable Assets Used In The Following Activities, lists assets used in certain activities, as described therein.

3. How to Use Table B (Publication 946)

In general, if the property is described in Table B-1, the recovery period shown in that table is the recovery period for the asset. However, if the property is specifically listed in Table B-2 under the type of activity in which the asset is used, the recovery period listed under the activity in Table B-2 should be used. Further direction on the use of these tables is explained below.

a. Table B-1, Specific Depreciable Assets Used In All Business Activities, Except As Noted

First, check Table B-1 to see if it contains a description of the asset in question. If the subject asset is described in Table B-1, then check Table B-2 to find the activity to which the property relates or in which it is being used. If the activity is described in Table B-2, read the text (if any) under the title to determine if the property is specifically included in the asset class listed in Table B-2. If it is, then use the recovery period shown in the appropriate column of Table B-2 following the description of that activity. If the activity to which the property relates is not described in Table B-2, then use the recovery period shown in the appropriate column following the description of the property in Table B-1. Also, if the activity is described in Table B-2, but the property either is not specifically included in or is specifically excluded from that asset class, then use the recovery period shown in the appropriate column following the description of the property in Table B-1.

b. Table B-2, Depreciable Assets Used in the Following Activities

If the asset is not listed in Table B-1, then check Table B-2 to find the activity to which the property relates or in which the property is primarily being used, and use the recovery period shown in the appropriate column following the asset description.

c. Property not in either table

If the property is not listed in Table B-1 and the activity to which it relates is not included in Table B-2, then check the end of Table B-2 to find "Certain Property for which Recovery periods Assigned (Personal PropertySection 1245 Real Property With No Class Life)." Property in this category generally has a recovery period of 7 years for GDS or 12 years for ADS. For residential rental property, and nonresidential real property, see Appendix A in Publication 946.

1. Examples (from Publication 946, Appendix B)

The following examples appear in Appendix B of Publication 946, and illustrate the use of these tables for determining the proper asset recovery period.

a. Example 1

Richard Green is a paper manufacturer. During the year, he made substantial improvements to the land on which his paper plant is located. He checks Table B-1 and finds land improvements under Asset Class 00.3. He then checks Table B-2 and finds his activity, paper manufacturing, under Asset Class 26.1, Manufacturer of Pulp and Paper.

If Richard had looked only at Table B-1, he would have incorrectly selected Asset Class 00.3, Land Improvements, and incorrectly used a recovery period of 15 years for GDS or 20 years for ADS. However, Richard uses the recovery period under Asset Class 26.1, because it specifically includes land improvements. The land improvements have a 13-year class life and a 7-year recovery period for GDS. If he elects to use ADS, the recovery period is 13 years.

[Note: It is presumed in this example that the subject land improvements are associated with the factory site or production process, in the likeness of effluent ponds and canals. Other land improvements, such as general parking lots, would fall into Asset Class 00.3 and have a 15-year recovery period under GDS.]

b. Example 2

Sam Plower produces rubber products. During the year, he made substantial improvements to the land on which his rubber plants are located. He checks Table B-1 and finds land improvements under Asset Class 00.3. He then checks Table B-2 and finds his activity, producing rubber products, under Asset Class 30.1, Manufacture of Rubber Products. Reading the headlines and descriptions under Asset Class 30.1, Sam finds that it does not include land improvements. Therefore, Sam uses the recovery period under Asset Class 00.3. The land improvements have a 20-year class life and a 15-year recovery period for GDS. If he elects to use ADS, the recovery period is 20 years.

c. Example 3

Pam Martin owns a retail-clothing store. During the year, she purchased a desk and a cash register for use in her business. She checks Table B-1 and finds office furniture under Asset Class 00.11. Cash registers are not specifically listed in any of the asset classes in Table B-1. She then checks Table B-2 and finds her activity, retail store, under Asset Class 57.0, Distributive Trades, and which includes assets used in wholesale and retail trade. This description for this asset class does not specifically list office furniture or a cash register.

She looks back at Table B-1 and uses Asset Class 00.11 for the desk, since it constitutes office furniture. The desk has a 10-year class life and a 7- year recovery period for GDS. If she elects to use ADS, the recovery period is 10 years. For the cash register, Pam uses Asset Class 57.0, because cash registers are not specifically listed in Table B-1 but are assets used in retail business. Accordingly, the cash register has a 9-year class life and a 5-year recovery period for GDS. If she elects to use the ADS method, the recovery period is 9 years.

1. General Rules for Classifying Assets

In most cases, a single industry asset guideline class will cover all the production machinery and equipment that is typically used in that particular industry. Asset Guideline Classes 1.1 through 80.0 (Table B-2) list depreciable assets used in specific, primary business activities (the "activity" category).

Specific depreciable assets used in and common to all business activities (the "asset" category) cross all industry lines and are covered by Asset Guideline Classes 00.11 through 00.4 (Table B-1). For most taxpayers, three or four asset class guidelines will encompass all of their depreciable assets, such as autos, computers, and furniture & fixtures. The rule is that these classes (from Table B-1) must be applied first to determine the asset classification before applying and determining the primary business asset class (the "activity" category).

The exception to this rule is that certain activity categories, such as those described in Asset Classes 48.11 and 57.1, specify the assets that are section 1245 or section 1250 property. Other activity classes, such as Asset Class 28.0, include all land improvements, which takes priority over the asset category, such as Asset Class 00.3. [Note: As in Example 1 on page 6.3-5, only those land improvements associated with the plant site or production process, such as effluent ponds and canals, should be included in Asset Class 28.0. General land improvements, such as parking lots, should be included in Asset Class 00.3.]

9. Application of Asset Classification Rules

Asset classification pursuant to the rules in Rev. Proc. 87-56 is not always a straight-forward determination, particularly where the taxpayer is involved in a number of related business activities. The proper steps to follow in assigning assets to the appropriate asset or activity or class may be summarized as follows:

1. Ascertain and fully understand the primary business activity of the taxpayer.

2. Determine the specific function and use of the assets in the taxpayer's business.

3. Apply the clear and plain language contained in the asset guideline classes of Rev. Proc. 87-56 with respect to the assets in question.

The application of these steps may be illustrated by the analysis used in a sampling of court cases, private letter rulings, and revenue rulings, which are summarized below. The analysis in each citation is based on a strict reading of Rev. Proc. 87-56, including historical reference to original asset and activity class descriptions from which later classes have been derived. Note that, for those instances in which a taxpayer was permitted to use an asset class that was different from its primary business activity, the taxpayer was able to demonstrate that it did, in fact, have a separate trade or business for that property item.

Revenue Ruling 77-476, 1977-2 C.B. 5

Conclusion: The primary business activity of the taxpayer determines the appropriate activity class.

Analysis: An oil pipeline owned by an electric utility company and used to transport oil between the company's dock and its inland generating facility is "public utility property" (Asset Guideline Class 49.13, Electric Utility Steam Production Plant). Since the taxpayer is not in the trade or business of transporting oil by pipeline, the pipeline should not be classified as "pipeline transportation property" (Asset Guideline Class 46.0, Pipeline Transportation).

Revenue Ruling 80-127, 1980-1 C.B. 53

Conclusion: Assets specifically excluded from a certain activity class must be classified in the appropriate asset class.

Analysis: The taxpayer leases shipping containers to a shipping company. The containers are designed to transport cargo over the road on trailers and by water on cargo ships and should be classified in Asset Guideline Class 00.27, which includes "trailer-mounted containers." Activity Guideline Class 44.0, Water Transportation, which describes assets used in the commercial and contract carrying of freight by water, specifically excludes assets included in classes with a 00.2 prefix. (Note: the result would be the same if the shipping company owned the containers.)

Private Letter Ruling 9101003 (Sept. 25, 1990)

Conclusion: Property is classified according to the primary business activity of the taxpayer, even though the activity in which such property is primarily used is insubstantial in relation to all the taxpayer's activities. In determining the primary business activity included in a current activity class, it is helpful and appropriate to analyze the historic business activities included in the classes from which it is derived.

Analysis: The taxpayer's business activities include the acquisition, processing, and sale of various types of scrap materials. Asset Guideline Class 57.0, Distributive Trades and Services, includes assets used in wholesale and retail trade. The description for this class includes no further detail. However, the predecessor to Asset Guideline Class 57.0 included Asset Guideline Class 50.0, Wholesale and Retail Trade, which included assets used in the acquisition and processing of goods at both the wholesale and retail level. The description for Asset Guideline Class 50.0 also specifically referenced the brokerage of scrap metal and various pre-sale processing activities.

Private Letter Rulings 9502001, 9502002, and 9502003 (June 30, 1994)

Conclusion: Property is included in the asset class in which the property is primarily used, even if it is used in more than one activity or the activity is not specifically defined.

Analysis: The taxpayer uses a factory trawler to harvest and process various species of fish. There is no specific Asset Guideline Class for the fishing industry. Asset Guideline Class 20.4 covers the Manufacture of Other Food and Kindred Products, but does not specifically list water vessels. However, Asset Guideline Class 00.28 includes Vessels, Barges, Tugs, and Similar Water Transportation. Accordingly, the trawler is a specific asset described in Asset Guideline Class 00.28, which includes all water vessels without regard to the business activity.

Private Letter Ruling 9548003 (July 31, 1995)

Conclusion: Assets engaged in more than one activity must be classified to the activity in which they are primarily used.

Analysis: The taxpayer is a public utility company supplying electric and gas utility service. Through a number of subsidiaries, the taxpayer also owns and operates several natural gas gathering systems, processing plants, and pipeline systems. Most of the pipelines are not connected to the taxpayer's processing plants; thus, the taxpayer is engaged in two separate business activities. The gathering pipelines are appropriately included in Asset Class 46.0 (Pipeline Transportation), while the processing plants are included in Asset Class 49.23 (Natural Gas Production Plant).

***Duke Energy Natural Gas Corporation v. Commissioner*, 109 T.C. 416 (1997), rev'd, 172 F.3d 1255 (10th Cir. 1999), nonacq., 1999-2 C.B. xvi.**

Conclusion: The class life of an asset is based on the asset's primary use in relationship to the classes in question.

Analysis: The taxpayer was a natural gas corporation. At issue was the classification of its natural gas gathering systems as either assets used in the production of gas or assets used in the transportation of gas. It was determined that the plain language of the asset descriptions supported the contention that the gathering systems constituted assets used in the taxpayer's production of natural gas.

***Saginaw Bay Pipeline Co., et al v. United States*, 124 F. Supp. 2d 465 (E.D. Mich. 2001), *rev'd and rem'd*, 2003 FED App. 0259P (6th Cir.) (No. 01-2599)**

Conclusion: The proper asset class is determined by the use of the property rather than the activity of the owner of the property.

Analysis: The 6th Circuit held that, because the taxpayer's underground natural gas pipelines were used primarily by natural gas producers and functioned as gathering pipelines in the natural gas production process, the taxpayer's underground natural gas pipelines are includible in Asset Class 13.2. The 6th Circuit reached this result, even though the taxpayer was not a producer of natural gas (that is, not engaged in the activity described in Asset Class 13.2).

***Clajon Gas Co. LP, et al v. Commissioner*, 119 T.C. 197 (2002), *rev'd*, 2004 U.S. App. LEXIS 284 (8th Cir. Mo. Jan. 12, 2004)**

Conclusion: Classification of property as to the proper asset class is based on the use of the property in a manner as described in an asset class.

Analysis: The taxpayer was not a natural gas producer and the taxpayer used the gathering lines to transport gas. At issue was the classification of taxpayer's gathering lines as either assets includible in Asset Class 13.2 (Exploration for and Production of Petroleum and Natural Gas Deposits), which has a MACRS recovery period of 7 years, or Asset Class 46.0 (Pipeline Transportation), which has a MACRS recovery period of 15 years. The 8th Circuit determined that Clajon primarily used the gathering system in a manner consistent with the description of Asset Class 13.2 (i.e., as gathering pipelines). The descriptive language of the asset class does not require that the producer be the owner of the gathering system assets. The result is that there is no distinction between the gathering system assets of producers and nonproducers, for purposes of depreciation deductions.

¶ 191

Rev. Proc. 87-56 (IRS Recovery Period Table for MACRS Assets)

The following text is from IRS Publication 946 (How to Depreciate Property) and explains how to use the table of class lives and recovery periods contained in Rev. Proc. 87-56. For additional information on how to determine an asset's recovery period under MACRS, see ¶ 190.

The *Table of Class Lives and Recovery Periods* has two sections. The first section, *Specific Depreciable Assets Used In All Business Activities, Except as Noted:,* generally lists assets used in all business activities. It is shown as Table B-1. The second section, *Depreciable Assets Used In The Following Activities:,* describes assets used only in certain activities. It is shown as Table B-2.

How To Use the Tables

You will need to look at both Table B-1 and B-2 to find the correct recovery period. Generally, if the property is listed in Table B-1 you use the recovery period shown in that table. However, if the property is specifically listed in Table B-2 under the type of activity in which it is used, you use the recovery period listed under the activity in that table. Use the tables in the order shown below to determine the recovery period of your depreciable property.

Table B-1. Check Table B-1 for a description of the property. If it is described in Table B-1, also check Table B-2 to find the activity in which the property is being used. If the activity is described in Table B-2, read the text (if any) under the title to determine if the property is specifically included in that asset class. If it is, use the recovery period shown in the appropriate column of Table B-2 following the description of the activity. If the activity is not described in Table B-2 or if the activity is described but property either is not specifically included in or is specifically excluded from that asset class, then use the recovery period shown in the appropriate column following the description of the property in Table B-1.

Table B-2. If the property is not listed in Table B-1, check Table B-2 to find the activity in which the property is being used and use the recovery period shown in the appropriate column following the description.

Property not in either table. If the activity or the property is not included in either table, check the end of Table B-2 to find *Certain Property for Which Recovery Periods Assigned.* This property generally has a recovery period of 7 years for GDS or 12 years for ADS. For residential rental property and nonresidential real property see Appendix A, Chart 2 or *Which Recovery Period Applies* in chapter 4 for recovery periods for both GDS and ADS.

Example (1): Richard Green is a paper manufacturer. During the year, he made substantial improvements to the land on which his paper plant is located. He checks Table B-1 and finds land improvements under asset class 00.3. He then checks Table B-2 and finds his activity, paper manufacturing, under asset class 26.1, *Manufacture of Pulp and Paper.* He uses the recovery period under this asset class because it specifically includes land improvements. The land improvements have a 13-year class life and a 7-year recovery period for GDS. If he elects to use ADS, the recovery period is 13 years. If Richard only looked at Table B-1, he would select asset class 00.3 *Land Improvements* and incorrectly use a recovery period of 15 years for GDS or 20 years for ADS.

Example (2): Sam Plower produces rubber products. During the year, he made substantial improvements to the land on which his rubber plant is located. He checks Table B-1 and finds land improvements under asset class 00.3. He then checks Table B-2 and finds his activity, producing rubber products, under asset class 30.1 *Manufacture of Rubber Products.* Reading the headings and descriptions under asset class 30.1, Sam finds that it does not include land improvements. Therefore, Sam uses the recovery period under asset class 00.3. The land improvements have a 20-year class life and a 15-year recovery period for GDS. If he elects to use the ADS method, the recovery period is 20 years.

Example (3): Pam Martin owns a retail clothing store. During the year, she purchased a desk and a cash register for use in her business. She checks Table B-1 and finds office furniture under asset class 00.11. Cash registers are not listed in any of the asset classes in Table B-1. She then checks Table B-2 and finds her activity, retail store, under asset class 57.0, *Distributive Trades and Services,* which includes **assets used in wholesale and retail trade**. This asset class does not specifically list office furniture or a cash register. She looks back at Table B-1 and uses asset class 00.11 for the desk. The desk has a 10-year class life and a 7-year recovery period for GDS. If she elects to use ADS, the recovery period is 10 years. For the cash register, she uses asset class 57.0 because cash registers are not listed in Table B-1 but it is an **asset** used in her retail business. The cash register has a 9-year class life and a 5-year recovery period for GDS. If she elects to use the ADS method, the recovery period is 9 years.

[End of IRS text.—CCH.]

The Tax Court has ruled (in accordance with the preceding IRS explanation) that the depreciation period of an asset that was specifically described in an asset group (Asset Classes 00.11 through 00.4, specific depreciable assets used in all business activities) but could also be included in an activity group (Asset Classes 01.1 through 80.0, depreciable assets used in specified activities), should be determined by reference to the asset group classification (*Norwest Corp. and Subsidiaries*, 111 TC 105, Dec. 52,830). The case involved office furniture used by a bank. Banking is an activity described in Asset Class 57.0. Asset Class 57.0 (five-year recovery period) includes "assets used in wholesale and retail trade, and personal and professional services." However, Asset Class 00.11 (seven-year recovery period) specifically includes "furniture and fixtures that are not a structural component of a building." Applying the priority rule, the furniture was classified as 7-year property (Asset Class 00.11). If the office furniture had also been specifically described as included in Asset Class 57.0, then it would have been treated as 5-year property, as the preceding IRS guidelines also dictate.

It is unclear from the decision whether any of the furniture involved was of a type suitable only for use in banks (for example, check writing stands). In an earlier decision involving the same taxpayer, the IRS conceded that this type of furniture was 5-year property (*Norwest Corp. and Subsidiaries,* 70 TCM 416, Dec. 50,834(M)). See ¶ 106.

Predecessors to Rev. Proc. 87-56

Useful insight into the development of the current asset classes contained in Rev. Proc. 87-56 may be obtained by referring to various predecessor revenue procedures and publications issued by the IRS.

Bulletin F (revised January 1942)—provides an asset-by-asset listing of useful lives;

Rev. Proc. 62-21, 1962-2 CB 418—provides useful lives ("guideline lives") for assets used by businesses in general and guideline lives for assets used in specified business activities ("guideline classes"). Supplement II, 1963-2 CB 744, which consists of Questions and Answers, was published to assist taxpayers in applying Rev. Proc. 62-21;

Rev. Proc. 71-25, 1971-2 CB 553—sets forth asset guideline classes, asset guideline periods, and asset depreciation ranges for purposes of the Asset Depreciation Range System (ADR);

Rev. Proc. 72-10, 1972-1 CB 721—supersedes Rev. Proc. 71-25 and updates asset guideline classes, asset guideline periods, and asset depreciation ranges. Also supersedes Rev. Proc. 62-21;

Rev. Proc. 77-10, 1977-1 CB 548—updates and supersedes Rev. Proc. 72-10; and

Rev. Proc. 83-35, 1983-1 CB 745—updates and supersedes Rev. Proc. 77-10. The asset guideline periods (midpoint class lives) set forth in Rev. Proc. 83-35 are also used in defining the classes of recovery property under the Accelerated Cost Recovery System (i.e., pre-MACRS Code Sec. 168 property).

Rev. Proc. 87-56 and its predecessors are based in large part on the Standard Industrial Classification Manual (SIC) published by the Office of Management and Budget. SIC has precise categorization by primary business activity using language very similar to that found in Rev. Proc. 87-56. The asset class numbers for the particular business activities described in Rev. Proc. 87-56 are largely taken from SIC. For example, in ruling that gaming devices such as slot machines are 7-year property (Asset Class 79.0 (relating to assets used in the provision of entertainment services)), the IRS cited the SIC classification numbers for operators of coin operated amusement devices and casino operations which fell within SIC asset class 79 (IRS Coordinated Issue Paper for the Gaming Industry, April 10, 2000). The SIC manual (1987 version) is reproduced at the following government web site:

http://www.osha.gov/oshstats

While SIC has precise categorization by primary business activity using language very similar to that found in Rev. Proc. 87-56, that revenue procedure departs dramatically from the categorization scheme of SIC by establishing the two broad categories of depreciable assets (viz., assets used in all business activities (Table B-1) and assets used in particular business activities (Table B-2). The asset class numbers for specific business activities, however, are largely taken from SIC.

Full Text of Rev. Proc. 87-56 Recovyer Period Tables

			Recovery Periods (in years)	
Asset class	*Description of assets included*	*Class Life (in years)*	*General Depreciation System*	*Alternative Depreciation System*
	[Table B-1]			
	SPECIFIC DEPRECIABLE ASSETS USED IN ALL BUSINESS ACTIVITIES, EXCEPT AS NOTED:			
00.11	**Office Furniture, Fixtures, and Equipment:** Includes furniture and fixtures that are not a structural component of a building. Includes such assets as desks, files, safes, and communications equipment. Does not include communications equipment that is included in other classes	10	7	10

Asset class	Description of assets included	Class Life (in years)	Recovery Periods (in years) General Depreciation System	Alternative Depreciation System
00.12	**Information Systems:** Includes computers and their peripheral equipment used in administering normal business transactions and the maintenance of business records, their retrieval and analysis. Information systems are defined as: 1) Computers: A computer is a programmable electronically activated device capable of accepting information, applying prescribed processes to the information, and supplying the results of these processes with or without human intervention. It usually consists of a central processing unit containing extensive storage, logic, arithmetic, and control capabilities. Excluded from this category are adding machines, electronic desk calculators, etc. and other equipment described in class 00.13. 2) Peripheral equipment consists of the auxiliary machines which are designed to be placed under control of the central processing unit. Nonlimiting examples are: Card readers, card punches, magnetic tape feeds, high speed printers, optical character readers, tape cassettes, mass storage units, paper tape equipment, keypunches, data entry devices, teleprinters, terminals, tape drives, disc drives, disc files, disc packs, visual image projector tubes, card sorters, plotters, and collators. Peripheral equipment may be used on-line or off-line. Does not include equipment that is an integral part of other capital equipment that is included in other classes of economic activity, i.e., computers used primarily for process or production control, switching, channeling, and automating distributive trades and services such as point of sale (POS) computer systems. Also, does not include equipment of a kind used primarily for amusement or entertainment of the user . .	6	5	5
00.13	**Data Handling Equipment, except Computers:** Includes only typewriters, calculators, adding and accounting machines, copiers, and duplicating equipment	6	5	6
00.21	**Airplanes (airframes and engines), except those used in commercial or contract carrying of passengers or freight, and all helicopters (airframes and engines)** . . .	6	5	6
00.22	**Automobiles, Taxis**	3	5	5
00.23	**Buses**	9	5	9
00.241	**Light General Purpose Trucks:** Includes trucks for use over the road (actual unloaded weight less than 13,000 pounds) .	4	5	5
00.242	**Heavy General Purpose Trucks:** Includes heavy general purpose trucks, concrete ready mix-truckers, and ore trucks, for use over the road (actual unloaded weight 13,000 pounds or more)	6	5	6

Asset class	Description of assets included	Class Life (in years)	Recovery Periods (in years) General Depreciation System	Alternative Depreciation System
00.25	**Railroad Cars and Locomotives, except those owned by railroad transportation companies**	15	7	15
00.26	**Tractor Units For Use Over-The-Road** . .	4	3	4
00.27	**Trailers and Trailer-Mounted Containers**	6	5	6
00.28	**Vessels, Barges, Tugs, and Similar Water Transportation Equipment, except those used in marine construction**	18	10	18
00.3	**Land Improvements:** Includes improvements directly to or added to land, whether such improvements are section 1245 property or section 1250 property, provided such improvements are depreciable. Examples of such assets might include sidewalks, roads, canals, waterways, drainage facilities, sewers (not including municipal sewers in Class 51), wharves and docks, bridges, fences, landscaping, shrubbery, or radio and television transmitting towers. Does not include land improvements that are explicitly included in any other class, and buildings and structural components as defined in section 1.48-1(e) of the regulations. Excludes public utility initial clearing and grading land improvements as specified in Rev. Rul. 72-403, 1972-2 C.B. 102.	20	15	20

Asset class	Description of assets included	Class Life (in years)	Recovery Periods (in years) General Depreciation System	Alternative Depreciation System
00.4	**Industrial Steam and Electric Generation and/or Distribution Systems:** Includes assets, whether such assets are section 1245 property or 1250 property, providing such assets are depreciable, used in the production and/or distribution of electricity with rated total capacity in excess of 500 Kilowatts and/or assets used in the production and/or distribution of steam with rated total capacity in excess of 12,500 pounds per hour for use by the taxpayer in its industrial manufacturing process or plant activity and not ordinarily available for sale to others. Does not include buildings and structural components as defined in section 1.48-1(e) of the regulations. Assets used to generate and/or distribute electricity or steam of the type described above but of lesser rated capacity are not included, but are included in the appropriate manufacturing equipment classes elsewhere specified. Also includes electric generating and steam distribution assets, which may utilize steam produced by a waste reduction and resource recovery plant, used by the taxpayer in its industrial manufacturing process or plant activity. Steam and chemical recovery boiler systems used for the recovery and regeneration of chemicals used in manufacturing, with rated capacity in excess of that described above, with specifically related distribution and return systems are not included but are included in appropriate manufacturing equipment classes elsewhere specified. An example of an excluded steam and chemical recovery boiler system is that used in the pulp and paper manufacturing industry	22	15	22

[Table B-2]

DEPRECIABLE ASSETS USED IN THE FOLLOWING ACTIVITIES:

Asset class	Description of assets included	Class Life (in years)	General Depreciation System	Alternative Depreciation System
01.1	**Agriculture:** Includes machinery and equipment, grain bins, and fences but no other land improvements, that are used in the production of crops or plants, vines, and trees; livestock; the operation of farm dairies, nurseries, greenhouses, sod farms, mushrooms cellars, cranberry bogs, apiaries, and fur farms; the performance of agriculture, animal husbandry, and horticultural services [new farm machinery and equipment placed in service in 2009 may qualify for a 5-year recovery period (Code Sec. 168(e)(3)(B)(vii)). See ¶ 118—CCH.]	10	7	10
01.11	**Cotton Ginning Assets**	12	7	12
01.21	**Cattle, Breeding or Dairy**	7	5	7
01.221	**Any breeding or work horse that is 12 years old or less at the time it is placed in service**[1]	10	7	10

Asset class	Description of assets included	Class Life (in years)	Recovery Periods (in years) General Depreciation System	Alternative Depreciation System
01.222	**Any breeding or work horse that is more than 12 years old at the time it is placed in service**[1]	10	3	10
01.223	**Any race horse that is more than 2 years old at the time it is placed in service** [Any race horse placed in service after December 31, 2008 and before January 1, 2014 is three-year property (Code Sec. 168(e)(3)(A)(i)). See ¶ 103—CCH.][1]	[2]	3	12
01.224	**Any horse that is more than 12 years old at the time it is placed in service and that is neither a race horse nor a horse described in class 01.222**[1]	[2]	3	12
01.225	**Any horse not described in classes 01.221, 01.222, 01.223, or 01.224**	[2]	7	12
01.23	**Hogs, Breeding**	3	3	3
01.24	**Sheep and Goats, Breeding**	5	5	5
01.3	**Farm buildings except structures included in Class 01.4**	25	20	25
01.4	**Single purpose agricultural or horticultural structures (within the meaning of section 168(i)(13) of the Code)**	15	10 [3]	15
10.0	**Mining:** Includes assets used in the mining and quarrying of metallic and nonmetallic minerals (including sand, gravel, stone, and clay) and the milling, beneficiation and other primary preparation of such materials	10	7	10
13.0	**Offshore Drilling:** Includes assets used in offshore drilling for oil and gas such as floating, self-propelled and other drilling vessels, barges, platforms, and drilling equipment and support vessels such as tenders, barges, towboats and crewboats. Excludes oil and gas production assets	7.5	5	7.5
13.1	**Drilling of Oil and Gas Wells:** Includes assets used in the drilling of onshore oil and gas wells and the provision of geophysical and other exploration services; and the provision of such oil and gas field services as chemical treatment, plugging and abandoning of wells and cementing or perforating well casings. Does not include assets used in the performance of any of these activities and services by integrated petroleum and natural gas producers for their own account	6	5	6

Asset class	Description of assets included	Class Life (in years)	Recovery Periods (in years): General Depreciation System	Alternative Depreciation System
13.2	**Exploration for and Production of Petroleum and Natural Gas Deposits:** Includes assets used by petroleum and natural gas producers for drilling wells and production of petroleum and natural gas, including gathering pipelines and related storage facilities. Also includes petroleum and natural gas offshore transportation facilities used by producers and others consisting of platforms (other than drilling platforms classified in Class 13.0), compression or pumping equipment, and gathering and transmission lines to the first onshore transshipment facility. The assets used in the first onshore transshipment facility are also included and consist of separation equipment (used for separation of natural gas, liquids, and solids), compression or pumping equipment (other than equipment classified in Class 49.23), and liquid holding or storage facilities (other than those classified in Class 49.25). Does not include support vessels	14	7	14
13.3	**Petroleum Refining:** Includes assets used for the distillation, fractionation, and catalytic cracking of crude petroleum into gasoline and its other components	16	10	16
15.0	**Construction:** Includes assets used in construction by general building, special trade, heavy and marine construction contractors, operative and investment builders, real estate subdividers and developers, and others except railroads	6	5	6
20.1	**Manufacture of Grain and Grain Mill Products:** Includes assets used in the production of flours, cereals, livestock feeds, and other grain and grain mill products	17	10	17
20.2	**Manufacture of Sugar and Sugar Products:** Includes assets used in the production of raw sugar, syrup, or finished sugar from sugar cane or sugar beets	18	10	18
20.3	**Manufacture of Vegetable Oils and Vegetable Oil Products:** Includes assets used in the production of oil from vegetable materials and the manufacture of related vegetable oil products	18	10	18
20.4	**Manufacture of Other Food and Kindred Products:** Includes assets used in the production of foods and beverages not included in classes 20.1, 20.2 and 20.3	12	7	12

Asset class	Description of assets included	Class Life (in years)	Recovery Periods (in years) General Depreciation System	Alternative Depreciation System
20.5	**Manufacture of Food and Beverages—Special Handling Devices:** Includes assets defined as specialized materials handling devices such as returnable pallets, palletized containers, and fish processing equipment including boxes, baskets, carts, and flaking trays used in activities as defined in classes 20.1, 20.2, 20.3 and 20.4. Does not include general purpose small tools such as wrenches and drills, both hand and power-driven, and other general purpose equipment such as conveyors, transfer equipment, and materials handling devices	4	3	4
21.0	**Manufacture of Tobacco and Tobacco Products:** Includes assets used in the production of cigarettes, cigars, smoking and chewing tobacco, snuff, and other tobacco products	15	7	15
22.1	**Manufacture of Knitted Goods:** Includes assets used in the production of knitted and netted fabrics and lace. Assets used in yarn preparation, bleaching, dyeing, printing, and other similar finishing processes, texturing, and packaging, are elsewhere classified	7.5	5	7.5
22.2	**Manufacture of Yarn, Thread, and Woven Fabric:** Includes assets used in the production of spun yarns including the preparing, blending, spinning, and twisting of fibers into yarns and threads, the preparation of yarns such as twisting, warping, and winding, the production of covered elastic yarn and thread, cordage, woven fabric, tire fabric, twisted jute for packaging, mattresses, pads, sheets, and industrial belts, and the processing of textile mill waste to recover fibers, flocks, and shoddies. Assets used to manufacture carpets, man-made fibers, and nonwovens, and assets used in texturing, bleaching, dyeing, printing, and other similar finishing processes, are elsewhere classified.	11	7	11

Asset class	Description of assets included	Class Life (in years)	Recovery Periods (in years): General Depreciation System	Recovery Periods (in years): Alternative Depreciation System
22.3	**Manufacture of Carpets, and Dyeing, Finishing, and Packaging of Textile Products and Manufacture of Medical and Dental Supplies:** Includes assets used in the production of carpets, rugs, mats, woven carpet backing, chenille, and other tufted products, and assets used in the joining together of backing with carpet yarn or fabric. Includes assets used in washing, scouring, bleaching, dyeing, printing, drying, and similar finishing processes applied to textile fabrics, yarns, threads, and other textile goods. Includes assets used in the production and packaging of textile products, other than apparel, by creasing, forming, trimming, cutting, and sewing, such as the preparation of carpet and fabric samples, or similar joining together processes (other than the production of scrim reinforced paper products and laminated paper products) such as the sewing and folding of hosiery and panty hose, and the creasing, folding, trimming, and cutting of fabrics to produce nonwoven products, such as disposable diapers and sanitary products. Also includes assets used in the production of medical and dental supplies other than drugs and medicines. Assets used in the manufacture of nonwoven carpet backing, and hard surface floor covering such as tile, rubber, and cork, are elsewhere classified .	9	5	9
22.4	**Manufacture of Textured Yarns:** Includes assets used in the processing of yarns to impart bulk and/or stretch properties to the yarn. The principal machines involved are falsetwist, draw, beam-to-beam, and stuffer box texturing equipment and related highspeed twisters and winders. Assets, as described above, which are used to further process man-made fibers are elsewhere classified when located in the same plant in an integrated operation with man-made fiber producing assets. Assets used to manufacture man-made fibers and assets used in bleaching, dyeing, printing, and other similar finishing processes, are elsewhere classified	8	5	8

Asset class	Description of assets included	Class Life (in years)	Recovery Periods (in years): General Depreciation System	Recovery Periods (in years): Alternative Depreciation System
22.5	**Manufacture of Nonwoven Fabrics:** Includes assets used in the production of nonwoven fabrics, felt goods including felt hats, padding, batting, wadding, oakum, and fillings, from new materials and from textile mill waste. Nonwoven fabrics are defined as fabrics (other than reinforced and laminated composites consisting of nonwovens and other products) manufactured by bonding natural and/or synthetic fibers and/or filaments by means of induced mechanical interlocking, fluid entanglement, chemical adhesion, thermal or solvent reaction, or by combination thereof other than natural hydration bonding as occurs with natural cellulose fibers. Such means include resin bonding, web bonding, and melt bonding. Specifically includes assets used to make flocked and needle punched products other than carpets and rugs. Assets, as described above, which are used to manufacture nonwovens are elsewhere classified when located in the same plant in an integrated operation with man-made fiber producing assets. Assets used to manufacture man-made fibers and assets used in bleaching, dyeing, printing, and other similar finishing processes, are elsewhere classified	10	7	10
23.0	**Manufacture of Apparel and Other Finished Products:** Includes assets used in the production of clothing and fabricated textile products by the cutting and sewing of woven fabrics, other textile products, and furs; but does not include assets used in the manufacture of apparel from rubber and leather	9	5	9
24.1	**Cutting of Timber:** Includes logging machinery and equipment and roadbuilding equipment used by logging and sawmill operators and pulp manufacturers for their own account	6	5	6
24.2	**Sawing of Dimensional Stock from Logs:** Includes machinery and equipment installed in permanent or well established sawmills .	10	7	10
24.3	**Sawing of Dimensional Stock from Logs:** Includes machinery and equipment installed in sawmills characterized by temporary foundations and a lack, or minimum amount, of lumberhandling, drying, and residue disposal equipment and facilities	6	5	6
24.4	**Manufacture of Wood Products, and Furniture:** Includes assets used in the production of plywood, hardboard, flooring, veneers, furniture, and other wood products, including the treatment of poles and timber	10	7	10

Asset class	Description of assets included	Class Life (in years)	Recovery Periods (in years) General Depreciation System	Alternative Depreciation System
26.1	**Manufacture of Pulp and Paper:** Includes assets for pulp materials handling and storage, pulp mill processing, bleach processing, paper and paperboard manufacturing, and on-line finishing. Includes pollution control assets and all land improvements associated with the factory site or production process such as effluent ponds and canals, provided such improvements are depreciable but does not include buildings and structural components as defined in section 1.48-1(e)(1) of the regulations. Includes steam and chemical recovery boiler systems, with any rated capacity, used for the recovery and regeneration of chemicals used in manufacturing. Does not include assets used either in pulpwood logging, or in the manufacture of hardboard	13	7	13
26.2	**Manufacture of Converted Paper, Paperboard, and Pulp Products:** Includes assets used for modification, or remanufacture of paper and pulp into converted products, such as paper coated off the paper machine, paper bags, paper boxes, cartons and envelopes. Does not include assets used for manufacture of nonwovens that are elsewhere classified	10	7	10
27.0	**Printing, Publishing, and Allied Industries:** Includes assets used in printing by one or more processes, such as letter-press, lithography, gravure, or screen; the performance of services for the printing trade, such as bookbinding, typesetting, engraving, photo-engraving, and electrotyping; and the publication of newspapers, books, and periodicals	11	7	11

Asset class	Description of assets included	Class Life (in years)	Recovery Periods (in years) General Depreciation System	Alternative Depreciation System
28.0	**Manufacture of Chemicals and Allied Products:** Includes assets used to manufacture basic organic and inorganic chemicals; chemical products to be used in further manufacture, such as synthetic fibers and plastics materials; and finished chemical products. Includes assets used to further process man-made fibers, to manufacture plastic film, and to manufacture nonwoven fabrics, when such assets are located in the same plant in an integrated operation with chemical products producing assets. Also includes assets used to manufacture photographic supplies, such as film, photographic paper, sensitized photographic paper, and developing chemicals. Includes all land improvements associated with plant site or production processes, such as effluent ponds and canals, provided such land improvements are depreciable but does not include buildings and structural components as defined in section 1.48-1(e) of the regulations. Does not include assets used in the manufacture of finished rubber and plastic products or in the production of natural gas products, butane, propane, and by-products of natural gas production plants	9.5	5	9.5
30.1	**Manufacture of Rubber Products:** Includes assets used for the production of products from natural, synthetic, or reclaimed rubber, gutta percha, balata, or gutta siak, such as tires, tubes, rubber footwear, mechanical rubber goods, heels and soles, flooring, and rubber sundries, and in the recapping, retreading, and rebuilding of tires	14	7	14
30.11[4]	**Manufacture of Rubber Products—Special Tools and Devices:** Includes assets defined as special tools, such as jigs, dies, mandrels, molds, lasts, patterns, specialty containers, pallets, shells; and tire molds, and accessory parts such as rings and insert plates used in activities as defined in class 30.1. Does not include tire building drums and accessory parts and general purpose small tools such as wrenches and drills, both power and hand-driven, and other general purpose equipment such as conveyors and transfer equipment.	4	3	4
30.2	**Manufacture of Finished Plastic Products:** Includes assets used in the manufacture of plastics products and the molding of primary plastics for the trade. Does not include assets used in the manufacture of basic plastics materials nor the manufacture of phonograph records	11	7	11

Asset class	Description of assets included	Class Life (in years)	Recovery Periods (in years) General Depreciation System	Alternative Depreciation System
30.21	**Manufacture of Finished Plastic Products—Special Tools:** Includes assets defined as special tools, such as jigs, dies, fixtures, molds, patterns, gauges, and specialty transfer and shipping devices, used in activities as defined in class 30.2. Special tools are specifically designed for the production or processing of particular parts and have no significant utilitarian value and cannot be adapted to further or different use after changes or improvements are made in the model design of the particular part produced by the special tools. Does not include general purpose small tools such as wrenches and drills, both hand and power-driven, and other general purpose equipment such as conveyors, transfer equipment, and materials handling devices	3.5	3	3.5
31.0	**Manufacture of Leather and Leather Products:** Includes assets used in the tanning, currying, and finishing of hides and skins; the processing of fur pelts; and the manufacture of finished leather products, such as footwear, belting, apparel, and luggage . . .	11	7	11
32.1	**Manufacture of Glass Products:** Includes assets used in the production of flat, blown, or pressed products of glass, such as float and window glass, glass containers, glassware and fiberglass. Does not include assets used in the manufacture of lenses . .	14	7	14
32.11	**Manufacture of Glass Products—Special Tools:** Includes assets defined as special tools such as molds, patterns, pallets, and specialty transfer and shipping devices such as steel racks to transport automotive glass, used in activities as defined in class 32.1. Special tools are specifically designed for the production or processing of particular parts and have no significant utilitarian value and cannot be adapted to further or different use after changes or improvements are made in the model design of the particular part produced by the special tools. Does not include general purpose small tools such as wrenches and drills, both hand and power-driven, and other general purpose equipment such as conveyors, transfer equipment, and materials handling devices	2.5	3	2.5
32.2	**Manufacture of Cement:** Includes assets used in the production of cement, but does not include any assets used in the manufacture of concrete and concrete products nor in any mining or extraction process	20	15	20

Asset class	Description of assets included	Class Life (in years)	Recovery Periods (in years) General Depreciation System	Alternative Depreciation System
32.3	**Manufacture of Other Stone and Clay Products:** Includes assets used in the manufacture of products from materials in the form of clay and stone, such as brick, tile, and pipe; pottery and related products, such as vitreous-china, plumbing fixtures, earthenware and ceramic insulating materials; and also includes assets used in manufacture of concrete and concrete products. Does not include assets used in any mining or extraction processes	15	7	15
33.2	**Manufacture of Primary Nonferrous Metals:** Includes assets used in the smelting, refining, and electrolysis of nonferrous metals from ore, pig, or scrap, the rolling, drawing, and alloying of nonferrous metals; the manufacture of castings, forgings, and other basic products of nonferrous metals; and the manufacture of nails, spikes, structural shapes, tubing, wire, and cable	14	7	14
33.21	**Manufacture of Primary Nonferrous Metals—Special Tools:** Includes assets defined as special tools such as dies, jigs, molds, patterns, fixtures, gauges, and drawings concerning such special tools used in the activities as defined in class 33.2, Manufacture of Primary Nonferrous Metals. Special tools are specifically designed for the production or processing of particular products or parts and have no significant utilitarian value and cannot be adapted to further or different use after changes or improvements are made in the model design of the particular part produced by the special tools. Does not include general purpose small tools such as wrenches and drills, both hand and power-driven, and other general purpose equipment such as conveyors, transfer equipment, and materials handling devices. Rolls, mandrels and refractories are not included in class 33.21 but are included in class 33.2	6.5	5	6.5
33.3	**Manufacture of Foundry Products:** Includes assets used in the casting of iron and steel, including related operations such as molding and coremaking. Also includes assets used in the finishing of castings and patternmaking when performed at the foundry, all special tools and related land improvements	14	7	14

Asset class	Description of assets included	Class Life (in years)	Recovery Periods (in years) General Depreciation System	Alternative Depreciation System
33.4	**Manufacture of Primary Steel Mill Products:** Includes assets used in the smelting, reduction, and refining of iron and steel from ore, pig, or scrap; the rolling, drawing and alloying of steel; the manufacture of nails, spikes, structural shapes, tubing, wire, and cable. Includes assets used by steel service centers, ferrous metal forges, and assets used in coke production, regardless of ownership. Also includes related land improvements and all special tools used in the above activities .	15	7	15
34.0	**Manufacture of Fabricated Metal Products:** Includes assets used in the production of metal cans, tinware, fabricated structural metal products, metal stampings, and other ferrous and nonferrous metal and wire products not elsewhere classified. Does not include assets used to manufacture non-electric heating apparatus	12	7	12
34.01	**Manufacturer of Fabricated Metal Products—Special Tools:** Includes assets defined as special tools such as dies, jigs, molds, patterns, fixtures, gauges, and returnable containers and drawings concerning such special tools used in the activities as defined in class 34.0. Special tools are specifically designed for the production or processing of particular machine components, products, or parts, and have no significant utilitarian value and cannot be adapted to further or different use after changes or improvements are made in the model design of the particular part produced by the special tools. Does not include general purpose small tools such as wrenches and drills, both hand and power-driven, and other general purpose equipment such as conveyors, transfer equipment, and materials handling devices	3	3	3

Asset class	Description of assets included	Class Life (in years)	Recovery Periods (in years) General Depreciation System	Alternative Depreciation System
35.0	**Manufacture of Electrical and Non-Electrical Machinery and Other Mechanical Products:** Includes assets used to manufacture or rebuild finished machinery and equipment and replacement parts thereof such as machine tools, general industrial and special industry machinery, electrical power generation, transmission, and distribution systems, space heating, cooling, and refrigeration systems, commercial and home appliances, farm and garden machinery, construction machinery, mining and oil field machinery, internal combustion engines (except those elsewhere classified), turbines (except those that power airborne vehicles), batteries, lamps and lighting fixtures, carbon and graphite products, and electromechanical and mechanical products including business machines, instruments, watches and clocks, vending and amusement machines, photographic equipment, medical and dental equipment and appliances, and ophthalmic goods. Includes assets used by manufacturers or rebuilders of such finished machinery and equipment in activities elsewhere classified such as the manufacture of castings, forgings, rubber and plastic products, electronic subassemblies or other manufacturing activities if the interim products are used by the same manufacturer primarily in the manufacture, assembly, or rebuilding of such finished machinery and equipment. Does not include assets used in mining, assets used in the manufacture of primary ferrous and nonferrous metals, assets included in class 00.11 through 00.4 and assets elsewhere classified	10	7	10

Asset class	Description of assets included	Class Life (in years)	Recovery Periods (in years) General Depreciation System	Alternative Depreciation System
36.0	**Manufacture of Electronic Components, Products, and Systems:** Includes assets used in the manufacture of electronic communication, computation, instrumentation and control system, including airborne applications, also includes assets used in the manufacture of electronic products such as frequency and amplitude modulated transmitters and receivers, electronic switching stations, television cameras, video recorders, record players and tape recorders, computers and computer peripheral machines, and electronic instruments, watches, and clocks; also includes assets used in the manufacture of components, provided their primary use is in products and systems defined above such as electron tubes, capacitors, coils, resistors, printed circuit substrates, switches, harness cables, lasers, fiber optic devices, and magnetic media devices. Specifically excludes assets used to manufacture electronic products and components, photocopiers, typewriters, postage meters and other electromechanical and mechanical business machines and instruments that are elsewhere classified. Does not include semiconductor manufacturing equipment included in class 36.1	6	5	6
36.1	**Manufacture of Semiconductors:** Any Semiconductor Manufacturing Equipment [Includes equipment used in the manufacturing of semiconductors if the primary use of the semiconductors so produced is in products and systems of the type defined in class 36.0 (IRS Pub. 946)] . .	5	5	5

Asset class	Description of assets included	Class Life (in years)	Recovery Periods (in years) General Depreciation System	Alternative Depreciation System
37.11	**Manufacture of Motor Vehicles:** Includes assets used in the manufacture and assembly of finished automobiles, trucks, trailers, motor homes, and buses. Does not include assets used in mining, printing and publishing, production of primary metals, electricity, or steam, or the manufacture of glass, industrial chemicals, batteries, or rubber products, which are classified elsewhere. Includes assets used in manufacturing activities elsewhere classified other than those excluded above, where such activities are incidental to and an integral part of the manufacture and assembly of finished motor vehicles such as the manufacture of parts and subassemblies of fabricated metal products, electrical equipment, textiles, plastics, leather, and foundry and forging operations. Does not include any assets not classified in manufacturing activity classes, e.g., does not include any assets classified in asset guideline classes 00.11 through 00.4. Activities will be considered incidental to the manufacture and assembly of finished motor vehicles only if 75 percent or more of the value of the products produced under one roof are used for the manufacture and assembly of finished motor vehicles. Parts that are produced as a normal replacement stock complement in connection with the manufacture and assembly of finished motor vehicles are considered used for the manufacture and assembly of finished motor vehicles. Does not include assets used in the manufacture of component parts if these assets are used by taxpayers not engaged in the assembly of finished motor vehicles . . .	12	7	12
37.12	**Manufacture of Motor Vehicles—Special Tools:** Includes assets defined as special tools, such as jigs, dies, fixtures, molds, patterns, gauges, and specialty transfer and shipping devices, owned by manufacturers of finished motor vehicles and used in qualified activities as defined in class 37.11. Special tools are specifically designed for the production or processing of particular motor vehicle components and have no significant utilitarian value, and cannot be adapted to further or different use, after changes or improvements are made in the model design of the particular part produced by the special tools. Does not include general purpose small tools such as wrenches and drills, both hand and powerdriven, and other general purpose equipment such as conveyors, transfer equipment, and materials handling devices .	3	3	3

Asset class	Description of assets included	Class Life (in years)	Recovery Periods (in years) General Depreciation System	Alternative Depreciation System
37.2	**Manufacture of Aerospace Products:** Includes assets used in the manufacture and assembly of airborne vehicles and their component parts including hydraulic, pneumatic, electrical, and mechanical systems. Does not include assets used in the production of electronic airborne detection, guidance, control, radiation, computation, test, navigation, and communication equipment or the components thereof	10	7	10
37.31	**Ship and Boat Building Machinery and Equipment:** Includes assets used in the manufacture and repair of ships, boats, caissons, marine drilling rigs, and special fabrications not included in asset classes 37.32 and 37.33. Specifically includes all manufacturing and repairing machinery and equipment, including machinery and equipment used in the operation of assets included in asset class 37.32. Excludes buildings and their structural components	12	7	12
37.32	**Ship and Boat Building Dry Docks and Land Improvements:** Includes assets used in the manufacture and repair of ships, boats, caissons, marine drilling rigs, and special fabrications not included in asset classes 37.31 and 37.33. Specifically includes floating and fixed dry docks, ship basins, graving docks, shipways, piers, and all other land improvements such as water, sewer, and electric systems. Excludes buildings and their structural components	16	10	16
37.33	**Ship and Boat Building—Special Tools:** Includes assets defined as special tools such as dies, jigs, molds, patterns, fixtures, gauges, and drawings concerning such special tools used in the activities defined in classes 37.31 and 37.32. Special tools are specifically designed for the production or processing of particular machine components, products, or parts, and have no significant utilitarian value and cannot be adapted to further or different use after changes or improvements are made in the model design of the particular part produced by the special tools. Does not include general purpose small tools such as wrenches and drills, both hand and power-driven, and other general purpose equipment such as conveyors, transfer equipment, and materials handling devices	6.5	5	6.5
37.41	**Manufacture of Locomotives:** Includes assets used in building or rebuilding railroad locomotives (including mining and industrial locomotives). Does not include assets of railroad transportation companies or assets of companies which manufacture components of locomotives but do not manufacture finished locomotives	11.5	7	11.5

Asset class	Description of assets included	Class Life (in years)	Recovery Periods (in years) General Depreciation System	Alternative Depreciation System
37.42	**Manufacture of Railroad Cars:** Includes assets used in building or rebuilding railroad freight or passenger cars (including rail transit cars). Does not include assets of railroad transportation companies or assets of companies which manufacture components of railroad cars but do not manufacture finished railroad cars	12	7	12
39.0	**Manufacture of Athletic, Jewelry and Other Goods:** Includes assets used in the production of jewelry; musical instruments; toys and sporting goods; motion picture and television films and tapes; and pens, pencils, office and art supplies, brooms, brushes, caskets, etc.	12	7	12
	Railroad Transportation: Classes with the prefix 40 include the assets identified below that are used in the commercial and contract carrying of passengers and freight by rail. Assets of electrified railroads will be classified in a manner corresponding to that set forth below for railroads not independently operated as electric lines. Excludes the assets included in classes with the prefix beginning 00.1 and 00.2 above, and also excludes any non-depreciable assets included in Interstate Commerce Commission accounts enumerated for this class.			
40.1	**Railroad Machinery and Equipment:** Includes assets classified in the following Interstate Commerce Commission accounts: **Roadway accounts:** (16) Station and office buildings (freight handling machinery and equipment only) (25) TOFC/COFC terminals (freight handling machinery and equipment only) (26) Communication systems (27) Signals and interlockers (37) Roadway machines (44) Shop machinery Equipment Accounts: (52) Locomotives (53) Freight train cars (54) Passenger train cars (57) Work equipment	14	7	14

Asset class	Description of assets included	Class Life (in years)	Recovery Periods (in years): General Depreciation System	Recovery Periods (in years): Alternative Depreciation System
40.2	**Railroad Structures and Similar Improvements:** Includes assets classified in the following Interstate Commerce Commission road accounts: (6) Bridges, trestles, and culverts (7) Elevated structures (13) Fences, snowsheds, and signs (16) Station and office buildings (stations and other operating structures only) (17) Roadway buildings (18) Water stations (19) Fuel stations (20) Shops and enginehouses (25) TOFC/COFC terminals (operating structures only) (31) Power transmission systems (35) Miscellaneous structures (39) Public improvements construction . . .	30	20	30
40.3	**Railroad Wharves and Docks:** Includes assets classified in the following Interstate Commerce accounts: (23) Wharves and docks (24) Coal and ore wharves	20	15	20
40.4	**Railroad Track**	10	7	10
40.51	**Railroad Hydraulic Electric Generating Equipment**	50	20	50
40.52	**Railroad Nuclear Electric Generating Equipment**	20	15	20
40.53	**Railroad Steam Electric Generating Equipment**	28	20	28
40.54	**Railroad Steam, Compressed Air, and Other Power Plant Equipment**	28	20	28
41.0	**Motor Transport-Passengers:** Includes assets used in the urban and interurban commercial and contract carrying of passengers by road, except the transportation assets included in classes with the prefix 00.2	8	5	8
42.0	**Motor Transport-Freight:** Includes assets used in the commercial and contract carrying of freight by road, except the transportation assets included in classes with the prefix 00.2	8	5	8
44.0	**Water Transportation:** Includes assets used in the commercial and contract carrying of freight and passengers by water except the transportation assets included in classes with the prefix 00.2. Includes all related land improvements . . .	20	15	20

Asset class	Description of assets included	Class Life (in years)	Recovery Periods (in years) General Depreciation System	Alternative Depreciation System
45.0	**Air Transport:** Includes assets (except helicopters) used in commercial and contract carrying of passengers and freight by air. For purposes of section 1.167(a)-11(d)(2)(iv)(*a*) of the regulations, expenditures for "repair, maintenance, rehabilitation, or improvement" shall consist of direct maintenance expenses (irrespective of airworthiness provisions or charges) as defined by Civil Aeronautics Board uniform accounts 5200, maintenance burden (exclusive of expenses pertaining to maintenance buildings and improvements) as defined by Civil Aeronautics Board uniform accounts 5300, and expenditures which are not "excluded additions" as defined in section 1.167(a)-11(d)(2)(vi) of the regulations and which would be charged to property and equipment accounts in the Civil Aeronautics Board uniform system of accounts	12	7	12
45.1	**Air Transport (restricted):** Includes each asset described in the description of class 45.0 which was held by the taxpayer on April 15, 1976, or is acquired by the taxpayer pursuant to a contract which was, on April 15, 1976, and at all times thereafter, binding on the taxpayer. This criterion of classification based on binding contract concept is to be applied in the same manner as under the general rules expressed in section 49(b)(1), (4), (5) and (8) of the Code (as in effect prior to its repeal by the Revenue Act of 1978, section § 12(c)(1), (d), 1978-3 C.B. 1, 60)	6	5	6
46.0	**Pipeline Transportation:** Includes assets used in the private, commercial, and contract carrying of petroleum, gas and other products by means of pipes and conveyors. The trunk lines and related storage facilities of integrated petroleum and natural gas producers are included in this class. Excludes initial clearing and grading land improvements as specified in Rev. Rul. 72-403, 1972-2 C.B. 102, but includes all other related land improvements	22	15	22
	Telephone Communications:[5] Includes the assets identified below and that are used in the provision of commercial and contract telephonic services such as:			
48.11	**Telephone Central Office Buildings:** Includes assets intended to house central office equipment, as defined in Federal Communications Commission Part 31 [32—CCH.]Account No. 212 whether section 1245 or section 1250 property	45	20	45

Asset class	Description of assets included	Class Life (in years)	Recovery Periods (in years) General Depreciation System	Recovery Periods (in years) Alternative Depreciation System
48.12	**Telephone Central Office Equipment:** Includes central office switching and related equipment as defined in Federal Communications Commission Part 31 [32—CCH.] Account No. 221. Does not include computer-based telephone central office switching equipment included in class 48.121. Does not include private branch exchange (PBX) equipment	18	10	18
48.121	**Computer-based Telephone Central Office Switching Equipment:** Includes equipment whose functions are those of a computer or peripheral equipment (as defined in section 168(i)(2)(B) of the Code) used in its capacity as telephone central office equipment. Does not include private branch exchange (PBX) equipment.	9.5	5	9.5
48.13	**Telephone Station Equipment:** Includes such station apparatus and connections as teletypewriters, telephones, booths, private exchanges, and comparable equipment as defined in Federal Communications Commission Part 31 [32—CCH.]Account Nos. 231, 232, and 234	10	7 [6]	10 [6]
48.14	**Telephone Distribution Plant:** Includes such assets as pole lines, cable, aerial wire, underground conduits, and comparable equipment, and related land improvements as defined in Federal Communications Commission Part 31 [32—CCH.]Account Nos. 241, 242.1, 242.2, 242.3, 242.4, 243, and 244	24	15	24
48.2	**Radio and Television Broadcasting:** Includes assets used in radio and television broadcasting, except transmitting towers . .	6	5	6
	Telegraph, Ocean Cable, and Satellite Communications (TOCSC) includes communications-related assets used to provide domestic and international radio-telegraph, wire-telegraph, ocean-cable, and satellite communications services; also includes related land improvements. If property described in Classes 48.31—48.45 is comparable to telephone distribution plant described in Class 48.14 and used for 2-way exchange of voice and data communication which is the equivalent of telephone communication, such property is assigned a class life of 24 years under this revenue procedure. Comparable equipment does not include cable television equipment used primarily for 1-way communication.			
48.31	**TOCSC-Electric Power Generating and Distribution Systems:** Includes assets used in the provision of electric power by generation, modulation, rectification, channelization, control, and distribution. Does not include these assets when they are installed on customers' premises	19	10	19

Asset class	Description of assets included	Class Life (in years)	Recovery Periods (in years) General Depreciation System	Alternative Depreciation System
48.32	**TOCSC-High Frequency Radio and Microwave Systems:** Includes assets such as transmitters and receivers, antenna supporting structures, antennas, transmission lines from equipment to antenna, transmitter cooling systems, and control and amplification equipment. Does not include cable and long-line systems . . .	13	7	13
48.33	**TOCSC-Cable and Long-line Systems:** Includes assets such as transmission lines, pole lines, ocean cables, buried cable and conduit, repeaters, repeater stations, and other related assets. Does not include high frequency radio or microwave systems . . .	26.5	20	26.5
48.34	**TOCSC-Central Office Control Equipment:** Includes assets for general control, switching, and monitoring of communications signals including electromechanical switching and channeling apparatus, multiplexing equipment, patching and monitoring facilities, in-house cabling, teleprinter equipment, and associated site improvements	16.5	10	16.5
48.35	**TOCSC-Computerized Switching, Channeling, and Associated Control Equipment:** Includes central office switching computers, interfacing computers, other associated specialized control equipment, and site improvements	10.5	7	10.5
48.36	**TOCSC-Satellite Ground Segment Property:** Includes assets such as fixed earth station equipment, antennas, satellite communications equipment, and interface equipment used in satellite communications. Does not include general purpose equipment or equipment used in satellite space segment property	10	7	10
48.37	**TOCSC-Satellite Space Segment Property:** Includes satellites and equipment used for telemetry, tracking, control, and monitoring when used in satellite communications . . .	8	5	8
48.38	**TOCSC-Equipment Installed on Customer's Premises:** Includes assets installed on customer's premises, such as computers, terminal equipment, power generation and distribution systems, private switching center, teleprinters, facsimile equipment, and other associated and related equipment . . .	10	7	10
48.39	**TOCSC-Support and Service Equipment:** Includes assets used to support but not engage in communications. Includes store, warehouse and shop tools, and test and laboratory assets	13.5	7	13.5

Asset class	Description of assets included	Class Life (in years)	Recovery Periods (in years) General Depreciation System	Alternative Depreciation System
	Cable Television (CATV): Includes communications-related assets used to provide cable television [(]community antenna services). Does not include assets used to provide subscribers with two-way communications services.			
48.41	**CATV-Headend:** Includes assets such as towers, antennas, preamplifiers, converters, modulation equipment, and program non-duplication systems. Does not include headend buildings and program origination assets	11	7	11
48.42	**CATV-Subscriber Connection and Distribution Systems:** Includes assets such as trunk and feeder cable, connecting hardware, amplifiers, power equipment, passive devices, directional taps, pedestals, pressure taps, drop cables, matching transformers, multiple set connector equipment, and converters	10	7	10
48.43	**CATV-Program Origination:** Includes assets such as cameras, film chains, video tape recorders, lighting, and remote location equipment excluding vehicles. Does not include buildings and their structural components	9	5	9
48.44	**CATV-Service and Test:** Includes assets such as oscilloscopes, field strength meters, spectrum analyzers, and cable testing equipment, but does not include vehicles	8.5	5	8.5
48.45	**CATV-Microwave Systems:** Includes assets such as towers, antennas, transmitting and receiving equipment, and broad band microwave assets if used in the provision of cable television services. Does not include assets used in the provision of common carrier services	9.5	5	9.5
	Electric, Gas, Water and Steam, Utility Services: Includes assets used in the production, transmission and distribution of electricity, gas, steam, or water for sale including related land improvements.			
49.11	**Electric Utility Hydraulic Production Plant:** Includes assets used in the hydraulic power production of electricity for sale, including related land improvements, such as dams, flumes, canals, and waterways	50	20	50
49.12	**Electric Utility Nuclear Production Plant:** Includes assets used in the nuclear power production and electricity for sale and related land improvements. Does not include nuclear fuel assemblies	20	15	20

Asset class	Description of assets included	Class Life (in years)	Recovery Periods (in years) General Depreciation System	Alternative Depreciation System
49.121	**Electric Utility Nuclear Fuel Assemblies:** Includes initial core and replacement core nuclear fuel assemblies (i.e., the composite of fabricated nuclear fuel and container) when used in a boiling water, pressurized water, or high temperature gas reactor used in the production of electricity. Does not include nuclear fuel assemblies used in breeder reactors	5	5	5
49.13	**Electric Utility Steam Production Plant:** Includes assets used in the steam power production of electricity for sale, combustion turbines operated in a combined cycle with a conventional steam unit and related land improvements. Also includes package boilers, electric generators and related assets such as electricity and steam distribution systems as used by a waste reduction and resource recovery plant if the steam or electricity is normally for sale to others	28	20	28
49.14	**Electric Utility Transmission and Distribution Plant:** Includes assets used in the transmission and distribution of electricity for sale and related land improvements. Excludes initial clearing and grading land improvements as specified in Rev. Rul. 72-403, 1972-2 C.B. 102	30	20 [6A]	30 [6A]
49.15	**Electric Utility Combustion Turbine Production Plant:** Includes assets used in the production of electricity for sale by the use of such prime movers as jet engines, combustion turbines, diesel engines, gasoline engines, and other internal combustion engines, their associated power turbines and/or generators, and related land improvements. Does not include combustion turbines operated in a combined cycle with a conventional steam unit	20	15	20
49.21	**Gas Utility Distribution Facilities:** Includes gas water heaters and gas conversion equipment installed by utility on customers' premises on a rental basis	35	20	35
49.221	**Gas Utility Manufactured Gas Production Plants:** Includes assets used in the manufacture of gas having chemical and/or physical properties which do not permit complete interchangeability with domestic natural gas. Does not include gas producing systems and related systems used in waste reduction and resource recovery plants which are elsewhere classified	30	20	30
49.222	**Gas Utility Substitute Natural Gas (SNG) Production Plant (naphtha or lighter hydrocarbon feedstocks):** Includes assets used in the catalytic conversion of feedstocks or naphtha or lighter hydrocarbons to a gaseous fuel which is completely interchangeable with domestic natural gas	14	7	14

Asset class	Description of assets included	Class Life (in years)	Recovery Periods (in years) General Depreciation System	Alternative Depreciation System
49.223	**Substitute Natural Gas-Coal Gasification:** Includes assets used in the manufacture and production of pipeline quality gas from coal using the basic Lurgi process with advanced methanation. Includes all process plant equipment and structures used in this coal gasification process and all utility assets such as cooling systems, water supply and treatment facilities, and assets used in the production and distribution of electricity and steam for use by the taxpayer in a gasification plant and attendant coal mining site processes but not for assets used in the production and distribution of electricity and steam for sale to others. Also includes all other related land improvements. Does not include assets used in the direct mining and treatment of coal prior to the gasification process itself	18	10	18
49.23	**Natural Gas Production Plant**	14	7	14
49.24	**Gas Utility Trunk Pipelines and Related Storage Facilities:** Excluding initial clearing and grading land improvements as specified in Rev. Rul. 72-403	22	15	22
49.25	**Liquefied Natural Gas Plant:** Includes assets used in the liquefaction, storage, and regasification of natural gas including loading and unloading connections, instrumentation equipment and controls, pumps, vaporizers and odorizers, tanks, and related land improvements. Also includes pipeline interconnections with gas transmission lines and distribution systems and marine terminal facilities	22	15	22
49.3	**Water Utilities:** Includes assets used in the gathering, treatment, and commercial distribution of water	50	20 or 25 [7]	50
49.4	**Central Steam Utility Production and Distribution:** Includes assets used in the production and distribution of steam for sale. Does not include assets used in waste reduction and resource recovery plants which are elsewhere classified	28	20	28

Asset class	Description of assets included	Class Life (in years)	Recovery Periods (in years) General Depreciation System	Alternative Depreciation System
49.5	**Waste Reduction and Resource Recovery Plants:** Includes assets used in the conversion of refuse or other solid waste or biomass to heat or to a solid, liquid, or gaseous fuel. Also includes all process plant equipment and structures at the site used to receive, handle, collect, and process refuse or other solid waste or biomass to a solid, liquid, or gaseous fuel or to handle and burn refuse or other solid waste or biomass in a waterwall combustion system, oil or gas pyrolysis system, or refuse derived fuel system to create hot water, gas, steam and electricity. Includes material recovery and support assets used in refuse or solid refuse or solid waste receiving, collecting, handling, sorting, shredding, classifying, and separation systems. Does not include any package boilers, or electric generators and related assets such as electricity, hot water, steam and manufactured gas production plants classified in classes 00.4, 49.13, 49.221, and 49.4. Does include, however, all other utilities such as water supply and treatment facilities, ash handling and other related land improvements of a waste reduction and resource recovery plant	10	7	10
50.0	**Municipal Wastewater Treatment Plant** .	24	15	24
51.0	**Municipal Sewer**	50	20 or [7] 25	50
57.0	**Distributive Trades and Services:** Includes assets used in wholesale and retail trade, and personal and professional services. Includes section 1245 assets used in marketing petroleum and petroleum products	9	5	9 [8]
57.1	**Distributive Trades and Services-Billboard, Service Station Buildings and Petroleum Marketing Land Improvements:** Includes section 1250 assets, including service station buildings [See ¶ 110—CCH.]and depreciable land improvements, whether section 1245 property or section 1250 property, used in the marketing of petroleum and petroleum products, but not including any of these facilities related to petroleum and natural gas trunk pipelines. Includes car wash buildings and related land improvements. Includes billboards, whether such assets are section 1245 property or section 1250 property. Excludes all other land improvements, buildings and structural components as defined in section 1.48-1(e) of the regulations	20	15	20

Asset class	Description of assets included	Class Life (in years)	Recovery Periods (in years) General Depreciation System	Alternative Depreciation System
79.0	**Recreation:** Includes assets used in the provision of entertainment services on payment of a fee or admission charge, as in the operation of bowling alleys, billiard and pool establishments, theaters, concert halls, and miniature golf courses. Does not include amusement and theme parks and assets which consist primarily of specialized land improvements or structures, such as golf courses, sports stadiums, race tracks, ski slopes, and buildings which house the assets used in entertainment services	10	7	10
80.0	**Theme and Amusement Parks:** Includes assets used in the provision of rides, attractions, and amusements in activities defined as theme and amusement parks, and include appurtenances associated with a ride, attraction, amusement or theme setting within the park such as ticket booths, facades, shop interiors, and props, special purpose structures, and buildings other than warehouses, administration buildings, hotels, and motels. Includes all land improvements for or in support of park activities, (e.g., parking lots, sidewalks, waterways, bridges, fences, landscaping, etc.) and support functions (e.g., food and beverage retailing, souvenir vending and other nonlodging accommodations) if owned by the park and provided exclusively for the benefit of park patrons. Theme and amusement parks are defined as combinations of amusements, rides, and attractions which are permanently situated on park land and open to the public for the price of admission. This guideline class is a composite of all assets used in this industry except transportation equipment (general purpose trucks, cars, airplanes, etc., which are included in asset guideline classes with the prefix 00.2), assets used in the provision of administrative services (asset classes with the prefix 00.1), and warehouses, administration buildings, hotels and motels [Race track facilities have been specifically excluded from Asset Class 80.0 (Act Sec. 704(e)(2) of P.L. 108-357). See ¶ 106.—CCH.]	12.5	7	12.5
	Certain Property for Which Recovery Periods Assigned			
	A. Personal Property With No Class Life . .		7	12
	Section 1245 Real Property With No Class Life		7	40
	B. Qualified Technological Equipment, as defined in section 168(i)(2)	[9]	5	5
	C. Property Used in Connection with Research and Experimentation referred to in section 168(e)(3)(B)	[9]	5	class life if no class life—12

Asset class	Description of assets included	Class Life (in years)	Recovery Periods (in years) General Depreciation System	Recovery Periods (in years) Alternative Depreciation System
	D. Alternative Energy Property described in sections 48(l)(3)(viii) or (iv), or section 48(l)(4) of the Code	[9]	5	class life if no class life—12
	E. Biomass property described in section 48(l)(15) and is a qualifying small production facility within the meaning of section 3(17)(c) of the Federal Power Act, (16 U.S.C. 796(17)(C)), as in effect on September 1, 1986	[9]	5	class life if no class life—12

[1] A horse is more than 2 (or 12) years old after the day that is 24 (or 144) months after its actual birthdate.

[2] Property described in asset classes 01.223, 01.224, and 01.225 are assigned recovery periods under either section 168(e)(3)(A) or section 168(g)(2)(C) but have no class lives.

[3] 7 if property was placed in service before 1989.

[4] [Asset Class 30.11 includes general rebuilding or rehabilitation costs for the special tools defined in class 30.11 that have been traditionally capitalized as the cost of a new asset, according to Rev. Proc. 87-56, section .05. This rule was incorporated from section 2.02 of Rev. Proc. 83-35.—CCH.]

[5] [References to Part 31 in Asset Classes 48.11—48.14 are to Vol. 47 Part 31 of the Code of Federal Regulations (CFR). However, Part 31 was replaced by Part 32, effective 1-1-88. See Vol. 52 Federal Register p. 43,499. Part 32 may be accessed through the FCC web site (www.fcc.gov).—CCH.]

[6] Property described in asset guideline class 48.13 which is qualified technological equipment as defined in section 168(i)(2) is assigned a 5-year recovery period for both the general and alternative depreciation systems.

[6A] [The recovery period for the cost of the initial clearing and grading land improvements pertaining to any electric utility transmission and distribution plant has been increased from seven years to 20 years, effective for property placed in service after October 22, 2004 (Code Sec. 168(e)(3)(F), as added by the 2004 Jobs Act (P.L. 108-357)). The ADS period is 25 years (Code Sec. 168(g)(3)(B), as amended by P.L. 108-357); Smart electric meters and grid systems placed in service after October 3, 2008 are 10-year property (Code Sec. 168(e)(3)(D)). See ¶ 108.—CCH.]

[7] [A 25-year recovery period applies to property placed in service after June 12, 1996. See ¶ 113.—CCH.]

[8] Any high technology medical equipment as defined in section 168(i)(2)(C) which is described in asset guideline class 57.0 is assigned a 5-year recovery period for the alternative depreciation system.

[9] The class life (if any) of property described in classes B, C, D, or E is determined by reference to the asset guideline classes in this revenue procedure. If an item of property described in paragraphs B, C, D, or E is not described in any asset guideline class, such item of property has no class life.

Rev. Proc. 87-56, 1987-2 CB 674, as clarified and modified by Rev. Proc. 88-22, 1988-1 CB 785.

Passenger Automobiles and Other Listed Property

Limitations on Depreciation Deductions

¶ 200

Passenger Automobiles

Specific dollar amount limits apply to annual depreciation deductions that may be claimed for "passenger automobiles" (Code Sec. 280F(a)). For this purpose, the Code Sec. 179 expense deduction and bonus depreciation allowance are treated as a depreciation deduction for the tax year in which a car is placed in service. Thus, the combined Code Sec. 179 deduction, bonus deduction, and regular first-year depreciation deduction is limited to the applicable first-year depreciation cap. Generally, the first year cap is exceeded even if the section 179 allowance is not claimed. See ¶ 487 for a complete discussion of this point, including formulas for determining the amount to expense under Code Sec. 179 so that the sum of regular depreciation and the 179 allowance do not exceed the first-year depreciation cap.

See ¶ 70 for calculation of the depreciable basis of a car.

List of vehicles in excess of 6,000 pounds GVWR. These annual limitations do not apply to trucks (including SUVs that are considered trucks) and vans with a gross vehicle weight rating (GVWR) (i.e., loaded weight rating) in excess of 6,000 pounds. See ¶ 208. See Quick Reference Chart section at end of this book (Tables I, II, and III) for a list of trucks, SUVs , and vans exempt under this rule.

$25,000 section 179 expensing cap on SUVs and certain vans in excess of 6,000 pounds and trucks in excess of 6,000 pounds with a bed length under six feet. If an SUV which is considered a truck has a GVWR in excess of 6,000 pounds and is therefore, exempt from the annual depreciation caps, no more than $25,000 of the cost may be expensed under Code Sec. 179. This rule also applies to pick-up trucks with a GVWR in excess of 6,000 pounds and an interior cargo bed length of less than six feet as well as to *certain* vans with a GVWR in excess of 6,000 pounds. This $25,000 limit applies to vehicles placed in service after October 22, 2004. See ¶ 201 for a discussion of the provision. See Table IV in the Quick Reference Chart section at the end of this book for a list of trucks exceeding 6,000 pounds with a bed length under 6 feet.

Passenger automobile and truck defined. In general, all passenger cars are "passenger automobiles" and subject to the depreciation caps. Trucks and vans are not considered passenger automobiles subject to the caps if they have a gross vehicle weight rating in excess of 6,000 pounds. According to informal guidance provided by the IRS to CCH, an SUV that is categorized by its manufacturer as a truck pursuant to Department of Transportation regulations is considered a truck. See ¶ 208.

Trade-ins and involuntary conversions. For the application of the luxury car caps on a vehicle received in a trade-in or involuntarily converted, see ¶ 214.

50 percent or less business use. The MACRS alternative depreciation system (ADS) must be used to depreciate a "passenger automobile" or other listed property if its business use is 50 percent or less. No Code Sec. 179 expense allowance or bonus depreciation (including New York Liberty Zone (¶ 127E), GO-Zone bonus depreciation (¶ 127F), Kansas Disaster Area bonus depreciation (¶ 127G), or Disaster Area bonus depreciation (¶ 127H)) may be claimed. If business use falls to 50 percent or less after the first tax year, depreciation recapture (including the section 179 allowance and bonus depreciation) is required. See ¶ 210. This recapture rule applies to trucks (including SUVs that are considered trucks) and vans that are exempt from the luxury car caps as a result of having a GVWR in excess of 6,000 pounds because such vehicles are still considered a type of listed property—specifically, they are considered a property used as a means of transportation. See ¶ 208.

Determining which set of caps applies. The applicable set of annual dollar amount limits depends on the calendar year in which the vehicle is placed in service for use in a trade or business or for the production of income. Thus, if a car is converted from personal use to business use, the dollar limits are those that are in effect in the calendar year that the car is placed in service for business use.

Example (1): Assume that a car is placed in service for business purposes on June 1, 2009. Based on the chart below, the dollar limits for the vehicle's five-year recovery period are $10,960 (first year if bonus depreciation claimed), $4,800 (second year), $2,850 (third year), and $1,775 (subsequent years). See, also, *"Fiscal-year taxpayers," below.*

Fiscal-year taxpayers. The appropriate limitation is determined by reference to the *calendar year* that the vehicle is first placed in service. For example, a corporation with a 2008-2009 fiscal year would apply the 2009 limitations to a vehicle placed in service in the 2009 calendar year.

Lessors. Taxpayers who are regularly engaged in the business of leasing automobiles are not subject to the annual caps. See ¶ 204.

Improvements to a vehicle. A taxpayer may make a major improvement to a vehicle (e.g., replace the engine). The improvement is separately depreciated as a new vehicle when placed in service. However, the sum of the depreciation claimed on the vehicle and the improvement may not exceed the applicable cap for the vehicle. A single cap applies (Temporary Reg.§ 1.280F-2T(f)).

The cost of an improvement made before the vehicle is placed in service, for example, an improvement made by the dealer at the purchaser's request, should be added the depreciable basis of the vehicle.

Post-recovery year deductions

A depreciation deduction that is disallowed during a particular recovery year because the cap for that year is smaller is combined with any disallowed deductions from other recovery years. The combined amount is then deducted at the applicable "Year 4 and later" cap (for example $1,775 per year for a car placed in service in 2009 assuming 100-percent business use) beginning with the first year following the end of the recovery period. See ¶ 202.

Separate depreciation caps for trucks and vans placed in service after 2002

If a truck or van (including an SUV that is consideref a truck) is placed in service after calendar-year 2002 and the truck or van is subject to the annual caps (generally because it has a gross vehicle weight rating of 6,000 pounds or less), the taxpayer must use a separate set of annual limitations that are somewhat higher than those that apply to other types of vehicles. The caps for trucks and vans placed in service after 2002 are reproduced in Table II below. Separate caps for trucks and vans are issued annually. Table II should only be used if the vehicle is built on a truck chassis (e.g., an SUV or minivan built on a truck chassis).

Separate lease inclusion tables are also provided for trucks and vans (including SUVs that are considered trucks) first leased after 2002. See ¶ 204.

Exclusion for trucks and vans unsuitable for personal use

Certain trucks and vans (including SUVs) placed in service after July 6, 2003, are not subject to the caps if, because of their design, they are not likely to be used for personal purposes. See ¶ 208.

TABLE I

Depreciation Limits on Passenger Automobiles (Other Than Trucks and Vans Placed in Service after 2002)

For Cars Placed in Service		*Depreciation Allowable in—*				
After	*Before*	*Year 1*	*Year 2*	*Year 3*	*Year 4, etc.*	*Authority*
6/18/84	1/1/85	$ 4,000	$6,000	$6,000	$6,000	Former 280F(a)(2)
12/31/84	4/3/85	4,100	6,200	6,200	6,200	Rev. Rul. 86-107
4/2/85	1/1/87	3,200	4,800	4,800	4,800	Former 280F(a)(2)
12/31/86	1/1/89	2,560	4,100	2,450	1,475	Current 280F(a)(2)
12/31/88	1/1/91	2,660	4,200	2,550	1,475	Rev. Proc. 89-64; Rev. Proc. 90-22
12/31/90	1/1/92	2,660	4,300	2,550	1,575	Rev. Proc. 91-30
12/31/91	1/1/93	2,760	4,400	2,650	1,575	Rev. Proc. 92-43
12/31/92	1/1/94	2,860	4,600	2,750	1,675	Rev. Proc. 93-35
12/31/93	1/1/95	2,960	4,700	2,850	1,675	Rev. Proc. 94-53 Rev. Proc. 95-9
12/31/94	1/1/97	3,060	4,900	2,950	1,775	Rev. Proc. 96-25
12/31/96	1/1/98	3,160	5,000	3,050	1,775	Rev. Proc. 97-20
12/31/97	1/1/99	3,160	5,000	2,950	1,775	Rev. Proc. 98-30
12/31/98	1/1/00	3,060	5,000	2,950	1,775	Rev. Proc. 99-14
12/31/99	9/11/01	3,060	4,900	2,950	1,775	Rev. Proc. 2000-18
9/10/01	5/6/03	7,660 [1] 3,060 [1]	4,900	2,950	1,775	Rev. Proc. 2003-75
5/5/03	1/1/04	10,710 [2] 3,060 [2]	4,900	2,950	1,775	Rev. Proc. 2003-75
12/31/03	1/1/05	10,610 [3] 2,960 [3]	4,800	2,850	1,675	Rev. Proc. 2004-20
12/31/04	1/1/06	2,960	4,700	2,850	1,675	Rev. Proc. 2005-13
12/31/05	1/1/07	2,960	4,800	2,850	1,775	Rev. Proc. 2006-18
12/31/06	1/1/08	3,060	4,900	2,850	1,775	Rev. Proc. 2007-30
12/31/07	1/1/09	10,960 [4] 2,960 [4]	4,800	2,850	1,775	Rev. Proc. 2008-22
12/31/08	1/1/10	10,960 [4] 2,960 [4]	4,800	2,850	1,775	Rev. Proc. 2009-24

[1] The $7,660 limit applies if the vehicle qualifies for 30-percent bonus depreciation and no election out is made. Otherwise, the limit is $3,060.

[2] $10,710 if vehicle qualifies for 50-percent bonus depreciation and no election out is made or if 30-percent bonus depreciation is elected in place of the 50-percent rate; $3,060 if vehicle does not qualify for bonus depreciation (for example, because it is used) or an election out of bonus depreciation is made.

[3] $10,610 if vehicle qualifies for 50-percent bonus depreciation and no election out is made or if 30-percent bonus depreciation is elected in place of the 50-percent rate; $2,960 if vehicle does not qualify for bonus depreciation (for example, because it is used) or an election out of bonus depreciation is made.

[4] $10,960 if vehicle qualifies for 50-percent bonus depreciation; $2,960 if vehicle does not qualify for bonus depreciation (for example, because it is used) or an election out of bonus depreciation is made.

TABLE II

Depreciation Limits on Trucks and Vans Placed in Service after 2002

For Vehicles Placed in Service After	*Before*	*Depreciation Allowable in—* *Year 1*	*Year 2*	*Year 3*	*Year 4, etc.*	*Authority*
12/31/08 .	1/1/10	11,060 [1] 3,060 [1]	4,900	2,950	1,775	Rev. Proc. 2009-24
12/31/07 .	1/1/09	11,160 [1] 3,160 [1]	5,100	3,050	1,875	Rev. Proc. 2008-22
12/31/06 .	1/1/08	3,260	5,200	3,050	1,875	Rev. Proc. 2007-30
12/31/05 .	1/1/07	3,260	5,200	3,150	1,875	Rev. Proc. 2006-18
12/31/04 .	1/1/06	3,260	5,200	3,150	1,875	Rev. Proc. 2005-13
12/31/03 .	1/1/05	10,910 [2] 3,260 [2]	5,300	3,150	1,875	Rev. Proc. 2004-20
12/31/02 .	1/1/04	$11,010 [3] 7,960 [3] 3,360 [3]	$5,400	$3,250	$1,975	Rev. Proc. 2003-75

[1] $11,160 (2008) and $11,060 (2009) if vehicle qualifies for 50-percent bonus depreciation and no election out is made. $3,160 (2008) and $3,060 (2009) if election out of bonus depreciation is made or vehicle does not qualify for bonus depreciation (for example, because it is used).

[2] $10,910 if vehicle qualifies for 50-percent bonus depreciation and no election out is made or if an election to use 30-percent in lieu of 50-percent bonus depreciation is made. $3,260 if election out of bonus depreciation is made or vehicle does not qualify for bonus depreciation (for example, because it is used).

[3] The $11,010 limit applies if the vehicle qualifies for 50-percent bonus depreciation and no election out is made or if an election to use 30-percent in lieu of 50-percent bonus depreciation is made. $7,960 if vehicle qualifies for 30-percent bonus depreciation and no election out is made. $3,360 if election out of bonus depreciation is made or vehicle does not qualify for bonus depreciation (for example, because it is used).

Example (2): A car costing $25,000 is placed in service on September 15, 2009. No amount is expensed under Code Sec. 179. The 50% bonus depreciation allowance is claimed. The car is used 100% for business and the half-year convention applies. Bonus depreciation is $12,500. The adjusted depreciable basis to which the table percentages (20%, 32%, 19.20%, 11.52%, 11.52%, and 5.76%) are applied is $12,500 ($25,000 – $12,500 bonus deduction). Allowable depreciation deductions during the recovery period are as follows:

Year	*Regular Deduction*	*Luxury Car Cap*	*Allowable Depreciation*
2009	$15,000	$10,960	$10,960
2010	$4,000	$4,800	$4,000
2011	$2,400	$2,850	$2,400
2012	$1,440	$1,775	$1,440
2013	$1,440	$1,775	$1,440
2014	$720	$1,775	$720
		TOTAL	$20,960

The $15,000 regular deduction for 2009 is the sum of the $12,500 bonus deduction and the $2,500 first-year depreciation deduction ($12,500 × 20%). 2009 is the only year during the recovery period that allowable depreciation is limited to the luxury car cap. The disallowed amount ($15,000 – $10,960) is $4,040. $1,775 of this amount may be deducted in 2015, $1,775 in 2016, and the remaining $490 may be deducted in 2017.

Example (3): A used car costing $25,000 is placed in service on September 15, 2009. Bonus depreciation is not claimed because the original use of the vehicle did not begin with the taxpayer (i.e., the car is used). No amount is expensed under Code Sec. 179. The car is used 100% for business and the half-year convention applies. The adjusted depreciable basis to which the table percentages (20%, 32%, 19.20%, 11.52%, 11.52%, and 5.76%) are applied is $25,000. Allowable depreciation deductions during the recovery period are as follows:

Year	*Regular Deduction*	*Luxury Car Cap*	*Allowable Depreciation*
2009	$5,000	$2,960	$2,960
2010	$8,000	$4,800	$4,800
2011	$4,800	$2,850	$2,850
2012	$2,880	$1,775	$1,775
2013	$2,880	$1,775	$1,775
2014	$1,440	$1,775	$1,440
		TOTAL	$15,600

The disallowed depreciation deduction is $9,400 ($25,000 – $15,600). This amount is deducted at the rate of $1,775 per year until used up.

See ¶ 202 for additional examples.

Bonus depreciation and bump-up in first-year cap

The 50 percent bonus depreciation deduction was reinstated effective for property acquired after December 31, 2007 and before January 1, 2010. The first-year depreciation cap for a vehicle placed in service in 2008 or 2009 is increased by $8,000 if bonus depreciation is claimed under Code Sec. 168(k) on the vehicle (Code Sec. 168(k)(2)(F), as amended by P.L. 110-185).

There are no bump-ups if bonus depreciation is claimed on a vehicle placed in service in the Gulf Opportunity Zone (i.e., GO Zone bonus depreciation was claimed on a vehicle placed in service before January 1, 2008 (¶ 127F), the Kansas Disaster Area (¶ 127G), or a federally declared disaster area (¶ 127H).

Pre-Stimulus Act bonus depreciation. If bonus depreciation was claimed on a new vehicle at the 30-percent rate, the basic first-year cap was increased by an additional $4,600. If the 50-percent rate applied (or the 30-percent rate was elected in place of the 50-percent rate), the basic first-year cap was increased by an additional $7,650 (Code Sec. 168(k)(2)(E)(i); Reg.§ 1.168(k)-1(f)(8); Rev. Proc. 2004-20). For example, the basic first-year cap for a vehicle other than a truck or van that was placed in service in 2004 was $2,960. If 50 percent bonus depreciation was claimed, this amount was increased by $7,650 to $10,610 (see Table I, above).

The bump-up amounts were tripled in the case of electric vehicles, as explained below. See Table III.

New York Liberty Zone. Special rules applied to used vehicles placed in service in the New York Liberty Zone. See below.

Partial business use

The maximum amounts indicated above apply when business/investment use is 100 percent and the amounts must be reduced to reflect the personal use of a vehicle in any tax year. The limit imposed on the maximum amount of depreciation deduction is redetermined by multiplying the amount of the limitation by the percentage of business/investment use (determined on an annual basis) during the tax year (Temporary Reg.§ 1.280F-2T(i)). See examples at ¶ 202.

Example (4): A calendar-year taxpayer purchases a car for $20,000 in August 2007 and uses it 60% for business. Before consideration of the Code Sec. 280F limitations, the amount of depreciation on such car under the general MACRS 200% declining-balance method over a 5-year recovery period using a half-year convention is $2,400 ($12,000 depreciable basis ($20,000 × 60% business use) × 20% (first-year percentage from Table 1 at ¶ 180 for 5-year property)). However, the maximum MACRS deduction allowed for

2007 under the Code Sec. 280F luxury car limitations is $1,876 ($3,060 maximum limit for car placed in service in 2007 × 60% (business use)). The 2008 deduction, assuming 60% business use and without regard to the second-year cap, is $3,840 ($12,000 depreciable basis × 32% second-year percentage). The 2008 deduction, however, is limited to $2,940 ($4,900 second-year cap for car placed in service in 2007 × 60%). See ¶ 202 for additional examples.

Short tax year

The limitation imposed upon the maximum amount of allowable depreciation deductions (including any Code Sec. 179 expense deduction) must be adjusted if there is a short tax year. The limitation is reduced by multiplying the dollar amount that would have applied if the tax year were not a short tax year by a fraction, the numerator of which is the number of months and partial months in the short tax year and the denominator of which is 12 (Temp. Reg. § 1.280F-2T(i) (2)).

Example (5): In August 2009, a corporation purchased and placed in service a used passenger automobile and used it 100% for business. The corporation's 2009 tax year is a short tax year consisting of six months. The maximum amount that the corporation may claim as a depreciation deduction for 2009 is $1,480 ($2,960 × 6⁄12). $2,960 is the first-year cap for a passenger car placed in service in 2009. See Table I, above.

Bonus deduction in short tax year. The Code Sec. 168(k) bonus depreciation deduction (¶ 127D) for vehicles placed in service before January 1, 2005 is allowed in full in a short tax year (Rev. Proc. 2002-33; Reg.§ 1.168(k)-1(d)(1)). The $4,600 and $7,650 bump-ups in the first-year depreciation caps for vehicles on which bonus depreciation is claimed are not reduced in a short tax year (Premable to T.D. 9283, filed with the Federal Register on August 28, 2006). The basic cap, however, is subject to the general rule which requires reduction in a short tax year. See "Bonus depreciation and bump-up in first year cap," above. Note that the bump-up does not apply if bonus depreciation on a car is claimed under the New York Liberty Zone, Gulf Opportunity Zone, Kansas Disaster Area, or Federally Declared Disaster Area bonus provisions, as explained above.

50 percent bonus depreciation has been reinstated for property acquired after 2007 and placed in service before January 1, 2010. An $8,000 first-year cap bump-up is provided (Code Sec. 168(k)(2)(F)(i)). The preceding rules apply to this bump-up.

Example (6): Assume the same facts as in *Example (5)*, except that the vehicle was new and qualifies for bonus depreciation at the 50-percent rate. The basic first-year cap for a car placed in service in 2009 is $2,960. The first-year depreciation cap for the short tax year is $9,480 (full $8,000 bump-up + reduced $1,480 basic cap).

Year of acquisition and disposition

The applicable depreciation limit is not reduced in the year that a vehicle is placed in service or disposed of, except to reflect personal use, if necessary. Thus, even though only one-half of a full year's depreciation may be claimed in the year of purchase or disposition (assuming the half-year convention applies and the vehicle is not sold in the same tax year it is acquired), no similar reduction is made to the depreciation cap.

Example (7): A new car costing $25,000 was purchased on January 1, 2007, and disposed of in 2009. The allowable depreciation deduction in 2009 without regard to the third-year cap is $2,400 ($25,000 × 19.2% third year table percentage × 50% (to reflect half-year convention)). Since $2,400 does not exceed the $2,850 third-year depreciation cap for a car placed in service in 2007, the allowable depreciation deduction is $2,400.

Example (8): Assume the same facts as in *Example (7)*, except that the business use percentage for 2009 is 80%. In this case, the allowable depreciation deduction without regard to the cap is $1,920 ($25,000 × 80% × 19.2% × 50%). The depreciation cap, as reduced to reflect personal use, is $2,280 ($2,850 × 80%). The taxpayer may claim $1,920 depreciation in 2009, since this is less than the adjusted $2,280 cap.

Electric vehicles

The annual depreciation caps are tripled for automobiles produced by an original equipment manufacturer to run primarily on electricity and placed in service after August 5, 1997, and before January 1, 2007 (Code Sec. 280F(a)(1)(C)). These are so-called "purpose built passenger vehicles" as defined in Code Sec. 4001(a)(2)(C)(ii). The IRS has announced the following depreciation caps are applicable for electric vehicles placed in service after August 5, 1997 and before January 1, 2007. For electric vehicles placed in service after 2006, the caps in Table I or Table II above, as appropriate, are used.

TABLE III
Depreciation Caps for Electric Cars

For Electric Cars Placed in Service After	*Before*	*Depreciation Allowable in—* *Year 1*	*Year 2*	*Year 3*	*Year 4, etc.*	*Authority*
8/5/97	1/1/98	$9,480	$15,100	$9,050	$5,425	Rev. Proc. 98-24
12/31/97	1/1/99	$9,380	$15,000	$8,950	$5,425	Rev. Proc. 98-30
12/31/98	1/1/00	$9,280	$14,900	$8,950	$5,325	Rev. Proc. 99-14
12/31/99	1/1/01	$9,280	$14,800	$8,850	$5,325	Rev. Proc. 2000-18
12/31/00	9/11/01	$9,280	$14,800	$8,850	$5,325	Rev. Proc. 2001-19
9/10/01	1/1/02	$23,080 * $9,280 *	$14,800	$8,850	$5,325	Rev. Proc. 2003-75
12/31/01	1/1/03	$22,980 * $9,180 *	$14,700	$8,750	$5,325	Rev. Proc. 2003-75
12/31/02	5/6/03	$22,880 * $9,080 *	$14,600	$8,750	$5,225	Rev. Proc. 2003-75
5/5/03	1/1/04	$32,030 * $9,080 *	$14,600	$8,750	$5,225	Rev. Proc. 2003-75
12/31/03	1/1/05	$31,830 * $8,880 *	$14,300	$8,550	$5,125	Rev. Proc. 2004-20
12/31/04	1/1/06	$8,880	$14,200	$8,450	$5,125	Rev. Proc. 2005-13
12/31/05	1/1/07	$8,980	$14,400	$8,650	$5,225	Rev. Proc. 2006-18

* The higher figure applies if the car qualifies for the additional bonus depreciation allowance and no election out is made. Otherwise, the lower limit is used.

Vehicles in the New York Liberty Zone

A new or used vehicle placed in service in the NYLZ after December 31, 2004, and before January 1, 2007, can only qualify for bonus depreciation at a 30-percent rate. The basic first-year luxury car cap amount, however, is not increased by any bump-up.

Used vehicles. A used vehicle does not qualify for bonus depreciation unless substantially all of the use of the vehicle is in the New York Liberty Zone (NYLZ) in the active conduct of a trade or business by the taxpayer in the NYLZ and the first use of the vehicle in the NYLZ commences with the taxpayer (Code Sec. 1400L(b)(2)(A)). A used vehicle placed in service in the NYLZ can only qualify for bonus depreciation at a 30-percent rate even if it is placed in service after May 5, 2003 when the rate under Code Sec. 168(k) increased to 50 percent. The $4,600 increase in the first-year basic cap that applies when bonus depreciation is claimed at the 30-percent rate does not apply to used vehicles placed in service in the NYLZ.

Thus, the first-year cap for a *qualifying* used vehicle placed in service in the NYLZ in 2004, 2005, or 2006 is $2,960 in the case of a nonelectric car placed (Table I) and $3,260 in the case of a truck or van (Table II). The cap on a used electric vehicle placed in service in the NYLZ in 2004 and 2005 is $8,880 and in 2006 is $8,980 (Table III).

New vehicles. New vehicles placed in service in the NYLZ qualify for bonus depreciation at the 30-percent rate if placed in service after September 10, 2001, and before May 6, 2003. The 50-percent rate applies if the new vehicle is placed in service after May 5, 2003, and before January 1, 2005. The bump-ups ($4,600 if the 30-percent bonus rate applies and $7,650 if the 50-percent rate applies) to the basic first-year cap apply to these new vehicles.

A new or used vehicle placed in service in the NYLZ after December 31, 2004, and before January 1, 2007, only qualifies for bonus depreciation at the 30-percent rate. The basic luxury car cap amount for the first year, however, is not increased by any bump-up.

Background of the rules. The root of these differences starts with the fact that there are two separate bonus depreciation provisions—the general provision of Code Sec. 168(k) and the more limited provision of Code Sec. 1400L(b), which only applies to "qualified New York Liberty Zone" property. The $4,600 and $7,650 bump-ups are only available if bonus depreciation is claimed pursuant to Code Sec. 168(k).

The definition of "qualified New York Liberty Zone property" excludes property that is eligible for bonus depreciation under Code Sec. 168(k) even if such property is placed in service in the New York Liberty Zone (Code Sec. 1400L(b)(2)(C)(i)).

New property placed in service in the NYLZ after September 10, 2001, and before January 1, 2005, qualifies for bonus depreciation under Code Sec. 168(k). New property placed in service in the NYLZ after December 31, 2004, and before January 1, 2007, however, only qualifies under Code Sec. 1400L(b) (Code Sec. 1400L(b)(2)(A) (last sentence)). Used property does not qualify for bonus depreciation under Code Sec. 168(k), but it may qualify under Code Sec. 1400L(b) if the taxpayer was the first person to use the property in the NYLZ (Code Sec. 1400L(b)(2)(A)(iii)). Consequently, there is no bump-up for used property or for new property placed in service after December 31, 2004, in the NYLZ. Furthermore, since the increase in the bonus depreciation rate from 30-percent to 50-percent only applies to property for which bonus depreciation is claimed under Code Sec. 168(k), the bonus rate on qualified New York Liberty Zone property, whether new or used, is always 30-percent (Code Sec. 168(k)(4)(B)).

Termination date for NYLZ bonus depreciation. New or used vehicles placed in service in the NYLZ after 2006 do not qualify for bonus depreciation.

Vehicles placed in service in Gulf Opportunity GO-Zone, Kansas Disaster Area, or Presidentially Declared Disaster Area

The regular luxury car depreciation caps apply to a vehicle that is placed in service in the Gulf Opportunity Zone (i.e., the GO-Zone) even if the 50 percent GO-Zone bonus deduction is claimed. There is no bump-up in the caps on account of the GO-Zone additional depreciation allowance available for qualifying property acquired after August 27, 2005 and placed in service before January 1, 2008. See ¶ 127F for a discussion of the Go-Zone bonus allowance.

There is also no bump-up if 50% bonus depreciation is claimed under Act § 15345 of the Heartland, Habitat, Harvest and Horticulture Acts of 2008 (P.L.

110-246)) on a vehicle acquired on or after May 5, 2007 and placed in service in the Kansas Disaster Area on or before December 31, 2008. See ¶ 127G. Likewise, the otherwise allowable first-year cap is not increased if a vehicle qualifies for 50% bonus depreciation under Code Sec. 168(n) as qualified disaster assistance property placed in service after December 31, 2007, with respect to a federal disaster declared after that date and occurring before January 1, 2010. See ¶ 127H.

¶ 201

$25,000 Expensing Limit on Heavy SUVs, Trucks, and Vans

Taxpayers who purchased and placed a sport utility vehicle that was exempt from the luxury car depreciation limitations because it had a gross vehicle weight rating (GVWR) in excess of 6,000 pounds were allowed to claim the Code Sec. 179 expense deduction without restriction in the case of vehicles placed in service before October 23, 2004. For example, for tax years beginning in 2004 up to $102,000 of the cost of such a vehicle purchased before October 23, 2004 could be deducted, assuming the vehicle otherwise qualified for expensing under Code Sec. 179 and that the investment and taxable income limitations described at ¶ 300 did not limit the deduction.

The American Jobs Creation Act of 2004, however, now limits the cost of an SUV that may be taken into account under Code Sec. 179 to $25,000 if the SUV is exempt from the Code Sec. 280F depreciation limitations. The provision is effective for vehicles placed in service after October 22, 2004 (Code Sec. 179(b)(6), as added by the 2004 Jobs Act). The limitation also applies to heavy pick-up trucks with a cargo bed under six feet that are exempt from the depreciation caps and certain heavy vans that are exempt from the depreciation caps.

The new law does not eliminate the exemption from the Code Sec. 280F luxury car depreciation limitations for sport utility vehicles that are considered trucks and have a gross vehicle weight rating in excess of 6,000 pounds (see ¶ 200. It simply prevents a taxpayer from expensing the maximum amount otherwise allowable under Code Sec. 179 (i.e., $250,000 for tax years beginning in 2008 and 2009) if the vehicle is exempt. Consequently, owners of heavy sport utility vehicles that are considered trucks are still be able to claim a significantly higher first-year depreciation deduction than owners of lighter vehicles that are not exempt from the limitations.

For example, if an SUV costs $100,000 and is subject to the half-year convention, 40-percent of the cost may be deducted in the first year, as opposed to about 3-percent of the cost of a lighter vehicle of the same price that is subject to the depreciation limitations (the first-year depreciation limitation on an SUV that is considered a truck if placed in service in calendar year 2007 is $3,160 (see Table 3 at ¶ 200)). A more typically priced heavy SUV will cost $50,000 or less. The first-year combined section 179 and regular depreciation deduction on such an SUV would be 60-percent of the cost ($25,000 expensing limit + ($50,000 − $25,000 × 20%) = $30,000 or 60-percent of $50,000). About 6-percent of the $50,000 cost ($3,160) would be deductible in the first year if the depreciation limitations applied.

Partial business use. Code Sec. 179(b)(6) states: "The cost of any sport utility vehicle for any taxable year which may be taken into account under this section shall not exceed $25,000." Presumably, the $25,000 limitation applies after the determination of cost that is attributable to business use.

> ***Example 1:*** An SUV that is exempt from the luxury car depreciation caps cost $100,000 and is used 51% for business. Basis attributable to business use is $51,000 ($100,000 × 51%). Since this does not exceed $25,000, a $25,000 expensing deduction

should be allowed. However, if the "cost taken into account" is first limited to $25,000 and the business percentage then applied, the maximum section 179 deduction would be limited to $12,750 ($25,000 × 51%).

The first, more favorable, interpretation seems to be supported by the manner in which similar language contained in Code Sec. 179(b)(1) is applied. Code Sec. 179(b)(1) states: "The aggregate cost which may be taken into account under subsection (a) for any taxable year shall not exceed [the applicable dollar limitation for the tax year]" (e.g., $250,000 for tax years beginning in 2008 or 2009). In determining the allowable section 179 deduction under subsection for a tax year, the cost is multiplied by the business percentage. This amount is deductible to the extent that it does not exceed the dollar limitation for the tax year.

Example 2: A taxpayer purchases a machine for $600,000 in 2009 and uses it 51% for business. Basis attributable to business use is $306,000 ($600,000 × 51%). Since $306,000 exceeds $250,0000, the taxpayer may deduct $250,000. The deduction is not limited to $127,500 ($250,000 × 51%).

Multiple vehicles purchased in single tax year. The $25,000 limit appears to apply to each separate vehicle. Code Sec. 176(b)96)(A) provides that the cost of "any" sport utility vehicle for any taxable year which may be taken into account under this section shall not exceed $25,000. If the limitation was not applied separately, this section should be drafted to state that the cost of "all" sport utility vehicles for any taxable year which may be taken into account under this section shall not exceed $25,000.

Sport utility vehicle defined. For purposes of the new provision, a "sport utility vehicle" is broadly defined as any four-wheeled vehicle:

(1) primarily designed or which can be used to carry passengers over public streets, roads, or highways (except any vehicle operated exclusively on a rail or rails);

(2) which is not subject to the Code Sec. 280F depreciation caps (i.e., the vehicle is considered a truck and has a GVWR in excess of 6,000 pounds or is otherwise exempt); and

(3) which has a GVWR of not more than 14,000 pounds (Code Sec. 179(b)(6)(B)(i), as added by the 2004 Jobs Act).

Because this definition would include all heavy pickup trucks, vans, and small buses in addition to sport utility vehicles that are considered trucks, the term "sport utility vehicle" is further defined to exclude any of the following vehicles:

(1) a vehicle designed to have a seating capacity of more than nine persons behind the driver's seat;

(2) a vehicle equipped with a cargo area of at least six feet in interior length that is an open area and is not readily accessible directly from the passenger compartment;

(3) a vehicle equipped with a cargo area of at least six feet in interior length that is designed for use as an open area but is enclosed by a cap and is not readily accessible directly from the passenger compartment; or

(4) a vehicle with an integral enclosure, fully enclosing the driver compartment and load carrying device, does not have seating rearward of the driver's seat, and has no body section protruding more than 30 inches ahead of the leading edge of the windshield (Code Sec. 179(b)(6)(B)(ii), as added by the 2004 Jobs Act).

Under this definition, the $25,000 limit applies to a passenger van with a GVWR in excess of 6000 pounds but which does not seat at least 10 persons behind the driver. Cargo vans are not subject to the limit if the requirements of item (4) are satisfied.

A few heavy pickup trucks with extended, quad, or crew cabs have a cargo bed shorter than six feet and, therefore, are subject to the $25,000 limit. ***A list of trucks with short beds is provided in a Quick Reference Table in the Appendix of this book. Other Quick Reference Tables also provide lists of SUVS, trucks, and vans that have a GVWR in excess of 6,000 pounds and are exempt from the depreciation caps.***

Although the definition of an SUV for purposes of the $25,000 limitation does not apply to a vehicle that weighs 6,000 pounds or less and is subject to the depreciation limitations, a taxpayer is already effectively prevented from claiming any expense allowance in most cases because regular first-year depreciation exceeds the first-year luxury car cap.

¶ 202

Post-recovery Period Deductions

If there is continued use of a vehicle for business purposes after expiration of the MACRS recovery period, a limited deduction (treated as a depreciation deduction) of the unrecovered basis resulting from application of the luxury car limits (¶ 200) is authorized by Code Sec. 280F(a)(1)(B). The authorized deduction may be claimed beginning in the first tax year after the tax year in which the recovery period ends. It would usually first be claimed in the seventh tax year after the car is placed in service since the recovery period of most vehicles extends over six tax years. The limited deduction is claimed annually after the recovery period ends until the unrecovered basis of the car is considered fully recovered. A car must continue to qualify as depreciable property in any year that a post-recovery period deduction is claimed.

The maximum post-recovery period deduction in each tax year depends on when the car was placed in service. The maximum deduction is indicated at ¶ 200 in the chart for the applicable set of annual dollar limits for the depreciation allowable under the column for "Year 4, etc."

The maximum deduction must be reduced for personal use and is subject to the short tax year adjustments indicated at ¶ 200.

Section 280F unrecovered basis

In determining how much post-recovery period basis remains available for deduction, the basis of a passenger automobile is reduced by the maximum allowable deduction as if the automobile were used 100 percent for business/investment use (Code Sec. 280F(d)(8)). Thus, the term "unrecovered basis" means the adjusted basis of the passenger automobile after reduction by the lesser of the amount of the full luxury car specific dollar limit or the depreciation deduction (assuming 100-percent business use even where, because of personal use, a smaller deduction was actually allowed).

> ***Example (1):*** On April 5, 2009, a calendar-year taxpayer purchased a used car for $20,000 and placed it in service. No amount is expensed under Code Sec. 179 or claimed as bonus depreciation. Business use of the car each year for the life of the car is 80%. Depreciation is computed under the general MACRS 200% declining-balance method over a 5-year recovery period using a half-year convention subject to limitation by Code Sec. 280F.
>
> The recovery period depreciation for 2009 through 2014 is computed as follows:

Year	*100% Business-Use MACRS Depreciation*	*Luxury Car Limit*	*80% of Lesser*	*Section 280F Unrecovered Basis*
2009	$4,000	$2,960	$2,368	$17,040
2010	6,400	4,800	3,840	12,240
2011	3,840	2,850	2,280	9,390
2012	2,304	1,775	1,420	7,615
2013	2,304	1,775	1,420	5,840
2014	1,152	1,775	922	4,688

The 100% business-use MACRS deductions are computed without regard to the Code Sec. 280F limitations using the applicable table percentages for 5-year property (Table 1 at ¶ 180). The allowable deduction (Column 3) for each year is the lesser of 80% of the MACRS deduction computed for the year based on 100% business use (Column 1) or 80% of the luxury car depreciation cap for the year (Column 2). The Sec. 280F unrecovered basis (Column 4) for each year is the original cost of the vehicle ($20,000) reduced by the accumulated depreciation that could have been claimed if business use for each year had been 100% (i.e., for each year, the lesser of Column 1 or Column 2). For example, 2009 unrecovered basis is $17,040 ($20,000 - $2,960). 2010 unrecovered basis is $12,240 ($20,000 - $2,960 - $4,800).

The $4,688 Section 280F unrecovered basis at the end of 2014 may be recovered in the post-recovery period years beginning in 2015. The allowable deduction for each post recovery period year is the lesser of: (1) the depreciation cap for post-recovery period years multiplied by the percentage of business use for the year ($1,420 ($1,775 × 80%)) or (2) the remaining Section 280F unrecovered basis at the beginning of the year multiplied by the percentage of business use. Section 280F unrecovered basis in each post-recovery year is reduced by the lesser of the full amount of the post-recovery period depreciation cap as if business use had been 100% or the Section 280F unrecovered basis at the beginning of the year.

Depreciation allowances for the years 2015 through 2017 after application of the luxury car limits are as follows, assuming 80% business use continues:

Year	*Section 280F Unrecovered Basis at Beginning of Year*	*Luxury Car Limit*	*80% of Lesser*	*Section 280F Unrecovered Basis at End of Year*
2015	$4,688	$1,775	$1,420	$2,913
2016	2,913	1,775	1,420	1,138
2017	1,138	1,775	910	0

The total depreciation claimed by the taxpayer from 2009 through 2017 is $16,000 (the sum of the Column 3 figures). This is the same amount of depreciation that would have been claimed during the regular recovery period (2009 - 2014) if the luxury car limits did not apply ($20,000 × 80%).

At first glance, one might conclude that the luxury car limits do not reduce overall depreciation (i.e., the depreciation that would be claimed if there were no luxury car caps) but rather simply increase the period over which otherwise allowable depreciation is claimed. However, this is not necessarily the case. For example, if the car in the preceding example had been converted to personal use for all of 2015 (the first-post recovery period year), no additional depreciation deductions would be allowed and no portion of the disallowed deductions attributable to application of the depreciation caps during the earlier years would be recovered (Code Sec. 280F(a)(1)(B)(iii), indicating that post-recovery period deductions are not allowed unless the property is depreciable).

Example (2): Assume the same facts in as in *Example (1)*, except that the business use percentages are 60% in 2015, 50% in 2016, and 10% in 2017. The post-recovery deductions would be computed as follows:

Year	*Section 280F Unrecovered Basis at Beginning of Year*	*Luxury Car Limit*	*Business% of Lesser*	*Section 280F Unrecovered Basis at End of Year*
2015	$4,688	$1,775	$1,065	$2,913
2016	2,913	1,775	888	1,138
2017	1,138	1,775	114	0

In this example (which modifies Example (1), above) the total depreciation claimed on the vehicle (the sum of the Column 3 figures for 2009-2017) is $14,317. If there were no luxury car caps the taxpayer could have claimed $16,000 ($20,000 × 80% business use for the regular recovery 2009-2014 recovery period).

The following example shows how the first-year bonus depreciation allowance is treated under the luxury car rules.

Example (3): On April 5, 2009, a calendar-year taxpayer purchased a new car for $30,000 and claimed the 50% bonus depreciation allowance under Code Sec. 168(k). See ¶ 127D. 2009 bonus depreciation without regard to the first-year cap ($10,960) and 80% business use would be $15,000 ($30,000 × 50%). Regular depreciation would be $3,000 (($30,000 - $15,000) × 20%). The sum of regular and bonus depreciation without regard to 80% business use is $18,000 ($15,000 + $3,000). Note that the basis used for computing the regular depreciation deductions is $15,000—the cost reduced by the bonus depreciation ($30,000 - $15,000).

The recovery period depreciation for 2009 through 2014 is computed as follows:

Year	*100% Business-Use MACRS Depreciation*	*Luxury Car Limit*	*80% of Lesser*	*Section 280F Unrecovered Basis*
2009	$18,000	$10,960	$8,768	$19,040
2010	4,800	4,800	3,840	14,240
2011	2,880	2,850	2,280	11,390
2012	1,728	1,775	1,382	9,662
2013	1,728	1,775	1,382	7,934
2014	864	1,775	691	7,070

The $7,070 unrecovered basis at the end of 2014 may be recovered in the post-recovery period years beginning in 2015 at the rate of $1,420 ($1,775 × 80%) per year, assuming business use continues at 80 percent. However, the unrecovered basis is reduced by $1,775 in each post recovery year. See Example (1).

¶ 204

Leased Automobiles and Other Listed Property

Lessors

Listed property (¶ 208) leased or held for leasing by a person regularly engaged in the business of leasing listed property is not subject to the listed property rules of Code Sec. 280F (Code Sec. 280F(c)(1)). A person is considered to be regularly engaged in the business of leasing cars only if contracts to lease cars are made with some frequency over a continuous period. Occasional or incidental leasing is not considered leasing activity. An employer that allows an employee to use the employer's car for personal purposes and charges the employee for such use is not regularly engaged in the business of leasing (Temp. Reg. § 1.280F-5T(c)).

Listed property leased or held for leasing by a person not regularly engaged in the business of leasing listed property is subject to the listed property rules of Code Sec. 280F.

Lessees

To prevent avoidance of the "listed property" luxury car rules (¶ 200) and the "listed property" business use rules (¶ 206 and ¶ 210) that apply to owned passenger automobiles and other listed property, a parallel system of limitations applies to leased passenger automobiles (discussed below) and to other leased listed property (see ¶ 212). The system applies to all lessees of passenger automobiles and other listed property regardless of whether the lessor is regularly engaged in the business of leasing.

The mechanics of providing comparable limitations on purchased property and leased property are accomplished by reducing the lessee's rental deductions by inclusion amounts. No inclusion amount is required if the lease term is less than 30 days (Code Sec. 280F(c)(2)).

Note that the lessee inclusion amounts that were included in income over the term of the lease are *not* deductible at the end of the lease term.

Under this system, a lessee who leases a passenger automobile for business may be required to include an amount in gross income, based on the price of the car, to offset rental deductions.

The inclusion amount is entered on Schedule C (Form 1040) by the self-employed, Form 2106 by employees, and on Schedule F (Form 1040) by farmers. On these forms, the inclusion amount is in effect included in gross income by reducing rental expense.

Post-1986 lease—Inclusion tables for passenger automobiles

If a taxpayer leases a passenger automobile after 1986, the inclusion amount for each tax year that the automobile is leased is determined by referring to the appropriate table (the tables for post-1999 leases are reproduced below) based on the calendar-year in which the lease term begins. The term "passenger automobile" includes pick-up trucks, SUVs, and vans with a gross vehicle weight rating of 6,000 pounds or less (see ¶ 208). These lease inclusion tables are only used if the vehicle would be subject to the depreciation caps if the lessee owned it. Beginning in 2003, the IRS is issuing separate lease inclusion tables for trucks (including SUVs that are considered trucks) and vans. From the appropriate table:

(1) Locate the dollar amounts for the years of the lease term based on the fair market value of the vehicle on the first day of the lease term.

(2) Select the dollar amount for the tax year in which the automobile is used under the lease.

(3) Prorate the dollar amount for the number of days of the lease term included in the tax year.

(4) Multiply the prorated dollar amount by the business/investment use for the tax year (Reg. § 1.280F-7(a)).

Dollar amount for last tax year. For the last tax year during any lease that does not begin and end in the same tax year, the dollar amount for the preceding year is used.

If a leased business car is converted to personal use, the dollar amount for the tax year in which business use ceases is the dollar amount for the preceding tax year. See *Example (12)* at ¶ 206.

Fair market value. With respect to fair market value, if the lease agreement provides a capitalized cost of the vehicle, that cost should be used as the fair market value. Otherwise, fmv is determined on the basis of what would be paid in an arms-length transaction. Similar sales at the time of the lease may be useful in determining fair market value.

If a car leased for personal purposes is later converted to business use, the fair market value is determined on the date of the conversion to business use. See *Example (10)* at ¶ 206.

FMV trigger points. Lease inclusion amounts are required in the case of leased vehicles (other than trucks and vans, including SUVs that are considered trucks and first leased after 2002) if the fair market value on the first day of the lease exceeds the following amounts:

Vehicles (Other Than Trucks and Vans First Leased after 2002)

Calendar year first leased	*FMV Over*	*Authority*
2009	$18,500	Rev. Proc. 2009-24
2008	$18,500	Rev. Proc. 2008-22
2007	$15,500	Rev. Proc. 2007-30
2006	$15,200	Rev. Proc. 2006-18
2005	$15,200	Rev. Proc. 2005-13
2004	$17,500	Rev. Proc. 2004-20
2003	$18,000	Rev. Proc. 2003-75
2002	$15,500	Rev. Proc. 2002-14
2001	$15,500	Rev. Proc. 2001-19

Lease inclusion tables for post-2004 leases are reproduced below. For earlier tables, refer to the authority cited above or IRS Publication 463 (Travel, Entertainment, Gift, and Car Expenses).

Trucks and vans first leased after 2002

Beginning in 2003, a separate lease inclusion table is provided for trucks (including SUVs that are considered trucks) and vans that are leased. A lease inclusion amount using this table is only required if the truck or van would be subject to the annual depreciation caps if it was owned by the lessee. Thus, no inclusion amount is required if the leased truck or van has a loaded gross vehicle weight of more than 6,000 pounds. The inclusion amount for a truck or van first leased in 2002 or earlier is determined using the table that applies to other types of nonelectric passenger automobiles.

Trucks and Vans

Calendar year first leased	*FMV Over*	*Authority*
2009	$18,500	Rev. Proc. 2009-24
2008	$19,000	Rev. Proc. 2008-22
2007	$16,400	Rev. Proc. 2007-30
2006	$16,700	Rev. Proc. 2006-18
2005	$16,700	Rev. Proc. 2005-13
2004	$18,000	Rev. Proc. 2004-20
2003	$18,500	Rev. Proc. 2003-75

Electric vehicles

Separate inclusion amount tables are provided for clean-air vehicles (see ¶ 200) first leased after August 5, 1997 and before 2007. For such vehicles first leased in 2007 and thereafter, the appropriate lease inclusion table above is used.

The lease inclusion amounts are required if the fair market value of the vehicle on the date of lease exceeds the following amounts:

Electric Vehicles first leased before 2007

Calendar year first leased	*FMV Over*	*Authority*
after 2006	Refer to tables above	
2006	$45,000	Rev. Proc. 2006-18
2005	$45,000	Rev. Proc. 2005-13
2004	$53,000	Rev. Proc. 2004-20
2003	$53,000	Rev. Proc. 2003-75
2002	$46,000	Rev. Proc. 2002-14
2001	$47,000	Rev. Proc. 2001-19
2000	$47,000	Rev. Proc. 2000-18
1999	$47,000	Rev. Proc. 99-14
1998	$47,000	Rev. Proc. 98-30
8/5/97 - 12/31/97	$47,000	Rev. Proc. 98-24

Reporting the inclusion amount

Employees who lease a vehicle report the inclusion amount on Form 2106, Section C. The self-employed use Schedule C (Form 1040), and farmers use Schedule F (Form 1040).

¶ 205
Automobile Lease Inclusion Tables

Lease Inclusion Table Index

LEASE INCLUSION TABLES FOR VEHICLES OTHER THAN TRUCKS AND VANS

January 1, 2009 to December 31, 2009 Leases of Vehicles Other than Trucks and Vans

The following table from Rev. Proc. 2009-24 governs computation of includible amounts for passenger automobiles (that are not trucks (including SUVs that are considered trucks) or vans) with a fair market value exceeding $18,500 and first leased in 2009. This table also applies to electric vehicles first leased in 2009 that are not a truck or van.

Dollar Amounts for Nonelectric Passenger Automobiles (Other than Trucks or Vans) First Leased in 2009

Fair Market Value of Automobile		*Tax Year During Lease**				
Over	*Not Over*	*1st*	*2nd*	*3rd*	*4th*	*5th and Later*
$ 18,500	$ 19,000	9	19	28	34	38
19,000	19,500	10	21	32	38	43
19,500	20,000	11	24	36	42	48
20,000	20,500	12	27	39	46	54
20,500	21,000	13	29	43	51	58
21,000	21,500	15	31	47	55	64
21,500	22,000	16	34	50	60	68
22,000	23,000	17	38	56	66	76
23,000	24,000	20	42	64	75	86
24,000	25,000	22	47	71	84	96
25,000	26,000	24	52	78	93	107
26,000	27,000	26	58	85	101	117
27,000	28,000	29	62	93	110	127
28,000	29,000	31	67	100	119	138
29,000	30,000	33	72	108	128	147
30,000	31,000	35	77	115	137	157
31,000	32,000	38	82	122	146	167
32,000	33,000	40	87	129	155	178
33,000	34,000	42	92	137	163	188
34,000	35,000	44	97	144	172	199
35,000	36,000	47	102	151	181	208
36,000	37,000	49	107	159	189	219
37,000	38,000	51	112	166	199	228
38,000	39,000	53	117	173	208	239
39,000	40,000	56	122	180	216	250
40,000	41,000	58	127	188	225	259
41,000	42,000	60	132	195	234	269
42,000	43,000	62	137	203	242	280
43,000	44,000	65	141	210	252	290
44,000	45,000	67	146	218	260	300
45,000	46,000	69	151	225	269	311
46,000	47,000	71	157	232	278	320
47,000	48,000	74	161	240	286	331
48,000	49,000	76	166	247	296	340
49,000	50,000	78	171	255	304	351

Fair Market Value of Automobile		*Tax Year During Lease**				
Over	*Not Over*	*1st*	*2nd*	*3rd*	*4th*	*5th and Later*
50,000	51,000	80	176	262	313	361
51,000	52,000	83	181	269	322	371
52,000	53,000	85	186	276	331	381
53,000	54,000	87	191	284	339	392
54,000	55,000	89	196	291	349	401
55,000	56,000	92	201	298	357	412
56,000	57,000	94	206	306	365	423
57,000	58,000	96	211	313	375	432
58,000	59,000	98	216	320	384	442
59,000	60,000	101	221	327	393	452
60,000	62,000	104	228	339	406	467
62,000	64,000	109	238	353	424	488
64,000	66,000	113	248	368	441	509
66,000	68,000	118	258	382	459	529
68,000	70,000	122	268	397	476	550
70,000	72,000	127	277	413	493	570
72,000	74,000	131	288	427	511	590
74,000	76,000	136	297	442	529	610
76,000	78,000	140	307	457	546	631
78,000	80,000	145	317	471	564	651
80,000	85,000	152	335	497	595	686
85,000	90,000	164	359	534	639	737
90,000	95,000	175	384	570	683	789
95,000	100,000	186	409	607	727	839
100,000	110,000	203	446	662	793	916
110,000	120,000	226	495	736	881	1,018
120,000	130,000	248	545	809	970	1,119
130,000	140,000	271	594	883	1,058	1,220
140,000	150,000	293	644	956	1,146	1,322
150,000	160,000	316	693	1,030	1,234	1,424
160,000	170,000	338	743	1,103	1,322	1,526
170,000	180,000	361	792	1,177	1,410	1,628
180,000	190,000	383	842	1,250	1,498	1,730
190,000	200,000	406	891	1,324	1,586	1,831
200,000	210,000	428	941	1,397	1,675	1,932
210,000	220,000	451	990	1,471	1,762	2,035
220,000	230,000	473	1,040	1,544	1,851	2,136
230,000	240,000	496	1,089	1,618	1,939	2,238
240,000	And up	518	1,139	1,691	2,027	2,340

* For the last tax year of the lease, use the dollar amount for the preceding tax year.

Example (1): A car with a fair market value of $34,500 is leased for a term of 3 years beginning on April 1, 2009. Assuming full business use by a calendar-year taxpayer, the includible amount for 2009 is $33.15 (275/365 × $44). The includible amount for 2010 is $97. The includible amount for 2011 is $144. The includible amount for 2012 is $35.51 ($144 × 90/365) (the dollar amount for the preceding tax year is used for the last tax year of the lease).

January 1, 2008 to December 31, 2008 Leases of Vehicles Other than Trucks and Vans

The following table from Rev. Proc. 2008-22 governs computation of includible amounts for passenger automobiles (that are not trucks (including SUVs that are considered trucks) or vans) with a fair market value exceeding $18,500 and first leased in 2008. This table also applies to electric vehicles first leased in 2008 that are not a truck or van.

Dollar Amounts for Nonelectric Passenger Automobiles (Other than Trucks or Vans) First Leased in 2008

Fair Market Value of Automobile		*Tax Year During Lease**				
Over	*Not Over*	*1st*	*2nd*	*3rd*	*4th*	*5th and Later*
$ 18,500	$ 19,000	20	42	62	73	84
19,000	19,500	22	47	71	83	94
19,500	20,000	25	53	78	93	106
20,000	20,500	27	58	87	102	117
20,500	21,000	30	63	95	112	128
21,000	21,500	32	69	103	122	139
21,500	22,000	34	75	111	131	151
22,000	23,000	38	83	123	146	167
23,000	24,000	43	94	139	165	190
24,000	25,000	48	105	155	185	212
25,000	26,000	53	115	172	204	235
26,000	27,000	58	126	188	223	257
27,000	28,000	63	137	204	243	279
28,000	29,000	68	148	220	262	302
29,000	30,000	73	159	236	282	324
30,000	31,000	78	170	252	301	347
31,000	32,000	83	181	268	321	368
32,000	33,000	88	192	284	340	391
33,000	34,000	93	202	301	359	414
34,000	35,000	98	213	317	379	436
35,000	36,000	103	224	333	398	459
36,000	37,000	108	235	349	418	481
37,000	38,000	113	246	365	437	503
38,000	39,000	118	257	381	457	525
39,000	40,000	123	268	397	476	548
40,000	41,000	128	279	413	495	571
41,000	42,000	133	289	430	515	593
42,000	43,000	137	301	446	534	615
43,000	44,000	142	312	462	553	638
44,000	45,000	147	323	478	573	659
45,000	46,000	152	333	495	592	682
46,000	47,000	157	344	511	611	705
47,000	48,000	162	355	527	631	727
48,000	49,000	167	366	543	650	750
49,000	50,000	172	377	559	670	772
50,000	51,000	177	388	575	689	794
51,000	52,000	182	399	591	709	816
52,000	53,000	187	410	607	728	839

Fair Market Value of Automobile		*Tax Year During Lease**				
Over	*Not Over*	*1st*	*2nd*	*3rd*	*4th*	*5th and Later*
53,000	54,000	192	420	624	747	862
54,000	55,000	197	431	640	767	884
55,000	56,000	202	442	657	785	906
56,000	57,000	207	453	673	805	928
57,000	58,000	212	464	689	824	951
58,000	59,000	217	475	705	844	973
59,000	60,000	222	486	721	863	996
60,000	62,000	229	502	746	892	1,029
62,000	64,000	239	524	778	931	1,074
64,000	66,000	249	546	810	970	1,118
66,000	68,000	259	567	843	1,008	1,164
68,000	70,000	269	589	875	1,047	1,209
70,000	72,000	279	611	907	1,086	1,253
72,000	74,000	289	633	939	1,125	1,298
74,000	76,000	299	654	972	1,164	1,342
76,000	78,000	309	676	1,004	1,203	1,387
78,000	80,000	319	698	1,036	1,242	1,432
80,000	85,000	336	736	1,093	1,309	1,511
85,000	90,000	361	791	1,173	1,406	1,623
90,000	95,000	386	845	1,255	1,503	1,734
95,000	100,000	410	900	1,335	1,600	1,846
100,000	110,000	448	981	1,457	1,745	2,014
110,000	120,000	497	1,090	1,619	1,939	2,238
120,000	130,000	547	1,199	1,780	2,133	2,462
130,000	140,000	597	1,308	1,942	2,327	2,685
140,000	150,000	646	1,417	2,103	2,521	2,910
150,000	160,000	696	1,526	2,265	2,715	3,133
160,000	170,000	745	1,635	2,427	2,908	3,357
170,000	180,000	795	1,744	2,588	3,103	3,581
180,000	190,000	845	1,853	2,750	3,296	3,805
190,000	200,000	894	1,962	2,912	3,490	4,028
200,000	210,000	944	2,071	3,073	3,684	4,252
210,000	220,000	994	2,179	3,235	3,878	4,476
220,000	230,000	1,043	2,289	3,396	4,072	4,700
230,000	240,000	1,093	2,397	3,559	4,265	4,924
240,000	and up	1,142	2,507	3,720	4,459	5,148

* For the last tax year of the lease, use the dollar amount for the preceding tax year.

Example (2): A car with a fair market value of $34,500 is leased for a term of 3 years beginning on April 1, 2008. Assuming full business use by a calendar-year taxpayer, the includible amount for 2008 is $73.83 (275/365 × $98). The includible amount for 2009 is $213. The includible amount for 2010 is $317. The includible amount for 2011 is $78.16 ($317 × 90/365) (the dollar amount for the preceding tax year is used for the last tax year of the lease).

January 1, 2007 to December 31, 2007 Leases of Vehicles Other than Trucks and Vans

The following table from Rev. Proc. 2007-30 governs computation of includible amounts for passenger automobiles (that are not trucks (including an SUV that is considered a truck) with a fair market value exceeding $15,500 and first leased in

2007. This table also applies to electric vehicles first leased in 2007 that are not electric trucks or vans.

Dollar Amounts for Passenger Automobiles (Other than Trucks or Vans) First Leased in 2007

Fair Market Value of Automobile		*Tax Year During Lease**				
Over	*Not Over*	*1st*	*2nd*	*3rd*	*4th*	*5th and Later*
$15,500	$15,800	2	5	11	11	13
15,800	16,100	4	10	17	19	22
16,100	16,400	6	14	24	28	31
16,400	16,700	9	18	31	35	41
16,700	17,000	11	23	37	43	50
17,000	17,500	13	29	46	54	62
17,500	18,000	17	37	56	68	77
18,000	18,500	20	44	68	81	93
18,500	19,000	24	51	80	94	108
19,000	19,500	27	59	90	108	124
19,500	20,000	30	67	101	121	139
20,000	20,500	34	74	113	134	154
20,500	21,000	37	82	123	148	170
21,000	21,500	41	89	135	161	185
21,500	22,000	44	97	146	174	201
22,000	23,000	49	108	163	194	224
23,000	24,000	56	123	185	221	255
24,000	25,000	63	138	207	248	285
25,000	26,000	70	153	229	275	316
26,000	27,000	77	168	251	302	347
27,000	28,000	83	183	274	328	378
28,000	29,000	90	198	296	355	409
29,000	30,000	97	213	318	382	439
30,000	31,000	104	228	341	408	470
31,000	32,000	111	243	363	435	501
32,000	33,000	118	258	385	461	532
33,000	34,000	125	273	407	488	563
34,000	35,000	131	288	430	515	593
35,000	36,000	138	303	452	542	624
36,000	37,000	145	318	474	568	656
37,000	38,000	152	333	496	595	686
38,000	39,000	159	348	519	621	717
39,000	40,000	166	363	541	648	748
40,000	41,000	172	378	564	674	779
41,000	42,000	179	393	586	701	810
42,000	43,000	186	408	608	728	840
43,000	44,000	193	423	630	755	871
44,000	45,000	200	438	652	782	902
45,000	46,000	207	453	674	809	933
46,000	47,000	213	468	697	835	964
47,000	48,000	220	483	719	862	995
48,000	49,000	227	498	742	888	1,025

Fair Market Value of Automobile		*Tax Year During Lease**				
Over	*Not Over*	*1st*	*2nd*	*3rd*	*4th*	*5th and Later*
49,000	50,000	234	513	764	915	1,056
50,000	51,000	241	528	786	942	1,087
51,000	52,000	248	543	808	969	1,117
52,000	53,000	254	558	831	995	1,148
53,000	54,000	261	573	853	1,022	1,179
54,000	55,000	268	588	875	1,049	1,210
55,000	56,000	275	603	897	1,076	1,241
56,000	57,000	282	618	920	1,102	1,271
57,000	58,000	289	633	942	1,128	1,303
58,000	59,000	296	648	964	1,155	1,334
59,000	60,000	302	663	987	1,182	1,364
60,000	62,000	313	685	1,020	1,222	1,411
62,000	64,000	326	716	1,064	1,276	1,472
64,000	66,000	340	746	1,108	1,329	1,534
66,000	68,000	354	775	1,154	1,382	1,595
68,000	70,000	367	806	1,198	1,435	1,657
70,000	72,000	381	836	1,242	1,489	1,719
72,000	74,000	395	865	1,287	1,543	1,780
74,000	76,000	408	896	1,331	1,596	1,842
76,000	78,000	422	926	1,376	1,649	1,903
78,000	80,000	436	955	1,421	1,703	1,965
80,000	85,000	460	1,008	1,498	1,796	2,074
85,000	90,000	494	1,083	1,610	1,929	2,228
90,000	95,000	528	1,158	1,721	2,063	2,382
95,000	100,000	562	1,233	1,833	2,196	2,536
100,000	110,000	614	1,346	1,999	2,396	2,767
110,000	120,000	682	1,496	2,222	2,663	3,075
120,000	130,000	750	1,646	2,444	2,931	3,383
130,000	140,000	819	1,796	2,667	3,197	3,692
140,000	150,000	887	1,946	2,890	3,464	4,000
150,000	160,000	956	2,096	3,112	3,731	4,308
160,000	170,000	1,024	2,246	3,335	3,998	4,616
170,000	180,000	1,093	2,396	3,557	4,266	4,924
180,000	190,000	1,161	2,546	3,780	4,532	5,233
190,000	200,000	1,229	2,696	4,003	4,799	5,541
200,000	210,000	1,298	2,846	4,225	5,067	5,848
210,000	220,000	1,366	2,996	4,448	5,333	6,157
220,000	230,000	1,435	3,146	4,671	5,600	6,465
230,000	240,000	1,503	3,296	4,893	5,867	6,774
240,000	and up	1,571	3,446	5,116	6,134	7,082

* For the last tax year of the lease, use the dollar amount for the preceding tax year.

Example (3): A car with a fair market value of $34,500 is leased for a term of 3 years beginning on April 1, 2007. Assuming full business use by a calendar-year taxpayer, the includible amount for 2007 is $98.70 (275/365 × $131). The includible amount for 2008 is $288. The includible amount for 2009 is $430. The includible amount for 2010 is $106.03 ($430 × 90/365) (the dollar amount for the preceding tax year is used for the last tax year of the lease).

January 1, 2006 to December 31, 2006 Leases of Nonelectric Vehicles Other than Trucks or Vans

The following table from Rev. Proc. 2006-18 governs computation of includible amounts for nonelectric passenger automobiles (that are not trucks (including SUVs that are considered trucks) or vans) with a fair market value exceeding $15,200 and first leased in 2006.

Dollar Amounts for Nonelectric Passenger Automobiles (Other than Trucks or Vans) First Leased in 2006

Fair Market Value of Automobile		*Tax Year During Lease**				
Over	*Not Over*	*1st*	*2nd*	*3rd*	*4th*	*5th and Later*
$15,200	$15,500	4	6	10	10	10
15,500	15,800	6	10	16	18	18
15,800	16,100	8	15	22	25	28
16,100	16,400	9	19	29	33	36
16,400	16,700	11	24	35	40	45
16,700	17,000	13	28	42	48	53
17,000	17,500	16	34	50	58	66
17,500	18,000	19	41	61	71	80
18,000	18,500	23	48	71	84	95
18,500	19,000	26	55	82	96	110
19,000	19,500	29	62	93	109	125
19,500	20,000	32	70	103	122	139
20,000	20,500	36	76	114	135	154
20,500	21,000	39	84	124	148	168
21,000	21,500	42	91	135	160	184
21,500	22,000	45	98	146	173	198
22,000	23,000	50	109	162	192	220
23,000	24,000	57	123	183	218	250
24,000	25,000	63	138	204	243	279
25,000	26,000	70	152	225	269	309
26,000	27,000	76	166	247	294	339
27,000	28,000	83	181	268	319	368
28,000	29,000	90	195	289	345	397
29,000	30,000	96	209	311	371	426
30,000	31,000	103	223	332	397	455
31,000	32,000	109	238	353	422	485
32,000	33,000	116	252	374	448	515
33,000	34,000	122	267	395	473	545
34,000	35,000	129	281	417	498	574
35,000	36,000	135	295	439	523	604
36,000	37,000	142	309	460	549	633
37,000	38,000	148	324	481	575	662
38,000	39,000	155	338	502	601	691
39,000	40,000	161	353	523	626	721
40,000	41,000	168	367	545	651	750
41,000	42,000	175	381	566	677	780
42,000	43,000	181	396	587	702	810
43,000	44,000	188	410	608	728	839

Fair Market Value of Automobile		*Tax Year During Lease**				
Over	*Not Over*	*1st*	*2nd*	*3rd*	*4th*	*5th and Later*
44,000	45,000	194	424	630	753	869
45,000	46,000	201	438	651	779	898
46,000	47,000	207	453	672	805	927
47,000	48,000	214	467	694	830	956
48,000	49,000	220	482	715	855	986
49,000	50,000	227	496	736	881	1,016
50,000	51,000	233	510	758	906	1,045
51,000	52,000	240	525	778	932	1,075
52,000	53,000	246	539	800	958	1,104
53,000	54,000	253	553	821	984	1,133
54,000	55,000	259	568	842	1,009	1,163
55,000	56,000	266	582	864	1,034	1,192
56,000	57,000	273	596	885	1,060	1,221
57,000	58,000	279	611	906	1,085	1,251
58,000	59,000	286	625	927	1,111	1,281
59,000	60,000	292	639	949	1,136	1,311
60,000	62,000	302	661	981	1,174	1,354
62,000	64,000	315	690	1,023	1,225	1,413
64,000	66,000	328	718	1,066	1,276	1,473
66,000	68,000	341	747	1,108	1,328	1,531
68,000	70,000	354	776	1,151	1,378	1,590
70,000	72,000	367	804	1,194	1,429	1,649
72,000	74,000	380	833	1,236	1,481	1,707
74,000	76,000	393	862	1,278	1,532	1,767
76,000	78,000	407	890	1,321	1,583	1,825
78,000	80,000	420	919	1,363	1,634	1,884
80,000	85,000	443	969	1,438	1,723	1,987
85,000	90,000	475	1,041	1,544	1,851	2,135
90,000	95,000	508	1,112	1,651	1,978	2,282
95,000	100,000	541	1,184	1,757	2,106	2,429
100,000	110,000	590	1,291	1,917	2,297	2,650
110,000	120,000	655	1,435	2,130	2,552	2,944
120,000	130,000	720	1,579	2,342	2,807	3,239
130,000	140,000	786	1,722	2,555	3,062	3,534
140,000	150,000	851	1,865	2,768	3,317	3,829
150,000	160,000	916	2,009	2,980	3,573	4,123
160,000	170,000	982	2,152	3,193	3,828	4,417
170,000	180,000	1,047	2,295	3,406	4,083	4,712
180,000	190,000	1,112	2,439	3,619	4,337	5,007
190,000	200,000	1,178	2,582	3,832	4,592	5,301
200,000	210,000	1,243	2,726	4,044	4,848	5,595
210,000	220,000	1,309	2,869	4,257	5,103	5,890
220,000	230,000	1,374	3,012	4,470	5,358	6,185
230,000	240,000	1,439	3,156	4,682	5,613	6,480
240,000	and up	1,505	3,299	4,895	5,868	6,774

* For the last tax year of the lease, use the dollar amount for the preceding tax year.

Example (4): A car with a fair market value of $34,500 is leased for a term of 3 years beginning on April 1, 2006. Assuming full business use by a calendar-year taxpayer, the includible amount for 2006 is $97.19 (275/365 × $129). The includible amount for 2007 is $281. The includible amount for 2008 is $417. The includible amount for 2009 is $102.82 ($417 × 90/365) (the dollar amount for the preceding tax year is used for the last tax year of the lease).

LEASE INCLUSION TABLES FOR TRUCKS, VANS, OR SUVs THAT ARE CONSIDERED TRUCKS

January 1, 2009 to December 31, 2009 Leases of Trucks or Vans

The following table from Rev. Proc. 2009-24 governs computation of includible amounts for trucks (including SUVs that are considered trucks) or vans with a GVWR of 6,000 pounds or less, a fair market value exceeding $18,500, and which are first leased in calendar-year 2009. This table should also be used for electric vehicles that are trucks or vans first leased in calendar-year 2009.

Dollar Amounts for Trucks or Vans First Leased in 2009

Fair Market Value of Automobile		*Tax Year During Lease**				
Over	*Not Over*	*1st*	*2nd*	*3rd*	*4th*	*5th and Later*
$ 18,500	$ 19,000	8	17	25	30	35
19,000	19,500	9	19	29	35	40
19,500	20,000	10	22	33	38	45
20,000	20,500	11	25	36	43	50
20,500	21,000	12	27	40	48	55
21,000	21,500	13	30	43	52	60
21,500	22,000	15	32	47	56	66
22,000	23,000	16	36	52	64	72
23,000	24,000	18	41	60	72	83
24,000	25,000	21	45	68	81	93
25,000	26,000	23	50	75	90	103
26,000	27,000	25	56	82	98	114
27,000	28,000	27	61	89	107	124
28,000	29,000	30	65	97	116	134
29,000	30,000	32	70	104	125	144
30,000	31,000	34	75	112	134	154
31,000	32,000	36	80	119	143	164
32,000	33,000	39	85	126	151	175
33,000	34,000	41	90	134	160	184
34,000	35,000	43	95	141	169	195
35,000	36,000	45	100	148	178	205
36,000	37,000	48	105	155	187	215
37,000	38,000	50	110	163	195	226
38,000	39,000	52	115	170	204	236
39,000	40,000	55	120	177	213	246
40,000	41,000	57	125	185	221	256
41,000	42,000	59	130	192	231	266
42,000	43,000	61	135	199	240	276
43,000	44,000	64	139	207	249	286
44,000	45,000	66	144	215	257	296

Fair Market Value of Automobile		*Tax Year During Lease**				
Over	*Not Over*	*1st*	*2nd*	*3rd*	*4th*	*5th and Later*
45,000	46,000	68	149	222	266	307
46,000	47,000	70	155	229	274	317
47,000	48,000	73	159	237	283	327
48,000	49,000	75	164	244	292	338
49,000	50,000	77	169	251	301	348
50,000	51,000	79	174	259	310	357
51,000	52,000	82	179	266	318	368
52,000	53,000	84	184	273	328	378
53,000	54,000	86	189	281	336	388
54,000	55,000	88	194	288	345	399
55,000	56,000	91	199	295	354	408
56,000	57,000	93	204	302	363	419
57,000	58,000	95	209	310	371	429
58,000	59,000	97	214	317	381	439
59,000	60,000	100	219	324	389	450
60,000	62,000	103	226	336	402	465
62,000	64,000	107	236	351	420	485
64,000	66,000	112	246	365	438	505
66,000	68,000	116	256	380	455	526
68,000	70,000	121	266	394	473	546
70,000	72,000	125	276	409	491	566
72,000	74,000	130	286	423	509	586
74,000	76,000	134	296	438	526	607
76,000	78,000	139	305	454	543	627
78,000	80,000	143	316	467	561	648
80,000	85,000	151	333	493	592	684
85,000	90,000	163	357	531	635	735
90,000	95,000	174	382	567	680	785
95,000	100,000	185	407	604	724	836
100,000	110,000	202	444	659	790	912
110,000	120,000	225	493	733	878	1,014
120,000	130,000	247	543	806	966	1,116
130,000	140,000	270	592	880	1,054	1,218
140,000	150,000	292	642	953	1,143	1,319
150,000	160,000	315	691	1,027	1,230	1,421
160,000	170,000	337	741	1,100	1,319	1,522
170,000	180,000	360	790	1,174	1,407	1,624
180,000	190,000	382	840	1,247	1,495	1,726
190,000	200,000	405	889	1,321	1,583	1,828
200,000	210,000	427	939	1,394	1,671	1,930
210,000	220,000	450	988	1,468	1,759	2,031
220,000	230,000	472	1,038	1,541	1,847	2,134
230,000	240,000	495	1,087	1,615	1,935	2,235
240,000	and up	517	1,137	1,688	2,024	2,336
240,000	and up	517	1,137	1,688	2,024	2,336

* For the last tax year of the lease, use the dollar amount for the preceding tax year.

Example (5): An SUV with a GVWR of 6,000 pounds or less and with a fair market value of $34,500 is leased for a term of 3 years beginning on April 1, 2009. The SUV is considered a truck. Assuming full business use by a calendar-year taxpayer, the includible amount for 2009 is $30.89 (275/365 × $41). The includible amount for 2010 is $90. The includible amount for 2011 is $134. The includible amount for 2012 is $33.04 ($134 × 90/365) (the dollar amount for the preceding tax year is used for the last tax year of the lease).

January 1, 2008 to December 31, 2008 Leases of Trucks or Vans

The following table from Rev. Proc. 2008-22 governs computation of includible amounts for trucks (including SUVs that are considered trucks) or vans with a GVWR of 6,000 pounds or less, a fair market value exceeding $19,000, and which are first leased in calendar-year 2008. This table should also be used for electric vehicles that are trucks or vans first leased in calendar-year 2008.

Dollar Amounts for Trucks or Vans First Leased in 2008

Fair Market Value of Automobile		*Tax Year During Lease**				
Over	*Not Over*	*1st*	*2nd*	*3rd*	*4th*	*5th and Later*
$ 19,000	$ 19,500	17	37	54	65	73
19,500	20,000	20	42	63	73	85
20,000	20,500	22	48	70	84	96
20,500	21,000	25	53	79	93	107
21,000	21,500	27	59	86	103	118
21,500	22,000	30	64	95	112	130
22,000	23,000	33	72	107	128	146
23,000	24,000	38	83	123	147	168
24,000	25,000	43	94	139	166	191
25,000	26,000	48	105	155	186	213
26,000	27,000	53	116	171	205	236
27,000	28,000	58	127	187	225	258
28,000	29,000	63	138	204	243	280
29,000	30,000	68	148	221	263	302
30,000	31,000	73	159	237	282	325
31,000	32,000	78	170	253	301	348
32,000	33,000	83	181	269	321	370
33,000	34,000	88	192	285	340	393
34,000	35,000	93	203	301	360	414
35,000	36,000	98	214	317	379	437
36,000	37,000	103	225	333	399	459
37,000	38,000	108	235	350	418	482
38,000	39,000	113	246	366	437	505
39,000	40,000	118	257	382	457	526
40,000	41,000	123	268	398	476	549
41,000	42,000	128	279	414	496	571
42,000	43,000	133	290	430	515	594
43,000	44,000	137	301	447	534	616
44,000	45,000	142	312	463	553	639
45,000	46,000	147	323	479	573	661
46,000	47,000	152	334	495	592	684
47,000	48,000	157	345	511	612	705
48,000	49,000	162	356	527	631	728
49,000	50,000	167	366	544	651	750

Fair Market Value of Automobile		*Tax Year During Lease**				
Over	*Not Over*	*1st*	*2nd*	*3rd*	*4th*	*5th and Later*
50,000	51,000	172	377	560	670	773
51,000	52,000	177	388	576	689	796
52,000	53,000	182	399	592	709	817
53,000	54,000	187	410	608	728	840
54,000	55,000	192	421	624	748	862
55,000	56,000	197	432	640	767	885
56,000	57,000	202	443	656	787	907
57,000	58,000	207	453	673	806	929
58,000	59,000	212	464	689	825	952
59,000	60,000	217	475	705	845	974
60,000	62,000	224	492	729	874	1,008
62,000	64,000	234	513	762	913	1,052
64,000	66,000	244	535	794	951	1,098
66,000	68,000	254	557	826	990	1,142
68,000	70,000	264	579	858	1,029	1,187
70,000	72,000	274	600	892	1,067	1,232
72,000	74,000	284	622	924	1,106	1,276
74,000	76,000	294	644	956	1,145	1,321
76,000	78,000	304	666	988	1,184	1,366
78,000	80,000	314	687	1,021	1,222	1,411
80,000	85,000	331	726	1,077	1,290	1,489
85,000	90,000	356	780	1,158	1,387	1,601
90,000	95,000	381	835	1,238	1,484	1,713
95,000	100,000	405	889	1,320	1,581	1,825
100,000	110,000	443	971	1,440	1,727	1,993
110,000	120,000	492	1,080	1,602	1,921	2,216
120,000	130,000	542	1,189	1,764	2,114	2,440
130,000	140,000	592	1,297	1,926	2,308	2,665
140,000	150,000	641	1,407	2,087	2,502	2,888
150,000	160,000	691	1,515	2,249	2,696	3,112
160,000	170,000	740	1,625	2,410	2,890	3,336
170,000	180,000	790	1,733	2,573	3,083	3,560
180,000	190,000	840	1,842	2,734	3,278	3,783
190,000	200,000	889	1,951	2,896	3,472	4,007
200,000	210,000	939	2,060	3,058	3,665	4,231
210,000	220,000	989	2,169	3,219	3,859	4,455
220,000	230,000	1,038	2,278	3,381	4,053	4,678
230,000	240,000	1,088	2,387	3,542	4,247	4,903
240,000	and up	1,137	2,496	3,704	4,441	5,126

* For the last tax year of the lease, use the dollar amount for the preceding tax year.

Example (6): An SUV with a GVWR of 6,000 pounds or less and with a fair market value of $34,500 is leased for a term of 3 years beginning on April 1, 2008. The SUV is considered a truck. Assuming full business use by a calendar-year taxpayer, the includible amount for 2008 is $70.06 (275/365 × $93). The includible amount for 2009 is $203. The includible amount for 2010 is $301. The includible amount for 2011 is $74.22 ($301 × 90/365) (the dollar amount for the preceding tax year is used for the last tax year of the lease).

January 1, 2007 to December 31, 2007 Leases of Trucks or Vans

The following table from Rev. Proc. 2007-30 governs computation of includible amounts for trucks (including SUVs that are considered trucks) or vans with a GVWR of 6,000 pounds or less, a fair market value exceeding $16,400, and which were first leased in calendar-year 2007. This table should also be used for electric vehicles that are trucks or vans and first leased in calendar-year 2007.

Dollar Amounts for Trucks or Vans First Leased in 2007

Fair Market Value of Automobile		*Tax Year During Lease**				
Over	*Not Over*	*1st*	*2nd*	*3rd*	*4th*	*5th and Later*
$16,400	$16,700	2	4	8	10	11
16,700	17,000	4	9	15	17	21
17,000	17,500	6	15	24	28	33
17,500	18,000	10	22	35	42	48
18,000	18,500	13	30	46	55	64
18,500	19,000	17	37	57	69	79
19,000	19,500	20	45	68	82	94
19,500	20,000	24	52	80	95	109
20,000	20,500	27	60	90	109	125
20,500	21,000	30	67	102	122	141
21,000	21,500	34	75	113	135	156
21,500	22,000	37	82	124	149	171
22,000	23,000	42	94	140	169	194
23,000	24,000	49	109	163	195	225
24,000	25,000	56	123	186	222	256
25,000	26,000	63	138	208	249	286
26,000	27,000	70	153	230	276	317
27,000	28,000	77	168	252	302	349
28,000	29,000	83	184	274	329	379
29,000	30,000	90	199	296	356	410
30,000	31,000	97	214	318	383	440
31,000	32,000	104	228	342	408	472
32,000	33,000	111	243	364	435	503
33,000	34,000	118	258	386	462	534
34,000	35,000	125	273	408	489	564
35,000	36,000	131	289	430	515	595
36,000	37,000	138	304	452	542	626
37,000	38,000	145	318	475	569	657
38,000	39,000	152	333	497	596	688
39,000	40,000	159	348	520	622	718
40,000	41,000	166	363	542	649	749
41,000	42,000	172	379	563	676	780
42,000	43,000	179	394	586	702	811
43,000	44,000	186	409	608	729	842
44,000	45,000	193	423	631	756	872
45,000	46,000	200	438	653	783	903
46,000	47,000	207	453	675	810	934
47,000	48,000	213	469	697	836	965
48,000	49,000	220	484	719	863	996

Fair Market Value of Automobile		*Tax Year During Lease**				
Over	*Not Over*	*1st*	*2nd*	*3rd*	*4th*	*5th and Later*
49,000	50,000	227	499	741	890	1,026
50,000	51,000	234	514	764	916	1,057
51,000	52,000	241	528	787	943	1,088
52,000	53,000	248	543	809	969	1,119
53,000	54,000	254	559	831	996	1,150
54,000	55,000	261	574	853	1,023	1,180
55,000	56,000	268	589	875	1,050	1,211
56,000	57,000	275	604	897	1,076	1,243
57,000	58,000	282	618	920	1,103	1,273
58,000	59,000	289	633	943	1,129	1,304
59,000	60,000	296	648	965	1,156	1,335
60,000	62,000	306	671	998	1,196	1,381
62,000	64,000	319	701	1,043	1,249	1,443
64,000	66,000	333	731	1,087	1,303	1,504
66,000	68,000	347	761	1,131	1,357	1,566
68,000	70,000	361	791	1,176	1,410	1,627
70,000	72,000	374	821	1,221	1,463	1,689
72,000	74,000	388	851	1,265	1,517	1,751
74,000	76,000	402	881	1,309	1,570	1,813
76,000	78,000	415	911	1,354	1,624	1,874
78,000	80,000	429	941	1,399	1,676	1,936
80,000	85,000	453	994	1,476	1,770	2,044
85,000	90,000	487	1,069	1,587	1,904	2,198
90,000	95,000	521	1,144	1,699	2,037	2,352
95,000	100,000	555	1,219	1,810	2,171	2,506
100,000	110,000	607	1,331	1,977	2,371	2,737
110,000	120,000	675	1,481	2,200	2,638	3,045
120,000	130,000	744	1,631	2,423	2,904	3,354
130,000	140,000	812	1,781	2,646	3,171	3,662
140,000	150,000	880	1,932	2,867	3,439	3,970
150,000	160,000	949	2,081	3,091	3,705	4,279
160,000	170,000	1,017	2,232	3,313	3,972	4,586
170,000	180,000	1,086	2,381	3,536	4,239	4,895
180,000	190,000	1,154	2,532	3,758	4,506	5,203
190,000	200,000	1,222	2,682	3,981	4,773	5,511
200,000	210,000	1,291	2,831	4,204	5,040	5,820
210,000	220,000	1,359	2,982	4,426	5,307	6,128
220,000	230,000	1,428	3,131	4,649	5,575	6,435
230,000	240,000	1,496	3,282	4,871	5,841	6,744
240,000	and up	1,565	3,431	5,095	6,108	7,052

* For the last tax year of the lease, use the dollar amount for the preceding tax year.

Example (7): An SUV that is considered a truck has a loaded GVWR of 6,000 pounds or less. It has a fair market value of $34,500 and is leased for a term of 3 years beginning on April 1, 2007. Assuming full business use by a calendar-year taxpayer, the includible amount for 2007 is $94.18 (275/365 × $125). The includible amount for 2008 is $273. The includible amount for 2009 is $408. The includible amount for 2010 is $100.60 ($408 × 90/365) (the dollar amount for the preceding tax year is used for the last tax year of the lease).

January 1, 2006 to December 31, 2006 Leases of Trucks and Vans

The following table from Rev. Proc. 2006-18 governs computation of includible amounts for nonelectric trucks (including SUVs that are considered trucks) and vans with a GVWR of 6,000 pounds or less, a fair market value exceeding $16,700, and which are first leased in calendar-year 2006.

Dollar Amounts for Nonelectric Trucks and Vans First Leased in 2006

Fair Market Value of Truck or Van		*Tax Year During Lease**				
Over	*Not Over*	*1st*	*2nd*	*3rd*	*4th*	*5th and Later*
$16,700	$17,000	4	8	12	14	16
17,000	17,500	6	14	20	24	29
17,500	18,000	9	21	31	37	43
18,000	18,500	13	28	42	49	58
18,500	19,000	16	36	52	62	72
19,000	19,500	19	43	63	75	87
19,500	20,000	23	50	73	88	102
20,000	20,500	26	57	84	101	116
20,500	21,000	29	64	95	113	131
21,000	21,500	32	72	105	126	146
21,500	22,000	36	78	116	139	161
22,000	23,000	41	89	132	158	183
23,000	24,000	47	104	153	183	213
24,000	25,000	54	118	174	209	242
25,000	26,000	60	132	196	235	271
26,000	27,000	67	146	217	261	300
27,000	28,000	73	161	238	286	330
28,000	29,000	80	175	260	311	359
29,000	30,000	86	190	281	336	389
30,000	31,000	93	204	302	362	418
31,000	32,000	99	219	323	388	447
32,000	33,000	106	233	344	413	478
33,000	34,000	112	247	366	439	506
34,000	35,000	119	261	387	465	536
35,000	36,000	125	276	408	490	566
36,000	37,000	132	290	430	515	595
37,000	38,000.	139	304	451	541	624
38,000	39,000	145	319	472	566	654
39,000	40,000	152	333	493	592	684
40,000	41,000	158	347	515	618	712
41,000	42,000	165	362	536	642	743
42,000	43,000	171	376	557	669	772
43,000	44,000	178	390	579	694	801
44,000	45,000	184	405	600	719	831
45,000	46,000	191	419	621	745	860
46,000	47,000	197	434	642	770	890
47,000	48,000	204	448	663	796	919
48,000	49,000	210	462	685	822	948
49,000	50,000	217	476	707	847	977
50,000	51,000	224	490	728	872	1,008

Fair Market Value of Truck or Van		*Tax Year During Lease**				
Over	*Not Over*	*1st*	*2nd*	*3rd*	*4th*	*5th and Later*
51,000	52,000	230	505	749	898	1,037
52,000	53,000	237	519	770	924	1,066
53,000	54,000	243	534	791	949	1,096
54,000	55,000	250	548	813	974	1,125
55,000	56,000	256	563	833	1,000	1,155
56,000	57,000	263	577	855	1,025	1,184
57,000	58,000	269	591	877	1,051	1,213
58,000	59,000	276	605	898	1,077	1,243
59,000	60,000	282	620	919	1,102	1,272
60,000	62,000	292	641	951	1,141	1,316
62,000	64,000	305	670	994	1,191	1,375
64,000	66,000	318	699	1,036	1,242	1,435
66,000	68,000	331	728	1,078	1,293	1,494
68,000	70,000	344	756	1,121	1,345	1,552
70,000	72,000	358	784	1,164	1,395	1,612
72,000	74,000	371	813	1,206	1,447	1,670
74,000	76,000	384	842	1,249	1,497	1,729
76,000	78,000	397	871	1,291	1,548	1,788
78,000	80,000	410	899	1,334	1,600	1,846
80,000	85,000	433	949	1,409	1,688	1,950
85,000	90,000	465	1,021	1,515	1,816	2,098
90,000	95,000	498	1,093	1,621	1,944	2,244
95,000	100,000	531	1,164	1,728	2,071	2,392
100,000	110,000	580	1,272	1,887	2,263	2,612
110,000	120,000	645	1,416	2,099	2,518	2,907
120,000	130,000	711	1,559	2,312	2,773	3,202
130,000	140,000	776	1,702	2,525	3,028	3,497
140,000	150,000	841	1,846	2,738	3,283	3,791
150,000	160,000	907	1,989	2,950	3,539	4,085
160,000	170,000	972	2,132	3,164	3,793	4,380
170,000	180,000	1,037	2,276	3,376	4,049	4,674
180,000	190,000	1,103	2,419	3,589	4,303	4,969
190,000	200,000	1,168	2,563	3,801	4,559	5,263
200,000	210,000	1,233	2,706	4,015	4,813	5,558
210,000	220,000	1,299	2,849	4,227	5,069	5,853
220,000	230,000	1,364	2,993	4,440	5,324	6,147
230,000	240,000	1,430	3,136	4,652	5,580	6,441
240,000	and up	1,495	3,279	4,866	5,834	6,736

* For the last tax year of the lease, use the dollar amount for the preceding tax year.

Example (8): A truck with a GVWR of 6,000 pounds or less and with a fair market value of $34,500 is leased for a term of 3 years beginning on April 1, 2006. Assuming full business use by a calendar-year taxpayer, the includible amount for 2006 is $89.65 (275/365 × $119). The includible amount for 2007 is $261. The includible amount for 2008 is $387. The includible amount for 2009 is $95.42 ($387 × 90/365) (the dollar amount for the preceding tax year is used for the last tax year of the lease).

LEASE INCLUSION TABLES FOR ELECTRIC VEHICLES

Leases of Electric Vehicles on or after January 1, 2007

Beginning in 2007, separate lease inclusion tables are not provided for electric vehicles. The tables above for passenger autos or trucks (including SUVs that are considered trucks) and vans are used, as appropriate.

January 1, 2006 to December 31, 2006 Leases of Electric Vehicles

The following table from Rev. Proc. 2006-18 governs computation of includible amounts for electric vehicles with a GVWR of 6,000 pounds or less, a fair market value exceeding $45,000, and which are first leased in calendar-year 2006.

DOLLAR AMOUNTS FOR ELECTRIC AUTOMOBILES WITH A LEASE TERM BEGINNING IN CALENDAR YEAR 2006

Fair Market Value of Automobile		*Tax Year During Lease**				
Over	*Not Over*	*1st*	*2nd*	*3rd*	*4th*	*5th and Later*
$45,000	$46,000	4	8	11	12	12
46,000	47,000	10	22	33	37	42
47,000	48,000	17	36	54	63	72
48,000	49,000	24	51	74	89	101
49,000	50,000	30	65	96	114	131
50,000	51,000	37	79	118	139	160
51,000	52,000	43	94	139	165	189
52,000	53,000	50	108	160	190	219
53,000	54,000	56	123	181	216	248
54,000	55,000	63	137	202	242	277
55,000	56,000	69	151	224	267	307
56,000	57,000	76	165	245	293	337
57,000	58,000	82	180	266	318	367
58,000	59,000	89	194	288	343	396
59,000	60,000	95	209	309	369	425
60,000	62,000	105	230	341	407	470
62,000	64,000	118	259	383	459	528
64,000	66,000	131	288	425	510	587
66,000	68,000	144	316	469	560	646
68,000	70,000	158	345	510	612	705
70,000	72,000	171	373	554	662	764
72,000	74,000	184	402	596	713	823
74,000	76,000	197	431	638	765	881
76,000	78,000	210	459	682	815	940
78,000	80,000	223	488	724	866	1,000
80,000	85,000	246	538	798	956	1,103
85,000	90,000	278	610	905	1,083	1,250
90,000	95,000	311	682	1,011	1,211	1,397
95,000	100,000	344	753	1,118	1,338	1,544
100,000	110,000	393	861	1,277	1,529	1,766
110,000	120,000	458	1,004	1,490	1,785	2,060
120,000	130,000	524	1,147	1,703	2,040	2,354
130,000	140,000	589	1,291	1,915	2,295	2,649
140,000	150,000	654	1,435	2,127	2,551	2,943

Fair Market Value of Automobile		*Tax Year During Lease**				
Over	*Not Over*	*1st*	*2nd*	*3rd*	*4th*	*5th and Later*
150,000	160,000	720	1,578	2,340	2,806	3,237
160,000	170,000	785	1,721	2,553	3,061	3,532
170,000	180,000	850	1,865	2,766	3,315	3,827
180,000	190,000	916	2,008	2,979	3,570	4,122
190,000	200,000	981	2,151	3,192	3,826	4,416
200,000	210,000	1,046	2,295	3,404	4,081	4,711
210,000	220,000	1,112	2,438	3,617	4,336	5,005
220,000	230,000	1,177	2,581	3,830	4,591	5,300
230,000	240,000	1,243	2,725	4,042	4,846	5,594
240,000	and up	1,308	2,868	4,255	5,102	5,888

* For the last tax year of the lease, use the dollar amount for the preceding tax year.

January 1, 2005 to December 31, 2005 Leases of Electric Vehicles

The following table from Rev. Proc. 2005-13 governs computation of includible amounts for electric vehicles with a GVWR of 6,000 pounds or less, a fair market value exceeding $45,000, and which are first leased in calendar-year 2005. Tables for electric vehicles first leased prior to 2005 can be found in IRS Publication 463.

DOLLAR AMOUNTS FOR ELECTRIC AUTOMOBILES WITH A LEASE TERM BEGINNING IN CALENDAR YEAR 2005

Fair Market Value of Automobile		*Tax Year During Lease**				
Over	*Not Over*	*1st*	*2nd*	*3rd*	*4th*	*5th and Later*
$45,000	$46,000	5	11	18	21	25
46,000	47,000	10	21	33	39	45
47,000	48,000	14	31	48	57	66
48,000	49,000	19	41	63	75	86
49,000	50,000	23	52	77	93	107
50,000	51,000	28	61	93	111	127
51,000	52,000	33	71	108	129	148
52,000	53,000	37	82	122	147	169
53,000	54,000	42	92	137	164	190
54,000	55,000	46	102	152	183	210
55,000	56,000	51	112	167	200	231
56,000	57,000	55	122	182	218	252
57,000	58,000	60	132	197	236	272
58,000	59,000	65	142	212	254	293
59,000	60,000	69	152	227	272	314
60,000	62,000	76	167	250	298	345
62,000	64,000	85	187	280	334	386
64,000	66,000	94	208	309	370	427
66,000	68,000	104	227	339	406	469
68,000	70,000	113	247	369	442	510
70,000	72,000	122	268	398	478	551
72,000	74,000	131	288	428	514	593

Fair Market Value of Automobile		*Tax Year During Lease**				
Over	*Not Over*	*1st*	*2nd*	*3rd*	*4th*	*5th and Later*
74,000	76,000	140	308	458	550	634
76,000	78,000	149	328	489	585	675
78,000	80,000	159	348	518	621	717
80,000	85,000	175	383	571	683	789
85,000	90,000	197	434	645	773	892
90,000	95,000	220	484	720	863	995
95,000	100,000	243	534	795	952	1,099
100,000	110,000	278	610	906	1,086	1,254
110,000	120,000	323	711	1,055	1,266	1,460
120,000	130,000	369	811	1,205	1,444	1,668
130,000	140,000	415	912	1,354	1,623	1,874
140,000	150,000	461	1,012	1,504	1,802	2,081
150,000	160,000	507	1,113	1,652	1,982	2,287
160,000	170,000	553	1,213	1,802	2,161	2,494
170,000	180,000	598	1,314	1,951	2,340	2,701
180,000	190,000	644	1,415	2,100	2,519	2,908
190,000	200,000	690	1,515	2,250	2,698	3,114
200,000	210,000	736	1,616	2,399	2,877	3,321
210,000	220,000	782	1,716	2,549	3,055	3,528
220,000	230,000	827	1,817	2,698	3,235	3,734
230,000	240,000	873	1,918	2,847	3,413	3,942
240,000	and up	919	2,018	2,997	3,592	4,148

* For the last tax year of the lease, use the dollar amount for the preceding tax year.

Full business use by fiscal-year taxpayer

Example (9): A car with a fair market value of $40,600 is leased for a term of 4 years beginning on February 14, 2009, by a February 1 through January 31 fiscal-year taxpayer. Assuming full business use, the includible amounts (from the table for vehicles (other than trucks and vans first first leased in 2009) are:

Tax Year	*Dollar Amount*	*Proration*	*Business Use*	*Inclusion Amount*
2009/2010 .	$ 58	352/365	100%	$ 56
2010/2009 .	$127	365/365	100%	$127
2011/2012 .	$188	365/365	100%	$188
2012/2013 .	$225	366/366	100%	$225
2013/2014 .	$259	13/365	100%	$ 9

352 is the number of days the car was leased in FY 2009/2010 (February 14–January 31). 13 is the number of days the car was leased in the FY 2013/2014 tax year (February 1–February 13). In the last tax year in which the car is leased, the dollar amount for the preceding tax year is used.

Partial business use by calendar-year taxpayer

Example (10): Same facts as above except the taxpayer is a calendar-year taxpayer and business use each year is 70%. The includible amounts are:

Tax Year	*Dollar Amount*	*Proration*	*Business Use*	*Inclusion Amount*
2009	$ 58	321/365	70%	$36
2010	$127	365/3665	70%	$89

Tax Year	*Dollar Amount*	*Proration*	*Business Use*	*Inclusion Amount*
2011	$188	365/365	70%	$132
2012	$225	366/366	70%	$158
2013	$259	44/365	70%	$ 22

321 is the number of days the car was leased in the 2009 tax year (February 14–December 31). 44 is the number of days the car was leased in the 2013 tax year (January 1–February 13). In the last tax year in which the car is leased, the dollar amount for the preceding tax year is used.

Vehicle converted to business use after lease term begins

If a car leased for personal purposes is later converted to business use, the fair market value is determined on the date of the conversion to business use. Use the lease inclusion table for the year in which the vehicle was converted to business use. That year is treated as the first year of the lease.

Example (11): A car is leased for 4 years for personal purposes by a calendar-year taxpayer in December 2007. On March 1, 2009, the car was converted to business use. The business-use percentage for the period March 1, 2009, through December 31, 2009, was 70%. The fair market value of the vehicle on March 1, 2009, was $25,500. The inclusion amount for 2009 is computed as follows:

Tax Year	*Dollar Amount*	*Proration*	*Business Use*	*Inclusion Amount*
2009	$24	306/365	70%	$14

306 is the number of days in the tax year that the car was leased (March 1–December 31). The 2009 table for vehicles (other than trucks and vans) is used and $24 is the dollar amount for the first year of a lease.

Vehicle converted from business use to personal use

If a leased business car is converted to personal use, the dollar amount for the tax year in which business use ceases is the dollar amount for the preceding tax year.

Example (12): A car with a fair market value of $28,100 is leased on September 1, 2008, by a calendar-year taxpayer and used for exclusively for business purposes. On March 1, 2009, the taxpayer's business operations are terminated and the car is used exclusively for personal purposes as of that date. The inclusion amounts are computed as follows:

Tax Year	*Dollar Amount*	*Proration*	*Business Use*	*Inclusion Amount*
2008	$68	122/366	100%	$23
2009	$68	60/365	100%	$ 11

122 is the number of days the car was leased and used for business in the 2008 tax year (September 1–December 31). 60 is the number of days the car was leased and used for business in the 2009 tax year (January 1–February 29).

¶ 206

Consequences of Listed Property Classification

Unless the qualified business use of an asset classified as listed property exceeds 50 percent, certain deductions for listed property are limited (Code Sec. 280F(b)(1)). Listed property that fails to meet this requirement in the year that it is placed in service does not qualify for the Code Sec. 179 expense deduction (¶ 302) or bonus depreciation (¶ 127D), including New York Liberty Zone bonus depreciation (¶ 127E) and Gulf Opportunity Zone bonus depreciation (127F), Kansas Disaster Area bonus depreciation (¶ 127G), or Presidentially-declared disaster area bonus depreciation (¶ 127H).

Listed property subject to MACRS that fails to meet this requirement in the year placed in service also must be depreciated under the alternative depreciation system (ADS) (¶ 150) for that tax year and all succeeding tax years. Further, failure to continuously meet this requirement during each year of the asset's ADS recovery period (which is usually longer than the regular recovery period) triggers the recapture of the amount by which the depreciation claimed prior to the recapture year (including the section 179 allowance and bonus depreciation) exceeded the amount that would have been allowable under ADS (without claiming the section 179 allowance or bonus depreciation) during the period prior to the recapture year. The recaptured amount is added back to the property's adjusted basis (Code Sec. 280F(b)(2)) and depreciation is computed using ADS during the recapture year and the remaining ADS recovery period as if ADS had been used since the asset was first placed in service. See ¶ 210 for examples of the required calculations.

Listed property subject to ACRS that fails to meet the business use requirement during any tax year must be depreciated under the ACRS straight-line method generally over the earnings and profits life (see ¶ 310) of the property for such year and all succeeding tax years (former Code Sec. 280F(b)(4)) (before repeal by the Tax Reform Act of 1986 (P.L. 99-514), which remains in effect for ACRS property). Depreciation claimed in previous tax years that exceeds the amount that would have been allowed under this method is recaptured.

The listed property limitations generally apply to property placed in service or leased after June 18, 1984, except for certain transitional property.

¶ 208

Categories of Listed Property

Code Sec. 280F(d)(4) sets forth the following specific categories of listed property:

(1) passenger automobiles,

(2) any other property used as a means of transportation (for exceptions relating to vehicles that are unlikely to be used for personal purposes, see discussion below),

(3) property of a type generally used for purposes of entertainment, recreation, or amusement (unless used either exclusively at the taxpayer's regular business establishment or in connection with the taxpayer's principal trade or business),

(4) computers or peripheral equipment (unless used exclusively at a regular business establishment and owned or leased by the operator of the establishment), and

(5) cellular telephones (or other similar telecommunications equipment).

The definition of listed property potentially extends to other types of property specified by the regulations, but, under the caption *"Other property,"* Temp. Reg. § 1.280F-6T(b)(4) has, so far, merely been reserved.

Improvements to listed property that must be capitalized are treated as new items of listed property.

Passenger automobiles, including trucks, vans, and SUVs

The luxury car depreciation caps only apply to a listed property that is a "passenger automobile." If any type of listed property, including a passenger automobile, is not used more than 50 percent for business, depreciation deductions must be computed under the MACRS alternative depreciation system (ADS) and recapture is required if the business use requirement is not satisfied after the first tax year that the property was placed in service. See ¶ 210.

For luxury car limitation and listed property purposes, a passenger automobile includes any four-wheeled vehicle manufactured primarily for use on public streets, roads, and highways that has an *unloaded gross* vehicle weight of 6,000 pounds or less (Code Sec. 280F(d)(5)(A)). A truck or van is included in such classification if it has a *gross* vehicle weight rating (GVWR) of 6,000 pounds or less. A recreational vehicle is considered a truck. See ¶ 104.

Treatment of Sport Utility Vehicles as Trucks. Beginning in 2003, the IRS indicated in its annual revenue procedure which updates of the annual depreciation caps for luxury automobiles that an SUV is considered a truck if it is built on a truck chassis (Rev. Proc. 2003-75, Section 2.01). Thus, if an SUV, was built on a unibody platform it could not qualify as a truck. Although the definition was applied in the context of qualification for the higher depreciation limits that apply to trucks and vans, this definition was subsequently used in various IRS publications and the instructions for Form 4562 in the context of the exemption from the depreciation caps for trucks and vans that have a gross vehicle weight rating in excess of 6,000 pounds. In its most recent update of the depreciation caps for 2008 (Rev. Proc. 2008-22) the language defining an SUV built on a truck chassis as a truck was dropped. CCH contacted the IRS and was told that this definition was intended as a safe harbor and not to exclude all unibody vehicles from truck classification. The determination of whether an SUV is a truck should be based on the manufacturer's classification of the vehicle in accordance with applicable Department of Transportation Standards.

Sport utility vehicle purchasers should check the manufacturer's specifications for their vehicle to determine if its gross vehicle weight exceeds 6,000 pounds and if it is classified as a truck by its manufacturer. CCH has prepared a list of vehicles with a GVWR in excess of 6,000 pounds. See the Quick Reference Table on page 1053.

The fact that an SUV or other vehicle may not be subject to the passenger automobile caps because its GVWR exceeds 6,000 pounds does not mean that the vehicle is not a listed property. This is because listed property includes property used as a means of transportation (see immediately below) whether or not the depreciation caps apply. An SUV, therefore, as a listed property, is subject to the listed property limitations discussed at ¶ 206 if qualified business use does not exceed 50 percent. Thus, if qualified business use falls to 50 percent or lower, depreciation must be computed using ADS and depreciation recapture applies.

Ambulances or hearses used directly in a trade or business, vehicles (such as a taxi or limo) used directly in the trade or business of transporting persons or property for hire, and commuter highway vehicles described in former Code Sec. 46(c)(6) (relating to vehicles with a seating capacity of at least eight persons plus the driver that are provided by an employer to transport employees to and from work) are not passenger automobiles subject to the depreciation caps (Code Sec. 280F(d)(5)(B)(iii); Temp. Reg. § 1.280F-6T(c)(3)). Note that a taxi or limo appears to be a "listed property" because it is used as a means of transportation (item 2) and is apparently capable of being used for personal purposes. See "*Property used for transportation*," below.

CCH EDITORS HAVE PREPARED A LIST OF TRUCKS, VANS, AND SUVS WITH GROSS VEHICLE WEIGHT RATINGS IN EXCESS OF 6,000 POUNDS. SEE THE QUICK REFERENCE TABLE ON PAGE 1053.

Web site for locating vehicle weights

The following web site contains specifications and vehicle weight information for most vehicles:

http://www.carsdirect.com

Qualified nonpersonal use trucks and vans placed in service after July 6, 2003

Effective for trucks (including SUVs that are considered trucks) and vans placed in service on or after July 7, 2003, any truck or van that is a qualified nonpersonal use vehicle as defined in Temp. Reg. § § 1.274-5T(k) is not considered a passenger automobile subject to the luxury car depreciation caps (Reg. § 1.280F-6(c)(3)(iii) and (f)). These are trucks and vans that have been modified in such a way that they are not likely to be used more than a de minimis amount for personal purposes. The regulation can also apply to trucks and vans placed in service before July 7, 2003. See Reg.§ 1.280F-6(f)(2).

Temp. Reg. § 1.274-5T(k)(7) only provides one example of a specially modified van that is not likely to be used more than a de minimus amount for personal purposes. That regulation describes a van that has a front bench for seating, has permanent shelving that fills most of the cargo area, constantly carries merchandise or equipment, and is specially painted with advertising or a company name. Other specially modified vans, however, should be able to qualify as nonpersonal use vehicles if they are not likely to be used more than a de minimis amount for personal purposes.

Temp. Reg. § 1.274-5T(k)(2)(ii) also provides a list of qualified nonpersonal use vehicles. Certain trucks or vans that could otherwise be considered passenger automobiles may be described in this list. These include a clearly marked police or fire vehicle, a delivery truck with seating only for the driver or only for the driver plus a folding jump seat, a flatbed truck, a refrigerated truck, and an unmarked vehicle used by law enforcement officers.

A vehicle that is either a passenger automobile or a property used as a means of transportation is considered a listed property. As noted immediately below, qualified nonpersonal use vehicles are not considered property used as a means of transportation (Temp. Reg. § 1.274-5T(k)). Thus, trucks and vans that are qualified nonpersonal use vehicles and that are placed in service on or after July 7, 2003 are no longer considered listed property. Consequently, in addition to being exempt from the depreciation caps applicable to passenger automobiles, such trucks and vans are not subject to the rules requiring the use of the MACRS alternative depreciation system (ADS) if business use of a listed property falls to 50 percent or less or the recapture of depreciation claimed in excess of the amount that would have been allowed under ADS. See ¶ 210.

Property used for transportation

The term listed property includes "property used as a means of transportation." Trucks, vans, buses, trains, boats, airplanes, motorcycles, and any other vehicles used for transporting persons or goods are generally regarded as other property used as a means of transportation, but exceptions are recognized for various kinds of vehicles, which by their nature are unlikely to receive more than minimal personal use. In this excluded category are clearly marked police and fire vehicles, ambulances and hearses used as such, any vehicle with a loaded gross vehicle weight over 14,000 pounds that is designed to carry cargo, bucket trucks ("cherry pickers"), cement mixers, combines, cranes, derricks, delivery trucks seating only the driver (except for one folding jump seat), dump trucks (garbage trucks included), flatbed trucks, forklifts, school buses, other buses that are used as buses and accommodate 20 or more passengers, qualified moving vans and specialized utility repair trucks, refrigerated trucks, tractors and other special purpose farm vehicles, and (subject to their authorized use) unmarked police cars (Reg. § 1.280F-6T(b)(2); Temp. Reg. § 1.274-5T(k)).

Code Sec. 280F(d)(4)(C) provides that, except to the extent provided in regulations, property used as a means of transportation does not include any property substantially all of the use of which is in a trade or business of providing unrelated persons services consisting of the transportation of persons or property for compensation or hire. At first blush, this exception would seem to apply to a taxicab or limo. However, the regulations defining property used as a means of transportation treat trucks, buses, trains, boats, airplanes, motorcycles, and any other vehicle for transporting persons or goods as a means of transportation, except that a "listed property" does not include a qualified nonpersonal use vehicle as defined in Code Sec. 274(i) and Temp. Reg. § 1.274-5T(k).

Although a truck (including an SUV that is considered a truck) or van is not a "passenger automobile," it may be a "means of transportation" and, therefore, a listed property. Thus, although the depreciation caps do not apply, depreciation recapture is required in a tax year that business use of a large truck, van, or SUV falls to 50 percent or less. Further, the MACRS alternative depreciation system (ADS) must be used if business use of such a vehicle is 50 percent or less (¶ 210). Also, if such a vehicle is leased, a lease inclusion amount is required in the tax year that business use is 50 percent or less (see ¶ 212). As noted above, however, trucks and vans that are not likely to be used for personal purposes are not considered a means of transportation and, therefore, would not be subject to these rules.

Property used for entertainment

Photographic, phonographic, communication, and video recording equipment exemplifies property generally regarded as used for purposes of entertainment, recreation, or amusement. However, such equipment is not considered listed property if it is used either exclusively at a regular business establishment or in connection with a principal trade or business. A regular business establishment includes a home office for which home office deductions may be claimed (Temp. Reg. § 1.280F-6T(b)(3)).

Under this category, it is possible for certain real property to be considered listed property (Reg. §§ 1.280F-3T(e)(1) and 1.280F-6T(b)(3)).

The IRS audit technique guide for the entertainment industry (April 1995) (reproduced at ¶ 204,500 in the CCH IRS POSITIONS REPORTER) indicates that horses may be listed property, apparently on the grounds that a horse is generally used for entertainment, recreation, or amusement.

Computers

As defined under Code Sec. 168(i)(2)(B), a "computer" is a programmable electronically activated device that is capable of accepting information, applying prescribed processes to such information, and supplying the results of these processes (with or without human intervention) and that consists of a central processing unit containing extensive storage, logic, arithmetic, and control capabilities. Related peripheral equipment is any auxiliary machine (either on-line or off-line) designed to be placed under the control of a computer's central processing unit. Typewriters, adding machines, copiers, duplicating equipment, and similar equipment, as well as equipment of a kind used primarily for the user's amusement or entertainment, are not regarded as computers or peripheral equipment.

The exception for computers and peripheral equipment used exclusively at a regular business establishment can extend to the use of such property at a portion of a dwelling unit, provided such an area meets the Code Sec. 280A(c)(1) requirements for home-office deductions.

Employees must meet the convenience-of-the-employer and the conditions-of-employment tests for listed property to be treated as used in a trade or business (Code Sec. 280F(d)(3)).

> ***Example:*** An aerospace engineer uses his home computer exclusively for job-related research and development. He bought the computer because he needed one for his job and the computers provided at work were frequently unavailable because of their use by others. According to the IRS (Rev. Rul. 86-129, 1986-2 CB 48), he cannot deduct depreciation on the computer even though it enables him to do his job more efficiently and his employer states in writing that purchasing the home computer was a condition of employment. Under the same rules that apply to employer-provided lodging, this falls short of the requisite clear showing that he could not perform his job with the computers at his workplace.

Cellular telephones

Cellular telephones are listed property and, if business use exceeds 50 percent, are depreciable over seven years (cell phones are considered MACRS 7-year property (Asset Class 00.11)). A 10-year recovery period and straight-line method apply under ADS if business use does not exceed 50 percent. See ¶ 206. As listed property, cell phones are subject to the recordkeeping and substantiation requirements of Code Sec. 274(d).

¶ 210

Qualified Business Use

In determining whether listed property has a business-use percentage in excess of 50 percent (and, thus, qualifies for regular MACRS deductions, see ¶ 206), use of an automobile or other means of transportation is allocated on the basis of mileage, and use of other property is allocated on the basis of time of actual use, as measured in terms of the most appropriate unit of time. For a computer, for example, the qualified business-use percentage is (hours of business use) divided by (total hours of use).

Although investment use may justify tax deductions, only business use may be counted in meeting the more-than-50-percent-business-use test (Temp. Reg. § 1.280F-6T(d)(2)).

> ***Example (1):*** Andrew uses his personal computer 150 hours in his part-time business operated out of his home, 100 hours in managing his investments, and 75 hours for his personal entertainment. Since his business use of the computer is only 46% (150/325), he must use the MACRS alternative depreciation system (i.e., straight-line method over ADS recovery period) in computing the depreciation allocable to his 77% (250/325) business/investment use of his computer.

Certain business use of listed property by five-percent owners and related persons is not from qualified business use (Code Sec. 280F(d)(6)). The exclusion applies if:

(A) The listed property is leased to a five-percent owner or related person;

(B) The use of listed property was provided as compensation for the performance of services by a five-percent owner or related person; or

(C) The use of listed property is provided as compensation for the performance of services by any person not described in (B), above, unless an amount is reported as income to such person and taxes are withheld (Temp. Reg. § 1.280F-6T(d) (2) (ii)).

For a corporation, a five-percent owner is any person who owns, or is considered to own, more than five percent of the outstanding stock of the corporation or stock possessing more than five percent of the total combined voting power of all stock in the corporation. For other types of business, a five-percent owner is a person who owns more than five percent of the capital or profits interest in the business (Code Sec. 416(i) (1) (B) (i)).

A related person is any person related to the taxpayer within the meaning of Code Sec. 267(b).

If the property involved is an airplane, the above-mentioned business use by five-percent owners and related persons is qualified business use if at least 25 percent of the total use during the tax year consists of other types of qualified business use.

A determination for purposes of Code Sec. 280F must be made on two levels: (1) total business/investment use and (2) qualified business use. For purposes of (1), a corporation or other business may treat all of the cost of a company car used partially for personal purposes by a five-percent owner or a related party as a trade or business use, provided the value of such personal use is included in the individual's income and taxes are withheld (Temp. Reg. § 1.280F-6T(d) (3) (iv)). This consideration affects the limitation on the maximum amount allowable as a depreciation deduction (Temp. Reg. § 1.280F-2T(i) (1)).

For purposes of (2), personal use of a company car by a five-percent owner or related person (as distinguished from other employees) is not considered a qualified business use under Code Sec. 280F even if the value of such personal use is included in income and taxes are withheld (Temp. Reg. § 1.280F-6T(d) (2) (ii) (A) (*2*) and (*3*)). Such personal use is, however, considered in determining whether an asset has a qualified business use percentage of at least 50 percent for purposes of determining the applicable depreciation method. Such method would be applied to the business/investment use portion of such asset.

Commuting is not a qualified business use even if accompanied by a business meeting in the car, a business call from the car, or an advertising display. However, commuting (and other personal use) by employees in employer-owned cars used for business is a qualified business use if reported as income on which taxes are withheld.

Example (2): A corporation owns several automobiles used by its employees for business purposes. The employees are allowed to take the automobiles home at night. However, the fair market value of the use of an automobile for any personal purpose, such as commuting to work, is reported by the corporation as income to the respective employee and taxes are withheld. The use of the automobiles by the employees, even for personal purposes, is a qualified business use provided that the employees are not 5% owners of the corporation.

Example (3): The owner of a business allows his employee-brother to use one of the company automobiles for personal use as part of his compensation. The employee-brother's use of the company automobile is not a qualified business use because the owner and his brother are related parties.

Example (4): Assume the owner in *Example (3)*, above, allowed an unrelated employee to use a company automobile as part of his compensation, but he neither includes the value of such use in the gross income of the employee nor withholds any tax. The unrelated employee's use of the company automobile is not business/investment use.

MACRS/section 179 listed property recapture

If a listed property such as a car satisfies the qualified business use test (more than 50-percent business use) in the tax year in which it is placed in service but fails to meet the test in a later tax year that would fall within the asset's recovery period under the MACRS alternative depreciation system (ADS), the MACRS deductions (including any Code Sec. 179 expense allowance and first-year bonus deduction under Code Sec. 168(k) (¶ 127D), the New York Liberty Zone provision (¶ 127E), the Gulf Opportunity Zone provision(¶ 127F), the Kansas Disaster Area provision (¶ 127G), or the Presidentially declared disaster area provision (¶ 127H)) are subject to recapture in the later year. The MACRS deductions for tax years preceding the tax year in which business use fell to 50 percent or less are recaptured to the extent that the MACRS deductions (including any Code Sec. 179 expense allowance and bonus deduction) for these years exceed the depreciation that would have been allowed under ADS (without claiming any section 179 deduction or bonus depreciation).

For the year of recapture and subsequent tax years during the asset's ADS recovery period, depreciation must be computed using ADS. ADS depreciation during the remaining ADS recovery period is computed as if it was originally elected and no amount was expensed under section 179 or claimed as bonus depreciation.

No Code Sec. 179 allowance or bonus-depreciation deduction of any type is allowed in the tax year that a listed property is placed in service if the 50 percent or greater qualified business use requirement is not satisfied in that year. The listed property must be depreciated beginning in the tax year that it is palced in service using ADS.

The section 179 allowance claimed on a property that is not a listed property is subject to recapture if business use falls to 50 percent or less during the regular MACRS recovery period. See ¶ 300.

The listed property recapture is computed on Part IV of Form 4797 (Sales of Business Property) and reported as "other income" on the form or schedule on which the depreciation deduction was claimed (e.g., Schedule C in the case of a sole proprietor).

The amount recaptured is added back to the property's adjusted basis for the first tax year in which the property is not predominantly used in a qualified business use (Temp. Reg. § 1.280F-3T(d)(1)). Property is predominantly used in a qualified business use if the percentage of its use in a trade or business exceeds 50 percent (Temp. Reg. § 1.280F-6T(d)(4)).

The listed property recapture rules only apply if the business use test is failed during the ADS recovery period that applies to the asset. There is no excess depreciation/section 179 expense to recapture under the listed property rules if the applicable ADS recovery period has expired.

If a taxpayer depreciates a listed property using ADS for regular tax purposes, there is no recapture if business use drops to 50 percent or less during the ADS recovery period unless a Code Sec. 179 expense allowance or bonus-depreciation allowance was also claimed.

Example (5): In June 2008, a calendar-year taxpayer purchases a computer for $5,000 and uses it at home 100% for business purposes in 2008. Assume that no home office deduction is allowable so that such computer is considered listed property. The computer has a 5-year recovery period for both general and alternative depreciation systems. The taxpayer recovers the cost of the computer under the general MACRS 200% declining-balance method using a half-year convention. Assume that no amount is expensed or claimed as bonus depreciation. The MACRS depreciation claimed for 2008 is $1,000 ($5,000 × 40% × ½). If the business use of the computer drops to 40% in 2009, a portion of the 2008 MACRS deduction claimed must be recaptured because the computer is listed property. The amount of the 2008 MACRS deduction that must be recaptured in 2009 is $500, the excess of $1,000 over $500 (what would have been allowed under the alternative depreciation system if such system had been used in 2008 ($5,000 × 20% × ½)).

Beginning in 2009, and for all later tax years, depreciation is computed using ADS. The depreciable basis of the computer for calculating the 2009 ADS deduction is $4,500 ($5,000 − $1,000 + $500 recapture amount). The 2009 ADS deduction is $400 ($4,500 × 22.22% (1/4.5 years remaining in recovery period (as explained at ¶ 179)) × 40% business use). Alternatively, the table percentages may be used by multiplying the product of the original basis ($5,000) and the second-year ADS table percentage (20%) (Table 8 at ¶ 180) for 5-year property by the business use percentage (40%) ($5,000 × 20% × 40% = $400).

Example (6): A 7-year listed property costing $10,000 is purchased in April 2009 and is used 100% for business purposes. The taxpayer expenses $1,000. Bonus depreciation is $4,500 ($10,000 − $1,000) × 50%). For purposes of computing the regular MACRS depreciation deductions the $10,000 basis is reduced to $4,500 ($10,000 − $1,000 − $4,500). The 2009 MACRS regular deduction is $643 ($4,500 × 14.29% first-year table percentage for seven-year property). Total first-year depreciation is $6,143 ($1,000 + $4,500 + $643). If business use falls to 40% in 2010, recapture is required. Assume that the ADS period is 10 years. The recapture amount is the $5,643 difference between the $6,143 depreciation claimed and the $500 depreciation deduction that would have been allowed in the first-year computing using ADS as if no section 179 expense allowance or bonus depreciation had been claimed ($10,000 × 5%). The 2010 depreciation deduction is $400 ($10,000 × 10% (second-year ADS table percentage) × 40% business use percentage).

ACRS listed property recapture

If ACRS recovery property that is also listed property satisfies the qualified business use test (more than 50-percent business use) in the tax year in which it is placed in service but fails to meet the test in a later tax year, ACRS deductions are subject to recapture in the later year. Depreciation deductions for tax years preceding the tax year in which business use fell to 50 percent or less are recaptured to the extent that the ACRS deductions for these years exceed the depreciation that would have been allowed under the straight-line method (with a half-year convention for personal recovery property) over the earnings and profits life of the property. For subsequent tax years, depreciation must be computed under the straight-line method over the earnings and profits life.

For ACRS purposes, the earnings and profits life recovery periods to be used under Code Sec. 280F where the business use of recovery property that is also listed property does not exceed 50 percent are at ¶ 310.

The table below shows the applicable percentages to be used under Code Sec. 280F for listed property that is recovery property other than 18- or 19-year real property where business use does not exceed 50 percent (Temp. Reg. § 1.280F-3T(e)).

Table A1

If the recovery year is:	*And the recovery period is (in yrs.):* 5	12	25	35
1	10 %	4 %	2 %	1 %
2 - 5	20	9	4	3
6	10	8	4	3
7 - 12		8	4	3
13		4	4	3
14 - 25			4	3
26			2	3
27 - 31				3
32 - 35				2
36				1

The table below shows the applicable percentages to be used under Code Sec. 280F for listed property that is 18- or 19-year recovery real property where business use does not exceed 50 percent (IRS Pub. 534).

Table A2

Year	*Month Placed in Service* 1	2	3	4	5	6	7	8	9	10	11	12
1st	2.4	2.2	2.0	1.8	1.6	1.4	1.1	0.9	0.7	0.5	0.3	0.1
2 - 40th	2.5	2.5	2.5	2.5	2.5	2.5	2.5	2.5	2.5	2.5	2.5	2.5
41st	0.1	0.3	0.5	0.7	0.9	1.1	1.4	1.6	1.8	2.0	2.2	2.4

¶ 212

Lessee's Inclusion Amount for Listed Property Other Than Passenger Automobiles

Lessees of listed property (other than passenger automobiles as defined at ¶ 208) are required to add an inclusion amount to gross income in the first tax year (and only in that year) in which qualified business use fails to exceed 50 percent. For example, this rule would apply to an SUV that is considered a truck and has a gross vehicle weight rating in excess of 6,000 pounds. Although such an SUV is not a "passenger automobile," it is a listed property because it is a "means of transportation" (see ¶ 208).

This particular lease inclusion rule is designed to place lessees on par with *owners* of listed property who are subject to depreciation recapture and required to use the MACRS alternative depreciation system (ADS) when business use falls to 50 percent or less (see ¶ 210).

The inclusion amount may not exceed the sum of all deductions related to the use of the listed property properly allocable to the lessee's tax year in which the inclusion amount is added to gross income (Temp. Reg. § 1.280F-5T(g)(3)).

Where a lease term begins within nine months of the end of the lessee's tax year, qualified business use is 50 percent or less, and the lease term continues into the next tax year, the inclusion amount is added to gross income in the lessee's subsequent tax year in an amount based on the average of the business/investment use for both tax years and the applicable percentage for the tax year in which the lease term begins (Temp. Reg. § 1.280F-5T(g)(1)).

If the lease term is for less than one year, the amount that must be added to gross income is an amount that bears the same ratio to the inclusion amount as the number of days in the lease term bears to 365 (Temp. Reg. § 1.280F-5T(g)(2)).

Post-1986 leases

The lessee's inclusion amount for listed property (other than passenger automobiles) leased after 1986 is the sum of the following (Reg. § 1.280F-7(b)(2)):

(1) the fair market value of the property on the first day of the lease term × the business/investment use for the first tax year in which the business use percentage is 50 percent or less × the applicable percentage from Table I, below; and

(2) the fair market value of the property on the first day of the lease term × the average business/investment use for all tax years in which the property is leased before the tax year in which the business use percentage is 50 percent or less × the applicable percentage from Table II, below.

Table I

Type of Property	First Taxable Year During Lease in Which Business Use Percentage Is 50% or Less											
	1	2	3	4	5	6	7	8	9	10	11	12 & Later
Property with a Recovery Period of Less Than 7 Years under the Alternative Depreciation System (Such as Computers, Trucks and Airplanes)	2.1%	−7.2%	−19.8%	−20.1%	−12.4%	−12.4%	−12.4%	−12.4%	−12.4%	−12.4%	−12.4%	−12.4%
Property with a 7- to 10-Year Recovery Period under the Alternative Depreciation System (Such as Recreation Property)	3.9%	−3.8%	−17.7%	−25.1%	−27.8%	−27.2%	−27.1%	−27.6%	−23.7%	−14.7%	−14.7%	−14.7%
Property with a Recovery Period of More Than 10 Years under the Alternative Depreciation System (Such as Certain Property with No Class Life)	6.6%	−1.6%	−16.9%	−25.6%	−29.9%	−31.1%	−32.8%	−35.1%	−33.3%	−26.7%	−19.7%	−12.2%

Table II

Type of Property	First Taxable Year During Lease in Which Business Use Percentage Is 50% or Less											
	1	2	3	4	5	6	7	8	9	10	11	12 & Later
Property with a Recovery Period of Less Than 7 Years under the Alternative Depreciation System (Such as Computers, Trucks and Airplanes)	0.0%	10.0%	22.0%	21.2%	12.7%	12.7%	12.7%	12.7%	12.7%	12.7%	12.7%	12.7%
Property with a 7- to 10-Year Recovery Period under the Alternative Depreciation System (Such as Recreation Property)	0.0%	9.3%	23.8%	31.3%	33.8%	32.7%	31.6%	30.5%	25.0%	15.0%	15.0%	15.0%
Property with a Recovery Period of More Than 10 Years under the Alternative Depreciation System (Such as Certain Property with No Class Life)	0.0%	10.1%	26.3%	35.4%	39.6%	40.2%	40.8%	41.4%	37.5%	29.2%	20.8%	12.5%

Example: On February 1, 2008, a calendar-year taxpayer leased and placed in service an SUV with a fair market value of $32,000. Assume that the SUV is listed property (a "means of transportation," ¶ 208) and the lease term is two years. The SUV is not a "passenger automobile" because its gross vehicle weight rating is in excess of 6,000 pounds and it is considered a truck. Qualified business use is 80% in 2008 and 40% in 2009. The lessee must add an inclusion amount to gross income for 2009, which was the first tax year in which qualified business use of the SUV did not exceed 50%. Since 2009 is the second tax year of the lease and the SUV has a 5-year recovery period, the applicable percentage from Table I is -7.2%, and the applicable percentage from Table II is 10%. The 2009 inclusion amount is $1,638, which is the sum of the amounts determined under the tables. The amount determined under Table I is -$922 ($32,000 × 40% × (-7.2%)), and the amount determined under Table II is $2,560 ($32,000 × 80% × 10%). As noted above, the amount of the $1,638 inclusion amount that is actually included in income is limited to a smaller amount if the business deductions (such as the deductible portion of the lease payment and deductible gas and insurance expenses) related to the vehicle in 2009 are less than $1,638 (Temp. Reg. § 1.280F-5T(g)(2)). If the SUV had a gross vehicle weight rating of 6,000 pounds or less, it would be a "passenger automobile" and annual lease inclusion amounts would be required regardless of the percentage of business use. These inclusion amounts would be computed annually using the lease inclusion tables at ¶ 204.

Pre-1987 leases

The lessee's inclusion amount for recovery property that is also listed property (other than passenger automobiles) leased after June 18, 1984, and before 1987 is the product of: the fair market value of the property on the first day of the lease term × the average business/investment use × the applicable percentage from the tables below.

The average business/investment use is the average of the combined business/investment use of the listed property for the first tax year in which the qualified business use percentage is 50 percent or less (see ¶ 210) and all previous tax years in which the property is leased (Temp. Reg. § 1.280F-5T(h)(3)). The following IRS tables provide the applicable percentages for five- and ten-year recovery property. The table for three-year recovery property is not reproduced because the applicable percentage is zero if business use fails to exceed 50 percent in the sixth tax year of the lease term or succeeding tax years.

5-year recovery property:
For the first tax year in which the business use percentage is 50 percent or less, the applicable percentage for such tax year is:

Tax year during lease term	1	2	3	4	5	6	7	8	9	10	11	12
For a lease term of:												
1 year	2.7 %											
2 years	5.3	1.2 %										
3 years	9.9	6.1	1.6 %									
4 years	14.4	11.1	7.3	2.3 %								
5 years	18.4	15.7	12.4	8.2	3.0 %							
6 or more years	21.8	19.6	16.7	13.5	9.6	5.25 %	4.4 %	3.6 %	2.8 %	1.8 %	1.0 %	0 %

10-year recovery property:
For the first tax year in which the business use percentage is 50 percent or less, the applicable percentage for such tax year is:

Tax year during lease term	1	2	3	4	5	6	7	8	9	10	11	12	13	14	15
For a lease term of:															
1 year	2.5 %														
2 years	5.1	.6 %													
3 years	9.8	5.6	1.0 %												
4 years	14.0	10.3	6.2	1.4 %											
5 years	17.9	14.5	10.9	6.7	1.8 %										
6 years	21.3	18.3	15.1	11.4	7.1	2.1 %									
7 years	21.9	19.0	15.9	12.4	8.4	3.9	2.4 %								
8 years	22.4	19.6	16.7	13.4	9.7	5.5	4.5	2.7 %							
9 years	22.9	20.2	17.4	14.3	10.9	7.0	6.4	5.1	3.0 %						
10 years	23.5	20.9	18.2	15.2	11.9	8.3	8.1	7.2	5.7	3.3 %					
11 years	23.9	21.4	18.8	16.0	12.8	9.3	9.4	8.9	7.7	5.9	3.1 %				
12 years	24.3	21.9	19.3	16.5	13.4	10.1	10.3	10.0	9.3	7.8	5.5	2.9 %			
13 years	24.7	22.2	19.7	16.9	14.0	10.7	11.1	11.0	10.4	9.2	7.4	5.2	2.7 %		
14 years	25.0	22.5	20.1	17.3	14.4	11.1	11.6	11.7	11.3	10.3	8.8	6.9	4.8	2.5 %	
15 or more years	25.3	22.8	20.3	17.5	14.7	11.5	12.0	12.2	11.9	11.1	9.8	8.2	6.5	4.5	2.3 %

¶ 214

Cars Involved in Trade-Ins or Involuntary Conversions

Cars, light general purpose trucks (for use over the road having actual unloaded weight of less than 13,000 pounds) and vehicles that share characteristics of both cars and light general purpose trucks (e.g., crossovers, sport utility vehicles, minivans, cargo vans and similar vehicles) are of like kind for purposes of Code Sec. 1031 (IRS Letter Ruling 200912004, December 2, 2008). Like-kind exchanges are reported on Form 8824.

Special rules govern the depreciation deductions claimed on a business vehicle received in a tax-deferred like-kind exchange (trade-in) under Code Sec. 1031 or involuntarily conversion under Code Sec. 1033 after January 2, 2000.

Pursuant to IRS Notice 2002-4 and subsequently issued regulations which implement the principles of that notice (which has been declared obsolete, effective February 27, 2004), depreciation on the carryover portion of the adjusted basis of the acquired automobile (the "exchanged basis"), is separately depreciated from the noncarryover basis ("excess basis"). The "excess basis" (e.g., cash paid) is depreciated as if it is newly acquired property. The exchanged basis and excess basis each qualify for bonus depreciation if the trade-in occurs in a tax year in which bonus depreciation is allowed. See ¶ 127D for a discussion of bonus depreciation. This bifurcated treatment only applies if the taxpayer used MACRS to depreciate the relinquished vehicle and will use MACRS to depreciate the replacement vehicle.

Notice 2000-4 did not explain the interplay with the Code Sec. 280F luxury car depreciation caps. The IRS did not issue any formal guidance on this point until temporary regulations (now finalized) were released on February 27, 2004 (T.D. 9115, filed with the Federal Register on February 27, 2004).

Effective date of regulations and transitional rules. Final regulations apply to like-kind exchanges and involuntary conversions of MACRS property for which the time of disposition and time of replacement both occur after February 27, 2004 (Reg. § 1.168(i)-6(k)(1)). A taxpayer may apply the final regulations to pre-February 27, 2004 transactions or rely on prior guidance issued by the IRS (e.g., Notice 2000-4) (Reg. § 1.168(i)-6(k)(2)). For additional discussion of effective date rules, see ¶ 167.

Election not to apply regulations. A taxpayer may elect not to apply the final regulations to a transaction occurring on or after the effective date (Reg. § 1.168(i)-6(i)(1)).

If the election not to apply the regulations is made, the exchanged (carryover) basis and excess basis (additional cash paid) in the acquired vehicle are treated as placed in service at the time of replacement and the adjusted depreciable basis (generally cost less depreciation claimed (including amounts expensed under section 179 and bonus depreciation)) of the relinquished vehicle is treated as disposed of by the taxpayer at the time of disposition. The election must be made by the due date (including extensions) of the tax return for the year of replacement in the manner provided in the instructions to Form 4562, Depreciation and Amortization. Once made, the election may only be revoked in extraordinary circumstances with IRS consent (Reg. § 1.168(i)-6(j)).

Depreciation computations if no election out is made. If no election out is made, a vehicle acquired in a like-kind exchange or involuntary conversion is treated as comprised of two separate components. The first component is the exchanged basis (generally, the adjusted basis of the relinquished vehicle immediately prior to the trade-in or involuntary conversion) and the second component is the excess basis (generally, the cash paid for the new vehicle, if any).

The exchanged basis in the acquired vehicle is determined after determining the depreciation deduction on the relinquished vehicle in the trade-in year. The exchanged basis is defined as the lesser of:

(a) the basis of the replacement property, determined under Code Sec. 1031(d) or Code Sec. 1033(b), as applicable; or

(b) the adjusted depreciable basis of the relinquished property (as defined in Reg. § 1.168(b)-1(a)(4)).

Adjusted depreciable basis is the basis for determining gain or loss (adjusted to reflect personal use during the tax year). This basis reflects basis reductions such as those for the Code Sec. 179 expense allowance, bonus depreciation, and regular depreciation deductions previously claimed.

Excess basis is defined as the difference between the basis in the replacement property (item (a), above) and the exchanged basis.

In the year of disposition the sum of the depreciation deductions for the relinquished MACRS passenger automobile and the replacement MACRS passenger automobile may not exceed the replacement automobile section 280F limit (Reg. § 1.168(i)-6(d)(3)(i)).

Depreciation deductions on the relinquished car in the year of disposition and the replacement car in the year of replacement (and each subsequent tax year) are allowed in the following order (Reg. § 1.168(i)-6(d)(3)):

(1) The depreciation deduction on the relinquished car (prior to the trade-in) in the year of disposition is allowed to the extent of the smaller of (a) the relinquished car's 280F limit (for the year of disposition) or (b) the replacement car's 280F limit for the year of disposition.

(If the replacement vehicle is not acquired in the year of trade-in or involuntary conversion, the depreciation deduction on the relinquished vehicle is limited solely by the relinquished car's 280F limit).

(2) Bonus depreciation on the remaining exchanged basis of the replacement vehicle (i.e., the carryover basis of replacement car) is allowed to the extent of the replacement car's 280F limit reduced by the depreciation claimed on the relinquished car prior to the trade-in (item 1). Thus, the bonus deduction on the remaining exchanged basis can be claimed without regard to the 280F cap for the relinquished vehicle. It is only limited by the 280F cap for the replacement vehicle as reduced by depreciation claimed on the relinquished vehicle prior to the trade in the trade-in year.

(3) The depreciation deduction on the depreciable exchanged basis of the replacement vehicle is allowed to the extent of the smaller of the replacement car's 280F limit or the relinquished car's 280F limit as reduced by items (1) and (2).

(4) Any section 179 deduction claimed on the excess basis of the replacement vehicle is allowed to the extent of the 280F limit for the replacement car as reduced by items (1), (2), and (3) above.

(5) The bonus deduction on the remaining excess basis of the replacement vehicle is allowed to the extent of the 280F limit for the replacement car as reduced by items (1), (2), (3), and (4), above.

(6) The depreciation deduction on the depreciable excess basis is allowed to the extent of the 280F limit for the replacement car as reduced by items (1), (2), (3), (4), and (5), above.

The regulations provide four examples of a trade-in (Reg. § 1.168(i)-6(d)(3)(iii)). None of the examples show computations after the trade-in year.

Example (1): Taxpayer purchases a car in 2000 for $30,000. In 2003 he exchanges the car plus $15,000 cash for a new vehicle. No bonus deduction or section 179 allowance was claimed on the relinquished vehicle in 2000.

Year Purchased	*Price*	*Bonus*	*Sec. 179*	*Method*	*Convention*	*Trade-in Year*
2000	$30,000	$0	$0	200DB	Half-Year	2003

Year	*Annual Limit*	*Deduction**	*Lesser*
2000	$3,060	$6,000	$3,060
2001	$4,900	$9,600	$4,900
2002	$2,950	$5,760	$2,950
2003	$1,775**	$3,818	$1,775

* $30,000 × 40% × 6/12 = $6,000
($30,000 – $6,000) × 40% = $9,600
($30,000 – $6,000 – $9,600) × 40% = $5,760
30,000 – $3,060 – $4,900 – $2,950) × 40% × 6/12 = $3,818
40% is the double declining Balance rate for 5-year property. 6/12 is used to reflect half-year convention in the acquisition year and trade-in year.

** The 280F limit for the relinquished vehicle ($1,775) is used because it is smaller than the 280F limit for the replacement vehicle (i.e., $10,710) (ordering rule 1).

In the IRS example, which does not show the relevant pre-trade calculations, the allowed depreciation deduction for 2003 prior to the trade-in is given as $1,775 (the applicable cap). $1,775 is correct if the pre-trade depreciation is computed on the "adjusted depreciable basis" of the vehicle as of the beginning of the year of disposition. Adjusted depreciable basis is defined by Reg. § 1.168(b)-1(a)(4), as the unadjusted depreciable basis (cost less bonus allowance) reduced by the adjustments described in Code Sec. 1016(a)(2) and Code Sec. 1016(a)(3) (i.e., depreciation allowed in computing taxable income). Thus, in the example, the adjusted depreciable basis would be $19,090 ($30,000 - $3,060 - $4,900 - $2,950). The regular fourth-year deduction on this amount is $3,818 ($19,090 × 40% × 6/12). Since $3,818 is greater than the $1,775 cap, the deduction is limited to the cap.

However, it is unclear why the regular pre-trade deduction is not $1,728 ($30,000 - $6,000 - $9,600 - $5,760) × 40% × 6/12 = $1,728). In this case, the allowed deduction would be $1,728 since this is less than the $1,775 cap. See IRS Publication 463 (Travel, Entertainment, Gift, and Car Expenses) (For use in preparing 2007 returns), showing how regular deductions are first computed without regard to the caps and then limited by the applicable cap if it is smaller.

The new regulations do not seem to support the use of the adjusted depreciable basis to make the pre-trade-in regular depreciation calculation. The regulations state that the depreciation deduction on the relinquished automobile in the year of disposition is determined under Reg. § 1.168(i)-6(c)(5)(i) (Reg. § 1.168(i)-6(d)(3)(ii)(A)). Reg. § 1.168(i)-6(c)(5)(i) indicates that the depreciation deduction for the year of disposition of a relinquished asset is computed by multiplying the "allowable depreciation deduction" for the property by 6/12 if the half-year convention applies. The term "allowable depreciation deduction" is not defined. Reg. § 1.168(i)-6(c)(5)(i), however, cross references to Reg. § 1.168(i)-6(e) if the optional tables are used. That regulation indicates that the deduction in the year of disposition is determined by multiplying the "unadjusted depreciable basis" (less any bonus allowance allowed or allowable) by the recovery percentage for the year of disposition. The product is then multiplied by 6/12 if the half-year convention applies. Unadjusted depreciable basis is defined by Reg. § 1.168(b)-1(a)(3) as the basis of the property for determining gain or loss, without reduction for depreciation (other than the Code Sec. 179 expense allowance). Thus, the table percentages are applied to the original cost less any amount a taxpayer elected to expense under Code Sec. 179 and claimed as a bonus depreciation allowance. In the above example, using the optional table percentages, the 2003 pre-trade deduction is $1,728 ($30,000 × 11.52% (fourth year table percentage) × 6/12 to reflect the half-year convention).

Interestingly, all three examples in Reg. § 1.168(i)-6(d)(iii) appear to make the pre-trade calculation on the adjusted depreciable basis of the vehicle as of the beginning of the 2003 tax year. The text of IRS Example (3), specifically refers to calculating the deduction on the "adjusted depreciable basis" of the relinquished automobile.

Since the IRS examples use the adjusted depreciable basis in computing regular depreciation on the relinquished vehicle in the trade-in year, this and the following examples will also use the adjusted depreciable basis.

The exchanged basis of the replacement vehicle is calculated by reducing the original cost of the acquired vehicle ($30,000) by the depreciation (including any section 179 expense and bonus allowance) actually allowed on the replacement vehicle prior to the trade-in.

The exchanged basis is therefore $17,315 ($30,000 - $3,060 - $4,900 - $2,950 - $1,775 = $17,315).

Bonus depreciation and regular first-year deduction are then computed on the exchanged basis without regard to any 280F limit. Note that exchanged basis (i.e., carryover basis) never qualifies for expensing under Code Sec. 179.

Bonus depreciation on the exchanged basis is $8,658 ($17,315 × 50% = $8,658). Regular depreciation is $1,731 (($17,315 - $8,658) × 40% × 6/12 = $1,731).

Under the second ordering rule, the bonus deduction ($8,658) is limited to $8,935. $8,935 is the replacement car's 280F limit ($10,710) reduced by the depreciation claimed on the relinquished car in 2003 prior to the trade-in ($1,775). Since the bonus deduction does not exceed the $8,935 section 280F limit, the bonus deduction may be claimed in its entirety.

Under the third ordering rule, the $1,731 regular depreciation deduction on the exchanged basis of the replacement car is allowed only to the extent of the relinquished car's 280F limit ($1,775) (since this is smaller than the replacement car's 280F limit ($10,710)) reduced by the depreciation allowed on the relinquished car in 2003 prior to the trade in ($1,775) and the bonus depreciation allowed on the exchanged basis after the trade in ($8,658). Since the sum of these two amounts already exceeds $1,775 ($1,775 + $8,658 = $10,433) no regular depreciation deduction may be claimed on the exchanged basis.

Next, the Code Sec. 179 allowance, bonus allowance, and regular first-year deduction are computed on the excess basis ($15,000 additional cash) without regard to any cap. Assume that no amount is expensed under Code Sec. 179.

The bonus deduction is $7,500 ($15,000 × 50%). The regular first-year deduction is $1,500 ($7,500 × 40% × 6/12).

The ordering rules are then applied.

The fourth ordering rule is not applicable since no Code Sec. 179 expense allowance is claimed on the excess basis.

Under the fifth ordering rule, the bonus deduction on the remaining excess basis of the replacement vehicle may only be claimed to the extent that the bonus deduction does not exceed the 280F limit for the replacement car ($10,710) as reduced by the regular depreciation deduction on the relinquished vehicle ($1,775), bonus depreciation on the exchanged basis ($8,658), depreciation on the exchanged basis ($0), and any amount of the excess basis that is expensed under Code Section 179 ($0).

The bonus deduction, is therefore limited to $277 ($10,710 – $1,775 – $8,658). Since the first-year cap is now used up, no amount of the regular depreciation ($1,500) may be claimed (ordering rule 6).

At the end of 2003, the adjusted depreciable basis of the acquired automobile is $23,380, comprised of the adjusted depreciable exchanged basis of $8,657 ($17,315 (exchanged basis) – $8,658 (bonus on exchanged basis) and the adjusted depreciable excess basis of $14,723 ($15,000 excess basis – $277 bonus on excess basis).

Example (2): Taxpayer purchases a vehicle costing $30,000 in 2002. The vehicle is exchanged in 2003 with an additional $15,000 cash paid for the acquired vehicle. No section 179 expense allowance is claimed on either vehicle and an election out of bonus depreciation was made for both vehicles.

Depreciable allowed in 2002 on the relinquished automobile is $3,060 (first-year cap) since this is less than the regular first-year deduction of $6,000 ($30,000 × 40% × 6/12).

In determining the depreciation allowed on the relinquished vehicle in 2003 prior to the trade-in, the applicable cap is $3,060. This cap is the smaller of the second-year cap for a vehicle placed in service in 2002 ($4,900) or the first-year cap for the acquired vehicle ($3,060 since no bonus is claimed on the acquired vehicle) (ordering rule 1).

According to the IRS example, the regular deduction on the relinquished automobile in 2003 prior to the trade-in, without regard to the $3,060 cap, is $5,388 ($30,000 – $3,060 × 40% × 6/12). Since this amount exceeds the applicable cap of $3,060, the depreciation deduction is limited to $3,060. As explained in the *Comment* above, the IRS computes the pre-trade depreciation in the trade-in year using the vehicle's adjusted depreciable basis. If the adjusted depreciable basis had not been used, the regular deduction on the relinquished vehicle without regard to the cap would have been $4,800 ($30,000 - $6,000 × 40% × 6/12). In either event, the depreciation deduction would be limited by the $3,060 cap.

In determining the depreciation allowed on the exchanged basis after the trade in, the applicable cap is $3,060 (the lesser of the cap on the relinquished car ($4,900) or the cap on the acquired car ($3,060)). Since no portion of the $3,060 first-year cap remains, no regular depreciation on the exchanged basis may be claimed (ordering rule 3).

Similarly, no regular depreciation deduction may be claimed on the excess basis ($15,000). The applicable cap for the excess basis is $3,060 (the first-year cap for a vehicle placed in service in 2003). This cap has already been reduced to zero (ordering rule 6).

Example (3): A vehicle costing $10,000 is purchased is 2000 and traded in 2003. An additional $14,000 cash is paid. The double declining balance method and half-year convention apply.

Deductions on relinquished vehicle prior to trade-in. No bonus claimed.

Year	*Annual Limit*	*Deduction**	*Lesser*
2000	$3,060	$2,000	$2,000
2001	$4,900	$3,200	$3,200
2002	$2,950	$1,920	$1,920
2003	$1,775**	$576***	$576***
Total depreciation allowed			$7,696

* ($10,000 × 40% × 6/12) = $2,000
($10,000 – $2,000) × 40% = $3,200
($10,000 – $2,000 – $3,200) × 40% = $1,920
($10,000 – $2,000 – $3,200 – $1,920) × 40% × 6/12 = $576

** The annual limit for 2003 is the lesser of the 2003 limit for the relinquished vehicle ($1,775) or the $10,710 first-year limit for the acquired vehicle (ordering rule 1).

*** The IRS example indicates that pre-trade depreciation of $576 in 2003 is computed on the relinquished car's adjusted depreciable basis. See *Comment* in *Example 1,* above.

Next, bonus depreciation is computed on the exchanged basis of $2,304 ($10,000 – $7,696). The bonus deduction is $1,152 ($2,304 × 50%) and may be claimed in full since it does not exceed $10,134 (the first-year depreciation cap for the acquired vehicle ($10,710) reduced by the depreciation claimed on the relinquished vehicle in 2003 prior to the trade-in ($576)) (ordering rule 2).

Next regular depreciation is computed on the depreciable exchanged basis of $1,152 ($2,304 exchanged basis - $1,152 bonus deduction). The regular depreciation deduction is $230 ($1,152 × 40% × 6/12). Since the 2003 $1,775 cap for the relinquished vehicle is the less than the $10,710 cap for the acquired vehicle, the depreciation deduction cannot exceed $47 ($1,775 – $576 – $1,152) and, therefore, is limited to $47 (ordering rule 3).

The next step is to compute the Code Sec. 179 expense deduction, bonus deduction, and regular depreciation deduction that may be claimed on the excess basis (i.e., $14,000 cash paid). These three items are first figured without regard to the cap. Assume that the taxpayer expenses $1,400. Bonus depreciation is $6,300 ($14,000 - $1,400) × 50%). Regular first-year depreciation is $1,260 ($14,000 – $1,400 – $6,300) × 40% × 6/12).

The applicable first-year cap for a vehicle placed in service in 2003 on which 50% bonus depreciation is claimed is $10,710. However, the cap must first be reduced by the amount of regular depreciation actually claimed on the relinquished vehicle in 2003 prior to the trade-in and the amount of bonus and regular depreciation claimed on the exchanged basis after the trade-in. The cap is, therefore, reduced to $8,935 ($10,710 – $576 – $1,152 – $47). Note that the deductions claimed on the relinquished vehicle and exchanged basis after the trade-in were limited to the $1,775 cap ($576 + $1,152 + $47 = $1,775).

The reduced cap ($8,935) is applied in the following order: First to any amount expensed under Code Sec. 179, then to any bonus deduction, then to the regular depreciation deduction (ordering rules 4, 5, and 6).

The $1,400 Code Sec. 179 deduction may be claimed in full ($8,935 - $1,400 = $7,535). The $6,300 bonus deduction is allowed in full ($7,535 - $6,300 = $1,235). The regular first-year deduction of $1,260, however, is limited to the remaining $1,235 first-year cap.

The IRS regulations do not provide examples of post-trade year calculations. It appears, however, that the depreciation computed on the exchanged basis would be limited to the applicable cap for the exchanged basis if it does not exceed the applicable cap for the excess basis (ordering rule 3). The depreciation deduction on the excess basis would be limited to the applicable cap for the excess basis reduced by the depreciation claimed on the exchanged basis (ordering rule 6).

Example (4): Assume the same facts as in *Example 3*. The depreciation deduction in 2004 on the exchanged basis is limited to the $1,775 (fourth year cap for a vehicle placed in service in 2000) since this is less than $4,900 (second-year cap for vehicle placed in service in 2003). The depreciation deduction on the excess basis is limited to $4,900 minus any depreciation allowed on the exchanged basis.

Partial business use. The rule requiring a special basis adjustment when a vehicle which had not been used 100 percent for business is involved in a trade-in (Temporary Reg. § 1.280F-2T(g)(2)) is unaffected by the new regulations.

The basis reduction is required for an acquired business automobile for the purpose of computing MACRS depreciation. The basis for gain or loss is not so reduced. The reduction amount is the excess, if any, of the total MACRS deductions that would have been allowable during the years before the trade if the exchanged or converted automobile had been used 100 percent for business/investment use over the total MACRS deductions actually allowed during those years.

Example (5): On January 1, 2002, a calendar-year taxpayer bought and placed in service a $30,000 car. The car was used 80% for business purposes each year. No Code Sec. 179 election was made. The taxpayer elected out of bonus depreciation. The car was depreciated under the general MACRS 200% declining balance method over a five-year recovery period using the half-year convention. In September 2003, a new car is purchased for $31,000 consisting of a $7,000 cash payment plus a trade-in allowance of $24,000 on the old car. MACRS deductions allowed on the old car for 2002 and 2003 are $2,448 ($3,060 × .8) and $3,840 ($30,000 × .32 × .5 × .8) since $3,840 does not exceed the second-year depreciation cap for a car placed in service in 2002 of $3,920 ($4,900 × .8), respectively. (Note: For the year of disposition of property subject to the half-year convention, generally one-half of the MACRS deduction computed in the regular manner for a full year adjusted for business use is compared with the Code Sec. 280F limit adjusted for business use but not adjusted for the fact that it is the year of disposition of property that is subject to the half-year convention.) No Code Sec. 179 election is made with respect to excess basis of the new car and the new car is depreciated under the general MACRS 200% declining balance method over a five-year recovery period using the half-year convention. The taxpayer elects not to take the additional 30% first-year depreciation under Code Sec. 168(k). The new car is used 100% for business purposes each year. The depreciable basis of the new car is determined as follows:

Original basis of old car		$30,000
Less: MACRS deductions allowed:		
2002	$2,448	
2003	3,840	6,288

Adjusted basis of old car		$23,712
New car:		
Adjusted basis of old car		$23,712
Plus: Additional amount paid		7,000
Total		$30,712
Less: Depreciation allowable assuming 100% business use:		
For 2002 and 2003 ($3,060 + $4,800*)	$7,860	
Less: MACRS deductions actually allowed	6,288	1,572
Depreciable basis of new car		$29,140

* The $4,800 figure is equal to $30,000 cost × .32 (second-year recovery percentage) × .5 (to take into account half-year convention). Since $4,800 does not exceed the $4,900 second-year depreciation cap for a car placed in service in 2002, $4,800 is treated as the 2003 deduction, assuming 100% business use.

Although the total depreciable basis of the new car is $29,140, the basis must be separated into two parts. The noncarryover basis (excess basis) ($7,000) is treated as newly purchased MACRS property. The carryover basis (exchanged basis) $22,140 ($29,140 – $7,000) (which is an adjusted amount that reflects 100 percent business use) must be depreciated over the remaining recovery period using the same MACRS depreciation method (IRS Publication 463, Travel, Entertainment, Gift, and Car Expenses (for use in preparing 2006 returns), p. 20, Example 1.)

Example (6): Assume the same facts as in Example 1 except that the relinquished vehicle was used 75 percent of the time during each tax year. The total allowable depreciation claimed on the relinquished auto is $9,513.75 ($2,295 for 2000 ($3,060 limit × .75), $3,675 for 2001 ($4,900 limit × .75), $2,212.50 for 2002 ($2,950 limit × .75), and $1,331.25 for 2003 ($1,775 limit × .75). However, the exchanged basis is reduced by the excess (if any) of the depreciation that would have been allowable if the exchanged automobile had been used solely for business over the depreciation that was allowable in those years. Thus, the exchanged basis, for purposes of computing depreciation, for the replacement vehicle is $17,315 (Reg. § 1.168(i)-6(d)(3)(iii), Example 2).

Mileage Allowances

¶ 217

Standard Mileage Rates, FAVR Allowances, and Mileage-Based Methods

Mileage allowance methods may be grouped into three categories: the standard mileage rate, the fixed and variable rate allowance (FAVR), and other mileage allowances that meet specified requirements.

Standard mileage rate

The standard mileage rate is adjusted annually by the IRS in a revenue procedure which is generally issued in November or December.

Standard Mileage Rate

Miles Driven During	*Rate Per Mile*	*Source*
1/1/09 - 12/31/09	55 cents	Rev. Proc. 2008-72
7/1/08 - 12/31/08	58.5 cents	Announcement 2008-63
1/1/08 - 6/30/08	50.5 cents	Rev. Proc. 2007-70, as modified by Announcement 2008-63
2007	48.5 cents	Rev. Proc. 2006-49
2006	44.5 cents	Rev. Proc. 2005-78
1/1/05 - 8/31/05	40.5 cents	Rev. Proc. 2004-64, as modified by Announcement 2005-71
9/1/05 - 12/31/05	48.5 cents	Rev. Proc. 2004-64, as modified by Announcement 2005-71
2004	37.5 cents	Rev. Proc. 2003-76
2003	36.0 cents	Rev. Proc. 2002-61
2002	36.5 cents	Rev. Proc. 2001-54
2001	34.5 cents	Rev. Proc. 2000-48
2000	32.5 cents	Rev. Proc. 99-38
4/1/99 - 12/31/99	31.0 cents	Rev. Proc. 98-63; Ann. 99-7
1/1/98 - 3/31/99	32.5 cents	Rev. Proc. 97-58; Ann. 99-7

Employees and self-employed individuals who use their own or leased cars (including vans, pickups, and panel trucks) cars for business may determine deductible car expenses under the standard mileage rate for estimating expenses based on the number of business miles that a car is driven. A deduction computed using the standard mileage rate for business miles is in place of operating and fixed costs of the automobile allocable to business (including depreciation or lease payments, tires, gas, and taxes thereon, oil, insurance, and license and registration fees. Parking fees, tolls, interest, and state and local taxes may be separately deductible).

Effective for tax years beginning after December 31, 1997, the standard mileage rate may not be used to compute deductible automobile expenses of postal employees in connection with the collection and delivery of mail on a rural route if the employee receives qualified reimbursements. These reimbursements will now be considered as equivalent to such an employee's expenses (Code Sec. 162(o), as added by P.L. 105-34). Previously, a standard mileage rate equal to 150 percent of the otherwise applicable standard mileage rate applied to these Postal workers (Act Sec. 6008 of P.L. 100-647 (Technical and Miscellaneous Revenue Act of 1998) prior to repeal by Act Sec. 1203(b) of P.L. 105-34 (Taxpayer Relief Act of 1997)).

Employees may use the standard mileage rate for computing expenses when they are not reimbursed by an employer or when the reimbursement is partial for purposes of claiming a miscellaneous itemized deduction.

Self-employed individuals may use the standard mileage rate to compute a deduction for expenses of operating a car in their business in arriving at adjusted gross income.

The standard mileage rate is not allowable in the following circumstances: the car is used for hire; five (two in 2003 and earlier) or more cars are used simultaneously in the same trade or business (for example, fleet operations); a depreciation method other than the straight-line method has been used; the taxpayer claimed a Code Sec. 179 expense deduction; or the car has been depreciated under ACRS or MACRS.

An election to use the standard mileage allowance to figure the actual expenses of operating a passenger car (including a van, pickup, or panel truck) is considered an election under Code Sec. 168(f)(1) to exclude the automobile from MACRS by using a method not based on a term of years in the first year that an asset is placed in service. An election under Code Sec. 168(f)(1) to exclude property from MACRS is irrevocable. See ¶ 140. Nevertheless, a taxpayer may switch from the standard mileage rate in a subsequent tax year to the actual cost method and depreciate the vehicle over the remaining useful life of the vehicle using the straight-line method. This is a non-MACRS method and, therefore, its use apparently is not considered to violate the rule that an election out of MACRS under Code Sec. 168(f)(1) is irrevocable.

The election must be made in the year that such vehicle is first placed in service. Thereafter, an annual election may be made to compute deductible transportation expenses by using the standard mileage rate allowance or actual costs. However, if the car is leased the election to use the standard mileage rate applies for the entire lease term. The election to use the standard mileage allowance precludes a Code Sec. 179 expense deduction and bonus depreciation deduction in the year that a car is placed in service as well as the use of MACRS or ACRS in such year and subsequent years. Rev. Proc. 2007-70, as well as IRS Publication 463, (Travel, Entertainment, Gift, and Car Expenses), provide that in the event of a subsequent-year switch from the standard mileage rate allowance to the actual cost method for determining allowable expenses by an owner, depreciation is computed under the straight-line method over the car's remaining estimated useful life (subject to the Code Sec. 280F depreciation limits for passenger automobiles).

FAVR (Fixed or Variable Rate) allowances

Employers having five or more employees who each drive cars, which they either own or lease, on company business for 5,000 or more miles (or if greater, 80 percent of the business miles projected by the employer for purposes of computing the FAVR variable mileage rate) may set up a FAVR allowance to reimburse employees (Rev. Proc. 2007-70). This method may not be established by employees or self-employed individuals, although employees may be covered by the method if a FAVR allowance is established by their employers.

An employer must designate a standard automobile (i.e., a car of specific make, model and year) and standard automobile cost for each FAVR that it sets up. The standard automobile cost may not exceed 95 percent of the sum of the retail dealer invoice cost of the standard automobile and any state and local sales or use taxes applicable on the purchase of the vehicle. The standard automobile cost is adjusted annually by the IRS in a revenue procedure which is generally issued in November or December.

Standard Automobile Cost

Year	*Cost*	*Source*
2009	$27,200	Rev. Proc. 2008-72
2008	$27,500	Rev. Proc. 2007-70
2007	$27,600	Rev. Proc. 2006-49
2006	$27,400	Rev. Proc. 2005-78
2005	$27,600	Rev. Proc. 2004-64
2004	$28,100	Rev. Proc. 2003-76
2003	$26,900	Rev. Proc. 2002-61
2002	$27,100	Rev. Proc. 2001-54
2001	$27,100	Rev. Proc. 2000-48
2000	$27,300	Rev. Proc. 99-38
1999	$27,100	Rev. Proc. 98-63
1998	$27,100	Rev. Proc. 97-58

An employee may not participate in a particular FAVR if the cost of his vehicle when new is less than 90 percent of the cost of the standard automobile. The employee's car does not have to be the same make and model as the standard automobile. However the employee's car may not be older than the number of calendar years that the employer determines that a standard automobile will be driven in connection with the performance of services as an employee before being replaced (i.e., the "retention period").

Amounts reimbursed under a FAVR arrangement are considered transportation expenses of the employer and are deductible as such. The allowance, which is determined by each employer using statistical methods based on local retail costs, consists of two component payments.

(1) Fixed payment. Projected fixed costs (including depreciation) for a standard automobile's projected retention period are prorated over the projected retention period and multiplied by the car's projected business use percentage (which may not exceed 75 percent). This amount must be paid to covered employees at least quarterly.

(2) Variable payment. This is a mileage allowance also paid at least quarterly to cover the operating costs for substantiated business miles. The mileage rate is the projected operating costs of a standard automobile for a computation period divided by projected miles driven for the period.

For purposes of (1), above, an employer may determine the projected business use percentage based on the following table instead of using other data.

(Projected) Annual business mileage	*(Projected) Business use percentage*
6,250 or more but less than 10,000	45%
10,000 or more but less than 15,000	55%
15,000 or more but less than 20,000	65%
20,000 or more	75%

Limits on depreciation component. The total amount of the depreciation component of the fixed payments for the retention period may not exceed the excess of the standard automobile cost over the residual value of the standard automobile at the end of the projected retention period. Residual value may be determined by the employer or may be determined by multiplying the standard automobile cost by one of the following percentages.

Retention period	*Residual value*
2 years	70%
3 years	60%
4 years	50%

Also, in no event may the total amount of the depreciation component exceed the sum of the annual Code Sec. 280F limits on depreciation (in effect at the beginning of the retention period) that apply to the standard automobile during the retention period.

An exception to these two limitations on the depreciation component of the fixed payments made to an employee has been added, effective for reimbursements for 1999 expenses. The exception takes the form of a business standard mileage test and is available to an employee who drives at least 80 percent of the "annual business mileage" of their standard automobile (Rev. Proc. 2006-49, section 8.04(3)). The annual business mileage of a standard automobile is the mileage that the employer projects that a standard automobile will be driven for business purposes during the calendar year. The exception applies in any year during which the total annual amount of the fixed and variable payments made to the qualifying employee do not exceed the amount obtained by multiplying 80 percent of the annual business mileage of the standard automobile by the applicable standard mileage rate for that year (50.5/58.5 cents in 2008).

Adjustments to basis

Employees and self-employed individuals whose car expenses are determined under one of the foregoing mileage allowances (whether in computing their own deductions or in determining the amount of a reimbursement) are required to reduce the basis of their cars as follows:

(1) *Standard mileage rate basis adjustment.* For each year the standard mileage rate has been used, the basis of an owned vehicle is reduced (not below zero) as follows:

Year method used	*Amount of adjustment (cents per mile)*
1980 - 81	7.0
1982	7.5
1983 - 85	8.0
1986	9.0
1987	10.0
1988	10.5
1989-91	11.0
1992 - 93	11.5
1994 - 99	12.0
2000	14.0
2001 - 02	15.0
2003 - 04	16.0
2005 - 2006	17.0
2007	19.0
2008 - 2009	21.0

Pre-1990 use of the car in excess of 15,000 miles in one year is disregarded for the purposes of basis adjustment, even if the actual business mileage was higher.

(2) *FAVR method.* The basis of a car subject to a FAVR allowance is reduced (not below zero) by the depreciation component of the periodic fixed payment, which the employer is required to report to the employee.

(3) *Other mileage allowances.* The basis of a car covered under an accountable plan by another type of permitted mileage allowance is reduced by the standard-mileage-rate basis adjustment (item (1), above) or, if the employee claims expenses on Form 2106 (Employee Business Expenses) in excess of reimbursement, basis is adjusted in accordance with the method used on Form 2106.

Mileage-based depreciation method

The IRS has approved a mileage based depreciation method used by a corporation which leased fleets of vehicles to corporate clients. The lessor was allowed to make an election out of MACRS pursuant to Code Sec. 168(f)(1) which allows the use of a permissible method not based on a term of years (IRS Letter Ruling 200046020, August 17, 2000).

The leases were for a term of one year with automatic monthly renewals after the first year. The average lease lasted 32 months and the average mileage logged per vehicle was 67,000 miles. Upon termination of a lease, the leased vehicle was sold. Based on historical information, the lessor determined the average mileage life of the leased vehicles and the average salvage (resale) value at the end of the lease term. The average mileage life and salvage value were reviewed annually and adjusted for any significant changes. The annual depreciation deduction was determined by multiplying a vehicle's cost (less salvage value) by a fraction, the numerator of which was the actual number of miles the vehicle was driven during the year and the denominator of which was the average mileage life of the vehicle. Depreciation was not claimed below salvage value.

ACRS

Accelerated Cost Recovery System

¶ 220

Rules for Recovery Property

The original version of the Accelerated Cost Recovery System (ACRS) (Code Sec. 168, prior to amendment by the 1986 Tax Reform Act (P.L. 99-514)), generally applicable to most tangible depreciable property placed in service after 1980 and before 1987, was born out of a consensus that further incentives were needed to stimulate capital investment. Inflation had diminished the value of previous depreciation allowances, and the need to upgrade technology had further increased the cost of replacing older equipment. The approach, as embodied in the Economic Recovery Tax Act of 1981, moved away from the useful-life concept and minimized exceptions and elections.

By 1984, economic priorities had changed, and the Tax Reform Act of 1984 increased the recovery period for what otherwise would have been 15-year real property to 18 years and introduced supplementary rules (see ¶ 200–214) for so-called mix-use property—cars and other specified kinds of property by their nature lending themselves to both business and personal use. P.L. 99-21 further increased the recovery period for what formerly would have been 15-year real property or 18-year property to 19 years, but the big overhaul was left to the Tax Reform Act of 1986, which, under the old system's name (the Accelerated Cost Recovery System), in effect, introduced a new system. The "old" system (ACRS) is discussed below. For an explanation of Modified ACRS (MACRS), see the discussion beginning at ¶ 80.

Since ACRS is not based on estimated useful lives, cost recovery under it may not, in a strict dictionary sense, qualify as depreciation. The ACRS rules are careful in this regard, defining "recovery property" as property that, among other things, is "of a character subject to the allowance for depreciation." Although the term "of a character subject to the allowance for depreciation" is undefined, the word depreciation means exhaustion or wear and tear (including a reasonable allowance for obsolescence). Thus, property must suffer exhaustion, wear and tear, or obsolescence in order to be depreciated (*R.L. Simon*, 103 TC 247, aff'd, CA-2, 95-2 USTC ¶ 50,552 (Nonacq., I.R.B. 1996-29, 4)). As a matter of convenience and practice, ACRS is considered a system of depreciation, but, given two similarly named systems, "recovery property" becomes a particularly useful term for purposes of distinguishing property subject to ACRS from MACRS property.

Just as the rules discussed at ¶ 264 prevent the "churning" of pre-1981 assets into recovery property, more recent anti-churning rules may thwart the churning of some recovery property into MACRS property. Thus, property placed in service after 1986 may still be recovery property. However, the latter rules are considerably narrower in scope than those fashioned for ACRS because, generally, MACRS is less generous than ACRS and the rules are, of course, not designed to benefit transferees of property from related taxpayers. Rules under which property placed in service after 1986 must be treated as recovery property are more fully discussed at ¶ 142.

¶ 222
Computation of ACRS Allowances

Under pre-1981 rules, basis, salvage value, and useful life were the three essential elements for computing depreciation. Under ACRS, only basis is essential. Salvage value is no longer a factor, and assets may be "depreciated" over periods considerably shorter than their estimated useful lives. In contrast to methods prescribed under Modified ACRS (see ¶ 80), recovery percentages are applied to unadjusted basis.

The unadjusted basis to which recovery percentages are applied does not include any portion of the basis of an asset for which there is an election to amortize or to rapidly depreciate (¶ 320–326), or to expense under Code Sec. 179 (¶ 300). For property placed in service after 1982 and before 1986, unadjusted basis may reflect a reduction for an investment tax credit.

Once basis has been determined, it is necessary to identify the class to which the asset belongs (see ¶ 230). A recovery period is prescribed for each class, and statutory recovery percentages are assigned for each year of the recovery period.

Then, the ACRS allowance is determined by multiplying the unadjusted basis of the asset by the appropriate recovery percentage for the tax year. Except for 15-year real property, 18-year real property, or 19-year real property, the same recovery percentage applies to all recovery property in the same class placed in service in the same tax year, and the applicable recovery percentage may be applied to the total unadjusted basis of such property.

No short tax year adjustment (¶ 290) is made merely because real recovery property is placed in service during a tax year, even if such tax year is a short tax year (Prop. Reg. § 1.168-2(f)(1)).

> ***Example:*** A corporation is formed on February 10, 1985, and engages in the rental real estate business. It acquires and places in service on March 31, 1985, 18-year real recovery property that has an unadjusted basis of $100,000. No optional ACRS straight-line method election is made. The corporation's normal tax year is a calendar-year tax year so it has a short tax year for the first recovery year. The recovery allowance for 1985, the year that the property is placed in service, is computed as though it were a full tax year. Because the recovery property would have been deemed placed in service in the third month of the corporation's normal calendar-year tax year, the corporation is entitled to a recovery deduction for the short tax year computed as if the 18-year property had been placed in service in the third month of a 12-month tax year. The ACRS deduction is $8,000 ($100,000 unadjusted basis × 8% (third month of year one ACRS percentage)).

Applicable recovery methods

As the names of the property classes indicate, the cost of ACRS property is generally recoverable in 3, 5, 10, 15, 18, or 19 years (¶ 230). Most personal property is 3-year or 5-year property. However, taxpayers who elect straight-line ACRS allowances may elect to recover their costs over specified longer periods (¶ 254). Except for 15-year real property, 18-year real property, or 19-year real property, the straight-line method is elected on a class-by-class basis (for any tax year), and the half-year convention applies (thus spreading the recovery of basis over one more tax year). These optional longer periods are also available to taxpayers restricted to the straight-line method because the property was financed with the proceeds of industrial development bonds (¶ 256).

If, under the rules discussed at ¶ 206–¶ 214, property is classified as listed and not used more than 50 percent for business, straight-line depreciation is mandated over generally longer periods.

Half-year convention

Under the regular method (for other than 15-year real property, 18-year real property, or 19-year real property), the half-year convention is mandatory and built into the applicable tables. For 5-year property, for example, 15 percent of the cost is recoverable in the first year irrespective of the day of the year in which it is placed in service. No deduction is allowed for the year of disposition. Recovery percentages for tangible personal property are designed to approximate the effect of the use of the 150-percent declining-balance method with a later-year switch to straight-line recovery.

Months

If 15-year real property, 18-year real property, or 19-year real property is involved, months figure in computations, both in years of acquisition and in years of disposition (¶ 242–246). The recovery percentages for such property other than low-income housing approximate the use of the 175-percent declining-balance method with an eventual switch to the straight-line method. The recovery percentages for low-income housing provide 200-percent declining-balance recovery with a switch to the straight-line method. Fifteen-year property is regarded as placed in service on the first day of the month, and a mid-month convention applies to 18-year real property placed in service after June 22, 1984, and to 19-year real property. Thus, in the case of 15-year real property, a full month's depreciation is allowed for the month that the property is placed in service and no depreciation is allowed for the month that the property is disposed of. In the case of 18- and 19-year real property subject to the mid-month convention, one-half month's depreciation is allowed for both the month that the property is placed in service and the month that the property is disposed of. The table percentages for the year that the property is placed in service reflect the applicable convention. However, the table percentages must be adjusted for the year that a property is disposed of.

> ***Example:*** ACRS 19-year real property with a depreciable basis of $100,000 is placed in service in February 1986 and disposed of in April of 1999 by a calendar-year taxpayer. 1999 is the 14th year of the recovery period. The 14th year recovery percentage for 19-year real property placed in service in February is 4.2%. The taxpayer is allowed to claim 3½ months depreciation in 1999 as the property is considered in service during January, February, March, and one-half of April under the mid-month convention. The allowable deduction for 1999 is $1,225 ($100,000 × 4.2% × 3.5/12). If the property was 15-year real property, it would be considered in service only during the months of January, February, and March. No depreciation would be allowed for the month of disposition under the applicable convention.

Component depreciation is eliminated (¶ 242). The recovery period and method used for such items as wiring and plumbing are the same as are used for the building (or the shell, as it sometimes is called), unless the recovery period is longer because the dates of placing the building in service and of placing components in service straddle the effective date of one of the increases in the generally applicable period for recovering the cost of real property.

Consistent with prior-law treatment, costs recovered under ACRS or expensed under Code Sec. 179 are not the costs that are used in computing earnings and profits available for dividend payments. The relevant rules are discussed at ¶ 310.

¶ 226

Property Placed in Service

Since property had to be placed in service after 1980 to be classified as recovery property, it is important to know when property has been placed in service. The IRS considers property to be placed in service when it is ready and available for a specifically assigned function (Prop. Reg. § 1.168-2(l)(2) at ¶ 525). No distinction is drawn between readiness and availability for use in a trade or business or for the production of income and readiness and availability for use in a personal or tax-exempt activity. Depreciation, on the other hand, begins when the property becomes ready for service in a trade or business or for the production of income.

The IRS illustrates the distinction with the simple example of a taxpayer who buys a house in 1975, lives in it until 1981, and then begins renting the home out. Having been placed in service in 1975, the residence is not recovery property. It should be noted, however, that a statutory exception to this general principle requires that real property used by a taxpayer for personal purposes prior to 1987 and converted to business use after 1986 be depreciated using MACRS (Act Sec. 1002(c)(3) of the Technical and Miscellaneous Revenue Act of 1988 (P.L. 100-647)).

Since property may be placed in service after use by a prior owner, specific rules prevent the conversion of pre-1981 property into recovery property through transfers to related parties. These so-called anti-churning rules are discussed at ¶ 264.

Changes in use

The recovery allowance for property converted from personal (or tax-exempt) use to business (or investment) use is computed as if the property is placed in service as recovery property as of the date of conversion. To the extent of an increase in business (or investment) use, an allowance becomes available as if property is placed in service in the year of the increase. For purposes of applying these rules, the basis of any such property may not exceed fair market value.

Example (1): In 1983, Harper purchases a car for $9,000 and, through 1985, uses it 80% for business. The car is 3-year property, and, for each of the three years included in the regular recovery period, he deducts recovery allowances based on the cost of the car, the applicable percentages, and his 80% business use. Beginning in 1986, his business use of the car, now worth $4,500, increases to 100%. Harper's allowable deduction for 1986 is $225, based on the car's fair market value at the beginning of the year ($4,500), 20% business use (the excess of 100% over 80%), and the applicable first-year percentage (25%). For 1987, the second-year percentage (38%) applies, and the allowable deduction is $342.

Example (2): The facts are the same as in Example (1) except that all the dates of all relevant facts are advanced by one year. The question that this variance presents is whether the deduction of the "post-recovery period" year is computed under ACRS or MACRS. Since the governing date of placement in service may relate to placement in service for personal (not just business) use, the car was deemed placed in service in 1986, and ACRS should be used to compute additional depreciation.

At the option of the taxpayer, similar treatment is available where property is reassigned to a class with a shorter recovery period or property ceases to be used outside the United States. However, if property is reassigned to a class with a longer recovery period (as, for example, where property ceases to be predominantly used in connection with research and experimentation), ceases to be low-income housing, or starts being used predominantly outside the United States, deductions are computed as if allowances had always been computed on the basis of present status, and not only must current deductions be determined under these principles, but the taxpayer must account for prior-year excess allowances. The following example is adapted from proposed regulations:

Example (3): A taxpayer pays $20,000 for property that, in the year of its purchase, is predominantly used for research and experimentation and qualifies as 3-year property. For the year it is placed in service, he deducts $5,000 (25% of $20,000). In the following year, the property ceases to be used for research and development and is treated as 5-year property. Not only is the second-year deduction limited to 22% (the applicable second-year percentage for 5-year property) of $20,000, but it is further reduced by the allocable portion of the prior year excess allowance. The excess first-year allowance is $2,000 (the excess of 25% of $20,000 over 15% of $20,000), and the portion of this amount allocable to the second recovery year is $518, determined by multiplying $20,000 by .15 (the first-year percentage for 5-year property) and dividing by .85 (the remaining unused applicable percentages). Thus, the second-year deduction is $3,882 (the excess of the regular allowance (22% of $20,000) over $518 (the allowable portion of the first-year excess allowance)).

Building placed in service in stages

The proposed ACRS regulations recognize that a building (for example, a high-rise) may be placed in service in stages. These regulations provide that each significant portion of a building should be separately depreciated as it is placed in service. Placed in service means made available for use in a finished condition, for example, as when a certificate of occupancy is issued. However, the same depreciation method must be used to depreciate the entire building. For example, this rule, when applied to MACRS residential rental property, would mean that a taxpayer could not depreciate one portion of the building over a 27.5 year period and elect ADS (40-year depreciation period) for another portion of the building. The regulations explain the allocation of basis among the completed portions and provides examples (Prop. Reg. § 1.168-2(e)(3) and (5) at ¶ 525).

The definition of "placed in service" is also discussed at ¶ 3.

¶ 228

What Is Recovery Property?

Property to which ACRS applies is called recovery property. Except as indicated below, recovery property is tangible property that is:

(1) of a depreciable character;

(2) placed in service after 1980 and before 1987; and

(3) used in a trade or business or held for the production of income.

Property may be new or used, but, as subsequently discussed, special rules are designed to thwart the conversion of pre-1981 property into recovery property through various kinds of transactions involving related parties.

Intangible depreciable property cannot be recovery property, and land is, of course, not depreciable. Consistent with a pre-ACRS revenue ruling that a work of art is generally nondepreciable even though its physical condition may influence its valuation (Rev. Rul. 68-232, 1968-1 CB 79; Reg. § 1.168-3(a)(1)), the IRS has ruled that an old and valuable cello of a Professor of Cello and a concert performer did not qualify as recovery property (IRS Letter Ruling 8641006, July 1, 1986). However, the courts have said otherwise with respect to valuable instruments that are used in a musician's trade or business and are subject to wear and tear. See ¶ 3.

Exceptions to the rules under which tangible depreciable property placed in service after 1980 and before 1987 is regarded as recovery property fall into the following categories:

(1) property depreciated under methods not based on a term of years and, at the election of the taxpayer, excluded from ACRS;

(2) certain public utility property;

(3) property that was pre-1981 property in the hands of a related owner or user;

(4) property acquired in any of various enumerated transactions in which no gain or loss is recognized;

(5) property placed in service after July 31, 1986, and before 1987 and, pursuant to the taxpayer's election, depreciated under MACRS (see ¶ 228); and

(6) some post-1986 property not qualifying for MACRS under rules similar to those (see ¶ 264) that prevent some post-1980 property from qualifying for ACRS.

Recovery property for which an expensing election is made under Code Sec. 179 (see ¶ 302) is, to the extent of that election, effectively removed from the general ACRS rules.

Property that is properly amortized pursuant to a valid election is also effectively removed from the general ACRS rules, see ¶ 320–326.

A video tape is not recovery property; nor is any motion picture film not created primarily for use as public entertainment or for educational purposes and not (1) placed in service before March 15, 1984, and treated as recovery property on a return filed before March 16, 1984, or (2) placed in service before 1985, treated as recovery property, and produced at a cost of which at least 20 percent was incurred before March 16, 1984.

Sound recordings placed in service after March 15, 1984, could, at the election of a taxpayer with whom the original use began, be treated as 3-year recovery property.

Property predominantly used outside the United States qualifies as recovery property, but separate rules apply for determining recovery periods. See ¶ 252.

Transitional rules

Although MACRS governs property generally placed in service after 1986, certain property placed in service before 1991 is governed by ACRS under transitional rules if certain action was taken by March 1, 1986.

Classes of ACRS Recovery Property

¶ 230

Relationship to "Present Class Life"

ACRS recovery property must be classified. Most qualifying personal property falls into the 5-year class, but cars, light-duty trucks, research and experimentation equipment, and certain other items are classified as 3-year property. Except for property used in connection with research or experimentation, a "present class life" of no more than four years is a prerequisite for qualifying as 3-year property. Except for low-income housing (see ¶ 248), manufactured homes, and railroad tank cars, real property with a "present class life" of more than 12.5 years is 15-year real property, 18-year real property, or 19-year real property. Certain variations apply to public utility property.

"Present class life" is a statutory term used to key recovery periods to prior-law asset guideline periods. It refers to the class life that would have applied to property had there been no ACRS rules and had an ADR election been made under former Code Sec. 167(m). Thus, the guideline classes provided in Rev. Proc. 83-35, 1983-1 CB 745, for ADR property still play a continuing role in classifying ACRS recovery property even though obsoleted for MACRS property.

As hereafter used with respect to the ACRS rules, "ADR class life" means the same as "present class life."

As originally conceived, the classes of recovery property were entirely governed by the nature of the property, and naming the classes by reference to the length of recovery periods clarified application of the rules. Subsequent legislation lengthened recovery periods for real property placed in service after specified dates, and, thus, under ACRS, the date of placement in service generally governs whether a building is 15-year real property, 18-year real property, or 19-year real property.

Notwithstanding some similar names, classes of recovery property must be distinguished from classes of property established under Modified ACRS (MACRS). For example, under ACRS, an automobile is 3-year property but, under MACRS, an automobile is 5-year property.

¶ 240

Personal Property

The ACRS classes for personal property are 3-year property, 5-year property, and 10-year property. (This property should be fully depreciated by now.)

In general, 3-year property included all Sec. 1245 class property with an ADR class life of no more than four years and machinery and equipment used in connection with research and experimentation.

Tangible personal property that was not 3-year property, 10-year property, or 15-year public utility property was included in the category of 5-year property.

Ten-year property includes

(1) public utility property (that is not Sec. 1250 class property or property that is 3-year property by reason of its use in connection with research and experimentation) with an "ADR class life" of more than 18 but not more than 25 years and

(2) Sec. 1250 class property with a "present class life" of not more than 12.5 years.

Theme and amusement park structures, manufactured (including mobile) homes, railroad tank cars, and qualified coal utilization property that would otherwise be 15-year public utility property are 10-year property. Under a special rule for theme parks, a building and its structural components with a present class life of no more than 12.5 years will not become 10-year or 15-year property by reason of conversion to a use other than its original use.

Assuming no straight-line election, recovery percentages for 10-year property are as follows:

Property	*Percentage*
Year 1	8
Year 2	14
Year 3	12
Year 4 - 6	10
Year 7 - 10	9

¶ 242

15-Year Real Property

Subject to when placed in service and the applicable transitional rules, Sec. 1250 class property with an "ADR class life" of more than 12.5 years is 15-year real property. Low-income housing must be distinguished from other 15-year real property because, in the early years, its costs are recoverable at a slightly faster rate. Separate tables are provided.

In general, 15-year real property must have been placed in service before March 16, 1984. However, otherwise eligible property qualified as 15-year real property if:

(1) it was purchased or constructed under a contract entered into before March 16, 1984, or construction began by that date; and

(2) the taxpayer placed the property in service before 1987.

This applied to a subsequent transferee so long as a qualified transferor had not yet placed the property in service.

Elevators and escalators are treated as 15-year real property even though they were also eligible for the investment credit.

Since the recovery percentages depend on the month on which an asset is placed in service, separate items of 15-year real property may be grouped together only if they are placed in service in both the same month and the same year.

The following recovery percentages were prescribed by the IRS for 15-year real property other than low-income housing:

If the Recovery Year Is	*The applicable percentage is (use the column representing the month in the first tax year the property is placed in service):*											
	1	*2*	*3*	*4*	*5*	*6*	*7*	*8*	*9*	*10*	*11*	*12*
1	12	11	10	9	8	7	6	5	4	3	2	1
2	10	10	11	11	11	11	11	11	11	11	11	12
3	9	9	9	9	10	10	10	10	10	10	10	10
4	8	8	8	8	8	8	9	9	9	9	9	9
5	7	7	7	7	7	7	8	8	8	8	8	8
6	6	6	6	6	7	7	7	7	7	7	7	7
7	6	6	6	6	6	6	6	6	6	6	6	6

If the Recovery Year Is	*The applicable percentage is (use the column representing the month in the first tax year the property is placed in service):*											
	1	*2*	*3*	*4*	*5*	*6*	*7*	*8*	*9*	*10*	*11*	*12*
8	6	6	6	6	6	6	5	6	6	6	6	6
9	6	6	6	6	5	6	5	5	5	6	6	6
10	5	6	5	6	5	5	5	5	5	5	6	5
11 - 15	5	5	5	5	5	5	5	5	5	5	5	5
16	—	—	1	1	2	2	3	3	4	4	4	5

Additions and improvements

Substantial improvements to a building are treated as a separate building under ACRS. This, for example, means that a new roof may qualify as recovery property even though the building itself may have to be depreciated under pre-1981 rules. (Note that this discussion relates to improvements placed in service after 1980 and before 1987. Additions and improvements placed in service after 1986 are depreciated under MACRS. See ¶ 126 for the applicable rules).

Two requirements must be met for an improvement to be "substantial":

(1) it must have been made three or more years after the building is placed in service; and

(2) the addition to the capital account for the building and its components during any 24-month period must be at least 25 percent of the building's adjusted basis (ignoring any adjustments for depreciation and amortization).

The 25-percent test is applied to the building's adjusted basis as of the first day of the 24-month period.

The general rule that the cost of a building's components—plumbing, wiring, storm windows, etc.—must be recovered in the same manner as the cost of the building itself is complicated by changes in the law that extended recovery periods and, eventually, replaced ACRS. Under a special transitional rule, applicable to the first component placed in service after 1980 on a building that was placed in service before 1981, the first such component was treated as a separate building. Thus, for components placed in service before March 16, 1984, either the statutory ACRS percentages for 15-year realty or straight-line ACRS allowances (¶ 254) had to be elected, and the method elected was mandatory for other components placed in service before March 16, 1984.

Consistent with this approach and subject to transitional rules, the first component placed in service after March 18, 1984, and before May 9, 1985, is treated as a separate building and classified as 18-year real property, and the first component placed in service after May 9, 1985, and not subject to MACRS is treated as a separate building and classified as 19-year real property. With regard to additions or improvements placed in service after July 31, 1986, and before 1987, a taxpayer could elect MACRS and treat what would otherwise be 19-year real property as, depending on which was applicable, 27.5-year residential rental property or 31.5-year nonresidential real property. Unless shielded by transitional rules, post-1986 improvements are MACRS property. See ¶ 126.

Example: In September of 1985, a new roof is placed in service for a pre-1985 office building. The new roof is treated as a new building, and is classified as 19-year real property.

¶ 244

18-Year Real Property

Eighteen-year real property is real property placed in service after March 15, 1984, and before May 9, 1985. Eighteen-year real property also includes real property placed in service before 1987 if either purchased or constructed under a binding contract entered into before May 9, 1985 or construction of the property began before May 9, 1985 (Act Sec. 105(b)(2), P.L. 99-121).

A variation in the applicable convention for such real property, in effect, creates two subclasses of 18-year real property. Eighteen-year real property placed in service before June 23, 1984, is regarded as placed in service on the first day of the month, and 18-year real property placed in service after June 22, 1984, is regarded as placed in service on the midpoint of the month. Therefore, separate recovery percentages are prescribed for each "subclass."

The following recovery percentages, assuming no mid-month convention, apply to 18-year real property placed in service before June 23, 1984.

If the Recovery Year Is:	*The applicable percentage is (use the column representing the month in the first tax year the property is placed in service):*											
	1	*2*	*3*	*4*	*5*	*6*	*7*	*8*	*9*	*10*	*11*	*12*
1	10	9	8	7	6	6	5	4	3	2	2	1
2	9	9	9	9	9	9	9	9	9	10	10	10
3	8	8	8	8	8	8	8	8	9	9	9	9
4	7	7	7	7	7	7	8	8	8	8	8	8
5	6	7	7	7	7	7	7	7	7	7	7	7
6	6	6	6	6	6	6	6	6	6	6	6	6
7	5	5	5	5	6	6	6	6	6	6	6	6
8 - 12	5	5	5	5	5	5	5	5	5	5	5	5
13	4	4	4	5	5	4	4	5	4	4	4	4
14 - 18	4	4	4	4	4	4	4	4	4	4	4	4
19			1	1	1	2	2	2	3	3	3	4

The following recovery percentages, reflecting the mid-month convention, apply to 18-year real property placed in service after June 22, 1984.

If the Recovery Year Is:	*The applicable percentage is (use the column representing the month in the first tax year the property is placed in service):*											
	1	*2*	*3*	*4*	*5*	*6*	*7*	*8*	*9*	*10*	*11*	*12*
1	9	9	8	7	6	5	4	4	3	2	1	0.4
2	9	9	9	9	9	9	9	9	9	10	10	10.0
3	8	8	8	8	8	8	8	8	9	9	9	9.0
4	7	7	7	7	7	8	8	8	8	8	8	8.0
5	7	7	7	7	7	7	7	7	7	7	7	7.0
6	6	6	6	6	6	6	6	6	6	6	6	6.0
7	5	5	5	5	6	6	6	6	6	6	6	6.0
8 - 12	5	5	5	5	5	5	5	5	5	5	5	5.0
13	4	4	4	5	4	4	5	4	4	4	5	5.0
14 - 17	4	4	4	4	4	4	4	4	4	4	4	4.0
18	4	3	4	4	4	4	4	4	4	4	4	4.0
19		1	1	1	2	2	2	3	3	3	3	3.6

¶ 246

19-Year Real Property

Real property placed in service after May 8, 1985 and before 1987 is generally classified as 19-year real property. Real property placed in service before 1991 may qualify as 19-year real property under transitional rules for binding contracts (Act Sec. 203(b)(1)(A) of P.L. 99-514) and self-constructed property (Act Sec. 203(b)(1)(B) of P.L. 99-514). The following recovery percentages, reflecting a mid-month convention, are prescribed for 19-year real property:

If the Recovery Year Is:	*The applicable percentage is (use the column representing the month in the first tax year the property is placed in service):*											
	1	*2*	*3*	*4*	*5*	*6*	*7*	*8*	*9*	*10*	*11*	*12*
1	8.8	8.1	7.3	6.5	5.8	5.0	4.2	3.5	2.7	1.9	1.1	0.4
2	8.4	8.5	8.5	8.6	8.7	8.8	8.8	8.9	9.0	9.0	9.1	9.2
3	7.6	7.7	7.7	7.8	7.9	7.9	8.0	8.1	8.1	8.2	8.3	8.3
4	6.9	7.0	7.0	7.1	7.1	7.2	7.3	7.3	7.4	7.4	7.5	7.6
5	6.3	6.3	6.4	6.4	6.5	6.5	6.6	6.6	6.7	6.8	6.8	6.9
6	5.7	5.7	5.8	5.9	5.9	5.9	6.0	6.0	6.1	6.1	6.2	6.2
7	5.2	5.2	5.3	5.3	5.3	5.4	5.4	5.5	5.5	5.6	5.6	5.6
8	4.7	4.7	4.8	4.8	4.8	4.9	4.9	5.0	5.0	5.1	5.1	5.1
9	4.2	4.3	4.3	4.4	4.4	4.5	4.5	4.5	4.5	4.6	4.6	4.7
10 - 19	4.2	4.2	4.2	4.2	4.2	4.2	4.2	4.2	4.2	4.2	4.2	4.2
20	0.2	0.5	0.9	1.2	1.6	1.9	2.3	2.6	3.0	3.3	3.7	4.0

¶ 248

Low-Income Housing

The cost of low-income housing is recovered in the same manner as the cost of ordinary real property except that recovery percentages are based on the use of the 200-percent declining-balance method. Property in this category includes federally assisted housing projects in which the mortgage is insured under the National Housing Act; housing financed or assisted under similar local law provisions; low-income rental housing for which rehabilitation expenditures qualified for depreciation deductions; low-income rental housing held for occupancy by families or persons who qualify for subsidies under the National Housing Act or local law that authorize similar subsidies; or housing that is insured or directly assisted under Title V of the Housing Act of 1949.

The IRS has prescribed the following recovery percentages:

(1) for low-income housing placed in service before May 9, 1985; and

(2) for low-income housing placed in service after May 8, 1985, and for which allowances are determined without regard to the mid-month convention.

If the Recovery Year Is:	*For low-income housing placed in service before May 9, 1985, the applicable percentage is (use the column representing the month in the first tax year the property is placed in service):*											
	1	*2*	*3*	*4*	*5*	*6*	*7*	*8*	*9*	*10*	*11*	*12*
1	13	12	11	10	9	8	7	6	4	3	2	1
2	12	12	12	12	12	12	12	13	13	13	13	13

If the Recovery Year Is:	*For low-income housing placed in service before May 9, 1985, the applicable percentage is (use the column representing the month in the first tax year the property is placed in service):*											
	1	*2*	*3*	*4*	*5*	*6*	*7*	*8*	*9*	*10*	*11*	*12*
3	10	10	10	10	11	11	11	11	11	11	11	11
4	9	9	9	9	9	9	9	9	10	10	10	10
5	8	8	8	8	8	8	8	8	8	8	8	9
6	7	7	7	7	7	7	7	7	7	7	7	7
7	6	6	6	6	6	6	6	6	6	6	6	6
8	5	5	5	5	5	5	5	5	5	5	6	6
9	5	5	5	5	5	5	5	5	5	5	5	5
10	5	5	5	5	5	5	5	5	5	5	5	5
11	4	5	5	5	5	5	5	5	5	5	5	5
12	4	4	4	5	4	5	5	5	5	5	5	5
13	4	4	4	4	4	4	5	4	5	5	5	5
14	4	4	4	4	4	4	4	4	4	5	4	4
15	4	4	4	4	4	4	4	4	4	4	4	4
16	—	—	1	1	2	2	2	3	3	3	4	4

If the Recovery Year Is:	*For low-income housing placed in service after May 8, 1985, and before 1987, the applicable percentage is (use the column representing the month in the first tax year the property is placed in service):*											
	1	*2*	*3*	*4*	*5*	*6*	*7*	*8*	*9*	*10*	*11*	*12*
1	13.3	12.2	11.1	10	8.9	7.8	6.6	5.6	4.4	3.3	2.2	1.1
2	11.6	11.7	11.9	12	12.1	12.3	12.5	12.6	12.7	12.9	13	13.2
3	10	10.1	10.2	10.4	10.5	10.7	10.8	10.9	11.1	11.2	11.3	11.4
4	8.7	8.8	8.9	9	9.1	9.2	9.3	9.5	9.6	9.7	9.8	9.9
5	7.5	7.6	7.7	7.8	7.9	8	8.1	8.2	8.3	8.4	8.5	8.6
6	6.5	6.6	6.7	6.8	6.9	6.9	7	7.1	7.2	7.3	7.4	7.4
7	5.7	5.7	5.8	5.9	5.9	6	6.1	6.1	6.2	6.3	6.4	6.5
8	4.9	5	5	5.1	5.2	5.2	5.3	5.3	5.4	5.5	5.5	5.6
9	4.6	4.6	4.6	4.6	4.6	4.6	4.6	4.6	4.6	4.7	4.8	4.8
10	4.6	4.6	4.6	4.6	4.6	4.6	4.6	4.6	4.6	4.6	4.6	4.6
11	4.6	4.6	4.6	4.6	4.6	4.6	4.6	4.6	4.6	4.6	4.6	4.6
12	4.5	4.6	4.6	4.6	4.6	4.6	4.6	4.6	4.6	4.6	4.6	4.6
13	4.5	4.5	4.6	4.5	4.6	4.6	4.6	4.6	4.6	4.5	4.6	4.6
14	4.5	4.5	4.5	4.5	4.5	4.5	4.5	4.6	4.6	4.5	4.5	4.5
15	4.5	4.5	4.5	4.5	4.5	4.5	4.5	4.5	4.5	4.5	4.5	4.5
16		0.4	0.7	1.1	1.5	1.9	2.3	2.6	3	3.4	3.7	4.1

Example: In May 1986, a calendar-year taxpayer purchases and places in service some property that qualifies as low-income rental housing. The purchase price is \$80,000, of which \$20,000 is allocable to land. For 1986, his deduction is \$5,340 (8.9% of \$60,000). For 1987, his deduction is \$7,260 (12.1% of \$60,000). If the property had not qualified as low-income property, his deductions are \$3,480 for 1986 and \$5,220 for 1987.

¶ 250

15-Year Public Utility Property

Public utility property that is not Sec. 1250 class property or 3-year property and that has an ADR class life of more than 25 years is classified as 15-year public utility property. It includes electric utility steam production plants, gas utility manufactured gas production plants, water utility property, and telephone distribution plants.

Except for the recovery period, 15-year public utility property is treated like 3-year, 5-year, or 10-year property rather than like 15-year real property. Recovery percentages are statutory, and the particular month in which property is placed in service does not affect computations.

Recovery percentages are as follows for 15-year public utility property:

Property	*Percentage*
Year 1	5
Year 2	10
Year 3	9
Year 4	8
Year 5	7
Year 6	7
Year 7 - 15	6

¶ 252

Property Used Outside the Country

Rules are modified for ACRS property that is predominantly used outside the United States. The cost of personal property is generally recoverable over its ADR class life. Absent such class life, a 12-year period applies. The cost of real property used predominantly outside the United States is generally recoverable over a 35-year period.

Property is regarded as used predominantly outside the United States if it is located outside the United States for more than 50 percent of the tax year or, if placed in service during the tax year, more than 50 percent of the period beginning on the day in which the property is placed in service and ending on the last day of the tax year. For a discussion of the effect of subsequent-year change of use, see ¶ 104.

The following tables, extracted from proposed regulations or Rev. Proc. 86-14, 1986-1 CB 542, provide recovery percentages for property predominantly used outside the United States.

Property Used Predominantly Outside The United States Other Than 15-, 18- or 19-Year Real Property

Accelerated Cost Recovery System

(200% Declining Balance)
(Half-Year Convention)

Recovery Period

Year	*2.5*	*3*	*3.5*	*4*	*5*	*6*	*6.5*	*7*	*7.5*	*8*	*8.5*	*9*	*9.5*	*10*	*10.5*	*11*	*11.5*	*12*	*12.5*	*13*	*13.5*	*14*	*15*
1	40	33	29	25	20	17	15	14	13	13	12	11	11	10	10	9	9	8	8	8	7	7	7
2	48	45	41	38	32	28	26	25	23	22	21	20	19	18	17	17	16	15	15	14	14	13	12
3	12	15	17	19	19	18	18	17	17	16	16	15	15	14	14	13	13	13	12	12	12	11	11
4		7	13	12	12	12	13	13	13	12	12	12	12	12	11	11	11	11	10	10	10	10	9
5				6	12	10	10	9	9	9	9	9	9	9	9	9	9	9	9	9	8	8	8
6					5	10	9	9	9	8	8	8	7	7	7	7	7	7	7	7	7	7	7
7						5	9	9	8	8	8	7	7	7	7	7	6	6	6	6	6	6	6
8								4	8	8	7	7	7	7	7	6	6	6	6	6	6	5	5
9										4	7	7	7	7	6	6	6	6	6	5	5	5	5
10												4	6	6	6	6	6	6	6	5	5	5	5
11														3	6	6	6	5	5	5	5	5	5
12																3	5	5	5	5	5	5	5
13																		3	5	5	5	5	5
14																				3	5	5	4
15																						3	4
16																							2

Property Used Predominantly Outside The United States
Other Than 15-, 18- or 19-Year Real Property

Accelerated Cost Recovery System

(200% Declining Balance)
(Half-Year Convention)

Recovery Period

Year	*16*	*16.5*	*17*	*18*	*19*	*20*	*22*	*25*	*26.5*	*28*	*30*	*35*	*45*	*50*
1	6	6	6	6	5	5	5	4	4	4	3	3	2	2
2	12	11	11	10	10	10	9	8	7	7	6	6	4	4
3	10	10	10	9	9	9	8	7	7	6	6	5	4	4
4	9	9	9	8	8	8	7	6	6	6	6	5	4	4
5	8	8	8	7	7	7	6	6	6	6	5	5	4	3
6	7	7	7	7	6	6	6	6	5	5	5	4	4	3
7	6	6	6	6	6	6	5	5	5	5	5	4	3	3
8	5	5	5	5	5	5	5	5	5	4	4	4	3	3
9	5	5	5	5	5	4	4	4	4	4	4	4	3	3
10	5	5	4	4	4	4	4	4	4	4	4	3	3	3
11	5	4	4	4	4	4	4	4	4	4	3	3	3	3
12	4	4	4	4	4	4	4	3	3	3	3	3	3	3
13	4	4	4	4	4	4	4	3	3	3	3	3	3	2
14	4	4	4	4	4	4	3	3	3	3	3	3	3	2
15	4	4	4	4	4	3	3	3	3	3	3	3	2	2
16	4	4	4	4	4	3	3	3	3	3	3	3	2	2

Accelerated Cost Recovery System

Recovery Period

Year	*16*	*16.5*	*17*	*18*	*19*	*20*	*22*	*25*	*26.5*	*28*	*30*	*35*	*45*	*50*
17	2	4	3	4	3	3	3	3	3	3	3	2	2	2
18			2	3	3	3	3	3	3	3	3	2	2	2
19				2	3	3	3	3	3	3	3	2	2	2
20					2	3	3	3	3	3	3	2	2	2
21						2	3	3	3	3	3	2	2	2
22							3	3	3	2	2	2	2	2
23							2	3	3	2	2	2	2	2
24-25								2	2	2	2	2	2	2
26								1	2	2	2	2	2	2
27									1	2	2	2	2	2
28										2	2	2	2	2
29										1	2	2	2	2
30											2	2	2	2
31											1	2	2	2
32-35												2	2	2
36												1	2	1
37-46													1	1
47-51														1

Low-Income Housing Used Predominantly Outside the United States (placed in service after December 31, 1980 and before May 9, 1985)
15-Year Real Property Used Predominantly Outside the United States (placed in service after December 31, 1980 and before March 16, 1984)
18-Year Real Property Used Predominantly Outside the United States (placed in service after March 15, 1984 and before June 23, 1984)

(35-Year 150% Declining Balance)
(Assuming No Mid-Month Convention)

	Month Placed in Service				
Year	**1**	**2-3**	**4-6**	**7-8**	**9-12**
1	4 %	4 %	3 %	2 %	1 %
2-5	4	4	4	4	4
6	3	3	3	4	4
7-24	3	3	3	3	3
25	3	2	3	2	3
26-35	2	2	2	2	2
36	.	1	1	2	2

18-Year Real Property Used Predominantly Outside the United States (placed in service after June 22, 1984 and before May 9, 1985)

(35-Year 150% Declining Balance)
(Assuming Mid-Month Convention)

	Month Placed in Service						
Year	**1**	**2**	**3**	**4-5**	**6-8**	**9-11**	**12**
1	4 %	4 %	3 %	3 %	2 %	1 %	0.2 %
2-5	4	4	4	4	4	4	4.0
6	3	3	3	3	4	4	4.0
7	3	3	3	3	3	3	3.8
8-24	3	3	3	3	3	3	3.0
25	3	2	3	2	2	3	3.0
26-35	2	2	2	2	2	2	2.0
36	.	1	1	2	2	2	2.0

19-Year Real Property Used Predominantly Outside the United States (placed in service after May 8, 1985 and before 1987)

(35-Year 150% Declining Balance)
(Assuming Mid-Month Convention)

	Month Placed in Service											
Year	**1**	**2**	**3**	**4**	**5**	**6**	**7**	**8**	**9**	**10**	**11**	**12**
1	4.1	3.7	3.4	3.0	2.7	2.3	2.0	1.6	1.3	0.9	0.5	0.2
2	4.1	4.1	4.1	4.2	4.2	4.2	4.2	4.2	4.2	4.3	4.3	4.3
3	3.9	4.0	4.0	4.0	4.0	4.0	4.0	4.0	4.1	4.1	4.1	4.1
4	3.8	3.8	3.8	3.8	3.8	3.8	3.9	3.9	3.9	3.9	3.9	3.9

19-Year Real Property Used Predominantly Outside the United States (placed in service after May 8, 1985 and before 1987)

(35-Year 150% Declining Balance)
(Assuming Mid-Month Convention)

	Month Placed in Service											
Year	1	2	3	4	5	6	7	8	9	10	11	12
5	3.6	3.6	3.6	3.6	3.7	3.7	3.7	3.7	3.7	3.8	3.7	3.7
6	3.5	3.5	3.5	3.5	3.5	3.5	3.5	3.5	3.5	3.6	3.6	3.6
7	3.3	3.3	3.3	3.3	3.3	3.4	3.4	3.4	3.4	3.4	3.4	3.4
8	3.2	3.2	3.2	3.2	3.2	3.2	3.2	3.2	3.3	3.3	3.3	3.3
9	3.0	3.0	3.0	3.1	3.1	3.1	3.1	3.1	3.1	3.1	3.1	3.1
10	2.9	2.9	2.9	2.9	2.9	2.9	3.0	3.0	3.0	3.0	3.0	3.0
11	2.8	2.8	2.8	2.8	2.8	2.8	2.8	2.8	2.9	2.9	2.9	2.9
12	2.6	2.7	2.7	2.7	2.7	2.7	2.7	2.7	2.7	2.7	2.8	2.8
13 - 29 ...	2.6	2.6	2.6	2.6	2.6	2.6	2.6	2.6	2.6	2.6	2.6	2.6
30 - 35 ...	2.5	2.5	2.5	2.5	2.5	2.5	2.5	2.5	2.5	2.5	2.5	2.5
36	0.0	0.2	0.5	0.7	0.9	1.2	1.3	1.7	1.7	1.8	2.2	2.5

Low-Income Housing Used Predominantly Outside the United States (placed in service after May 8, 1985 and before 1987)

(35-Year 150% Declining Balance)
(Assuming No Mid-Month Convention)

	Month Placed in Service											
Year	1	2	3	4	5	6	7	8	9	10	11	12
1	4.2	3.9	3.6	3.2	2.8	2.5	2.1	1.8	1.4	1.1	0.7	0.4
2	4.1	4.1	4.1	4.2	4.2	4.2	4.2	4.2	4.2	4.2	4.3	4.3
3	3.9	3.9	4.0	4.0	4.0	4.0	4.0	4.0	4.0	4.1	4.1	4.1
4	3.8	3.8	3.8	3.8	3.8	3.8	3.8	3.8	3.9	3.9	3.9	3.9
5	3.6	3.6	3.6	3.6	3.7	3.7	3.7	3.7	3.7	3.7	3.7	3.7
6	3.4	3.5	3.5	3.5	3.5	3.5	3.5	3.5	3.5	3.6	3.6	3.6
7	3.3	3.3	3.3	3.3	3.3	3.4	3.4	3.4	3.4	3.4	3.4	3.4
8	3.2	3.2	3.2	3.2	3.2	3.2	3.2	3.2	3.3	3.3	3.3	3.3
9	3.0	3.0	3.0	3.1	3.1	3.1	3.1	3.1	3.1	3.1	3.1	3.1
10	2.9	2.9	2.9	2.9	2.9	2.9	3.0	3.0	3.0	3.0	3.0	3.0
11	2.8	2.8	2.8	2.8	2.8	2.8	2.8	2.8	2.8	2.8	2.9	2.9
12	2.6	2.7	2.7	2.7	2.7	2.7	2.7	2.7	2.7	2.7	2.7	2.8
13 - 28 ...	2.6	2.6	2.6	2.6	2.6	2.6	2.6	2.6	2.6	2.6	2.6	2.6
29	2.6	2.5	2.5	2.5	2.6	2.6	2.6	2.6	2.6	2.6	2.6	2.6
30 - 35 ...	2.5	2.5	2.5	2.5	2.5	2.5	2.5	2.5	2.5	2.5	2.5	2.5
36	0.0	0.2	0.4	0.6	0.8	1.0	1.3	1.6	1.8	1.9	2.1	2.3

Straight-Line ACRS

¶ 254

Straight-Line Elections

Taxpayers who may prefer slower recovery of the cost of ACRS property are not locked into the generally prescribed recovery percentages or the generally applicable recovery periods. They may elect a straight-line recovery method over the following optional recovery periods. For the classes of property indicated, straight-line recovery periods are elected in accordance with the following table:

3-year property	3, 5, or 12 years
5-year property	5, 12, 25 years
10-year property	10, 25, or 35 years
15-year real property (or low-income housing)	15, 35, or 45 years
15-year public utility property	15, 35, or 45 years
18-year real property	18, 35, or 45 years
19-year real property	19, 35, or 45 years

For real property in general, a straight-line election averted ordinary income recapture treatment if the property is subsequently sold at a gain. However, for residential real property, this is less of a consideration because the recapture rules limit ordinary income treatment to the excess of ACRS deductions over costs that would have been recovered under the straight-line method based on the applicable recovery period.

Except for most real property, a taxpayer may not pick and choose. An election must apply to all property of the same class placed in service in the same year. Property of a separate class or placed in service in a separate year qualifies for separate treatment. In the case of 15-year, 18-year, or 19-year real property, any election is made on an asset-by-asset basis.

For other than most real property, the half-year convention applies if the straight-line method is elected. Thus, in the case of 5-year property, the taxpayer may claim a half year's recovery in the first year, a full year's recovery in the next four years, and a half year's recovery in the sixth year. Straight-line percentages for property other than most real property are as follows for the recovery periods indicated:

Recovery Period	*First Year*	*Annual Percentage*	*Last Year*
3 Years	16.667	33.333	16.667
5 Years	10.000	20.000	10.000
10 Years	5.000	10.000	5.000
12 Years	4.167	8.333	4.170
15 Years	3.333	6.667	3.329
25 Years	2,000	4.000	2.000
35 Years	1.429	2.857	1.433
45 Years	1.111	2.222	1.121

Consistent with the general ACRS rules applying to most real property, computations must reflect the number of months in which such property is in service during the tax year. The annual percentages for 15, 35 and 45 years as well as the first year and last year percentages based on the month the real property is placed in service are provided in decimal form at ¶ 610.

In the case of property used outside the United States, straight-line recovery periods may be elected in accordance with the following table:

In the case of	*The taxpayer may elect a recovery period of*
3-year property	The ADR class life, 5 or 12 years
5-year property	The ADR class life, 12 or 25 years
10-year property	The ADR class life, 25 or 35 years
15-year, 18-year, or 19-year real property	The ADR class life, 35 or 45 years
15-year public utility property	The ADR class life, 35 or 45 years

The annual percentages and the first-year and last-year percentages for 5, 12, 25, 35, and 45 years for property other than 15-year real property can be obtained from the above table of percentages for such property. If the applicable ADR class life is not included in the above table of percentages, the annual percentage and the first year and last-year percentages can be found in decimal form in the tables at ¶ 610 by using the "S-L" and the 6-month columns (half-year convention applies). The annual percentages for 35 and 45 years are provided in decimal form at ¶ 610.

An election is made on the return for the year in which the property is placed in service. Once made, it may not be revoked without IRS consent.

To the same extent that a tax-free exchange, a transfer between related parties, or a leaseback may not convert pre-1981 property into recovery property, such a transaction may not free recovery property from the consequences of a straight-line election. The transferee inherits the transferor's accounting method and recovery period. For the effect of "boot," see Example (2) at ¶ 264.

15-Year Real Property
(Placed in Service After December 31, 1980, and Before March 16, 1984)
and Low-Income Housing For Which Alternate ACRS Method
Over a 15-Year Period Is Elected
(No Mid-Month Convention)

Year	*Month Placed in Service*						
	1	*2–3*	*4*	*5–6*	*7–8*	*9–10*	*11–12*
1st	7%	6%	5%	4%	3%	2%	1%
2–10th	7%	7%	7%	7%	7%	7%	7%
11–15th	6%	6%	6%	6%	6%	6%	6%
16th		1%	2%	3%	4%	5%	6%

15-Year Real Property, 18-Year Real Property
(Placed in Service After March 15, 1984 and Before June 23, 1984),
and Low-Income Housing (Placed in Service Before May 9, 1985)
For Which Alternate ACRS Method Over a 35-Year Period Is Elected
(No Mid-Month Convention)

	Month Placed in Service		
Year	*1–2*	*3–6*	*7–12*
1st	3%	2%	1%
2–30th	3%	3%	3%
31–35th	2%	2%	2%
36th		1%	2%

15-Year Real Property, 18-Year Real Property (Placed in Service After March 15, 1984 and Before June 23, 1984), and Low-Income Housing Placed in Service After December 31, 1980 For Which Alternate ACRS Method Over a 45-Year Period Is Elected (No Mid-Month Convention)

	Month Placed in Service											
Year	*1*	*2*	*3*	*4*	*5*	*6*	*7*	*8*	*9*	*10*	*11*	*12*
1st	2.3%	2%	1.9%	1.7%	1.5%	1.3%	1.2%	0.9%	0.7%	0.6%	0.4%	0.2%
2–10th	2.3%	2.3%	2.3%	2.3%	2.3%	2.3%	2.3%	2.3%	2.3%	2.3%	2.3%	2.3%
11–45th	2.2%	2.2%	2.2%	2.2%	2.2%	2.2%	2.2%	2.2%	2.2%	2.2%	2.2%	2.2%
46th		0.3%	0.4%	0.6%	0.8%	1%	1.1%	1.4%	1.6%	1.7%	1.9%	2.1%

18-Year Real Property (Placed in Service After March 15 and Before June 23, 1984) For Which Alternate ACRS Method Over an 18-Year Period Is Elected (No Mid-Month Convention)

	Month Placed in Service						
Year	*1*	*2–3*	*4–5*	*6–7*	*8–9*	*10–11*	*12*
1st	6%	5%	4%	3%	2%	1%	0.5%
2–10th	6%	6%	6%	6%	6%	6%	6%
11th	5%	5%	5%	5%	5%	5%	5.5%
12–18th	5%	5%	5%	5%	5%	5%	5%
19th		1%	2%	3%	4%	5%	5%

Low-Income Housing (Placed in Service After May 8, 1985) For Which Alternate ACRS Method Over a 35-Year Period Is Elected (No Mid-Month Convention)

	Month Placed in Service											
Year	*1*	*2*	*3*	*4*	*5*	*6*	*7*	*8*	*9*	*10*	*11*	*12*
1st	2.9%	2.6%	2.4%	2.1%	1.9%	1.7%	1.4%	1.2%	1.0%	0.7%	0.5%	0.2%
2–20th	2.9%	2.9%	2.9%	2.9%	2.9%	2.9%	2.9%	2.9%	2.9%	2.9%	2.9%	2.9%
21–35th	2.8%	2.8%	2.8%	2.8%	2.8%	2.8%	2.8%	2.8%	2.8%	2.8%	2.8%	2.8%
36th		0.3%	0.5%	0.8%	1.0%	1.2%	1.5%	1.7%	1.9%	2.2%	2.4%	2.7%

The following straight-line recovery percentages are provided for real property subject to the mid-month convention.

18-Year Real Property (Placed in Service After June 22, 1984)
For Which Alternate ACRS Method Over an
18-Year Period Is Elected
(Mid-Month Convention)

Year	*Month Placed in Service*					
	1–2	*3–4*	*5–7*	*8–9*	*10–11*	*12*
1st	5%	4%	3%	2%	1%	0.2%
2–10th	6%	6%	6%	6%	6%	6%
11th	5%	5%	5%	5%	5%	5.8%
12–18th	5%	5%	5%	5%	5%	5%
19th	1%	2%	3%	4%	5%	5%

18-Year Real Property
(Placed in Service After June 22, 1984)
For Which Alternate ACRS Method Over a
35-Year Period Is Elected
(Mid-Month Convention)

Year	*Month Placed in Service*				
	1–2	*3–6*	*7–10*	*11*	*12*
1st	3%	2%	1%	0.4%	0.1%
2–30th	3%	3%	3%	3%	3%
31st	2%	2%	2%	2.6%	2.9%
32–35th	2%	2%	2%	2%	2%
36th		1%	2%	2%	2%

18-Year Real Property
(Placed in Service After June 22, 1984)
19-Year Real Property
For Which Alternate ACRS Method Over a
45-Year Period Is Elected
(Mid-Month Convention)

Year	*Month Placed in Service*											
	1	*2*	*3*	*4*	*5*	*6*	*7*	*8*	*9*	*10*	*11*	*12*
1st	2.1%	1.9%	1.8%	1.6%	1.4%	1.2%	1%	0.8%	0.6%	0.5%	0.3%	0.1%
2–11th	2.3%	2.3%	2.3%	2.3%	2.3%	2.3%	2.3%	2.3%	2.3%	2.3%	2.3%	2.3%
12–45th	2.2%	2.2%	2.2%	2.2%	2.2%	2.2%	2.2%	2.2%	2.2%	2.2%	2.2%	2.2%
46th	0.1%	0.3%	0.4%	0.6%	0.8%	1%	1.2%	1.4%	1.6%	1.7%	1.9%	2.1%

The following table provides the general straight-line recovery percentages for 19-year real property.

19-Year Real Property
For Which Alternate ACRS Method Over a 19-Year Period Is Elected
(Mid-Month Convention)

Year	*Month Placed in Service*											
	1	*2*	*3*	*4*	*5*	*6*	*7*	*8*	*9*	*10*	*11*	*12*
1st	5.0%	4.6%	4.2%	3.7%	3.3%	2.9%	2.4	2.0%	1.5%	1.1%	0.7%	0.2%
2–13th	5.3%	5.3%	5.3%	5.3%	5.3%	5.3%	5.3%	5.3%	5.3%	5.3%	5.3%	5.3%
14–19th	5.2%	5.2%	5.2%	5.2%	5.2%	5.2%	5.2%	5.2%	5.2%	5.2%	5.2%	5.2%
20th	0.2%	0.6%	1.0%	1.5%	1.9%	2.3%	2.8%	3.2%	3.7%	4.1%	4.5%	5.0%

If, for 19-year real property, a 45-year period is elected, the recovery percentages are the same as they are for 18-year real property placed in service after June 22, 1984. If a 35-year period is elected, the following percentages apply:

19-Year Real Property
For Which Alternate ACRS Method Over a 35-Year Period Is Elected
(Mid-Month Convention)

Year	*Month Placed in Service*											
	1	*2*	*3*	*4*	*5*	*6*	*7*	*8*	*9*	*10*	*11*	*12*
1st	2.7%	2.5%	2.3%	2.0%	1.8%	1.5%	1.3	1.1%	0.8%	0.6%	0.4%	0.1%
2–20th	2.9%	2.9%	2.9%	2.9%	2.9%	2.9%	2.9%	2.9%	2.9%	2.9%	2.9%	2.9%
21–35th	2.8%	2.8%	2.8%	2.8%	2.8%	2.8%	2.8%	2.8%	2.8%	2.8%	2.8%	2.8%
36th	0.2%	0.4%	0.6%	0.9%	1.1%	1.4%	1.6%	1.8%	2.1%	2.3%	2.5%	2.8%

¶ 256

Property Financed with Tax-Exempt Bonds

To the extent that property placed in service after 1983 was financed by the proceeds from the issue of post-October 18, 1983, tax-exempt industrial development bonds, the straight-line ACRS method was required to be used to recover cost (or other basis). However, residential rental projects for low-or-moderate-income individuals were not subject to this restriction.

The cost of low-income housing financed with IDBs is recoverable over 15 years under regular ACRS with the month of placement in service counting as one full month. The cost of residential rental projects that are financed with IDBs but are not low-income housing are recovered under the ACRS straight-line method over a 19-year recovery period (instead of the former 15-year recovery period) for property placed in service after May 8, 1985, and before 1987.

The cost of tax-exempt financed ACRS 3-, 5-, 10-, and 15-year public utility property is recoverable over 3-, 5-, 10-, and 15-year recovery periods.

Taxpayers required to use the straight-line method for property that was financed with industrial development bonds were not precluded from using the longer optional recovery periods available to those who elect straight-line ACRS.

ACRS Leasehold Improvements

¶ 258

Lessee's and Lessor's Deductions

An improvement made by a lessee after 1980 and before 1987 is depreciated under ACRS if the recovery period of the improvement is less than the remaining term of the lease when the improvement is placed in service (former Code Sec. 168(f)(6); Prop. Reg. § 1.168-5(d)). In determining the length of the lease term, the rules of Code Sec. 178 (prior to amendment by the 1986 Tax Reform Act (P.L. 99-514)) apply.

If the statutory recovery period is shorter than the lease term, ACRS allowances should be claimed over the recovery period. If the lease term is shorter, amortization should be claimed over the lease term.

If the statutory recovery period is shorter than the lease term, the taxpayer may elect a longer recovery period in connection with a straight-line ACRS election (¶ 254) if he wishes to claim amortization over the lease term or cost recovery over a longer period.

If, after the improvements are completed, the term remaining on the lease (excluding renewal periods) is less than 60 percent of the recovery period (former Code Sec. 178), and it cannot be shown that the lease will not be renewed, renewal periods must be counted in determining the term of the lease.

> ***Example:*** In 1985, a lessee put up a building on land on which his lease would expire in 1993. He also had an option to renew the lease for five additional years. The building is 15-year property. Since the eight years remaining on the lease were less than 60% of the 15-year recovery period, the renewal period must be counted as time remaining on the lease. Thus, the cost of the building is amortized over a period extending into 1998.

An improvement made by (i.e., owned by) the lessor is depreciated using ACRS regardless of the term of the lease (Prop. Reg. § 1.168-5(d)).

See ¶ 126 for leasehold improvements under MACRS.

Excluded Property

¶ 260

Specially Depreciated Property

If the taxpayer elects to depreciate property under the unit-of-production method (¶ 360), an income forecast method (¶ 364), or any other method not expressed in a term of years, the property will be excluded from ACRS. The election must be made for the first taxable year for which an ACRS deduction for the property would otherwise be allowable.

¶ 262

Certain Public Utility Property

Subject to general requirements, public utility property qualifies as ACRS recovery property only if accounting is normalized for purposes of setting rates and reflecting operating results in regulated books of account. In theory, regulatory agencies set utility rates at levels that permit a fair rate of return on investments, and normalization (as opposed to "flow-through" accounting) limits the conversion of ACRS benefits into rate reductions for customers. Prior law imposed a similar limitation with respect to the accelerated depreciation methods and the 20-percent ADR useful life variance available to certain utilities.

As under prior law, regulatory agencies may treat any taxes deferred as zero-cost capital or as reductions in the rate base. Amounts so treated, however, may not exceed the amount of the taxes deferred as a result of the methods and recovery periods that were actually used to compute recovery allowances.

Post-1980 property that does not qualify as recovery property due to lack of normalization is not depreciated under the rules that apply to pre-1981 property. Depreciation must be based on the method used by the regulatory agency for rate-making purposes. Any averaging conventions and salvage value limitations are part of the regulatory agency's method. Useful lives must be at least as long as those used by the regulatory agency.

¶ 264

The Anti-churning Rules

Two sets of rules—one for Sec. 1245 class property (generally, all personal property) and one for Sec. 1250 class property—prevent transfers, *other than by reason of death,* to related persons from "churning" pre-1981 assets into ACRS recovery property.

The first set of rules denies ACRS treatment to Sec. 1245 class property acquired by a taxpayer after 1980 if the property was:

(1) owned or used by the taxpayer or a related person at any time during 1980;

(2) acquired from a person who owned it at any time during 1980, and, as part of the transaction, the user remains the same;

(3) leased by the taxpayer to a person (or a person related to such person) who owned or used it at any time during 1980; or

(4) acquired in a transaction in which the user does not change and in which, due to (2) or (3), above, the property was not recovery property in the hands of the transferor.

Example (1): Smith rents a computer in 1980 and buys it in 1986. It is not ACRS property because he used it in 1980.

The second set of rules denies ACRS treatment to Sec. 1250 class property that was acquired by a taxpayer after 1980 if the property was:

(1) owned by the taxpayer (or a party related to the taxpayer) during 1980;

(2) leased back to a person that owned the property (or a person related to such person) during 1980; or

(3) acquired in certain like-kind exchanges and reacquisitions.

The exchanges and reacquisitions referred to in (3), above, are like-kind exchanges of property held for productive use in a trade or business or for investment (under Code Sec. 1031), involuntary conversions (under Code Sec. 1033), repossessions (under Code Sec. 1038), and rollovers of low-income housing (under Code Sec. 1039, repealed effective November 5, 1990). However, ACRS treatment is denied (and the old depreciation rules govern) only to so much of the basis of the property acquired as represents the basis of the property exchanged. To the extent of any "boot" (money or other property) that is given, ACRS applies.

Example (2): In 1986, a taxpayer exchanges an office building acquired before 1981 plus $120,000 for another office building. The office building exchanged had an adjusted basis of $180,000. To the extent that the basis of the building acquired is attributable to the adjusted basis ($180,000) of the building exchanged, ACRS is inapplicable. To the extent of the "boot" ($120,000), ACRS applies.

Pre-1981 ownership of property under construction will not bar ACRS treatment. For anti-churning rule purposes, the property is not treated as owned until it is placed in service.

Sec. 1245 class property transferred incidentally to the transfer of Sec. 1250 class property will be subject to the rules for the latter class of property. However, committee reports indicate that a transfer is not incidental if the Sec. 1245 class property is a "significant portion" of the transferred property.

¶ 266

Related Persons

For purposes of the ACRS anti-churning rules (¶ 264), related persons are:

(1) brothers and sisters (half or full), spouses, ancestors, and lineal descendants;

(2) a corporation and an individual owning more than 10 percent of the value of the corporation's outstanding stock;

(3) two corporations if the same individual owns more than 10 percent of the value of each corporation's outstanding stock, if either corporation was a personal holding company for the preceding tax year;

(4) a grantor and a fiduciary of any trust;

(5) fiduciaries of separate trusts if the trusts have the same grantor;

(6) a fiduciary and a beneficiary of the same trust;

(7) a fiduciary of one trust and a beneficiary of another if the trusts have the same grantor;

(8) a fiduciary of a trust and a corporation of which more than a specified value of the outstanding stock is owned by or for the trust or for the grantor of the trust;

(9) certain tax-exempt educational or charitable organizations and a controlling individual or a member of a controlling family;

(10) a partnership and partner owning more than 10 percent of the partnership capital or profits;

(11) two partnerships if the same person owns (directly or indirectly) more than 10 percent of each partnership's capital or profits; and

(12) organizations engaged in trades or businesses under common control ("organization" here means a sole proprietorship, a partnership, a trust, an estate, or a corporation).

Where a partnership is considered terminated by reason of a sale or exchange within a 12-month period of at least 50 percent of an interest in partnership capital and profits, the relationship of an acquiring partnership is determined as of immediately before the terminating event. Thus, the antichurning rules are inapplicable to the acquisition of more than 90 percent of partnership interests by parties unrelated to the selling partners.

Relationships are determined as of the date of acquisition of the property, and ex-spouses are not related parties. These rules benefited a taxpayer who, under a settlement agreement, obtained a half interest in a condominium (*J.H. Drake II,* DC Ill., 86-2 USTC ¶ 9746).

¶ 268

Tax-Free Exchanges

As might be expected, there are rules to prevent tax-free exchanges from conferring ACRS benefits on pre-1981 property. These rules list the following categories of nonrecognition transactions by reference to the Code Secs. indicated:

(1) complete liquidations of subsidiaries (Code Sec. 332);

(2) transfers to controlled corporations (Code Sec. 351);

(3) exchanges, pursuant to plans of reorganization, solely for stock or securities of other corporations (Code Sec. 361);

(4) reorganizations in certain bankruptcy and receivership proceedings (Code Sec. 371, repealed effective November 5, 1990);

(5) certain railroad reorganizations (Code Sec. 374, repealed effective November 5, 1990);

(6) contributions to partners in exchange for partnership interests (Code Sec. 721); and

(7) distributions by partnerships to partners (Code Sec. 731).

As in the case of a leaseback or an acquisition from a related party, a transferee in a tax-free exchange is generally bound by the transferor's method and period of depreciation. If "boot" is involved, however, ACRS may apply to the same extent as explained at ¶ 264 with respect to the anti-churning rules.

For property placed in service after 1985, the "step-in-the-shoes rules" have been shored up for property acquired from related parties (other than in nonrecognition transactions) or leased back to transferors. To the extent of the transferor's adjusted basis in the hands of the transferee, the transferee is bound by a transferor's election of straight-line depreciation and, if applicable, longer recovery periods (however, so much of the basis of 15-year real property subject to the technically corrected rules would be recoverable over the applicable longer period). Furthermore, such basis is recovered over a new recovery period.

Safe-Harbor Leases

¶ 278

Transitional Rules

So-called safe-harbor leasing rules—under which transactions meeting certain requirements were assured of being treated as leases—proved controversial and were repealed for "leases" entered into after 1983. Moreover, for agreements entered into or property placed in service after July 1, 1982 (except where the lessee had already acquired, commenced to construct, or contracted to acquire or commence to construct the property), some safe-harbor requirements were stiffened, and, for safe-harbor leases, some tax benefits were reduced. Some of the tax benefit reductions are related to ACRS. Leases created during the period the safe harbor lease rules apply and for which the safe harbor lease election was made are controlled by such rules for the duration of the lease.

Recovery periods and percentages

Under safe-harbor leases subject to the more stringent rules, recovery periods were extended and recovery percentages were based on the 150-percent declining-balance method with an appropriately timed switch to the straight-line method. The cost of three-year property was recoverable over a five-year period, the cost of five-year property was recoverable over an eight-year period, and the cost of 10-year property was recoverable over a 15-year period. The recovery percentages for three-year and five-year property subject to safe-harbor leases (which are fully depreciated) are not reproduced. For 10-year property still subject to these more stringent rules, the recovery percentage is six percent for recovery years 7 through 15.

Lessor's tax liability

Under safe-harbor leases subject to the more stringent rules, a lessor could not reduce liability for federal income tax (corporate minimum tax included) by more than 50 percent through the use of safe-harbor lease benefits. Application of this limitation requires computation of tax liability without regard to the relevant rental income, interest and ACRS deductions, and investment tax credits.

> ***Example:*** A lessor's tax liability is $100,000 if rental income, deductions for interest and depreciation, and investment credit from safe-harbor leases are excluded but is $30,000 if such leasing benefits are included. The 50% limit would apply in such case, and the lessor's liability would be $50,000 (50% of $100,000).

Safe-harbor lease deductions and credits that are not utilized in the current tax year because of such limitation on tax liability may only be carried forward.

Although the 50-percent limitation does not apply to safe-harbor leases not subject to the new rules (generally leases covering property placed in service before July 2, 1982), those leases must be taken into account in computing the limitation.

Finance leases

The repeal of the safe-harbor lease rules was accompanied by the enactment of a new set of rules that, for post-1983 leases qualifying as "finance leases," would likewise entitle third parties to qualify as lessors and deduct ACRS allowances. These new rules were subsequently deferred and eventually repealed, so that, with exceptions for transition property, "true" leases are once again distinguishable from mere tax-motivated arrangements under the same nonstatutory rules that apply to pre-ACRS property. Transition property is:

(1) new investment credit farming-use property leased under qualifying arrangements entered into after July 1, 1982, and before 1988 (provided that the aggregate cost for a taxable year of all such farming-use property subject to a finance lease entered into by a lessee does not exceed $150,000);

(2) up to $150 million of qualifying automobile manufacturing property; and

(3) property that a lessee was bound to acquire or construct, or had acquired, or on which construction had begun by or for the lessee, before March 7, 1984.

Dispositions of ACRS Recovery Property

¶ 280

Early Dispositions

The treatment of the early disposition of ACRS recovery property to a large extent flows from the general rules for such property. Thus, dispositions of real property, for which computations must reflect actual months in service, must be distinguished from dispositions of other classes of recovery property. A disposition is the permanent withdrawal of property from use in a trade or business or in the production of income, and a disposition is early if it precedes the end of the applicable recovery period. An early disposition may arise from the sale, exchange, retirement, abandonment, or destruction of the property. The adjusted basis of abandoned property is deductible.

Generally, no part of the cost of 3-year, 5-year or 10-year property, or 15-year public utility property is recovered in the year of disposition or retirement. The relevant basis for determining gain or loss is the basis of the property as of the first day of the year in which disposition occurs.

> ***Example (1):*** In May of 1986, a construction contractor places in service an electric saw for which he paid $180. The saw was 5-year property, and, for 1986, the contractor deducts $27 (15% of $180). No other 5-year property was placed in service during 1986. For 1987, he deducts $40 (22% of $180), and, for 1988, he deducts $38 (21% of $180). In 1989, the contractor sells the saw. For 1989, there is no ACRS deduction for the saw, and $75 ($180 - $27 - $40 - $38) is the basis of the saw for determining gain or loss.

> ***Example (2):*** The facts are the same as in Example (1) except that the contractor (1) purchased several other items of 5-year property in 1986 at a total cost of $500 and (2) sold the saw in 1987 (rather than in 1989). For 1987, there was no deduction for the saw, the basis for determining gain or loss on the sale of the saw was $153 ($180 - $27), and (assuming no election to depreciate any eligible 1986 property under MACRS) $110 (22% of the unadjusted basis of all the 5-year property other than the saw placed in service in 1986) was deductible as depreciation. Assuming no dispositions, his deduction for either 1988 or 1989 is $105 (21% of $500).

Cost recovery would be computed in a similar manner (substituting the appropriate percentages) even if the taxpayer had elected to recover the cost of the property under the straight-line method.

If 15-year, 18-year, or 19-year real property is sold, there will probably be no need for the kind of adjustment illustrated in Example (2) (because separate items of such property may not be grouped together unless they are placed in service in both the same month and year). However, months in service are taken into account.

A partial recovery of the cost of 15-year, 18-year, or 19-year real recovery property is permitted in the year of disposition before the end of the recovery period (Prop. Reg. § 1.168-2(a)(3)).

(1) Disposition in first recovery year

The recovery allowance for real recovery property in this situation is determined for a full year and then prorated based on the number of months of business use divided by the number of months in the taxpayer's tax year after the recovery property was placed in service (including the month that the property was placed in service). This rule is applied in conjunction with the mid-month convention, if applicable.

(2) Disposition in year other than first recovery year

The recovery allowance for real recovery property in this situation is determined for a full year and then prorated based on the number of months of business use divided by 12. This rule is applied in conjunction with the mid-month convention, if applicable.

> ***Example (3):*** In May of 1986, a taxpayer purchases an office building for $150,000 (exclusive of the cost of the land) and immediately places it in service as 19-year real property. He does not elect the straight-line method, and, for 1986, the ACRS deduction is $8,700 (5.8% of $150,000—see the table at ¶ 246). The deduction for 1987 is $13,050 (8.7% of $150,000), for 1988 it is $11,850 (7.9% of $150,000), for 1989 it is $10,650 (7.1% of $150,000), for 1990 it is $9,750 (6.5% of $150,000), for 1991 it is $8,850 (5.9% of $150,000), for 1992 it is $7,950 (5.3% of $150,000), for 1993 it is $7,200 (4.8% of $150,000), for 1994 it is $6,600 (4.4% of $150,000), and for each year 1995—1998 it is $6,300 (4.2% of $150,000). He sells the building in September 1999, and his deduction for that year is $4,463. This represents 4.2% (the fifth-month percentage for the fourteenth year of service) of $150,000 with a proration (multiplying by 8.5/12) to reflect 1999 months of service.

Computations for 18-year real property placed in service after June 22, 1984, or as in the above example, 19-year real property, vary slightly from computations for 15-year real property or 18-year real property placed in service before June 23, 1984, to reflect the mid-month convention.

> ***Example (4):*** The facts are the same as in *Example (3)* except that the property was purchased in May of 1984 and is classified as 18-year property. Since the property was placed in service before June 22, 1984, the appropriate table (at ¶ 244) does not reflect the mid-month convention, and 8/12 (rather than 8.5/12) is the appropriate fraction for computing year-of-disposition recovery.

(3) Disposition in short tax year

Although a disposition of real recovery property occurs in a short tax year, no ACRS short tax year adjustment is made because the short tax year rule (¶ 290) does not apply to the year of disposition of real recovery property. The ACRS deduction is determined under (2), above.

In situations where a short tax year arises because, for example, the taxpayer dies or is a corporation that becomes a member or ceases being a member of an affiliated group filing a consolidated return, the ACRS deduction on real recovery property disposed of in the short tax year is determined under (2), above, but the denominator is modified to represent the number of months in the taxpayer's tax year (Prop. Reg. § 1.168-2(a)(3)).

> ***Example (5):*** An individual, who is a calendar-year taxpayer, acquired 18-year real recovery property for $100,000 in March 1985. The property is sold in February 1999, and the individual dies in March 1999. The 1999 short tax year recovery allowance for such property is $2,000 ($100,000 unadjusted basis × 4% (fifteenth-year percentage for 18-year real property placed in service in the third month of a full tax year) × 1.5 ÷ 3).

Provision is made under which, pursuant to regulations, year-of-disposition recovery is permissible with respect to transactions in which gain or loss is not recognized or to certain related-party transfers, sale-leasebacks, and tax-free transfers in which a transferee is bound by the transferor's recovery period and method of depreciation.

In the event of recapture of a basis-reducing credit, basis for gain or loss is correspondingly adjusted.

Recapture

Gain on the disposition of Sec. 1245 recovery property is recaptured as ordinary income to the extent of all ACRS deductions. Gain on the disposition of nonresidential real recovery property is recaptured to the extent of all ACRS deductions, but there is no recapture if the straight-line ACRS method was elected. Gain on the disposition of recovery property that is residential rental property, is recaptured to the extent of the excess of accelerated depreciation over straight-line depreciation. If there is a disposition of recovery property before it is held more than one year, all ACRS allowances are recaptured to the extent of gain. See, also ¶ 488.

¶ 282

Mass Asset Accounts

As an alternative to calculating gain on each disposition of an item of ACRS property from a mass asset account, a taxpayer may elect to recognize gain on the entire proceeds and recover the cost of the item in the same manner as if it still remained in the account. This may be practical for dispositions of a few of the items in a large group of items that are relatively minor in value and burdensome to identify separately. Candidates for such treatment might include minor fixtures or items of furniture. Such treatment is elected by reporting the total disposition proceeds (on Form 4797, Supplemental Schedule of Gains and Losses) as ordinary income and recovering the cost of the item or items, together with the cost of all the other items in the mass asset account, over the appropriate recovery period.

Items in any mass asset account need not be homogeneous, but they must have the same present class life, and they must be placed in service in the same taxable year. The election is made for the year in which the assets are placed in service. It is binding with respect to those assets, but has no bearing on similar assets placed in service in other years.

If an early disposition of an item in a mass asset account triggers a recapture of an investment credit, then any basis adjustment (generally 50 percent of the amount recaptured) is added to the account. However, if records are consistent with prior practice and good accounting and engineering practices, proposed regulations indicate that a taxpayer may construct a mortality dispersion table for identifying dispositions. Alternatively, the proposed regulations provide a standard table.

¶ 284

Recordkeeping

Although 2009 Form 4562, Depreciation and Amortization, provides only line 16 for "ACRS and other depreciation" (including depreciation of pre-ACRS assets), and no attachments are necessary, the basis and amounts claimed for depreciation should be part of your permanent books and records. A sample Depreciation Summary contained in IRS Publication 534, Depreciation (and a substantially similar Depreciation Record from IRS Publication 583, Taxpayers Starting a Business), provides headings for the following information: "Description of Property," "Date Placed in Service," "Cost or Other Basis," "Business Use %," "Section 179 Deduction," "Depreciation for Prior Years," "Basis for Depreciation," "Depreciation Method/Convention," "Recovery Period or Useful Life," "Rate or Table Percentage," and "Depreciation Deduction for Current Year."

With regard to listed property, any deduction for a year beginning after 1985 is contingent on substantiation by adequate records or sufficient evidence corroborating a taxpayer's statement. However, for any listed property, records must be maintained for any year in which recapture may still occur. For example, in the case of a car (3-year property) depreciated under ACRS and placed in service after June

18, 1984, but before 1985, records must be kept for six years even if the full cost of the car is recovered in only three.

Maintaining adequate records means keeping an account book, diary, log, statement of expense, trip sheet, or similar record and documentary evidence. Information reflected on receipts need not be entered in such records so long as the records and receipt complement each other in an orderly manner.

ACRS Short Tax Year

¶ 290

Allocation Required

In computing an ACRS recovery allowance for a tax year of less than 12 months, certain adjustments must be made depending on whether property is personal recovery property or 15-year, 18-year, or 19-year real recovery property. Recovery allowances for years in a recovery period following a short tax year are determined without regard to the short tax year.

Personal recovery property

For other than 15-year, 18-year, or 19-year real recovery property, the recovery allowance for a short tax year is determined by multiplying the deduction that would have been allowable if the recovery year was not a short tax year by a fraction the numerator of which is the number of months and part-months in the short tax year and the denominator of which is 12 (Prop. Reg. § 1.168-2(f)(1)).

Any unrecovered allowance (the difference between the recovery allowance properly allowed for the short tax year and the recovery allowance that would have been allowable if such year were not a short tax year) is claimed in the tax year following the last year in the recovery period (Prop. Reg. § 1.168-2(f)(3)). However, there is a maximum limitation on the amount of an unrecovered allowance that may be claimed in a tax year. The unrecovered allowance claimed as a recovery allowance in the tax year following the last year of the recovery period may not exceed the amount of the recovery allowance permitted for the last year of the recovery period, assuming that such year consists of 12 months. Any remaining unrecovered allowance is carried forward to the following tax years until the allowance is exhausted.

> ***Example (1):*** In January 1986, a calendar-year corporation purchases a railroad tank car (10-year ACRS recovery property). For 1986, the corporation deducts $8,000 (8% of $100,000) and, for 1987, the corporation deducts $14,000 (14% of $100,000). Pursuant to a change in accounting period, the corporation files a return for a short tax year ending October 31, 1988. But for the short tax year, the third-year recovery allowance would have been $12,000 (12% of $100,000). To reflect the short tax year, the corporation must multiply this regular third-year amount by a fraction of which the numerator is the number of months in the year (10) and the denominator is 12. Thus, for the short tax year, the corporation deducts $10,000 (10/12 of $12,000). Assuming no dispositions or further short tax years, the corporation deducts $10,000 (10% of $100,000) for each of the tax years ending October 31, 1989 through 1991, and $9,000 (9% of $100,000) for each of the tax years ending October 31, 1992 through 1995. The remaining $2,000 ($100,000 – $98,000 depreciation deducted) is recoverable for the tax year ending October 31, 1996.

In the case of automobiles depreciated under ACRS subject to the luxury car rules (see ¶ 200), ceilings must be similarly scaled down.

For depreciation purposes, a year does not begin until the first month in which a person engages in a trade or business or holds property for the production of income. An employee may be regarded as engaging in a trade or business merely by reason of his employment—but only with regard to recovery property used for purposes of employment.

For purposes of depreciating property, a taxable year may commence before a business is acquired if the taxpayer is already engaged in a trade or business. Moreover the trade or business in which the taxpayer was engaged need not be the same trade or business in which the property is used—or even the same kind of trade or business.

Example (2): A calendar-year corporation engaged in selling appliances purchases a fast food restaurant. No short-year computation is required in depreciating the restaurant's assets irrespective of the month in which the restaurant is acquired.

According to the IRS, the benefit of the rule that is illustrated in the above example does not extend to a person engaging in a small amount of trade or business activity if:

(1) this activity is conducted to avoid the short-year requirements, and

(2) the subsequent placing in service of the assets in issue represents a substantial increase in the level of business activity.

Corresponding rules apply with regard to depreciating property held for the production of income.

Real recovery property

If ACRS 15-year, 18-year, or 19-year real recovery property is placed in service or disposed of during a short tax year, the cost recovery deduction for the short tax year is computed as if the property was placed in service or disposed of during a full calendar year. See ¶ 222 and ¶ 280 for rules explaining the manner of computing recovery allowances on real property acquired or disposed of during a tax year.

If the short tax year occurs after real recovery property is placed in service, recovery allowances for the short tax year and subsequent tax years during the recovery period are computed in the same manner applicable to personal recovery property.

Example (3): A calendar-year taxpayer acquires and places in service 18-year real recovery property in March 1985. The taxpayer changes to a June through May fiscal year beginning June 1, 2000. As a result there is a short tax year beginning January 1, 1999 and ending May 31, 2000. Assuming the unadjusted basis of the property is \$100,000, depreciation for the short tax year is \$1,667 (\$100,000 × 4%) (fifteenth-year percentage for 18-year real property placed in service in the third month of a full tax year) × 5⁄12 (reflecting the number of months in the short tax year). The sixteenth-year table percentage (4%) is used to compute depreciation for the 2000-2001 fiscal year.

The unrecovered basis of the property (\$100,000 × 4% × 7⁄12) is recovered beginning in the tax year after the end of the recovery period as explained under the rules for personal property.

Special Expensing Election (Code Sec. 179)

Annual Expensing Election

¶ 300

Expensing Alternative

Taxpayers other than estates, trusts, and certain noncorporate lessors may claim a current deduction under Code Sec. 179 for a specified amount of the cost of qualifying MACRS section 1245 property acquired by purchase during the tax year and used more than 50 percent in the active conduct of the taxpayer's trade or business (¶ 302). The portion of any property used for investment does not qualify for expensing and is not counted toward the greater than 50 percent business use requirement.

The Code Sec. 179 deduction reduces the basis of property before the Code Sec. 168(k) bonus depreciation deduction is computed on the property. See ¶ 127D.

A taxpayer may also be able to write-off the cost of depreciable items without regard to Code Sec. 179 on the basis of relative immateriality under a de minimis rule commonly recognized by IRS auditors. See ¶ 307.

Maximum annual dollar cost limitation

The following chart summarizes the maximum allowable Code Sec. 179 deduction for tax years since 1982 (Code Sec. 179(b)(1); Reg.§ 1.179-2(b)(1)).

Maximum expense deduction for tax years beginning in:

1982–1986	$5,000
1987–1992	$10,000
1993–1996	$17,500
1997	$18,000
1998	$18,500
1999	$19,000
2000	$20,000
2001 or 2002	$24,000
2003	$100,000
2004	$102,000
2005	$105,000
2006	$108,000
2007	$125,000
2008	$250,000
2009	$250,000
2010	$134,000
2011 or thereafter	$25,000

The $100,000 dollar limitation is adjusted for inflation in tax years beginning in 2004 through 2006. The inflation-adjusted limitation is $108,000 in 2006 (Rev. Proc. 2005-70), $105,000 in 2005 (Rev. Proc. 2004-71), and $102,000 in 2004 (Rev. Proc. 2003-85). The expense deduction was temporarily increased from $125,000 to $250,000 (P.L. 110-185), effective for property placed in service in tax years beginning in 2008 and 2009 (Code Sec. 179(b)(7), as added by P.L. 110-185 and amended by P.L. 111-5; Rev. Proc. 2007-66, as amended by Rev. Proc. 2008-65). The 2010 inflation-adjusted limitation is $134,000 (Rev. Proc. 2009-50).

The expense deduction that may be claimed on SUVs, trucks with cargo beds less than six-feet long, and certain vans is limited to $25,000 if the vehicle is exempt from the luxury car depreciation limits. See ¶ 201.

Partial business use. To qualify for expensing under Code Sec. 179, the property must be used more than 50 percent for business purposes (¶ 302). If business use falls to 50 percent or less in a tax year after the deduction is claimed, recapture is required, as explained below.

If business use is greater than 50 percent but less than 100 percent, the allowable Code Sec. 179 deduction is computed with respect to the percentage of the basis that is used for business purposes. For example, if a qualifying asset costing $300,000 is placed in service in 2009 and used 60 percent for business purposes, the maximum section 179 deduction is $180,000 ($300,000 cost × 60%) (since this less than the $250,000 dollar limit for 2009) and *not* $150,000 ($250,000 (2009 dollar limit) × 60%).

Section 179 tax planning. See ¶ 487 for Code Sec. 179 tax planning strategies.

Enterprise zones. An enterprise zone business (Code Sec. 1397C) located within a government-designated empowerment zone may increase the applicable annual dollar limitation ($250,000 in 2008 and 2009) by the lesser of $35,000 or the cost of Sec. 179 property that is qualified zone property (as defined in Code Sec. 1397D) (Code Sec. 1397A). This maximum amount is reduced (but not below zero) by the excess investment over the applicable investment limitation ($800,000 in tax years beginning in 2008 and 2009). However, in applying this investment limitation, only one-half of the cost of qualified zone property is taken into account (the full cost of Code Sec. 179 property that is not qualified zone property is taken into account). This maximum amount is also subject to the taxable income limitation discussed below. If the property ceases to be used in an empowerment zone by the enterprise zone business, the benefit of the increased portion of the section 179 allowance is subject to recapture under the rules described below (Code Sec. 1397A(b)). The standard allowance remains subject to recapture if business use in or outside of the zone decreases to 50 percent or less.

Farm businesses in an empowerment zone which own or lease assets with a total value in excess of $500,000 do not qualify as enterprise zone businesses and are ineligible for this increased Code Sec. 179 annual dollar limitation (Code Sec. 1397C(d)(5)).

The original use of the qualified zone property in the empowerment zone must begin with the taxpayer. In addition to being section 179 property as defined in Code Sec. 179(d) (see ¶ 302), the property must be eligible for depreciation under Code Sec. 168 (i.e. under MACRS). Computer software which is section 179 property (see Code Sec. 179(d)(1)(A)(ii))) does not qualify for the increased section 179 allowance because it is depreciable over three years under Code Sec. 167(f) and the $35,000 bump-up only applies to property eligible for depreciation under Code Sec. 168 (see ¶ 48 for a discussion of computer software).

Renewal communities. Rules that apply to an enterprise zone business also apply to a renewal community business that acquires qualified renewal property by purchase (as defined in Code Sec. 179(d)(2)) after December 31, 2001 and before January 1, 2010 and places the property in service in a renewal community (Code Sec. 1400J)). The IRS has issued a revenue procedure that explains how a taxpayer may make a retroactive election to deduct the increased section 179 expensing allowance for qualified renewal property that is placed in service in an expanded area of a renewal community (i.e., a contiguous tract to a renewal community based on 2000 census data) that is authorized by Code Sec. 1400E(g), as added by the American Jobs Creation Act (P.L. 108-357) (Rev. Proc. 2006-16, I.R.B. 2006-9).

Qualified disaster assistance property. The Code Sec. 179 expense deduction ($250,000 for 2008 and 2009) is increased by the lesser of $100,000 or the cost of disaster assistance property placed in service during the tax year that is also section 179 property. The investment limitation ($800,000 for 2008 and 2009) is increased by the lesser of $600,000 or the cost of qualified section 179 disaster assistance property placed in service during the tax year. Qualified disaster assistance property must rehabilitate property damaged, or replace property destroyed or condemned, as a result of a federally declared disaster. This provision applies to property placed in service after December 31, 2007, with respect to federally declared disasters declared after such date and occurring before January 1, 2010 (Code Sec. 179(e), as added by the Emergency Economic Stabilization Act of 2008 (P.L. 110-343)). Recapture is required if business use in the disaster area falls to less than 80 percent and, therefore, ceases to be qualified disaster assistance property. Also, if overall business use (whether inside or outside of the disaster area) falls to 50 percent or below, then the entire section 179 expenses allowance (the regular allowance (e.g., $250,000 in 2009) plus the $100,000 increase (or portion thereof claimed)) is subject to recapture under the rules described below. See ¶ 306B.

Gulf Opportunity Zone. A $100,000 increase in the section 179 allowance applies to qualifying section 179 property placed in service in the Gulf Opportunity Zone placed in service before January 1, 2008. The investment limit is increased by up to $600,000. This portion of the section 179 allowance is subject to recapture by applying the rules below if business use in the GO Zone drops below 80 percent and, therefore, no longer qualifies as Gulf Opportunity Zone property (Code Sec. 1400N(e)(4)). Also, if overall business use (whether inside or outside of the Zone falls to 50 percent or below), then the entire section 179 expenses allowance (the regular allowance (e.g., $125,000 in 2007) plus the $100,000 increase (or portion thereof claimed)) is subject to recapture under the rules described below. See ¶ 306.

Kansas disaster area. The same increases in the dollar and investment limitations for section 179 property that is Gulf Opportunity Zone property also apply to property placed in service in the Kansas disaster area if such property is section 179 property and would also qualify for the bonus depreciation deduction for property placed in service in the Kansas disaster area (Act § 15345(d)(2) of the Heartland, Habitat, Harvest and Horticulture Acts of 2008 (P.L. 110-246)). The property must be acquired by purchase on or after May 5, 2007 and placed in service on or before December 31, 2008. The original use of the property in the Kansas disaster area must commence with the taxpayer on or after May 5, 2007. No binding contract for acquisition of the property may be in effect before May 5, 2007. Recapture of the $100,000 increase in the dollar limitation is required if business use in the disaster area falls to less than 80 percent and, therefore, no the longer qualifies as Kansas Disaster area property. Also, if overall business use (whether inside or outside of the Kansas disaster area) falls to 50 percent or less, then the entire section 179 expenses allowance is subject to recapture under the rules described below. See ¶ 305A.

New York Liberty Zone. Qualifying property placed in service in the New York Liberty Zone is also eligible for a $35,000 increase in the otherwise applicable dollar limitation and only 50 percent of the cost of qualifying property is taken into account in applying the investment limitation. The additional $35,000 bump-up is subject to recapture if the property ceases to be used in the New York Liberty Zone

(Code Sec. 1400L(f)(3)). Also, if overall business use (whether inside or outside of the New York Liberty Zone area) falls to 50 percent or less, then the entire section 179 expenses allowance is subject to recapture under the rules described below. See ¶ 305.

Short tax year. A taxpayer with a short tax year is entitled to claim the full maximum deduction (subject to the investment and taxable income limitations described below) (Reg. § 1.179-1(c)(1)).

Basis adjustment. The depreciable basis of a property for which an expense deduction is claimed is reduced by the amount of its cost that is expensed. No depreciation deduction may be claimed for this amount. The cost of more than one item of qualifying property may be expensed, but the total amount expensed may not exceed the maximum ceiling.

Investment limitation

The following chart summarizes the Code Sec. 179 investment limitation for tax years since 1987 (Code Sec. 179(b)(2)).

Maximum investment limitation for tax years beginning in:	
1987–2002	$200,000
2003	$400,000
2004	$410,000
2005	$420,000
2006	$430,000
2007	$500,000
2008	$800,000
2009	$800,000
2010	$530,000
2011 or thereafter	$200,000

In a tax year that begins in 2003 through 2006, the maximum annual dollar limitation is reduced (but not below zero) by the excess of the cost of qualified Sec. 179 property placed in service during the tax year over $400,000 (adjusted for inflation in 2004 through 2006). This investment limitation increases to $500,000 in tax years beginning in 2007, to $800,000 in tax years beginning in 2008 and 2009, and $530,000 in tax years beginning in 2010. Any amount of the dollar limitation ($250,000 in 2008 and 2009) disallowed under this rule is lost and may not be carried over to another tax year. The investment limitation is reduced to $200,000 in tax years that begin in 2011 and thereafter. This is when the maximum annual dollar limitation will be reduced to $25,000.

> ***Example (1):*** A taxpayer places $810,000 of qualifying property in service in 2009. The maximum dollar limitation for 2009 ($250,000) must be reduced by $10,000 ($810,000 - $800,000) to $240,000. The $10,000 disallowed is not carried forward for deduction in later tax years.

If the cost of qualifying property placed in service in 2009 equals or exceeds $1,050,000 ($250,000 dollar limitation - ($1,050,000 - $800,000 investment limitation) = 0) then no amount may be expensed under Code Sec. 179.

No attribution to partners and S shareholders. In determining the excess section 179 property placed in service by a partner in a tax year, the cost of section 179 property placed in service by the partnership is not attributed to any partner (Reg.§ 1.179-2(b)(3)). A similar rule applies to S shareholders (Reg. § 1.179-2(b)(4)).

Taxable income limitation

The expense deduction may not exceed the total amount of taxable income that is derived from the active conduct of all of the trades or businesses that a taxpayer engaged in during the tax year. This rule is applied after application of the investment limitation.

Taxable income is computed without regard to the expense deduction, any net operating loss carryback or carryforward, the deduction against gross income for one-half of self-employment tax liability for the self-employed, and deductions suspended under any Code provision (such as the limitation on a partner's share of partnership loss under Code Sec. 704(d)) (Reg. § 1.179-2(c)(1)). However, income items derived from the active conduct of a trade or business include Code Sec. 1231 gains or losses and interest from working capital of a trade or business.

Taxable income attributable to services performed by an employee is considered taxable income from the active conduct of a trade or business (Reg. § 1.179-2(c)(6)(iv)). Thus, wages, salaries, tips, and other compensation (not reduced by unreimbursed employee business expenses) derived as an employee are included in taxable income.

Computation of the aggregate amount of taxable income derived from the active conduct of any trade or business during the tax year includes the following: wages and salaries derived as an employee; net profit or loss from a sole proprietorship in which the taxpayer's involvement constitutes the active conduct of a trade or business; net profit or loss from the active conduct of rental real estate activities; and net distributable profit or loss from pass through entities (such as a partnership or S corporation) in which the taxpayer is an active participant (IRS Letter Ruling 9126014, March 29, 1991).

The taxable income (or loss) derived by a partnership or S corporation from the active conduct of a trade or business is computed by aggregating the net income (or loss) from all the trades or businesses actively conducted by the entity during the tax year.

Partnership net income is generally defined for this purpose as the aggregate amount of the partnership items of income and expense described in Code Sec. 702(a), other than credits, tax-exempt income, the section 179 expense deduction, and guaranteed payments under Code Sec. 707(c) (Reg. § 1.179-2(c)(2)).

S corporation net income is generally defined for this purpose as the aggregate amount of the S corporation items of income and expense described in Code Sec. 1366(a), other than credits, tax-exempt income, the section 179 expense deduction, and deductions for compensation paid to an S corporation's shareholder-employees (Reg. § 1.179-2(c)(3)).

C corporation taxable income is generally defined for purposes of the taxable income limitation as the aggregate amount of taxable income before the section 179 expense deduction, net operating loss deduction and special deductions, (excluding items of income or deduction that were not derived from a trade or business actively conducted by the corporation during the tax year) (Reg. § 1.179-2(c)(4)).

The taxable income limitation is applied to a husband and wife who file a joint return by aggregating the taxable income of each spouse (Reg. § 1.179-2(c)(7)). Even though an individual has a loss from a sole proprietorship, a Sec. 179 expense deduction may be claimed if a joint return is filed and there is sufficient taxable income from the spouse's active trade or business.

Carryforward

The amount disallowed as a result of the taxable income limitation is carried forward to succeeding tax years. The deduction for carryovers and the amounts expensed for qualifying property placed in service in carryover years, however, may not exceed the maximum annual dollar cost ceiling, investment limitation, or, if less, the taxable income limitation.

Any outstanding carryover of unused Sec. 179 allowance arising because of the taxable income limitation may not be transferred in a sale or exchange of Sec. 179 property, in a nonrecognition transaction (including a transfer at death and certain corporate acquisitions under Code Sec. 381), or in the sale of an interest in a partnership or S corporation (Reg. § 1.179-3(f)(1) and (h)(2)). In these situations, the basis of the property (or basis in the partnership interest or the S corporation stock) is increased by the amount of the unused carryover immediately before the transfer. Thus, the unused deduction is not available to either the transferor or the transferee.

Section 179 recapture

For recapture purposes, the Code Sec. 179 expense deduction is treated as a depreciation deduction. The applicable recapture rule depends on the event that triggers recapture and the nature of the property.

The section 179 deduction (and bonus depreciation) is treated like a regular depreciation deduction for purposes of the section 1245 depreciation recapture rules. Thus, gain on the disposition of property on which a Code Sec. 179 expense deduction was claimed is generally recaptured as ordinary income to the extent of the regular depreciation deductions (including bonus depreciation) and the amount expensed under section 179. This recapture rule has priority over the other recapture rules discussed below (Reg. § 1.179-1(e)(3)).

The Code Sec. 1245 recapture rules apply not only to sales but to other types of dispositions including like-kind exchanges and involuntary conversions.

See ¶ 160 and ¶ 488 for a discussion of the MACRS depreciation recapture rules.

Business use 50 percent or less. A portion of the Code Sec. 179 expense deduction is recaptured in any tax year of any asset's recovery period that business use fails to exceed 50 percent (Code Sec. 179(d)(10) (Reg. § 1.179-1(e)(1)). For listed property (defined at ¶ 208), such as a car, the applicable recapture rule is provided in Code Sec. 280F(b)(2) and takes precedence over the recapture rule discussed here. The recapture rule for listed property is discussed at ¶ 210.

A change from trade or business use to production of income use is treated as a change to personal use for purposes of the section 179 recapture rules and can trigger recapture (Reg. § 1.179-1(e)(2)).

The Code Sec. 179 expense deduction on non-listed property is recaptured as ordinary income in the tax year during the recovery period that business use fails to exceed 50 percent. The recapture amount included in income is the difference between the Code Sec. 179 expense allowance claimed and the depreciation (including Code Sec. 168(k) bonus depreciation if applicable (see *Example 5*, below)) that would have been allowed on the Code Sec. 179 amount for prior tax years and the tax year of recapture (Reg. § 1.179-1(e)).

The recapture amount is computed in Part IV of Form 4797.

Although Code Sec. 179(d)(10) provides that the IRS shall issue regulations to provide for recapture with respect to any property which is not used predominantly in a trade or business at *any* time, Reg. § 1.179-1(e)(1) only requires recapture if the predominant business use test is not met during an asset's recovery (i.e., depreciation) period (e.g., GDS recovery period unless an election was made to depreciate the asset under the MACRS alternative depreciation period (ADS)) which generally provides for a longer recovery period than GDS). This is because once the recovery period has ended, the basis of the asset would have been fully recovered even if no Sec. 179 expense allowance had been claimed.

Example (2): Sam Jones bought an item of 7-year MACRS property (not a listed property) in 2006 that cost $22,000. He expensed $10,000 of the cost and used the property in his trade or business (100% business use). In 2009, he converted the property to Code Sec. 212 production of income use. This triggers the recapture of the Code Sec. 179 expense allowance.

To determine the recapture amount, Sam must subtract from the expense allowance claimed ($10,000), the amount of depreciation that could have been claimed on the amount expensed during 2006, 2007, 2008, and 2009.

Section 179 deduction claimed (2006)		$10,000
Allowable depreciation deduction on $10,000 expensed amount:		
2006 = $10,000 × 14.29%	$1,429	
2007 = $10,000 × 24.49%	2,449	
2008 = $10,000 × 17.49%	1,749	
2009 = $10,000 × 12.49%	1,249	6,876
2009 recapture amount		$3,124

The depreciation deductions for the years 2006 through 2009 are computed on $12,000 (the $22,000 cost of the property as reduced by the $10,000 expense deduction).

MACRS deductions through recapture year:	
2006 = $12,000 × 14.29%	$1,715
2007 = $12,000 × 24.49%	2,939
2008 = $12,000 × 17.49%	2,098
2009 = $12,000 × 12.49%	1,499

Beginning in 2010, the MACRS deductions are computed as if the Code Sec. 179 expense allowance had not been claimed. Thus, the table percentages are applied to the original $22,000 cost.

MACRS deductions after recapture year:	
2010 = $22,000 × 8.93%	$1,965
2011 = $22,000 × 8.92%	1,962
2012 = $22,000 × 8.93%	1,965
2013 = $22,000 × 4.46%	981

Note that the sum of all of the MACRS deductions actually claimed ($15,124) plus the unrecaptured expense deduction ($6,876) allowance is equal to the $22,000 amount that would have been allowed if no amount had been expensed under Code Sec. 179.

Example (3): Donald Reed purchased 5-year property (not a listed-property) in April 2007 for $22,000. He expensed $10,000. In 2009, business use declined to 40%.

The recapture amount is computed as follows:

Section 179 deduction claimed (2007)		$10,000
Allowable depreciation deduction on $10,000 expensed amount:		
2007 = $10,000 × 20%	$2,000	
2008 = $10,000 × 32%	3,200	
2009 = $10,000 × 19.2% × 40%	1,920	7,120
2009 recapture amount		$2,880

MACRS deductions through recapture year:

2007 = $12,000 × 20%	$2,400
2008 = $12,000 × 32%	3,840
2009 = $12,000 × 19.20% × 40%	922

MACRS deductions after recapture year assuming business use is 40%:

2010 = $22,000 × 11.52% × 40%	$1,014
2011 = $22,000 × 11.52% × 40%	1,014
2012 = $22,000 × 5.76% × 40%	507

Note that the sum of the MACRS deductions actually claimed ($9,697) plus the unrecaptured expense allowance ($7,120) is the same as the MACRS deductions that would have been allowed if no amount had been expensed taking into account the reduction in business use ($16,817).

Example (4): Assume the same facts as in Example (3) except that the property was converted to 100% personal use in 2009. In this case, $4,800 ($10,000 – $5,200) is recaptured in 2009. No depreciation is allowed in 2009 or thereafter assuming that the asset continues to be used only for personal purposes.

Interaction of bonus depreciation with section 179 recapture. If a taxpayer claimed Code Sec. 168(k) (¶ 127D) bonus depreciation on a non-listed property in the tax year that the expensed asset was placed in service, then in computing the Code Sec. 179 recapture amount, the bonus deduction that would have been allowed on the expensed amount should be taken into account in computing the section 179 recapture upon a decline in business use to 50 percent or less. However, if Gulf Zone bonus depreciation (¶ 127F), Kansas Disaster Area bonus depreciation (¶ 127G), or Disaster Area Assistance property (¶ 127H) was claimed the bonus deprecation is also subject to recapture under the rule unique to these provisions that requires bonus depreciation recapture if business use within the zone or area drops to less than 80 percent (i.e. the property ceases to be qualified GO Zone property, qualified Kansas Disaster Assistance property, or qualified Disaster Area Assistance property). A decline in business use does not trigger recapture of the Code Sec. 168(k) bonus allowance (¶ 127D) unless the decline is to 50 percent or less and the property is a listed property such as a car (Code Sec. 168(k)(2)(F)(ii)). For section 179 and bonus depreciation recapture rules that apply to listed property (¶ 208), see ¶ 210.

Example (5): A calendar-year taxpayer places 5-year property (not a listed property) costing $150,000 in service on August 1, 2009, and uses it 100% for business purposes. She expenses $100,000 of the cost and claims a bonus depreciation deduction under Code Sec. 168(k) (¶ 127D) of $25,000 (($150,000 – $100,000) × 50%). In 2010, business use drops to 40%. The recapture amount is the difference between the $100,000 expensed and the depreciation (including bonus deprecation) that could have been claimed on that amount during 2009 and 2010. Bonus depreciation for 2009 would have been $50,000 ($100,000 × 50%). 2009 regular depreciation would have been $10,000 ($100,000 – $50,000 bonus) × 20%). 2010 depreciation would have been $6,400 ($100,000 – $50,000 bonus × 32% second-year table percentage × 40%). The 2010 recapture amount is $33,600 ($100,000 – $50,000 – $10,000 – $6,400).

If, in the preceding example, the asset had cost $100,000 and the entire amount had been expensed, depreciation recapture should be computed by taking bonus depreciation into account, assuming no formal election out of bonus depreciation was made for 5-year property placed in service in 2009. Note that if bonus depreciation is taken into account in computing the recapture amount, the recapture amount is significantly reduced when the decline in business use occurs early in an asset's recovery period.

Basis add-back

The basis of property on which the Code Sec. 179 expense deduction is recaptured under the 50 percent or less business use recapture rule provided in Code Sec. 179(d)(10) is increased immediately before the recapture event by the amount recaptured (Reg. § 1.179-1(e)(3)).

> ***Example (6):*** Assume the same facts as in *Example 3*. The adjusted basis of the asset at the end of 2009 (the recapture year) is $7,718 ($22,000 cost – $10,000 section 179 expense allowance + $2,880 recapture amount – $2,400 – $3,840 – $922).

See, also, *Example (9)* and related discussion at ¶ 487.

Married persons filing separately

Married persons filing separately are treated as one taxpayer for purposes of computing the allowable deduction and may elect to allocate the maximum allowable deduction between themselves in any proportion. Thus, for purposes of the dollar limitation (e.g., $250,000 in tax years beginning in 2008 and 2009) and the investment limitation (e.g., $800,000 in 2008 and 2009), the cost of all section 179 property purchased by each is aggregated to determine the combined deduction that is allocated between the spouses. However, the rule limiting the Sec. 179 expense deduction to taxable income is applied separately to each spouse without regard to the other spouse's taxable income. If no election is made or only one spouse makes an election or the sum of the amounts elected by both spouses exceeds 100 percent, the deduction is divided equally (i.e., each spouse will receive 50 percent of the deduction). (Code Sec. 179(b)(4); Reg. § 1.179-2(b)(6); Reg. § 1.179-2(c)(8)).

> ***Example 6A:*** John and Mary file separate returns in 2009. Their combined purchases of section 179 property in 2009 equal $1 million. The section 179 deduction computed jointly and without regard to the taxable income limitation is $50,000 ($250,000 – ($1,000,000 – $800,000)). Unless an election is made to allocate the deduction differently, John and Mary are each entitled to deduct $25,000 subject to the taxable income limitation which is computed separately by each.

Partnerships and S corporations

The maximum dollar limit ($250,000 in tax years beginning in 2008 and 2009), investment limitation ($800,000 in 2008 and 2009), and the taxable income limitation are applied separately at the partnership and partner levels (Reg. § 1.179-2(b) and (c)). Thus, a partnership may elect to expense up to the maximum annual dollar cost limitation of the cost of qualifying property (assuming the taxable income and investment limitations do not reduce the ceiling), and the partner may not claim an expense deduction in excess of the maximum annual dollar cost limitation, taking into account his allocated share of the amount expensed by the partnership. A similar rule applies to S corporations and S shareholders (Reg. § 1.179-2(b) and (c)).

The amount allocated by a partnership to a partner (or allocated by an S corporation to an S shareholder) is not considered in determining whether the partner (or S shareholder) placed more than the applicable investment limit (e.g., $800,000 in tax years beginning in 2008 or 2009) of qualifying property into service during the tax year (Reg. § 1.179-2(b)(3) and Reg. § 1.179-2(b)(4)).

Partners and S corporation shareholders are required to reduce the basis of their partnership or S corporation interest by the full amount of an expense deduction allocated to them by the respective entity even though part of the deduction must be carried over because of the partner or S corporation shareholder's taxable income limitation or is disallowed because of the dollar limitation (Rev. Rul. 89-7, 1989-1 CB 178; (Reg. § 1.179-3(h)(1)).

> ***Example (7):*** S is a 50% calendar-year partner in three separate calendar-year partnerships, A, B, and C. In 2009, S received a $125,000 share of a Code Sec. 179 expense deduction from each partnership that satisfied the $250,000 dollar limit, the $800,000 investment limit, and the aggregate taxable income limit at the partnership level. In 2009, S is engaged in other business activities that generate losses and has a total aggregate taxable income for the year, including the partnership income allocations, of $15,000.
>
> For 2009, S's expense deduction is limited to the aggregate taxable income of $15,000 and there is a $235,000 ($250,000 - $15,000) carryover. Although S received a total allocation of $375,000 from the three partnerships, only $250,000 (subject to the taxable income limitation) may be taken into account. The $125,000 excess is disregarded, and this amount may not be carried over.

A partner's distributive share of a partnership's Code Sec. 179 expenses for a partnership's tax year is taken into account in the partnership's tax year that ends with or within the partner's tax year (Reg.§ 1.179-2(b)(3)(iv)). The same rule applies to an S corporation and its shareholders (Reg.§ 1.179-2(b)(4)). Thus, when the tax years of a pass-thru and its owners differ, each is subject to a different dollar and investment limitation (Rev. Proc. 2008-54).

> ***Example 8A:*** ABC partnership has a fiscal year beginning on June 1, 2007. A is a calendar-year partner. ABC is subject to the $125,000 dollar limit that applies to tax years beginning in 2007 with respect to property placed in service in its fiscal year and A is subject the $250,000 limit that applies to tax years beginning in 2008. ABC may expense no more than $125,000 of property in its 2007 fiscal year. A's distributive share of the amount expensed by ABC in its 2007 fiscal year is taken into account in A's 2008 calendar year because ABC's 2007 fiscal year ends in A's 2008 calendar year. Thus, A's distributive share of ABC's 2007 fiscal-year expense amount is applied toward A's 2008 calendar year limit of $250,000.

Controlled group

All members of a controlled group of corporations are treated as a single taxpayer for purposes of the maximum annual dollar cost limitation, the investment limitation, and the taxable income limitation (Code Sec. 179(d)(6)). "Controlled group" is defined by reference to the definition at Code Sec. 1563(a), relating to consolidated returns; however, the phrase "more than 50 percent" is substituted for the phrase "at least 80 percent" that would otherwise apply with respect to stock ownership requirements.

The maximum annual dollar cost limitation may be claimed by any one member of the consolidated group or allocated among the members of the group by the parent of the group if a consolidated return is filed for all component members. If separate returns are filed, the amount must be allocated by agreement among the members (or by the parent of members filing a consolidated return and members that file separately). The amount allocated to any group member may not exceed the cost of the qualifying property placed in service by that group member (Reg. § 1.179-2(b)(7)). Property transferred between members of a controlled group may not be expensed (Reg. § 1.179-4(c)).

Noncorporate lessors

A lessor who is not a corporation may not claim the section 179 deduction on leased property unless the property was manufactured or produced by the lessor, or the term of the lease is less than one-half of the property's class life (¶ 180) and for the 12-month period following the date that the leased property is transferred to the lessee, the total Code Sec. 162 business deductions allowed to the lessor for the property exceed 15 percent of the rental income produced by the property (Code Sec. 179(d)(5); Reg. § 1.179-1(i)(2)). An S corporation is treated as a noncorporate lessor (i.e., a lessor other than a corporation) for purposes of this rule.

Farmers

Farmers who elect to deduct preproductive period costs of certain plants rather than capitalize them under Code Sec. 263A(d)(3) and consequently are required to depreciate farm property placed in service during the year of the election under the MACRS alternative depreciation system (see ¶ 150) are not precluded from claiming a Code Sec. 179 expense deduction (Temp. Reg. § 1.263A-4T(c)(6)(vi)).

¶ 302
Eligible Property

Property (new or used) is eligible for the Code Sec. 179 expensing election if it is (1) tangible Sec. 1245 property as defined in Code Sec. 1245(a)(3), (2) depreciable under Code Sec. 168 (MACRS), and (3) acquired by purchase for use in the active conduct of the taxpayer's trade or business (Code Sec. 179(d)(1); Reg. § 1.179-4).

Off-the-shelf computer software placed in service in tax years beginning in 2003 through 2010 may be expensed under Code Sec. 179 (Code Sec. 179(d)(1)(A); Reg.§ 1.179-4(a)). Off-the-shelf computer software is software that is readily available for purchase by the general public, is subject to a nonexclusive license, and has not been substantially modified (Code Sec. 197(e)(3)(A)(i) and (e)(3)(B)). Such software is amortizable over three years. See 48. This temporary rule is an exception to the requirement that only tangible property which is depreciable under MACRS may be expensed.

Investment use. The trade or business limitation makes it clear that there is no expensing allowance for property that is held merely for the production of income. To qualify for expensing, property must be used more than 50 percent in the active conduct of the taxpayer's trade or business and cannot qualify by reason of being held by the taxpayer for the production of income (Reg.§ 1.179-2(c)(6)). If a property is used more than 50 percent for business and also for investment, the investment portion still does not qualify for the expensing allowance.

Section 1245(a)(3) property defined. In general, property described in Code Sec. 1245(a)(3) is tangible personal property and other types of tangible property described below. Reg. § 1.1245-3(b) defines tangible personal property by cross reference to the definition contained in Reg. § 1.48-1(c) of the investment tax credit regulations. See ¶ 116, ¶ 127 and ¶ 127C for a detailed discussion of the definition of tangible personal property.

Sec. 1245(a)(3) property also includes livestock. The term livestock includes horses, cattle, hogs, sheep, goats, mink, and other furbearing animals (Reg. § 1.1245-3(a)(4)). Thus, livestock may be expensed under Code Sec. 179 if it is depreciable and acquired by purchase.

In addition to tangible personal property, Code Sec. 1245(a)(3) property eligible for expensing includes "other tangible property" that is not personal property. Other tangible property is tangible property used as an integral part of manufacturing, production, or extraction or of furnishing transportation, communications, electrical energy, gas, water, or sewage disposal services (Reg.§ 1.48-1(d)); research facilities used in connection with any of these activities; facilities used in connection with any of these activities for the bulk storage of fungible commodities (including commodities in a liquid or gaseous state); single purpose livestock or horticultural structures (¶ 108); petroleum storage facilities (if they are neither buildings nor structural components thereof); railroad gradings and tunnel bores; and certain livestock (Code Sec. 1245(a)(3)). The definition of other tangible property is discussed at ¶ 110 and ¶ 127C.

For example, grape vines and trees of a fruit orchard or grove although not considered tangible personal property can be considered property used as an integral part of a production activity and, thus, are eligible for expensing under Code Sec. 179 if the trees or vines are depreciable and acquired by purchase. Rev. Rul. 67-51, 1967-1 CB 68, which holds that fruit trees are not eligible for expensing was based on a prior-law definition of section 179 property that did not include property held for manufacturing, production, or extraction. The IRS Audit Guide for Farmers erroneously indicates, based on this ruling, that fruit trees are not eligible section 179 property. Section 179 deductions claimed with respect to such property are subject to recapture under Code Sec. 1245 as ordinary income if a taxpayer made an election out of Code Sec. 263A, as described at ¶ 150. Special election rules apply to a citrus or almond grove (Code Sec. 263A(e)(1); Reg.§ 1.263A-4(d)). Grape vines and fruit trees are considered placed in service when they bear fruit in commercial quantitities. However, a taxpayer that acquires an existing commerically viable orchard is considered to have placed the orchard trees or vines in service in the year of acquisition. If the trees or vines have been planted but are not commercially viable when purchased then they are considered placed in service when they begin to produce fruit in commercial quantities. See ¶ 108 for additional information, including rules regarding depreciation.

The following property does not qualify for the Code Sec. 179 expense deduction:

(1) property described in Code Sec. 50(b), relating to the investment tax credit (generally, property used predominantly outside of the U.S., property used predominantly to furnish lodging or used predominantly in connection with the furnishing of lodging, property used by certain tax-exempt organizations unless used in connection with the production of income subject to the tax on unrelated trade or business income, and property used by governments and foreign persons);

(2) air conditioning units; and

(3) heating units (including space heaters) (Code Sec. 179(d)(1)).

The exclusion for air conditioning and heating units is intended, according the legislative history of the provision, to apply to portable units. This legislative history states that an air conditioner or heating system (HVAC) may be treated as personal property and could be eligible for expensing, if it relates to the temperature or humidity requirements of machinery or equipment or the processing of foodstuffs. See ¶ 127A.

Lodging facilities. Property used in the living quarters of a lodging facility, including beds and other furniture, refrigerators, ranges, and other equipment is considered as used predominantly to furnish lodging (item (1), above). Examples of property used in connection with the furnishing of a lodging facility include lobby furniture, office equipment, and laundry and swimming pool equipment. Property used in furnishing electrical energy, water, sewage disposal services, gas, telephone service or similar services is not treated as used in connection with the furnishing of lodging (Reg. § 1.48-1(h)).

The term lodging facility includes an apartment building or house, hotel, motel, dormitory, or (subject to certain exceptions) any other facility or part of a facility where sleeping accommodations are provided and let (Reg. § 1.48-1(h)). However, property used by a hotel, motel, inn, or other similar establishment is not considered used in connection with the furnishing of lodging if more than half of the living quarters are used to accommodate tenants on a transient basis (rental periods of 30 days or less) (Code Sec. 50(b)(2)(B); Reg. § 1.48-1(h)).

Commercial facilities, such as grocery stores and restaurants, that are located within a lodging facility are not considered lodging facilities if nontenants have equal access. Thus, property used within such commercial facilities can qualify for the expensing allowance. Similarly, vending machines that are equally available to nontenants can qualify (Reg. § 1.48-1(h)(2)).

A lodging facility does not include a facility used primarily as a means of transportation (such as an aircraft, a vessel, or a railroad car) or used primarily to provide medical or convalescent services, even though sleeping accommodations are provided (Reg. § 1.48-1(h)(1)(i)). The IRS has ruled that a motor home (RV) used by a railroad employee in connection with traveling to and lodging at temporary duty stations for as short as one week and as long as several months was used predominantly for lodging (Technical Advice Memorandum 8546005, August 20, 1985; GCM 39443, November 12, 1985; *Union Pacific Corporation*, 91 TC 771, CCH Dec. 44,886). The IRS stated that if a motor home is used at least as many days for lodging as it is for transportation, its predominant use is for lodging, particularly where the mileage driven is relatively low.

The IRS has ruled that furniture rented directly to owners of apartment buildings, duplex houses, and similar establishments that lease to tenants for periods of more than 30 days was considered property used in connection with the furnishing of lodging and was not eligible for the investment tax credit. However, if the furniture had been leased directly to the tenants instead, it would not have been considered used in connection with the furnishing of lodging because the tenants did not furnish lodging to themselves (Rev. Rul. 81-133, 1981-1 CB 21).

Energy property is not disqualified even though used in connection with the furnishing of lodging (Code Sec. 50(b)(2)(D))). See IRS Publication 946 (Depreciation and Amortization) for a definition of energy property.

Purchase requirement. Property does not qualify for expensing unless it is acquired by purchase. Property is not considered acquired by purchase if it (Code Sec. 179(d)(2)):

(1) is acquired from a person whose relationship to the taxpayer would bar recognition of a loss in any transaction between them under Code Sec. 267 or 707(b);

(2) is transferred between members of a controlled group of corporations (substituting 50 percent for the 80 percent that would otherwise apply with respect to stock ownership requirements);

(3) will have a substituted basis (in whole or in part); or

(4) has a basis determined under Code Sec. 1014(a) relating to inherited property (Reg. § 1.179-4(c)).

Carryover basis. The portion of the basis of property that is attributable to the basis of property that was previously held by the taxpayer (e.g., carryover basis in a trade-in or involuntary conversion) does not qualify for the expense deduction (Code Sec. 179(d)(3)).

Property converted from personal to business use. Eligibility for expensing is determined as of the first year in which the property is placed in service.

Example: A car purchased for personal use in 2007 is converted to business use in 2008. Since it could not be expensed in 2007 when it was first placed in service for personal use, the purchaser cannot expense it in 2008.

¶ 304
Elections

A Code Sec. 179 election to expense the cost of qualifying property must specify the items of property to which the election applies and the portion of the cost of each of these items to be deducted currently. The election is made on Form 4562 (Depreciation and Amortization) by claiming the expense allowance. The specification of property for which the election is made is made on line 6 of 2008 Form 4562. For partnerships and S corporations—which, up to the annual ceiling, may expense qualifying property and pass the deduction through to their partners or shareholders—the total amount expensed is carried to Schedules K and K-1 of Form 1065 or 1120S.

Time for making and revoking an election for property placed in service in tax years beginning in 2003-2010. As explained below, an election to expense under Code Sec. 179 is generally revocable only with IRS consent (Code Sec. 179(c)(2)). However, the rule is temporarily suspended and any election or specification made for property placed in service in a tax year beginning in 2003-2010 may be revoked by a taxpayer without IRS consent. The revocation, once made, is irrevocable (Code Sec. 179(c)(2)).

The IRS intends to update Reg.§ 1.179-5(c)(1) to provide that a taxpayer may revoke a section 179 election for any tax year beginning after 2002 and *before 2011* (Section 7 of Rev. Proc. 2008-54). The regulation currently provides that the rule applies to tax years before 2008 and does not reflect extension of the provision by P.L. 109-122 to tax years beginning before 2011.

Although Code Sec. 179(c)(2), as amended, only refers to the "revocation" of a Code Sec. 179 election without IRS consent, the related committee report states that a taxpayer may also "make" an election on an amended return without IRS consent under the provision. Final and temporary regulations which explain the provision adopt this position (T.D. 9209, filed with the Federal Register on July 12, 2005; Reg.§ 1.179-5; T.D. 9146, filed with the Federal Register on August 4, 2004; Temporary Reg.§ 1.179-5T).

The amended return must be filed before expiration of the applicable limitations period for filing an amended return for the tax year that the property was placed in service (Reg.§ 1.179-5(c)(1)). The amended return must include the adjustment to taxable income caused by the election or revocation of the expense deduction as well as any collateral adjustments to taxable income or tax liability. Amended returns must also be filed for any subsequent affected tax years (Reg.§ 1.179-5(c)(2)(i) and (c)(3)(i)).

Generally, an amended return must be filed within three years from the date the original return was filed. For this purpose, a return that is filed early is considered filed on the due date. See instructions for Form 1040-X.

An election on an amended return to expense the entire cost of an asset or any portion of an asset that was not expensed on the original return is not considered a revocation of a Code Sec. 179 election (Reg.§ 1.179-5(c)(2)(i)). Thus, the rule which prohibits the revocation of a revocation (Code Sec. 179(c)(2); Reg.§ 1.179-5(c)(3)(ii)) is not applicable and a taxpayer may revoke an election made on an original or amended return (if the period for filing an amended return to make the revocation has not expired).

If a taxpayer elects to expense a portion of the cost of an item of section 179 property placed in service in a tax year beginning in 2003 through 2010, the taxpayer may file an amended return (within the limitations period) to expense any or all of the cost basis that was not expensed. If no election was made to expense a particular item of property placed in service in a tax year beginning in 2003-2010, an amended return may be filed to expense any portion or all of its cost basis (Reg.§ 1.179-5(c)(2)(ii)).

A revocation may be made with respect to any portion of an election to expense an item of section 179 property placed in service in a tax year beginning in 2003-2010 whether the election was made on an original or an amended return. The revocation may be made without IRS consent by filing an amended return within the limitations period and designating the dollar amount that the revocation applies to. The revocation is irrevocable. Thus, to the extent that a revocation applies to the cost basis of an item of property, no new election may be made to expense that property (Reg.§ 1.179-5(c)(3)).

Example (1): John Adams purchases a table saw in 2007 for $5,000. He only elects to expense $3,000 of its cost on the 2007 tax return filed on April 15, 2008. In November 2009, he decides to revoke the 2007 election. John may file an amended 2007 return to revoke the election since 2007 is still an open year under the statute of limitations. This election is irrevocable. He will also need to file an amended 2008 return since this is an affected year (he has to claim second-year depreciation on the $3,000 and make any other necessary adjustments). In June 2010, after filing his 2009 return, John decides that he wants to make an election to expense the $2,000 portion of the machine's cost that was not expensed in 2007. John may make the election on an amended 2007 return. He will also need to file amended returns for 2008 and 2009 since these are affected tax years. John may later revoke the election to expense the $2,000 (or any portion of the $2,000) by filing an amended 2007 return (and amended returns for subsequent affected tax years) before the expiration of the statute of limitations for amending the 2007 return.

The new election/revocation process allows small businesses more time to consider whether making the section Code Sec. 179 election is to their advantage. For example, because an election to expense reduces adjusted gross income and taxable income it may also reduce exemptions and deductions, social security coverage of the self-employed, and certain tax credits.

An election out of bonus depreciation cannot be made without IRS consent. See ¶ 127D. Thus, if a taxpayer revokes a Code Sec. 179 expense election, bonus depreciation may not be claimed on the revoked amount if an election out of bonus depreciation applied to the property in the year it was placed in service.

Example (2): Jack placed office furniture (seven-year MACRS property) in service in 2009 and expensed the entire cost. The furniture cost $100,000. He also placed other seven-year property in service in 2009 and made an election out of bonus depreciation for seven-year property. If Jack files an amended 2009 return to revoke the Code Sec. 179 expense election he may not claim a bonus depreciation deduction on the office furniture. The amended return will reflect the addition of a depreciation deduction of $1,429 ($100,000 × 14.29% first-year table percentage) and the elimination of the $100,000 expense deduction. Note that revocation is not considered a change in accounting method and no Code Sec. 481(a) adjustment is made.

Making section 179 election and revocation for property placed in service in tax years that begin before 2003 or after 2010. The election for property placed in service in a tax year that begins before 2003 or after 2010 must be made by filing Form 4562 with either (1) the taxpayer's first return (whether or not timely filed) for the tax year in which the property is placed in service or (2) with an amended return that is filed prior to the due date (including extensions) for filing the taxpayer's return for that tax year (Code Sec. 179(c); Reg. § 1.179-5(a)).

In addition, a taxpayer who timely files an original return without making the election is permitted to make an election on an amended return filed within six months of the due date of the original return (excluding extensions) (2003 Form 4562 (Depreciation and Amortization) instructions).

The election is revocable only with IRS consent. Consent is only granted in extraordinary circumstances. IRS consent is also required to change the designation of the property expensed (Code Sec. 179(c)(2); Reg.§ 1.179-5(b)). A late revocation or election is made by filing a letter ruling and cannot be made through a request under Code Sec. 446(e) to change a method of accounting (T.D. 9209; Reg.§ 1.179-5(d)).

Special relief for tax year that includes September 11, 2001. Certain taxpayers who failed to claim bonus depreciation on a tax return that included September 11, 2001 were allowed to change their Code Sec. 179 election for that year on an amended return filed by December 31, 2003.

Court decisions. A taxpayer who elects to expense specific property cannot later substitute other property for the election without the consent of the IRS (*B.B. King*, 60 TCM 1048, CCH Dec. 46,938(M)).

The Tax Court determined that the IRS did not abuse its discretion when it refused to allow a taxpayer to claim the Code Sec. 179 expense allowance on property which, as the result of an audit, was reclassified as depreciable (*S.H. Patton*, 116 TC 206, CCH Dec. 54,307). Similarly, *M.A. McGrath*, T.C. Memo. 2002-231, CCH Dec. 54,873(M), aff'd per curiam on another issue, CA-5, 2003-2 USTC ¶ 50,663).

The inclusion of property in cost of goods sold is not the equivalent of an election under section 179 (*M. Visin*, 86 TCM 279, T.C. Memo. 2003-246, CCH Dec. 55,269(M), aff'd, CA-9 (unpublished opinion), 2005-1 USTC ¶ 50,199.

¶ 305

New York Liberty Zone Property

The maximum dollar limitation on Code Sec. 179 property ($125,000 in 2007) is increased by an amount equal to $35,000 for Code Sec. 179 property which is "qualified New York Liberty Zone property" (as defined below) (Code Sec. 1400L(f), as amended by the Working Families Tax Relief Act of 2004 (P.L. 108-311)). The $35,000 increase applies to qualified NYLZ property acquired after September 10, 2001 and placed into service before January 1, 2007.

The amendment made by the Working Families Tax Relief Act retroactively clarifies that the term qualified New York Liberty Zone Property for purposes of the additional $35,000 expense allowance includes property which would be NYLZ property for purposes of the Code Sec. 1400L(b) NYLZ bonus depreciation allowance but for the fact that it qualifies for the 30-percent or 50-percent bonus depreciation allowance under Code Sec. 168(k). The amendment is particularly significant because most property placed in service in the NYLZ qualifies for bonus depreciation under Code Sec. 168(k) rather than Code Sec. 1400L(b) and, therefore, is not considered qualified New York Liberty Zone property. This point is discussed at ¶ 127E.

Taking the $35,000 increase into account, the maximum amount of qualified NYLZ property placed in service before January 1, 2007 that may be expensed is $143,000 for tax years beginning in 2006 ($108,000 (inflation-adjusted dollar limit) +

$35,000) and $140,000 for tax years beginning in 2005 ($105,000 (inflation-adjusted dollar limit) + $35,000). The $35,000 bump-up is not adjusted for inflation. The $35,000 increase does not apply to property placed in service after December 31, 2006.

In addition to the increased expensing allowance, the deduction phaseout rule based on a taxpayer's total investments (the "investment limitation") for the tax year is modified to take into account only 50 percent of the taxpayer's investment in Code Sec. 179 property that qualifies (or would qualify) as New York Liberty Zone property (Code Sec. 1400L(f) (1) (B)). See "*Investment limitation modified*," below.

Because the $35,000 bump-up provision was enacted after many taxpayers had already filed their 2000 (fiscal-year) or 2001 return, some taxpayers may not have claimed the additional section 179 allowance on qualifying Liberty Zone property. These taxpayers were directed to file an amended return by December 31, 2003 (Rev. Proc. 2003-50, I.R.B. 2003-29).

Qualified New York Liberty Zone property

The additional expensing allowance is limited to the cost of qualified New York Liberty Zone property placed in service during the tax year. Qualified New York Liberty Zone property has the same meaning as the definition used for purposes of the 30-percent additional first-year depreciation allowance (bonus depreciation allowance) for qualified New York Liberty Zone property provided for in Code Sec. 1400L(b) (2). However, the requirement in Code Sec. 1400L(b) (2) (C) (i) that the property not be eligible for expensing under the more general bonus depreciation provision of Code Sec. 168(k) (2) does not apply (Code Sec. 1400L(f) (2), as amended by the Working Families Tax Relief Act of 2004 (P.L. 108-311). The definition of qualified New York Liberty Zone property for bonus depreciation purposes is described at ¶ 127E.

In addition to being qualified NYLZ property, the property must also qualify as Section 179 property (i.e., it must be the type of property that the Section 179 expense allowance can be claimed on without regard to the provision which increases the expense amount by $35,000). Thus, for example, section 1250 property which is eligible for bonus depreciation does not qualify for either the $35,000 increase or the $100,000 basic section 179 allowance.

Other requirements for claiming the additional Liberty Zone expensing allowance are:

(1) the property must have an MACRS recovery period of 20 years or less;

(2) the property must be acquired by the taxpayer by purchase (within the meaning of Code Sec. 179(d) (2)) after September 10, 2001, and placed in service before January 1, 2007;

(3) the original use of the property in the Liberty Zone must commence with the taxpayer after September 10, 2001; and

(4) substantially all (80 percent or more) of the use of the property must be in the New York Liberty Zone in the active conduct of a trade or business by the taxpayer in the Zone (Code Sec. 1400L(f) (2); Code Sec. 1400L(b) (2)).

Mandatory ADS property does not qualify

Property for which the MACRS alternative depreciation system (ADS) is mandatory (¶ 152) does not qualify for the increased Code Sec. 179 allowance (Code Sec. 1400L(f) (2); Code Sec. 1400L(b) (2) (C) (ii)).

Leasehold improvements

New York Liberty Zone leasehold improvement property (see ¶ 124A) does not qualify for the $35,000 increased expensing allowance (Code Sec. 1400L(f)(2); Code Sec. 1400L(b)(2)(C)(iii)). Furthermore, leasehold improvement property that is a structural component (Section 1250 real property) does not qualify for the basic $100,000 Code Sec. 179 deduction amount. See ¶ 124A.

New York Liberty Zone defined

The New York Liberty Zone is the area located on or south of Canal Street, East Broadway (east of its intersection with Canal Street), or Grand Street (east of its intersection with East Broadway) in the Borough of Manhattan in New York City (Code Sec. 1400L(h)).

Acquisition by purchase after September 10, 2001

The property must be acquired by purchase within the meaning of Code Sec. 179(d)(2) after September 10, 2001 and placed in service before January 1, 2007 (Code Sec. 1400L(b)(2)(A)(iv)). Under Code Sec. 179(d)(2), property is not considered purchased by the taxpayer if it is acquired from a related party or by a member of a controlled group, has a substituted basis or is acquired from a decedent with a fair market value basis. See ¶ 302. Property will not qualify if a binding written contract for the acquisition of the property was in effect before September 11, 2001.

Self-produced property

Property manufactured, constructed, or produced by a taxpayer for the taxpayer's own use is treated as acquired after September 10, 2001, if the taxpayer began manufacturing, constructing, or producing the property after September 10, 2001 (Code Sec. 1400L(b)(2)(D)). The Joint Committee Explanation states that property manufactured, constructed, or produced for the taxpayer by another person under a contract entered into prior to the manufacture, construction, or production of the property is considered manufactured, constructed, or produced by the taxpayer (Joint Committee on Taxation, *Technical Explanation of the "Job Creation and Worker Assistance Act of 2002"* (JCX-12-02), March 6, 2002).

Original use requirement

The original use of the property in the New York Liberty Zone must commence with the taxpayer after September 10, 2001 (Code Sec. 1400L(b)(2)(A)(iii)). The Joint Committee Explanation indicates that used property may qualify as long as it was not previously used in the Liberty Zone. The Explanation further states that additional capital expenditures incurred to recondition or rebuild property for which the original use in the Liberty Zone began with the taxpayer will also satisfy the original use requirement (Joint Committee on Taxation, *Technical Explanation of the "Job Creation and Worker Assistance Act of 2002"* (JCX-12-02), March 6, 2002).

Investment limitation modified

The Code Sec. 179 allowance is generally reduced for taxpayers with investments above $400,000 (adjusted for inflation) during the year. The reduction is $1 for each $1 of investment over $400,000 (¶ 300). For qualifying Liberty Zone property, the expensing limitation is reduced by the excess of (1) 50 percent of the cost of Code Sec. 179 property that is qualified Liberty Zone property placed in service during the tax year plus the total amount of any other Code Sec. 179 property placed in service during the tax year, over (2) $400,000 ($410,000 in 2004, $420,000 in 2005, and $430,000 in 2006). For Liberty Zone property placed in service in a tax year that begins in 2004, the deduction will be completely phased out once the amount invested amount equals or exceeds $1,094,000 ($1,094,000/2 - $410,000 = the deduction limit of $137,000). The phaseout is reached at $1,120,000 ($1,120,000/2 - $420,000 = the deduction limit of $140,000) in 2005 and at $1,146,000 ($1,146,000/2 - $430,000 = the deduction limit of $143,000) in 2006.

Other Code Sec. 179 provisions apply

Other than the increased dollar amount limitation and increased investment limitation phaseout range, the provisions of Code Sec. 179 are applied to Liberty Zone property in the same manner as they are applied to other businesses.

Recapture

The $35,000 additional section 179 dollar amount for New York Liberty Zone property is subject to recapture if the qualified New York Liberty Zone property ceases to be used in the New York Liberty Zone by applying rules similar to Code Sec. 179(d)(10) (relating to recapture when business use of section 179 property drops to 50 percent or less) (Code Sec. 1400L(f)(3)). See ¶ 300 for a discussion of these recapture rules.

For example, removal of the property from the Liberty Zone for continued business use outside of the Zone would result in recapture with respect to the $35,000 additional Code Sec. 179 allowance but not the standard Code Sec. 179 allowance ($108,000 is 2006). The sum of both components of the allowance, however, would be subject to recapture in the year that the property is not used predominantly for business purposes (i.e., more than 50 percent) even if the property remains in the Zone.

Expiration date

Property placed in service after December 31, 2006, does not qualify for the additional $35,000 expense allowance (Code Sec. 1400L(b)(2)(A)(v)).

¶ 306

Gulf Opportunity Zone Property

The maximum allowable Code Sec. 179 expense allowance ($125,000 for tax years beginning in 2007 and $250,000 for tax years beginning in 2008) is increased by the lesser of $100,000 or the cost of qualified section 179 Gulf Opportunity Zone property placed in service in the tax year. The investment limit ($500,000 for tax years beginning in 2007 and $800,000 for tax years beginning in 2008) is increased by the lesser of $600,000 or the amount of qualified section 179 Gulf Opportunity Zone property placed in service during the tax year (Code Sec. 1400N(e), as added by the Gulf Opportunity Zone Act of 2005 (P.L. 109-135); Section 6.01(1) of Rev. Proc. 2008-54)). The $100,000 increase in the dollar limitation and the $600,000 increase in the investment limitation are not adjusted for inflation.

The increases in the dollar and investment limits apply to qualified section 179 Gulf Opportunity Zone property acquired on or after August 28, 2005, and placed in service before January 1, 2008 (Code Sec. 1400N(d)(2)(A), (e)(2)). However, the placed-in-service deadline is extended an additional year for section 179 Gulf Opportunity Zone property placed in service in certain specified counties and parishes within the Gulf Opportunity Zone where more than 60 percent of the housing was destroyed by hurricanes in 2005 (Code Sec. 1400N(e)(2)(B)). Thus, the qualifying property located in one of these parishes or counties must be placed in service before January 1, 2009. These counties and parishes are referred to as "specified portions" of the GO Zone. This is the only type of GO Zone property placed in service in 2008 that qualifies for an increased section 179 allowance (Rev. Proc. 2008-54).

See ¶ 127F for a discussion of the Gulf Opportunity Go Zone 50 percent bonus depreciation deduction.

The specified portions of the GO Zone are (Notice 2007-36, I.R.B. 2007-17):

- **Alabama**: No counties
- **Louisiana**: The parishes of Calcasieu, Cameron, Orleans, Plaquemines, St. Bernard, St. Tammany, and Washington
- **Mississippi**: The counties of Hancock, Harrison, Jackson, Pearl River, and Stone

Note that property may be acquired before it is considered placed in service. For example, a machine may be acquired before it is completely assembled and integrated into a manufacturing process for use in its assigned function (i.e., placed in service). See ¶ 3.

Taking into account these increases, the maximum dollar amounts for qualifying section 179 Gulf Opportunity Zone property acquired on or after August 28, 2005 and placed in service within a particular tax year are:

- $205,000 ($105,000 + $100,000) for property acquired on or after August 28, 2005 and placed in service in tax years beginning in 2005
- $208,000 ($108,000 + $100,000) for property placed in service in tax years beginning in 2006.
- $225,000 ($125,000 + $100,000) for property placed in service before January 1, 2008 in tax years beginning in 2007.
- $350,000 ($250,000 + $100,000) for property placed in service before January 1, 2009 in tax years beginning in 2008 (in a specified portion of the GO Zone).

The dollar amount begins to be reduced by reason of the investment limitation (if at least $600,000 of qualifying zone property is placed in service) at:

- $1,020,000 ($420,000 + $600,000) for property acquired on or after August 28, 2005 and placed in service in tax years beginning in 2005
- $1,030,000 ($430,000 + $600,000) for property placed in service in tax years beginning in 2006
- $1,100,000 ($500,000 + $600,000) for property placed in service before January 1, 2008 in tax years beginning in 2007
- $1,400,000 ($800,000 + $600,000) for property placed in service before January 1, 2009 in tax years beginning in 2008 (applies to specified portions of the GO Zone)

The dollar amount is completely phased out by reason of the investment limitation at:

- $1,225,000 ($205,000 – ($1,225,000 – ($420,000 + $600,000)) = $0) for property acquired on or after August 28, 2005 and placed in service in tax years beginning in 2005.
- $1,238,000 ($208,000 – ($1,238,000 – ($430,000 + $600,000)) = $0) for property placed in service in tax years beginning in 2006
- $1,325,000 ($225,000 – ($1,325,000 – ($500,000 + $600,000)) = $0) for property placed in service before January 1, 2008 in tax years beginning in 2007

• $1,750,000 ($350,000 – ($1,750,000 – ($800,000 + $600,000)) = $0) for property placed in service before January 1, 2009 in tax years beginning in 2008 (applies to specified portions of the GO Zone)

Example (1): In 2008, a calendar-year taxpayer places $500,000 of qualified section 179 Gulf Opportunity Zone property in service in a specified county and $950,000 of other qualifying section 179 property in service. The dollar limitation is $350,000 ($250,000 + $100,000). The investment limitation is $1,300,000 ($800,000 basic limit + $500,000 amount of qualified section 179 Gulf Opportunity Zone property placed in service since this is less than $600,000). Because the total amount of section 179 property placed in service ($1,450,000) exceeds the investment limit by $150,000 ($1,450,000 –$1,300,000), the dollar limit is reduced to $200,000 ($350,000 – $150,000) and this amount is claimed as the deduction under Code Sec. 179 subject to the taxable income limitation.

Example (2): XYZ corporation, a calendar-year taxpayer, places $1,200,000 of new machinery in service in 2007. The machinery is qualified section 179 Gulf Opportunity Zone property. XYZ places no other section 179 property in service in 2007. Under the dollar limitation, only $225,000 ($125,000 basic limit + $100,000 bump-up for section 179 Gulf Opportunity Zone property) of the total $1,200,000 of machinery placed in service may be expensed. The investment limit is $1,100,000 ($500,000 basic limit + $600,000 maximum increase since this is less than the cost of qualifying section 179 zone property placed in service). The dollar limit must be reduced by $100,000 ($1,200,000 cost of section 179 property placed in service –$1,100,000 investment limit). Thus, XYZ's section 179 deduction for 2007 is $125,000 ($225,000 dollar limit – $100,000), assuming that XYZ's taxable income is at least $125,000.

Property must be both section 179 property and qualified zone property

For the increased limits to apply, the property must be both section 179 property and qualified Gulf Opportunity Zone property. If the property is not section 179 property, then no amount may be expensed under Code Sec. 179. To qualify as section 179 property, the property must be new or used tangible section 1245 property that is depreciable under MACRS (subject to an exception for off-the-shelf computer software) and used predominantly (more than 50 percent) in the active conduct of a trade or business. In addition, the property must be acquired by "purchase" from an unrelated person (Code Sec. 179(d)(2)). See ¶ 302 for a discussion of the definition of qualifying section 179 property.

Certain qualified Gulf Opportunity Zone property, most notably, residential rental and nonresidential real property will not qualify for any expensing under Code Sec. 179 because section 1250 property is not section 179 property. Most used property will not qualify for the increase in the dollar amount because such property cannot be qualified zone property unless the original use in the zone commences with the taxpayer. Used property, however, may constitute section 179 property and qualify for the basic section 179 allowance.

Qualifying Gulf Opportunity Zone property

Property that otherwise qualifies for expensing under Code Sec. 179 (i.e., section 179 property as defined in Code Sec. 179(d); see ¶ 302) will qualify for the increased section 179 limitations if it is Gulf Opportunity Zone property as defined for purposes of the 50-percent additional depreciation allowance (see ¶ 127F). In general, property is Gulf Opportunity Zone property if (Code Sec. 1400N(d)(2)):

• It is depreciable under MACRS and has a recovery period of 20 years or less

• Substantially all (80 percent or greater) of the property is used in the active conduct of a trade or business by the taxpayer within the Gulf Opportunity Zone (as defined in Code Sec. 1400M(1))

- The original use of the property within the zone commences with the taxpayer on or after August 28, 2005, and the property is placed in service before January 1, 2008 (January 1, 2009 in specified areas of the GO Zone, as previously explained)

- It acquired by purchase (within the meaning of Code Sec. 179(d)(2); see ¶ 302) on or after August 28, 2005

- No written binding contract for the acquisition of the property was in effect before August 28, 2005

If the first use of used property within the Gulf Opportunity Zone commences with the taxpayer, then the used property may qualify for the increased allowance. If the section 179 property was previously used by another taxpayer within the Zone, it will only remain eligible for the standard section 179 allowance ($105,000 in tax years beginning in 2005, $108,000 in 2006, and $125,000 in 2007, and $250,000 in 2008).

Gulf Opportunity Zone property does not include property that must be depreciated using the MACRS alternative depreciation system (ADS) (see ¶ 152) or property financed to any extent with state and local tax-exempt bonds that generate tax-exempt interest under Code Sec. 103 (Code Sec. 1400N(d)(2)(B)). Property which a taxpayer elects to depreciate under ADS may qualify.

The additional section 179 allowance may not be claimed on property used in connection with: a private or commercial golf course, a country club, a massage parlor, a hot tub facility, a suntan facility, a liquor store, or a gambling or animal racing property (Code Sec. 1400N(p); see ¶ 127F).

Recapture if business use declines to less than 80 percent

Code Sec. 1400N(e)(4) provides that: "For purposes of this subsection, rules similar to the rules under section 179(d)(10) shall apply with respect to any qualified section 179 Gulf Opportunity Zone property which ceases to be qualified section 179 Gulf Opportunity Zone property." Thus, recapture of the additional section 179 expense allowance allowed by Code Sec. 1400N(e) is required if the property ceases to be substantially used for business in the GO Zone (i.e., business use in the Zone is not 80 percent or greater or the property is removed from the zone) since this would cause the property to lose its status as Gulf Opportunity Zone property. The standard section 179 deduction ($125,000 in 2007 and $250,000 in 2008) (as well as the additional section 179 deduction) is subject to recapture under the generally applicable rule if business use, whether in or outside the GO Zone, drops to 50 percent or less. The recapture rules of Code Sec. 179(d)(10) are described at ¶ 300.

Recapture upon disposition

The Code Sec. 179 expense allowance (including the increased section 179 allowance for qualifying Gulf Zone property) is treated as a depreciation deduction for section 1245 recapture purposes upon the disposition of the property. See ¶ 300.

Coordination with increased expense allowance for empowerment zones and renewal communities

If qualifying section 179 Gulf Opportunity Property is placed in service within an empowerment zone or renewal community located within the Gulf Opportunity Zone, a taxpayer may not also claim the benefit of the additional $35,000 expense allowance provided for qualifying property placed in service in an empowerment zone (Code Sec. 1397A or a renewal community (Code Sec. 1400J; see ¶ 300) unless the taxpayer elects not to claim the additional $100,000 allowance provided for section 179 Gulf Opportunity Zone property (Code Sec. 1400N(e)(3)).

Generally, it will be preferable to take advantage of the $100,000 bump-up provided for qualified section 179 Gulf Opportunity Zone property since the additional allowance for empowerment zone and renewal community property is only $35,000 (e.g., $160,000 total in 2007 ($125,000 + $35,000)) as compared to $100,000 for Gulf Opportunity Zone property (e.g., $225,000 total in 2007 ($125,000 + $100,000)).

¶ 306A

Kansas Disaster Area Recovery Assistance Property

Taxpayers other than estates, trusts, and certain noncorporate lessors may elect to claim a Code Sec. 179 expense deduction on the cost of qualifying section 179 property acquired by purchase (see ¶ 302). The maximum allowable Code Sec. 179 expense allowance ($125,000 for tax years beginning in 2007 and $250,000 for tax years beginning in 2008) is increased by the lesser of $100,000 or the cost of qualified section 179 Recovery Assistance property placed in service in the tax year. The investment limit ($500,000 for tax years beginning in 2007 and $800,000 for tax years beginning in 2008) is increased by the lesser of $600,000 or the amount of qualified section 179 Recovery Assistance property placed in service during the tax year (Act Sec. 15345(d)(2) of the Heartland, Habitat, Harvest, and Horticulture Act of 2008 (P.L. 110-246), applying Code Sec. 1400N(e), as added by the Gulf Opportunity Zone Act of 2005 (P.L. 109-135); Section 6.01(1)(a) of Rev. Proc. 2008-54). The $100,000 increase in the dollar limitation and the $600,000 increase in the investment limitation are not adjusted for inflation.

The increases in the dollar and investment limits apply to qualified section 179 Recovery Assistance property acquired on or after May 5, 2007, and placed in service before January 1, 2009 in the Kansas disaster area (Act Sec. 15345(d)(1) and (2) of the Heartland, Habitat, Harvest, and Horticulture Act of 2008 (P.L. 110-246), applying Code Sec. 1400N(e)(2) and Code Sec. 1400N(d)(2)(A), (e)(2)).

The Kansas disaster area is an area with respect to which a major disaster has been declared by the President under section 401 of the Robert T. Stafford Disaster Relief and Emergency Assistance Act (FEMA-1699-DR, as in effect on the date of the enactment (May 5, 2008) by reason of severe storms and tornados beginning on May 4, 2007, and determined by the President to warrant individual or individual and public assistance from the Federal Government under such Act with respect to damages attributable to such storms and tornados (Act § 15345 of the Heartland, Habitat, Harvest and Horticulture Act of 2008, P.L. 110-246). The Kansas disaster area is comprised of the following counties: Barton, Clay, Cloud, Comanche, Dickinson, Edwards, Ellsworth, Kiowa, Leavenworth, Lyon, McPherson, Osage, Osborne, Ottawa, Phillips, Pottawatomie, Pratt, Reno, Rice, Riley, Saline, Shawnee, Smith, and Stafford. (Notice 2008-67, I.R.B. 2008-32).

Note that property may be acquired before it is considered placed in service. For example, a machine may be acquired before it is completely assembled and integrated into a manufacturing process for use in its assigned function (i.e., placed in service). See ¶ 3.

Taking into account these increases, the maximum dollar amounts for qualifying section 179 Recovery Assistance property acquired on or after May 5, 2007 are:

- $208,000 ($108,000 + $100,000) for property placed in service in tax years beginning in 2006.

- $225,000 ($125,000 + $100,000) for property placed in service in tax years beginning in 2007.
- $350,000 ($250,000 + $100,000) for property placed in service before January 1, 2009 in tax years beginning in 2008.

The dollar amount begins to be reduced by reason of the investment limitation (if at least $600,000 of qualifying Recovery Assistance property is placed in service) at:

- $1,030,000 ($430,000 + $600,000) for tax years beginning in 2006
- $1,100,000 ($500,000 + $600,000) for property placed in service in tax years beginning in 2007
- $1,400,000 ($800,000 + $600,000) for property placed in service before January 1, 2009 in tax years beginning in 2008

The dollar amount is completely phased out by reason of the investment limitation (assuming at least $100,000 of Recovery Assistance property is placed in service during the tax year) at:

- $1,238,000 ($208,000 – ($1,238,000 – ($430,000 + $600,000)) = $0) for tax years beginning in 2006
- $1,325,000 ($225,000 – ($1,325,000 – ($500,000 + $600,000)) = $0) for property placed in service in tax years beginning in 2007
- $1,750,000 ($350,000 – ($1,750,000 – ($800,000 + $600,000)) = $0) for property placed in service before January 1, 2009 in tax years beginning in 2008

Example (1): In 2007, a calendar-year taxpayer places $200,000 of qualified section 179 Recovery Assistance property in service after May 5, 2007 and $550,000 of other qualifying section 179 property in service during 2007. The dollar limitation is $225,000 ($125,000 for 2007 + $100,000). The investment limitation is $700,000 ($500,000 basic limit + $200,000 amount of qualified section 179 Recovery Assistance property placed in service since this is less than $600,000). Because the total amount of section 179 property placed in service ($750,000) exceeds the investment limit by $50,000 ($750,000 - $700,000), the dollar limit is reduced to $175,000 ($225,000 - $50,000) and this amount is claimed as the deduction under Code Sec. 179 subject to the taxable income limitation. The 50% bonus depreciation is $12,500 (($200,000 - $175,000) × 50%) (see ¶ 125G).

Example (2): XYZ corporation, a calendar-year taxpayer, places $1,500,000 of new machinery in service in 2008. The machinery is qualified section 179 Recovery Assistance property. XYZ places no other section 179 property in service in 2008. Under the dollar limitation, only $350,000 ($250,000 basic limit for 2008 + $100,000 bump-up for section 179 Recovery Assistance property) of the total $1,500,000 of machinery placed in service may be expensed. The investment limit is $1,400,000 ($800,000 basic limit for 2008 + $600,000). The dollar limit must be reduced by $100,000 ($1,500,000 cost of section 179 property placed in service - $1,400,000 investment limit). Thus, XYZ's section 179 deduction for 2008 is $250,000 ($350,000 dollar limit - $100,000), assuming that XYZ's taxable income is at least $250,000. XYZ's 50-percent additional depreciation allowance is $625,000 ($1,500,000 - $250,000) × 50%).

Property must be both section 179 property and qualified Recovery Assistance property

For the increased limits to apply, the property must be both section 179 property and qualified Recovery Assistance property. If the property is not section 179 property, then no amount may be expensed under Code Sec. 179. To qualify as section 179 property, the property must be new or used tangible section 1245 property that is depreciable under MACRS (subject to an exception for off-the-shelf computer software) and used predominantly (more than 50 percent) in the active conduct of a trade or business. In addition, the property must be acquired by "purchase" from an unrelated person (Code Sec. 179(d)(2)). See ¶ 302 for a discussion of the definition of qualifying section 179 property.

Certain qualified Recovery Assistance property, most notably, residential rental and nonresidential real property will not qualify for any expensing under Code Sec. 179 because section 1250 property is not section 179 property. Most used property will not qualify for the increase in the dollar amount because such property cannot be qualified Recovery Assistance property unless the original use in the zone commences with the taxpayer. Used property, however, may constitute section 179 property and qualify for the basic allowance.

Qualifying Recovery Assistance property

Property that otherwise qualifies for expensing under Code Sec. 179 (i.e., section 179 property as defined in Code Sec. 179(d); see ¶ 302) will qualify for the increased section 179 limitations if it is Recovery Assistance Property as defined for purposes of the 50-percent additional depreciation allowance for Recovery Assistance Property (see ¶ 127G). In general, property is Recovery Assistance property if:

- It is depreciable under MACRS and has a recovery period of 20 years or less
- Substantially all (80 percent or greater) of the property is used in the active conduct of a trade or business by the taxpayer within the Kansas disaster area
- The original use of the property commences with the taxpayer in the Kansas disaster area on or after May 5, 2007, and the property is placed in service before January 1, 2009
- It acquired by purchase (within the meaning of Code Sec. 179(d)(2); see ¶ 302) on or after May 5, 2007
- No written binding contract for the acquisition of the property was in effect before May 5, 2007

If the first use of used property within the Kansas disaster area commences with the taxpayer, then the used property may qualify for the increased allowance. If the section 179 property was previously used by another taxpayer within the disaster area, it will only remain eligible for the standard section 179 allowance ($125,000 in 2007 and $250,000 in 2008).

Recovery Assistance property does not include property that must be depreciated using the MACRS alternative depreciation system (ADS) (see ¶ 152) (including listed property (¶ 208), such as a vehicle, used less than 50 percent for business purposes) or property financed to any extent with state and local tax-exempt bonds that generate tax-exempt interest under Code Sec. 103 (Code Sec. 1400N(d)(2)(B)). Property which a taxpayer elects to depreciate under ADS may qualify.

It appears that property used in connection with: a private or commercial golf course, a country club, a massage parlor, a hot tub facility, a suntan facility, a liquor store, or a gambling or animal racing property may qualify as Recovery Assistance property; see ¶ 127G).

Recapture if business use declines 80 percent or less

Rules similar to the rules Code Sec. 179(d)(10) apply with respect to any qualified section 179 Recovery Assistance property which ceases to be qualified section 179 Recovery Assistance Property (Act Sec. 15345(d)(2) of the Heartland, Habitat, Harvest, and Horticulture Act of 2008 (P.L. 110-246), applying Code Sec. 1400N(e)(4)). Thus, recapture of the $100,000 additional section 179 expense allowance is required if the property ceases to be substantially used in the Kansas disaster area (i.e., business use in the disaster area is not 80 percent or greater or the property is removed from the disaster area) since this would cause the property to lose its status as Recovery Assistance property. Both the standard section 179 deduction ($125,000 in 2007 and $250,000 in 2008) and additional section 179 deduction for recovery assistance property would be subject to recapture under the generally applicable rule if business use, whether inside or outside the Kansas disaster area , dropped to 50 percent or less during the tax year. The recapture rules of Code Sec. 179(d)(10) are described at ¶ 300.

Recapture upon disposition

The Code Sec. 179 expense allowance (including the increase for qualifying Recovery Assistance property) is treated as a depreciation deduction for section 1245 recapture purposes upon the disposition of the property. See ¶ 300.

Coordination with increased expense allowance for empowerment zones and renewal communities

If qualifying section 179 Recovery Assistance property is placed in service within an empowerment zone or renewal community located within the Kansas Disaster Area, a taxpayer may not also claim the benefit of the additional $35,000 expense allowance provided for qualifying property placed in service in an empowerment zone (Code Sec. 1397A) or a renewal community (Code Sec. 1400J) (see ¶ 300) unless the taxpayer elects not to claim the additional $100,000 allowance provided for section 179 Recovery Assistance property (Act Sec. 15345(d)(2) of the Heartland, Habitat, Harvest, and Horticulture Act of 2008 (P.L. 110-246), applying Code Sec. 1400N(e)(3)).

Generally, it will be preferable to take advantage of the $100,000 bump-up provided for qualified section 179 Recovery Assistance property since the additional allowance for empowerment zone and renewal community property is only $35,000 (e.g., $285,000 total in 2008 ($250,000 + $35,000)) as compared to $350,000 for Recovery Assistance property (e.g., $375,000 total in 2008 ($250,000 + $100,000)).

¶ 306B

Disaster Assistance Property

The Code Sec. 179 expense dollar limitation and investment limitation (¶ 300) are increased for section 179 property (i.e., eligible property as defined at ¶ 302) that is "disaster assistance property" placed in service after December 31, 2007, with respect to disasters declared after December 31, 2007 and occurring before January 1, 2010 (Code Sec. 179(e), as added by the Emergency Economic Stabilization Act of 2008 (P.L. 110-343)).

- The Code Sec. 179 expense deduction ($250,000 for tax years beginning in 2008 and 2009) is increased by the lesser of $100,000 or the cost of qualified section 179 disaster assistance property placed in service during the tax year (Code Sec. 179(e)(1)(A), as added by P.L. 110-343).

- The amount of the investment limitation ($800,000 for tax years beginning in 2008 and 2009) is increased by the lesser of $600,000 or the cost of qualified section 179 disaster assistance property placed in service during the tax year (Code Sec. 179(e)(1)(B), as added by P.L. 110-343).

These increases mean that for qualified Section 179 disaster assistance property placed in service during 2008 or 2009, the maximum allowable Code Sec. 179 expense deduction is $350,000, and the investment limitation is $1,400,000.

Eligible property

Qualified Section 179 disaster assistance property is Section 179 property (as defined at ¶ 302) that is qualified disaster assistance property (Code Sec. 179(e)(2), as added by P.L. 110-343).

Qualified disaster assistance property defined

Qualified disaster assistance property must meet all of the following tests:

- The property must be described in Code Sec. 168(k)(2)(A)(i) (i.e., MACRS recovery property with an recovery period of 20 years or less, computer software that is depreciable over three years, water utility property, or qualified leasehold improvement property) or be nonresidential real property or residential rental property (note: Code Sec. 179 applies to section 1245 property and does not apply to section 1250 (i.e. real) property).

- Substantially all (80 percent or more) of the use of the property must be in a disaster area with respect to a federally declared disaster occurring before January 1, 2010, and in the active conduct of the taxpayer's trade or business in that disaster area.

- The property must rehabilitate property damaged, or replace property destroyed or condemned, as a result of the disaster. Property is treated as replacing property destroyed or condemned if, as part of an integrated plan, it replaces property that is included in a continuous area that includes real property destroyed or condemned. The property must also be similar in nature to, and located in the same county as, the property being rehabilitated or replaced.

- The original use of the property in the disaster area must commence with an eligible taxpayer on or after the applicable disaster date.

- The property must be acquired by the eligible taxpayer by purchase on or after the applicable disaster date, but only if no written binding contract for the acquisition was in effect before that date. A purchase is defined by reference to the definition in Code Sec. 179(d); therefore, it cannot be a transaction between related parties or members of the same controlled group, and the transferee's basis in the property cannot be determined by reference to the transferor's basis.

- The property must be placed in service by the eligible taxpayer on or before the date that is the last day of the third calendar year following the applicable disaster date (or the fourth calendar year in the case of nonresidential real property and residential rental property) (Code Sec. 168(n)(2)(A), as added by the Emergency Economic Act of 2008).

Qualified disaster assistance property does not include (Code Sec. 168(n)(2)(B), as added by P.L. 110-343):

- any property that is eligible for bonus depreciation under Code Sec. 168(k) (without regard to any election under Code Sec. 168(k)(4) to forgo bonus depreciation in favor of an accelerated research or AMT credit), cellulosic biomass ethanol plant property (Code Sec. 168(l)), and qualified refuse and recycling property (Code Sec. 168(m));

- property that qualifies for bonus depreciation under the special rules for the Gulf Opportunity (GO) Zone (Code Sec. 1400N(d));

• any property used in connection with any private or commercial golf course, country club, massage parlor, hot tub facility, or suntan facility; any store whose principal business is the sale of alcoholic beverages for consumption off premises; or any gambling or animal racing property (i.e., property described in Code Sec. 1400N(p)(3));

• property that must be depreciated under the MACRS alternative depreciation system (ADS) (not including property for which an ADS election is made);

• property financed by tax-exempt bonds;

• qualified revitalization buildings for which the taxpayer has elected the Code Sec. 1400I commercial revitalization deduction; and

Federally declared disaster

The term federally declared disaster means any disaster subsequently determined by the President of the United States to warrant assistance by the Federal Government under the Robert T. Stafford Disaster Relief and Emergency Assistance Act. The term disaster area means the area so determined to warrant such assistance (Code Sec. 165(h)(3)(C))).

Recapture

If any qualified Section 179 disaster assistance property ceases to be qualified Section 179 disaster assistance property, then recapture of the tax benefit received is required under the section Code Sec. 179(d)(10) recapture rules described at ¶ 300 (Code Sec. 179(e)(4), as added by P.L. 110-343; see Code Sec. 179(d)(10)). Thus, in the year that property ceases to be qualified Section 179 disaster assistance property, the taxpayer must generally include in income the amount of tax benefit derived from the additional amount of the Code Sec. 179 deduction claimed in the year that the property was placed in service. In general, property will lose its status as disaster assistance property if it is removed from the disaster zone or it is not used 80 percent or more for business purposes within the zone. Both the standard section 179 deduction ($250,000 for 2008 and 2009) and additional section 179 allowance for disaster assistance property are recaptured in a tax year that business use (whether inside or outside of the disaster zone) drops to 50 percent or less. See ¶ 300.

Limitations

Qualified Section 179 disaster assistance property cannot be treated as qualified zone property for purposes of the empowerment zone rules in Code Sec. 1397A, or as qualified renewal property for purposes of the renewal community rules in Code Sec. 1400J, unless the taxpayer elects not to take qualified section 179 disaster assistance property into account for purposes of the increased expensing amount and investment limitation (Code Sec. 179(e)(3), as added by P.L. 110-343).

¶ 307

De Minimis Expensing Rule for Immaterial Purchases

Strictly speaking, other than Code Sec. 179, there is no authority for immediately expensing or writing off the cost of assets which meet the criteria for depreciation. For example, in a Chief Counsel Advice (IRS Letter Ruling 199952010, September 29, 1999), the IRS rejected a taxpayer's request to change its method of accounting for assets such as machinery, equipment, furniture, and fixtures. The taxpayer's present method of accounting was not to capitalize and depreciate such assets if an asset was valued at $1,000 or less. The taxpayer requested to increase the minimum threshold amount to $2,000. The request was denied and the taxpayer informed that its present method of accounting was unacceptable. Said the IRS: "All property used in a trade or business (except land and inventory) that has a useful life of more than one year must be capitalized and depreciated. Taxpayers are not permitted to treat such items as current expenses simply because the particular item has a certain minimum value or less."

Nevertheless, the IRS recognizes and approves a practice by its auditors that allows taxpayers to write-off the cost of low-cost depreciable assets on the basis of relative immateriality. Certain court cases, discussed below, also lend support to taxpayers who expense immaterial amounts.

This unofficial de minimis rule applied by IRS auditors was described in the preamble to proposed regulations issued under Code Sec. 263. The relevant portion of the preamble is quoted in italics below (NPRM REG-168745-03, published in the Federal Register on August 21, 2006). These proposed regulations did not include a de minimis rule. The August 2006 proposals were withdrawn and reissued (NPRM REG-168745-03, published in the Federal Register on March 10, 2008). The reissued proposed regulations now include a proposed de minimis rule (Proposed Reg.§ 1.263(a)-2(d)(4)) which is described below. The proposed de minimis rule now included in the proposed regulations may not be relied upon until the regulations are finalized.

Even if a de minimis rule does not apply in a taxpayer's particular situation, it may be possible to alleviate some of the record-keeping difficulties by setting up MACRS general asset accounts. However, each account may contain only assets that are placed in service in the same tax year and have the same asset class, recovery period, and depreciation method and convention. See ¶ 128.

Current De minimis rule as described in August 2006 preamble of withdrawn proposed regulations

"In Notice 2004-6, the IRS and Treasury Department requested comments on whether the regulations should provide a de minimis rule. Because the notice refers to the application of section 263(a) to amounts paid to repair, improve, or rehabilitate tangible property, most commentators focused on a de minimis rule for the cost of repairs rather than the cost to acquire property. However, one commentator requested that the regulations specifically provide a de minimis rule for acquisition costs, but allow taxpayers to continue to use their current method if they have reached a working agreement with their IRS examining agent regarding a de minimis rule.

The IRS and Treasury Department recognize that for regulatory or financial accounting purposes, taxpayers often have a policy for deducting an amount paid below a certain dollar threshold for the acquisition of tangible property (de minimis rule). For Federal income tax purposes, the taxpayer generally would be required to capitalize the amount paid if the property has a useful life substantially beyond the taxable year. However, in this context some courts have permitted the use of a de minimis rule for Federal income tax purposes. See Union Pacific R.R. Co. v. United States, 524 F.2d 1343 (Ct. Cl. 1975) (permitting the use of the taxpayer's $500 de minimis rule, which was in accordance with the Interstate Commerce Commission (ICC) minimum rule and generally accepted accounting principles); Cincinnati, N.O. & Tex. Pac. Ry. v. United States, 424 F.2d 563 (Ct. Cl. 1970) (same). But see Alacare Home Health Services, Inc. v. Commissioner, T.C. Memo 2001-149 (disallowing the taxpayer's use of a $500 de minimis rule because it distorted income).

The proposed regulations do not include a de minimis rule for acquisition costs. However, the IRS and Treasury Department recognize that taxpayers often reach an agreement with IRS examining agents that, as an administrative matter, based on risk analysis and/or materiality, the IRS examining agents do not select certain items for review such as the acquisition of tangible assets with a small cost. This often is referred to by taxpayers and IRS examining agents as a de minimis rule. The absence of a de minimis rule in the proposed regulations is not intended to change this practice.

The IRS and Treasury Department considered including a de minimis rule in the proposed regulations. The de minimis rule considered would have provided that taxpayers are not required to capitalize certain de minimis amounts paid for the acquisition or production of a unit of property. Under the rule considered, if a taxpayer had written accounting procedures in place treating as an expense on its applicable financial statement (AFS) amounts paid for property costing less than a certain dollar amount, and treated the amounts paid during the taxable year as an expense on its AFS in accordance with those written accounting procedures, the taxpayer would not have been required to capitalize those amounts if they did not exceed a certain dollar threshold. A taxpayer that did not meet these criteria (for example, a taxpayer that did not have an AFS) would not have been required to capitalize amounts paid for a unit of property that did not exceed the established dollar threshold. Because taxpayers without an AFS generally are smaller than taxpayers with an AFS, the dollar threshold for the de minimis rule that would have applied to them would have been lower than the threshold for taxpayers with an AFS (although the de minimis rule for taxpayers with an AFS also would have been limited to the amount treated as an expense on their AFS). The de minimis rule considered by the IRS and Treasury Department would not have applied to inventory property, improvements, land, or a component of a unit of property.

The de minimis rule considered also would have provided that property to which a taxpayer applies the de minimis rule is treated upon sale or disposition similar to section 179 property. Thus, de minimis property would have been property of a character subject to depreciation and amounts paid that were not capitalized under the de minimis rule would have been treated as amortization subject to recapture under section 1245. Thus, gain on disposition of the property would have been ordinary income to the taxpayer to the extent of the amount treated as amortization for purposes of section 1245.

The IRS and Treasury Department decided to not include a de minimis rule in the proposed regulations but instead to request comments on whether such a rule should be included in the final regulations or whether to continue to rely on the current administrative practice of IRS examining agents. Therefore, the IRS and Treasury Department request comments on whether a de minimis rule for acquisition costs should be included in the final regulations, and, if so, whether the de minimis rule should be the rule described above and what dollar thresholds are appropriate.

The IRS and Treasury Department also request comments on the scope of costs that should be included in a de minimis rule if one is provided in the final regulations and on the character of de minimis rule property. For example, the de minimis rule considered by the IRS and Treasury Department would have applied to the aggregate of amounts paid for the acquisition or production (including any amounts paid to facilitate the acquisition or production) of a unit of property and including amounts paid for improvements prior to the unit of property being placed in service. If a de minimis rule should be provided in the final regulations, the IRS and Treasury Department request comments on what, if any, type of rule should be provided to prevent a distortion of income when taxpayers acquire a large number of assets, each of which individually is within the de minimis rule (for example, the purchase by a taxpayer of 2,000 personal computers).

If a de minimis rule for acquisition costs should be provided in the final regulations, the IRS and Treasury Department request comments on whether the rule should permit IRS examining agents and taxpayers to agree to the use of higher de minimis thresholds on the basis of materiality and risk analysis and, if so, under what circumstances a higher threshold should be allowed. The IRS and Treasury Department also request comments on whether, if a de minimis rule should be provided in the final regulations, changes to begin using a de minimis rule or changes to a higher dollar amount within a de minimis rule should be treated as changes in a method of accounting."

De minimis rule as proposed in revised proposed regulations

Proposed Reg.§ 1.263(a)-2(d)(4), which will only be effective upon issuance as a final regulation, provides that a taxpayer does not capitalize amounts paid for the acquisition or production of property if:

(1) the taxpayer has an applicable financial statement;

(2) the taxpayer has at the beginning of the tax year, written accounting procedures that expenses for non-tax purposes amounts paid for property that costs less than a certain dollar amount;

(3) the amounts are treated as expenses on the applicable financial statement; and

(4) the amounts expensed do not distort taxable income for the year.

The de minimis rule does not apply to amount paid to improve property, amounts paid for property that is or is intended to be included in property produced or acquired for resale, or amounts paid for land.

A taxpayer may elect not to apply the de minimis rule with respect to some or all of the property that it could otherwise expense under this provision. This election may be made, for example, with respect to some property in order to prevent the expensing of the remainder of the property from distorting taxable income or in order to ensure qualification under the safe harbor described below. In general, this election to capitalize is made separately for each asset by treating the amount paid as a capital expenditure on the tax return.

The cost of property to which a taxpayer properly applies the de minimis rule is not required to be capitalized under Code Sec. 263A as a separate unit of property, but may be required to be capitalized as a cost incurred by reason of the production of other property.

Under this safe harbor, the amount expensed will not be treated as distorting taxable income if the sum of the amount expensed plus any amount deducted as materials and supplies for units of property costing $100 or less under Proposed Reg.§ 1.162-3(d)(1)(iii) is no greater than the lesser of (a) 0.1 percent of the taxpayer's gross receipts for the tax year or (b) 2 percent of the of the taxpayers total depreciation and amortization expense for the tax year as determined in its applicable financial statement.

An applicable financial statement is defined as:

(1) A financial statement required to be filed with the SEC (viz., a 10K or Annual Statement to Shareholders);

(2) A certified audited financial statement that is accompanied by the report of an independent CPA and which is used for specified purposes; or

(3) A financial statement (but not a tax return) required to be provided to the Federal or state government or any agency thereof other than the SEC or IRS.

Gain on the sale or disposition of property accounted for under the de minimis rule is not treated as gain resulting from the sale or disposition of a capital asset under Code Sec. 1221 or as property used in the trade or business under Code Sec. 1231.

Taxpayers are required to keep books and records sufficient to establish their eligibility to use the de minimis rule.

The proposed regulations include examples of the de minimis expensing rule.

Courts' position on de minimis expensing

Courts that have considered the issue have rejected the hard-line IRS position taken in Chief Counsel Advice (IRS Letter Ruling 199952010, September 29, 1999 (discussed above), instead relying on a clear-reflection of income standard set forth in Code Sec. 446(a) and (b). In general, the amount expensed is compared to other significant income and balance sheet figures to determine whether an expensing policy distorts or does not clearly reflect income.

In *Alacare Home Health Services Inc.*, 81 TCM 1794, TC Memo 2001-149, CCH Dec. 54,378(M), a Medicare-certified home health care agency capitalized office and computer items costing less than $500. This treatment was permitted for non-tax purposes under the accounting guidelines contained in the Medicare Provider Reimbursement Manual (HCFA Publication 15-1) issued by the Federal Health Care Financing Administration (HCFA). The court, however, concluded that the taxpayer's treatment did not clearly reflect income for tax purposes. In making this determination, the court compared the ratios of the expensed items to various other balance sheet and income tax figures. In the two tax years at issue, the expensed items amounted to 165 percent and 83.5 percent of taxable income; 288 percent and 189 percent of its total depreciation deductions; .85 percent and .71 percent of its gross receipts; and .84 percent and 1.12 percent of total operating expenses.

The taxpayer in *Alacare* relied upon *Cincinnati, New Orleans & Tex. Pac. Ry. Co.*, CtCls, 70-1 USTC ¶ 9344, 424 F2d 563. In the *Cincinnati* case (which involved three tax years), the railroad followed the Interstate Commerce Commission's prescribed financial accounting convention which required the current deduction of equipment costing less than $500 (the "minimum rule"). The expensed items were less than one percent of the taxpayer's net income each year; less than two percent of total depreciation claimed year; .04 percent, .03 percent, and .07 percent of gross receipts; and .06 percent, .04 percent, and .01 percent of total operating expenses. These ratios were substantially lower than those in *Alacare*.

The *Alacare* court noted several additional factors that favored the taxpayer in the *Cincinnati* case. The taxpayer in *Cincinnati* presented 17 years of data (only two years were presented in *Alacare*) for the court's consideration and presented evidence that the Interstate Commerce Commission adopted an expensing policy only after specifically concluding that it would not cause a railroad's financial statement to not clearly reflect income. The taxpayer in *Cincinnati* also presented evidence that its expensing method complied with generally accepted accounting principles (GAAP). The *Alacare* taxpayer presented no evidence on these points.

The court also placed significance on the fact that the ICC required railroads to comply with its expensing policy for regulatory accounting purposes. The HCFA's expensing policy was not mandatory. In this regard the court cited *Idaho Power Co.*, SCt, 74-2 USTC ¶ 9521, 418 US 1 (where a taxpayer's generally accepted method of accounting is made compulsory by a regulatory agency and that method clearly reflects income, it is almost presumptively controlling for Federal tax purposes (depreciation on equipment used by a utility to build capital improvements had to be capitalized)).

Five years following its decision in the *Cincinnati* case, the Court of Claims allowed another railroad to expense items under $500 pursuant to the same ICC accounting standards at issue in the *Cincinnati* decision (*Union Pacific Railroad Co., Inc.*, CtCls, 75-2 USTC ¶ 9800, rehearing denied 76-1 USTC ¶ 9308, 524 F2d 1343, cert. denied 429 US 827). The ratio of expensed items to total investment account was .026 percent (compared to .014 percent for *Cincinnati*) and the ratio of expensed items to total operating expense was .052 percent (.059 percent for *Cincinnati*).

In *R.G. Galazin*, 38 TCM 851, TC Memo. 1979-206, CCH Dec. 36,094(M), the Tax Court allowed a salesman to claim a current deduction for a calculator costing $52.45 and with an agreed upon useful life of two years. The court noted that the *Cincinnati* case did not sanction a blanket rule for the expensing of low-cost items but rather applied in situations involving a large number of expensed items that are relatively inexpensive. Nevertheless, the court, allowed the deduction of the calculator on the basis of Reg. § 1.162-6 (adopted by T.D. 6291, 4-3-58) which provides that "Amounts currently paid or accrued for books, furniture, and professional instruments and equipment, the useful life of which is short, may be deducted." An interesting contrast to the puzzling *Galazin* decision, is the Tax Court's decision in *G.O. Klutz* (38 TCM 724, TC Memo. 1979-169, CCH Dec. 36,043(M)) in which a used adding machine costing $75 was required to be depreciated over five years.

Corporate Earnings and Profits

Effect of Depreciation

¶ 310

Straight-Line Method Required

The straight-line method is required for computing corporate earnings and profits. This prevents rapid cost recovery from converting what would otherwise be taxable dividends (payable only out of earnings and profits) into nontaxable distributions or capital gain.

MACRS property

The MACRS alternative (straight-line) depreciation system (ADS) (¶ 150) must be used to depreciate MACRS property for purposes of computing corporate earnings and profits (Code Sec. 312(k)(3) and (4)).

Bonus depreciation

Bonus depreciation is not allowed in computing earnings and profits (Reg.§ 1.168(k)-1(f)(7)). See below for treatment of the Code Sec. 179 expense deduction.

ACRS recovery property

A corporation's depreciation on ACRS recovery property is computed using the straight-line method over the earnings and profits recovery period. In the case of personal recovery property, a half-year convention applies. In the case of real property, the full-month or mid-month convention applies depending upon whether the property is 15-year, 18-year, or 19-year real property. Salvage value is disregarded in making the earnings and profits straight-line depreciation computation.

The following recovery periods are prescribed for making the straight-line depreciation computation unless a longer period was elected under the ACRS optional straight-line method for regular tax purposes:

In the case of:	*E & P recovery period:*
3-year recovery property	5 years
5-year recovery property	12 years
10-year recovery property	25 years
15-year real property	35 years
18-year real property	35 or 40 years
19-year real property	40 years
15-year public utility property	35 years

A 35-year earnings and profits recovery period applies to 18-year real property placed in service after March 15, 1984, in a tax year beginning before October 1, 1984 (Act Secs. 61(b) and 111(e)(5) of P.L. 98-369 (Tax Reform Act of 1984)).

The earnings and profits recovery period for low-income housing (recovery property) placed in service in tax years beginning after September 30, 1984 is 40 years. A 35-year recovery period applies to low-income housing placed in service after March 15, 1984 in a tax year beginning before October 1, 1984.

If a corporation elects to depreciate an item of recovery property for regular tax purposes using the ACRS optional straight-line method (¶ 254) or elects one of the optional recovery periods prescribed for property used predominantly outside of the U.S. (¶ 252) and the elected recovery period is longer than the recovery period that would otherwise apply for earnings and profits purposes, earnings and profits are computed using the longer optional recovery period (Code Sec. 312(k)(3)(C) (before repeal by the Tax Reform Act of 1986 (P.L. 99-514))).

No ACRS depreciation is claimed on personal recovery property for earnings and profits purposes in the year the property is disposed of. The full-month or mid-month convention is used to determine the allowable deduction for ACRS real property (including low-income housing) in the year of disposition.

The table below shows the applicable percentages (ACRS straight-line method over the earnings and profits life recovery period using a half-year convention) for Code Sec. 280F listed property that is ACRS recovery property (other than 18- or 19-year real property) where business use does not exceed 50 percent (Reg. § 1.280F-3T(e)).

If the recovery year is:	*And the recovery period is (in yrs.):*			
	5	12	25	35
1	10 %	4 %	2 %	1%
2-5	20	9	4	3
6	10	8	4	3
7-12		8	4	3
13		4	4	3
14-25			4	3
26			2	3
27-31				3
32-35				2
36				1

The table below shows the applicable percentages (ACRS straight-line method over a 40-year earnings and profits life recovery period using a mid-month convention) for Code Sec. 280F listed property that is ACRS 18- or 19-year recovery real property where business use does not exceed 50 percent.

	Month Placed in Service											
Year	*1*	*2*	*3*	*4*	*5*	*6*	*7*	*8*	*9*	*10*	*11*	*12*
1st	2.4%	2.2%	2.0%	1.8%	1.6%	1.4%	1.1%	0.9%	0.7%	0.5%	0.3%	0.1%
2-40th	2.5%	2.5%	2.5%	2.5%	2.5%	2.5%	2.5%	2.5%	2.5%	2.5%	2.5%	2.5%
41st	0.1%	0.3%	0.5%	0.7%	0.9%	1.1%	1.4%	1.6%	1.8%	2.0%	2.2%	2.4%

Sec. 179 expense allowance

In figuring earnings and profits, any amount deducted under Code Sec. 179 in computing taxable income is considered deducted ratably over a five-year period beginning with the tax year that the cost is expensed (Code Sec. 312(k)(3)(B)). The amount deducted under Code Sec. 179 for taxable income purposes reduces the basis of the asset for purposes of computing the depreciation allowable under ACRS or MACRS for earnings and profits purposes.

Assets placed in service before 1981

The straight-line method is used to compute depreciation or amortization on an asset placed in service by a corporation before 1981 in a tax year beginning after June 30, 1972 (Code Sec. 312(k)(1)). The straight-line method also applies to an asset placed in service after 1980 but which is not depreciable under ACRS or MACRS.

If an ADR election was made, straight-line depreciation is computed in accordance with ADR Reg. § 1.167(a)-11(g)(3). The provisions of Reg. § 1.167(b)-1 control the manner of computing straight-line depreciation on property not depreciable under ADR.

Any election to reduce salvage value or any convention adopted under ADR or the general pre-1981 rules with respect to additions or retirements from multiple-asset accounts for purposes of computing taxable income apply in computing straight-line earnings and profits depreciation.

Method not based on a term of years

A corporation that uses a method not based on a term of years (for example, the unit-of-production method) to compute depreciation for income tax purposes must also use that method for earnings and profits purposes (Code Sec. 312(k)(2); Reg. § 1.167-1(b)).

ITC basis adjustment

The depreciation allowance computed for earnings and profits purposes is determined without regard to any investment tax credit basis reduction required under Code Sec. 50(c) (formerly Code Sec. 48(q)) to the depreciated property (Code Sec. 312(k)(5)).

Roundup of Selected Rules for Pre-1981 Property

Elements Needed to Compute Depreciation

¶ 330

Basis, Salvage Value, Useful Life

Under the rules that apply to property placed in service before 1981 (and post-1980 assets that do not qualify for ACRS or MACRS), three items are essential for computing depreciation. These are the basis of the asset for depreciation purposes, the estimated salvage value at the end of the useful life of the asset, and the estimated useful life of the asset. The basis reduced by salvage value is the amount to be depreciated. The useful life determines the period over which the asset is depreciated.

¶ 332

Basis for Depreciation

The basis for depreciation is the same as the adjusted basis for determining gain on the sale or other disposition of the asset (see ¶ 70).

¶ 336

Salvage Value

Salvage value is the amount a taxpayer expected to receive in cash or trade-in allowance upon disposition of an asset at the end of its useful life. This could be a large amount for property customarily disposed of while still in good operating condition. Or it could be junk value if the asset is used until it is worn out.

Under the straight-line and sum of the years-digits methods, salvage value is subtracted from the depreciation basis before applying the depreciation rate. See ¶ 346 and ¶ 352. This is not so under the declining-balance method (¶ 348). In any event, no asset may be depreciated below its salvage value.

Net salvage is salvage value minus the cost of removal and disposition. Either salvage or net salvage could have been used in figuring depreciation allowances, but the practice had to be consistent and the treatment of the costs of removal had to be consistent with the practice adopted.

¶ 338

Election of Salvage Reduction Increases Depreciation

The salvage value of personal property (other than livestock) with a useful life of at least three years may, at the taxpayer's election, be reduced by an amount not exceeding 10 percent of the original depreciation basis (Code Sec. 167(f) before repeal by the Omnibus Budget Reconciliation Act of 1990 (P.L. 101-508)). This is 10 percent of the basis, which, for pre-1981 property, was before reduction for additional first-year depreciation.

As already noted at ¶ 336, no asset may be depreciated below its salvage value. This election to reduce salvage also applies for this purpose. Thus, the election increased the total depreciation that can be deducted. If the salvage value of an asset costing $10,000 is $800, salvage value can be completely ignored if the election was made. Depreciation deductions totaling $10,000 can be claimed (including additional first-year depreciation). Without the election, the maximum depreciation that could be claimed would be $9,200 ($10,000 – $800 salvage value).

If a change is made from the declining-balance method (in which salvage is not taken into account) to the straight-line method (in which salvage is taken into account), the election to reduce salvage may be made in the changeover year. If the estimated useful life (see ¶ 340) is redetermined, the salvage value may also be redetermined at the same time.

Of course, the reduction in salvage value reduces the basis at the end of useful life and increases the gain (or decreases the loss) upon disposition of the asset.

If a taxpayer elected ADR or CLS depreciation of equipment, salvage value is not considered in the computation of depreciation since the ADR and CLS rates were set up by taking salvage value into account. Also, salvage value for ADR purposes is gross salvage, not net salvage (¶ 446).

¶ 340

Estimated Useful Life

The rate of depreciation depends upon the estimated useful life of the property. This is the period over which the asset may reasonably be expected to be useful *in the taxpayer's trade or business* or in the production of income. It is not necessarily its expected physical life.

Here are some factors affecting useful life:

(1) wear, tear, decay or decline from natural causes;

(2) the normal progress of the art, economic changes, inventions, and current developments within the industry and the taxpayer's trade or business;

(3) the effect of climate and other local conditions peculiar to the taxpayer's trade or business; and

(4) the taxpayer's policy as to repairs, renewals, and replacements.

If a taxpayer's experience was inadequate for determining useful life, it was permissible to use the general experience in the industry.

Methods of Computing Depreciation

¶ 344

Consistent Method Required

Any reasonable method of computing depreciation was permissible, so long as that method was used consistently. This means only that the method has to be consistent for the specific item (or items in a group account) being depreciated. It does not mean that the same method has to be used for all assets. Nor does a method chosen for depreciation of property in one year have to be adopted for similar property acquired in a later year.

Generally, the depreciation method for an asset may not be changed without the Commissioner's consent. However, a change from an acceptable declining-balance method to the straight-line method may be made without his consent (Reg. § 1.167(e)-1(b)). Also, a number of other depreciation method changes will be automatically permitted if the change meets the conditions in Rev. Proc. 2002-9 (Appendix Section 2.02). See ¶ 75.

There are three primary methods: straight-line, declining-balance, and sum of the years-digits.

¶ 346

Straight-Line Method

The depreciation deduction under this method is calculated by reducing the basis by the salvage value and either dividing the remainder by the useful life or multiplying it by the straight-line rate.

> ***Example:*** An asset costing $10,000 had a 20-year useful life with an expected $500 salvage value at the end of that period. If the taxpayer elected to reduce salvage by up to 10% of cost, annual depreciation allowances would be $500 ($10,000 ÷ 20). The deduction could also have been figured by multiplying the $10,000 by the 5% straight-line rate (1 ÷ 20).
>
> If there was no election to ignore salvage, annual deductions would be $475—5% of $9,500 ($10,000 cost less $500 salvage value).

¶ 348

Declining-Balance Method

The deduction under this method is determined by reducing the basis by any previously deducted depreciation and multiplying the balance by the declining-balance rate.

New tangible assets acquired after 1953 (and placed in service before 1981) qualified for rates up to twice the straight-line rates (double declining-balance method). Rates not in excess of one and one-half the straight-line rates (150-percent declining-balance method) were permissible for used assets acquired after 1953 and for new and used assets acquired before 1954. Special limitations applied in the case of real estate depreciation.

An asset was treated as new if its original use began with the taxpayer. An asset's original use was the first use to which it was put, whether or not that use corresponded to the use to which the taxpayer put it (Reg. § 1.167(c)-1(a)(2)).

> ***Example:*** New farm machinery with a 10-year useful life was bought for $100,000. Under the 200% declining-balance method, the first five years' depreciation at the 20% rate (twice the 10% straight-line rate) is calculated as follows:

Year	Remaining Basis	Declining-Balance Rate	Depreciation Allowance
First	$100,000	20%	$20,000
Second	80,000	20%	16,000
Third	64,000	20%	12,800
Fourth	51,200	20%	10,240
Fifth	40,960	20%	8,192

The declining-balance method applies only to tangible assets with a useful life of three or more years. Although salvage value is not taken into account in determining the deduction under this method, an asset may not be depreciated below its salvage value.

¶ 350

Declining-Balance Method with Change to Straight-Line

If the declining-balance method were followed throughout the life of an asset, the asset would in many cases not be fully depreciated down to salvage value. As a result, it is a common practice to change over to the straight-line method at the point where this method would give a larger deduction than the declining-balance method. The CCH depreciation decimal tables in the appendix to this GUIDE indicate when the change occurs.

The straight-line rate in the changeover year is based on the remaining useful life at the beginning of the year and is applied to the adjusted basis at the beginning of the year (cost or other basis less depreciation deducted) reduced by salvage value.

> ***Example:*** After depreciating the farm machinery for the first 5 years of the 10-year life in the example at ¶ 348, above, under the double declining-balance method, the farmer had a remaining adjusted basis of $32,768 ($40,960 basis at the beginning of the fifth year minus $8,192 depreciation for that year). The straight-line rate based on the remaining useful life of five years is 20%. Assuming that salvage value is less than $10,000 (10% of $100,000) and the farmer elects to ignore it, straight-line depreciation for the sixth year is $6,554 (20% of $32,768).

¶ 352

Sum of the Years-Digits Method

Under this method, the years of useful life are numbered and these numbers are totaled. The result is the sum of the years-digits. The deduction under this method is figured by reducing the basis by the salvage value and multiplying the remainder by a fraction. The fraction has the remaining useful life at the beginning of the year as its numerator and the sum of the years-digits as its denominator.

> ***Example:*** An automobile with a three-year life to the taxpayer was bought for $3,600. Salvage value was estimated to be $300. The sum of the years-digits is 6 (1 + 2 + 3).

His deductions would be—

1st year ($3,300 × 3/6)	$1,650
2nd year ($3,300 × 2/6)	1,100
3rd year ($3,300 × 1/6)	550
Total	$3,300

A speedy way to find the sum of the years-digits for an asset with a long useful life is to square the useful life, add the useful life to the result, and divide by two. Thus, the sum of the years-digits for an asset with a 40-year life would be 820—the sum of 1,600 (40 × 40) and 40 divided by 2.

The sum of the years-digits method was applicable only to new tangible assets with a useful life of three years or more.

¶ 354

Sum of the Years-Digits Remaining Life Method

Another way to compute years-digits depreciation was by applying rates based on the remaining life to the undepreciated basis at the beginning of the year (cost minus salvage value minus depreciation previously deducted). A remaining life rate is equal to the remaining life divided by the sum of the years-digits for the remaining life.

> ***Example:*** In the example at ¶ 352, above, the computation of the first year's depreciation would be the same under the remaining life method. For the second year, the remaining life is 2 years and the sum of the years-digits for that life is 3 (1 + 2). The deduction for the second year would be ⅔ of the $1,800 undepreciated basis ($3,600 cost less $1,800 first year's depreciation), or $1,200.

¶ 356

Other Consistent Methods

In addition to the straight-line, declining-balance, and the sum of the years-digits methods, any other method was permissible for new assets so long as it was consistently applied as explained at ¶ 344 and the accumulated allowances at the end of any tax year during the first two-thirds of the useful life are not more than those that would accumulate under the 200-percent declining-balance method.

¶ 358

Depreciation in Year of Purchase or Sale

If an asset was bought or sold during the year, only a fractional part of a year's depreciation was deducted, depending on the number of months the asset was held during the year.

In determining depreciation in the year of acquisition, it was proper to treat an asset as having been held a full month if it was acquired on or before the 15th of the month. If it was acquired after the 15th, the month was not counted. Consistently, it was proper to count the disposition month only if the asset was disposed of after the 15th of the month. Thus, an asset bought on May 14 by a calendar year taxpayer would get 8 months' first year depreciation (8/12 of first full year's depreciation). If acquired on May 17, only 7 months' depreciation was allowed.

Another possible way to handle this was to count the month of acquisition and exclude the month of disposition (regardless of the day acquired or disposed of).

Also, the taxpayer could compute the exact amount of depreciation on the basis of the number of days held during the year.

If the sum of the years-digits method was used, allocations must be made throughout the useful life of the asset. Thus, if an asset was held three months in the year it was bought, 3/12 of the first full year's depreciation was deductible in that year. In the second taxable year held, 9/12 of the first full year's depreciation and 3/12 of the second full year's depreciation were deductible. This procedure must be followed for the asset's entire useful life.

¶ 360

Methods Keyed to Production

There are several depreciation methods which prorate the cost over an asset's production life.

Under the machine-hour method, the useful life is estimated in machine hours. An hourly rate is then found by dividing the depreciable cost by the total hours of useful life. The deduction is equal to the total hours of use times the rate.

Similar to this is the operating-day method, except that the life is estimated in days.

The unit-of-production method is mainly for equipment used in exploiting natural resources (mines, wells, etc.). This method prorates the cost according to the ratio of the units produced for the year to the total expected units to be produced. The space above a landfill or dump may be depreciated using the unit-of-production method (*H.K. Sanders*, 75 TC 157, CCH Dec. 37,348).

It should be noted that property depreciable under the unit-of-production method (or any other method not expressed in a term of years) may, if the taxpayer elects, be depreciated under this method even if it was placed in service after 1980. See ¶ 140 (MACRS) and ¶ 264 (ACRS).

¶ 364

Income Forecast Method

The usefulness of certain tangible or intangible assets used in a trade or business is more accurately measured by the stream of income produced rather than over the passage of time. An irrevocable election may be made to depreciate these assets using the income forecast method. Under this method, which has been allowed since the early 1960s, the depreciable basis of a property is recovered over the anticipated income to be earned from the property. The depreciation deductions follow the uneven flow of income in order to avoid a distortion of income.

> ***Comment:*** *The American Jobs Creation Act of 2004 (P.L. 108-357) includes a new provision that allows a taxpayer to elect to treat the cost of any qualified film or television production as a currently deductible expense. In the case of a production commencing after October 22, 2004 and on or before December 31, 2007, the election applies only to qualifying film productions with an aggregate cost that does not exceed $15 million ($20 million in the case of productions filmed in certain low-income or distressed areas). In the case of a production commencing after December 31, 2007 and on or before January 1, 2010, the election applies regardless of the cost of the film and the first $15 million or $20 million of production costs are deductible. The election must be made by the due date (including extensions) for filing the taxpayer's tax return for the tax year in which costs of the production are first incurred. Once the election is made, the election may not be revoked without IRS consent (Code Sec. 181, as added by P.L. 108-357 and amended by the Emergency Economic Stabilization Act of 2008 (P.L. 110-343)). Election guidance is provided in Temporary Reg. § 1.181-2T, incorporating election guidance previously provided in Notice 2006-47. Note that the temporary regulations do not reflect the law changes made by P..L. 110-343.*
>
> *See also ¶ 67 for rules allowing 15-year amortization of film indusrty creative property costs.*

This depreciation method was developed by the IRS in response to a determination that a distortion of income occurred where producers of motion picture and television films did not report taxable income until the income from these assets exceeded costs incurred.

For tangible property, an election to depreciate property under the income forecast method (a method not expressed in a term of years) constitutes an election to exclude such property from MACRS (Code Sec. 168(f)(1)) (see also ¶ 140). This election must be made in the year that the property is placed in service (IRS Letter Ruling 9323007, March 8, 1993). The election to use the income forecast method is made on a property-by-property basis. Income forecast method depreciation is entered on line 16 ("Other depreciation") of Form 4562 (line reference to 2006 Form).

Property eligible for income forecast method.

Effective for property placed in service after August 5, 1997, the income forecast method (or any similar method) may only be used with respect to film, video tape, sound recordings, copyrights, books, patents, and other property to be specified in IRS regulations (Code Sec. 167(g)(6), as added by the Taxpayer Relief Act of 1997 (P.L. 105-34)). This provision essentially codifies the previous IRS position.

The income forecast method may not be elected to depreciate intangible assets that are amortizable Sec. 197 intangibles (Code Sec. 197(b); Code 167(g)(6)).

Prior to the 1997 Act, use of the income forecast method of depreciation was approved by the IRS for the following property: television films (Rev. Rul. 60-358, 1960-2 CB 68); motion picture films and video tapes (Rev. Rul. 64-273, 1964-2 CB 62; Code Sec. 168(f)(3)); sound recordings (Rev. Rul. 60-358, 1960-2 CB 680; Code Sec. 168(f)(4)); book manuscript rights, patents, and master recordings (Rev. Rul. 79-285, 1979-1 CB 91); copyrighted musical works (IRS Letter Ruling 8501006, 9-24-84); rental videocassettes (Rev. Rul. 89-62, 1989-1 CB 78 (see also ¶ 140)); video game machines (IRS Letter Ruling 9323007, 3-8-93), and other property of a similar character.

Musical compositions and copyrights thereto. A taxpayer may elect five-year amortization of capitalized expenses paid or incurred in creating or acquiring a musical composition (including the accompanying words) or a copyright to a musical composition if the expenses could otherwise be recovered using the income forecast method (Code Sec. 167(g)(8), as added by the Tax Increase Prevention and Reconciliation Act of 2005 (P.L. 109-222)).

Rent-to-own property. The Tax Court had ruled that the income forecast method may not be used to depreciate consumer durables (appliances, furniture, televisions, stereos, and video cassette recorders) leased under rent-to-own contracts (*ABC Rentals of San Antonio, Inc.*, 68 TCM 1362, TC Memo. 1994-601, CCH Dec. 50,278(M), affirmed *per curiam* under the name *El Charo TV Rentals*, CA-5, 97-1 USTC ¶ 50,140; Rev. Rul. 95-52, 1955-2 CB 27) because the property had a determinable useful life. The Tax Court decision, however, was also appealed by certain petitioners to the Court of Appeals for the Tenth Circuit, which held that the income forecast method could apply to the rented consumer durables (and presumably to other types of property) if the method meets certain standards of reasonableness set forth in Code Sec. 167 and the regulations. Since the IRS conceded that the income forecast method was a reasonable method, the taxpayers were entitled to use that method provided that the proper procedures were followed in electing out of MACRS under Code Sec. 168(f)(1) and the method was properly applied to produce reasonable allowances (*ABC Rentals of San Antonio, Inc.*, CA-10, 98-1 USTC ¶ 50,340). The case was remanded to the Tax Court to determine these two issues (see *ABC Rentals of San Antonio, Inc.*, et al., 77 TCM 1229, TC Memo. 1999-14, CCH Dec. 53,217(M) which found in favor of certain taxpayers and against others on these issues).

The 1997 Taxpayer Relief Act (P.L. 105-34), added a provision which treats rent-to-own property (property held by a rent-to-own dealer for purposes of being subject to a rent-to-own contract) as 3-year MACRS property, effective for property placed in service after August 5, 1997. Such property is assigned a four-year recovery period under the alternative depreciation system (ADS). (Code Sec. 168(e)(3); Code Sec. 168(g)(3); and Code Sec. 168(i)(14), as amended by P.L. 105-34)). Rent-to-own property placed in service before August 6, 1997, was treated by the IRS as 5-year MACRS property.

Formula for computing income forecast depreciation.

Under the income forecast method, the cost of an asset placed in service after September 13, 1995, is multiplied by a fraction, the numerator of which is the net income from the asset for the tax year, and the denominator of which is the total net income to be derived from the asset before the close of the tenth tax year *following* the tax year in which the asset is placed in service (Code Sec. 167(g)(1)(A), as added by the Small Business Job Protection Act of 1996 (P.L. 104-188)). The unrecovered adjusted basis of the property as of the beginning of the tenth tax year is claimed as a depreciation deduction in the tenth tax year after the year in which the property is placed in service (Code Sec. 167(g)(1)(C), as added by P.L. 104-188).

If, in a later year, the outlook for the income forecast changes, the formula for computing depreciation would be as follows: the unrecovered depreciable cost of the asset at the beginning of the tax year of revision multiplied by a fraction, the numerator of which is the net income from the asset for the tax year of revision and the denominator of which is the revised forecasted total net income from the asset for the year of revision and the remaining years before the close of the tenth tax year following the tax year in which the asset was placed in service.

Denominator of formula. For purposes of the denominator in the formula, the total forecasted net income from the asset is based on the conditions known to exist at the end of the current tax year (Rev. Rul. 60-358, 1960-2 CB 68). There must be evidence to support the forecast of total net income from the asset or a depreciation deduction will be denied (*E.D. Abramson*, 86 TC 360, CCH Dec. 42,919). The amount of the denominator cannot be less than any nonrecourse loan secured by the asset (Rev. Rul. 78-28, 1978-1 CB 61).

Income projections must be made for each asset subject to this method. Videocassettes and video game machines may be grouped by title (but not by a broader grouping) for income projection purposes (Rev. Rul. 89-62, 1989-1 CB 78; IRS Letter Ruling 9323007, 3-8-93).

The types of income taken into account in the income forecast depreciation formula were significantly expanded by the Small Business Job Protection Act (P.L. 104-188), effective for property placed in service after September 13, 1995. Estimated income from films and TV shows include, but is not limited to, estimated income from foreign and domestic sources, theatrical releases, television releases and syndications, and video tape releases, sales, rentals and syndications. Estimated income also includes amounts derived from unrelated taxpayers with respect to the financial exploitation of characters, designs, scripts, scores, and other incidental income associated with the films (Code Sec. 167(g)(5)(C)).

When a taxpayer produces a TV series and initially does not anticipate syndicating the series, the forecasted income for the episodes of the first three years of the series need not take into account any future syndication fees. This rules does not apply if the taxpayer enters into a syndication agreement for the shows during the three-year period (Code Sec. 167(g)(5)(B)).

Numerator of formula. For purposes of the numerator in the formula, income from the asset means the actual net income from the asset determined without considering depreciation expense (Rev. Rul. 60-358, 1960-2 CB 68; *L. Greene*, 81 TC 132, CCH Dec. 40,390). No depreciation is allowed if there is no income from the asset during the tax year.

Income utilized in the numerator used to compute depreciation must reflect the same gross income used to compute taxable income from the asset for the same period under the taxpayer's method of accounting (Rev. Rul. 78-28, 1978-1 CB 61). Thus, a cash-basis entity could not include an accrued income amount in the numerator for depreciation purposes because the amount was not received before the end of the tax year and was not includible in gross income or taxable income for such year (Rev. Rul. 78-28, 1978-1 CB 61; *L. Greene*, 81 TC 132, CCH Dec. 40,390).

The new law also clarifies that the term "income from the property" is the taxpayer's gross income from the property (Code Sec. 167(g)(5)(E), as added by the American Jobs Creation Act of 2004 (P.L. 108-357)). This definition precludes taxpayers from taking distribution costs into account for purposes of determining current (numerator of formula) and total forecasted income (denominator of the formula) with respect to a property (Conference Committee Report (H.R. Conf. Rep. No. 108-755)).

Cost basis under income forecast method—participations and residuals.

The cost basis of an asset depreciated under the income forecast method is determined in a unique manner. Because forecasted total net income is used in the formula, the Ninth Circuit has ruled that estimated costs dependent on such amount are includible in cost basis (*Transamerica Corp.*, CA-9, 93-2 USTC ¶ 50,388). This is necessary so that all costs are included and spread evenly over the flow of income derived from the asset. Thus, estimated percentages (participations) to be paid based on the forecasted future gross receipts and net profits from a motion picture as well as percentages (residuals) to be paid stemming from forecasted future revenue received from the movie's television exhibition were includible in the cost basis of the property for purposes of computing depreciation under the income forecast method.

Since the *Transamerica* decision was decided prior to the enactment of the economic performance rules of Code Sec. 461(h), it has been unclear what effect the economic performance rules would have had on its outcome since the payments involved were contingent on the occurrence of future events. The Small Business Job Protection Act of 1996, however, specifically provides that the basis of a film or other property depreciated under the income forecast method only includes amounts that satisfy the economic performance standard of Code Sec. 461(h) (Code Sec. 167(g)(1)(B), as added by P.L. 104-188, generally effective for property placed in service after September 13, 1995)). The IRS has taken the position in its proposed regulations, discussed below, that the economic performance requirement precludes the inclusion of contingent expenses in the basis of income forecast property.

Effective for property placed in service after October 22, 2004, a taxpayer may include participations and residuals in the basis of a film in the tax year that it is placed in service, but only to the extent that the participations and residuals relate to income estimated to be earned in connection with the film before the close of the tenth tax year after the tax year the property was placed in service (Code Sec. 167(g)(7)(A), as added by the American Jobs Creation Act of 2004 (P.L. 108-357)). This provision is not intended to create an inference regarding the proper treatment of participations and residuals paid in connections with films placed in service before the effective date.

As an alternative to including such participations and residuals in the basis of the film and recovering their cost over a 10-year period, a taxpayer may exclude the participations and residuals from basis and deduct them in full in the year that they are actually paid (Code Sec. 167(g)(7)(D)(i), as added by the 2004 Jobs Act). The Conference Committee Report (H.R. Conf. Rep. No. 108-755) states that the decision to currently deduct these expenses may be made on a property-by-property basis but must be applied consistently with respect to a given property thereafter.

The method of treating participations and residuals is considered an election. The election must be made by the due date (including extensions) for filing the return for the taxable year the income forecast property is placed in service. Election procedures (including rules for taxpayers who filed returns before June 15, 2006 for a tax year ending after October 22, 2004 without making the election) are provided in Notice 2006-47, I.R.B. 2006-20.

The Large and Mid-Size Business (LMSB) Division of the IRS has issued guidance regarding issues raised during examinations of taxpayers using the income forecast method (IRS LMSB Memo on Disposition of Income Forecast Method Issues, January 6, 2005). The most common issues during examination are net versus gross and participation/residuals. The net versus gross issue concerns whether income in the income forecast fraction includes distribution costs. Taxpayers using the net method could exclude distribution costs under Rev. Rul. 60-358, 1960-2 CB 68. However, under Code Sec. 167(g)(5)(E), as amended by the American Jobs Creation Act of 2004 (P.L. 108-357), taxpayers must use the gross method and include distribution costs in the income forecast fraction.

The participation/residual issue concerns the proper time for adding these payments to a film's basis. The IRS had taken the position that participations/residuals are deferred compensation under Code Sec. 404 and may not be added to a film's basis until the recipient includes the payment in income. Changes to Code Sec. 167(g)(7)(A), however, permit a taxpayer to include participations/residuals in basis for the tax year in which the property is placed in service for purposes of determining depreciation under the income forecast method. Alternatively, Code Sec. 167(g)(7)(D)(i) allows a taxpayer to claim a deduction for depreciation of the participations/residuals in the tax year in which they are paid. The memo further details how examining agents should deal with net versus gross and participations/residuals issues that arise during an examination in light of the recent changes to Code Sec. 167.

Interest computation under look-back rule.

Effective for property placed in service after September 13, 1995, taxpayers that claim depreciation under the income-forecast method are required to pay (or may be entitled to receive) interest based on the recalculation of deprecation using actual income figures. This look-back calculation is required during a recomputation year. In general, a recomputation year is the third and tenth tax years beginning after the tax year in which the film or other property was placed in service (Code Sec. 167(g)(2)). The look-back rule does not apply to property that had a cost basis of $100,000 or less or if the taxpayer's income projections were within 10 percent of the income actually earned (Code Sec. 167(g)(3)).

Form 8866 for look-back interest computatoin. The IRS released Form 8866 (Interest Computation Under the Look-Back Method for Property Depreciated Under the Income Forecast Method) in early 1999 to compute the interest due or owed during a recomputation year.

Proposed income forecast depreciation regulations

The IRS has issued proposed income forecast depreciation regulations which reflect the addition of Code Sec. 167(g) by the Small Business Job Protection Act of 1996 (P.L. 104-188) and the amendment of Code Sec. 167(g) by the Taxpayer Relief Act of 1997 (P.L. 105-34) to limit the use of the income forecast method to specified types of property (Prop. Reg. § 1.167(n)-1 through 7).

The proposed regulations will apply to property placed in service on or after the date that final regulations are published in the Federal Register (Prop. Reg. § 1.167(n)-7).

Property eligible for the income forecast method

Under the proposed regulations, the following property is the only property eligible for the income forecast method (Prop. Reg. § 1.167(n)-5(a)):

(1) film, video tape, and sound recordings (property described in Code Sec. 168(f)(3) and (4));

(2) copyrights;

(3) books;

(4) patents;

(5) theatrical productions; and

(6) any other property designed by the IRS in published guidance.

With the exception of theatrical productions, these are the same items listed in Code Sec. 167(g)(6).

The income forecast method does not apply to any amortizable section 197 intangible as defined in Code Sec. 197(c) and Reg. § 1.197-2(d) (Code Sec. 167(g)(6); Prop. Reg. § 1.167(n)-5(b)).

Computation

Under Code Sec. 167(g) the depreciable basis of an income forecast property is generally recovered over an 11-year period beginning in the year that the income forecast property is placed in service.

The income-forecast method depreciation deduction is generally equal to:

$$\frac{\text{depreciable basis} \times \text{current year income}}{\text{forecasted total income}}$$

Example (1): Income forecast property with a depreciable basis of $100,000 is placed in service in Year 1. Current-year income is $30,000. Forecasted total income to be received from the property before the close of the tenth tax year after the year the asset is placed in service is estimated at the end of Year 1 to be $200,000. Year 1 depreciation is $15,000 ($100,000 × $30,000/$200,000). If current-year income in Year 2 is $25,000, the depreciation deduction for Year 2 is $12,500 ($100,000 × $25,000/$200,000).

As explained below, in tax years after the tax year that the income forecast method property is placed in service it may be necessary to compute income forecast depreciation deductions using revise forecasted total income if the original estimate of forecasted income changes sufficiently. Revised forecasted total income for a tax year is the sum of current-year income for the tax year and all prior tax years, plus all income from the income forecast method property that the taxpayer reasonably believes will be included in current-year income in tax years after the current tax year up to and including the tenth tax year after the tax year in which the income forecast method property was placed in service.

In a tax year in which forecasted total income is revised, the income forecast method deduction is equal to:

$$\frac{\text{unrecovered depreciable basis} \times \text{current year income}}{\text{revised forecasted total income} - \text{current year income from prior years}}$$

Safe harbor. The revised computation may be used in any year that revised forecasted total income differs from forecasted total income. However, a taxpayer is *required* to use the revised computation if forecasted total income (revised forecasted total income if the taxpayer previously revised its income projections) in the immediately preceding tax year is either:

(1) Less than 90 percent of revised forecasted total income for the tax year; or

(2) Greater than 110 percent of revised forecasted total income for the tax year (Prop. Reg. § 1.167(n)-4(b)(2)).

Example (2): Assume same facts as in *Example (1)*, except that at the end of Year 3 the taxpayer estimates that $210,000 of income will be recognized over the remaining 8 years in the 11-year depreciation period. Assuming the current-year income for Year 3 is $35,000, the revised forecasted income is $300,000 ($30,000 + $25,000 + $35,000 + $210,000). The safe harbor does not apply because the taxpayer's original forecasted total income ($200,000) is less than 90% of the revised forecasted total income for Year 3 ($300,000). The taxpayer, therefore, must compute the Year 3 and later deductions based on the revised forecasted income amount. Revised forecasted income less actual income from years prior to the revision year is $245,000 ($300,000 – $30,000 – $25,000). The undepreciated basis at the beginning of Year 3 is $72,500 ($100,000 – $15,000 – $12,500). The Year 3 income forecast depreciation deduction is $10,357 ($72,500 × $35,000/$245,000). If Year 4 current income is $40,000, the Year 4 depreciation deduction is $11,837 ($72,500 × $40,000/$245,000).

Computation if basis of property increases. The depreciable basis of an income forecast method property is increased by capital expenses paid or incurred with respect to the property in a tax year after it is placed in service (Prop. Reg. § 1.167(n)-2(a)(2)). The increased basis is referred to as the "redetermined basis." The amount of the increase is referred to as the "basis redetermination amount."

In the tax year that the basis is redetermined, a taxpayer is entitled to an additional depreciation deduction (a "catch-up" deduction) equal to the portion of the basis increase (the basis redetermination amount) that would have been recovered in prior tax years if the redetermination amount had originally been included in depreciable basis (Prop. Reg. § 1.167(n)-4(c)(1)).

In the tax year that the basis is increased and in subsequent tax years, the redetermined basis is used to determine the regular income forecast depreciation deductions (Prop. Reg. § 1.167(n)-2(b)).

The catch up deduction is not allowed with respect to basis increases that occur in the last tax year of the depreciation period (i.e., the tenth tax year following the tax year that the income forecast method property was placed in service). Instead, the full amount of the basis increase is deducted, as explained below.

Example (3): A movie producer agrees to pay a book author 5% of a movie's income in excess of $500,000. Forecasted total income is $1 million. The basis of the film is $500,000. The payments will be determined and made within one month after the end of each tax year.

Year	*Current Year Income*	*Regular Deduction*
1	$300,000	$150,000 (500,000 × 300,000/1,000,000)
2	$150,000	$ 75,000 (500,000 × 150,000/1,000,000)
3	$100,000	$ 50,000 (500,000 × 100,000/1,000,000)

In the first month of Year 4, the producer pays the author $2,500 ($50,000 earnings in excess of $500,000 at end of Year 3 × 5%). Beginning in Year 4 the basis of the film is increased by $2,500 (see timing rule for deferred compensation payments under the heading "*Determining depreciable basis,*" below.).

Year	*Current Year Income*	*Regular Deduction*
4	$90,000	$45,225 (502,500 × 90,000/1,000,000)

Year	*Additional Deduction*
4	$ 750 (2,500 × 300,000/1,000,000)
	375 (2,500 × 150,000/1,000,000)
	250 (2,500 × 100,000/1,000,000)
	$1,375

The additional deduction can also be determined by multiplying the basis redetermination amount ($2,500) by the ratio of the $550,000 cumulative prior-year incomes ($300,000 + $150,000 + $100,000) to $1,000,000 forecasted total income ($2,500 × $550,000/$1,000,000 = $1,375).

In the first month of Year 5, the producer pays the author an additional $4,500 ($90,000 × 5%). In Year 5, the basis of the film is increased by $4,500 to $507,000 ($502,500 + $4,500). An additional depreciation deduction of $2,970 can be claimed.

Year	*Current Year Income*	*Regular Deduction*
5	$110,000	$55,770 (507,000 × 110,000/1,000,000)

Year	*Additional Deduction*
5	$1,350 (4,500 × 300,000/1,000,000)
	675 (4,500 × 150,000/1,000,000)
	450 (4,500 × 100,000/1,000,000)
	495 (4,500 × 110,000/1,000,000)
	$2,970

The same computational process would be followed for each subsequent year of the 11-year depreciation period other than the final year.

Certain significant basis increases may be treated as a separate item of income forecast property. See "*Costs treated as separate property,*" below.

Undepreciated basis recovered in final year. The depreciation period for an item of income forecast property is generally 11 years—the tax year that the property is placed in service and ten additional tax years. Thus, the final year that a depreciation deduction is claimed is usually the tenth tax year following the tax year that the property is placed in service. The entire undepreciated basis of the property can be claimed in this year. However, if in an earlier tax year, a taxpayer reasonably believes, based on the conditions known to exist at the end of the earlier tax year, that no additional income will be earned in the remaining years of the 11-year depreciation period, the remaining basis (including any basis redetermination amount for that year (i.e., basis increase)) may be deducted in that year (Prop. Reg. § 1.167(n)-4(d)(1) and (2)).

A taxpayer may pay or incur expenses with respect to an income forecast property in a tax year after the final depreciation deduction is claimed. These expenses may be deducted in full as depreciation in the year paid or incurred if they would have constituted a basis redetermination amount (Prop. Reg. § 1.167(n)-4(d)(2)). If the additional expense will generate significant income, then it may be necessary to depreciate the expense as a separate item of income forecast property. See "*Costs treated as separate property*," below.

Depreciation in year of disposition. If an income forecast property is sold or otherwise disposed of prior to the end of the 11-year recovery period, the depreciation allowance for the year of disposition is equal to (Prop. Reg. § 1.167(n)-4(d)(3))):

$$\frac{\text{depreciable (or redetermined) basis} \times \text{current year income}}{\text{amount realized} + \text{current year income} + \text{current year income from all prior years}}$$

The rule allowing the deduction of the full amount of the remaining basis in the final year of depreciation does not apply in this situation.

See "*Income from dispositions*," below.

Determining depreciable basis

The starting basis used to compute depreciation under the income forecast method is the basis for determining gain or loss under Code Sec. 1011 (Prop. Reg. § 1.167(n)-2(a)(1)).

Salvage value. Although Rev. Rul. 60-358, which had governed the computation of income forecast depreciation prior to the enactment of Code Sec. 167(g) required the reduction of basis by salvage value, the proposed regulations contain no such requirement. The introduction to the proposed regulations explains this change by concluding that Congress intended to allow the recovery of the *entire* basis of income forecast method property within ten tax years after the income forecast method property is placed in service.

All events tests. In the case of an accrual method taxpayer, costs are included in basis in the tax year that all events have occurred that establish the fact of the liability, the amount of the liability can be determined with reasonable accuracy, and economic performance (within the meaning of Code Sec. 461(h)) has occurred (Code Sec. 167(g)(1)(B); Prop. Reg. § 1.167(n)-2(a)(2)). These three requirements are referred to as the all events test. The basis of income forecast property produced by a taxpayer is determined under the uniform capitalization rules of Code Sec. 263A. Amounts are not taken into account under the UNICAP rules until the preceding all events test is satisfied (Reg. § 1.263A-1(c)(2)(ii)).

If any Code Section requires a liability of an accrual method taxpayer to be deducted later than the time that the all events test would otherwise be considered satisfied, then the depreciable basis is not increased until that later time (Reg. § 1.461-1(a)(2)(iii)(A)).

Contingent payments. Under the all events tests, contingent payments are not included in the basis of income forecast property until the tax year they are actually paid or incurred even if it is nearly certain that the forecasted total income used in the income forecast method computation method will be sufficient to satisfy the contingency (Prop. Reg. § 1.167(n)-2(a)(2)). However, participations and residuals may be included in basis or currently deducted, effective for films placed in service after October 22, 2004.

Deferred compensation payments. Deferred compensation payments which are subject to Code Sec. 404 (relating to employer contributions to a plan of deferred compensation) do not satisfy the economic performance requirement and, therefore, are not included in basis of income forecast method property, until the amount is deductible under Code Sec. 404 (Reg. § 1.461-1(a)(2)(3)(D)).

> ***Example (4):*** An accrual method studio contracts to pay an actor 5% of gross movie income in excess of $20 million. At the end of the third tax year after the movie is placed in service cumulative gross film revenue reaches $21 million. The studio makes a $50,000 payment to the actor 20 days after the end of the third tax year. The studio may increase the film's basis in the fourth tax year when the $50,000 is paid. Although the studio had a fixed liability to pay the actor $50,000 in the third tax year, the requirements for deductibility under Code Sec. 404 were not satisfied until the liability was actually paid.

Separate property. Certain amounts paid or incurred in a tax year after income forecast method property is placed in service are treated as separate items of property which are separately depreciated using the income forecast method (Prop. Reg. § 1.167(n)-5(c)). See "*Costs treated as separate property,*" below.

Basis redeterminations. Assuming that a capitalizable amount paid or incurred in a tax year after the income forecast property is placed in service is not treated as a separate property, the basis of the income forecast property is increased by the additional capitalizable amount (Prop. Reg. § 1.167(n)-2(b)).

The redetermined basis is used to computed the income forecast method deduction in the tax year that the basis is redetermined and in later tax years. However, an additional "catch up" deduction is allowed in the tax year that the basis of income forecast property is redetermined (Reg. § 1.167(n)-4(c)). See "*Computation if basis of property increases,*" above.

Unrecovered depreciable basis. The unrecovered depreciable basis of an item of income forecast property for any tax year is the depreciable basis of the property less prior depreciation deductions (Reg. § 1.167(n)-2(c)).

Income from the property

Under the income forecast method the depreciation allowance is generally computed by multiplying the basis of the income forecast method property by the ratio of current-year income to forecasted total income.

Forecasted total income (computed in the tax year the property is placed in service) and revised forecasted total income (computed in later tax years) are determined based on conditions known to exist at the end of the tax year of the computation.

Current-year income. Generally, current-year income is all income from the income forecast method property for the current year determined in accordance with the taxpayer's method of accounting. Current-year income may be reduced by any distribution costs for the year (Prop. Reg. § 1.167(n)-3(a)(1)). However, a new rule applies to films placed in service after October 22, 2004. See "*Distribution costs*" below.

In the tax year that an income forecast method property is placed in service, current-year income includes any amount connected with the property that was included in gross income in a prior tax year (i.e., advance payments) (Prop. Reg. § 1.167(n)-3(a)(2)).

Films, television shows, and similar property. The proposed regulations provide that current-year income includes (but is not limited to) (Prop. Reg. § 1.167(n)-3(a)(1):

> (1) Income from foreign and domestic theatrical, television, and other releases and syndications;

(2) Income from releases, sales, rentals, and syndications of video tape, DVD, and other media; and

(3) Incidental income associated with the property.

Incidental income includes, but is not limited to, income from the financial exploitation of characters, designs, titles, scripts, and scores provided the income is not received from a related person within the meaning of Code Sec. 267(b).

The proposed regulations provide a special rule for income from the syndication of a television series produced for distribution on television networks. The rule provides that syndication income does not need to be included in current-year income, forecasted total income, or revised forecasted total income until the earlier of the fourth tax year beginning after the date that the first episode is placed in service or the earliest tax year in which the taxpayer has an arrangement relating to the syndication of the series. An arrangement relating to the syndication of a series means any arrangement other than the first run exhibition agreement (Prop. Reg. § 1.167(n)-3(d)(2)).

Forecasted total income. Forecasted total income is sum of the current-year income for the year that the income forecast method property is placed in service and the total amount of current-year income that the taxpayer reasonably believes will be included in current-year income for the next 10 tax years. Forecasted total income includes any amounts that will be earned by any subsequent owner during the 11-year depreciation period (Prop. Reg. § 1.167(n)-3(b)).

Revised forecasted total income. A taxpayer must recompute forecasted total income in any tax year that information reveals that forecasted total income is inaccurate. However, a taxpayer is not required to actually use revised forecasted income in making the depreciation calculations unless the forecasted total income in the immediately preceding tax year is less than 90 percent or greater than 110 percent of the revised forecasted income (Prop. Reg. § 1.167(n)-4(b)(2)).

If revised forecasted total income was used to compute income forecast deprecation in the immediately preceding tax year, revised forecasted total income for the preceding year is compared to revised forecasted income for the current tax year for purposes of the 90/110 percent test.

Revised forecasted total income for a tax year is the sum of current-year income for the tax year of revision and all prior tax years, plus all income from the income forecast property that the taxpayer reasonably believes will be included in current-year income through the end of the tenth tax year following the tax year that the income forecast property was placed in service (Prop. Reg. § 1.167(n)-3(c)).

Special rules for the computation of the income forecast deduction apply if forecasted total income is revised. See *Example (2)*, above.

Distribution costs. Effective for films placed in service after October 22, 2004, distribution costs are not taken into account in computing current year and total forecasted income (Code Sec. 167(g)(5)(E), as added by the American Jobs Creation Act of 2004 (P.L. 108-357)). For the treatment of distribution costs prior to this provision see IRS Letter Ruling 200252028, August 7, 2002.

Income from dispositions. Income from the sale or other disposition of income forecast property is not included in current-year income. Anticipated income from the future sale of income forecast property is not included in forecasted total income. Such income is included in revised forecasted total income in the year of sale for purposes of computing depreciation in the year of disposition and for purposes of applying the look-back rule discussed below. When computing forecasted total income or revised forecasted total income, the entire anticipated income for the 11-year depreciation period (the tax year the income forecast depreciation property is placed in service plus the next 10 years) is taken into account even if a sale prior to the close of the depreciation period is reasonably anticipated (Prop. Reg. § 1.167(n)-3(d)(1)).

> ***Example (5):*** Art Tistick produces a feature film that is placed in service in 2004. Art reasonably anticipates selling the film on the last day of 2011 for $2 million. Income earned in 2004 is $5 million. Art estimates that $15 million will be earned in 2005 through 2011. Estimated income from 2012 through 2014 is $3 million. Therefore, in computing depreciation for 2004, forecasted total income is $23 million ($5M + $15M + $3M) and does not include the estimated sales proceeds. In computing depreciation for 2011 (year of the sale), revised forecasted total income is equal to the amounts actually earned through 2011 plus the sales proceeds. The sales proceeds, however, are not included in current-year income in 2011 when making the 2011 depreciation calculation. See, also, Prop. Reg. § 1.167(n)-3(d)(4), *Example 2.*

Apportionment of income. Income from a particular source may relate to more than one income forecast property. For example, income from the sale or license of merchandise that features the image of a movie character may relate to more than one film. The regulations require a reasonable allocation of the income among the income forecast properties based on all relevant factors (Prop. Reg. § 1.167(n)-3(d)(3)).

Costs treated as separate property

Any amount paid or incurred after an income forecast property is placed in service (but before the property is fully depreciated) must be treated as a separate item of income forecast property rather than an increase in basis (basis redetermination amount) if the cost is:

(1) significant and

(2) gives rise to an increase in income that is significant and which was not included in either forecasted total income or revised forecasted total income in a prior tax year (Code Sec. 167(g)(5)(A))ii); Prop. Reg. § 1.167(n)-5(c)).

An amount treated as a separate item of income forecast property is considered placed in service in the year the amount is paid or incurred.

For purposes of item (1), a cost is not significant if it less than the lesser of five percent of depreciable basis (as of the date the cost is paid or incurred) or $100,000.

For purposes of item (2), whether an increase in income is significant is determined by comparing the amount that would be considered revised forecasted total income from the amounts treated as separate property to the most recent estimate of forecasted total income or revised forecasted total income used in calculating an allowance for depreciation with respect to the income forecast property.

> ***Example (6):*** A film which was released in 2006 is prepared in 2009 for future rerelease as a DVD. The costs attributable to rerelease as a DVD exceed $100,000 and 5% of the film's depreciable basis. Assuming that no amount of the anticipated DVD revenue was originally included in the prior-year income projections (assume the DVD release was unanticipated) and that the DVD release income will be significant in relation to the forecasted total income used in calculating the 2008 depreciation allowance on the film, the additional expenditures are treated as a separate item of income forecast depreciation property beginning in 2009 when the expenditures are paid or incurred.

Any amount paid or incurred with respect to an income forecast property in a tax year after the tax year in which a final-year income forecast depreciation allowance has been claimed (see above) is deductible when paid or incurred as a basis redetermination amount unless the amount is expected to give rise to a significant increase in current-year income in any tax year (Prop. Reg. § 1.167(n)-5(c)(3)).

> ***Example (7):*** Assume the same facts as in *Example (6)*, except that the DVD preparation costs are in incurred in 2023 and that the film was fully depreciated under the income forecast method in 2016. If income from the DVD release will be significant in relation to the revised forecasted total income used in calculating depreciation in 2016, the cost of preparing the release is separately depreciated as an income forecast property. If the anticipated income is not significant, the cost is fully deductible in 2023.

Permissible aggregations of multiple properties

The proposed regulations only allow aggregations of multiple properties as a single item of income forecast property in the following four situations (Prop. Reg. § 1.167(n)-5(d)):

(1) Multiple episodes of a single television series produced in the same tax year;

(2) Multiple episodes of a single television series that are produced as a single season of episodes and placed in service over a period not in excess of twelve consecutive calendar months;

(3) Multiple interests in specifically identified income forecast properties acquired for broadcast pursuant to a single contract; and

(4) Multiple copies of the same title of videocassettes and DVDs purchased or licensed in the same tax year for rental to the public.

If a taxpayer chooses one of these aggregations, the additional depreciation allowance provided in Prop. Reg. § 1.167(n)-4(c)(1) for a basis redetermination (basis increase) in a tax year after the property is placed in service and before the tenth tax year following the tax year that the property was placed in service is not allowed. Thus, the amount of depreciation that would have been recovered if the basis redetermination amount had originally been included in the depreciable basis of the property when it was placed in service may not be claimed.

The aggregation of multiple properties is considered an adoption of an accounting method that can only be changed with IRS permission.

Look back method

Effective for property placed in service after September 13, 1995, taxpayers that claim depreciation under the income-forecast method are required to pay (or may be entitled to receive) interest based on hypothetical increases and decreases in tax liability attributable to the recalculation of deprecation using actual income figures (Code Sec. 167(g)(2); Prop. Reg. § 1.167(n)-6).

A look-back calculation is required during each recomputation year. In general, a recomputation year is the third and tenth tax years beginning after the tax year in which the film or other property was placed in service. The look-back method also applies in the tax-year income from the income forecast property ceases with respect to a taxpayer (Code Sec. 167(g)(4); Prop. Reg. § 1.167(n)-6(e)).

The computation of look-back interest is made on Form 8866 (Interest Computation Under the Look-Back Method for Property Depreciated Under the Income Forecast Method (January 1999)).

The look-back rule does not apply to property that had a cost basis (unadjusted basis) of $100,000 or less at the end of the recomputation year or the taxpayer's income projections for each year before the recomputation year were within 10 percent of the income actually earned (Code Sec. 167(g)(3) and (4)). See "*De minimus exceptions to look-back rule*," below.

The look-back method applies separately to each income forecast property or group of properties which were aggregated pursuant to the special rules described above in Prop. Reg. § 1.167(n)-5(d).

Pass-through entities are required to use a simplified look-back method. See "*Simplified look-back method for certain pass-through entities*," below.

Computational steps

A taxpayer is entitled to receive interest if total income expected to be earned with respect to a property was overestimated, thereby causing a reduction in the depreciation allowances that should have been claimed and an increased tax liability. Interest is owed if total income was underestimated.

The following computational steps apply (Prop. Reg. § 1.167(n)-6(b)(1)):

(1) Recompute depreciation allowances for each year prior to the recomputation year using revised forecasted total income (i.e., the sum of current-year income for the recomputation year and all prior tax years plus a reasonable estimate of current-year income for future tax years through the end of the tenth tax year following the tax year that the income forecast property was placed in service).

(2) Substituting the recomputed depreciation allowances for the allowances allowed (or allowable), redetermine the tax liability for each prior year. The redetermined tax liability for each prior year is a "hypothetical" tax liability used only for purposes of computing whether interest is paid (too much depreciation was claimed) or received (too little depreciation was claimed).

(3) For each prior year, compare the hypothetical tax liability with the actual tax liability and compute the interest on the difference as explained below.

Syndication income from television series. Syndication income from a television series that was excluded from forecasted total income (or revised forecasted total income) in any prior tax year is excluded from revised forecasted total income for purposes of computing look-back interest (Prop. Reg. § 1.167(n)-6(c)(2)(ii)).

Look-back computation in year of disposition. Look-back interest must be computed in the year that an income forecast property is sold or otherwise disposed of if the disposition occurs prior to the end of the tenth tax year after the property is placed in service. Income from the disposition of income forecast property is included in the revised forecasted total income amount used in computing look-back interest. Thus, revised forecasted total income is the sum of the amount realized on the disposition plus all amounts included in current-year income in the year of disposition and prior years (Prop. Reg. § 1.167(n)-6(c)(2)(iii)).

Treatment of basis redetermination amounts. An amount paid or incurred after the property was placed in service which increased the basis of the property (i.e., a basis redetermination amount) may be taken into account by discounting the basis redetermination amount to its value as of the date the property was placed in service. The discounted basis redetermination amount is computing using the Federal mid-term rate (determined under Code Sec. 1274(d)) at the time the cost was paid or incurred. A taxpayer may elect not to discount the basis redetermination amount simply by making the look-back calculation without a discount (Prop. Reg. § 1.167(n)-6(c)).

Computation of hypothetical overpayment or underpayment of tax

For each prior year, a taxpayer must calculate a hypothetical overpayment or underpayment of tax by comparing the actual tax liability (as originally reported or subsequently adjusted on examination or by amended return) and hypothetical tax liability for the prior year (Prop. Reg. § 1.167(n)-6(d)(2)(i)). A hypothetical income tax liability must be determined for any prior tax year that income tax liability would be affected by a recalculated depreciation allowance. This rule includes changes in net operating losses that would be affected by a recalculated depreciation allowance. For example, if a recalculated depreciation allowance in the year that the income forecast property was placed in service reduces, increases, or results in a net operating loss carryforward in the following year, a hypothetical income tax liability must be recomputed for the following year that takes into account the change in the NOL carryforward.

The hypothetical tax liability for each prior year must be computed by taking into account all applicable additions to tax, credits, and net operating loss carrybacks and carryforwards. Any alternative minimum tax must also be taken into account.

The hypothetical tax liability for each prior year is compared to the actual tax liability for the prior year determined as of the latest of the following dates:

(1) The original due date of the return (including extensions);

(2) The date of a subsequently amended return;

(3) The date a return is adjusted by examination; or

(4) The date of the previous application of the look-back method.

When the look-back method is used for a second time (e.g., in the tenth tax year following the year the income forecast property was placed in service), the hypothetical tax liability for each prior tax year is compared to the hypothetical tax liability previously computed for those years the first time that the look-back method was applied.

Computation of interest

The adjusted overpayment rate under Code Sec. 460(b)(7)), compounded daily, is applied to the overpayment or underpayment for each prior tax year for the period beginning with the due date of the return (excluding extensions) for the prior year and ending on the earlier of the due date of the return (excluding extensions) for the recomputation year or the first date by which both the income tax return for the recomputation year is filed and the tax for that year has been paid in full (Prop. Reg. § 1.167(n)-6(d)(2)(ii)).

The amounts of interest on overpayments are then netted against interest on underpayments to arrive at the look-back interest payable or receivable.

Measurement of interest if recomputed depreciation changes net operating loss carryback or carryforward. If a recomputation of income forecast depreciation results in an increase or decrease to a net operating loss carryback, the interest a taxpayer is entitled to receive or required to pay must be computed on the decrease or increase in tax attributable to the change to the carryback only from the due date (not including extensions) of the return for the prior tax year that generated the carryback (Prop. Reg. § 1.167(n)-6(d)(2)(iii)).

In the case of a change in the amount of a carryforward, interest is computed from the due date of the return for the years in which the carryforward was absorbed.

Measurement of interest if prior-year tax liability was refunded as the result of a loss or credit carryback. A special rule applies if the hypothetical tax liability for a prior tax year is less than the amount of the actual tax liability for the prior year and any portion of the prior-year tax liability was refunded as the result of a loss or credit carryback that arose in a later tax year. In this situation, interest is computed on the amount of any refund in excess of the hypothetical income tax liability for the prior year only until the due date (not including extensions) of the return for the year in which the carryback arose (Prop. Reg. § 1.167(n)-(6)(d)(iv)).

Example (8): Assume that Year 3 is a recomputation year. In Year 1 actual tax liability before an NOL carryback from Year 2 is $1,000. The tax liability after an NOL carryback from Year 2 is $800 and the taxpayer receives a $200 refund for Year 1 taxes paid in Year 2. If the hypothetical tax liability for Year 1 is $850, the taxpayer has made a hypothetical overpayment of $150 ($1,000 less $850). Since the $200 refund does not exceed the $850 hypothetical tax liability, interest is credited on the $150 hypothetical overpayment from the due date of the Year 1 return to the due date of the Year 3 return for the recomputation year.

Example (9): Assume the same facts as in *Example (8)* except that the taxpayer received a $1,000 refund in Year 1. Since the amount of the refund ($1,000), exceeds the hypothetical tax liability for Year 1 ($850) by $150, the taxpayer is only entitled to interest on the $150 hypothetical overpayment from the due date of the Year 1 return to the due date of the Year 2 return.

Example (10): Assume the same facts as in *Example (8)*, except that the taxpayer received a $950 refund in Year 1. Since the amount of the refund ($950) exceeds the hypothetical tax liability ($850) by $100, interest is credited to the taxpayer on $100 of the hypothetical overpayment from the due date of the Year 1 return to the due date of the Year 2 return. Interest is credited on the remaining $50 of the hypothetical overpayment from the due date of the Year 1 return to the due date of the Year 3 return.

Simplified look-back method for certain pass-through entities

Pass-through entities that are not closely-held must use a simplified method to compute their hypothetical overpayment or underpayment for each prior year in which depreciation deductions were claimed. The pass-through entity applies the simplified method at the entity level and the owners do not calculate look-back interest (Reg. § 1.167(n)-(d)(3)). A pass-through entity only includes a partnership, S corporation, estate, or trust. A closely-held pass-through entity is one that, at any time during any year for which depreciation is recomputed, 50 percent or more (by value) of the beneficial interests in the entity are held (directly or indirectly) by or for five or fewer persons (Prop. Reg. § 1.167(n)-(d)(4)).

The proposed regulations do not require or allow other taxpayers to use the simplified method. However, the IRS requests comments on whether the method should be extended to other taxpayers.

Under the simplified method, look-back interest is computed for each prior year by applying a set tax rate to the net change in the depreciation allowance for that year.

Depreciation allowances are recomputed in the same manner as they are using the nonsimplified method described above. The recomputed depreciation allowances are compared with the depreciation allowances allowed (or allowable) for each prior tax year. For each prior tax year, the net change is multiplied by the highest rate in effect for corporations under Code Sec. 11 (35 percent) to arrive at the hypothetical underpayment or overpayment of tax for that year. The highest tax rate imposed on individuals under Code Sec. 1 (35 percent in 2003) is used if, at all times during all prior tax years more than 50 percent of the interests in the entity were held by individuals directly or through one or more pass-through entities. The highest rate of tax imposed on individuals is determined without regard to any additional tax imposed for the purpose of phasing out multiple tax brackets or exemptions.

When multiple properties are subject to the look-back method in any prior year, the changes in depreciation allowances attributable to each income forecast property are cumulated or netted against one another to arrive at a net change in income forecast depreciation for purposes of computing the hypothetical overpayment or underpayment attributable to the year.

Look-back recomputation years

There are a maximum of two recomputation years. Generally, these are the third and tenth tax years beginning after the tax year that the income forecast property is placed in service. However, if income from the income forecast property ceases with respect to the taxpayer before the tenth tax year after the property is placed in service, the tax year the income ceases is a recomputation year. For example, if the taxpayer sells the property in the first or second tax year after the property is placed in service, then that second tax year is the only recomputation year. If the property is sold after the third tax year and before the tenth tax year, then the third tax year and the tax year that the income ceases are the computation years (Prop. Reg. § 1.167(n)-(e)(1)).

In determining whether income from a property has ceased, the income must cease with respect to all persons treated a single taxpayer under rules similar to Code Sec. 41(f)(1) (relating to single taxpayer treatment of members of controlled groups and trades or businesses under common control for purposes of the research credit).

De minimum exceptions to look-back rule

No look-back interest calculation is required in any tax year that would otherwise be a recomputation year if one of two de minimus exceptions apply in the recomputation year.

Under the first exception, the look-back method does not apply to any income forecast property with a basis of $100,000 or less in a look-back (recomputation) year. The basis is determined without reduction for prior depreciation allowed or allowable (Code Sec. 167(g)(3); Prop. Reg. § 1.167(n)-6(f)).

The second exception requires that the taxpayer's income projections be within 10 percent of the income actually received (Code Sec. 167(g)(4); Prop. Reg. § 1.167(n)-6(e)(2)). Specifically, the 10-percent test is met if forecasted total income (and revised forecasted total income, if applicable) for each year prior to the look-back (recomputation) year is:

(1) greater than 90 percent of revised forecasted total income for the look-back year; and

(2) less than 110 percent of revised forecasted total income for the look-back year.

If the look-back method applied in the first recomputation year (i.e., third tax year after the income forecast property was placed in service) the amount of the forecasted total income or the revised forecasted total income for each tax year up to and including the third tax year after the year the property was placed in service is deemed equal to the revised forecasted total income that was used for purposes of applying the look-back rule in the third tax year.

Treatment of look-back interest

A taxpayer who fails to report look-back interest when due is subject to any penalties imposed under Subtitle F of the Internal Revenue Code (other than estimated tax penalties) attributable to the failure to report and pay a tax liability (Prop. Reg. § 1.167(n)-6(g)(1)).

Look-back interest is treated as interest arising from an underpayment of income tax under Subtitle A of the Internal Revenue Code, even though it is treated as an income tax liability for penalty purposes. Thus, look-back interest that is paid by an individual (or by a pass-through entity on behalf of an individual owner under the simplified method) is nondeductible personal interest.

The determination of whether look-back interest is treated as an income tax under Subtitle A, is determined on a net basis for each look-back (recomputation) year. Thus, in the recomputation year, the taxpayer nets the deemed overpayments or underpayments that are computed for each of the prior tax years, taking into account all income forecast property for which the look-back method is required in the recomputation year.

Interest received is treated as taxable interest rather than a reduction in tax liability.

Interest determined at the entity level is allocated among the owners (or beneficiaries) for reporting purposes in the same manner that interest income and interest expense are allocated to owners (or beneficiaries). The allocation rules generally applicable to the entity also apply.

Interest on look-back payments

Look-back interest is computed on the hypothetical increase or decrease in the liability only until the initial due date of the return (without regard to extensions) for the look-back year. Interest is charged on the amount of look-back interest payable by a taxpayer from the initial due date of the return (without regard to extensions) for the look-back year through the date the return is actually filed unless the taxpayer has a refund that fully offsets the amount of interest due. If look-back interest is refundable to the taxpayer, interest on the look-back amount is credited to the taxpayer from the initial due date of the return through the date the return is filed (Prop. Reg. § 1.167(n)-6(g)(2)).

Computing Depreciation on Multiple-Asset Accounts

¶ 370

Group, Classified and Composite Accounts

A group account is one that includes assets that are similar in kind and have roughly the same useful lives. The classified and composite accounts segregate assets without regard to useful lives—the classified account covering specific classes of assets (such as machinery and equipment or furniture and fixtures) and the composite account including more than one class of assets (such as all the assets of a business in one account).

Group, classified or composite accounts could be either open-end or year's acquisition accounts. An open-end account is one to which additions and from which retirements are made as they occur—a feature now substantially restricted since most property placed in service after 1980 must be treated as ACRS recovery property or MACRS property. An account that includes all the assets acquired in a year for a group or class of assets is a year's acquisition account.

¶ 372

Averaging Conventions

Where many assets are acquired or disposed of during a taxable year, depreciation may be computed on an average balance, unless the deduction is materially distorted for a particular year.

One popular averaging convention assumes that additions and retirements occur uniformly during the year so that depreciation is computed on the average of the beginning and ending balances of the asset account. This is the same as the "half-year" convention under ADR at ¶ 428.

Another permissible averaging convention assumes that additions and retirements in the first half of the year occur on the first day of that year and that second-half additions and retirements occur on the first day of the next year. Thus, a full year's depreciation is taken on first-half additions and second-half retirements. No depreciation is taken on first-half retirements and second-half additions.

A different version of this convention, called the "modified half-year convention," is available under ADR, as explained at ¶ 428.

Of course, there can no longer be additions to such pre-1981 multiple-asset accounts. Only retirements will affect computations under these conventions.

¶ 374

Straight-Line Depreciation on Multiple-Asset Account

Since useful lives of assets in a group account are roughly the same, the straight-line rate can be determined by averaging the useful lives of the assets.

In a classified or composite account, however, assets are grouped without regard to useful lives. To find the straight-line rate, one year's straight-line depreciation on each asset in the account is computed and the total annual depreciation is divided by the total basis of those assets. The average rate so obtained may continue to be used as long as the relative proportions of different types of assets in the account remain the same.

If an averaging convention was used that assumed uniform additions and retirements throughout the year, straight-line depreciation on an open-end, multiple-asset account may be computed by applying the average rate, adjusted for salvage, to the average of the beginning and ending balances of the asset account for the year.

¶ 376

Declining-Balance Depreciation on Multiple-Asset Account

The deduction under this method may be computed by applying 200 percent (or, for used assets, 150 percent) of the straight-line rate, *not* adjusted for salvage, to the average balance in the account reduced by the average reserve (before depreciation for the year).

¶ 378

Sum of the Years-Digits Depreciation on Multiple-Asset Account

The deduction under this method for an open-end account may be computed by using the complex remaining life plan prescribed by Reg. § 1.167(b)-3. Two rates are required, a years-digits rate based on the estimated *remaining* useful life of the account and a years-digits rate based on the *average* useful lives of the assets in the account. Here is a simplified explanation and illustration of how to compute the deduction:

(1) Multiply the *remaining life* rate by the beginning asset balance as adjusted for salvage and reduced by the beginning reserve.

(2) Multiply the rate based on *average life* by one-half of the additions during the year, adjusted for salvage.

(3) The sum of (1) and (2) is the deduction.

The sum of the years-digits deduction for a year's acquisition account can be determined by executing step (1) only of the remaining life plan, since there are no additions to the account after the first year, only retirements.

Retirement of Depreciated Property

¶ 380

Retirements from Item Accounts

Where depreciable property is retired from an item account through a sale, any gain or loss will be recognized to the extent of the difference between the selling price and the adjusted basis of the asset (Reg. § 1.167(a)-8).

Where the retirement is through an exchange, recognition of any gain or loss will depend on whether the exchange is wholly or partially "tax-free." If a gain or loss is recognized, it is the difference between the fair market value of the property received and the adjusted basis of the asset given in exchange.

If an asset is retired through actual physical abandonment, any loss will be recognized and it is measured by the adjusted basis of the asset at the time of abandonment. To qualify for a recognition of the loss, however, the taxpayer must intend to irrevocably abandon or discard the asset so that he will not use it again or retrieve it for sale or other disposition.

A depreciable asset may be withdrawn from productive use without a disposition. For instance, it could be placed in a supplies or scrap account. If a depreciated asset is retired from an item account without any disposition, any gain will not be recognized at that time. A loss, however, will be recognized to the extent of the excess of the adjusted basis of the asset at the time of retirement over the estimated salvage value. But if the fair market value of the retired asset is greater than the estimated salvage value, then the loss deduction is limited to the excess of the adjusted basis at retirement over the fair market value.

Special rule for item accounts

A loss on the normal retirement of an asset in a multiple asset account is not allowable where the depreciation rate is based upon the average useful life of the assets in the account. See ¶ 382. A taxpayer who sets up single item accounts for a few depreciable assets which cover a relatively narrow range of useful lives and which use an average useful life for such assets will generally not be treated as if a multiple-asset account has been set up (Reg. § 1.167(a)-8(d)).

ACRS and MACRS

See ¶ 162 for a rules regarding retirements and abandonments of ACRS and MACRS property, as well as a general discussion of what constitutes a retirement or abandonment.

ADR

For treatment of retirements from item vintage accounts under the ADR System, see ¶ 480.

¶ 382

Retirements from Multiple-Asset Accounts

Where depreciable property is retired from a multiple-asset account because of a sale, exchange, or abandonment, the rules for recognition of gain or loss are basically the same as those for retirements from an item account.

If an asset is retired from a multiple-asset account without disposing of it, any gain will not be recognized at that time. And a loss will be recognized only on abnormal retirements. Losses on such abnormal retirements are computed in the same way as losses on retirements (without disposition) from an item account, as discussed at ¶ 380.

The adjusted basis for determining a gain or loss on any type of retirement from a multiple-asset account, however, depends on whether the retirement is normal or abnormal. A normal retirement is one which occurs within the normal range of years considered in fixing the depreciation rate. The condition of the retired asset should be similar to that of assets customarily retired from use in the business.

If the retirement is a normal one, the adjusted basis for gain or loss purposes is the amount of the estimated salvage value.

Example (1): A machine in a multiple-asset account is sold for $35. The sale is a normal retirement. The original cost of the asset was $1,000 and estimated salvage value is $50. A loss of $15 is recognized on the sale—$50 adjusted basis (the estimated salvage value) minus $35 selling price.

If the retirement is an abnormal one, the adjusted basis for gain or loss is the original cost of the asset minus the depreciation which would have been proper had the asset been depreciated in an item account at the rate used for the multiple-asset account.

Example (2): A machine costing $1,000 was recorded in a multiple-asset account with an average life of 10 years and a 10% salvage factor. The straight-line method was used to compute depreciation. After the asset is held 3 years, it is accidentally damaged beyond repair. The machine is sold as scrap for $50. If the machine had been depreciated in an item account using the multiple-asset account rates, annual depreciation would have been $90 ($1,000 - $100 salvage (10%) × 10%). The adjusted basis of the machine for gain or loss purposes is $730—$1,000 cost minus $270 depreciation ($90 × 3)—and a $680 loss is recognized on the sale ($730 - $50 scrap proceeds).

Where acquisitions and retirements are numerous, accounting for individual retirements becomes quite detailed. In such cases, the Internal Revenue Service permits taxpayers to handle retirements in either of the following ways, provided that the one used is consistently followed and income is clearly reflected:

(1) Charge the full cost of retirements and credit the salvage proceeds to the reserve.

(2) Reduce both the asset and the reserve accounts by the cost of retirements and report all receipts from salvage as ordinary income.

See ¶ 380 for rules regarding retirements from item accounts.

See ¶ 162 for rules regarding retirements and abandonments of ACRS and MACRS property, as well as a general discussion of what constitutes a retirement or abandonment.

For rules under the ADR System for retirements from multiple-asset vintage accounts, see ¶ 462–¶ 478.

¶ 384

Item Accounts Treated as Multiple-Asset Accounts

The Regulations provide that if a separate account is set up for each asset and the depreciation rate is based on the average useful life of the assets (so that the same life is used for each account), the taxpayer may be subject to the rules governing losses on retirement from multiple-asset accounts.

Class Life ADR System

ADR System for Classes of Assets

¶ 400

ADR System Grew Out of Guidelines

The Class Life Asset Depreciation Range System (ADR), effective for assets placed in service after 1970 (but inapplicable to most property placed in service after 1980) was a direct offshoot of the depreciation guidelines in Rev. Proc. 62-21,[1] 1962-2 CB 418 (Code Sec. 167(m), prior to repeal by P.L. 101-508). The ADR System was similarly intended to minimize conflict over individual asset lives and to liberalize depreciation rates.

The ADR System is also based on broad industry classes of assets. Basically, the Rev. Proc. 62-21 guideline classes for which guideline lives were specified were used initially under ADR (¶ 406).

In the case of classes for land improvements, a class life is given (called an "asset guideline period" (¶ 420)). For all other classes of assets, a range of years (called "asset depreciation range" (¶ 422)) is given in addition to the class life. The upper and lower limits of the range are about 20 percent above and below the class life. For each asset in a class that has a range in effect, the taxpayer could select a depreciation period from that range.

The ADR regulations refer to the "asset depreciation period" rather than the "useful life" in explaining how to compute ADR depreciation. This is because such depreciation period can be shorter than the actual useful life. However, the depreciation period is treated as the useful life for all income tax purposes (with a few exceptions), including the computation of depreciation (¶ 424).

A taxpayer using the ADR System does not have to justify his retirement and replacement policies. A depreciation period selected for an asset cannot be changed by either the taxpayer or the IRS during the remaining period of use of the asset.

The election to use the ADR System is an annual one (Reg. § 1.167(a)-11(a)(1)). If made it applies to all eligible assets placed in service in the trade or business during the year of election. The ADR System does not apply to assets first placed in service before 1971 (or to property placed in service after 1980 if depreciable under ACRS or MACRS) or in a year in which an ADR election was not made (Reg. § 1.167(a)-11(a)(1)). See ¶ 406–412 as to the eligibility of assets for ADR depreciation and ¶ 442 for a discussion of when an asset is first placed in service.

¶ 402

A Survey of the ADR System

For land improvements, the class life is treated as the useful life for computing depreciation. For assets in other classes, the depreciation period selected by the taxpayer from the appropriate range is used to compute depreciation. Permissible depreciation methods under ADR include the straight-line, declining-balance and sum of the years-digits methods, with a special exception (¶ 426).

---

[1] As amplified by Rev. Proc. 68-27, 1968-2 CB 911, and supplemented by Rev. Procs. 65-13, 1965-1 CB 795; 66-18, 1966-1 CB 646; 66-39, 1966-2 CB 1244; and 68-35, 1968-2 CB 921.

ADR requires the use of either of two first-year averaging conventions (¶ 428). One is the half-year convention, in which a half year's depreciation can be taken on all assets first placed in service during the tax year. The other is the modified half-year convention, which allows a full year's depreciation on first-half additions and no depreciation on second-half additions. Any period prior to the month in which the taxpayer begins engaging in a trade or business or holding depreciable property for the production of income is not part of the taxable year for purposes of either convention. Employees by virtue of employment or, to a limited extent, persons engaging in a small amount of trade or business activity are not regarded as engaged in a trade or business. The latter limitation applies only so far as it prevents a small amount of trade or business from justifying a disproportionately large depreciation deduction for the year of the placing in service of assets that substantially increase the level of the taxpayer's business activity.

Assets must be accounted for in item accounts or multiple-asset accounts by year placed in service. These accounts by year placed in service are called "vintage accounts" (see ¶ 440).

Salvage value under the ADR System is gross salvage value, unreduced by the cost of removal, dismantling, demolition, or similar operations (¶ 446). These costs are currently deductible under the ADR System.

Generally, gain or loss on retirement from multiple-asset vintage accounts is not recognized under ADR unless the retirement is an "extraordinary" one—that is, a retirement because of casualty or because of discontinuance or curtailment of a sizable part of a business operation (¶ 462–¶ 466). Ordinary retirements are handled by adding the retirement proceeds to the depreciation reserve. These and other adjustments to the reserve may possibly result in the realization of gain during the life of the vintage account (¶ 476) or loss upon the termination of the account when the last asset is retired (¶ 478).

Assets Eligible for ADR Depreciation

¶ 406

Assets Generally Eligible Under ADR System

The ADR System may be elected for all Code Sec. 1245 and Code Sec. 1250 property that was first placed in service after 1970 (and that is not ACRS recovery property or depreciable under MACRS) for which a class and class life were in effect for the year of election. The classes and class lives are determined generally under Rev. Proc. 77-10, 1977-1 CB 548 (superseded by Rev. Proc. 83-35, 1983-1 CB 745) for applicable years ending after March 20, 1977, and under Rev. Proc. 72-10, 1972-1 CB 721 for applicable years ending before March 21, 1977 (superseded by Rev. Proc. 77-10).

Eligible property includes Sec. 1245 or 1250 property that was new property, used property (see ¶ 408), a property improvement (Reg. § 1.167(a)-11(d)(2)(vii)(*a*)), or an excluded addition (Reg. § 1.167(a)-11(d)(2)(vi)). Further, property qualified even if depreciation on it had to be capitalized, such as property used for self-construction of fixed assets.

If the ADR System is elected for any year, the election covers all eligible property first placed in service in that year by the taxpayer (Reg. § 1.167(a)-11(b)(5)(ii)). This is so whether the assets are used in a trade or business or held for the production of income. Thus, except as indicated at ¶ 408, the election cannot be made for all the assets put into operation in one trade or business for a year without making the election for those placed in service in any other trade or business of the same taxpayer or for those placed in service and held by him for the production of income in that same year.

Property received from a related person in a transfer that did not trigger an investment credit recapture and was not described in Code Sec. 381(a) (carryovers in certain corporate acquisitions) may have been ineligible for ADR depreciation. In the case of such a transfer, the transferred property was not eligible for the ADR election if the depreciation period used by the transferor in computing his investment credit is not within the range for the class in which the transferred asset falls. The question of whether a person is related is determined under Code Sec. 267 (disallowance of losses, etc., between related persons), except that brothers and sisters are not considered related. This rule also applies to transfers between controlled partnerships (or a partnership and its controlling partner) under Code Sec. 707(b) and transfers between corporate members of the same affiliated group (affiliation determined on the basis of a 50-percent rather than an 80-percent stock ownership test). However, if property was ineligible under this rule, the transferor may have recomputed any investment credit for the year the transferred asset was placed in service, using a depreciation period within the range for the class (this would be beneficial only if the initial depreciation period is below the range) (Reg. § 1.167(a)-11(e)(3)(iv)).

¶ 408

Used Assets and the 10-Percent Rule

The ADR System applies to used assets as well as new assets. But if the unadjusted basis of used Sec. 1245 property first placed in service in a trade or business during the tax year for which there is no specific used property asset guideline class in effect is over 10 percent of the unadjusted basis of all the Sec. 1245 property placed in service in that year, the taxpayer can elect to apply ADR to only the new Sec. 1245 property and determine the useful lives of the used Sec. 1245 property by other means (Reg. § 1.167(a)-11(b)(5)(iii)(*a*)).

This same 10-percent rule applies separately in the case of used Sec. 1250 property (Reg. § 1.167(a)-11(b)(5)(iii)(*b*)).

The "unadjusted basis" means the cost or other basis of an asset without adjustment for regular depreciation or amortization, but with other adjustments required under Code Sec. 1016 or other applicable provisions. Thus, the cost or other basis of a Sec. 1245 asset had to be reduced by any 20-percent additional first-year depreciation claimed for property placed in service before 1981 to arrive at its unadjusted basis (Reg. § 1.167(a)-11(c)(1)(v)(*a*)).

An election may be made for either the Sec. 1245 or Sec. 1250 category to have the lives of both new and used assets determined under ADR even though over 10 percent of the assets placed in service in that category during the year were used.

Used assets are those whose original use did not begin with the taxpayer (Reg. § 1.167(a)-11(b)(5)(iii)(*c*)). This means that assets transferred in a tax-free transaction (such as a transfer to a controlled corporation) must be treated as used assets (but the transferred assets do not qualify for ADR if they were placed in service by the transferor before 1971 or are recovery property). Thus, the manner in which the transferred assets are depreciated depends on whether the transferee elected ADR for the year it placed the transferred assets in service and whether it elected the 10-percent used asset rule for either the Sec. 1245 or the Sec. 1250 property.

If Code Sec. 381(a) applied to a transfer, however, the transferee is bound by the transferor's election or failure to elect the ADR System for assets placed in service in pre-transfer years. See ¶ 450.

For the purpose of determining whether the used assets are more than 10 percent of the total assets placed in service during the year, any assets subject to special depreciation or amortization provisions (see ¶ 410) and any assets acquired in a transaction to which Sec. 381(a) applies are treated as used assets (Reg. § 1.167(a)-11(b)(5)(iii)(*c*)).

¶ 410

Property Subject to Special Amortization or Depreciation

The ADR System does not apply to certain assets that are given special depreciation or amortization treatment.

If ADR was claimed in the first year an asset was placed in service, the ADR election for that asset was subject to termination at the beginning of any later year in which the taxpayer elected one of these special provisions (Reg. § 1.167(a)-11(b)(5)(v)). See ¶ 452 on how to account for such a termination.

¶ 412

Public Utilities

The use of accelerated depreciation and the 20-percent ADR useful life variance by most public utilities (electric, water, sewage, gas distribution or pipeline, steam, or telephone companies) is conditioned on "normalized" accounting in setting the rates charged to customers. Rate-fixing generally reflects straight-line depreciation and ADR midpoint lives. The effect of these rules may be viewed as interest-free loans to utilities, but regulatory bodies are not prevented from passing through the tax benefits to customers by treating some capital as cost-free or by excluding some assets from a utility's rate base. This is distinguishable from "flow-through" accounting, under which the benefits are passed through in the form of accelerated methods and shorter useful lives.

A failure to "normalize" accounting in setting utility rates may terminate an ADR election. See ¶ 452 on how to account for any such termination.

For the treatment of public utility property under ACRS, see ¶ 262.

Computation of ADR Depreciation

¶ 418

Classifying Assets Under the ADR System

ADR elections cover all eligible property placed in service by the taxpayer during the taxable year. Computations reflect guideline classes into which such property falls. An asset guideline is an ADR class of assets for which a separate class life is in effect under Rev. Proc. 83-35, superseding Rev. Proc. 77-10. An asset for which no separate class life is provided is ineligible for ADR treatment and must be depreciated under the general depreciation rules.

Omission of classes pertaining to buildings in Rev. Proc. 77-10 (superseded by Rev. Proc. 83-35), which reorganized and reclassified assets that qualified for the ADR System, made buildings placed in service for certain relevant years subject to depreciation under the general rules. However, P.L. 93-625 provided transitional rules under which taxpayers electing ADR could determine the class life of Sec. 1250 property either under the guidelines in effect on December 31, 1970, or on the basis of facts and circumstances. A represcribed guideline brought land improvements under ADR.

Property is classified according to the activity in which it is primarily used (Reg. § 1.167(a)-11(b)(4)(iii)(*b*)). This is the case even though the primary activity is insubstantial in relation to all the taxpayer's activities. Once classified, an asset stays in the same class even if there is a change in its primary use after the ADR election year. This includes a change in primary use that causes Sec. 1250 property to become Sec. 1245 property.

Similarly, leased property is classified as if it were owned by the lessee (unless there is a class in effect for lessors of such property) (Reg. § 1.167(a)-11(e)(3)(iii)). However, property is classified without regard to the lessee's activity if the class covers property based upon type (trucks or railroad cars) as distinguished from the activity in which used.

An incorrect classification of property does not revoke an ADR election for an asset. The classification is corrected. See ¶ 448.

¶ 420

Class Life (Asset Guideline Period)

The average class life given for each class is called an "asset guideline period" in the ADR Regulations and applicable revenue procedures. Herein, however, it is referred to as the "class life." Where a class has a class life in effect for the tax year but does not have a range (¶ 422) in effect for that year, depreciation is computed on the assets in that class by using the class life as the depreciation period (¶ 424). (Reg. § 1.167(a)-11(b)(4)(i)(*a*).) ("Present class life" under ACRS and the streamlined but similarly defined "class life" under Modified ACRS are statutory terms having particular meaning under the rules that apply to the classification of most property placed in service after 1980. See ¶ 230.)

The class lives are set forth in applicable revenue procedures.

The class life for an ADR election year is the one that was in effect on the last day of the year. But it cannot be longer than it was on the first day of the tax year (or later date during the year when a class was first established). Thus, a taxpayer can take advantage of changes during a tax year resulting in a shorter class life but will not have a class life lengthened because of changes during the year (Reg. § 1.167(a)-11(b)(4)(ii)).

A change in the length of a class life after the year in which a vintage account is established is not effective for that account unless the supplement or revision making the change expressly permits change for the revision and succeeding years.

Assets used predominantly outside the United States in the year first placed in service were treated as if they were in separate classes from the assets used predominantly within the United States. Consequently, each class was divided into a class for assets used predominantly within the U.S. and a class for those used predominantly outside the U.S. Each class that includes only assets used predominantly outside the U.S. is treated as if the class life for the class is in effect but the range is not in effect. Depreciation on the assets in such a class is computed by using the class life as the depreciation period (¶ 424). And the depreciation period will not be changed in any later year because of a change in predominant use after the close of the ADR election tax year.

¶ 422

Asset Depreciation Range

The asset depreciation range for a class is a range of years from 20 percent below to 20 percent above the class life (¶ 420), rounded to the nearest whole or half year. The lower limit of the range is 80 percent and the upper limit is 120 percent of the class life. The ranges for the various classes are set forth in Rev. Proc. 83-35. From the range for a class, the taxpayer selects a depreciation period (¶ 424) over which depreciation for an asset or group of assets in the class would be claimed.

The range for an ADR election year is the one that is in effect on the last day of the year. But the lower limit of the range cannot be longer than it was on the first day of the tax year (or later date during the year when a class was first established). This means that the taxpayer can take advantage of changes during a tax year resulting in shorter lower limits but cannot have a lower limit lengthened because of changes during the year (Reg. § 1.167(a)-11(b)(4)(ii)).

A change in the limits of a range after the year in which a vintage account is established is not effective for that account unless the supplement or revision making the change expressly permits change for the revision and succeeding years.

Lessors figuring ADR depreciation on leased property determine the range and the depreciation period without regard to the period for which the property is leased, including any extensions or renewals (Reg. § 167(a)-11(e)(3)(iii)).

¶ 424

Asset Depreciation Period

The asset depreciation period is the period over which the taxpayer depreciates an asset. If the asset is in a class with a class life but no range in effect, the depreciation period is equal to the class life (¶ 420). If it is in a class with a range in effect, it is the period for depreciation selected from the range (¶ 422).

Any period which is a whole number of years or a whole number of years plus a half year may be selected (Reg. § 1.167(a)-11(b)(4)(i)(*b*)). If property is transferred from a related person in a transfer that does not trigger an investment credit recapture and is not described in Code Sec. 381(a) (see ¶ 406), however, the period selected by the transferee may not be shorter than the period used by the transferor in computing his investment credit (Reg. § 1.167(a)-11(e)(3)(iv)). (This interpretation is reached in spite of an ambiguous reference to the word "taxpayer" in the first sentence of subdivision (iv). In the first part of the sentence, "taxpayer" refers to the transferor. In the latter part of the sentence, it appears that the "taxpayer" means the transferee.) See ¶ 142 and ¶ 264 for rules that prevent transfers between related parties or tax-free exchanges from bringing pre-1987 property under the Modified Accelerated Cost Recovery System (MACRS) and pre-1981 property under the Accelerated Cost Recovery System (ACRS).

The depreciation period is used as if it were the useful life. Depreciation is then computed on the basis of that period, which may actually be shorter than the useful life.

Generally, the depreciation period must be treated as if it were the useful life for all other income tax purposes (Reg. § 1.167(a)-11(g)(1)) (for exceptions, such as the period used in estimating salvage value, see Reg. § 1.167(a)-11(g)(1)(ii)).

For example, if the depreciation period is less than six years, additional first-year depreciation may not have been claimed. If it is less than three years, accelerated depreciation could not be claimed and salvage value may not be ignored to the extent of 10 percent of the basis of the asset. If ADR is elected, the depreciation period chosen for improvements to leased assets is compared to the lease term in determining whether the lessee deducts depreciation based on the depreciation period or amortization based on the lease term (Reg. § 1.162-11). If the appropriate range lower limit is equal to or less than the lease term, it would seem to be advisable to select a depreciation period equal to or shorter than the lease term, if possible. If amortization is based on the lease term, an accelerated method of depreciation is not available.

If accelerated depreciation is taken under the ADR System on personal property subject to a lease, straight-line depreciation based on the depreciation period selected and computed according to ADR rules is subtracted from the ADR depreciation deducted for the asset in determining the minimum tax preference item (¶ 170) for noncorporate taxpayers and personal holding companies (see the example at Reg. § 1.167(a)-11(g)(3)(ii)).

The following three determinations are made, however, without regard to the depreciation period (Reg. § 1.167(a)-11(g)(1)(ii)):

(1) determination of the anticipated period of use for estimating salvage value at the end of the vintage year;

(2) determination of whether an expense prolongs the life of an asset (this is to be done on the basis of the anticipated period of use, estimated at the close of the vintage year); and

(3) determination of whether a transaction is a sale or a lease.

¶ 426

Depreciation Methods Under ADR

If ADR is elected, the straight-line, the sum of the years-digits, or any acceptable declining-balance method must be applied to each asset properly included in the ADR election (Reg. § 1.167(a)-11(b)(5)(v)(*a*)). Thus, for new eligible property, the straight-line, the 200-percent declining-balance or the sum of the years-digits method may be used. For used eligible property, the straight-line or the 150-percent declining-balance method may be used. Accelerated depreciation on realty is limited.

There is an exception, however. A taxpayer has the option of using a different method or methods for assets consisting of 75 percent or more of the unadjusted basis of all assets placed in service during the tax year in a class and excluding all the assets in that class from the ADR election. The different method must be continued for these excluded assets unless the Commissioner consents to a change.

Use of an ineligible method for an asset cancels the privilege of making the ADR election for all the assets in the same class unless there was a good faith misclassification (see ¶ 448).

The ADR System assumes that the depreciation period chosen already takes salvage value into account (Reg. § 1.167(a)-11(c)(1)(i)), just as did the depreciation guideline lives in Rev. Proc. 62-21, 1962-2 CB 418. Accordingly, the straight-line and sum of the years-digits depreciation computations under ADR do not take salvage value into account.

Straight-line ADR depreciation is computed by dividing the unadjusted basis of the asset (unreduced by salvage value) by the number of years in the depreciation period (Reg. § 1.167(a)-11(c)(1)(i)(*b*)). Alternatively, the unadjusted basis may be multiplied by a straight-line rate based on the depreciation period.

Sum of the years-digits ADR depreciation is calculated by multiplying the unadjusted basis of the asset (unreduced by salvage value) by a sum of the years-digits fraction (or its decimal equivalent) based on the depreciation period.

Example (1): An item of equipment cost $10,000 and had an estimated salvage value of $900. A depreciation period of 5 years was selected for the determination of ADR depreciation. Straight-line depreciation under ADR for the first year the asset was placed in service (assuming a full year's depreciation) was $2,000 ($10,000 unadjusted basis either divided by 5 or multiplied by 20%). If the sum of the years-digits method was elected, the first year's depreciation was $3,333—5/15 of $10,000 unadjusted basis. The numerator of the fraction is the number of years remaining in the 5-year depreciation period at the beginning of the tax year. The denominator is the sum of the years-digits for a depreciation period of 5 years.

Where the depreciation period is a whole number of years plus a half year, the sum of the years-digits is the sum of the remaining depreciation periods at the beginning of each year of the period. Thus, the sum of the years-digits for a 5.5-year period is 18 (5.5 + 4.5 + 3.5 + 2.5 + 1.5 + .5). A quick way to determine the sum of the years-digits where the depreciation period is a whole number of years plus a half year is to square the next higher whole number and divide the result by two. Thus, the sum of the years-digits for the 5.5-year period could have been found by squaring six (36) and dividing by two (18).

The unadjusted basis of an asset had to be reduced by any 20-percent bonus depreciation before computing the straight-line or sum of the years-digits depreciation.

The 200-percent declining-balance rate under ADR is double the straight-line rate based on the depreciation period. The 150-percent declining-balance rate is 1½ times the straight-line rate based on the depreciation period. To compute depreciation under either the 150-percent or 200-percent declining-balance method, the proper rate is applied to the adjusted basis of the asset. The adjusted basis is the excess of the unadjusted basis over the depreciation reserve. In essence, this excess is the undepreciated basis of the asset.

Example (2): If 200% declining-balance depreciation were claimed under ADR for the asset described in Example (1), the amount of the deduction would have been $4,000 for the first year ($10,000 × 40% (double the 20% straight-line rate based on the 5-year depreciation period)) and $2,400 for the next year (40% of the $6,000 adjusted basis (unadjusted basis of $10,000 minus $4,000 depreciation reserve)).

Where the tax year is less than 12 months, ADR depreciation is allowed only for the actual number of months in the tax year. In such a case, a full year's depreciation should be first computed and then prorated according to the percentage that the actual number of months during the year is of 12. (Reg. § 1.167(a)-11(c)(2)(iv).) The Tax Court has ruled that this does not bar a taxpayer commencing activity after the beginning of the month (and, in this case, electing the modified half-year convention discussed at ¶ 428) from treating the commencement month as a full month for purposes of computing depreciation in a short taxable year (*L.D. Greenbaum,* 53 TCM 708, Dec. 43,884(M)).

In no instance, however, may an asset be depreciated below salvage value (Reg. § 1.167(a)-11(d)(1)(iv)). Accordingly, depreciation for any tax year under ADR may not be greater than the excess at the beginning of the tax year of the unadjusted basis of the account over the sum of the depreciation reserve and the salvage value of the account (Reg. § 1.167(a)-11(c)(1)(i)(*a*)). For the determination of salvage value under ADR, see ¶ 446.

Post-1980 improvements to pre-1981 property are generally subject to ACRS or MACRS rules. However, the original property and pre-1981 improvements remain subject to ADR elections. Thus, improved property may be only partially subject to the Class Life ADR System.

¶ 428

First-Year Convention Required Under ADR

In computing ADR depreciation, the taxpayer must use one of two first-year conventions:

Half-year convention

Under this convention, a half year's depreciation is taken on all assets put in service during the year. This is done on the assumption that all property is placed in service on the first day of the second half of the tax year (July 1 of a calendar year) (Reg. § 1.167(a)-11(c)(2)(iii)).

The consumption of only a half year's depreciation in the first tax year does not affect the computation of the straight-line and declining-balance depreciation in succeeding tax years. Under the straight-line method, the full ADR rate is applied to the unadjusted basis of the account. Declining-balance depreciation is computed by applying the full declining-balance ADR rate to the adjusted basis of the account (total unadjusted basis less depreciation previously deducted).

However, the using up of a half year's depreciation in the first tax year affects the sum of the years-digits computation for the second and following years. This is because it is necessary that the years-digits rate reflect the proration required where only a partial year's depreciation was allowed in the first year. See ¶ 358. Thus, the second tax year's fraction would be set up to provide half of the first full year's depreciation and half of the second full year's depreciation. This could be done conveniently by averaging the years-digits fractions for the two tax years involved. Accordingly, the fractions for the first two full depreciation years of a 10-year depreciation period would be 10/55 and 9/55. The fraction for the first tax year would be 5/55, half of the first year's fraction. The fraction for the second tax year would be 9.5/55, the average of 10/55 and 9/55. The third tax year's fraction would be 8.5/55, etc. The fraction for the second or later year is applied to the total unadjusted basis of the account.

The modified half-year convention

If the taxpayer elects this convention, it is assumed that first-half additions are made on the first day of the year and second-half additions are made on the first day of the succeeding year. Thus, depreciation for the first year is computed by applying the full ADR rate (straight-line, declining-balance or sum of the years-digits) to the first-half additions. This has the effect of giving a full year's depreciation on first-half additions and no depreciation on second-half additions.

In determining the second and following years' depreciation, it is assumed that a half year's depreciation has been allowed for the first tax year (full rate applied to only first-half additions obviously is considered the equivalent of a half year's depreciation). Consequently, the second tax year's depreciation is computed in basically the same manner as under the half-year convention. The full straight-line ADR rate is applied to the total unadjusted basis of the account. The full declining-balance ADR rate is applied to the adjusted basis of the account. The years-digits fraction for the second or later tax year (determined by averaging the fractions for the two tax years involved, as above) is applied to the total unadjusted basis of the account.

Each of these two conventions applies to both item and multiple-asset vintage accounts.

If one of these two conventions was elected under ADR for any year, it must be used for all eligible assets (see ¶ 406–¶ 412) placed in service in that year. However, the other convention may be elected for another ADR election year.

Example (1): Of $80,000 of production machinery and equipment placed in service in 1980, $50,000 was charged to a multiple-asset vintage account and $30,000 was the cost of one piece of equipment recorded in an item account. From the range of eight to 12 years, the taxpayer selected an 8-year depreciation period for the $50,000 multiple-asset account and a 10-year period for the $30,000 item account. The assets in the $50,000 account were placed in service on January 15, 1980. The equipment in the item account was installed and began operating on August 15, 1980. The taxpayer elected ADR and the modified half-year convention for 1980, the double declining-balance method for the multiple-asset account, and the sum of the years-digits method for the item account.

The 200% declining-balance ADR rate for the multiple-asset account is 25%, double the 12.5% straight-line ADR rate (based on an 8-year depreciation period). Depreciation on this account for 1980 is $12,500—25% of $50,000—since a full year's depreciation was allowed under the modified half-year convention (put in service in the first half of 1980).

No depreciation was allowed on the item account for 1980 since the equipment was placed in service in the second half of the year.

Example (2): If the taxpayer in *Example (1)* had chosen the half-year convention for 1980, only a half year's depreciation would have been allowable on the assets in the $50,000 account which were placed in service in the first half of the year. Depreciation on this account for 1980 under the half-year convention would have been $6,250 ($50,000 × 25% × ½). Likewise, a half year's depreciation was allowable on the $30,000 item account for 1980. This amounted to $2,727: 18.181% (10/55) × $30,000 × ½.

Example (3): Double declining-balance depreciation for 1981 on the $50,000 multiple-asset account in *Example (1)* under the modified half-year convention would have been $9,375: $37,500 adjusted basis ($50,000 unadjusted basis – $12,500 first-year deduction) × 25% double declining-balance ADR rate. Thus, assuming no intervening shift to straight-line depreciation, the deduction for 1982 would have been $7,031 (25% of $28,125) and for 1983 would be $5,274 (25% of $21,094).

Sum of the years-digits depreciation for 1981 on the $30,000 item account in *Example (1)* under the modified half-year convention would have been $5,182: $30,000 unadjusted basis × 9.5/55.

Example (4): Double declining-balance depreciation for 1981 on the $50,000 multiple-asset account in *Example (2)* under the half-year convention would have been $10,938: $43,750 adjusted basis ($50,000 unadjusted basis – $6,250 first-year deduction) × 25% double declining-balance ADR rate. Thus, assuming no intervening switch to straight-line depreciation, the deduction for 1982 would have been $8,203 (25% of $32,812) and for 1983 would be $6,152 (25% of $24,609).

Sum of the years-digits depreciation for 1981 on the $30,000 item account in *Example (2)* under the half-year convention would have been $5,182, computed the same way as in *Example (3)* ($30,000 unadjusted basis × 9.5/55).

In applying these two half-year conventions, the first half of the year was considered as expiring at the close of the last day of a calendar month which was the closest such last day to the middle of the tax year. The second half of the year begins the day after the expiration of the first half of the tax year. (Reg. § 1.167(a)-11(c)(2)(iv).)

Example (5): A taxpayer has a short tax year beginning February 1 and ending December 31. There are 334 days in this tax year and the midpoint is midnight of the 167th day. The 30th of June is the 150th day and the 31st of July is the 181st day of the tax year. July 31 is the day on which the first half of the tax year expires since it is closer to the middle of the year (13 days) than June 30 (17 days). Accordingly, the second half of the year begins on August 1.

In applying the above rule, however, there may be instances in which the middle of the tax year is exactly equidistant from the last day of the two calendar months.

Example (6): If a year begins May 1 and ends November 30, the tax year consists of 214 days. The midpoint of the year is 12:00 midnight of the 107th day, which is August 15. This is exactly 15 days apart from both July 31 and August 31. The ADR regulations do not address this problem, although Reg. § 1.1250-5(f)(1), dealing with an analogous problem under the realty depreciation recapture rules, arbitrarily selects the earliest of two such days that are equidistant from the middle of the year.

If a taxable year consisted of only one calendar month, the first day of the second half of the taxable year begins on the fifteenth day of a 28-day month, the sixteenth day of a 29-day or 30-day month, and the seventeenth day of a 31-day month (Reg. § 1.167(a)-11(c)(2)(iv)).

¶ 430

Effect of Retirements on Depreciation Computation

In the case of an ordinary retirement (see ¶ 462), the retired asset is not removed from a multiple-asset vintage account. Instead, the retirement proceeds are added to the depreciation reserve. See ¶ 464. Accordingly, the computation of straight-line and sum of the years-digits depreciation on the account from which the asset was retired is unaffected by the retirement except to the extent that the increase in the depreciation reserve limits the amount of depreciation that can be deducted. Since the increase in the depreciation reserve by the retirement proceeds decreases the adjusted basis of the account, declining-balance depreciation is reduced by an ordinary retirement.

An extraordinarily retired asset (see ¶ 462), however, is removed from a multiple-asset vintage account. See ¶ 466. Consequently, the amount of depreciation deductible in the retirement year is affected in a majority of cases. Whether and how much it is affected depends on which first-year convention was elected for the year the vintage account was established.

Under the half-year convention, extraordinary retirements are considered as occurring on the first day of the second half of the year. Hence, a half year's depreciation is allowed in the year of retirement.

Under the modified half-year convention, an extraordinary retirement gets a full year's depreciation, a half year's depreciation or no depreciation, depending on the time of year when the asset was acquired and retired. A first-half addition that is retired in the first half of the year gets no depreciation (assumption that the retirement occurred on the first day of the year). A half year's depreciation is allowed if a first-half addition is retired in the second half of the year or a second-half addition is retired in the first half of the year (assumption that the retirement occurred on the first day of the second half of the year). A full year's depreciation is granted if a second-half addition is retired in the second half of the year (assumption that the retirement occurred on the first day of the next tax year).

¶ 432

Depreciation of Mass Assets

It may not have been practical to maintain records as to the vintage of mass assets or the time of the year in which such assets were placed in service. In such an instance, the computation of the first tax year's depreciation could have been based on the amount spent on such mass assets during the year under the half-year convention. Under the modified half-year convention, the calculation could have been based on the amount spent during the first half of the year.

If an ordinary retirement of mass assets occurs, there is no problem in computing depreciation since the retirement proceeds are simply added to the related depreciation reserve.

In the case of an extraordinary retirement, however, it becomes necessary to determine the vintage of the retired assets so as to figure out the vintage account and related reserve from which the assets and accumulated depreciation are to be removed. The vintage of the retired assets is also necessary in order to calculate the amount of accumulated depreciation.

If a taxpayer adopted reasonable recordkeeping practices for mass assets, their vintage may be determined upon retirement by an appropriate mortality dispersion table (Reg. § 1.167(a)-11(d)(3)(v)*(d)*). It may be based on an acceptable sampling of the taxpayer's experience or other acceptable statistical or engineering techniques. Or, a standard table prescribed by the Commissioner may be used, but the table must continue to be used in later years unless consent to change is obtained.

Where the allocation is apportioned to a year in which the half-year convention was elected, a half-year's depreciation is allowed for the retirement year as indicated at ¶ 430.

In order to compute depreciation in the retirement year for mass assets allocated to a year in which the modified half-year convention was elected, they must be separated into first-half and second-half retirements. The first-half retirements are then divided into first-half additions and second-half additions of the allocation year. This apportionment is made according to the respective percentages that the actual first-half additions and second-half additions are of the total actual additions for the allocation year (Reg. § 1.167(a)-11(c)(2)(v)). Next, the same type of apportionment is made for the second-half retirements. With the resulting information, depreciation for the retirement year is computed in accordance with the rules at ¶ 430.

Example (1): Two years after electing the modified half-year convention, a taxpayer has mass asset extraordinary retirements from a class. By means of an appropriate mortality dispersion table, he determines that $9,000 of these retirements are allocable to the year of the election. Of this amount, $4,000 were first-half retirements and the remaining $5,000 were second-half retirements. In the election year, there were actual mass asset additions of $10,000 in the first half of the year and $15,000 in the second half of the year.

Of the $4,000 first-half retirements allocated to the election year, $1,600 is treated as first-half additions ($10,000/$25,000 × $4,000) and the remaining $2,400 balance is treated as second-half additions. Of the $5,000 second-half retirements so allocated, $2,000 is treated as first-half additions ($10,000/$25,000 × $5,000) and the remaining $3,000 balance is treated as second-half additions.

Accordingly, no depreciation is taken for the post-retirement year on the $1,600 first-half retirements treated as first-half additions. A half-year's depreciation is claimed on the $2,400 of first-half retirements treated as second-half additions and the $2,000 of second-half retirements treated as first-half additions. A full-year's depreciation may be deducted for the $3,000 of second-half retirements treated as second-half additions.

Example (2): If the taxpayer in *Example (1)* had elected the half-year convention in the election year, a half-year's depreciation would be claimed on the post-retirement year on the $9,000 of the mass asset retirements in that were allocated to the year of the election.

¶ 434

Depreciation Method Changes Under ADR Without Consent

Consent of the Commissioner is not needed under the ADR System to change from the declining-balance method to the sum of the years-digits method and from either a declining-balance method or the sum of the years-digits method to the straight-line method (Reg. § 1.167(a)-11(c)(1)(iii)). Although the Regulation does not specifically state that more than one change can be made without consent for the same vintage account, it appears that a taxpayer could start depreciating a vintage account with the 200-percent declining-balance method, change to the sum of the years-digits method, and change again to the straight-line method.

A statement must be furnished with the income tax return for the year of change setting forth the vintage accounts for which change is made.

As to public utility property, any changes required or permitted under Sec. 167(l) (prior to repeal by P.L. 101-508) are permissible under ADR rules.

Further, where changes are required or allowed because realty does or does not qualify as residential rental property, these changes are likewise permissible under ADR. Such a change causes a removal of the asset to a separate vintage account, however (see ¶ 440).

The above changes are the only ones available under ADR for which the Commissioner's consent is not necessary.

In determining the remaining portion of a depreciation period at the beginning of the year of change, it will be assumed that a half year's depreciation was taken in the year the asset was first placed in service regardless of which first-year convention was adopted by the taxpayer.

Where the change is to the straight-line method, the annual depreciation allowance beginning with the year of change is determined by dividing the adjusted basis (unadjusted basis less depreciation reserve) of the vintage account (unreduced by salvage value) by the number of years remaining in its depreciation period as of the beginning of the year of change. Or the adjusted basis could be multiplied by a straight-line rate based on the remaining depreciation period.

Example (1): An item of equipment costs $10,000, has an estimated salvage value of $900, and is placed in service in the first half of the tax year. The taxpayer elects the modified half-year convention and selects a 5-year depreciation period. Double declining-balance depreciation is $4,000 for the first year (40% ADR double declining-balance rate × $10,000) and $2,400 for the second year (40% × $6,000 adjusted basis ($10,000 – $4,000 depreciation reserve)). If the taxpayer changes to the straight-line method in the third year, the asset will be treated as having a 3.5-year remaining depreciation period even though two full years' depreciation has been deducted under the modified half-year convention. Thus, depreciation for the year of change under the straight-line method would be $1,029: $3,600 adjusted basis/3.5.

If it is assumed that the above item of equipment is placed in service in the second half of the tax year, no depreciation is deductible in the year placed in service and $4,000 is deductible in the second year under the modified half-year convention. If the taxpayer changes to the straight-line method in the third year, the asset will be treated as having a 3.5-year remaining depreciation period even though only one full year's depreciation has been deducted. Depreciation for the year of change would be $1,714: $6,000 adjusted basis/3.5.

The amount of straight-line depreciation allowable after such a change may not be more than the annual ADR straight-line allowance based on the original depreciation period (unadjusted basis of account, without reduction for salvage value, divided by the number of years in the original depreciation period).

Where the change is from a declining-balance method to the sum of the years-digits method, depreciation for the year of change would be computed by applying a sum of the years-digits fraction or rate based on the remaining depreciation period to the adjusted basis of the asset at the beginning of the year of change.

Example (2): Assume that depreciation on the asset placed in service in the first half of the year in *Example (1)* is changed to the sum of the years-digits method (instead of to the straight-line method) in the third year. The sum of the years-digits for the remaining 3.5-year depreciation period is 8 ($4^2 \div 2$) (see ¶ 426). The depreciation allowance for the year of change under the sum of the years-digits method is $1,575 – 3.5/8 × $3,600 adjusted basis. The years-digits fraction for the following years would be 2.5/8, 1.5/8 and .5/8.

Depreciation Accounting Under ADR

¶ 440

Vintage Accounts Required

As already observed at ¶ 400, a taxpayer electing ADR for any tax year must include all eligible assets (¶ 406–¶ 412) first placed in service in that year in either item or multiple-asset accounts by the year placed in service. These accounts by the year placed in service are called "vintage accounts." (Reg. § 1.167(a)-11(b)(3).)

Each vintage account must include only assets within a single class (¶ 418). It may not include assets from more than one class. However, more than one account of the same vintage (for the same tax year) may be established for different assets of the same class.

Certain kinds of assets may not be included in the same vintage account. Sec. 1245 and 1250 property may not be placed in the same account. New and used assets require separate accounts. Where Code Sec. 381(a) applies to transferred assets, see ¶ 450. (Reg. § 1.167(a)-11(b)(3)(ii).)

If a change in depreciation method is required for realty because it does or does not qualify as residential rental property, the realty must be removed from the vintage account and placed in a separate item vintage account (Reg. § 1.167(a)-11(b)(4)(iii)(*e*)). Similarly, accumulated depreciation allowances on the property must be subtracted from the related depreciation reserve and placed in a separate reserve. The amount accumulated is figured by using the method, rate and averaging convention selected, in the same way as accumulated depreciation is computed on extraordinary retirements, illustrated in the example at ¶ 466.

Also, salvage value for the multiple-asset vintage account may be decreased by the salvage value of the removed property. If separate salvage value was not otherwise established for the removed property, the amount of salvage value for it may be determined by multiplying the total salvage value for the account by the ratio of the unadjusted basis of the removed property to the unadjusted basis of the entire vintage account (before removal). (Reg. § 1.167(a)-11(d)(3)(vii)(*c*) and (*e*).)

¶ 442

Determining the Vintage of an Asset

The vintage account in which an asset is recorded depends on the vintage of the asset. That vintage depends on when the taxpayer first placed the asset in service.

An asset is first placed in service when it is first placed in a condition or state of readiness and availability for a specifically assigned function. This definition applies whether the asset is used in a trade or business, in the production of income, in a tax-exempt activity, or in a personal activity (Reg. § 1.167(a)-11(e)(1)).

The determination of the date on which property was first placed in service is not influenced by the date on which depreciation was treated as beginning under a first-year convention or a particular method of depreciation, such as the unit of production method or the retirement method.

The time when an asset was first placed in service is also significant in determining ADR depreciation under the modified half-year convention (¶ 428). The amount of depreciation in the first year depended on the half of the year in which the asset was first placed in service. The time during the year in which the asset was first placed in service does not affect depreciation computations under the half-year convention.

In the case of mass assets where it is impracticable to keep track of each individual asset, it is necessary to determine the vintage of these assets upon their retirement. If a taxpayer has followed reasonable recordkeeping practices, he may determine their vintage by means of an appropriate mortality dispersion table. See ¶ 432.

¶ 444

Depreciation Reserve for Vintage Account

Each vintage account under ADR must have a depreciation reserve. The amount of the reserve for each vintage account must be stated on each income tax return on which ADR depreciation is claimed on that vintage account (Reg. § 1.167(a)-11(c)(1)(ii)).

The balance in a depreciation reserve is affected by a number of retirement adjustments on which gain (¶ 476) or loss (¶ 478) may be recognized. Moreover, this balance must be reduced by accumulated depreciation on an asset that must be removed from the related vintage account if a change in depreciation method is required for realty because it does or does not qualify as residential rental property. Termination of an ADR election for an asset upon election of rapid amortization or depreciation may also require or have required an adjustment.

¶ 446

Salvage Value Under ADR

Many of the general depreciation rules apply in determining salvage value for a vintage account under ADR. Salvage value must be determined for each vintage account upon the basis of all the facts and circumstances existing at the close of the ADR election year. The estimated salvage value will not be redetermined merely because of price level fluctuations. Estimated salvage proceeds are the approximate amount that the taxpayer can be expected to receive on the disposition of an asset that is no longer useful in the taxpayer's trade or business and is to be disposed of or retired. This means that the resale value may be more than mere junk value if the asset would be relatively new at the time it is expected to be retired. (Reg. § 1.167(a)-11(d)(1)(i) and (iii).)

In the case of an ADR vintage account, however, *net* salvage value may not be used. Salvage value of a vintage account is its *gross* salvage value unreduced by the cost of removal, dismantling, demolition, or similar operations (Reg. § 1.167(a)-11(d)(1)(i) and (ii)). These costs are deductible as current expenses in the year paid or incurred (¶ 482).

¶ 448

Correction of Asset Misclassification

Where an asset has been placed in the wrong class or has not been placed in a vintage account because of an incorrect classification or characterization, the classification or characterization shall be corrected. The asset shall be placed in a proper vintage account. A depreciation period is to be selected from the range for the proper class. The new depreciation period is to be specified on the return for the tax year in which the improper classification or characterization is found. (Reg. § 1.167(a)-11(b)(4)(iii)(*c*).)

Adjustments will be made to correct the unadjusted basis, adjusted basis, salvage value, and depreciation reserve of all vintage accounts affected and the amount of the depreciation deductions for all open tax years involved.

Example (1): An asset costing $10,000 but not qualifying as ACRS recovery property was placed in service in 1981. It was included in class 24.3 with a range of 5 to 7 years. Depreciation for 1981 and 1982 of $2,000 per year was claimed, based on a 5-year depreciation period and the straight-line method. As of January 1, 1983, the adjusted basis of the asset was $6,000—$10,000 unadjusted basis less $4,000 depreciation reserve. It was discovered in a 1983 IRS audit that the proper classification for the asset is class 24.4 with a depreciation range of 8 to 12 years. For 1983, the asset is included in class 24.4 and an 8-year depreciation period is selected by the taxpayer. The depreciation deductions for 1981 and 1982 are each reduced by $750 ($2,000 annual deduction based on 5-year depreciation period minus $1,250 deduction based on 8-year depreciation period). The depreciation reserve is decreased by the $1,500 total adjustment for the 2 years. The adjusted basis, accordingly, is increased by $1,500, to $7,500 (as of January 1, 1983). Depreciation for 1983 is $1,250.

Further, if this asset is included in a multiple-asset vintage account in class 24.4, the estimated salvage value for that vintage account is increased by the estimated salvage value for that asset.

Where an ineligible depreciation method is applied to an asset, all the assets in the same class become ineligible for ADR depreciation (Reg. § 1.167(a)-11(b)(4)(iii)(*d*)). But if the taxpayer can show that the use of the ineligible method is the result of a good faith misclassification, he can save the ADR election for that class. The asset can be reclassified and adjustments made to reflect the new depreciation period selected by the taxpayer from the correct range.

Example (2): A taxpayer depreciated property included in one class on the machine-hour basis. He depreciated property included in another class under the ADR System using the sum of the years-digits method. One asset was depreciated under the machine-hour method because of a good faith misclassification of the asset in the former class. In the year the erroneous classification is brought to light, the taxpayer may include the asset in the latter class, depreciate the asset under the sum of the years-digits method using a depreciation period selected from the range for that class, and make adjustments for prior open years as explained above.

If the misclassified assets for which an ineligible method was used have a combined unadjusted basis that is at least 75 percent of the total unadjusted basis of all the assets in the class in which they belong (including the unadjusted basis of the misclassified assets), however, the taxpayer may elect to condone the use of the ineligible method for the misclassified assets and exclude the remaining assets in that same class from the ADR election. See ¶ 410 and ¶ 426.

¶ 450

Successor Corporation Subject to Predecessor's Elections

Where depreciable property is received by a successor corporation in a transfer to which Code Sec. 381(a) applies, the successor must follow the depreciation elections of its predecessor. Thus, ADR depreciation cannot be claimed on the transferred assets unless the predecessor elected ADR for those assets (Reg. § 1.167(a)-11(e)(3)(i)).

The receiving corporation must separate the eligible property (for which the predecessor elected ADR depreciation) into vintage accounts as nearly coextensive as possible with the predecessor's vintage accounts identified by the year originally placed in service. The depreciation period for each vintage account of the predecessor must be used by the successor. Similarly, the same method of depreciation used by the predecessor must be continued by the successor unless the Commissioner's consent is obtained or a change is permissible (see ¶ 434).

See ¶ 142 and ¶ 264–¶ 268 for comparable rules de signed to prevent various transactions between related taxpayers or tax-free exchanges from bringing pre-1981 property under the Accelerated Cost Recovery System (ACRS) or Modified ACRS (MACRS).

¶ 452

Termination of ADR Election for an Asset

An ADR election for an asset will be terminated if rapid amortization or depreciation is elected (¶ 410) and is subject to termination if the property is public utility property and the utility fails to normalize any tax deferral resulting from the ADR election (¶ 412). Termination of an election for an asset requires the removal of the asset's unadjusted basis from the vintage account in which it was recorded.

The depreciation reserve for the vintage account must also be reduced by the depreciation attributable to the terminated asset. The depreciation attributable to the terminated asset is computed by applying the method and rate used for the vintage account to the unadjusted basis of the asset for the number of depreciation periods the vintage account has been depreciated before the beginning of the year of termination (Reg. § 1.167(a)-11, subsections (b)(5)(v)(*b*), (b)(6)(iii), and (c)(1)(v)(*b*)).

The ADR election for a property improvement (Reg. § 1.167(a)-11(d)(2)(vii)(*a*)) is apparently not terminated just because the related asset's ADR election is terminated. Termination occurs if the reason for termination applies to the property improvement.

Where an ADR election is terminated for an asset and it is removed from its vintage account, the salvage value for the account may be decreased by the salvage value for the removed asset. If separate salvage value was not otherwise established for the removed asset, the salvage value for it may be determined by multiplying the total salvage value for the vintage account by the ratio of the unadjusted basis of the removed asset to the unadjusted basis of the entire vintage account. (Reg. § 1.167(a)-11(d)(3)(vii)(*c*) and (*e*)).

Retirements Under ADR

¶ 460

Retirements from Multiple-Asset or Item Accounts

While the rules on retirements from vintage accounts under Reg. § 1.167(a)-11(d)(3) are designed primarily for multiple-asset vintage accounts, pertinent portions of these rules also apply to item vintage accounts.

The more complex rules for retirements from multiple-asset vintage accounts are explained at ¶ 462–¶ 478. The easier rules for retirements from item vintage accounts are covered at ¶ 480.

¶ 462

Ordinary and Extraordinary Retirements Distinguished

Generally, a retirement is defined the same way for ADR purposes as it is under the regular depreciation provisions in Reg. § 1.167(a)-8. An asset is treated as retired when it is permanently withdrawn from use in the business or the production of income. This can be accomplished by a sale or exchange of the asset, physical abandonment of it, or transfer of it to supplies or scrap. Aside from these similarities, however, ADR retirements have a completely different set of rules. The requirements of Reg. § 1.167(a)-8 do not apply.

Under ADR, retirements are separated into two categories—ordinary retirements and extraordinary retirements.

All retirements other than extraordinary retirements are ordinary retirements. Extraordinary retirements include—

(1) retirements of Sec. 1250 property;

(2) retirements of Sec. 1245 property as a direct result of fire, storm, shipwreck or other casualty where the taxpayer chooses to consistently treat such retirements as extraordinary;

(3) retirements of Sec. 1245 property as a direct result of the cessation, termination, curtailment or disposition of a business, manufacturing, or other income-producing process, operation, facility or unit; or

(4) retirements after 1980 of Sec. 1245 property by means of a charitable contribution for which a deduction is allowable.

A type (3) retirement event will result in extraordinary retirements, however, only if the unadjusted basis of the assets retired from a vintage account because of such an event is greater than 20 percent of the entire unadjusted basis of the account immediately before the event. Accounts from which type (3) retirements are made are grouped together and treated as a single vintage account for this 20-percent determination to the extent that they are in the same class and have the same vintage (Reg. § 1.167(a)-11(d)(3)(ii)).

Example: A taxpayer has a type (3) retirement event. He has eight accounts from which retirements are made as a result of this event. Six of them are four-year-old accounts and two are three-year-old accounts. For purposes of the 20% test, there are two combined vintage accounts—one for the six four-year-old accounts and one for the two three-year-old accounts. Thus, if the total unadjusted basis of the retirements from the four-year-old accounts is more than 20% of the total unadjusted basis of those six accounts, the retirements from the four-year-old accounts are extraordinary. The retirements from the four-year-old accounts are ordinary if their total unadjusted basis is 20% or less of the total unadjusted basis of the six accounts. A similar comparison would be made for the three-year-old accounts.

Further, a type (3) retirement must be made other than by a transfer to supplies or scrap (sale, exchange, or other disposition, or physical abandonment of the asset would qualify).

A type (4) retirement removes the unadjusted basis of the contributed property from the vintage account, and the depreciation reserve is adjusted.

The transfer of property to a related person in the tax year in which it is first placed in service is treated as an extraordinary retirement regardless of the above rules. This exception applies to transfers between persons who would have losses, etc. disallowed under Code Sec. 267 (except for brothers and sisters), transfers between controlled partnerships or a partner and its controlling partner under Code Sec. 707(b), and transfers between corporate members of the same affiliated group (affiliation determined on the basis of a 50-percent rather than an 80-percent stock ownership test). (Reg. § 1.167(a)-11(d)(3)(v)(*c*).)

¶ 464

Ordinary Retirements Handled Through Reserve

Generally, gain or loss is not recognized upon an ordinary retirement. The retirement proceeds are added to the depreciation reserve of the vintage account from which the asset is retired (Reg. § 1.167(a)-11(d)(3)(iii)). However, gain may be recognized if the depreciation reserve after adjustment exceeds the unadjusted basis of the vintage account (see ¶ 476).

Additions to the depreciation reserve for ordinary retirements made during the tax year are effective as of the beginning of that year (Reg. § 1.167(a)-11(c)(1)(ii)). See ¶ 430 for the effect this has on the computation of depreciation for the retirement year.

¶ 466

Extraordinary Retirements Removed from Accounts

Unless a nonrecognition provision of the Code applies (see ¶ 474), gain or loss is recognized on an extraordinary retirement (Reg. § 1.167(a)-11(d)(3)(iv)). The gain or loss is recognized in the year of retirement.

The nature of the gain or loss depends on the type of retirement event involved. A sale or exchange could bring Code Sec. 1231 and either Code Sec. 1245 or Code Sec. 1250 into play. Any casualty loss would be determined under Code Sec. 165.

Where the asset extraordinarily retired is the only or the last asset in a vintage account, the account is terminated. Where the retirement is from a multiple-asset vintage account and the asset retired is not the last asset in the account, the unadjusted basis of the retired asset must be removed from the vintage account in which it was included. The accumulated depreciation allowances must be subtracted from the related depreciation reserve. The amount of accumulated depreciation for an asset is determined by applying the depreciation method, the ADR rate, and the ADR averaging convention selected (Reg. § 1.167(a)-11(c)(1)(v)(*b*)). Extraordinary retirements are considered made on the date specified by the averaging convention (¶ 428) adopted (see Reg. § 1.167(a)-11(c)(1)(ii)).

Example: An asset in a 1985 vintage account has an unadjusted basis of $50,000. The account contains assets which were excluded from ACRS by reason of the anti-churning rules. The 200% declining-balance method, the half-year convention, and a 20-year depreciation period were chosen for the account. The asset is sold for $16,000 in an extraordinary retirement in 2002. Depreciation accumulated for the asset upon retirement is determined to be $41,639, as follows:

Depreciation for—	
1985 ($50,000 × 10% ADR DDB method rate × one-half)	$2,500
1986 ($47,500 adjusted basis × 10% rate)	4,750
1987 ($42,750 adjusted basis × 10% rate)	4,275
1988 ($38,475 adjusted basis × 10% rate)	3,848
1989 ($34,627 adjusted basis × 10% rate)	3,463
1990 ($31,164 adjusted basis × 10% rate)	3,116
1991 ($28,048 adjusted basis × 10% rate)	2,805
1992 ($25,243 adjusted basis × 10% rate)	2,524
1993 ($22,719 adjusted basis × 10% rate)	2,272
1994 ($20,447 adjusted basis × 10% rate)	2,045
1995 ($18,402 adjusted basis × 10% rate)	1,840
1996 ($16,562 adjusted basis × 10% rate)	1,656
1997 ($14,906 adjusted basis × 10% rate)	1,491
1998 ($13,415 adjusted basis × 10% rate)	1,342
1999 ($12,073 adjusted basis × 10% rate)	1,207
2000 ($10,866 adjusted basis × 10% rate)	1,087
2001 ($ 9,779 adjusted basis × 10% rate)	978
2002 ($ 8,801 adjusted basis × 10% rate × one-half)	440
Total depreciation accumulated	$41,639

Accordingly, the adjusted basis of the asset is $8,361 ($50,000 unadjusted basis less $41,639 depreciation accumulated), a $7,639 ($16,000 - $8,361) Sec. 1245 gain is recognized, and a $440 depreciation expense is deductible for 2002. The $50,000 unadjusted basis is removed from the vintage account, and the $41,639 depreciation accumulated is removed from the reserve for the vintage account.

Also, accumulated depreciation includes, to the extent identifiable, the amount added to the depreciation reserve for the proceeds from a previous ordinary retirement of a part of the asset extraordinarily retired.

¶ 468

Salvage Value May Be Decreased by Retirements

When retirements are made from a vintage account, there are three choices as to the effect the retirement has on the estimated salvage value for the account (Reg. § 1.167(a)-11(d)(3)(vii)(*a*) and (*b*)):

(1) Leave salvage value as it is and not reduce it.

(2) Diminish salvage value by the portion related to each retired asset (for both ordinary and extraordinary retirements).

(3) Decrease salvage value by the portion related to each extraordinary retirement (and not ordinary retirements).

The salvage option chosen for a vintage account must be consistently followed. Since the Regulations require consistent treatment "for a vintage account," it appears that different options may be selected for different vintage accounts.

If option (1) above is selected for a vintage account and does not reduce salvage value, there may be a loss deduction when the last asset is retired from the account. See ¶ 478. The same would be true if option (3) is selected and salvage value is not reduced for ordinary retirements.

If salvage for a vintage account is reduced under option (2) or (3) for a retired asset, the amount of salvage value for the asset may be calculated as a pro rata portion of the total salvage for the account or by any other method consistently applied that reasonably reflects the original salvage related to the retired asset (Reg. § 1.167(a)-11(d)(3)(vii)(*c*)). The pro rata allocation is made by multiplying the total salvage value for the vintage account by the ratio of the unadjusted basis of the retired asset to the total unadjusted basis for the account. Thus, if an account has a total salvage value of $1,000 and a total unadjusted basis of $10,000, the pro rata reduction for retirement of an asset with a $500 unadjusted basis would be $50—$500/$10,000 × $1,000. Of course, if salvage is determined on an asset-by-asset basis, no allocation method is necessary.

Further, where adjustments to the depreciation reserve for ordinary retirements increase it to an amount greater than the depreciable basis of the account (unadjusted basis less salvage value), salvage value is reduced by the excess of the reserve over such depreciable basis (Reg. § 1.167(a)-11(d)(3)(iii)).

> ***Example:*** A multiple-asset vintage account has an unadjusted basis of $1,000 and estimated salvage value of $100. If ordinary retirement proceeds increase the depreciation reserve above $900, the excess over $900 reduces the salvage value. If the reserve is increased to $1,000, the salvage value is reduced to zero.

For special rules on ordinary retirements made by transfers to supplies or scrap accounts, see ¶ 472.

¶ 470

How to Account for Retirements from Casualties

A retirement resulting from a fire, storm, shipwreck or other casualty is an ordinary retirement unless an election is made to treat it as an extraordinary retirement (¶ 462). In such case the casualty loss rules apply in determining the amount of deductible loss or, possibly, taxable gain (Reg. § 1.167(a)-11(d)(3)(iv)).

If the asset is transferred to a supplies or scrap account (see ¶ 472) after the casualty, its tax basis in that account for later sale, exchange, other disposition, or physical abandonment is also determined under the casualty loss rules.

For purposes of the casualty loss rules, the adjusted basis of the retired asset just before the casualty is the excess of its unadjusted basis over its accumulated depreciation (computed as explained at ¶ 466).

If an election is made to treat casualty losses as ordinary retirements, any salvage proceeds are added to the depreciation reserve (¶ 464).

¶ 472

How to Handle Ordinary Retirements to Supplies or Scrap Account

As already explained at ¶ 464, gain or loss is not recognized on an ordinary retirement. If the ordinary retirement is the result of a transfer to a supplies or scrap account, the basis of the asset in that account depends on whether an election was made to reduce the salvage value of the vintage account as ordinary retirements occur (see ¶ 468).

If there was no election to reduce salvage value, it would appear that the asset would have a zero basis in the supplies account since the salvage value would be recovered through a possible loss when the last asset in the vintage account is retired (see ¶ 478). Any amount realized on a later disposition from the supplies account would seem to be fully taxable.

If an election was made to reduce salvage value, one of three consistent practices may be followed (Reg. § 1.167(a)-11(d)(3)(vii)(*d*) and (viii)):

(1) Reduce the salvage value of the vintage account by the retired asset's salvage value (as illustrated at ¶ 468). Nothing is added to the depreciation

reserve as in practices (2) and (3) below. The basis of the asset in the supplies account is zero. Any proceeds of a later sale of the asset are fully taxable.

(2) Reduce the salvage value of the vintage account by the retired asset's salvage value and add the amount of the reduction to the depreciation reserve. The basis of the asset in the supplies account is the amount of the reserve addition. Under this practice, the reserve may not be increased above an amount equal to the unadjusted basis of the vintage account. Accordingly, if the reserve addition is less than the salvage value reduction or is zero because of this limitation, the basis of the asset in the supplies account is the lesser amount or zero. Gain or loss is recognized on any later disposition to the extent of the difference between the amount realized and the asset's basis in that account.

(3) Determine the value of the retired asset by any reasonable method consistently applied, add that value to the depreciation reserve, and subtract that value from the salvage value of the vintage account (to the extent thereof). (Although the Regulations state that the reserve addition should be the greater of the salvage value reduction or the retired asset's value, it appears that, as a practical matter, the retired asset's value will never be smaller than the salvage value reduction.) Acceptable valuation methods include average cost, conditioned cost, or fair market value. The method used must be adequately identified in the books and records. The basis of the asset in the supplies account is the amount added to the reserve. Under this practice, the reserve may exceed the unadjusted basis of the vintage account. If this happens, gain is recognized to the extent of the excess and the reserve is reduced by such excess (¶ 476). Again, gain or loss is recognized on any later disposition to the extent of the difference between the amount realized and the asset's basis in that account.

Any depreciation reserve adjustments made under practice (2) or (3) are considered made as of the beginning of the tax year in which the ordinary retirement is made (Reg. § 1.167(a)-11(c)(ii)). This may possibly affect the amount of the retirement year's depreciation deduction. See ¶ 430.

¶ 474

Nonrecognition of Gain or Loss on Retirements

Where gain or loss on a retirement is not recognized in whole or in part because of a special Code provision, such as like-kind exchanges under Code Sec. 1031, the retirement is treated as an extraordinary retirement (Reg. § 1.167(a)-11(d)(3)(iv) and (v)). No portion of the retirement proceeds is to be added to the depreciation reserve for the vintage account.

The retired asset's unadjusted basis is removed from the vintage account. The depreciation reserve is decreased by the asset's accumulated depreciation. The amount of an asset's accumulated depreciation is calculated in the same way as for an extraordinary retirement. See ¶ 466.

Example: Corporation X has a 1980 vintage account consisting of machines A, B and C. Each has an unadjusted basis of $1,000. The unadjusted basis of the account is $3,000. Depreciation accumulated on the account at the end of 1982 is $2,100. At the beginning of 1987, machine A is transferred to wholly owned Corporation Y for stock of Y valued at $1,200 and $200 in cash.

The transaction qualifies as a transfer to a controlled corporation under Code Sec. 351. Gain of $1,100 is realized: $1,400 realized – $300 adjusted basis ($1,000 unadjusted basis – $700 depreciation). However, gain is recognized only to the extent of the $200 cash received.

Although this was an ordinary retirement, it is handled as an extraordinary retirement. The proceeds are not added to the depreciation reserve. The $1,000 unadjusted basis of machine A is removed from the vintage account and the $700 accumulated depreciation is taken out of the depreciation reserve.

If a depreciable asset is received in exchange, for the retired asset and its basis is determined by reference to the retired asset (such as in a like-kind exchange), it would appear that the basis for the asset received in exchange, as determined under the nonrecognition provision, would be the unadjusted basis of the asset for ADR purposes and could be recorded in a vintage account for the year of exchange if ADR is elected for that year.

If a depreciable asset is not received in exchange, it would seem that the taxpayer would simply record the nonrecognized (and any recognizable) gain or loss on the retirement.

Where a retirement results because of a transaction between affiliated corporations, the retirement is treated as extraordinary and handled separately under the provisions of Reg. § 1.1502-13. No proceeds are added to the depreciation reserve of the vintage account from which the asset was retired. (Reg. § 1.167(a)-11(d)(3)(v)(*b*).)

¶ 476

Gain May Result from Adjustments to Reserve

A number of retirement and other adjustments affect the balance in a depreciation reserve for a multiple-asset vintage account for Sec. 1245 property. The reserve must be—

(1) increased by the proceeds of ordinary retirements (see ¶ 464);

(2) increased by adjustments for reduction of the salvage value of a vintage account because of ordinary retirements to a supplies or scrap account (see practices (2) and (3) at ¶ 472);

(3) decreased by any adjustments for extraordinary retirements (see ¶ 466) and retirements on which gain or loss is fully or partially not recognized (see ¶ 474); and

(4) decreased by depreciation attributable to an asset removed from a vintage account because it is no longer eligible for ADR depreciation (see ¶ 452).

For a depreciation reserve regarding Sec. 1250 property, adjustment (3) applies. Also, the reserve is decreased by depreciation accumulated for residential rental property that must be placed in a separate vintage account (see ¶ 440).

The reserve may not be decreased below zero.

Where retirement adjustments (1) and (2) above for Sec. 1245 property increase the reserve to an amount in excess of the depreciable basis (unadjusted basis minus estimated salvage value) of the account, the salvage value is reduced by the excess of the reserve over such depreciable basis (see ¶ 468). If the reserve is increased to an amount in excess of the unadjusted basis of the vintage account, that excess is recognized as gain during the tax year (Reg. § 1.167(a)-11(d)(3)(ix)). The gain is treated as Sec. 1245 ordinary income to the extent of depreciation allowances accumulated in the reserve, reduced by any Code Sec. 1245 ordinary income previously recognized for that account.

Where gain results because retirement adjustments increase the reserve to an amount in excess of the unadjusted basis, the reserve is then reduced by the gain recognized (Reg. § 1.167(a)-11(c)(1)(ii)). This brings the reserve back to an amount equal to the unadjusted basis of the vintage account.

Example: A multiple-asset vintage account has an unadjusted basis of $1,000 and an estimated salvage value of $100. If the depreciation reserve for that vintage account is increased by proceeds of ordinary retirements to $1,100, salvage will be decreased to zero (see example at ¶ 468) and a $100 gain will be recognized. The reserve will then be decreased by the $100 gain back to a $1,000 balance.

If the ordinary retirement proceeds increase the reserve to $1,800 (instead of $1,100) and it is assumed that $600 of the reserve balance represents depreciation allowances, a gain of $800 would be recognized, $600 of which would be a Code Sec. 1245 gain and $200 of which would be a Code Sec. 1231 gain. The reserve would then be reduced by $800 back to a $1,000 balance.

¶ 478

Loss May Result on Retirement of Last Asset in Vintage Account

When the last asset in a vintage account for Sec. 1245 property is retired, any excess of the unadjusted basis of the account over the depreciation reserve is deductible as a loss under Code Sec. 165 or as depreciation under Code Sec. 167. If the retirement is a sale or exchange on which gain or loss is recognized, the excess is a Code Sec. 1231 loss. (Reg. § 1.167(a)-11(d)(3)(ix)(*b*).)

Upon retirement of the last asset, the vintage account terminates.

¶ 480

Simplified Rules for Retirements from Item Vintage Accounts

The rules explained at ¶ 462–478 are for retirements from multiple-asset vintage accounts. The rules for retirements from item vintage accounts are less complex.

A retirement from an item vintage account results in recognition of gain or loss to the extent of the difference between the unadjusted basis of the vintage account and the depreciation reserve balance.

If it is an extraordinary retirement, gain or loss is specifically recognized unless a nonrecognition provision applies (¶ 474). If the extraordinary retirement is by transfer to a supplies or scrap account as a result of a casualty loss, the casualty loss rules apply in determining the amount of deductible casualty loss (or possibly taxable gain) and the basis of the asset in the supplies account.

Although gain or loss is not recognized on ordinary retirements (¶ 464), gain is recognized if the addition of the retirement proceeds to the depreciation reserve makes it larger than the unadjusted basis of the asset (¶ 476). Also, since the retirement of the asset is from an item vintage account, it is the last asset in the account. Therefore, any excess of the unadjusted basis of the account over the depreciation reserve (as adjusted by retirement proceeds) is recognized as a loss or an additional depreciation deduction (¶ 478). If the ordinary retirement is the result of a transfer to a supplies or scrap account, the asset has a zero basis in that account since the excess of the unadjusted basis of the asset over the reserve is recognized as a loss upon retirement. The proceeds of a later sale of the asset are fully taxable.

Where a taxpayer uses item accounts for Sec. 1245 property as if they were a multiple-asset account by assigning the same depreciation period and method to each asset in the same class with the same vintage, these item accounts would be treated like a multiple-asset vintage account for purposes of determining loss upon retirement of the last asset from a vintage account (Reg. § 1.167(a)-11(d)(3)(xi)).

This has the effect of recognizing gains from retirement as they occur and of deferring losses until the last of those assets is retired.

¶ 482

Cost of Dismantling, Demolishing or Removing Asset

When an asset is retired from a vintage account, the cost of dismantling, demolishing or removing it is deductible as a current expense. This cost is not subtracted from the depreciation reserve for a multiple-asset vintage account. (Reg. § 1.167(a)-11(d)(3)(x).) Therefore, a taxpayer should maintain adequate records of these costs and carefully distinguish them from costs of maintenance and repair.

ADR Elections

¶ 483

How the System Is Elected

Elections to use ADR are made on an annual basis and apply only to eligible assets first placed in service in the election year. Subject to certain options, provisions of the system are available on an all or nothing basis (Reg. § 1.167(a)-11(a)(1)). For assets included in the election, vintage accounts must be established and depreciation periods selected. The first-year convention to be used also has to be selected.

Taxpayers who elect ADR must maintain books and records that specify the information required under Reg. § 1.167(a)-11(f)(4) and any other required information. Failure to do so will not render an election invalid where the taxpayer has in good faith substantially complied with requirements.

Any election becomes irrevocable after the last day for filing it (Reg. § 1.167(a)-11(a)(1), (b)(5)(i), and (f)(3)). Different vintage accounts, different depreciation periods, or different first-year conventions may not thereafter be used for assets to which it applies. Thus, a lessor could not retreat from the selection of the lower asset depreciation range for a ship even though subsequent legislation made the depreciation resulting from the difference between the lower range and the middle range a tax preference item subject to the minimum tax (Rev. Rul. 82-22, 1982-1 CB 33). However, provision is made for correcting misclassifications (see ¶ 448).

A taxpayer electing the Class Life Asset Depreciation Range System for assets that do not qualify for ACRS or MACRS (and filing Form 4562) must attach a statement to timely (extensions included) returns that specifies the still applicable items from Reg. § 1.167(a)-11(f)(2). In addition to the taxpayer's consent to the general regulatory requirements, required information includes the asset guideline class for each vintage account, the first-year convention adopted, and whether any specially amortized or depreciated property was excluded from the election.

¶ 484

ADR Strategy

Present recovery of cost under the ADR System may reflect prior ADR strategy. Insofar as this strategy centered on such items as depreciation periods or half-year conventions, it has no current application. However, for property subject to an ADR election, it remains important to maximize tax deferral by appropriate changes in methods of depreciating ADR property.

The ADR Regulations permit automatic changes (1) from a break method to the sum of the years-digits method or (2) from a break method or the sum of the years-digits method to the straight-line method.

To maximize the depreciation tax deferral, the 200-percent declining-balance method should be used for the first two years with a change to the sum of the years-digits method in the third year. This is true whether the half-year convention or the modified half-year convention is used.

Although the Regulations do not specifically say that two depreciation method changes can be made for the same vintage account, it would appear that this can be done. See Reg. § 1.167(a)-11(c)(1)(iii). Thus, a taxpayer who has changed from the 200-percent declining-balance method to the sum of the years-digits method could probably change again in a later year to the straight-line method. This might be advisable if he is trying to level out the latter years' deductions and avoid very small deductions in the final years.

¶ 485

Class Life System for Pre-1971 Assets

Along with the Class Life ADR System for post-1970 assets, the Treasury Department provided an elective class life system (CLS) for post-1970 depreciation on pre-1971 assets. The classes were the same as initially set forth for post-1970 assets except that no ranges were specified. Class lives were as originally set forth in Rev. Proc. 72-10 unless shorter lives were prescribed in revisions or supplements and expressly made applicable to pre-1971 assets.

Under CLS, property could be depreciated under the straight-line, declining-balance, or sum of the years-digits method. Assets could be accounted for in any number of item or multiple-asset accounts. Salvage value had to be established for all assets for which CLS was elected. The rules for retirement of assets were generally the same as under ADR.

Depreciation Planning

Acquisitions and Dispositions

¶ 486

Choosing the Best MACRS Depreciation Method and Period

A taxpayer has some flexibility in choosing a depreciation method and recovery period under MACRS. Generally, these choices allow the selection of a slower recovery method (such as the straight-line method) and/or a longer recovery period than would otherwise apply. These choices may offer certain tax planning opportunities as discussed below.

Overview of MACRS methods and periods

Under the MACRS general depreciation system (GDS) the 200-percent declining-balance method is used to depreciate MACRS 3-, 5-, 7-, and 10-year property over their respective 3-, 5-, 7-, and 10-year recovery periods. However, the 150-percent declining-balance method applies to 3-, 5-, 7-, and 10-year farm property.

The 150-percent declining-balance method also applies to MACRS 15-and 20-year property over their respective 15- and 20-year recovery periods under GDS. The straight-line method is used to depreciate residential rental property over a 27.5-year recovery period and nonresidential real property over a 39-year recovery period (31.5 years for property placed in service before May 13, 1993).

MACRS offers four elections that can defer depreciation deductions into later tax years. Situations in which depreciation deferral could be beneficial are discussed below.

First, a taxpayer may make an irrevocable election to use the 150-percent declining-balance method to depreciate 3-, 5-, 7-, or 10-year property that would otherwise be depreciable using the 200-percent declining-balance method (Code Sec. 168(b)(2)(C)). The election is made on a property class by property class basis. If the election is made for property placed in service after December 31, 1998, the recovery period for a particular property within a property class is the regular recovery period that applies under GDS. For property placed in service before January 1, 1999, the recovery period is the same period that would apply if the property was depreciated under the MACRS alternative depreciation system (ADS). In general, the ADS recovery period is equal to the Class Life of the property (or a specially assigned recovery period) which is longer than the regular period that applies under the GDS 200-percent declining-balance method.

The 150-percent declining-balance method and the ADS recovery period are used to compute AMT depreciation on MACRS personal (section 1245) property placed in service before January 1, 1999. The 150-percent declining-balance method and depreciation period used for regular tax purposes applies for AMT purposes to personal property placed in service after December 31, 1998 (Code Sec. 56(a)(1)(A)). As a result, a taxpayer making the 150-percent election for regular income tax purposes would not need to make an AMT depreciation adjustment for the property to which the election applies. If a taxpayer claims bonus depreciation (127D) then the bonus depreciation deduction and regular depreciation deductions are allowed in full for AMT purposes.

A taxpayer may also make an irrevocable election to depreciate 3-, 5-, 7-, 10-, 15-, or 20-year property classes using the straight-line method over the regularly applicable 3-, 5-, 7-, 10-, 15-, or 20-year recovery period (¶ 84). This election, which is also made on a property class by property class basis, does not apply to residential and nonresidential real property since the straight-line method is always used to depreciate such property (Code Sec. 168(b)(3)(D)). If a taxpayer makes this election, allowable AMT depreciation is computed using the straight-line method and applicable ADS recovery period for property placed in service before January 1, 1999. No AMT adjustment is required on property for which the straight-line election is made and which is placed in service after December 31, 1998 (Code Sec. 56(a)(1)(A).

A taxpayer may elect the MACRS alternative depreciation system (ADS) (¶ 150). This irrevocable election applies to all property within the same class for which an election is made and which is placed in service during the tax year of the election. However, in the case of residential rental and nonresidential real property, the election is made on an asset-by-asset basis. The cost of property depreciated under ADS is recovered using the straight-line method over the class life of the asset or an assigned recovery period. ADS provides the slowest cost recovery under MACRS (Code Sec. 168(g)(7)). ADS is used to compute allowable AMT depreciation on MACRS Code Sec. 1250 real property placed in service before January 1, 1999. No AMT adjustment is required for Code Sec. 1250 real property which is depreciated using the straight-line method and placed in service after December 31, 1998. Thus, no AMT adjustment is required on MACRS residential rental and nonresidential real property placed in service after 1998 and depreciated over the regular 27.5 or 39-year recovery periods or the 40-year period prescribed under ADS for such property (Code Sec. 56(a)(1)(A)(i)).

Most new MACRS property acquired after 2007 and placed in service before 2010 with a recovery period of 20 years or less is eligible for a Code Sec. 168(k) bonus depreciation allowance equal to 50 percent of its cost computed after reducing the cost by any amount expensed under Code Sec. 179. See ¶ 127D. If it makes tax sense to defer depreciation deductions then an election out of bonus depreciation should be made (and no amount should be expensed under Code Sec. 179 if the property qualifies for expensing). However, the election out may trigger an AMT liability. To further minimize depreciation deductions claimed in the early years of the recovery period (and avoid an AMT depreciation adjustment), the taxpayer may also make the ADS, straight-line, or 150-percent declining-balance elections described above in conjunction with an election out of bonus depreciation.

Planning considerations in choosing a recovery period

In most instances, taxpayers will reap the greatest tax benefit by recovering the cost of their depreciable MACRS property as quickly as possible. Thus, the election of the 150-percent declining-balance method, MACRS straight-line method or the ADS method in lieu of GDS is generally not advisable since these methods delay cost recovery when compared to GDS. Similarly, an election out of bonus depreciation is generally not advantageous, since the amount of bonus depreciation that could otherwise be claimed in the first year of the recovery period will be deducted over the entire recovery period.

> ***Example (1):*** An individual taxpayer purchases machinery (5-year property) costing $100,000 in 2009. Assume that the ADS recovery period is 10 years and that the half-year convention applies. The taxpayer will deduct $100,000 (including bonus depreciation) over six years using GDS. If he elects ADS (and elects out of bonus depreciation), he will only deduct $55,000 under ADS during the same period. The remaining $45,000 will be deducted over an additional 5 years.

Some factors, however, may result in a greater tax savings by delaying the rate at which depreciation deductions are claimed. Most notably, a taxpayer may be in a low tax bracket during the first years after an asset is placed in service but expect to be in a higher tax bracket in the later years of the asset's recovery period. Deferring depreciation deductions to later years to offset ordinary income subject to higher tax rates by electing out of bonus depreciation (if available), not claiming a section 179 expense allowance (if available), and electing the MACRS straight-line method or ADS could make sense in this situation. For example, if the individual in the preceding example is in the 15-percent tax bracket during the first six years and is in the 35-percent tax bracket during the next five years, the ADS election could result in a greater overall tax savings.

Another wrinkle that could work in favor of deferring depreciation deductions to high-bracket years is that recaptured depreciation that is claimed against ordinary income in low-bracket years could be taxed as ordinary income at a higher rate in the year of disposition if the asset is sold at a gain. As a result, the tax paid on the ordinary income recapture could exceed the tax saved when the depreciation was claimed against ordinary income in the low-bracket years. See ¶ 487.

MACRS mid-quarter convention planning

The mid-quarter convention (¶ 92) treats property placed in service during any quarter of the tax year (or disposed of during any quarter of the tax year) as placed in service (or disposed of) at the midpoint of the quarter. Thus, one and one-half months' depreciation is allowed for the quarter in which an MACRS asset subject to this convention is placed in service or disposed of.

The mid-quarter convention applies if the sum of the aggregate basis of MACRS property placed in service during the last three months (i.e., quarter) of the tax year is more than 40 percent of the sum of the total bases of all MACRS property placed in service during the entire tax year. The mid-quarter convention, however, does not apply to residential rental property and nonresidential real property. Furthermore, this property is not taken into account in determining whether the 40-percent test is met. Any amount expensed under Code Sec. 179 is also excluded from the calculation of total bases.

As a rule of thumb, a taxpayer is subject to the midquarter convention if more than 66.66 percent of the aggregate basis of all property placed in service in the first three quarters is placed in service in the fourth quarter. For example, if the property placed in service during the first three quarters has an aggregate basis of \$100, fourth quarter additions must be no more than \$66.66 (\$166.66 × 40% = \$66.66).

The MACRS deduction for property subject to the mid-quarter convention may be determined by figuring depreciation for a full tax year and then multiplying that amount by the following percentages for the quarter of the tax year in which the property is placed in service:

Quarter of tax year	*Percentage*
First	87.5%
Second	62.5%
Third	37.5%
Fourth	12.5%

A taxpayer may be able to control whether the mid-quarter convention applies in a particular tax year by taking the 40-percent test into consideration when timing the purchases of depreciable property. The Code Sec. 179 expense allowance can also provide an excellent tool for avoiding the midquarter convention. Since amounts expensed under Code Sec. 179 are not taken into account in determining whether the convention applies, it may be possible to avoid the convention by expensing assets placed in service in the fourth quarter. Conversely, it may be possible to trigger its application by expensing assets placed in service in the first, second, or third quarters. This planning technique does not apply to the bonus depreciation deduction. Unlike the Code Sec. 179 expense allowance, the bonus depreciation allowance (¶ 127D) does not reduce the basis of an asset for purposes of applying the 40-percent test.

It is not always desirable, however, to avoid the mid-quarter convention. When several assets are placed in service in the same tax year, the mid-quarter convention can produce an overall first-year depreciation deduction that is larger than the aggregate depreciation deduction that would otherwise result if the half-year convention applied.

> ***Example (2):*** Three-year MACRS property costing $550 is placed in service in the first quarter of 2009. Ten-year MACRS property costing $450 is placed in service in the fourth quarter. Since the mid-quarter convention applies, total depreciation (assuming no bonus depreciation is claimed) is $332 (($550 × 66.67% × 87.5%)+ ($450 × 20% × 12.5%)).
>
> However, if the half-year convention had applied, total depreciation would be $228 (($550 × 66.67% × 50%) + ($450 × 20% × 50%)).

Since the amount of bonus depreciation that a taxpayer may claim is not affected by application of the mid-quarter convention, the bonus deduction somewhat diminishes the potential acceleration of depreciation that the mid-quarter convention can sometimes offer.

> ***Example (3):*** Assume the same facts as in *Example (2)*, except that bonus depreciation is claimed. Bonus depreciation on the 3-year property is $275 ($550 × 50%). The basis of the 3-year property for purposes of computing the regular depreciation deductions under either the half-year or mid-quarter convention is reduced to $275 ($550 – $275). Bonus depreciation on the 10-year property is $225 ($450 × 50%) and the basis is reduced to $225 ($450 – $225). If the mid-quarter convention applies, total depreciation (including bonus depreciation) is $666 ($275 + $225 + ($275 × 66.67% × 87.5%) + ($225 × 20% × 12.5%)). If the half-year convention had applied, total depreciation (including bonus depreciation) would be $615 ($275 + $225 + ($275 × 66.67% × 50%) + ($225 × 20% × 50%)).

The mid-quarter convention produces the best potential for tax savings when assets with the shortest recovery periods and highest costs (but not in excess of 60 percent of the total cost of all assets placed in service during the tax year) are placed in service during the first quarter. This can readily be seen by examining the applicable table percentages for the mid-quarter convention at ¶ 180 (Tables 2 through 5). For example, in the case of 5-year property subject to the mid-quarter convention, 35 percent of depreciable basis is recovered if the property is placed in service in the first quarter, 25 percent if placed in service in the second quarter, 15 percent if placed in service in the third quarter, and five percent if placed in service in the fourth quarter. Under the half-year convention, 20 percent of depreciable basis is recovered regardless of the quarter the property is placed in service.

For further discussion of mid-quarter convention planning opportunities, see ¶ 487.

Planning for sales of depreciable business property at a loss

Differentials between the ordinary income and capital gains tax rates may play a role in deciding whether to depreciate an asset using GDS or an elective MACRS method. If nonrecaptured gains from Sec. 1231 assets (real property and depreciable personal property held for more than one year and used in a trade or business or for the production of rents or royalties) exceed the losses from Sec. 1231 assets sold or disposed of during the tax year, the net gain (gains in excess of the losses) is treated as a long-term capital gain. When losses from Sec. 1231 assets exceed the gains from Sec. 1231 assets, the net loss is treated as an ordinary loss which is deductible in full against ordinary income. However, net gain is treated as ordinary income to the extent of any unrecaptured net loss incurred in the five preceding tax years.

Example (4): An individual taxpayer in the highest tax bracket purchases used machinery (5-year property that does not qualify for bonus depreciation) costing $100,000 and sells it in the third-year of the recovery period. Assume that the taxpayer remains in the highest tax bracket and that the straight-line ADS recovery period is 10 years. Using the MACRS GDS (200% declining-balance method, 5-year recovery period, and half-year convention), the taxpayer's total depreciation deductions are $61,600 ($20,000 for year 1, $32,000 for year 2 and $9,600 for year 3). Using the ADS depreciation system (straight-line method, 10-year recovery period, and half-year convention), the taxpayer's total depreciation deductions are $20,000 ($5,000 for year 1, $10,000 for year 2, and $5,000 for year 3).

Assume that the taxpayer sells the machinery for $38,400 in year 3. Under GDS, no gain or loss is recognized, and no depreciation deductions are recaptured as ordinary income because the taxpayer's adjusted basis is also $38,400 ($100,000 - $61,600). Under ADS, the taxpayer's adjusted basis is $80,000 ($100,000 – $20,000). Therefore, the taxpayer has a $41,600 ($80,000 – $38,400) Sec. 1231 loss and no depreciation recapture. This loss, assuming that there are no Sec. 1231 gains to offset, is deductible in full against ordinary income. However, the benefit of the ordinary income offset is subject to recapture if the taxpayer has net Sec. 1231 gains during the next five tax years. Disregarding this possibility, the benefit of GDS is limited to the increased depreciation deductions claimed in the tax years prior to the disposition.

Example (5): Assume that the taxpayer in the preceding *Example* also had $41,600 in Sec. 1231 gains. This situation tips the scales a bit further against the ADS election. Instead of deducting the $41,600 Sec. 1231 loss against an equal amount of ordinary income taxed at the highest individual rate, the taxpayer is required to offset the Sec. 1231 gain, which would otherwise be taxed at the lower maximum capital gains rate for individuals.

Planning for sales of depreciable business property at a gain

In the case of the sale of Sec. 1245 property, depreciation is recaptured as ordinary income to the extent of any gain. The remaining gain is treated as Sec. 1231 gain. Gain from the sale of Sec. 1250 property is generally subject to recapture as ordinary income to the extent of accelerated depreciation in excess of straight-line depreciation.

When selling depreciable business property at a gain, taxpayers need to consider that Sec. 1231 gains generated by the sale will offset Sec. 1231 losses that might otherwise be deductible against ordinary income. Sec. 1231 gains, however, could be beneficial if they can be used to offset capital losses which would otherwise go unused during the tax year.

See ¶ 488, for additional details.

Planning for the alternative minimum tax

The tax benefits of depreciation deductions claimed in computing a taxpayer's regular income tax liability can be effectively reduced or eliminated if a taxpayer is subject to the alternative minimum tax. The alternative minimum tax depreciation adjustments and preferences apply to both corporate and noncorporate taxpayers.

Briefly, in the case of MACRS residential rental and nonresidential real property placed in service after 1986 and before January 1, 1999, MACRS depreciation is a minimum tax *adjustment* to the extent it exceeds the depreciation that would have been claimed under the MACRS (straight-line) alternative depreciation system

(ADS). Section 1250 property, other than residential rental and nonresidential real property, that is not depreciated using the straight-line method for regular tax purposes is also depreciated using ADS. In the case of MACRS section 1245 property placed in service after 1986 and before January 1, 1999 the AMT adjustment is the excess of the depreciation claimed over the amount of depreciation that would have been claimed using the 150-percent declining-balance method over the recovery period that would have applied under ADS. However, if an item of MACRS section 1245 property is depreciated for regular tax purposes using the MACRS straight-line method over the regular MACRS recovery period or using ADS, then AMT depreciation for that asset is computed using ADS (i.e., the straight-line method over the ADS recovery period) (Code Sec. 56(a)(1)).

In the case of MACRS property placed in service *after December 31, 1998*, the following rules apply. No AMT adjustment is required for MACRS residential rental and nonresidential real property and, if the straight-line method was used for regular depreciation purposes, any other type of section 1250 property. No AMT adjustment is required for MACRS section 1245 property (i.e., personal property) depreciated using the straight-line method, ADS, or the 150-percent declining-balance method for regular tax purposes. An AMT adjustment will continue to be computed on MACRS 3-, 5-, 7-, and 10-year section 1245 property which is depreciated by a taxpayer using the 200-percent declining-balance method for regular tax purposes. For AMT purposes, such property must be depreciated using the 150-percent declining-balance method and the recovery period used by the taxpayer for regular tax purposes. AMT depreciation on any section 1250 property which is not depreciated for regular tax purposes using the straight-line method (e.g., certain land improvements) must be computed using the straight-line method and the depreciation period that applied for regular tax purposes (Code Sec. 56(a)(1), as amended by the Taxpayer Relief Act of 1997 (P.L. 105-34)).

If bonus depreciation under Code Sec. 168(k) was claimed on any asset, then AMT and regular tax depreciation are the same throughout the asset's recovery period provided the depreciable basis of the asset is the same for AMT and regular tax purposes, as is usually the case. No AMT adjustment is required (Code Sec. 168(k)(2)(F)). See ¶ 127D. The bonus deduction is also allowed in full for AMT purposes. These rules also apply if bonus depreciation is claimed on New York Liberty Zone Property (¶ 127E), Gulf Opportunity Zone Property (¶ 127F), Kansas Disaster Area Property (¶ 127G), and Disaster Assistance Property (¶ 127H).

The following charts show how AMT tax depreciation is computed when regular tax depreciation is computed as shown.

MACRS PROPERTY FOR WHICH BONUS DEPRECIATION CLAIMED

If bonus depreciation is claimed in the first year of an asset's recovery period then regular tax depreciation and AMT depreciation is computed in the same manner throughout the asset's recovery period. Further, the bonus depreciation allowance is allowed in full for AMT purposes.

MACRS PROPERTY PLACED IN SERVICE AFTER 1998

MACRS Regular Tax Depreciation Method (¶84)	*MACRS AMT Tax Depreciation Method*
200-percent declining-balance method (*3-*, *5-*, *7-*, *10-*year property that is not section 1250 property)	Use 150-percent declining-balance method and regular tax depreciation period
150-percent declining-balance method (*15-*, *20-*year property that is not section 1250 property)	No adjustment required, compute AMT and regular tax depreciation the same way
150-percent declining-balance method election (*3-*, *5-*, *7-*, *10*, *15*, *20-*year property that is not section 1250 property)	No adjustment required, compute AMT and regular tax depreciation the same way
Straight-line (*27.5-*year residential rental and *31.5-* or *39-*year nonresidential real property and other section 1250 property)	No adjustment required, compute AMT and regular tax depreciation the same way
Straight-line election (*3-*, *5-*, *7-*, *10-*, *15-*, *20-*year property)	No adjustment required, compute AMT and regular tax depreciation the same way
MACRS ADS method (elective or nonelective)	No adjustment required, compute AMT and regular tax depreciation the same way on real and personal property
Section 1250 property if straight-line method not used	Compute AMT depreciation using straight-line method and regular tax depreciation period

MACRS PROPERTY PLACED IN SERVICE AFTER 1986 AND BEFORE 1999

MACRS Regular Tax Depreciation Method (¶84)	*MACRS AMT Tax Depreciation Method*
200-percent declining-balance method (*3-*, *5-*, *7-*, *10-*year property that is not section 1250 property)	Use 150-percent declining-balance method and ADS recovery period
150-percent declining-balance method (*15-*, *20-*year property that is not section 1250 property)	Use 150-percent declining-balance method and ADS recovery period
150-percent declining-balance method election (*3-*, *5-*, *7-*, *10*, *15*, *20-*year property that is not section 1250 property)	No adjustment required, compute AMT and regular tax depreciation the same way
Straight-line (*27.5-*year residential rental property and *31.5-* or *39-*year nonresidential real property)	Use ADS (recovery period 40 years)
Section 1250 property not depreciated using straight-line	Use straight-line method and ADS recovery period
Straight-line election (*3-*, *5-*, *7-*, *10-*, *15-*, *20-*year property)	Use ADS
MACRS ADS method (elective or nonelective)	No adjustment required, compute AMT and regular tax depreciation the same way on real and personal property

Accelerated depreciation in excess of straight-line depreciation claimed on ACRS real property or pre-ACRS real property is an item of AMT *tax preference*. Accelerated deprecation in excess of straight-line depreciation claimed on personal property which is placed in service before 1987 and depreciated under ACRS or a pre-ACRS method is generally not an item of tax preference unless the property is leased (Code Sec. 57(a)(7); Code Sec. 57(a)(3) and (12) (prior to amendment by the 1986 Tax Reform Act).

Taxpayers with the option of electing out of MACRS by adopting a depreciation method not expressed in a term of years, such as the unit-of-production method, should consider in making the decision, that these methods do not give rise to AMT adjustments (Code Sec. 56(a)(1)(B)).

In most instances a taxpayer will have more than one item of MACRS property on which to compute the required AMT adjustment. The AMT adjustment is the difference between the total amount of MACRS depreciation claimed on all MACRS assets for regular tax purposes and the total amount of depreciation allowed on all MACRS assets for AMT purposes.

The allowable AMT deduction for a particular item of property may exceed the depreciation claimed for regular tax purposes. In this case, the difference is taken into account as a negative adjustment in computing the AMT adjustment and will reduce alternative minimum taxable income. This benefit only applies to property depreciated under MACRS. AMT depreciation in excess of ACRS or pre-ACRS depreciation may not be used to offset ACRS or pre-ACRS depreciation in excess of allowable AMT depreciation when computing the AMT depreciation preference for such property.

In the case of MACRS real property placed in service before 1999, allowable AMT depreciation will only exceed regular tax depreciation beginning with the final year of the applicable 27.5-, 31.5-,or 39-year recovery period and extending through the 40-year AMT (i.e., ADS) recovery period for such property. However, in the case of personal property, AMT depreciation can begin to exceed regular tax depreciation well prior to the end of the standard recovery period.

Example (6): A lumber company purchases equipment for $100,000 and places it in service in 2005. No bonus depreciation is claimed. The equipment is 7-year MACRS property. The half-year convention applies. Regular MACRS depreciation using the 200% DB method and 7-year recovery period for 2009 is $8,920 ($100,000 × 8.92%). Allowable, AMT depreciation using the 150% DB method and 7-year recovery period is $12,250 ($100,000 × 12.25%). The company is entitled to a negative (favorable) AMT depreciation adjustment on Form 4626 (assuming that it has no other depreciable MACRS property) of $3,330 ($12,250 – $8,920).

Although the company is benefiting from the negative adjustment, if it sells or disposes of the property in a later tax year, the benefit would in effect be recaptured. This is because the amount of gain or loss recognized for AMT purposes is determined using the basis of the asset as adjusted for AMT depreciation. See, below.

A taxpayer can avoid keeping two sets of depreciation records and calculating MACRS AMT depreciation adjustments by electing the applicable AMT method for regular tax purposes when an asset is placed in service. Except for residential rental and nonresidential real property, however, an election applies to all property in the same property class placed in service during the tax year.

In the case of section 1250 property placed in service after December 31, 1998, on which bonus depreciation is not claimed, record-keeping for AMT purposes will generally only be a concern with respect to 3-, 5-, 7-, and 10-year section 1245 property which is depreciated using the 200-percent declining-balance method for regular tax purposes because the MACRS method and depreciation period used for regular tax purposes for all other section 1245 property is the same method and period used for AMT purposes. In the case of 3-, 5-, 7-, and 10-year section 1245 property on which bonus depreciation is not claimed, the 150-percent declining-balance method and depreciation period that apply for regular tax purposes (i.e., 3-, 5-, 7-, and 10-years) will be used for AMT purposes if the 200-percent declining-balance method is used for regular tax purposes. If the taxpayer elects the straight-line method, ADS method, or 150-percent declining-balance method for such property, a taxpayer claims the same amount of AMT depreciation as claimed for regular tax purposes whether or not bonus depreciation is claimed.

Notwithstanding potential savings in record-keeping costs, the decision to elect an AMT depreciation method for regular tax purposes would normally be made by comparing the additional regular income tax savings (if any) with the additional AMT liability resulting from the use of an MACRS method that results in an AMT depreciation adjustment. To the extent possible, the decision should take into account not only the impact of the AMT depreciation adjustment in the tax year that an asset is placed in service but also on the AMT impact in future years.

For example, while use of the 200-percent declining-balance method for MACRS section 1245 property (which does not qualify for bonus depreciation or with respect to which an election out is made) could trigger or increase AMT liability in the tax year the depreciable assets are placed in service, a taxpayer may anticipate claiming a Code Sec. 53 credit for prior-year AMT tax liability in the following year and having no additional AMT liability during the remaining GDS recovery period of the assets. In this situation, an election to depreciate using an allowable AMT method could result in a taxpayer claiming reduced depreciation deductions against regular tax liability in the immediately succeeding years when the 200-percent declining-balance method would not cause or increase AMT tax liability. Here, the additional AMT liability paid in one year as the result of using the 200-percent declining-balance method could be less than the value of income tax savings attributable to accelerated deductions claimed in succeeding non-AMT years against taxable income.

At the other extreme, a taxpayer may be in a "permanent" state of AMT liability and unable to recover its tax credit for prior-year AMT liability within the foreseeable future. Here, an election to depreciate using the applicable AMT method for regular tax purposes would allow the taxpayer to claim the entire cost of the depreciable assets against regular taxable income (if any) without increasing AMT tax liability. Note that a special election allows a corporation to forgo bonus depreciation in order to release locked up AMT and research credits. See ¶ 127D.

Adjusted AMT gain or loss

When depreciated property is sold or exchanged the amount of gain or loss recognized for regular tax purposes must be redetermined for AMT purposes. The difference between the regular tax gain or loss and AMT gain or loss is taken into account as a positive or negative adjustment. The AMT gain or loss is determined by reducing the adjusted basis of the property by the amount of allowable AMT depreciation (and any other AMT basis adjustments) (Code Sec. 56(a)(7)). If the total amount of AMT depreciation allowed is less than the total deprecation claimed for regular tax purposes, the gain recognized for AMT purposes will be less than the regular tax gain, thereby reducing alternative minimum tax liability. However, the gain recognized for AMT purposes will be increased if the depreciation allowed under the AMT exceeds the depreciation claimed for regular tax purposes.

Example (7): MACRS machinery is purchased for $10,000. Assume that its adjusted basis as the result of claiming MACRS depreciation is $4,000. Assume that for

AMT purposes, the machinery's adjusted basis is $6,000, taking into account allowable AMT depreciation. If the machinery is sold for $7,000, the gain for regular tax purposes is $3,000 ($7,000 - $4,000) but its gain for AMT purposes is $1,000 ($7,000 - $6,000). Since the AMT gain is less than the regular tax gain, the difference ($2,000) is a negative AMT adjustment in favor of the taxpayer.

¶ 487

Code Sec. 179 Expense and Bonus Depreciation Planning

Code Sec. 179 provides an election to treat a specified amount of new or used qualifying property ("section 179 property") as a current expense in the tax year that the section 179 property is placed in service. See, also, ¶ 300.

For a tax year beginning in 2008 and 2009, the maximum expense deduction is $250,000. The limit is $134,000 for tax years beginning in 2010 (Rev. Proc. 2009-50). See ¶ 300 for other tax years.

In general, section 179 property is depreciable personal property (more specifically, property described in Code Sec. 1245(a)(3)) that is acquired by purchase from an unrelated party for use in the active conduct of a trade or business (Code Sec. 179(d)(1)). Property held for personal use or for the production of income does not qualify as section 179 property. Property owned by a taxpayer and used for personal purposes does not qualify if it is converted to business use since it was not acquired for use in a trade or business.

A taxpayer can allocate the maximum allowable expense deduction to a single qualifying property or among several qualifying properties placed in service during the same tax year. The amount by which an item is expensed reduces its basis for depreciation, as well as for determining gain or loss. In general, the greatest benefit is derived by allocating the deduction to qualifying property with the longest recovery period. However, as noted below, amounts expensed under Code Sec. 179 are subject to recapture if business use of the property during a tax year falls to 50 percent or less (assuming that the MACRS recovery period for the asset has not ended).

Example (1): Wanda Williams purchases qualifying 3-year property costing $250,000 and qualifying 10-year property costing $250,000 in 2009. If she expenses the 10-year property in 2009, she will have deducted $250,000 by 2012 (the last year of the recovery period for the 3-year property). If Williams elects to expense the cost of the 3-year property in 2009, she will not recover the full cost of the machinery until 2019 (the last year of the recovery period for the 10-year property).

In order to maximize the Code Sec. 168(k) first-year bonus depreciation allowance (¶ 127D), a taxpayer who has purchased new and used property should first allocate the expense allowance to the used property because the bonus allowance is only available for new property placed in service in the 2009 calendar year and in computing the bonus allowance, cost is first reduced by any amount expensed under Code Sec. 179.

Example (1A): A calendar-year taxpayer purchases $250,000 of new property and $250,000 of used property 2009. The used property does not qualify for the bonus deduction. If the taxpayer expenses $250,000 of new property, no bonus depreciation may be claimed. If the used property is expensed, the bonus allowance on the new property is $112,500.

The Code Sec. 179 expense deduction and bonus allowance are not prorated on the basis of the length of time that a qualifying asset is in service during the tax year. For example, up to $250,000 of the cost of a qualifying asset placed in service on the last day of the 2009 tax year can be deducted under Code Sec. 179. Also, no proration is required on account of a short tax year (Reg. § 1.179-1(c)(1);

Reg.§ 1.168(k)-1(d)(1)). MACRS depreciation allowances (other than the first-year bonus-depreciation allowance), however, are prorated in a short tax year. Thus, the section 179 allowance and bonus depreciation deduction can be particularly beneficial in comparison to a regular depreciation deduction in a short tax year.

Like-kind exchanges and involuntary conversions

The portion of the basis of property received in a Code Sec. 1031 like-kind exchange (for example, a purchase involving a "trade-in") or acquired as replacement property in a Code Sec. 1033 involuntary conversion that is determined by reference to the basis of the property given in the exchange or replaced does not qualify for the Code Sec. 179 expense allowance (Code Sec. 179(d)(3)).

> ***Example (2):*** John Jones purchases machinery costing $20,000 for use in his business but is granted a $5,000 trade-in allowance on old machinery so his cash outlay is $15,000. The old machinery has an adjusted basis of $3,000. The adjusted basis of the new machinery is $18,000 ($20,000 – $5,000 + $3,000). However, only $15,000 of the adjusted basis may be expensed under Code Sec. 179 since $3,000 of the $18,000 adjusted basis is determined by reference to the adjusted basis of the old machinery (i.e., is a carryover basis).

Although the carryover basis of property received in a like-kind exchange or involuntary conversion cannot be expensed under Code Sec. 179, bonus depreciation may be claimed on the entire adjusted basis of the property received (i.e., on both the carryover and noncarryover basis) (Reg. § 1.168(k)-1(f)(5)). This may serve as an incentive to engage in like-kind exchanges if the property received qualifies for bonus depreciation. However, if property is acquired and exchanged for other like-kind property in the same tax year, no depreciation or bonus deduction may be claimed on the originally acquired property (Reg. § 1.168(k)-1(f)(5)(iii)(B)).

> ***Example (2A):*** A private corporate aircraft (5-year property) costing $100,000 is purchased in August 2008 and used entirely for business purposes. Bonus depreciation is $50,000 ($100,000 × 50%) and regular first year depreciation is $10,000 (($100,000 – $50,000) × 40% (200% DB rate for five-year property) × 50% to reflect half-year convention). The aircraft is traded in January 2009 for another aircraft that qualifies for bonus depreciation. Depreciation for 2009 on the aircraft prior to the trade-in is $8,000 (($50,000 – $10,000) × 40% × 50% to reflect half-year convention). The carryover basis is $32,000 ($100,000 – $50,000 – $8,000). Bonus depreciation on the carryover basis following the trade-in is $16,000 ($32,000 × 50%). Depreciation on the carryover basis following the trade-in is $3,200 (($32,000 – $16,000) × 40% × 50% to reflect half-year convention). Total depreciation claimed on the $100,000 aircraft and its carryover basis over two tax years is $87,200 ($50,000 + $10,000 + $8,000 + $16,000 + $3,200).

See ¶ 167 for rules concerning the depreciation of property received in a like-kind exchange or an involuntary conversion.

Alternative minimum taxuniform capitalization rules

The Code Sec. 179 expense allowance is not an item of alternative minimum tax adjustment or preference. Depreciation deductions in excess of allowable AMT depreciation increase alternative minimum taxable income. Amounts expensed under Code Sec. 179 are also not subject to the uniform capitalization rules of Code Sec. 263A (Reg. § 1.179-1(j)).

Bonus depreciation is allowed for AMT purposes. However, if the AMT basis of the asset on which bonus depreciation is claimed is different than the regular tax basis, the AMT bonus deduction is the applicable percentage (i.e., 50 percent) of the AMT basis (Reg. § 1.168(k)-1(d)(2)).

Investment limitation

The maximum expense deduction ($250,000 for tax years beginning in 2008 and in 2009) is reduced by the amount that the cost of all qualifying property placed in service during the tax year exceeds $800,000 for tax years beginning in 2008 and in 2009. In 2008 and in 2009, no amount may be expensed if $1,050,000 of section 179 property is placed in service ($1,050,000 – $800,000 = $250,000). The amount by which the Code Sec. 179 expense deduction is reduced under this "investment limitation" rule is lost and may not be carried forward and deducted in later tax years (Code Sec. 179(b)(2)). Thus, if possible, a taxpayer should attempt to time the placing of property in service in such a way as to avoid the investment limitation.

Example (3): A calendar-year corporation purchases various machinery costing $1,050,000 in 2009 and places the machinery in service in the same year. The corporation may not claim a Code Sec. 179 expense allowance. If possible, the corporation should have delayed purchasing $250,000 of the machinery until 2010 (or delayed placing $250,000 of the machinery into service until 2010) so that its investment in section 179 property would not have exceeded $800,000. If only $800,000 of equipment had been placed in service in 2009, a $250,000 expense allowance could have been claimed in 2009.

For tax years beginning in 2010, the maximum expense deduction is $134,000 and the investment limitation is $530,000 (Rev. Proc. 2009-50). No amount may be expensed if $664,000 of section 179 property is placed in service in 2010 ($664,000 – $530,000 = $134,000).

Taxable income limitation

The "taxable income limitation" may also reduce the maximum expense deduction allowed for the tax year. Under this limitation, the total cost of section 179 property deducted in a tax year may not exceed the total amount of the taxable income of the taxpayer that is derived during the year from the active conduct of any trade or business. Taxable income for this purpose is determined without regard to the section 179 expense deduction, the Code Sec. 164(f) deduction for one-half of self-employment taxes paid, net operating loss carrybacks and carryforwards, and deductions suspended under other provisions of the Code. The taxable income limitation is applied after the "investment limitation" discussed above (Code Sec. 179(b)(3); Reg. § 1.179-2(c)(1); Reg. § 1.179-2(c)(6)).

A taxpayer whose Sec. 179 expense allowance would be reduced by the taxable income limitation should consider the possible advantage of accelerating the recognition of income in order to avoid the limitation.

Because amounts disallowed under the taxable income limitation may be carried forward indefinitely (Code Sec. 179(b)(3); Reg. § 1.179-2(c)(1)), it can be beneficial to elect the expense deduction even if no amount is currently deductible. In deciding whether to create a Sec. 179 carryforward, however, a taxpayer needs to consider the possibility that the taxable income limitation and dollar limitation can prevent its deduction in carryforward years. Note that a section 179 deduction disallowed by reason of the taxable income limitation is carried forward. It may not be carried back, either separately or as part of a NOL sustained during the tax year.

Example (4): Acme Inc., expenses $250,000 in 2009 but the entire deduction is carried forward to 2010 due to the taxable income limitation. In 2010, Acme places $134,000 of depreciable property in service and elects to expense the entire cost. Assume that Acme's 2010 taxable income is at least $134,000. Acme's Code Sec. 179 expense deduction is limited to $134,000 (the dollar limitation for 2010) and it continues to have a carryforward from 2009 to 2011 of $250,000.

If Acme's taxable income had been $50,000 in 2010, its carryforward to 2011 would have been $334,000 ($250,000 from 2009 + $84,000 ($134,000 – $50,000) from 2010).

If Acme had placed $664,000 of qualifying property in service in 2010, its dollar limitation for 2010 would have been reduced to zero. It would not have been able to deduct any amount in 2010 and its carryforward to 2011 would have been $250,000 (from 2009).

Taxable income from the active conduct of a trade or business is determined by aggregating the net income (or loss) from all of the trades or businesses actively conducted by the taxpayer during the tax year. Sec. 1231 gains (or losses) from an actively conducted trade or business and interest from working capital of an actively conducted trade or business are taken into account in computing taxable income from the active conduct of the trade or business (Reg. § 1.179-2(c)(1)). Wages, salaries, tips, and other compensation (not reduced by unreimbursed employee business expenses) are treated as taxable income from the active conduct of a trade or business (Reg.§ 1.179-2(c)(6)(iv)).

Dollar limitation and pass-through entities

Amounts that are disallowed as the result of the dollar limitation (e.g., $250,000 in 2008 and in 2009) may not be carried forward and deducted in future years. This rule has particular relevance in the case of a taxpayer with an interest in more than one flow-through entity such as an S-corporation, partnership, or limited liability company. The dollar limitation applies at both the entity level and the flow-through owner's level. Thus, in determining whether the dollar limitation is exceeded, a taxpayer must aggregate the amounts received from each flow-through entity as well as any amounts elected by the taxpayer, for example, with respect to assets purchased through a business operation run as a sole proprietorship. If a taxpayer anticipates that the dollar limitation will be exceeded as a result of amounts received through flow-through entities, it may be possible for the taxpayer to convince one or more of the entities to reduce the amount that it elects to expense so as to avoid exceeding the limitation. It should also be noted that the owner's basis in a flow-through entity is reduced by the amount of the expense allocated to the owner even if the expense cannot be deducted by the owner because of the dollar limitation. This means that the owner will recognize increased gain (or reduced loss) upon the sale of the interest even though no benefit was derived from the Code Sec. 179 deduction which was passed through.

Taxable income limitation and pass-through entities

In the case of a partner, taxable income (for purposes of the taxable income limitation) includes the partner's allocable share of taxable income derived from the active conduct by the partnership of any trade or business if the partner actively conducts a trade or business of the partnership by meaningfully participating in the management or operations of at least one of the partnership's trades or businesses (Reg. § 1.179-2(c)(2)(v); Reg. § 1.179-2(c)(6)(ii)). A similar standard applies to S shareholders in determining whether income or loss from an S corporation is included in the S shareholder's taxable income for purposes of the taxable income limitation (Reg. § 1.179-2(c)(3)).

Investment limitation and pass-through entities

In determining the excess section 179 property placed in service by a partner in a tax year, the cost of section 179 property placed in service by the partnership is not attributed to any partner (Reg. § 1.179-2(b)(3)(i)). A similar standard applies to S shareholders (Reg. § 1.179-2(b)(4)).

What is the active conduct of a trade or business?

The determination of whether a trade or business is actively conducted by a taxpayer is based on all of the facts and circumstances. The purpose of the standard is to prevent a passive investor in a trade or business from deducting section 179 expenses against taxable income derived from that trade or business (Reg. § 1.179-2(c)(6)(ii)). Although not stated in the Code Sec. 179 regulations, the preamble to the regulations (T.D. 8455, filed with the *Federal Register* 122392) indicates that the terms "active" and "passive" do not have the same meaning as in Code Sec. 469 (relating to passive activity losses) and that the definition of the Code Sec. 179 active conduct standard is different than the material participation standard of Code Sec. 469. Thus, it appears likely that a taxpayer can take rental activities into account in determining the taxable income limitation if the actively conducted standard of Code Sec. 179 is satisfied even though rental activities are generally considered *per se* passive under Code Sec. 469. The rule is a double-edged sword, however, insofar as losses from rental activities could reduce the taxable income limitation.

Mid-quarter convention planning

Generally, MACRS personal property is deprecated using the half-year convention. However, the mid-quarter convention applies to all property placed in service during the year if more than 40 percent of the aggregate adjusted bases of all assets (other than residential rental and nonresidential real property) placed in service during the year are placed in service during the last quarter of the year. The mid-quarter convention usually decreases the overall depreciation that would otherwise be claimed if the half-year convention applied but may, in some instances, result in an increased overall depreciation deduction. This point is discussed at ¶ 486.

Since the adjusted basis of an asset taken into account in determining whether the mid-quarter convention applies does not include amounts expensed under Code Sec. 179, a taxpayer may be able to avoid the mid-quarter depreciation convention by expensing assets placed in service in the fourth quarter of the tax year or, conversely, trigger the convention by expensing assets placed in service in the first three quarters.

Example (5): John Jefferson, a calendar-year taxpayer, purchases MACRS 5-year property costing $400,000 and places it in service in January 2009 (quarter one). Jefferson also places 5-year property costing $400,000 in service in December 2009 (quarter four). If Jefferson expenses $180,000 of the cost of the 5-year property placed in service in December and $70,000 of the property placed in service in January (the 2009 expense allowance dollar limit is $250,000), the mid-quarter convention will not apply since only 40% of the adjusted bases of all assets placed in service during the year were placed in service in quarter four ($400,000 – $180,000/$400,000 – $180,000 + $400,000 – $70,000 = 40%). If John allocates more than $70,000 of the Sec. 179 expense allowance to the 5-year property placed in service in January, the mid-quarter convention would apply.

In determining whether the mid-quarter convention applies, the amount of bonus depreciation that may be claimed on an asset is not a factor in applying the 40-percent test. Note also that the full amount of bonus depreciation may be claimed on any asset subject to the mid-quarter convention.

If the mid-quarter convention applies, the greatest benefit from the Code Sec. 179 expense allowance is obtained by allocating the allowance to assets placed in service in the fourth quarter when all of the assets placed in service in the fourth quarter have recovery periods equal to or longer than the recovery period of any asset placed in service in prior quarters.

Example (6): Assume that 3-year property costing $50,000 is placed in service in January 2009 (quarter one), 3-year property costing $47,000 is placed in service in November (quarter four), and 3-year property costing $315,000 is placed in service in December (quarter four). In this case, the mid-quarter convention will apply regardless of how the Sec. 179 expense allowance is allocated among the assets. (Even if the entire $250,000 expense allowance for 2009 is allocated to assets placed in service in the fourth quarter, 69% ($47,000 + $315,000 – $250,000/$47,000 + $315,000 – $250,000 + $50,000 = 69%) of the total adjusted basis of all assets will have been placed in service in the fourth quarter and the mid-quarter convention will apply).

Under the mid-quarter convention, 58.33% of the depreciable basis of the 3-year property placed in service in the first quarter is depreciable in the year placed in service (Table 2 at ¶ 180). However, for 3-year property placed in service in the fourth quarter, the applicable recovery percentage is only 8.33% (Table 5 at ¶ 180).

The tax benefit of expensing assets placed in service in the fourth quarter is maximized if the allowance is allocated to assets with long recovery periods because the applicable fourth quarter recovery percentage becomes smaller as the recovery period for the property increases. For example, if one of the assets placed in service in the fourth quarter in the preceding example was 20-year property, the first-year recovery percentage is only 0.938 percent.

Allocating the expense deduction to fourth quarter assets will not necessarily produce the greatest overall tax savings if the allowance can be allocated to property placed in service in an earlier quarter with a longer recovery period than any of the fourth quarter assets. For example, suppose 20-year property is placed in service in the first quarter and 3-year property is placed in service in the fourth quarter. Here, the allocation of the expense allowance to the 20-year property will produce the greatest overall tax savings. The difference between the first-year recovery percentages for the 3- and 20-year property (8.33 percent for 3-year property placed in service in the fourth quarter and 6.563 percent for 20-year property placed in service in the first quarter) is not nearly significant enough justify allocation to the 3-year property.

Tax bracket considerations

It may be advisable to forego the Code Sec. 179 expense election (and elect out of bonus depreciation if available) if a taxpayer anticipates falling into a higher-income tax bracket in later tax years. For example, if an individual is in the 15-percent tax bracket in 2009 but will be in the highest individual tax bracket in 2010 and later tax years, it may be possible to derive a greater overall tax benefit by recovering the cost that would otherwise be expensed in 2009 over the entire recovery period of the asset. The election of the MACRS straight-line method or ADS will also operate to reduce the first-year depreciation deduction and thereby defer depreciation deductions into the later, higher tax bracket years.

Earned income credit, social security coverage, exemptions and deductions

The election to expense under Code Sec. 179 (or not elect out of bonus depreciation) can reduce a taxpayer's earned income credit, reduce coverage under social security, and reduce exemptions and deductions that are based on adjusted gross income or taxable income.

On the other hand, reduction of adjusted gross income or taxable income can prevent the phase-out of certain deductions, exemptions, and credits.

Self-employment tax savings

The Code Sec. 179 expense deduction provides a self-employed person with the double benefit of reducing income tax liability and self-employment tax liability assuming that the deduction offsets self-employment income below the applicable base amount ($106,800 in 2009 and 2010) on which the tax (15.3 percent) is imposed. However, if a loss is reported on Schedule C (without regard to Code Sec. 179), the benefit of the section 179 election with respect to a Schedule C asset is limited to a reduction in income tax liability (assuming the taxpayer has taxable income from non-Schedule C sources). If the self-employed person anticipates being subject to SE tax in subsequent years, it may be preferable to depreciate rather than expense because the depreciation deductions claimed in later years could reduce both income tax and self-employment tax liability. On the other hand, if the taxable income limitation prevents the self-employed person from claiming an expense deduction, a Code Sec. 179 election made for the purpose of obtaining a section 179 carryforward could be even more beneficial assuming that the carryforward can be quickly deducted.

Example (7): Joan Jackson, a sole proprietor, places 3-year property costing $100,000 into service in 2009. She reports a 2009 Schedule C loss without regard to the depreciable property and has no self-employment tax liability. Assume that the taxable income limitation is satisfied because Joan's spouse has significant wage income. If Joan makes the Code Sec. 179 election, the $100,000 expense deduction will reduce the taxable income on the couple's joint return but will not save self-employment taxes. In this case, it may be preferable to not elect to claim the section 179 expense allowance in 2009 and to minimize depreciation deductions in 2009 by electing ADS or the MACRS straight-line method to depreciate the asset in order to reduce both income and self-employment taxes during the immediately following years if Joan will be subject to SE tax in those years.

Example (8): Assume the same facts as in the preceding *Example* except that the taxable income limitation cannot be satisfied. Joan elects to expense the 3-year property and, as a result, has a $100,000 section 179 carryforward. Assume that Joan will have $100,000 of self-employment income in 2010 (without regard to the carryforward) and will not place any additional depreciable assets in service in 2010. In this case, Joan benefits by making the Code Sec. 179 election, since the entire carryforward can be deducted in 2010 and will reduce both taxable income and self-employment income. However, Joan may still want to elect the MACRS straight-line or ADS in order to defer first-year depreciation deductions into later years of the recovery period. Note that regular depreciation could create a net operating loss for immediate carryback.

Collateral impact on AGI based items

Code Sec. 179 expense deductions or first-year bonus depreciation allowances that reduce an individual's adjusted gross income may allow an individual to claim increased deductions, exclusions, credits, and other tax benefits that are tied to a taxpayer's adjusted gross income level (e.g., casualty losses, medical expense deductions, individual retirement account contributions, miscellaneous itemized deductions, itemized deductions of high-income taxpayers, savings bond interest exclusion, adoption credit, child credit, and dependent care credit).

Recapture upon decline in business use

The tax benefit received from the Sec. 179 expense deduction claimed on property placed in service after 1986 is recaptured as ordinary income during any tax year in which the trade or business use of the property falls to 50 percent or less prior to the end of the property's recovery period. The recapture amount included in income is the difference between the Sec. 179 expense deduction claimed and the depreciation that would have been allowed on the Sec. 179 amount for prior tax years and the year of recapture (Code Sec. 179(d)(10); Reg. § 1.179-1(e)). See ¶ 300 for examples of the calculation.

The additional portion of the section 179 allowance allowed for qualifying section 179 Gulf Opportunity Zone property (¶ 306), Kansas Disaster Area property

(¶ 306A), and Disaster Assistance Property (¶ 306B) are also subject to recapture in a tax year during the property's recovery period that it is no longer substantially used in a trade or business in the Gulf Zone, Kansas Disaster Area, or Presidentially-declared disaster area (i.e., business use in the zone or area falls below 80 percent). The additional section 179 allowance that may be claimed on qualifying section 179 New York Liberty Zone property (see¶ 305) is subject to recapture if the property ceases to be used in the New York Liberty Zone regardless of the percentage of business use. Note that these section 179 bump-ups are also subject to recapture along with the standard section 179 deduction (e.g., $250,000 for 2009) if business use within or outside the zone or area fall to 50 percent or less.

> ***Example:*** A taxpayer claims a $350,000 section 179 expense allowance for section 179 property placed in service in a Presidentially declared disaster area in 2009 ($250,000 standard section 179 allowance for 2009 plus $100,000 bump-up for Disaster Assistance Property). If business use in the disaster area falls below 80 percent but remains above 50 percent, only the $100,000 bump-up is subject to section 179 recapture. If business use in or outside of the disaster area falls to 50 percent or lower, the entire $350,000 section 179 expense allowance is subject to recapture.

The bonus depreciation deduction on Gulf Opportunity Zone property is subject to recapture in a tax year during an asset's recovery period that business use in the Gulf Zone is not 80 percent or greater (¶ 127F). A similar rule applies to Kansas disaster area bonus depreciation (¶ 127G) and bonus depreciation for disaster assistance property (¶ 127H). A decline in business use does not trigger bonus depreciation recapture in the case of New York Liberty Zone property (¶ 127E) or bonus depreciation claimed under Code Sec. 168(k) (¶ 127D).

In the case of a listed property such as a car or truck (¶ 200 and following), bonus depreciation claimed under Code Sec. 168(k) is subject to recapture (along with any amount expensed under section 179) if business use during the asset's recovery period under ADS does not exceed 50 percent (Code Sec. 168(k)(2)(F)(ii)). The recapture amount is the difference between the amount of bonus depreciation, section 179 expense, and regular depreciation deductions that exceed that amount of depreciation that would have been allowed under the MACRS alternative depreciation system. See Example (5) at ¶ 300.

Recapture amounts are added to the basis of the property. No recapture for decline in business use is required if the property is sold or disposed of in a transaction that triggers Sec. 1245 recapture. However, amounts expensed under Code Sec. 179 are treated as depreciation for purposes of Code Sec. 1245 recapture (Reg. § 1.179-1(e)(3)).

If a taxpayer expenses the entire cost of a property, the amount of depreciation that would have been allowed is presumably computed using the MACRS method that would have applied if the asset had not been expensed. This will usually be the MACRS general depreciation system (GDS) (i.e., regular table percentages). However, if an election is made to depreciate other property in the same class as the property expensed using an alternate method (e.g., the MACRS straight-line method, the MACRS 150-percent DB method, or MACRS alternative straight-line method), presumably that method is used to compute recapture since it would have applied to the property if it had not been expensed. Furthermore, the applicable recovery period during which recapture could be triggered is presumably the recovery period that would have applied under the elective method.

These rules dictate that when claiming a Code Sec. 179 expense allowance, a taxpayer should consider that allocation to an asset that is depreciated (or would be depreciated if the entire cost is expensed) under an elective MACRS depreciation system that uses a longer recovery period than applies under GDS will result in a longer recapture period.

Example (9): A taxpayer expensed the entire cost an item of 5-year property placed in service in 2009 and elected the MACRS alternative straight-line system (ADS) for all other 5-year property placed in service in 2009. The ADS recovery period for the expensed asset is 10 years. If business use of the expensed property falls to 50% or less after expiration of the 5-year GDS recovery period but prior to the expiration of the 10-year ADS recovery period, recapture is computed using ADS even though no recapture would apply under GDS.

Code Sec. 179 recapture amounts are computed on Form 4797. The recapture amount is reported as "other income" on the same form or schedule on which the deduction was claimed. Thus, for example, if the deduction was claimed on Form 1040 Schedule C by a sole proprietor, the recapture would be entered on that form and increase the amount of the sole proprietor's self-employment income. In contrast, amounts recaptured under Code Sec. 1245 are reported directly by individuals on Form 1040 as "other income" and are not subject to self-employment tax (Code Sec. 1402(a)(3)).

Relationship of section 179 deduction to luxury car depreciation caps

The Code Sec. 179 expense deduction is treated as a depreciation deduction for purposes of the depreciation caps imposed by the Code Sec. 280F luxury car rules (Code Sec. 280F(d)(1)). Consequently, the sum of the regular first-year depreciation deduction (including bonus allowance) and the Code Sec. 179 expense allowance may not exceed the applicable first-year depreciation cap. See ¶ 200 for applicable caps.

If the first-year depreciation deduction on a car is less than the applicable first-year depreciation cap, the expense deduction may be claimed only to the extent necessary to reach the first-year cap. The instructions for Part V of Form 4562, on which passenger automobile depreciation is reported, indicate that the sum of the depreciation deduction entered on line 26, and the expense deduction elected and entered on line 26 may not exceed the applicable first-year cap.

Formula for determining appropriate section 179 expense deduction on cars if bonus depreciation not claimed

In most situations the first-year depreciation on a used car will exceed the applicable first-year cap that applies to cars on which bonus depreciation is not claimed. (Bonus depreciation may not be claimed on used property or if an election out is made). Thus, generally it is not necessary to elect to expense any portion under Code Sec. 179. For example, for a used car placed in service in calendar-year 2009, the first-year depreciation deduction (assuming half-year convention, 200-percent declining-balance method, five-year recovery period) on a used vehicle that costs at least $14,800 will equal or exceed the $2,960 first-year cap for cars placed in service in calendar year 2009 ($14,800 × 20% first-year depreciation percentage under half-year convention = $2,960 first year cap if bonus depreciation claimed)). See ¶ 200 for applicable first-year caps.

If the mid-quarter convention applies and the applicable first-year cap is $2,960, the vehicle must cost less than the following amounts before any amount of the vehicle's cost is expensed under section 179:

- First quarter $8,457 ($8,457 × 35% = $2,960)
- Second quarter $11,840 ($11,840 × 25% = $2,960)
- Third quarter $19,733 ($19,733 × 15% = $2,960)
- Fourth quarter $59,200 ($59,200 × 5% = $2,960)

If the cost of a car does not exceed these amounts, a formula may be used to determine the amount to expense under Code Sec. 179 so that the sum of the regular depreciation allowance plus the amount expensed under Code Sec. 179 is exactly equal to the applicable first-year cap. The formulas for the half-year and mid-quarter conventions are provided below. Note that if a taxpayer has placed other property in service that qualifies for the Code Sec. 179 expense allowance, the tax savings will be greater if the allowance is first allocated to other property with a recovery period that is longer than five years. See comments at the beginning of this explanation paragraph.

Assuming that a car will be depreciated under the MACRS general depreciation system (i.e., five-year recovery period, 200-percent DB method) and that the half-year convention applies and that bonus depreciation will not be claimed, the amount of Sec. 179 expense allowance to claim on a car in order to reach the first-year cap may be determined by (1) reducing the amount of the first-year cap by 20 percent of the cost or other depreciable basis of the vehicle (determined without regard to the expense deduction) and (2) dividing the amount determined in (1) by .8.

> ***Example (10):*** Assume that the depreciable basis of a used car is $12,000. The used car is used 100% for business purposes and is placed in service in 2009. The applicable first-year depreciation cap for 2009 is $2,960. The purchaser should expense $700 (($2,960 – ($12,000 × 20%))/.8). If the purchaser expenses $700, the sum of the first year depreciation allowance plus the expensed amount will exactly equal the applicable first-year cap (($12,000 – $700) × 20% + $700 = $2,960).

If the mid-quarter convention applies to a car on which bonus depreciation is not claimed (and the first-year depreciation deduction does not exceed the first-year cap ($2,960 for a vehicle placed in service in the 2009 calendar year if bonus depreciation is not claimed), the formula is applied by substituting the applicable mid-quarter convention recovery percentage for 20 percent and substituting the difference between 1 and the applicable mid-quarter recovery percentage (expressed as a decimal) for .8.

> ***Example (11):*** Assume the same facts as in the preceding *Example*, except that the mid-quarter convention applies and the car is placed in service in the fourth quarter of 2009. The mid-quarter recovery percentage for 5-year property placed in service in the fourth quarter is 5%. The purchaser in this case should expense $2,484 (($2,960 – ($12,000 × 5%))/(1 – .05)). If the purchaser expenses $2,484, the sum of the first year depreciation allowance plus the expensed amount will equal the applicable first-year cap (($12,000 – $2,484) × 5% + $2,484 = $2,960).

Formula for determining appropriate section 179 expense deduction on cars if bonus depreciation is claimed

In most situations the first-year depreciation on a new car placed in service in calendar-year 2009 on which bonus depreciation is claimed will exceed the applicable first-year cap. Thus, it is not necessary to elect to expense any portion under Code Sec. 179. For example, for a car placed in service in 2009, the first-year depreciation deduction (including bonus allowance) (assuming half-year convention, 200-percent declining-balance method, five-year recovery period, and bonus depreciation) on a vehicle that costs at least $18,266 will equal or exceed the $10,960 first-year cap for cars placed in service in calendar year 2009 ($9,133 bonus depreciation (($18,266 - $9,133) × 20% first-year depreciation percentage under half-year convention = $10,960 first year cap if bonus depreciation claimed)). See ¶ 200 for applicable first-year caps.

If bonus depreciation is claimed and the price of a car is less than $18,266 and the half-year convention applies, the amount to expense under section 179 is determined by (1) reducing the first-year cap ($10,960 for a car placed in service in calendar year 2009) by 60 percent of the cost of the vehicle and (2) dividing the amount determined in (1) by 40 percent.

The 200 percent declining balance method is used to depreciate a car unless a taxpayer elects to use another method. The first-year table percentage is 20% if the 200 percent declining balance method applies.

> ***Example (12):*** A new car is purchased for $16,000 in 2009. The half-year convention and 200 percent declining balance method applies. The applicable first-year cap is $10,960. The purchaser should expense $3,400 (($10,960 – ($16,000 × 60%))/.40). If the purchaser expenses $3,400, the sum of the expensed amount ($3,400), bonus depreciation deduction ($6,300) (($16,000 – $3,400) × 50%), and regular first-year depreciation deduction ($1,260) (($16,000 – $3,400 – $6,300) × 20%) will exactly equal the $10,960 cap.

If the midquarter convention applies and 50 percent bonus depreciation is claimed on a vehicle placed in service in 2009, the vehicle must cost no more than the following amounts to make it necessary to claim a section 179 deduction in order to reach the $10,960 cap applicable in to vehicles placed in service in calendar-year 2009:

- First quarter $16,237 (($16,237 × 50%) + ($8,118.50 × 35%) = $10,960)
- Second quarter $17,536 (($17,536 × 50%) + ($8,768 × 25%) = $10,960)
- Third quarter $19,061 (($19,061 × 50%) + ($9,530 × 15%) = $10,960)
- Fourth quarter $20,876 (($20,876 × 50%) + ($10,438 × 5%) = $10,960)

If the mid-quarter convention applies and bonus depreciation is claimed at the 50-percent rate, the formula is applied by reducing the first-year cap ($10,960 for a car placed in service in 2009) by 67.5 percent if placed in service in the first quarter, by 62.5 percent if placed in service in the second quarter, by 57.5 percent if placed in service in the third quarter, and by 52.5 percent of the cost if placed in service in the fourth quarter. The amount so determined is divided by .325 if the car was placed in service in the first quarter, .375 for the second quarter, .425 for the third quarter, and .475 for the fourth quarter.

> ***Example (13):*** A new car is purchased in the first quarter of 2009 for $15,500. The applicable first-year cap is $10,960. The purchaser should expense $1,530 ($10,960 – ($15,500 × 67.5%)/.325). If the purchaser expenses $1,530, the sum of the expensed amount ($1,530), bonus depreciation deduction ($6,985) ($15,500 – $1,530 × 50%), and regular first-year depreciation deduction ($2,445) ($15,500 – $1,530 – $6,985 × 35% (table percentage for 5-year property placed in service in first quarter)) is equal to the $10,960 cap.

Note that if the taxpayer in *Example (13)* placed other qualifying bonus depreciation property in service in later quarters of the tax year for which the first-year table percentage is lower than 35 percent, the section 179 allowance could produce greater tax savings if allocated to that property. If a taxpayer placed property in service which does not qualify for bonus depreciation and property which does qualify, it is also generally preferable to allocate the section 179 deduction to the nonqualifying property in order to maximize depreciation, bonus, and section 179 deductions claimed during the tax year.

¶ 488

Planning for Depreciation Recapture

When acquiring or disposing of a depreciable asset, taxpayers need to consider that some or all of the depreciation claimed or allowable on the asset may be recaptured as ordinary income.

Recapture may be limited to actual depreciation claimed if adequate records are maintained. See "*Keep records to reduce depreciation recapture—allowed or allowable rule,*" below.

The amount of depreciation subject to recapture depends primarily on the type of asset (for example, real (Sec. 1250) or personal (Sec. 1245) property), the depreciation system used to depreciate the asset (MACRS, ACRS, or pre-ACRS), and the depreciation method used under that system (declining-balance or straight-line). Recapture is reported on Form 4797.

Generally, depreciation recapture is associated with the sale or exchange of a depreciable property. However, depreciation recapture can also apply to other types of dispositions in which no gain is recognized. For example, a corporation that transfers depreciable property as a dividend may need to recognize recapture income even though the transfer would otherwise be tax-free. See ¶ 160.

Overview of recapture rules

In general, all gain from the sale, exchange, or involuntary conversion of Sec. 1245 property (primarily personal property) that is depreciated under MACRS is recaptured as ordinary income to the extent of previously allowed or allowable depreciation deductions (including the Code Sec. 179 expense deduction and bonus depreciation deduction) regardless of whether the cost of the property is recovered using the MACRS general depreciation system (GDS) or an elective MACRS method which slows the rate of cost recovery (Code Sec. 1245(a)). Depreciation recapture, however, is not required with respect to MACRS residential rental property or MACRS nonresidential real property held for more than one year. See ¶ 160. However, all MACRS depreciation deductions claimed on Sec. 1250 real property are subject to recapture if the property is held for one year or less (Code Sec. 1250(b)(1); Reg. § 1.1250-4).

Bonus depreciation claimed on section 1250 property (e.g., section 1250 land improvements, MACRS qualified 15-year leasehold improvement property, and 15-year restaurant improvement property, as well as certain residential and nonresidential real property) is treated as accelerated depreciation for purposes of the section 1250 recapture rules. Thus, the difference between the bonus deduction and straight-line depreciation is subject to recapture. See ¶ 160.

Gain recognized on the sale of ACRS Sec. 1245 property is subject to recapture as ordinary income to the extent of previously claimed depreciation regardless of whether the property was depreciated using an accelerated or straight-line method. ACRS real property is treated as Sec. 1245 property for recapture purposes. However, ACRS 15-, 18-, and 19-year property that is residential rental property, any 15-, 18-, or 19-year nonresidential property that is depreciated under the ACRS straight-line method, and any low-income housing is treated as Sec. 1250 property for purposes of recapture (Code Sec. 1245(a)(5), prior to amendment by the 1986 Tax Reform Act). Gain on the sale or disposition of Sec. 1250 ACRS property is recaptured to the extent that the depreciation allowed exceeds the amount allowable under the ACRS straight-line method using the applicable 15-, 18-, or 19-year recovery period.

The recapture of gain on the sale of ACRS 15-year low-income housing is phased out after the property has been held for a prescribed number of months, at the rate of one percentage point per month (Code Sec. 168(c)(2)(F) (prior to amendment by the 1986 Tax Reform Act); Code Sec. 1250(a)(1)(B)).

Gain on the sale of Sec. 1245 property placed in service before 1981 is treated as ordinary income to the extent of prior depreciation allowed or allowable. Gain on the disposition of nonresidential real property is generally recaptured only to the extent that the depreciation claimed after 1969 exceeds the amount that would have been allowed after 1969 under the straight-line method. Gain on residential rental property is subject to recapture to the extent that accelerated depreciation claimed after 1975 exceeds straight-line depreciation. Special recapture rules apply to low-income housing.

See ¶ 160 for a discussion of the MACRS recapture rules.

Additional corporate real property recapture

A corporation (other than an S corporation) which disposes of Sec. 1250 property at a gain may be required to recapture up to 20 percent of its previously claimed depreciation even though recapture is not otherwise required. Specifically, in the case of section 1250 property which is disposed of during the tax year, 20 percent of the excess (if any) of the amount that would be treated as ordinary income if the property was Section 1245 property over the amount (if any) recaptured as ordinary income under Code Sec. 1250 is treated as ordinary income (Code Sec. 291(a)).

Example (1): A corporation places MACRS residential real property costing $100,000 in service in 1999 and sells the property in 2009 for $130,000. Assume $40,000 of depreciation was claimed on the property. The depreciation is not subject to recapture under Code Sec. 1250. However, if the property was Code Sec. 1245 property the $40,000 of depreciation claimed would have been subject to recapture as ordinary income since the gain on the sale ($70,000 ($130,000 amount realized – $60,000 adjusted basis) exceeded the depreciation claimed ($40,000). Thus, under Code Sec. 291, $8,000 (20% × $40,000) is recaptured as ordinary income.

Code Sec. 291(a) recapture is in addition to any recapture otherwise required under Code Sec. 1250, for example, with respect to ACRS real property depreciated using an accelerated method.

Purpose of recapture

The recapture provisions were enacted to prevent taxpayers from obtaining favorable capital gains tax rates on gain attributable to depreciation deductions which were used to offset ordinary income.

Current law generally limits the maximum capital gains tax rate of an individual, estate, or trust to 15, 25 or 28 percent while ordinary income is subject to a maximum tax rate of 35 percent. The maximum capital gains rate of a corporation is currently set at 35 percent. This rate, however, is the same as the maximum tax rate on a corporation's ordinary income (the special tax rates in excess of 35 percent imposed on high-income corporations to phase-out the benefit of lower tax-brackets are not taken into account in determining whether the maximum 35-percent capital gains tax rate applies).

Unrecaptured section 1250 gain—25-percent capital gains rate

In the case of individuals, estates, and trusts, a 25-percent capital gains tax rate applies to "unrecaptured section 1250 gain." In general, unrecaptured section 1250 gain is the amount of depreciation claimed on section 1250 property which is not recaptured as ordinary income. Unrecaptured depreciation taken into account in computing unrecaptured section 1250 gain cannot exceed the amount of gain recognized on the property after the gain is reduced by any ordinary income recapture. Any gain in excess of the amount treated as unrecaptured section 1250 gain is eligible for the 15-percent capital gains rate.

Since MACRS residential rental and nonresidential real property is not subject to ordinary income recapture, all depreciation on such property, to the extent of gain, is potentially characterized as unrecaptured section 1250 gain.

It should be kept in mind that depreciable property and nondepreciable real property (e.g., land) used in a trade or business and held for more than one year is section 1231 property. As a result, unrecaptured section 1250 gain is not subject to the 25-percent rate unless a taxpayer has a net section 1231 gain for the year—that is, gains in excess of ordinary income depreciation recapture from section 1231 real and personal property must exceed losses from such property. If a taxpayer has a net section 1231 gain, each section 1231 gain and loss is treated as a long-term capital gain and loss and is combined with any other capital gains and losses for the year in accordance with prescribed capital gain and loss netting rules. A net section 1231 loss, on the other hand, is deductible in full against ordinary income.

> ***Example (2):*** Sam Jones receives $150,000 for depreciable MACRS real estate acquired for $100,000. He has claimed $30,000 of depreciation on the property. Sam also receives $7,000 for a fully depreciated machine, which cost $5,000. The $5,000 depreciation claimed on the machine is recaptured as ordinary income under Code Sec. 1245. Sam has a net section 1231 gain of $52,000 ($50,000 gain from the real estate plus $2,000 unrecaptured gain from the machine), which is treated as long-term capital gain. The $2,000 gain from the machine is treated as 15% rate gain. $30,000 of the gain from the real estate is treated as 25% unrecaptured section 1250 gain. The remaining $50,000 of gain from the real estate is treated as 15% rate gain. These gains will be combined with any other capital gains and losses for the year in accordance with the capital gain and loss netting rules.

The recapture provisions can have an adverse impact on individuals or corporations even when there is no differential between ordinary income and capital gains rates. The following paragraphs point out possible pitfalls associated with the recapture provisions and techniques for avoiding them.

Sell recapture assets in low-bracket tax year

Recaptured depreciation is taxed at the ordinary income tax rate in effect in the year of recapture. The recapture provisions can operate as a penalty against taxpayers who offset ordinary income in low-bracket tax years (or have an operating loss) and then dispose of the asset in a high-bracket tax year.

> ***Example (3):*** Melinda Jones is in the 15% tax bracket in the year she purchases 5-year MACRS property for $20,000. Assume that she sells the property for $20,000 in the third year of the recovery period when she is in the 35% tax bracket. Under GDS, Jones would claim $4,000 ($20,000 × 20%) depreciation in Year 1 and $6,400 ($20,000 × 32%) in Year 2. The tax benefit of the deductions, without regard to present value considerations, is $1,560 ($10,400×15%). In Year 3, when the asset is sold, the $10,400 of depreciation is recaptured as ordinary income and an additional tax of $3,640 is imposed ($10,400 × 35% rate).
>
> Note: Year 3 depreciation is not considered in the example since it will offset ordinary income taxed at a 35% tax rate and is subject to recapture as ordinary income at a 35% tax rate in the same year.

The result in the preceding example could have been avoided if the taxpayer had delayed sale to a low-bracket tax year or a tax year in which a net operating loss was sustained. Another possibility, which could have mitigated the result somewhat, would have been to elect the MACRS alternative depreciation system (ADS), so that less depreciation would have been claimed in the earlier years when the benefit of the deductions were minimal. Also, it may have been possible to avoid immediate recapture by disposing of the asset in a Code Sec. 1031 like-kind exchange.

Maximizing capital loss deductions

In general, noncorporate taxpayers deduct capital losses to the extent of capital gains. Capital losses in excess of capital gains can offset up to $3,000 ($1,500 for a married person filing separately) of ordinary income per year. The nondeductible portion of the loss can be carried forward indefinitely (Code Sec. 1211(b)). Corporations may only deduct capital losses against capital gains (Code Sec. 1211(a)).

Even where there is no tax rate differential between a taxpayer's ordinary income tax rate and capital gains tax rate, the conversion of Sec. 1231 gain (see ¶ 496) to ordinary income under the recapture provisions can be significant for purposes of planning the deduction of capital losses. For example, the Sec. 1231 capital gain available for offset against capital losses may be reduced or eliminated.

> ***Example (4):*** John Jones recognizes a short-term capital loss of $15,000 on the sale of XYZ stock. He also sells depreciable Sec. 1245 business property at a gain of $15,000. Assume that he has claimed $15,000 of depreciation on the property and that the entire amount is recaptured as ordinary income. If Jones has no other capital gains or losses, he may only deduct $3,000 of the short-term capital loss against ordinary income. The remaining $12,000 of the short-term capital loss must be carried forward. If the recapture provisions did not apply, the entire $15,000 of Sec. 1231 gain would have been treated as long-term capital gain and would have offset the entire short-term capital loss.

Note that if the taxpayer in the preceding example were a corporation, then the entire short-term capital loss would have been carried forward since a corporation may only deduct capital gains against capital losses (Code Sec. 1211(a)).

Utilize net operating losses

In general, net operating losses can be carried forward for 20 years (15 years for NOLs arising in tax years beginning before August 6, 1997). Rather than lose the tax benefit of an expiring NOL, a taxpayer who owns a depreciated asset which can readily be sold at a gain may be able to use the NOL to absorb ordinary income recapture that would otherwise be subject to tax in a later year.

Anticipate installment sale recaptures

The recapture provisions are important to a taxpayer selling depreciable property (or a partnership interest in a partnership with depreciable property) and reporting income using the installment method because all depreciation recapture is reported as ordinary income *in the year of sale* (Code Sec. 453(i)). As a result, it may be advisable that the seller receives an initial payment in the year of sale sufficient to satisfy the additional tax liability caused by recapture.

This rule is not a concern with respect to the disposition of MACRS real property, as MACRS real property is not subject to depreciation recapture. However, special rules apply in determining what portion of an installment payment is considered attributable to the 25-percent capital-gains rate on unrecaptured section 1250 gain. See Reg. § 1.453-12.

> ***Example (5):*** John sells his raised dairy cows, machinery, and equipment to Jake for $260,000. The cows are valued at $120,000 and the machinery at $140,000. Jake pays $20,000 down and $80,000 plus interest annually for 3 years. John's machinery and equipment have an adjusted basis of $64,000; its original cost was $200,000. John's gain on the sale of the machinery and equipment is $76,000 (($140,000 – $64,000). The entire gain is recaptured as ordinary income under Code Sec. 1245 in the year of sale because the gain is less than the $136,000 ($200,000 – $64,000) of depreciation claimed in prior years. John will report the $120,000 cattle sale on the installment method.
>
> If John and Jake are related and Jake resells the cattle within two years, then John may be required to recognized all of the gain from the cattle sale in the resale year. See Code Sec. 453(e).

Delay sale of MACRS real property held for one year or less

Depreciation recapture on Sec. 1250 real property is generally limited to the difference between accelerated depreciation claimed and straight-line depreciation. However, if the Sec. 1250 real property is held for one year or less all depreciation is subject to recapture (up to the amount of gain realized from the sale or disposition) (Code Sec. 1250(b)(1)). Although MACRS residential rental and nonresidential real property is not normally subject to recapture because it is depreciated using the straight-line method, all MACRS deductions on such property are subject to recapture if the property is not held for more than one year prior to the date of sale or disposition. Moreover, any gain not recaptured as ordinary income, would also not qualify for favorable treatment as Sec. 1231 gain. Thus, where possible, it may be advantageous to delay the sale of MACRS real property which would otherwise be sold within one year.

Since a taxpayer may not claim MACRS on a property that is acquired and disposed of in the same tax year (Reg. § 1.168(d)-1(b)(3)(ii)), the full recapture rule for property held for one year or less only has implications where the property is acquired in one tax year, disposed of in the following tax year, and held for one year of less.

Allocate purchase price favorably

When a taxpayer sells a group of assets (or a business) for a single price certain allocations of the purchase price may prove advantageous. For example, to the extent that the fair market value of assets are unclear or otherwise subject to negotiation, a seller may be able to allocate the purchase price to those assets that are not subject to depreciation recapture, such as MACRS real property or nondepreciable property. Allocations causing ordinary gain (recapture gain, for example) should be minimized if possible. This strategy could maximize capital gains recognition (generally taxable at a favorable rate) and reduce ordinary income recapture.

On the other hand, a purchaser may benefit by maximizing allocation of the purchase price to depreciable property with the shortest recovery periods in order to obtain larger depreciation deductions during the early years of the asset's recovery period. The present value of the tax-benefit of the current write-off will normally offset the negative impact of any future ordinary income recapture upon the sale of the depreciable asset if it is sold at a gain. A purchaser, however, also needs to consider whether the tax benefit of its depreciation deductions could be negatively impacted by an alternative minimum tax liability arising from accelerated depreciation on Sec. 1245 personal property or whether it may be in a higher income tax bracket in later tax years, in which case reduced depreciation deductions in earlier tax years may be warranted.

Related party recapture trap

When an asset is sold to a related party at a loss, Code Sec. 267 generally disallows the loss but allows the related purchaser to reduce the amount of gain otherwise recognizable on a subsequent sale by the amount of the previously disallowed loss. The reduction in subsequent gain is authorized by Code Sec. 267(d). However, the recapture regulations for Code Sec. 1245 and Code Sec. 1250 specifically override Code Sec. 267(d) (Reg. § 1.1245-6(b) and Reg. § 1.1250-1(c)(2)). Thus, the full amount of the subsequent gain without reduction for the disallowed loss is subject to recapture as ordinary income.

Example (6): John James sells Sec. 1245 machinery to his wholly-owned corporation for $100,000. His basis in the machinery is $120,000. Since he is related to the corporation the $20,000 loss is disallowed. Assume that the corporation claims $40,000 of depreciation on the asset and then sells it to an unrelated party for $90,000. The corporation's gain is $30,000 ($90,000 – ($100,000 – $40,000)). If Code Sec. 267(d) applied, the corporation's gain would be reduced by $20,000 and only $10,000 would be recaptured as ordinary income. However, because Code Sec. 267(d) does not apply, the entire $30,000 gain is recaptured as ordinary income.

Recapture on sales to or by controlled entities and certain other related persons

All gain on the sale or exchange of property that is depreciable in the hands of certain related transferees is taxed as ordinary income to the transferor (Code Sec. 1239). In general, the following transferors and transferees are related for purposes of this rule:

(1) a person and a person's controlled entity;

(2) a taxpayer and a trust in which the taxpayer (or the taxpayer's spouse) is a beneficiary (other than a beneficiary with a remote contingent interest);

(3) an employer and the employer's controlled welfare benefit fund (Code Sec. 1239(d)); and

(4) an executor and a beneficiary of an estate, unless the sale or exchange is in satisfaction of a pecuniary bequest.

A corporation is controlled for purposes of this rule if a person owns (directly or indirectly) more than 50 percent of the value of its stock. A partnership is controlled if a person owns (directly or indirectly) more than 50 percent of the capital or profits interest in the partnership.

The rule also applies to two corporations that are members of the same controlled group (certain modifications apply to the Code Sec. 1563(a) definition of a controlled group); two S corporations, if the same persons own more than 50 percent in value of the outstanding stock of each corporation; and two corporations, one of which is an S corporation, if the same persons own more than 50 percent in value of the outstanding stock of each corporation.

A patent application is treated as depreciable property for purposes of this recapture rule (Code Sec. 1239(e)).

Retire structural components

Although the sale or retirement of ACRS 15-, 18-, or 19-year real property can trigger depreciation recapture, ACRS proposed regulations provide that the retirement of a structural component of such property is not considered a disposition (Code Sec. 168(d)(2)(C) (prior to amendment by the 1986 Tax Reform Act); Prop. Reg. § 1.168-2(l)(1)). Accordingly, retirement and replacement of a defective or worn component may be preferable to the sale of the entire structure where ordinary recapture income or Sec. 1231 gain would be recognized. This strategy applies to MACRS residential rental and nonresidential real property insofar as it would defer the recognition of Sec. 1231 gain. Depreciation on MACRS residential rental and nonresidential real property is not subject to recapture.

Gift and death transfer exceptions to recapture

Certain types of dispositions and transfers will not cause depreciation recapture or will at least result in a limitation on the amount otherwise recaptured.

Recapture can be avoided if a depreciable property is disposed of by gift or transferred on account of death (Code Sec. 1245(b)(1) and Code Sec. 1245(b)(2); Code Sec. 1250(d)(1) and (2)). Thus, if a taxpayer plans on making a death or gift transfer and has the choice between transferring recapture property or nonrecapture property, it may be advantageous to transfer the recapture property. However, as noted below, the donee of a gift may be required to recognize recapture on a later sale or disposition of the property.

The exception from recapture for transfers at death does not apply to income in respect of a decedent (Code Sec. 1245(b)(2) and Code Sec. 1250(d)(2)). Thus, when a decedent sells property under the installment method prior to death, all recapture income would be reported in the year of the disposition (for example, on the decedent's final return) (Code Sec. 453(i)). The basis of the installment obligation, however, is stepped up to reflect the recapture income reported by the decedent.

It should be noted that in the case of a gift, the donee generally takes the donor's adjusted basis for purposes of computing gain (see ¶ 70). If the donee later sells the property in a disposition that is subject to recapture (e.g., sells the property at a gain), the donee must determine ordinary income recapture as if he had claimed the depreciation deducted by the donor (Code Sec. 1015). If the transfer of the depreciable property is for less than its fair market value, the transfer is considered part sale and part gift. The transferor will recognize gain to the extent that the amount realized exceeds the adjusted basis of the property. Prior depreciation on Sec. 1245 property (accelerated depreciation in excess of straight-line in the case of Sec. 1250 property) is subject to recapture to the extent of the gain. If the gain is not sufficient to offset the full amount of the otherwise recapturable depreciation, the balance must be taken into account by the transferee upon any later disposition (Reg. § 1.1001-1(e); Reg. § 1.1015-4; Reg. § 1.1245-4(a)(3); Reg. § 1.1250-3(a)(2)).

Example (7): Joan Dilliard transfers depreciable personal property with a fair market value of $10,000 to her son for $6,500. She has claimed $7,000 of depreciation on the property which has an adjusted basis of $2,000. Joan is considered to have made a gift of $3,500 ($10,000 – $6,500). Her taxable gain on the transfer is $4,500 ($6,500 – $2,000). This gain is recaptured as ordinary income. The unrecaptured depreciation ($2,500 ($7,000 – $4,500)) is "carried over" to the son and is subject to recapture if he sells or disposes of the property at a gain.

In the case of a gift of depreciable real or personal property to a charity, the fair market value of the property for purposes of determining the amount of the contribution is reduced by the amount of depreciation that would have been recaptured if the property had been sold at its fair market value. The fair market value may also have to be reduced by any Sec. 1231 gain that would have resulted if the property had been sold (Code Sec. 170(e)(1); Reg. § 1.170A-1(c); Reg. § 1.170A-4(a) and (b)).

Special rules apply to bargain sales to charity (Reg. § 1.1011-2(a)(1)).

Transfers to a spouse (if an election was made) or former spouse incident to a divorce are treated as gifts under Code Sec. 1041 (Code Sec. 1041(b)). Code Sec. 1041 is generally effective for property received after July 18, 1984, under a divorce or separation instrument in effect after that date. It also applies to all other property received after 1983 if an election was made (Temp. Reg. § 1.1041-1T(g)).

The basis to the recipient spouse for determining gain or loss is the adjusted basis of the transferor. This basis applies regardless of the fair market value at the time of the transfer or any consideration paid (Temp. Reg. § 1.1041-1T(d), Q&A-11).

The transfer does not trigger depreciation recapture. However, depreciation claimed by the transferor is subject to recapture when the transferee disposes of the property.

Although the regulations under Code Sec. 1041 provide for the recapture of the investment tax credit if, upon or after the transfer, the property is disposed of by, or ceases to be Code Sec. 38 property with respect to, the transferee (Temp. Reg. § 1.1041-1T). The regulations under Code Secs. 179 and 1041 do not provide for a recapture of the Code Sec. 179 expense allowance if the transferee spouse uses the property 50 percent or less for business purposes. Presumably, therefore, no recapture is required. The IRS Publications also make no mention of this issue.

Since a Code Sec. 1041 transfer is treated as a gift, the transferee should compute depreciation as if the property were newly acquired, by reference to the carryover basis. However, no Code Sec. 179 expense allowance is permitted because only property acquired by purchase qualifies for the expense deduction. Property with a carryover basis is specifically disqualified. See ¶ 302.

Like-kind exchange and involuntary conversion exception

Depreciation recapture is not triggered in a like-kind exchange (Code Sec. 1031) or an involuntary conversion (Code Sec. 1033) unless (1) gain is recognized because money or property other than like-kind (Code Sec. 1031) or similar or related (Code Sec. 1033) property was also received or (2) the like-kind, similar, or related property given-up and acquired are not both section 1245 personal property or both section 1250 real property.

The recapture potential, however, attaches to the acquired property. For example, if a fully depreciated machine that cost $100 and has a fair market value of $1,000 is traded for another machine with a fair market value of $1,000, the basis of the acquired machine is $0. However, $100 of any gain recognized upon its subsequent sale is recaptured as ordinary income (Reg. § 1.1245-2(c)(4)).

Like-kind exchanges are reported on Form 8824. The amount recaptured as ordinary income is carried over from line 21 of 2006 Form 8824 to line 16 of 2006 Form 4797. Involuntary conversions are reported directly on Form 4797.

Section 1245 property exchanged. In the case of a like-kind exchange (Code Sec. 1031) or an involuntary conversion (Code Sec. 1033) of depreciated Sec. 1245 personal property, the amount of depreciation subject to recapture as ordinary income is limited to the sum of:

(1) the gain (if any) recognized under Code Sec. 1031 or Code Sec. 1033 because money or property other than like-kind, similar, or related property was also received; plus

(2) the fair market value of like-kind, similar, or related property acquired in the transaction which is Sec. 1250 property (Code Sec. 1245(b)(4)).

Example (8): A taxpayer exchanges MACRS machinery with an original cost of $2,000, an adjusted (depreciated) basis of $200 and a fmv of $1,000 for another new machine with a fmv of $800 and $200 cash. Gain of $800 is *realized* ($1,000 ($800 fmv of machine received + $200 cash) - $200 adjusted basis of machine given up) but *recognized gain* is limited to the $200 cash received. The recognized gain is treated as ordinary income under the recapture rules. The taxpayer's basis in the machine received is $400 ($200 adjusted basis + $200 recognized gain). Under the rules explained at ¶ 167, the taxpayer will continue to depreciate $200 of the $400 adjusted basis of the acquired property as if the exchange had not taken place. This $200 carryover basis does not qualify for the section 179 expense allowance but does qualify for bonus depreciation if the exchange took place during a tax year in which bonus depreciation applies). The additional $200 noncarryover basis is treated as newly purchased MACRS property for purposes of computing MACRS depreciation and qualifies for the Code Sec. 179 expense allowance (and bonus depreciation).

Summary of section 1245 for section 1245 exchange.

Machinery Exchanged			Machinery Received	Cash Received
Cost	*Adjusted Basis*	*FMV*	*FMV*	
$2,000	$200	$1,000	$800	$200

Amount realized: $800 ($800 + $200 cash – $200 adjusted basis)
Amount recognized: $200 (cash received) (recaptured as ordinary income)
Basis of machine received: $400 ($200 adjusted basis + $200 cash)

ACRS real property, other than residential rental property and low-income housing, for which accelerated depreciation has been claimed is treated as section 1245 property for purposes of depreciation recapture. See "*Overview of recapture rules*" above. If such ACRS section 1245 property is exchanged for or involuntarily converted into MACRS real property which is section 1250 property, then item (2), above, would appear to require the recapture of the depreciation claimed on the ACRS property to the extent of the fair market value of the MACRS real property acquired.

Another situation in which item (2) would apply is an involuntary conversion in which the qualifying replacement property is stock (i.e., nondepreciable personal property).

Example (9): ACRS commercial property (Section 1245 property) that cost $1.5 million has an adjusted basis of $100,000 and a fair market value of $1 million is exchanged for MACRS commercial property with a fair market value of $1 million. The taxpayer will recognize $1 million of ordinary income recapture (an amount equal to the fair market value of the section 1250 property received in exchange for the ACRS Sec. 1245 property). The remaining $400,000 of unrecaptured ordinary income ($1.5 million cost – $100,000 adjusted basis – $1 million recaptured ordinary income) attaches to the MACRS property and will be recaptured as ordinary income to the extent of gain recognized on its later disposition. The basis of the MACRS property received in the exchange is $1,100,000 ($100,000 carryover basis + $1 million recapture gain). The entire basis is depreciated as newly acquired MACRS commercial real property since this is an ACRS for MACRS property exchange and is not covered by the rule described at ¶ 167.

Summary of section 1245 for section 1250 exchange.

1245 Property Exchanged			1250 Property Received
Cost	*Adjusted Basis*	*FMV*	*FMV*
$1.5M	$100,000	$1M	$1M

Recapture Potential: $1.4M ($1.5 – $100,000)
Recapture Required: $1.0M (FMV of Sec. 1250 property received)
Basis of Section 1250 Property: $1.1M ($100,000 + $1M recaptured gain)

The taxpayer could have avoided the recapture by exchanging the ACRS property for MACRS Sec. 1245 property. This, however, may not be a practical solution if the taxpayer wishes to trade for real property since real property is generally Sec. 1250 property under MACRS.

Section 1250 property exchanged. In the case of a like-kind exchange or an involuntary conversion of Sec. 1250 real property depreciated under an accelerated ACRS or pre-ACRS method, the amount of accelerated depreciation in excess of straight-line depreciation subject to recapture as ordinary income is limited to the larger of:

(1) the gain (if any) recognized under Code Sec. 1031 or Code Sec. 1033 because money or property other than like-kind, similar, or related property was also received; or

(2) the gain that would have been reported as ordinary income because of the depreciation recapture provisions if the transaction had been a cash sale, *less* (in the case of an involuntary conversion) the cost of the depreciable property acquired or (in the case of a like-kind exchange) the fair market value of the depreciable real property received (Code Sec. 1250(d)(4); Reg. § 1.1250-3(d)).

For purposes of item (1) gain is increased by the fair market value of stock purchased as replacement property in acquiring control of a corporation.

Example (10): A taxpayer exchanges section 1250 real property placed in service in 1980 (land and a building) plus $300,000 cash for other section 1250 real property (land and a building) in a qualifying like-kind exchange. The adjusted basis of the land is $50,000 and its fair market value is $100,000. The building has a depreciated basis of $250,000 and a fair market value of $500,000. Additional depreciation subject to recapture is $150,000. The fair market value of the building acquired is $50,000, while the fair market value of the land acquired is $850,000.

Since the taxpayer received no cash or other boot, no gain is recognized under the like-kind exchange provisions of Code Sec. 1031. However, ordinary income that must be recaptured is the larger of (1) the gain that must be reported under the Code Sec. 1031 rules (but only to the extent attributable to the structure) ($0) or (2) the ordinary income depreciation that would have been recaptured ($150,000) if this had been a cash sale *less* the fair market value of the depreciable real property acquired ($50,000). Thus, $100,000 ($150,000 – $50,000) is recaptured as ordinary income.

If this had been a cash sale, the taxpayer would have received $500,000 for the structure. The adjusted basis of the structure is $250,000. The recognized gain would have been $250,000 ($500,000 – $250,000 adjusted basis). Since the potential recognized gain exceeds the $150,000 subject to recapture, the entire $150,000 would have been recaptured as ordinary income.

Ordinary income recapture which is not required to be reported in the year of the disposition is carried over as additional depreciation to the depreciable real property acquired in the like-kind exchange or involuntary conversion and may be taxed as ordinary income on a later disposition (Code Sec. 1250(d)(4)(E)).

If the ordinary income reported as additional depreciation is limited, the basis of the property acquired is its fair market value (its cost if purchased to replace property involuntarily converted to cash), minus the gain postponed.

If MACRS Sec. 1250 property is replaced or exchanged before it has been held for one year, then the entire amount of MACRS depreciation claimed is subject to recapture as ordinary income to the extent of the larger of (1) or (2). See Reg. § 1.1250-4 for rules regarding the determination of the holding period.

Sale of principal residence

Code Sec. 121 allows qualifying taxpayers to exclude up to $500,000 gain ($250,000 for taxpayers who do not file jointly) when a principal residence is sold. The exclusion, however, does not apply to the extent of any depreciation claimed or allowable on the residence that is attributable to periods after May 6, 1997 (Code Sec. 121(d)(6)). For example, the rule applies to depreciation claimed with respect to a home office, day care business, or the rental of the property.

> ***Example (11):*** John sells his residence for a $30,000 gain in 2008. He used the residence as a home office starting in 2004 and claimed $1,500 of depreciation. The maximum amount that John may exclude is $28,500. The remaining $1,500 gain is taxable. Note that the IRS formerly did not allow any portion of gain attributable to a home office to be excluded under Code Sec. 121. Gain was computed separately on the home office and the remaining portion of the residence. The new rule, which is contained in Reg. § 1.121-1(e), is generally effective for sales and exchanges after December 24, 2002 (Reg. § 1.121-1(f)). However, a taxpayer may elect to apply the rule retroactively to any tax year that is not barred by the statute of limitations (Reg. § 1.121-4(j)). This affords an amended return opportunity.

A significant planning consideration may affect a taxpayer whose spouse has died where a house that was held jointly has significantly appreciated. In order to take advantage of the $500,000 exclusion, the requirements for qualifying for the $500,000 exclusion must have been satisfied before the death of the spouse and the taxpayer must sell the residence within two years of the date of the death. If the house is not sold within this period, the exclusion drops to $250,000 (Code Sec. 121(b)(4)). To determine whether a sale is worthwhile, however, consideration must be given to the step-up basis rules.

For joint interests acquired after 1976, (property held in joint tenancy by a married couple with a right of survivorship or as tenants by the entirety) the basis of one-half of the property is stepped-up to its fair market value regardless of the amount contributed by either spouse toward the purchase price since only one-half of the property is included in the deceased spouse's gross estate (Code Sec. 2040(b)). The surviving spouse's basis of the remaining half is the amount contributed by him or her toward the purchase price. The IRS position is that the same rule applies to joint interests acquired before 1977. However, all courts that have considered the issue, including the Tax Court (*T. Hahn,* 110 TC 140, CCH Dec. 52,606), have ruled that the amount of pre-1977 jointly held property included in a deceased spouse's estate is based on the decedent's contribution. Thus, if the deceased spouse was considered to have paid for 100 percent of the property, the entire value is included in his or her gross estate. Due to the unlimited marital deduction, this is of no particular significance from an estate tax perspective. However, if 100 percent is included in the gross estate, then the surviving spouse is entitled to a full basis step-up. Conversely, if the surviving spouse contributed 100 percent of the cost, no amount is included in the deceased spouse's estate and there is no basis-step up for the survivor. Thus, the current state of affairs allows a taxpayer to whipsaw the IRS by choosing the rule (IRS position or court position) which best suits their situation.

Keep records to reduce depreciation recapture—allowed or allowable rule

Generally, recapture is based on the amount of allowable depreciation even though a taxpayer actually claimed less than the full amount of depreciation to which the taxpayer was entitled. Recapture can be limited to the actual amount of depreciation claimed on Sec. 1245 property, however, if the taxpayer can establish by adequate records or other sufficient evidence that the amount claimed was less than the amount allowable (Code Sec. 1245(a)(2)(B); Reg. §1.1245-2(a)(7)). Recordkeeping requirements are set forth in Reg. §1.1245-2(b)). A similar rule applies in the case of Sec. 1250 property (Reg. §1.1250-2(d)(4)). The allowed or allowable rule is less important now because the IRS will permit a taxpayer who has sold an asset without claiming the full amount of depreciation to request an accounting method change on Form 3115 and claim an adjustment on the return for the year of sale, as noted immediately below.

Computing gain or loss on dispositions—greater of allowed or allowable depreciation rule

Gain on the sale or disposition of a depreciable asset is equal to its cost reduced by the greater of the depreciation actually claimed or the depreciation actually allowable. Thus, the rule in the preceding paragraph does not reduce the amount of gain recognized; it only reduces the amount of gain that is subject to recapture as ordinary income.

Previously, a taxpayer who sold a depreciable asset without having claimed the full amount of allowable depreciation could not request an accounting method change in order to claim the full amount of allowable depreciation unless the taxpayer owned the property at the beginning of the year of change (¶ 75). The IRS, however, now allows a taxpayer to file a request for a change in accounting method any time prior to expiration of the Code Sec. 6501(a) limitations period for assessments for the tax year of the disposition. The revenue procedure generally applies to a taxpayer that is changing from an impermissible to a permissible method of accounting in situations where no depreciation or insufficient depreciation was claimed. Note that a math or posting error is not considered an accounting method. See ¶ 75. Thus, this change of accounting method procedure does not apply to posting and math errors.

Originally, the effective date for this change was generally for Forms 3115 filed for tax years ending on or after December 30, 2003. However, the original procedure was revised to also extend its application to dispositions of depreciable property occurring in tax years ending before December 30, 2003. An additional changes clarifies that the change in accounting method may also be made by filing Form 3115 with a timely filed original return for the year of disposition. The entire Code Sec. 481 adjustment for the unclaimed depreciation is taken into account on the original or amended return filed for the year of the disposition (Rev. Proc. 2007-16, modifying and superseding Rev. Proc. 2004-11, and modifying and amplifying Rev. Proc. 2002-9). Exceptions apply to certain property held by tax-exempt organizations, property disposed of in any nonrecognition transactions (unless, in the case of a Code Sec. 1033 (involuntary converions) or Code Sec. 1031 (like-kind exchanges) transaction, the taxpayer elected to depreciatie the entire basis of the replacement property as newly acquired property. See ¶ 167.

Appendices of Selected Final, Temporary, and Proposed Regulations

Code Sec. 167 Regulations

¶ 509

Reg. § 1.167(a)-3

»»→ ***Caution: Reg. § 1.167(a)-3 does not reflect recent law changes. For details, see ¶ 509.01.***

§ 1.167(a)-3. **Intangibles.**—(a) *In general.*—If an intangible asset is known from experience or other factors to be of use in the business or in the production of income for only a limited period, the length of which can be estimated with reasonable accuracy, such an intangible asset may be the subject of a depreciation allowance. Examples are patents and copyrights. An intangible asset, the useful life of which is not limited, is not subject to the allowance for depreciation. No allowance will be permitted merely because, in the unsupported opinion of the taxpayer, the intangible asset has a limited useful life. No deduction for depreciation is allowable with respect to good will. For rules with respect to organizational expenditures, see section 248 and the regulations thereunder. For rules with respect to trademark and trade name expenditures, see section 177 and the regulations thereunder. See sections 197 and 167(f) and, to the extent applicable, § § 1.197-2 and 1.167(a)-14 for amortization of goodwill and certain other intangibles acquired after August 10, 1993, or after July 25, 1991, if a valid retroactive election under § 1.197-1T has been made.

(b) *Safe harbor amortization for certain intangible assets.*—(1) *Useful life.*—Solely for purposes of determining the depreciation allowance referred to in paragraph (a) of this section, a taxpayer may treat an intangible asset as having a useful life equal to 15 years unless —

(i) An amortization period or useful life for the intangible asset is specifically prescribed or prohibited by the Internal Revenue Code, the regulations thereunder (other than by this paragraph (b)), or other published guidance in the Internal Revenue Bulletin (see § 601.601(d)(2) of this chapter);

(ii) The intangible asset is described in § 1.263(a)-4(c) (relating to intangibles acquired from another person) or § 1.263(a)-4(d)(2) (relating to created financial interests);

(iii) The intangible asset has a useful life the length of which can be estimated with reasonable accuracy; or

(iv) The intangible asset is described in § 1.263(a)-4(d)(8) (relating to certain benefits arising from the provision, production, or improvement of real property), in which case the taxpayer may treat the intangible asset as having a useful life equal to 25 years solely for purposes of determining the depreciation allowance referred to in paragraph (a) of this section.

(2) *Applicability to acquisitions of a trade or business, changes in the capital structure of a business entity, and certain other transactions.*—The safe harbor useful life provided by paragraph (b)(1) of this section does not apply to an amount required to be capitalized by § 1.263(a)-5 (relating to amounts paid to facilitate an acquisition of a trade or business, a change in the capital structure of a business entity, and certain other transactions).

(3) *Depreciation method.*—A taxpayer that determines its depreciation allowance for an intangible asset using the 15-year useful life prescribed by paragraph (b)(1) of this section (or the 25-year useful life in the case of an intangible asset described in § 1.263(a)-4(d)(8)) must determine the allowance by amortizing the basis of the intangible asset (as determined under section 167(c) and without regard to salvage value) ratably over the useful life beginning on the first day of the

»»→ Caution: Reg. § 1.167(a)-3 does not reflect recent law changes. For details, see ¶ 509.01.

month in which the intangible asset is placed in service by the taxpayer. The intangible asset is not eligible for amortization in the month of disposition.

(4) *Effective date.*—This paragraph (b) applies to intangible assets created on or after December 31, 2003. [Reg. § 1.167(a)-3.]

.01 Historical Comment: Proposed 11/11/55. Adopted 6/11/56 by T.D. 6182. Amended 2/3/60 by T.D. 6452, 1/20/2000 by T.D. 8865 and 12/31/2003 by T.D. 9107. [Reg. § 1.167(a)-3 does not reflect P.L. 100-647 (1988) or P.L. 103-66 (1993). See ¶ 11,250.13 and ¶ 12,450.70.]

¶ 510

Reg. § 1.167(a)-14

§ 1.167(a)-14. **Treatment of certain intangible property excluded from section 197.**—(a) *Overview.*—This section provides rules for the amortization of certain intangibles that are excluded from section 197 (relating to the amortization of goodwill and certain other intangibles). These excluded intangibles are specifically described in § 1.197-2(c)(4), (6), (7), (11), and (13) and include certain computer software and certain other separately acquired rights, such as rights to receive tangible property or services, patents and copyrights, certain mortgage servicing rights, and rights of fixed duration or amount. Intangibles for which an amortization amount is determined under section 167(f) and intangibles otherwise excluded from section 197 are amortizable only if they qualify as property subject to the allowance for depreciation under section 167(a).

(b) *Computer software.*—(1) *In general.*—The amount of the deduction for computer software described in section 167(f)(1) and § 1.197-2(c)(4) is determined by amortizing the cost or other basis of the computer software using the straight line method described in § 1.167(b)-1 (except that its salvage value is treated as zero) and an amortization period of 36 months beginning on the first day of the month that the computer software is placed in service. Before determining the amortization deduction allowable under this paragraph (b), the cost or other basis of computer software that is section 179 property, as defined in section 179(d)(1)(A)(ii), must be reduced for any portion of the basis the taxpayer properly elects to treat as an expense under section 179. In addition, the cost or other basis of computer software that is qualified property under section 168(k)(2) or § 1.168(k)-1, 50-percent bonus depreciation property under section 168(k)(4) or § 1.168(k)-1, or qualified New York Liberty Zone property under section 1400L(b) or § 1.1400L(b)-1, must be reduced by the amount of the additional first year depreciation deduction allowed or allowable, whichever is greater, under section 168(k) or section 1400L(b) for the computer software. If costs for developing computer software that the taxpayer properly elects to defer under section 174(b) result in the development of property subject to the allowance for depreciation under section 167, the rules of this paragraph (b) will apply to the unrecovered costs. In addition, this paragraph (b) applies to the cost of separately acquired computer software if the cost to acquire the software is separately stated and the cost is required to be capitalized under section 263(a).

(2) *Exceptions.*—Paragraph (b)(1) of this section does not apply to the cost of computer software properly and consistently taken into account under § 1.162-11. The cost of acquiring an interest in computer software that is included, without being separately stated, in the cost of the hardware or other tangible property is treated as part of the cost of the hardware or other tangible property that is capitalized and depreciated under other applicable sections of the Internal Revenue Code.

(3) *Additional rules.*—Rules similar to those in § 1.197-2(f)(1)(iii), (f)(1)(iv), and (f)(2) (relating to the computation of amortization deductions and the treatment of contingent amounts) apply for purposes of this paragraph (b).

(c) *Certain interests or rights not acquired as part of a purchase of a trade or business.*—(1) *Certain rights to receive tangible property or services.*—The amount of the deduction for a right (other than a right acquired as part of a purchase of a trade or business) to receive tangible property or services under a contract or from a governmental unit (as specified in section 167(f)(2) and § 1.197-2(c)(6)) is determined as follows:

(i) *Amortization of fixed amounts.*—The basis of a right to receive a fixed amount of tangible property or services is amortized for each taxable year by multiplying the basis of the right by a fraction, the numerator of which is the amount of tangible property or services received during the taxable year and the denominator of which is the total amount of tangible property or services received or to be received under the terms of the contract or governmental grant. For example, if a taxpayer acquires a favorable contract right to receive a fixed amount of raw materials during an unspecified period, the taxpayer must amortize the cost of acquiring the contract right by multiplying the total cost by a fraction, the numerator of which is the amount of raw materials received under the contract during the taxable year and the denominator of which is the total amount of raw materials received or to be received under the contract.

(ii) *Amortization of unspecified amount over fixed period.*—The cost or other basis of a right to receive an unspecified amount of tangible property or services over a fixed period is amortized ratably over the period of the right. (See paragraph (c)(3) of this section regarding renewals).

(iii) *Amortization in other cases.*—[Reserved]

(2) *Rights of fixed duration or amount.*—The amount of the deduction for a right (other than a right acquired as part of a purchase of a trade or business) of fixed duration or amount received under a contract or granted by a governmental unit (specified in section 167(f)(2) and § 1.197-2(c)(13)) and not covered by paragraph (c)(1) of this section is determined as follows:

(i) *Rights to a fixed amount.*—The basis of a right to a fixed amount is amortized for each taxable year by multiplying the basis by a fraction, the numerator of which is the amount received during the taxable year and the denominator of which is the total amount received or to be received under the terms of the contract or governmental grant.

(ii) *Rights to an unspecified amount over fixed duration of less than 15 years.*—The basis of a right to an unspecified amount over a fixed duration of less than 15 years is amortized ratably over the period of the right.

(3) *Application of renewals.*—(i) For purposes of paragraphs (c)(1) and (2) of this section, the duration of a right under a contract (or granted by a governmental unit) includes any renewal period if, based on all of the facts and circumstances in existence at any time during the taxable year in which the right is acquired, the facts clearly indicate a reasonable expectancy of renewal.

(ii) The mere fact that a taxpayer will have the opportunity to renew a contract right or other right on the same terms as are available to others, in a competitive auction or similar process that is designed to reflect fair market value and in which the taxpayer is not contractually advantaged, will generally not be taken into account in determining the duration of such right provided that the bidding produces a fair market value price comparable to the price that would be obtained if the rights were purchased immediately after renewal from a person (other than the person granting the renewal) in an arm's-length transaction.

(iii) The cost of a renewal not included in the terms of the contract or governmental grant is treated as the acquisition of a separate intangible asset.

(4) *Patents and copyrights.*—If the purchase price of a interest (other than an interest acquired as part of a purchase of a trade or business) in a patent or copyright described in section 167(f)(2) and § 1.197-2(c)(7) is payable on at least an annual basis as either a fixed amount per use or a fixed percentage of the revenue derived from the use of the patent or copyright, the depreciation deduction for a taxable year is equal to the amount of the purchase price paid or incurred during the year. Otherwise, the basis of such patent or copyright (or an interest therein) is depreciated either ratably over its remaining useful life or under section 167(g) (income forecast method). If a patent or copyright becomes valueless in any year before its legal expiration, the adjusted basis may be deducted in that year.

(5) *Additional rules.*—The period of amortization under paragraphs (c)(1) through (4) of this section begins when the intangible is placed in service, and rules similar to those in § 1.197-2(f)(2) apply for purposes of this paragraph (c).

(d) *Mortgage servicing rights.*—(1) *In general.*—The amount of the deduction for mortgage servicing rights described in section 167(f)(3) and § 1.197-2(c)(11) is determined by using the straight line method described in § 1.167(b)-1 (except that the salvage value is treated as zero) and an amortization period of 108 months beginning on the first day of the month that the rights are placed in service. Mortgage servicing rights are not depreciable to the extent the rights are stripped coupons under section 1286.

(2) *Treatment of rights acquired as a pool.*—(i) *In general.*—Except as provided in paragraph (d)(2)(ii) of this section, all mortgage servicing rights acquired in the same transaction or in a series of related transactions are treated as a single asset (the pool) for purposes of determining the depreciation deduction under this paragraph (d) and any gain or loss from the sale, exchange, or other disposition of the rights. Thus, if some (but not all) of the rights in a pool become worthless as a result of prepayments, no loss is recognized by reason of the prepayment and the adjusted basis of the pool is not affected by the unrecognized loss. Similarly, any amount realized from the sale or exchange of some (but not all) of the mortgage servicing rights is included in income and the adjusted basis of the pool is not affected by the realization.

(ii) *Multiple accounts.*—If the taxpayer establishes multiple accounts within a pool at the time of its acquisition, gain or loss is recognized on the sale or exchange of all mortgage servicing rights within any such account.

(3) *Additional rules.*—Rules similar to those in § 1.197-2(f)(1)(iii), (f)(1)(iv), and (f)(2) (relating to the computation of amortization deductions and the treatment of contingent amounts) apply for purposes of this paragraph (d).

(e) *Effective dates.*—(1) *In general.*—This section applies to property acquired after January 25, 2000, except that § 1.167(a)-14(c)(2) (depreciation of the cost of certain separately acquired rights) and so much of § 1.167(a)-14(c)(3) as relates to § 1.167(a)-14(c)(2) apply to property acquired after August 10, 1993 (or July 25, 1991, if a valid retroactive election has been made under § 1.197-1T).

(2) *Change in method of accounting.*—See § 1.197-2(l)(4) for rules relating to changes in method of accounting for property to which § 1.167(a)-14 applies. However, see § 1.168(k)-1(g)(4) or 1.1400L(b)-1(g)(4) for rules relating to changes in method of accounting for computer software to which the third sentence in § 1.167(a)-14(b)(1) applies.

(3) *Qualified property, 50-percent bonus depreciation property, qualified New York Liberty Zone property, or section 179 property.*—This section also applies to computer software that is qualified property under section 168(k)(2) or qualified New York Liberty Zone property under section 1400L(b) acquired by a taxpayer after September 10, 2001, and to computer software that is 50-percent bonus depreciation property under section 168(k)(4) acquired by a taxpayer after May 5, 2003. This section also applies to computer software that is section 179 property placed in service by a taxpayer in a taxable year beginning after 2002 and before 2010. [Reg. § 1.167(a)-14.]

.01 Historical Comment: Proposed 1/16/97. Adopted 1/20/2000 by T.D. 8865. Amended 9/5/2003 by T.D. 9091 and 8/28/2006 by T.D. 9283.

ACRS Regulations

¶ 520

Proposed Reg. § 1.168-1

Proposed Regulations

»»→ Note: The text of the Preamble to the Proposed Regulation is at ¶ 49,032 in the CCH Standard Federal Tax Reporter.

§ 1.168-1. **Accelerated Cost Recovery System; in general,** LR-185-81, 2/16/84, LR-92-73, 12/19/85.

(a) *Cost recovery deduction allowed.*—Section 168 of the Internal Revenue Code of 1954 provides a system for determining cost recovery deductions for recovery property, the Accelerated Cost Recovery System ("ACRS"). The deduction allowable under section 168 is deemed to constitute the reasonable allowance for depreciation allowed as a deduction under section 167(a). Operating rules regarding determination of the allowable cost recovery deduction are provided in § 1.168-2. The definition of recovery property and the classification of recovery property into recovery categories of 3, 5, 10, and 15 years are provided in § 1.168-3. ACRS must be applied with respect to recovery property placed in service after December 31, 1980, except for certain property which does not qualify under section 168 or which may be excluded from ACRS; § 1.168-4 provides rules regarding such exclusions and non-qualifications. Special rules regarding ACRS are provided in § 1.168-5. Rules relating to the recognition of gain or loss on dispositions are provided in § 1.168-6.

(b) *Cross references.*—See § 1.167(a)-11(d)(2) regarding the election after 1980 of the repair allowance for certain property. See § 1.178-1 regarding the availability of ACRS deductions for, or the amortization of, improvements on leased property. See § 1.1016-3(a)(3) regarding the basis adjustment for the amount allowable where no ACRS deduction is claimed. [Reg. § 1.168-1.]

¶ 525

Proposed Reg. § 1.168-2

Proposed Regulations

»»→ Note: The text of the Preamble to the Proposed Regulation is at ¶ 49,032 in the CCH Standard Federal Tax Reporter.

§ 1.168-2. **Amount of deduction for recovery property,** LR-185-81, 2/16/84. [On 1/29/98, paragraph (n) was withdrawn by REG-209682-94.]

(a) *Computation of recovery allowance.*—(1) *General rule.*—Except as otherwise provided in section 168 and the regulations thereunder, the recovery allowance for any taxable year equals the aggregate amount determined by multiplying the unadjusted basis (as defined in § 1.168-2(d)) of recovery property (as defined in § 1.168-3) by the appropriate applicable percentage provided in paragraph (b) of this section. For purposes of determining the recovery allowance, salvage value shall be disregarded.

(2) *No allowance in year of disposition.*—Except for 15-year real property and except as otherwise provided in § 1.168-5, no recovery allowance shall be allowed in the year of disposition of recovery property.

(3) *Proration of allowance in year of disposition of 15-year real property.*—In the taxable year in which 15-year real property is disposed of, the recovery allowance shall be determined by multiplying the allowance (determined without regard to this subparagraph) by a fraction, the numerator of which equals the number of months in the taxable year that the property is in service in the taxpayer's trade or business or for the production of income and the denominator of which is 12. In the case of 15-year real property that is disposed of in the first recovery year, the denominator shall equal the number of months in the taxpayer's taxable year after the recovery property was placed in service by the taxpayer (including the month the property was placed in service). If

Proposed Regulations

the recovery allowance for the taxable year is limited by reason of the short taxable year rules of section 168(f)(5) and paragraph (f) of this section (*e.g.,* if the taxpayer dies, or if the taxpayer is a corporation which becomes a member, or ceases being a member, of an affiliated group of corporations filing a consolidated return), then the denominator shall equal the number of months in the taxpayer's taxable year. For purposes of this subparagraph, 15-year real property shall be treated as disposed of as of the last day of the month preceding the month in which it is withdrawn from service.

(b) *Applicable percentage.*—(1) *Property other than 15-year real property.*—The applicable percentage for recovery property, other than 15-year real property, is as follows:

If the recovery year is:	*And the class of property is:*			
	3-year	*5-year*	*10-year*	*15-year Public Utility*
	The applicable percentage is:			
1	25	15	8	5
2	38	22	14	10
3	37	21	12	9
4		21	10	8
5		21	10	7
6			10	7
7			9	6
8			9	6
9			9	6
10			9	6
11				6
12				6
13				6
15				6

(2) *15-year real property.*—(i) The applicable percentage for 15-year real property, other than low-income housing is as follows:

If the recovery year is:	*And the month in the 1st recovery year the property is placed in service is:*											
	1	*2*	*3*	*4*	*5*	*6*	*7*	*8*	*9*	*10*	*11*	*12*
	The applicable percentage is:											
1	12	11	10	9	8	7	6	5	4	3	2	1
2	10	10	11	11	11	11	11	11	11	11	11	12
3	9	9	9	9	10	10	10	10	10	10	10	10
4	8	8	8	8	8	8	9	9	9	9	9	9
5	7	7	7	7	7	7	8	8	8	8	8	8
6	6	6	6	6	7	7	7	7	7	7	7	7
7	6	6	6	6	6	6	6	6	6	6	6	6
8	6	6	6	6	6	6	5	6	6	6	6	6
9	6	6	6	6	5	6	5	5	5	6	6	6
10	5	6	5	6	5	5	5	5	5	5	6	5
11	5	5	5	5	5	5	5	5	5	5	5	5
12	5	5	5	5	5	5	5	5	5	5	5	5
13	5	5	5	5	5	5	5	5	5	5	5	5
14	5	5	5	5	5	5	5	5	5	5	5	5
15	5	5	5	5	5	5	5	5	5	5	5	5
16	—	—	1	1	2	2	3	3	4	4	4	5

(ii) The applicable percentage for 15-year real property that is low-income housing is as follows:

Proposed Regulations

If the recovery year is:	*And the month in the 1st recovery year the property is placed in service is:*											
	1	*2*	*3*	*4*	*5*	*6*	*7*	*8*	*9*	*10*	*11*	*12*
	The applicable percentage is:											
1	13	12	11	10	9	8	7	6	4	3	2	1
2	12	12	12	12	12	12	12	13	13	13	13	13
3	10	10	10	10	11	11	11	11	11	11	11	11
4	9	9	9	9	9	9	9	9	10	10	10	10
5	8	8	8	8	8	8	8	8	8	8	8	9
6	7	7	7	7	7	7	7	7	7	7	7	7
7	6	6	6	6	6	6	6	6	6	6	6	6
8	5	5	5	5	5	5	5	5	5	5	6	6
9	5	5	5	5	5	5	5	5	5	5	5	5
10	5	5	5	5	5	5	5	5	5	5	5	5
11	4	5	5	5	5	5	5	5	5	5	5	5
12	4	4	4	5	4	5	5	5	5	5	5	5
13	4	4	4	4	4	4	5	4	5	5	5	5
14	4	4	4	4	4	4	4	4	4	5	4	4
15	4	4	4	4	4	4	4	4	4	4	4	4
16	—	—	1	1	2	2	2	3	3	3	4	4

(iii) For purposes of this section, the term "low-income housing" means property described in clause (i), (ii), (iii), or (iv) of section 1250(a)(1)(B).

(iv) For purposes of this subparagraph (2), 15-year real property placed in service on or after the first day of a month shall be treated as placed in service in that month.

(c) *Election of optional recovery percentage.*—(1) *Straight line method.*—Except as provided by section 168(f)(2) and § 1.168-2(g) (relating to property used predominantly outside the United States), in lieu of using the applicable percentages prescribed in section 168(b)(1) and (2) and § 1.168-2(b), the taxpayer may elect (in accordance with § 1.168-5(e)), for recovery property placed in service during the taxable year, to determine the recovery allowance by using the straight line method over one of the recovery periods elected by the taxpayer and set forth in the following table:

Class of property	*Recovery periods*
3-year property	3, 5, or 12 years
5-year property	5, 12, or 25 years
10-year property	10, 25, or 35 years
15-year real property	15, 35, or 45 years
15-year public utility property	15, 35, or 45 years

Such election is irrevocable without the consent of the Commissioner. See subparagraph (4) of this paragraph for tables containing the applicable percentages to be used in computing the recovery allowance.

(2) *Election for property other than 15-year real property.*—Except in the case of 15-year real property, a single recovery period must be elected under this paragraph for all recovery property which is in the same recovery class and which is placed in service in the same taxable year. A different recovery period may be elected (or the tables provided in section 168(b)(1) and § 1.168-2(b)(1) may be used) for recovery property in different recovery classes placed in service during the same taxable year, or for recovery property placed in service in different taxable years, whether or not in the same recovery class.

(3) *Election for 15-year real property.*—In the case of 15-year real property, the election provided in paragraph (c)(1) may be made separately with respect to each property.

Proposed Regulations

(4) *Applicable percentage.*—(i) For property other than 15-year real property—

If the recovery year is:	*And the period elected is:* 3	5	10	12	15	25	35	45
	The applicable percentage is:							
1	17	10	5	4	3	2	1	1.1
2	33	20	10	9	7	4	3	2.3
3	33	20	10	9	7	4	3	2.3
4	17	20	10	9	7	4	3	2.3
5		20	10	9	7	4	3	2.3
6		10	10	8	7	4	3	2.3
7			10	8	7	4	3	2.3
8			10	8	7	4	3	2.3
9			10	8	7	4	3	2.3
10			10	8	7	4	3	2.3
11			5	8	7	4	3	2.3
12				8	6	4	3	2.2
13				4	6	4	3	2.2
14					6	4	3	2.2
15					6	4	3	2.2
16					3	4	3	2.2
17						4	3	2.2
18						4	3	2.2
19						4	3	2.2
20						4	3	2.2
21						4	3	2.2
22						4	3	2.2
23						4	3	2.2
24						4	3	2.2
25						4	3	2.2
26						2	3	2.2
27							3	2.2
28							3	2.2
29							3	2.2
30							3	2.2
31							3	2.2
32							2	2.2
33							2	2.2
34							2	2.2
35							2	2.2
36							1	2.2
37								2.2
38								2.2
39								2.2
40								2.2
41								2.2
42								2.2
43								2.2
44								2.2
45								2.2
46								1.1

(ii) For 15-year real property—

(A) For which a 15-year period is elected—

Proposed Regulations

If the recovery year is:	*And the month in the 1st recovery year that the property is placed in service is:*						
	1	*2-3*	*4*	*5-6*	*7-8*	*9-10*	*11-12*
	The applicable percentage is:						
1	7	6	5	4	3	2	1
2	7	7	7	7	7	7	7
3	7	7	7	7	7	7	7
4	7	7	7	7	7	7	7
5	7	7	7	7	7	7	7
6	7	7	7	7	7	7	7
7	7	7	7	7	7	7	7
8	7	7	7	7	7	7	7
9	7	7	7	7	7	7	7
10	7	7	7	7	7	7	7
11	6	6	6	6	6	6	6
12	6	6	6	6	6	6	6
13	6	6	6	6	6	6	6
14	6	6	6	6	6	6	6
15	6	6	6	6	6	6	6
16		1	2	3	4	6	6

(B) For which a 35-year period is elected—

If the recovery year is:	*And the month in the 1st recovery year that the property is placed in service is:*		
	1-2	*3-6*	*7-12*
	The applicable percentage is:		
1	3	2	1
2	3	3	3
3	3	3	3
4	3	3	3
5	3	3	3
6	3	3	3
7	3	3	3
8	3	3	3
9	3	3	3
10	3	3	3
11	3	3	3
12	3	3	3
13	3	3	3
14	3	3	3
15	3	3	3
16	3	3	3
17	3	3	3
18	3	3	3
19	3	3	3
20	3	3	3
21	3	3	3
22	3	3	3
23	3	3	3
24	3	3	3
25	3	3	3
26	3	3	3

Proposed Regulations

If the recovery year is:	*And the month in the 1st recovery year that the property is placed in service is:*		
	1-2	*3-6*	*7-12*
	The applicable percentage is:		
27	3	3	3
28	3	3	3
29	3	3	3
30	3	3	3
31	2	2	2
32	2	2	2
33	2	2	2
34	2	2	2
35	2	2	2
36		1	2

(C) For which a 45-year period is elected—

If the recovery year is:	*And the month in the 1st recovery year that the property is placed in service is:*											
	1	*2*	*3*	*4*	*5*	*6*	*7*	*8*	*9*	*10*	*11*	*12*
	The applicable percentage is:											
1	2.3	2.0	1.9	1.7	1.5	1.3	1.2	.9	.7	.6	.4	.2
2	2.3	2.3	2.3	2.3	2.3	2.3	2.3	2.3	2.3	2.3	2.3	2.3
3	2.3	2.3	2.3	2.3	2.3	2.3	2.3	2.3	2.3	2.3	2.3	2.3
4	2.3	2.3	2.3	2.3	2.3	2.3	2.3	2.3	2.3	2.3	2.3	2.3
5	2.3	2.3	2.3	2.3	2.3	2.3	2.3	2.3	2.3	2.3	2.3	2.3
6	2.3	2.3	2.3	2.3	2.3	2.3	2.3	2.3	2.3	2.3	2.3	2.3
7	2.3	2.3	2.3	2.3	2.3	2.3	2.3	2.3	2.3	2.3	2.3	2.3
8	2.3	2.3	2.3	2.3	2.3	2.3	2.3	2.3	2.3	2.3	2.3	2.3
9	2.3	2.3	2.3	2.3	2.3	2.3	2.3	2.3	2.3	2.3	2.3	2.3
10	2.3	2.3	2.3	2.3	2.3	2.3	2.3	2.3	2.3	2.3	2.3	2.3
11	2.2	2.2	2.2	2.2	2.2	2.2	2.2	2.2	2.2	2.2	2.2	2.2
12	2.2	2.2	2.2	2.2	2.2	2.2	2.2	2.2	2.2	2.2	2.2	2.2
13	2.2	2.2	2.2	2.2	2.2	2.2	2.2	2.2	2.2	2.2	2.2	2.2
14	2.2	2.2	2.2	2.2	2.2	2.2	2.2	2.2	2.2	2.2	2.2	2.2
15	2.2	2.2	2.2	2.2	2.2	2.2	2.2	2.2	2.2	2.2	2.2	2.2
16	2.2	2.2	2.2	2.2	2.2	2.2	2.2	2.2	2.2	2.2	2.2	2.2
17	2.2	2.2	2.2	2.2	2.2	2.2	2.2	2.2	2.2	2.2	2.2	2.2
18	2.2	2.2	2.2	2.2	2.2	2.2	2.2	2.2	2.2	2.2	2.2	2.2
19	2.2	2.2	2.2	2.2	2.2	2.2	2.2	2.2	2.2	2.2	2.2	2.2
20	2.2	2.2	2.2	2.2	2.2	2.2	2.2	2.2	2.2	2.2	2.2	2.2
21	2.2	2.2	2.2	2.2	2.2	2.2	2.2	2.2	2.2	2.2	2.2	2.2
22	2.2	2.2	2.2	2.2	2.2	2.2	2.2	2.2	2.2	2.2	2.2	2.2
23	2.2	2.2	2.2	2.2	2.2	2.2	2.2	2.2	2.2	2.2	2.2	2.2
24	2.2	2.2	2.2	2.2	2.2	2.2	2.2	2.2	2.2	2.2	2.2	2.2
25	2.2	2.2	2.2	2.2	2.2	2.2	2.2	2.2	2.2	2.2	2.2	2.2
26	2.2	2.2	2.2	2.2	2.2	2.2	2.2	2.2	2.2	2.2	2.2	2.2
27	2.2	2.2	2.2	2.2	2.2	2.2	2.2	2.2	2.2	2.2	2.2	2.2
28	2.2	2.2	2.2	2.2	2.2	2.2	2.2	2.2	2.2	2.2	2.2	2.2
29	2.2	2.2	2.2	2.2	2.2	2.2	2.2	2.2	2.2	2.2	2.2	2.2
30	2.2	2.2	2.2	2.2	2.2	2.2	2.2	2.2	2.2	2.2	2.2	2.2
31	2.2	2.2	2.2	2.2	2.2	2.2	2.2	2.2	2.2	2.2	2.2	2.2
32	2.2	2.2	2.2	2.2	2.2	2.2	2.2	2.2	2.2	2.2	2.2	2.2

Proposed Regulations

If the recovery year is:	*And the month in the 1st recovery year that the property is placed in service is:*											
	1	*2*	*3*	*4*	*5*	*6*	*7*	*8*	*9*	*10*	*11*	*12*
	The applicable percentage is:											
33	2.2	2.2	2.2	2.2	2.2	2.2	2.2	2.2	2.2	2.2	2.2	2.2
34	2.2	2.2	2.2	2.2	2.2	2.2	2.2	2.2	2.2	2.2	2.2	2.2
35	2.2	2.2	2.2	2.2	2.2	2.2	2.2	2.2	2.2	2.2	2.2	2.2
36	2.2	2.2	2.2	2.2	2.2	2.2	2.2	2.2	2.2	2.2	2.2	2.2
37	2.2	2.2	2.2	2.2	2.2	2.2	2.2	2.2	2.2	2.2	2.2	2.2
38	2.2	2.2	2.2	2.2	2.2	2.2	2.2	2.2	2.2	2.2	2.2	2.2
39	2.2	2.2	2.2	2.2	2.2	2.2	2.2	2.2	2.2	2.2	2.2	2.2
40	2.2	2.2	2.2	2.2	2.2	2.2	2.2	2.2	2.2	2.2	2.2	2.2
41	2.2	2.2	2.2	2.2	2.2	2.2	2.2	2.2	2.2	2.2	2.2	2.2
42	2.2	2.2	2.2	2.2	2.2	2.2	2.2	2.2	2.2	2.2	2.2	2.2
43	2.2	2.2	2.2	2.2	2.2	2.2	2.2	2.2	2.2	2.2	2.2	2.2
44	2.2	2.2	2.2	2.2	2.2	2.2	2.2	2.2	2.2	2.2	2.2	2.2
45	2.2	2.2	2.2	2.2	2.2	2.2	2.2	2.2	2.2	2.2	2.2	2.2
46		.3	.4	.6	.8	1.0	1.1	1.4	1.6	1.7	1.9	2.1

(iii) For purposes of this paragraph, 15-year real property that is placed in service on or after the first day of a month shall be treated as placed in service in that month.

(5) *Property financed with the proceeds of industrial development bonds.*—If, in accordance with section 168(f)(12) and § 1.168-2(m), the recovery allowance for property financed with the proceeds of an industrial development bond (as described in section 103(b)) is determined using the straight line method, then an election as provided in section 168(b)(3) and this paragraph shall be deemed to have been made with respect to such property.

(d) *Unadjusted basis.*—(1) *Computation.*—Except as provided in paragraph (j)(6)(ii) of this section (relating to change of status), the unadjusted basis of recovery property is equal to the difference between—

(i) The basis of the property for purposes of determining gain under sections 1011 through 1024 but without regard to any adjustments to basis described in section 1016(a)(2) and (3), and

(ii) Any portion of the basis for which the taxpayer properly elects amortization in lieu of cost recovery (*e.g.,* under section 167(k)) or treatment as an expense under section 179.

The unadjusted basis of recovery property shall be first taken into account under this section for the taxable year in which the property is placed in service (as defined in paragraph (l)(2) of this § 1.168-2) as recovery property.

(2) *Reductions in basis.*—(i) If an investment tax credit is determined under section 46(a)(2) with respect to recovery property, then, unless the taxpayer makes an election provided under section 48(q)(4), for purposes of this section the unadjusted basis shall be reduced by 50 percent of the amount of the credit so determined. In the case of a credit determined under section 46(a)(2) for any qualified rehabilitation expenditure made in connection with a qualified rehabilitated building (other than a certified historic structure), the unadjusted basis shall be reduced by 100 percent of the amount of the credit so determined. See section 48(q) and the regulations thereunder. For rules relating to the treatment of such basis adjustment upon the disposition of an asset from a mass asset account, see § 1.168-2(h)(4).

(ii) Subject to the rules of other applicable provisions of the Code (*e.g.,* section 280A), for recovery property which is used in the taxpayer's trade or business (or for the production of income) as well as in a personal or tax-exempt activity throughout a taxable year, the unadjusted basis shall be determined by multiplying the unadjusted basis (determined without regard to this subdivision) by a fraction, the numerator of which equals the taxpayer's use of the property during the taxable year in his trade or business (or for the production of income) and the denominator of which equals the

Proposed Regulations

taxpayer's total use of the property during the taxable year. For property converted from personal or tax-exempt use to use in the taxpayer's trade or business (or for the production of income), or for property devoted to increased use in the taxpayer's trade or business (or for the production of income), see § 1.168-2(j).

Example. In 1981, A, a calendar year taxpayer, purchases a car for $10,000 to be used in his business as well as for his personal enjoyment. During 1981, A drives the car a total of 20,000 miles of which 8,000 miles (*i.e.,* 40 percent) is in the course of A's business. During 1982, A drives the car a total of 30,000 miles of which 21,000 miles (*i.e.,* 70 percent) is in the course of A's business. During 1983, A drives the car a total of 10,000 miles of which 3,000 miles (*i.e.,* 30 percent) is in the course of A's business. The optional straight line method provided under § 1.168-2(c) is not elected. Thus, A's recovery allowance in 1981 equals $1,000 (*i.e.,* ($10,000 × .40) × .25), in 1982 equals $2,660 (*i.e.,* ($10,000 × .70) × .38) and in 1983 equals $1,110 (*i.e.,* ($10,000 × .30) × .37). If A continues to use the car in his business after 1983, additional recovery may be allowed. See § 1.168-2(j).

(3) *Redeterminations.*—(i) For the taxable year (and subsequent taxable years) in which the unadjusted basis of recovery property is redetermined (*e.g.,* due to contingent purchase price or discharge of indebtedness), the recovery allowance shall be the amount determined by multiplying the redetermined adjusted basis by the redetermined applicable percentage. For purposes of this subparagraph, the redetermination adjusted basis is the unadjusted basis reduced by the recovery allowance previously allowed or allowable to the taxpayer with respect to the property and adjusted to reflect the redetermination. The redetermined applicable percentage is the percentage determined by dividing the applicable percentage otherwise provided in paragraph (b), (c), (g), or (m) of § 1.168-2 for the recovery year by an amount equal to the unrecovered percentage (*i.e.,* 100 percent minus the applicable percentage for recovery years prior to the year in which the basis is redetermined). Thus, the increase or decrease in basis shall be accounted for over the remaining recovery years beginning with the recovery year in which the basis is redetermined.

(ii) The following examples illustrate the provisions of this subparagraph (3):

Example (1). On July 15, 1984, A places in service 5-year recovery property with an unadjusted basis of $100,000. In order to purchase the property, A borrowed $80,000 from B. On December 1, 1984, B forgives $10,000 of the indebtedness. A makes the election provided in section 108(d)(4). The recovery allowance for the property in 1984 is $15,000. Under section 1017(a), as of January 1, 1985, the adjusted basis of the property is $75,000. In 1985 the recovery allowance is $19,411.77 (*i.e.,* .22÷(1.00 – .15) × ($100,000 – ($10,000 + $15,000))). In 1986, 1987, and 1988 the recovery allowance is $18,529.41 in each year (*i.e.,* .21÷(1.00 – .15) × ($100,000 – ($10,000 + $15,000))).

Example (2). On July 15, 1984, C purchases and places in service 5-year recovery property with an unadjusted basis of $100,000. In addition to the $100,000, C agrees to pay the seller 25 percent of the gross profits from the operation of the property in the first year. On July 15, 1985, C pays to the seller an additional $10,000. The recovery allowance for the property in 1984 is $15,000. In 1985 the recovery allowance is $24,588.23 (*i.e.,* .22÷(1.00 – .15) × ($100,000 + ($10,000 – $15,000))). In 1986, 1987, and 1988 the recovery allowance is $23,470.59 in each year (*i.e.,* .21÷(1.00 – .15) × ($100,000 + ($10,000 – $15,000))).

(e) *Components and improvements.*—(1) *Component cost recovery not permitted.*—In general, the unadjusted basis of structural components (as defined in § 1.48-1(e)(2)) of a building must be recovered as a whole. Thus, the same recovery period and method must be used for all structural components, and such components must be recovered as constituent parts of the building of which they are a part. The recovery period for a component begins on the later of the first day of the month in which the component is placed in service as recovery property or the first day of the month in which the building of which the component is a part is placed in service as recovery property. See subparagraph (3) of this paragraph for the treatment of components of a building which is made available in stages.

(2) *Treatment of amounts added to capital account.*—(i) Sections 162, 212, and 263 provide rules for the treatment of certain expenditures for the repair, maintenance, rehabilitation, or improvement of property. An expenditure which is treated as a capital

Proposed Regulations

expenditure under such sections (after application of the repair allowance rules of § 1.167(a)-11(d)(2)) is treated as the purchase of recovery property if the improvement for which the expenditure is made is placed in service after December 31, 1980. The recovery of such expenditure shall begin when the improvement is placed in service. See subparagraph (3) of this paragraph for the treatment of a building which is made available in stages.

(ii) For capital expenditures (which are section 1250 class property) made with respect to an improvement of a building which is recovery property, the taxpayer must use the same recovery period and method as are used with respect to the building, unless the improvement qualifies as a substantial improvement. See subparagraph (4) of this paragraph. If capital expenditures (which are section 1250 class property) are made with respect to improvements of a building which is not recovery property under section 168(e) and § 1.168-4, then the taxpayer may select any applicable recovery period and method for the recovery of the first of such expenditures. The recovery period and method so selected shall apply to each subsequent expenditure (unless the improvement qualifies as a substantial improvement).

(iii) A capital expenditure made with respect to the improvement of property, other than a building, is assigned to the same recovery class (as defined in § 1.168-3(b)) as the property of which the improvement is a part. For such an expenditure, the taxpayer need not use the same recovery period and method as are used with respect to the property of which the improvement is a part.

(3) *Recovery for a building which is made available in stages.*—This subparagraph (3) (and not subparagraphs (1) and (2) of this paragraph) applies to a building which is made available in stages. For purposes of this section, a building shall be considered placed in service (and, therefore, recovery will begin) only when a significant portion is made available for use in a finished condition (*e.g.,* when a certificate of occupancy is issued with respect to such portion). If less than the entire building is made available, then the unadjusted basis which is taken into account under this section shall be that amount of the unadjusted basis of the building (including capital expenditures for any components) as is properly allocable to the portion made available. If another portion of the building is subsequently made available, then that amount of the unadjusted basis (including capital expenditures for any components) as is properly allocable to the ensuing portion shall be taken into account under this section when such portion becomes available. The taxpayer must use the same recovery period and method for all portions of the building.

(4) *Substantial improvements.*—(i) A substantial improvement to a building shall be treated as a separate building. Thus, the taxpayer may use a different period and method for computing the recovery allowance for the substantial improvement than are used for computing the allowance for the building.

(ii) An improvement is a substantial improvement if—

(A) Over 24 consecutive months the aggregate expenditures properly chargeable to the capital account for a building equal at least 25 percent of the adjusted basis of the building (disregarding adjustments provided in section 1016(a)(2) and (3)) as of the day on which the first expenditure is made, and

(B) All expenditures for the improvement are made 3 or more years after the building is placed in service by the taxpayer.

For purposes of the preceding sentence, a building acquired in a transaction to which section 1031 or 1033 applies is considered placed in service when the building that was replaced was placed in service. Similarly, a building acquired in a transaction to which section 168(f)(10)(A) applies is deemed placed in service by the transferee when such building was placed in service by the transferor. An expenditure which is allocated to a 24-month period shall not be allocated to another 24-month period. For example, an expenditure may not be part of one substantial improvement when considered together with an expenditure incurred 15 months earlier and also be part of another substantial improvement when combined with an expenditure incurred 10 months later.

(iii) It is possible that an improvement will not be part of a substantial improvement in the taxable year in which the improvement is placed in service but will become part of a substantial improvement in a subsequent taxable year. In such case, if the taxpayer uses a different method and recovery period with respect to the substantial improvement, then the tax return filed for the taxable year in which the first improvement is placed in service shall be amended accordingly.

Proposed Regulations

(5) *Examples.*—The provisions of this paragraph may be illustrated by the following examples:

Example (1). In 1985, A spends $10,000 to improve machinery used in his trade or business. The $10,000 is added to capital account under the principles of sections 162, 212, and 263. The machinery would be 5-year property if placed in service after 1980. The $10,000 expenditure is treated as the purchase of 5-year recovery property, placed in service in 1985. Any election made by A with respect to the underlying machinery will not affect the recovery allowance for the improvement.

Example (2). B, a calendar year taxpayer, begins constructing a 10-story office building in 1982. All floors will have approximately the same amount of usable floor space. By 1983, B has paid or incurred $10 million for the building's shell (and other items not directly related to any specific portion of the building), $4 million for work with respect to the first three floors, and $5 million for work directly related to other floors (including installation of components). In March 1983, B receives a certificate of occupancy for the first three floors and begins offering the floors for rental to tenants. The building is considered placed in service in March 1983. No deduction is allowable under this section with respect to the building for 1982. No election is made under § 1.168-2(c) to use the optional recovery percentages. B's recovery for 1983 is the properly allocable unadjusted basis times the applicable percentage (10 percent). The properly allocable unadjusted basis is $7 million, consisting of the amount of unadjusted basis directly related to the portion of the building which is made available for use ($4 million), plus that amount of the unadjusted basis which is not directly related to any specific portion of the building ($10 million) properly allocable to the portion which is made available for use (*i.e.,* 3 floors/10 floors equals 30 percent or $3 million). No deduction is allowable in 1983 for the $5 million paid or incurred for work directly related to portions of the building not made available for use. B will recover the $7 million unadjusted basis over the 15-year recovery period, beginning in March 1983.

Example (3). The facts are the same as in example (2) except that, in January 1984, B receives a certificate of occupancy for the remaining seven floors and begins offering them for rental to tenants. B has spent an additional $7 million to complete the building as of the date on which the remaining seven floors are offered for rental. In January 1984, B takes into account as unadjusted basis the $12 million not previously taken into account, plus the $7 million of later expenditures. B will recover the $19 million unadjusted basis over a 15-year recovery period beginning in January 1984. B may not use a different recovery period and method for such amount than were used for the amount taken into account in March 1983.

Example (4). The facts are the same as in examples (2) and (3) except that in 1990 B spends $1 million, which is added to capital account to rehabilitate certain portions of the building. The $1 million is treated as the purchase by B of 15-year real property in 1990. B must use the same recovery period and method with respect to that improvement as were used for the underlying building. The improvement has a 15-year recovery period, and the recovery begins when the improvement is placed in service.

Example (5). In 1983 C spends $1 million, which is added to capital account, to rehabilitate certain portions of a building placed in service by C in 1975. The $1 million is treated as the purchase by C of 15-year real property in 1983. C may use any applicable recovery period and method with respect to such expenditure, and the recovery begins when the improvement is placed in service. The recovery period and method selected with respect to such expenditure, however, will apply to all ensuing capital expenditures made by C with respect to the building, unless an expenditure qualifies as part of a substantial improvement. The result in this example would be the same if the building were placed in service by C after 1980, but did not qualify as recovery property by reason of the provisions of section 168(e)(4) and § 1.168-4(d).

(f) *Short taxable years.*—(1) *General rule.*—For any recovery year in which there are less than 12 months (hereinafter in this section referred to as a "short taxable year"), the recovery allowance shall be determined by multiplying the deduction which would have been allowable if the recovery year were not a short taxable year by a fraction the numerator of which equals the number of months and part-months in the short taxable year and the denominator of which is 12. This paragraph shall not apply to 15-year real property for the year the property is placed in service or disposed of.

Proposed Regulations

(2) *Subsequent years' allowance.*—Recovery allowances for years in a recovery period following a short taxable year shall be determined in accordance with paragraph (a), (c), (g), or (m) of this section without reference to the short taxable year.

(3) *Unrecovered allowance.*—In the taxable year following the last year in the recovery period, a recovery allowance is permitted to the extent of any unrecovered allowance. If the optional recovery percentages are elected under § 1.168-2(c) or (g)(3) and the short taxable year is the last recovery year, then the unrecovered allowance shall be allowed in the year following the short taxable year. The term "unrecovered allowance" means the difference between—

(i) The recovery allowance properly allowed for the short taxable year, and

(ii) The recovery allowance which would have been allowable if such year were not a short taxable year.

In no event shall the recovery allowance for any taxable year following the last year in the recovery period be greater than what the recovery allowance would be for the last year in the recovery period assuming that such year consists of 12 months. Any amount in excess of such recovery allowance for the last year in the recovery period shall be taken into account in the following taxable year or years in the same manner as provided in this subparagraph (3).

(4) *When a taxable year begins.*—For purposes of this section, a taxable year of a person placing property in service does not include any month prior to the month in which the person begins engaging in a trade or business or holding recovery or depreciable property for the production of income. For purposes of applying the preceding sentence to an employee, an employee is not considered engaged in a trade or business by virtue of his employment except that, for purposes of applying this section to recovery property used for purposes of employment, the taxable year includes any month during which a person is engaged in trade or business as an employee. In addition, if a person engages in a small amount of trade or business activity for the purpose of obtaining a disproportionately large recovery allowance for assets for the taxable year in which they are placed in service, and if placing those assets in service represents a substantial increase in the person's level of business activity, then for purposes of the recovery allowance for such assets the person will not be treated as beginning a trade or business until the increased amount of business activity begins. For property held for the production of income, the principle of the preceding sentence also applies.

(5) *Successive short taxable years.*—In applying the rule of subparagraph (1) of this paragraph, no month shall be taken into account more than once. Thus, if a taxpayer has successive short taxable years, with one taxable year ending and the following taxable year beginning in the same calendar month, then the recovery year which is ending shall not include the month in which the taxable year terminates.

(6) *Examples.*—The following examples illustrate the application of this paragraph:

Example (1). On October 10, 1983, A and B enter into an agreement to form a partnership (P), for the purpose of leasing sailboats. The partnership adopts a calendar year as its taxable year pursuant to § 1.706-1(b)(1). On November 5, 1983, P purchases four sailboats for a total of $20,000 and places the sailboats in service immediately. For purposes of section 168, P's taxable year begins on November 5, 1983. Sailboats are 5-year recovery property as defined in section 168(c)(2). No straight line election is made under § 1.168-2(c). The recovery allowance for the sailboats in 1983, a short taxable year, is $500 (*i.e.,* .15 × $20,000 × 2/12). In 1984, the recovery allowance is $4,400 (.22 × $20,000). In 1985, 1986, and 1987, the recovery allowance is $4,200 annually (.21 × $20,000). In 1988, the taxable year following the last year in the recovery period, the unrecovered allowance equal to $2,500 may be deducted by A and B.

Example (2). In November 1984, Corporation L is incorporated and places in service two race horses which it acquired for a total of $18,500. The corporation adopts a calendar year as its taxable year. For purposes of section 168, the race horses are 3-year recovery property. No straight line election is made under § 1.168-2(c). In 1984, the recovery allowance permitted to L for the race horses is $770.83 (*i.e.,* (.25 × $18,500) × 2/12). At the close of business on June 30, 1985, all of the stock of L is acquired by Corporation M. M elects in accordance with section 1501 to file a consolidated return with respect to M and L. M's taxable year begins on July 1. By reason of becoming included in the consolidated return, under § 1.1502-76 L's second taxable year ending

Proposed Regulations

June 30, 1985, is also a short taxable year containing 6 months. In the second taxable year, L is permitted a recovery allowance equal to $3,515 (*i.e.,* .38 × $18,500 × 6/12). In the third taxable year ending June 30, 1986, L is entitled to a recovery allowance of $6,845 (*i.e.,* .37 × $18,500). Thus, the unrecovered allowance as of July 1, 1986, equals $7,369.17. Since the unrecovered allowance exceeds the recovery allowance for the third recovery year (the last year in the recovery period), the recovery allowance for the taxable year ending June 30, 1987, equals the allowance for such year, $6,845. The recovery allowance in the taxable year ending June 30, 1988, equals $524.17, the remaining unrecovered allowance.

Example (3). On August 1, 1984, Partnership M is formed and places in service a warehouse which will be leased to an unrelated person. M acquires the warehouse for $250,000. M adopts a calendar year as its taxable year pursuant to § 1.706-1(b)(1). In 1984, M has a short taxable year within the meaning of § 1.168-2(f)(1). Since the property is 15-year real property, however, the recovery allowance is computed as though 1984 were a full taxable year. Because the recovery property would have been placed in service in the eighth month of M's normal taxable year, the recovery property is deemed placed in service in the eighth month of the first recovery year. The recovery allowance in 1984 is $12,500 (*i.e.,* .05 × $250,000).

Example (4). In July 1983, D, who has been an employee of Corporation N since 1982, purchases an automobile for use in the performance of his employment for N. On June 5, 1984, D purchases a truck for use in another business. D begins the new business on June 5, 1984. In 1984, D holds no other depreciable or recovery property for the production of income. D does not have a short taxable year for the automobile purchased in 1983 since the automobile is used by D in his trade or business as an employee. Since an employee is not considered engaged in a trade or business by virtue of employment, however, for purposes of determining when a taxable year begins with respect to property not used in the trade or business of employment, D has a short taxable year in 1984 for the truck purchased in that year. The recovery allowance permitted D in 1984 with respect to the truck must be adjusted in accordance with the provisions of § 1.168-2(f).

Example (5). A has been actively engaged in the trade or business of selling used cars since 1981. On July 1, 1983, A accepts employment with Corporation M and on that same date purchases a truck for $10,000 for use in the performance of his employment for M. A does not have a short taxable year for the truck because the taxable year of a person placing property in service includes all months during which that person is engaged in a trade or business.

Example (6). In 1983, C graduates from college and on July 1, 1983, is employed by N. On that same day, C purchases an automobile for $10,000 for use in the performance of his employment for N. C has a short taxable year for the automobile purchased in 1983. Although, for recovery property used for purposes of employment, the taxable year includes any month during which a person is an employee, C does not begin that trade or business until July. In addition, C is engaged in no other trade or business (and does not hold any depreciable or recovery property for the production of income) during the taxable year. The recovery allowance permitted C in 1983 with respect to the automobile must be adjusted in accordance with the provisions of § 1.168-2(f).

Example (7). Corporation X, a calendar year taxpayer, has been in the trade or business of selling household appliances since 1979. On July 1, 1983, X purchases a restaurant. On that same day, X purchases restaurant equipment for use in its new business. X does not have a short taxable year for the restaurant equipment because the taxable year of a person placing property in service includes all months during which that person is engaged in a trade or business.

(g) *Special rules for property used predominantly outside the United States.*—(1) *General rule.*—(i) In lieu of the deduction allowed under paragraphs (a) and (c) of this § 1.168-2, except as provided in subparagraphs (3) and (4) of this paragraph, and except as otherwise provided in section 168 and the regulations thereunder, the recovery allowance for recovery property used predominantly outside the United States (as described in § 1.168-2(g)(5)) during the taxable year equals the aggregate amount determined by multiplying the unadjusted basis (as defined in § 1.168-2(d)) of such recovery property by the applicable percentage provided in paragraph (g)(2) of this section. For purposes of determining the recovery allowance, salvage value shall be disregarded.

Proposed Regulations

(ii) The recovery period for recovery property used predominantly outside the United States, other than 15-year real property, shall be the present class life. For recovery property (other than 15-year real property) which is not assigned a present class life, the recovery period shall be 12 years. For 15-year real property used predominantly outside the United States, the recovery period shall be 35 years.

(iii) Except for 15-year real property and except as otherwise provided in § 1.168-5, no recovery allowance shall be allowed in the year of disposition of recovery property described in this paragraph.

(iv) For purposes of this paragraph, rules similar to the rules of paragraph (e) of this section shall apply.

(2) *Applicable percentages.*—(i) For property other than 15-year real property—

If the recovery year is:	*And the recovery period is:*									
	2.5	*3*	*3.5*	*4*	*5*	*6*	*6.5*	*7*	*7.5*	*8*
	The applicable percentage is:									
1	40	33	29	25	20	17	15	14	13	13
2	48	45	41	38	32	28	26	25	23	22
3	12	15	17	19	19	18	18	17	17	16
4		7	13	12	12	12	13	13	13	12
5				6	12	10	10	9	9	9
6					5	10	9	9	9	8
7						5	9	9	8	8
8								4	8	8
9										4

If the recovery year is:	*And the recovery period is:*									
	8.5	*9*	*9.5*	*10*	*10.5*	*11*	*11.5*	*12*	*12.5*	*13*
	The applicable percentage is:									
1	12	11	11	10	10	9	9	8	8	8
2	21	20	19	18	17	17	16	15	15	14
3	16	15	15	14	14	13	13	13	12	12
4	12	12	12	12	11	11	11	11	10	10
5	9	9	9	9	9	9	9	9	9	9
6	8	8	7	7	7	7	7	7	7	7
7	8	7	7	7	7	7	6	6	6	6
8	7	7	7	7	7	6	6	6	6	6
9	7	7	7	7	6	6	6	6	6	5
10		4	6	6	6	6	6	6	6	5
11				3	6	6	6	5	5	5
12						3	5	5	5	5
13								3	5	5
14										3

If the recovery year is:	*And the recovery period is:*									
	13.5	*14*	*15*	*16*	*16.5*	*17*	*18*	*19*	*20*	*22*
	The applicable percentage is:									
1	7	7	7	6	6	6	6	5	5	5
2	14	13	12	12	11	11	10	10	10	9
3	12	11	11	10	10	10	9	9	9	8
4	10	10	9	9	9	9	8	8	8	7
5	8	8	8	8	8	8	7	7	7	6

Proposed Regulations

If the recovery year is:	*And the recovery period is:*									
	13.5	*14*	*15*	*16*	*16.5*	*17*	*18*	*19*	*20*	*22*
	The applicable percentage is:									
6	7	7	7	7	7	7	7	6	6	6
7	6	6	6	6	6	6	6	6	6	5
8	6	5	5	5	5	5	5	5	5	5
9	5	5	5	5	5	5	5	5	4	4
10	5	5	5	5	5	4	4	4	4	4
11	5	5	5	5	4	4	4	4	4	4
12	5	5	5	4	4	4	4	4	4	4
13	5	5	5	4	4	4	4	4	4	4
14	5	5	4	4	4	4	4	4	4	3
15		3	4	4	4	4	4	4	3	3
16			2	4	4	4	4	4	3	3
17				2	4	3	4	3	3	3
18						2	3	3	3	3
19							2	3	3	3
20								2	3	3
21									2	3
22										3
23										2

If the recovery year is:	*And the recovery period is:*						
	25	*26.5*	*28*	*30*	*35*	*45*	*50*
	The applicable percentage is:						
1	4	4	4	3	3	2	2
2	8	7	7	6	6	4	4
3	7	7	6	6	5	4	4
4	6	6	6	6	5	4	4
5	6	6	6	5	5	4	3
6	6	5	5	5	4	4	3
7	5	5	5	5	4	3	3
8	5	5	4	4	4	3	3
9	4	4	4	4	4	3	3
10	4	4	4	4	3	3	3
11	4	4	4	3	3	3	3
12	3	3	3	3	3	3	3
13	3	3	3	3	3	3	2
14	3	3	3	3	3	3	2
15	3	3	3	3	3	2	2
16	3	3	3	3	3	2	2
17	3	3	3	3	2	2	2
18	3	3	3	3	2	2	2
19	3	3	3	3	2	2	2
20	3	3	3	3	2	2	2
21	3	3	3	3	2	2	2
22	3	3	2	2	2	2	2
23	3	3	2	2	2	2	2
24	2	2	2	2	2	2	2
25	2	2	2	2	2	2	2

Proposed Regulations

If the recovery year is:	*And the recovery period is:*						
	25	*26.5*	*28*	*30*	*35*	*45*	*50*
	The applicable percentage is:						
26	1	2	2	2	2	2	2
27		1	2	2	2	2	2
28			2	2	2	2	2
29			1	2	2	2	2
30				2	2	2	2
31				1	2	2	2
32					2	2	2
33					2	2	2
34					2	2	2
35					2	2	2
36					1	2	1
37						1	1
38						1	1
39						1	1
40						1	1
41						1	1
42						1	1
43						1	1
44						1	1
45						1	1
46						1	1
47							1
48							1
49							1
50							1
51							1

(ii) For 15-year real property—

If the recovery year is	*And the month in the 1st recovery year in which the property is placed in service is:*				
	1	*2,3*	*4,5,6*	*7,8*	*9,10,11,12*
	The applicable percentage is:				
1	4	4	3	2	1
2	4	4	4	4	4
3	4	4	4	4	4
4	4	4	4	4	4
5	4	4	4	4	4
6	3	3	3	4	4
7	3	3	3	3	3
8	3	3	3	3	3
9	3	3	3	3	3
10	3	3	3	3	3
11	3	3	3	3	3
12	3	3	3	3	3
13	3	3	3	3	3
14	3	3	3	3	3
15	3	3	3	3	3
16	3	3	3	3	3

Proposed Regulations

If the recovery year is	*And the month in the 1st recovery year in which the property is placed in service is:* 1	2,3	4,5,6	7,8	9,10,11,12
	The applicable percentage is:				
17	3	3	3	3	3
18	3	3	3	3	3
19	3	3	3	3	3
20	3	3	3	3	3
21	3	3	3	3	3
22	3	3	3	3	3
23	3	3	3	3	3
24	3	3	3	3	3
25	3	2	3	2	3
26	2	2	2	2	2
27	2	2	2	2	2
28	2	2	2	2	2
29	2	2	2	2	2
30	2	2	2	2	2
31	2	2	2	2	2
32	2	2	2	2	2
33	2	2	2	2	2
34	2	2	2	2	2
35	2	2	2	2	2
36		1	1	2	2

(3) *Election of optional recovery percentage method.*—(i) In lieu of the applicable percentage provided by subparagraphs (1) and (2), the taxpayer may elect (in accordance with § 1.168-5(e)), for recovery property used predominantly outside the United States that is placed in service during the taxable year, to determine the recovery allowance by using the straight line method over one of the recovery periods elected by the taxpayer and set forth in the following table:

CLASS OF PROPERTY	RECOVERY PERIOD
3-year property	5 or 12 years or present class life
5-year property	12 or 25 years or present class life
10-year property	25 or 35 years or present class life
15-year real property	35 or 45 years
15-year public utility property	35 or 45 years or present class life

Such election is irrevocable without the consent of the Commissioner. See subdivision (iv) of this subparagraph for tables containing the applicable percentages to be used in computing the recovery allowance.

(ii) Except in the case of 15-year real property, a single recovery period must be elected under this subparagraph for all recovery property placed in service in the same taxable year which is in the same recovery class and which has the same present class life. For property other than 15-year real property the recovery period elected may not be shorter than the present class life (or, if none, 12 years). A different recovery period may be elected (or the tables provided in subparagraph (2) may be used) for recovery property in different recovery classes, or with different present class lives, placed in service during the taxable year, or for recovery property placed in service in a different taxable year, whether or not in the same recovery class or with the same present class life.

(iii) In the case of 15-year real property, the election provided by this subparagraph may be made separately with respect to each property.

(iv) (A) For property other than 15-year real property—

If the recovery year is:	*And the period elected is:* 2.5	3	3.5	4	5	6	6.5	7	7.5
	The applicable percentage is:								
1	20	17	14	13	10	8	8	8	7
2	40	33	29	25	20	17	16	14	14
3	40	33	29	25	20	17	16	14	14
4		17	28	25	20	17	15	14	13
5				12	20	17	15	14	13
6					10	17	15	14	13
7						7	15	14	13
8								8	13

If the recovery year is:	*And the period elected is:* 8	8.5	9	9.5	10	10.5	11	11.5	12
	The applicable percentage is:								
1	6	6	6	5	5	5	5	4	4
2	13	12	11	11	10	10	9	9	9
3	13	12	11	11	10	10	9	9	9
4	13	12	11	11	10	10	9	9	9
5	13	12	11	11	10	10	9	9	9
6	12	12	11	11	10	10	9	9	8
7	12	12	11	10	10	9	9	9	8
8	12	11	11	10	10	9	9	9	8
9	6	11	11	10	10	9	9	9	8
10			6	10	10	9	9	8	8
11					5	9	9	8	8
12							5	8	8
13									4

If the recovery year is:	*And the period elected is:* 12.5	13	13.5	14	15	16	16.5	17	18
	The applicable percentage is:								
1	4	4	4	4	3	3	3	3	3
2	8	8	8	8	7	7	7	6	6
3	8	8	8	7	7	7	6	6	6
4	8	8	8	7	7	7	6	6	6
5	8	8	8	7	7	7	6	6	6
6	8	8	8	7	7	6	6	6	6
7	8	8	7	7	7	6	6	6	6
8	8	8	7	7	7	6	6	6	6
9	8	8	7	7	7	6	6	6	6
10	8	8	7	7	7	6	6	6	6
11	8	7	7	7	7	6	6	6	6
12	8	7	7	7	6	6	6	6	5
13	8	7	7	7	6	6	6	6	5
14		3	7	7	6	6	6	6	5
15				4	6	6	6	6	5
16					3	6	6	6	5
17						3	6	5	5

Proposed Regulations

If the recovery year is:	*And the period elected is:*								
	12.5	*13*	*13.5*	*14*	*15*	*16*	*16.5*	*17*	*18*
	The applicable percentage is:								
18								2	5
19									2

If the recovery year is:	*And the period elected is:*							
	19	*20*	*22*	*25*	*26.5*	*28*	*30*	*35*
	The applicable percentage is:							
1	3	3	2	2	2	2	2	1
2	6	5	5	4	4	4	4	3
3	6	5	5	4	4	4	4	3
4	6	5	5	4	4	4	4	3
5	6	5	5	4	4	4	4	3
6	6	5	5	4	4	4	4	3
7	5	5	5	4	4	4	4	3
8	5	5	5	4	4	4	4	3
9	5	5	5	4	4	4	4	3
10	5	5	5	4	4	4	4	3
11	5	5	5	4	4	4	3	3
12	5	5	5	4	4	4	3	3
13	5	5	5	4	4	4	3	3
14	5	5	4	4	4	4	3	3
15	5	5	4	4	4	4	3	3
16	5	5	4	4	4	4	3	3
17	5	5	4	4	4	3	3	3
18	5	5	4	4	4	3	3	3
19	5	5	4	4	4	3	3	3
20	2	5	4	4	4	3	3	3
21		2	4	4	4	3	3	3
22			4	4	3	3	3	3
23			2	4	3	3	3	3
24				4	3	3	3	3
25				4	3	3	3	3
26				2	3	3	3	3
27					3	3	3	3
28						3	3	3
29						2	3	3
30							3	3
31							2	3
32								2
33								2
34								2
35								2
36								1

Proposed Regulations

If the recovery year is:	*And the period elected is:* 45	50
	The applicable percentage is:	
1	1.1	1
2	2.3	2
3	2.3	2
4	2.3	2
5	2.3	2
6	2.3	2
7	2.3	2
8	2.3	2
9	2.3	2
10	2.3	2
11	2.3	2
12	2.2	2
13	2.2	2
14	2.2	2
15	2.2	2
16	2.2	2
17	2.2	2
18	2.2	2
19	2.2	2
20	2.2	2
21	2.2	2
22	2.2	2
23	2.2	2
24	2.2	2
25	2.2	2
26	2.2	2
27	2.2	2
28	2.2	2
29	2.2	2
30	2.2	2
31	2.2	2
32	2.2	2
33	2.2	2
34	2.2	2
35	2.2	2
36	2.2	2
37	2.2	2
38	2.2	2
39	2.2	2
40	2.2	2
41	2.2	2
42	2.2	2
43	2.2	2
44	2.2	2
45	2.2	2
46	1.1	2
47		2
48		2
49		2

Proposed Regulations

If the recovery year is:	*And the period elected is:* 45	50
	The applicable percentage is:	
50		2
51		1

(B) *For 15-year real property.—(1)* If a 35-year period is elected—

If the recovery year is:	*And the month in the 1st recovery year the property is placed in service is:* 1-2	3-6	7-12
		The applicable percentage is:	
1	3	2	1
2	3	3	3
3	3	3	3
4	3	3	3
5	3	3	3
6	3	3	3
7	3	3	3
8	3	3	3
9	3	3	3
10	3	3	3
11	3	3	3
12	3	3	3
13	3	3	3
14	3	3	3
15	3	3	3
16	3	3	3
17	3	3	3
18	3	3	3
19	3	3	3
20	3	3	3
21	3	3	3
22	3	3	3
23	3	3	3
24	3	3	3
25	3	3	3
26	3	3	3
27	3	3	3
28	3	3	3
29	3	3	3
30	3	3	3
31	2	2	2
32	2	2	2
33	2	2	2
34	2	2	2
35	2	2	2
36		1	2

(2) If a 45-year period is elected—

Proposed Regulations

If the recovery year is:	*And the month in the 1st recovery year the property is placed in service is:*											
	1	*2*	*3*	*4*	*5*	*6*	*7*	*8*	*9*	*10*	*11*	*12*
	The applicable percentage is:											
1	2.3	2.0	1.9	1.7	1.5	1.3	1.2	.9	.7	.6	.4	.2
2	2.3	2.3	2.3	2.3	2.3	2.3	2.3	2.3	2.3	2.3	2.3	2.3
3	2.3	2.3	2.3	2.3	2.3	2.3	2.3	2.3	2.3	2.3	2.3	2.3
4	2.3	2.3	2.3	2.3	2.3	2.3	2.3	2.3	2.3	2.3	2.3	2.3
5	2.3	2.3	2.3	2.3	2.3	2.3	2.3	2.3	2.3	2.3	2.3	2.3
6	2.3	2.3	2.3	2.3	2.3	2.3	2.3	2.3	2.3	2.3	2.3	2.3
7	2.3	2.3	2.3	2.3	2.3	2.3	2.3	2.3	2.3	2.3	2.3	2.3
8	2.3	2.3	2.3	2.3	2.3	2.3	2.3	2.3	2.3	2.3	2.3	2.3
9	2.3	2.3	2.3	2.3	2.3	2.3	2.3	2.3	2.3	2.3	2.3	2.3
10	2.3	2.3	2.3	2.3	2.3	2.3	2.3	2.3	2.3	2.3	2.3	2.3
11	2.2	2.2	2.2	2.2	2.2	2.2	2.2	2.2	2.2	2.2	2.2	2.2
12	2.2	2.2	2.2	2.2	2.2	2.2	2.2	2.2	2.2	2.2	2.2	2.2
13	2.2	2.2	2.2	2.2	2.2	2.2	2.2	2.2	2.2	2.2	2.2	2.2
14	2.2	2.2	2.2	2.2	2.2	2.2	2.2	2.2	2.2	2.2	2.2	2.2
15	2.2	2.2	2.2	2.2	2.2	2.2	2.2	2.2	2.2	2.2	2.2	2.2
16	2.2	2.2	2.2	2.2	2.2	2.2	2.2	2.2	2.2	2.2	2.2	2.2
17	2.2	2.2	2.2	2.2	2.2	2.2	2.2	2.2	2.2	2.2	2.2	2.2
18	2.2	2.2	2.2	2.2	2.2	2.2	2.2	2.2	2.2	2.2	2.2	2.2
19	2.2	2.2	2.2	2.2	2.2	2.2	2.2	2.2	2.2	2.2	2.2	2.2
20	2.2	2.2	2.2	2.2	2.2	2.2	2.2	2.2	2.2	2.2	2.2	2.2
21	2.2	2.2	2.2	2.2	2.2	2.2	2.2	2.2	2.2	2.2	2.2	2.2
22	2.2	2.2	2.2	2.2	2.2	2.2	2.2	2.2	2.2	2.2	2.2	2.2
23	2.2	2.2	2.2	2.2	2.2	2.2	2.2	2.2	2.2	2.2	2.2	2.2
24	2.2	2.2	2.2	2.2	2.2	2.2	2.2	2.2	2.2	2.2	2.2	2.2
25	2.2	2.2	2.2	2.2	2.2	2.2	2.2	2.2	2.2	2.2	2.2	2.2
26	2.2	2.2	2.2	2.2	2.2	2.2	2.2	2.2	2.2	2.2	2.2	2.2
27	2.2	2.2	2.2	2.2	2.2	2.2	2.2	2.2	2.2	2.2	2.2	2.2
28	2.2	2.2	2.2	2.2	2.2	2.2	2.2	2.2	2.2	2.2	2.2	2.2
29	2.2	2.2	2.2	2.2	2.2	2.2	2.2	2.2	2.2	2.2	2.2	2.2
30	2.2	2.2	2.2	2.2	2.2	2.2	2.2	2.2	2.2	2.2	2.2	2.2
31	2.2	2.2	2.2	2.2	2.2	2.2	2.2	2.2	2.2	2.2	2.2	2.2
32	2.2	2.2	2.2	2.2	2.2	2.2	2.2	2.2	2.2	2.2	2.2	2.2
33	2.2	2.2	2.2	2.2	2.2	2.2	2.2	2.2	2.2	2.2	2.2	2.2
34	2.2	2.2	2.2	2.2	2.2	2.2	2.2	2.2	2.2	2.2	2.2	2.2
35	2.2	2.2	2.2	2.2	2.2	2.2	2.2	2.2	2.2	2.2	2.2	2.2
36	2.2	2.2	2.2	2.2	2.2	2.2	2.2	2.2	2.2	2.2	2.2	2.2
37	2.2	2.2	2.2	2.2	2.2	2.2	2.2	2.2	2.2	2.2	2.2	2.2
38	2.2	2.2	2.2	2.2	2.2	2.2	2.2	2.2	2.2	2.2	2.2	2.2
39	2.2	2.2	2.2	2.2	2.2	2.2	2.2	2.2	2.2	2.2	2.2	2.2
40	2.2	2.2	2.2	2.2	2.2	2.2	2.2	2.2	2.2	2.2	2.2	2.2
41	2.2	2.2	2.2	2.2	2.2	2.2	2.2	2.2	2.2	2.2	2.2	2.2
42	2.2	2.2	2.2	2.2	2.2	2.2	2.2	2.2	2.2	2.2	2.2	2.2
43	2.2	2.2	2.2	2.2	2.2	2.2	2.2	2.2	2.2	2.2	2.2	2.2
44	2.2	2.2	2.2	2.2	2.2	2.2	2.2	2.2	2.2	2.2	2.2	2.2
45	2.2	2.2	2.2	2.2	2.2	2.2	2.2	2.2	2.2	2.2	2.2	2.2
46		.3	.4	.6	.8	1.0	1.1	1.4	1.6	1.7	1.9	2.1

(4) *Rules for year of disposition and placement in service of 15-year real property.*—(i) In the taxable year in which 15-year real property is disposed of, the recovery

Proposed Regulations

allowance shall be determined by multiplying the allowance (determined without regard to this subdivision) by a fraction, the numerator of which equals the number of months in the taxable year that the property is in service in the taxpayer's trade or business or for the production of income and the denominator of which is 12. In the case of 15-year real property that is disposed of during the first recovery year, the denominator shall equal the number of months in the taxpayer's taxable year after the property was placed in service by the taxpayer (including the month the property was placed in service). If the recovery allowance for the taxable year is limited by reason of the short taxable year rules of section 168(f)(5) and paragraph (f) of this section (*e.g.,* if the taxpayer dies, or if the taxpayer is a corporation which becomes a member, or ceases being a member, of an affiliated group of corporations filing a consolidated return), then the denominator shall equal the number of months in the taxpayer's taxable year.

(ii) For purposes of this paragraph—

(A) 15-year real property that is placed in service on or after the first day of a month shall be treated as placed in service in that month; and

(B) 15-year real property that is disposed of during the recovery year shall be treated as disposed of as of the last day of the month preceding the month in which it is withdrawn from service.

(5) *Determination of whether property is used predominantly outside the United States.*—(i) The determination of whether property is used predominantly outside the United States (as defined in section 7701(a)(9)) during the taxable year shall be made by comparing the period in such year during which the property is physically located outside of the United States with the period during which the property is physically located within the United States. If the property is physically located outside the United States during more than 50 percent of the taxable year, such property shall be considered used predominantly outside the United States during the year. If property is placed in service after the first day of the taxable year, the determination of whether such property is physically located outside the United States during more than 50 percent of the taxable year shall be made with respect to the period beginning on the date on which the property is placed in service and ending on the last day of such taxable year.

(ii) This paragraph applies whether recovery property is used predominantly outside the United States by the owner or by the lessee of the property. For recovery property which is leased, the determination of whether such property is physically located outside the United States during the taxable year shall be made with respect to the taxable year of the lessor.

(iii) For purposes of this § 1.168-2(g), the following property is not "property used predominantly outside the United States":

(A) Any aircraft which is registered by the Administrator of the Federal Aviation Agency, and which (*1*) is operated, whether on a scheduled or nonscheduled basis, to and from the United States, or (*2*) is operated under contract with the United States, provided that the use of the aircraft under the contract constitutes its principal use outside the United States during the taxable year. The term "to and from the United States" shall not exclude an aircraft which makes flights from one point in a foreign country to another such point, as long as such aircraft returns to the United States with some degree of frequency;

(B) Rolling stock which is used within and without the United States and which is (*1*) of a domestic railroad corporation subject to part I of the Interstate Commerce Act or (*2*) of a United States person (other than a corporation subject to part I of the Interstate Commerce Act) but only if the rolling stock is not leased to one or more foreign persons for periods totaling more than 12 months in any 24-month period. For purposes of this subdivision (iii)(B), the term "rolling stock" means locomotives, freight and passenger train cars, floating equipment, and miscellaneous transportation equipment on wheels, the expenditures for which are of the type chargeable to the equipment investment accounts in the uniform system of accounts for railroad companies prescribed by the Interstate Commerce Commission.

(C) Any vessel documented under the laws of the United States which is operated in the foreign or domestic commerce of the United States. A vessel is documented under the laws of the United States if it is registered, enrolled, or licensed under the laws of the United States by the Commandant, United States Coast Guard. Vessels operated in the foreign or domestic commerce of the United States include those documented for use in foreign trade, coast-wise trade, or fisheries;

Proposed Regulations

(D) Any motor vehicle of a United States person (as defined in section 7701(a)(30)) which is operated to and from the United States with some degree of frequency;

(E) Any container of a United States person which is used in the transportation of property to and from the United States;

(F) Any property (other than a vessel or an aircraft) of a United States person which is used for the purpose of exploring for, developing, removing, or transporting resources from the Outer Continental Shelf (within the meaning of section 2 of the Outer Continental Shelf Lands Act, as amended and supplemented, 43 U.S.C. section 1331), *e.g.*, offshore drilling equipment;

(G) Any property which (*1*) is owned by a domestic corporation (other than a corporation which has an election in effect under section 936 or which is entitled to the benefits of section 934(b)), by a United States citizen (other than a citizen entitled to the benefits of section 931, 932, 933, or 934(c)), or by a domestic partnership, all of whose partners are domestic corporations (none of which has an election in effect under section 936 or is entitled to the benefits of section 934(b)) or United States citizens (none of whom is entitled to the benefits of section 931, 932, 933, or 934(c)), and (*2*) which is used predominantly in a possession of the United States during the taxable year by such a corporation, citizen, or partnership, or by a corporation created or organized in, or under the law of, a possession of the United States. The determination of whether property is used predominantly in a possession of the United States during the taxable year shall be made under principles similar to those described in subdivision (i) of this subparagraph. For example, if a machine is placed in service in a possession of the United States on July 1, 1981, by a calendar year taxpayer and if it is physically located in such a possession during more than 50 percent of the period beginning on July 1, 1981, and ending on December 31, 1981, then such machine shall be considered used predominantly in a possession of the United States during the taxable year 1981;

(H) Any communications satellite (as defined in section 103(3) of the Communications Satellite Act of 1962, 47 U.S.C. section 702(3)), or any interest therein, of a United States person;

(I) Any cable, or any interest therein, of a domestic corporation engaged in furnishing telephone service to which section 46(c)(3)(B)(iii) applies (or of a wholly owned domestic subsidiary of such corporation), if such cable is part of a submarine cable system which constitutes part of a communications link exclusively between the United States and one or more foreign countries;

(J) Any property (other than a vessel or an aircraft) of a United States person which is used in international or territorial waters within the northern portion of the Western Hemisphere for the purpose of exploring for, developing, removing, or transporting resources from ocean waters or deposits under such waters. The term "northern portion of the Western Hemisphere" means the area lying west of the 30th meridian west of Greenwich, east of the international dateline, and north of the Equator, but not including any foreign country which is a country of South America; and

(K) Any property described in section 48(l)(3)(A)(ix) which is owned by a United States person and which is used in international or territorial waters to generate energy for use in the United States.

(h) *Mass asset accounts.*—(1) *In general.*—In accordance with the provisions of § 1.168-5(e), a taxpayer may elect to account for mass assets (as defined in § 1.168-2(h)(2)) in the same mass asset account, as though such assets were a single asset. If such treatment is elected, the taxpayer, upon disposition of an asset in the account, shall include as ordinary income (as defined in section 64) all proceeds realized to the extent of the unadjusted basis in the account (as defined in paragraph (d) of this section), less any amounts previously so included, and shall include as capital gain any excess, unless gain on such disposition is not recognized under another provision of the Code. With respect to the recovery allowance, the account shall be treated as though the asset were not disposed of.

(2) *Definition.*—For purposes of this section, the term "mass assets" means a mass or group of individual items of recovery property (i) not necessarily homogenous, (ii) each of which is minor in value relative to the total value of such mass or group, (iii) numerous in quantity, (iv) usually accounted for only on a total dollar or quantity basis, (v) with respect to which separate identification is impracticable, (vi) with the same present class life, and (vii) placed in service in the same taxable year.

Proposed Regulations

(3) *Election.*—The election under this paragraph shall be made for the taxable year in which the assets in the account are placed in service. The election shall apply, with respect to the account, throughout the applicable recovery period and for all subsequent taxable years. The taxpayer is not bound by such election with respect to assets placed in service in other taxable years, or with respect to other assets placed in service in the same taxable year, which may properly be included in another mass asset account (*e.g.,* assets with a different present class life).

(4) *Recovery of an increase in basis.*—To the extent that § 1.168-2(d)(2)(i) (relating to reductions in basis) applies, if as a result of early disposition of an asset in a mass asset account (determined in accordance with the provision of subparagraph (5) of this paragraph), the investment tax credit is recaptured (in accordance with section 47 and the regulations thereunder), then the basis of the account shall be increased by an amount equal to one-half of the amount of the recapture. Such increase shall be treated in a manner similar to § 1.168-2(d)(3), relating to redeterminations. For purposes of subparagraph (1) of this paragraph, such increase will be taken into account as unadjusted basis in determining the inclusion of proceeds as ordinary income.

(5) *Identification of dispositions for purposes of basis increase.*—For purposes of subparagraph (4) of this paragraph, disposition of assets from a mass asset account shall be determined by the use of an appropriate mortality dispersion table. If the taxpayer adopts recordkeeping practices consistent with his prior practices and consonant with good accounting and engineering practices, and supplies such reasonable information as may be required by the Commissioner, the mortality dispersion table may be based upon an acceptable sampling of the taxpayer's actual experience or other acceptable statistical or engineering techniques. Alternatively, the taxpayer may use the following standard mortality dispersion table:

STANDARD MORTALITY DISPERSION TABLE
PERCENTAGE OF BASIS OF MASS ASSET ACCOUNT CONSIDERED
DISPOSED OF EACH 12-MONTH PERIOD AFTER THE
ACCOUNT IS PLACED IN SERVICE

Present Class Life	*1st (1)*	*2nd (2)*	*3rd (3)*	*4th (4)*	*5th (5)*	*6th (6)*	*7th (7)*	*8th (8)*	*9th (9)*	*10th (10)*
2.5	3.59	23.84	45.14	23.84	3.59	.	.	.	.	..
3	2.28	13.59	34.13	34.13	13.59	2.28	.	.	.	..
3.5	1.62	8.23	23.51	33.28	23.51	8.23	1.62	.	.	..
4	1.22	5.46	15.98	27.34	27.34	15.98	5.46	1.22	.	..
5	.82	2.77	7.92	15.91	22.58	22.58	15.91	7.92	2.77	.82
6	.62	1.66	4.40	9.19	14.98	19.15	19.15	14.98	9.19	4.40
6.5	.55	1.33	3.38	7.25	12.00	16.39	18.20	16.39	12.00	7.25
7	.51	1.11	2.74	5.49	9.64	13.87	16.64	16.64	13.87	9.64
7.5	.47	.92	2.20	4.49	7.79	11.55	14.65	15.86	14.65	11.55
8	.44	.78	1.85	3.61	6.46	9.52	12.91	14.43	14.43	12.91
8.5	.40	.70	1.52	2.97	5.16	8.19	10.87	13.05	14.28	13.05
9	.38	.61	1.29	2.47	4.43	6.69	9.27	11.93	12.93	12.93
9.5	.37	.52	1.13	2.07	3.69	5.57	8.13	10.44	11.72	12.72
10 and 10.5	.35	.47	.97	1.80	3.09	4.83	6.90	9.01	10.79	11.79
11 and 11.5	.32	.39	.75	1.35	2.24	3.64	5.10	6.82	8.51	10.24
12 and 12.5	.30	.32	.60	1.06	1.73	2.67	3.88	5.31	6.79	8.19
13 and 13.5	.28	.27	.49	.84	1.34	2.04	3.12	4.13	5.37	6.63
14	.27	.24	.40	.71	1.06	1.68	2.32	3.17	4.38	5.26
15	.26	.21	.35	.57	.89	1.31	1.89	2.60	3.43	4.36
16 and 16.5	.25	.18	.29	.49	.75	1.10	1.48	2.13	2.83	3.83
17	.24	.16	.28	.42	.60	.92	1.30	1.67	2.34	2.82
18	.23	.15	.24	.37	.51	.78	1.08	1.39	1.93	2.50
19	.23	.14	.20	.32	.47	.66	.92	1.15	1.61	2.08
20-24	.22	.13	.19	.28	.40	.57	.77	1.03	1.36	1.73

Proposed Regulations

Present Class Life	*1st (1)*	*2nd (2)*	*3rd (3)*	*4th (4)*	*5th (5)*	*6th (6)*	*7th (7)*	*8th (8)*	*9th (9)*	*10th (10)*
25-29	.20	.09	.12	.18	.23	.31	.41	.53	.67	.85
30-50	.19	.07	.09	.12	.15	.20	.25	.32	.40	.49

Present Class Life	*11th (11)*	*12th (12)*	*13th (13)*	*14th (14)*	*15th (15)*	*16th (16)*	*17th (17)*	*18th (18)*	*19th (19)*	*20th (20)*
2.5	.	.	.	.	.	.	.	.	.	. .
3	.	.	.	.	.	.	.	.	.	. .
3.5	.	.	.	.	.	.	.	.	.	. .
4	.	.	.	.	.	.	.	.	.	. .
5	.	.	.	.	.	.	.	.	.	. .
6	1.66	.62	.	.	.	.	.	.	.	. .
6.5	3.38	1.33	.55	.	.	.	.	.	.	. .
7	5.49	2.74	1.11	.51	.	.	.	.	.	. .
7.5	7.70	4.49	2.20	.92	.47	.	.	.	.	. .
8	9.52	6.46	3.61	1.85	.78	.44	.	.	.	. .
8.5	10.87	8.19	5.16	2.97	1.52	.70	.40	.	.	. .
9	11.93	9.27	6.69	4.43	2.47	1.29	.61	.38	.	. .
9.5	11.72	10.44	8.13	5.57	3.69	2.07	1.13	.52	.37	. .
10 and 10.5	11.79	10.79	9.01	6.90	4.83	3.09	1.80	.97	.47	.35
11 and 11.5	10.64	10.64	10.24	8.51	6.82	5.10	3.64	2.24	1.35	.75
12 and 12.5	9.28	9.87	9.87	9.28	8.19	6.79	5.31	3.88	2.67	1.73
13 and 13.5	7.77	8.62	9.10	9.10	8.62	7.77	6.63	5.37	4.13	3.12
14	6.62	7.25	8.32	8.32	8.32	8.32	7.25	6.62	5.26	4.38
15	5.32	6.23	7.04	7.61	7.93	7.93	7.61	7.04	6.23	5.32
16 and 16.5	4.22	5.30	6.11	6.80	6.89	7.54	7.54	6.89	6.80	6.11
17	3.71	4.48	4.94	5.93	6.51	6.54	7.14	7.14	6.54	6.51
18	3.12	3.57	4.46	4.81	5.71	6.19	6.21	6.75	6.75	6.21
19	2.60	2.97	3.76	4.37	4.96	5.48	5.53	6.19	6.36	6.36
20-24	2.17	2.66	3.18	3.72	4.25	4.76	5.22	5.57	5.83	5.96
25-29	1.06	1.29	1.55	1.85	2.18	2.50	2.84	3.19	3.54	3.84
30-50	.59	.72	.87	1.02	1.20	1.40	1.60	1.83	2.86	2.30

STANDARD MORTALITY DISPERSION TABLE
PERCENTAGE OF BASIS OF MASS ASSET ACCOUNT CONSIDERED DISPOSED OF EACH 12-MONTH PERIOD AFTER THE ACCOUNT IS PLACED IN SERVICE

Present Class Life	*21st (21)*	*22nd (22)*	*23rd (23)*	*24th (24)*	*25th (25)*	*26th (26)*	*27th (27)*	*28th (28)*	*29th (29)*	*30th (30)*
2.5	.	.	.	.	.	.	.	.	.	. .
3	.	.	.	.	.	.	.	.	.	. .
3.5	.	.	.	.	.	.	.	.	.	. .
4	.	.	.	.	.	.	.	.	.	. .
5	.	.	.	.	.	.	.	.	.	. .
6	.	.	.	.	.	.	.	.	.	. .
6.5	.	.	.	.	.	.	.	.	.	. .
7	.	.	.	.	.	.	.	.	.	. .
7.5	.	.	.	.	.	.	.	.	.	. .
8	.	.	.	.	.	.	.	.	.	. .
8.5	.	.	.	.	.	.	.	.	.	. .
9	.	.	.	.	.	.	.	.	.	. .

Proposed Regulations

Present Class Life	*21st (21)*	*22nd (22)*	*23rd (23)*	*24th (24)*	*25th (25)*	*26th (26)*	*27th (27)*	*28th (28)*	*29th (29)*	*30th (30)*
9.5	.	.	.	.	.	.	.	.	.	..
10 and 10.5	.	.	.	.	.	.	.	.	.	..
11 and 11.5	.39	.32	.	.	.	.	.	.	.	..
12 and 12.5	1.06	.60	.32	.30	.	.	.	.	.	..
13 and 13.5	2.04	1.34	.84	.49	.27	.28	.	.	.	..
14	3.17	2.32	1.68	1.06	.71	.40	.24	.27	.	..
15	4.36	3.43	2.60	1.89	1.31	.89	.57	.35	.21	.26
16 and 16.5	5.30	4.22	3.83	2.83	2.13	1.48	1.10	.75	.49	.29
17	5.93	4.94	4.48	3.71	2.82	2.34	1.67	1.30	.92	.60
18	6.19	5.71	4.81	4.46	3.57	3.12	2.50	1.93	1.39	1.08
19	6.19	5.53	5.48	4.96	4.37	3.76	2.97	2.60	2.08	1.61
20-24	5.96	5.83	5.57	5.22	4.76	4.25	3.72	3.18	2.66	2.17
25-29	4.13	4.38	4.58	4.70	4.78	4.78	4.70	4.58	4.38	4.13
30-50	2.54	2.78	3.01	3.23	3.42	3.61	3.75	3.86	3.95	3.98

For purposes of applying the standard mortality dispersion table, all assets in a mass asset account placed in service during a taxable year are considered to be placed in service on the same day. If the taxpayer uses the standard mortality dispersion table for a taxable year, such table must be used for all subsequent taxable years unless the taxpayer obtains the consent of the Commissioner.

(6) *Transitional rule.*—Unless the taxpayer establishes to the contrary (by statistical methods or otherwise), all proceeds realized upon the disposition of assets from one or more mass asset accounts shall be considered realized with respect to accounts placed in service by the taxpayer after December 31, 1980.

(i) [Reserved]

(j) *Changes in use.*—(1) *Conversion from personal use or use in tax-exempt activity.*—If property which was previously used by the taxpayer for personal purposes or in a tax-exempt activity is converted to use in a trade or business or for the production of income during the taxable year, then the recovery allowance for the taxable year (and subsequent taxable years) shall be determined as though the property were placed in service by the taxpayer as recovery property on the date on which the conversion occurs. Thus, the recovery allowance shall be determined by multiplying the unadjusted basis (as provided in subparagraph (6)(ii) of this paragraph) by the applicable percentage.

(2) *Increased business use of property.*—If a taxpayer uses property in a trade or business (or for the production of income) and for personal (or tax-exempt) purposes during a recovery period, and increases the business (or income-producing) use of such property after the recovery for that period is completed, then a recovery allowance shall continue to be allowed with respect to such property. The amount of the allowance shall be determined as though, to the extent of the increase in business (or income-producing) use, the property were placed in service by the taxpayer as recovery property at the beginning of the taxable year in which such increased use occurs. Thus, the recovery allowance for the taxable year shall be determined first by multiplying the unadjusted basis (as provided in subparagraph (6)(ii) of this paragraph) by the applicable percentage, and then by the excess of the percentage of the business (or income-producing) use during the taxable year over the average of such use during the prior recovery period (or periods). The combined recovery under this subpara graph and subparagraph (1) shall not exceed the original cost of the property. See Example (2) of subparagraph (7) of this paragraph.

(3) *Domestic property changing recovery classes.*—(i) When the class of recovery property not used predominantly outside the United States changes during the taxable year, and the property continues to be used as recovery property by the taxpayer (*e.g.,* when property ceases to be used predominantly in connection with research and experimentation) the following rules apply:

(A) If the change results in the property's being assigned to a class with a shorter recovery period, then the recovery allowance for the taxable year in which

Proposed Regulations

the change occurs (and subsequent taxable years) shall be determined as though the property were placed in service as recovery property in the year of the change. Thus, the recovery allowance shall be determined by multiplying the unadjusted basis (as provided in subparagraph (6)(ii) of this paragraph) by the applicable percentage. Alternatively, the taxpayer may continue to treat the property as though the change had not occurred.

(B) If the change results in the property's being assigned to a class with a longer recovery period, then the recovery allowance for the taxable year of the change (and subsequent taxable years) shall be determined as though the property had originally been assigned to that longer recovery class. Proper adjustment shall be made under the principles of § 1.168-2(d)(3) (relating to redeterminations) to account for the deductions allowable to the taxpayer with respect to the property prior to the year of the change in excess of those which would have been allowable had the taxpayer used the applicable percentages for the longer recovery class for those years.

(4) *Foreign property.*—(i) If recovery property ceases being used predominantly outside the United States during a taxable year, and the property continues to be used as recovery property by the taxpayer, then the recovery allowance for the taxable year (and subsequent taxable years) shall be determined as though the property were placed in service as recovery property in the year of the cessation. Thus, the recovery allowance shall be determined by multiplying the unadjusted basis (as provided in subparagraph (6)(ii) of this paragraph) by the applicable percentage. Alternatively, the taxpayer may continue to treat the property as though the cessation had not occurred. See § § 1.168-5(e)(5) and 1.1016-3(a)(3)(iii) and (iv).

(ii) If the recovery property begins to be used by the taxpayer predominantly outside the United States during a taxable year after having been used otherwise by the taxpayer as recovery property in the previous taxable year, then the recovery allowance for the taxable year in which the change occurs (and subsequent years) shall be determined as though the property had originally been placed in service by the taxpayer as recovery property used predominantly outside the United States. Proper adjustment shall be made under the principles of § 1.168-2(d)(3) to account for the difference between the deductions allowable with respect to the property prior to the year of the change and those which would have been allowable had the taxpayer used the applicable percentages for property used predominantly outside the United States for those years.

(5) *Low income housing.*—If 15-year real property begins or ceases to be low income housing (as defined in § 1.168-2(b)(2) (iii)) during a taxable year, then the recovery allowance for the taxable year in which the change occurs (and subsequent taxable years) shall be determined under the principles of paragraph (j)(3)(i)(B) and (4)(ii) of this section.

(6) *Special rules.*—(i) For purposes of this paragraph, if, prior to a change in status, the taxpayer used the optional applicable percentages (under paragraph (c) or (g)(3) of this section) with respect to recovery property, then similar optional percentages shall be used with respect to the property after the change.

(ii) For purposes of subparagraphs (1) and (2) of this paragraph, the unadjusted basis shall be the lesser of the fair market value or the adjusted basis of the property (taking into account the adjustments described in section 1016(a)(3)) at the time of the conversion to use in the taxpayer's trade or business (or for the production of income), or at the beginning of the taxable year in which the increase in business (or income-producing) use occurs, as the case may be. For purposes of subparagraphs (3)(i)(A) and (4)(i) of this paragraph, the unadjusted basis shall be the adjusted basis of the property (taking into account the adjustments described in section 1016(a)(2) and (3)) at the beginning of the year in which the change or cessation occurs.

(7) *Examples.*—The following examples illustrate the application of this paragraph:

Example (1). A, a calendar year taxpayer, purchases a house in 1981 which he occupies as his principal residence. In June 1985, A ceases to occupy the house and converts it to rental property. Under paragraph (j)(1) of this section, for purposes of determining the recovery allowance, A is deemed to have placed the house in service as recovery property in June 1985. A does not elect to compute the recovery allowance by use of the optional recovery method provided in § 1.168-2(c). Thus, A's recovery allowance under section 168 for 1985 is determined by multiplying the unadjusted basis of the

Proposed Regulations

property by .07. Under paragraph (j)(6)(ii) of this section, the unadjusted basis is the lesser of the property's basis or its fair market value in June 1985. See also section 280A and the regulations thereunder.

Example (2). In 1981, B (a calendar year taxpayer) purchases an automobile for $10,000. In taxable years 1981 through 1983, B's business use of the automobile is 60 percent of his total use. B does not elect use of the optional percentages provided in § 1.168-2(c). The fair market value of the automobile at the beginning of 1984 is $7,500. In 1984, B's business use of the automobile is 70 percent of the total. B's allowable deduction for 1984 is $187.50, computed as follows: $7,500 (lesser of basis or fair market value) × .25 (applicable percentage) × .10 (increase in the percentage business use in 1984 (70 percent) over the average business use during 1981-1983 (60 percent)). In 1985, B's business use of the automobile is 50 percent of the total. B is entitled to no recovery allowance with respect to the automobile for 1985 since B's business use of the automobile in that year does not exceed the average business use during 1981-1983 (60 percent). In 1986, B's business use of the automobile is 75 percent of the total. B's allowable deduction for 1986 is $416.25 computed as follows: $7,500 (lesser of basis or fair market value in 1984) × .37 (applicable percentage) × .15 (increase in the percentage business use in 1986 (75 percent) over the average business use during 1981-1983 (60 percent)).

Example (3). In 1981 C, a calendar year taxpayer, purchases for $20,000 and places in service section 1245 class property used predominantly in connection with research and experimentation. C does not elect to compute the recovery allowance by use of the optional method as provided in § 1.168-2(c). In 1981 C's allowable deduction is $5,000 (*i.e.,* .25 × $20,000). In 1982 C continues to use the property as recovery property, but not predominantly in connection with research and experimentation. As a result, in 1982 the property is treated as 5-year property. C's recovery allowance for 1982 (and subsequent taxable years) is determined as though C had placed the property in service in 1981 as 5-year property. The excess recovery allowance allowed in 1981 is accounted for in accordance with § 1.168-2(d)(3). Thus, the difference between the recovery allowance which would have been allowed had the applicable percentage for 5-year property been used (*i.e.,* .15 × $20,000 = $3,000) and the recovery allowance allowed in 1981 (*i.e.,* .25 × $20,000 = $5,000) equals $2,000 and is accounted for as follows:

Unadjusted basis × applicable percentage for second recovery year ($20,000.00 × .22)	$4,400.00
Excess allowance × applicable percentage for second recovery year ÷ the sum of the remaining unused applicable percentages (($2,000.00 × .22)/.85)	- 517.65
Difference—allowable deduction for 1982	$3,882.35

Example (4). In 1981 D, a calendar year taxpayer, places in service 5-year recovery property with an unadjusted basis of $100,000 and a present class life of 8 years. D uses the property predominantly outside the United States in 1981, 1982, and 1983. D does not elect to compute the recovery allowance by use of the optional method as provided in § 1.168-2(g)(3). In 1984 D uses the property as recovery property but not predominantly outside the United States. D's allowable deduction for 1984 (and subsequent taxable years) is determined as though D placed the property in service in 1984 as recovery property not used predominantly outside the United States. The basis of the property is deemed to be the adjusted basis in 1984. Thus, D's allowable deduction for 1984 is $7,350 (*i.e.,* .15 × $49,000 (basis)) and for 1985 is $10,780 (*i.e.,* .22 × $49,000 (basis)). If D elected to use the optional method based on the present class life, D would use the optional percentages based on a 5-year recovery period. Alternatively, D may continue to treat the property as though it continued to be used predominantly outside the United States. If so treated D's allowable deductions for 1984 and 1985 would be $12,000 (*i.e.,* .12 × $100,000) and $9,000 (.09 × $100,000), respectively.

Example (5). The facts are the same as in example (4) except that the recovery property is not used predominantly outside the United States for 1981 through 1983. In 1984, however, D begins using the property predominantly outside the United States. D's allowable deduction for 1984 is determined as though D placed the property in service in 1981 as property used predominantly outside the United States. Additionally, D accounts for the difference between the recovery allowance for 1981 through 1983 ($58,000) and the allowance which would have been allowable for those years had the applicable percentages for property used predominantly outside the United States been used

Proposed Regulations

($51,000) in accordance with § 1.168-2(d)(3). Thus, the recovery allowance in 1984 is $10,285.71, determined as follows:

Unadjusted basis × applicable percentage for 4th recovery year for property with an 8-year present class life ($100,000.00 × .12)	$12,000.00
Excess recovery from 1981 through 1983 × applicable percentage for 4th recovery year ÷ the sum of the remaining unused applicable percentages (($7,000.00 × .12)/.49)	- 1,714.29
Difference	$10,285.71

If, for 1981 through 1983, D elected to use the optional method based on a 5-year recovery period, then the allowable deduction for 1984 and subsequent taxable years would be determined using the optional percentages over the 8-year present class life.

(k) *Ratable inclusion rule.*—(1) *General rule.*—In general, the recovery allowance provided by section 168 and this section shall be considered as accruing ratably over the taxable year. Thus, for example, the distributive share of the recovery allowance for each partner in a partnership in which a partner's partnership interest varies so as to be subject to section 706(c)(2)(B) shall be determined by allocating to each partner a pro rata share of such allowance for the entire taxable year of the partnership. This paragraph does not apply, however, in determining the recovery allowance for the taxable year in which 15-year real property is placed in service or disposed of.

(2) *Example.*—The provisions of this subparagraph are illustrated by the following example:

Example. In 1978 A and B each acquire 50 percent interests in partnership P which is in the business of renting and managing beach resort property. On December 1, 1983, C and D each acquire from the partnership 25 percent interests in the partnership. On December 15, 1983, the partnership acquires for rental and places in service two sailboats (5-year recovery property) for $10,000 each. No election is made to use the optional recovery percentages provided by § 1.168-2(c). The recovery allowance for P for the sailboats in 1983 equals $3,000 (*i.e.,* .15 × $20,000). The recovery allowance, however, must be allocated pro rata over the taxable year. As such, the distributive share of the recovery allowance for A and B is $1,437.50 each. The distributive share of the recovery allowance for C and D is $62.50 each.

(l) *Definitions.*—For purposes of section 168 and § § 1.168-1 through 1.168-6—

(1) *Disposition.*—The term "disposition" means the permanent withdrawal of property from use in the taxpayer's trade or business or use for the production of income. Withdrawal may be made in several ways, including sale, exchange, retirement, abandonment, or destruction. A disposition does not include a transfer of property by gift or by reason of the death of the taxpayer. See § 1.168-5(f)(3) and (4). A disposition also does not include the retirement of a structural component of 15-year real property. The manner of disposition (*e.g.,* ordinary retirement, abnormal retirement) is not a consideration. For rules relating to nonrecognition transactions see section 168(f)(7) and (10)) and the regulations thereunder. For rules relating to the recognition of gain or loss on dispositions, see § 1.168-6.

(2) *Placed in service.*—The term "placed in service" means the time that property is first placed by the taxpayer in a condition or state of readiness and availability for a specifically assigned function, whether for use in a trade or business, for the production of income, in a tax-exempt activity, or in a personal activity. In the case of a building which is intended to house machinery and equipment, such readiness and availability shall be determined without regard to whether the machinery or equipment which the building houses, or is intended to house, has been placed in service. However, in an appropriate case, as, for example, where the building is essentially an item of machinery or equipment, or the use of the building is so closely related to the use of the machinery or equipment that it clearly can be expected to be replaced or retired when the property it initially houses is replaced or retired, the determination of readiness or availability of the building shall be made by taking into account the readiness and availability of such machinery or equipment. For a building which becomes available for use in separate stages, see paragraph (e)(3) of this section.

Proposed Regulations

(3) *Recovery year.*—The term "recovery year" means the taxable year during which recovery property is placed in service by the taxpayer and each subsequent taxable year for which a deduction is allowable to the taxpayer under this section with respect to such property.

(4) *Recovery period.*—The term "recovery period" means the actual period of years assigned, or elected by the taxpayer, for the computation under this section of the recovery allowance with respect to the unadjusted basis of the recovery property (*e.g.,* 3 years, 5 years, 12 years, present class life). The recovery period does not include any year after the end of the period assigned or elected, even though under paragraph (c), (g)(3), or (m) of this section a year following the recovery period may be a recovery year (as defined in subparagraph (3)).

(m) *Limitation on property financed with proceeds of industrial development bonds.*—[Reserved]

(n) [Withdrawn]

[Reg. § 1.168-2.]

¶ 530

Proposed Reg. § 1.168-3

Proposed Regulations

§ 1.168-3. **Recovery property,** LR-185-81, 2/16/84.

(a) *Recovery property.*—(1) *In general.*—Except as provided in § 1.168-4, "recovery property" to which ACRS applies means tangible property of a character subject to the allowance for depreciation which is—

(i) Used in a trade or business, or

(ii) Held for the production of income. Property is considered recovery property only if such property would have been depreciable under section 167. Thus, ACRS applies only to that part of the property which is subject to wear and tear, to decay or decline from natural causes, to exhaustion, and to obsolescence. ACRS does not apply to inventories or stock in trade, works of art, or to land apart from the improvements or physical development added to it. ACRS does not apply to natural resources which are subject to the allowance for depletion provided in section 611. No deduction shall be allowed under ACRS for automobiles or other vehicles used solely for pleasure, for a building used by the taxpayer solely as his residence, or for furniture or furnishings therein, personal effects, or clothing; but properties and costumes used exclusively in a business, such as a theatrical business, may be recovery property. For rules regarding the recovery allowance for property which is used partly for business and partly for personal purposes, or which is converted from personal to business use, see §§ 1.168-2(d)(2)(ii) and 1.168-2(j)(1) and (2).

(2) *Intangible property.*—[Reserved]

(3) *Boilers fueled by oil or gas.*—The term "recovery property" includes property described in section 167(p), relating to boilers fueled by oil or gas, if such property otherwise qualifies as "recovery property" under section 168 and subparagraph (1) of this paragraph.

(b) *Classes of recovery property.*—Each item of recovery property shall be assigned to one of the following classes of property:

(1) 3-year property,

(2) 5-year property,

(3) 10-year property,

(4) 15-year real property, or

(5) 15-year public utility property.

Any property which is treated as included in a class of property by reason of paragraph (c)(1), (2), (3), (4), or (5) of this § 1.168-3 shall not be treated as property included in any other class.

Proposed Regulations

(c) *3-, 5-, 10-, and 15-year recovery property; definitions.*—(1) *3-year property.*—The following recovery property is included in the 3-year class:

(i) Section 1245 class property (as defined in paragraph (c)(6) of this § 1.168-3) with a present class life (as defined in paragraph (c)(8)) of 4 years or less,

(ii) Section 1245 class property predominantly used in connection with research and experimentation (as described in section 174 and § 1.174-2(a)). Property is used in connection with research and experimentation if the property is used (A) by its owner to conduct research and experimentation in its owner's trade or business, (B) by its owner to conduct research and experimentation for another person, (C) by a lessee to conduct research and experimentation in its trade or business, or (D) by the lessee to conduct research and experimentation for another person, and

(iii) Any race horse which is more than 2 years old at the time the horse is placed in service and any other horse which is more than 12 years old at the time the horse is placed in service. A horse is more than 2 (or 12) years old after 24 (or 144) months after its actual birthdate.

Examples of 3-year recovery property are automobiles and light-duty trucks.

(2) *5-year property.*—The following recovery property is included in the 5-year class: Section 1245 class property which is not 3-year property (as defined in paragraph (c)(1)), or 10-year property (as defined in paragraph (c)(3)), or 15-year public utility property (as defined in paragraph (c)(5) and (10)). Included in the 5-year recovery property class are horses which are not included in the 3-year recovery property class, property which, prior to January 1, 1981, may have been depreciated under the retirement-replacement-betterment method (subject to the provisions of § 1.168-5(a)), single-purpose agricultural and horticultural structures, and storage facilities (other than buildings and their structural components) used in connection with the distribution of petroleum or any of its primary products. Primary products of petroleum are products described in § 1.993-3(g)(3)(i).

(3) *10-year property.*—The following recovery property is included in the 10-year class:

(i) Public utility property with a present class life of more than 18 years but not more than 25 years, other than section 1250 class property (as defined in paragraph (c)(7)) or 3-year property,

(ii) Section 1250 class property with a present class life of 12.5 years or less,

(iii) Railroad tank cars,

(iv) Manufactured homes (as defined in 42 U.S.C. section 5402(6)) which are section 1250 class property used as dwelling units, and

(v) Qualified coal utilization property (as defined in paragraph (c)(9)) which would otherwise be 15-year public utility property.

A building (and its structural components, if any) is not treated as having a present class life of 12.5 years or less if, in its original use (as defined in paragraph (c)(11) of this § 1.168-3), the building (and its structural components, if any) does not have a present class life of 12.5 years or less. Thus, for example, a theme park structure is considered 10-year property only if the original use of such structure is as a theme park structure.

(4) *15-year real property.*—Fifteen-year real property is section 1250 class property which does not have a present class life of 12.5 years or less (including section 1250 class property which does not have a present class life). Examples of 15-year real property are office buildings and elevators and escalators.

(5) *15-year public utility property.*—Fifteen-year public utility property is public utility property, other than section 1250 class property or 3-year property, with a present class life of more than 25 years. Examples of 15-year public utility property are: most property in electric utility steam production plants, gas utility manufactured gas production plants, water utility property, and telephone distribution plants.

(6) *Section 1245 class property defined.*—For purposes of section 168 and §§ 1.168-1 through 1.168-6, section 1245 class property is tangible property described in section 1245(a)(3) (other than subparagraphs (C) and (D)). See § 1.168-4 for exclusion of certain "section 1245 class property" from recovery property.

Proposed Regulations

(7) *Section 1250 class property defined.*—For purposes of section 168 and §§1.168-1 through 1.168-6, section 1250 class property is property described in section 1250(c) and property described in section 1245(a)(3)(C). See §1.168-4 for exclusion of certain "section 1250 class property" from recovery property.

(8) *Present class life defined.*—(i) For purposes of section 168 and §§1.168-1 through 1.168-6, present class life is the asset depreciation range (ADR) class life ("midpoint" or "asset guideline period") (if any) applicable with respect to the property as of January 1, 1981, published in Rev. Proc. 83-35. No changes will be made to the classes or class lives which are set forth in Rev. Proc. 83-35.

(ii) The application of subdivision (i) may be illustrated by the following example:

Example. X purchases a light-duty truck to be used in his trade or business. The ADR midpoint life of this asset as of January 1, 1981, determined under Rev. Proc. 83-35 is 4 years. Since this truck is section 1245 class property with a present class life of 4 years or less, it is 3-year recovery property under section 168.

(9) *Qualified coal utilization property.*—See section 168(g)(8) for the definition of "qualified coal utilization property".

(10) *Public utility property.*—(i) For purposes of section 168 and §§1.168-1 through 1.168-6, the term "public utility property" means property used predominantly in the trade or business of the furnishing or sale of—

(A) Electrical energy, water, or sewage disposal services,

(B) Gas or steam through a local distribution system,

(C) Telephone services, or other communication services if furnished or sold by the Communications Satellite Corporation for purposes authorized by the Communications Satellite Act of 1962 (47 U.S.C. section 701), or

(D) Transportation of gas or steam by pipeline, if the rates for such furnishing or sale, as the case may be, are regulated, *i.e.,* are established or approved by a State (including the District of Columbia) or political subdivision thereof, by any agency or instrumentality of the United States, or by a public service or public utility commission or other similar body of any State or political subdivision thereof. A taxpayer's rates are "regulated" if they are established or approved on a rate-of-return basis. Rates regulated on a rate-of-return basis are an authorization to collect revenues that cover the taxpayer's cost of providing goods or services, including a fair return on the taxpayer's investment in providing such goods or services, where the taxpayer's costs and investment are determined by use of a uniform system of accounts prescribed by the regulatory body. A taxpayer's rates are not "regulated" if they are established or approved on the basis of maintaining competition within an industry, insuring adequate service to customers of an industry, insuring adequate security for loans, or charging "reasonable" rates within an industry since the taxpayer is not authorized to collect revenues based on the taxpayer's cost of providing goods or services. Rates are considered to be "established or approved" if a schedule of rates is filed with a regulatory body that has the power to approve such rates, even though the regulatory body takes no action on the filed schedule or generally leaves undisturbed rates filed by the taxpayer.

(ii) Public utility property includes property which is leased to others by a taxpayer, where the leasing of such property is part of the lessor's public utility activity, as described in subdivision (i). Public utility property also includes property leased to a person who uses such property predominantly in a public utility activity, as described in subdivision (i).

(11) *"Original use".*—The term "original use" means the first use to which the property is put, whether or not such use corresponds to the use of such property by the taxpayer. [Reg. §1.168-3.]

¶ 535

Proposed Reg. § 1.168-4

Proposed Regulations

»»→ ***Note: The text of the Preamble to the Proposed Regulation is at ¶ 49,045.***

§ 1.168-4. **Exclusions from ACRS,** LR-185-81, 2/16/84.

(a) *Property placed in service by the taxpayer before January 1, 1981.*—ACRS does not apply with respect to property placed in service by the taxpayer before January 1, 1981. See § 1.168-2(l)(2) for when property is placed in service. As provided in paragraph (d) of this section, ACRS does not apply with respect to property placed in service before January 1, 1981, which is transferred in certain "churning" transactions. If property is excluded from ACRS, the provisions of section 167 (and related provisions) apply in determining the allowable depreciation deduction with respect to such property.

(b) *Property amortized or depreciated other than in terms of years.*—(1) *Depreciation.*—If—

(i) Property can properly be depreciated under a method not expressed in a term of years (such as unit-of-production) which, before January 1, 1981, was a recognized method within the particular industry for the type of property in question, and

(ii) The taxpayer properly elects such treatment for such property in accordance with section 168(f)(4) and § 1.168-5(e) for the first taxable year for which an ACRS deduction would (but for this election) be allowable with respect to such property in the hands of the taxpayer,

then such property shall be entirely excluded from ACRS so long as it remains in the hands of such taxpayer. A taxpayer may elect to apply a depreciation method not expressed in a term of years (and thereby exclude the property from ACRS) with respect to some or all property within the same recovery class and placed in service in the same taxable year.

(2) *Amortization.*—If—

(i) The basis of a recovery property may be amortized, in lieu of being depreciated, under any section of the Code (such as section 167(k), relating to expenditures to rehabilitate low-income rental housing, or section 169, relating to pollution control facilities), and

(ii) The taxpayer properly elects to amortize such property in accordance with the relevant amortization provision,

then the amount subject to such amortization shall be excluded from the property's unadjusted basis as defined in section 168(d)(1)(A) and § 1.168-2(d). A taxpayer may elect amortization with respect to one property (or a portion thereof) and apply ACRS with respect to other property (or the remaining portion) within the same recovery class and placed in service in the same taxable year.

(c) *Special rule for public utility property.*—[Reserved]

(d) *Anti-churning rules for certain transactions in property placed in service before 1981.*—(1) *In general.*—To be eligible for ACRS, property must be placed in service by the taxpayer after 1980. The anti-churning rules of section 168(e)(4) and this paragraph (d) are designed generally to deny ACRS to property in service before 1981 in the absence of a significant change in ownership or use.

(2) *Section 1245 class property.*—(i) *In general.*—Section 1245 class property, as defined in section 168(g)(3) and § 1.168-3(c)(6), acquired by the taxpayer after December 31, 1980, will not qualify for ACRS if—

(A) The property was owned or used at any time during 1980 by the taxpayer or a related person,

(B) The property is acquired from a person who owned such property at any time during 1980, and, as part of the transaction, the user of the property does not change,

(C) The property is leased by the taxpayer for more than 3 months to a person (or a person related to such person) who owned or used such property at any time during 1980, or

Proposed Regulations

(D) The property is acquired in a transaction in which the user of such property does not change, and the property does not qualify for ACRS in the hands of the person from whom the property is so acquired due to subdivisions (B) and (C) of this paragraph (d)(2)(i).

See section 168(e)(4)(D) and subparagraph (6) of this paragraph (d) for definition of the term "related person". See subparagraph (3) of this paragraph (d) for the treatment of the acquisition of section 1245 class property acquired incidental to the acquisition of section 1250 class property. See subparagraph (4) of this paragraph (d) for other special rules.

(ii) *Change in user.*—For purposes of subdivision (i) of this paragraph (d)(2), the user of a section 1245 class property shall not be considered to have changed as part of a transaction if the property is physically used, for more than 3 months after its transfer, by the same person (or a related person) who used such property before the transfer, or if such person, pursuant to a plan, resumes use of the property after the transfer. If the former owner (or a related person) continues to operate section 1245 class property through an arrangement such as a management contract for more than 3 months after the transfer, then all facts and circumstances will be taken into account in determining whether the user of the property has changed as part of such transaction for purposes of section 168(e)(4)(A) and subdivision (i) of this paragraph (d)(2). Among the factors which would indicate that the user of section 1245 property has changed in such case are—

(A) The arrangement in question is a customary commercial practice,

(B) The transaction in question has been arranged at arm's length, and

(C) The new owner has assumed all benefits and burdens of ownership. For purposes of this subdivision (ii)(C), the former owner will not be considered to have retained any benefits and burdens of ownership solely by reason of receiving contingent payments if such payments—

(1) Represent the real value of services rendered,

(2) Are reasonable in amount, and

(3) Are ordinary and customary in both nature and amount within the industry and region for the transaction in question.

(3) *Section 1250 class property.*—A section 1250 class property, as defined in section 168(g)(4) and § 1.168-3(c)(7), acquired by the taxpayer after December 31, 1980, will not qualify for ACRS if—

(i) The property was owned at any time during 1980 by the taxpayer or a related person,

(ii) The property is leased by the taxpayer for more than 3 months to a person (or a person related to such person) who owned such property at any time during 1980, or

(iii) The property is acquired in an exchange described in section 1031 (relating to exchange of property held for productive use or investment), section 1033 (relating to involuntary conversions), section 1038 (relating to certain reacquisitions of real property), or section 1039 (relating to certain sales of low-income housing projects), to the extent that the basis of such property includes an amount representing the adjusted basis of other property owned by the taxpayer or a related person at any time during 1980. The excess of the basis of the property acquired over the adjusted basis of such other property shall be considered a separate item of property, eligible for ACRS, provided that the exchange is not otherwise treated as a "churning" transaction under section 168(e)(4) and this paragraph. Property which does not qualify for ACRS under this subdivision shall be considered, for purposes of this section, as owned by the taxpayer during 1980.

See section 168(e)(4)(D) and subparagraph (6) of this paragraph (d) for definition of the term "related person". If, in a transaction, section 1245 class property is acquired incidental to the acquisition of section 1250 class property, then the rules of section 168(e)(4)(B) and this subparagraph shall apply with respect to the section 1245 property acquired in such transaction instead of the rules of section 168(e)(4)(A) and paragraph (d)(2) of this section. The preceding sentence will not apply in transactions where section 1245 property constitutes a significant portion of the property acquired.

Proposed Regulations

(4) *Special rules.*—(i) *Property under construction during 1980.*—For purposes of paragraph (d)(2) and (3) of this section, a taxpayer shall not be deemed to own property under construction during 1980 until it is placed in service, as described in § 1.168-2(1)(2).

(ii) *Entire property excluded.*—Except as provided in paragraph (d)(3)(iii) of this section (relating to excess basis in substituted basis transactions), subdivision (iii) of this paragraph (d)(4) (relating to the lease of a portion of section 1250 class property), and paragraph (d)(6)(ii)(C) of this section (relating to transactions between persons related by reason of the application of § 1.267(b)-1(b)), if property is acquired in a transaction described in paragraph (d)(2) or (3) of this section, the entire property shall be excluded from ACRS.

(iii) *Lease of portion of section 1250 class property.*—Paragraph (d)(3)(ii) of this section (relating to the lease of section 1250 class property) shall apply only with respect to that portion of the property (determined on a fair market value basis) that is leased to the person (or to a person related to such person) who owned the property during 1980. The portion of the property excluded from ACRS shall not exceed the portion of the property which was owned by the lessee (or a person related to the lessee) during 1980.

(iv) *Undivided interests.*—Subject to the provisions of paragraph (d)(7) of this section (relating to avoidance), if an undivided interest in property is acquired, and the resulting arrangement is not a partnership for tax purposes, then such interest shall be treated as a separate item of property for purposes of paragraph (d)(2) and (3) of this section.

(v) *Acquisition by or lease to 1980 owner or user.*—If recovery property is acquired by, or leased to, its 1980 owner (or, in the case of section 1245 class property, its 1980 owner or user), or a related person, then the property shall cease to qualify for ACRS.

(vi) *Sale-leaseback of disqualified property.*—If property which does not qualify for ACRS under this section becomes the subject of a sale-leaseback transaction, then the property shall not become ACRS property by virtue of that transaction.

(5) *Certain nonrecognition transactions.*—(i) *In general.*—With respect to property placed in service by the transferor or distributor before January 1, 1981, and which is acquired by the taxpayer after December 31, 1980, in a nonrecognition transaction described in section 168(e)(4)(C) and in subdivision (ii) of this paragraph (d)(5), ACRS shall not apply to the extent that the property's basis in the hands of the taxpayer is determined by reference to its basis in the hands of the transferor or distributor. In such a transaction, the taxpayer shall be treated as the transferor or distributor for purposes of computing the depreciation allowance under section 167 with respect to so much of the basis of the acquired property in the hands of the taxpayer as does not exceed its adjusted basis in the hands of the transferor or distributor. However, the taxpayer shall treat the portion of the basis of the acquired property which exceeds the adjusted basis in the hands of the transferor or distributor as a separate item of property, eligible for ACRS, provided that sale or exchange of such property by the transferor or distributor to the taxpayer would not be treated as a "churning" transaction under section 168(e)(4) and this paragraph.

(ii) *Nonrecognition transactions affected.*—Subdivision (i) of this paragraph (d)(5) applies to transactions described in any of the following provisions:

(A) Section 332 (relating to distributions in complete liquidation of an 80 percent or more controlled subsidiary corporation) except where the basis of the assets distributed is determined under section 334(b)(2) (as in effect on August 31, 1982);

(B) Section 351 (relating to transfer to a corporation controlled by transferor);

(C) Section 361 (relating to exchanges pursuant to certain corporate reorganizations);

(D) Section 371(a) (relating to exchanges pursuant to certain receivership and bankruptcy proceedings);

Proposed Regulations

(E) Section 374(a) (relating to exchanges pursuant to certain railroad reorganizations);

(F) Section 721 (relating to transfers to a partnership in exchange for a partnership interest); and

(G) Section 731 (relating to distributions by a partnership to a partner).

A distribution of property by a partnership to a partner in liquidation of the partner's interest in the partnership (where the basis of the distributed property to the partner is determined under section 732(b)) is not a transaction described in section 168(e)(4)(C) and this subdivision (ii) since, in such case, the basis of the property is determined by reference to the partner's adjusted basis in his interest in the partnership and not by reference to the basis of the property in the hands of the partnership. However, such distribution may be described in paragraph (d)(2) or (3) of this section.

(iii) *Successive application.*—Property which does not qualify for ACRS by reason of its acquisition in a nonrecognition transaction will not qualify for ACRS if it is subsequently transferred in another nonrecognition transaction. The preceding sentence shall apply to the extent that the basis of the property in the hands of the transferee does not exceed the basis that does not qualify for ACRS in the hands of the transferor.

(6) *Related person defined.*—(i) *In general.*—For purposes of this paragraph (d) except as provided in section 168(e)(4)(E) and in subparagraph (11) of this paragraph (d), persons are related if—

(A) They bear a relationship specified in section 267(b) or section 707(b)(1) and the regulations thereunder, or

(B) They are engaged in trades or businesses under common control (as defined by subsections (a) and (b) of section 52 and the regulations thereunder).

For purposes of applying section 267(b) and 707(b)(1) with respect to this paragraph (d)(6), "10 percent" shall be substituted for "50 percent".

(ii) *Special rules.*—(A) In general, persons are related if they are related either immediately before or immediately after the taxpayer's acquisition of the property in question. When a partnership's acquisition of property results from the termination of another partnership under section 708(b)(1)(B), whether the acquiring partnership is related to such other partnership shall be determined by comparing the ownership of the acquiring partnership immediately after the acquisition with that of the terminated partnership as it existed immediately before the event resulting in such termination occurs. Similarly, when the acquisition of property by a partner results from the termination of a partnership under section 708(b)(1)(A), whether the acquiring person is related to the partnership shall be determined immediately before the event resulting in such termination occurs.

(B) If a person would be related to a corporation, partnership, or trust which owned (or, in the case of section 1245 class property, owned or used) property during 1980 but for the fact that such corporation, partnership, or trust is no longer in existence when the taxpayer acquires such property, then, for purposes of this subparagraph (6), such corpora tion, partnership, or trust is deemed to be in existence when the taxpayer acquires such property. Similarly, when a taxpayer leases property to a newly-created corporation, partnership, or trust, and a person who owned (or, in the case of section 1245 class property, owned or used) such property during 1980 would be related to the lessee but for the fact that such corporation, partnership, or trust is not in existence when the taxpayer acquires such property, then, for purposes of this subparagraph (6), such corporation, partnership, or trust is deemed to be in existence when the taxpayer acquires such property.

(C) If persons are related by reason of the application of § 1.267(b)-1(b), then only a portion of the property shall be excluded from ACRS, consistent with the principles of § 1.267(b)-1(b). See, however, paragraph (d)(7) of this section (relating to avoidance).

(D) If persons are not considered to be engaged in trades or businesses under common control (as defined by subsections (a) and (b) of section 52 and the regulations thereunder), but are considered to be related persons by substituting "10 percent" for "50 percent" within the provisions of section 267(b) or 707(b)(1), then such persons are considered to be related persons for purposes of this subparagraph (6).

Proposed Regulations

(7) *Avoidance purpose indicated.*—Property acquired by the taxpayer after December 31, 1980, does not qualify for ACRS if it is acquired in a transaction one of whose principal purposes is to avoid the operation of the effective date rule of section 168(e)(1) and the "anti-churning" rules of section 168(e)(4), and the rules of this section. A transaction will be presumed to have a principal purpose of avoidance if it does not effect a significant change in ownership or use of property in service before 1981 commensurate with that otherwise required for ACRS to apply. Among the circumstances in which a principal avoidance purpose may be indicated, and in which the property involved in the transfer may therefore be ineligible for ACRS, are—

(i) The same person owns (other than as a nominee), directly or indirectly, more than a 10 percent interest in the taxpayer (or the taxpayer's lessee) and in a person who owned (or, in the case of section 1245 class property, owned or used) the property during 1980;

(ii) There is a mere change in form of the ownership of property owned by a person during 1980 (such as from a partnership to undivided interests);

(iii) The taxpayer (or the taxpayer's lessee) and a person who owned (or, in the case of section 1245 class property, owned or used) the property during 1980 are engaged in trades or businesses under common control within the meaning of section 52(a) and (b) and the regulations thereunder, substituting a 25 percent test for the 50 percent tests of § 1.52-1, or there is a similar 25 percent common ownership in the property (or in a leasehold of the property) and in a person who owned (or, in the case of section 1245 class property, owned or used) the property during 1980;

(iv) The taxpayer (or the taxpayer's lessee) is related during 1980 to the person who owned (or, in the case of section 1245 class property, owned or used) the property during 1980;

(v) Section 1250 class property is operated by a person who owned such property during 1980 (or by a related person) under a management contract and, had such property been section 1245 class property instead of section 1250 class property, the user would be considered not to have changed as part of the transaction (see § 1.168-4(d)(2)(ii));

(vi) The taxpayer leases section 1250 class property to a person and, through one or more subleases, the property is leased to a person who owned such property during 1980 (or to a related person); or

(vii) Section 1245 class property is acquired in an exchange described in section 1031, relating to exchange of property held for productive use or investment, to the extent that the basis of such property includes an amount representing the adjusted basis of other property owed by the taxpayer or a related person at any time during 1980. In the case of property which does not qualify for ACRS under this subdivision, rules similar to those of paragraph (d)(3)(iii) of this section shall apply.

In general, the avoidance intent indicated in subdivisions (i) through (vii) may be rebutted by evidence of an overriding business purpose (or purposes) for the transaction. However, even if the taxpayer demonstrates an overriding business purpose (or purposes) for the transaction, the property will not qualify for ACRS if the Internal Revenue Service establishes that one of the principal purposes of the transaction is to avoid the operation of the effective date rule of section 168(e)(1) and the "anti-churning" rules of section 168(e)(4), and the rules of this section.

(8) *Adjustment to basis of partnership property.*—ACRS shall not apply with respect to any adjustment to the basis of partnership property made under section 734(b) (relating to the optional adjustment to the basis of undistributed partnership property) or section 743(b) (relating to the optional adjustment to the basis of partnership property) if the partnership property itself does not qualify for ACRS because of section 168(e) and this section. If a partnership has property which qualifies for ACRS, see § 1.168-2(n) for the application of ACRS to the adjustments, pursuant to section 734(b) or 743(b), to the basis of such property.

(9) *Acquisitions by reason of death.*—Property acquired by the taxpayer after December 31, 1980, by reason of death, for which the basis is determined under section 1014(a), is eligible for ACRS.

(10) *Reduction in unadjusted basis.*—The unadjusted basis of property for purposes of section 168(d)(1) and § 1.168-2(d) shall be reduced to the extent that such property does not qualify for ACRS due to the application of this paragraph (d). The basis

Proposed Regulations

not taken into account for ACRS purposes pursuant to the preceding sentence shall be taken into account by the taxpayer for purposes of other provisions of the Code.

(11) *Certain corporate transactions.*—For purposes of section 168(e)(4) and § 1.168-4(d)(6), a corporation is not related to a distributee (or, in the case of a transaction described in section 338, the new target corporation) if—

(i) Such corporation is a distributing corporation in a transaction to which section 334(b)(2)(B) (as in effect on August 31, 1982) applies, or is a target corporation for which an election under section 338 is made, and at least 80 percent of the stock of such corporation (as described in section 334(b)(2)(B) or 338(d)(3)) is acquired by purchase after December 31, 1980, or

(ii) Such corporation is a distributing corporation in a complete liquidation to which section 331(a) applies, or a partial liquidation to which section 331(a) (as in effect on August 31, 1982) applies, or to which section 302(b)(4) applies, and the distributee (or a related person) by himself or together with one or more persons acquires the amount of stock specified in subdivision (i) of this paragraph (d)(11) by purchase after December 31, 1980.

(e) *Examples.*—The application of this section may be illustrated by the following examples:

Example (1). In 1978 A buys a house which he uses as his family residence. In 1983, A's family moves out, and A converts the house into rental property. A may not use ACRS with respect to the property because he placed it in service before 1981. A must depreciate the property in accordance with section 167 and the regulations thereunder, subject to the other applicable provisions of the Code.

Example (2). In 1982 X Corp. purchases and places in service two major pieces of manufacturing equipment. One is newly constructed, while the other is a used machine expected to produce only 5,000 additional units. X elects to depreciate the used machine under the unit-of-production method. Such method was properly used within X's industry before 1981. Assuming that X has met the requirements of section 168(f)(4) and § 1.168-5(e), the used machine will not be recovery property as defined in section 168(c)(1) and § 1.168-3(a). X will apply ACRS with respect to the new machine even though it properly elected to apply the unit-of-production method with respect to the used machine.

Example (3). On November 15, 1984, B, a calendar year taxpayer, places in service a 10-unit apartment building for individuals and families of low income under section 8 of the United States Housing Act of 1937. B acquired the building for $100,000 and has incurred an additional $100,000 of expenditures for its rehabilitation, which B elects to amortize under section 167(k). In 1984, B is entitled to an allowance under ACRS of $2,000 (*i.e.*, .02 × $100,000). The $100,000 which B amortizes under section 167(k) is not included in the unadjusted basis and therefore is not recovered under the provisions of ACRS.

Example (4). C is an individual engaged in the trucking business. On February 1, 1983, C purchases a new truck from a dealer. As is his normal business practice, C financed the transaction partly by trading in a truck C had used in his business for the previous 3 years. Although this transaction is described in section 1031, it does not have as one of its principal purposes avoidance of the rules of section 168(e)(1) and (4). C therefore will use ACRS with respect to the entire unadjusted basis of the truck purchased in 1983, including cash paid, indebtedness incurred, and the amount attributable to the adjusted basis of the used truck traded in.

Example (5). On June 1, 1983, in a transaction described in section 1031, Corporation M exchanges a corporate jet, acquired before 1981, for a very similar corporate jet owned and also acquired before 1981 by unrelated Corporation N. There is no significant difference to M or N in the use of the jet acquired from that of the jet exchanged, and the operations of each corporation do not change significantly as a result of the transaction. These facts and circumstances indicate that one of the principal purposes of this transaction is to avoid the principles of paragraphs (1) and (4) of section 168(e). Thus, absent evidence of an overriding business purpose (or purposes) for the transaction, neither of the jets will be treated as recovery property. Further, even if an overriding business purpose (or purposes) for the transaction is (or are) demonstrated, the property will not be eligible for ACRS if the Internal Revenue Service establishes that one of the principal purposes of the transaction is to avoid the principles of paragraphs (1) and (4) of section 168(e). The result in this example would be the same if, after the exchange, M

Proposed Regulations

or N sold the acquired property and leased it back, or sold the property to a related person.

Example (6). Z Corp., owner and largest occupant of the Z Building since 1965, sells this building to an institutional investor, M Corp., on May 1, 1983. After this sale, 25 percent of the Z Building is leased to Z until May 1, 1985. Because 25 percent of the Z Building is leased for more than 3 months by Z, which owned the building during 1980, M may not take ACRS deductions with respect to this 25 percent portion. Such portion must be depreciated in accordance with section 167. However, ACRS will apply with respect to the portion of the Z Building which is not leased by Z for more than 3 months after the above-described sale. If Z had leased the building only until July 31, 1983, then M Corp. would apply ACRS with respect to the entire building.

Example (7). During 1980 O Corp. undertakes construction of a department store which becomes available for its assigned business function on April 1, 1981. For purposes of section 168(e)(4)(B), O is not treated as owning the department store building under construction until it placed it in service on April 1, 1981. Accordingly, ACRS will apply with respect to the building, beginning on the day it is placed in service.

Example (8). On June 1, 1983, P Corp. sells an undivided 70 percent interest in a building it has owned since March 1, 1980, to Q Corp. which is not related to P. R Corp., which is not related to P, has occupied the building as a tenant since June 1980 and will continue to occupy it after this sale. P and Q will own the building as tenants-in-common. Q, but not P, will take ACRS deductions with respect to its portion of the building. The fact that the user of the building did not change will not affect this result. However, if P and Q had formed a partnership which owned the building after the sale, no portion of the building would qualify for ACRS because the taxpayer acquiring the property after 1980 (the partnership) would be related under section 168(e)(4)(D) to a person (P) which owned the building in 1980.

Example (9). On January 1, 1984, D, a 20 percent partner in Partnership W, sells his entire partnership interest to E for $400,000. Partnership W has one asset, a building it placed in service before 1981. D's adjusted basis in his partnership interest, allocable entirely to the building, is $200,000 when it is sold. A valid election under section 754 is in effect with respect to the sale of the partnership interest. Accordingly, Partnership W makes an adjustment pursuant to section 743(b) to increase the basis of the building with respect to E from $200,000 to $400,000. Under the provisions of § 1.168-4(d)(8) no portion of the increase in the basis of the partnership property with respect to E is eligible for ACRS because the partnership property itself does not qualify for ACRS due to the provisions of section 168(e)(1) and § 1.168-4(a).

Example (10). In 1983, F, an individual, sells a piece of business equipment he placed in service in 1980 to X, a partnership in which F owns a 20 percent interest. No portion of such equipment will qualify for ACRS since it was acquired after 1980 by the taxpayer (Partnership X) and was owned during 1980 by a related person (partner P). The result in this example would not be changed if F owned no interest in X in 1980.

Example (11). G, an individual, has owned an apartment building containing furnished apartments since 1979. On June 1, 1983, G sells the building and its furnishings to unrelated Partnership Y. The furniture was purchased by G before 1981. Most of these apartments will continue to be occupied by the same tenants who occupied them before the sale. For purposes of section 168(e)(4)(I) and § 1.168-4(d)(3), the furniture is acquired incidental to the acquisition of the building. Therefore, ACRS will apply with respect to the furniture, notwithstanding that many of the tenants who use the furniture do not change as part of the transaction.

Example (12). On June 1, 1983, Partnership Z purchases a factory which has been leased by Corporation S, an unrelated person, since 1979. Corporation S continues to use this factory for more than 3 months after the sale. The pre-1981 section 1245 class property transferred in this transaction, such as machinery and equipment, represents a significant portion of the unadjusted basis of the property purchased by Z. Since the unadjusted basis of such section 1245 class property is significant in relation to the factory's unadjusted basis, for purposes of section 168(e)(4)(I) and § 1.168-4(d)(3), the machinery and equipment are not acquired incidental to the acquisition of the factory. Since the user of such machinery and equipment does not change as part of the transaction, Partnership Z may not use ACRS with respect to such section 1245 class property. However, Z will use ACRS with respect to the factory and the other section 1250 class property acquired.

Proposed Regulations

Example (13). Partnership W, in which Partner E holds a 25 percent interest, has as its sole asset an office building it placed in service in 1980. On May 1, 1983, E dies, and his partnership interest, whose basis is determined under section 1014, passes to his daughter, D. ACRS is not available with respect to any increase in the basis of the partnership property with respect to D, because the partnership property itself does not qualify for ACRS due to the provisions of section 168(e)(1) and § 1.168-4(a).

Example (14). On July 1, 1983, Corporation X sells a building it had owned in 1980 to Corporation Y, an unrelated person. X retains an option to repurchase this building within 5 years. This building qualifies as recovery property in Y's hands, and Y will take ACRS deductions under section 168 with respect to it. On July 1, 1985, X exercises its option and repurchases the building. When X repurchases the building, it ceases to be recovery property because the taxpayer (X) owned the building during 1980. X may not take ACRS deductions with respect to the repurchased building. Instead, X must depreciate it under section 167 and the regulations thereunder.

Example (15). F, an individual, sells his business (including section 1245 class property owned in 1980) to G, on August 1, 1983. Under their arrangement, F continues to manage the business for G, using the same equipment he had previously used. F receives as compensation for managing the business a fixed salary plus 5 percent of the gross profits. The arrangement follows customary commercial practice and was negotiated by F and G at arm's length. In addition, the amounts received (including the 5 percent of gross profits) represent the real value of the services rendered by F and are reasonable in amount. Further, receipt of 5 percent of gross profits under these circumstances is an ordinary and customary feature in the sale of a business in the industry and region in question. This arrangement results in a sufficient change in the ownership and use of the equipment that G will recover the cost of such equipment under ACRS.

Example (16). Individuals J and K each own a 50 percent interest in Partnership X, whose only asset is a building placed in service before 1981. On August 1, 1983, H, an individual, purchases a 25 percent interest each from J and K. Partnership X is deemed under section 708(b)(1)(B) to have terminated when H purchases the 50 percent interest. The building is not eligible for ACRS because the taxpayer acquiring the property after 1980 (the new partnership formed by H, J, and K) is related to the person who owned the property during 1980 (the old partnership), since J and K own more than a 10 percent interest in each of the two partnerships.

Example (17). In 1980, individual A owns all of the stock of Corporation T, which in turn owns depreciable property. In 1982, A sells the stock of T to unrelated Corporation V. Shortly thereafter, T sells some of the depreciable property it owned in 1980 to A. Under section 168(e)(4)(D), the property is not owned during 1980 by a person related to the taxpayer (A) since A is not related to the 1980 owner (T) when A acquires the property. However, an avoidance purpose is indicated under § 1.168-4(d)(7)(iv) since A was related in 1980 to the 1980 owner (T). Also, A broke the relationship with T shortly before acquiring the property. Accordingly, A may not use ACRS with respect to the property acquired, unless he can demonstrate an overriding business purpose (or purposes) for the transaction. Further, even if an overriding business purpose (or purposes) for the transaction is (or are) demonstrated, the property will not be eligible for ACRS if the Internal Revenue Service establishes that one of the principal purposes of the transaction is to avoid the principles of paragraphs (1) and (4) of section 168(e).

Example (18). In 1980, individual B owns all of the stock of Corporations X and Y. In 1980, X owns depreciable property. In 1981, X liquidates. In 1982, B sells to Y property owned by X in 1980. Y may not use ACRS with respect to the acquired property. Since the taxpayer (Y) would be related to the 1980 owner (X) but for the fact that X is no longer in existence when Y acquires the property, then, under § 1.168-4(d)(6)(ii)(B), X is considered to be in existence for purposes of determining whether the property was owned (or used) by a related person during 1980.

Example (19). In 1980, individual C owns all of the stock of Corporation M, which in turn owns all of the stock of Corporation N. In 1980, N owns depreciable property. In 1981, N distributes such 1980 property to M. In 1982, M sells the N stock to an unrelated person. In 1983, M distributes to C the property it received from N. Under section 168(e)(4)(D), the property is not owned during 1980 by a person related to the taxpayer (C), since C is not related to the 1980 owner (N) when C acquires the property. However, under § 1.168-4(d)(7)(iv) an avoidance purpose is indicated since the taxpayer (C) is related in 1980 to the 1980 owner (N). Also, upon acquisition, C is related to the person from whom the property is acquired (M). Therfore, C may not use ACRS with respect to

Proposed Regulations

the property unless he demonstrates an overriding business purpose (or purposes) for the transaction. Further, even if an overriding business purpose (or purposes) for the transaction is (or are) demonstrated, the property will not be eligible for ACRS if the Internal Revenue Service establishes that one of the principal purposes of the transaction is to avoid the principles of paragraphs (1) and (4) of section 168(e).

Example (20). D owns 20 percent of Corporation X and a 20 percent interest in Partnership P. X owns depreciable property in 1980. In 1981, X sells the property to P. Under § 1.267(b)-1(b), the sale is considered as occurring between X and the members of the partnership (including D) separately. Accordingly, under the principles of § 1.267(b)-1(b), 20 percent of the unadjusted basis of the property is excluded from ACRS. In addition, under § 1.168-4(d)(7)(i) an avoidance purpose is indicated since D owns more than a 10 percent interest in the taxpayer (P) and the person who owned the property during 1980 (X). Therefore, ACRS is not available with respect to the remainder of the unadjusted basis of the property unless an overriding business purpose (or purposes) for the transaction is (or are) demonstrated. Further, even if an overriding business purpose (or purposes) for the transaction is (or are) demonstrated, the property will not be eligible for ACRS if the Internal Revenue Service establishes that one of the principal purposes of the transaction is to avoid the principles of paragraphs (1) and (4) of section 168(e).

Example (21). In 1980, E leases section 1245 class property to F. In 1982, at the termination of the lease, F purchases the property from E and continues to use it for more than 3 months after the sale. F is not entitled to use ACRS with respect to the property since, as part of the transaction, the user of the property did not change. The result in this example would be the same if, instead of selling the property to F, E sold the property to G, subject to F's lease, with F's use continuing for more than 3 months after the sale.

Example (22). In 1980, H and I each own section 1245 class property which they use in their respective businesses. In 1981, H and I swap titles to the property, with the parties continuing to use the same property as before the exchange. Neither H nor I is entitled to use ACRS with respect to the acquired property, since the user of the property does not change as part of the transaction.

Example (23). A owns section 1250 class property in 1980. In 1981, A sells the property to B who leases it back to A. B later sells the property to C, subject to A's lease. ACRS is not available with respect to the property in the hands of C since the taxpayer (C) leases the property to a person who owned it during 1980 (A).

Example (24). D owns section 1250 class property in 1980. In 1981, D transfers the property to E (an unrelated person) in exchange for property of a like kind in a transaction described in section 1031. Subsequently, D sells to and leases back from F the property acquired from E. Under § 1.168-4(d)(3)(iii), the property acquired from E is considered to have been owned by D in 1980. Therefore, ACRS is not available with respect to such property in the hands of F since the taxpayer (F) leases the property to a person who owned it during 1980 (D). The result in this example would be the same if, instead of selling the property to F, D sold it to G (regardless of whether G leased it back to D), a person related to D under section 168(e)(4)(D) and § 1.168-4(d)(6).

Example (25). In 1980, Corporation X places in service section 1245 class property. In 1981, X merges into Corporation Y in a transaction described in section 368(a)(1)(A). Subsequently, Y sells to and leases back from Z the 1980 section 1245 class property acquired from X in the merger. Under § 1.168-4(d)(4)(vi), ACRS is not available with respect to the property in the hands of Z. [Reg. § 1.168-4.]

¶ 537

Reg. § 1.168-5

§ 1.168-5. **Special rules.**—(a) *Retirement-replacement-betterment (RRB) property.*—(1) *RRB replacement property placed in service before January 1, 1985.*—(i) Except as provided in paragraph (a)(1)(ii) of this section, the recovery deduction for the taxable year for retirement-replacement-betterment (RRB) replacement property (as defined in paragraph (a)(3) of this section) placed in service before January 1, 1985, shall be (in lieu of the amount determined under section 168(b)) an amount determined by applying to the unadjusted basis (as defined in section

168(d)(1) and regulations thereunder) of such property the applicable percentage determined in accordance with the following table:

If the recovery year is:	*And the year the property is placed in service is:*			
	1981	*1982*	*1983*	*1984*
	The applicable percentage is:			
1	100	50	33	25
2		50	45	38
3			22	25
4				12

(ii) The provisions of paragraph (a)(1)(i) of this section do not apply to any taxpayer who did not use the RRB method of depreciation under section 167 as of December 31, 1980. In such case, RRB replacement property placed in service by the taxpayer after December 31, 1980, shall be treated as other 5-year recovery property under section 168.

(2) *RRB replacement property placed in service after December 31, 1984.*—RRB replacement property placed in service after December 31, 1984, is treated as other 5-year recovery property under section 168.

(3) *RRB replacement property defined.*—RRB replacement property, for purposes of section 168, means replacement track material (including rail, ties, other track material, and ballast) installed by a railroad (including a railroad switching or terminal company) if—

(i) The replacement is made pursuant to a scheduled program for replacement,

(ii) The replacement is made pursuant to observations by maintenance-of-way personnel of specific track material needing replacement,

(iii) The replacement is made pursuant to the detection by a rail-test car of specific track material needing replacement, or

(iv) The replacement is made as a result of a casualty.

Replacements made as a result of a casualty shall be RRB replacement property only to the extent that, in the case of each casualty, the replacement cost with respect to the replacement track material exceeds $50,000.

(4) *Recovery of adjusted basis of RRB property as of December 31, 1980.*—The taxpayer shall recover the adjusted basis of RRB property (as defined in section 168(g)(6)) as of December 31, 1980, over a period of not less than 5 years and not more than 50 years, using a rate of recovery consistent with any method described in section 167(b), including the method described in section 167(b)(2), switching to the method described in section 167(b)(3) at a time to maximize the deduction. For purposes of determining the recovery allowance under this subparagraph, salvage value shall be disregarded and, in the case of a taxpayer that depreciated RRB property placed in service before January 1, 1981, using the RRB method consistently for all periods after February 28, 1913, the adjusted basis of RRB property is the adjusted basis for purposes of determining the deduction for retirements under the RRB method, with no adjustment for depreciation sustained prior to March 1, 1913.

(5) *RRB property (which is not RRB replacement property) placed in service after December 31, 1980.*—Property placed in service by the taxpayer after December 31, 1980, which is not RRB replacement property and which, under the taxpayer's method of depreciation as of December 31, 1980, would have been depreciated by the taxpayer under the RRB method, is treated as other property under section 168.

(b)-(f) [Reserved] [Reg. § 1.168-5.]

.01 Historical Comment: Proposed 2/16/84. Adopted 12/23/86 by T.D. 8116.

¶ 540

Proposed Reg. § 1.168-5

Proposed Regulations

»»→ Note: The text of the Preamble to the Proposed Regulation is at ¶ 49,032 in the CCH Standard Federal Tax Reporter.

§ 1.168-5. **Special rules,** LR-185-81, 2/16/84.

(a) [Paragraph (a) was adopted by T.D. 8116.]

(b) *Transferee bound by transferor's period and method in certain transactions.*—(1) *In general.*—In the case of recovery property which is transferred in a transaction described in section 168(f)(10)(B) and subparagraph (2) of this § 1.168-5(b), the transferee shall be treated as the transferor for purposes of computing the recovery allowance under section 168(a) and § 1.168-2 with respect to so much of the basis of such property in the hands of the transferee as does not exceed its adjusted basis (determined before the application of the section 48(q)(2) adjustment, if any) in the hands of the transferor immediately before the transfer.

(2) *Transactions covered.*—The provisions of subparagraph (1) of this paragraph (b) apply to the following transactions:

(i) A transaction described in—

(A) Section 332 (relating to distributions in complete liquidation of an 80 percent or more controlled subsidiary corporation) except where the basis of the assets distributed is determined under section 334(b)(2) (as in effect on August 31, 1982);

(B) Section 351 (relating to transfer to a corporation controlled by transferor);

(C) Section 361 (relating to exchanges pursuant to certain corporate reorganizations);

(D) Section 371(a) (relating to exchanges pursuant to certain receivership and bankruptcy proceedings);

(E) Section 374(a) (relating to exchanges pursuant to certain railroad reorganizations);

(F) Section 721 (relating to transfers to a partnership in exchange for a partnership interest); and

(G) Section 731 (relating to distributions by a partnership to a partner);

(ii) An acquisition (other than one described in subdivision (i) of this paragraph (2)) from a related person (as defined in section 168(e)(4)(D) and § 1.168-4(d)(6)). Property acquired from a decedent is not property acquired in a transaction included in this subdivision (ii); and

(iii) An acquisition followed by a leaseback to the person from whom the property is acquired. A leaseback does not exist for purposes of this subdivision (iii) if the former owner in turn subleases the property to another person.

(3) *Transactions excluded.*—The provisions of section 168(f)(10)(A) and paragraph (b)(1) of this section do not apply—

(i) To recovery property which is transferred within 12 months after the property is placed in service by the transferor. The exception of this subdivision (i) shall not apply in the case of a transaction also described in section 168(f)(7) (*i.e.,* a transaction in which gain or loss is not recognized in whole or in part); or

(ii) To any transaction described in section 168(e)(4) and § 1.168-4(d).

(4) *Allowable deduction when transferor and transferee are calendar year taxpayers or have the same fiscal year.*—When the transferor and transferee are calendar year taxpayers or when both the transferee and transferor have the same fiscal year—

(i) *Allowable deduction in year of transfer.*—The allowable deduction for the recovery year in which the property is transferred shall be prorated between the

Proposed Regulations

transferor and the transferee on a monthly basis. For property other than 15-year real property, the transferor's deduction for such year is the deduction allowable to the transferor (determined without regard to this subdivision) multiplied by a fraction, the numerator of which is the number of months in the transferor's taxable year before the month in which the transfer occurs, and the denominator of which is the total number of months in the transferor's taxable year. The remaining portion of the transferor's allowable deduction for the taxable year of the transfer (determined without regard to this subdivision) shall be allocated to the transferee. For property transferred in a transaction described in section 332, 361, 371(a), 374(a), or 731, the two preceding sentences shall be applied by disregarding that the taxable year of the transferor may end on the date of the transfer. In the case of 15-year real property, the transferor's deduction for the year of the transfer is the deduction allowable to the transferor under the disposition rules of § 1.168-2(a)(3) or (g)(4) (as the case may be). The remaining portion of the transferor's allowable deduction for the taxable year of the transfer (determined as if the transfer had not occurred) shall be allocated to the transferee. See subdivision (ii) of this paragraph (4) for a special rule applicable to certain nonrecognition transactions.

(ii) *Special rule for certain nonrecognition transactions occurring as of the close of business on the last day of any calendar month.*—For purposes of this paragraph (b), in the case of a transaction described in section 168(f)(10(B)(i) and paragraph (b)(2)(i) of this section, if the transfer occurs as of the close of business on the last day of any calendar month, such transfer is deemed to occur on the first day of the next calendar month.

(iii) *Transferee's allowable deduction for a taxable year subsequent to the year of transfer.*—The allowable deduction to the transferee for taxable years subsequent to the year of transfer shall be determined as if the cost of the property were being recovered in the transferor's hands (*i.e.,* by multiplying the transferor's applicable recovery percentage for the current recovery year by the transferor's unadjusted basis in the transferred property).

Thus, for example, A, a calendar year taxpayer, purchases for $30,000 and places in service 15-year real property (other than low income housing) on February 15, 1981, and transfers the property to partnership B, a calendar year partnership, on March 15, 1981, in a transaction described in section 721. A does not elect to use the optional recovery percentages provided in § 1.168-2(c). For 1981, A's allowable deduction is $300 (*i.e.,* $30,000 × .11 × 1/11). B's allowable deductions for 1981 and 1982 are $3,000 (*i.e.,* $3,300 - $300) and $3,000 (*i.e.,* .10 × $30,000), respectively.

(5) *Allowable deduction when transferor and transferee have different taxable years.*—When the transferor and the transferee have different taxable years—

(i) *Transferor's allowable deduction.*—The allowable deduction to the transferor for any taxable year in which the property is transferred shall be determined as under paragraph (b)(4)(i) and (ii) of this section.

(ii) *Transferee's allowable deduction.*—In computing the transferee's allowable deduction for the year of transfer and for subsequent taxable years, the property shall similarly be treated as if its cost were being recovered by the transferor. However, the allowable deduction for any taxable year shall be allocated to the transferee based on the transferee's taxable year.

Thus, for example, B, a calendar year taxpayer, purchases for $30,000 and places in service 15-year real property (other than low income housing) on February 15, 1981. B's allowable deduction for 1981 is $3,300 (*i.e.,* .11 × $30,000). B transfers the property to C on March 15, 1982. C's taxable year is a fiscal year ending June 30. For 1982, B's allowable deduction is $500 (*i.e.,* $30,000 × .10 × 2/12). For fiscal year 1982, C's allowable deduction is $1,000 (*i.e.,* the remainder of B's 1982 deduction ($2,500), allocated to the period March 1 through June 30, 1982 (4 months/10 months)). For fiscal year 1983, C's allowable deduction is $2,850 (*i.e.,* the remainder of B's allowable 1982 deduction ($1,500), plus $1,350 which is B's allowable 1983 deduction of $2,700 ($30,000 × .09) allocated to the period January 1 through June 30, 1983 (*i.e.,* $2,700 × 6 months/12 months).

(6) *Transferee's basis lower than transferor's.*—If the adjusted basis of the property in the hands of the transferee is lower than the adjusted basis of the property in the

Proposed Regulations

hands of the transferor immediately before the transfer, see § 1.168-2 (d) (3) for rules relating to redeterminations of basis.

(7) *Portion of basis in hands of transferee which exceeds transferor's adjusted basis.*—The transferee shall treat as newly purchased ACRS property that portion of the basis of the property in the hands of the transferee that exceeds the adjusted basis (determined before the application of the section 48 (q) (2) adjustment, if any) of the property in the hands of the transferor immediately before the transfer. Thus, such excess shall be treated as recovery property placed in service by the transferee in the year of the transfer. The transferee may choose any applicable recovery period and recovery method with respect to such excess and need not use the transferor's recovery period and recovery method.

(8) *Examples.*—The application of this paragraph (b) may be illustrated by the following examples:

Example (1). In 1981, A, a calendar year taxpayer, purchases for $12,000 and places in service 3-year recovery property. Under section 168 (b) (1) and § 1.168-2 (b) (1), the recovery allowances for the first and second recovery years are $3,000 (*i.e.,* .25 × $12,000) and $4,560 (*i.e.,* .38 × $12,000), respectively. On February 15, 1983, A transfers the property to M Corporation, a calendar year taxpayer, in exchange for M's stock and $2,000 cash in a transaction described in section 351. A's recovery allowance for 1983 is $370 (*i.e.,* (1/12 × .37) × $12,000). A's adjusted basis immediately before the exchange is $4,070 (*i.e.,* $12,000 – $7,930). Assume A recognizes gain of $2,000 on the transaction. The basis attributable to the property under section 362 is determined to be $6,070 in the hands of M Corporation. Under the provisions of section 168 (f) (10) (A) and this paragraph (b), M, the transferee, is treated the same as A, the transferor, with respect to $4,070, which is so much of M's basis as does not exceed A's adjusted basis. However, in computing the deduction allowable with respect to such basis, A's unadjusted basis ($12,000) is used. Thus, in the third recovery year, M may deduct $4,070 (*i.e.,* (11/12 × .37) × $12,000) under section 168 (f) (10) (A) and § 1.168-5 (b) (1) and (4). The remaining $2,000 of basis in the property is treated as newly purchased ACRS property placed in service in 1983. M may choose any applicable recovery period and recovery method with respect to such $2,000 and need not use A's recovery period and recovery method.

Example (2). In 1983, B, a calendar year taxpayer, purchases for $12,000 and places in service 5-year recovery property. Under section 46, B's investment tax credit for such property is $1,200. Under section 48 (q) (1) and § 1.168-2 (d) (2), B reduces his basis of $600 (*i.e.,* .50 × $1,200). Therefore, B's unadjusted basis for purposes of section 168 is $11,400 (*i.e.,* $12,000 – $600). Under section 168 (b) (1) and § 1.168-2 (b) (1), the recovery allowances for the first and second recovery years are $1,710 (*i.e.,* .15 × $11,400) and $2,508 (*i.e.,* .22 × $11,400), respectively. On February 15, 1985, B sells the property for $13,000 to C, a related party (as defined in section 168 (e) (4) (D) and § 1.168-4 (d) (6)) who is a calendar year taxpayer. B's recovery allowance for 1985 is $199.50 (*i.e.,* (1/12 × .21) × $11,400). B's adjusted basis (determined without regard to the section 48 (q) (2) adjustment), immediately before the sale is $6,982.50 (*i.e.,* $11,400 – $4,417.50). The basis of the property under section 1012 is $13,000 in C's hands. Under the provisions of section 168 (f) (10) (A) and this paragraph (b), C, the transferee, is treated the same as B, the transferor, with respect to $6,982.50, which is so much of C's basis as does not exceed B's adjusted basis. However, in computing the deduction allowable with respect to such basis, B's unadjusted basis ($11,400) is used. Thus, in the third recovery year, C may deduct $2,194.50 (*i.e.,* (11/12 × .21) × $11,400) under section 168 (f) (10) (A) and § 1.168-5 (b) (1) and (4). In the fourth and fifth recovery years, C may deduct $2,394 (*i.e.,* .21 × $11,400) each year. The remaining basis of $6,017.50 (*i.e.,* $13,000 – $6,982.50) in property is treated as newly purchased ACRS property placed in service in 1985. C may choose any applicable period and recovery method with respect to such amount and need not use B's recovery period and recovery method.

Example (3). In 1981, D, a calendar year taxpayer, purchases for $12,000 and places in service 5-year recovery property. Under section 168 (b) (1) and § 1.168-2 (b) (1), the recovery allowances for the first and second recovery years are $1,800 (*i.e.,* .15 × $12,000) and $2,640 (*i.e.,* .22 × $12,000), respectively. On March 15, 1983, D transfers the property to N Corporation, a taxpayer having a fiscal year ending June 30, in exchange for N's stock and $2,000 cash in a transaction described in section 351. D's recovery allowance for 1983 is $420 (*i.e.,* (2/12 × .21) × $12,000). D's adjusted basis in the

Proposed Regulations

property immediately before the exchange is $7,140 (*i.e.,* $12,000 – $4,860). Assume D recognizes gain of $2,000 on the transaction. The basis attributable to the property under section 362 is determined to be $9,140 in the hands of N Corporation. Under the provisions of section 168(f) (10) (A) and this paragraph (b), N, the transferee, is treated the same as D, the transferor, with respect to $7,140, which is so much of N's basis as does not exceed D's adjusted basis. However, in computing the deduction allowable with respect to such basis, D's unadjusted basis ($12,000) is used. Thus, for fiscal year 1983, N Corporation's allowable deduction with respect to the carryover basis is $840 (*i.e.,* (4/12 × .21) × $12,000). For fiscal years 1984 and 1985, N Corporation's allowable deduction is $2,520 (*i.e.,* [(6/12 × .21) + (6/12 × .21)] × $12,000). For fiscal year 1986, N Corporation's allowable deduction is $1,260 (*i.e.,* (6/12 × .21) × $12,000). The remaining $2,000 of basis in the property is treated as newly purchased ACRS property. N may choose any applicable recovery period and recovery method with respect to such basis and need not use D's recovery period and recovery method. N elects to use the optional recovery percentage based on a 5-year recovery period with respect to the $2,000 of basis which is treated as newly purchased ACRS property. For fiscal years 1983, 1984, 1985, 1986, 1987, and 1988, N's recovery allowance with respect to such $2,000 basis are $200, $400, $400, $400, $400, and $200, respectively. If N's fiscal year ending June 30, 1983, were a short taxable year, the provisions of § 1.168-2(f) would apply with respect to the $2,000 considered newly purchased ACRS property, but not with respect to N's basis carried over from D.

Example (4). On May 1, 1981, E, a calendar year taxpayer, purchases for $100,000 and places in service 5-year recovery property. On April 1, 1982, E sells the property for $100,000 to F who leases it back to E. Under the provisions of paragraph (b) (3), section 168 (f) (10) (A) and § 1.168-5 (b) (1) do not apply. Thus, F may choose any applicable recovery period and recovery method with respect to its unadjusted basis of $100,000, with recovery beginning in 1982.

Example (5). Assume the same facts as in example (4) except that the property is sold to F and leased back to E on June 15, 1982. Assume further that F's fiscal year ends on July 31, 1982. For 1981, E's allowable deduction is $15,000 (*i.e.,* .15 × $100,000), and for 1982 is $9,166.67 (*i.e.,* $100,000 × .22 × 5/12). E's adjusted basis in the property immediately before the transfer is $75,833.33 (*i.e.,* $100,000 – $24,166.67). Under the provisions of section 168(f)(10)(A) and this paragraph (b), F, the transferee, is treated the same as E, the transferor, with respect to $75,833.33 which is so much of F's basis as does not exceed E's adjusted basis. However, in computing the deduction allowable with respect to such basis, E's unadjusted basis ($100,000) is used. Thus, for the fiscal year ending July 31, 1982, F's allowable deduction with respect to the carryover basis is $3,666.66 (*i.e.,* 2/12 × .22 × $100,000). For fiscal year 1983, F's allowable deduction is $21,416.67 (*i.e.,* (5/12 × .22 × $100,000) + (7/12 × .21 × $100,000)). For fiscal years 1984 and 1985, F's allowable deductions are $21,000 (*i.e.,* (.21 × 5/12 × $100,000) + (.21 × 7/12 × $100,000)). For the fiscal year ending July 31, 1986, F's allowable deduction is $8,750 (*i.e.,* 5/12 × .21 × $100,000). The remaining $24,166.67 of basis is treated as newly-purchased property, placed in service by F in 1981. F may choose any applicable recovery period and method for such amount and need not use E's recovery period and method.

Example (6). On January 1, 1981, G, a calendar year taxpayer, purchases for $1 million and places in service 15-year real property (other than low income housing). On July 15, 1988, G sells the property to H for $1.5 million, who leases it back to G. H's taxable year is a fiscal year ending September 30. G does not elect use of the optional percentages provided by § 1.168-2(c). For 1988, G's allowable deduction is $30,000 (*i.e.,* .06 × $1,000,000 × 6/12). H is treated the same as G with respect to $390,000, which is so much of the basis of the property in the hands of H as does not exceed its adjusted basis to G immediately before the transfer (*i.e.,* $1,000,000 – $610,000). H's allowable deduction for its fiscal year ending September 30, 1988, with respect to such basis is $15,000 (*i.e.,* the remainder of G's allowable deduction for 1988 ($30,000) allocated to the period July 1 through September 30, 1988 (3 months/6 months)). For H's fiscal year ending September 30, 1989, H's allowable deduction is $60,000 (*i.e.,* the remainder of G's allowable 1988 deduction ($15,000) plus G's allowable 1989 deduction ($60,000) allocated to the period January 1 through September 30, 1989 (9 months/12 months) or $45,000). For H's fiscal year ending September 30, 1990, H's allowable deduction is $52,500 (*i.e.,* the remainder of G's allowable deduction for 1989 ($15,000), plus G's allowable deduction for 1990 ($50,000), allocated to the period January 1 through September 30, 1990 (9 months/12 months), or $37,500). For H's fiscal year ending September 30, 1996, H is entitled to G's allowable deduction for 1995 ($50,000), allocated to the period October 1 through December 31, 1995 (3 months/12 months), or $12,500. The amount of H's basis in excess of G's adjusted basis (*i.e.,* $1,500,000 less $390,000, or $1,110,000) is treated as newly purchased ACRS property placed in service by H on July 15, 1988. H may use any applicable recovery period and method with respect to such basis. Thus, assuming H does not elect the optional percentages provided by § 1.168-2(c), H has an additional allowable deduction for its year ending September 30, 1988, of $33,300 (*i.e.,* .03 × $1,110,000). For its fiscal year ending September 30, 1989, H's allowable deduction with respect to such basis is $122,100 (*i.e.,* .11 × $1,110,000).

Example (7). On January 1, 1981, partnership P, a calendar year taxpayer, purchases for $1,000,000 and places in service 15-year real property (other than low income housing) which is the only asset of the partnership. At no time does the partnership have an election under section 754 in effect. P is owned equally by partners A, B, and C. On April 18, 1985, individual D purchases the interests of B and C for $1,500,000, thereby terminating the partnership under section 708(b) (1) (B). The deduction allowable with respect to the property for 1985 prior to the termination is $17,500 (*i.e.,* $1,000,000 × .07 × 3⁄12). The partnership's adjusted basis in the property immediately before the termination is $592,500 (*i.e.,* $1,000,000 – $407,500). Under the provisions of section 168(f) (10) (A) and § 1.168-5(b) (1), the new partnership which is created by A and D is treated the same as the old partnership with respect to $592,500, which is so much of the adjusted basis of the property to the new partnership as does not exceed its adjusted basis to the old partnership. However, in computing the allowable deduction with respect to such basis the old partnership's unadjusted basis ($1,000,000) is used. Thus, for 1985, the deduction allowable to the new partnership with respect to such basis is $52,500 (*i.e.,* $1,000,000 × .07 × 9⁄12) and for 1986 is $60,000 (*i.e.,* $1,000,000 × .06). This result would be the same if D purchased a 95 percent interest in the partnership. Recovery of such basis will be completed in 1995. The new partnership's basis in the property in excess of that of the old partnership is taken into account under ACRS as if it were newly-purchased recovery property placed in service in 1985. Any applicable period and method may be used with respect to such basis.

Example (8). In 1981, Corporation X, a calendar year taxpayer, purchases for $100,000 and places in service 5-year recovery property. Under section 168(b) (1) and § 1.168-2(b) (1), X's recovery allowance for 1981 is $15,000. On March 15, 1982, X merges into Corporation Y in a transaction described in section 368(a) (1) (A) solely in exchange for Y stock. Y's taxable year is a fiscal year ending August 31. X's recovery allowance for 1982 is $3,666.66 (*i.e.,* 2⁄12 × .22 × $100,000). Under section 362, Y's basis in the property is the same as the property's adjusted basis in the hands of X immediately before the transfer. Therefore, for fiscal year 1982, Y's allowable deduction is $11,000 which is the remainder of X's allowable deduction for 1982, $18,333.34 (*i.e.,* $22,000 – $3,666.66) allocated to the period March 1, 1982, through August 31, 1982 (*i.e.,* 6 months/10 months). For fiscal year 1983, Y's allowable deduction is $21,333.34 which is the remainder of X's allowable deduction for 1982 ($7,333.34) plus the deduction which would be allowable to X in 1983 (*i.e.,* $100,000 × .21, or $21,000) allocated to the period January 1 through August 31, 1983 (*i.e.,* $21,000 × 8 months/12 months or $14,000). In computing the deductions allowable to X and Y, the fact that X's taxable year ends on the date of the merger is disregarded.

(c) *Recovery property reacquired by the taxpayer.*—(1) *In general.*—Recovery property which is disposed of and then reacquired by the taxpayer shall be treated (for purposes of computing the allowable deduction under section 168(a) and § 1.168-2) as if such property had not been disposed of by the taxpayer. This paragraph (c) (1) generally applies only to so much of the taxpayer's adjusted basis in the reacquired property as does not exceed his adjusted basis at the time he disposed of the property.

(2) *Taxpayers to whom provisions apply.*—The provisions of section 168(f) (10) (C) and paragraph (c) (1) of this section apply only to a taxpayer who, at the time of the disposition of the property, anticipates a reacquisition of the same property.

(3) *Exceptions.*—Section 168(f) (10) (C) and paragraph (c) (1) of this section shall not apply—

(i) To recovery property which is disposed of during the same taxable year that the property is placed in service by the taxpayer, or

(ii) To any transaction described in section 168(e) (4) and § 1.168-4(d).

Proposed Regulations

(4) *Taxpayer resumes prior recovery.*—For purposes of paragraph (c)(1) of this § 1.168-5, the reacquiring taxpayer shall resume the recovery under § 1.168-2 applicable at the time of the disposition. For example, if the taxpayer originally uses a 3-year recovery period and the applicable percentages prescribed in section 168(b)(1) and § 1.168-2(b)(1), in the year of reacquisition the recovery allowance is computed by applying the applicable percentage for the year of disposition to the original unadjusted basis (*i.e.,* the unadjusted basis at the time the taxpayer originally placed the recovery property in service).

(5) *Portion of unadjusted basis in reacquired property which exceeds taxpayer's adjusted basis at the time of disposition.*—That part of the unadjusted basis in the reacquired property which exceeds the taxpayer's adjusted basis in the property at the time of disposition shall be treated generally as newly purchased ACRS property. For property other than a building, any appropriate recovery period and method may be used with respect to such excess. For a building, the taxpayer must use the same recovery period and method with respect to such excess as are used for the building, unless such excess would qualify as a substantial improvement under § 1.168-2(e)(4) if paid or incurred by the taxpayer for an improvement if he had continued to own the building.

(6) *Unadjusted basis in reacquired property lower than taxpayer's adjusted basis at time of disposition.*—If the unadjusted basis in the reacquired property is lower than the taxpayer's adjusted basis in the property at the time of disposition, see § 1.168-2(d)(3) for rules relating to redetermination of basis.

(7) *Examples.*—The provisions of this paragraph may be illustrated by the following examples:

Example (1). In 1981 A, a calendar year taxpayer, purchases for $6,000 and places in service 3-year recovery property. A does not elect an optional recovery percentage under § 1.168-2(c). Under section 168(b)(1) and § 1.168-2(b)(1), A's recovery allowance for 1981 is $1,500 (*i.e.,* .25 × $6,000). A wants to change his method of cost recovery from the use of the accelerated percentages to the use of the optional straight line percentages. To effectuate this change, A sells the property to B in 1982 for $7,000 anticipating that B will sell the property back to A. B does not elect to use an optional recovery percentage. B's recovery deduction for 1982 is $1,750 (*i.e.,* .25 × $7,000). In 1983 A reacquires the property from B for $9,000. With respect to that portion of A's unadjusted basis in the reacquired property which does not exceed the adjusted basis at the time of disposition (*i.e.,* $4,500), A's recovery allowance for 1983 is determined as if A had not disposed of the property, that is, by applying the percentage (38 percent) applicable for the second recovery year (*i.e.,* 1982, the year of disposition) to the original unadjusted basis ($6,000). Thus, A's allowable deduction is $2,280 (*i.e.,* .38 × $6,000). That portion of the unadjusted basis in the reacquired property which exceeds A's adjusted basis at the time of disposition (*i.e.,* $4,500) is treated as newly purchased ACRS property placed in service in 1983. A may use any appropriate recovery period and method for such excess. Thus, if A uses the tables under § 1.168-2(b)(1), A's recovery allowance for 1983 also includes $1,125 (*i.e.,* .25 × $4,500). A's recovery allowances for 1984 are $2,220 (*i.e.,* .37 × $6,000) plus $1,710 (*i.e.,* .38 × $4,500). A's recovery allowance for 1985 is $1,665 (*i.e.,* .37 × $4,500).

Example (2). In 1981 C, a calendar year taxpayer, purchases for $15,000 and places in service 3-year recovery property and elects under § 1.168-2(c) the optional 5-year recovery period using the straight line method. Under § 1.168-2(c)(4), C's recovery allowance for 1981 is $1,500 (*i.e.,* .10 × $15,000). C wants to change his method of cost recovery from the use of the optional straight line percentages to the use of the accelerated percentages. Consent to change is not granted to C under section 168(f)(4). Therefore, C tries to effectuate this change by selling the property to D in 1982 for $16,000 anticipating that D will sell the property back to C. D does not elect to use the optional recovery percentages. D's recovery allowance for 1982 is $4,000 (*i.e.,* .25 × $16,000). In 1983, C reacquires the property from D for $17,000. With respect to that portion of C's unadjusted basis in the reacquired property that does not exceed the adjusted basis at the time of disposition (*i.e.,* $13,500), C must use the option recovery percentages originally elected. C's recovery allowances for 1983, 1984, 1985, 1986, and 1987 are determined as if C had not disposed of the property, that is, by applying the applicable percentages beginning in the second recovery year to the original unadjusted basis ($15,000). Thus, C's allowable deductions are $3,000, $3,000, $3,000, $3,000, and $1,500, respectively. With respect to that portion of the unadjusted basis in the reac-

Proposed Regulations

quired property which exceeds C's adjusted basis at the time of disposition (*i.e.*, $3,500), C may use any appropriate recovery period and method. Cost recovery for this portion of the reacquired property begins in 1983 as if C placed the property in service in that year.

Example (3). On February 15, 1981, E, a calendar year taxpayer, purchases for $30,000 and places in service 15-year real property (other than low income housing) and does not elect the optional straight line percentages under § 1.168-2(c). Under § 1.168-2(b)(2), E's recovery allowance for 1981 is $3,000 (*i.e.*, .11 × $30,000). E wants to change his method of cost recovery from the use of the accelerated percentages to the use of the optional straight line percentages. To effectuate this change, E sells the property to F on February 15, 1983, anticipating that F will sell the property back to E. E's recovery allowance for 1982 is $3,000 (*i.e.*, .10 × $30,000) and for 1983 is $225 (*i.e.*, .09 × 1⁄12 × $30,000). In 1985 E reacquires the property from F for $28,000. With respect to that portion of E's unadjusted basis in the reacquired property which does not exceed the adjusted basis at the time of disposition (*i.e.*, $23,475) E's recovery allowance for 1985 is determined as if E had not disposed of the property, that is, by applying the percentage (9 percent) applicable for the third recovery year to the original unadjusted basis ($30,000). The recovery for the year of reacquisition must be adjusted to reflect the number of months the property is used by the taxpayer in that year as recovery property. Thus, if E reacquired the property in July, E's recovery allowance for 1985 would be $1,350 (*i.e*, .09 × 6⁄12 × $30,000). The unrecovered allowance for the third recovery year, $1,125 ($30,000 × .09 × 5⁄12), must be recovered in the year following the last recovery year. With respect to that portion of the unadjusted basis in the reacquired property which exceeds E's adjusted basis at the time of disposition (*i.e.*, $4,525), E may not elect an optional recovery period. Cost recovery for this portion of the reacquired property will begin in 1985. Thus, if the reacquisition occurred in July, E's allowable deduction for 1985 with respect to this portion would be $271.50 (*i.e.*, .06 × $4,525).

(d) *Treatment of leasehold improvements.*—(1) *In general.*—Capital expenditures made by a lessee for the erection of buildings or the construction of other permanent improvements on leased property are recoverable through ACRS deductions or amortization deductions. If the recovery period of such improvements in the hands of the taxpayer is equal to or shorter than the remaining period of the lease, the allowances shall take the form of ACRS deductions under section 168. If, on the other hand, the recovery period of such property in the hands of the taxpayer would be longer than the remaining period of such lease, the allowances shall take the form of annual deductions from gross income in an amount equal to the unrecovered cost of such capital expenditures divided by the number of years remaining on the term of the lease. Such deductions shall be in lieu of ACRS deductions. See section 162 and the regulations thereunder.

(2) *Determination of recovery period.*—For purposes of determining whether the recovery period is longer than the lease term, an election of an optional recovery period under section 168(b)(3) or (f)(2)(C) shall be taken into account.

(3) *Determination of the effect given to lease renewal options; related lessee and lessor.*—Section 178 governs the effect to be given renewal options in determining whether the recovery period of the improvements exceeds the remaining period of the lease. Section 178 also provides rules for determining the period of a lease when the lessee and lessor are related. In making any determination under section 178, the "recovery period" of the improvement shall be taken into account in lieu of its useful life. See § 1.178-1.

(4) *Improvements made by lessor.*—If a lessor makes an improvement to the leased property, the cost of the improvement must be recovered under the general provisions of section 168. The provisions of 168(f)(6) and this Paragraph (d) do not apply to improvements made by the lessor.

(5) *Example.*—The application of this paragraph may be illustrated by the following example:

Example. In 1981, A leases B's land for a term of 99 years. The lease provisions do not include any options to renew the lease. In 2034, A places in service 15-year real property which he built on the leased premises. Since the remaining term of the lease (46 years) is longer than any recovery period which A could select under section 168 (*i.e.*, 15, 35, or 45 years), A must recover the costs of the improvement under section 168.

Proposed Regulations

(e) *Manner and time for making election.*—(1) *Elections to which this paragraph applies.*—The rules in this paragraph apply to the following elections provided under section 168:

(i) Section 168(b)(3)(A) and (B)(i) and § 1.168-2(c)(1) and (2), relating to election of optional recovery percentage with respect to property in the same recovery class (*i.e.,* all 3-year recovery property);

(ii) Section 168(b)(3)(A) and (B)(ii) and § 1.168-2(c)(1) and (3), relating to election of optional recovery percentage on a property-by-property basis for 15-year real property;

(iii) Section 168(d)(2)(A) and § 1.168-2(h), relating to election to account for mass assets in the same mass asset account and to include in income all proceeds realized on disposition;

(iv) Section 168(e)(2) and § 1.168-4(b), relating to election to exclude property from ACRS by use of a method of depreciation not expressed in a term of years;

(v) Section 168(f)(2)(C)(i) and (ii)(I) and § 1.168-2(g)(3)(i) and (ii), relating to election of optional recovery percentage for property used predominantly outside the United States in the same recovery class and with the same present class life (*e.g.,* 3-year recovery property with a present class life of 4 years); and

(vi) Section 168(f)(2)(C)(i) and (ii)(II) and § 1.168-2(g)(3)(i) and (iii), relating to election of optional recovery percentage on a property-by-property basis for 15-year real property used predominantly outside the United States.

Use by a taxpayer of a method of cost recovery described in section 168(b)(1) and (2) and § 1.168-2(b)(1) and (2) or section 168(f)(2)(A) and (B) and § 1.168-2(g)(1) and (2) (relating to the use of the accelerated percentages) is not an election for purposes of section 168 and this paragraph (e). Thus, no consent will be granted to change from such a method to another method described in section 168. The provisions of section 168(f)(4) and this paragraph (e) do not apply to elections which must be made under another section of the Code. Thus, for example, if a taxpayer wants to amortize property under section 167(k), the rules under section 167(k) apply with respect to such election and the revocation of such election.

(2) *Time for making elections.*—Except as provided in subparagraph (4) or (5), the elections specified in subparagraph (1) of this paragraph (e) shall be made on the taxpayer's income tax return filed for the taxable year in which the property is placed in service as recovery property (as defined in § 1.168-3(a)) by the taxpayer. If the taxpayer does not file a timely return (taking into account extensions of the time for filing) for such taxable year, the election shall be made at the time the taxpayer files his first return for such year. The election may be made on a return, as amended, filed within the time prescribed by law (including extensions) for filing the return for such taxable year. A separate election may be made for each corporation which is a member of an affiliated group (as defined in section 1504) and which joins in the making of a consolidated return in accordance with section 1502 and the regulations thereunder. See § 1.1502-77.

(3) *Manner of making elections.*—Except as provided in subparagraph (5), Form 4562 is provided for making an election under this paragraph and for submitting the information required. The taxpayer must specify in the election—

(i) The name of the taxpayer;

(ii) The taxpayer's identification number;

(iii) The year the recovery property was placed in service (or, in the case of 15-year real property, the month the property was placed in service);

(iv) The unadjusted basis of the recovery property; and

(v) Such other information as may be required.

An election will not be rendered invalid so long as there is substantial compliance, in good faith, with the requirements of this subparagraph (3).

(4) *Special rule for qualified rehabilitated buildings.*—In the case of any qualified rehabilitated building (as defined in section 48(g)(1)), an election under section 168(b)(3) and § 1.168-2(c) (relating to election of optional recovery percentage) may be made at any time before the date 3 years after the building was placed in service by the taxpayer.

(5) *Special rule for foreign taxpayers.*—(i) *Foreign corporations subject to section 964.*—In the case of a foreign corporation whose earnings and profits are determined

Proposed Regulations

under section 964, the elections specified in subparagraph (1) of this paragraph (e) shall be made at the time and in the manner provided in § 1.964-1(c). Except as provided in the regulations under section 952 and section 1248, any election made under this subdivision (i) shall apply with respect to the recovery property affected by the election from the taxable year in which such property is placed in service. Such election may be revoked only as provided in § 1.964-1(c)(7) and subparagraph (9) of this paragraph.

(ii) *Foreign taxpayers other than corporations subject to section 964.*—In the case of a foreign taxpayer other than a corporation described in subdivision (i) of this subparagraph (5), the elections specified in subparagraph (1) of this paragraph (e) shall be made at the time and in the manner provided in subparagraphs (2) and (3) of this paragraph, except that the election shall be made on the taxpayer's income tax return for the later of the taxable year in which the property is placed in service as recovery property by the taxpayer or the first taxable year in which the taxpayer is subject to United States tax. Any election made under this subdivision (ii) shall apply with respect to the recovery property affected by the election from the taxable year in which such property is placed in service. Such election may be revoked only as provided in subparagraph (9) of this paragraph. No election may be made under this subdivision (ii) by a taxpayer who was required to, but did not make the election at the time and in the manner prescribed under subdivision (i). For purposes of this subdivision (ii)—

(A) "Foreign taxpayer" means a taxpayer that is not a United States person as defined in section 7701(a)(30), and

(B) "United States tax" means tax under subtitle A of the Code (relating to income taxes) other than sections 871(a)(1) and 881 thereof.

(6) *Failure to elect optional recovery percentages.*—If a taxpayer does not elect to use the optional recovery percentages within the time and in the manner prescribed in subpara graphs (2), (3), (4), and (5) (or is not considered to have elected under § 1.168-2(c)(5)), the amount allowable under section 168 must be determined under section 168(b)(1) or (2) (or under section 168(f)(2)(A) or (B), where applicable) for the year in which the recovery property is placed in service and for all subsequent recovery years. Thus, no election to use such optional percentages may be made by the taxpayer in any other manner (*e.g.,* through a request under section 446(e) to change the taxpayer's method of accounting).

(7) *Individuals, partnerships, trusts, estates, and corporations.*—Except as provided in subparagraph (8) of this paragraph with respect to transactions to which section 168(f)(10)(A) and (B) applies, and subject to other applicable provisions of the Code and regulations, if recovery property is placed in service by an individual, trust, estate, partnership, or corporation, an election under this paragraph shall be made by the individual, trust, estate, partnership, or corporation placing such property in service.

(8) *Transactions to which section 168(f)(10)(A) and (B) applies.*—In a transaction to which section 168(f)(10)(A) and (B) and paragraph (b) of this § 1.168-5 apply, the transferee is bound by the transferor's election (or nonelection) under this paragraph with respect to the property so acquired. The rule of the preceding sentence shall apply with respect to so much of the basis of the property in the hands of the transferee as does not exceed the adjusted basis of the property in the hands of the transferor immediately before the transfer.

(9) *Revocation of election.*—An election under this paragraph, once made, may be revoked only with the consent of the Commissioner. Such consent will be granted only in extraordinary circumstances. Requests for consent must be filed with the Commissioner of Internal Revenue, Washington, D.C. 20224.

(f) *Treatment of certain nonrecognition transactions.*—(1) *Section 1033 transactions.*—(i) *Allowable deduction for section 1033 converted property.*—For any taxable year in which a transaction described in section 1033 occurs, the full year's allowable deduction shall be prorated on a monthly basis under the principles of paragraph (b)(4)(i) of this section. Thus, for example, on March 3, 1981, A, a calendar year taxpayer, purchases for $25,000 and places in service 3-year recovery property. On August 14, 1981, the property is converted. A's 1981 allowable deduction for the converted property is $3,645.83 (*i.e.,* $25,000 × .25 × 7/12). If the property were 15-year real property (other than low income housing) A's 1981 allowable deduction for the converted property would be $1,250 (*i.e.,* $25,000 × .10 × 5/10).

Proposed Regulations

(ii) *Allowable deduction for section 1033 replacement property in year of replacement and subsequent taxable years.*—(A) Replacement property acquired in a transaction to which section 1033 applies, which qualifies as recovery property, shall be treated the same as the converted property. Thus, the replacement property shall be recovered over the remaining recovery period using the same recovery method as the converted property. The preceding sentence applies only with respect to so much of the basis (as determined under section 1033(b)) in the replacement property as does not exceed the adjusted basis in the converted property. Any excess of the unadjusted basis of the replacement property over the adjusted basis of the converted property shall be treated as newly purchased ACRS property. Any excess of the adjusted basis of the converted property over the unadjusted basis of the replacement property shall be recovered under the principles of § 1.168-2(d)(3) (relating to redeterminations).

(B) The allowable deduction for the replacement property in the year of replacement (whether such replacement year is the same as the year of conversion or a later year) shall be based on the number of months the replacement property is in service as recovery property during the replacement year.

(1) If the number of months in the conversion year after the property is converted (including the month of conversion) is greater than or equal to the number of months the replacement property is in service during the replacement year, the allowable deduction for the replacement year shall equal—

$$(a/b \times c) \times d$$

where

a = number of months replacement property is in service as recovery property during replacement year,

b = 12 or, in the case of 15-year real property converted in the first recovery year, the number of months in the taxpayer's taxable year after the converted property was placed in service by the taxpayer (including the month the property was placed in service),

c = applicable recovery percentage for converted property in year of conversion, and

d = unadjusted basis of converted property.

An allowance is permitted to the extent of any unrecovered allowance in the taxable year following the final recovery year. The term "unrecovered allowance" means the difference between—

(i) The sum of recovery allowances for the year of the conversion and the year of the replacement, and

(ii) The recovery allowance which would have been allowable in the year of conversion had such conversion not occurred.

In a year following the year of replacement, the allowable deduction shall be computed by multiplying the applicable recovery percentage for the next recovery year to the unadjusted basis of the converted property.

(2) If the number of months in the conversion year after the property is converted (including the month of conversion) is less than the number of months the replacement property is in service during the replacement year, the allowable deduction for the replacement year shall equal—

$$[(a/b \times c) + (d/12 \times e)] \times f$$

where

a = number of months in conversion year after the property is converted (including the month of conversion),

b = 12 or, in the case of 15-year real property converted in the first recovery year, the number of months in the taxpayer's taxable year after the converted property was placed in service by the taxpayer (including the month the property was placed in service),

c = applicable recovery percentage for converted property in the year of conversion,

d = number of months replacement property is in service as recovery property during replacement year minus a,

Proposed Regulations

e = applicable recovery percentage for the next recovery year, and

f = unadjusted basis of converted property.

An allowance is permitted to the extent of any unrecovered allowance in the taxable year following the final recovery year. The term "unrecovered allowance" means the difference between—

(i) The sum of the recovery allowances for the year of conversion and the year of replacement, and

(ii) The sum of the recovery allowances which would have been allowable in the year of conversion and the next recovery year had such conversion not occurred.

In a year following the year of replacement, the allowable deduction shall be computed by multiplying the unadjusted basis of the converted property by the applicable recovery percentage for the second recovery year after the year of conversion.

(iii) *Examples.*—The provisions of paragraph (f)(1)(i) and (ii) may be illustrated by the following examples:

Example (1). On January 1, 1981, A, a calendar year taxpayer, purchases for $40,000 and places in service recovery property which is 15-year real property (other than low income housing). Under section 168(b)(2) and § 1.168-2(b)(2), the allowable deductions for the first and second recovery years are $4,800 (*i.e.,* .12 × $40,000) and $4,000 (*i.e.,* .10 × $40,000). On March 3, 1983, A's property is involuntarily converted. Under the provisions of subdivision (i), A's 1983 allowable deduction for the converted property is $600 (*i.e.,* 2/12 × .09 × $40,000). On May 15, 1984, A acquires replacement property. A's unadjusted basis in the replacement property is the same as his adjusted basis in the converted property (*i.e.,* $30,600). Under the provisions of subdivision (ii), the replacement property is treated the same as the converted property with respect to such $30,600 of basis. However, in computing the allowable deduction with respect to such basis, A's unadjusted basis in the converted property ($40,000) is used. Thus, A's allowable deduction for 1984 is $2,400 (*i.e.,* 8/12 × .09 × $40,000). Under the provisions of subdivision (ii)(B)(*1*), the unrecovered allowance is $600 (*i.e.,* $3,600 – $3,000), and it must be recovered in the taxable year following the final recovery year, that is, in the taxable year following the fifteenth recovery year. A's allowable deduction for 1985 is $3,200 (*i.e.,* .08 × $40,000).

Example (2). Assume the same facts as in example (1) except that A acquires the replacement property on January 1, 1984. A's allowable deduction for 1984 is $3,533.33 (*i.e.,* [(10/12 × .09) = (2/12 × .08)] × $40,000). Under the provisions of subdivision (ii)(B)(*2*), the unrecovered allowance is $2,666.67 (*i.e.,* $6,800 – $4,133.33), and it must be recovered in the taxable year following the final recovery year, that is, in the taxable year following the fifteenth recovery year. A's allowance deduction for 1985 is $2,800 (*i.e.,* .07 × $40,000).

Example (3). Assume the same facts as in example (1) except that A acquires the replacement property on the same day as the conversion (March 3, 1983). A's allowable deduction for 1983 for the converted property is $600 (*i.e.,* (2/12 × .09) × $40,000). A's allowable deduction for 1983 for the replacement property is $3,000 (*i.e.,* (10/12 × .09) × $40,000). A's allowable deduction for 1984 is $3,200 (*i.e.,* $40,000 × .08).

Example (4). On February 3, 1981, B, a calendar year taxpayer, purchases for $100,000 and places in service recovery property which is 15-year real property (other than low income housing). On June 25, 1981, B's property is involuntarily converted. On that same day B acquires replacement property with the same basis as the converted property. B's allowable deduction for 1981 for the converted property is $4,000 (*i.e.,* 4/11 × .11 × $100,000). B's allowable deduction for 1981 for the replacement property is $7,000 (*i.e.,* 7/11 × .11 × $100,000). B's allowable deduction for 1982 is $10,000 (*i.e.,* $100,000 × .10).

(2) *Section 1031 transactions.*—(i) *Allowable deductions.*—In a transaction to which section 1031 applies, the allowable deduction for the exchanged and acquired properties shall be determined under the principles of subparagraph (1) of this paragraph. Similarly, any excess of the unadjusted basis of the acquired property over the adjusted basis of the exchanged property shall be treated as newly purchased ACRS property, and any excess of the adjusted basis of the exchanged property over the unadjusted basis of the acquired property shall be recovered under the principles of § 1.168-2(d)(3) (relating to redeterminations).

Proposed Regulations

(ii) *Examples.*—The provisions of paragraph (f) (2) (i) may be illustrated by the following examples:

Example (1). In 1981 A, a calendar year taxpayer, purchases for $12,000 and places in service recovery property which is 3-year recovery property. Under section 168(b) (1) and § 1.168-2(b) (1), the allowable deductions for the first and second recovery years are $3,000 (*i.e.,* .25 × $12,000) and $4,560 (*i.e.,* .38 × $12,000), respectively. On March 3, 1983, A exchanges this property and $1,000 cash for property of a "like kind." A's 1983 allowable deduction for the exchanged property is $740 (*i.e.,* 2/12 × .37 × $12,000). A's basis in the acquired property is $4,700. The acquired property is treated the same as the exchanged property with respect to $3,700, which is so much of the basis in the acquired property as does not exceed the adjusted basis in the exchanged property. However, in computing the allowable deduction with respect to such basis, A's unadjusted basis in the exchanged property ($12,000) is used. Therefore, A's 1983 allowable deduction for the acquired property with respect to the substituted basis is $3,700 (*i.e.,* 10/12 × .37 × $12,000). The remaining $1,000 of basis in the acquired property is treated as newly purchased ACRS property placed in service in 1983. A may choose any applicable recovery period and recovery method for such basis and need not use the same recovery period and recovery method used for the exchanged property. If A uses the tables provided in section 168(b) (1) and § 1.168-2(b) (1), for 1983, 1984, and 1985, A is entitled to additional allowable deductions of $250, $380, and $370, respectively.

Example (2). On February 8, 1981, B, a calendar year taxpayer, purchases for $80,000 and places in service 15-year real property (other than low income housing). Under the provisions of section 168(b) (2) and § 1.168-2(b) (2), the allowable deduction for 1981 is $8,800 (*i.e.,* .11 × $80,000). On March 3, 1982, B exchanges this property and $20,000 cash for property of a "like kind." B's 1982 allowable deduction for the exchanged property is $1,333.33 (*i.e.,* 2/12 × .10 × $80,000). B's basis in the acquired property is $89,866.67. The acquired property is treated the same as the exchanged property with respect to $69,866.67, which is so much of the basis in the acquired property as does not exceed the adjusted basis in the exchanged property. However, in computing the allowable deduction with respect to such basis, B's unadjusted basis in the exchanged property ($80,000) is used. Therefore, B's 1982 and 1983 allowable deductions for the acquired property with respect to the substituted basis are $6,666.66 (*i.e.,* 10/12 × .10 × $80,000) and $7,200 (*i.e.,* .09 × $80,000), respectively. The remaining $20,000 of basis in the acquired property is treated as newly purchased ACRS property placed in service in March 1982. B may choose any applicable recovery period and recovery method for this basis and need not use the same period and method used for the exchanged property. If B uses the tables prescribed in § 1.168-2(b) (2), B's 1982 allowable deduction for this basis is $2,000 (*i.e.,* $20,000 × .10).

(3) *Transfers of property by gift.*—(i) *Allowable deductions.*—With respect to recovery property which is transferred by gift (where the donee's basis is determined under section 1015), the allowable deduction for the taxable year of the gift shall be apportioned between the donor and donee under the principles of paragraphs (b) (including paragraph (b) (4) (ii)) and (f) (1) of this section, and the donee shall be treated as the donor for subsequent taxable years to the extent that the donee's basis is carried over from the donor. That portion of the donee's basis (as determined under section 1015) in the property that exceeds the donor's adjusted basis immediately preceding the gift shall be treated as newly purchased ACRS property. The donee may choose any applicable recovery period and recovery method with respect to such excess and need not use the donor's recovery period and recovery method.

(ii) *Example.*—The provisions of paragraph (f) (3) (i) may be illustrated by the following example:

Example. In 1981 A, a calendar year taxpayer, purchases for $12,000 and places in service 5-year recovery property. Under section 168(b) (1) and § 1.168-2(b) (1), the allowable deduction for 1981 is $1,800 (*i.e.,* .15 × $12,000). On March 15, 1982, A transfers the property by gift to B (another calendar year taxpayer) who continues to use it as recovery property. A's 1982 allowable deduction is $440 (*i.e.,* 2/12 × .22 × $12,000). Under section 1015, B's basis in the property is determined to be $11,000. In the hands of B, the donee, the property is treated the same as in the hands of the donor with respect to $9,760, which is so much of the carryover basis as does not exceed the donor's adjusted basis in the property immediately preceding the gift. However, in computing the allowable deduction with respect to such basis, the donor's unadjusted basis ($12,000) is

Proposed Regulations

used. Therefore, B's 1982 allowable deduction with respect to such basis is $2,200 (*i.e.,* 10/12 × .22 × $12,000). The remaining $1,240 (*i.e.,* $11,000 – $9,760) of basis is treated as newly purchased ACRS property. B may choose any applicable recovery period and recovery method for such basis and need not use the donor's recovery period and recovery method.

(4) *Transfers of property by reason of death.*—Where recovery property is transferred by reason of the death of the taxpayer, the allowable deduction for the taxpayer's taxable year which ends upon his death shall be governed by the rules applicable to short taxable years. See § 1.168-2(f). [Reg. § 1.168-5.]

¶ 545

Proposed Reg. § 1.168-6

Proposed Regulations

»»→ *Note: The text of the Preamble to the Proposed Regulation is at ¶ 49,032 in the CCH Standard Federal Tax Reporter.*

§ 1.168-6. **Gain or loss on dispositions,** LR-185-81, 2/16/84.

(a) *General rule.*—Except as provided in § 1.168-2(h) (relating to mass assets), where recovery property is disposed of during a taxable year, the following rules shall apply:

(1) If the asset is disposed of by sale or exchange, gain or loss shall be recognized as provided under the applicable provisions of the Code.

(2) If the asset is disposed of by physical abandonment, loss shall be recognized in the amount of the adjusted basis of the asset at the time of the abandonment. For a loss to qualify for recognition under this subparagraph (2), the taxpayer must intend to discard the asset irrevocably so that he will neither use the asset again, nor retrieve it for sale, exchange, or other disposition.

(3) If the asset is disposed of other than by sale or exchange or physical abandonment (as, for example, where the asset is transferred to a supplies or scrap account), gain shall not be recognized. Loss shall be recognized in the amount of the excess of the adjusted basis of the asset over its fair market value at the time of the disposition. No loss shall be recognized upon the conversion of property to personal use.

(b) *Definitions.*—(1) See § 1.168-2(l)(1) for the definition of "disposition," which excludes the retirement of a structural component of 15-year real property. Thus, no loss shall be recognized on such retirement, and the unadjusted basis of the property under § 1.168-2(d) shall not be reduced. For example, if a taxpayer replaces the roof on 15-year real property, no loss is recognized upon the retirement of the replaced roof, and the unadjusted basis of the property continues to be recovered over the remaining period. For determination of the deductions allowable under section 168 with respect to the expenditures paid or incurred to replace the roof, see § 1.168-2(e).

(2) The adjusted basis of an asset at the time of its disposition is its unadjusted basis, as provided in § 1.168-2, adjusted as prescribed in § 1.1011-1. [Reg. § 1.168-6.]

MACRS Regulations

¶ 550

Reg. § 1.168(a)-1

§ 1.168(a)-1. **Modified accelerated cost recovery system.**—(a) Section 168 determines the depreciation allowance for tangible property that is of a character subject to the allowance for depreciation provided in section 167(a) and that is placed in service after December 31, 1986 (or after July 31, 1986, if the taxpayer made an election under section 203(a)(1)(B) of the Tax Reform Act of 1986; 100 Stat. 2143). Except for property excluded from the application of section 168 as a result of section 168(f) or as a result of a transitional rule, the provisions of section 168 are mandatory for all eligible property. The allowance for depreciation under section 168 constitutes the amount of depreciation allowable under section 167(a). The determination of whether tangible property is property of a character subject to the allowance for depreciation is made under section 167 and the regulations under section 167.

(b) This section is applicable on and after February 27, 2004. [Reg. § 1.168(a)-1.]

.01 Historical Comment: Proposed 3/1/2004. Adopted 2/26/2007 by T.D. 9314.

¶ 551

Reg. § 1.168(b)-1

1.168(b)-1. **Definitions.**—(a) *Definitions.*—For purposes of section 168 and the regulations under section 168, the following definitions apply:

(1) *Depreciable property* is property that is of a character subject to the allowance for depreciation as determined under section 167 and the regulations under section 167.

(2) *MACRS property* is tangible, depreciable property that is placed in service after December 31, 1986 (or after July 31, 1986, if the taxpayer made an election under section 203(a)(1)(B) of the Tax Reform Act of 1986; 100 Stat. 2143) and subject to section 168, except for property excluded from the application of section 168 as a result of section 168(f) or as a result of a transitional rule.

(3) *Unadjusted depreciable basis* is the basis of property for purposes of section 1011 without regard to any adjustments described in section 1016(a)(2) and (3). This basis reflects the reduction in basis for the percentage of the taxpayer's use of property for the taxable year other than in the taxpayer's trade or business (or for the production of income), for any portion of the basis the taxpayer properly elects to treat as an expense under section 179, section 179C, or any similar provision, and for any adjustments to basis provided by other provisions of the Internal Revenue Code and the regulations under the Code (other than section 1016(a)(2) and (3)) (for example, a reduction in basis by the amount of the disabled access credit pursuant to section 44(d)(7)). For property subject to a lease, see section 167(c)(2).

(4) *Adjusted depreciable basis* is the unadjusted depreciable basis of the property, as defined in § 1.168(b)-1(a)(3), less the adjustments described in section 1016(a)(2) and (3).

(b) *Effective date.*—This section is applicable on or after February 27, 2004. [Reg. § 1.168(b)-1.]

.01 Historical Comment: Proposed 3/1/2004. Adopted 2/26/2007 by T.D. 9314.

¶ 559

Reg. § 1.168(d)-0

§ 1.168(d)-0. **Table of contents for the applicable convention rules.**—This section lists the major paragraphs in § 1.168(d)-1.

 [Reg. § 1.168(d)-0.]

.01 Historical comment: Proposed 12/31/90. Adopted 10/28/92 by T.D. 8444.

¶ 560

Reg. § 1.168(d)-1

§ 1.168(d)-1. **Applicable conventions—Half-year and mid-quarter conventions.**—(a) *In general.*—Under section 168(d), the half-year convention applies to depreciable property (other than certain real property described in section 168(d)(2)) placed in service during a taxable year, unless the mid-quarter convention applies to the property. Under section 168(d)(3)(A), the mid-quarter convention applies to depreciable property (other than certain real property described in section 168(d)(2)) placed in service during a taxable year if the aggregate basis of property placed in service during the last three months of the taxable year exceeds 40 percent of the aggregate basis of property placed in service during the taxable year ("the 40-percent test"). Thus, if the depreciable property is placed in service during a taxable year that consists of three months or less, the mid-quarter convention applies to the property. Under section 168(d)(3)(B)(i), the depreciable basis of nonresidential real property, residential rental property, and any railroad grading or tunnel bore is disregarded in applying the 40-percent test. For rules regarding property that is placed in service and disposed of in the same taxable year, see paragraph (b)(3) of this section. For the definition of "aggregate basis of property," see paragraph (b)(4) of this section.

(b) *Applicable conventions—half-year and mid-quarter conventions.*—(1) *Property described in section 168(f).*—In determining whether the 40-percent test is satisfied for a taxable year, the depreciable basis of property described in section 168(f) (property to which section 168 does not apply) is not taken into account.

(2) *Listed property.*—The depreciable basis of listed property (as defined in section 280F(d)(4) and the regulations thereunder) placed in service during a taxable year is taken into account (unless otherwise excluded) in applying the 40-percent test.

(3) *Property placed in service and disposed of in the same taxable year.*—(3) (i) Under section 168(d) (3) (B) (ii), the depreciable basis of property placed in service and disposed of in the same taxable year is not taken into account in determining whether the 40-percent test is satisfied. However, the depreciable basis of property placed in service, disposed of, subsequently reacquired, and again placed in service, by the taxpayer in the same taxable year must be taken into account in applying the 40-percent test, but the basis of the property is only taken into account on the later of the dates that the property is placed in service by the taxpayer during the taxable year. Further, see §§1.168(i)-6(c) (4) (v) (B) and 1.168(i)-6(f) for rules relating to property placed in service and exchanged or involuntarily converted during the same taxable year.

(ii) The applicable convention, as determined under this section, applies to all depreciable property (except nonresidential real property, residential rental property, and any railroad grading or tunnel bore) placed in service by the taxpayer during the taxable year, excluding property placed in service and disposed of in the same taxable year. However, see §§1.168(i)-6(c) (4) (v) (A) and 1.168(i)-6(f) for rules relating to MACRS property that has a basis determined under section 1031(d) or section 1033(b). No depreciation deduction is allowed for property placed in service and disposed of during the same taxable year. However, see §1.168(k)-1(f) (1) for rules relating to qualified property or 50-percent bonus depreciation property, and §1.1400L(b)-1(f) (1) for rules relating to qualified New York Liberty Zone property, that is placed in service by the taxpayer in the same taxable year in which either a partnership is terminated as a result of a technical termination under section 708(b) (1) (B) or the property is transferred in a transaction described in section 168(i) (7).

»»→ Caution: Reg. §1.168(d)-1(b)(4) does not reflect recent law changes. For details, see ¶560.01.

(4) *Aggregate basis of property.*—For purposes of the 40-percent test, the term "aggregate basis of property" means the sum of the depreciable bases of all items of depreciable property that are taken into account in applying the 40-percent test. "Depreciable basis" means the basis of depreciable property for purposes of determining gain under sections 1011 through 1024. The depreciable basis for the taxable year the property is placed in service reflects the reduction in basis for—

(i) Any portion of the basis the taxpayer properly elects to treat as an expense under section 179;

(ii) Any adjustment to basis under section 48(q); and

(iii) The percentage of the taxpayer's use of property for the taxable year other than in the taxpayer's trade or business (or for the production of income), but is determined before any reduction for depreciation under section 167(a) for that taxable year.

(5) *Special rules for affiliated groups.*—(i) In the case of a consolidated group (as defined in §1.1502-1(h)), all members of the group that are included on the consolidated return are treated as one taxpayer for purposes of applying the 40-percent test. Thus, the depreciable bases of all property placed in service by members of a consolidated group during a consolidated return year are taken into account (unless otherwise excluded) in applying the 40-percent test to determine whether the mid-quarter convention applies to property placed in service by the members during the consolidated return year. The 40-percent test is applied separately to the depreciable bases of property placed in service by any member of an affiliated group that is not included in a consolidated return for the taxable year in which the property is placed in service.

(ii) In the case of a corporation formed by a member or members of a consolidated group and that is itself a member of the consolidated group ("newly-formed subsidiary"), the depreciable bases of property placed in service by the newly-formed subsidiary in the consolidated return year in which it is formed is included with the depreciable bases of property placed in service during the consolidated return year by the other members of the consolidated group in applying the 40-percent test. If depreciable property is placed in service by a newly-formed subsidiary during the consolidated return year in which it was formed, the newly-formed subsidiary is considered as being in existence for the entire consolidated return year for purposes of applying the applicable convention to determine when the recovery period begins.

(iii) The provisions of paragraph (b)(5)(ii) of this section are illustrated by the following example.

Example. Assume a member of a consolidated group that files its return on a calendar-year basis forms a subsidiary on August 1. The subsidiary places depreciable property in service on August 5. If the mid-quarter convention applies to property placed in service by the members of the consolidated group (including the newly-formed subsidiary), the property placed in service by the subsidiary on August 5 is deemed placed in service on the mid-point of the third quarter of the consolidated return year (*i.e.,* August 15). If the mid-quarter convention does not apply, the property is deemed placed in service on the mid-point of the consolidated return year (*i.e.,* July 1).

(iv) In the case of a corporation that joins or leaves a consolidated group, the depreciable bases of property placed in service by the corporation joining or leaving the group during the portion of the consolidated return year that the corporation is a member of the consolidated group is included with the depreciable bases of property placed in service during the consolidated return year by the other members in applying the 40-percent test. The depreciable bases of property placed in service by the joining or leaving member in the taxable year before it joins or after it leaves the consolidated group is not taken into account by the consolidated group in applying the 40-percent test for the consolidated return year. If a corporation leaves a consolidated group and joins another consolidated group, each consolidated group takes into account, in applying the 40-percent test, the depreciable bases of property placed in service by the corporation while a member of the group.

(v) The provisions of paragraph (b)(5)(iv) of this section are illustrated by the following example.

Example. Assume Corporations A and B file a consolidated return on a calendar-year basis. Corporation C, also a calendar-year taxpayer, enters the consolidated group on July 1 and is included on the consolidated return for that taxable year. The depreciable bases of property placed in service by C during the period of July 1 to December 31 is included with the depreciable bases of property placed in service by A and B during the entire consolidated return year in applying the 40-percent test. The depreciable bases of property placed in service by C from January 1 to June 30 is not taken into account by the consolidated group in applying the 40-percent test. If C was a member of another consolidated group during the period from January 1 to June 30, that consolidated group would include the depreciable bases of property placed in service by C during that period.

(vi) A corporation that joins or leaves a consolidated group during a consolidated year is considered as being a member of the consolidated group for the entire consolidated return year for purposes of applying the applicable convention to determine when the recovery period begins for depreciable property placed in service by the corporation during the portion of the consolidated return year that the corporation is a member of the group.

(vii) If depreciable property is placed in service by a corporation in the taxable year ending immediately before it joins a consolidated group or beginning immediately after it leaves a consolidated group, the applicable convention is applied to the property under either the full taxable year rules or the short taxable year rules, as applicable.

(viii) The provisions of paragraphs (d)(5)(vi) and (vii) of this section are illustrated by the following example.

Example. Assume that on July 1, C, a calendar-year corporation, joins a consolidated group that files a return on a calendar-year basis. The short taxable year rules apply to C for the period of January 1 to June 30. However, in applying the applicable convention to determine when the recovery period begins for depreciable property placed in service for the period of July 1 to December 31, C is considered as being a member of the consolidated group for the entire consolidated return year. Thus, if the half-year convention applies to depreciable property placed in service by the consolidated group (taking into account the depreciable bases of property placed in service by C after June 30), the property is deemed placed in service on the mid-point of the consolidated return year (*i.e.*, July 1, if the group did not have a short taxable year).

(ix) In the case of a transfer of depreciable property between members of a consolidated group, the following special rules apply for purposes of applying the 40-percent test. Property that is placed in service by one member of a consolidated group and transferred to another member of the same group is considered as placed in service on the date that it is placed in service by the transferor member, and the date it is placed in service by the transferee member is disregarded. In the case of multiple transfers of property between members of a consolidated group, the property is considered as placed in service on the date that the first member places the property in service, and the dates it is placed in service by other members are disregarded. The depreciable basis of the transferred property that is taken into account in applying the 40-percent test is the depreciable basis of the property in the hands of the transferor member (as determined under paragraph (b)(4) of this section), or, in the case of multiple transfers of property between members, the depreciable basis in the hands of the first member that placed the property in service.

(x) The provisions of paragraph (b)(5)(ix) of this section are illustrated by the following example.

Example. Assume the ABC consolidated group files its return on a calendar-year basis. A, a member of the consolidated group, purchases depreciable property costing $50,000 and places the property in service on January 5, 1991. On December 1, 1991, the property is transferred for $75,000 to B, another member of the consolidated group. In applying the 40-percent test to the members of the consolidated group for 1991, the property is considered as placed in service on January 5, the date that A placed the property in service, and the depreciable basis of the property that is taken into account is $50,000.

(6) *Special rule for partnerships and S corporations.*—In the case of property placed in service by a partnership or an S corporation, the 40-percent test is generally applied at the partnership or corporate level. However, if a partnership or an S corporation is formed or availed of for the principal purpose of either avoiding the application of the mid-quarter convention or having the mid-quarter convention apply where it otherwise would not, the 40-percent test is applied at the partner, shareholder, or other appropriate level.

(7) *Certain nonrecognition transactions.*—(i) Except as provided in paragraph (b)(6) of this section, if depreciable property is transferred in a transaction described in section 168(i)(7)(B)(i) (other than in a transaction between members of a consolidated group) in the same taxable year that the property is placed in service by the transferor, the 40-percent test is applied by treating the transferred property as placed in service by the transferee on the date of transfer. Thus, if the aggregate basis of property (including the transferred property) placed in service

by the transferee during the last three months of its taxable year exceeds 40 percent of the aggregate basis of property (including the transferred property) placed in service by the transferee during the taxable year, the mid-quarter convention applies to the transferee's depreciable property, including the transferred property. The depreciable basis of the transferred property is not taken into account by the transferor in applying the 40-percent test for the taxable year that the transferor placed the property in service.

(ii) In applying the applicable convention to determine when the recovery period for the transferred property begins, the date on which the transferor placed the property in service must be used. Thus, for example, if the mid-quarter convention applies, the recovery period for the transferred property begins on the mid-point of the quarter of the taxable year that the transferor placed the property in service. If the transferor placed the transferred property in service in a short taxable year, then for purposes of applying the applicable convention and allocating the depreciation deduction between the transferor and the transferee, the transferor is treated as having a full 12-month taxable year commencing on the first day of the short taxable year. The depreciation deduction for the transferor's taxable year in which the property was placed in service is allocated between the transferor and the transferee based on the number of months in the transferor's taxable year that each party held the property in service. For purposes of allocating the depreciation deduction, the transferor takes into account the month in which the property was placed in service but does not take into account the month in which the property was transferred. The transferee is allocated the remaining portion of the depreciation deduction for the transferor's taxable year in which the property was transferred. For the remainder of the transferee's current taxable year (if the transferee has a different taxable year than the transferor) and for subsequent taxable years, the depreciation deduction for the transferee is calculated by allocating to the transferee's taxable year the depreciation attributable to each recovery year, or portion thereof, that falls within the transferee's taxable year.

(iii) If the applicable convention for the transferred property has not been determined by the time the transferor files its income tax return for the year of transfer because the transferee's taxable year has not ended, the transferor may use either the mid-quarter or the half-year convention in determining the depreciation deduction for the property. However, the transferor must specify on the depreciation form filed for the taxable year that the applicable convention has not been determined for the property. If the transferee determines that a different convention applies to the transferred property, the transferor should redetermine the depreciation deduction on the property, and, within the period of limitation, should file an amended income tax return for the taxable year and pay any additional tax due plus interest.

(iv) The provisions of this paragraph (b)(7) are illustrated by the following example.

Example. (i) During 1991, C, a calendar-year taxpayer, purchases satellite equipment costing $100,000, and computer equipment costing $15,000. The satellite equipment is placed in service in January, and the computer equipment in February. On October 1, C transfers the computer equipment to Z Partnership in a transaction described in section 721. During 1991, Z, a calendar-year partnership, purchases 30 office desks for a total of $15,000. The desks are placed in service in June. These are the only items of depreciable property placed in service by C and Z during 1991.

(ii) In applying the 40-percent test, because C transferred the computer equipment in a transaction described in section 168(i)(7)(B)(i) in the same taxable year that C placed it in service, the computer equipment is treated as placed in service by the transferee, Z, on the date of transfer, October 1. The 40-percent test is satisfied with respect to Z, because the computer equipment is placed in service during the last three months of Z's taxable year and its basis ($15,000) exceeds 40 percent of the aggregate basis of property placed in service by Z during the taxable year (desks and computer equipment with an aggregate basis of $30,000).

(iii) In applying the mid-quarter convention to determine when the computer equipment is deemed to be placed in service, the date on which C placed the property in service is used. Accordingly, because C placed the computer equipment in service during the first quarter of its taxable year, the computer equipment is deemed placed in service on February 15, 1991, the mid-point of the first quarter of C's taxable year. The depreciation deduction allowable for C's 1991 taxable year, $5,250 ($15,000 × 40 percent × 10.5⁄12), is allocated between C and Z based on the number of months in C's taxable year that C and Z held the property in service. Thus, because the property was in service for 11 months during C's 1991 taxable year and C held it for 8 of those 11 months, C is allocated $3,818 (8⁄11 × $5,250). Z is allocated $1,432, the remaining 3⁄11 of the $5,250 depreciation deduction for C's 1991 taxable year. For 1992, Z's depreciation deduction for the computer equipment is $3,900, the sum of the remaining 1.5 months of depreciation deduction for the first recovery year and 10.5 months of depreciation deduction for the second recovery year (($15,000 × 40 percent × 1.5⁄12) + ($9,000 × 40 percent × 10.5/12)).

(c) *Disposition of property subject to the half-year or mid-quarter convention.*—(1) *In general.*—If depreciable property is subject to the half-year (or mid-quarter) convention in the taxable year in which it is placed in service, it also is subject to the half-year (or mid-quarter) convention in the taxable year in which it is disposed of.

(2) *Example.*—The provisions of paragraph (c)(1) of this section are illustrated by the following example.

Example. In October 1991, B, a calendar-year taxpayer, purchases and places in service a light general purpose truck costing $10,000. B does not elect to expense any part of the cost of the truck, and this is the only item of depreciable property placed in service by B during 1991. The 40-percent test is satisfied and the mid-quarter convention applies, because the truck is placed in service during the last three months of the taxable year and no other assets are placed in service in that year. In April 1993 (prior to the end of the truck's recovery period), B sells the truck. The mid-quarter convention applies in determining the depreciation deduction for the truck in 1993, the year of disposition.

(d) *Effective dates.*—(1) *In general.*—This section applies to depreciable property placed in service in taxable years ending after January 30, 1991. For depreciable property placed in service after December 31, 1986, in taxable years ending on or before January 30, 1991, a taxpayer may use a method other than the method provided in this section in applying the 40-percent test and the applicable convention, provided the method is reasonable and is consistently applied to the taxpayer's property.

(2) *Qualified property, 50-percent bonus depreciation property, or qualified New York Liberty Zone property.*—This section also applies to qualified property under section 168(k)(2) or qualified New York Liberty Zone property under section 1400L(b) acquired by a taxpayer after September 10, 2001, and to 50-percent percent bonus depreciation property under section 168(k)(4) acquired by a taxpayer after May 5, 2003.

(3) *Like-kind exchanges and involuntary conversions.*—(3) Like-kind exchanges and involuntary conversions.—The last sentence in paragraph (b)(3)(i) and the second sentence in paragraph (b)(3)(ii) of this section apply to exchanges to which section 1031 applies, and involuntary conversions to which section 1033

applies, of MACRS property for which the time of disposition and the time of replacement both occur after February 27, 2004. [Reg. 1.168(d)-1.]

.01 Historical Comment: Proposed 12/31/90. Adopted 10/28/92 by T.D. 8444. Amended 9/5/2003 by T.D. 9091, 2/27/2004 by T.D. 9115, 8/28/2006 by T.D. 9283 and 2/26/2007 by T.D. 9314. [Reg. § 1.168(d)-1(b)(4) does not reflect P.L. 96-223(1980) and P.L. 101-508 (1990).]

¶ 562

Reg. § 1.168(h)-1

§ 1.168(h)-1. **Like-kind exchanges involving tax-exempt use property.**—(a) *Scope.*—(1) This section applies with respect to a direct or indirect transfer of property among related persons, including transfers made through a qualified intermediary (as defined in § 1.1031(k)-1(g)(4)) or other unrelated person, (a transfer) if—

(i) Section 1031 applies to any party to the transfer or to any related transaction; and

(ii) A principal purpose of the transfer or any related transaction is to avoid or limit the application of the alternative depreciation system (within the meaning of section 168(g)).

(2) For purposes of this section, a person is related to another person if they bear a relationship specified in section 267(b) or section 707(b)(1).

(b) *Allowable depreciation deduction for property subject to this section.*—(1) *In general.*—Property (tainted property) transferred directly or indirectly to a taxpayer by a related person (related party) as part of, or in connection with, a transaction in which the related party receives tax-exempt use property (related tax-exempt use property) will, if the tainted property is subject to an allowance for depreciation, be treated in the same manner as the related tax-exempt use property for purposes of determining the allowable depreciation deduction under section 167(a). Under this paragraph (b), the tainted property is depreciated by the taxpayer over the remaining recovery period of, and using the same depreciation method and convention as that of, the related tax-exempt use property.

(2) *Limitations.*—(i) *Taxpayer's basis in related tax-exempt use property.*—The rules of this paragraph (b) apply only with respect to so much of the taxpayer's basis in the tainted property as does not exceed the taxpayer's adjusted basis in the related tax-exempt use property prior to the transfer. Any excess of the taxpayer's basis in the tainted property over its adjusted basis in the related tax-exempt use property prior to the transfer is treated as property to which this section does not apply. This paragraph (b)(2)(i) does not apply if the related tax-exempt use property is not acquired from the taxpayer (e.g., if the taxpayer acquires the tainted property for cash but section 1031 nevertheless applies to the related party because the transfer involves a qualified intermediary).

(ii) *Application of section 168(i)(7).*—This section does not apply to so much of the taxpayer's basis in the tainted property as is subject to section 168(i)(7).

(c) *Related tax-exempt use property.*—(1) For purposes of paragraph (b) of this section, related tax-exempt use property includes—

(i) Property that is tax-exempt use property (as defined in section 168(h)) at the time of the transfer; and

(ii) Property that does not become tax-exempt use property until after the transfer if, at the time of the transfer, it was intended that the property become tax-exempt use property.

(2) For purposes of determining the remaining recovery period of the related tax-exempt use property in the circumstances described in paragraph (c)(1)(ii) of this section, the related tax-exempt use property will be treated as having, prior to the transfer, a lease term equal to the term of any lease that causes such property to become tax-exempt use property.

(d) *Examples.*—The following examples illustrate the application of this section. The examples do not address common law doctrines or other authorities that may apply to recharacterize or alter the effects of the transactions described therein. Unless otherwise indicated, parties to the transactions are not related to one another.

Example 1. (i) X owns all of the stock of two subsidiaries, B and Z. X, B and Z do not file a consolidated federal income tax return. On May 5, 1995, B purchases an aircraft (*FA*) for $1 million and leases it to a foreign airline whose income is not subject to United States taxation and which is a tax-exempt entity as defined in section 168(h)(2). On the same date, Z owns an aircraft (*DA*) with a fair market value of $1 million, which has been, and continues to be, leased to an airline that is a United States taxpayer. Z's adjusted basis in DA is $0. The next day, at a time when each aircraft is still worth $1 million, B transfers FA to Z (subject to the lease to the foreign airline) in exchange for DA (subject to the lease to the airline that is a United States taxpayer). Z realizes gain of $1 million on the exchange, but that gain is not recognized pursuant to section 1031(a) because the exchange is of like-kind properties. Assume that a principal purpose of the transfer of DA to B or of FA to Z is to avoid the application of the alternative depreciation system. Following the exchange, Z has a $0 basis in FA pursuant to section 1031(d). B has a $1 million basis in DA.

(ii) B has acquired property from Z, a related person; Z's gain is not recognized pursuant to section 1031(a); Z has received tax-exempt use property as part of the transaction; and a principal purpose of the transfer of DA to B or of FA to Z is to avoid the application of the alternative depreciation system. Accordingly, the transaction is within the scope of this section. Pursuant to paragraph (b) of this section, B must recover its $1 million basis in DA over the remaining recovery period of, and using the same depreciation method and convention as that of, FA, the related tax-exempt use property.

(iii) If FA did not become tax-exempt use property until after the exchange, it would still be related tax-exempt use property and paragraph (b) of this section would apply if, at the time of the exchange, it was intended that FA become tax-exempt use property.

Example 2. (i) X owns all of the stock of two subsidiaries, B and Z. X, B and Z do not file a consolidated federal income tax return. B and Z each own identical aircraft. B's aircraft (*FA*) is leased to a tax-exempt entity as defined in section 168(h)(2) and has a fair market value of $1 million and an adjusted basis of $500,000. Z's aircraft (DA) is leased to a United States taxpayer and has a fair market value of $1 million and an adjusted basis of $10,000. On May 1, 1995, B and Z exchange aircraft, subject to their respective leases. B realizes gain of $500,000 and Z realizes gain of $990,000, but neither person recognizes gain because of the operation of section 1031(a). Moreover, assume that a principal purpose of the transfer of DA to B or of FA to Z is to avoid the application of the alternative depreciation system.

(ii) As in *Example 1,* B has acquired property from Z, a related person; Z's gain is not recognized pursuant to section 1031(a); Z has received tax-exempt use property as part of the transaction; and a principal purpose of the transfer of DA to B or of FA to Z is to avoid the application of the alternative depreciation system. Thus, the transaction is within the scope of this section even though B has held tax-exempt use property for a period of time and, during that time, has used the alternative depreciation system with respect to such property. Pursuant to paragraph (b) of this section, B, which has a substituted basis determined pursuant to section 1031(d) of $500,000 in DA, must depreciate the aircraft over the remaining recovery period of FA, using the same depreciation method and convention. Z holds tax-exempt use property with a basis of $10,000, which must be depreciated under the alternative depreciation system.

(iii) Assume the same facts as in paragraph (i) of this *Example 2*, except that B and Z are members of an affiliated group that files a consolidated federal income tax return. Of B's $500,000 basis in DA, $10,000 is subject to section 168(i)(7) and therefore not subject to this section. The remaining $490,000 of basis is subject to this section. But see § 1.1502-80(f) making section 1031 inapplicable to intercompany transactions occurring in consolidated return years beginning on or after July 12, 1995.

(e) *Effective date.*—This section applies to transfers made on or after April 20, 1995. [Reg. § 1.168(h)-1.]

.01 Historical Comment: Proposed 4/21/95. Adopted 4/26/96 by T.D. 8667.

¶ 564

Reg. § 1.168(i)-0

§ 1.168(i)-0. **Table of contents for the general asset account rules.**—This section lists the major paragraphs contained in Reg. § 1.168(i)-1.

§ 1.168(i)-1. General asset accounts.

(a) Scope.
(b) Definitions.
  (1) Unadjusted depreciable basis.
  (2) Unadjusted depreciable basis of the general asset account.
  (3) Adjusted depreciable basis of the general asset account.
  (4) Expensed cost.
(c) Establishment of general asset accounts.
  (1) Assets eligible for general asset accounts.
    (i) General rules.
    (ii) Special rules for assets generating foreign source income.
  (2) Grouping assets in general asset accounts.
    (i) General rules.
    (ii) Special rules.
(d) Determination of depreciation allowance.
  (1) In general.
  (2) Special rule for passenger automobiles.
(e) Disposition of an asset from a general asset account.
  (1) Scope.
  (2) General rules for a disposition.
    (i) No immediate recovery of basis.
    (ii) Treatment of amount realized.
    (iii) Effect of disposition on a general asset account.
    (iv) Coordination with nonrecognition provisions.
    (v) Examples.
  (3) Special rules.
    (i) In general.
    (ii) Disposition of all assets remaining in a general asset account.
    (iii) Disposition of an asset in a qualifying disposition.
    (iv) Transactions subject to section 168(i)(7).

(v) Transactions subject to section 1031 or 1033.
(vi) Anti-abuse rule.
(f) Assets generating foreign source income.
(1) In general.
(2) Source of ordinary income, gain, or loss.
(i) Source determined by allocation and apportionment of depreciation allowed.
(g) Assets subject to recapture.
(h) Changes in use.
(1) Conversion to personal use.
(2) Change in use results in a different recovery period and/or depreciation method.
(i) No effect on general asset account election.
(ii) Asset is removed from the general asset account.
(iii) New general asset account is established.
(i) Identification of disposed or converted asset.
(j) Effect of adjustments on prior dispositions.
(k) Election.
(1) Irrevocable election.
(2) Time for making election.
(3) Manner of making election.
(l) Effective date.
(1) In general.
(2) Exceptions.
(3) Like-kind exchanges and involuntary conversions.

[Reg. § 1.168(i)-0.]

.01 Historical Comment: Proposed 8/31/92. Adopted 10/7/94 by T.D. 8566. Amended 2/27/2004 by T.D. 9115, 6/16/2004 by T.D. 9132 and 2/26/2007 by T.D. 9314.

¶ 565

Reg. § 1.168(i)-1

§ 1.168(i)-1. **General asset accounts.**—(a) *Scope.*—This section provides rules for general asset accounts under section 168(i)(4). The provisions of this section apply only to assets for which an election has been made under paragraph (k) of this section.

(b) *Definitions.*—For purposes of this section, the following definitions apply:

(1) *Unadjusted depreciable basis* is the basis of an asset for purposes of section 1011 without regard to any adjustments described in section 1016(a)(2) and (3). This basis reflects the reduction in basis for the percentage of the taxpayer's use of property for the taxable year other than in the taxpayer's trade or business (or for the production of income), for any portion of the basis the taxpayer properly elects to treat as an expense under section 179, and for any adjustments to basis provided by other provisions of the Internal Revenue Code and the regulations under the Internal Revenue Code (other than section 1016(a)(2) and (3)) (for example, a reduction in basis by the amount of the disabled access credit pursuant to section 44(d)(7)). For property subject to a lease, see section 167(c)(2).

(2) *Unadjusted depreciable basis of the general asset account.*—is the sum of the unadjusted depreciable bases of all assets included in the general asset account.

(3) *Adjusted depreciable basis of the general asset account.*—is the unadjusted depreciable basis of the general asset account less the adjustments to basis described in sections 1016(a)(2) and (3).

(4) *Expensed cost.*—is the amount of any allowable credit or deduction treated as a deduction allowable for depreciation or amortization for purposes of section 1245 (for example, a credit allowable under section 30 or a deduction allowable under section 179, 179A, or 190).

(c) *Establishment of general asset accounts.*—(1) *Assets eligible for general asset accounts.*—(i) *General rules.*—Assets that are subject to either the general depreciation system of section 168(a) or the alternative depreciation system of section 168(g) may be accounted for in one or more general asset accounts. An asset may be included in a general asset account only to the extent of the asset's unadjusted depreciable basis (for example, if, in 1995, a taxpayer places in service an asset that costs $20,000 and elects under section 179 to expense $17,500 of that asset's cost, the unadjusted depreciable basis of the asset is $2,500 and, therefore, only $2,500 of the asset's cost may be included in a general asset account). However, an asset is not to be included in a general asset account if the asset is used both in a trade or business (or for the production of income) and in a personal activity at any time during the taxable year in which the asset is first placed in service by the taxpayer.

(ii) *Special rules for assets generating foreign source income.*—(A) Assets that generate foreign source income, both United States and foreign source income, or combined gross income of a FSC (as defined in section 922), DISC (as defined in section 992(a)), or possessions corporation (as defined in section 936) and its related supplier, may be included in a general asset account if the requirements of paragraph (c)(2)(i) of this section are satisfied. If, however, the inclusion of these assets in a general asset account results in a substantial distortion of income, the Commissioner may disregard the general asset account election and make any reallocations of income or expense necessary to clearly reflect income.

(B) A general asset account shall be treated as a single asset for purposes of applying the rules in § 1.861-9T(g)(3) (relating to allocation and apportionment of interest expense under the asset method). A general asset account that generates income in more than one grouping of income (statutory and residual) is a multiple category asset (as defined in § 1.861-9T(g)(3)(ii)), and the income yield from the general asset account must be determined by applying the rules for multiple category assets as if the general asset account were a single asset.

(2) *Grouping assets in general asset accounts.*—(i) *General rules.*—If a taxpayer makes the election under paragraph (k) of this section, assets that are subject to the election are grouped into one or more general asset accounts. Assets that are eligible to be grouped into a single general asset account may be divided into more than one general asset account. Each general asset account must include only assets that—

(A) Have the same asset class (for further guidance, see Rev. Proc. 87-56, 1987-2 CB 674, and § 601.601(d)(2)(ii)(*b*) of this chapter);

(B) Have the same applicable depreciation method;

(C) Have the same applicable recovery period;

(D) Have the same applicable convention; and

(E) Are placed in service by the taxpayer in the same taxable year.

(ii) *Special rules.*—In addition to the general rules in paragraph (c)(2)(i) of this section, the following rules apply when establishing general asset accounts—

(A) Assets without an asset class, but with the same characteristics described in paragraphs (c)(2)(i)(B), (C), (D), and (E) of this section, may be grouped into a general asset account;

(B) Assets subject to the mid-quarter convention may only be grouped into a general asset account with assets that are placed in service in the same quarter of the taxable year;

(C) Assets subject to the mid-month convention may only be grouped into a general asset account with assets that are placed in service in the same month of the taxable year;

(D) Passenger automobiles for which the depreciation allowance is limited under section 280F(a) must be grouped into a separate general asset account; and

(E) Assets subject to paragraph (h)(2)(iii)(A) of this section (change in use results in a shorter recovery period and/or a more accelerated depreciation method) for which the depreciation allowance for the year of change (as defined in § 1.168(i)-4(a)) is not determined by using an optional depreciation table must be grouped into a separate general asset account.

(d) *Determination of depreciation allowance.*—(1) *In general.*—Depreciation allowances are determined for each general asset account by using the applicable depreciation method, recovery period, and convention for the assets in the account. The depreciation allowances are recorded in a depreciation reserve account for each general asset account. The allowance for depreciation under this section constitutes the amount of depreciation allowable under section 167(a).

(2) *Special rule for passenger automobiles.*—For purposes of applying section 280F(a), the depreciation allowance for a general asset account established for passenger automobiles is limited for each taxable year to the amount prescribed in section 280F(a) multiplied by the excess of the number of automobiles originally included in the account over the number of automobiles disposed of during the taxable year or in any prior taxable year in a transaction described in paragraph (e)(3)(iii) (disposition of an asset in a qualifying disposition), (e)(3)(iv) (transactions subject to section 168(i)(7)), (e)(3)(v) (transactions subject to section 1031 or 1033), (e)(3)(vi) (anti-abuse rule), (g) (assets subject to recapture), or (h)(1) (conversion to personal use) of this section.

(e) *Disposition of an asset from a general asset account.*—(1) *Scope.*—This paragraph (e) provides rules applicable to dispositions of assets included in a general asset account. For purposes of this paragraph (e), an asset in a general asset account is disposed of when ownership of the asset is transferred or when the asset is permanently withdrawn from use either in the taxpayer's trade or business or in the production of income. A disposition includes the sale, exchange, retirement, physical abandonment, or destruction of an asset. A disposition also occurs when an asset is transferred to a supplies, scrap, or similar account. A disposition does not include, however, the retirement of a structural component of real property.

(2) *General rules for a disposition.*—(i) *No immediate recovery of basis.*—Immediately before a disposition of any asset in a general asset account, the asset is treated as having an adjusted basis of zero for purposes of section 1011. Therefore, no loss is realized upon the disposition of an asset from the general asset account. Similarly, where an asset is disposed of by transfer to a supplies, scrap, or similar account, the basis of the asset in the supplies, scrap, or similar account will be zero.

(ii) *Treatment of amount realized.*—Any amount realized on a disposition is recognized as ordinary income (notwithstanding any other provision of subtitle A of the Internal Revenue Code (Code) to the extent the sum of the unadjusted depreciable basis of the general asset account and any expensed cost (as defined in paragraph (b)(4) of this section) for assets in the account exceeds any amounts previously recognized as ordinary income upon the disposition of other assets in the account. The recognition and character of any excess amount realized are determined under other applicable provisions of the Code (other than sections 1245 and 1250 or provisions of the Code that treat gain on a disposition as subject to section 1245 or 1250).

(iii) *Effect of disposition on a general asset account.*—The unadjusted depreciable basis and the depreciation reserve of the general asset account are not affected as a result of a disposition of an asset from the general asset account.

(iv) *Coordination with nonrecognition provisions.*—For purposes of determining the basis of an asset acquired in a transaction described in paragraph (e)(3)(iii)(B)(*4*) of this section (relating to certain nonrecognition provisions), the amount of ordinary income recognized under this paragraph (e)(2) is treated as the amount of gain recognized on the disposition.

(v) *Examples.*—The following examples illustrate the application of this paragraph (e)(2).

Example 1. (i) *R*, a calendar-year corporation, maintains one general asset account for ten machines. The machines cost a total of $10,000 and were placed in service in June 1995. Of the ten machines, one machine costs $8,200 and nine machines cost a total of $1,800. Assume this general asset account has a depreciation method of 200 percent declining balance, a recovery period of 5 years, and a half-year convention. *R* does not make a section 179 election for any of the machines. As of January 1, 1996, the depreciation reserve of the account is $2,000 [(($10,000 – $0) × 40%) / 2].

(ii) On February 8, 1996, *R* sells the machine that cost $8,200 to an unrelated party for $9,000. Under paragraph (e)(2)(i) of this section, this machine has an adjusted basis of zero.

(iii) On its 1996 tax return, *R* recognizes the amount realized of $9,000 as ordinary income because such amount does not exceed the unadjusted depreciable basis of the general asset account ($10,000), plus any expensed cost for assets in the account ($0), less amounts previously recognized as ordinary income ($0). Moreover, the unadjusted depreciable basis and depreciation reserve of the account are not affected by the disposition of the machine. Thus, the depreciation allowance for the account in 1996 is $3,200 (($10,000 – $2,000) × 40%).

Example 2. (i) The facts are the same as in *Example 1.* In addition, on June 4, 1997, *R* sells seven machines to an unrelated party for a total of $1,100. In accordance with paragraph (e)(2)(i) of this section, these machines have an adjusted basis of zero.

(ii) On its 1997 tax return, *R* recognizes $1,000 as ordinary income (the unadjusted depreciable basis of $10,000, plus the expensed cost of $0, less the amount of $9,000 previously recognized as ordinary income). The recognition and character of the excess amount realized of $100 ($1,100 – $1,000) are determined under applicable provisions of the Code other than section 1245 (such as section 1231). Moreover, the unadjusted depreciable basis and depreciation reserve of the account are not affected by the disposition of the machines. Thus, the depreciation allowance for the account in 1997 is $1,920 (($10,000 – $5,200) × 40%).

(3) *Special rules.*—(i) *In general.*—This paragraph (e)(3) provides the rules for terminating general asset account treatment upon certain dispositions. While the rules under paragraphs (e)(3)(ii) and (iii) of this section are optional rules, the rules under paragraphs (e)(3)(iv), (v), and (vi) of this section are mandatory rules. A taxpayer applies paragraph (e)(3)(ii) or (iii) of this section by reporting the gain, loss, or other deduction on the taxpayer's timely filed Federal income tax return (including extensions) for the taxable year in which the disposition occurs. For purposes of applying paragraph (e)(3)(iii) through (vi) of this

section, see paragraph (i) of this section for identifying the unadjusted depreciable basis of a disposed asset.

(ii) *Disposition of all assets remaining in a general asset account.*—(A) *Optional termination of a general asset account.*—Upon the disposition of all of the assets, or the last asset, in a general asset account, a taxpayer may apply this paragraph (e)(3)(ii) to recover the adjusted depreciable basis of the general asset account (rather than having paragraph (e)(2) of this section apply). Under this paragraph (e)(3)(ii), the general asset account terminates and the amount of gain or loss for the general asset account is determined under section 1001(a) by taking into account the adjusted depreciable basis of the general asset account at the time of the disposition. The recognition and character of the gain or loss are determined under other applicable provisions of the Code, except that the amount of gain subject to section 1245 (or section 1250) is limited to the excess of the depreciation allowed or allowable for the general asset account, including any expensed cost (or the excess of the additional depreciation allowed or allowable for the general asset account), over any amounts previously recognized as ordinary income under paragraph (e)(2) of this section.

(B) *Example.*—The following example illustrates the application of this paragraph (e)(3)(ii).

Example. (i) *T*, a calendar-year corporation, maintains a general asset account for 1,000 calculators. The calculators cost a total of $60,000 and were placed in service in 1995. Assume this general asset account has a depreciation method of 200 percent declining balance, a recovery period of 5 years, and a half-year convention. *T* does not make a section 179 election for any of the calculators. In 1996, *T* sells 200 of the calculators to an unrelated party for a total of $10,000 and recognizes the $10,000 as ordinary income in accordance with paragraph (e)(2) of this section.

(ii) On March 26, 1997, *T* sells the remaining calculators in the general asset account to an unrelated party for $35,000. *T* chooses to apply paragraph (e)(3)(ii) of this section. As a result, the account terminates and gain or loss is determined for the account.

(iii) On the date of disposition, the adjusted depreciable basis of the account is $23,040 (unadjusted depreciable basis of $60,000 less the depreciation allowed or allowable of $36,960). Thus, in 1997, *T* recognizes gain of $11,960 (amount realized of $35,000 less the adjusted depreciable basis of $23,040). The gain of $11,960 is subject to section 1245 to the extent of the depreciation allowed or allowable for the account (plus the expensed cost for assets in the account) less the amounts previously recognized as ordinary income ($36,960 + $0 - $10,000 = $26,960). As a result, the entire gain of $11,960 is subject to section 1245.

(iii) *Disposition of an asset in a qualifying disposition.*—(A) *Optional determination of the amount of gain, loss, or other deduction.*—In the case of a qualifying disposition of an asset (described in paragraph (e)(3)(iii)(B) of this section), a taxpayer may apply this paragraph (e)(3)(iii) (rather than having paragraph (e)(2) of this section apply). Under this paragraph (e)(3)(iii), general asset account treatment for the asset terminates as of the first day of the taxable year in which the qualifying disposition occurs, and the amount of gain, loss, or other deduction for the asset is determined by taking into account the asset's adjusted basis. The adjusted basis of the asset at the time of the disposition equals the unadjusted depreciable basis of the asset less the depreciation allowed or allowable for the asset, computed by using the depreciation method, recovery period, and convention applicable to the general asset account in which the asset was included. The recognition and character of the gain, loss, or other deduction are determined under other applicable provisions of the Code, except that the amount of gain subject to section 1245 (or section 1250) is limited to the lesser of—

(1) The depreciation allowed or allowable for the asset, including any expensed cost (or the additional depreciation allowed or allowable for the asset); or

(2) The excess of—

(i) The original unadjusted depreciable basis of the general asset account plus, in the case of section 1245 property originally included in the general asset account, any expensed cost; over

(ii) The cumulative amounts of gain previously recognized as ordinary income under either paragraph (e)(2) of this section or section 1245 (or section 1250).

(B) *Qualifying dispositions.*—A qualifying disposition is a disposition that does not involve all the assets, or the last asset, remaining in a general asset account and that is—

(1) A direct result of a fire, storm, shipwreck, or other casualty, or from theft;

(2) A charitable contribution for which a deduction is allowable under section 170;

(3) A direct result of a cessation, termination, or disposition of a business, manufacturing or other income producing process, operation, facility, plant, or other unit (other than by transfer to a supplies, scrap, or similar account); or

(4) A transaction, other than a transaction described in paragraphs (e)(3)(iv) (pertaining to transactions subject to section 168(i)(7)) and (e)(3)(v) (pertaining to transactions subject to section 1031 or 1033) of this section, to which a nonrecognition section of the Code applies (determined without regard to this section).

(C) *Effect of a qualifying disposition on a general asset account.*—If the taxpayer applies this paragraph (e)(3)(iii) to a qualifying disposition of an asset, then—

(1) The asset is removed from the general asset account as of the first day of the taxable year in which the qualifying disposition occurs;

(2) The unadjusted depreciable basis of the general asset account is reduced by the unadjusted depreciable basis of the asset as of the first day of the taxable year in which the disposition occurs;

(3) The depreciation reserve of the general asset account is reduced by the depreciation allowed or allowable for the asset as of the end of the taxable year immediately preceding the year of disposition, computed by using the depreciation method, recovery period, and convention applicable to the general asset account in which the asset was included; and

(4) For purposes of determining the amount of gain realized on subsequent dispositions that is subject to ordinary income treatment under paragraph (e)(2)(ii) of this section, the amount of any expensed cost with respect to the asset is disregarded.

(D) *Example.*—The provisions of this paragraph (e)(3)(iii) are illustrated by the following example.

Example. (i) *Z*, a calendar-year corporation, maintains one general asset account for 12 machines. Each machine costs $15,000 and was placed in service in 1995. Of the 12 machines, nine machines that cost a total of $135,000 are used in *Z*'s Kentucky plant, and three machines that cost a total of $45,000 are used in *Z*'s Ohio plant. Assume this general asset account has a depreciation method of 200 percent declining balance, a recovery period of 5 years, and a half-year convention. *Z* does not make a section 179 election for any of the machines. As of January 1, 1997, the depreciation reserve for the account is $93,600.

(ii) On May 27, 1997, *Z* sells its entire manufacturing plant in Ohio to an unrelated party. The sales proceeds allocated to each of the three machines at the Ohio plant is $5,000. Because this transaction is a qualifying disposition under paragraph (e)(3)(iii)(B)(*3*) of this section, *Z* chooses to apply paragraph (e)(3)(iii) of this section.

(iii) For *Z*'s 1997 return, the depreciation allowance for the account is computed as follows. As of December 31, 1996, the depreciation allowed or allowable for the three machines at the Ohio plant is $23,400. Thus, as of January 1, 1997, the unadjusted depreciable basis of the account is reduced from $180,000 to $135,000 ($180,000 less the unadjusted depreciable basis of $45,000 for the three machines), and the depreciation reserve of the account is decreased from $93,600 to $70,200 ($93,600 less the depreciation allowed or allowable of $23,400 for the three machines as of December 31, 1996). Consequently, the depreciation allowance for the account in 1997 is $25,920 (($135,000 – $70,200) × 40%).

(iv) For *Z*'s 1997 return, gain or loss for each of the three machines at the Ohio plant is determined as follows. The depreciation allowed or allowable in 1997 for each machine is $1,440 [(($15,000 – $7,800) × 40%) / 2]. Thus, the adjusted basis of each machine under section 1011 is $5,760 (the adjusted depreciable basis of $7,200 removed from the account less the depreciation allowed or allowable of $1,440 in 1997). As a result, the loss recognized in 1997 for each machine is $760 ($5,000 – $5,760), which is subject to section 1231.

(iv) *Transactions subject to section 168(i)(7).*—If an asset in a general asset account is transferred in a transaction described in section 168(i)(7)(B) (pertaining to treatment of transferees in certain nonrecognition transactions), the transferor must remove the transferred asset from the general asset account as of the first day of the taxable year in which the transaction occurs. In addition, the adjustments to the general asset account described in paragraph (e)(3)(iii)(C)(*2*) through (*4*) of this section must be made. The transferee is bound by the transferor's election under paragraph (k) of this section with respect to so much of the asset's basis in the hands of the transferee as does not exceed the asset's adjusted basis in the hands of the transferor. If all of the assets, or the last asset, in a general asset account are transferred, the transferee's basis in the assets or asset transferred is equal to the adjusted depreciable basis of the general asset account as of the beginning of the transferor's taxable year in which the transaction occurs, decreased by the amount of depreciation allocable to the transferor for the year of the transfer.

(v) *Transactions subject to section 1031 or section 1033.*—(A) *Like-kind exchange or involuntary conversion of all assets remaining in a general asset account.*—If all the assets, or the last asset, in a general asset account are transferred by a taxpayer in a like-kind exchange (as defined under § 1.168-6(b)(11)) or in an involuntary conversion (as defined under § 1.168-6(b)(12)), the taxpayer must apply this paragraph (e)(3)(v)(A) (instead of applying paragraph (e)(2), (e)(3)(ii), or (e)(3)(iii) of this section). Under this paragraph (e)(3)(v)(A), the general asset account terminates as of the first day of the year of disposition (as defined in § 1.168(i)-6(b)(5)) and—

(1) The amount of gain or loss for the general asset account is determined under section 1001(a) by taking into account the adjusted depreciable basis of the general asset account at the time of disposition (as defined in § 1.168(i)-6(b)(3)). The depreciation allowance for the general asset account in the year of disposition is determined in the same manner as the depreciation allowance for the relinquished MACRS property (as defined in § 1.168(i)-6(b)(2)) in the year of disposition is determined under § 1.168(i)-6. The recognition and character of gain or loss are determined in accordance with paragraph (e)(3)(ii)(A) of this

section (notwithstanding that paragraph (e)(3)(ii) of this section is an optional rule); and

(2) The adjusted depreciable basis of the general asset account at the time of disposition is treated as the adjusted depreciable basis of the relinquished MACRS property.

(B) *Like-kind exchange or involuntary conversion of less than all assets remaining in a general asset account.*—If an asset in a general asset account is transferred by a taxpayer in a like-kind exchange or in an involuntary conversion and if paragraph (e)(3)(v)(A) of this section does not apply to this asset, the taxpayer must apply this paragraph (e)(3)(v)(B) (instead of applying paragraph (e)(2), (e)(3)(ii), or (e)(3)(iii) of this section). Under this paragraph (e)(3)(v)(B), general asset account treatment for the asset terminates as of the first day of the year of disposition (as defined in § 1.168(i)-6(b)(5)), and—

(1) The amount of gain or loss for the asset is determined by taking into account the asset's adjusted basis at the time of disposition (as defined in § 1.168(i)-6(b)(3)). The adjusted basis of the asset at the time of disposition equals the unadjusted depreciable basis of the asset less the depreciation allowed or allowable for the asset, computed by using the depreciation method, recovery period, and convention applicable to the general asset account in which the asset was included. The depreciation allowance for the asset in the year of disposition is determined in the same manner as the depreciation allowance for the relinquished MACRS property (as defined in § 1.168(i)-6(b)(2)) in the year of disposition is determined under § 1.168(i)-6. The recognition and character of the gain or loss are determined in accordance with paragraph (e)(3)(iii)(A) of this section (notwithstanding that paragraph (e)(3)(iii) of this section is an optional rule); and

(2) As of the first day of the year of disposition, the taxpayer must remove the relinquished asset from the general asset account and make the adjustments to the general asset account described in paragraph (e)(3)(iii)(C)(*2*) through (*4*) of this section.

(vi) *Anti-abuse rule.*—(A) *In general.*—If an asset in a general asset account is disposed of by a taxpayer in a transaction described in paragraph (e)(3)(vi)(B) of this section, general asset account treatment for the asset terminates as of the first day of the taxable year in which the disposition occurs. Consequently, the taxpayer must determine the amount of gain, loss, or other deduction attributable to the disposition in the manner described in paragraph (e)(3)(iii)(A) of this section (notwithstanding that paragraph (e)(3)(iii)(A) of this section is an optional rule) and must make the adjustments to the general asset account described in paragraph (e)(3)(iii)(C)(*1*) through (*4*) of this section.

(B) *Abusive transactions.*—A transaction is described in this paragraph (e)(3)(vi)(B) if the transaction is not described in paragraph (e)(3)(iv) or (e)(3)(v) of this section and the transaction is entered into, or made, with a principal purpose of achieving a tax benefit or result that would not be available absent an election under this section. Examples of these types of transactions include—

(1) A transaction entered into with a principal purpose of shifting income or deductions among taxpayers in a manner that would not be possible absent an election under this section in order to take advantage of differing effective tax rates among the taxpayers; or

(2) An election made under this section with a principal purpose of disposing of an asset from a general asset account in order to utilize an expiring net operating loss or credit. The fact that a taxpayer with a net operating loss carryover or a credit carryover transfers an asset to a related person or

transfers an asset pursuant to an arrangement where the asset continues to be used (or is available for use) by the taxpayer pursuant to a lease (or otherwise) indicates, absent strong evidence to the contrary, that the transaction is described in this paragraph (e)(3)(vi)(B).

(f) *Assets generating foreign source income.*—(1) In general.—This paragraph (f) provides the rules for determining the source of any income, gain, or loss recognized, and the appropriate section 904(d) separate limitation category or categories for any foreign source income, gain, or loss recognized, on a disposition (within the meaning of paragraph (e)(1) of this section) of an asset in a general asset account that consists of assets generating both United States and foreign source income. These rules apply only to a disposition to which paragraph (e)(2) (general disposition rules), (e)(3)(ii) (disposition of all assets remaining in a general asset account), (e)(3)(iii) (disposition of an asset in a qualifying disposition), (e)(3)(v) (transactions subject to section 1031 or 1033), or (e)(3)(vi) (anti-abuse rule) of this section applies.

(2) *Source of ordinary income, gain, or loss.*—(i) *Source determined by allocation and apportionment of depreciation allowed.*—The amount of any ordinary income, gain, or loss that is recognized on the disposition of an asset in a general asset account must be apportioned between United States and foreign sources based on the allocation and apportionment of the—

(A) Depreciation allowed for the general asset account as of the end of the taxable year in which the disposition occurs if paragraph (e)(2) of this section applies to the disposition;

(B) Depreciation allowed for the general asset account as of the time of disposition if the taxpayer applies paragraph (e)(3)(ii) of this section to the disposition of all assets, or the last asset, in the general asset account, or if all the assets, or the last asset, in the general asset account are disposed of in a transaction described in paragraph (e)(3)(v)(A) of this section; or

(C) Depreciation allowed for the disposed asset for only the taxable year in which the disposition occurs if the taxpayer applies paragraph (e)(3)(iii) of this section to the disposition of the asset in a qualifying disposition, if the asset is disposed of in a transaction described in paragraph (e)(3)(v)(B) of this section (like-kind exchange or involuntary conversion), or if the asset is disposed in a transaction described in paragraph (e)(3)(vi) of this section (anti-abuse rule).

(ii) *Formula for determining foreign source income, gain, or loss.*—The amount of ordinary income, gain, or loss recognized on the disposition that shall be treated as foreign source income, gain, or loss must be determined under the formula in this paragraph (f)(2)(ii). For purposes of this formula, the allowed depreciation deductions are determined for the applicable time period provided in paragraph (f)(2)(i) of this section. The formula is:

$$\text{Foreign Source Income, Gain, or Loss from the Disposition of an Asset} = \text{Total Ordinary Income, Gain, or Loss from Disposition of an Asset} \times \frac{\text{Allowed Depreciation Deductions Allocated and Apportioned to Foreign Source Income}}{\text{Total Allowed Depreciation Deductions for the General Asset Account or for the Disposed Asset (as applicable)}}$$

(3) *Section 904(d) separate categories.*—If the assets in the general asset account generate foreign source income in more than one separate category under section 904(d)(1) or another section of the Code (for example, income treated as foreign source income under section 904(g)(10)), or under a United States income tax treaty that requires the foreign tax credit limitation to be determined separately for specified types of income, the amount of "foreign source income, gain, or loss

from the disposition of an asset" (as determined under the formula in paragraph (f)(2)(ii) of this section) must be allocated and apportioned to the applicable separate category or categories under the formula in this paragraph (f)(3). For purposes of this formula, the allowed depreciation deductions are determined for the applicable time period provided in paragraph (f)(2)(i) of this section. The formula is:

$$\text{Foreign Source Income, Gain, or Loss In a Separate Category} = \text{Foreign Source Income, Gain, or Loss from the Disposition of an Asset} \times \frac{\text{Allowed Depreciation Deductions Allocated and Apportioned to a Separate Category}}{\text{Total Allowed Depreciation Deductions Allocated and Apportioned to Foreign Source Income}}$$

(g) *Assets subject to recapture.*—If the basis of an asset in a general asset account is increased as a result of the recapture of any allowable credit or deduction (for example, the basis adjustment for the recapture amount under section 30(d)(2), 50(c)(2), 179(d)(10), or 179A(e)(4)), general asset account treatment for the asset terminates as of the first day of the taxable year in which the recapture event occurs. Consequently, the taxpayer must remove the asset from the general asset account as of that day and must make the adjustments to the general asset account described in paragraph (e)(3)(iii)(C)(*2*) through (*4*) of this section.

(h) *Changes in use.*—(1) *Conversion to personal use.*—An asset in a general asset account becomes ineligible for general asset account treatment if a taxpayer uses the asset in a personal activity during a taxable year. Upon a conversion to personal use, the taxpayer must remove the asset from the general asset account as of the first day of the taxable year in which the change in use occurs (the year of change) and must make the adjustments to the general asset account described in paragraph (e)(3)(iii)(C)(*2*) through (*4*) of this section.

(2) *Change in use results in a different recovery period and/or depreciation method.*—(i) *No effect on general asset account election.*—A change in the use described in §1.168(i)-4(d) (change in use results in a different recovery period and/or depreciation method) of an asset in a general asset account shall not cause or permit the revocation of the election made under this section.

(ii) *Asset is removed from the general asset account.*—Upon a change in the use described in §1.168(i)-4(d), the taxpayer must remove the asset from the general asset account as of the first day of the year of change and must make the adjustments to the general asset account described in paragraphs (e)(3)(iii)(C)(*2*) through (*4*) of this section. If, however, the result of the change in use is described in §1.168(i)-4(d)(3) (change in use results in a shorter recovery period and/or a more accelerated depreciation method) and the taxpayer elects to treat the asset as though the change in use had not occurred pursuant to §1.168(i)-4(d)(3)(ii), no adjustment is made to the general asset account upon the change in use.

(iii) *New general asset account is established.*—(A) *Change in use results in a shorter recovery period and/or a more accelerated depreciation method.*—If the result of the change in use is described in §1.168(i)-4(d)(3) (change in use results in a shorter recovery period and/or a more accelerated depreciation method) and adjustments to the general asset account are made pursuant to paragraph (h)(2)(ii) of this section, the taxpayer must establish a new general asset account for the asset in the year of change in accordance with the rules in paragraph (c) of this section, except that the adjusted depreciable basis of the asset as of the first day of the year of change is included in the general asset account. For purposes of paragraph (c)(2) of this section, the applicable depreciation method, recovery period, and convention are determined under § 1.168(i)-4(d)(3)(i).

(B) *Change in use results in a longer recovery period and/or a slower depreciation method.*—If the result of the change in use is described in § 1.168(i)-4(d)(4) (change in use results in a longer recovery period and/or a slower depreciation method), the taxpayer must establish a separate general asset account for the asset in the year of change in accordance with the rules in paragraph (c) of this section, except that the unadjusted depreciable basis of the asset, and the greater of the depreciation of the asset allowed or allowable in accordance with section 1016(a)(2), as of the first day of the year of change are included in the newly established general asset account. Consequently, this general asset account as of the first day of the year of change will have a beginning balance for both the unadjusted depreciable basis and the depreciation reserve of the general asset account. For purposes of paragraph (c)(2) of this section, the applicable depreciation method, recovery period, and convention are determined under § 1.168(i)-4(d)(4)(ii).

(i) Identification of disposed on converted asset..—A taxpayer may use any reasonable method that is consistently applied to the taxpayer's general asset accounts for purposes of determining the unadjusted depreciable basis of a disposed or converted asset in a transaction described in paragraph (e)(3)(iii) (disposition of an asset in a qualifying disposition), (e)(3)(iv) (transactions subject to section 168(i)(7)), (e)(3)(v) (transactions subject to section 1031 or 1033), (e)(3)(vi) (anti-abuse rule), (g) (assets subject to recapture), or (h)(1) (conversion to personal use) of this section.

(j) Effect of adjustments in prior dispositions.—The adjustments to a general asset account under paragraph (e)(3)(iii), (e)(3)(iv), (e)(3)(v), (e)(3)(vi), (g), or (h)(1) of this section have no effect on the recognition and character of prior dispositions subject to paragraph (e)(2) of this section.

(k) *Election.*—(1) *Irrevocable election.*—If a taxpayer makes an election under this paragraph (k), the taxpayer consents to, and agrees to apply, all of the provisions of this section to the assets included in a general asset account. Except as provided in paragraph (c)(1)(ii)(A), (e)(3), (g), or (h) of this section, an election made under this section is irrevocable and will be binding on the taxpayer for computing taxable income for the taxable year for which the election is made and for all subsequent taxable years. An election under this paragraph (k) is made separately by each person owning an asset to which this section applies (for example, by each member of a consolidated group, at the partnership level (and not by the partner separately), or at the S corporation level (and not by the shareholder separately)).

(2) *Time for making election.*—The election to apply this section shall be made on the taxpayer's timely filed (including extensions) income tax return for the taxable year in which the assets included in the general asset account are placed in service by the taxpayer.

(3) *Manner of making election.*—In the year of election, a taxpayer makes the election under this section by typing or legibly printing at the top of the Form 4562, "GENERAL ASSET ACCOUNT ELECTION MADE UNDER SECTION 168(i)(4)," or in the manner provided for on Form 4562 and its instructions. The taxpayer shall maintain records (for example, "General Asset Account #1—all 1995 additions in asset class 00.11 for Salt Lake City, Utah facility") that identify the assets included in each general asset account, that establish the unadjusted depreciable basis and depreciation reserve of the general asset account, and that reflect the amount realized during the taxable year upon dispositions from each general

asset account. (But see section 179(c) and § 1.179-5 for the recordkeeping requirements for section 179 property.) The taxpayer's recordkeeping practices should be consistently applied to the general asset accounts. If Form 4562 is revised or renumbered, any reference in this section to that form shall be treated as a reference to the revised or renumbered form.

(l) *Effective dates.*—(1) *In general.*—Except as provided in paragraphs (l)(2) and (l)(3) of this section, this section applies to depreciable assets placed in service in taxable years ending on or after October 11, 1994. For depreciable assets placed in service after December 31, 1986, in taxable years ending before October 11, 1994, the Internal Revenue Service will allow any reasonable method that is consistently applied to the taxpayer's general asset accounts.

(2) *Exceptions.*—(i) *In general.*—(A) Paragraph (b)(1) of this section applies on or after June 17, 2004. For the applicability of § 1.168(i)-1(b)(1) before June 17, 2004, see § 1.168(i)-1(b)(1) in effect prior to June 17, 2004 (§ 1.168(i)-1(b)(1) as contained in 26 CFR part 1 edition revised as of April 1, 2004).

(B) Paragraphs (c)(2)(ii)(E) and (h)(2) of this section apply to any change in the use of depreciable assets pursuant to § 1.168(i)-4(d) in a taxable year ending on or after June 17, 2004. For any change in the use of depreciable assets as described in § 1.168(i)-4(d) after December 31, 1986, in a taxable year ending before June 17, 2004, the Internal Revenue Service will allow any reasonable method that is consistently applied to the taxpayer's general asset accounts or the taxpayer may choose, on an asset-by-asset basis, to apply paragraphs (c)(2)(ii)(E) and (h)(2) of this section.

(ii) *Change in method of accounting.*—(A) *In general.*—If a taxpayer adopted a method of accounting for general asset account treatment due to a change in the use of depreciable assets pursuant to § 1.168(i)-4(d) in a taxable year ending on or after December 30, 2003, and the method adopted is not in accordance with the method of accounting provided in paragraphs (c)(2)(ii)(E) and (h)(2) of this section, a change to the method of accounting provided in paragraphs (c)(2)(ii)(E) and (h)(2) of this section is a change in method of accounting to which the provisions of section 446(e) and the regulations under section 446(e) apply. However, if a taxpayer adopted a method of accounting for general asset account treatment due to a change in the use of depreciable assets pursuant to § 1.168(i)-4(d) after December 31, 1986, in a taxable year ending before December 30, 2003, and the method adopted is not in accordance with the method of accounting provided in paragraphs (c)(2)(ii)(E) and (h)(2) of this section, the taxpayer may treat the change to the method of accounting provided in paragraphs (c)(2)(ii)(E) and (h)(2) of this section as a change in method of accounting to which the provisions of section 446(e) and the regulations under section 446(e) apply.

(B) *Automatic consent to change method of accounting.*—A taxpayer changing its method of accounting in accordance with this paragraph (l)(2)(ii) must follow the applicable administrative procedures issued under § 1.446-1(e)(3)(ii) for obtaining the Commissioner's automatic consent to a change in method of accounting (for further guidance, for example, see Rev. Proc. 2002-9 (2002-1 C.B. 327), (see § 601.601(d)(2)(ii)(*b*) of this chapter)). Because this change does not change the adjusted depreciable basis of the asset, the method change is made on a cut-off basis and, therefore, no adjustment under section 481(a) is required or allowed. For purposes of Form 3115, *Application for Change in Accounting Method*, the designated number for the automatic accounting method change authorized by this paragraph (l)(2)(ii) is "87." If Form 3115 is revised or renumbered, any reference in this section to that form is treated as a reference to the revised or renumbered form.

(3) *Like-kind exchanges and involuntary conversions.*—This section applies for an asset transferred by a taxpayer in a like-kind exchange (as defined under § 1.168-6(b)(11)) or in an involuntary conversion (as defined under § 1.168-6(b)(12)) for which the time of disposition (as defined in § 1.168(i)-6(b)(3)) and the time of replacement (as defined in § 1,168(i)-6(b)(4)) both occur after February 27, 2004. For an asset transferred by a taxpayer in a like-kind exchange or in an involuntary conversion for which the time of disposition, the time of replacement, or both occur on or before February 27, 2004, see § 1.168(i)-1 in effect prior to February 27, 2004 (§ 1.168(i)-1 as contained in 26 CFR part 1 edition revised as of April 1, 2003). [Reg. 1.168(i)-1.]

.01 Historical Comment: Proposed 8/31/92. Adopted 10/7/94 by T.D. 8566 (corrected 12/15/94). Amended 2/27/2004 by T.D. 9115, 6/16/2004 by T.D. 9132 and 2/26/2007 by T.D. 9314.

¶ 566

Reg. § 1.168(i)-2

§ 1.168(i)-2. **Lease term.**—(a) *In general.*—For purposes of section 168, a lease term is determined under all the facts and circumstances. Paragraph (b) of this section and § 1.168(j)-1T, Q&A 17, describe certain circumstances that will result in a period of time not included in the stated duration of an original lease (additional period) nevertheless being included in the lease term. These rules do not prevent the inclusion of an additional period in the lease term in other circumstances.

(b) *Lessee retains financial obligation.*—(1) *In general.*—An additional period of time during which a lessee may not continue to be the lessee will nevertheless be included in the lease term if the lessee (or a related person)—

(i) Has agreed that one or both of them will or could be obligated to make a payment of rent or a payment in the nature of rent with respect to such period; or

(ii) Has assumed or retained any risk of loss with respect to the property for such period (including, for example, by holding a note secured by the property).

(2) *Payments in the nature of rent.*—For purposes of paragraph (b)(1)(i) of this section, a payment in the nature of rent includes a payment intended to substitute for rent or to fund or supplement the rental payments of another. For example, a payment in the nature of rent includes a payment of any kind (whether denominated as supplemental rent, as liquidated damages, or otherwise) that is required to be made in the event that—

(i) The leased property is not leased for the additional period;

(ii) The leased property is leased for the additional period under terms that do not satisfy specified terms and conditions;

(iii) There is a failure to make a payment of rent with respect to such additional period; or

(iv) Circumstances similar to those described in paragraph (b)(2)(i), (ii), or (iii) of this section occur.

(3) *De minimis rule.*—For the purposes of this paragraph (b), obligations to make de minimis payments will be disregarded.

(c) *Multiple leases or subleases.*—If property is subject to more than one lease (including any sublease) entered into as part of a single transaction (or a series of related transactions), the lease term includes all periods described in one or more of such leases. For example, if one taxable corporation leases property to another taxable corporation for a 20-year term and, as part of the same transaction, the lessee subleases the property to a tax-exempt entity for a 10-year term, then the lease term of the property for purposes of section 168 is 20 years. During the period of tax-exempt use, the property must be depreciated under the alternative depreciation system using the straight line method over the greater of its class life or 25 years (125 percent of the 20-year lease term).

(d) *Related person.*—For purposes of paragraph (b) of this section, a person is related to the lessee if such person is described in section 168(h)(4).

(e) *Changes in status.*—Section 168(i)(5) (changes in status) applies if an additional period is included in a lease term under this section and the leased property ceases to be tax-exempt use property for such additional period.

(f) *Example.*—The following example illustrates the principles of this section. The example does not address common law doctrines or other authorities that may apply to cause an additional period to be included in the lease term or to recharacterize a lease as a conditional sale or otherwise for federal income tax purposes. Unless otherwise indicated, parties to the transactions are not related to one another.

Example. Financial obligation with respect to an additional period—(i) *Facts.* X, a taxable corporation, and Y, a foreign airline whose income is not subject to United States taxation, enter into a lease agreement under which X agrees to lease an aircraft to Y for a period of 10 years. The lease agreement provides that, at the end of the lease period, Y is obligated to find a subsequent lessee (replacement lessee) to enter into a subsequent lease (replacement lease) of the aircraft from X for an additional 10-year period. The provisions of the lease agreement require that any replacement lessee be unrelated to Y and that it not be a tax-exempt entity as defined in section 168(h)(2). The provisions of the lease agreement also set forth the basic terms and conditions of the replacement lease, including its duration and the required rental payments. In the event Y fails to secure a replacement lease, the lease agreement requires Y to make a payment to X in an amount determined under the lease agreement.

(ii) *Application of this section.* The lease agreement between X and Y obligates Y to make a payment in the event the aircraft is not leased for the period commencing after the initial 10-year lease period and ending on the date the replacement lease is scheduled to end. Accordingly, pursuant to paragraph (b) of this section, the term of the lease between X and Y includes such additional period, and the lease term is 20 years for purposes of section 168.

(iii) *Facts modified.* Assume the same facts as in paragraph (i) of this *Example,* except that Y is required to guarantee the payment of rentals under the 10-year replacement lease and to make a payment to X equal to the present value of any excess of the replacement lease rental payments specified in the lease agreement between X and Y, over the rental payments actually agreed to be paid by the replacement lessee. Pursuant to paragraph (b) of this section, the term of the lease between X and Y includes the additional period, and the lease term is 20 years for purposes of section 168.

(iv) *Changes in status.* If, upon the conclusion of the stated duration of the lease between X and Y, the aircraft either is returned to X or leased to a replacement lessee that is not a tax-exempt entity as defined in section 168(h)(2), the subsequent method of depreciation will be determined pursuant to section 168(i)(5).

(g) *Effective date.*—(1) *In general.*—Except as provided in paragraph (g)(2) of this section, this section applies to leases entered into on or after April 20, 1995.

(2) *Special rules.*—Paragraphs (b)(1)(ii) and (c) of this section apply to leases entered into after April 26, 1996. [Reg. § 1.168(i)-2.]

.01 Historical Comment: Proposed 4/21/95. Adopted 4/26/96 by T.D. 8667.

¶ 568

Reg. § 1.168(i)-4

§ 1.168(i)-4. **Changes in use.**—(a) *Scope.*—This section provides the rules for determining the depreciation allowance for MACRS property (as defined in § 1.168(b)-1T(a)(2)) for which the use changes in the hands of the same taxpayer (change in the use). The allowance for depreciation under this section constitutes the amount of depreciation allowable under section 167(a) for the year of change and any subsequent taxable year. For purposes of this section, the year of change is the taxable year in which a change in the use occurs.

(b) *Conversion to business or income-producing use.*—(1) *Depreciation deduction allowable.*—This paragraph (b) applies to property that is converted from personal use to use in a taxpayer's trade or business, or for the production of income, during a taxable year. This conversion includes property that was previously used by the taxpayer for personal purposes, including real property (other than land) that is acquired before 1987 and converted from personal use to business or income-producing use after 1986, and depreciable property that was previously used by a tax-exempt entity before the entity changed to a taxable entity. Except as otherwise provided by the Internal Revenue Code or regulations under the Internal Revenue Code, upon a conversion to business or income-producing use, the depreciation allowance for the year of change and any subsequent taxable year is determined as though the property is placed in service by the taxpayer on the date on which the conversion occurs. Thus, except as otherwise provided by the Internal Revenue Code or regulations under the Internal Revenue Code, the taxpayer must use any applicable depreciation method, recovery period, and convention prescribed under section 168 for the property in the year of change, consistent with any election made under section 168 by the taxpayer for that year (see, for example, section 168(b)(5)). See §§ 1.168(k)-1T(f)(6)(iii) and 1.1400L(b)-1T(f)(6) for the additional first year depreciation deduction rules applicable to a conversion to business or income-producing use. The depreciable basis of the property for the year of change is the lesser of its fair market value or its adjusted depreciable basis (as defined in § 1.168(b)-1T(a)(4)), as applicable, at the time of the conversion to business or income-producing use.

(2) *Example.*—The application of this paragraph (b) is illustrated by the following example:

Example. A, a calendar-year taxpayer, purchases a house in 1985 that she occupies as her principal residence. In February 2004, *A* ceases to occupy the house and converts it to residential rental property. At the time of the conversion to residential rental property, the house's fair market value (excluding land) is $130,000 and adjusted depreciable basis attributable to the house (excluding land) is $150,000. Pursuant to this paragraph (b), *A* is considered to have placed in service residential rental property in February 2004 with a depreciable basis of $130,000. *A* depreciates the residential rental property under the general depreciation system by using the straight-line method, a 27.5-year recovery period, and the mid-month convention. Pursuant to §§ 1.168(k)-1T(f)(6)(iii)(B) or 1.1400L(b)-1T(f)(6), this property is not eligible for the additional first year depreciation deduction provided by section 168(k) or section 1400L(b). Thus, the depreciation allowance for the house for 2004 is $4,137, after taking into account the mid-month convention (($130,000 adjusted depreciable basis multiplied by the applicable depreciation rate of 3.636% (1/27.5)) multiplied by the mid-month convention fraction of 10.5/12). The amount of depreciation computed under section 168, however, may be limited under other provisions of the Internal Revenue Code, such as, section 280A.

(c) *Conversion to personal use.*—The conversion of MACRS property from business or income-producing use to personal use during a taxable year is treated as a disposition of the property in that taxable year. The depreciation allowance for MACRS property for the year of change in which the property is treated as being disposed of is determined by first multiplying the adjusted depreciable basis of the property as of the first day of the year of change by the applicable depreciation rate for that taxable year (for further guidance, for example, see section 6 of Rev. Proc. 87-57 (1987-2 C. B. 687, 692) (see § 601.601(d)(2)(ii)(*b*) of this chapter)). This amount is then multiplied by a fraction, the numerator of which is the number of months (including fractions of months) the property is deemed to be placed in service during the year of change (taking into account the applicable convention) and the denominator of which is 12. No depreciation deduction is allowable for MACRS property placed in service and disposed of in the same taxable year. See § § 1.168(k)-1T(f)(6)(ii) and 1.1400L(b)-1T(f)(6) for the additional first year depreciation deduction rules applicable to property placed in service and converted to personal use in the same taxable year. Upon the conversion to personal use, no gain, loss, or depreciation recapture under section 1245 or section 1250 is recognized. However, the provisions of section 1245 or section 1250 apply to any disposition of the converted property by the taxpayer at a later date. For listed property (as defined in section 280F(d)(4)), see section 280F(b)(2) for the recapture of excess depreciation upon the conversion to personal use.

(d) *Change in the use results in a different recovery period and/or depreciation method.*—(1) *In general.*—This paragraph (d) applies to a change in the use of MACRS property during a taxable year subsequent to the placed-in-service year, if the property continues to be MACRS property owned by the same taxpayer and, as a result of the change in the use, has a different recovery period, a different depreciation method, or both. For example, this paragraph (d) applies to MACRS property that—

(i) Begins or ceases to be used predominantly outside the United States;

(ii) Results in a reclassification of the property under section 168(e) due to a change in the use of the property; or

(iii) Begins or ceases to be tax-exempt use property (as defined in section 168(h)).

(2) *Determination of change in the use.*—(i) *In general.*—Except as provided in paragraph (d)(2)(ii) of this section, a change in the use of MACRS property occurs when the primary use of the MACRS property in the taxable year is different from its primary use in the immediately preceding taxable year. The primary use of MACRS property may be determined in any reasonable manner that is consistently applied to the taxpayer's MACRS property.

(ii) *Alternative depreciation system property.*—(A) *Property used within or outside the United States.*—A change in the use of MACRS property occurs when a taxpayer begins or ceases to use MACRS property predominantly outside the United States during the taxable year. The determination of whether MACRS property is used predominantly outside the United States is made in accordance with the test in § 1.48-1(g)(1)(i) for determining predominant use.

(B) *Tax-exempt bond financed property.*—A change in the use of MACRS property occurs when the property changes to tax-exempt bond financed property, as described in section 168(g)(1)(C) and (g)(5), during the taxable year. For purposes of this paragraph (d), MACRS property changes to tax-exempt bond financed property when a tax-exempt bond is first issued after the MACRS property is placed in service. MACRS property continues to be tax-exempt bond financed property in the hands of the taxpayer even if the tax-exempt bond (including any refunding issue) is no longer outstanding or is redeemed.

(C) *Other mandatory alternative depreciation system property.*—A change in the use of MACRS property occurs when the property changes to, or changes from, property described in section 168(g)(1)(B) (tax-exempt use property) or (D) (imported property covered by an Executive order) during the taxable year.

(iii) *Change in the use deemed to occur on first day of the year of change.*—If a change in the use of MACRS property occurs under this paragraph (d)(2), the depreciation allowance for that MACRS property for the year of change is determined as though the use of the MACRS property changed on the first day of the year of change.

(3) *Change in the use results in a shorter recovery period and/or a more accelerated depreciation method.*—(i) *Treated as placed in service in the year of change.*—(A) *In general.*—If a change in the use results in the MACRS property changing to a shorter recovery period and/or a depreciation method that is more accelerated than the method used for the MACRS property before the change in the use, the depreciation allowances beginning in the year of change are determined as though the MACRS property is placed in service by the taxpayer in the year of change.

(B) *Computation of depreciation allowance.*—The depreciation allowances for the MACRS property for any 12-month taxable year beginning with the year of change are determined by multiplying the adjusted depreciable basis of the MACRS property as of the first day of each taxable year by the applicable depreciation rate for each taxable year. In determining the applicable depreciation rate for the year of change and subsequent taxable years, the taxpayer must use any applicable depreciation method and recovery period prescribed under section 168 for the MACRS property in the year of change, consistent with any election made under section 168 by the taxpayer for that year (see, for example, section 168(b)(5)). If there is a change in the use of MACRS property, the applicable convention that applies to the MACRS property is the same as the convention that applied before the change in the use of the MACRS property. However, the depreciation allowance for the year of change for the MACRS property is determined without applying the applicable convention, unless the MACRS property is disposed of during the year of change. See paragraph (d)(5) of this section for the rules relating to the computation of the depreciation allowance under the optional depreciation tables. If the year of change or any subsequent taxable year is less than 12 months, the depreciation allowance determined under this paragraph (d)(3)(i) must be adjusted for a short taxable year (for further guidance, for example, see Rev. Proc. 89-15 (1989-1 C.B. 816) (see § 601.601(d)(2)(ii)(*b*) of this chapter)).

(C) *Special rules.*—MACRS property affected by this paragraph (d)(3)(i) is not eligible in the year of change for the election provided under section 168(f)(1), 179, or 1400L(f), or for the additional first year depreciation deduction provided in section 168(k) or 1400L(b). See §§ 1.168(k)-1T(f)(6)(iv) and 1.1400L(b)-1T(f)(6) for other additional first year depreciation deduction rules applicable to a change in the use of MACRS property subsequent to its placed-in-service year. For purposes of determining whether the mid-quarter convention applies to other MACRS property placed in service during the year of change, the unadjusted depreciable basis (as defined in § 1.168(b)-1T(a)(3)) or the adjusted depreciable basis of MACRS property affected by this paragraph (d)(3)(i) is not taken into account.

(ii) *Option to disregard the change in the use.*—In lieu of applying paragraph (d)(3)(i) of this section, the taxpayer may elect to determine the depreciation allowance as though the change in the use had not occurred. The taxpayer elects this option by claiming on the taxpayer's timely filed (including extensions) Federal income tax return for the year of change the depreciation allowance for the property as though the change in the use had not occurred. See paragraph (g)(2) of this section for the manner for revoking this election.

(4) *Change in the use results in a longer recovery period and/or a slower depreciation method.*—(i) *Treated as originally placed in service with longer recovery period and/or slower depreciation method.*—If a change in the use results in a longer recovery period and/or a depreciation method for the MACRS property that is less accelerated than the method used for the MACRS property before the change in the use, the depreciation allowances beginning with the year of change are determined as though the MACRS property had been originally placed in service by the taxpayer with the longer recovery period and/or the slower depreciation method. MACRS property affected by this paragraph (d)(4) is not eligible in the year of change for the election provided under section 168(f)(1), 179, or 1400L(f), or for the additional first year depreciation deduction provided in section 168(k) or 1400L(b). See §§1.168(k)-1T(f)(6)(iv) and 1.1400L(b)-1T(f)(6) for other additional first year depreciation deduction rules applicable to a change in the use of MACRS property subsequent to its placed-in-service year.

(ii) *Computation of the depreciation allowance.*—The depreciation allowances for the MACRS property for any 12-month taxable year beginning with the year of change are determined by multiplying the adjusted depreciable basis of the MACRS property as of the first day of each taxable year by the applicable depreciation rate for each taxable year. If there is a change in the use of MACRS property, the applicable convention that applies to the MACRS property is the same as the convention that applied before the change in the use of the MACRS property. If the year of change or any subsequent taxable year is less than 12 months, the depreciation allowance determined under this paragraph (d)(4)(ii) must be adjusted for a short taxable year (for further guidance, for example, see Rev. Proc. 89-15 (1989-1 C.B. 816) (see §601.601(d)(2)(ii)(*b*) of this chapter)). See paragraph (d)(5) of this section for the rules relating to the computation of the depreciation allowance under the optional depreciation tables. In determining the applicable depreciation rate for the year of change and any subsequent taxable year—

(A) The applicable depreciation method is the depreciation method that would apply in the year of change and any subsequent taxable year for the MACRS property had the taxpayer used the longer recovery period and/or the slower depreciation method in the placed-in-service year of the property. If the 200- or 150-percent declining balance method would have applied in the placed-in-service year but the method would have switched to the straight line method in the year of change or any prior taxable year, the applicable depreciation method beginning with the year of change is the straight line method; and

(B) The applicable recovery period is either—

(1) The longer recovery period resulting from the change in the use if the applicable depreciation method is the 200- or 150-percent declining balance method (as determined under paragraph (d)(4)(ii)(A) of this section) unless the recovery period did not change as a result of the change in the use, in which case the applicable recovery period is the same recovery period that applied before the change in the use; or

(2) The number of years remaining as of the beginning of each taxable year (taking into account the applicable convention) had the taxpayer used the longer recovery period in the placed-in-service year of the property if the applicable depreciation method is the straight line method (as determined under

paragraph (d)(4)(ii)(A) of this section) unless the recovery period did not change as a result of the change in the use, in which case the applicable recovery period is the number of years remaining as of the beginning of each taxable year (taking into account the applicable convention) based on the recovery period that applied before the change in the use.

(5) *Using optional depreciation tables.*—(i) *Taxpayer not bound by prior use of table.*—If a taxpayer used an optional depreciation table for the MACRS property before a change in the use, the taxpayer is not bound to use the appropriate new table for that MACRS property beginning in the year of change (for further guidance, for example, see section 8 of Rev. Proc. 87-57 (1987-2 C.B. 687, 693) (see § 601.601(d)(2)(ii)(*b*) of this chapter)). If a taxpayer did not use an optional depreciation table for MACRS property before a change in the use and the change in the use results in a shorter recovery period and/or a more accelerated depreciation method (as described in paragraph (d)(3)(i) of this section), the taxpayer may use the appropriate new table for that MACRS property beginning in the year of change. If a taxpayer chooses not to use the optional depreciation table, the depreciation allowances for the MACRS property beginning in the year of change are determined under paragraph (d)(3)(i) or (4) of this section, as applicable.

(ii) *Taxpayer chooses to use optional depreciation table after a change in the use.*—If a taxpayer chooses to use an optional depreciation table for the MACRS property after a change in the use, the depreciation allowances for the MACRS property for any 12-month taxable year beginning with the year of change are determined as follows:

(A) *Change in the use results in a shorter recovery period and/or a more accelerated depreciation method.*—If a change in the use results in a shorter recovery period and/or a more accelerated depreciation method (as described in paragraph (d)(3)(i) of this section), the depreciation allowances for the MACRS property for any 12-month taxable year beginning with the year of change are determined by multiplying the adjusted depreciable basis of the MACRS property as of the first day of the year of change by the annual depreciation rate for each recovery year (expressed as a decimal equivalent) specified in the appropriate optional depreciation table. The appropriate optional depreciation table for the MACRS property is based on the depreciation system, depreciation method, recovery period, and convention applicable to the MACRS property in the year of change as determined under paragraph (d)(3)(i) of this section. The depreciation allowance for the year of change for the MACRS property is determined by taking into account the applicable convention (which is already factored into the optional depreciation tables). If the year of change or any subsequent taxable year is less than 12 months, the depreciation allowance determined under this paragraph (d)(5)(ii)(A) must be adjusted for a short taxable year (for further guidance, for example, see Rev. Proc. 89-15 (1989-1 C.B. 816) (see § 601.601(d)(2)(ii)(*b*) of this chapter)).

(B) *Change in the use results in a longer recovery period and/or a slower depreciation method.*—*(1) Determination of the appropriate optional depreciation table.*—If a change in the use results in a longer recovery period and/or a slower depreciation method (as described in paragraph (d)(4)(i) of this section), the depreciation allowances for the MACRS property for any 12-month taxable year beginning with the year of change are determined by choosing the optional depreciation table that corresponds to the depreciation system, depreciation method, recovery period, and convention that would have applied to the MACRS property in the placed-in-service year had that property been originally placed in service by the taxpayer with the longer recovery period and/or the slower depreciation method. If there is a change in the use of MACRS property, the applicable convention that applies to the MACRS property is the same as the convention that applied before the change in the use of the MACRS property. If the year of change or any subsequent taxable year is less than 12 months, the depreciation allowance determined under this paragraph (d)(5)(ii)(B) must be adjusted for a short taxable year (for further guidance, for example, see Rev. Proc. 89-15 (1989-1 C.B. 816) (see § 601.601(d)(2)(ii)(*b*) of this chapter)).

(2) Computation of the depreciation allowance.—The depreciation allowances for the MACRS property for any 12-month taxable year beginning with the year of change are computed by first determining the appropriate recovery year in the table identified under paragraph (d)(5)(ii)(B)(*1*) of this section. The appropriate recovery year for the year of change is the year that corresponds to the year of change. For example, if the recovery year for the year of change would have been Year 4 in the table that applied before the change in the use of the MACRS property, then the recovery year for the year of change is Year 4 in the table identified under paragraph (d)(5)(ii)(B)(*1*) of this section. Next, the annual depreciation rate (expressed as a decimal equivalent) for each recovery year is multiplied by a transaction coefficient. The transaction coefficient is the formula (1 / (1 - x)) where x equals the sum of the annual depreciation rates from the table identified under paragraph (d)(5)(ii)(B)(*1*) of this section (expressed as a decimal equivalent) for the taxable years beginning with the placed-in-service year of the MACRS property through the taxable year immediately prior to the year of change. The product of the annual depreciation rate and the transaction coefficient is multiplied by the adjusted depreciable basis of the MACRS property as of the beginning of the year of change.

(6) *Examples.*—The application of this paragraph (d) is illustrated by the following examples:

Example 1. Change in the use results in a shorter recovery period and/or a more accelerated depreciation method and optional depreciation table is not used—(i) *X*, a calendar-year corporation, places in service in 1999 equipment at a cost of $100,000 and uses this equipment from 1999 through 2003 primarily in its *A* business. *X* depreciates the equipment for 1999 through 2003 under the general depreciation system as 7-year property by using the 200-percent declining balance method (which switched to the straight-line method in 2003), a 7-year recovery period, and a half-year convention. Beginning in 2004, *X* primarily uses the equipment in its *B* business. As a result, the classification of the equipment under section 168(e) changes from 7-year property to 5-year property and the recovery period of the equipment under the general depreciation system changes from 7 years to 5 years. The depreciation method does not change. On January 1, 2004, the adjusted depreciable basis of the equipment is $22,311. *X* depreciates its 5-year recovery property placed in service in 2004 under the general depreciation system by using the 200-percent declining balance method and a 5-year recovery period. *X* does not use the optional depreciation tables.

(ii) Under paragraph (d)(3)(i) of this section, *X*'s allowable depreciation deduction for the equipment for 2004 and subsequent taxable years is determined as though *X* placed the equipment in service in 2004 for use primarily in its *B* business. The depreciable basis of the equipment as of January 1, 2004, is $22,311 (the adjusted depreciable basis at January 1, 2004). Because *X* does not use the optional depreciation tables, the depreciation allowance for 2004 (the deemed placed-in-service year) for this equipment only is computed without taking into account the half-year convention. Pursuant to paragraph (d)(3)(i)(C) of this section, this equipment is not eligible for the additional first year depreciation deduction provided by section 168(k) or section 1400L(b). Thus, *X*'s allowable depreciation deduction for the equipment for 2004 is $8,924 ($22,311 adjusted depreciable basis at January 1, 2004, multiplied by the applicable depreciation rate of 40% (200/5)).

X's allowable depreciation deduction for the equipment for 2005 is $5,355 ($13,387 adjusted depreciable basis at January 1, 2005, multiplied by the applicable depreciation rate of 40% (200/5)).

(iii) Alternatively, under paragraph (d)(3)(ii) of this section, *X* may elect to disregard the change in the use and, as a result, may continue to treat the equipment as though it is used primarily in its *A* business. If the election is made, *X*'s allowable depreciation deduction for the equipment for 2004 is $8,924 ($22,311 adjusted depreciable basis at January 1, 2004, multiplied by the applicable depreciation rate of 40% (1/2.5 years remaining at January 1, 2004)). *X*'s allowable depreciation deduction for the equipment for 2005 is $8,925 ($13,387 adjusted depreciable basis at January 1, 2005, multiplied by the applicable depreciation rate of 66.67% (1/1.5 years remaining at January 1, 2005)).

Example 2. Change in the use results in a shorter recovery period and/or a more accelerated depreciation method and optional depreciation table is used—(i) Same facts as in *Example 1*, except that *X* used the optional depreciation tables for computing depreciation for 1999 through 2003. Pursuant to paragraph (d)(5) of this section, *X* chooses to continue to use the optional depreciation table for the equipment. *X* does not make the election provided in paragraph (d)(3)(ii) of this section to disregard the change in use.

(ii) In accordance with paragraph (d)(5)(ii)(A) of this section, *X* must first identify the appropriate optional depreciation table for the equipment. This table is table 1 in Rev. Proc. 87-57 because the equipment will be depreciated in the year of change (2004) under the general depreciation system using the 200-percent declining balance method, a 5-year recovery period, and the half-year convention (which is the convention that applied to the equipment in 1999). Pursuant to paragraph (d)(3)(i)(C) of this section, this equipment is not eligible for the additional first year depreciation deduction provided by section 168(k) or section 1400L(b). For 2004, *X* multiplies its adjusted depreciable basis in the equipment as of January 1, 2004, of $22,311, by the annual depreciation rate in table 1 for recovery year 1 for a 5-year recovery period (.20), to determine the depreciation allowance of $4,462. For 2005, *X* multiplies its adjusted depreciable basis in the equipment as of January 1, 2004, of $22,311, by the annual depreciation rate in table 1 for recovery year 2 for a 5-year recovery period (.32), to determine the depreciation allowance of $7,140.

Example 3. Change in the use results in a longer recovery period and/or a slower depreciation method—(i) *Y*, a calendar-year corporation, places in service in January 2002, equipment at a cost of $100,000 and uses this equipment in 2002 and 2003 only within the United States. *Y* elects not to deduct the additional first year depreciation under section 168(k). *Y* depreciates the equipment for 2002 and 2003 under the general depreciation system by using the 200-percent declining balance method, a 5-year recovery period, and a half-year convention. Beginning in 2004, *Y* uses the equipment predominantly outside the United States. As a result of this change in the use, the equipment is subject to the alternative depreciation system beginning in 2004. Under the alternative depreciation system, the equipment is depreciated by using the straight line method and a 9-year recovery period. The adjusted depreciable basis of the equipment at January 1, 2004, is $48,000.

(ii) Pursuant to paragraph (d)(4) of this section, *Y*'s allowable depreciation deduction for 2004 and subsequent taxable years is determined as though the equipment had been placed in service in January 2002, as property used predominantly outside the United States. Further, pursuant to paragraph (d)(4)(i) of this section, the equipment is not eligible in 2004 for the additional first year depreciation deduction provided by section 168(k) or section 1400L(b). In determining the applicable depreciation rate for 2004, the applicable depreciation method is the straight line method and the applicable recovery period is 7.5 years, which is the number of years remaining at January 1, 2004, for property placed in service in 2002 with a 9-year recovery period (taking into account the half-year convention). Thus, the depreciation allowance for 2004 is $6,398 ($48,000 adjusted depreciable basis at January 1, 2004, multiplied by the applicable depreciation rate of 13.33% (1/7.5 years)). The depreciation allowance for 2005 is $6,398 ($41,602 adjusted depreciable basis at January 1, 2005, multiplied by the applicable depreciation rate of 15.38% (1/6.5 years remaining at January 1, 2005)).

Example 4. Change in the use results in a longer recovery period and/or a slower depreciation method and optional depreciation table is used—(i) Same facts as in *Example 3*, except that *Y* used the optional depreciation tables for computing depreciation in 2002 and 2003. Pursuant to paragraph (d)(5) of this section, *Y* chooses to continue to use the optional depreciation table for the equipment. Further, pursuant to paragraph (d)(4)(i) of this section, the equipment is not eligible in 2004 for the additional first year depreciation deduction provided by section 168(k) or section 1400L(b).

(ii) In accordance with paragraph (d)(5)(ii)(B) of this section, *Y* must first determine the appropriate optional depreciation table for the equipment pursuant to paragraph (d)(5)(ii)(B)(*1*) of this section. This table is table 8 in Rev. Proc. 87-57, which corresponds to the alternative depreciation system, the straight line method, a 9-year recovery period, and the half-year convention (because *Y* depreciated 5-year property in 2002 using a half-year convention). Next, *Y* must determine the appropriate recovery year in table 8. Because the year of change is 2004, the depreciation allowance for the equipment for 2004 is determined using recovery year 3 of table 8. For 2004, *Y* multiplies its adjusted depreciable basis in the equipment as of January 1, 2004, of $48,000, by the product of the annual depreciation rate in table 8 for recovery year 3 for a 9-year recovery period (.1111) and the transaction coefficient of 1.200 [1/(1-(.0556 (table 8 for recovery year 1 for a 9-year recovery period) +.1111 (table 8 for recovery year 2 for a 9-year recovery period)))], to determine the depreciation allowance of $6,399. For 2005, *Y* multiplies its adjusted depreciable basis in the equipment as of January 1, 2004, of $48,000, by the product of the annual depreciation rate in table 8 for recovery year 4 for a 9-year recovery period (.1111) and the transaction coefficient (1.200), to determine the depreciation allowance of $6,399.

(e) *Change in the use of MACRS property during the placed-in-service year.*—(1) *In general.*—Except as provided in paragraph (e)(2) of this section, if a change in the use of MACRS property occurs during the placed-in-service year and the property continues to be MACRS property owned by the same taxpayer, the depreciation allowance for that property for the placed-in-service year is determined by its primary use during that year. The primary use of MACRS property may be determined in any reasonable manner that is consistently applied to the taxpayer's MACRS property. For purposes of this paragraph (e), the determination of whether the mid-quarter convention applies to any MACRS property placed in service during the year of change is made in accordance with § 1.168(d)-1.

(2) *Alternative depreciation system property.*—(i) *Property used within and outside the United States.*—The depreciation allowance for the placed-in-service year for MACRS property that is used within and outside the United States is determined by its predominant use during that year. The determination of whether MACRS property is used predominantly outside the United States during the placed-in-service year shall be made in accordance with the test in § 1.48-1(g)(1)(i) for determining predominant use.

(ii) *Tax-exempt bond financed property.*—The depreciation allowance for the placed-in-service year for MACRS property that changes to tax-exempt bond financed property, as described in section 168(g)(1)(C) and (g)(5), during that taxable year is determined under the alternative depreciation system. For purposes of this paragraph (e), MACRS property changes to tax-exempt bond financed property when a tax-exempt bond is first issued after the MACRS property is placed in service. MACRS property continues to be tax-exempt bond financed property in the hands of the taxpayer even if the tax-exempt bond (including any refunding issue) is not outstanding at, or is redeemed by, the end of the placed-in-service year.

(iii) *Other mandatory alternative depreciation system property.*—The depreciation allowance for the placed-in-service year for MACRS property that changes to, or changes from, property described in section 168(g)(1)(B) (tax-exempt use property) or (D) (imported property covered by an Executive order) during that taxable year is determined under—

(A) The alternative depreciation system if the MACRS property is described in section 168(g)(1)(B) or (D) at the end of the placed-in-service year; or

(B) The general depreciation system if the MACRS property is not described in section 168(g)(1)(B) or (D) at the end of the placed-in-service year, unless other provisions of the Internal Revenue Code or regulations under the Internal Revenue Code require the depreciation allowance for that MACRS property to be determined under the alternative depreciation system (for example, section 168(g)(7)).

(3) *Examples.*—The application of this paragraph (e) is illustrated by the following examples:

Example 1. (i) *Z*, a utility and calendar-year corporation, acquires and places in service on January 1, 2004, equipment at a cost of $100,000. *Z* uses this equipment in its combustion turbine production plant for 4 months and then uses the equipment in its steam production plant for the remainder of 2004. *Z*'s combustion turbine production plant assets are classified as 15-year property and are depreciated by *Z* under the general depreciation system using a 15-year recovery period and the 150-percent declining balance method of depreciation. *Z*'s steam production plant assets are classified as 20-year property and are depreciated by *Z* under the general depreciation system using a 20-year recovery period and the 150-percent declining balance method of depreciation. *Z* uses the optional depreciation tables. The equipment is 50-percent bonus depreciation property for purposes of section 168(k).

(ii) Pursuant to this paragraph (e), *Z* must determine depreciation based on the primary use of the equipment during the placed-in-service year. *Z* has consistently determined the primary use of all of its MACRS properties by comparing the number of full months in the taxable year during which a MACRS property is used in one manner with the number of full months in that taxable year during which that MACRS property is used in another manner. Applying this approach, *Z* determines the depreciation allowance for the equipment for 2004 is based on the equipment being classified as 20-year property because the equipment was used by *Z* in its steam production plant for 8 months in 2004. If the half-year convention applies in 2004, the appropriate optional depreciation table is table 1 in Rev. Proc. 87-57, which is the table for MACRS property subject to the general depreciation system, the 150-percent declining balance method, a 20-year recovery period, and the half-year convention. Thus, the depreciation allowance for the equipment for 2004 is $51,875, which is the total of $50,000 for the 50-percent additional first year depreciation deduction allowable (the unadjusted depreciable basis of $100,000 multiplied by .50), plus $1,875 for the 2004 depreciation allowance on the remaining adjusted depreciable basis of $50,000 [(the unadjusted depreciable basis of $100,000 less the additional first year depreciation deduction of $50,000) multiplied by the annual depreciation rate of .0375 in table 1 for recovery year 1 for a 20-year recovery period].

Example 2. T, a calendar year corporation, places in service on January 1, 2004, several computers at a total cost of $100,000. *T* uses these computers within the United States for 3 months in 2004 and then moves and uses the computers outside the United States for the remainder of 2004. Pursuant to § 1.48-1(g)(1)(i), the computers are considered as used predominantly outside the United States in 2004. As a result, for 2004, the computers are required to be depreciated under the alternative depreciation system of section 168(g) with a recovery period of 5 years pursuant to section 168(g)(3)(C). *T* uses the optional depreciation tables. If the half-year convention applies in 2004, the appropriate optional depreciation table is table 8 in Rev. Proc. 87-57, which is the table for MACRS property subject to the alternative depreciation system, the straight line method, a 5-year recovery period, and the half-year convention. Thus, the depreciation allowance for the computers for 2004 is $10,000, which is equal to the unadjusted depreciable basis of $100,000 multiplied by the annual depreciation rate of .10 in table 8 for recovery year 1 for a 5-year recovery period. Because the computers are required to be depreciated under the alternative depreciation system in their placed-in-service year, pursuant to section 168(k)(2)(C)(i) and § 1.168(k)-1T(b)(2)(ii), the computers are not eligible for the additional first year depreciation deduction provided by section 168(k).

(f) *No change in accounting method.*—A change in computing the depreciation allowance in the year of change for property subject to this section is not a change in method of accounting under section 446(e). See § 1.446-1(e)(2)(ii)(*d*)(*3*)(*ii*).

(g) *Effective dates.*—(1) *In general.*—This section applies to any change in the use of MACRS property in a taxable year ending on or after June 17, 2004. For any change in the use of MACRS property after December 31, 1986, in a taxable year ending before June 17, 2004, the Internal Revenue Service will allow any reasonable method of depreciating the property under section 168 in the year of change and the subsequent taxable years that is consistently applied to any property for which the use changes in the hands of the same taxpayer or the taxpayer may choose, on a property-by-property basis, to apply the provisions of this section.

(2) *Change in method of accounting.*—(i) *In general.*—If a taxpayer adopted a method of accounting for depreciation due to a change in the use of MACRS property in a taxable year ending on or after December 30, 2003, and the method adopted is not in accordance with the method of accounting for depreciation provided in this section, a change to the method of accounting for depreciation provided in this section is a change in method of accounting to which the provisions of sections 446(e) and 481 and the regulations under sections 446(e) and 481 apply. Also, a revocation of the election provided in paragraph (d)(3)(ii) of this section to disregard a change in the use is a change in method of accounting to which the provisions of sections 446(e) and 481 and the regulations under sections 446(e) and 481 apply. However, if a taxpayer adopted a method of accounting for depreciation due to a change in the use of MACRS property after December 31, 1986, in a taxable year ending before December 30, 2003, and the method adopted is not in accordance with the method of accounting for depreciation provided in this section, the taxpayer may treat the change to the method of accounting for depreciation provided in this section as a change in method of accounting to which the provisions of sections 446(e) and 481 and the regulations under sections 446(e) and 481 apply.

(ii) *Automatic consent to change method of accounting.*—A taxpayer changing its method of accounting in accordance with this paragraph (g)(2) must follow the applicable administrative procedures issued under § 1.446-1(e)(3)(ii) for obtaining the Commissioner's automatic consent to a change in method of accounting (for further guidance, for example, see Rev. Proc. 2002-9 (2002-1 C.B. 327) (see § 601.601(d)(2)(ii)(*b*) of this chapter)). Any change in method of accounting made under this paragraph (g)(2) must be made using an adjustment under section 481(a). For purposes of Form 3115, *Application for Change in Accounting Method,* the designated number for the automatic accounting method change authorized by this paragraph (g)(2) is "88." If Form 3115 is revised or renumbered, any reference in this section to that form is treated as a reference to the revised or renumbered form. [Reg. § 1.168(i)-4.]

.01 Historical Comment: Proposed 7/21/2003. Adopted 6/16/2004 by T.D. 9132. Amended 12/22/2006 by T.D. 9307.

¶ 568A

Reg. § 1.168(i)-5

§ 1.168(i)-5. **Table of contents.**—This section lists the major paragraphs contained in § 1.168(i)-6.

(5) Year of disposition and year of replacement.
(i) Relinquished MACRS property.
(A) General rule.
(B) Special rule.
(ii) Replacement MACRS property.
(A) Remaining recovery period of the replacement MACRS property.
(B) Year of replacement is 12 months.
(iii) Year of disposition or year of replacement is less than 12 months.
(iv) Deferred transactions.
(A) In general.
(B) Allowable depreciation for a qualified intermediary.
(v) Remaining recovery period.
(6) Examples.
(d) Special rules for determining depreciation allowances.
(1) Excess basis.
(i) In general.
(ii) Example.
(2) Depreciable and nondepreciable property.
(3) Depreciation limitations for automobiles.
(i) In general.
(ii) Order in which limitations on depreciation under section 280F(a) are applied.
(iii) Examples.
(4) Involuntary conversion for which the replacement MACRS property is acquired and placed in service before disposition of relinquished MACRS property.
(e) Use of optional depreciation tables.
(1) Taxpayer not bound by prior use of table.
(2) Determination of the depreciation deduction.
(i) Relinquished MACRS property.
(ii) Replacement MACRS property.
(A) Determination of the appropriate optional depreciation table.
(B) Calculating the depreciation deduction for the replacement MACRS property.
(iii) Unrecovered basis.
(3) Excess basis.
(4) Examples.
(f) Mid-quarter convention.
(1) Exchanged basis.
(2) Excess basis.
(3) Depreciable property acquired for nondepreciable property.
(g) Section 179 election.
(h) Additional first year depreciation deduction.
(i) Elections.
(1) Election not to apply this section.
(2) Election to treat certain replacement property as MACRS property.
(j) Time and manner of making election under paragraph (i)(1) of this section.
(1) In general.
(2) Time for making election.
(3) Manner of making election.

(4) Revocation.

(k) Effective date.

(1) In general.

(2) Application to pre-effective date like-kind exchanges and involuntary conversions.

(3) Like-kind exchanges and involuntary conversions where the taxpayer made the election under section 168(f)(1) for the relinquished property. [Reg. § 1.168(i)-5.]

.01 Historical Comment: Proposed 3/1/2004. Adopted 2/26/2007 by T.D. 9314.

¶ 568B

Reg. § 1.168(i)-6

§ 1.168(i)-6. **Like-kind exchanges and involuntary conversions.**—(a) *Scope.*—This section provides the rules for determining the depreciation allowance for MACRS property acquired in a like-kind exchange or an involuntary conversion, including a like-kind exchange or an involuntary conversion of MACRS property that is exchanged or replaced with other MACRS property in a transaction between members of the same affiliated group. The allowance for depreciation under this section constitutes the amount of depreciation allowable under section 167(a) for the year of replacement and any subsequent taxable year for the replacement MACRS property and for the year of disposition of the relinquished MACRS property. The provisions of this section apply only to MACRS property to which § 1.168(h)-1 (like-kind exchanges of tax-exempt use property) does not apply. Additionally, paragraphs (c) through (f) of this section apply only to MACRS property for which an election under paragraph (i) of this section has not been made.

(b) *Definitions.*—For purposes of this section, the following definitions apply:

(1) *Replacement MACRS property* is MACRS property (as defined in § 1.168(b)-1(a)(2)) in the hands of the acquiring taxpayer that is acquired for other MACRS property in a like-kind exchange or an involuntary conversion.

(2) *Relinquished MACRS property* is MACRS property that is transferred by the taxpayer in a like-kind exchange, or in an involuntary conversion.

(3) *Time of disposition* is when the disposition of the relinquished MACRS property takes place under the convention, as determined under § 1.168(d)-1, that applies to the relinquished MACRS property.

(4) *Time of replacement* is the later of—

(i) When the replacement MACRS property is placed in service under the convention, as determined under this section, that applies to the replacement MACRS property; or

(ii) The time of disposition of the exchanged or involuntarily converted property.

(5) *Year of disposition* is the taxable year that includes the time of disposition.

(6) *Year of replacement* is the taxable year that includes the time of replacement.

(7) *Exchanged basis* is determined after the depreciation deductions for the year of disposition are determined under paragraph (c)(5)(i) of this section and is the lesser of—

(i) The basis in the replacement MACRS property, as determined under section 1031(d) and the regulations under section 1031(d) or section 1033(b) and the regulations under section 1033(b); or

(ii) The adjusted depreciable basis (as defined in § 1.168(b)-1(a)(4)) of the relinquished MACRS property.

(8) *Excess basis* is any excess of the basis in the replacement MACRS property, as determined under section 1031(d) and the regulations under section 1031(d) or section 1033(b) and the regulations under section 1033(b), over the exchanged basis as determined under paragraph (b)(7) of this section.

(9) *Depreciable exchanged basis* is the exchanged basis as determined under paragraph (b)(7) of this section reduced by—

(i) The percentage of such basis attributable to the taxpayer's use of property for the taxable year other than in the taxpayer's trade or business (or for the production of income); and

(ii) Any adjustments to basis provided by other provisions of the Internal Revenue Code (Code) and the regulations under the Code (including section 1016(a)(2) and (3), for example, depreciation deductions in the year of replacement allowable under section 168(k) or 1400L(b)).

(10) *Depreciable excess basis* is the excess basis as determined under paragraph (b)(8) of this section reduced by—

(i) The percentage of such basis attributable to the taxpayer's use of property for the taxable year other than in the taxpayer's trade or business (or for the production of income);

(ii) Any portion of the basis the taxpayer properly elects to treat as an expense under section 179; and

(iii) Any adjustments to basis provided by other provisions of the Code and the regulations under the Code (including section 1016(a)(2) and (3), for example, depreciation deductions in the year of replacement allowable under section 168(k) or 1400L(b)).

(11) *Like-kind exchange* is an exchange of property in a transaction to which section 1031(a)(1), (b), or (c) applies.

(12) *Involuntary conversion* is a transaction described in section 1033(a)(1) or (2) that resulted in the nonrecognition of any part of the gain realized as the result of the conversion.

(c) *Determination of depreciation allowance.*—(1) *Computation of the depreciation allowance for depreciable exchanged basis beginning in the year of replacement.*—(i) *In general.*—This paragraph (c) provides rules for determining the applicable recovery period, the applicable depreciation method, and the applicable convention used to determine the depreciation allowances for the depreciable exchanged basis beginning in the year of replacement. See paragraph (c)(5) of this section for rules relating to the computation of the depreciation allowance for the year of disposition and for the year of replacement. See paragraph (d)(1) of this section for rules relating to the computation of the depreciation allowance for depreciable excess basis. See paragraph (d)(4) of this section if the replacement MACRS property is acquired before disposition of the relinquished MACRS property in a transaction to which section 1033 applies. See paragraph (e) of this section for rules relating to the computation of the depreciation allowance using the optional depreciation tables.

(ii) *Applicable recovery period, depreciation method, and convention.*—The recovery period, depreciation method, and convention determined under this paragraph (c) are the only permissible methods of accounting for MACRS property within the scope of this section unless the taxpayer makes the election under paragraph (i) of this section not to apply this section.

(2) *Effect of depreciation treatment of the replacement MACRS property by previous owners of the acquired property.*—If replacement MACRS property is acquired by a taxpayer in a like-kind exchange or an involuntary conversion, the depreciation treatment of the replacement MACRS property by previous owners has no effect on the determination of depreciation allowances for the replacement

MACRS property in the hands of the acquiring taxpayer. For example, a taxpayer exchanging, in a like-kind exchange, MACRS property for property that was depreciated under section 168 of the Internal Revenue Code of 1954 (ACRS) by the previous owner must use this section because the replacement property will become MACRS property in the hands of the acquiring taxpayer. In addition, elections made by previous owners in determining depreciation allowances for the replacement MACRS property have no effect on the acquiring taxpayer. For example, a taxpayer exchanging, in a like-kind exchange, MACRS property that the taxpayer depreciates under the general depreciation system of section 168(a) for other MACRS property that the previous owner elected to depreciate under the alternative depreciation system pursuant to section 168(g)(7) does not have to continue using the alternative depreciation system for the replacement MACRS property.

(3) *Recovery period and/or depreciation method of the properties are the same, or both are not the same.*—(i) *In general.*—For purposes of paragraphs (c)(3) and (c)(4) of this section in determining whether the recovery period and the depreciation method prescribed under section 168 for the replacement MACRS property are the same as the recovery period and the depreciation method prescribed under section 168 for the relinquished MACRS property, the recovery period and the depreciation method for the replacement MACRS property are considered to be the recovery period and the depreciation method that would have applied under section 168, taking into account any elections made by the acquiring taxpayer under section 168(b)(5) or 168(g)(7), had the replacement MACRS property been placed in service by the acquiring taxpayer at the same time as the relinquished MACRS property.

(ii) *Both the recovery period and the depreciation method are the same.*—If both the recovery period and the depreciation method prescribed under section 168 for the replacement MACRS property are the same as the recovery period and the depreciation method prescribed under section 168 for the relinquished MACRS property, the depreciation allowances for the replacement MACRS property beginning in the year of replacement are determined by using the same recovery period and depreciation method that were used for the relinquished MACRS property. Thus, the replacement MACRS property is depreciated over the remaining recovery period (taking into account the applicable convention), and by using the depreciation method, of the relinquished MACRS property. Except as provided in paragraph (c)(5) of this section, the depreciation allowances for the depreciable exchanged basis for any 12-month taxable year beginning with the year of replacement are determined by multiplying the depreciable exchanged basis by the applicable depreciation rate for each taxable year (for further guidance, for example, see section 6 of Rev. Proc. 87-57 (1987-2 CB 687, 692) and § 601.601(d)(2)(ii)(*b*) of this chapter).

(iii) *Either the recovery period or the depreciation method is the same, or both are not the same.*—If either the recovery period or the depreciation method prescribed under section 168 for the replacement MACRS property is the same as the recovery period or the depreciation method prescribed under section 168 for the relinquished MACRS property, the depreciation allowances for the depreciable exchanged basis beginning in the year of replacement are determined using the recovery period or the depreciation method that is the same as the relinquished MACRS property. See paragraph (c)(4) of this section to determine the depreciation allowances when the recovery period or the depreciation method of the replacement MACRS property is not the same as that of the relinquished MACRS property.

(4) *Recovery period or depreciation method of the properties is not the same.*—If the recovery period prescribed under section 168 for the replacement MACRS property (as determined under paragraph (c)(3)(i) of this section) is not the same as the recovery period prescribed under section 168 for the relinquished MACRS property, the depreciation allowances for the depreciable exchanged basis beginning in the year of replacement are determined under this paragraph (c)(4). Similarly, if the depreciation method prescribed under section 168 for the replacement MACRS property (as determined under paragraph (c)(3)(i) of this section) is not the same as the depreciation method prescribed under section 168 for the relinquished MACRS property, the depreciation method used to determine the depreciation allowances for the depreciable exchanged basis beginning in the year of replacement is determined under this paragraph (c)(4).

(i) *Longer recovery period.*—If the recovery period prescribed under section 168 for the replacement MACRS property (as determined under paragraph (c)(3)(i) of this section) is longer than that prescribed for the relinquished MACRS property, the depreciation allowances for the depreciable exchanged basis beginning in the year of replacement are determined as though the replacement MACRS property had originally been placed in service by the acquiring taxpayer in the same taxable year the relinquished MACRS property was placed in service by the acquiring taxpayer, but using the longer recovery period of the replacement MACRS property (as determined under paragraph (c)(3)(i) of this section) and the convention determined under paragraph (c)(4)(v) of this section. Thus, the depreciable exchanged basis is depreciated over the remaining recovery period (taking into account the applicable convention) of the replacement MACRS property.

(ii) *Shorter recovery period.*—If the recovery period prescribed under section 168 for the replacement MACRS property (as determined under paragraph (c)(3)(i) of this section) is shorter than that of the relinquished MACRS property, the depreciation allowances for the depreciable exchanged basis beginning in the year of replacement are determined using the same recovery period as that of the relinquished MACRS property. Thus, the depreciable exchanged basis is depreciated over the remaining recovery period (taking into account the applicable convention) of the relinquished MACRS property.

(iii) *Less accelerated depreciation method.*—(A) If the depreciation method prescribed under section 168 for the replacement MACRS property (as determined under paragraph (c)(3)(i) of this section) is less accelerated than that of the relinquished MACRS property at the time of disposition, the depreciation allowances for the depreciable exchanged basis beginning in the year of replacement are determined as though the replacement MACRS property had originally been placed in service by the acquiring taxpayer at the same time the relinquished MACRS property was placed in service by the acquiring taxpayer, but using the less accelerated depreciation method. Thus, the depreciable exchanged basis is depreciated using the less accelerated depreciation method.

(B) Except as provided in paragraph (c)(5) of this section, the depreciation allowances for the depreciable exchanged basis for any 12-month taxable year beginning in the year of replacement are determined by multiplying the adjusted depreciable basis by the applicable depreciation rate for each taxable year. If, for example, the depreciation method of the replacement MACRS property in the year of replacement is the 150-percent declining balance method and the depreciation method of the relinquished MACRS property in the year of replacement is the 200-percent declining balance method, and neither method had been switched to the straight line method in the year of replacement or any prior taxable year, the applicable depreciation rate for the year of replacement and subsequent taxable years is determined by using the depreciation rate of the replacement MACRS property as if the replacement MACRS property was placed in service by the acquiring taxpayer at the same time the relinquished MACRS property was placed in service by the acquiring taxpayer, until the 150-percent declining balance method has been switched to the straight line method. If, for example, the depreciation method of the replacement MACRS property is the straight line method, the applicable depreciation rate for the year of replacement is determined by using the remaining recovery period at the beginning of the year of disposition (as determined under this paragraph (c)(4) and taking into account the applicable convention).

(iv) *More accelerated depreciation method.*—(A) If the depreciation method prescribed under section 168 for the replacement MACRS property (as determined under paragraph (c)(3)(i) of this section) is more accelerated than that of the relinquished MACRS property at the time of disposition, the depreciation allowances for the replacement MACRS property beginning in the year of replacement are determined using the same depreciation method as the relinquished MACRS property.

(B) Except as provided in paragraph (c)(5) of this section, the depreciation allowances for the depreciable exchanged basis for any 12-month taxable year beginning in the year of replacement are determined by multiplying the adjusted depreciable basis by the applicable depreciation rate for each taxable year. If, for example, the depreciation method of the relinquished MACRS property in the year of replacement is the 150-percent declining balance method and the depreciation method of the replacement MACRS property in the year of replacement is the 200-percent declining balance method, and neither method had been switched to the straight line method in the year of replacement or any prior taxable year, the applicable depreciation rate for the year of replacement and subsequent taxable years is the same depreciation rate that applied to the relinquished MACRS property in the year of replacement, until the 150-percent declining balance method has been switched to the straight line method. If, for example, the depreciation method is the straight line method, the applicable depreciation rate for the year of replacement is determined by using the remaining recovery period at the beginning of the year of disposition (as determined under this paragraph (c)(4) and taking into account the applicable convention).

(v) *Convention.*—The applicable convention for the exchanged basis is determined under this paragraph (c)(4)(v).

(A) *Either the relinquished MACRS property or the replacement MACRS property is mid-month property.*—If either the relinquished MACRS property or the replacement MACRS property is property for which the applicable convention (as determined under section 168(d)) is the mid-month convention, the exchanged basis must be depreciated using the mid-month convention.

(B) *Neither the relinquished MACRS property nor the replacement MACRS property is mid-month property.*—If neither the relinquished MACRS property nor the replacement MACRS property is property for which the applicable convention (as determined under section 168(d)) is the mid-month convention, the applicable convention for the exchanged basis is the same convention that applied to the relinquished MACRS property. If the relinquished MACRS property is placed in service in the year of disposition, and the time of replacement is also in the year of disposition, the convention that applies to the relinquished MACRS property is determined under paragraph (f)(1)(i) of this section. If, however, relinquished MACRS property was placed in service in the year of disposition and the time of replacement is in a taxable year subsequent to the year of disposition, the convention that applies to the exchanged basis is the convention that applies in that subsequent taxable year (see paragraph (f)(1)(ii) of this section).

(5) *Year of disposition and year of replacement.*—No depreciation deduction is allowable for MACRS property disposed of by a taxpayer in a like-kind exchange or involuntary conversion in the same taxable year that such property was placed in service by the taxpayer. If replacement MACRS property is disposed of by a taxpayer during the same taxable year that the relinquished MACRS property is placed in service by the taxpayer, no depreciation deduction is allowable for either MACRS property. Otherwise, the depreciation allowances for the year of disposition and for the year of replacement are determined as follows:

(i) *Relinquished MACRS property.*—(A) *General rule.*—Except as provided in paragraphs (c)(5)(i)(B), (c)(5)(iii), (e), and (i) of this section, the depreciation allowance in the year of disposition for the relinquished MACRS property is computed by multiplying the allowable depreciation deduction for the property for that year by a fraction, the numerator of which is the number of months (including fractions of months) the property is deemed to be placed in service during the year of disposition (taking into account the applicable convention of the relinquished MACRS property), and the denominator of which is 12. In the case of termination under § 1.168(i)-1(e)(3)(v) of general asset account treatment of an asset, or of all the assets remaining, in a general asset account, the allowable depreciation deduction in the year of disposition for the asset or assets for which general asset account treatment is terminated is determined using the depreciation method, recovery period, and convention of the general asset account. This allowable depreciation deduction is adjusted to account for the period the asset or assets is deemed to be in service in accordance with this paragraph (c)(5)(i).

(B) *Special rule.*—If, at the beginning of the year of disposition, the remaining recovery period of the relinquished MACRS property, taking into account the applicable convention of such property, is less than the period between the beginning of the year of disposition and the time of disposition, the depreciation deduction for the relinquished MACRS property for the year of disposition is equal to the adjusted depreciable basis of the relinquished MACRS property at the beginning of the year of disposition. If this paragraph applies, the exchanged basis is zero and no depreciation is allowable for the exchanged basis in the replacement MACRS property.

(ii) *Replacement MACRS property.*—(A) *Remaining recovery period of the replacement MACRS property.*—The replacement MACRS property is treated as placed in service at the time of replacement under the convention that applies to the replacement MACRS property as determined under this paragraph (c)(5)(ii). The remaining recovery period of the replacement MACRS property at the time of replacement is the excess of the recovery period for the replacement MACRS property, as determined under paragraph (c) of this section, over the period of time that the replacement MACRS property would have been in service if it had been placed in service when the relinquished MACRS property was placed in service and removed from service at the time of disposition of the relinquished MACRS property. This period is determined by using the convention that applied to the relinquished MACRS property to determine the date that the relinquished MACRS property is deemed to have been placed in service and the date that it is deemed to have been disposed of. The length of time the replacement MACRS property would have been in service is determined by using these dates and the convention that applies to the replacement MACRS property.

(B) *Year of replacement is 12 months.*—Except as provided in paragraphs (c)(5)(iii), (e), and (i) of this section, the depreciation allowance in the year of replacement for the depreciable exchanged basis is determined by—

(1) Calculating the applicable depreciation rate for the replacement MACRS property as of the beginning of the year of replacement taking

into account the depreciation method prescribed for the replacement MACRS property under paragraph (c)(3) of this section and the remaining recovery period of the replacement MACRS property as of the beginning of the year of disposition as determined under this paragraph (c)(5)(ii);

(2) Calculating the depreciable exchanged basis of the replacement MACRS property, and adding to that amount the amount determined under paragraph (c)(5)(i) of this section for the year of disposition; and

(3) Multiplying the product of the amounts determined under paragraphs (c)(5)(ii)(B)(*1*) and (B)(*2*) of this section by a fraction, the numerator of which is the number of months (including fractions of months) the property is deemed to be in service during the year of replacement (in the year of replacement the replacement MACRS property is deemed to be placed in service by the acquiring taxpayer at the time of replacement under the convention determined under paragraph (c)(4)(v) of this section), and the denominator of which is 12.

(iii) *Year of disposition or year of replacement is less than 12 months.*—If the year of disposition or the year of replacement is less than 12 months, the depreciation allowance determined under paragraph (c)(5)(ii)(A) of this section must be adjusted for a short taxable year (for further guidance, for example, see Rev. Proc. 89-15 (1989-1 CB 816) and § 601.601(d)(2)(ii)(*b*) of this chapter).

(iv) *Deferred transactions.*—(A) *In general.*—If the replacement MACRS property is not acquired until after the disposition of the relinquished MACRS property, taking into account the applicable convention of the relinquished MACRS property and replacement MACRS property, depreciation is not allowable during the period between the disposition of the relinquished MACRS property and the acquisition of the replacement MACRS property. The recovery period for the replacement MACRS property is suspended during this period. For purposes of paragraph (c)(5)(ii) of this section, only the depreciable exchanged basis of the replacement MACRS property is taken into account for calculating the amount in paragraph (c)(5)(ii)(B)(*2*) of this section if the year of replacement is a taxable year subsequent to the year of disposition.

(B) *Allowable depreciation for a qualified intermediary.*—[Reserved].

(v) *Remaining recovery period.*—The remaining recovery period of the replacement MACRS property is determined as of the beginning of the year of disposition of the relinquished MACRS property. For purposes of determining the remaining recovery period of the replacement MACRS property, the replacement MACRS property is deemed to have been originally placed in service under the convention determined under paragraph (c)(4)(v) of this section but at the time the relinquished MACRS property was deemed to be placed in service under the convention that applied to it when it was placed in service.

(6) *Examples.*—The application of this paragraph (c) is illustrated by the following examples:

Example 1. A1, a calendar-year taxpayer, exchanges Building M, an office building, for Building N, a warehouse in a like-kind exchange. Building M is relinquished in July 2004 and Building N is acquired and placed in service in October 2004. A1 did not make any elections under section 168 for either Building M or Building N. The unadjusted depreciable basis of Building M was $4,680,000 when placed in service in July 1997. Since the recovery period and depreciation method prescribed under section 168 for Building N (39 years, straight line method) are the same as the recovery period and depreciation method prescribed under section 168 for Building M (39 years, straight line method), Building N is depreciated over the remaining recovery period of, and using the same depreciation method and convention as that of, Building M. Applying the applicable convention, Building M is deemed disposed of on July 15, 2004, and Building N is placed in service on October 15, 2004. Thus, Building N will be depreciated using the straight line method over a remaining recovery period of 32 years beginning in October 2004 (the remaining recovery period of 32 years and 6.5 months at the beginning of 2004, less the 6.5 months of depreciation taken prior to the disposition of the exchanged MACRS property (Building M) in 2004). For 2004, the year in which the transaction takes place, the depreciation allowance for Building M is ($120,000) (6.5/12) which equals $65,000. The depreciation allowance for Building N for 2004 is ($120,000) (2.5/12) which equals $25,000. For 2005 and subsequent years, Building N is depreciated over the remaining recovery period of, and using the same depreciation method and convention as that of, Building M. Thus, the depreciation allowance for Building N is the same as Building M, namely $10,000 per month.

Example 2. B, a calendar-year taxpayer, placed in service Bridge P in January 1998. Bridge P is depreciated using the half-year convention. In January 2004, B exchanges Bridge P for Building Q, an apartment building, in a like-kind exchange. Pursuant to paragraph (k) (2) (i) of this section, B decided to apply § 1.168(i)-6 to the exchange of Bridge P for Building Q, the replacement MACRS property. B did not make any elections under section 168 for either Bridge P or Building Q. Since the recovery period prescribed under section 168 for Building Q (27.5 years) is longer than that of Bridge P (15 years), Building Q is depreciated as if it had originally been placed in service in July 1998 and disposed of in July 2004 using a 27.5 year recovery period. Additionally, since the depreciation method prescribed under section 168 for Building Q (straight line method) is less accelerated than that of Bridge P (150-percent declining balance method), then the depreciation allowance for Building Q is computed using the straight line method. Thus, when Building Q is acquired and placed in service in 2004, its basis is depreciated over the remaining 21.5 year recovery period using the straight line method of depreciation and the mid-month convention beginning in July 2004.

Example 3. C, a calendar-year taxpayer, placed in service Building R, a restaurant, in January 1996. In January 2004, C exchanges Building R for Tower S, a radio transmitting tower, in a like-kind exchange. Pursuant to paragraph (k) (2) (i) of this section, C decided to apply § 1.168(i)-6 to the exchange of Building R for Tower S, the replacement MACRS property. C did not make any elections under section 168 for either Building R or Tower S. Since the recovery period prescribed under section 168 for Tower S (15 years) is shorter than that of Building R (39 years), Tower S is depreciated over the remaining recovery period of Building R. Additionally, since the depreciation method prescribed under section 168 for Tower S (150% declining balance method) is more accelerated than that of Building R (straight line method), then the depreciation allowance for Tower S is also computed using the same depreciation method as Building R. Thus, Tower S is depreciated over the remaining 31 year recovery period of Building R using the straight line method of depreciation and the mid-month convention. Alternatively, C may elect under paragraph (i) of this section to treat Tower S as though it is placed in service in January 2004. In such case, C uses the applicable recovery period, depreciation method, and convention prescribed under section 168 for Tower S.

Example 4. (i) In February 2002, D, a calendar-year taxpayer and manufacturer of rubber products, acquired for $60,000 and placed in service Asset T (a special tool) and depreciated Asset T using the straight line method election under section 168(b) (5) and the mid-quarter convention over its 3-year recovery period. D elected not to deduct the additional first year depreciation for 3-year property placed in service in 2002. In June 2004, D exchanges Asset T for Asset U (not a special tool) in a like-kind exchange. D elected not to deduct the additional first year depreciation for 7-year property placed in service in 2004. Since the recovery period prescribed under section 168 for Asset U (7 years) is longer than that of Asset T (3 years), Asset U is depreciated as if it had originally been placed in service in February 2002 using a 7-year recovery period. Additionally, since the depreciation method prescribed under section 168 for Asset U (200-percent declining balance method) is more accelerated than that of Asset T (straight line method) at the time of disposition, the depreciation allowance for Asset U is computed using the straight line method. Asset U is depreciated over its remaining recovery period of 4.75 years using the straight line method of depreciation and the mid-quarter convention.

(ii) The 2004 depreciation allowance for Asset T is $7,500 ($20,000 allowable depreciation deduction for 2004) × 4.5 months ÷ 12).

(iii) The depreciation rate in 2004 for Asset U is 0.1951 (1 ÷ 5.125 years (the length of the applicable recovery period remaining as of the beginning of 2004)). Therefore, the depreciation allowance for Asset U in 2004 is $2,744 (0.1951 × $22,500 (the sum of the $15,000 depreciable exchanged basis of Asset U ($22,500 adjusted depreciable basis at the beginning of 2004 for Asset T, less the $7,500 depreciation allowable for Asset T for 2004) and the $7,500 depreciation allowable for Asset T for 2004) × 7.5 months ÷ 12).

Example 5. The facts are the same as in *Example 4* except that D exchanges Asset T for Asset U in June 2005, in a like-kind exchange. Under these facts, the remaining recovery period of Asset T at the beginning of 2005 is 1.5 months and, as a result, is less than the 5-month period between the beginning of 2005 (year of disposition) and June 2005 (time of disposition). Accordingly, pursuant to paragraph (c)(5)(i)(B) of this section, the 2005 depreciation allowance for Asset T is $2,500 ($2,500 adjusted depreciable basis at the beginning of 2005 ($60,000 original basis minus $17,500 depreciation deduction for 2002 minus $20,000 depreciation deduction for 2003 minus $20,000 depreciation deduction for 2004)). Because the exchanged basis of asset U is $0.00 no depreciation is allowable for asset U.

Example 6. On January 1, 2004, E, a calendar-year taxpayer, acquired and placed in service Canopy V, a gas station canopy. The purchase price of Canopy V was $60,000. On August 1, 2004, Canopy V was destroyed in a hurricane and was therefore no longer usable in E's business. On October 1, 2004, as part of the involuntary conversion, E acquired and placed in service new Canopy W with the insurance proceeds E received due to the loss of Canopy V. E elected not to deduct the additional first year depreciation for 5-year property placed in service in 2004. E depreciates both canopies under the general depreciation system of section 168(a) by using the 200-percent declining balance method of depreciation, a 5-year recovery period, and the half-year convention. No depreciation deduction is allowable for Canopy V. The depreciation deduction allowable for Canopy W for 2004 is $12,000 ($60,000 × the annual depreciation rate of .40 × ½ year). For 2005, the depreciation deduction for Canopy W is $19,200 ($48,000 adjusted basis × the annual depreciation rate of .40).

Example 7. The facts are the same as in *Example 6,* except that E did not make the election out of the additional first year depreciation for 5-year property placed in service in 2004. E depreciates both canopies under the general depreciation system of section 168(a) by using the 200-percent declining balance method of depreciation, a 5-year recovery period, and the half-year convention. No depreciation deduction is allowable for Canopy V. For 2004, E is allowed a 50-percent additional first year depreciation deduction of $30,000 for Canopy W (the unadjusted depreciable basis of $60,000 multiplied by .50), and a regular MACRS depreciation deduction of $6,000 for Canopy W (the depreciable exchanged basis of $30,000 multiplied by the annual depreciation rate of .40 × ½ year). For 2005, E is allowed a regular MACRS depreciation deduction of $9,600 for Canopy W (the depreciable exchanged basis of $24,000 ($30,000 minus regular 2003 depreciation of $6,000) multiplied by the annual depreciation rate of .40).

Example 8. In January 2001, F, a calendar-year taxpayer, places in service a paved parking lot, Lot W, and begins depreciating Lot W over its 15-year recovery period. F's unadjusted depreciable basis in Lot W is $1,000x. On April 1, 2004, F disposes of Lot W in a like-kind exchange for Building X, which is nonresidential real property. Lot W is depreciated using the 150 percent declining balance method and the half-year convention. Building X is depreciated using the straight-line method with a 39-year recovery period and using the mid-month convention. Both Lot W and Building X were in service at the time of the exchange. Because Lot W was depreciated using the half-year convention, it is deemed to have been placed in service on July 1, 2001, the first day of the second half of 2001, and to have been disposed of on July 1, 2004, the first day of the second half of 2004. To determine the remaining recovery period of Building X at the time of replacement, Building X is deemed to have been placed in service on July 1, 2001, and removed from service on July 1, 2004. Thus, Building X is deemed to have been in service, at the time of replacement, for 3 years (36 months=5.5 months in 2001 + 12 months in 2002 + 12 months in 2003 + 6.5 months in 2004) and its remaining recovery period is 36 years (39 - 3). Because Building X is deemed to be placed in service at the time of replacement, July 1, 2004, the first day of the second half of 2004, Building X is depreciated for 5.5 months in 2004. However, at the beginning of the year of replacement the remaining recovery period for Building X is 36 years and 6.5 months (39 years - 2 years and 5.5 months (5.5 months in 2001 + 12 months in 2002 + 12 months in 2003)). The depreciation rate for building X for 2004 is 0.02737 (= 1/(39-2-5.5/12)). For 2005, the depreciation rate for Building X is 0.02814 (= 1/(39-3-5.5/12)).

Example 9. The facts are the same as in *Example 8.* F did not make the election under paragraph (i) of this section for Building Y in the initial exchange. In January 2006, F exchanges Building Y for Building Z, an office building, in a like-kind exchange. F did not make any elections under section 168 for either Building Y or Building Z. Since the recovery period prescribed for Building Y as a result of the initial exchange (39 years) is longer than that of Building Z (27.5 years), Building Z is depreciated over the remaining 33 years of the recovery period of Building Y. The depreciation methods are the same for both Building Y and Building Z so F's exchanged basis in Building Z is depreciated over 33 years, using the straight-line method and the mid-month convention, beginning in January 2006. Alternatively, F could have made the election under paragraph (i) of this section. If F makes such election, Building Z is treated as placed in service by F when acquired in January 2006 and F would recover its exchanged basis in Building Z over 27.5 years, using the straight line method and the mid-month convention, beginning in January 2006.

(d) *Special rules for determining depreciation allowances.*—(1) *Excess basis.*—(i) *In general.*—Any excess basis in the replacement MACRS property is treated as property that is placed in service by the acquiring taxpayer in the year of replacement. Thus, the depreciation allowances for the depreciable excess basis are determined by using the applicable recovery period, depreciation method, and convention prescribed under section 168 for the property at the time of replacement. However, if replacement MACRS property is disposed of during the same taxable year the relinquished MACRS property is placed in service by the acquiring taxpayer, no depreciation deduction is allowable for either MACRS property. See paragraph (g) of this section regarding the application of section 179. See paragraph (h) of this section regarding the application of section 168(k) or 1400L(b).

(ii) *Example.*—The application of this paragraph (d)(1) is illustrated by the following example:

Example. In 1989, G placed in service a hospital. On January 16, 2004, G exchanges this hospital plus $2,000,000 cash for an office building in a like-kind exchange. On January 16, 2004, the hospital has an adjusted depreciable basis of $1,500,000. After the exchange, the basis of the office building is $3,500,000. Pursuant to paragraph (k)(2)(i) of this section, G decided to apply § 1.168(i)-6 to the exchange of the hospital for the office building, the replacement MACRS property. The depreciable exchanged basis of the office building is depreciated in accordance with paragraph (c) of this section. The depreciable excess basis of $2,000,000 is treated as being placed in service by G in 2004 and, as a result, is depreciated using the applicable depreciation method, recovery period, and convention prescribed for the office building under section 168 at the time of replacement.

(2) *Depreciable and nondepreciable property.*—(i) If land or other nondepreciable property is acquired in a like-kind exchange for, or as a result of an involuntary conversion of, depreciable property, the land or other nondepreciable property is not depreciated. If both MACRS and nondepreciable property are acquired in a like-kind exchange for, or as part of an involuntary conversion of, MACRS property, the basis allocated to the nondepreciable property (as determined under section 1031(d) and the regulations under section 1031(d) or section 1033(b) and the regulations under section 1033(b)) is not depreciated and the basis allocated to the replacement MACRS property (as determined under section 1031(d) and the regulations under section 1031(d) or section 1033(b) and the regulations under section 1033(b)) is depreciated in accordance with this section.

(ii) If MACRS property is acquired, or if both MACRS and nondepreciable property are acquired, in a like-kind exchange for, or as part of an involuntary conversion of, land or other nondepreciable property, the basis in the replacement MACRS property that is attributable to the relinquished nondepreciable property is treated as though the replacement MACRS property is placed in service by the acquiring taxpayer in the year of replacement. Thus, the depreciation allowances for the replacement MACRS property are determined by using the applicable recovery period, depreciation method, and convention prescribed under section 168 for the replacement MACRS property at the time of replacement. See paragraph (g) of this section regarding the application of section 179. See paragraph (h) of this section regarding the application of section 168(k) or 1400L(b).

(3) *Depreciation limitations for automobiles.*—(i) *In general.*—Depreciation allowances under section 179 and section 167 (including allowances under sections 168 and 1400L(b)) for a passenger automobile, as defined in section 280F(d)(5), are subject to the limitations of section 280F(a). The depreciation allowances for a passenger automobile that is replacement MACRS property (replacement MACRS passenger automobile) generally are limited in any taxable year to the replacement automobile section 280F limit for the taxable year. The taxpayer's basis in the replacement MACRS passenger automobile is treated as being comprised of two separate components. The first component is the exchanged basis and the second component is the excess basis, if any. The depreciation allowances for a passenger automobile that is relinquished MACRS property (relinquished MACRS passenger automobile) for the taxable year generally are limited to the relinquished automobile section 280F limit for that taxable year. In the year of disposition the sum of the depreciation deductions for the relinquished MACRS passenger automobile and the replacement MACRS passenger automobile may not exceed the replacement automobile section 280F limit unless the taxpayer makes the election under § 1.168(i)-6(i). 6(i). For purposes of this paragraph (d)(3), the following definitions apply:

(A) *Replacement automobile section 280F limit* is the limit on depreciation deductions under section 280F(a) for the taxable year based on the time of replacement of the replacement MACRS passenger automobile (including the effect of any elections under section 168(k) or section 1400L(b), as applicable).

(B) *Relinquished automobile section 280F limit* is the limit on depreciation deductions under section 280F(a) for the taxable year based on when the relinquished MACRS passenger automobile was placed in service by the taxpayer.

(ii) *Order in which limitations on depreciation under section 280F(a) are applied.*—Generally, depreciation deductions allowable under section 280F(a) reduce the basis in the relinquished MACRS passenger automobile and the exchanged basis of the replacement MACRS passenger automobile, before the excess basis of the replacement MACRS passenger automobile is reduced. The depreciation deductions for the relinquished MACRS passenger automobile in the year of disposition and the replacement MACRS passenger automobile in the year of replacement and each subsequent taxable year are allowable in the following order:

(A) The depreciation deduction allowable for the relinquished MACRS passenger automobile as determined under paragraph (c)(5)(i) of this section for the year of disposition to the extent of the smaller of the replacement automobile section 280F limit and the relinquished automobile section 280F limit, if the year of disposition is the year of replacement. If the year of replacement is a taxable year subsequent to the year of disposition, the depreciation deduction allowable for the relinquished MACRS passenger automobile for the year of disposition is limited to the relinquished automobile section 280F limit.

(B) The additional first year depreciation allowable on the remaining exchanged basis (remaining carryover basis as determined under § 1.168(k)-1(f)(5) or § 1.1400L(b)-1(f)(5), as applicable) of the replacement MACRS passenger automobile, as determined under § 1.168(k)-1(f)(5) or § 1.1400L(b)-1(f)(5), as applicable, to the extent of the excess of the replacement automobile section 280F limit over the amount allowable under paragraph (d)(3)(ii)(A) of this section.

(C) The depreciation deduction allowable for the taxable year on the depreciable exchanged basis of the replacement MACRS passenger automobile determined under paragraph (c) of this section to the extent of any excess over the sum of the amounts allowable under paragraphs (d)(3)(ii)(A) and (B) of this section of the smaller of the replacement automobile section 280F limit and the relinquished automobile section 280F limit.

(D) Any section 179 deduction allowable in the year of replacement on the excess basis of the replacement MACRS passenger automobile to the extent of the excess of the replacement automobile section 280F limit over the sum of the amounts allowable under paragraphs (d)(3)(ii)(A), (B), and (C) of this section.

(E) The additional first year depreciation allowable on the remaining excess basis of the replacement MACRS passenger automobile, as determined under § 1.168(k)-1(f)(5) or § 1.1400L(b)-1(f)(5), as applicable, to the extent of the excess of the replacement automobile section 280F limit over the sum of the amounts allowable under paragraphs (d)(3)(ii)(A), (B), (C), and (D) of this section.

(F) The depreciation deduction allowable under paragraph (d) of this section for the depreciable excess basis of the replacement MACRS passenger automobile to the extent of the excess of the replacement automobile section 280F limit over the sum of the amounts allowable under paragraphs (d)(3)(ii)(A), (B), (C), (D), and (E) of this section.

(iii) *Examples.*—The application of this paragraph (d)(3) is illustrated by the following examples:

Example 1. H, a calendar-year taxpayer, acquired and placed in service Automobile X in January 2000 for $30,000 to be used solely for H's business.

In December 2003, H exchanges, in a like-kind exchange, Automobile X plus $15,000 cash for new Automobile Y that will also be used solely in H's business. Automobile Y is 50-percent bonus depreciation property for purposes of section 168(k)(4). Both automobiles are depreciated using the double declining balance method, the half-year convention, and a 5-year recovery period. Pursuant to § 1.168(k)-1(g(3)(ii) and paragraph (k)(2)(i) of this section, H decided to apply § 1.168(i)-6 to the exchange of Automobile X for Automobile Y, the replacement MACRS property. The relinquished automobile section 280F limit for 2003 for Automobile X is $1,775. The replacement automobile section 280F limit for Automobile Y is $10,710. The exchanged basis for Automobile Y is $17,315 ($30,000 less total depreciation allowable of $12,685 (($3,060 for 2000, $4,900 for 2001, $2,950 for 2002, and $1,775 for 2003)). Without taking section 280F into account, the additional first year depreciation deduction for the remaining exchanged basis is $8,658 ($17,315 × 0.5). Because this amount is less than $8,935 ($10,710 (the replacement automobile section 280F limit for 2003 for Automobile Y) - $1,775 (the depreciation allowable for Automobile X for 2003)), the additional first year depreciation deduction for the exchanged basis is $8,658. No depreciation deduction is allowable in 2003 for the depreciable exchanged basis because the depreciation deductions taken for Automobile X and the remaining exchanged basis exceed the exchanged automobile section 280F limit. An additional first year depreciation deduction of $277 is allowable for the excess basis of $15,000 in Automobile Y. Thus, at the end of 2003 the adjusted depreciable basis in Automobile Y is $23,379 comprised of adjusted depreciable exchanged basis of $8,657 ($17,315 (exchanged basis) — $8,658 (additional first year depreciation for exchanged basis)) and of an adjusted depreciable excess basis of $14,723 ($15,000 (excess basis) - $277 (additional first year depreciation for 2003)).

Example 2. The facts are the same as in *Example 1,* except that H used Automobile X only 75 percent for business use. As such, the total allowable depreciation for Automobile X is reduced to reflect that the automobile is only used 75 percent for business. The total allowable depreciation of Automobile X is $9,513.75 ($2,295 for 2000 ($3,060 limit × .75), $3,675 for 2001 ($4,900 limit × .75), $2,212.50 for 2002 ($2,950 limit × .75), and $1,331.25 for 2003 ($1,775 limit × .75). However, under § 1.280F-2T(g)(2)(ii)(A), the exchanged basis is reduced by the excess (if any) of the depreciation that would have been allowable if the exchanged automobile had been used solely for business over the depreciation that was allowable in those years. Thus, the exchanged basis, for purposes of computing depreciation, for Automobile Y is $17,315.

Example 3. The facts are the same as in *Example 1,* except that H placed in service Automobile X in January 2002, and H elected not to claim the additional first year depreciation deduction for 5-year property placed in service in 2002 and 2003. The relinquished automobile section 280F limit for Automobile X for 2003 is $4,900. Because the replacement automobile section 280F limit for 2003 for Automobile Y ($3,060) is less than the relinquished automobile section 280F limit for Automobile X for 2003 and is less than $5,388 (($30,000 (cost) - $3,060 (depreciation allowable for 2002)) × 0.4 × 6/12), the depreciation that would be allowable for Automobile X (determined without regard to section 280F) in the year of disposition, the depreciation for Automobile X in the year of disposition is limited to $3,060. For 2003 no depreciation is allowable for the excess basis and the exchanged basis in Automobile Y.

Example 4. AB, a calendar-year taxpayer, purchased and placed in service Automobile X1 in February 2000 for $10,000. X1 is a passenger automobile subject to section 280F(a) and is used solely for AB's business. AB depreciated X1 using a 5-year recovery period, the double declining balance method, and the half-year convention. As of January 1, 2003, the adjusted depreciable basis of X1 was $2,880 ($10,000 original cost minus $2,000 depreciation deduction for 2000, minus

$3,200 depreciation deduction for 2001, and $1,920 depreciation deduction for 2002). In November 2003, AB exchanges, in a like-kind exchange, Automobile X1 plus $14,000 cash for new Automobile Y1 that will be used solely in AB's business. Automobile Y1 is 50-percent bonus depreciation property for purposes of section 168(k)(4) and qualifies for the expensing election under section 179. Pursuant to paragraph § 1.168(k)-1(g)(3)(ii) and paragraph (k)(2)(i) of this section, AB decided to apply § 1.168(i)-6 to the exchange of Automobile X1 for Automobile Y1, the replacement MACRS property. AB also makes the election under section 179 for the excess basis of Automobile Y1. AB depreciates Y1 using a five-year recovery period, the double declining balance method and the half-year convention. For 2003, the relinquished automobile section 280F limit for Automobile X1 is $1,775 and the replacement automobile section 280F limit for 2003 for Automobile Y1 is $10,710.

(i) The 2003 depreciation deduction for Automobile X1 is $576. The depreciation deduction calculated for X1 is $576 (the adjusted depreciable basis of Automobile X1 at the beginning of 2003 of $2,880 × 40% × ½ year), which is less than the relinquished automobile section 280F limit and the replacement automobile section 280F limit.

(ii) The additional first year depreciation deduction for the exchanged basis is $1,152. The additional first year depreciation deduction of $1,152 (remaining exchanged basis of $2,304 ($2,880 adjusted basis of Automobile X1 at the beginning of 2003 minus $576) × 0.5)) is less than the replacement automobile section 280F limit minus $576.

(iii) AB's MACRS depreciation deduction allowable in 2003 for the remaining exchanged basis of $1,152 is $47 (the relinquished automobile section 280F limit of $1,775 less the depreciation deduction of $576 taken for Automobile X1 less the additional first year depreciation deduction of $1,152 taken for the exchanged basis) which is less than the depreciation deduction calculated for the depreciable exchanged basis.

(iv) For 2003, AB takes a $1,400 section 179 deduction for the excess basis of Automobile Y1. AB must reduce the excess basis of $14,000 by the section 179 deduction of $1,400 to determine the remaining excess basis of $12,600.

(v) For 2003, AB is allowed a 50-percent additional first year depreciation deduction of $6,300 (the remaining excess basis of $12,600 multiplied by .50).

(vi) For 2003, AB's depreciation deduction for the depreciable excess basis is limited to $1,235. The depreciation deduction computed without regard to the replacement automobile section 280F limit is $1,260 ($6,300 depreciable excess basis × 0.4 × 6/12). However the depreciation deduction for the depreciable excess basis is limited to $1,235 ($10,710 (replacement automobile section 280F limit) - $576 (depreciation deduction for Automobile X1) - $1,152 (additional first year depreciation deduction for the exchanged basis) - $47 (depreciation deduction for exchanged basis) $1,400 (section 179 deduction) - $6,300 (additional first year depreciation deduction for remaining excess basis)).

(4) *Involuntary conversion for which the replacement MACRS property is acquired and placed in service before disposition of relinquished MACRS property.*—If, in an involuntary conversion, a taxpayer acquires and places in service the replacement MACRS property before the date of disposition of the relinquished MACRS property, the taxpayer depreciates the unadjusted depreciable basis of the replacement MACRS property under section 168 beginning in the taxable year when the replacement MACRS property is placed in service by the taxpayer and by using the applicable depreciation method, recovery period, and convention prescribed under section 168 for the replacement MACRS property at the placed-in-service date. However, at the time of disposition of the relinquished MACRS property, the taxpayer determines the exchanged basis and the excess basis of the replacement MACRS property and begins to depreciate the depreciable exchanged basis of the

replacement MACRS property in accordance with paragraph (c) of this section. The depreciable excess basis of the replacement MACRS property continues to be depreciated by the taxpayer in accordance with the first sentence of this paragraph (d)(4). Further, in the year of disposition of the relinquished MACRS property, the taxpayer must include in taxable income the excess of the depreciation deductions allowable on the unadjusted depreciable basis of the replacement MACRS property over the depreciation deductions that would have been allowable to the taxpayer on the depreciable excess basis of the replacement MACRS property from the date the replacement MACRS property was placed in service by the taxpayer (taking into account the applicable convention) to the time of disposition of the relinquished MACRS property. However, see § 1.168(k)-1(f)(5)(v) for replacement MACRS property that is qualified property or 50-percent bonus depreciation property and § 1.1400L(b)-1(f)(5) for replacement MACRS property that is qualified New York Liberty Zone property.

(e) *Use of optional depreciation tables.*—(1) *Taxpayer not bound by prior use of table.*—If a taxpayer used an optional depreciation table for the relinquished MACRS property, the taxpayer is not required to use an optional table for the depreciable exchanged basis of the replacement MACRS property. Conversely, if a taxpayer did not use an optional depreciation table for the relinquished MACRS property, the taxpayer may use the appropriate table for the depreciable exchanged basis of the replacement MACRS property. If a taxpayer decides not to use the table for the depreciable exchanged basis of the replacement MACRS property, the depreciation allowance for this property for the year of replacement and subsequent taxable years is determined under paragraph (c) of this section. If a taxpayer decides to use the optional depreciation tables, no depreciation deduction is allowable for MACRS property placed in service by the acquiring taxpayer and subsequently exchanged or involuntarily converted by such taxpayer in the same taxable year, and, if, during the same taxable year, MACRS property is placed in service by the acquiring taxpayer, exchanged or involuntarily converted by such taxpayer, and the replacement MACRS property is disposed of by such taxpayer, no depreciation deduction is allowable for either MACRS property.

(2) *Determination of the depreciation deduction.*—(i) *Relinquished MACRS property.*—In the year of disposition, the depreciation allowance for the relinquished MACRS property is computed by multiplying the unadjusted depreciable basis (less the amount of the additional first year depreciation deduction allowed or allowable, whichever is greater, under section 168(k) or section 1400L(b), as applicable) of the relinquished MACRS property by the annual depreciation rate (expressed as a decimal equivalent) specified in the appropriate table for the recovery year corresponding to the year of disposition. This product is then multiplied by a fraction, the numerator of which is the number of months (including fractions of months) the property is deemed to be placed in service during the year of the exchange or involuntary conversion (taking into account the applicable convention) and the denominator of which is 12. However, if the year of disposition is less than 12 months, the depreciation allowance determined under this paragraph (e)(2)(i) must be adjusted for a short taxable year (for further guidance, for example, see Rev. Proc. 89-15 (1989-1 CB 816) and § 601.601(d)(2)(ii)(*b*) of this chapter).

(ii) *Replacement MACRS property.*—(A) *Determination of the appropriate optional depreciation table.*—If a taxpayer chooses to use the appropriate optional depreciation table for the depreciable exchanged basis, the depreciation allowances for the depreciable exchanged basis beginning in the year of replacement are determined by choosing the optional depreciation table that corresponds to the recovery period, depreciation method, and convention of the replacement MACRS property determined under paragraph (c) of this section.

(B) *Calculating the depreciation deduction for the replacement MACRS property.*—(1) The depreciation deduction for the taxable year is computed by first determining the appropriate recovery year in the table identified under paragraph (e)(2)(ii)(A) of this section. The appropriate recovery year for the year of replacement is the same as the recovery year for the year of disposition, regardless of the taxable year in which the replacement property is acquired. For example, if the recovery year for the year of disposition would have been year 4 in the table that applied before the disposition of the relinquished MACRS property, then the recovery year for the year of replacement is Year 4 in the table identified under paragraph (e)(2)(ii)(A) of this section.

(2) Next, the annual depreciation rate (expressed as a decimal equivalent) for each recovery year is multiplied by a transaction coefficient. The transaction coefficient is the formula (1 / (1 - x)) where x equals the sum of the annual depreciation rates from the table identified under paragraph (e)(2)(ii)(A) of this section (expressed as a decimal equivalent) corresponding to the replacement MACRS property (as determined under paragraph (e)(2)(ii)(A) of this section) for the taxable years beginning with the placed-in-service year of the relinquished MACRS property through the taxable year immediately prior to the year of disposition. The product of the annual depreciation rate and the transaction coefficient is multiplied by the depreciable exchanged basis (taking into account paragraph (e)(2)(i) of this section). In the year of replacement, this product is then multiplied by a fraction, the numerator of which is the number of months (including fractions of months) the property is deemed to be placed in service by the acquiring taxpayer during the year of replacement (taking into account the applicable convention) and the denominator of which is 12. However, if the year of replacement is the year the relinquished MACRS property is placed in service by the acquiring taxpayer, the preceding sentence does not apply. In addition, if the year of replacement is less than 12 months, the depreciation allowance determined under paragraph (e)(2)(ii) of this section must be adjusted for a short taxable year (for further guidance, for example, see Rev. Proc. 89-15 (1989-1 CB 816) and §601.601(d)(2)(ii)(*b*) of this chapter).

(iii) *Unrecovered basis.*—If the replacement MACRS property would have unrecovered depreciable basis after the final recovery year (for example, due to a deferred exchange), the unrecovered basis is an allowable depreciation deduction in the taxable year that corresponds to the final recovery year unless the unrecovered basis is subject to a depreciation limitation such as section 280F.

(3) *Excess basis.*—As provided in paragraph (d)(1) of this section, any excess basis in the replacement MACRS property is treated as property that is placed in service by the acquiring taxpayer at the time of replacement. Thus, if the taxpayer chooses to use the appropriate optional depreciation table for the depreciable excess basis in the replacement MACRS property, the depreciation allowances for the depreciable excess basis are determined by multiplying the depreciable excess basis by the annual depreciation rate (expressed as a decimal equivalent) specified in the appropriate table for each taxable year. The appropriate table for the depreciable excess basis is based on the depreciation method, recovery period, and convention applicable to the depreciable excess basis under section 168 at the time of replacement. However, If the year of replacement is less than 12 months, the depreciation allowance determined under this paragraph (e)(3) must be adjusted for a short taxable year (for further guidance, for example, see Rev. Proc. 89-15 (1989-1 CB 816) and §601.601(d)(2)(ii)(*b*) of this chapter).

(4) *Examples.*—The application of this paragraph (e) is illustrated by the following examples:

Example 1. J, a calendar-year taxpayer, acquired 5-year property for $10,000 and placed it in service in January 2001. J uses the optional tables to depreciate the property. J uses the half-year convention and did not make any elections for the property. In December 2003, J exchanges the 5-year property for used 7-year property in a like-kind exchange. Pursuant to paragraph (k)(2)(i) of this section, J decided to apply § 1.168(i)-6 to the exchange of the 5-year property for the 7-year property, the replacement MACRS property. The depreciable exchanged basis of the 7-year property equals the adjusted depreciable basis of the 5-year property at the time of disposition of the relinquished MACRS property, namely $3,840 ($10,000 less $2,000 depreciation in 2001, $3,200 depreciation in 2002, and $960 depreciation in 2003). J must first determine the appropriate optional depreciation table pursuant to paragraph (c) of this section. Since the replacement MACRS property has a longer recovery period and the same depreciation method as the relinquished MACRS property, J uses the optional depreciation table corresponding to a 7-year recovery period, the 200% declining balance method, and the half-year convention (because the 5-year property was depreciated using a half-year convention). Had the replacement MACRS property been placed in service in the same taxable year as the placed-in-service year of the relinquished MACRS property, the depreciation allowance for the replacement MACRS property for the year of replacement would be determined using recovery year 3 of the optional table. The depreciation allowance equals the depreciable exchanged basis ($3,840) multiplied by the annual depreciation rate for the current taxable year (.1749 for recovery year 3) as modified by the transaction coefficient [1 / (1 - (.1429 + .2449))] which equals 1.6335. Thus, J multiplies $3,840, its depreciable exchanged basis in the replacement MACRS property, by the product of .1749 and 1.6335, and then by one-half, to determine the depreciation allowance for 2003, $549. For 2004, J multiples its depreciable exchanged basis in the replacement MACRS property determined at the time of replacement of $3,840 by the product of the modified annual depreciation rate for the current taxable year (.1249 for recovery year 4) and the transaction coefficient (1.6335) to determine its depreciation allowance of $783.

Example 2. K, a calendar-year taxpayer, acquired used Asset V for $100,000 and placed it in service in January 1999. K depreciated Asset V under the general depreciation system of section 168(a) by using a 5-year recovery period, the 200-percent declining balance method of depreciation, and the half-year convention. In December 2003, as part of the involuntary conversion, Asset V is involuntarily converted due to an earthquake. In October 2005, K purchases used Asset W with the insurance proceeds from the destruction of Asset V and places Asset W in service to replace Asset V. Pursuant to paragraph (k)(2)(i) of this section, K decided to apply § 1.168(i)-6 to the involuntary conversion of Asset V with the replacement of Asset W, the replacement MACRS property. If Asset W had been placed in service when Asset V was placed in service, it would have been depreciated using a 7-year recovery period, the 200-percent declining balance method, and the half-year convention. K uses the optional depreciation tables to depreciate Asset V and Asset W. For 2003 (recovery year 5 on the optional table), the depreciation deduction for Asset V is $5,760 ((0.1152)($100,000)(1/2)). Thus, the adjusted depreciable basis of Asset V at the time of replacement is $11,520 ($100,000 less $20,000 depreciation in 1999, $32,000 depreciation in 2000, $19,200 depreciation in 2001, $11,520 depreciation in 2002, and $5,760 depreciation in 2003). Under the table that applied to Asset V, the year of disposition was recovery year 5 and the depreciation deduction was determined under the straight line method. The table that applies for Asset W is the table that applies the straight line depreciation method, the half-year convention, and a 7-year recovery period. The appropriate recovery year under this table is recovery year 5. The depreciation deduction for Asset W for 2005 is $1,646 (($11,520)(0.1429)(1/(1- 0.5))(1/2)). Thus, the depreciation deduction for Asset W in 2006 (recovery year 6) is $3,290 ($11,520)(0.1428)(1/(1-0.5)). The depreciation deduction for 2007 (recovery year 7) is $3,292 (($11,520)(.1429)(1/(1-.5))). The depreciation deduction for 2008 (recovery year 8) is $3292 ($11,520 less allowable depreciation for Asset W for 2005 through 2007 ($1,646 + $3,290 + $3,292)).

Example 3. L, a calendar-year taxpayer, placed in service used Computer X in January 2002 for $5,000. L depreciated Computer X under the general depreciation system of section 168(a) by using the 200-percent declining balance method of depreciation, a 5-year recovery period, and the half-year convention. Computer X is destroyed in a fire in March 2004. For 2004, the depreciation deduction allowable for Computer X equals $480 ([($5,000)(.1920)] × (1/2)). Thus, the adjusted depreciable basis of Computer X was $1,920 when it was destroyed ($5,000 unadjusted depreciable basis less $1,000 depreciation for 2002, $1,600 depreciation for 2003, and $480 depreciation for 2004). In April 2004, as part of the involuntary conversion, L acquired and placed in service used Computer Y with insurance proceeds received due to the loss of Computer X. Computer Y will be depreciated using the same depreciation method, recovery period, and convention as Computer X. L elected to use the optional depreciation tables to compute the depreciation allowance for Computer X and Computer Y. The depreciation deduction allowable for 2004 for Computer Y equals $384 ([$1,920 × (.1920)(1/(1-.52))] × (1/2)).

(f) *Mid-quarter convention.*—For purposes of applying the 40-percent test under section 168(d) and the regulations under section 168(d), the following rules apply:

(1) *Exchanged basis.*—If, in a taxable year, MACRS property is placed in service by the acquiring taxpayer (but not as a result of a like-kind exchange or involuntary conversion) and—

(i) In the same taxable year, is disposed of by the acquiring taxpayer in a like-kind exchange or an involuntary conversion and replaced by the acquiring taxpayer with replacement MACRS property, the exchanged basis (determined without any adjustments for depreciation deductions during the taxable year) of the replacement MACRS property is taken into account in the year of replacement in the quarter the relinquished MACRS property was placed in service by the acquiring taxpayer; or

(ii) In the same taxable year, is disposed of by the acquiring taxpayer in a like-kind exchange or an involuntary conversion, and in a subsequent taxable year is replaced by the acquiring taxpayer with replacement MACRS property, the exchanged basis (determined without any adjustments for depreciation deductions during the taxable year) of the replacement MACRS property is taken into account in the year of replacement in the quarter the replacement MACRS property was placed in service by the acquiring taxpayer; or

(iii) In a subsequent taxable year, disposed of by the acquiring taxpayer in a like-kind exchange or involuntary conversion, the exchanged basis of the replacement MACRS property is not taken into account in the year of replacement.

(2) *Excess basis.*—Any excess basis is taken into account in the quarter the replacement MACRS property is placed in service by the acquiring taxpayer.

(3) *Depreciable property acquired for nondepreciable property.*—Both the exchanged basis and excess basis of the replacement MACRS property described in paragraph (d)(2)(ii) of this section (depreciable property acquired for nondepreciable property), are taken into account for determining whether the mid-quarter convention applies in the year of replacement.

(g) *Section 179 election.*—In applying the section 179 election, only the excess basis, if any, in the replacement MACRS property is taken into account. If the replacement MACRS property is described in paragraph (d)(2)(ii) of this section (depreciable property acquired for nondepreciable property), only the excess basis in the replacement MACRS property is taken into account.

(h) *Additional first year depreciation deduction.*—See § 1.168(k)-1(f)(5) (for qualified property or 50-percent bonus depreciation property) and § 1.1400L(b)-1(f)(5) (for qualified New York Liberty Zone property).

(i) *Elections.*—(1) *Election not to apply this section.*—A taxpayer may elect not to apply this section for any MACRS property involved in a like-kind exchange or involuntary conversion. An election under this paragraph (i)(1) applies only to the taxpayer making the election and the election applies to both the relinquished MACRS property and the replacement MACRS property. If an election is made under this paragraph (i)(1), the depreciation allowances for the replacement MACRS property beginning in the year of replacement and for the relinquished MACRS property in the year of disposition are not determined under this section (except as otherwise provided in this paragraph). Instead, for depreciation purposes only, the sum of the exchanged basis and excess basis, if any, in the replacement MACRS property is treated as property placed in service by the taxpayer at the time of replacement and the adjusted depreciable basis of the relinquished MACRS property is treated as being disposed of by the taxpayer at the time of disposition. While the relinquished MACRS property is treated as being disposed of at the time of disposition for depreciation purposes, the election not to apply this section does not affect the application of sections 1031 and 1033 (for example, if a taxpayer does not make the election under this paragraph (i)(1) and does not recognize gain or loss under section 1031, this result would not change if the taxpayer chose to make the election under this paragraph (i)(1)). In addition, the election not to apply this section does not affect the application of sections 1245 and 1250 to the relinquished MACRS property. Paragraphs (c)(5)(i) (determination of depreciation for relinquished MACRS property in the year of disposition), (c)(5)(iii) (rules for deferred transactions), (g) (section 179 election), and (h) (additional first year depreciation deduction) of this section apply to property to which this paragraph (i)(1) applies. See paragraph (j) of this section for the time and manner of making the election under this paragraph (i)(1).

(2) *Election to treat certain replacement property as MACRS property.*—If the tangible depreciable property acquired by a taxpayer in a like-kind exchange or involuntary conversion (the replacement property) replaces tangible depreciable property for which the taxpayer made a valid election under section 168(f)(1) to exclude it from the application of MACRS (the relinquished property), the taxpayer may elect to treat, for depreciation purposes only, the sum of the exchanged basis and excess basis, if any, of the replacement property as MACRS property that is placed in service by the taxpayer at the time of replacement. An election under this paragraph (i)(2) applies only to the taxpayer making the election and the election applies to both the relinquished property and the replacement property. If an election is made under this paragraph (i)(2), the adjusted depreciable basis of the relinquished property is treated as being disposed of by the taxpayer at the time of disposition. Rules similar to those provided in §§ 1.168(i)-6(b)(3) and (4) apply for purposes of determining the time of disposition and time of replacement under this paragraph (i)(2). While the relinquished property is treated as being disposed of at the time of disposition for depreciation purposes, the election under this paragraph (i)(2) does not affect the application of sections 1031 and 1033, and the application of sections 1245 and 1250 to the relinquished property. If an election is made under this paragraph (i)(2), rules similar to those provided in paragraphs (c)(5)(iii) (rules for deferred transactions), (g) (section 179 election), and (h) (additional first year depreciation deduction) of this section apply to property. Except as provided in paragraph (k)(3)(ii) of this section, a taxpayer makes the election under this paragraph (i)(2) by claiming the depreciation allowance as determined under

MACRS for the replacement property on the taxpayer's timely filed (including extensions) original Federal tax return for the placed-in-service year of the replacement property as determined under this paragraph (i)(2).

(j) *Time and manner of making election under paragraph (i)(1) of this section.*—(1) *In general.*—The election provided in paragraph (i)(1) of this section is made separately by each person acquiring replacement MACRS property. The election is made for each member of a consolidated group by the common parent of the group, by the partnership (and not by the partners separately) in the case of a partnership, or by the S corporation (and not by the shareholders separately) in the case of an S corporation. A separate election under paragraph (i)(1) of this section is required for each like-kind exchange or involuntary conversion. The election provided in paragraph (i)(1) of this section must be made within the time and manner provided in paragraph (j)(2) and (3) of this section and may not be made by the taxpayer in any other manner (for example, the election cannot be made through a request under section 446(e) to change the taxpayer's method of accounting), except as provided in paragraph (k)(2) of this section.

(2) *Time for making election.*—The election provided in paragraph (i)(1) of this section must be made by the due date (including extensions) of the taxpayer's Federal tax return for the year of replacement.

(3) *Manner of making election.*—The election provided in paragraph (i)(1) of this section is made in the manner provided for on Form 4562, Depreciation and Amortization, and its instructions. If Form 4562 is revised or renumbered, any reference in this section to that form is treated as a reference to the revised or renumbered form.

(4) *Revocation.*—The election provided in paragraph (i)(1) of this section, once made, may be revoked only with the consent of the Commissioner of Internal Revenue. Such consent will be granted only in extraordinary circumstances. Requests for consent are requests for a letter ruling and must be filed with the Commissioner of Internal Revenue, Washington, DC, 20224. Requests for consent may not be made in any other manner (for example, through a request under section 446(e) to change the taxpayer's method of accounting).

(k) *Effective date.*—(1) *In general.*—Except as provided in paragraph (k)(3) of this section, this section applies to a like-kind exchange or an involuntary conversion of MACRS property for which the time of disposition and the time of replacement both occur after February 27, 2004.

(2) *Application to pre-effective date like-kind exchanges and involuntary conversions.*—For a like-kind exchange or an involuntary conversion of MACRS property for which the time of disposition, the time of replacement, or both occur on or before February 27, 2004, a taxpayer may—

(i) Apply the provisions of this section. If a taxpayer's applicable Federal tax return has been filed on or before February 27, 2004, and the taxpayer has treated the replacement MACRS property as acquired, and the relinquished MACRS property as disposed of, in a like-kind exchange or an involuntary conversion, the taxpayer changes its method of accounting for depreciation of the replacement MACRS property and relinquished MACRS property in accordance with this paragraph (k)(2)(i) by following the applicable administrative procedures issued under § 1.446-1(e)(3)(ii) for obtaining the Commissioner's automatic consent to a change in method of accounting (for further guidance, see Rev. Proc. 2002-9 (2002-1 CB 327) and § 601.601(d)(2)(ii)(*b*) of this chapter); or

(ii) Rely on prior guidance issued by the Internal Revenue Service for determining the depreciation deductions of replacement MACRS property and relinquished MACRS property (for further guidance, for example, see Notice 2000-4

(2001-1 CB 313) and § 601.601(d)(2)(ii)(*b*) of this chapter). In relying on such guidance, a taxpayer may use any reasonable, consistent method of determining depreciation in the year of disposition and the year of replacement. If a taxpayer's applicable Federal tax return has been filed on or before February 27, 2004, and the taxpayer has treated the replacement MACRS property as acquired, and the relinquished MACRS property as disposed of, in a like-kind exchange or an involuntary conversion, the taxpayer changes its method of accounting for depreciation of the replacement MACRS property and relinquished MACRS property in accordance with this paragraph (k)(2)(ii) by following the applicable administrative procedures issued under § 1.446-1(e)(3)(ii) for obtaining the Commissioner's automatic consent to a change in method of accounting (for further guidance, see Rev. Proc. 2002-9 (2002-1 CB 327) and § 601.601(d)(2)(ii)(*b*) of this chapter).

(3) *Like-kind exchanges and involuntary conversions where the taxpayer made the election under section 168(f)(1) for the relinquished property.*—(i) *In general.*—If the tangible depreciable property acquired by a taxpayer in a like-kind exchange or involuntary conversion (the replacement property) replaces tangible depreciable property for which the taxpayer made a valid election under section 168(f)(1) to exclude it from the application of MACRS (the relinquished property), paragraph (i)(2) of this section applies to such relinquished property and replacement property for which the time of disposition and the time of replacement (both as determined under paragraph (i)(2) of this section) both occur after February 26, 2007.

(ii) *Application of paragraph (i)(2) of this section to pre-February 26, 2007 like-kind exchanges and involuntary conversions.*—If the tangible depreciable property acquired by a taxpayer in a like-kind exchange or involuntary conversion (the replacement property) replaces tangible depreciable property for which the taxpayer made a valid election under section 168(f)(1) to exclude it from the application of MACRS (the relinquished property), the taxpayer may apply paragraph (i)(2) of this section to the relinquished property and the replacement property for which the time of disposition, the time of replacement (both as determined under paragraph (i)(2) of this section), or both occur on or before February 26, 2007. If the taxpayer wants to apply paragraph (i)(2) of this section and the taxpayer's applicable Federal tax return has been filed on or before February 26, 2007, the taxpayer must change its method of accounting for depreciation of the replacement property and relinquished property in accordance with this paragraph (k)(3)(ii) by following the applicable administrative procedures issued under § 1.446-1(e)(3)(ii) for obtaining the Commissioner's automatic consent to a change in method of accounting (for further guidance, see Rev. Proc. 2002-9 (2002-1 CB 327) and § 601.601(d)(2)(ii)(*b*) of this chapter). [Reg. § 1.168(i)-6.]

.01 Historical Comment: Proposed 3/1/2004. Adopted 2/26/2007 by T.D. 9314.

¶ 569

Reg. § 1.168(k)-0

§ 1.168(k)-0. **Table of contents.**—This section lists the headings that appear in § 1.168(k)-1.

(i) In general.

(ii) Property not eligible for additional first year depreciation deduction.

(A) Property that is not qualified property.

(B) Property that is not 50-percent bonus depreciation property.

(3) Original use.

(i) In general.

(ii) Conversion to business or income-producing use.

(iii) Sale-leaseback, syndication, and certain other transactions.

(A) Sale-leaseback transaction.

(B) Syndication transaction and certain other transactions.

(C) Sale-leaseback transaction followed by a syndication transaction and certain other transactions.

(iv) Fractional interests in property.

(v) Examples.

(4) Acquisition of property.

(i) In general.

(A) Qualified property.

(B) 50-percent bonus depreciation property.

(ii) Definition of binding contract.

(A) In general.

(B) Conditions.

(C) Options.

(D) Supply agreements.

(E) Components.

(iii) Self-constructed property.

(A) In general.

(B) When does manufacture, construction, or production begin.

(1) In general.

(2) Safe harbor.

(C) Components of self-constructed property.

(1) Acquired components.

(2) Self-constructed components.

(iv) Disqualified transactions.

(A) In general.

(B) Related party defined.

(v) Examples.

(5) Placed-in-service date.

(i) In general.

(ii) Sale-leaseback, syndication, and certain other transactions.

(A) Sale-leaseback transaction.

(B) Syndication transaction and certain other transactions.

(C) Sale-leaseback transaction followed by a syndication transaction and certain other transactions.

(iii) Technical termination of a partnership.

(iv) Section 168(i)(7) transactions.

(v) Example.

(c) Qualified leasehold improvement property.

(1) In general.

(2) Certain improvements not included.

(3) Definitions.

(d) Computation of depreciation deduction for qualified property or 50-percent bonus depreciation property.

(1) Additional first year depreciation deduction.

(i) In general.

(ii) Property having a longer production period.

(iii) Alternative minimum tax.

(2) Otherwise allowable depreciation deduction.

(i) In general.

(ii) Alternative minimum tax.

(3) Examples.

(e) Election not to deduct additional first year depreciation.

(1) In general.

(i) Qualified property.

(ii) 50-percent bonus depreciation property.

(2) Definition of class of property.

(3) Time and manner for making election.

(i) Time for making election.

(ii) Manner of making election.

(4) Special rules for 2000 or 2001 returns.

(5) Failure to make election.

(6) Alternative minimum tax.

(7) Revocation.

(i) In general.

(ii) Automatic 6-month extension.

(f) Special rules.

(1) Property placed in service and disposed of in the same taxable year.

(i) In general.

(ii) Technical termination of a partnership.

(iii) Section 168(i)(7) transactions.

(iv) Examples.

(2) Redetermination of basis.

(i) Increase in basis.

(ii) Decrease in basis.

(iii) Definition.

(iv) Examples.

(3) Section 1245 and 1250 depreciation recapture.

(4) Coordination with section 169.

(5) Like-kind exchanges and involuntary conversions.

(i) Scope.

(ii) Definitions.

(iii) Computation.

(A) In general.

(B) Year of disposition and year of replacement.

(C) Property having a longer production period.

(D) Alternative minimum tax.

(iv) Sale-leasebacks.

(v) Acquired MACRS property or acquired computer software that is acquired and placed in service before disposition of involuntarily converted MACRS property or involuntarily converted computer software.

(A) Time of replacement.

(B) Depreciation of acquired MACRS property or acquired computer software.

(vi) Examples.

(6) Change in use.

(i) Change in use of depreciable property.

(ii) Conversion to personal use.

(iii) Conversion to business or income-producing use.

(A) During the same taxable year.

(B) Subsequent to the acquisition year.

(iv) Depreciable property changes use subsequent to the placed-in-service year.

(v) Examples.

(7) Earnings and profits.

(8) Limitation of amount of depreciation for certain passenger automobiles.

(9) Section 754 election.

(10) Coordination with section 47.

(11) Coordination with section 514(a)(3).

(g) Effective date.

(1) In general.

(2) Technical termination of a partnership or section 168(i)(7) transactions.

(3) Like-kind exchanges and involuntary conversions.

(4) Change in method of accounting.

(i) Special rules for 2000 or 2001 returns.

(ii) Like-kind exchanges and involuntary conversions.

(5) Revisions to paragraphs (b)(3)(ii)(B) and (b)(5)(ii)(B).

(6) Rehabilitation credit. [Reg. § 1.168(k)-0.]

.01 Historical Comment: Adopted 9/5/2003 by T.D. 9091. Amended 8/28/2006 by T.D. 9283.

¶ 570

Reg. § 1.168(k)-1

§ 1.168(k)-1. **Additional first year depreciation deduction.**—(a) *Scope and definitions.*—(1) *Scope.*—This section provides the rules for determining the 30-percent additional first year depreciation deduction allowable under section 168(k)(1) for qualified property and the 50-percent additional first year depreciation deduction allowable under section 168(k)(4) for 50-percent bonus depreciation property.

(2) *Definitions.*—For purposes of section 168(k) and this section, the following definitions apply:

(i) *Depreciable property.*—is property that is of a character subject to the allowance for depreciation as determined under section 167 and the regulations thereunder.

(ii) *MACRS property.*—is tangible, depreciable property that is placed in service after December 31, 1986 (or after July 31, 1986, if the taxpayer made an election under section 203(a)(1)(B) of the Tax Reform Act of 1986; 100 Stat. 2143) and subject to section 168, except for property excluded from the application of section 168 as a result of section 168(f) or as a result of a transitional rule.

(iii) *Unadjusted depreciable basis* is the basis of property for purposes of section 1011 without regard to any adjustments described in section 1016(a)(2) and (3). This basis reflects the reduction in basis for the percentage of the taxpayer's use of property for the taxable year other than in the taxpayer's trade or business (or for the production of income), for any portion of the basis the taxpayer properly elects to treat as an expense under section 179 or section 179C, and for any adjustments to basis provided by other provisions of the Internal Revenue Code and the regulations thereunder (other than section 1016(a)(2) and (3)) (for example, a reduction in basis by the amount of the disabled access credit pursuant to section 44(d)(7)). For property subject to a lease, see section 167(c)(2).

(iv) *Adjusted depreciable basis* is the unadjusted depreciable basis of the property, as defined in § 1.168(k)-1(a)(2)(iii), less the adjustments described in section 1016(a)(2) and (3).

(b) *Qualified property or 50-percent bonus depreciation property.*—(2) *Description of qualified property or 50-percent bonus depreciation property.*—(i) *In general.*— Depreciable property will meet the requirements of this paragraph (b)(2) if the property is—

(A) MACRS property (as defined in § 1.168(k)-1(a)(2)(ii)) that has a recovery period of 20 years or less. For purposes of this paragraph (b)(2)(i)(A) and section 168(k)(2)(B)(i)(ll) and 168(k)(4)(C), the recovery period is determined in accordance with section 168(c) regardless of any election made by the taxpayer under section 168(g)(7);

(B) Computer software as defined in, and depreciated under, section 167(f)(1) and the regulations thereunder;

(C) Water utility property as defined in section 168(e)(5) and depreciated under section 168; or

(D) Qualified leasehold improvement property as defined in paragraph (c) of this section and depreciated under section 168.

(ii) *Property not eligible for additional first year depreciation deduction.*—(A) *Property that is not qualified property.*—For purposes of the 30-percent additional first year depreciation deduction, depreciable property will not meet the requirements of this paragraph (b)(2) if the property is—

(1) Described in section 168(f);

(2) Required to be depreciated under the alternative depreciation system of section 168(g) pursuant to section 168(g)(1)(A) through (D) or other provisions of the Internal Revenue Code (for example, property described in section 263A(e)(2)(A) if the taxpayer (or any related person as defined in section 263A(e)(2)(B)) has made an election under section 263A(d)(3), or property described in section 280F(b)(1)).

(3) Included in any class of property for which the taxpayer elects not to deduct the 30-percent additional first year depreciation (for further guidance, see paragraph (e) of this section); or

(4) Qualified New York Liberty Zone leasehold improvement property as defined in section 1400L(c)(2).

(B) *Property that is not 50-percent bonus depreciation property.*— For purposes of the 50-percent additional first year depreciation deduction, depreciable property will not meet the requirements of this paragraph (b)(2) if the property is—

(1) Described in paragraph (b)(2)(ii)(A)(*1*), (*2*), or (*4*) of this section; or

(2) Included in any class of property for which the taxpayer elects the 30-percent, instead of the 50-percent, additional first year depreciation deduction or elects not to deduct any additional first year depreciation (for further guidance, see paragraph (e) of this section).

(3) *Original use.*—(i) *In general.*—For purposes of the 30-percent additional first year depreciation deduction, depreciable property will meet the requirements of this paragraph (b)(3) if the original use of the property commences with the taxpayer after September 10, 2001. For purposes of the 50-percent additional first year depreciation deduction, depreciable property will meet the requirements of this paragraph (b)(3) if the original use of the property commences with the taxpayer after May 5, 2003. Except as provided in paragraphs (b)(3)(iii) and (iv) of this section, original use means the first use to which the property is put, whether or not that use corresponds to the use of the property by the taxpayer. Thus, additional capital expenditures incurred by a taxpayer to recondition or rebuild property acquired or owned by the taxpayer satisfies the original use requirement. However, the cost of reconditioned or rebuilt property does not satisfy the original use requirement. The question of whether property is reconditioned or rebuilt property is a question of fact. For purposes of this paragraph (b)(3)(i), property that contains used parts will not be treated as reconditioned or rebuilt if the cost of the used parts is not more than 20 percent of the total cost of the property, whether acquired or self-constructed.

(ii) *Conversion to business or income-producing use.*—(A) *Personal use to business or income-producing use.*—If a taxpayer initially acquires new property for personal use and subsequently uses the property in the taxpayer's trade or business or for the taxpayer's production of income, the taxpayer is considered the original user of the property. If a person initially acquires new property for personal use and a taxpayer subsequently acquires the property from the person for use in the taxpayer's trade or business or for the taxpayer's production of income, the taxpayer is not considered the original user of the property.

(B) *Inventory to business or income-producing use.*—If a taxpayer initially acquires new property and holds the property primarily for sale to customers in the ordinary course of the taxpayer's business and subsequently withdraws the property from inventory and uses the property primarily in the taxpayer's trade or business or primarily for the taxpayer's production of income, the taxpayer is considered the original user of the property. If a person initially acquires new property and holds the property primarily for sale to customers in the ordinary course of the person's business and a taxpayer subsequently acquires the property from the person for use primarily in the taxpayer's trade or business or primarily for the taxpayer's production of income, the taxpayer is considered the original user of the property. For purposes of this paragraph (b)(3)(ii)(B), the original use of the property by the taxpayer commences on the date on which the taxpayer uses the property primarily in the taxpayer's trade or business or primarily for the taxpayer's production of income.

(iii) *Sale-leaseback, syndication, and certain other transactions.*—(A) *Sale-leaseback transaction.*—If new property is originally placed in service by a person after September 10, 2001 (for qualified property), or after May 5, 2003 (for 50-percent bonus depreciation property), and is sold to a taxpayer and leased back to the person by the taxpayer within three months after the date the property was originally placed in service by the person, the taxpayer-lessor is considered the original user of the property.

(B) *Syndication transaction and certain other transactions.*—If new property is originally placed in service by a lessor (including by operation of paragraph (b)(5)(ii)(A) of this section) after September 10, 2001 (for qualified property), or after May 5, 2003 (for 50-percent bonus depreciation property), and is sold by the lessor or any subsequent purchaser within three months after the date the property was originally placed in service by the lessor (or, in the case of multiple units of property subject to the same lease, within three months after the date the final unit is placed in service, so long as the period between the time the first unit is placed in service and the time the last unit is placed in service does not exceed 12 months), and the user of the property after the last sale during the three-month period remains the same as when the property was originally placed in service by the lessor, the purchaser of the property in the last sale during the three-month period is considered the original user of the property.

(C) *Sale-leaseback transaction followed by a syndication transaction and certain other transactions.*—If a sale-leaseback transaction that satisfies the requirements in paragraph (b)(3)(iii)(A) of this section is followed by a transaction that satisfies the requirements in paragraph (b)(3)(iii)(B) of this section, the original user of the property is determined in accordance with paragraph (b)(3)(iii)(B) of this section.

(iv) *Fractional interests in property.*—If, in the ordinary course of its business, a taxpayer sells fractional interests in property to third parties unrelated to the taxpayer, each first fractional owner of the property is considered as the original user of its proportionate share of the property. Furthermore, if the taxpayer uses the property before all of the fractional interests of the property are sold but the property continues to be held primarily for sale by the taxpayer, the original use of any fractional interest sold to a third party unrelated to the taxpayer subsequent to the taxpayer's use of the property begins with the first purchaser of that fractional interest. For purposes of this paragraph (b)(3)(iv), persons are not related if they do not have a relationship described in section 267(b) or 707(b) and the regulations thereunder.

(v) *Examples.*—The application of this paragraph (b)(3) is illustrated by the following examples:

Example 1. On August 1, 2002, *A* buys from *B* for $20,000 a machine that has been previously used by *B* in *B's* trade or business. On March 1, 2003, *A* makes a $5,000 capital expenditure to recondition the machine. The $20,000 purchase price does not qualify for the additional first year depreciation deduction because the original use requirement of this paragraph (b)(3) is not met. However, the $5,000 expenditure satisfies the original use requirement of this paragraph (b)(3) and, assuming all other requirements are met, qualifies for the 30-percent additional first year depreciation deduction, regardless of whether the $5,000 is added to the basis of the machine or is capitalized as a separate asset.

Example 2. *C*, an automobile dealer, uses some of its automobiles as demonstrators in order to show them to prospective customers. The automobiles that are used as demonstrators by *C* are held by *C* primarily for sale to customers in the ordinary course of its business. On September 1, 2002, *D* buys from *C* an automobile that was previously used as a demonstrator by *C*. *D* will use the automobile solely for business purposes. The use of the automobile by *C* as a demonstrator does not constitute a "use" for purposes of the original use requirement and, therefore, *D* will be considered the original user of the automobile for purposes of this paragraph (b)(3). Assuming all other requirements are met, *D's* purchase price of the automobile qualifies for the 30-percent additional first year depreciation deduction for *D*, subject to any limitation under section 280F.

Example 3. On April 1, 2000, *E* acquires a horse to be used in *E's* thoroughbred racing business. On October 1, 2003, *F* buys the horse from *E* and will use the horse in *F's* horse breeding business. The use of the horse by *E* in its racing business prevents the original use of the horse from commencing with *F*. Thus, *F's* purchase price of the horse does not qualify for the additional first year depreciation deduction.

Example 4. In the ordinary course of its business, *G* sells fractional interests in its aircraft to unrelated parties. *G* holds out for sale eight equal fractional interests in an aircraft. On January 1, 2003, *G* sells five of the eight fractional interests in the aircraft to *H*, an unrelated party, and *H* begins to use its proportionate share of the aircraft immediately upon purchase. On June 1, 2003, G sells to I, an unrelated party to G, the remaining unsold 3/8 fractional interests in the aircraft. *H* is considered the original user as to its 5/8 fractional interest in the aircraft and *I* is considered the original user as to its 3/8 fractional interest in the aircraft. Thus, assuming all other requirements are met, *H's* purchase price for its 5/8 fractional interest in the aircraft qualifies for the 30-percent additional first year depreciation deduction and *I's* purchase price for its 3/8 fractional interest in the aircraft qualifies for the 50-percent additional first year depreciation deduction.

Example 5. On September 1, 2001, *JJ*, an equipment dealer, buys new tractors that are held by *JJ* primarily for sale to customers in the ordinary course of its business. On October 15, 2001, *JJ* withdraws the tractors from inventory and begins to use the tractors primarily for producing rental income. The holding of the tractors by *JJ* as inventory does not constitute a "use" for purposes of the original use requirement and, therefore, the original use of the tractors commences with *JJ* on October 15, 2001, for purposes of paragraph (b) (3) of this section. However, the tractors are not eligible for the additional first year depreciation deduction because *JJ* acquired the tractors before September 11, 2001.

(4) *Acquisition of property.*—(i) *In general.*—(A) *Qualified property.*—For purposes of the 30-percent additional first year depreciation deduction, depreciable property will meet the requirements of this paragraph (b) (4) if the property is—

(1) Acquired by the taxpayer after September 10, 2001, and before January 1, 2005, but only if no written binding contract for the acquisition of the property was in effect before September 11, 2001; or

(2) Acquired by the taxpayer pursuant to a written binding contract that was entered into after September 10, 2001, and before January 1, 2005.

(B) *50-percent bonus depreciation property.*—For purposes of the 50-percent additional first year depreciation deduction, depreciable property will meet the requirements of this paragraph (b) (4) if the property is

(1) Acquired by the taxpayer after May 5, 2003, and before January 1, 2005, but only if no written binding contract for the acquisition of the property was in effect before May 6, 2003; or

(2) Acquired by the taxpayer pursuant to a written binding contract that was entered into after May 5, 2003, and before January 1, 2005.

(ii) *Definition of binding contract.*—(A) *In general.*—A contract is binding only if it is enforceable under State law against the taxpayer or a predecessor, and does not limit damages to a specified amount (for example, by use of a liquidated damages provision). For this purpose, a contractual provision that limits damages to an amount equal to at least 5 percent of the total contract price will not be treated as limiting damages to a specified amount. In determining whether a contract limits damages, the fact that there may be little or no damages because the contract price does not significantly differ from fair market value will not be taken into account. For example, if a taxpayer entered into an irrevocable written contract to purchase an asset for $100 and the contract contained no provision for liquidated damages, the contract is considered binding notwithstanding the fact that the asset had a fair market value of $99 and under local law the seller would only recover the difference in the event the purchaser failed to perform. If the contract provided for a full refund of the purchase price in lieu of any damages allowable by law in the event of breach or cancellation, the contract is not considered binding.

(B) *Conditions.*—A contract is binding even if subject to a condition, as long as the condition is not within the control of either party or a predecessor. A contract will continue to be binding if the parties make insubstantial changes in its terms and conditions or because any term is to be determined by a standard beyond the control of either party. A contract that imposes significant obligations on the taxpayer or a predecessor will be treated as binding notwithstanding the fact that certain terms remain to be negotiated by the parties to the contract.

(C) *Options.*—An option to either acquire or sell property is not a binding contract.

(D) *Supply agreements.*—A binding contract does not include a supply or similar agreement if the amount and design specifications of the property to be purchased have not been specified. The contract will not be a binding contract for the property to be purchased until both the amount and the design specifications are specified. For example, if the provisions of a supply or similar agreement state the design specifications of the property to be purchased, a purchase order under the agreement for a specific number of assets is treated as a binding contract.

(E) *Components.*—A binding contract to acquire one or more components of a larger property will not be treated as a binding contract to acquire the larger property. If a binding contract to acquire the component does not satisfy the requirements of this paragraph (b)(4), the component does not qualify for the 30-percent or 50-percent additional first year depreciation deduction, as applicable.

(iii) *Self-constructed property.*—(A) *In general.*—If a taxpayer manufactures, constructs, or produces property for use by the taxpayer in its trade or business (or for its production of income), the acquisition rules in paragraph (b)(4)(i) of this section are treated as met for qualified property if the taxpayer begins manufacturing, constructing, or producing the property after September 10, 2001, and before January 1, 2005, and for 50-percent bonus depreciation property if the taxpayer begins manufacturing, constructing, or producing the property after May 5, 2003, and before January 1, 2005. Property that is manufactured, constructed, or produced for the taxpayer by another person under a written binding contract (as defined in paragraph (b)(4)(ii) of this section) that is entered into prior to the manufacture, construction, or production of the property for use by the taxpayer in its trade or business (or for its production of income) is considered to be manufactured, constructed, or produced by the taxpayer. If a taxpayer enters into a written binding contract (as defined in paragraph (b)(4)(ii) of this section) after September 10, 2001, and before January 1, 2005, with another person to manufacture, construct, or produce property described in section 168(k)(2)(B) (longer production period property) or section 168(k)(2)(C) (certain aircraft) and the manufacture, construction, or production of this property begins after December 31, 2004, the acquisition rule in paragraph (b)(4)(i)(A)(*2*) or (b)(4)(i)(B)(*2*) of this section is met.

(B) *When does manufacture, construction, or production begin.*—*(1) In general.*—For purposes of paragraph (b)(4)(iii) of this section, manufacture, construction, or production of property begins when physical work of a significant nature begins. Physical work does not include preliminary activities such as planning or designing, securing financing, exploring, or researching. The determination of when physical work of a significant nature begins depends on the facts and circumstances. For example, if a retail motor fuels outlet or other facility is to be constructed on-site, construction begins when physical work of a significant nature commences at the site; that is, when work begins on the excavation for footings, pouring the pads for the outlet, or the driving of foundation pilings into the ground. Preliminary work, such as clearing a site, test drilling to determine soil condition, or excavation to change the contour of the land (as distinguished from excavation for footings) does not constitute the beginning of construction. However, if a retail motor fuels outlet or other facility is to be assembled on-site from modular units manufactured off-site and delivered to the site where the outlet will be used, manufacturing begins when physical work of a significant nature commences at the off-site location.

(2) Safe harbor.—For purposes of paragraph (b)(4)(iii)(B)(*1*) of this section, a taxpayer may choose to determine when physical work of a significant nature begins in accordance with this paragraph (b)(4)(iii)(B)(*2*). Physical work of a significant nature will not be considered to begin before the taxpayer incurs (in the case of an accrual basis taxpayer) or pays (in the case of a cash basis taxpayer) more than 10 percent of the total cost of the property (excluding the cost of any land and preliminary activities such as planning or designing, securing financing, exploring, or researching). When property is manufactured, constructed, or produced for the taxpayer by another person, this safe harbor test must be satisfied by the taxpayer. For example, if a retail motor fuels outlet or other facility is to be constructed for an accrual basis taxpayer by another person for the total cost of $200,000 (excluding the cost of any land and preliminary activities such as planning or designing, securing financing, exploring, or researching), construction is deemed to begin for purposes of this paragraph (b)(4)(iii)(B)(*2*) when the taxpayer has incurred more than 10 percent (more than $20,000) of the total cost of the property. A taxpayer chooses to apply this paragraph (b)(4)(iii)(B)(*2*) by filing an income tax return for the placed-in-service year of the property that determines when physical work of a significant nature begins consistent with this paragraph (b)(4)(iii)(B)(*2*).

(C) *Components of self-constructed property.—(1) Acquired components.*—If a binding contract (as defined in paragraph (b)(4)(ii) of this section) to acquire a component does not satisfy the requirements of paragraph (b)(4)(i) of this section, the component does not qualify for the 30-percent or 50-percent additional first year depreciation deduction, as applicable. A binding contract (as defined in paragraph (b)(4)(ii) of this section) to acquire one or more components of a larger self-constructed property will not preclude the larger self-constructed property from satisfying the acquisition rules in paragraph (b)(4)(iii)(A) of this section. Accordingly, the unadjusted depreciable basis of the larger self-constructed property that is eligible for the 30-percent or 50-percent additional first year depreciation deduction, as applicable (assuming all other requirements are met), must not include the unadjusted depreciable basis of any component that does not satisfy the requirements of paragraph (b)(4)(i) of this section. If the manufacture, construction, or production of the larger self-constructed property begins before September 11, 2001, for qualified property, or before May 6, 2003, for 50-percent bonus depreciation property, the larger self-constructed property and any acquired components related to the larger self-constructed property do not qualify for the 30-percent or 50-percent additional first year depreciation deduction, as applicable. If a binding contract to acquire the component is entered into after September 10, 2001, for qualified property, or after May 5, 2003, for 50-percent bonus depreciation property, and before January 1, 2005, but the manufacture, construction, or production of the larger self-constructed property does not begin before January 1, 2005, the component qualifies for the additional first year depreciation deduction (assuming all other requirements are met) but the larger self-constructed property does not.

(2) Self-constructed components.—If the manufacture, construction, or production of a component does not satisfy the requirements of paragraph (b)(4)(iii)(A) of this section, the component does not qualify for the 30-percent or 50-percent additional first year depreciation deduction, as applicable. However, if the manufacture, construction, or production of a component does not satisfy the requirements of paragraph (b)(4)(iii)(A) of this section, but the manufacture, construction, or production of the larger self-constructed property satisfies the

requirements of paragraph (b)(4)(iii)(A) of this section, the larger self-constructed property qualifies for the 30-percent or 50-percent additional first year depreciation deduction, as applicable (assuming all other requirements are met) even though the component does not qualify for the 30-percent or 50-percent additional first year depreciation deduction. Accordingly, the unadjusted depreciable basis of the larger self-constructed property that is eligible for the 30-percent or 50-percent additional first year depreciation deduction, as applicable (assuming all other requirements are met), must not include the unadjusted depreciable basis of any component that does not qualify for the 30-percent or 50-percent additional first year depreciation deduction. If the manufacture, construction, or production of the larger self-constructed property began before September 11, 2001, for qualified property, or before May 6, 2003, for 50-percent bonus depreciation property, the larger self-constructed property and any self-constructed components related to the larger self-constructed property do not qualify for the 30-percent or 50-percent additional first year depreciation deduction, as applicable. If the manufacture, construction, or production of a component begins after September 10, 2001, for qualified property, or after May 5, 2003, for 50-percent bonus depreciation property, and before January 1, 2005, but the manufacture, construction, or production of the larger self-constructed property does not begin before January 1, 2005, the component qualifies for the additional first year depreciation deduction (assuming all other requirements are met) but the larger self-constructed property does not.

(iv) *Disqualified transactions.*—(A) *In general.*—Property does not satisfy the requirements of this paragraph (b)(4) if the user of the property as of the date on which the property was originally placed in service (including by operation of paragraphs (b)(5)(ii), (iii), and (iv) of this section), or a related party to the user or to the taxpayer, acquired, or had a written binding contract (as defined in paragraph (b)(4)(ii) of this section) in effect for the acquisition of the property at any time before September 11, 2001 (for qualified property), or before May 6, 2003 (for 50-percent bonus depreciation property). In addition, property manufactured, constructed, or produced for the use by the user of the property or by a related party to the user or to the taxpayer does not satisfy the requirements of this paragraph (b)(4) if the manufacture, construction, or production of the property for the user or the related party began at any time before September 11, 2001 (for qualified property), or before May 6, 2003 (for 50-percent bonus depreciation property).

(B) *Related party defined.*—For purposes of this paragraph (b)(4)(iv), persons are related if they have a relationship specified in section 267(b) or 707(b) and the regulations thereunder.

(v) *Examples.*—The application of this paragraph (b)(4) is illustrated by the following examples:

Example 1. On September 1, 2001, *J*, a corporation, entered into a written agreement with *K*, a manufacturer, to purchase 20 new lamps for $100 each within the next two years. Although the agreement specifies the number of lamps to be purchased, the agreement does not specify the design of the lamps to be purchased. Accordingly, the agreement is not a binding contract pursuant to paragraph (b)(4)(ii)(D) of this section.

Example 2. Same facts as *Example 1.* On December 1, 2001, *J* placed a purchase order with *K* to purchase 20 new model XPC5 lamps for $100 each for a total amount of $2,000. Because the agreement specifies the number of lamps to be purchased and the purchase order specifies the design of the lamps to be purchased, the purchase order placed by *J* with *K* on December 1, 2001, is a binding contract pursuant to paragraph (b)(4)(ii)(D) of this section. Accordingly, the cost of the 20 lamps qualifies for the 30-percent additional first year depreciation deduction.

Example 3. Same facts as *Example 1* except that the written agreement between *J* and *K* is to purchase 100 model XPC5 lamps for $100 each within the next two years. Because this agreement specifies the amount and design of the lamps to be purchased, the agreement is a binding contract pursuant to paragraph (b)(4)(ii)(D) of this section. Accordingly, because the agreement was entered into before September 11, 2001, any lamp acquired by *J* under this contract does not qualify for the additional first year depreciation deduction.

Example 4. On September 1, 2001, *L* began constructing an electric generation power plant for its own use. On November 1, 2002, *L* ceases construction of the power plant prior to its completion. Between September 1, 2001, and November 1, 2002, *L* incurred $3,000,000 for the construction of the power plant. On May 6, 2003, *L* resumed construction of the power plant and completed its construction on August 31, 2003. Between May 6, 2003, and August 31, 2003, *L* incurred another $1,600,000 to complete the construction of the power plant and, on September 1, 2003, *L* placed the power plant in service. None of *L's* total expenditures of $4,600,000 qualify for the additional first year depreciation deduction because, pursuant to paragraph (b)(4)(iii)(A) of this section, *L* began constructing the power plant before September 11, 2001.

Example 5. Same facts as *Example 4* except that *L* began constructing the electric generation power plant for its own use on October 1, 2001. *L's* total expenditures of $4,600,000 qualify for the additional first year depreciation deduction because, pursuant to paragraph (b)(4)(iii)(A) of this section, *L* began constructing the power plant after September 10, 2001, and placed the power plant in service before January 1, 2005. Accordingly, the additional first year depreciation deduction for the power plant will be $1,380,000, computed as $4,600,000 multiplied by 30 percent.

Example 6. On August 1, 2001, *M* entered into a written binding contract to acquire a new turbine. The new turbine is a component part of a new electric generation power plant that is being constructed on *M's* behalf. The construction of the new electric generation power plant commenced in November 2001, and the new electric generation power plant was completed in November 2002. Because *M* entered into a written binding contract to acquire a component part (the new turbine) prior to September 11, 2001, pursuant to paragraph (b)(4)(iii)(C) of this section, the component part does not qualify for the additional first year depreciation deduction. However, pursuant to paragraphs (b)(4)(iii)(A) and (C) of this section, the new plant constructed for *M* will qualify for the 30-percent additional first year depreciation deduction because construction of the new plant began after September 10, 2001, and before May 6, 2003. Accordingly, the unadjusted depreciable basis of the new plant that is eligible for the 30-percent additional first year depreciation deduction must not include the unadjusted depreciable basis of the new turbine.

Example 7. Same facts as *Example 6* except that *M* entered into the written binding contract to acquire the new turbine on September 30, 2002, and construction of the new plant commenced on August 1, 2001. Because *M* began construction of the new plant prior to September 11, 2001, pursuant to paragraphs (b)(4)(iii)(A) and (C) of this section, neither the new plant constructed for *M* nor the turbine will qualify for the additional first year depreciation deduction because self-construction of the new plant began prior to September 11, 2001.

Example 8. On September 1, 2001, *N* began constructing property for its own use. On October 1, 2001, *N* sold its rights to the property to *O*, a related party under section 267(b). Pursuant to paragraph (b)(4)(iv) of this section, the property is not eligible for the additional first year depreciation deduction because *N* and *O* are related parties and construction of the property by *N* began prior to September 11, 2001.

Example 9. On September 1, 2001, *P* entered into a written binding contract to acquire property. On October 1, 2001, *P* sold its rights to the property to *Q*, a related party under section 267(b). Pursuant to paragraph (b)(4)(iv) of this section, the property is not eligible for the additional first year depreciation deduction because *P* and *Q* are related parties and a written binding contract for the acquisition of the property was in effect prior to September 11, 2001.

Example 10. Prior to September 11, 2001, *R* began constructing an electric generation power plant for its own use. On May 1, 2003, prior to the completion of the power plant, *R* transferred the rights to own and use this power plant to *S*, an unrelated party, for $6,000,000. Between May 6, 2003, and June 30, 2003, S, a calendar-year taxpayer, began construction, and incurred another $1,200,000 to complete the construction, of the power plant and, on August 1, 2003, S placed the power plant in service. Because *R* and *S* are not related parties, the transaction between *R* and *S* will not be a disqualified transaction pursuant to paragraph (b)(4)(iv) of this section. Accordingly, *S's* total expenditures of $7,200,000 for the power plant qualify for the additional first year depreciation deduction. *S's* additional first year depreciation deduction for the power plant will be $2,400,000, computed as $6,000,000 multiplied by 30 percent, plus $1,200,000 multiplied by 50 percent. The $6,000,000 portion of the total $7,200,000 unadjusted depreciable basis qualifies for the 30-percent additional first year depreciation deduction because that portion of the total unadjusted depreciable basis was acquired by *S* after September 10, 2001, and before May 6, 2003. However, because *S* began construction to complete the power plant after May 5, 2003, the $1,200,000 portion of the total $7,200,000 unadjusted depreciable basis qualifies for the 50-percent additional first year depreciation deduction.

Example 11. On September 1, 2001, *T* acquired and placed in service equipment. On October 15, 2001, *T* sells the equipment to *U*, an unrelated party, and leases the property back from *U* in a sale-leaseback transaction. Pursuant to paragraph (b)(4)(iv) of this section, the equipment does not qualify for the additional first year depreciation deduction because *T*, the user of the equipment, acquired the equipment prior to September 11, 2001. In addition, the sale-leaseback rules in paragraphs (b)(3)(iii)(A) and (b)(5)(ii)(A) of this section do not apply because the equipment was originally placed in service by T before September 11, 2001.

Example 12. On July 1, 2001, KK began constructing property for its own use. KK placed this property in service on September 15, 2001. On October 15, 2001, KK sells the property to LL, an unrelated party, and leases the property back from LL in a sale-leaseback transaction. Pursuant to paragraph (b)(4)(iv) of this section, the property does not qualify for the additional first year depreciation deduction because the property was constructed for KK, the user of the property, and that construction began prior to September 11, 2001.

Example 13. On June 1, 2004, MM decided to construct property described in section 168(k)(2)(B) for its own use. However, one of the component parts of the property had to be manufactured by another person for MM. On August 15, 2004, MM entered into a written binding contract with NN to acquire this component part of the property for $100,000. The manufacture of the component part commenced on September 1, 2004, and MM received the completed component part on February 1, 2005. The cost of this component part is 9 percent of the total cost of the property to be constructed by MM. MM began constructing the property described in section 168(k)(2)(B) on January 15, 2005, and placed this property (including all component parts) in service on November 1, 2005. Pursuant to paragraph (b)(4)(iii)(C)(*2*) of this section, the self-constructed component part of $100,000 manufactured by NN for MM is eligible for the additional first year depreciation deduction (assuming all other requirements are met) because the manufacturing of the component part began after September 10, 2001, and before

January 1, 2005, and the property described in section 168(k)(2)(B), the larger self-constructed property, was placed in service by MM before January 1, 2006. However, pursuant to paragraph (b)(4)(iii)(A) of this section, the cost of the property described in section 168(k)(2)(B) (excluding the cost of the self-constructed component part of $100,000 manufactured by NN for MM) is not eligible for the additional first year depreciation deduction because construction of the property began after December 31, 2004.

Example 14. On December 1, 2004, OO entered into a written binding contract (as defined in paragraph (b)(4)(ii) of this section) with PP to manufacture an aircraft described in section 168(k)(2)(C) for use in OO's trade or business. PP begins to manufacture the aircraft on February 1, 2005. OO places the aircraft in service on August 1, 2005. Pursuant to paragraph (b)(4)(iii)(A) of this section, the aircraft meets the requirements of paragraph (b)(4)(i)(B)(*2*) of this section because the aircraft was acquired by OO pursuant to a written binding contract entered into after May 5, 2003, and before January 1, 2005.

(5) *Placed-in-service date.*—(i) *In general.*—Depreciable property will meet the requirements of this paragraph (b)(5) if the property is placed in service by the taxpayer for use in its trade or business or for production of income before January 1, 2005, or, in the case of property described in section 168(k)(2)(B) or (C), is placed in service by the taxpayer for use in its trade or business or for production of income before January 1, 2006 (or placed in service by the taxpayer for use in its trade or business or for production of income before January 1, 2007, in the case of property described in section 168(k)(2)(B) or (C) to which section 105 of the Gulf Opportunity Zone Act of 2005 (Public Law 109-135, 119 Stat. 2577) applies (for further guidance, see Announcement 2006-29 (2006-19 I.R.B. 879) and §601.601(d)(2)(ii)(*b*) of this chapter)).

(ii) *Sale-leaseback, syndication, and certain other transactions.*—(A) *Sale-leaseback transaction.*—If qualified property is originally placed in service after September 10, 2001, or 50-percent bonus depreciation property is originally placed in service after May 5, 2003, by a person and sold to a taxpayer and leased back to the person by the taxpayer within three months after the date the property was originally placed in service by the person, the property is treated as originally placed in service by the taxpayer-lessor not earlier than the date on which the property is used by the lessee under the leaseback.

(B) *Syndication transaction and certain other transactions.*—If qualified property is originally placed in service after September 10, 2001, or 50-percent bonus depreciation property is originally placed in service after May 5, 2003, by a lessor (including by operation of paragraph (b)(5)(ii)(A) of this section) and is sold by the lessor or any subsequent purchaser within three months after the date the property was originally placed in service by the lessor (or, in the case of multiple units of property subject to the same lease, within three months after the date the final unit is placed in service, so long as the period between the time the first unit is placed in service and the time the last unit is placed in service does not exceed 12 months), and the user of the property after the last sale during this three-month period remains the same as when the property was originally placed in service by the lessor, the property is treated as originally placed in service by the purchaser of the property in the last sale during the three-month period but not earlier than the date of the last sale.

(C) *Sale-leaseback transaction followed by a syndication transaction and certain other transactions.*—If a sale-leaseback transaction that satisfies the requirements in paragraph (b)(5)(ii)(A) of this section is followed by a transaction that satisfies the requirements in paragraph (b)(5)(ii)(B) of this section, the placed-in-service date of the property is determined in accordance with paragraph (b)(5)(ii)(B) of this section.

(iii) *Technical termination of a partnership.*—For purposes of this paragraph (b)(5), in the case of a technical termination of a partnership under section 708(b)(1)(B), qualified property or 50-percent bonus depreciation property placed in service by the terminated partnership during the taxable year of termination is treated as originally placed in service by the new partnership on the date the qualified property or the 50-percent bonus depreciation property is contributed by the terminated partnership to the new partnership.

(iv) *Section 168(i)(7) transactions.*—For purposes of this paragraph (b)(5), if qualified property or 50-percent bonus depreciation property is transferred in a transaction described in section 168(i)(7) in the same taxable year that the qualified property or the 50-percent bonus depreciation property is placed in service by the transferor, the transferred property is treated as originally placed in service on the date the transferor placed in service the qualified property or the 50-percent bonus depreciation property, as applicable. In the case of multiple transfers of qualified property or 50-percent bonus depreciation property in multiple transactions described in section 168(i)(7) in the same taxable year, the placed in service date of the transferred property is deemed to be the date on which the first transferor placed in service the qualified property or the 50-percent bonus depreciation property, as applicable.

(v) *Example.*—The application of this paragraph (b)(5) is illustrated by the following example:

Example. On September 15, 2004, QQ acquired and placed in service new equipment. This equipment is not described in section 168(k)(2)(B) or (C). On December 1, 2004, QQ sells the equipment to RR and leases the equipment back from RR in a sale-leaseback transaction. On February 15, 2005, RR sells the equipment to TT subject to the lease with QQ. As of February 15, 2005, QQ is still the user of the equipment. The sale-leaseback transaction of December 1, 2004, between QQ and RR satisfies the requirements of paragraph (b)(5)(ii)(A) of this section. The sale transaction of February 15, 2005, between RR and TT satisfies the requirements of paragraph (b)(5)(ii)(B) of this section. Consequently, pursuant to paragraph (b)(5)(ii)(C) of this section, the equipment is treated as originally placed in service by TT on February 15, 2005. Further, pursuant to paragraph (b)(3)(iii)(C) of this section, TT is considered the original user of the equipment. Accordingly, the equipment is not eligible for the additional first year depreciation deduction.

(c) *Qualified leasehold improvement property.*—(1) *In general.*—For purposes of section 168(k), qualified leasehold improvement property means any improvement, which is section 1250 property, to an interior portion of a building that is nonresidential real property if—

(i) The improvement is made under or pursuant to a lease by the lessee (or any sublessee) of the interior portion, or by the lessor of that interior portion;

(ii) The interior portion of the building is to be occupied exclusively by the lessee (or any sublessee) of that interior portion; and

(iii) The improvement is placed in service more than 3 years after the date the building was first placed in service by any person.

(2) *Certain improvements not included.*—Qualified leasehold improvement property does not include any improvement for which the expenditure is attributable to:

(i) The enlargement of the building;

(ii) Any elevator or escalator;

(iii) Any structural component benefiting a common area; or

(iv) The internal structural framework of the building.

(3) *Definitions.*—For purposes of this paragraph (c), the following definitions apply:

(i) *Building* has the same meaning as that term is defined in § 1.48-1(e)(1).

(ii) *Common area* means any portion of a building that is equally available to all users of the building on the same basis for uses that are incidental to the primary use of the building. For example, stairways, hallways, lobbies, common seating areas, interior and exterior pedestrian walkways and pedestrian bridges, loading docks and areas, and rest rooms generally are treated as common areas if they are used by different lessees of a building.

(iii) *Elevator* and *escalator* have the same meanings as those terms are defined in § 1.48-1(m)(2).

(iv) *Enlargement* has the same meaning as that term is defined in § 1.48-12(c)(10).

(v) *Internal structural framework* has the same meaning as that term is defined in § 1.48-12(b)(3)(i)(D)(iii).

(vi) *Lease* has the same meaning as that term is defined in section 168(h)(7). In addition, a commitment to enter into a lease is treated as a lease, and the parties to the commitment are treated as lessor and lessee. However, a lease between related persons is not considered a lease. For purposes of the preceding sentence, related persons are—

(A) Members of an affiliated group (as defined in section 1504 and the regulations thereunder); and

(B) Persons having a relationship described in section 267(b) and the regulations thereunder. For purposes of applying section 267(b), the language "80 percent or more" is used instead of "more than 50 percent."

(vii) *Nonresidential real property* has the same meaning as that term is defined in section 168(e)(2)(B).

(viii) *Structural component* has the same meaning as that term is defined in § 1.48-1(e)(2).

(d) *Computation of depreciation deduction for qualified property or 50-percent bonus depreciation property.*—(1) *Additional first year depreciation deduction.*—(i) *In general.*—Except as provided in paragraph (f) of this section, the additional first year depreciation deduction is allowable in the first taxable year in which the qualified property or 50-percent bonus depreciation property is placed in service by the taxpayer for use in its trade or business or for the production of income. Except as provided in paragraph (f)(5) of this section, the allowable additional first year depreciation deduction for qualified property is determined by multiplying the unadjusted depreciable basis (as defined in § 1.168(k)-1(a)(2)(iii)) of the qualified property by 30 percent. Except as provided in paragraph (f)(5) of this section, the allowable additional first year depreciation deduction for 50-percent bonus depreciation property is determined by multiplying the unadjusted depreciable basis (as defined in § 1.168(k)-1(a)(2)(iii)) of the 50-percent bonus depreciation property by 50 percent. Except as provided in paragraph (f)(1) of this section, the 30-percent or 50-percent additional first year depreciation deduction is not affected by a taxable year of less than 12 months. See paragraph (f)(1) of this section for qualified property or 50-percent bonus depreciation property placed in service and disposed of in the same taxable year. See paragraph (f)(5) of this section for qualified property or 50-percent bonus depreciation property acquired in a like-kind exchange or as a result of an involuntary conversion.

(ii) *Property having a longer production period.*—For purposes of paragraph (d)(1)(i) of this section, the unadjusted depreciable basis (as defined in § 1.168(k)-1(a)(2)(iii)) of qualified property or 50-percent bonus depreciation property described in section 168(k)(2)(B) is limited to the property's unadjusted depreciable basis attributable to the property's manufacture, construction, or production after September 10, 2001 (for qualified property), or May 5, 2003 (for 50-percent bonus depreciation property), and before January 1, 2005.

(iii) *Alternative minimum tax.*—The 30-percent or 50-percent additional first year depreciation deduction is allowed for alternative minimum tax purposes for the taxable year in which the qualified property or the 50-percent bonus depreciation property is placed in service by the taxpayer. In general, the 30-percent or 50-percent additional first year depreciation deduction for alternative minimum tax purposes is based on the unadjusted depreciable basis of the property for alternative minimum tax purposes. However, see paragraph (f)(5)(iii)(D) of this section for qualified property or 50-percent bonus depreciation property acquired in a like-kind exchange or as a result of an involuntary conversion.

(2) *Otherwise allowable depreciation deduction.*—(i) *In general.*—Before determining the amount otherwise allowable as a depreciation deduction for the qualified property or the 50-percent bonus depreciation property for the placed-in-service year and any subsequent taxable year, the taxpayer must determine the remaining adjusted depreciable basis of the qualified property or the 50-percent bonus depreciation property. This remaining adjusted depreciable basis is equal to the unadjusted depreciable basis of the qualified property or the 50-percent bonus depreciation property reduced by the amount of the additional first year depreciation allowed or allowable, whichever is greater. The remaining adjusted depreciable basis of the qualified property or the 50-percent bonus depreciation property is then depreciated using the applicable depreciation provisions under the Internal Revenue Code for the qualified property or the 50-percent bonus depreciation property. The remaining adjusted depreciable basis of the qualified property or the 50-percent bonus depreciation property that is MACRS property is also the basis to which the annual depreciation rates in the optional depreciation tables apply (for further guidance, see section 8 of Rev. Proc. 87-57 (1987-2 C.B. 687) and § 601.601(d)(2)(ii)(*b*) of this chapter). The depreciation deduction allowable for the remaining adjusted depreciable basis of the qualified property or the 50-percent bonus depreciation property is affected by a taxable year of less than 12 months.

(ii) *Alternative minimum tax.*—For alternative minimum tax purposes, the depreciation deduction allowable for the remaining adjusted depreciable basis of the qualified property or the 50-percent bonus depreciation property is based on the remaining adjusted depreciable basis for alternative minimum tax purposes. The remaining adjusted depreciable basis of the qualified property or the 50-percent bonus depreciable property for alternative minimum tax purposes is depreciated using the same depreciation method, recovery period (or useful life in the case of computer software), and convention that apply to the qualified property or the 50-percent bonus depreciation property for regular tax purposes.

(3) *Examples.*—This paragraph (d) is illustrated by the following examples:

Example 1. On March 1, 2003, *V*, a calendar-year taxpayer, purchased and placed in service qualified property that costs $1 million and is 5-year property under section 168(e). *V* depreciates its 5-year property placed in service in 2003 using the optional depreciation table that corresponds with the general depreciation system, the 200-percent declining balance method, a 5-year recovery period, and the half-year convention. For 2003, *V* is allowed a 30-percent additional first year depreciation deduction of $300,000 (the unadjusted depreciable basis of $1 million multiplied by .30). Next, *V* must reduce the unadjusted depreciable basis of $1 million by the additional first year depreciation deduction of $300,000 to determine the remaining adjusted depreciable basis of $700,000. Then, *V's* depreciation deduction allowable in 2003 for the remaining adjusted depreciable basis of $700,000 is $140,000 (the remaining adjusted depreciable basis of $700,000 multiplied by the annual depreciation rate of .20 for recovery year 1).

Example 2. On June 1, 2003, *W*, a calendar-year taxpayer, purchased and placed in service 50-percent bonus depreciation property that costs $126,000. The property qualifies for the expensing election under section 179 and is 5-year property under section 168(e). *W* did not purchase any other section 179 property in 2003. *W* makes the election under section 179 for the property and depreciates its 5-year property placed in service in 2003 using the optional depreciation table that corresponds with the general depreciation system, the 200-percent declining balance method, a 5-year recovery period, and the half-year convention. For 2003, *W* is first allowed a $100,000 deduction under section 179. Next, *W* must reduce the cost of $126,000 by the section 179 deduction of $100,000 to determine the unadjusted depreciable basis of $26,000. Then, for 2003, *W* is allowed a 50-percent additional first year depreciation deduction of $13,000 (the unadjusted depreciable basis of $26,000 multiplied by .50). Next, *W* must reduce the unadjusted depreciable basis of $26,000 by the additional first year depreciation deduction of $13,000 to determine the remaining adjusted depreciable basis of $13,000. Then, *W's* depreciation deduction allowable in 2003 for the remaining adjusted depreciable basis of $13,000 is $2,600 (the remaining adjusted depreciable basis of $13,000 multiplied by the annual depreciation rate of .20 for recovery year 1).

(e) *Election not to deduct additional first year depreciation.*—(1) *In general.*—If a taxpayer makes an election under this paragraph (e), the election applies to all qualified property or 50-percent bonus depreciation property, as applicable, that is in the same class of property and placed in service in the same taxable year. The rules of this paragraph (e) apply to the following elections provided under section 168(k):

(i) *Qualified property.*—A taxpayer may make an election not to deduct the 30-percent additional first year depreciation for any class of property that is qualified property placed in service during the taxable year. If this election is made, no additional first year depreciation deduction is allowable for the property placed in service during the taxable year in the class of property.

(ii) *50-percent bonus depreciation property.*—For any class of property that is 50-percent bonus depreciation property placed in service during the taxable year, a taxpayer may make an election—

(A) To deduct the 30-percent, instead of the 50-percent, additional first year depreciation. If this election is made, the allowable additional first year depreciation deduction is determined as though the class of property is qualified property under section 168(k)(2); or

(B) Not to deduct both the 30-percent and the 50-percent additional first year depreciation. If this election is made, no additional first year depreciation deduction is allowable for the class of property.

(2) *Definition of class of property.*—For purposes of this paragraph (e), the term class of property means:

(i) Except for the property described in paragraphs (e)(2)(ii) and (iv) of this section, each class of property described in section 168(e) (for example, 5-year property);

(ii) Water utility property as defined in section 168(e)(5) and depreciated under section 168;

(iii) Computer software as defined in, and depreciated under, section 167(f)(1) and the regulations thereunder; or

(iv) Qualified leasehold improvement property as defined in paragraph (c) of this section and depreciated under section 168.

(3) *Time and manner for making election.*—(i) *Time for making election.*—Except as provided in paragraph (e)(4) of this section, any election specified in paragraph (e)(1) of this section must be made by the due date (including extensions) of the Federal tax return for the taxable year in which the qualified property or the 50-percent bonus depreciation property, as applicable, is placed in service by the taxpayer.

(ii) *Manner of making election.*—Except as provided in paragraph (e)(4) of this section, any election specified in paragraph (e)(1) of this section must be made in the manner prescribed on Form 4562, "Depreciation and Amortization," and its instructions. The election is made separately by each person owning qualified property or 50-percent bonus depreciation property (for example, for each member of a consolidated group by the common parent of the group, by the partnership, or by the S corporation). If Form 4562 is revised or renumbered, any reference in this section to that form shall be treated as a reference to the revised or renumbered form.

(4) *Special rules for 2000 or 2001 returns.*—For the election specified in paragraph (e)(1)(i) of this section for qualified property placed in service by the taxpayer during the taxable year that included September 11, 2001, the taxpayer should refer to the guidance provided by the Internal Revenue Service for the time and manner of making this election on the 2000 or 2001 Federal tax return for the taxable year that included September 11, 2001 (for further guidance, see sections 3.03(3) and 4 of Rev. Proc. 2002-33 (2002-1 C.B. 963), Rev. Proc. 2003-50 (2003-29 I.R.B. 119), and § 601.601(d)(2)(ii)(*b*) of this chapter).

(5) *Failure to make election.*—If a taxpayer does not make the applicable election specified in paragraph (e)(1) of this section within the time and in the manner prescribed in paragraph (e)(3) or (4) of this section, the amount of depreciation allowable for that property under section 167(f)(1) or under section 168, as applicable, must be determined for the placed-in-service year and for all subsequent taxable years by taking into account the additional first year depreciation deduction. Thus, any election specified in paragraph (e)(1) of this section shall not be made by the taxpayer in any other manner (for example, the election cannot be made through a request under section 446(e) to change the taxpayer's method of accounting).

(6) *Alternative minimum tax.*—If a taxpayer makes an election specified in paragraph (e)(1) of this section for a class of property, the depreciation adjustments under section 56 and the regulations under section 56 apply to the property to which that election applies for purposes of computing the taxpayer's alternative minimum taxable income.

(7) *Revocation of election.*—(i) *In general.*—Except as provided in paragraph (e)(7)(ii) of this section, an election specified in paragraph (e)(1) of this section, once made, may be revoked only with the written consent of the Commissioner of Internal Revenue. To seek the Commissioner's consent, the taxpayer must submit a request for a letter ruling.

(ii) *Automatic 6-month extension.*—If a taxpayer made an election specified in paragraph (e)(1) of this section for a class of property, an automatic extension of 6 months from the due date of the taxpayer's Federal tax return (excluding extensions) for the placed-in-service year of the class of property is granted to revoke that election, provided the taxpayer timely filed the taxpayer's Federal tax return for the placed-in-service year of the class of property and, within this 6-month extension period, the taxpayer (and all taxpayers whose tax liability would be affected by the election) files an amended Federal tax return for the placed-in-service year of the class of property in a manner that is consistent with the revocation of the election.

(f) *Special rules.*—(1) *Property placed in service and disposed of in the same taxable year.*—(i) *In general.*—Except as provided in paragraphs (f)(1)(ii) and (iii) of this section, the additional first year depreciation deduction is not allowed for qualified property or 50-percent bonus depreciation property placed in service and disposed of during the same taxable year. Also if qualified property or 50-percent bonus depreciation property is placed in service and disposed of during the same taxable year and then reacquired and again placed in service in a subsequent taxable year, the additional first year depreciation deduction is not allowable for the property in the subsequent taxable year.

(ii) *Technical termination of a partnership.*—In the case of a technical termination of a partnership under section 708(b)(1)(B), the additional first year depreciation deduction is allowable for any qualified property or 50-percent bonus depreciation property placed in service by the terminated partnership during the taxable year of termination and contributed by the terminated partnership to the new partnership. The allowable additional first year depreciation deduction for the qualified property or the 50-percent bonus depreciation property shall not be claimed by the terminated partnership but instead shall be claimed by the new partnership for the new partnership's taxable year in which the qualified property or the 50-percent bonus depreciation property was contributed by the terminated partnership to the new partnership. However, if qualified property or 50-percent bonus depreciation property is both placed in service and contributed to a new partnership in a transaction described in section 708(b)(1)(B) by the terminated partnership during the taxable year of termination, and if such property is disposed of by the new partnership in the same taxable year the new partnership received such property from the terminated partnership, then no additional first year depreciation deduction is allowable to either partnership.

(iii) *Section 168(i)(7) transactions.*—If any qualified property or 50-percent bonus depreciation property is transferred in a transaction described in section 168(i)(7) in the same taxable year that the qualified property or the 50-percent bonus depreciation property is placed in service by the transferor, the additional first year depreciation deduction is allowable for the qualified property or the 50-percent bonus depreciation property. The allowable additional first year depreciation deduction for the qualified property or the 50-percent bonus depreciation property for the transferor's taxable year in which the property is placed in service is allocated between the transferor and the transferee on a monthly basis. This allocation shall be made in accordance with the rules in § 1.168(d)-1(b)(7)(ii) for allocating the depreciation deduction between the transferor and the transferee. However, if qualified property or 50-percent bonus depreciation property is both placed in service and transferred in a transaction described in section 168(i)(7) by the transferor during the same taxable year, and if such property is disposed of by the transferee (other than by a transaction described in section 168(i)(7)) during the same taxable year the transferee received such property from the transferor, then no additional first year depreciation deduction is allowable to either party.

(iv) *Examples.*—The application of this paragraph (f)(1) is illustrated by the following examples:

Example 1. X and *Y* are equal partners in *Partnership XY*, a general partnership. On February 1, 2002, *Partnership XY* purchased and placed in service new equipment at a cost of $30,000. On March 1, 2002, *X* sells its entire 50 percent interest to *Z* in a transfer that terminates the partnership under section 708(b)(1)(B). As a result, terminated *Partnership XY* is deemed to have contributed the equipment to new *Partnership XY*. Pursuant to paragraph (f)(1)(ii) of this section, new *Partnership XY*, not terminated *Partnership XY*, is eligible to claim the 30-percent additional first year depreciation deduction allowable for the equipment for the taxable year 2002 (assuming all other requirements are met).

Example 2. On January 5, 2002, *BB* purchased and placed in service new office desks for a total amount of $8,000. On August 20, 2002, *BB* transferred the office desks to *Partnership BC* in a transaction described in section 721. *BB* and *Partnership BC* are calendar-year taxpayers. Because the transaction between *BB* and *Partnership BC* is a transaction described in section 168(i)(7), pursuant to paragraph (f)(1)(iii) of this section the 30-percent additional first year depreciation deduction allowable for the desks is allocated between *BB* and *Partnership BC* in accordance with the rules in § 1.168(d)-1(b)(7)(ii) for allocating the depreciation deduction between the transferor and the transferee. Accordingly, the 30-percent additional first year depreciation deduction allowable for the desks for 2002 of $2,400 (the unadjusted depreciable basis of $8,000 multiplied by .30) is allocated between *BB* and *Partnership BC* based on the number of months that *BB* and *Partnership BC* held the desks in service. Thus, because the desks were held in service by *BB* for 7 of 12 months, which includes the month in which *BB* placed the desks in service but does not include the month in which the desks were transferred, *BB* is allocated $1,400 (7/12 × $2,400 additional first year depreciation deduction). *Partnership BC* is allocated $1,000, the remaining 5/12 of the $2,400 additional first year depreciation deduction allowable for the desks.

(2) *Redetermination of basis.*—If the unadjusted depreciable basis (as defined in § 1.168(k)-1(a)(2)(iii)) of qualified property or 50-percent bonus depreciation property is redetermined (for example, due to contingent purchase price or discharge of indebtedness) before January 1, 2005, or, in the case of property described in section 168(k)(2)(B) or (C), is redetermined before January 1, 2006 (or redetermined before January 1, 2007, in the case of property described in section 168(k)(2)(B) or (C) to which section 105 of the Gulf Opportunity Zone Act of 2005 (Public Law 109-135, 119 Stat. 2577) applies (for further guidance, see Announcement 2006-29 (2006-19 I.R.B. 879) and § 601.601(d)(2)(ii)(*b*) of this chapter)), the additional first year depreciation deduction allowable for the qualified property or the 50-percent bonus depreciation property is redetermined as follows:

(i) *Increase in basis.*—For the taxable year in which an increase in basis of qualified property or 50-percent bonus depreciation property occurs, the taxpayer shall claim an additional first year depreciation deduction for qualified property by multiplying the amount of the increase in basis for this property by 30 percent or, for 50-percent bonus depreciation property, by multiplying the amount of the increase in basis for this property by 50 percent. For purposes of this paragraph (f)(2)(i), the 30-percent additional first year depreciation deduction applies to the increase in basis if the underlying property is qualified property and the 50-percent additional first year depreciation deduction applies to the increase in basis if the underlying property is 50-percent bonus depreciation property. To determine the amount otherwise allowable as a depreciation deduction for the increase in basis of qualified property or 50-percent bonus depreciation property, the amount of the increase in basis of the qualified property or the 50-percent bonus depreciation property must be reduced by the additional first year depreciation deduction allowed or allowable, whichever is greater, for the increase in basis and the remaining increase in basis of—

(A) Qualified property or 50-percent bonus depreciation property (except for computer software described in paragraph (b)(2)(i)(B) of this section) is depreciated over the recovery period of the qualified property or the 50-percent bonus depreciation property, as applicable, remaining as of the beginning of the taxable year in which the increase in basis occurs, and using the same depreciation method and convention applicable to the qualified property or 50-percent bonus depreciation property, as applicable, that applies for the taxable year in which the increase in basis occurs; and

(B) Computer software (as defined in paragraph (b)(2)(i)(B) of this section) that is qualified property or 50-percent bonus depreciation property is depreciated ratably over the remainder of the 36-month period (the useful life under section 167(f)(1)) as of the beginning of the first day of the month in which the increase in basis occurs.

(ii) *Decrease in basis.*—For the taxable year in which a decrease in basis of qualified property or 50-percent bonus depreciation property occurs, the taxpayer shall include in the taxpayer's income the excess additional first year depreciation deduction previously claimed for the qualified property or the 50-percent bonus depreciation property. This excess additional first year depreciation deduction for qualified property is determined by multiplying the amount of the decrease in basis for this property by 30 percent. The excess additional first year depreciation deduction for 50-percent bonus depreciation property is determined by multiplying the amount of the decrease in basis for this property by 50 percent. For purposes of this paragraph (f)(2)(ii), the 30-percent additional first year depreciation deduction applies to the decrease in basis if the underlying property is qualified property and the 50-percent additional first year depreciation deduction applies to the decrease in basis if the underlying property is 50-percent bonus depreciation property. Also, if the taxpayer establishes by adequate records or other sufficient evidence that the taxpayer claimed less than the additional first year depreciation deduction allowable for the qualified property or the 50-percent bonus depreciation property before the decrease in basis or if the taxpayer claimed more than the additional first year depreciation deduction allowable for the qualified property or the 50-percent bonus depreciation property before the decrease in basis, the excess additional first year depreciation deduction is determined by multiplying the amount of the decrease in basis by the additional first year depreciation deduction percentage actually claimed by the taxpayer for the qualified property or the 50-percent bonus depreciation property, as applicable, before the decrease in basis. To determine the amount includible in the taxpayer's income for the excess depreciation previously claimed (other than the additional first year depreciation deduction) resulting from the decrease in basis of the qualified property or the 50-percent bonus depreciation property, the amount of the decrease in basis of the qualified property or the 50-percent bonus depreciation property must be adjusted by the excess additional first year depreciation deduction includible in the taxpayer's income (as determined under this paragraph) and the remaining decrease in basis of—

(A) Qualified property or 50-percent bonus depreciation property (except for computer software described in paragraph (b)(2)(i)(B) of this section) is included in the taxpayer's income over the recovery period of the qualified property or the 50-percent bonus depreciation property, as applicable, remaining as of the beginning of the taxable year in which the decrease in basis occurs, and using the same depreciation method and convention of the qualified property or 50-percent bonus depreciation property, as applicable, that applies in the taxable year in which the decrease in basis occurs; and

(B) Computer software (as defined in paragraph (b)(2)(i)(B) of this section) that is qualified property or 50-percent bonus depreciation property is included in the taxpayer's income ratably over the remainder of the 36-month period (the useful life under section 167(f)(1)) as of the beginning of the first day of the month in which the decrease in basis occurs.

(iii) *Definition.*—Except as otherwise expressly provided by the Internal Revenue Code (for example, section 1017(a)), the regulations under the Internal Revenue Code, or other guidance published in the Internal Revenue Bulletin (see § 601.601(d)(2)(ii)(*b*) of this chapter), for purposes of this paragraph (f)(2)—

(A) An increase in basis occurs in the taxable year an amount is taken into account under section 461; and

(B) A decrease in basis occurs in the taxable year an amount would be taken into account under section 451.

(iv) *Examples.*—The application of this paragraph (f)(2) is illustrated by the following examples:

Example 1. (i) On May 15, 2002, *CC*, a cash-basis taxpayer, purchased and placed in service qualified property that is 5-year property at a cost of $200,000. In addition to the $200,000, *CC* agrees to pay the seller 25 percent of the gross profits from the operation of the property in 2002. On May 15, 2003, *CC* paid to the seller an additional $10,000. *CC* depreciates the 5-year property placed in service in 2002 using the optional depreciation table that corresponds with the general depreciation system, the 200-percent declining balance method, a 5-year recovery period, and the half-year convention.

(ii) For 2002, *CC* is allowed a 30-percent additional first year depreciation deduction of $60,000 (the unadjusted depreciable basis of $200,000 multiplied by .30). In addition, *CC's* depreciation deduction for 2002 for the remaining adjusted depreciable basis of $140,000 (the unadjusted depreciable basis of $200,000 reduced by the additional first year depreciation deduction of $60,000) is $28,000 (the remaining adjusted depreciable basis of $140,000 multiplied by the annual depreciation rate of .20 for recovery year 1).

(iii) For 2003, *CC's* depreciation deduction for the remaining adjusted depreciable basis of $140,000 is $44,800 (the remaining adjusted depreciable basis of $140,000 multiplied by the annual depreciation rate of .32 for recovery year 2). In addition, pursuant to paragraph (f)(2)(i) of this section, *CC* is allowed an additional first year depreciation deduction for 2003 for the $10,000 increase in basis of the qualified property. Consequently, *CC* is allowed an additional first year depreciation deduction of $3,000 (the increase in basis of $10,000 multiplied by .30). Also, *CC* is allowed a depreciation deduction for 2003 attributable to the remaining increase in basis of $7,000 (the increase in basis of $10,000 reduced by the additional first year depreciation deduction of $3,000). The depreciation deduction allowable for 2003 attributable to the remaining increase in basis of $7,000 is $3,111 (the remaining increase in basis of $7,000 multiplied by .4444, which is equal to 1/remaining recovery period of 4.5 years at January 1, 2003, multiplied by 2). Accordingly, for 2003, *CC's* total depreciation deduction allowable for the qualified property is $50,911.

Example 2. (i) On May 15, 2002, DD, a calendar-year taxpayer, purchased and placed in service qualified property that is 5-year property at a cost of $400,000. To purchase the property, DD borrowed $250,000 from Bank2. On May 15, 2003, Bank2 forgives $50,000 of the indebtedness. DD makes the election provided in section 108(b)(5) to apply any portion of the reduction under section 1017 to the basis of the depreciable property of the taxpayer. DD depreciates the 5-year property placed in service in 2002 using the optional depreciation table that corresponds with the general depreciation system, the 200-percent declining balance method, a 5-year recovery period, and the halfyear convention.

(ii) For 2002, DD is allowed a 30-percent additional first year depreciation deduction of $120,000 (the unadjusted depreciable basis of $400,000 multiplied by .30). In addition, DD's depreciation deduction allowable for 2002 for the remaining adjusted depreciable basis of $280,000 (the unadjusted depreciable basis of $400,000 reduced by the additional first year depreciation deduction of $120,000) is $56,000 (the remaining adjusted depreciable basis of $280,000 multiplied by the annual depreciation rate of .20 for recovery year 1).

(iii) For 2003, DD's deduction for the remaining adjusted depreciable basis of $280,000 is $89,600 (the remaining adjusted depreciable basis of $280,000 multiplied by the annual depreciation rate .32 for recovery year 2). Although Bank2 forgave the indebtedness in 2003, the basis of the property is reduced on January 1, 2004, pursuant to sections 108(b)(5) and 1017(a) under which basis is reduced at the beginning of the taxable year following the taxable year in which the discharge of indebtedness occurs.

(iv) For 2004, DD's deduction for the remaining adjusted depreciable basis of $280,000 is $53,760 (the remaining adjusted depreciable basis of $280,000 multiplied by the annual depreciation rate .192 for recovery year 3). However, pursuant to paragraph (f)(2)(ii) of this section, DD must reduce the amount otherwise allowable as a depreciation deduction for 2004 by the excess depreciation previously claimed for the $50,000 decrease in basis of the qualified property. Consequently, DD must reduce the amount of depreciation otherwise allowable for 2004 by the excess additional first year depreciation of $15,000 (the decrease in basis of $50,000 multiplied by .30). Also, DD must reduce the amount of depreciation otherwise allowable for 2004 by the excess depreciation attributable to the remaining decrease in basis of $35,000 (the decrease in basis of $50,000 reduced by the excess additional first year depreciation of $15,000). The reduction in the amount of depreciation otherwise allowable for 2004 for the remaining decrease in basis of $35,000 is $19,999 (the remaining decrease in basis of $35,000 multiplied by .5714, which is equal to 1/remaining recovery period of 3.5 years at January 1, 2004, multiplied by 2). Accordingly, assuming the qualified property is the only depreciable property owned by DD, for 2004, DD's total depreciation deduction allowable for the qualified property is $18,761 ($53,760 minus $15,000 minus $19,999).

(3) *Section 1245 and 1250 depreciation recapture.*—For purposes of section 1245 and the regulations thereunder, the additional first year depreciation deduction is an amount allowed or allowable for depreciation. Further, for purposes of section 1250(b) and the regulations thereunder, the additional first year depreciation deduction is not a straight line method.

(4) *Coordination with section 169.*—The additional first year depreciation deduction is allowable in the placed-in-service year of a certified pollution control facility (as defined in § 1.169-2(a)) that is qualified property or 50-percent bonus depreciation property, even if the taxpayer makes the election to amortize the certified pollution control facility under section 169 and the regulations thereunder in the certified pollution control facility's placed-in-service year.

(5) *Like-kind exchanges and involuntary conversions.*—(i) *Scope.*—The rules of this paragraph (f)(5) apply to acquired MACRS property or acquired computer software that is qualified property or 50-percent bonus depreciation property at the time of replacement provided the time of replacement is after September 10, 2001, and before January 1, 2005, or, in the case of acquired MACRS property or acquired computer software that is qualified property, or 50-percent bonus depreciation property, described in section 168(k)(2)(B) or (C), the time of replacement is after September 10, 2001, and before January 1, 2006 (or the time of replacement is after September 10, 2001, and before January 1, 2007, in the case of property described in section 168(k)(2)(B) or (C) to which section 105 of the Gulf Opportunity Zone Act of 2005 (Public Law 109-135, 119 Stat. 2577) applies (for further guidance, see Announcement 2006-29 (2006-19 I.R.B. 879) and § 601.601(d)(2)(ii)(*b*) of this chapter)).

(ii) *Definitions.*—For purposes of this paragraph (f)(5), the following definitions apply:

(A) *Acquired MACRS property* is MACRS property in the hands of the acquiring taxpayer that is acquired in a transaction described in section 1031(a), (b), or (c) for other MACRS property or that is acquired in connection with an involuntary conversion of other MACRS property in a transaction to which section 1033 applies.

(B) *Exchanged or involuntarily converted MACRS property* is MACRS property that is transferred by the taxpayer in a transaction described in section 1031(a), (b), or (c), or that is converted as a result of an involuntary conversion to which section 1033 applies.

(C) *Acquired computer software* is computer software (as defined in paragraph (b)(2)(i)(B) of this section) in the hands of the acquiring taxpayer that is acquired in a like-kind exchange under section 1031 or as a result of an involuntary conversion under section 1033.

(D) *Exchanged or involuntarily converted computer software* is computer software (as defined in paragraph (b)(2)(i)(B) of this section) that is transferred by the taxpayer in a like-kind exchange under section 1031 or that is converted as a result of an involuntary conversion under section 1033.

(E) *Time of disposition* is when the disposition of the exchanged or involuntarily converted MACRS property or the exchanged or involuntarily converted computer software, as applicable, takes place.

(F) Except as provided in paragraph (f)(5)(v) of this section, the *time of replacement* is the later of—

(1) When the acquired MACRS property or acquired computer software is placed in service; or

(2) The time of disposition of the exchanged or involuntarily converted property.

(G) *Carryover basis* is the lesser of:

(1) the basis in the acquired MACRS property or acquired computer software, as applicable and as determined under section 1031(d) or 1033(b) and the regulations thereunder; or

(2) the adjusted depreciable basis of the exchanged or involuntarily converted MACRS property or the exchanged or involuntarily converted computer software, as applicable.

(H) *Excess basis* is any excess of the basis in the acquired MACRS property or acquired computer software, as applicable and as determined under section 1031(d) or 1033(b) and the regulations thereunder, over the carryover basis as determined under paragraph (f)(5)(ii)(G) of this section.

(I) *Remaining carryover basis* is the carryover basis as determined under paragraph (f)(5)(ii)(G) of this section reduced by—

(1) The percentage of the taxpayer's use of property for the taxable year other than in the taxpayer's trade or business (or for the production of income); and

(2) Any adjustments to basis provided by other provisions of the Code and the regulations thereunder (including section 1016(a)(2) and (3)) for periods prior to the disposition of the exchanged or involuntarily converted property.

(J) *Remaining excess basis* is the excess basis as determined under paragraph (f)(5)(ii)(H) of this section reduced by—

(1) The percentage of the taxpayer's use of property for the taxable year other than in the taxpayer's trade or business (or for the production of income);

(2) Any portion of the basis the taxpayer properly elects to treat as an expense under section 179 or section 179C;

(3) Any adjustments to basis provided by other provisions of the Code and the regulations thereunder.

(K) *Year of disposition* is the taxable year that includes the time of disposition.

(L) *Year of replacement* is the taxable year that includes the time of replacement.

(iii) *Computation.*—(A) *In general.*—Assuming all other requirements of section 168(k) and this section are met, the remaining carryover basis for the year of replacement and the remaining excess basis, if any, for the year of replacement for the acquired MACRS property or the acquired computer software, as applicable, are eligible for the additional first year depreciation deduction. The 30-percent additional first year depreciation deduction applies to the remaining carryover basis and the remaining excess basis, if any, of the acquired MACRS property or the acquired computer software if the time of replacement is after September 10, 2001, and before May 6, 2003, or if the taxpayer made the election provided in paragraph (e)(1)(ii)(A) of this section. The 50-percent additional first year depreciation deduction applies to the remaining carryover basis and the remaining excess basis, if any, of the acquired MACRS property or the acquired computer software if the time of replacement is after May 5, 2003, and before January 1, 2005, or, in the case of acquired MACRS property or acquired computer software that is 50-percent bonus depreciation property described in section 168(k)(2)(B) or (C), the time of replacement is after May 5, 2003, and before January 1, 2006 (or the time of replacement is after May 5, 2003, and before January 1, 2007, in the case of 50-percent bonus depreciation property described in section 168(k)(2)(B) or (C) to which section 105 of the Gulf Opportunity Zone Act of 2005 (Public Law 109-135, 119 Stat. 2577) applies (for further guidance, see Announcement 2006-29 (2006-19 I.R.B. 879) and § 601.601(d)(2)(ii)(*b*) of this chapter)). The additional first year depreciation deduction is computed separately for the remaining carryover basis and the remaining excess basis.

(B) *Year of disposition and year of replacement.*—The additional first year depreciation deduction is allowable for the acquired MACRS property or acquired computer software in the year of replacement. However, the additional first year depreciation deduction is not allowable for the exchanged or involuntarily converted MACRS property or the exchanged or involuntarily converted computer software if the exchanged or involuntarily converted MACRS property or the exchanged or involuntarily converted computer software, as applicable, is placed in service and disposed of in an exchange or involuntary conversion in the same taxable year.

(C) *Property having a longer production period.*—For purposes of paragraph (f)(5)(iii)(A) of this section, the total of the remaining carryover basis and the remaining excess basis, if any, of the acquired MACRS property that is qualified property or 50-percent bonus depreciation property described in section 168(k)(2)(B) is limited to the total of the property's remaining carryover basis and remaining excess basis, if any, attributable to the property's manufacture, construction, or production after September 10, 2001 (for qualified property), or May 5, 2003 (for 50-percent bonus depreciation property), and before January 1, 2005.

(D) *Alternative minimum tax.*—The 30-percent or 50-percent additional first year depreciation deduction is allowed for alternative minimum tax purposes for the year of replacement of acquired MACRS property or acquired computer software that is qualified property or 50-percent bonus depreciation property. The 30-percent or 50-percent additional first year depreciation deduction for alternative minimum tax purposes is based on the remaining carryover basis and the remaining excess basis, if any, of the acquired MACRS property or the acquired computer software for alternative minimum tax purposes.

(iv) *Sale-leaseback transaction.*—For purposes of this paragraph (f)(5), if MACRS property or computer software is sold to a taxpayer and leased back to a person by the taxpayer within three months after the time of disposition of the MACRS property or computer software, as applicable, the time of replacement for this MACRS property or computer software, as applicable, shall not be earlier than the date on which the MACRS property or computer software, as applicable, is used by the lessee under the leaseback.

(v) *Acquired MACRS property or acquired computer software that is acquired and placed in service before disposition of involuntarily converted MACRS property or involuntarily converted computer software.*—If, in an involuntary conversion, a taxpayer acquires and places in service the acquired MACRS property or the acquired computer software before the time of disposition of the involuntarily converted MACRS property or the involuntarily converted computer software and the time of disposition of the involuntarily converted MACRS property or the involuntarily converted computer software is after December 31, 2004, or, in the case of property described in section 168(k)(2)(B) or (C), after December 31, 2005 (or after December 31, 2006, in the case of property described in section 168(k)(2)(B) or (C) to which section 105 of the Gulf Opportunity Zone Act of 2005 (Public Law 109-135, 119 Stat. 2577) applies (for further guidance, see Announcement 2006-29 (2006-19 I.R.B. 879) and § 601.601(d)(2)(ii)(*b*) of this chapter)), then—

(A) *Time of replacement.*—The time of replacement for purposes of this paragraph (f)(5) is when the acquired MACRS property or acquired computer software is placed in service by the taxpayer, provided the threat or imminence of requisition or condemnation of the involuntarily converted MACRS property or involuntarily converted computer software existed before January 1, 2005, or, in the case of property described in section 168(k)(2)(B) or (C), existed before January 1, 2006 (or existed before January 1, 2007, in the case of property described in section 168(k)(2)(B) or (C) to which section 105 of the Gulf Opportunity Zone Act of 2005 (Public Law 109-135, 119 Stat. 2577) applies (for further guidance, see Announcement 2006-29 (2006-19 I.R.B. 879) and § 601.601(d)(2)(ii)(*b*) of this chapter)); and

(B) *Depreciation of acquired MACRS property or acquired computer software.*—The taxpayer depreciates the acquired MACRS property or acquired computer software in accordance with paragraph (d) of this section. However, at the time of disposition of the involuntarily converted MACRS property, the taxpayer determines the exchanged basis (as defined in § 1.168(i)-6(b)(7)) and the excess basis (as defined in § 1.168(i)-6(b)(8)) of the acquired MACRS property and begins to depreciate the depreciable exchanged basis (as defined in § 1.168(i)-6(b)(9) of the acquired MACRS property in accordance with § 1.168(i)-6(c). The depreciable excess basis (as defined in § 1.168(i)-6(b)(10)) of the acquired MACRS property continues to be depreciated by the taxpayer in accordance with the first sentence of this paragraph (f)(5)(v)(B). Further, in the year of disposition of the involuntarily converted MACRS property, the taxpayer must include in taxable income the excess of the depreciation deductions allowable, including the additional first year depreciation deduction allowable, on the unadjusted depreciable basis of the acquired MACRS property over the additional first year depreciation deduction that would have been allowable to the taxpayer on the remaining carryover basis of the acquired MACRS property at the time of replacement (as defined in paragraph (f)(5)(v)(A) of this section) plus the depreciation deductions that would have been allowable, including the additional first year depreciation deduction allowable, to the taxpayer on the depreciable excess basis of the acquired MACRS property from the date the acquired MACRS property was placed in service by the taxpayer (taking into account the applicable convention) to the time of disposition of the involuntarily converted MACRS property. Similar rules apply to acquired computer software.

(vi) *Examples.*—The application of this paragraph (f)(5) is illustrated by the following examples:

Example 1. (i) In December 2002, EE, a calendar-year corporation, acquired for $200,000 and placed in service Canopy V1, a gas station canopy. Canopy V1 is qualified property under section 168(k)(1) and is 5-year property under section 168(e). EE depreciated Canopy V1 under the general depreciation system of section 168(a) by using the 200-percent declining balance method of depreciation, a 5-year recovery period, and the half-year convention. EE elected to use the optional depreciation tables to compute the depreciation allowance for Canopy V1. On January 1, 2003, Canopy V1 was destroyed in a fire and was no longer usable in EE's business. On June 1, 2003, in an involuntary conversion, EE acquired and placed in service new Canopy W1 with all of the $160,000 of insurance proceeds EE received due to the loss of Canopy V1. Canopy W1 is 50-percent bonus depreciation property under section 168(k)(4) and is 5-year property under section 168(e). Pursuant to paragraph (g)(3)(ii) of this section and § 1.168(i)-6(k)(2)(i), EE decided to apply § 1.168(i)-6 to the involuntary conversion of Canopy V1 with the replacement of Canopy W1, the acquired MACRS property.

(ii) For 2002, EE is allowed a 30-percent additional first year depreciation deduction of $60,000 for Canopy V1 (the unadjusted depreciable basis of $200,000 multiplied by .30), and a regular MACRS depreciation deduction of $28,000 for Canopy V1 (the remaining adjusted depreciable basis of $140,000 multiplied by the annual depreciation rate of .20 for recovery year 1).

(iii) For 2003, EE is allowed a regular MACRS depreciation deduction of $22,400 for Canopy V1 (the remaining adjusted depreciable basis of $140,000 multiplied by the annual depreciation rate of .32 for recovery year 2 × ½ year).

(iv) Pursuant to paragraph (f)(5)(iii)(A) of this section, the additional first year depreciation deduction allowable for Canopy W1 equals $44,800 (.50 of Canopy W1's remaining carryover basis at the time of replacement of $89,600 (Canopy V1's remaining adjusted depreciable basis of $140,000 minus 2002 regular MACRS depreciation deduction of $28,000 minus 2003 regular MACRS depreciation deduction of $22,400).

Example 2. (i) Same facts as in *Example 1,* except EE elected not to deduct the additional first year depreciation for 5-year property placed in service in 2002. EE deducted the additional first year depreciation for 5-year property placed in service in 2003.

(ii) For 2002, EE is allowed a regular MACRS depreciation deduction of $40,000 for Canopy V1 (the unadjusted depreciable basis of $200,000 multiplied by the annual depreciation rate of .20 for recovery year 1).

(iii) For 2003, EE is allowed a regular MACRS depreciation deduction of $32,000 for Canopy V1 (the unadjusted depreciable basis of $200,000 multiplied by the annual depreciation rate of .32 for recovery year 2 × ½ year).

(iv) Pursuant to paragraph (f)(5)(iii)(A) of this section, the additional first year depreciation deduction allowable for Canopy W1 equals $64,000 (.50 of Canopy W1's remaining carryover basis at the time of replacement of $128,000 (Canopy V1's unadjusted depreciable basis of $200,000 minus 2002 regular MACRS depreciation deduction of $40,000 minus 2003 regular MACRS depreciation deduction of $32,000)).

Example 3. (i) In December 2001, FF, a calendar-year corporation, acquired for $10,000 and placed in service Computer X2. Computer X2 is qualified property under section 168(k)(1) and is 5-year property under section 168(e). FF depreciated Computer X2 under the general depreciation system of section 168(a) by using the 200-percent declining balance method of depreciation, a 5-year recovery period, and the half-year convention. FF elected to use the optional depreciation tables to compute the depreciation allowance for Computer X2. On January 1, 2002, FF acquired new Computer Y2 by exchanging Computer X2 and $1,000 cash in a like-kind exchange. Computer Y2 is qualified property under section 168(k)(1) and is 5-year property under section 168(e). Pursuant to paragraph (g)(3)(ii) of this section and § 1.168(i)-6(k)(2)(i), FF decided to apply § 1.168(i)-6 to the exchange of Computer X2 for Computer Y2, the acquired MACRS property.

(ii) For 2001, FF is allowed a 30-percent additional first year depreciation deduction of $3,000 for Computer X2 (unadjusted basis of $10,000 multiplied by .30), and a regular MACRS depreciation deduction of $1,400 for Computer X2 (the remaining adjusted depreciable basis of $7,000 multiplied by the annual depreciation rate of .20 for recovery year 1).

(iii) For 2002, FF is allowed a regular MACRS depreciation deduction of $1,120 for Computer X2 (the remaining adjusted depreciable basis of $7,000 multiplied by the annual depreciation rate of .32 for recovery year 2 × ½ year).

(iv) Pursuant to paragraph (f)(5)(iii)(A) of this section, the 30-percent additional first year depreciation deduction for Computer Y2 is allowable for the remaining carryover basis at the time of replacement of $4,480 (Computer X2's unadjusted depreciable basis of $10,000 minus additional first year depreciation deduction allowable of $3,000 minus 2001 regular MACRS depreciation deduction of $1,400 minus 2002 regular MACRS depreciation deduction of $1,120) and for the remaining excess basis at the time of replacement of $1,000 (cash paid for Computer Y2). Thus, the 30-percent additional first year depreciation deduction for the remaining carryover basis at the time of replacement equals $1,344 ($4,480 multiplied by .30) and for the remaining excess basis at the time of replacement equals $300 ($1,000 multiplied by .30), which totals $1,644.

Example 4. (i) In September 2002, GG, a June 30 year-end corporation, acquired for $20,000 and placed in service Equipment X3. Equipment X3 is qualified property under section 168(k)(1) and is 5-year property under section 168(e). GG depreciated Equipment X3 under the general depreciation system of section 168(a) by using the 200-percent declining balance method of depreciation, a 5-year recovery period, and the half-year convention. GG elected to use the optional depreciation tables to compute the depreciation allowance for Equipment X3. In December 2002, GG acquired new Equipment Y3 by exchanging Equipment X3 and $5,000 cash in a like-kind exchange. Equipment Y3 is qualified property under section 168(k)(1) and is 5-year property under section 168(e). Pursuant to paragraph (g)(3)(ii) of this section and § 1.168(i)-6(k)(2)(i), GG decided to apply § 1.168(i)-6 to the exchange of Equipment X3 for Equipment Y3, the acquired MACRS property.

(ii) Pursuant to paragraph (f)(5)(iii)(B) of this section, no additional first year depreciation deduction is allowable for Equipment X3 and, pursuant to § 1.168(d)-1T(b)(3)(ii), no regular depreciation deduction is allowable for Equipment X3, for the taxable year ended June 30, 2003.

(iii) Pursuant to paragraph (f)(5)(iii)(A) of this section, the 30-percent additional first year depreciation deduction for Equipment Y3 is allowable for the remaining carryover basis at the time of replacement of $20,000 (Equipment X3's unadjusted depreciable basis of $20,000) and for the remaining excess basis at the time of replacement of $5,000 (cash paid for Equipment Y3). Thus, the 30-percent additional first year depreciation deduction for the remaining carryover basis at the time of replacement equals $6,000 ($20,000 multiplied by .30) and for the remaining excess basis at the time of replacement equals $1,500 ($5,000 multiplied by .30), which totals $7,500.

Example 5. (i) Same facts as in *Example 4.* GG depreciated Equipment Y3 under the general depreciation system of section 168(a) by using the 200-percent declining balance method of depreciation, a 5-year recovery period, and the half-year convention. GG elected to use the optional depreciation tables to compute the depreciation allowance for Equipment Y3. On July 1, 2003, GG acquired new Equipment Z1 by exchanging Equipment Y3 in a like-kind exchange. Equipment Z1 is 50-percent bonus depreciation property under section 168(k)(4) and is 5-year property under section 168(e). Pursuant to paragraph (g)(3)(ii) of this section and § 1.168(i)-6(k)(2)(i), GG decided to apply § 1.168(i)-6 to the exchange of Equipment Y3 for Equipment Z1, the acquired MACRS property.

(ii) For the taxable year ending June 30, 2003, the regular MACRS depreciation deduction allowable for the remaining carryover basis at the time of replacement (after taking into account the additional first year depreciation deduction) of Equipment Y3 is $2,800 (the remaining carryover basis at the time of replacement of $20,000 minus the additional first year depreciation deduction of $6,000, multiplied by the annual depreciation rate of .20 for recovery year 1) and for the remaining excess basis at the time of replacement (after taking into account the additional first year depreciation deduction) of Equipment Y3 is $700 (the remaining excess basis at the time of replacement of $5,000 minus the additional first year depreciation deduction of $1,500, multiplied by the annual depreciation rate of .20 for recovery year 1), which totals $3,500.

(iii) For the taxable year ending June 30, 2004, the regular MACRS depreciation deduction allowable for the remaining carryover basis (after taking into account the additional first year depreciation deduction) of Equipment Y3 is $2,240 (the remaining carryover basis at the time of replacement of $20,000 minus the additional first year depreciation deduction of $6,000, multiplied by the annual depreciation rate of .32 for recovery year 2 × ½ year) and for the remaining excess basis (after taking into account the additional first year depreciation deduction) of Equipment Y3 is $560 (the remaining excess basis at the time of replacement of $5,000 minus the additional first year depreciation deduction of $1,500, multiplied by the annual depreciation rate of .32 for recovery year 2 × ½ year), which totals $2,800.

(iv) For the taxable year ending June 30, 2004, pursuant to paragraph (f)(5)(iii)(A) of this section, the 50-percent additional first year depreciation deduction for Equipment Z1 is allowable for the remaining carryover basis at the time of replacement of $11,200 (Equipment Y3's unadjusted depreciable basis of $25,000 minus the total additional first year depreciation deduction of $7,500 minus the total 2003 regular MACRS depreciation deduction of $3,500 minus the total 2004 regular depreciation deduction (taking into account the half-year convention) of $2,800). Thus, the 50-percent additional first year depreciation deduction for the remaining carryover basis at the time of replacement equals $5,600 ($11,200 multiplied by .50).

(6) *Change in use.*—(i) *Change in use of depreciable property.*—The determination of whether the use of depreciable property changes is made in accordance with section 168(i)(5) and regulations thereunder.

(ii) *Conversion to personal use.*—If qualified property or 50-percent bonus depreciation property is converted from business or income-producing use to personal use in the same taxable year in which the property is placed in service by a taxpayer, the additional first year depreciation deduction is not allowable for the property.

(iii) *Conversion to business or income-producing use.*—(A) *During the same taxable year.*—If, during the same taxable year, property is acquired by a taxpayer for personal use and is converted by the taxpayer from personal use to business or income-producing use, the additional first year depreciation deduction is allowable for the property in the taxable year the property is converted to business or income-producing use (assuming all of the requirements in paragraph (b) of this section are met). See paragraph (b)(3)(ii) of this section relating to the original use rules for a conversion of property to business or income-producing use.

(B) *Subsequent to the acquisition year.*—If property is acquired by a taxpayer for personal use and, during a subsequent taxable year, is converted by the taxpayer from personal use to business or income-producing use, the additional first year depreciation deduction is allowable for the property in the taxable year the property is converted to business or income-producing use (assuming all of the requirements in paragraph (b) of this section are met). For purposes of paragraphs (b)(4) and (5) of this section, the property must be acquired by the taxpayer for personal use after September 10, 2001 (for qualified property), or after May 5, 2003 (for 50-percent bonus depreciation property), and converted by the taxpayer from personal use to business or income-producing use by January 1, 2005. See paragraph (b)(3)(ii) of this section relating to the original use rules for a conversion of property to business or income-producing use.

(iv) *Depreciable property changes use subsequent to the placed-in-service year.*—(A) If the use of qualified property or 50-percent bonus depreciation property changes in the hands of the same taxpayer subsequent to the taxable year the qualified property or the 50-percent bonus depreciation property, as applicable, is placed in service and, as a result of the change in use, the property is no longer qualified property or 50-percent bonus depreciation property, as applicable, the additional first year depreciation deduction allowable for the qualified property or the 50-percent bonus depreciation property, as applicable, is not redetermined.

(B) If depreciable property is not qualified property or 50-percent bonus depreciation property in the taxable year the property is placed in service by the taxpayer, the additional first year depreciation deduction is not allowable for the property even if a change in the use of the property subsequent to the taxable year the property is placed in service results in the property being qualified property or 50-percent bonus depreciation property in the taxable year of the change in use.

(v) *Examples.*—The application of this paragraph (f)(6) is illustrated by the following examples:

Example 1. (i) On January 1, 2002, *HH*, a calendar year corporation, purchased and placed in service several new computers at a total cost of $100,000. *HH* used these computers within the United States for 3 months in 2002 and then moved and used the computers outside the United States for the remainder of 2002. On January 1, 2003, *HH* permanently returns the computers to the United States for use in its business.

(ii) For 2002, the computers are considered as used predominantly outside the United States in 2002 pursuant to § 1.48-1(g)(1)(i). As a result, the computers are required to be depreciated under the alternative depreciation system of section 168(g). Pursuant to paragraph (b)(2)(ii)(A)(*2*) of this section, the computers are not qualified property in 2002, the placed-in-service year. Thus, pursuant to (f)(6)(iv)(B) of this section, no additional first year depreciation deduction is allowed for these computers, regardless of the fact that the computers are permanently returned to the United States in 2003.

Example 2. (i) On February 8, 2002, *II*, a calendar year corporation, purchased and placed in service new equipment at a cost of $1,000,000 for use in its California plant. The equipment is 5-year property under section 168(e) and is qualified property under section 168(k). *II* depreciates its 5-year property placed in service in 2002 using the optional depreciation table that corresponds with the general depreciation system, the 200-percent declining balance method, a 5-year recovery period, and the half-year convention. On June 4, 2003, due to changes in *II's* business circumstances, *II* permanently moves the equipment to its plant in Mexico.

(ii) For 2002, *II* is allowed a 30-percent additional first year depreciation deduction of $300,000 (the adjusted depreciable basis of $1,000,000 multiplied by .30). In addition, *II's* depreciation deduction allowable in 2002 for the remaining adjusted depreciable basis of $700,000 (the unadjusted depreciable basis of $1,000,000 reduced by the additional first year depreciation deduction of $300,000) is $140,000 (the remaining adjusted depreciable basis of $700,000 multiplied by the annual depreciation rate of .20 for recovery year 1).

(iii) For 2003, the equipment is considered as used predominantly outside the United States pursuant to § 1.48-1(g)(1)(i). As a result of this change in use, the adjusted depreciable basis of $560,000 for the equipment is required to be depreciated under the alternative depreciation system of section 168(g) beginning in 2003. However, the additional first year depreciation deduction of $300,000 allowed for the equipment in 2002 is not redetermined.

(7) *Earnings and profits.*—The additional first year depreciation deduction is not allowable for purposes of computing earnings and profits.

(8) *Limitation of amount of depreciation for certain passenger automobiles.*—For a passenger automobile as defined in section 280F(d)(5), the limitation under section 280F(a)(1)(A)(i) is increased by—

(i) $4,600 for qualified property acquired by a taxpayer after September 10, 2001, and before May 6, 2003; and

(ii) $7,650 for qualified property or 50-percent bonus depreciation property acquired by a taxpayer after May 5, 2003.

(9) *Section 754 election.*—In general, for purposes of section 168(k) any increase in basis of qualified property or 50-percent bonus depreciation property due to a section 754 election is not eligible for the additional first year depreciation deduction. However, if qualified property or 50-percent bonus depreciation property is placed in service by a partnership in the taxable year the partnership terminates under section 708(b)(1)(B), any increase in basis of the qualified property or the 50-percent bonus depreciation property due to a section 754 election is eligible for the additional first year depreciation deduction.

(10) *Coordination with section 47.*—(i) *In general.*—If qualified rehabilitation expenditures (as defined in section 47(c)(2) and § 1.48-12(c)) incurred by a taxpayer with respect to a qualified rehabilitated building (as defined in section 47(c)(1) and § 1.48-12(b)) are qualified property or 50-percent bonus depreciation property, the taxpayer may claim the rehabilitation credit provided by section 47(a) (provided the requirements of section 47 are met)—

(A) With respect to the portion of the basis of the qualified rehabilitated building that is attributable to the qualified rehabilitation expenditures if the taxpayer makes the applicable election under paragraph (e)(1)(i) or (e)(1)(ii)(B) of this section not to deduct any additional first year depreciation for the class of property that includes the qualified rehabilitation expenditures; or

(B) With respect to the portion of the remaining rehabilitated basis of the qualified rehabilitated building that is attributable to the qualified rehabilitation expenditures if the taxpayer claims the additional first year depreciation deduction on the unadjusted depreciable basis (as defined in paragraph (a)(2)(iii) of this section but before the reduction in basis for the amount of the rehabilitation credit) of the qualified rehabilitation expenditures and the taxpayer depreciates the remaining adjusted depreciable basis (as defined in paragraph (d)(2)(i) of this section) of such expenditures using straight line cost recovery in accordance with section 47(c)(2)(B)(i) and § 1.48-12(c)(7)(i). For purposes of this paragraph (f)(10)(i)(B), the remaining rehabilitated basis is equal to the unadjusted depreciable basis (as defined in paragraph (a)(2)(iii) of this section but before the reduction in basis for the amount of the rehabilitation credit) of the qualified rehabilitation expenditures that are qualified property or 50-percent bonus depreciation property reduced by the additional first year depreciation allowed or allowable, whichever is greater.

(ii) *Example.*—The application of this paragraph (f)(10) is illustrated by the following example.

Example. (i) Between February 8, 2004, and June 4, 2004, UU, a calendar-year taxpayer, incurred qualified rehabilitation expenditures of $200,000 with respect to a qualified rehabilitated building that is nonresidential real property under section 168(e). These qualified rehabilitation expenditures are 50-percent bonus depreciation property and qualify for the 10-percent rehabilitation credit under section 47(a)(1). UU's basis in the qualified rehabilitated building is zero before incurring the qualified rehabilitation expenditures and UU placed the qualified rehabilitated building in service in July 2004. UU depreciates its nonresidential real property placed in service in 2004 under the general depreciation system of section 168(a) by using the straight line method of depreciation, a 39-year recovery period, and the mid-month convention. UU elected to use the optional depreciation tables to compute the depreciation allowance for its depreciable property placed in service in 2004. Further, for 2004, UU did not make any election under paragraph (e) of this section.

(ii) Because UU did not make any election under paragraph (e) of this section, UU is allowed a 50-percent additional first year depreciation deduction of $100,000 for the qualified rehabilitation expenditures for 2004 (the unadjusted depreciable basis of $200,000 (before reduction in basis for the rehabilitation credit) multiplied by .50). For 2004, UU also is allowed to claim a rehabilitation credit of $10,000 for the remaining rehabilitated basis of $100,000 (the unadjusted depreciable basis (before reduction in basis for the rehabilitation credit) of $200,000 less the additional first year depreciation deduction of $100,000). Further, UU's depreciation deduction for 2004 for the remaining adjusted depreciable basis of $90,000 (the unadjusted depreciable basis (before reduction in basis for the rehabilitation credit) of $200,000 less the additional first year depreciation deduction of $100,000 less the rehabilitation credit of $10,000) is $1,059.30 (the remaining adjusted depreciable basis of $90,000 multiplied by the depreciation rate of .01177 for recovery year 1, placed in service in month 7).

(11) *Coordination with section 514(a)(3).*—The additional first year depreciation deduction is not allowable for purposes of section 514(a)(3).

(g) *Effective date.*—(1) *In general.*—Except as provided in paragraphs (g)(2), (3), and (5) of this section, this section applies to qualified property under section 168(k)(2) acquired by a taxpayer after September 10, 2001, and to 50-percent bonus depreciation property under section 168(k)(4) acquired by a taxpayer after May 5, 2003.

(2) *Technical termination of a partnership or section 168(i)(7) transactions.*—If qualified property or 50 percent bonus depreciation property is transferred in a technical termination of a partnership under section 708(b)(1)(B) or in a transaction described in section 168(i)(7) for a taxable year ending on or before September 8, 2003, and the additional first year depreciation deduction allowable for the property was not determined in accordance with paragraph (f)(1)(ii) or (iii) of this section, as applicable, the Internal Revenue Service will allow any reasonable method of determining the additional first year depreciation deduction allowable for

the property in the year of the transaction that is consistently applied to the property by all parties to the transaction.

(3) *Like-kind exchanges and involuntary conversions.*—(i) If a taxpayer did not claim on a federal tax return for a taxable year ending on or before September 8, 2003, the additional first year depreciation deduction for the remaining carryover basis of qualified property or 50-percent bonus depreciation property acquired in a transaction described in section 1031(a), (b), or (c), or in a transaction to which section 1033 applies and the taxpayer did not make an election not to deduct the additional first year depreciation deduction for the class of property applicable to the remaining carryover basis, the Internal Revenue Service will treat the taxpayer's method of not claiming the additional first year depreciation deduction for the remaining carryover basis as a permissible method of accounting and will treat the amount of the additional first year depreciation deduction allowable for the remaining carryover basis as being equal to zero, provided the taxpayer does not claim the additional first year depreciation deduction for the remaining carryover basis in accordance with paragraph (g)(4)(ii) of this section.

(ii) Paragraphs (f)(5)(ii)(F)(*2*) and (f)(5)(v) of this section apply to a like-kind exchange or an involuntary conversion of MACRS property and computer software for which the time of disposition and the time of replacement both occur after February 27, 2004. For a like-kind exchange or an involuntary conversion of MACRS property for which the time of disposition, the time of replacement, or both occur on or before February 27, 2004, see § 1.168(i)-6(k)(2)(ii). For a like-kind exchange or involuntary conversion of computer software for which the time of disposition, the time of replacement, or both occur on or before February 27, 2004, a taxpayer may rely on prior guidance issued by the Internal Revenue Service for determining the depreciation deductions of the acquired computer software and the exchanged or involuntarily converted computer software (for further guidance, see § 1.168(k)-1T(f)(5) published in the **Federal Register** on September 8, 2003 (68 FR 53000)). In relying on such guidance, a taxpayer may use any reasonable, consistent method of determining depreciation in the year of disposition and the year of replacement.

(4) *Change in method of accounting.*—(i) *Special rules for 2000 or 2001 returns.*—If a taxpayer did not claim on the Federal tax return for the taxable year that included September 11, 2001, any additional first year depreciation deduction for a class of property that is qualified property and did not make an election not to deduct the additional first year depreciation deduction for that class of property, the taxpayer should refer to the guidance provided by the Internal Revenue Service for the time and manner of claiming the additional first year depreciation deduction for the class of property (for further guidance, see section 4 of Rev. Proc. 2002-33 (2002-1 C.B. 963), Rev. Proc. 2003-50 (2003-29 I.R.B. 119), and § 601.601(d)(2)(ii)(*b*) of this chapter).

(ii) *Like-kind exchanges and involuntary conversions.*—If a taxpayer did not claim on a federal tax return for any taxable year ending on or before September 8, 2003, the additional first year depreciation deduction allowable for the remaining carryover basis of qualified property or 50-percent bonus depreciation property acquired in a transaction described in section 1031(a), (b), or (c), or in a transaction to which section 1033 applies and the taxpayer did not make an election not to deduct the additional first year depreciation deduction for the class of property applicable to the remaining carryover basis, the taxpayer may claim the additional first year depreciation deduction allowable for the remaining carryover basis in accordance with paragraph (f)(5) of this section either:

(A) by filing an amended return (or a qualified amended return, if applicable (for further guidance, see Rev. Proc. 94-69 (1994-2 C.B. 804) and

§ 601.601(d)(2)(ii)(*b*) of this chapter)) on or before December 31, 2003, for the year of replacement and any affected subsequent taxable year; or,

(B) by following the applicable administrative procedures issued under § 1.446-1(e)(3)(ii) for obtaining the Commissioner's automatic consent to a change in method of accounting (for further guidance, see Rev. Proc. 2002-9 (2002-1 C.B. 327) and § 601.601(d)(2)(ii)(*b*) of this chapter).

(5) *Revision to paragraphs (b)(3)(iii)(B) and (b)(5)(ii)(B) of this section.*—The addition of "(or, in the case of multiple units of property subject to the same lease, within three months after the date the final unit is placed in service, so long as the period between the time the first unit is placed in service and the time the last unit is placed in service does not exceed 12 months)" to paragraphs (b)(3)(iii)(B) and (b)(5)(ii)(B) of this section applies to property sold after June 4, 2004.

(6) *Rehabilitation credit.*—If a taxpayer did not claim on a Federal tax return for any taxable year ending on or before September 1, 2006, the rehabilitation credit provided by section 47(a) with respect to the portion of the basis of a qualified rehabilitated building that is attributable to qualified rehabilitation expenditures and the qualified rehabilitation expenditures are qualified property or 50-percent bonus depreciation property, and the taxpayer did not make the applicable election specified in paragraph (e)(1)(i) or (e)(1)(ii)(B) of this section for the class of property that includes the qualified rehabilitation expenditures, the taxpayer may claim the rehabilitation credit for the remaining rehabilitated basis (as defined in paragraph (f)(10)(i)(B) of this section) of the qualified rehabilitated building that is attributable to the qualified rehabilitation expenditures (assuming all the requirements of section 47 are met) in accordance with paragraph (f)(10)(i)(B) of this section by filing an amended Federal tax return for the taxable year for which the rehabilitation credit is to be claimed. The amended Federal tax return must include the adjustment to the tax liability for the rehabilitation credit and any collateral adjustments to taxable income or to the tax liability (for example, the amount of depreciation allowed or allowable in that taxable year for the qualified rehabilitated building). Such adjustments must also be made on amended Federal tax returns for any affected succeeding taxable years. [Reg. § 1.168(k)-1.]

.01 Historical Comment: Adopted 9/5/2003 by T.D. 9091 (corrected 11/7/2003). Amended 2/27/2004 by T.D. 9115 (corrected 4/2/2004), 8/28/2006 by T.D. 9283 and 2/27/2007 by T.D. 9314.

Code Sec. 179 Expensing Regulations

¶ 576

Reg. § 1.179-0

§ 1.179-0. **Table of contents for section 179 expensing rules.**

This section lists captioned paragraphs contained in §§ 1.179-1 through 1.179-6.

(i) In general.
(ii) Joint returns filed after separate returns.
(iii) Example.
(6) Married individuals filing separately.
(i) In general.
(ii) Example.
(7) Component members of a controlled group.
(i) In general.
(ii) Statement to be filed.
(iii) Revocation.
(c) Taxable income limitation.
(1) In general.
(2) Application to partnerships and partners.
(i) In general.
(ii) Taxable year.
(iii) Example.
(iv) Taxable income of a partnership.
(v) Partner's share of partnership taxable income.
(3) S corporations and S corporation shareholders.
(i) In general.
(ii) Taxable income of an S corporation.
(iii) Shareholder's share of S corporation taxable income.
(4) Taxable income of a corporation other than an S corporation.
(5) Ordering rule for certain circular problems.
(i) In general.
(ii) Example.
(6) Active conduct by the taxpayer of a trade or business.
(i) Trade or business.
(ii) Active conduct.
(iii) Example.
(iv) Employees.
(7) Joint returns.
(i) In general.
(ii) Joint returns filed after separate returns.
(8) Married individuals filing separately.
(d) Examples.

§ 1.179-3 Carryover of disallowed deduction.

(a) In general.
(b) Deduction of carryover of disallowed deduction.
(1) In general.
(2) Cross references.
(c) Unused section 179 expense allowance.
(d) Example.
(e) Recordkeeping requirement and ordering rule.
(f) Dispositions and other transfers of section 179 property.
(1) In general.
(2) Recapture under section 179(d)(10).
(g) Special rules for partnerships and S corporations.
(1) In general.
(2) Basis adjustment.

(3) Dispositions and other transfers of section 179 property by a partnership or an S corporation.

(4) Example.

(h) Special rules for partners and S corporation shareholders.

(1) In general.

(2) Dispositions and other transfers of a partner's interest in a partnership or a shareholder's interest in an S corporation.

(3) Examples.

§ 1.179-4 Definitions.

(a) Section 179 property.

(b) Section 38 property.

(c) Purchase.

(d) Cost.

(e) Placed in service.

(f) Controlled group of corporations and component member of controlled group.

§ 1.179-5 Time and manner of making election.

(a) Election.

(b) Revocation.

(c) Section 179 property placed in service by the taxpayer in a taxable year beginning after 2002 and before 2008.

(d) Election or revocation must not be made in any other manner.

§ 1.179-6 Effective dates.

(a) In general.

(b) Section 179 property placed in service by the taxpayer in a taxable year beginning after 2002 and before 2008.

(c) Application of § 1.179-5(d).

[Reg. § 1.179-0.]

.01 Historical Comment: Proposed 3/28/91. Adopted 12/23/92 by T.D. 8455. Amended 8/3/2004 by T.D. 9146 and 7/12/2005 by T.D. 9209.

¶ 577

Reg. § 1.179-1

§ 1.179-1. **Election to expense certain depreciable assets.**—(a) *In general.*—Section 179(a) allows a taxpayer to elect to expense the cost (as defined in § 1.179-4(d)), or a portion of the cost, of section 179 property (as defined in § 1.179-4(a)) for the taxable year in which the property is placed in service (as defined in § 1.179-4(e)). The election is not available for trusts, estates, and certain noncorporate lessors. See paragraph (i)(2) of this section for rules concerning noncorporate lessors. However, section 179(b) provides certain limitations on the amount that a taxpayer may elect to expense in any one taxable year. See §§ 1.179-2 and 1.179-3 for rules relating to the dollar and taxable income limitations and the carryover of disallowed deduction rules. For rules describing the time and manner of making an election under section 179, see § 1.179-5. For the effective date, see § 1.179-6.

(b) *Cost subject to expense.*—The expense deduction under section 179 is allowed for the entire cost or a portion of the cost of one or more items of section 179 property. This expense deduction is subject to the limitations of section 179(b) and § 1.179-2. The taxpayer may select the properties that are subject to the election as well as the portion of each property's cost to expense.

(c) *Proration not required.*—(1) *In general.*—The expense deduction under section 179 is determined without any proration based on—

(i) The period of time the section 179 property has been in service during the taxable year; or

(ii) The length of the taxable year in which the property is placed in service.

(2) *Example.*—The following example illustrates the provisions of paragraph (c)(1) of this section.

Example. On December 1, 1991, X, a calendar-year corporation, purchases and places in service section 179 property costing $20,000. For the taxable year ending December 31, 1991, X may elect to claim a section 179 expense deduction on the property (subject to the limitations imposed under section 179(b)) without proration of its cost for the number of days in 1991 during which the property was in service.

(d) *Partial business use.*—(1) *In general.*—If a taxpayer uses section 179 property for trade or business as well as other purposes, the portion of the cost of the property attributable to the trade or business use is eligible for expensing under section 179 provided that more than 50 percent of the property's use in the taxable year is for trade or business purposes. The limitations of section 179(b) and § 1.179-2 are applied to the portion of the cost attributable to the trade or business use.

(2) *Example.*—The following example illustrates the provisions of paragraph (d)(1) of this section.

Example. A purchases section 179 property costing $10,000 in 1991 for which 80 percent of its use will be in A's trade or business. The cost of the property adjusted to reflect the business use of the property is $8,000 (80 percent × $10,000). Thus, A may elect to expense up to $8,000 of the cost of the property (subject to the limitations imposed under section 179(b) and § 1.179-2).

(3) *Additional rules that may apply.*—If a section 179 election is made for "listed property" within the meaning of section 280F(d)(4) and there is personal use of the property, section 280F (d)(1), which provides rules that coordinate section 179 with the section 280F limitation on the amount of depreciation, may apply. If section 179 property is no longer predominantly used in the taxpayer's trade or business, paragraphs (e)(1) through (4) of this section, relating to recapture of the section 179 deduction, may apply.

(e) *Change in use; recapture.*—(1) *In general.*—If a taxpayer's section 179 property is not used predominantly in a trade or business of the taxpayer at any time before the end of the property's recovery period, the taxpayer must recapture in the taxable year in which the section 179 property is not used predominantly in a trade or business any benefit derived from expensing such property. The benefit derived from expensing the property is equal to the excess of the amount expensed under this section over the total amount that would have been allowable for prior taxable years and the taxable year of recapture as a deduction under section 168 (had section 179 not been elected) for the portion of the cost of the property to which the expensing relates (regardless of whether such excess reduced the taxpayer's tax liability). For purposes of the preceding sentence, (i) the "amount expensed under this section" shall not include any amount that was not allowed as a deduction to a taxpayer because the taxpayer's aggregate amount of allowable section 179 expenses exceeded the section 179(b) dollar limitation, and (ii) in the case of an individual who does not elect to itemize deductions under section 63(g) in the taxable year of recapture, the amount allowable as a deduction under section 168 in the taxable year of recapture shall be determined by treating property used in the production of income other than rents or royalties as being property used for personal purposes. The amount to be recaptured shall be treated as ordinary income for the taxable year in which the property is no longer used predominantly in a trade or business of the taxpayer. For taxable years following the year of recapture, the taxpayer's deductions under section 168(a) shall be determined as if no section 179 election with respect to the property had been made. However, see section 280F(d)(1) relating to the coordination of section 179 with the limitation on the amount of depreciation for luxury automobiles and where certain property is used for personal purposes. If the recapture rules of both section 280F(b)(2) and this paragraph (e)(1) apply to an item of section 179 property, the amount of recapture for such property shall be determined only under the rules of section 280F(b)(2).

(2) *Predominant use.*—Property will be treated as not used predominantly in a trade or business of the taxpayer if 50 percent or more of the use of such property during any taxable year within the recapture period is for a use other than in a trade or business of the taxpayer. If during any taxable year of the recapture period the taxpayer disposes of the property (other than in a disposition to which section 1245(a) applies) or ceases to use the property in a trade or business in a manner that had the taxpayer claimed a credit under section 38 for such property such disposition or cessation in use would cause recapture under section 47, the property will be treated as not used in a trade or business of the taxpayer. However, for purposes of applying the recapture rules of section 47 pursuant to the preceding sentence, converting the use of the property from use in a trade or business to use in the production of income will be treated as a conversion to personal use.

(3) *Basis; application with section 1245.*—The basis of property with respect to which there is recapture under paragraph (e)(1) of this section shall be increased immediately before the event resulting in such recapture by the amount recaptured. If section 1245(a) applies to a disposition of property, there is no recapture under paragraph (e)(1) of this section.

(4) *Carryover of disallowed deduction.*—See § 1.179-3 for rules on applying the recapture provisions of this paragraph (e) when a taxpayer has a carryover of disallowed deduction.

(5) *Example.*—The following example illustrates the provisions of paragraphs (e)(1) through (e)(4) of this section.

Example. A, a calendar-year taxpayer, purchases and places in service on January 1, 1991, section 179 property costing $15,000. The property is 5-year property for section 168 purposes and is the only item of depreciable property placed in service by A during 1991. A properly elects to expense $10,000 of the cost and elects under section 168(b)(5) to depreciate the remaining cost under the straight-line method. On January 1, 1992, A converts the property from use in A's business to use for the production of income, and A uses the property in the latter capacity for the entire year. A elects to itemize deductions for 1992. Because the property was not predominantly used in A's trade or business in 1992, A must recapture any benefit derived from expensing the property under section 179. Had A not elected to expense the $10,000 in 1991, A would have been entitled to deduct, under section 168, 10 percent of the $10,000 in 1991, and 20 percent of the $10,000 in 1992. Therefore, A must include $7,000 in ordinary income for the 1992 taxable year, the excess of $10,000 (the section 179 expense amount) over $3,000 (30 percent of $10,000).

(f) *Basis.*—(1) *In general.*—A taxpayer who elects to expense under section 179 must reduce the depreciable basis of the section 179 property by the amount of the section 179 expense deduction.

(2) *Special rules for partnerships and S corporations.*—Generally the basis of a partnership or S corporation's section 179 property must be reduced to reflect

the amount of section 179 expense elected by the partnership or S corporation. This reduction must be made in the basis of partnership or S corporation property even if the limitations of section 179(b) and § 1.179-2 prevent a partner in a partnership or a shareholder in an S corporation from deducting all or a portion of the amount of the section 179 expense allocated by the partnership or S corporation. See § 1.179-3 for rules on applying the basis provisions of this paragraph (f) when a person has a carryover of disallowed deduction.

(3) *Special rules with respect to trusts and estates which are partners or S corporation shareholders.*—Since the section 179 election is not available for trusts or estates, a partner or S corporation shareholder that is a trust or estate, may not deduct its allocable share of the section 179 expense elected by the partnership or S corporation. The partnership or S corporation's basis in section 179 property shall not be reduced to reflect any portion of the section 179 expense that is allocable to the trust or estate. Accordingly, the partnership or S corporation may claim a depreciation deduction under section 168 or a section 38 credit (if available) with respect to any depreciable basis resulting from the trust or estate's inability to claim its allocable portion of the section 179 expense.

(g) *Disallowance of the section 38 credit.*—If a taxpayer elects to expense under section 179, no section 38 credit is allowable for the portion of the cost expensed. In addition, no section 38 credit shall be allowed under section 48(d) to a lessee of property for the portion of the cost of the property that the lessor expensed under section 179.

(h) *Partnerships and S corporations.*—(1) *In general.*—In the case of property purchased and placed in service by a partnership or an S corporation, the determination of whether the property is section 179 property is made at the partnership or S corporation level. The election to expense the cost of section 179 property is made by the partnership or the S corporation. See sections 703(b), 1363(c), 6221, 6231(a)(3), 6241, and 6245.

(2) *Example.*—The following example illustrates the provisions of paragraph (h)(1) of this section.

Example. A owns certain residential rental property as an investment. A and others form ABC partnership whose function is to rent and manage such property. A and ABC partnership file their income tax returns on a calendar-year basis. In 1991, ABC partnership purchases and places in service office furniture costing $20,000 to be used in the active conduct of ABC's business. Although the office furniture is used with respect to an investment activity of A, the furniture is being used in the active conduct of ABC's trade or business. Therefore, because the determination of whether property is section 179 property is made at the partnership level, the office furniture is section 179 property and ABC may elect to expense a portion of its cost under section 179.

(i) *Leasing of section 179 property.*—(1) *In general.*—A lessor of section 179 property who is treated as the owner of the property for Federal tax purposes will be entitled to the section 179 expense deduction if the requirements of section 179 and the regulations thereunder are met. These requirements will not be met if the lessor merely holds the property for the production of income. For certain leases entered prior to January 1, 1984, the safe harbor provisions of section 168(f)(8) apply in determining whether an agreement is treated as a lease for Federal tax purposes.

(2) *Noncorporate lessor.*—In determining the class of taxpayers (other than an estate or trust) for which section 179 is applicable, section 179(d)(5) provides that if a taxpayer is a noncorporate lessor (*i.e.*, a person who is not a corporation and is a lessor), the taxpayer shall not be entitled to claim a section 179

expense for section 179 property purchased and leased by the taxpayer unless the taxpayer has satisfied all of the requirements of section 179(d)(5)(A) or (B).

(j) *Application of sections 263 and 263A.*—Under section 263(a)(1)(G), expenditures for which a deduction is allowed under section 179 and this section are excluded from capitalization under section 263(a). Under this paragraph (j), amounts allowed as a deduction under section 179 and this section are excluded from the application of the uniform capitalization rules of section 263A.

(k) *Cross references.*—See section 453(i) and the regulations thereunder with respect to installment sales of section 179 property. See section 263(a)(1)(H) and the regulations thereunder with respect to capitalizing section 179 property. [Reg. § 1.179-1.]

.01 Historical Comment: Proposed 9/26/85. Adopted 1/5/87 by T.D. 8121. Amended 12/23/92 by T.D. 8455.

¶ 578

Reg. § 1.179-2

Caution: Reg. § 1.179-2 does not reflect recent law changes. For details, see ¶ 578.01.

§ 1.179-2. **Limitations on amount subject to section 179 election.**—(a) *In general.*—Sections 179(b)(1) and (2) limit the aggregate cost of section 179 property that a taxpayer may elect to expense under section 179 for any one taxable year (dollar limitation). See paragraph (b) of this section. Section 179(b)(3)(A) limits the aggregate cost of section 179 property that a taxpayer may deduct in any taxable year (taxable income limitation). See paragraph (c) of this section. Any cost that is elected to be expensed but that is not currently deductible because of the taxable income limitation may be carried forward to the next taxable year (carryover of disallowed deduction). See § 1.179-3 for rules relating to carryovers of disallowed deductions. See also sections 280F(a), (b), and (d)(1) relating to the coordination of section 179 with the limitations on the amount of depreciation for luxury automobiles and other listed property. The dollar and taxable income limitations apply to each taxpayer and not to each trade or business in which the taxpayer has an interest.

(b) *Dollar limitation.*—(1) *In general.*—The aggregate cost of section 179 property that a taxpayer may elect to expense under section 179 for any taxable year beginning in 2003 and thereafter is $25,000 ($100,000 in the case of taxable years beginning after 2002 and before 2008 under section 179(b)(1), indexed annually for inflation under section 179(b)(5) for taxable years beginning after 2003 and before 2008), reduced (but not below zero) by the amount of any excess section 179 property (described in paragraph (b)(2) of this section) placed in service during the taxable year.

(2) *Excess section 179 property.*—The amount of any excess section 179 property for a taxable year equals the excess (if any) of—

(i) The cost of section 179 property placed in service by the taxpayer in the taxable year; over

(ii) $200,000 ($400,000 in the case of taxable years beginning after 2002 and before 2008 under section 179(b)(2), indexed annually for inflation under section 179(b)(5) for taxable years beginning after 2003 and before 2008).

(3) *Application to partnerships.*—(i) *In general.*—The dollar limitation of this paragraph (b) applies to the partnership as well as to each partner. In applying the dollar limitation to a taxpayer that is a partner in one or more partnerships, the partner's share of section 179 expenses allocated to the partner from each partnership is aggregated with any nonpartnership section 179 expenses of the taxpayer

»»→ *Caution: Reg. § 1.179-2 does not reflect recent law changes. For details, see ¶ 578.01.*

for the taxable year. However, in determining the excess section 179 property placed in service by a partner in a taxable year, the cost of section 179 property placed in service by the partnership is not attributed to any partner.

(ii) *Example.*—The following example illustrates the provisions of paragraph (b) (3) (i) of this section.

Example. During 1991, CD, a calendar-year partnership, purchases and places in service section 179 property costing $150,000 and elects under section 179(c) and § 1.179-5 to expense $10,000 of the cost of that property. CD properly allocates to C, a calendar-year taxpayer and a partner in CD, $5,000 of section 179 expenses (C's distributive share of CD's section 179 expenses for 1991). In applying the dollar limitation to C for 1991, C must include the $5,000 of section 179 expenses allocated from CD. However, in determining the amount of any excess section 179 property C placed in service during 1991, C does not include any of the cost of section 179 property placed in service by CD, including the $5,000 of cost represented by the $5,000 of section 179 expenses allocated to C by the partnership.

(iii) *Partner's share of section 179 expenses.*—Section 704 and the regulations thereunder govern the determination of a partner's share of a partnership's section 179 expenses for any taxable year. However, no allocation among partners of the section 179 expenses may be modified after the due date of the partnership return (without regard to extensions of time) for the taxable year for which the election under section 179 is made.

(iv) *Taxable year.*—If the taxable years of a partner and the partnership do not coincide, then for purposes of section 179, the amount of the partnership's section 179 expenses attributable to a partner for a taxable year is determined under section 706 and the regulations thereunder (generally the partner's distributive share of partnership section 179 expenses for the partnership year that ends with or within the partner's taxable year).

(v) *Example.*—The following example illustrates the provisions of paragraph (b) (3) (iv) of this section.

Example. AB partnership has a taxable year ending January 31. A, a partner of AB, has a taxable year ending December 31. AB purchases and places in service section 179 property on March 10, 1991, and elects to expense a portion of the cost of that property under section 179. Under section 706 and § 1.706-1(a) (1), A will be unable to claim A's distributive share of any of AB's section 179 expenses attributable to the property placed in service on March 10, 1991, until A's taxable year ending December 31, 1992.

(4) *S Corporations.*—Rules similar to those contained in paragraph (b) (3) of this section apply in the case of S corporations (as defined in section 1361(a)) and their shareholders. Each shareholder's share of the section 179 expenses of an S corporation is determined under section 1366.

(5) *Joint returns.*—(i) *In general.*—A husband and wife who file a joint income tax return under section 6013(a) are treated as one taxpayer in determining the amount of the dollar limitation under paragraph (b) (1) of this section, regardless of which spouse purchased the property or placed it in service.

(ii) *Joint returns filed after separate returns.*—In the case of a husband and wife who elect under section 6013(b) to file a joint income tax return for a taxable year after the time prescribed by law for filing the return for such taxable

Caution: Reg. § 1.179-2 does not reflect recent law changes. For details, see ¶ 578.01.

year has expired, the dollar limitation under paragraph (b)(1) of this section is the lesser of—

(A) The dollar limitation (as determined under paragraph (b)(5)(i) of this section); or

(B) The aggregate cost of section 179 property elected to be expensed by the husband and wife on their separate returns.

(iii) *Example.*—The following example illustrates the provisions of paragraph (b)(5)(ii) of this section.

Example. During 1991, Mr. and Mrs. B, both calendar-year taxpayers, purchase and place in service section 179 property costing $100,000. On their separate returns for 1991, Mr. B elects to expense $3,000 of section 179 property as an expense and Mrs. B elects to expense $4,000. After the due date of the return they elect under section 6013(b) to file a joint income tax return for 1991. The dollar limitation for their joint income tax return is $7,000, the lesser of the dollar limitation ($10,000) or the aggregate cost elected to be expensed under section 179 on their separate returns ($3,000 elected by Mr. B plus $4,000 elected by Mrs. B, or $7,000).

(6) *Married individuals filing separately.*—(i) *In general.*—In the case of an individual who is married but files a separate income tax return for a taxable year, the dollar limitation of this paragraph (b) for such taxable year is the amount that would be determined under paragraph (b)(5)(i) of this section if the individual filed a joint income tax return under section 6013(a) multiplied by either the percentage elected by the individual under this paragraph (b)(6) or 50 percent. The election in the preceding sentence is made in accordance with the requirements of section 179(c) and § 1.179-5. However, the amount determined under paragraph (b)(5)(i) of this section must be multiplied by 50 percent if either the individual or the individual's spouse does not elect a percentage under this paragraph (b)(6) or the sum of the percentages elected by the individual and the individual's spouse does not equal 100 percent. For purposes of this paragraph (b)(6), marital status is determined under section 7703 and the regulations thereunder.

(ii) *Example.*—The following example illustrates the provisions of paragraph (b)(6)(i) of this section.

Example. Mr. and Mrs. D, both calendar-year taxpayers, file separate income tax returns for 1991. During 1991, Mr. D places $195,000 of section 179 property in service and Mrs. D places $9,000 of section 179 property in service. Neither of them elects a percentage under paragraph (b)(6)(i) of this section. The 1991 dollar limitation for both Mr. D and Mrs. D is determined by multiplying by 50 percent the dollar limitation that would apply had they filed a joint income tax return. Had Mr. and Mrs. D filed a joint return for 1991, the dollar limitation would have been $6,000, $10,000 reduced by the excess section 179 property they placed in service during 1991 ($195,000 placed in service by Mr. D plus $9,000 placed in service by Mrs. D less $200,000, or $4,000). Thus, the 1991 dollar limitation for Mr. and Mrs. D is $3,000 each ($6,000 multiplied by 50 percent).

(7) *Component members of a controlled group.*—(i) *In general.*—Component members of a controlled group (as defined in § 1.179-4(f)) on a December 31 are treated as one taxpayer in applying the dollar limitation of sections 179(b)(1) and (2) and this paragraph (b). The expense deduction may be taken by any one component member or allocated (for the taxable year of each member that includes that December 31) among the several members in any manner. Any allocation of the expense deduction must be pursuant to an allocation by the common parent corporation if a consolidated return is filed for all component members of the

»»→ *Caution: Reg. § 1.179-2 does not reflect recent law changes. For details, see ¶ 578.01.*

group, or in accordance with an agreement entered into by the members of the group if separate returns are filed. If a consolidated return is filed by some component members of the group and separate returns are filed by other component members, the common parent of the group filing the consolidated return must enter into an agreement with those members that do not join in filing the consolidated return allocating the amount between the group filing the consolidated return and the other component members of the controlled group that do not join in filing the consolidated return. The amount of the expense allocated to any component member, however, may not exceed the cost of section 179 property actually purchased and placed in service by the member in the taxable year. If the component members have different taxable years, the term "taxable year" in sections 179(b)(1) and (2) means the taxable year of the member whose taxable year begins on the earliest date.

(ii) *Statement to be filed.*—If a consolidated return is filed, the common parent corporation must file a separate statement attached to the income tax return on which the election is made to claim an expense deduction under section 179. See § 1.179-5. If separate returns are filed by some or all component members of the group, each component member not included in a consolidated return must file a separate statement attached to the income tax return on which an election is made to claim a deduction under section 179. The statement must include the name, address, employer identification number, and the taxable year of each component member of the controlled group, a copy of the allocation agreement signed by persons duly authorized to act on behalf of the component members, and a description of the manner in which the deduction under section 179 has been divided among the component members.

(iii) *Revocation.*—If a consolidated return is filed for all component members of the group, an allocation among such members of the expense deduction under section 179 may not be revoked after the due date of the return (including extensions of time) of the common parent corporation for the taxable year for which an election to take an expense deduction is made. If some or all of the component members of the controlled group file separate returns for taxable years including a particular December 31 for which an election to take the expense deduction is made, the allocation as to all members of the group may not be revoked after the due date of the return (including extensions of time) of the component member of the controlled group whose taxable year that includes such December 31 ends on the latest date.

(c) *Taxable income limitation.*—(1) *In general.*—The aggregate cost of section 179 property elected to be expensed under section 179 that may be deducted for any taxable year may not exceed the aggregate amount of taxable income of the taxpayer for such taxable year that is derived from the active conduct by the taxpayer of any trade or business during the taxable year. For purposes of section 179(b)(3) and this paragraph (c), the aggregate amount of taxable income derived from the active conduct by an individual, a partnership, or an S corporation of any trade or business is computed by aggregating the net income (or loss) from all of the trades or businesses actively conducted by the individual, partnership, or S corporation during the taxable year. Items of income that are derived from the active conduct of a trade or business include section 1231 gains (or losses) from the trade or business and interest from working capital of the trade or business. Taxable income derived from the active conduct of a trade or business is computed without regard to the deduction allowable under section 179, any section 164(f) deduction, any net operating loss carryback or carryforward, and deductions suspended under any section of the Code. See paragraph (c)(6) of this section for rules

»»→ Caution: Reg. § 1.179-2 does not reflect recent law changes. For details, see ¶ 578.01.

on determining whether a taxpayer is engaged in the active conduct of a trade or business for this purpose.

(2) *Application to partnerships and partners.*—(i) *In general.*—The taxable income limitation of this paragraph (c) applies to the partnership as well as to each partner. Thus, the partnership may not allocate to its partners as a section 179 expense deduction for any taxable year more than the partnership's taxable income limitation for that taxable year, and a partner may not deduct as a section 179 expense deduction for any taxable year more than the partner's taxable income limitation for that taxable year.

(ii) *Taxable year.*—If the taxable year of a partner and the partnership do not coincide, then for purposes of section 179, the amount of the partnership's taxable income attributable to a partner for a taxable year is determined under section 706 and the regulations thereunder (generally the partner's distributive share of partnership taxable income for the partnership year that ends with or within the partner's taxable year).

(iii) *Example.*—The following example illustrates the provisions of paragraph (c) (2) (ii) of this section.

Example. AB partnership has a taxable year ending January 31. A, a partner of AB, has a taxable year ending December 31. For AB's taxable year ending January 31, 1992, AB has taxable income from the active conduct of its trade or business of $100,000, $90,000 of which was earned during 1991. Under section 706 and § 1.706-1 (a) (1), A includes A's entire share of partnership taxable income in computing A's taxable income limitation for A's taxable year ending December 31, 1992.

(iv) *Taxable income of a partnership.*—The taxable income (or loss) derived from the active conduct by a partnership of any trade or business is computed by aggregating the net income (or loss) from all of the trades or businesses actively conducted by the partnership during the taxable year. The net income (or loss) from a trade or business actively conducted by the partnership is determined by taking into account the aggregate amount of the partnership's items described in section 702 (a) (other than credits, tax-exempt income, and guaranteed payments under section 707 (c)) derived from that trade or business. For purposes of determining the aggregate amount of partnership items, deductions and losses are treated as negative income. Any limitation on the amount of a partnership item described in section 702 (a) which may be taken into account for purposes of computing the taxable income of a partner shall be disregarded in computing the taxable income of the partnership.

(v) *Partner's share of partnership taxable income.*—A taxpayer who is a partner in a partnership and is engaged in the active conduct of at least one of the partnership's trades or businesses includes as taxable income derived from the active conduct of a trade or business the amount of the taxpayer's allocable share of taxable income derived from the active conduct by the partnership of any trade or business (as determined under paragraph (c) (2) (iv) of this section).

(3) *S corporations and S corporation shareholders.*—(i) *In general.*—Rules similar to those contained in paragraphs (c) (2) (i) and (ii) of this section apply in the case of S corporations (as defined in section 1361 (a)) and their shareholders. Each shareholder's share of the taxable income of an S corporation is determined under section 1366.

»»→ Caution: Reg. § 1.179-2 does not reflect recent law changes. For details, see ¶ 578.01.

(ii) *Taxable income of an S corporation.*—The taxable income (or loss) derived from the active conduct by an S corporation of any trade or business is computed by aggregating the net income (or loss) from all of the trades or businesses actively conducted by the S corporation during the taxable year. The net income (or loss) from a trade or business actively conducted by an S corporation is determined by taking into account the aggregate amount of the S corporation's items described in section 1366(a) (other than credits, tax-exempt income, and deductions for compensation paid to an S corporation's shareholder-employees) derived from that trade or business. For purposes of determining the aggregate amount of S corporation items, deductions and losses are treated as negative income. Any limitation on the amount of an S corporation item described in section 1366(a) which may be taken into account for purposes of computing the taxable income of a shareholder shall be disregarded in computing the taxable income of the S corporation.

(iii) *Shareholder's share of S corporation taxable income.*—Rules similar to those contained in paragraph (c)(2)(v) and (c)(6)(ii) of this section apply to a taxpayer who is a shareholder in an S corporation and is engaged in the active conduct of the S corporation's trades or businesses.

(4) *Taxable income of a corporation other than an S corporation.*—The aggregate amount of taxable income derived from the active conduct by a corporation other than an S corporation of any trade or business is the amount of the corporation's taxable income before deducting its net operating loss deduction and special deductions (as reported on the corporation's income tax return), adjusted to reflect those items of income or deduction included in that amount that were not derived by the corporation from a trade or business actively conducted by the corporation during the taxable year.

(5) *Ordering rule for certain circular problems.*—(i) *In general.*—A taxpayer who elects to expense the cost of section 179 property (the deduction of which is subject to the taxable income limitation) also may have to apply another Internal Revenue Code section that has a limitation based on the taxpayer's taxable income. Except as provided in paragraph (c)(1) of this section, this section provides rules for applying the taxable income limitation under section 179 in such a case. First, taxable income is computed for the other section of the Internal Revenue Code. In computing the taxable income of the taxpayer for the other section of the Internal Revenue Code, the taxpayer's section 179 deduction is computed by assuming that the taxpayer's taxable income is determined without regard to the deduction under the other Internal Revenue Code section. Next, after reducing taxable income by the amount of the section 179 deduction so computed, a hypothetical amount of deduction is determined for the other section of the Internal Revenue Code. The taxable income limitation of the taxpayer under section 179(b)(3) and this paragraph (c) then is computed by including that hypothetical amount in determining taxable income.

(ii) *Example.*—The following example illustrates the ordering rule described in paragraph (c)(5)(i) of this section.

Example. X, a calendar-year corporation, elects to expense $10,000 of the cost of section 179 property purchased and placed in service during 1991. Assume X's dollar limitation is $10,000. X also gives a charitable contribution of $5,000 during the taxable year. X's taxable income for purposes of both sections 179 and 170(b)(2), but without regard to any deduction allowable under either section 179 or section 170, is $11,000. In determining X's taxable income limitation under section 179(b)(3) and this paragraph (c), X must first compute its section 170

»»→ Caution: Reg. § 1.179-2 does not reflect recent law changes. For details, see ¶ 578.01.

deduction. However, section 170(b)(2) limits X's charitable contribution to 10 percent of its taxable income determined by taking into account its section 179 deduction. Paragraph (c)(5)(i) of this section provides that in determining X's section 179 deduction for 1991, X first computes a hypothetical section 170 deduction by assuming that its section 179 deduction is not affected by the section 170 deduction. Thus, in computing X's hypothetical section 170 deduction, X's taxable income limitation under section 179 is $11,000 and its section 179 deduction is $10,000. X's hypothetical section 170 deduction is $100 (10 percent of $1,000 ($11,000 less $10,000 section 179 deduction)). X's taxable income limitation for section 179 purposes is then computed by deducting the hypothetical charitable contribution of $100 for 1991. Thus, X's section 179 taxable income limitation is $10,900 ($11,000 less hypothetical $100 section 170 deduction), and its section 179 deduction for 1991 is $10,000. X's section 179 deduction so calculated applies for all purposes of the Code, including the computation of its actual section 170 deduction.

(6) *Active conduct by the taxpayer of a trade or business.*—(i) *Trade or business.*—For purposes of this section and § 1.179-4(a), the term "trade or business" has the same meaning as in section 162 and the regulations thereunder. Thus, property held merely for the production of income or used in an activity not engaged in for profit (as described in section 183) does not qualify as section 179 property and taxable income derived from property held for the production of income or from an activity not engaged in for profit is not taken into account in determining the taxable income limitation.

(ii) *Active conduct.*—For purposes of this section, the determination of whether a trade or business is actively conducted by the taxpayer is to be made from all the facts and circumstances and is to be applied in light of the purpose of the active conduct requirement of section 179(b)(3)(A). In the context of section 179, the purpose of the active conduct requirement is to prevent a passive investor in a trade or business from deducting section 179 expenses against taxable income derived from that trade or business. Consistent with this purpose, a taxpayer generally is considered to actively conduct a trade or business if the taxpayer meaningfully participates in the management or operations of the trade or business. Generally, a partner is considered to actively conduct a trade or business of the partnership if the partner meaningfully participates in the management or operations of the trade or business. A mere passive investor in a trade or business does not actively conduct the trade or business.

(iii) *Example.*—The following example illustrates the provisions of paragraph (c)(6)(ii) of this section.

Example. A owns a salon as a sole proprietorship and employs B to operate it. A periodically meets with B to review developments relating to the business. A also approves the salon's annual budget that is prepared by B. B performs all the necessary operating functions, including hiring beauticians, acquiring the necessary beauty supplies, and writing the checks to pay all bills and the beauticians' salaries. In 1991, B purchased, as provided for in the salon's annual budget, equipment costing $9,500 for use in the active conduct of the salon. There were no other purchases of section 179 property during 1991. A's net income from the salon, before any section 179 deduction, totaled $8,000. A also is a partner in PRS, a calendar-year partnership, which owns a grocery store. C, a partner in PRS, runs the grocery store for the partnership, making all the management and operating decisions. PRS did not purchase any section 179 property during 1991. A's allocable share of partnership net income was $6,000. Based on the facts and circumstances, A meaningfully participates in the management of the salon. However, A does not meaningfully participate in the management or operations of the trade or business of PRS. Under section 179(b)(3)(A) and this paragraph (c), A's aggregate taxable income derived from the active conduct by A of any trade or business is $8,000, the net income from the salon.

(iv) *Employees.*—For purposes of this section, employees are considered to be engaged in the active conduct of the trade or business of their employment. Thus, wages, salaries, tips, and other compensation (not reduced by unreimbursed employee business expenses) derived by a taxpayer as an employee are included in the aggregate amount of taxable income of the taxpayer under paragraph (c)(1) of this section.

(7) *Joint returns.*—(i) *In general.*—The taxable income limitation of this paragraph (c) is applied to a husband and wife who file a joint income tax return under section 6013(a) by aggregating the taxable income of each spouse (as determined under paragraph (c)(1) of this section).

(ii) *Joint returns filed after separate returns.*—In the case of a husband and wife who elect under section 6013(b) to file a joint income tax return for a taxable year after the time prescribed by law for filing the return for such taxable year, the taxable income limitation of this paragraph (c) for the taxable year for which the joint return is filed is determined under paragraph (c)(7)(i) of this section.

(8) *Married individuals filing separately.*—In the case of an individual who is married but files a separate tax return for a taxable year, the taxable income limitation for that individual is determined under paragraph (c)(1) of this section by treating the husband and wife as separate taxpayers.

(d) *Examples.*—The following examples illustrate the provisions of paragraphs (b) and (c) of this section.

Example 1. (i) During 1991, PRS, a calendar-year partnership, purchases and places in service $50,000 of section 179 property. The taxable income of PRS derived from the active conduct of all its trades or businesses (as determined under paragraph (c)(1) of this section) is $8,000.

(ii) Under the dollar limitation of paragraph (b) of this section, PRS may elect to expense $10,000 of the cost of section 179 property purchased in 1991. Assume PRS elects under section 179(c) and § 1.179-5 to expense $10,000 of the cost of section 179 property purchased in 1991.

(iii) Under the taxable income limitation of paragraph (c) of this section, PRS may allocate to its partners as a deduction only $8,000 of the cost of section 179 property in 1991. Under section 179(b)(3)(B) and § 1.179-3(a), PRS may carry forward the remaining $2,000 it elected to expense, which would have been deductible under section 179(a) for 1991 absent the taxable income limitation.

Example 2. (i) The facts are the same as in *Example 1*, except that on December 31, 1991, PRS allocates to A, a calendar-year taxpayer and a partner in PRS, $7,000 of section 179 expenses and $2,000 of taxable income. A was engaged in the active conduct of a trade or business of PRS during 1991.

(ii) In addition to being a partner in PRS, A conducts a business as a sole proprietor. During 1991, A purchases and places in service $201,000 of section 179 property in connection with the sole proprietorship. A's 1991 taxable income derived from the active conduct of this business is $6,000.

(iii) Under the dollar limitation, A may elect to expense only $9,000 of the cost of section 179 property purchased in 1991, the $10,000 limit reduced by $1,000 (the amount by which the cost of section 179 property placed in service during 1991 ($201,000) exceeds $200,000). Under paragraph (b)(3)(i) of this section, the $7,000

»»→ ***Caution: Reg. § 1.179-2 does not reflect recent law changes. For details, see ¶ 578.01.***

of section 179 expenses allocated from PRS is subject to the $9,000 limit. Assume that A elects to expense $2,000 of the cost of section 179 property purchased by A's sole proprietorship in 1991. Thus, A has elected to expense under section 179 an amount equal to the dollar limitation for 1991 ($2,000 elected to be expensed by A's sole proprietorship plus $7,000, the amount of PRS's section 179 expenses allocated to A in 1991).

(iv) Under the taxable income limitation, A may only deduct $8,000 of the cost of section 179 property elected to be expensed in 1991, the aggregate taxable income derived from the active conduct of A's trades or businesses in 1991 ($2,000 from PRS and $6,000 from A's sole proprietorship). The entire $2,000 of taxable income allocated from PRS is included by A as taxable income derived from the active conduct by A of a trade or business because it was derived from the active conduct of a trade or business by PRS and A was engaged in the active conduct of a trade or business of PRS during 1991. Under section 179(b)(3)(B) and § 1.179-3(a), A may carry forward the remaining $1,000 A elected to expense, which would have been deductible under section 179(a) for 1991 absent the taxable income limitation. [Reg. § 1.179-2.]

.01 Historical Comment: Proposed 9/26/85. Adopted 1/5/87 by T.D. 8121. Amended 12/23/92 by T.D. 8455, 8/3/2004 by T.D. 9146 and 7/12/2005 by T.D. 9209. [Reg. § 1.179-2 does not reflect P.L. 109-222 (2006) and P.L.110-28 (2007). See ¶ 12,120.031 and ¶ 12,120.03.]

¶ 579

Reg. § 1.179-3

§ 1.179-3. **Carryover of disallowed deduction.**—(a) *In general.*—Under section 179(b)(3)(B), a taxpayer may carry forward for an unlimited number of years the amount of any cost of section 179 property elected to be expensed in a taxable year but disallowed as a deduction in that taxable year because of the taxable income limitation of section 179(b)(3)(A) and § 1.179-2(c) ("carryover of disallowed deduction"). This carryover of disallowed deduction may be deducted under section 179(a) and § 1.179-1(a) in a future taxable year as provided in paragraph (b) of this section.

(b) *Deduction of carryover of disallowed deduction.*—(1) *In general.*—The amount allowable as a deduction under section 179(a) and § 1.179-1(a) for any taxable year is increased by the lesser of—

(i) The aggregate amount disallowed under section 179(b)(3)(A) and § 1.179-2(c) for all prior taxable years (to the extent not previously allowed as a deduction by reason of this section); or

(ii) The amount of any unused section 179 expense allowance for the taxable year (as described in paragraph (c) of this section).

(2) *Cross references.*—See paragraph (f) of this section for rules that apply when a taxpayer disposes of or otherwise transfers section 179 property for which a carryover of disallowed deduction is outstanding. See paragraph (g) of this section for special rules that apply to partnerships and S corporations and paragraph (h) of this section for special rules that apply to partners and S corporation shareholders.

(c) *Unused section 179 expense allowance.*—The amount of any unused section 179 expense allowance for a taxable year equals the excess (if any) of—

(1) The maximum cost of section 179 property that the taxpayer may deduct under section 179 and § 1.179-1 for the taxable year after applying the limitations of section 179(b) and § 1.179-2; over

(2) The amount of section 179 property that the taxpayer actually elected to expense under section 179 and § 1.179-1(a) for the taxable year.

(d) *Example.*—The following example illustrates the provisions of paragraphs (b) and (c) of this section.

Example. A, a calendar-year taxpayer, has a $3,000 carryover of disallowed deduction for an item of section 179 property purchased and placed in service in 1991. In 1992, A purchases and places in service an item of section 179 property costing $25,000. A's 1992 taxable income from the active conduct of all A's trades or businesses is $100,000. A elects, under section 179(c) and § 1.179-5, to expense $8,000 of the cost of the item of section 179 property purchased in 1992. Under paragraph (b) of this section, A may deduct $2,000 of A's carryover of disallowed deduction from 1991 (the lesser of A's total outstanding carryover of disallowed deductions ($3,000), or the amount of any unused section 179 expense allowance for 1992 ($10,000 limit less $8,000 elected to be expensed, or $2,000)). For 1993, A has a $1,000 carryover of disallowed deduction for the item of section 179 property purchased and placed in service in 1991.

(e) *Recordkeeping requirement and ordering rule.*—The properties and the apportionment of cost that will be subject to a carryover of disallowed deduction are selected by the taxpayer in the year the properties are placed in service. This selection must be evidenced on the taxpayer's books and records and be applied consistently in subsequent years. If no selection is made, the total carryover of disallowed deduction is apportioned equally over the items of section 179 property elected to be expensed for the taxable year. For this purpose, the taxpayer treats any section 179 expense amount allocated from a partnership (or an S corporation) for a taxable year as one item of section 179 property. If the taxpayer is allowed to deduct a portion of the total carryover of disallowed deduction under paragraph (b) of this section, the taxpayer must deduct the cost of section 179 property carried forward from the earliest taxable year.

(f) *Dispositions and other transfers of section 179 property.*—(1) *In general.*—Upon a sale or other disposition of section 179 property, or a transfer of section 179 property in a transaction in which gain or loss is not recognized in whole or in part (including transfers at death), immediately before the transfer the adjusted basis of the section 179 property is increased by the amount of any outstanding carryover of disallowed deduction with respect to the property. This carryover of disallowed deduction is not available as a deduction to the transferor or the transferee of the section 179 property.

(2) *Recapture under section 179(d)(10).*—Under § 1.179-1(e), if a taxpayer's section 179 property is subject to recapture under section 179(d)(10), the taxpayer must recapture the benefit derived from expensing the property. Upon recapture, any outstanding carryover of disallowed deduction with respect to the property is no longer available for expensing. In determining the amount subject to recapture under section 179(d)(10) and § 1.179-1(e), any outstanding carryover of disallowed deduction with respect to that property is not treated as an amount expensed under section 179.

(g) *Special rules for partnerships and S corporations.*—(1) *In general.*—Under section 179(d)(8) and § 1.179-2(c), the taxable income limitation applies at the partnership level as well as at the partner level. Therefore, a partnership may have a carryover of disallowed deduction with respect to the cost of its section 179 property. Similar rules apply to S corporations. This paragraph (g) provides special rules that apply when a partnership or an S corporation has a carryover of disallowed deduction.

(2) *Basis adjustment.*—Under § 1.179-1(f)(2), the basis of a partnership's section 179 property must be reduced to reflect the amount of section 179 expense elected by the partnership. This reduction must be made for the taxable year for which the election is made even if the section 179 expense amount, or a portion

thereof, must be carried forward by the partnership. Similar rules apply to S corporations.

(3) *Dispositions and other transfers of section 179 property by a partnership or an S corporation.*—The provisions of paragraph (f) of this section apply in determining the treatment of any outstanding carryover of disallowed deduction with respect to section 179 property disposed of, or transferred in a nonrecognition transaction, by a partnership or an S corporation.

(4) *Example.*—The following example illustrates the provisions of this paragraph (g).

Example. ABC, a calendar-year partnership, owns and operates a restaurant business. During 1992, ABC purchases and places in service two items of section 179 property—a cash register costing $4,000 and office furniture costing $6,000. ABC elects to expense under section 179(c) the full cost of the cash register and the office furniture. For 1992, ABC has $6,000 of taxable income derived from the active conduct of its restaurant business. Therefore, ABC may deduct only $6,000 of section 179 expenses and must carry forward the remaining $4,000 of section 179 expenses at the partnership level. ABC must reduce the adjusted basis of the section 179 property by the full amount elected to be expensed. However, ABC may not allocate to its partners any portion of the carryover of disallowed deduction until ABC is able to deduct it under paragraph (b) of this section.

(h) *Special rules for partners and S corporation shareholders.*—(1) *In general.*—Under section 179(d)(8) and § 1.179-2(c), a partner may have a carryover of disallowed deduction with respect to the cost of section 179 property elected to be expensed by the partnership and allocated to the partner. A partner who is allocated section 179 expenses from a partnership must reduce the basis of his or her partnership interest by the full amount allocated regardless of whether the partner may deduct for the taxable year the allocated section 179 expenses or is required to carry forward all or a portion of the expenses. Similar rules apply to S corporation shareholders.

(2) *Dispositions and other transfers of a partner's interest in a partnership or a shareholder's interest in an S corporation.*—A partner who disposes of a partnership interest, or transfers a partnership interest in a transaction in which gain or loss is not recognized in whole or in part (including transfers of a partnership interest at death), may have an outstanding carryover of disallowed deduction of section 179 expenses allocated from the partnership. In such a case, immediately before the transfer the partner's basis in the partnership interest is increased by the amount of the partner's outstanding carryover of disallowed deduction with respect to the partnership interest. This carryover of disallowed deduction is not available as a deduction to the transferor or transferee partner of the section 179 property. Similar rules apply to S corporation shareholders.

(3) *Examples.*—The following examples illustrate the provisions of this paragraph (h).

Example 1. (i) G is a general partner in GD, a calendar-year partnership, and is engaged in the active conduct of GD's business. During 1991, GD purchases and places section 179 property in service and elects to expense a portion of the cost of the property under section 179. GD allocates $2,500 of section 179 expenses and $15,000 of taxable income (determined without regard to the section 179 deduction) to G. The income was derived from the active conduct by GD of a trade or business.

(ii) In addition to being a partner in GD, G conducts a business as a sole proprietor. During 1991, G purchases and places in service office equipment costing $25,000 and a computer costing $10,000 in connection with the sole proprietorship. G elects under section 179(c) and § 1.179-5 to expense $7,500 of the cost of the office equipment. G has a taxable loss (determined without regard to the section 179 deduction) derived from the active conduct of this business of $12,500.

(iii) G has no other taxable income (or loss) derived from the active conduct of a trade or business during 1991. G's taxable income limitation for 1991 is $2,500 ($15,000 taxable income allocated from GD less $12,500 taxable loss from the sole proprietorship). Therefore, G may deduct during 1991 only $2,500 of the $10,000 of section 179 expenses. G notes on the appropriate books and records that G expenses the $2,500 of section 179 expenses allocated from GD and carries forward the $7,500 of section 179 expenses with respect to the office equipment purchased by G's sole proprietorship.

(iv) On January 1, 1992, G sells the office equipment G's sole proprietorship purchased and placed in service in 1991. Under paragraph (f) of this section, immediately before the sale G increases the adjusted basis of the office equipment by $7,500, the amount of the outstanding carryover of disallowed deduction with respect to the office equipment.

Example 2. (i) Assume the same facts as in *Example 1*, except that G notes on the appropriate books and records that G expenses $2,500 of section 179 expenses relating to G's sole proprietorship and carries forward the remaining $5,000 of section 179 expenses relating to G's sole proprietorship and $2,500 of section 179 expenses allocated from GD.

(ii) On January 1, 1992, G sells G's partnership interest to A. Under paragraph (h)(2) of this section, immediately before the sale G increases the adjusted basis of G's partnership interest by $2,500, the amount of the outstanding carryover of disallowed deduction with respect to the partnership interest. [Reg. § 1.179-3.]

.01 Historical Comment: Adopted 12/23/92 by T.D. 8455.

¶ 580

Reg. § 1.179-4

»»→ Caution: Reg. § 1.179-4 does not reflect recent law changes. For details, see ¶ 580.01.

§ 1.179-4. **Definitions.**—The following definitions apply for purposes of section 179 and § § 1.179-1 through 1.179-6:

(a) *Section 179 property.*—The term *section 179 property* means any tangible property described in section 179(d)(1) that is acquired by purchase for use in the active conduct of the taxpayer's trade or business (as described in § 1.179-2(c)(6)). For taxable years beginning after 2002 and before 2008, the term *section 179 property* includes computer software described in section 179(d)(1) that is placed in service by the taxpayer in a taxable year beginning after 2002 and before 2008 and is acquired by purchase for use in the active conduct of the taxpayer's trade or business (as described in § 1.179-2(c)(6)). For purposes of this paragraph (a), the term *trade or business* has the same meaning as in section 162 and the regulations under section 162.

(b) *Section 38 property.*—The term "section 38 property" shall have the same meaning assigned to it in section 48(a) and the regulations thereunder.

(c) *Purchase.*—(1)(i) Except as otherwise provided in paragraph (d)(2) of this section, the term "purchase" means any acquisition of the property, but only if all the requirements of paragraphs (d)(1)(ii), (iii), and (iv) of this section are satisfied.

(ii) Property is not acquired by purchase if it is acquired from a person whose relationship to the person acquiring it would result in the disallowance of losses under section 267 or 707(b). The property is considered not acquired

»»→ Caution: Reg. § 1.179-4 does not reflect recent law changes. For details, see ¶ 580.01.

by purchase only to the extent that losses would be disallowed under section 267 or 707(b). Thus, for example, if property is purchased by a husband and wife jointly from the husband's father, the property will be treated as not acquired by purchase only to the extent of the husband's interest in the property. However, in applying the rules of section 267(b) and (c) for this purpose, section 267(c)(4) shall be treated as providing that the family of an individual will include only his spouse, ancestors, and lineal descendants. For example, a purchase of property from a corporation by a taxpayer who owns, directly or indirectly, more than 50 percent in value of the outstanding stock of such corporation does not qualify as a purchase under section 179(d)(2); nor does the purchase of property by a husband from his wife. However, the purchase of section 179 property by a taxpayer from his brother or sister does qualify as a purchase for purposes of section 179(d)(2).

(iii) The property is not acquired by purchase if acquired from a component member of a controlled group of corporations (as defined in paragraph (g) of this section) by another component member of the same group.

(iv) The property is not acquired by purchase if the basis of the property in the hands of the person acquiring it is determined in whole or in part by reference to the adjusted basis of such property in the hands of the person from whom acquired, or is determined under section 1014(a), relating to property acquired from a decedent. For example, property acquired by gift or bequest does not qualify as property acquired by purchase for purposes of section 179(d)(2); nor does property received in a corporate distribution the basis of which is determined under section 301(d)(2)(B), property acquired by a corporation in a transaction to which section 351 applies, property acquired by a partnership through contribution (section 723), or property received in a partnership distribution which has a carryover basis under section 732(a)(1).

(2) Property deemed to have been acquired by a new target corporation as a result of a section 338 election (relating to certain stock purchases treated as asset acquisitions) will be considered acquired by purchase.

(d) *Cost.*—The cost of section 179 property does not include so much of the basis of such property as is determined by reference to the basis of other property held at any time by the taxpayer. For example, X Corporation purchases a new drill press costing $10,000 in November 1984 which qualifies as section 179 property, and is granted a trade-in allowance of $2,000 on its old drill press. The old drill press had a basis of $1,200. Under the provisions of sections 1012 and 1031(d), the basis of the new drill press is $9,200 ($1,200 basis of old drill press plus cash expended of $8,000). However, only $8,000 of the basis of the new drill press qualifies as cost for purposes of the section 179 expense deduction; the remaining $1,200 is not part of the cost because it is determined by reference to the basis of the old drill press.

(e) *Placed in service.*—The term "placed in service" means the time that property is first placed by the taxpayer in a condition or state of readiness and availability for a specifically assigned function, whether for use in a trade or business, for the production of income, in a tax-exempt activity, or in a personal activity. See § 1.46-3(d)(2) for examples regarding when property shall be considered in a condition or state of readiness and availability for a specifically assigned function.

(f) *Controlled group of corporations and component member of controlled group.*—The terms "controlled group of corporations" and "component member" of a controlled group of corporations shall have the same meaning assigned to those terms in section 1563(a) and (b), except that the phrase "more than 50 percent"

»»→ Caution: Reg. § 1.179-4 does not reflect recent law changes. For details, see ¶ 580.01.

shall be substituted for the phrase "at least 80 percent" each place it appears in section 1563(a)(1). [Reg. § 1.179-4.]

.01 Historical Comment: Proposed 9/26/85. Adopted 1/5/87 by T.D. 8121. Amended 12/23/92 by T.D. 8455, 8/3/2004 by T.D. 9146 and 7/12/2005 by T.D. 9209. [Reg. § 1.179-4 does not reflect P.L. 109-222 (2006) and P.L.110-28 (2007). See ¶ 12,120.031 and ¶ 12,120.03.]

¶ 581

Reg. § 1.179-5

»»→ Caution: Reg. § 1.179-5 does not reflect recent law changes. For details, see ¶ 581.01.

§ 1.179-5. **Time and manner of making election.**—(a) *Election.*—A separate election must be made for each taxable year in which a section 179 expense deduction is claimed with respect to section 179 property. The election under section 179 and § 1.179-1 to claim a section 179 expense deduction for section 179 property shall be made on the taxpayer's first income tax return for the taxable year to which the election applies (whether or not the return is timely) or on an amended return filed within the time prescribed by law (including extensions) for filing the return for such taxable year. The election shall be made by showing as a separate item on the taxpayer's income tax return the following items:

(1) The total section 179 expense deduction claimed with respect to all section 179 property selected; and

(2) The portion of that deduction allocable to each specific item.

The person shall maintain records which permit specific identification of each piece of section 179 property and reflect how and from whom such property was acquired and when such property was placed in service. However, for this purpose a partner (or an S corporation shareholder) treats partnership (or S corporation) section 179 property for which section 179 expenses are allocated from a partnership (or an S corporation) as one item of section 179 property. The election to claim a section 179 expense deduction under this section, with respect to any property, is irrevocable and will be binding on the taxpayer with respect to such property for the taxable year for which the election is made and for all subsequent taxable years, unless the Commissioner consents to the revocation of the election. Similarly, the selection of section 179 property by the taxpayer to be subject to the expense deduction and apportionment scheme must be adhered to in computing the taxpayer's taxable income for the taxable year for which the election is made and for all subsequent taxable years, unless consent to change is given by the Commissioner.

(b) *Revocation.*—Any election made under section 179, and any specification contained in such election, may not be revoked except with the consent of the Commissioner. Such consent will be granted only in extraordinary circumstances. Requests for consent must be filed with the Commissioner of Internal Revenue, Washington, D.C., 20224. The request must include the name, address, and taxpayer identification number of the taxpayer and must be signed by the taxpayer or his duly authorized representative. It must be accompanied by a statement showing the year and property involved, and must set forth in detail the reasons for the request.

(c) *Section 179 property placed in service by the taxpayer in a taxable year beginning after 2002 and before 2008.*—(1) *In general.*—For any taxable year beginning after 2002 and before 2008, a taxpayer is permitted to make or revoke an election under section 179 without the consent of the Commissioner on an amended Federal tax return for that taxable year. This amended return must be

»»→ Caution: Reg. § 1.179-5 does not reflect recent law changes. For details, see ¶ 581.01.

filed within the time prescribed by law for filing an amended return for such taxable year.

(2) *Election.*—(i) *In general.*—For any taxable year beginning after 2002 and before 2008, a taxpayer is permitted to make an election under section 179 on an amended Federal tax return for that taxable year without the consent of the Commissioner. Thus, the election under section 179 and § 1.179-1 to claim a section 179 expense deduction for section 179 property may be made on an amended Federal tax return for the taxable year to which the election applies. The amended Federal tax return must include the adjustment to taxable income for the section 179 election and any collateral adjustments to taxable income or to the tax liability (for example, the amount of depreciation allowed or allowable in that taxable year for the item of section 179 property to which the election pertains). Such adjustments must also be made on amended Federal tax returns for any affected succeeding taxable years.

(ii) *Specifications of elections.*—Any election under section 179 must specify the items of section 179 property and the portion of the cost of each such item to be taken into account under section 179(a). Any election under section 179 must comply with the specification requirements of section 179(c)(1)(A), § 1.179-1(b), and § 1.179-5(a). If a taxpayer elects to expense only a portion of the cost basis of an item of section 179 property for a taxable year beginning after 2002 and before 2008 (or did not elect to expense any portion of the cost basis of the item of section 179 property), the taxpayer is permitted to file an amended Federal tax return for that particular taxable year and increase the portion of the cost of the item of section 179 property to be taken into account under section 179(a) (or elect to expense any portion of the cost basis of the item of section 179 property if no prior election was made) without the consent of the Commissioner. Any such increase in the amount expensed under section 179 is not deemed to be a revocation of the prior election for that particular taxable year.

(3) *Revocation.*—(i) *In general.*—Section 179(c)(2) permits the revocation of an entire election or specification, or a portion of the selected dollar amount of a specification. The term *specification* in section 179(c)(2) refers to both the selected specific item of section 179 property subject to a section 179 election and the selected dollar amount allocable to the specific item of section 179 property. Any portion of the cost basis of an item of section 179 property subject to an election under section 179 for a taxable year beginning after 2002 and before 2008 may be revoked by the taxpayer without the consent of the Commissioner by filing an amended Federal tax return for that particular taxable year. The amended Federal tax return must include the adjustment to taxable income for the section 179 revocation and any collateral adjustments to taxable income or to the tax liability (for example, allowable depreciation in that taxable year for the item of section 179 property to which the revocation pertains). Such adjustments must also be made on amended Federal tax returns for any affected succeeding taxable years. Reducing or eliminating a specified dollar amount for any item of section 179 property with respect to any taxable year beginning after 2002 and before 2008 results in a revocation of that specified dollar amount.

(ii) *Effect of revocation.*—Such revocation, once made, shall be irrevocable. If the selected dollar amount reflects the entire cost of the item of section 179 property subject to the section 179 election, a revocation of the entire selected dollar amount is treated as a revocation of the section 179 election for that item of section 179 property and the taxpayer is unable to make a new section 179 election with respect to that item of property. If the selected dollar amount is a portion of the

»»→ *Caution: Reg. § 1.179-5 does not reflect recent law changes. For details, see ¶ 581.01.*

cost of the item of section 179 property, revocation of a selected dollar amount shall be treated as a revocation of only that selected dollar amount. The revoked dollars cannot be the subject of a new section 179 election for the same item of property.

(4) *Examples*.—The following examples illustrate the rules of this paragraph (c):

Example 1. Taxpayer, a sole proprietor, owns and operates a jewelry store. During 2003, Taxpayer purchased and placed in service two items of section 179 property — a cash register costing $4,000 (5-year MACRS property) and office furniture costing $10,000 (7-year MACRS property). On his 2003 Federal tax return filed on April 15, 2004, Taxpayer elected to expense under section 179 the full cost of the cash register and, with respect to the office furniture, claimed the depreciation allowable. In November 2004, Taxpayer determines it would have been more advantageous to have made an election under section 179 to expense the full cost of the office furniture rather than the cash register. Pursuant to paragraph (c)(1) of this section, Taxpayer is permitted to file an amended Federal tax return for 2003 revoking the section 179 election for the cash register, claiming the depreciation allowable in 2003 for the cash register, and making an election to expense under section 179 the cost of the office furniture. The amended return must include an adjustment for the depreciation previously claimed in 2003 for the office furniture, an adjustment for the depreciation allowable in 2003 for the cash register, and any other collateral adjustments to taxable income or to the tax liability. In addition, once Taxpayer revokes the section 179 election for the entire cost basis of the cash register, Taxpayer can no longer expense under section 179 any portion of the cost of the cash register.

Example 2. Taxpayer, a sole proprietor, owns and operates a machine shop that does specialized repair work on industrial equipment. During 2003, Taxpayer purchased and placed in service one item of section 179 property — a milling machine costing $135,000. On Taxpayer's 2003 Federal tax return filed on April 15, 2004, Taxpayer elected to expense under section 179 $5,000 of the cost of the milling machine and claimed allowable depreciation on the remaining cost. Subsequently, Taxpayer determines it would have been to Taxpayer's advantage to have elected to expense $100,000 of the cost of the milling machine on Taxpayer's 2003 Federal tax return. In November 2004, Taxpayer files an amended Federal tax return for 2003, increasing the amount of the cost of the milling machine that is to be taken into account under section 179(a) to $100,000, decreasing the depreciation allowable in 2003 for the milling machine, and making any other collateral adjustments to taxable income or to the tax liability. Pursuant to paragraph (c)(2)(ii) of this section, increasing the amount of the cost of the milling machine to be taken into account under section 179(a) supplements the portion of the cost of the milling machine that was already taken into account by the original section 179 election made on the 2003 Federal tax return and no revocation of any specification with respect to the milling machine has occurred.

Example 3. Taxpayer, a sole proprietor, owns and operates a real estate brokerage business located in a rented storefront office. During 2003, Taxpayer purchases and places in service two items of section 179 property — a laptop computer costing $2,500 and a desktop computer costing $1,500. On Taxpayer's 2003 Federal tax return filed on April 15, 2004, Taxpayer elected to expense under section 179 the full cost of the laptop computer and the full cost of the desktop computer. Subsequently, Taxpayer determines it would have been to Taxpayer's advantage to have originally elected to expense under section 179 only $1,500 of the cost of the laptop computer on Taxpayer's 2003 Federal tax return. In November 2004, Taxpayer files an amended Federal tax return for 2003 reducing the amount of the cost of the laptop computer that was taken into account under section 179(a)

»»→ Caution: Reg. § 1.179-5 does not reflect recent law changes. For details, see ¶ 581.01.

to $1,500, claiming the depreciation allowable in 2003 on the remaining cost of $1,000 for that item, and making any other collateral adjustments to taxable income or to the tax liability. Pursuant to paragraph (c)(3)(ii) of this section, the $1,000 reduction represents a revocation of a portion of the selected dollar amount and no portion of those revoked dollars may be the subject of a new section 179 election for the laptop computer.

Example 4. Taxpayer, a sole proprietor, owns and operates a furniture making business. During 2003, Taxpayer purchases and places in service one item of section 179 property — an industrial-grade cabinet table saw costing $5,000. On Taxpayer's 2003 Federal tax return filed on April 15, 2004, Taxpayer elected to expense under section 179 $3,000 of the cost of the saw and, with respect to the remaining $2,000 of the cost of the saw, claimed the depreciation allowable. In November 2004, Taxpayer files an amended Federal tax return for 2003 revoking the selected $3,000 amount for the saw, claiming the depreciation allowable in 2003 on the $3,000 cost of the saw, and making any other collateral adjustments to taxable income or to the tax liability. Subsequently, in December 2004, Taxpayer files a second amended Federal tax return for 2003 selecting a new dollar amount of $2,000 for the saw, including an adjustment for the depreciation previously claimed in 2003 on the $2,000, and making any other collateral adjustments to taxable income or to the tax liability. Pursuant to paragraph (c)(2)(ii) of this section, Taxpayer is permitted to select a new selected dollar amount to expense under section 179 encompassing all or a part of the initially non-elected portion of the cost of the elected item of section 179 property. However, no portion of the revoked $3,000 may be the subject of a new section 179 dollar amount selection for the saw. In December 2005, Taxpayer files a third amended Federal tax return for 2003 revoking the entire selected $2,000 amount with respect to the saw, claiming the depreciation allowable in 2003 for the $2,000, and making any other collateral adjustments to taxable income or to the tax liability. Because Taxpayer elected to expense, and subsequently revoke, the entire cost basis of the saw, the section 179 election for the saw has been revoked and Taxpayer is unable to make a new section 179 election with respect to the saw.

(d) *Election or revocation must not be made in any other manner.*—Any election or revocation specified in this section must be made in the manner prescribed in paragraphs (a), (b), and (c) of this section. Thus, this election or revocation must not be made by the taxpayer in any other manner (for example, an election or a revocation of an election cannot be made through a request under section 446(e) to change the taxpayer's method of accounting), except as otherwise expressly provided by the Internal Revenue Code, the regulations under the Code, or other guidance published in the Internal Revenue Bulletin. [Reg. § 1.179-5.]

.01 Historical Comment: Proposed 9/26/85. Adopted 1/5/87 by T.D. 8121. Amended 12/23/92 by T.D. 8455, 8/3/2004 by T.D. 9146 and 7/12/2005 by T.D. 9209. [Reg. § 1.179-5 does not reflect P.L. 109-222 (2006) and P.L.110-28 (2007). See ¶ 12,120.031 and ¶ 12,120.03.]

¶ 582

Reg. § 1.179-6

»»→ Caution: Reg. § 1.179-6 does not reflect recent law changes. For details, see¶ 582.01.

§ 1.179-6. **Effective dates.**—(a) *In general.*—Except as provided in paragraphs (b) and (c) of this section, the provisions of §§ 1.179-1 through 1.179-5 apply for property placed in service by the taxpayer in taxable years ending after January 25, 1993. However, a taxpayer may apply the provisions of §§ 1.179-1 through 1.179-5 to property placed in service by the taxpayer after December 31,

»»→ Caution: Reg. § 1.179-6 does not reflect recent law changes. For details, see¶ 582.01.

1986, in taxable years ending on or before January 25, 1993. Otherwise, for property placed in service by the taxpayer after December 31, 1986, in taxable years ending on or before January 25, 1993, the final regulations under section 179 as in effect for the year the property was placed in service apply, except to the extent modified by the changes made to section 179 by the Tax Reform Act of 1986 (100 Stat. 2085), the Technical and Miscellaneous Revenue Act of 1988 (102 Stat. 3342) and the Revenue Reconciliation Act of 1990 (104 Stat. 1388-400). For that property, a taxpayer may apply any reasonable method that clearly reflects income in applying the changes to section 179, provided the taxpayer consistently applies the method to the property.

(b) *Section 179 property placed in service by the taxpayer in a taxable year beginning after 2002 and before 2008.*—The provisions of § 1.179-2(b)(1) and (b)(2)(ii), the second sentence of § 1.179-4(a), and the provisions of § 1.179-5(c), reflecting changes made to section 179 by the Jobs and Growth Tax Relief Reconciliation Act of 2003 (117 Stat. 752) and the American Jobs Creation Act of 2004 (118 Stat. 1418), apply for property placed in service in taxable years beginning after 2002 and before 2008.

(c) *Application of § 1.179-5(d).*—Section 1.179-5(d) applies on or after July 12, 2005. [Reg. § 1.179-6.]

.01 Historical Comment: Adopted 8/3/2004 by T.D. 9146. Amended and redesignated 7/12/2005 by T.D. 9209. [Reg. § 1.179-6 does not reflect P.L. 109-222 (2006) and P.L.110-28 (2007). See ¶ 12,120.031 and ¶ 12,120.03.]

Code Sec. 197 Intangible Regulations

¶ 585

Reg. § 1.197-0

§ 1.197-0. **Table of contents.**—This section lists the headings that appear in § 1.197-2.

(2) Exception for self-created intangibles.
(i) In general.
(ii) Created by the taxpayer.
(A) Defined.
(B) Contracts for the use of intangibles.
(C) Improvements and modifications.
(iii) Exceptions.
(3) Exception for property subject to anti-churning rules.
(e) Purchase of a trade or business.
(1) Goodwill or going concern value.
(2) Franchise, trademark, or trade name.
(i) In general.
(ii) Exceptions.
(3) Acquisitions to be included.
(4) Substantial portion.
(5) Deemed asset purchases under section 338.
(6) Mortgage servicing rights.
(7) Computer software acquired for internal use.
(f) Computation of amortization deduction.
(1) In general.
(2) Treatment of contingent amounts.
(i) Amounts added to basis during 15-year period.
(ii) Amounts becoming fixed after expiration of 15-year period.
(iii) Rules for including amounts in basis.
(3) Basis determinations for certain assets.
(i) Covenants not to compete.
(ii) Contracts for the use of section 197 intangibles; acquired as part of a trade or business.
(A) In general.
(B) Know-how and certain information base.
(iii) Contracts for the use of section 197 intangibles; not acquired as part of a trade or business.
(iv) Applicable rules.
(A) Franchises, trademarks, and trade names.
(B) Certain amounts treated as payable under a debt instrument.
(1) In general.
(2) Rights granted by governmental units.
(3) Treatment of other parties to transaction.
(4) Basis determinations in certain transactions.
(i) Certain renewal transactions.
(ii) Transactions subject to section 338 or 1060.
(iii) Certain reinsurance transactions.
(g) Special rules.
(1) Treatment of certain dispositions.
(i) Loss disallowance rules.
(A) In general.
(B) Abandonment or worthlessness.
(C) Certain nonrecognition transfers.
(ii) Separately acquired property.
(iii) Disposition of a covenant not to compete.

(iv) Taxpayers under common control.

(A) In general.

(B) Treatment of disallowed loss.

(2) Treatment of certain nonrecognition and exchange transactions.

(i) Relationship to anti-churning rules.

(ii) Treatment of nonrecognition and exchange transactions generally.

(A) Transfer disregarded.

(B) Application of general rule.

(C) Transactions covered.

(iii) Certain exchanged-basis property.

(iv) Transfers under section 708(b)(1).

(A) In general.

(B) Termination by sale or exchange of interest.

(C) Other terminations.

(3) Increase in the basis of partnership property under section 732(b), 734(b), 743(b), or 732(d).

(4) Section 704(c) allocations.

(i) Allocations where the intangible is amortizable by the contributor.

(ii) Allocations where the intangible is not amortizable by the contributor.

(5) Treatment of certain insurance contracts acquired in an assumption reinsurance transaction.

(i) In general.

(ii) Determination of adjusted basis of amortizable section 197 intangible resulting from an assumption reinsurance transaction.

(A) In general.

(B) Amount paid or incurred by acquirer (reinsurer) under the assumption reinsurance transaction.

(C) Amount required to be capitalized under section 848 in connection with the transaction.

(1) In general.

(2) Required capitalization amount.

(3) General deductions allocable to the assumption reinsurance transaction.

(4) Treatment of a capitalization shortfall allocable to the reinsurance agreement.

(i) In general.

(ii) Treatment of additional capitalized amounts as the result of an election under § 1.848-2(g)(8).

(5) Cross references and special rules.

(D) Examples

(E) Effective/applicability date.

(iii) Application of loss disallowance rule upon a disposition of an insurance contract acquired in an assumption reinsurance transaction.

(A) Disposition.

(1) In general.

(2) Treatment of indemnity reinsurance transactions.

(B) Loss.

(C) Examples.

(iv) Effective dates.

(A) In general.

(B) Application to pre-effective date acquisitions and dispositions.

(C) Change in method of accounting.

(1) In general.

(2) Acquisitions and dispositions on or after effective date.

(3) Acquisitions and dispositions before the effective date.

(6) Amounts paid or incurred for a franchise, trademark, or trade name.

(7) Amounts properly taken into account in determining the cost of property that is not a section 197 intangible.

(8) Treatment of amortizable section 197 intangibles as depreciable property.

(h) Anti-churning rules.

(1) Scope and purpose.

(i) Scope.

(ii) Purpose.

(2) Treatment of section 197(f)(9) intangibles.

(3) Amounts deductible under section 1253(d) or § 1.162-11.

(4) Transition period.

(5) Exceptions.

(6) Related person.

(i) In general.

(ii) Time for testing relationships.

(iii) Certain relationships disregarded.

(iv) De minimis rule.

(A) In general.

(B) Determination of beneficial ownership interest.

(7) Special rules for entities that owned or used property at any time during the transition period and that are no longer in existence.

(8) Special rules for section 338 deemed acquisitions.

(9) Gain-recognition exception.

(i) Applicability.

(ii) Effect of exception.

(iii) Time and manner of election.

(iv) Special rules for certain entities.

(v) Effect of nonconforming elections.

(vi) Notification requirements.

(vii) Revocation.

(viii) Election Statement.

(ix) Determination of highest marginal rate of tax and amount of other Federal income tax on gain.

(A) Marginal rate.

(1) Noncorporate taxpayers.

(2) Corporations and tax-exempt entities.

(B) Other Federal income tax on gain.

(x) Coordination with other provisions.

(A) In general.

(B) Section 1374.

(C) Procedural and administrative provisions.

(D) Installment method.

(xi) Special rules for persons not otherwise subject to Federal income tax.

(10) Transactions subject to both anti-churning and nonrecognition rules.
(11) Avoidance purpose.
(12) Additional partnership anti-churning rules
(i) In general.
(ii) Section 732(b) adjustments. [Reserved]
(iii) Section 732(d) adjustments.
(iv) Section 734(b) adjustments. [Reserved]
(v) Section 743(b) adjustments.
(vi) Partner is or becomes a user of partnership intangible.
(A) General rule.
(B) Anti-churning partner.
(C) Effect of retroactive elections.
(vii) Section 704(c) elections.
(A) Allocations where the intangible is amortizable by the contributor.
(B) Allocations where the intangible is not amortizable by the contributor.
(viii) Operating rule for transfers upon death.
(i) Reserved
(j) General anti-abuse rule.
(k) Examples.
(l) Effective dates.
(1) In general.
(2) Application to pre-effective date acquisitions.
(3) Application of regulation project REG-209709-94 to pre-effective date acquisitions.
(4) Change in method of accounting.
(i) In general.
(ii) Application to pre-effective date transactions.
(iii) Automatic change procedures.

[Reg. § 1.197-0.]

.01 Historical Comment: Proposed 1/16/97. Adopted 1/20/2000 by T.D. 8865. Amended 4/7/2006 by T.D. 9257 and 1/22/2008 by T.D. 9377.

¶ 586

Temporary Reg. § 1.197-1T

»»→ Caution: Temporary Reg. § 1.197-1T does not reflect recent law changes. For details, see ¶ 586.01.

§ 1.197-1T. **Certain elections for intangible property (Temporary).**—(a) *In general*.—This section provides rules for making the two elections under section 13261 of the Omnibus Budget Reconciliation Act of 1993 (OBRA '93). Paragraph (c) of this section provides rules for making the section 13261(g)(2) election (the retroactive election) to apply the intangibles provisions of OBRA '93 to property acquired after July 25, 1991, and on or before August 10, 1993 (the date of enactment of OBRA '93). Paragraph (d) of this section provides rules for making the section 13261(g)(3) election (binding contract election) to apply prior law to property acquired pursuant to a written binding contract in effect on August 10, 1993, and at all times thereafter before the date of acquisition. The provisions of this section apply only to property for which an election is made under paragraph (c) or (d) of this section.

(b) *Definitions and special rules*.—(1) *Intangibles provisions of OBRA '93*.—The intangibles provisions of OBRA '93 are sections 167(f) and 197 of the Internal

»»→ Caution: Temporary Reg. § 1.197-1T does not reflect recent law changes. For details, see ¶ 586.01.

Revenue Code (Code) and all other pertinent provisions of section 13261 of OBRA '93 (e.g., the amendment of section 1253 in the case of a franchise, trademark, or trade name).

(2) *Transition period property* .—The transition period property of a taxpayer is any property that was acquired by the taxpayer after July 25, 1991, and on or before August 10, 1993.

(3) *Eligible section 197 intangibles* .—The eligible section 197 intangibles of a taxpayer are any section 197 intangibles that—

(i) Are transition period property; and

(ii) Qualify as amortizable section 197 intangibles (within the meaning of section 197(c)) if an election under section 13261(g)(2) of OBRA '93 applies.

(4) *Election date* .—The election date is the date (determined after application of section 7502(a)) on which the taxpayer files the original or amended return to which the election statement described in paragraph (e) of this section is attached.

(5) *Election year* .—The election year is the taxable year of the taxpayer that includes August 10, 1993.

(6) *Common control* .—A taxpayer is under common control with the electing taxpayer if, at any time after August 2, 1993, and on or before the election date (as defined in paragraph (b)(4) of this section), the two taxpayers would be treated as a single taxpayer under section 41(f)(1)(A) or (B).

(7) *Applicable convention for sections 197 and 167(f) intangibles* .—For purposes of computing the depreciation or amortization deduction allowable with respect to transition period property described in section 167(f)(1) or (3) or with respect to eligible section 197 intangibles—

(i) Property acquired at any time during the month is treated as acquired as of the first day of the month and is eligible for depreciation or amortization during the month; and

(ii) Property is not eligible for depreciation or amortization in the month of disposition.

(8) *Application to adjustment to basis of partnership property under section 734(b) or 743(b)* .—Any increase in the basis of partnership property under section 734(b) (relating to the optional adjustment to basis of undistributed partnership property) or section 743(b) (relating to the optional adjustment to the basis of partnership property) will be taken into account under this section by a partner as if the increased portion of the basis were attributable to the partner's acquisition of the underlying partnership property on the date the distribution or transfer occurs. For example, if a section 754 election is in effect and, as a result of its acquisition of a partnership interest, a taxpayer obtains an increased basis in an intangible held through the partnership, the increased portion of the basis in the intangible will be treated as an intangible asset newly acquired by that taxpayer on the date of the transaction.

(9) *Former member* .—A former member of a consolidated group is a corporation that was a member of the consolidated group at any time after July 25, 1991, and on or before August 2, 1993, but that is not under common control with the common parent of the group for purposes of paragraph (c)(1)(ii) of this section.

(c) *Retroactive election* .—(1) *Effect of election* .—(i) *On taxpayer* .—Except as provided in paragraph (c)(1)(v) of this section, if a taxpayer makes the retroac-

»»→ Caution: Temporary Reg. § 1.197-1T does not reflect recent law changes. For details, see ¶ 586.01.

tive election, the intangibles provisions of OBRA '93 will apply to all the taxpayer's transition period property. Thus, for example, section 197 will apply to all the taxpayer's eligible section 197 intangibles.

(ii) *On taxpayers under common control* .—If a taxpayer makes the retroactive election, the election applies to each taxpayer that is under common control with the electing taxpayer. If the retroactive election applies to a taxpayer under common control, the intangibles provisions of OBRA '93 apply to that taxpayer's transition period property in the same manner as if that taxpayer had itself made the retroactive election. However, a retroactive election that applies to a non-electing taxpayer under common control is not treated as an election by that taxpayer for purposes of re-applying the rule of this paragraph (c)(1)(ii) to any other taxpayer.

(iii) *On former members of consolidated group* .—A retroactive election by the common parent of a consolidated group applies to transition period property acquired by a former member while it was a member of the consolidated group and continues to apply to that property in each subsequent consolidated or separate return year of the former member.

(iv) *On transferred assets* .—(A) *In general* .—If property is transferred in a transaction described in paragraph (c)(1)(iv)(C) of this section and the intangibles provisions of OBRA '93 applied to such property in the hands of the transferor, the property remains subject to the intangibles provisions of OBRA '93 with respect to so much of its adjusted basis in the hands of the transferee as does not exceed its adjusted basis in the hands of the transferor. The transferee is not required to apply the intangibles provisions of OBRA '93 to any other transition period property that it owns, however, unless such provisions are otherwise applicable under the rules of this paragraph (c)(1).

(B) *Transferee election* .—If property is transferred in a transaction described in paragraph (c)(1)(iv)(C)(*1*) of this section and the transferee makes the retroactive election, the transferor is not required to apply the intangibles provisions of OBRA '93 to any of its transition period property (including the property transferred to the transferee in the transaction described in paragraph (c)(1)(iv)(C)(*1*) of this section), unless such provisions are otherwise applicable under the rules of this paragraph (c)(1).

(C) *Transactions covered* .—This paragraph (c)(1)(iv) applies to—

(1) Any transaction described in section 332, 351, 361, 721, 731, 1031, or 1033; and

(2) Any transaction between corporations that are members of the same consolidated group immediately after the transaction.

(D) *Exchanged basis property* .—In the case of a transaction involving exchanged basis property (e.g., a transaction subject to section 1031 or 1033)—

(1) Paragraph (c)(1)(iv)(A) of this section shall not apply; and

(2) If the intangibles provisions of OBRA '93 applied to the property by reference to which the exchanged basis is determined (the predecessor property), the exchanged basis property becomes subject to the intangibles provisions of OBRA '93 with respect to so much of its basis as does not exceed the predecessor property's basis.

»»→ Caution: Temporary Reg. § 1.197-1T does not reflect recent law changes. For details, see ¶ 586.01.

(E) *Acquisition date* .—For purposes of paragraph (b)(2) of this section (definition of transition period property), property (other than exchanged basis property) acquired in a transaction described in paragraph (c)(1)(iv)(C)(*1*) of this section generally is treated as acquired when the transferor acquired (or was treated as acquiring) the property (or predecessor property). However, if the adjusted basis of the property in the hands of the transferee exceeds the adjusted basis of the property in the hands of the transferor, the property, with respect to that excess basis, is treated as acquired at the time of the transfer. The time at which exchanged basis property is considered acquired is determined by applying similar principles to the transferee's acquisition of predecessor property.

(v) *Special rule for property of former member of consolidated group* .—(A) *Intangibles provisions inapplicable for certain periods* .—If a former member of a consolidated group makes a retroactive election pursuant to paragraph (c)(1)(i) of this section or if an election applies to the former member under the common control rule of paragraph (c)(1)(ii) of this section, the intangibles provisions of OBRA '93 generally apply to all transition period property of the former member. The intangibles provisions of OBRA '93 do not apply, however, to the transition period property of a former member (including a former member that makes or is bound by a retroactive election) during the period beginning immediately after July 25, 1991, and ending immediately before the earlier of—

(1) The first day after July 25, 1991, that the former member was not a member of a consolidated group; or

(2) The first day after July 25, 1991, that the former member was a member of a consolidated group that is otherwise required to apply the intangibles provisions of OBRA '93 to its transition period property (e.g., because the common control election under paragraph (c)(1)(ii) of this section applies to the group).

(B) *Subsequent adjustments* .—See paragraph (c)(5) of this section for adjustments when the intangibles provisions of OBRA '93 first apply to the transition period property of the former member after the property is acquired.

(2) *Making the election* .—(i) *Partnerships, S corporations, estates, and trusts* .—Except as provided in paragraph (c)(2)(ii) of this section, in the case of transition period property of a partnership, S corporation, estate, or trust, only the entity may make the retroactive election for purposes of paragraph (c)(1)(i) of this section.

(ii) *Partnerships for which a section 754 election is in effect* .—In the case of increased basis that is treated as transition period property of a partner under paragraph (b)(8) of this section, only that partner may make the retroactive election for purposes of paragraph (c)(1)(i) of this section.

(iii) *Consolidated groups* .—An election by the common parent of a consolidated group applies to members and former members as described in paragraphs (c)(1)(ii) and (iii) of this section. Further, for purposes of paragraph (c)(1)(ii) of this section, an election by the common parent is not treated as an election by any subsidiary member. A retroactive election cannot be made by a corporation that is a subsidiary member of a consolidated group on August 10, 1993, but an election can be made on behalf of the subsidiary member under paragraph (c)(1)(ii) of this section (e.g., by the common parent of the group). See paragraph (c)(1)(iii) of this section for rules concerning the effect of the common parent's election on transition period property of a former member.

→ Caution: Temporary Reg. § 1.197-1T does not reflect recent law changes. For details, see ¶ 586.01.

(3) *Time and manner of election*.—(i) *Time*.—In general, the retroactive election must be made by the due date (including extensions of time) of the electing taxpayer's Federal income tax return for the election year. If, however, the taxpayer's original Federal income tax return for the election year is filed before April 14, 1994, the election may be made by amending that return no later than September 12, 1994.

(ii) *Manner*.—The retroactive election is made by attaching the election statement described in paragraph (e) of this section to the taxpayer's original or amended income tax return for the election year. In addition, the taxpayer must—

(A) Amend any previously filed return when required to do so under paragraph (c)(4) of this section; and

(B) Satisfy the notification requirements of paragraph (c)(6) of this section.

(iii) *Effect of nonconforming elections*.—An attempted election that does not satisfy the requirements of this paragraph (c)(3) (including an attempted election made on a return for a taxable year prior to the election year) is not valid.

(4) *Amended return requirements*.—(i) *Requirements*.—A taxpayer subject to this paragraph (c)(4) must amend all previously filed income tax returns as necessary to conform the taxpayer's treatment of transition period property to the treatment required under the intangibles provisions of OBRA '93. See paragraph (c)(5) of this section for certain adjustments that may be required on the amended returns required under this paragraph (c)(4) in the case of certain consolidated group member dispositions and tax-free transactions.

(ii) *Applicability*.—This paragraph (c)(4) applies to a taxpayer if—

(A) The taxpayer makes the retroactive election; or

(B) Another person's retroactive election applies to the taxpayer or to any property acquired by the taxpayer.

(5) *Adjustment required with respect to certain consolidated group member dispositions and tax-free transactions*.—(i) *Application*.—This paragraph (c)(5) applies to transition period property if the intangibles provisions of OBRA '93 first apply to the property while it is held by the taxpayer but do not apply to the property for some period (the "interim period") after the property is acquired (or considered acquired) by the taxpayer. For example, this paragraph (c)(5) may apply to transition period property held by a former member of a consolidated group if a retroactive election is made by or on behalf of the former member but is not made by the consolidated group. See paragraph (c)(1)(v) of this section.

(ii) *Required adjustment to income*.—If this paragraph (c)(5) applies, an adjustment must be taken into account in computing taxable income of the taxpayer for the taxable year in which the intangibles provisions of OBRA '93 first apply to the property. The amount of the adjustment is equal to the difference for the transition period property between—

(A) The sum of the depreciation, amortization, or other cost recovery deductions that the taxpayer (and its predecessors) would have been permitted if the intangibles provisions of OBRA '93 applied to the property during the interim period; and

(B) The sum of the depreciation, amortization, or other cost recovery deductions that the taxpayer (and its predecessors) claimed during that interim period.

»»→ *Caution: Temporary Reg. § 1.197-1T does not reflect recent law changes. For details, see ¶ 586.01.*

(iii) *Required adjustment to basis* .—The taxpayer also must make a corresponding adjustment to the basis of its transition period property to reflect any adjustment to taxable income with respect to the property under this paragraph (c)(5).

(6) *Notification requirements* .—(i) *Notification of commonly controlled taxpayers* .—A taxpayer that makes the retroactive election must provide written notification of the retroactive election (on or before the election date) to each taxpayer that is under common control with the electing taxpayer.

(ii) *Notification of certain former members, former consolidated groups, and transferees* .—This paragraph (c)(6)(ii) applies to a common parent of a consolidated group that makes or is notified of a retroactive election that applies to transition period property of a former member, a corporation that makes or is notified of a retroactive election that affects any consolidated group of which the corporation is a former member, or a taxpayer that makes or is notified of a retroactive election that applies to transition period property the taxpayer transfers in a transaction described in paragraph (c)(1)(iv)(C) of this section. Such common parent, former member, or transferor must provide written notification of the retroactive election to any affected former member, consolidated group, or transferee. The written notification must be provided on or before the election date in the case of an election by the common parent, former member, or transferor, and within 30 days of the election date in the case of an election by a person other than the common parent, former member, or transferor.

(7) *Revocation* .—Once made, the retroactive election may be revoked only with the consent of the Commissioner.

(8) *Examples* .—The following examples illustrate the application of this paragraph (c).

Example 1. (i) *X* is a partnership with 5 equal partners, *A* through *E*. *X* acquires in 1989, as its sole asset, intangible asset *M*. *X* has a section 754 election in effect for all relevant years. *F*, an unrelated individual, purchases *A*'s entire interest in the *X* partnership in January 1993 for $700. At the time of *F*'s purchase, *X*'s inside basis for *M* is $2,000, and its fair market value is $3,500.

(ii) Under section 743(b), *X* makes an adjustment to increase *F*'s basis in asset *M* by $300, the difference between the allocated purchase price and *M*'s inside basis ($700 - $400 = $300). Under paragraphs (b)(8) and (c)(2)(ii) of this section, if *F* makes the retroactive election, the section 743(b) basis increase of $300 in *M* is an amortizable section 197 intangible even though asset *M* is not an amortizable section 197 intangible in the hands of *X*. *F's* increase in the basis of asset *M* is amortizable over 15 years beginning with the month of *F*'s acquisition of the partnership interest. With respect to the remaining $400 of basis, *F* is treated as stepping into *A*'s shoes and continues *A*'s amortization (if any) in asset *M*. *F*'s retroactive election applies to all other intangibles acquired by *F* or a taxpayer under common control with *F*.

Example 2. *A*, a calendar year taxpayer, is under common control with *B*, a June 30 fiscal year taxpayer. *A* files its original election year Federal income tax return on March 15, 1994, and does not make either the retroactive election or the binding contract election. *B* files its election year tax return on September 15, 1994, and makes the retroactive election. *B* is required by paragraph (c)(6)(i) of this section to notify *A* of its election. Even though *A* had already filed its election year return, *A* is bound by *B*'s retroactive election under the common control rules. Additionally, if *A* had made a binding contract election, it would have been negated by *B*'s retroactive election. Because of *B*'s retroactive election, *A* must comply with

»»→ Caution: Temporary Reg. § 1.197-1T does not reflect recent law changes. For details, see ¶ 586.01.

the requirements of this paragraph (c), and file amended returns for the election year and any affected prior years as necessary to conform the treatment of transition period property to the treatment required under the intangibles provisions of OBRA '93.

Example 3. (i) *P* and *Y*, calendar year taxpayers, are the common parents of unrelated calendar year consolidated groups. On August 15, 1991, *S*, a subsidiary member of the *P* group, acquires a section 197 intangible with an unadjusted basis of $180. Under prior law, no amortization or depreciation was allowed with respect to the acquired intangible. On November 1, 1992, a member of the *Y* group acquires the *S* stock in a taxable transaction. On the *P* group's 1993 consolidated return, *P* makes the retroactive election. The *P* group also files amended returns for its affected prior years. *Y* does not make the retroactive election for the *Y* group.

(ii) Under paragraph (c)(1)(iii) of this section, a retroactive election by the common parent of a consolidated group applies to all transition period property acquired by a former member while it was a member of the group. The section 197 intangible acquired by *S* is transition period property that *S*, a former member of the *P* group, acquired while a member of the *P* group. Thus, *P*'s election applies to the acquired asset. *P* must notify *S* of the election pursuant to paragraph (c)(6)(ii) of this section.

(iii) *S* amortizes the unadjusted basis of its eligible section 197 intangible ($180) over the 15-year amortization period using the applicable convention beginning as of the first day of the month of acquisition (August 1, 1991). Thus, the *P* group amends its 1991 consolidated tax return to take into account $5 of amortization ($180/15 years × 5/12 year = $5) for *S*.

(iv) For 1992, *S* is entitled to $12 of amortization ($180/15). Assume that under § 1.1502-76, $10 of *S*' s amortization for 1992 is allocated to the *P* group's consolidated return and $2 is allocated to the *Y* group's return. The *P* group amends its 1992 consolidated tax return to reflect the $10 deduction for *S*. The *Y* group must amend its 1992 return to reflect the $2 deduction for *S*.

Example 4. (i) The facts are the same as in *Example 3*, except that the retroactive election is made for the *Y* group, not for the *P* group.

(ii) The *Y* group amends its 1992 consolidated return to claim a section 197 deduction of $2 ($180/15 years × 2/12 year = $2) for *S*.

(iii) Under paragraph (c)(1)(ii) of this section, the retroactive election by *Y* applies to all transition period property acquired by *S*. However, under paragraph (c)(1)(v)(A) of this section, the intangibles provisions of OBRA '93 do not apply to *S*'s transition period property during the period when it held such property as a member of *P* group. Instead, these provisions become applicable to *S*'s transition period property beginning on November 1, 1992, when *S* becomes a member of *Y* group.

(iv) Because the *P* group did not make the retroactive election, there is an interim period during which the intangibles provisions of OBRA '93 do not apply to the asset acquired by *S*. Thus, under paragraph (c)(5) of this section, the *Y* group must take into account in computing taxable income in 1992 an adjustment equal to the difference between the section 197 deduction that would have been permitted if the intangibles provisions of OBRA '93 applied to the property for the interim period (i.e., the period for which *S* was included in the *P* group's 1991 and 1992 consolidated returns) and any amortization or depreciation deductions claimed by *S* for the transferred intangible for that period. The retroactive election does not affect the *P* group, and the *P* group is not required to amend its returns.

Example 5. The facts are the same as in *Example 3*, except that both *P* and *Y* make the retroactive election. *P* must notify *S* of its election pursuant to paragraph (c)(6)(ii) of this section. Further, both the *P* and *Y* groups must file

»»→ Caution: Temporary Reg. § 1.197-1T does not reflect recent law changes. For details, see ¶ 586.01.

amended returns for affected prior years. Because there is no period of time during which the intangibles provisions of OBRA '93 do not apply to the asset acquired by *S*, the *Y* group is permitted no adjustment under paragraph (c)(5) of this section for the asset.

(d) *Binding contract election* .—(1) *General rule* .—(i) *Effect of election* .—If a taxpayer acquires property pursuant to a written binding contract in effect on August 10, 1993, and at all times thereafter before the acquisition (an eligible acquisition) and makes the binding contract election with respect to the contract, the law in effect prior to the enactment of OBRA '93 will apply to all property acquired pursuant to the contract. A separate binding contract election must be made with respect to each eligible acquisition to which the law in effect prior to the enactment of OBRA '93 is to apply.

(ii) *Taxpayers subject to retroactive election* .—A taxpayer may not make the binding contract election if the taxpayer or a person under common control with the taxpayer makes the retroactive election under paragraph (c) of this section.

(iii) *Revocation* .—A binding contract election, once made, may be revoked only with the consent of the Commissioner.

(2) *Time and manner of election* .—(i) *Time* .—In general, the binding contract election must be made by the due date (including extensions of time) of the electing taxpayer's Federal income tax return for the election year. If, however, the taxpayer's original Federal income tax return for the election year is filed before April 14, 1944, the election may be made by amending that return no later than September 12, 1944.

(ii) *Manner* .—The binding contract election is made by attaching the election statement described in paragraph (e) of this section to the taxpayer's original or amended income tax return for the election year.

(iii) *Effect of nonconforming election* .—An attempted election that does not satisfy the requirements of this paragraph (d)(2) is not valid.

(e) *Election statement* .—(1) *Filing requirements* .—For an election under paragraph (c) or (d) of this section to be valid, the electing taxpayer must:

(i) File (with its Federal income tax return for the election year and with any affected amended returns required under paragraph (c)(4) of this section) a written election statement, as an attachment to Form 4562 (Depreciation and Amortization), that satisfies the requirements of paragraph (e)(2) of this section; and

(ii) Forward a copy of the election statement to the Statistics Branch (QAM:S:6111), IRS Ogden Service Center, ATTN: Chief, Statistics Branch, P.O. Box 9941, Ogden, UT 84409.

(2) *Content of the election statement* .—The written election statement must include the information in paragraphs (e)(2)(i) through (vi) and (ix) of this section in the case of a retroactive election, and the information in paragraphs (e)(2)(i) and (vii) through (ix) of this section in the case of a binding contract election. The required information should be arranged and identified in accordance with the following order and numbering system—

(i) The name, address and taxpayer identification number (TIN) of the electing taxpayer (and the common parent if a consolidated return is filed).

(ii) A statement that the taxpayer is making the retroactive election.

»»→ Caution: Temporary Reg. § 1.197-1T does not reflect recent law changes. For details, see ¶ 586.01.

(iii) Identification of the transition period property affected by the retroactive election, the name and TIN of the person from which the property was acquired, the manner and date of acquisition, the basis at which the property was acquired, and the amount of depreciation, amortization, or other cost recovery under section 167 or any other provision of the Code claimed with respect to the property.

(iv) Identification of each taxpayer under common control (as defined in paragraph (b)(6) of this section) with the electing taxpayer by name, TIN, and Internal Revenue Service Center where the taxpayer's income tax return is filed.

(v) If any persons are required to be notified of the retroactive election under paragraph (c)(6) of this section, identification of such persons and certification that written notification of the election has been provided to such persons.

(vi) A statement that the transition period property being amortized under section 197 is not subject to the anti-churning rules of section 197(f)(9).

(vii) A statement that the taxpayer is making the binding contract election.

(viii) Identification of the property affected by the binding contract election, the name and TIN of the person from which the property was acquired, the manner and date of acquisition, the basis at which the property was acquired, and whether any of the property is subject to depreciation under section 167 or to amortization or other cost recovery under any other provision of the Code.

(ix) The signature of the taxpayer or an individual authorized to sign the taxpayer's Federal income tax return.

(f) *Effective date* .—These regulations are effective March 15, 1994. [Temporary Reg. § 1.197-1T.]

.01 Historical Comment: Adopted 3/10/94 by T.D. 8528. [Temporary Reg. § 1.197-1T(c) was modified by Notice 94-90.]

¶ 587

Reg. § 1.197-2

§ 1.197-2. **Amortization of goodwill and certain other intangibles.**—(a) *Overview* .—(1) *In general* .—Section 197 allows an amortization deduction for the capitalized costs of an amortizable section 197 intangible and prohibits any other depreciation or amortization with respect to that property. Paragraphs (b), (c), and (e) of this section provide rules and definitions for determining whether property is a section 197 intangible, and paragraphs (d) and (e) of this section provide rules and definitions for determining whether a section 197 intangible is an amortizable section 197 intangible. The amortization deduction under section 197 is determined by amortizing basis ratably over a 15-year period under the rules of paragraph (f) of this section. Section 197 also includes various special rules pertaining to the disposition of amortizable section 197 intangibles, nonrecognition transactions, anti-churning rules, and anti-abuse rules. Rules relating to these provisions are contained in paragraphs (g), (h), and (j) of this section. Examples demonstrating the application of these provisions are contained in paragraph (k) of this section. The effective date of the rules in this section is contained in paragraph (l) of this section.

(2) *Section 167(f) property* .—Section 167(f) prescribes rules for computing the depreciation deduction for certain property to which section 197 does not apply. See § 1.167(a)-14 for rules under section 167(f) and paragraphs (c)(4), (6),

(7), (11), and (13) of this section for a description of the property subject to section 167(f).

(3) *Amounts otherwise deductible* .—Section 197 does not apply to amounts that are not chargeable to capital account under paragraph (f)(3) (relating to basis determinations for covenants not to compete and certain contracts for the use of section 197 intangibles) of this section and are otherwise currently deductible. For this purpose, an amount described in § 1.162-11 is not currently deductible if, without regard to § 1.162-11, such amount is properly chargeable to capital account.

(b) *Section 197 intangibles; in general* .—Except as otherwise provided in paragraph (c) of this section, the term *section 197 intangible* means any property described in section 197(d)(1). The following rules and definitions provide guidance concerning property that is a section 197 intangible unless an exception applies:

(1) *Goodwill* .—Section 197 intangibles include goodwill. Goodwill is the value of a trade or business attributable to the expectancy of continued customer patronage. This expectancy may be due to the name or reputation of a trade or business or any other factor.

(2) *Going concern value* .—Section 197 intangibles include going concern value. Going concern value is the additional value that attaches to property by reason of its existence as an integral part of an ongoing business activity. Going concern value includes the value attributable to the ability of a trade or business (or a part of a trade or business) to continue functioning or generating income without interruption notwithstanding a change in ownership, but does not include any of the intangibles described in any other provision of this paragraph (b). It also includes the value that is attributable to the immediate use or availability of an acquired trade or business, such as, for example, the use of the revenues or net earnings that otherwise would not be received during any period if the acquired trade or business were not available or operational.

(3) *Workforce in place* .—Section 197 intangibles include workforce in place. Workforce in place (sometimes referred to as agency force or assembled workforce) includes the composition of a workforce (for example, the experience, education, or training of a workforce), the terms and conditions of employment whether contractual or otherwise, and any other value placed on employees or any of their attributes. Thus, the amount paid or incurred for workforce in place includes, for example, any portion of the purchase price of an acquired trade or business attributable to the existence of a highly-skilled workforce, an existing employment contract (or contracts), or a relationship with employees or consultants (including, but not limited to, any key employee contract or relationship). Workforce in place does not include any covenant not to compete or other similar arrangement described in paragraph (b)(9) of this section.

(4) *Information base* .—Section 197 intangibles include any information base, including a customer-related information base. For this purpose, an information base includes business books and records, operating systems, and any other information base (regardless of the method of recording the information) and a customer-related information base is any information base that includes lists or other information with respect to current or prospective customers. Thus, the amount paid or incurred for information base includes, for example, any portion of the purchase price of an acquired trade or business attributable to the intangible value of technical manuals, training manuals or programs, data files, and accounting or inventory control systems. Other examples include the cost of acquiring

customer lists, subscription lists, insurance expirations, patient or client files, or lists of newspaper, magazine, radio, or television advertisers.

(5) *Know-how, etc* .—Section 197 intangibles include any patent, copyright, formula, process, design, pattern, know-how, format, package design, computer software (as defined in paragraph (c)(4)(iv) of this section), or interest in a film, sound recording, video tape, book, or other similar property. (See, however, the exceptions in paragraph (c) of this section.)

(6) *Customer-based intangibles* .—Section 197 intangibles include any customer-based intangible. A customer-based intangible is any composition of market, market share, or other value resulting from the future provision of goods or services pursuant to contractual or other relationships in the ordinary course of business with customers. Thus, the amount paid or incurred for customer-based intangibles includes, for example, any portion of the purchase price of an acquired trade or business attributable to the existence of a customer base, a circulation base, an undeveloped market or market growth, insurance in force, the existence of a qualification to supply goods or services to a particular customer, a mortgage servicing contract (as defined in paragraph (c)(11) of this section), an investment management contract, or other relationship with customers involving the future provision of goods or services. (See, however, the exceptions in paragraph (c) of this section.) In addition, customer-based intangibles include the deposit base and any similar asset of a financial institution. Thus, the amount paid or incurred for customer-based intangibles also includes any portion of the purchase price of an acquired financial institution attributable to the value represented by existing checking accounts, savings accounts, escrow accounts, and other similar items of the financial institution. However, any portion of the purchase price of an acquired trade or business attributable to accounts receivable or other similar rights to income for goods or services provided to customers prior to the acquisition of a trade or business is not an amount paid or incurred for a customer-based intangible.

(7) *Supplier-based intangibles* .—Section 197 intangibles include any supplier-based intangible. A supplier-based intangible is the value resulting from the future acquisition, pursuant to contractual or other relationships with suppliers in the ordinary course of business, of goods or services that will be sold or used by the taxpayer. Thus, the amount paid or incurred for supplier-based intangibles includes, for example, any portion of the purchase price of an acquired trade or business attributable to the existence of a favorable relationship with persons providing distribution services (such as favorable shelf or display space at a retail outlet), the existence of a favorable credit rating, or the existence of favorable supply contracts. The amount paid or incurred for supplier-based intangibles does not include any amount required to be paid for the goods or services themselves pursuant to the terms of the agreement or other relationship. In addition, see the exceptions in paragraph (c) of this section, including the exception in paragraph (c)(6) of this section for certain rights to receive tangible property or services from another person.

(8) *Licenses, permits, and other rights granted by governmental units* .—Section 197 intangibles include any license, permit, or other right granted by a governmental unit (including, for purposes of section 197, an agency or instrumentality thereof) even if the right is granted for an indefinite period or is reasonably expected to be renewed for an indefinite period. These rights include, for example, a liquor license, a taxi-cab medallion (or license), an airport landing or takeoff right (sometimes referred to as a slot), a regulated airline route, or a television or radio broadcasting license. The issuance or renewal of a license, permit, or other right granted by a governmental unit is considered an acquisition of the license, permit,

or other right. (See, however, the exceptions in paragraph (c) of this section, including the exceptions in paragraph (c)(3) of this section for an interest in land, paragraph (c)(6) of this section for certain rights to receive tangible property or services, paragraph (c)(8) of this section for an interest under a lease of tangible property, and paragraph (c)(13) of this section for certain rights granted by a governmental unit. See paragraph (b)(10) of this section for the treatment of franchises.)

(9) *Covenants not to compete and other similar arrangements* .—Section 197 intangibles include any covenant not to compete, or agreement having substantially the same effect, entered into in connection with the direct or indirect acquisition of an interest in a trade or business or a substantial portion thereof. For purposes of this paragraph (b)(9), an acquisition may be made in the form of an asset acquisition (including a qualified stock purchase that is treated as a purchase of assets under section 338), a stock acquisition or redemption, and the acquisition or redemption of a partnership interest. An agreement requiring the performance of services for the acquiring taxpayer or the provision of property or its use to the acquiring taxpayer does not have substantially the same effect as a covenant not to compete to the extent that the amount paid under the agreement represents reasonable compensation for the services actually rendered or for the property or use of the property actually provided.

(10) *Franchises, trademarks, and trade names* .—(i) Section 197 intangibles include any franchise, trademark, or trade name. The term *franchise* has the meaning given in section 1253(b)(1) and includes any agreement that provides one of the parties to the agreement with the right to distribute, sell, or provide goods, services, or facilities, within a specified area. The term *trademark* includes any word, name, symbol, or device, or any combination thereof, adopted and used to identify goods or services and distinguish them from those provided by others. The term *trade name* includes any name used to identify or designate a particular trade or business or the name or title used by a person or organization engaged in a trade or business. A license, permit, or other right granted by a governmental unit is a franchise if it otherwise meets the definition of a franchise. A trademark or trade name includes any trademark or trade name arising under statute or applicable common law, and any similar right granted by contract. The renewal of a franchise, trademark, or trade name is treated as an acquisition of the franchise, trademark, or trade name.

(ii) Notwithstanding the definitions provided in paragraph (b)(10)(i) of this section, any amount that is paid or incurred on account of a transfer, sale, or other disposition of a franchise, trademark, or trade name and that is subject to section 1253(d)(1) is not included in the basis of a section 197 intangible. (See paragraph (g)(6) of this section.)

(11) *Contracts for the use of, and term interests in, section 197 intangibles* .—Section 197 intangibles include any right under a license, contract, or other arrangement providing for the use of property that would be a section 197 intangible under any provision of this paragraph (b) (including this paragraph (b)(11)) after giving effect to all of the exceptions provided in paragraph (c) of this section. Section 197 intangibles also include any term interest (whether outright or in trust) in such property.

(12) *Other similar items* .—Section 197 intangibles include any other intangible property that is similar in all material respects to the property specifically described in section 197(d)(1)(C)(i) through (v) and paragraphs (b)(3) through (7) of this section. (See paragraph (g)(5) of this section for special rules regarding certain reinsurance transactions.)

(c) *Section 197 intangibles; exceptions* .—The term *section 197 intangible* does not include property described in section 197(e). The following rules and definitions provide guidance concerning property to which the exceptions apply:

(1) *Interests in a corporation, partnership, trust, or estate* .—Section 197 intangibles do not include an interest in a corporation, partnership, trust, or estate. Thus, for example, amortization under section 197 is not available for the cost of acquiring stock, partnership interests, or interests in a trust or estate, whether or not the interests are regularly traded on an established market. (See paragraph (g)(3) of this section for special rules applicable to property of a partnership when a section 754 election is in effect for the partnership.)

(2) *Interests under certain financial contracts* .—Section 197 intangibles do not include an interest under an existing futures contract, foreign currency contract, notional principal contract, interest rate swap, or other similar financial contract, whether or not the interest is regularly traded on an established market. However, this exception does not apply to an interest under a mortgage servicing contract, credit card servicing contract, or other contract to service another person's indebtedness, or an interest under an assumption reinsurance contract. (See paragraph (g)(5) of this section for the treatment of assumption reinsurance contracts. See paragraph (c)(11) of this section and § 1.167(a)-14(d) for the treatment of mortgage servicing rights.)

(3) *Interests in land* .—Section 197 intangibles do not include any interest in land. For this purpose, an interest in land includes a fee interest, life estate, remainder, easement, mineral right, timber right, grazing right, riparian right, air right, zoning variance, and any other similar right, such as a farm allotment, quota for farm commodities, or crop acreage base. An interest in land does not include an airport landing or takeoff right, a regulated airline route, or a franchise to provide cable television service. The cost of acquiring a license, permit, or other land improvement right, such as a building construction or use permit, is taken into account in the same manner as the underlying improvement.

(4) *Certain computer software* .—(i) *Publicly available* .—Section 197 intangibles do not include any interest in computer software that is (or has been) readily available to the general public on similar terms, is subject to a nonexclusive license, and has not been substantially modified. Computer software will be treated as readily available to the general public if the software may be obtained on substantially the same terms by a significant number of persons that would reasonably be expected to use the software. This requirement can be met even though the software is not available through a system of retail distribution. Computer software will not be considered to have been substantially modified if the cost of all modifications to the version of the software that is readily available to the general public does not exceed the greater of 25 percent of the price at which the unmodified version of the software is readily available to the general public or $2,000. For the purpose of determining whether computer software has been substantially modified—

(A) Integrated programs acquired in a package from a single source are treated as a single computer program; and

(B) Any cost incurred to install the computer software on a system is not treated as a cost of the software. However, the costs for customization, such as tailoring to a user's specifications (other than embedded programming options) are costs of modifying the software.

(ii) *Not acquired as part of trade or business* .—Section 197 intangibles do not include an interest in computer software that is not acquired as part of a purchase of a trade or business.

(iii) *Other exceptions* .—For other exceptions applicable to computer software, see paragraph (a)(3) of this section (relating to otherwise deductible amounts) and paragraph (g)(7) of this section (relating to amounts properly taken into account in determining the cost of property that is not a section 197 intangible).

(iv) *Computer software defined* .—For purposes of this section, computer software is any program or routine (that is, any sequence of machine-readable code) that is designed to cause a computer to perform a desired function or set of functions, and the documentation required to describe and maintain that program or routine. It includes all forms and media in which the software is contained, whether written, magnetic, or otherwise. Computer programs of all classes, for example, operating systems, executive systems, monitors, compilers and translators, assembly routines, and utility programs as well as application programs, are included. Computer software also includes any incidental and ancillary rights that are necessary to effect the acquisition of the title to, the ownership of, or the right to use the computer software, and that are used only in connection with that specific computer software. Such incidental and ancillary rights are not included in the definition of trademark or trade name under paragraph (b)(10)(i) of this section. For example, a trademark or trade name that is ancillary to the ownership or use of a specific computer software program in the taxpayer's trade or business and is not acquired for the purpose of marketing the computer software is included in the definition of computer software and is not included in the definition of trademark or trade name. Computer software does not include any data or information base described in paragraph (b)(4) of this section unless the data base or item is in the public domain and is incidental to a computer program. For this purpose, a copyrighted or proprietary data or information base is treated as in the public domain if its availability through the computer program does not contribute significantly to the cost of the program. For example, if a word-processing program includes a dictionary feature used to spell-check a document or any portion thereof, the entire program (including the dictionary feature) is computer software regardless of the form in which the feature is maintained or stored.

(5) *Certain interests in films, sound recordings, video tapes, books, or other similar property* .—Section 197 intangibles do not include any interest (including an interest as a licensee) in a film, sound recording, video tape, book, or other similar property (such as the right to broadcast or transmit a live event) if the interest is not acquired as part of a purchase of a trade or business. A film, sound recording, video tape, book, or other similar property includes any incidental and ancillary rights (such as a trademark or trade name) that are necessary to effect the acquisition of title to, the ownership of, or the right to use the property and are used only in connection with that property. Such incidental and ancillary rights are not included in the definition of trademark or trade name under paragraph (b)(10)(i) of this section. For purposes of this paragraph (c)(5), computer software (as defined in paragraph (c)(4)(iv) of this section) is not treated as other property similar to a film, sound recording, video tape, or book. (See section 167 for amortization of excluded intangible property or interests.)

(6) *Certain rights to receive tangible property or services* .—Section 197 intangibles do not include any right to receive tangible property or services under a contract or from a governmental unit if the right is not acquired as part of a purchase of a trade or business. Any right that is described in the preceding sentence is not treated as a section 197 intangible even though the right is also described in section 197(d)(1)(D) and paragraph (b)(8) of this section (relating to certain governmental licenses, permits, and other rights) and even though the right fails to meet one or more of the requirements of paragraph (c)(13) of this section

(relating to certain rights of fixed duration or amount). (See § 1.167(a)-14(c)(1) and (3) for applicable rules.)

(7) *Certain interests in patents or copyrights* .—Section 197 intangibles do not include any interest (including an interest as a licensee) in a patent, patent application, or copyright that is not acquired as part of a purchase of a trade or business. A patent or copyright includes any incidental and ancillary rights (such as a trademark or trade name) that are necessary to effect the acquisition of title to, the ownership of, or the right to use the property and are used only in connection with that property. Such incidental and ancillary rights are not included in the definition of trademark or trade name under paragraph (b)(10)(i) of this section. (See § 1.167(a)-14(c)(4) for applicable rules.)

(8) *Interests under leases of tangible property* .—(i) *Interest as a lessor* .—Section 197 intangibles do not include any interest as a lessor under an existing lease or sublease of tangible real or personal property. In addition, the cost of acquiring an interest as a lessor in connection with the acquisition of tangible property is taken into account as part of the cost of the tangible property. For example, if a taxpayer acquires a shopping center that is leased to tenants operating retail stores, any portion of the purchase price attributable to favorable lease terms is taken into account as part of the basis of the shopping center and in determining the depreciation deduction allowed with respect to the shopping center. (See section 167(c)(2).)

(ii) *Interest as a lessee* .—Section 197 intangibles do not include any interest as a lessee under an existing lease of tangible real or personal property. For this purpose, an airline lease of an airport passenger or cargo gate is a lease of tangible property. The cost of acquiring such an interest is taken into account under section 178 and § 1.162-11(a). If an interest as a lessee under a lease of tangible property is acquired in a transaction with any other intangible property, a portion of the total purchase price may be allocable to the interest as a lessee based on all of the relevant facts and circumstances.

(9) *Interests under indebtedness* .—(i) *In general* .—Section 197 intangibles do not include any interest (whether as a creditor or debtor) under an indebtedness in existence when the interest was acquired. Thus, for example, the value attributable to the assumption of an indebtedness with a below-market interest rate is not amortizable under section 197. In addition, the premium paid for acquiring a debt instrument with an above-market interest rate is not amortizable under section 197. See section 171 for rules concerning the treatment of amortizable bond premium.

(ii) *Exceptions* .—For purposes of this paragraph (c)(9), an interest under an existing indebtedness does not include the deposit base (and other similar items) of a financial institution. An interest under an existing indebtedness includes mortgage servicing rights, however, to the extent the rights are stripped coupons under section 1286.

(10) *Professional sports franchises* .—Section 197 intangibles do not include any franchise to engage in professional baseball, basketball, football, or any other professional sport, and any item (even though otherwise qualifying as a section 197 intangible) acquired in connection with such a franchise.

(11) *Mortgage servicing rights* .—Section 197 intangibles do not include any right described in section 197(e)(7) (concerning rights to service indebtedness secured by residential real property that are not acquired as part of a purchase of a trade or business). (See § 1.167(a)-14(d) for applicable rules.)

(12) *Certain transaction costs* .—Section 197 intangibles do not include any fees for professional services and any transaction costs incurred by parties to a transaction in which all or any portion of the gain or loss is not recognized under part III of subchapter C of the Internal Revenue Code.

(13) *Rights of fixed duration or amount* .—(i) Section 197 intangibles do not include any right under a contract or any license, permit, or other right granted by a governmental unit if the right—

(A) Is acquired in the ordinary course of a trade or business (or an activity described in section 212) and not as part of a purchase of a trade or business;

(B) Is not described in section 197(d)(1)(A), (B), (E), or (F);

(C) Is not a customer-based intangible, a customer-related information base, or any other similar item; and

(D) Either—

(1) Has a fixed duration of less than 15 years; or

(2) Is fixed as to amount and the adjusted basis thereof is properly recoverable (without regard to this section) under a method similar to the unit-of-production method.

(ii) See § 1.167(a)-14(c)(2) and (3) for applicable rules.

(d) *Amortizable section 197 intangibles* .—(1) *Definition* .—Except as otherwise provided in this paragraph (d), the term *amortizable section 197 intangible* means any section 197 intangible acquired after August 10, 1993 (or after July 25, 1991, if a valid retroactive election under § 1.197-1T has been made), and held in connection with the conduct of a trade or business or an activity described in section 212.

(2) *Exception for self-created intangibles* .—(i) *In general* .—Except as provided in paragraph (d)(2)(iii) of this section, amortizable section 197 intangibles do not include any section 197 intangible created by the taxpayer (a self-created intangible).

(ii) *Created by the taxpayer* .—(A) *Defined* .—A section 197 intangible is created by the taxpayer to the extent the taxpayer makes payments or otherwise incurs costs for its creation, production, development, or improvement, whether the actual work is performed by the taxpayer or by another person under a contract with the taxpayer entered into before the contracted creation, production, development, or improvement occurs. For example, a technological process developed specifically for a taxpayer under an arrangement with another person pursuant to which the taxpayer retains all rights to the process is created by the taxpayer.

(B) *Contracts for the use of intangibles* .—A section 197 intangible is not a self-created intangible to the extent that it results from the entry into (or renewal of) a contract for the use of an existing section 197 intangible. Thus, for example, the exception for self-created intangibles does not apply to capitalized costs, such as legal and other professional fees, incurred by a licensee in connection with the entry into (or renewal of) a contract for the use of know-how or similar property.

(C) *Improvements and modifications* .—If an existing section 197 intangible is improved or otherwise modified by the taxpayer or by another person under a contract with the taxpayer, the existing intangible and the capitalized costs (if any) of the improvements or other modifications are each treated as a separate section 197 intangible for purposes of this paragraph (d).

(iii) *Exceptions* .—(A) The exception for self-created intangibles does not apply to any section 197 intangible described in section 197(d)(1)(D) (relating to licenses, permits or other rights granted by a governmental unit), 197(d)(1)(E) (relating to covenants not to compete), or 197(d)(1)(F) (relating to franchises, trademarks, and trade names). Thus, for example, capitalized costs incurred in the development, registration, or defense of a trademark or trade name do not qualify for the exception and are amortized over 15 years under section 197.

(B) The exception for self-created intangibles does not apply to any section 197 intangible created in connection with the purchase of a trade or business (as defined in paragraph (e) of this section).

(C) If a taxpayer disposes of a self-created intangible and subsequently reacquires the intangible in an acquisition described in paragraph (h)(5)(ii) of this section, the exception for self-created intangibles does not apply to the reacquired intangible.

(3) *Exception for property subject to anti-churning rules* .—Amortizable section 197 intangibles do not include any property to which the anti-churning rules of section 197(f)(9) and paragraph (h) of this section apply.

(e) *Purchase of a trade or business* .—Several of the exceptions in section 197 apply only to property that is not acquired in (or created in connection with) a transaction or series of related transactions involving the acquisition of assets constituting a trade or business or a substantial portion thereof. Property acquired in (or created in connection with) such a transaction or series of related transactions is referred to in this section as property acquired as part of (or created in connection with) a purchase of a trade or business. For purposes of section 197 and this section, the applicability of the limitation is determined under the following rules:

(1) *Goodwill or going concern value* .—An asset or group of assets constitutes a trade or business or a substantial portion thereof if their use would constitute a trade or business under section 1060 (that is, if goodwill or going concern value could under any circumstances attach to the assets). See § 1.1060-1(b)(2). For this purpose, all the facts and circumstances, including any employee relationships that continue (or covenants not to compete that are entered into) as part of the transfer of the assets, are taken into account in determining whether goodwill or going concern value could attach to the assets.

(2) *Franchise, trademark, or trade name* .—(i) *In general* .—The acquisition of a franchise, trademark, or trade name constitutes the acquisition of a trade or business or a substantial portion thereof.

(ii) *Exceptions* .—For purposes of this paragraph (e)(2)—

(A) A trademark or trade name is disregarded if it is included in computer software under paragraph (c)(4) of this section or in an interest in a film, sound recording, video tape, book, or other similar property under paragraph (c)(5) of this section;

(B) A franchise, trademark, or trade name is disregarded if its value is nominal or the taxpayer irrevocably disposes of it immediately after its acquisition; and

(C) The acquisition of a right or interest in a trademark or trade name is disregarded if the grant of the right or interest is not, under the principles of section 1253, a transfer of all substantial rights to such property or of an undivided interest in all substantial rights to such property.

(3) *Acquisitions to be included* .—The assets acquired in a transaction (or series of related transactions) include only assets (including a beneficial or other indirect interest in assets where the interest is of a type described in paragraph (c)(1) of this section) acquired by the taxpayer and persons related to the taxpayer from another person and persons related to that other person. For purposes of this

paragraph (e)(3), persons are related only if their relationship is described in section 267(b) or 707(b) or they are engaged in trades or businesses under common control within the meaning of section 41(f)(1).

(4) *Substantial portion* .—The determination of whether acquired assets constitute a substantial portion of a trade or business is to be based on all of the facts and circumstances, including the nature and the amount of the assets acquired as well as the nature and amount of the assets retained by the transferor. The value of the assets acquired relative to the value of the assets retained by the transferor is not determinative of whether the acquired assets constitute a substantial portion of a trade or business.

(5) *Deemed asset purchases under section 338* .—A qualified stock purchase that is treated as a purchase of assets under section 338 is treated as a transaction involving the acquisition of assets constituting a trade or business only if the direct acquisition of the assets of the corporation would have been treated as the acquisition of assets constituting a trade or business or a substantial portion thereof.

(6) *Mortgage servicing rights* .—Mortgage servicing rights acquired in a transaction or series of related transactions are disregarded in determining for purposes of paragraph (c)(11) of this section whether the assets acquired in the transaction or transactions constitute a trade or business or substantial portion thereof.

(7) *Computer software acquired for internal use* .—Computer software acquired in a transaction or series of related transactions solely for internal use in an existing trade or business is disregarded in determining for purposes of paragraph (c)(4) of this section whether the assets acquired in the transaction or series of related transactions constitute a trade or business or substantial portion thereof.

(f) *Computation of amortization deduction* .—(1) *In general* .—Except as provided in paragraph (f)(2) of this section, the amortization deduction allowable under section 197(a) is computed as follows:

(i) The basis of an amortizable section 197 intangible is amortized ratably over the 15-year period beginning on the later of—

(A) The first day of the month in which the property is acquired; or

(B) In the case of property held in connection with the conduct of a trade or business or in an activity described in section 212, the first day of the month in which the conduct of the trade or business or the activity begins.

(ii) Except as otherwise provided in this section, basis is determined under section 1011 and salvage value is disregarded.

(iii) Property is not eligible for amortization in the month of disposition.

(iv) The amortization deduction for a short taxable year is based on the number of months in the short taxable year.

(2) *Treatment of contingent amounts* .—(i) *Amounts added to basis during 15-year period* .—Any amount that is properly included in the basis of an amortizable section 197 intangible after the first month of the 15-year period described in paragraph (f)(1)(i) of this section and before the expiration of that period is amortized ratably over the remainder of the 15-year period. For this purpose, the remainder of the 15-year period begins on the first day of the month in which the basis increase occurs.

(ii) *Amounts becoming fixed after expiration of 15-year period* .—Any amount that is not properly included in the basis of an amortizable section 197 intangible until after the expiration of the 15-year period described in paragraph (f)(1)(i) of this section is amortized in full immediately upon the inclusion of the amount in the basis of the intangible.

(iii) *Rules for including amounts in basis* .—See §§1.1275-4(c)(4) and 1.483-4(a) for rules governing the extent to which contingent amounts payable under a debt instrument given in consideration for the sale or exchange of an amortizable section 197 intangible are treated as payments of principal and the time at which the amount treated as principal is included in basis. See §1.461-1(a)(1) and (2) for rules governing the time at which other contingent amounts are taken into account in determining the basis of an amortizable section 197 intangible.

(3) *Basis determinations for certain assets* .—(i) *Covenants not to compete* .—In the case of a covenant not to compete or other similar arrangement described in paragraph (b)(9) of this section (a covenant), the amount chargeable to capital account includes, except as provided in this paragraph (f)(3), all amounts that are required to be paid pursuant to the covenant, whether or not any such amount would be deductible under section 162 if the covenant were not a section 197 intangible.

(ii) *Contracts for the use of section 197 intangibles; acquired as part of a trade or business* .—(A) *In general* .—Except as provided in this paragraph (f)(3), any amount paid or incurred by the transferee on account of the transfer of a right or term interest described in paragraph (b)(11) of this section (relating to contracts for the use of, and term interests in, section 197 intangibles) by the owner of the property to which such right or interest relates and as part of a purchase of a trade or business is chargeable to capital account, whether or not such amount would be deductible under section 162 if the property were not a section 197 intangible.

(B) *Know-how and certain information base* .—The amount chargeable to capital account with respect to a right or term interest described in paragraph (b)(11) of this section is determined without regard to the rule in paragraph (f)(3)(ii)(A) of this section if the right or interest relates to property (other than a customer-related information base) described in paragraph (b)(4) or (5) of this section and the acquiring taxpayer establishes that—

(1) The transfer of the right or interest is not, under the principles of section 1235, a transfer of all substantial rights to such property or of an undivided interest in all substantial rights to such property; and

(2) The right or interest was transferred for an arm's-length consideration.

(iii) *Contracts for the use of section 197 intangibles; not acquired as part of a trade or business* .—The transfer of a right or term interest described in paragraph (b)(11) of this section by the owner of the property to which such right or interest relates but not as part of a purchase of a trade or business will be closely scrutinized under the principles of section 1235 for purposes of determining whether the transfer is a sale or exchange and, accordingly, whether amounts paid on account of the transfer are chargeable to capital account. If under the principles of section 1235 the transaction is not a sale or exchange, amounts paid on account of the transfer are not chargeable to capital account under this paragraph (f)(3).

(iv) *Applicable rules* .—(A) *Franchises, trademarks, and trade names* .—For purposes of this paragraph (f)(3), section 197 intangibles described in paragraph (b)(11) of this section do not include any property that is also described in paragraph (b)(10) of this section (relating to franchises, trademarks, and trade names).

(B) *Certain amounts treated as payable under a debt instrument .—(1) In general* .—For purposes of applying any provision of the Internal Revenue Code to a person making payments of amounts that are otherwise chargeable to capital account under this paragraph (f)(3) and are payable after the acquisition of the section 197 intangible to which they relate, such amounts are treated as payable under a debt instrument given in consideration for the sale or exchange of the section 197 intangible.

(2) Rights granted by governmental units .—For purposes of applying any provision of the Internal Revenue Code to any amounts that are otherwise chargeable to capital account with respect to a license, permit, or other right described in paragraph (b)(8) of this section (relating to rights granted by a governmental unit or agency or instrumentality thereof) and are payable after the acquisition of the section 197 intangible to which they relate, such amounts are treated, except as provided in paragraph (f)(4)(i) of this section (relating to renewal transactions), as payable under a debt instrument given in consideration for the sale or exchange of the section 197 intangible.

(3) Treatment of other parties to transaction .—No person shall be treated as having sold, exchanged, or otherwise disposed of property in a transaction for purposes of any provision of the Internal Revenue Code solely by reason of the application of this paragraph (f)(3) to any other party to the transaction.

(4) Basis determinations in certain transactions .—(i) Certain renewal transactions .—The costs paid or incurred for the renewal of a franchise, trademark, or trade name or any license, permit, or other right granted by a governmental unit or an agency or instrumentality thereof are amortized over the 15-year period that begins with the month of renewal. Any costs paid or incurred for the issuance, or earlier renewal, continue to be taken into account over the remaining portion of the amortization period that began at the time of the issuance, or earlier renewal. Any amount paid or incurred for the protection, expansion, or defense of a trademark or trade name and chargeable to capital account is treated as an amount paid or incurred for a renewal.

(ii) Transactions subject to section 338 or 1060 .—In the case of a section 197 intangible deemed to have been acquired as the result of a qualified stock purchase within the meaning of section 338(d)(3), the basis shall be determined pursuant to section 338(b)(5) and the regulations thereunder. In the case of a section 197 intangible acquired in an applicable asset acquisition within the meaning of section 1060(c), the basis shall be determined pursuant to section 1060(a) and the regulations thereunder.

(iii) Certain reinsurance transactions .—See paragraph (g)(5)(ii) of this section for special rules regarding the adjusted basis of an insurance contract acquired through an assumption reinsurance transaction.

(g) *Special rules* .—(1) *Treatment of certain dispositions* .—(i) *Loss disallowance rules* .—(A) *In general* .—No loss is recognized on the disposition of an amortizable section 197 intangible if the taxpayer has any retained intangibles. The retained intangibles with respect to the disposition of any amortizable section 197 intangible (the transferred intangible) are all amortizable section 197 intangibles, or rights to use or interests (including beneficial or other indirect interests) in amortizable section 197 intangibles (including the transferred intangible) that were acquired in the same transaction or series of related transactions as the transferred intangible and are retained after its disposition. Except as otherwise provided in paragraph (g)(1)(iv)(B) of this section, the adjusted basis of each of the retained intangibles is increased by the product of—

(1) The loss that is not recognized solely by reason of this rule; and

(2) A fraction, the numerator of which is the adjusted basis of the retained intangible on the date of the disposition and the denominator of which is the total adjusted bases of all the retained intangibles on that date.

(B) *Abandonment or worthlessness* .—The abandonment of an amortizable section 197 intangible, or any other event rendering an amortizable section 197 intangible worthless, is treated as a disposition of the intangible for purposes of this paragraph (g)(1), and the abandoned or worthless intangible is disregarded (that is, it is not treated as a retained intangible) for purposes of applying this paragraph (g)(1) to the subsequent disposition of any other amortizable section 197 intangible.

(C) *Certain nonrecognition transfers* .—The loss disallowance rule in paragraph (g)(1)(i)(A) of this section also applies when a taxpayer transfers an amortizable section 197 intangible from an acquired trade or business in a transaction in which the intangible is transferred basis property and, after the transfer, retains other amortizable section 197 intangibles from the trade or business. Thus, for example, the transfer of an amortizable section 197 intangible to a corporation in exchange for stock in the corporation in a transaction described in section 351, or to a partnership in exchange for an interest in the partnership in a transaction described in section 721, when other amortizable section 197 intangibles acquired in the same transaction are retained, followed by a sale of the stock or partnership interest received, will not avoid the application of the loss disallowance provision to the extent the adjusted basis of the transferred intangible at the time of the sale exceeds its fair market value at that time.

(ii) *Separately acquired property* .—Paragraph (g)(1)(i) of this section does not apply to an amortizable section 197 intangible that is not acquired in a transaction or series of related transactions in which the taxpayer acquires other amortizable section 197 intangibles (a separately acquired intangible). Consequently, a loss may be recognized upon the disposition of a separately acquired amortizable section 197 intangible. However, the termination or worthlessness of only a portion of an amortizable section 197 intangible is not the disposition of a separately acquired intangible. For example, neither the loss of several customers from an acquired customer list nor the worthlessness of only some information from an acquired data base constitutes the disposition of a separately acquired intangible.

(iii) *Disposition of a covenant not to compete* .—If a covenant not to compete or any other arrangement having substantially the same effect is entered into in connection with the direct or indirect acquisition of an interest in one or more trades or businesses, the disposition or worthlessness of the covenant or other arrangement will not be considered to occur until the disposition or worthlessness of all interests in those trades or businesses. For example, a covenant not to compete entered into in connection with the purchase of stock continues to be amortized ratably over the 15-year recovery period (even after the covenant expires or becomes worthless) unless all the trades or businesses in which an interest was acquired through the stock purchase (or all the purchaser's interests in those trades or businesses) also are disposed of or become worthless.

(iv) *Taxpayers under common control* .—(A) *In general* .—Except as provided in paragraph (g)(1)(iv)(B) of this section, all persons that would be treated as a single taxpayer under section 41(f)(1) are treated as a single taxpayer under this paragraph (g)(1). Thus, for example, a loss is not recognized on the disposition of an amortizable section 197 intangible by a member of a controlled group of corporations (as defined in section 41(f)(5)) if, after the disposition, another member retains other amortizable section 197 intangibles acquired in the same transaction as the amortizable section 197 intangible that has been disposed of.

(B) *Treatment of disallowed loss* .—If retained intangibles are held by a person other than the person incurring the disallowed loss, only the adjusted basis of intangibles retained by the person incurring the disallowed loss is increased, and only the adjusted basis of those intangibles is included in the denominator of the fraction described in paragraph (g)(1)(i)(A) of this section. If none of the retained intangibles are held by the person incurring the disallowed loss, the loss is allowed ratably, as a deduction under section 197, over the remainder of the period during which the intangible giving rise to the loss would have been amortizable, except that any remaining disallowed loss is allowed in full on the first date on which all other retained intangibles have been disposed of or become worthless.

(2) *Treatment of certain nonrecognition and exchange transactions* .—(i) *Relationship to anti-churning rules* .—This paragraph (g)(2) provides rules relating to the treatment of section 197 intangibles acquired in certain transactions. If these rules apply to a section 197(f)(9) intangible (within the meaning of paragraph (h)(1)(i) of this section), the intangible is, notwithstanding its treatment under this paragraph (g)(2), treated as an amortizable section 197 intangible only to the extent permitted under paragraph (h) of this section.

(ii) *Treatment of nonrecognition and exchange transactions generally* .—(A) *Transfer disregarded* .—If a section 197 intangible is transferred in a transaction described in paragraph (g)(2)(ii)(C) of this section, the transfer is disregarded in determining—

(1) Whether, with respect to so much of the intangible's basis in the hands of the transferee as does not exceed its basis in the hands of the transferor, the intangible is an amortizable section 197 intangible; and

(2) The amount of the deduction under section 197 with respect to such basis.

(B) *Application of general rule* .—If the intangible described in paragraph (g)(2)(ii)(A) of this section was an amortizable section 197 intangible in the hands of the transferor, the transferee will continue to amortize its adjusted basis, to the extent it does not exceed the transferor's adjusted basis, ratably over the remainder of the transferor's 15-year amortization period. If the intangible was not an amortizable section 197 intangible in the hands of the transferor, the transferee's adjusted basis, to the extent it does not exceed the transferor's adjusted basis, cannot be amortized under section 197. In either event, the intangible is treated, with respect to so much of its adjusted basis in the hands of the transferee as exceeds its adjusted basis in the hands of the transferor, in the same manner for purposes of section 197 as an intangible acquired from the transferor in a transaction that is not described in paragraph (g)(2)(ii)(C) of this section. The rules of this paragraph (g)(2)(ii) also apply to any subsequent transfers of the intangible in a transaction described in paragraph (g)(2)(ii)(C) of this section.

(C) *Transactions covered* .—The transactions described in this paragraph (g)(2)(ii)(C) are—

(1) Any transaction described in section 332, 351, 361, 721, or 731; and

(2) Any transaction between corporations that are members of the same consolidated group immediately after the transaction.

(iii) *Certain exchanged-basis property* .—This paragraph (g)(2)(iii) applies to property that is acquired in a transaction subject to section 1031 or 1033 and is permitted to be acquired without recognition of gain (replacement property). Replacement property is treated as if it were the property by reference to which its basis is determined (the predecessor property) in determining whether, with respect to so much of its basis as does not exceed the basis of the predecessor property, the replacement property is an amortizable section 197 intangible and the amortization period under section 197 with respect to such basis. Thus, if the predecessor property was an amortizable section 197 intangible, the taxpayer will amortize the adjusted basis of the replacement property, to the extent it does not exceed the adjusted basis of the predecessor property, ratably over the remainder of the 15-year amortization period for the predecessor property. If the predecessor property was not an amortizable section 197 intangible, the adjusted basis of the replacement property, to the extent it does not exceed the adjusted basis of the predecessor property, may not be amortized under section 197. In either event, the replacement property is treated, with respect to so much of its adjusted basis as exceeds the adjusted basis of the predecessor property, in the same manner for purposes of section 197 as property acquired from the transferor in a transaction that is not subject to section 1031 or 1033.

(iv) *Transfers under section 708(b)(1)* .—(A) *In general* .—Paragraph (g)(2)(ii) of this section applies to transfers of section 197 intangibles that occur or are deemed to occur by reason of the termination of a partnership under section 708(b)(1).

(B) *Termination by sale or exchange of interest* .—In applying paragraph (g)(2)(ii) of this section to a partnership that is terminated pursuant to section 708(b)(1)(B) (relating to deemed terminations from the sale or exchange of an interest), the terminated partnership is treated as the transferor and the new partnership is treated as the transferee with respect to any section 197 intangible held by the terminated partnership immediately preceding the termination. (See paragraph (g)(3) of this section for the treatment of increases in the bases of property of the terminated partnership under section 743(b).)

(C) *Other terminations* .—In applying paragraph (g)(2)(ii) of this section to a partnership that is terminated pursuant to section 708(b)(1)(A) (relating to cessation of activities by a partnership), the terminated partnership is treated as the transferor and the distributee partner is treated as the transferee with respect to any section 197 intangible held by the terminated partnership immediately preceding the termination.

(3) *Increase in the basis of partnership property under section 732(b), 734(b), 743(b), or 732(d)* .—Any increase in the adjusted basis of a section 197 intangible under sections 732(b) or 732(d) (relating to a partner's basis in property distributed by a partnership), section 734(b) (relating to the optional adjustment to the basis of undistributed partnership property after a distribution of property to a partner), or section 743(b) (relating to the optional adjustment to the basis of partnership property after transfer of a partnership interest) is treated as a separate section 197 intangible. For purposes of determining the amortization period under section 197 with respect to the basis increase, the intangible is treated as having been acquired at the time of the transaction that causes the basis increase, except as provided in § 1.743-1(j)(4)(i)(B)(*2*). The provisions of paragraph (f)(2) of this section apply to the extent that the amount of the basis increase is determined by reference to contingent payments. For purposes of the effective date and anti-churning provisions (paragraphs (l)(1) and (h) of this section) for a basis increase under section 732(d), the intangible is treated as having been acquired by the transferee partner at the time of the transfer of the partnership interest described in section 732(d). The provisions of paragraph (f)(2) of this section apply to the extent that the amount of the basis increase is determined by reference to contingent

payments. For purposes of the effective date and anti-churning provisions (paragraphs (l)(1) and (h) of this section) for a basis increase under section 732(d), the intangible is treated as having been acquired by the transferee partner at the time of the transfer of the partnership interest described in section 732(d).

(4) *Section 704(c) allocations* .—(i) *Allocations where the intangible is amortizable by the contributor* .—To the extent that the intangible was an amortizable section 197 intangible in the hands of the contributing partner, a partnership may make allocations of amortization deductions with respect to the intangible to all of its partners under any of the permissible methods described in the regulations under section 704(c). See § 1.704-3.

(ii) *Allocations where the intangible is not amortizable by the contributor* .—To the extent that the intangible was not an amortizable section 197 intangible in the hands of the contributing partner, the intangible is not amortizable under section 197 by the partnership. However, if a partner contributes a section 197 intangible to a partnership and the partnership adopts the remedial allocation method for making section 704(c) allocations of amortization deductions, the partnership generally may make remedial allocations of amortization deductions with respect to the contributed section 197 intangible in accordance with § 1.704-3(d). See paragraph (h)(12) of this section to determine the application of the anti-churning rules in the context of remedial allocations.

(5) *Treatment of certain insurance contracts acquired in an assumption reinsurance transaction* .—(i) *In general* .—Section 197 generally applies to insurance and annuity contracts acquired from another person through an assumption reinsurance transaction. See § 1.809-5(a)(7)(ii) for the definition of assumption reinsurance. The transfer of insurance or annuity contracts and the assumption of related liabilities deemed to occur by reason of a section 338 election for a target insurance company is treated as an assumption reinsurance transaction. The transfer of a reinsurance contract by a reinsurer (transferor) to another reinsurer (acquirer) is treated as an assumption reinsurance transaction if the transferor's obligations are extinguished as a result of the transaction.

(ii) Determination of adjusted basis of amortizable section 197 intangible resulting from an assumption reinsurance transaction—

(A) *In general.*—Section 197(f)(5) determines the basis of an amortizable section 197 intangible for insurance or annuity contracts acquired in an assumption reinsurance transaction. The basis of such intangible is the excess, if any, of—

(1) The amount paid or incurred by the acquirer (reinsurer) under the assumption reinsurance transaction; over

(2) The amount, if any, required to be capitalized under section 848 in connection with such transaction.

(B) *Amount paid or incurred by acquirer (reinsurer) under the assumption reinsurance transaction.*—The amount paid or incurred by the acquirer (reinsurer) under the assumption reinsurance transaction is—

(1) In a deemed asset sale resulting from an election under section 338, the amount of the adjusted grossed-up basis (AGUB) allocable thereto (see § § 1.338-6 and 1.338-11(b)(2));

(2) In an applicable asset acquisition within the meaning of section 1060, the amount of the consideration allocable thereto (see § § 1.338-6, 1.338-11(b)(2), and 1.1060-1(c)(5)); and

(3) In any other transaction, the excess of the increase in the reinsurer's tax reserves resulting from the transaction (computed in accordance

with sections 807, 832(b)(4)(B), and 846) over the value of the net assets received from the ceding company in the transaction.

(C) *Amount required to be capitalized under section 848 in connection with the transaction.*—(1) *In general.*—The amount required to be capitalized under section 848 for specified insurance contracts (as defined in section 848(e)) acquired in an assumption reinsurance transaction is the lesser of—

(i) The reinsurer's required capitalization amount for the assumption reinsurance transaction; or

(ii) The reinsurer's general deductions (as defined in section 848(c)(2)) allocable to the transaction.

(2) *Required capitalization amount.*—The reinsurer determines the required capitalization amount for an assumption reinsurance transaction by multiplying the net positive or net negative consideration for the transaction by the applicable percentage set forth in section 848(c)(1) for the category of specified insurance contracts acquired in the transaction. See § 1.848-2(g)(5). If more than one category of specified insurance contracts is acquired in an assumption reinsurance transaction, the required capitalization amount for each category is determined as if the transfer of the contracts in that category were made under a separate assumption reinsurance transaction. See § 1.848-2(f)(7).

(3) *General deductions allocable to the assumption reinsurance transaction.*—The reinsurer determines the general deductions allocable to the assumption reinsurance transaction in accordance with the procedure set forth in § 1.848-2(g)(6). Accordingly, the reinsurer must allocate its general deductions to the amount required under section 848(c)(1) on specified insurance contracts that the reinsurer has issued directly before determining the general deductions allocable to the assumption reinsurance transaction. For purposes of allocating its general deductions under § 1.848-2(g)(6), the reinsurer includes premiums received on the acquired specified insurance contracts after the assumption reinsurance transaction in determining the amount required under section 848(c)(1) on specified insurance contracts that the reinsurer has issued directly. If the reinsurer has entered into multiple reinsurance agreements during the taxable year, the reinsurer determines the general deductions allocable to each reinsurance agreement (including the assumption reinsurance transaction) by allocating the general deductions allocable to reinsurance agreements under § 1.848-2(g)(6) to each reinsurance agreement with a positive required capitalization amount.

(4) *Treatment of a capitalization shortfall allocable to the reinsurance agreement.*—(i) *In general.*—The reinsurer determines any capitalization shortfall allocable to the assumption reinsurance transaction in the manner provided in §§ 1.848-2(g)(4) and 1.848-2(g)(7). If the reinsurer has a capitalization shortfall allocable to the assumption reinsurance transaction, the ceding company must reduce the net negative consideration (as determined under § 1.848-2(f)(2)) for the transaction by the amount described in § 1.848-2(g)(3) unless the parties make the election provided in § 1.848-2(g)(8) to determine the amounts capitalized under section 848 in connection with the transaction without regard to the general deductions limitation of section 848(c)(2).

(ii) *Treatment of additional capitalized amounts as the result of an election under § 1.848-2(g)(8).*—The additional amounts capitalized by the reinsurer as the result of the election under § 1.848-2(g)(8) reduce the adjusted basis of any amortizable section 197 intangible with respect to specified insurance contracts acquired in the assumption reinsurance transaction. If the additional capitalized amounts exceed the adjusted basis of the amortizable section 197 intangible, the reinsurer must reduce its deductions under section 805 or section 832 by the amount of such excess. The additional capitalized amounts are treated as specified policy acquisition expenses attributable to the premiums and other consideration on the assumption reinsurance transaction and are deducted ratably over a 120-month period as provided under section 848(a)(2).

(5) *Cross references and special rules.*—In general, for rules applicable to the determination of specified policy acquisition expenses, net premiums, and net consideration, see section 848(c) and (d), and § 1.848-2(a) and (f). However, the following special rules apply for purposes of this paragraph (g)(5)(ii)(C)—

(i) The amount required to be capitalized under section 848 in connection with the assumption reinsurance transaction cannot be less than zero;

(ii) For purposes of determining the company's general deductions under section 848(c)(2) for the taxable year of the assumption reinsurance transaction, the reinsurer takes into account a tentative amortization deduction under section 197(a) as if the entire amount paid or incurred by the reinsurer for the specified insurance contracts were allocated to an amortizable section 197 intangible with respect to insurance contracts acquired in an assumption reinsurance transaction; and

(iii) Any reduction of specified policy acquisition expenses pursuant to an election under § 1.848-2(i)(4) (relating to an assumption reinsurance transaction with an insolvent insurance company) is disregarded.

(D) *Examples.*—The following examples illustrate the principles of this paragraph (g)(5)(ii):

Example 1. (i) Facts. On January 15, 2006, P acquires all of the stock of T, an insurance company, in a qualified stock purchase and makes a section 338 election for T. T issues individual life insurance contracts which are specified insurance contracts as defined in section 848(e)(1). P and new T are calendar year taxpayers. Under § § 1.338-6 and 1.338-11(b)(2), the amount of AGUB allocated to old T's individual life insurance contracts is $300,000. On the acquisition date, the tax reserves for old T's individual life insurance contracts are $2,000,000. After the acquisition date, new T receives $1,000,000 of net premiums with respect to new and renewal individual life insurance contracts and incurs $100,000 of general deductions under section 848(c)(2) through December 31, 2006. New T engages in no other reinsurance transactions other than the assumption reinsurance transaction treated as occurring by reason of the section 338 election.

(ii) Analysis. The transfer of insurance contracts and the assumption of related liabilities deemed to occur by reason of the election under section 338 is treated as an assumption reinsurance transaction. New T determines the adjusted basis under section 197(f)(5) for the life insurance contracts acquired in the assumption reinsurance transaction as follows. The amount paid or incurred for the individual life insurance contracts is $300,000. To determine the amount required to be capitalized under section 848 in connection with the assumption reinsurance transaction, new T compares the required capitalization amount for the assumption reinsurance transaction with the general deductions allocable to the transaction. The required capitalization amount for the assumption reinsurance transaction is $130,900, which is determined by multiplying the $1,700,000 net positive consideration for the transaction ($2,000,000 reinsurance premium less $300,000 ceding commission) by the applicable percentage under section 848(c)(1) for the acquired individual life insurance contracts (7.7 percent). To determine its general deductions, new T takes into account a tentative amortization deduction under section 197(a) as if the entire amount paid or incurred for old T's individual life insurance contracts ($300,000) were allocable to an amortizable section 197 intangible with respect to insurance contracts acquired in the assumption reinsurance transaction. Accordingly, for the year of the assumption reinsurance transaction, new T is treated as having general deductions under section 848(c)(2) of $120,000 ($100,000 + $300,000/15). Under § 1.848-2(g)(6), these general deductions are first allocated to the $77,000 capitalization requirement for new T's directly written business ($1,000,000 × .077). Thus, $43,000 ($120,000 – $77,000) of the general deductions are allocable to the assumption reinsurance transaction. Because the general deductions allocable to the assumption reinsurance transaction ($43,000) are less than the required capitalization amount for the transaction ($130,900), new T has a capitalization shortfall of $87,900 ($130,900 – $43,000) with regard to the transaction. Under § 1.848-2(g), this capitalization shortfall would cause old T to reduce the net negative consideration taken into account with respect to the assumption reinsurance transaction by $1,141,558 ($87,900 ÷ .077) unless the parties make the election under § 1.848-2(g)(8) to capitalize specified policy acquisition expenses in connection with the assumption reinsurance transaction without regard to the general deductions limitation. If the parties make the election, the amount capitalized by new T under section 848 in connection with the assumption reinsurance transaction would be $130,900. The $130,900 capitalized by new T under section 848 would reduce new T's adjusted basis of the amortizable section 197 intangible with respect to the specified insurance contracts acquired in the assumption reinsurance transaction. Accordingly, new T would have an adjusted basis under section 197(f)(5) with respect to the individual life insurance contracts acquired from old T of $169,100 ($300,000 – $130,900). New T's actual amortization deduction under section 197(a) with respect to the amortizable section 197 intangible for insurance contracts acquired in the assumption reinsurance transaction would be $11,273 ($169,100 ÷15).

Example 2. (i) Facts. The facts are the same as Example 1, except that T only issues accident and health insurance contracts that are qualified long-term care contracts under section 7702B. Under section 7702B(a)(5), T's qualified long-term care insurance contracts are treated as guaranteed renewable accident and health insurance contracts, and, therefore, are considered specified insurance contracts under section 848(e)(1). Under §§ 1.338-6 and 1.338-11(b)(2), the amount of AGUB allocable to T's qualified long-term care insurance contracts is $250,000. The amount of T's tax reserves for the qualified long-term care contracts on the acquisition date is $7,750,000. Following the acquisition, new T receives net premiums of $500,000 with respect to qualified long-term care contracts and incurs general deductions of $75,000 through December 31, 2006.

(ii) Analysis. The transfer of insurance contracts and the assumption of related liabilities deemed to occur by reason of the election under section 338 is treated as an assumption reinsurance transaction. New T determines the adjusted basis under section 197(f)(5) for the insurance contracts acquired in the assumption reinsurance transaction as follows. The amount paid or incurred for the insurance contracts is $250,000. To determine the amount required to be capitalized under section 848 in connection with the assumption reinsurance transaction, new T compares the required capitalization amount for the assumption reinsurance transaction with the general deductions allocable to the transaction. The required capitalization amount for the assumption reinsurance transaction is $577,500, which is determined by multiplying the $7,500,000 net positive consideration for the transaction ($7,750,000 reinsurance premium less $250,000 ceding commission) by the applicable percentage under section 848(c)(1) for the acquired insurance contracts (7.7 percent). To determine its general deductions, new T takes into account a tentative amortization deduction under section 197(a) as if the entire amount paid or incurred for old T's insurance contracts ($250,000) were allocable to an amortizable section 197 intangible with respect to insurance contracts acquired in the assumption reinsurance transaction. Accordingly, for the year of the assumption reinsurance transaction, new T is treated as having general deductions under section 848(c)(2) of $91,667 ($75,000 + $250,000/15). Under § 1.848-2(g)(6), these general deductions are first allocated to the $38,500 capitalization requirement for new T's directly written business ($500,000 × .077). Thus, $53,167 ($91,667 – $38,500) of general deductions are allocable to the assumption reinsurance transaction. Because the general deductions allocable to the assumption reinsurance transaction ($53,167) are less than the required capitalization amount for the transaction ($577,500), new T has a capitalization shortfall of $524,333 ($577,500 - $53,167) with regard to the transaction. Under § 1.848-2(g), this capitalization shortfall would cause old T to reduce the net negative consideration taken into account with respect to the assumption reinsurance transaction by $6,809,519 ($524,333 + .077) unless the parties make the election under § 1.848-2(g)(8) to capitalize specified policy acquisition expenses in connection with the assumption reinsurance transaction without regard to the general deductions limitation. If the parties make the election, the amount capitalized by new T under section 848 in connection with the assumption reinsurance transaction would increase from $53,167 to $577,500. Pursuant to paragraph (g)(5)(ii)(C)(4) of this section, the additional $524,333 ($577,500 - $53,167) capitalized by new T under section 848 would reduce new T's adjusted basis of the amortizable section 197 intangible with respect to the insurance contracts acquired in the assumption reinsurance transaction. Accordingly, new T's adjusted basis of the section 197 intangible with regard to the insurance contracts is reduced from $196,833 ($250,000 - $53,167) to $0. Because the additional $524,333 capitalized pursuant to the § 1.848-2(g)(8) election exceeds the $196,833 adjusted basis of the section 197 intangible before the reduction, new T is required to reduce its deductions under section 805 by the $327,500 ($524,333 - $196,833).

(E) *Effective/applicability date.*—This section applies to acquisitions and dispositions of insurance contracts on or after April 10, 2006.

(iii) *Application of loss disallowance rule upon a disposition of an insurance contract acquired in an assumption reinsurance transaction* .—The following rules apply for purposes of applying the loss disallowance rules of section 197(f)(1)(A) to the disposition of a section 197(f)(5) intangible. For this purpose, a section 197(f)(5) intangible is an amortizable section 197 intangible the basis of which is determined under section 197(f)(5).

(A) *Disposition .—(1) In general* .—A disposition of a section 197 intangible is any event as a result of which, absent section 197, recovery of basis is otherwise allowed for Federal income tax purposes.

(2) *Treatment of indemnity reinsurance transactions* .—The transfer through indemnity reinsurance of the right to the future income from the insurance contracts to which a section 197(f)(5) intangible relates does not preclude the recovery of basis by the ceding company, provided that sufficient economic rights relating to the reinsured contracts are transferred to the reinsurer. However, the ceding company is not permitted to recover basis in an indemnity reinsurance transaction if it has a right to experience refunds reflecting a significant portion of the future profits on the reinsured contracts, or if it retains an option to reacquire a significant portion of the future profits on the reinsured contracts through the exercise of a recapture provision. In addition, the ceding company is not permitted to recover basis in an indemnity reinsurance transaction if the reinsurer assumes only a limited portion of the ceding company's risk relating to the reinsured contracts (excess loss reinsurance).

(B) *Loss* .—The loss, if any, recognized by a taxpayer on the disposition of a section 197(f)(5) intangible equals the amount by which the taxpayer's adjusted basis in the section 197(f)(5) intangible immediately before the disposition exceeds the amount, if any, that the taxpayer receives from another person for the future income right from the insurance contracts to which the section 197(f)(5) intangible relates. In determining the amount of the taxpayer's loss on the disposition of a section 197(f)(5) intangible through a reinsurance transaction, any effect of the transaction on the amounts capitalized by the taxpayer as specified policy acquisition expenses under section 848 is disregarded.

(C) *Examples* .—The following examples illustrate the principles of this paragraph (g)(5)(iii):

Example 1. (i) *Facts.* In a prior taxable year, as a result of a section 338 election with respect to T, new T was treated as purchasing all of old T's insurance contracts that were in force on the acquisition date in an assumption reinsurance transaction. Under §§1.338-6 and 1.338-11(b)(2), the amount of AGUB allocable to the future income right from the purchased insurance contracts was $15, net of the amounts required to be capitalized under section 848 as a result of the assumption reinsurance transaction. At the beginning of the current taxable year, as a result of amortization deductions allowed by section 197(a), new T's adjusted basis in the section 197(f)(5) intangible resulting from the assumption reinsurance transaction is $12. During the current taxable year, new T enters into an indemnity reinsurance agreement with R, another insurance company, in which R assumes 100 percent of the risk relating to the insurance contracts to which the section 197(f)(5) intangible relates. In the indemnity reinsurance transaction, R agrees to pay new T a ceding commission of $10 in exchange for the future profits on the underlying reinsured policies. Under the indemnity reinsurance agreement, new T continues to administer the reinsured policies, but transfers investment assets equal to the required reserves for the reinsured policies together with all future premiums to R. The indemnity reinsurance agreement does not contain an experience refund provision or a provision allowing new T to terminate the reinsurance agreement at its sole option. New T retains the insurance licenses and other amortizable section 197 intangibles acquired in the deemed asset sale and continues to underwrite and issue new insurance contracts.

(ii) *Analysis.* The indemnity reinsurance agreement constitutes a disposition of the section 197(f)(5) intangible because it involves the transfer of sufficient economic rights attributable to the insurance contracts to which the section 197(f)(5) intangible relates such that recovery of basis is allowed. For purposes of applying the loss disallowance rules of section 197(f)(1) and paragraph (g) of this section, new T's loss is $2 (new T's adjusted basis in the section 197(f)(5) intangible immediately before the disposition ($12) less the ceding commission ($10)). Therefore, new T applies $10 of the adjusted basis in the section 197(f)(5) intangible against the amount received from R for the future income right on the reinsured policies and increases its basis in the amortizable section 197 intangibles that it acquired and retained from the deemed asset sale by $2, the amount of the disallowed loss. The amount of new T's disallowed loss under section 197(f)(1)(A) is determined without regard to the effect of the indemnity reinsurance transaction on the amounts capitalized by new T as specified policy acquisition expenses under section 848.

Example 2. (i) *Facts.* Assume the same facts as in *Example 1*, except that under the indemnity reinsurance agreement R agrees to pay new T a ceding commission of $5 with respect to the underlying reinsured contracts. In addition, under the indemnity reinsurance agreement, new T is entitled to an experience refund equal to any future profits on the reinsured contracts in excess of the ceding commission plus an annual risk charge. New T also has a right to recapture the business at any time after R has recovered an amount equal to the ceding commission.

(ii) *Analysis.* The indemnity reinsurance agreement between new T and R does not represent a disposition because it does not involve the transfer of sufficient economic rights with respect to the future income on the reinsured contracts. Therefore, new T may not recover its basis in the section 197(f)(5) intangible to which the contracts relate and must continue to amortize ratably the adjusted basis of the section 197(f)(5) intangible over the remainder of the 15-year recovery period and cannot apply any portion of this adjusted basis to offset the ceding commission received from R in the indemnity reinsurance transaction.

(iv) *Effective dates* .—(A) *In general* .—This paragraph (g)(5) applies to acquisitions and dispositions on or after April 10, 2006. For rules applicable to acquisitions and dispositions before that date, see § 1.197-2 in effect before that date (see 26 CFR part 1, revised April 1, 2001).

(B) *Application to pre-effective date acquisitions and dispositions* .—A taxpayer may choose, on a transaction-by-transaction basis, to apply the provisions of this paragraph (g)(5) to property acquired and disposed of before April 10, 2006.

(C) *Change in method of accounting* .—*(1) In general* .—A change in a taxpayer's treatment of all property acquired and disposed under paragraph (g)(5) is a change in method of accounting to which the provisions of sections 446 and 481 and the regulations thereunder apply.

(2) Acquisitions and dispositions on or after effective date .—A Taxpayer is granted the consent of the Commissioner under section 446(e) to change its method of accounting to comply with this paragraph (g)(5) for acquisitions and dispositions on or after April 10, 2006. The change must be made on a cut-off basis with no section 481(a) adjustment. Notwithstanding § 1.446-1(e)(3), a taxpayer should not file a Form 3115, "Application for Change in Accounting Method," to obtain the consent of the Commissioner to change its method of accounting under this paragraph (g)(5)(iv)(C)(*2*). Instead, a taxpayer must make the change by using the new method on its federal income tax returns.

(3) Acquisitions and dispositions before the effective date .—For the first taxable year ending after April 10, 2006, a taxpayer is granted consent of the Commissioner to change its method of accounting for all property acquired in transactions described in paragraph (g)(5)(iv)(B) to comply with this paragraph (g)(5) unless the proper treatment of any such property is an issue under consideration in an examination, before an Appeals office, or before a Federal Court. (For the definition of when an issue is under consideration, see, Rev. Proc. 97-27 (1997-1 C.B. 680); and, § 601.601(d)(2) of this chapter). A taxpayer changing its method of accounting in accordance with this paragraph (g)(5)(iv)(C)(*3*) must follow the applicable administrative procedures for obtaining the Commissioner's automatic consent to a change in method of accounting (for further guidance, see, for example, Rev. Proc. 2002-9 (2002-1 C.B. 327) as modified and clarified by Announcement 2002-17 (2002-1 C.B. 561), modified and amplified by Rev. Proc. 2002-19 (2002-1 C.B. 696), and amplified, clarified and modified by Rev. Proc. 2002-54 (2002-2 C.B. 432); and, § 601.601(d)(2) of this chapter), except, for purposes of this paragraph (g)(5)(iv)(C)(*3*), any limitations in such administrative procedures for obtaining the automatic consent of the Commissioner shall not apply. However, if the taxpayer is under examination, before an appeals office, or before a Federal court, the taxpayer must provide a copy of the application to the examining agent(s), appeals officer, or counsel for the government, as appropriate, at the same time that it files the copy of the application with the National Office. The application must contain the name(s) and telephone number(s) of the examining agent(s), appeals officer, or counsel for the government, as appropriate. For purposes of From 3115, "Application for Change in Accounting Method," the designated number for the automatic accounting method change authorized by this paragraph (g)(5)(iv)(C)(*3*) is "98". A change in method of accounting in accordance with this paragraph (g)(5)(iv)(C)(*3*) requires an adjustment under section 481(a).

(6) *Amounts paid or incurred for a franchise, trademark, or trade name .*—If an amount to which section 1253(d) (relating to the transfer, sale, or other disposition of a franchise, trademark, or trade name) applies is described in section 1253(d)(1)(B) (relating to contingent serial payments deductible under section 162), the amount is not included in the adjusted basis of the intangible for purposes of section 197. Any other amount, whether fixed or contingent, to which section 1253(d) applies is chargeable to capital account under section 1253(d)(2) and is amortizable only under section 197.

(7) *Amounts properly taken into account in determining the cost of property that is not a section 197 intangible .*—Section 197 does not apply to an amount that is properly taken into account in determining the cost of property that is not a section 197 intangible. The entire cost of acquiring the other property is included in its basis and recovered under other applicable Internal Revenue Code provisions. Thus, for example, section 197 does not apply to the cost of an interest in computer software to the extent such cost is included, without being separately stated, in the cost of the hardware or other tangible property and is consistently treated as part of the cost of the hardware or other tangible property.

(8) *Treatment of amortizable section 197 intangibles as depreciable property .*—An amortizable section 197 intangible is treated as property of a character subject to the allowance for depreciation under section 167. Thus, for example, an amortizable section 197 intangible is not a capital asset for purposes of section 1221, but if used in a trade or business and held for more than one year, gain or loss on its disposition generally qualifies as section 1231 gain or loss. Also, an amortizable section 197 intangible is section 1245 property and section 1239 applies to any gain recognized upon its sale or exchange between related persons (as defined in section 1239(b)).

(h) *Anti-churning rules .*—(1) *Scope and purpose .*—(i) *Scope .*—This paragraph (h) applies to section 197(f)(9) intangibles. For this purpose, section 197(f)(9) intangibles are goodwill and going concern value that was held or used at any time during the transition period and any other section 197 intangible that was held or used at any time during the transition period and was not depreciable or amortizable under prior law.

(ii) *Purpose .*—To qualify as an amortizable section 197 intangible, a section 197 intangible must be acquired after the applicable date (July 25, 1991, if the acquiring taxpayer has made a valid retroactive election pursuant to § 1.197-1T; August 10, 1993, in all other cases). The purpose of the anti-churning rules of section 197(f)(9) and this paragraph (h) is to prevent the amortization of section 197(f)(9) intangibles unless they are transferred after the applicable effective date in a transaction giving rise to a significant change in ownership or use. (Special rules apply for purposes of determining whether transactions involving partnerships give rise to a significant change in ownership or use. See paragraph (h)(12) of this section.) The anti-churning rules are to be applied in a manner that carries out their purpose.

(2) *Treatment of section 197(f)(9) intangibles .*—Except as otherwise provided in this paragraph (h), a section 197(f)(9) intangible acquired by a taxpayer after the applicable effective date does not qualify for amortization under section 197 if—

(i) The taxpayer or a related person held or used the intangible or an interest therein at any time during the transition period;

(ii) The taxpayer acquired the intangible from a person that held the intangible at any time during the transition period and, as part of the transaction, the user of the intangible does not change; or

(iii) The taxpayer grants the right to use the intangible to a person that held or used the intangible at any time during the transition period (or to a person related to that person), but only if the transaction in which the taxpayer grants the right and the transaction in which the taxpayer acquired the intangible are part of a series of related transactions.

(3) *Amounts deductible under section 1253(d) or § 1.162-11* .—For purposes of this paragraph (h), deductions allowable under section 1253(d)(2) or pursuant to an election under section 1253(d)(3) (in either case as in effect prior to the enactment of section 197) and deductions allowable under § 1.162-11 are treated as deductions allowable for amortization under prior law.

(4) *Transition period* .—For purposes of this paragraph (h), the transition period is July 25, 1991, if the acquiring taxpayer has made a valid retroactive election pursuant to § 1.197-1T and the period beginning on July 25, 1991, and ending on August 10, 1993, in all other cases.

(5) *Exceptions* .—The anti-churning rules of this paragraph (h) do not apply to —

(i) The acquisition of a section 197(f)(9) intangible if the acquiring taxpayer's basis in the intangible is determined under section 1014(a); or

(ii) The acquisition of a section 197(f)(9) intangible that was an amortizable section 197 intangible in the hands of the seller (or transferor), but only if the acquisition transaction and the transaction in which the seller (or transferor) acquired the intangible or interest therein are not part of a series of related transactions.

(6) *Related person* .—(i) *In general* .—Except as otherwise provided in paragraph (h)(6)(ii) of this section, a person is related to another person for purposes of this paragraph (h) if—

(A) The person bears a relationship to that person that would be specified in section 267(b) (determined without regard to section 267(e)) and, by substitution, section 267(f)(1), if those sections were amended by substituting 20 percent for 50 percent; or

(B) The person bears a relationship to that person that would be specified in section 707(b)(1) if that section were amended by substituting 20 percent for 50 percent; or

(C) The persons are engaged in trades or businesses under common control (within the meaning of section 41(f)(1)(A) and (B)).

(ii) *Time for testing relationships* .—Except as provided in paragraph (h)(6)(iii) of this section, a person is treated as related to another person for purposes of this paragraph (h) if the relationship exists—

(A) In the case of a single transaction, immediately before or immediately after the transaction in which the intangible is acquired; and

(B) In the case of a series of related transactions (or a series of transactions that together comprise a qualified stock purchase within the meaning of section 338(d)(3)), immediately before the earliest such transaction or immediately after the last such transaction.

(iii) *Certain relationships disregarded* .—In applying the rules in paragraph (h)(7) of this section, if a person acquires an intangible in a series of related transactions in which the person acquires stock (meeting the requirements of section 1504(a)(2)) of a corporation in a fully taxable transaction followed by a liquidation of the acquired corporation under section 331, any relationship created as part of such series of transactions is disregarded in determining whether any person is related to such acquired corporation immediately after the last transaction.

(iv) *De minimis rule* .—(A) *In general* .—Two corporations are not treated as related persons for purposes of this paragraph (h) if—

(1) The corporations would (but for the application of this paragraph (h)(6)(iv)) be treated as related persons solely by reason of substituting "more than 20 percent" for "more than 50 percent" in section 267(f)(1)(A); and

(2) The beneficial ownership interest of each corporation in the stock of the other corporation represents less than 10 percent of the total combined voting power of all classes of stock entitled to vote and less than 10 percent of the total value of the shares of all classes of stock outstanding.

(B) *Determination of beneficial ownership interest* .—For purposes of this paragraph (h)(6)(iv), the beneficial ownership interest of one corporation in the stock of another corporation is determined under the principles of section 318(a), except that—

(1) In applying section 318(a)(2)(C), the 50-percent limitation contained therein is not applied; and

(2) Section 318(a)(3)(C) is applied by substituting "20 percent" for "50 percent".

(7) *Special rules for entities that owned or used property at any time during the transition period and that are no longer in existence* .—A corporation, partnership, or trust that owned or used a section 197 intangible at any time during the transition period and that is no longer in existence is deemed, for purposes of determining whether a taxpayer acquiring the intangible is related to such entity, to be in existence at the time of the acquisition.

(8) *Special rules for section 338 deemed acquisitions* .—In the case of a qualified stock purchase that is treated as a deemed sale and purchase of assets pursuant to section 338, the corporation treated as purchasing assets as a result of an election thereunder (new target) is not considered the person that held or used the assets during any period in which the assets were held or used by the corporation treated as selling the assets (old target). Thus, for example, if a corporation (the purchasing corporation) makes a qualified stock purchase of the stock of another corporation after the transition period, new target will not be treated as the owner during the transition period of assets owned by old target during that period even if old target and new target are treated as the same corporation for certain other purposes of the Internal Revenue Code or old target and new target are the same corporation under the laws of the State or other jurisdiction of its organization. However, the anti-churning rules of this paragraph (h) may nevertheless apply to a deemed asset purchase resulting from a section 338 election if new target is related (within the meaning of paragraph (h)(6) of this section) to old target.

(9) *Gain-recognition exception* .—(i) *Applicability* .—A section 197(f)(9) intangible qualifies for the gain-recognition exception if—

(A) The taxpayer acquires the intangible from a person that would not be related to the taxpayer but for the substitution of 20 percent for 50 percent under paragraph (h)(6)(i)(A) of this section; and

(B) That person (whether or not otherwise subject to Federal income tax) elects to recognize gain on the disposition of the intangible and agrees, notwithstanding any other provision of law or treaty, to pay for the taxable year in which the disposition occurs an amount of tax on the gain that, when added to any other Federal income tax on such gain, equals the gain on the disposition multiplied by the highest marginal rate of tax for that taxable year.

(ii) *Effect of exception* .—The anti-churning rules of this paragraph (h) apply to a section 197(f)(9) intangible that qualifies for the gain-recognition exception only to the extent the acquiring taxpayer's basis in the intangible exceeds the gain recognized by the transferor.

(iii) *Time and manner of election* .—The election described in this paragraph (h)(9) must be made by the due date (including extensions of time) of the electing taxpayer's Federal income tax return for the taxable year in which the disposition occurs. The election is made by attaching an election statement satisfying the requirements of paragraph (h)(9)(viii) of this section to the electing taxpayer's original or amended income tax return for that taxable year (or by filing the statement as a return for the taxable year under paragraph (h)(9)(xi) of this section). In addition, the taxpayer must satisfy the notification requirements of paragraph (h)(9)(vi) of this section. The election is binding on the taxpayer and all parties whose Federal tax liability is affected by the election.

(iv) *Special rules for certain entities* .—In the case of a partnership, S corporation, estate or trust, the election under this paragraph (h)(9) is made by the entity rather than by its owners or beneficiaries. If a partnership or S corporation makes an election under this paragraph (h)(9) with respect to the disposition of a section 197(f)(9) intangible, each of its partners or shareholders is required to pay a tax determined in the manner described in paragraph (h)(9)(i)(B) of this section on the amount of gain that is properly allocable to such partner or shareholder with respect to the disposition.

(v) *Effect of nonconforming elections* .—An attempted election that does not substantially comply with each of the requirements of this paragraph (h)(9) is disregarded in determining whether a section 197(f)(9) intangible qualifies for the gain-recognition exception.

(vi) *Notification requirements* .—A taxpayer making an election under this paragraph (h)(9) with respect to the disposition of a section 197(f)(9) intangible must provide written notification of the election on or before the due date of the return on which the election is made to the person acquiring the section 197 intangible. In addition, a partnership or S corporation making an election under this paragraph (h)(9) must attach to the Schedule K-1 furnished to each partner or shareholder a written statement containing all information necessary to determine the recipient's additional tax liability under this paragraph (h)(9).

(vii) *Revocation* .—An election under this paragraph (h)(9) may be revoked only with the consent of the Commissioner.

(viii) *Election Statement* .—An election statement satisfies the requirements of this paragraph (h)(9)(viii) if it is in writing and contains the information listed below. The required information should be arranged and identified in accordance with the following order and numbering system:

(A) The name and address of the electing taxpayer.

(B) Except in the case of a taxpayer that is not otherwise subject to Federal income tax, the taxpayer identification number (TIN) of the electing taxpayer.

(C) A statement that the taxpayer is making the election under section 197(f)(9)(B).

(D) Identification of the transaction and each person that is a party to the transaction or whose tax return is affected by the election (including, except in the case of persons not otherwise subject to Federal income tax, the TIN of each such person).

(E) The calculation of the gain realized, the applicable rate of tax, and the amount of the taxpayer's additional tax liability under this paragraph (h)(9).

(F) The signature of the taxpayer or an individual authorized to sign the taxpayer's Federal income tax return.

(ix) *Determination of highest marginal rate of tax and amount of other Federal income tax on gain* .—(A) *Marginal rate* .—The following rules apply for purposes of determining the highest marginal rate of tax applicable to an electing taxpayer:

(1) Noncorporate taxpayers .—In the case of an individual, estate, or trust, the highest marginal rate of tax is the highest marginal rate of tax in effect under section 1, determined without regard to section 1(h).

(2) Corporations and tax-exempt entities .—In the case of a corporation or an entity that is exempt from tax under section 501(a), the highest marginal rate of tax is the highest marginal rate of tax in effect under section 11, determined without regard to any rate that is added to the otherwise applicable rate in order to offset the effect of the graduated rate schedule.

(B) *Other Federal income tax on gain* .—The amount of Federal income tax (other than the tax determined under this paragraph (h)(9)) imposed on any gain is the lesser of—

(1) The amount by which the taxpayer's Federal income tax liability (determined without regard to this paragraph (h)(9)) would be reduced if the amount of such gain were not taken into account; or

(2) The amount of the gain multiplied by the highest marginal rate of tax for the taxable year.

(x) *Coordination with other provisions* .—(A) *In general* .—The amount of gain subject to the tax determined under this paragraph (h)(9) is not reduced by any net operating loss deduction under section 172(a), any capital loss under section 1212, or any other similar loss or deduction. In addition, the amount of tax determined under this paragraph (h)(9) is not reduced by any credit of the taxpayer. In computing the amount of any net operating loss, capital loss, or other similar loss or deduction, or any credit that may be carried to any taxable year, any gain subject to the tax determined under this paragraph (h)(9) and any tax paid under this paragraph (h)(9) is not taken into account.

(B) *Section 1374* .—No provision of paragraph (h)(9)(iv) of this section precludes the application of section 1374 (relating to a tax on certain built-in gains of S corporations) to any gain with respect to which an election under this paragraph (h)(9) is made. In addition, neither paragraph (h)(9)(iv) nor paragraph (h)(9)(x)(A) of this section precludes a taxpayer from applying the provisions of section 1366(f)(2) (relating to treatment of the tax imposed by section 1374 as a loss sustained by the S corporation) in determining the amount of tax payable under paragraph (h)(9) of this section.

(C) *Procedural and administrative provisions* .—For purposes of subtitle F, the amount determined under this paragraph (h)(9) is treated as a tax imposed by section 1 or 11, as appropriate.

(D) *Installment method* .—The gain subject to the tax determined under paragraph (h)(9)(i) of this section may not be reported under the method described in section 453(a). Any such gain that would, but for the application of this paragraph (h)(9)(x)(D), be taken into account under section 453(a) shall be taken into account in the same manner as if an election under section 453(d) (relating to the election not to apply section 453(a)) had been made.

(xi) *Special rules for persons not otherwise subject to Federal income tax* .—If the person making the election under this paragraph (h)(9) with respect to a disposition is not otherwise subject to Federal income tax, the election statement satisfying the requirements of paragraph (h)(9)(viii) of this section must be filed with the Philadelphia Service Center. For purposes of this paragraph (h)(9) and subtitle F, the statement is treated as an income tax return for the calendar year in which the disposition occurs and as a return due on or before March 15 of the following year.

(10) *Transactions subject to both anti-churning and nonrecognition rules* .—If a person acquires a section 197(f)(9) intangible in a transaction described in paragraph (g)(2) of this section from a person in whose hands the intangible was an amortizable section 197 intangible, and immediately after the transaction (or series of transactions described in paragraph (h)(6)(ii)(B) of this section) in which such intangible is acquired, the person acquiring the section 197(f)(9) intangible is related to any person described in paragraph (h)(2) of this section, the intangible is, notwithstanding its treatment under paragraph (g)(2) of this section, treated as an amortizable section 197 intangible only to the extent permitted under this paragraph (h). (See, for example, paragraph (h)(5)(ii) of this section.)

(11) *Avoidance purpose* .—A section 197(f)(9) intangible acquired by a taxpayer after the applicable effective date does not qualify for amortization under section 197 if one of the principal purposes of the transaction in which it is acquired is to avoid the operation of the anti-churning rules of section 197(f)(9) and this paragraph (h). A transaction will be presumed to have a principal purpose of avoidance if it does not effect a significant change in the ownership or use of the intangible. Thus, for example, if section 197(f)(9) intangibles are acquired in a transaction (or series of related transactions) in which an option to acquire stock is issued to a party to the transaction, but the option is not treated as having been exercised for purposes of paragraph (h)(6) of this section, this paragraph (h)(11) may apply to the transaction.

(12) *Additional partnership anti-churning rules* .—(i) *In general* .—In determining whether the anti-churning rules of this paragraph (h) apply to any increase in the basis of a section 197(f)(9) intangible under section 732(b), 732(d), 734(b), or 743(b), the determinations are made at the partner level and each partner is treated as having owned and used the partner's proportionate share of partnership property. In determining whether the anti-churning rules of this paragraph (h) apply to any transaction under another section of the Internal Revenue Code, the determinations are made at the partnership level, unless under § 1.701-2(e) the Commissioner determines that the partner level is more appropriate.

(ii) *Section 732(b) adjustments* .—(A) *In general* .—The anti-churning rules of this paragraph (h) apply to any increase in the adjusted basis of a section 197(f)(9) intangible under section 732(b) to the extent that the basis increase exceeds the total unrealized appreciation from the intangible allocable to—

(1) Partners other than the distributee partner or persons related to the distributee partner;

(2) The distributee partner and persons related to the distributee partner if the distributed intangible is a section 197(f)(9) intangible acquired by the partnership on or before August 10, 1993, to the extent that—

(i) The distributee partner and related persons acquired an interest or interests in the partnership after August 10, 1993;

(ii) Such interest or interests were held after August 10, 1993, by a person or persons other than either the distributee partner or persons who were related to the distributee partner; and

(iii) The acquisition of such interest or interests by such person or persons was not part of a transaction or series of related transactions in which the distributee partner (or persons related to the distributee partner) subsequently acquired such interest or interests; and

(3) The distributee partner and persons related to the distributee partner if the distributed intangible is a section 197(f)(9) intangible acquired by the partnership after August 10, 1993, that is not amortizable with respect to the partnership, to the extent that—

(i) The distributee partner and persons related to the distributee partner acquired an interest or interests in the partnership after the partnership acquired the distributed intangible;

(ii) Such interest or interests were held after the partnership acquired the distributed intangible, by a person or persons other than either the distributee partner or persons who were related to the distributee partner; and

(iii) The acquisition of such interest or interests by such person or persons was not part of a transaction or series of related transactions in which the distributee partner (or persons related to the distributee partner) subsequently acquired such interest or interests.

(B) *Effect of retroactive elections* .—For purposes of paragraph (h)(12)(ii)(A) of this section, references to August 10, 1993, are treated as references to July 25, 1991, if the relevant party made a valid retroactive election under § 1.197-1T.

(C) *Intangible still subject to anti-churning rules* .—Notwithstanding paragraph (h)(12)(ii) of this section, in applying the provisions of this paragraph (h) with respect to subsequent transfers, the distributed intangible remains subject to the provisions of this paragraph (h) in proportion to a fraction (determined at the time of the distribution), as follows—

(1) The numerator of which is equal to the sum of—

(i) The amount of the distributed intangible's basis that is nonamortizable under paragraph (g)(2)(ii)(B) of this section; and

(ii) The total unrealized appreciation inherent in the intangible reduced by the amount of the increase in the adjusted basis of the distributed intangible under section 732(b) to which the anti-churning rules do not apply; and

(2) The denominator of which is the fair market value of such intangible.

(D) *Partner's allocable share of unrealized appreciation from the intangible* .—The amount of unrealized appreciation from an intangible that is allocable to a partner is the amount of taxable gain that would have been allocated to that partner if the partnership had sold the intangible immediately before the distribution for its fair market value in a fully taxable transaction.

(E) *Acquisition of partnership interest by contribution* .—Solely for purposes of paragraphs (h)(12)(ii)(A)(*2*) and (*3*) of this section, a partner who acquires an interest in a partnership in exchange for a contribution of property to the partnership is deemed to acquire a pro rata portion of that interest in the partnership from each person who is a partner in the partnership at the time of the contribution based on each partner's respective proportionate interest in the partnership.

(iii) *Section 732(d) adjustments* .—The anti-churning rules of this paragraph (h) do not apply to an increase in the basis of a section 197(f)(9) intangible under section 732(d) if, had an election been in effect under section 754 at the time of the transfer of the partnership interest, the distributee partner would have been able to amortize the basis adjustment made pursuant to section 743(b).

(iv) *Section 734(b) adjustments* .—(A) *In general* .—The anti-churning rules of this paragraph (h) do not apply to a continuing partner's share of an increase in the basis of a section 197(f)(9) intangible held by a partnership under section 734(b) to the extent that the continuing partner is an eligible partner.

(B) *Eligible partner* .—For purposes of this paragraph (h)(12)(iv), eligible partner means—

(1) A continuing partner that is not the distributee partner or a person related to the distributee partner;

(2) A continuing partner that is the distributee partner or a person related to the distributee partner, with respect to any section 197(f)(9) intangible acquired by the partnership on or before August 10, 1993, to the extent that—

(i) The distributee partner's interest in the partnership was acquired after August 10, 1993;

(ii) Such interest was held after August 10, 1993 by a person or persons who were not related to the distributee partner; and

(iii) The acquisition of such interest by such person or persons was not part of a transaction or series of related transactions in which the distributee partner or persons related to the distributee partner subsequently acquired such interest; or

(3) A continuing partner that is the distributee partner or a person related to the distributee partner, with respect to any section 197(f)(9) intangible acquired by the partnership after August 10, 1993, that is not amortizable with respect to the partnership, to the extent that—

(i) The distributee partner's interest in the partnership was acquired after the partnership acquired the relevant intangible;

(ii) Such interest was held after the partnership acquired the relevant intangible by a person or persons who were not related to the distributee partner; and

(iii) The acquisition of such interest by such person or persons was not part of a transaction or series of related transactions in which the distributee partner or persons related to the distributee partner subsequently acquired such interest.

(C) *Effect of retroactive elections* .—For purposes of paragraph (h)(12)(iv)(A) of this section, references to August 10, 1993, are treated as references to July 25, 1991, if the distributee partner made a valid retroactive election under § 1.197-1T.

(D) *Partner's share of basis increase* .—*(1) In general* .—Except as provided in paragraph (h)(12)(iv)(D)(*2*) of this section, for purposes of this paragraph (h)(12)(iv), a continuing partner's share of a basis increase under section 734(b) is equal to—

(i) The total basis increase allocable to the intangible; multiplied by

(ii) A fraction the numerator of which is the amount of the continuing partner's post-distribution capital account (determined immediately after the distribution in accordance with the capital accounting rules of § 1.704-1(b)(2)(iv)), and the denominator of which is the total amount of the post-

distribution capital accounts (determined immediately after the distribution in accordance with the capital accounting rules of § 1.704-1(b)(2)(iv)) of all continuing partners.

(2) Exception where partnership does not maintain capital accounts .—If a partnership does not maintain capital accounts in accordance with § 1.704-1(b)(2)(iv), then for purposes of this paragraph (h)(12)(iv), a continuing partner's share of a basis increase is equal to—

(i) The total basis increase allocable to the intangible; multiplied by

(ii) The partner's overall interest in the partnership as determined under § 1.704-1(b)(3) immediately after the distribution.

(E) *Interests acquired by contribution .—(1) Application of paragraphs (h)(12)(iv)(B)(2) and (3) of this section* .—Solely for purposes of paragraphs (h)(12)(iv)(B)(*2*) and (*3*) of this section, a partner who acquires an interest in a partnership in exchange for a contribution of property to the partnership is deemed to acquire a pro rata portion of that interest in the partnership from each person who is a partner in the partnership at the time of the contribution based on each such partner's proportionate interest in the partnership.

(2) Special rule with respect to paragraph (h)(12)(iv)(B)(1) of this section .—Solely for purposes of paragraph (h)(12)(iv)(B)(*1*) of this section, if a distribution that gives rise to an increase in the basis under section 734(b) of a section 197(f)(9) intangible held by the partnership is undertaken as part of a series of related transactions that include a contribution of the intangible to the partnership by a continuing partner, the continuing partner is treated as related to the distributee partner in analyzing the basis adjustment with respect to the contributed section 197(f)(9) intangible.

(F) *Effect of section 734(b) adjustments on partners' capital accounts* .—If one or more partners are subject to the anti-churning rules under this paragraph (h) with respect to a section 734(b) adjustment allocable to an intangible asset, taxpayers may use any reasonable method to determine amortization of the asset for book purposes, provided that the method used does not contravene the purposes of the anti-churning rules under section 197 and this paragraph (h). A method will be considered to contravene the purposes of the anti-churning rules if the effect of the book adjustments resulting from the method is such that any portion of the tax deduction for amortization attributable to the section 734 adjustment is allocated, directly or indirectly, to a partner who is subject to the anti-churning rules with respect to such adjustment.

(v) *Section 743(b) adjustments* .—(A) *General rule* .—The anti-churning rules of this paragraph (h) do not apply to an increase in the basis of a section 197 intangible under section 743(b) if the person acquiring the partnership interest is not related to the person transferring the partnership interest. In addition, the anti-churning rules of this paragraph (h) do not apply to an increase in the basis of a section 197 intangible under section 743(b) to the extent that—

(1) The partnership interest being transferred was acquired after August 10, 1993, provided—

(i) The section 197(f)(9) intangible was acquired by the partnership on or before August 10, 1993;

(ii) The partnership interest being transferred was held after August 10, 1993, by a person or persons (the post-1993 person or persons) other than the person transferring the partnership interest or persons who were related to the person transferring the partnership interest; and

(iii) The acquisition of such interest by the post-1993 person or persons was not part of a transaction or series of related transactions in which the person transferring the partnership interest or persons related to the person transferring the partnership interest acquired such interest; or

(2) The partnership interest being transferred was acquired after the partnership acquired the section 197(f)(9) intangible, provided—

(i) The section 197(f)(9) intangible was acquired by the partnership after August 10, 1993, and is not amortizable with respect to the partnership;

(ii) The partnership interest being transferred was held after the partnership acquired the section 197(f)(9) intangible by a person or persons (the post-contribution person or persons) other than the person transferring the partnership interest or persons who were related to the person transferring the partnership interest; and

(iii) The acquisition of such interest by the post-contribution person or persons was not part of a transaction or series of related transactions in which the person transferring the partnership interest or persons related to the person transferring the partnership interest acquired such interest.

(B) *Acquisition of partnership interest by contribution* .—Solely for purposes of paragraph (h)(12)(v)(A)(*1*) and (*2*) of this section, a partner who acquires an interest in a partnership in exchange for a contribution of property to the partnership is deemed to acquire a pro rata portion of that interest in the partnership from each person who is a partner in the partnership at the time of the contribution based on each such partner's proportionate interest in the partnership.

(C) *Effect of retroactive elections* .—For purposes of paragraph (h)(12)(v)(A) of this section, references to August 10, 1993, are treated as references to July 25, 1991, if the transferee partner made a valid retroactive election under § 1.197-1T.

(vi) *Partner is or becomes a user of partnership intangible* .—(A) *General rule* .—If, as part of a series of related transactions that includes a transaction described in paragraph (h)(12)(ii), (iii), (iv), or (v) of this section, an anti-churning partner or related person (other than the partnership) becomes (or remains) a direct user of an intangible that is treated as transferred in the transaction (as a result of the partners being treated as having owned their proportionate share of partnership assets), the anti-churning rules of this paragraph (h) apply to the proportionate share of such intangible that is treated as transferred by such anti-churning partner, notwithstanding the application of paragraph (h)(12)(ii), (iii), (iv), or (v) of this section.

(B) *Anti-churning partner* .—For purposes of this paragraph (h)(12)(vi), anti-churning partner means—

(1) With respect to all intangibles held by a partnership on or before August 10, 1993, any partner, but only to the extent that

(i) The partner's interest in the partnership was acquired on or before August 10, 1993, or

(ii) The interest was acquired from a person related to the partner on or after August 10, 1993, and such interest was not held by any person other than persons related to such partner at any time after August 10, 1993 (disregarding, for this purpose, a person's holding of an interest if the acquisition of such interest was part of a transaction or series of related transactions in which the partner or persons related to the partner subsequently acquired such interest),

(2) With respect to any section 197(f)(9) intangible acquired by a partnership after August 10, 1993, that is not amortizable with respect to the partnership, any partner, but only to the extent that

(i) The partner's interest in the partnership was acquired on or before the date the partnership acquired the section 197(f)(9) intangible, or

(ii) The interest was acquired from a person related to the partner on or after the date the partnership acquired the section 197(f)(9) intangible, and such interest was not held by any person other than persons related to such partner at any time after the date the partnership acquired the section 197(f)(9) intangible (disregarding, for this purpose, a person's holding of an interest if the acquisition of such interest was part of a transaction or series of related transactions in which the partner or persons related to the partner subsequently acquired such interest).

(C) *Effect of retroactive elections*.—For purposes of paragraph (h)(12)(vi)(B) of this section, references to August 10, 1993, are treated as references to July 25, 1991, if the relevant party made a valid retroactive election under § 1.197-1T.

(vii) *Section 704(c) allocations*.—(A) *Allocations where the intangible is amortizable by the contributor*.—The anti-churning rules of this paragraph (h) do not apply to the curative or remedial allocations of amortization with respect to a section 197(f)(9) intangible if the intangible was an amortizable section 197 intangible in the hands of the contributing partner (unless paragraph (h)(10) of this section applies so as to cause the intangible to cease to be an amortizable section 197 intangible in the hands of the partnership).

(B) *Allocations where the intangible is not amortizable by the contributor*.—If a section 197(f)(9) intangible was not an amortizable section 197 intangible in the hands of the contributing partner, a non-contributing partner generally may receive remedial allocations of amortization under section 704(c) that are deductible for Federal income tax purposes. However, such a partner may not receive remedial allocations of amortization under section 704(c) if that partner is related to the partner that contributed the intangible or if, as part of a series of related transactions that includes the contribution of the section 197(f)(9) intangible to the partnership, the contributing partner or related person (other than the partnership) becomes (or remains) a direct user of the contributed intangible. Taxpayers may use any reasonable method to determine amortization of the asset for book purposes, provided that the method used does not contravene the purposes of the anti-churning rules under section 197 and this paragraph (h). A method will be considered to contravene the purposes of the anti-churning rules if the effect of the book adjustments resulting from the method is such that any portion of the tax deduction for amortization attributable to section 704(c) is allocated, directly or indirectly, to a partner who is subject to the anti-churning rules with respect to such adjustment.

(viii) *Operating rule for transfers upon death*.—For purposes of this paragraph (h)(12), if the basis of a partner's interest in a partnership is determined under section 1014(a), such partner is treated as acquiring such interest from a person who is not related to such partner, and such interest is treated as having previously been held by a person who is not related to such partner.

(i) [Reserved]

(j) *General anti-abuse rule*.—The Commissioner will interpret and apply the rules in this section as necessary and appropriate to prevent avoidance of the purposes of section 197. If one of the principal purposes of a transaction is to achieve a tax result that is inconsistent with the purposes of section 197, the Commissioner will recast the transaction for Federal tax purposes as appropriate to achieve tax results that are consistent with the purposes of section 197, in light of the applicable statutory and regulatory provisions and the pertinent facts and circumstances.

(k) *Examples* .—The following examples illustrate the application of this section:

Example 1. Advertising costs. (i) Q manufactures and sells consumer products through a series of wholesalers and distributors. In order to increase sales of its products by encouraging consumer loyalty to its products and to enhance the value of the goodwill, trademarks, and trade names of the business, Q advertises its products to the consuming public. It regularly incurs costs to develop radio, television, and print advertisements. These costs generally consist of employee costs and amounts paid to independent advertising agencies. Q also incurs costs to run these advertisements in the various media for which they were developed.

(ii) The advertising costs are not chargeable to capital account under paragraph (f) (3) of this section (relating to costs incurred for covenants not to compete, rights granted by governmental units, and contracts for the use of section 197 intangibles) and are currently deductible as ordinary and necessary expenses under section 162. Accordingly, under paragraph (a) (3) of this section, section 197 does not apply to these costs.

Example 2. Computer software. (i) X purchases all of the assets of an existing trade or business from Y. One of the assets acquired is all of Y's rights in certain computer software previously used by Y under the terms of a nonexclusive license from the software developer. The software was developed for use by manufacturers to maintain a comprehensive accounting system, including general and subsidiary ledgers, payroll, accounts receivable and payable, cash receipts and disbursements, fixed asset accounting, and inventory cost accounting and controls. The developer modified the software for use by Y at a cost of $1,000 and Y made additional modifications at a cost of $500. The developer does not maintain wholesale or retail outlets but markets the software directly to ultimate users. Y's license of the software is limited to an entity that is actively engaged in business as a manufacturer.

(ii) Notwithstanding these limitations, the software is considered to be readily available to the general public for purposes of paragraph (c) (4) (i) of this section. In addition, the software is not substantially modified because the cost of the modifications by the developer and Y to the version of the software that is readily available to the general public does not exceed $2,000. Accordingly, the software is not a section 197 intangible.

Example 3. Acquisition of software for internal use. (i) B, the owner and operator of a worldwide package-delivery service, purchases from S all rights to software developed by S. The software will be used by B for the sole purpose of improving its package-tracking operations. B does not purchase any other assets in the transaction or any related transaction.

(ii) Because B acquired the software solely for internal use, it is disregarded in determining for purposes of paragraph (c) (4) (ii) of this section whether the assets acquired in the transaction or series of related transactions constitute a trade or business or substantial portion thereof. Since no other assets were acquired, the software is not acquired as part of a purchase of a trade or business and under paragraph (c) (4) (ii) of this section is not a section 197 intangible.

Example 4. Governmental rights of fixed duration. (i) City M operates a municipal water system. In order to induce X to locate a new manufacturing business in the city, M grants X the right to purchase water for 16 years at a specified price.

(ii) The right granted by M is a right to receive tangible property or services described in section 197(e) (4) (B) and paragraph (c) (6) of this section and, thus, is not a section 197 intangible. This exclusion applies even though the right does not qualify for exclusion as a right of fixed duration or amount under section 197(e)(4)(D) and paragraph (c)(13) of this section because the duration exceeds 15 years and the right is not fixed as to amount. It is also immaterial that the right would not qualify for exclusion as a self-created intangible under section 197(c)(2) and paragraph (d)(2) of this section because it is granted by a governmental unit.

Example 5. Separate acquisition of franchise. (i) S is a franchiser of retail outlets for specialty coffees. G enters into a franchise agreement (within the meaning of section 1253(b)(1)) with S pursuant to which G is permitted to acquire and operate a store using the S trademark and trade name at the location specified in the agreement. G agrees to pay S $100,000 upon execution of the agreement and also agrees to pay, throughout the term of the franchise, additional amounts that are deductible under section 1253(d)(1). The agreement contains detailed specifications for the construction and operation of the business, but G is not required to purchase from S any of the materials necessary to construct the improvements at the location specified in the franchise agreement.

(ii) The franchise is a section 197 intangible within the meaning of paragraph (b)(10) of this section. The franchise does not qualify for the exclusion relating to self-created intangibles described in section 197(c)(2) and paragraph (d)(2) of this section because the franchise is described in section 197(d)(1)(F). In addition, because the acquisition of the franchise constitutes the acquisition of an interest in a trade or business or a substantial portion thereof, the franchise may not be excluded under section 197(e)(4). Thus, the franchise is an amortizable section 197 intangible, the basis of which must be recovered over a 15-year period. However, the amounts that are deductible under section 1253(d)(1)are not subject to the provisions of section 197 by reason of section 197(f)(4)(C) and paragraph (b)(10)(ii) of this section.

Example 6. Acquisition and amortization of covenant not to compete. (i) As part of the acquisition of a trade or business from C, B and C enter into an agreement containing a covenant not to compete. Under this agreement, C agrees that it will not compete with the business acquired by B within a prescribed geographical territory for a period of three years after the date on which the business is sold to B. In exchange for this agreement, B agrees to pay C $90,000 per year for each year in the term of the agreement. The agreement further provides that, in the event of a breach by C of his obligations under the agreement, B may terminate the agreement, cease making any of the payments due thereafter, and pursue any other legal or equitable remedies available under applicable law. The amounts payable to C under the agreement are not contingent payments for purposes of § 1.1275-4. The present fair market value of B's rights under the agreement is $225,000. The aggregate consideration paid excluding any amount treated as interest or original issue discount under applicable provisions of the Internal Revenue Code, for all assets acquired in the transaction (including the covenant not to compete) exceeds the sum of the amount of Class I assets and the aggregate fair market value of all Class II, Class III, Class IV, Class V, and Class VI assets by $50,000. See § 1.338-6(b) for rules for determining the assets in each class.

(ii) Because the covenant is acquired in an applicable asset acquisition (within the meaning of section 1060(c)), paragraph (f)(4)(ii) of this section applies and the basis of B in the covenant is determined pursuant to section 1060(a) and the regulations thereunder. Under § § 1.1060-1(c)(2) and 1.338-6(c)(1), B's basis in the covenant cannot exceed its fair market value. Thus, B's basis in the covenant immediately after the acquisition is $225,000. This basis is amortized ratably over the 15-year period beginning on the first day of the month in which the agreement is entered into. All of the remaining consideration after allocation to the covenant and other Class VI assets, ($50,000) is allocated to Class VII assets (goodwill and going concern value). See § § 1.1060-1(c)(2) and 1.338-6(b).

Example 7. Stand-alone license of technology. (i) X is a manufacturer of consumer goods that does business throughout the world through subsidiary corporations organized under the laws of each country in which business is conducted. X licenses to Y, its subsidiary organized and conducting business in Country K, all of the patents, formulas, designs, and know-how necessary for Y to manufacture the same products that X manufactures in the United States. Assume that the license is not considered a sale or exchange under the principles of section 1235. The license is for a term of 18 years, and there are no facts to indicate that the license does not have a fixed duration. Y agrees to pay X a royalty equal to a specified, fixed percentage of the revenues obtained from selling products manufactured using the licensed technology. Assume that the royalty is reasonable and is not subject to adjustment under section 482. The license is not entered into in connection with any other transaction. Y incurs capitalized costs in connection with entering into the license.

(ii) The license is a contract for the use of a section 197 intangible within the meaning of paragraph (b)(11) of this section. It does not qualify for the exception in section 197(e)(4)(D) and paragraph (c)(13) of this section (relating to rights of fixed duration or amount) because it does not have a term of less than 15 years, and the other exceptions in section 197(e) and paragraph (c) of this section are also inapplicable. Accordingly, the license is a section 197 intangible.

(iii) The license is not acquired as part of a purchase of a trade or business. Thus, under paragraph (f)(3)(iii) of this section, the license will be closely scrutinized under the principles of section 1235 for purposes of determining whether the transfer is a sale or exchange and, accordingly, whether the payments under the license are chargeable to capital account. Because the license is not a sale or exchange under the principles of section 1235, the royalty payments are not chargeable to capital account for purposes section 197. The capitalized costs of entering into the license are not within the exception under paragraph (d)(2) of this section for self-created intangibles, and thus are amortized under section 197.

Example 8. License of technology and trademarks. (i) The facts are the same as in *Example 7*, except that the license also includes the use of the trademarks and trade names that X uses to manufacture and distribute its products in the United States. Assume that under the principles of section 1253 the transfer is not a sale or exchange of the trademarks and trade names or an undivided interest therein and that the royalty payments are described in section 1253(d)(1)(B).

(ii) As in *Example 7*, the license is a section 197 intangible. Although the license conveys an interest in X's trademarks and trade names to Y, the transfer of the interest is disregarded for purposes of paragraph (e)(2) of this section unless the transfer is considered a sale or exchange of the trademarks and trade names or an undivided interest therein. Accordingly, the licensing of the technology and the trademarks and trade names is not treated as part of a purchase of a trade or business under paragraph (e)(2) of this section.

(iii) Because the technology license is not part of the purchase of a trade or business, it is treated in the manner described in *Example 7*. The royalty payments for the use of the trademarks and trade names are deductible under section 1253(d)(1) and, under section 197(f)(4)(C) and paragraph (b)(10)(ii) of this section, are not chargeable to capital account for purposes of section 197. The capitalized costs of entering into the license are treated in the same manner as in example 7.

Example 9. Disguised sale. (i) The facts are the same as in *Example 7*, except that Y agrees to pay X, in addition to the contingent royalty, a fixed minimum royalty immediately upon entering into the agreement and there are sufficient facts present to characterize the transaction, for federal tax purposes, as a transfer of ownership of the intellectual property from X to Y.

(ii) The purported license of technology is, in fact, an acquisition of an intangible described in section 197(d)(1)(C)(iii) and paragraph (b)(5) of this section (relating to know-how, etc.). As in *Example 7*, the exceptions in section 197(e) and paragraph (c) of this section do not apply to the transfer. Accordingly, the transferred property is a section 197 intangible. Y's basis in the transferred intangible includes the capitalized costs of entering into the agreement and the fixed minimum royalty payment payable at the time of the transfer. In addition, except to the extent that a portion of any payment will be treated as interest or original issue discount under applicable provisions of the Internal Revenue Code, all of the contingent payments under the purported license are properly chargeable to capital account for purposes of section 197 and this section. The extent to which such payments are treated as payments of principal and the time at which any amount treated as a payment of principal is taken into account in determining basis are determined under the rules of § 1.1275-4(c)(4) or 1.483-4(a), whichever is applicable. Any contingent amount that is included in basis after the month in which the acquisition occurs is amortized under the rules of paragraph (f)(2)(i) or (ii) of this section.

Example 10. License of technology and customer list as part of sale of a trade or business. (i) X is a computer manufacturer that produces, in separate operating divisions, personal computers, servers, and peripheral equipment. In a transaction that is the purchase of a trade or business for purposes of section 197, Y (who is unrelated to X) purchases from X all assets of the operating division producing personal computers, except for certain patents that are also used in the division manufacturing servers and customer lists that are also used in the division manufacturing peripheral equipment. As part of the transaction, X transfers to Y the right to use the retained patents and customer lists solely in connection with the manufacture and sale of personal computers. The transfer agreement requires annual royalty payments contingent on the use of the patents and also requires a payment for each use of the customer list. In addition, Y incurs capitalized costs in connection with entering into the licenses.

(ii) The rights to use the retained patents and customer lists are contracts for the use of section 197 intangibles within the meaning of paragraph (b)(11) of this section. The rights do not qualify for the exception in 197(e)(4)(D) and paragraph (c)(13) of this section (relating to rights of fixed duration or amount) because they are transferred as part of a purchase of a trade or business and the other exceptions in section 197(e) and paragraph (c) of this section are also inapplicable. Accordingly, the licenses are section 197 intangibles.

(iii) Because the right to use the retained patents is described in paragraph (b)(11) of this section and the right is transferred as part of a purchase of a trade or business, the treatment of the royalty payments is determined under paragraph (f)(3)(ii) of this section. In addition, however, the retained patents are described in paragraph (b)(5) of this section. Thus, the annual royalty payments are chargeable to capital account under the general rule of paragraph (f)(3)(ii)(A) of this section unless Y establishes that the license is not a sale or exchange under the principles of section 1235 and the royalty payments are an arm's length consideration for the rights transferred. If these facts are established, the exception in paragraph (f)(3)(ii)(B) of this section applies and the royalty payments are not chargeable to capital account for purposes of section 197. The capitalized costs of entering into the license are treated in the same manner as in Example 7.

(iv) The right to use the retained customer list is also described in paragraph (b)(11) of this section and is transferred as part of a purchase of a trade or business. Thus, the treatment of the payments for use of the customer list is also determined under paragraph (f)(3)(ii) of this section. The customer list, although described in paragraph (b)(6) of this section, is a customer-related information base. Thus, the exception in paragraph (f)(3)(ii)(B) of this section does not apply.

Accordingly, payments for use of the list are chargeable to capital account under the general rule of paragraph (f)(3)(ii)(A) of this section and are amortized under section 197. In addition, the capitalized costs of entering into the contract for use of the customer list are treated in the same manner as in *Example 7*.

Example 11. Loss disallowance rules involving related persons. (i) Assume that X and Y are treated as a single taxpayer for purposes of paragraph (g)(1) of this section. In a single transaction, X and Y acquired from Z all of the assets used by Z in a trade or business. Z had operated this business at two locations, and X and Y each acquired the assets used by Z at one of the locations. Three years after the acquisition, X sold all of the assets it acquired, including amortizable section 197 intangibles, to an unrelated purchaser. The amortizable section intangibles are sold at a loss of $120,000.

(ii) Because X and Y are treated as a single taxpayer for purposes of the loss disallowance rules of section 197(f)(1) and paragraph (g)(1) of this section, X's loss on the sale of the amortizable section 197 intangibles is not recognized. Under paragraph (g)(1)(iv)(B) of this section, X's disallowed loss is allowed ratably, as a deduction under section 197, over the remainder of the 15-year period during which the intangibles would have been amortized, and Y may not increase the basis of the amortizable section 197 intangibles that it acquired from Z by the amount of X's disallowed loss.

Example 12. Disposition of retained intangibles by related person. (i) The facts are the same as in *Example 11*, except that 10 years after the acquisition of the assets by X and Y and 7 years after the sale of the assets by X, Y sells all of the assets acquired from Z, including amortizable section 197 intangibles, to an unrelated purchaser.

(ii) Under paragraph (g)(1)(iv)(B) of this section, X may recognize, on the date of the sale by Y, any loss that has not been allowed as a deduction under section 197. Accordingly, X recognizes a loss of $50,000, the amount obtained by reducing the loss on the sale of the assets at the end of the third year ($120,000) by the amount allowed as a deduction under paragraph (g)(1)(iv)(B) of this section during the 7 years following the sale by X ($70,000).

Example 13. Acquisition of an interest in partnership with no section 754 election. (i) A, B, and C each contribute $1,500 for equal shares in general partnership P. On January 1, 1998, P acquires as its sole asset an amortizable section 197 intangible for $4,500. P still holds the intangible on January 1, 2003, at which time the intangible has an adjusted basis to P of $3,000, and A, B, and C each have an adjusted basis of $1,000 in their partnership interests. D (who is not related to A) acquires A's interest in P for $1,600. No section 754 election is in effect for 2003.

(ii) Because there is no change in the basis of the intangible under section 743(b), D merely steps into the shoes of A with respect to the intangible. D's proportionate share of P's adjusted basis in the intangible is $1,000, which continues to be amortized over the 10 years remaining in the original 15-year amortization period for the intangible.

Example 14. Acquisition of an interest in partnership with a section 754 election. (i) The facts are the same as in *Example 13*, except that a section 754 election is in effect for 2003.

(ii) Pursuant to paragraph (g)(3) of this section, for purposes of section 197, D is treated as if P owns two assets. D's proportionate share of P's adjusted basis in one asset is $1,000, which continues to be amortized over the 10 years remaining in the original 15-year amortization period. For the other asset, D's proportionate share of P's adjusted basis is $600 (the amount of the basis increase under section 743 as a result of the section 754 election), which is amortized over a new 15-year period beginning January 2003. With respect to B and C, P's remaining $2,000 adjusted basis in the intangible continues to be amortized over the 10 years remaining in the original 15-year amortization period.

Example 15. Payment to a retiring partner by partnership with a section 754 election. (i) The facts are the same as in *Example 13*, except that a section 754 election is in effect for 2003 and, instead of D acquiring A's interest in P, A retires from P. A, B, and C are not related to each other within the meaning of paragraph (h)(6) of this section. P borrows $1,600, and A receives a payment under section 736 from P of such amount, all of which is in exchange for A's interest in the intangible asset owned by P. (Assume, for purposes of this example, that the borrowing by P and payment of such funds to A does not give rise to a disguised sale of A's partnership interest under section 707(a)(2)(B).) P makes a positive basis adjustment of $600 with respect to the section 197 intangible under section 734(b).

(ii) Pursuant to paragraph (g)(3) of this section, because of the section 734 adjustment, P is treated as having two amortizable section 197 intangibles, one with a basis of $3,000 and a remaining amortization period of 10 years and the other with a basis of $600 and a new amortization period of 15 years.

Example 16. Termination of partnership under section 708(b)(1)(B). (i) A and B are partners with equal shares in the capital and profits of general partnership P. P's only asset is an amortizable section 197 intangible, which P had acquired on January 1, 1995. On January 1, 2000, the asset had a fair market value of $100 and a basis to P of $50. On that date, A sells his entire partnership interest in P to C, who is unrelated to A, for $50. At the time of the sale, the basis of each of A and B in their respective partnership interests is $25.

(ii) The sale causes a termination of P under section 708(b)(1)(B). Under section 708, the transaction is treated as if P transfers its sole asset to a new partnership in exchange for the assumption of its liabilities and the receipt of all of the interests in the new partnership. Immediately thereafter, P is treated as if it is liquidated, with B and C each receiving their proportionate share of the interests in the new partnership. The contribution by P of its asset to the new partnership is governed by section 721, and the liquidating distributions by P of the interests in the new partnership are governed by section 731. C does not realize a basis adjustment under section 743 with respect to the amortizable section 197 intangible unless P had a section 754 election in effect for its taxable year in which the transfer of the partnership interest to C occurred or the taxable year in which the deemed liquidation of P occurred.

(iii) Under section 197, if P had a section 754 election in effect, C is treated as if the new partnership had acquired two assets from P immediately preceding its termination. Even though the adjusted basis of the new partnership in the two assets is determined solely under section 723, because the transfer of assets is a transaction described in section 721, the application of sections 743(b) and 754 to P immediately before its termination causes P to be treated as if it held two assets for purposes of section 197. See paragraph (g)(3) of this section. B's and C's proportionate share of the new partnership's adjusted basis is $25 each in one asset, which continues to be amortized over the 10 years remaining in the original 15-year amortization period. For the other asset, C's proportionate share of the new partnership's adjusted basis is $25 (the amount of the basis increase resulting from the application of section 743 to the sale or exchange by A of the interest in P), which is amortized over a new 15-year period beginning in January 2000.

(iv) If P did not have a section 754 election in effect for its taxable year in which the sale of the partnership interest by A to C occurred or the taxable year in which the deemed liquidation of P occurred, the adjusted basis of the new partnership in the amortizable section 197 intangible is determined solely under section 723, because the transfer is a transaction described in section 721, and P does not have a basis increase in the intangible. Under section 197(f)(2) and paragraph (g)(2)(ii) of this section, the new partnership continues to amortize the intangible over the 10 years remaining in the original 15-year amortization period. No additional amortization is allowable with respect to this asset.

Example 17. Disguised sale to partnership. (i) E and F are individuals who are unrelated to each other within the meaning of paragraph (h)(6) of this section. E has been engaged in the active conduct of a trade or business as a sole proprietor since 1990. E and F form EF Partnership. E transfers all of the assets of the business, having a fair market value of $100, to EF, and F transfers $40 of cash to EF. E receives a 60 percent interest in EF and the $40 of cash contributed by F, and F receives a 40 percent interest in EF, under circumstances in which the transfer by E is partially treated as a sale of property to EF under § 1.707-3(b).

(ii) Under § 1.707-3(a)(1), the transaction is treated as if E had sold to EF a 40 percent interest in each asset for $40 and contributed the remaining 60 percent interest in each asset to EF in exchange solely for an interest in EF. Because E and EF are related persons within the meaning of paragraph (h)(6) of this section, no portion of any transferred section 197(f)(9) intangible that E held during the transition period (as defined in paragraph (h)(4) of this section) is an amortizable section 197 intangible pursuant to paragraph (h)(2) of this section. Section 197(f)(9)(E) and paragraph (g)(3) of this section do not apply to any portion of the section 197 intangible in the hands of EF because the basis of EF in these assets was not increased under any of sections 732, 734, or 743.

Example 18. Acquisition by related person in nonrecognition transaction. (i) A owns a nonamortizable intangible that A acquired in 1990. In 2000, A sells a one-half interest in the intangible to B for cash. Immediately after the sale, A and B, who are unrelated to each other, form partnership P as equal partners. A and B each contribute their one-half interest in the intangible to P.

(ii) P has a transferred basis in the intangible from A and B under section 723. The nonrecognition transfer rule under paragraph (g)(2)(ii) of this section applies to A's transfer of its one-half interest in the intangible to P, and consequently P steps into A's shoes with respect to A's nonamortizable transferred basis. The anti-churning rules of paragraph (h) of this section apply to B's transfer of its one-half interest in the intangible to P, because A, who is related to P under paragraph (h)(6) of this section immediately after the series of transactions in which the intangible was acquired by P, held B's one-half interest in the intangible during the transition period. Pursuant to paragraph (h)(10) of this section, these rules apply to B's transfer of its one-half interest to P even though the nonrecognition transfer rule under paragraph (g)(2)(ii) of this section would have permitted P to step into B's shoes with respect to B's otherwise amortizable basis. Therefore, P's entire basis in the intangible is nonamortizable. However, if A (not B) elects to recognize gain under paragraph (h)(9) of this section on the transfer of each of the one-half interests in the intangible to B and P, then the intangible would be amortizable by P to the extent provided in section 197(f)(9)(B) and paragraph (h)(9) of this section.

Example 19. Acquisition of partnership interest following formation of partnership. (i) The facts are the same as in *Example 18* except that, in 2000, A formed P with an affiliate, S, and contributed the intangible to the partnership and except that in a subsequent year, in a transaction that is properly characterized as a sale of a partnership interest for Federal tax purposes, B purchases a 50 percent interest in P from A. P has a section 754 election in effect and holds no assets other than the intangible and cash.

(ii) For the reasons set forth in *Example 16*(iii), B is treated as if P owns two assets. B's proportionate share of P's adjusted basis in one asset is the same as A's proportionate share of P's adjusted basis in that asset, which is not amortizable under section 197. For the other asset, B's proportionate share of the remaining adjusted basis of P is amortized over a new 15-year period.

Example 20. Acquisition by related corporation in nonrecognition transaction. (i) The facts are the same as *Example 18,* except that A and B form corporation P as equal owners.

(ii) P has a transferred basis in the intangible from A and B under section 362. Pursuant to paragraph (h)(10) of this section, the application of the nonrecognition transfer rule under paragraph (g)(2)(ii) of this section and the anti-churning rules of paragraph (h) of this section to the facts of this *Example 18* is the same as in *Example 16.* Thus, P's entire basis in the intangible is nonamortizable.

Example 21. Acquisition from corporation related to purchaser through remote indirect interest. (i) X, Y, and Z are each corporations that have only one class of issued and outstanding stock. X owns 25 percent of the stock of Y and Y owns 25 percent of the outstanding stock of Z. No other shareholder of any of these corporations is related to any other shareholder or to any of the corporations. On June 30, 2000, X purchases from Z section 197(f)(9) intangibles that Z owned during the transition period (as defined in paragraph (h)(4) of this section).

(ii) Pursuant to paragraph (h)(6)(iv)(B) of this section, the beneficial ownership interest of X in Z is 6.25 percent, determined by treating X as if it owned a proportionate (25 percent) interest in the stock of Z that is actually owned by Y. Thus, even though X is related to Y and Y is related to Z, X and Z are not considered to be related for purposes of the anti-churning rules of section 197.

Example 22. Gain recognition election. (i) B owns 25 percent of the stock of S, a corporation that uses the calendar year as its taxable year. No other shareholder of B or S is related to each other. S is not a member of a controlled group of corporations within the meaning of section 1563(a). S has section 197(f)(9) intangibles that it owned during the transition period. S has a basis of $25,000 in the intangibles. In 2001, S sells these intangibles to B for $75,000. S recognizes a gain of $50,000 on the sale and has no other items of income, deduction, gain, or loss for the year, except that S also has a net operating loss of $20,000 from prior years that it would otherwise be entitled to use in 2001 pursuant to section 172(b). S makes a valid gain recognition election pursuant to section 197(f)(9)(B) and paragraph (h)(9) of this section. In 2001, the highest marginal tax rate applicable to S is 35 percent. But for the election, all of S's taxable income would be taxed at a rate of 15 percent.

(ii) If the gain recognition election had not been made, S would have taxable income of $30,000 for 2001 and a tax liability of $4,500. If the gain were not taken into account, S would have no tax liability for the taxable year. Thus, the amount of tax (other than the tax imposed under paragraph (h)(9) of this section) imposed on the gain is also $4,500. The gain on the disposition multiplied by the highest marginal tax rate is $17,500 ($50,000 × .35). Accordingly, S's tax liability for the year is $4,500 plus an additional tax under paragraph (h)(9) of this section of $13,000 ($17,500 – $4,500).

(iii) Pursuant to paragraph (h)(9)(x)(A) of this section, S determines the amount of its net operating loss deduction in subsequent years without regard to the gain recognized on the sale of the section 197 intangible to B. Accordingly, the entire $20,000 net operating loss deduction that would have been available in 2001 but for the gain recognition election may be used in 2002, subject to the limitations of section 172.

(iv) B has a basis of $75,000 in the section 197(f)(9) intangibles acquired from S. As the result of the gain recognition election by S, B may amortize $50,000 of its basis under section 197. Under paragraph (h)(9)(ii) of this section, the remaining basis does not qualify for the gain-recognition exception and may not be amortized by B.

Example 23. Section 338 election. (i) Corporation P makes a qualified stock purchase of the stock of T corporation from two shareholders in July 2000, and a section 338 election is made by P. No shareholder of either T or P owns stock in both of these corporations, and no other shareholder is related to any other shareholder of either corporation.

(ii) Pursuant to paragraph (h)(8) of this section, in the case of a qualified stock purchase that is treated as a deemed sale and purchase of assets pursuant to section 338, the corporation treated as purchasing assets as a result of an election thereunder (new target) is not considered the person that held or used the assets during any period in which the assets were held or used by the corporation treated as selling the assets (old target). Because there are no relationships described in paragraph (h)(6) of this section among the parties to the transaction, any nonamortizable section 197(f)(9) intangible held by old target is an amortizable section 197 intangible in the hands of new target.

(iii) Assume the same facts as set forth in paragraph (i) of this *Example 23*, except that one of the selling shareholders is an individual who owns 25 percent of the total value of the stock of each of the T and P corporation.

(iv) Old target and new target (as these terms are defined in § 1.338-2(c)(17)) are members of a controlled group of corporations under section 267(b)(3), as modified by section 197(f)(9)(C)(i), and any nonamortizable section 197(f)(9) intangible held by old target is not an amortizable section 197 intangible in the hands of new target. However, a gain recognition election under paragraph (h)(9) of this section may be made with respect to this transaction.

Example 24. Relationship created as part of public offering. (i) On January 1, 2001, Corporation X engages in a series of related transactions to discontinue its involvement in one line of business. X forms a new corporation, Y, with a nominal amount of cash. Shortly thereafter, X transfers all the stock of its subsidiary conducting the unwanted business (Target) to Y in exchange for 100 shares of Y common stock and a Y promissory note. Target owns a nonamortizable section 197(f)(9) intangible. Prior to January 1, 2001, X and an underwriter (U) had entered into a binding agreement pursuant to which U would purchase 85 shares of Y common stock from X and then sell those shares in a public offering. On January 6, 2001, the public offering closes. X and Y make a section 338(h)(10) election for Target.

(ii) Pursuant to paragraph (h)(8) of this section, in the case of a qualified stock purchase that is treated as a deemed sale and purchase of assets pursuant to section 338, the corporation treated as purchasing assets as a result of an election thereunder (new target) is not considered the person that held or used the assets during any period in which the assets were held or used by the corporation treated as selling the assets (old target). Further, for purposes of determining whether the nonamortizable section 197(f)(9) intangible is acquired by new target from a related person, because the transactions are a series of related transactions, the relationship between old target and new target must be tested immediately before the first transaction in the series (the formation of Y) and immediately after the last transaction in the series (the sale to U and the public offering). See paragraph (h)(6)(ii)(B) of this section. Because there was no relationship between old target and new target immediately before the formation of Y (because the section 338 election had not been made) and only a 15% relationship between old target and new target immediately after, old target is not related to new target for purposes of applying the anti-churning rules of paragraph (h) of this section. Accordingly, Target may amortize the section 197 intangible.

Example 25. Other transfers to controlled corporations. (i) In 2001, Corporation A transfers a section 197(f)(9) intangible that it held during the transition period to X, a newly formed corporation, in exchange for 15% of X's stock. As part of the same transaction, B transfers property to X in exchange for the remaining 85% of X stock.

(ii) Because the acquisition of the intangible by X is part of a qualifying section 351 exchange, under section 197(f)(2) and paragraph (g)(2)(ii) of this section, X is treated in the same manner as the transferor of the asset. Accordingly, X may not amortize the intangible. If, however, at the time of the exchange, B has a binding commitment to sell 25 percent of the X stock to C, an unrelated third party, the exchange, including A's transfer of the section 197(f)(9) intangible, would fail to qualify as a section 351 exchange. Because the formation of X, the transfers of property to X, and the sale of X stock by B are part of a series of related transactions, the relationship between A and X must be tested immediately before the first transaction in the series (the transfer of property to X) and immediately after the last transaction in the series (the sale of X stock to C). See paragraph (h)(6)(ii)(B) of this section. Because there was no relationship between A and X immediately before and only a 15% relationship immediately after, A is not related to X for purposes of applying the anti-churning rules of paragraph (h) of this section. Accordingly, X may amortize the section 197 intangible.

Example 26. Relationship created as part of stock acquisition followed by liquidation. (i) In 2001, Partnership P purchases 100 percent of the stock of Corporation X. P and X were not related prior to the acquisition. Immediately after acquiring the X stock, and as part of a series of related transactions, P liquidates X under section 331. In the liquidating distribution, P receives a section 197(f)(9) intangible that was held by X during the transition period.

(ii) Because the relationship between P and X was created pursuant to a series of related transactions where P acquires stock (meeting the requirements of section 1504(a)(2)) in a fully taxable transaction followed by a liquidation under section 331, the relationship immediately after the last transaction in the series (the liquidation) is disregarded. See paragraph (h)(6)(iii) of this section. Accordingly, P is entitled to amortize the section 197(f)(9) intangible.

Example 27. Section 743(b) adjustment with no change in user. (i) On January 1, 2001, A forms a partnership (PRS) with B in which A owns a 60-percent, and B owns a 40-percent, interest in profits and capital. A contributes a nonamortizable section 197(f)(9) intangible with a value of $80 and an adjusted basis of $0 to PRS in exchange for its PRS interest and B contributes $120 cash. At the time of the contribution, PRS licenses the section 197(f)(9) intangible to A. On February 1, 2001, A sells its entire interest in PRS to C, an unrelated person, for $80. PRS has a section 754 election in effect.

(ii) The section 197(f)(9) intangible contributed to PRS by A is not amortizable in the hands of PRS. Pursuant to section (g)(2)(ii) of this section, PRS steps into the shoes of A with respect to A's nonamortizable transferred basis in the intangible.

(iii) When A sells the PRS interest to C, C will have a basis adjustment in the PRS assets under section 743(b) equal to $80. The entire basis adjustment will be allocated to the intangible because the only other asset held by PRS is cash. Ordinarily, under paragraph (h)(12)(v) of this section, the anti-churning rules will not apply to an increase in the basis of partnership property under section 743(b) if the person acquiring the partnership interest is not related to the person transferring the partnership interest. However, A is an anti-churning partner under paragraph (h)(12)(vi)(B)(*2*)(*i*) of this section. As a result of the license agreement, A remains a direct user of the section 197(f)(9) intangible after the transfer to C. Accordingly, paragraph (h)(12)(vi)(A) of this section will cause the anti-churning rules to apply to the entire basis adjustment under section 743(b).

Example 28. Distribution of section 197(f)(9) intangible to partner who acquired partnership interest prior to the effective date. (i) In 1990, A, B, and C each contribute $150 cash to form general partnership ABC for the purpose of engaging in a consulting business and a software manufacturing business. The partners agree to share partnership profits and losses equally. In 2000, the partnership distributes the consulting business to A in liquidation of A's entire interest in ABC. The only asset of the consulting business is a nonamortizable intangible, which has a fair market value of $180 and a basis of $0. At the time of the distribution, the adjusted basis of

A's interest in ABC is $150. A is not related to B or C. ABC does not have a section 754 election in effect.

(ii) Under section 732(b), A's adjusted basis in the intangible distributed by ABC is $150, a $150 increase over the basis of the intangible in ABC's hands. In determining whether the anti-churning rules apply to any portion of the basis increase, A is treated as having owned and used A's proportionate share of partnership property. Thus, A is treated as holding an interest in the intangible during the transition period. Because the intangible was not amortizable prior to the enactment of section 197, the section 732(b) increase in the basis of the intangible may be subject to the anti-churning provisions. Paragraph (h)(12)(ii) of this section provides that the anti-churning provisions apply to the extent that the section 732(b) adjustment exceeds the total unrealized appreciation from the intangible allocable to partners other than A or persons related to A, as well as certain other partners whose purchase of their interests meet certain criteria. Because B and C are not related to A, and A's acquisition of its partnership interest does not satisfy the necessary criteria, the section 732(b) basis increase is subject to the anti-churning provisions to the extent that it exceeds B and C's proportionate share of the unrealized appreciation from the intangible. B and C's proportionate share of the unrealized appreciation from the intangible is $120 (⅔ of $180). This is the amount of gain that would be allocated to B and C if the partnership sold the intangible immediately before the distribution for its fair market value of $180. Therefore, $120 of the section 732(b) basis increase is not subject to the anti-churning rules. The remaining $30 of the section 732(b) basis increase is subject to the anti-churning rules. Accordingly, A is treated as having two intangibles, an amortizable section 197 intangible with an adjusted basis of $120 and a new amortization period of 15 years and a nonamortizable intangible with an adjusted basis of $30.

(iii) In applying the anti-churning rules to future transfers of the distributed intangible, under paragraph (h)(12)(ii)(C) of this section, one-third of the intangible will continue to be subject to the anti-churning rules, determined as follows: The sum of the amount of the distributed intangible's basis that is nonamortizable under paragraph (g)(2)(ii)(B) of this section ($0) and the total unrealized appreciation inherent in the intangible reduced by the amount of the increase in the adjusted basis of the distributed intangible under section 732(b) to which the anti-churning rules do not apply ($180–$120=$60), over the fair market value of the distributed intangible ($180).

Example 29. Distribution of section 197(f)(9) intangible to partner who acquired partnership interest after the effective date. (i) The facts are the same as in *Example 28*, except that B and C form ABC in 1990. A does not acquire an interest in ABC until 1995. In 1995, A contributes $150 to ABC in exchange for a one-third interest in ABC. At the time of the distribution, the adjusted basis of A's interest in ABC is $150.

(ii) As in *Example 28*, the anti-churning rules do not apply to the increase in the basis of the intangible distributed to A under section 732(b) to the extent that it does not exceed the unrealized appreciation from the intangible allocable to B and C. Under paragraph (h)(12)(ii) of this section, the anti-churning provisions also do not apply to the section 732(b) basis increase to the extent of A's allocable share of the unrealized appreciation from the intangible because A acquired the ABC interest from an unrelated person after August 10, 1993, and the intangible was acquired by the partnership before A acquired the ABC interest. Under paragraph (h)(12)(ii)(E) of this section, A is deemed to acquire the ABC partnership interest from an unrelated person because A acquired the ABC partnership interest in exchange for a contribution to the partnership of property other than the distributed intangible and, at the time of the contribution, no partner in the partnership was related to A. Consequently, the increase in the basis of the intangible under section 732(b) is not subject to the anti-churning rules to the extent of the total unrealized appreciation from the intangible allocable to A, B, and C. The total unrealized appreciation from the intangible allocable to A, B, and C is $180 (the gain the partnership would have recognized if it had sold the intangible for its fair market value immediately before the distribution). Because this amount exceeds the section 732(b) basis increase of $150, the entire section 732(b) basis increase is amortizable.

(iii) In applying the anti-churning rules to future transfers of the distributed intangible, under paragraph (h)(12)(ii)(C) of this section, one-sixth of the intangible will continue to be subject to the anti-churning rules, determined as follows: The sum of the amount of the distributed intangible's basis that is nonamortizable under paragraph (g)(2)(ii)(B) of this section ($0) and the total unrealized appreciation inherent in the intangible reduced by the amount of the increase in the adjusted basis of the distributed intangible under section 732(b) to which the anti-churning rules do not apply ($180–$150=$30), over the fair market value of the distributed intangible ($180).

Example 30. Distribution of section 197(f)(9) intangible contributed to the partnership by a partner. (i) The facts are the same as in *Example 29*, except that C purchased the intangible used in the consulting business in 1988 for $60 and contributed the intangible to ABC in 1990. At that time, the intangible had a fair market value of $150 and an adjusted tax basis of $60. When ABC distributes the intangible to A in 2000, the intangible has a fair market value of $180 and a basis of $60.

(ii) As in *Examples 28* and *29*, the adjusted basis of the intangible in A's hands is $150 under section 732(b). However, the increase in the adjusted basis of the intangible under section 732(b) is only $90 ($150 adjusted basis after the distribution compared to $60 basis before the distribution). Pursuant to paragraph (g)(2)(ii)(B) of this section, A steps into the shoes of ABC with respect to the $60 of A's adjusted basis in the intangible that corresponds to ABC's basis in the intangible and this portion of the basis is nonamortizable. B and C are not related to A, A acquired the ABC interest from an unrelated person after August 10, 1993, and the intangible was acquired by ABC before A acquired the ABC interest. Therefore, under paragraph (h)(12)(ii) of this section, the section 732(b) basis increase is amortizable to the extent of A, B, and C's allocable share of the unrealized appreciation from the intangible. The total unrealized appreciation from the intangible that is allocable to A, B, and C is $120. If ABC had sold the intangible immediately before the distribution to A for its fair market value of $180, it would have recognized gain of $120, which would have been allocated $10 to A, $10 to B, and $100 to C under section 704(c). Because A, B, and C's allocable share of the unrealized appreciation from the intangible exceeds the section 732(b) basis increase in the intangible, the entire $90 of basis increase is amortizable by A. Accordingly, after the distribution, A will be treated as having two intangibles, an amortizable section 197 intangible with an adjusted basis of $90 and a new amortization period of 15 years and a nonamortizable intangible with an adjusted basis of $60.

(iii) In applying the anti-churning rules to future transfers of the distributed intangible, under paragraph (h)(12)(ii)(C) of this section, one-half of the intangible will continue to be subject to the anti-churning rules, determined as follows: The sum of the amount of the distributed intangible's basis that is nonamortizable under paragraph (g)(2)(ii)(B) of this section ($60) and the total unrealized appreciation inherent in the intangible reduced by the amount of the increase in the adjusted basis of the distributed intangible under section 732(b) to which the anti-churning rules do not apply ($120–$90=$30), over the fair market value of the distributed intangible ($180).

Example 31. Partnership distribution causing section 734(b) basis adjustment to section 197(f)(9) intangible. (i) On January 1, 2001, A, B, and C form a partnership (ABC) in which each partner shares equally in capital and income, gain, loss, and deductions. On that date, A contributes a section 197(f)(9) intangible with a zero basis and a value of $150, and B and C each contribute $150 cash. A and B are related, but neither A nor B is related to C. ABC does not adopt the remedial allocation method for making section 704(c) allocations of amortization expenses with respect to the intangible. On December 1, 2004, when the value of the intangible has increased to $600, ABC distributes $300 to B in complete redemption of B's interest in the partnership. ABC has an election under section 754 in effect for the taxable year that includes December 1, 2004. (Assume that, at the time of the distribution, the basis of A's partnership interest remains zero, and the basis of each of B's and C's partnership interest remains $150.)

(ii) Immediately prior to the distribution, the assets of the partnership are revalued pursuant to § 1.704-1(b)(2)(iv)(*f*), so that the section 197(f)(9) intangible is reflected on the books of the partnership at a value of $600. B recognizes $150 of gain under section 731(a)(1) upon the distribution of $300 in redemption of B's partnership interest. As a result, the adjusted basis of the intangible held by ABC increases by $150 under section 734(b). A does not satisfy any of the tests set forth under paragraph (h)(12)(iv)(B) and thus is not an eligible partner. C is not related to B and thus is an eligible partner under paragraph (h)(12)(iv)(B)(*1*) of this section. The capital accounts of A and C are equal immediately after the distribution, so, pursuant to paragraph (h)(12)(iv)(D)(*1*) of this section, each partner's share of the basis increase is equal to $75. Because A is not an eligible partner, the anti-churning rules apply to A's share of the basis increase. The anti-churning rules do not apply to C's share of the basis increase.

(iii) For book purposes, ABC determines the amortization of the asset as follows: First, the intangible that is subject to adjustment under section 734(b) will be divided into three assets: the first, with a basis and value of $75 will be amortizable for both book and tax purposes; the second, with a basis and value of $75 will be amortizable for book, but not tax purposes; and a third asset with a basis of zero and a value of $450 will not be amortizable for book or tax purposes. Any subsequent revaluation of the intangible pursuant to § 1.704-1(b)(2)(iv)(*f*) will be made solely with respect to the third asset (which is not amortizable for book purposes). The book and tax attributes from the first asset (i.e., book and tax amortization) will be specially allocated to C. The book and tax attributes from the second asset (i.e., book amortization and non-amortizable tax basis) will be specially allocated to A. Upon disposition of the intangible, each partner's share of gain or loss will be determined first by allocating among the partners an amount realized equal to the book value of the intangible attributable to such partner, with any remaining amount realized being allocated in accordance with the partnership agreement. Each partner then will compare its share of the amount realized with its remaining basis in the intangible to arrive at the gain or loss to be allocated to such partner. This is a reasonable method for amortizing the intangible for book purposes, and the results in allocating the income, gain, loss, and deductions attributable to the intangible do not contravene the purposes of the anti-churning rules under section 197 or paragraph (h) of this section.

(l) *Effective dates* .—(1) *In general* .—This section applies to property acquired after January 25, 2000, except that paragraph (c)(13) of this section (exception from section 197 for separately acquired rights of fixed duration or amount) applies to property acquired after August 10, 1993 (or July 25, 1991, if a valid retroactive election has been made under § 1.197-IT), and paragraphs (h)(12)(ii), (iii), (iv), (v), (vi)(A), and (vii)(B) of this section (anti-churning rules applicable to partnerships) apply to partnership transactions occurring on or after November 20, 2000.

(2) *Application to pre-effective date acquisitions* .—A taxpayer may choose, on a transaction-by-transaction basis, to apply the provisions of this section and § 1.167(a)-14 to property acquired (or partnership transactions occurring) after August 10, 1993 (or July 25, 1991, if a valid retroactive election has been made under § 1.197-1T) and—

(i) On or before January 25, 2000; or

(ii) With respect to paragraphs (h)(12)(ii), (iii), (iv), (v), (vi)(A), and (vii)(B) of this section, before November 20, 2000.

(3) *Application of regulation project REG-209709-94 to pre-effective date acquisitions* .—A taxpayer may rely on the provisions of regulation project REG-209709-94 (1997-1 C.B. 731) for property acquired after August 10, 1993 (or July 25, 1991, if a valid retroactive election has been made under § 1.197-1T) and on or before January 25, 2000.

(3) *Application of regulation project REG-209709-94 to pre-effective date acquisitions* .—A taxpayer may rely on the provisions of regulation project REG-209709-94 (1997-1 C.B. 731) for property acquired after August 10, 1993 (or July 25, 1991, if a valid retroactive election has been made under § 1.197-1T) and on or before January 25, 2000.

(4) *Change in method of accounting* .—(i) *In general* .—For the first taxable year ending after January 25, 2000, a taxpayer that has acquired property to which the exception in § 1.197-2(c)(13) applies is granted consent of the Commissioner to change its method of accounting for such property to comply with the provisions of this section and § 1.167(a)-14 unless the proper treatment of such property is an issue under consideration (within the meaning of Rev. Proc. 97-27 (1997-21 IRB 10)(see § 601.601(d)(2) of this chapter)) in an examination, before an Appeals office, or before a Federal court.

(ii) *Application to pre-effective date acquisitions* .—For the first taxable year ending after January 25, 2000, a taxpayer is granted consent of the Commissioner to change its method of accounting for all property acquired in transactions described in paragraph (l)(2) of this section to comply with the provisions of this section and § 1.167(a)-14 unless the proper treatment of any such property is an issue under consideration (within the meaning of Rev. Proc. 97-27 (1997-21 IRB 10)(see § 601.601(d)(2) of this chapter)) in an examination, before an Appeals office, or before a Federal court.

(iii) *Automatic change procedures* .—A taxpayer changing its method of accounting in accordance with this paragraph (l)(4) must follow the automatic change in accounting method provisions of Rev. Proc. 99-49 (1999-52 IRB 725)(see § 601.601(d)(2) of this chapter) except, for purposes of this paragraph (l)(4), the scope limitations in section 4.02 of Rev. Proc. 99-49 (1999-52 IRB 725) are not applicable. However, if the taxpayer is under examination, before an appeals office, or before a federal court, the taxpayer must provide a copy of the application to the examining agent(s), appeals officer, or counsel for the government, as appropriate, at the same time that it files the copy of the application with the National Office. The application must contain the name(s) and telephone number(s) of the examining agent(s), appeals officer, or counsel for the government, as appropriate. [Reg. § 1.197-2.]

.01 Historical Comment: Proposed 1/16/97. Adopted 1/20/2000 by T.D. 8865 (corrected 3/27/2000 and 10/11/2000). Amended 11/17/2000 by T.D. 8907, 2/12/2001 by T.D. 8940, 4/7/2006 by T.D. 9257 and 1/22/2008 by T.D. 9377.

New York Liberty Zone Property Regulations

¶ 599

Reg. § 1.1400L(b)-1

§ 1.1400L(b)-1. **Additional first year depreciation deduction for qualified New York Liberty Zone property.**—(a) *Scope.*—This section provides the rules for determining the 30-percent additional first year depreciation deduction allowable under section 1400L(b) for qualified New York Liberty Zone property.

(b) *Definitions.*—For purposes of section 1400L(b) and this section, the definitions of the terms in § 1.168(k)-1(a)(2) apply and the following definitions also apply:

(1) *Building* and *structural components* have the same meanings as those terms are defined in § 1.48-1(e).

(2) *New York Liberty Zone* is the area located on or south of Canal Street, East Broadway (east of its intersection with Canal Street), or Grand Street (east of its intersection with East Broadway) in the Borough of Manhattan in the City of New York, New York.

(3) *Nonresidential real property* and *residential rental property* have the same meanings as those terms are defined in section 168(e)(2).

(4) *Real property* is a building or its structural components, or other tangible real property.

(c) *Qualified New York Liberty Zone property.*—(1) *In general.*—Qualified New York Liberty Zone property is depreciable property that meets all the following requirements in the first taxable year in which the property is subject to depreciation by the taxpayer whether or not depreciation deductions for the property are allowable—

(i) The requirements in § 1.1400L(b)-1(c)(2) (description of property);

(ii) The requirements in § 1.1400L(b)-1(c)(3) (substantial use);

(iii) The requirements in § 1.1400L(b)-1(c)(4) (original use);

(iv) The requirements in § 1.1400L(b)-1(c)(5) (acquisition of property by purchase); and

(v) The requirements in § 1.1400L(b)-1(c)(6) (placed-in-service date).

(2) *Description of qualified New York Liberty Zone property.*—(i) *In general.*—Depreciable property will meet the requirements of this paragraph (c)(2) if the property is—

(A) Described in § 1.168(k)-1(b)(2)(i); or

(B) Nonresidential real property or residential rental property depreciated under section 168, but only to the extent it rehabilitates real property damaged, or replaces real property destroyed or condemned, as a result of the terrorist attacks of September 11, 2001. Property is treated as replacing destroyed or condemned property if, as part of an integrated plan, the property replaces real property that is included in a continuous area that includes real property destroyed or condemned. For purposes of this section, real property is considered as destroyed or condemned only if an entire building or structure was destroyed or condemned as a result of the terrorist attacks of September 11, 2001. Otherwise, the real property is considered damaged real property. For example, if certain structural components (for example, walls, floors, and plumbing fixtures) of a building are damaged or destroyed as a result of the terrorist attacks of September

11, 2001, but the building is not destroyed or condemned, then only costs related to replacing the damaged or destroyed structural components qualify under this paragraph (c) (2) (i) (B).

(ii) *Property not eligible for additional first year depreciation deduction.*—Depreciable property will not meet the requirements of this paragraph (c) (2) if—

(A) Section 168(k) or § 1.168(k)-1 applies to the property;

(B) The property is described in section 168(f);

(C) The property is required to be depreciated under the alternative depreciation system of section 168(g) pursuant to section 168(g) (1) (A) through (D) or other provisions of the Internal Revenue Code (for example, property described in section 263A(e) (2) (A) if the taxpayer (or any related person) has made an election under section 263A(d) (3), or property described in section 280F(b) (1));

(D) The property is included in any class of property for which the taxpayer elects not to deduct the additional first year depreciation under paragraph (e) of this section; or

(E) The property is qualified New York Liberty Zone leasehold improvement property as described in section 1400L(c) (2).

* * *

(3) *Substantial use.*—Depreciable property will meet the requirements of this paragraph (c) (3) if substantially all of the use of the property is in the New York Liberty Zone and is in the active conduct of a trade or business by the taxpayer in New York Liberty Zone. For purposes of this paragraph (c) (3), "substantially all" means 80 percent or more.

(4) *Original use.*—Depreciable property will meet the requirements of this paragraph (c) (4) if the original use of the property commences with the taxpayer in the New York Liberty Zone after September 10, 2001. The original use rules in § 1.168(k)-1 (b) (3) apply for purposes of this paragraph (c) (4). In addition, used property will satisfy the original use requirement in this paragraph (c) (4) so long as the property has not been previously used within the New York Liberty Zone.

(5) *Acquisition of property by purchase.*—(i) *In general.*—Depreciable property will meet the requirements of this paragraph (c) (5) if the property is acquired by the taxpayer by purchase (as defined in section 179(d) and § 1.179-4(c)) after September 10, 2001, but only if no written binding contract for the acquisition of the property was in effect before September 11, 2001. For purposes of this paragraph (c) (5), the rules in § 1.168(k)-1 (b) (4) (ii) (binding contract), the rules in § 1.168(k)-1 (b) (4) (iii) (self-constructed property), and the rules in § 1.168(k)-1 (b) (4) (iv) (disqualified transactions) apply. For purposes of the preceding sentence, the rules in § 1.168(k)-1T(b) (4) (iii) shall be applied without regard to 'and before January 1, 2005.

(ii) *Exception for certain transactions.*—For purposes of this section, the new partnership of a transaction described in § 1.168(k)-1 (f) (1) (ii) (technical termination of a partnership) or the transferee of a transaction described in § 1.168(k)-1 (f) (1) (iii) (section 168(i) (7) transactions) is deemed to acquire the depreciable property by purchase.

(6) *Placed-in-service date.*—Depreciable property will meet the requirements of this paragraph (c) (6) if the property is placed in service by the taxpayer on

or before December 31, 2006. However, nonresidential real property and residential rental property described in paragraph (c)(2)(i)(B) of this section must be placed in service by the taxpayer on or before December 31, 2009. The rules in § 1.168(k)-1T(b)(5)(ii) (relating to sale-leaseback and syndication transactions), the rules in § 1.168(k)-1(b)(5)(iii) (relating to a technical termination of a partnership under section 708(b)(1)(B)), and the rules in § 1.168(k)-1(b)(5)(iv) (relating to section 168(i)(7) transactions) apply for purposes of this paragraph (c)(6).

(d) *Computation of depreciation deduction for qualified New York Liberty Zone property.*—The computation of the allowable additional first year depreciation deduction and the otherwise allowable depreciation deduction for qualified New York Liberty Zone property is made in accordance with the rules for qualified property in § 1.168(k)-1(d)(1)(i) and (2).

(e) *Election not to deduct additional first year depreciation.*—(1) *In general.*—A taxpayer may make an election not to deduct the 30-percent additional first year depreciation for any class of property that is qualified New York Liberty Zone property placed in service during the taxable year. If a taxpayer makes an election under this paragraph (e), the election applies to all qualified New York Liberty Zone property that is in the same class of property and placed in service in the same taxable year, and no additional first year depreciation deduction is allowable for the class of property.

(2) *Definition of class of property.*—For purposes of this paragraph (e), the term class of property means—

(i) Except for the property described in paragraphs (e)(2)(ii), (iv), and (v) of this section, each class of property described in section 168(e) (for example, 5-year property);

(ii) Water utility property as defined in section 168(e)(5) and depreciated under section 168;

(iii) Computer software as defined in, and depreciated under, section 167(f)(1) and the regulations thereunder;

(iv) Nonresidential real property as defined in paragraph (b)(3) of this section and as described in paragraph (c)(2)(B) of this section; or

(v) Residential rental property as defined in paragraph (b)(3) of this section and as described in paragraph (c)(2)(B) of this section.

(3) *Time and manner for making election.*—(i) *Time for making election.*—Except as provided in paragraph (e)(4) of this section, the election specified in paragraph (e)(1) of this section must be made by the due date (including extensions) of the federal tax return for the taxable year in which the qualified New York Liberty Zone property is placed in service by the taxpayer.

(ii) *Manner of making election.*—Except as provided in paragraph (e)(4) of this section, the election specified in paragraph (e)(1) of this section must be made in the manner prescribed on Form 4562, "Depreciation and Amortization," and its instructions. The election is made separately by each person owning qualified New York Liberty Zone property (for example, for each member of a consolidated group by the common parent of the group, by the partnership, or by the S corporation). If Form 4562 is revised or renumbered, any reference in this section to that form shall be treated as a reference to the revised or renumbered form.

(4) *Special rules for 2000 or 2001 returns.*—For the election specified in paragraph (e)(1) of this section for qualified New York Liberty Zone property

placed in service by the taxpayer during the taxable year that included September 11, 2001, the taxpayer should refer to the guidance provided by the Internal Revenue Service for the time and manner of making this election on the 2000 or 2001 federal tax return for the taxable year that included September 11, 2001 (for further guidance, see sections 3.03(3) and 4 of Rev. Proc. 2002-33 (2002-1 C.B. 963), Rev. Proc. 2003-50 (2003-29 I.R.B. 119), and § 601.601(d)(2)(ii)(*b*) of this chapter).

(5) *Failure to make election.*—If a taxpayer does not make the election specified in paragraph (e)(1) of this section within the time and in the manner prescribed in paragraph (e)(3) or (e)(4) of this section, the amount of depreciation allowable for that property under section 167(f)(1) or under section 168, as applicable, must be determined for the placed-in-service year and for all subsequent taxable years by taking into account the additional first year depreciation deduction. Thus, the election specified in paragraph (e)(1) of this section shall not be made by the taxpayer in any other manner (for example, the election cannot be made through a request under section 446(e) to change the taxpayer's method of accounting).

(6) *Alternative minimum tax.*—If a taxpayer makes an election under this paragraph (e) for a class of property, the depreciation adjustments under section 56 and the regulations under section 56 apply to the property to which the election applies for purposes of computing the taxpayer's alternative minimum taxable income.

(7) *Revocation of election.*—(i) *In general.*—Except as provided in paragraph (e)(7)(ii) of this section, an election under this paragraph (e), once made, may be revoked only with the written consent of the Commissioner of Internal Revenue. To seek the Commissioner's consent, the taxpayer must submit a request for a letter ruling.

(ii) *Automatic 6-month extension.*—If a taxpayer made an election under this paragraph (e) for a class of property, an automatic extension of 6 months from the due date of the taxpayer's Federal tax return (excluding extensions) for the placed-in-service year of the class of property is granted to revoke that election, provided the taxpayer timely filed the taxpayer's Federal tax return for the placed-in-service year of the class of property and, within this 6-month extension period, the taxpayer (and all taxpayers whose tax liability would be affected by the election) files an amended Federal tax return for the placed-inservice year of the class of property in a manner that is consistent with the revocation of the election.

(f) *Special rules.*—(1) *Property placed in service and disposed of in the same taxable year.*—Rules similar to those provided in § 1.168(k)-1(f)(1) apply for purposes of this paragraph (f)(1).

(2) *Redetermination of basis.*—If the unadjusted depreciable basis (as defined in § 1.168(k)-1(a)(2)(iii)) of qualified New York Liberty Zone property is redetermined (for example, due to contingent purchase price or discharge of indebtedness) on or before December 31, 2006 (or on or before December 31, 2009, for nonresidential real property and residential rental property described in paragraph (c)(2)(i)(B) of this section), the additional first year depreciation deduction allowable for the qualified New York Liberty Zone property is redetermined in accordance with the rules provided in § 1.168(k)-1(f)(2).

(3) *Section 1245 and 1250 depreciation recapture.*—The rules provided in § 1.168(k)-1(f)(3) apply for purposes of this paragraph (f)(3).

(4) *Coordination with section 169.*—Rules similar to those provided in § 1.168(k)-1(f)(4) apply for purposes of this paragraph (f)(4).

(5) *Like-kind exchanges and involuntary conversions.*—This paragraph (f)(5) applies to acquired MACRS property (as defined in § 1.168(k)-1(f)(5)(ii)(A)) or acquired computer software (as defined in § 1.168(k)-1(f)(5)(ii)(C)) that is eligible for the additional first year depreciation deduction under section 1400L(b) at the time of replacement provided the time of replacement is after September 10, 2001, and on or before December 31, 2006, or in the case of acquired MACRS property or acquired computer software that is qualified New York Liberty Zone property described in paragraph (c)(2)(i)(B) of this section, the time of replacement is after September 10, 2001, and on or before December 31, 2009. The rules and definitions similar to those provided in § 1.168(k)-1(f)(5) apply for purposes of this paragraph (f)(5).

(6) *Change in use.*—Rules similar to those provided in § 1.168(k)-1(f)(6) apply for purposes of this paragraph (f)(6).

(7) *Earnings and profits.*—The rule provided in § 1.168(k)-1(f)(7) applies for purposes of this paragraph (f)(7).

(8) *Section 754 election.*—Rules similar to those provided in § 1.168(k)-1(f)(9) apply for purposes of this paragraph (f)(8).

(9) *Coordination with section 47.*—Rules similar to those provided in § 1.168(k)-1(f)(10) apply for purposes of this paragraph (f)(9).

(10) *Coordination with section 514(a)(3).*—Rules similar to those provided in § 1.168(k)-1(f)(11) apply for purposes of this paragraph (f)(10).

(g) *Effective date.*—(1) *In general.*—Except as provided in paragraphs (g)(2), (3), and (5) of this section, this section applies to qualified New York Liberty Zone property acquired by a taxpayer after September 10, 2001.

* * *

(2) *Technical termination of a partnership or section 168(i)(7) transactions.*—If qualified New York Liberty Zone property is transferred in a technical termination of a partnership under section 708(b)(1)(B) or in a transaction described in section 168(i)(7) for a taxable year ending on or before September 8, 2003, and the additional first year depreciation deduction allowable for the property was not determined in accordance with paragraph (f)(1) of this section, the Internal Revenue Service will allow any reasonable method of determining the additional first year depreciation deduction allowable for the property in the year of the transaction that is consistently applied to the property by all parties to the transaction.

(3) *Like-kind exchanges and involuntary conversions.*—If a taxpayer did not claim on a federal tax return for a taxable year ending on or before September 8, 2003, the additional first year depreciation deduction for the remaining carryover basis of qualified New York Liberty Zone property acquired in a transaction described in section 1031(a), (b), or (c), or in a transaction to which section 1033 applies and the taxpayer did not make an election not to deduct the additional first year depreciation deduction for the class of property applicable to the remaining carryover basis, the Internal Revenue Service will treat the taxpayer's method of not claiming the additional first year depreciation deduction for the remaining carryover basis as a permissible method of accounting and will treat the amount of the

additional first year depreciation deduction allowable for the remaining carryover basis as being equal to zero, provided the taxpayer does not claim the additional first year depreciation deduction for the remaining carryover basis in accordance with paragraph (g)(4)(ii) of this section.

(4) *Change in method of accounting.*—(i) *Special rules for 2000 or 2001 returns.*—If a taxpayer did not claim on the federal tax return for the taxable year that included September 11, 2001, any additional first year depreciation deduction for a class of property that is qualified New York Liberty Zone property and did not make an election not to deduct the additional first year depreciation deduction for that class of property, the taxpayer should refer to the guidance provided by the Internal Revenue Service for the time and manner of claiming the additional first year depreciation deduction for the class of property (for further guidance, see section 4 of Rev. Proc. 2002-33 (2002-1 C.B. 963), Rev. Proc. 2003-50 (2003-29 I.R.B. 119), and § 601.601(d)(2)(ii)(*b*) of this chapter).

(ii) *Like-kind exchanges and involuntary conversions.*—If a taxpayer did not claim on a federal tax return for any taxable year ending on or before September 8, 2003, the additional first year depreciation deduction allowable for the remaining carryover basis of qualified New York Liberty Zone property acquired in a transaction described in section 1031(a), (b), or (c), or in a transaction to which section 1033 applies and the taxpayer did not make an election not to deduct the additional first year depreciation deduction for the class of property applicable to the remaining carryover basis, the taxpayer may claim the additional first year depreciation deduction allowable for the remaining carryover basis in accordance with paragraph (f)(5) of this section either—

(A) By filing an amended return (or a qualified amended return, if applicable (for further guidance, see Rev. Proc. 94-69 (1994-2 C.B. 804) and § 601.601(d)(2)(ii)(*b*) of this chapter)) on or before December 31, 2003, for the year of replacement and any affected subsequent taxable year; or,

(B) By following the applicable administrative procedures issued under § 1.446-1(e)(3)(ii) for obtaining the Commissioner's automatic consent to a change in method of accounting (for further guidance, see Rev. Proc. 2002-9 (2002-1 C.B. 327) and § 601.601(d)(2)(ii)(*b*) of this chapter).

(iii) *Revisions made in paragraphs (b)(4) and (c)(2)(ii) of this section.*—If a taxpayer did not claim on a Federal tax return for a taxable year ending on or after September 11, 2001, and on or before September 1, 2006, any additional first year depreciation deduction for qualified New York Liberty Zone property because of the application of § 1.1400L(b)-1T(b)(4) or because the taxpayer made an election under § 1.168(k)-1T(e)(1) for a class of property that included such qualified New York Liberty Zone property, the taxpayer may claim the additional first year depreciation deduction for such qualified New York Liberty Zone property under this section in accordance with the applicable administrative procedures issued under § 1.446-1(e)(3)(ii) for obtaining the Commissioner's consent to a change in method of accounting. Section 481(a) applies to a request to claim the additional first year depreciation deduction for such qualified New York Liberty Zone property under this paragraph (g)(4)(iii).

(5) *Revision to paragraphs (b)(4) and (b)(6).*—The addition of "(or, in the case of multiple units of property subject to the same lease, within three months after the date the final unit is placed in service, so long as the period between the time the first unit is placed in service and the time the last unit is placed in service does not exceed 12 months)" to § 1.168(k)-1(b)(3)(iii)(B) and

§ 1.168(k)-1(b)(5)(ii)(B) applies to property sold after June 4, 2004, for purposes of paragraphs (b)(4) and (b)(6) of this section.

(6) *Rehabilitation credit.*—If a taxpayer did not claim on a Federal tax return for a taxable year ending on or before September 1, 2006, the rehabilitation credit provided by section 47(a) with respect to the portion of the basis of a qualified rehabilitated building that is attributable to qualified rehabilitation expenditures and the qualified rehabilitation expenditures are qualified New York Liberty Zone property, and the taxpayer did not make the election specified in paragraph (e)(1) of this section for the class of property that includes the qualified rehabilitation expenditures, the taxpayer may claim the rehabilitation credit for the remaining rehabilitated basis (as defined in § 1.168(k)-1(f)(10)(i)(B)) of the qualified rehabilitated building that is attributable to the qualified rehabilitation expenditures (assuming all the requirements of section 47 are met) in accordance with paragraph (f)(9) of this section by filing an amended Federal tax return for the taxable year for which the rehabilitation credit is to be claimed. The amended Federal tax return must include the adjustment to the tax liability for the rehabilitation credit and any collateral adjustments to taxable income or to the tax liability (for example, the amount of depreciation allowed or allowable in that taxable year for the qualified rehabilitated building). Such adjustments must also be made on amended Federal tax returns for any affected succeeding taxable years. [Reg. § 1.1400L(b)-1.]

.01 Historical Comment: Adopted 9/5/2003 by T.D. 9091 (corrected 11/7/2003). Amended 8/28/2006 by T.D. 9283.

Depreciation Decimal Tables

¶ 601

Applying Decimals to Original Cost

The CCH-prepared tables of decimals at ¶ 610–¶ 640 are furnished to shorten depreciation calculation time. These tables are particularly easy to use because the decimals are to be applied to the original cost reduced by any additional first-year depreciation deducted and any salvage value taken into account (depending on the method of depreciation used and whether the taxpayer elects to ignore salvage value up to 10 percent of the cost).

Included are tables for straight-line depreciation (¶ 610), sum of the years-digits depreciation (¶ 620), double declining-balance depreciation with change to straight-line at the optimum point (¶ 640), and 150-percent declining-balance depreciation with change to straight-line at the optimum point (¶ 630).

The tables for the declining-balance methods with change to straight-line depreciation assume that the salvage is 10 percent or less of the cost of the asset and is ignored by the taxpayer in figuring depreciation. If any salvage value were taken into account, the optimum straight-line changeover point would occur later in the useful life than it does in the tables.

If the depreciation deduction is computed to the nearest penny, the total depreciation claimed using the decimals in these tables will be equal to the exact amount being depreciated (original cost less bonus depreciation and any salvage value taken into account). If the deductions are rounded off to the nearest dollar or a larger amount, however, the total depreciation claimed may be more or less than the basis being depreciated. Adjustment should be made in such case so that the taxpayer claims the proper amount of depreciation.

Although these tables were constructed for use in connection with property depreciated under pre-1981 rules, they, to a limited degree, may be useful in computing depreciation under ACRS and Modified ACRS (MACRS).

¶ 610

Straight-Line Decimals

The table on page 965 gives the straight-line decimals for the first tax year according to the number of months an asset was held in that year. (As to the number of months an asset is held, see ¶ 358.) The straight-line rates column is to be used where the asset is held 12 months in the first year. The straight-line rate is to be used for the second and all remaining years of useful life except the last year. The table on page 967 gives the straight-line decimals for the last year of useful life according to the number of months the asset is held in that year. Since the columns in the last-year table are in reverse order from those in the first-year table, the column to be used in finding the last-year decimal will be immediately below the column used for the first year (for example, the eight-month column for the last year is just below the four-month column for the first year).

These decimals are to be applied to original cost reduced by any additional first-year depreciation claimed and any salvage value taken into account.

> ***Example:*** An asset with a six-year life was held four months in the first taxable year. The first year's decimal is .05556, in the four-months column, the six-year life row in the first-year table on page 965. The decimal for the next five years is .16667, the straight-line rate in the six-year life row of the same table (from the column labeled "S-L

Rates"). The last year's decimal is .11109, in the eight-months column, the six-year life row in the last-year table on page 967.

If the asset has a depreciable basis (cost less bonus depreciation less any salvage value taken into account) of $10,000, straight-line depreciation without rounding would be as follows:

1st year	$555.60
2nd year	1,666.70
3rd year	1,666.70
4th year	1,666.70
5th year	1,666.70
6th year	1,666.70
7th year	1,110.90
Total depreciation	$10,000.00

Depreciation figured by rounding to the nearest dollar would be as follows:

1st year	$556
2nd year	1,667
3rd year	1,667
4th year	1,667
5th year	1,667
6th year	1,667
7th year	1,111
Total depreciation	$10,002

The above result could be adjusted to make the total depreciation come out even by making the third and fifth years' depreciation $1,666 instead of $1,667. Alternatively, the adjustment could be made in the last year, deducting the remaining basis of $1,109 at that time.

STRAIGHT-LINE DECIMALS

Years	S-L Rates	First-Year Decimals by Months Held 1	2	3	4	5	6	7	8	9	10	11
3	.33333	.02778	.05556	.08333	.11111	.13889	.16667	.19444	.22222	.25000	.27778	.30556
4	.25000	.02083	.04167	.06250	.08333	.10417	.12500	.14583	.16667	.18750	.20833	.22917
5	.20000	.01667	.03333	.05000	.06667	.08333	.10000	.11667	.13333	.15000	.16667	.18333
6	.16667	.01389	.02778	.04167	.05556	.06944	.08333	.09722	.11111	.12500	.13889	.15278
7	.14286	.01190	.02381	.03571	.04762	.05952	.07143	.08333	.09524	.10714	.11905	.13095
8	.12500	.01042	.02083	.03125	.04167	.05208	.06250	.07292	.08333	.09375	.10417	.11458
9	.11111	.00926	.01852	.02778	.03704	.04630	.05556	.06481	.07407	.08333	.09259	.10185
10	.10000	.00833	.01667	.02500	.03333	.04167	.05000	.05833	.06667	.07500	.08333	.09167
11	.09091	.00758	.01515	.02273	.03030	.03788	.04545	.05303	.06061	.06818	.07576	.08333
12	.08333	.00694	.01389	.02083	.02778	.03472	.04167	.04861	.05556	.06250	.06944	.07639
13	.07692	.00641	.01282	.01923	.02564	.03205	.03846	.04487	.05128	.05769	.06410	.07051
14	.07143	.00595	.01190	.01786	.02381	.02976	.03571	.04167	.04762	.05357	.05952	.06548
15	.06667	.00556	.01111	.01667	.02222	.02778	.03333	.03889	.04444	.05000	.05556	.06111
16	.06250	.00521	.01042	.01563	.02083	.02604	.03125	.03646	.04167	.04688	.05208	.05729
17	.05882	.00490	.00980	.01471	.01961	.02451	.02941	.03431	.03922	.04412	.04902	.05392
18	.05556	.00463	.00926	.01389	.01852	.02315	.02778	.03241	.03704	.04167	.04630	.05093
19	.05263	.00439	.00877	.01316	.01754	.02193	.02632	.03070	.03509	.03947	.04386	.04825
20	.05000	.00417	.00833	.01250	.01667	.02083	.02500	.02917	.03333	.03750	.04167	.04583
22	.04545	.00379	.00758	.01136	.01515	.01894	.02273	.02652	.03030	.03409	.03788	.04167
25	.04000	.00333	.00667	.01000	.01333	.01667	.02000	.02333	.02667	.03000	.03333	.03667
28	.03571	.00298	.00595	.00893	.01190	.01488	.01786	.02083	.02381	.02679	.02976	.03274
30	.03333	.00278	.00556	.00833	.01111	.01389	.01667	.01944	.02222	.02500	.02778	.03056
33	.03030	.00253	.00505	.00758	.01010	.01263	.01515	.01768	.02020	.02273	.02525	.02778
35	.02857	.00238	.00476	.00714	.00952	.01190	.01429	.01667	.01905	.02143	.02381	.02619
40	.02500	.00208	.00417	.00625	.00833	.01042	.01250	.01458	.01667	.01875	.02083	.02292
45	.02222	.00185	.00370	.00556	.00741	.00926	.01111	.01296	.01481	.01667	.01852	.02037

Years	S-L Rates	First-Year Decimals by Months Held										
		1	2	3	4	5	6	7	8	9	10	11
50	.02000	.00167	.00333	.00500	.00667	.00833	.01000	.01167	.01333	.01500	.01667	.01833
60	.01667	.00139	.00278	.00417	.00556	.00694	.00833	.00972	.01111	.01250	.01389	.01528
		Last-Year Decimals by Months Held										
Years	12	11	10	9	8	7	6	5	4	3	2	1
3	.33334	.30556	.27778	.25001	.22223	.19445	.16667	.13890	.11112	.08334	.05556	.02778
4	.25000	.22917	.20833	.18750	.16667	.14583	.12500	.10417	.08333	.06250	.04167	.02083
5	.20000	.18333	.16667	.15000	.13333	.11667	.10000	.08333	.06667	.05000	.03333	.01667
6	.16665	.15276	.13887	.12498	.11109	.09721	.08332	.06943	.05554	.04165	.02776	.01387
7	.14284	.13094	.11903	.10713	.09522	.08332	.07141	.05951	.04760	.03570	.02379	.01189
8	.12500	.11458	.10417	.09375	.08333	.07292	.06250	.05208	.04167	.03125	.02083	.01042
9	.11112	.10186	.09260	.08334	.07408	.06482	.05556	.04631	.03705	.02779	.01853	.00927
10	.10000	.09167	.08333	.07500	.06667	.05833	.05000	.04167	.03333	.02500	.01667	.00833
11	.09090	.08332	.07575	.06817	.06060	.05302	.04545	.03787	.03029	.02272	.01514	.00757
12	.08337	.07643	.06948	.06254	.05559	.04865	.04170	.03476	.02781	.02087	.01393	.00698
13	.07696	.07055	.06414	.05773	.05132	.04491	.03850	.03209	.02568	.01927	.01286	.00645
14	.07141	.06546	.05951	.05355	.04760	.04165	.03570	.02974	.02379	.01784	.01189	.00593
15	.06662	.06106	.05551	.04995	.04440	.03884	.03329	.02773	.02218	.01662	.01106	.00551
16	.06250	.05729	.05208	.04688	.04167	.03646	.03125	.02604	.02083	.01563	.01042	.00521
17	.05888	.05398	.04908	.04417	.03927	.03437	.02947	.02457	.01966	.01476	.00986	.00496
18	.05548	.05085	.04622	.04159	.03696	.03233	.02770	.02307	.01844	.01381	.00918	.00455
19	.05266	.04827	.04389	.03950	.03512	.03073	.02634	.02196	.01757	.01319	.00880	.00441
20	.05000	.04583	.04167	.03750	.03333	.02917	.02500	.02083	.01667	.01250	.00833	.00417
22	.04555	.04176	.03797	.03419	.03040	.02661	.02282	.01903	.01525	.01146	.00767	.00388
25	.04000	.03667	.03333	.03000	.02667	.02333	.02000	.01667	.01333	.01000	.00667	.00333
28	.03583	.03285	.02988	.02690	.02393	.02095	.01797	.01500	.01202	.00904	.00607	.00309
30	.03343	.03065	.02787	.02510	.02232	.01954	.01676	.01399	.01121	.00843	.00565	.00287
33	.03040	.02787	.02535	.02282	.02030	.01777	.01525	.01272	.01020	.00767	.00515	.00262

Last-Year Decimals by Months Held

Years	12	11	10	9	8	7	6	5	4	3	2	1
35	.02862	.02624	.02386	.02148	.01910	.01672	.01433	.01195	.00957	.00719	.00481	.00243
40	.02500	.02292	.02083	.01875	.01667	.01458	.01250	.01042	.00833	.00625	.00417	.00208
45	.02232	.02047	.01862	.01676	.01491	.01306	.01121	.00936	.00751	.00565	.00380	.00195
50	.02000	.01833	.01667	.01500	.01333	.01167	.01000	.00833	.00667	.00500	.00333	.00167
60	.01647	.01508	.01369	.01230	.01091	.00953	.00814	.00675	.00536	.00397	.00258	.00119

¶ 620

Years-Digits Decimals Allocate Fractional Years

If an asset was held less than a full year in the taxable year of acquisition, a special allocation is required under the sum of the years-digits method. See ¶ 358. The decimals provided in the following tables accomplish this allocation. These tables are to be used by applying the decimals in the column headed by the number of months the asset is held in the first year to the original cost reduced by any additional first-year depreciation deducted and any salvage value taken into account. (As to the number of months an asset is held, see ¶ 358.)

Example: An asset with a seven-year useful life is held five months in the first tax year. The sum of the years-digits decimals for this asset are indicated in the seven-year life table on page 970 in the five-months column. The decimals are: 1st year, .10417; 2nd year, .23512; 3rd year, .19940; 4th year, .16369; 5th year, .12798; 6th year, .09226; 7th year, .05655; and 8th year, .02083.

If the asset has a depreciable basis (original cost reduced by any bonus depreciation claimed and any salvage value taken into account) of $10,000, depreciation without rounding would be as follows:

1st year	$1,041.70
2nd year	2,351.20
3rd year	1,994.00
4th year	1,636.90
5th year	1,279.80
6th year	922.60
7th year	565.50
8th year	208.30

If depreciation were computed by rounding to the nearest dollar, total depreciation would be $10,001 and an adjustment would have to be made so as not to claim too much depreciation.

SUM OF THE YEARS-DIGITS DECIMALS

Months Held in First Year

Years	1	2	3	4	5	6	7	8	9	10	11	12
3 YEAR LIFE (Sum of the Years-Digits)												
1	.04167	.08333	.12500	.16667	.20833	.25000	.29167	.33333	.37500	.41667	.45833	.50000
2	.48611	.47222	.45833	.44444	.43056	.41667	.40278	.38889	.37500	.36111	.34722	.33333
3	.31944	.30556	.29167	.27778	.26389	.25000	.23611	.22222	.20833	.19444	.18056	.16667
4	.15278	.13889	.12500	.11111	.09722	.08333	.06944	.05556	.04167	.02778	.01389	
4 YEAR LIFE (Sum of the Years-Digits)												
1	.03333	.06667	.10000	.13333	.16667	.20000	.23333	.26667	.30000	.33333	.36667	.40000
2	.39167	.38333	.37500	.36667	.35833	.35000	.34167	.33333	.32500	.31667	.30833	.30000
3	.29167	.28333	.27500	.26667	.25833	.25000	.24167	.23333	.22500	.21667	.20833	.20000
4	.19167	.18333	.17500	.16667	.15833	.15000	.14167	.13333	.12500	.11667	.10833	.10000
5	.09166	.08334	.07500	.06666	.05834	.05000	.04166	.03334	.02500	.01666	.00834	
5 YEAR LIFE (Sum of the Years-Digits)												
1	.02778	.05556	.08333	.11111	.13889	.16667	.19444	.22222	.25000	.27778	.30556	.33333
2	.32778	.32222	.31667	.31111	.30556	.30000	.29444	.28889	.28333	.27778	.27222	.26667
3	.26111	.25556	.25000	.24444	.23889	.23333	.22778	.22222	.21667	.21111	.20556	.20000
4	.19444	.18889	.18333	.17778	.17222	.16667	.16111	.15556	.15000	.14444	.13889	.13333
5	.12778	.12222	.11667	.11111	.10556	.10000	.09444	.08889	.08333	.07778	.07222	.06667
6	.06111	.05555	.05000	.04445	.03888	.03333	.02779	.02222	.01667	.01111	.00555	

6 YEAR LIFE (Sum of the Years-Digits)

1	.02381	.04762	.07143	.09524	.11905	.14286	.16667	.19048	.21429	.23810	.26190	.28571
2	.28175	.27778	.27381	.26984	.26587	.26190	.25794	.25397	.25000	.24603	.24206	.23810
3	.23413	.23016	.22619	.22222	.21825	.21429	.21032	.20635	.20238	.19841	.19444	.19048
4	.18651	.18254	.17857	.17460	.17063	.16667	.16270	.15873	.15476	.15079	.14683	.14286
5	.13889	.13492	.13095	.12698	.12302	.11905	.11508	.11111	.10714	.10317	.09921	.09524
6	.09127	.08730	.08333	.07937	.07540	.07143	.06746	.06349	.05952	.05556	.05159	.04761
7	.04364	.03968	.03572	.03175	.02778	.02380	.01983	.01587	.01191	.00794	.00397	

7 YEAR LIFE (Sum of the Years-Digits)

1	.02083	.04167	.06250	.08333	.10417	.12500	.14583	.16667	.18750	.20833	.22917	.25000
2	.24702	.24405	.24107	.23810	.23512	.23214	.22917	.22619	.22321	.22024	.21726	.21429
3	.21131	.20833	.20536	.20238	.19940	.19643	.19345	.19048	.18750	.18452	.18155	.17857
4	.17560	.17262	.16964	.16667	.16369	.16071	.15774	.15476	.15179	.14881	.14583	.14286
5	.13988	.13690	.13393	.13095	.12798	.12500	.12202	.11905	.11607	.11310	.11012	.10714
6	.10417	.10119	.09821	.09524	.09226	.08929	.08631	.08333	.08036	.07738	.07440	.07143
7	.06845	.06548	.06250	.05952	.05655	.05357	.05060	.04762	.04464	.04167	.03869	.03571
8	.03274	.02976	.02679	.02381	.02083	.01786	.01488	.01190	.00893	.00595	.00298	

8 YEAR LIFE (Sum of the Years-Digits)

1	.01852	.03704	.05556	.07407	.09259	.11111	.12963	.14815	.16667	.18519	.20370	.22222
2	.21991	.21759	.21528	.21296	.21065	.20833	.20602	.20370	.20139	.19907	.19676	.19444
3	.19213	.18981	.18750	.18519	.18287	.18056	.17824	.17593	.17361	.17130	.16898	.16667
4	.16435	.16204	.15972	.15741	.15509	.15278	.15046	.14815	.14583	.14352	.14120	.13889
5	.13657	.13426	.13194	.12963	.12731	.12500	.12269	.12037	.11806	.11574	.11343	.11111
6	.10880	.10648	.10417	.10185	.09954	.09722	.09491	.09259	.09028	.08796	.08565	.08333
7	.08102	.07870	.07639	.07407	.07176	.06944	.06713	.06481	.06250	.06019	.05787	.05556

8	.05324	.05093	.04861	.04630	.04398	.04167	.03935	.03704	.03472	.03241	.03009	.02778
9	.02546	.02315	.02083	.01852	.01621	.01389	.01157	.00926	.00694	.00462	.00232	

8 YEAR LIFE (Sum of the Years-Digits)

9 YEAR LIFE (Sum of the Years-Digits)

1	.01667	.03333	.05000	.06667	.08333	.10000	.11667	.13333	.15000	.16667	.18333	.20000
2	.19815	.19630	.19444	.19259	.19074	.18889	.18704	.18519	.18333	.18148	.17963	.17778
3	.17593	.17407	.17222	.17037	.16852	.16667	.16481	.16296	.16111	.15926	.15741	.15556
4	.15370	.15185	.15000	.14815	.14630	.14444	.14259	.14074	.13889	.13704	.13519	.13333
5	.13148	.12963	.12778	.12593	.12407	.12222	.12037	.11852	.11667	.11481	.11296	.11111
6	.10926	.10741	.10556	.10370	.10185	.10000	.09815	.09630	.09444	.09259	.09074	.08889
7	.08704	.08519	.08333	.08148	.07963	.07778	.07593	.07407	.07222	.07037	.06852	.06667
8	.06481	.06296	.06111	.05926	.05741	.05556	.05370	.05185	.05000	.04815	.04630	.04444
9	.04259	.04074	.03889	.03704	.03519	.03333	.03148	.02963	.02778	.02593	.02407	.02222
10	.02037	.01852	.01667	.01481	.01296	.01111	.00926	.00741	.00556	.00370	.00185	

10 YEAR LIFE (Sum of the Years-Digits)

1	.01515	.03030	.04545	.06061	.07576	.09091	.10606	.12121	.13636	.15152	.16667	.18182
2	.18030	.17879	.17727	.17576	.17424	.17273	.17121	.16970	.16818	.16667	.16515	.16364
3	.16212	.16061	.15909	.15758	.15606	.15455	.15303	.15152	.15000	.14848	.14697	.14545
4	.14394	.14242	.14091	.13939	.13788	.13636	.13485	.13333	.13182	.13030	.12879	.12727
5	.12576	.12424	.12273	.12121	.11970	.11818	.11667	.11515	.11364	.11212	.11061	.10909
6	.10758	.10606	.10455	.10303	.10152	.10000	.09848	.09697	.09545	.09394	.09242	.09091
7	.08939	.08788	.08636	.08485	.08333	.08182	.08030	.07879	.07727	.07576	.07424	.07273
8	.07121	.06970	.06818	.06667	.06515	.06364	.06212	.06061	.05909	.05758	.05606	.05455
9	.05303	.05152	.05000	.04848	.04697	.04545	.04394	.04242	.04091	.03939	.03788	.03636
10	.03485	.03333	.03182	.03030	.02879	.02727	.02576	.02424	.02273	.02121	.01970	.01818
11	.01667	.01515	.01364	.01212	.01060	.00909	.00758	.00606	.00455	.00303	.00151	

11 YEAR LIFE (Sum of the Years-Digits)

1	.01389	.02778	.04167	.05556	.06944	.08333	.09722	.11111	.12500	.13889	.15278	.16667
2	.16540	.16414	.16288	.16162	.16035	.15909	.15783	.15657	.15530	.15404	.15278	.15152
3	.15025	.14899	.14773	.14646	.14520	.14394	.14268	.14141	.14015	.13889	.13763	.13636
4	.13510	.13384	.13258	.13131	.13005	.12879	.12753	.12626	.12500	.12374	.12247	.12121
5	.11995	.11869	.11742	.11616	.11490	.11364	.11237	.11111	.10985	.10859	.10732	.10606
6	.10480	.10354	.10227	.10101	.09975	.09848	.09722	.09596	.09470	.09343	.09217	.09091
7	.08965	.08838	.08712	.08586	.08460	.08333	.08207	.08081	.07955	.07828	.07702	.07576
8	.07449	.07323	.07197	.07071	.06944	.06818	.06692	.06566	.06439	.06313	.06187	.06061
9	.05934	.05808	.05682	.05556	.05429	.05303	.05177	.05051	.04924	.04798	.04672	.04545
10	.04419	.04293	.04167	.04040	.03914	.03788	.03662	.03535	.03409	.03283	.03157	.03030
11	.02904	.02778	.02652	.02525	.02399	.02273	.02146	.02020	.01894	.01768	.01641	.01515
12	.01390	.01262	.01135	.01010	.00885	.00758	.00631	.00505	.00379	.00252	.00126	

12 YEAR LIFE (Sum of the Years-Digits)

1	.01282	.02564	.03846	.05128	.06410	.07692	.08974	.10256	.11538	.12821	.14103	.15385
2	.15278	.15171	.15064	.14957	.14850	.14744	.14637	.14530	.14423	.14316	.14209	.14103
3	.13996	.13889	.13782	.13675	.13568	.13462	.13355	.13248	.13141	.13034	.12927	.12821
4	.12714	.12607	.12500	.12393	.12286	.12179	.12073	.11966	.11859	.11752	.11645	.11538
5	.11432	.11325	.11218	.11111	.11004	.10897	.10791	.10684	.10577	.10470	.10363	.10256
6	.10150	.10043	.09936	.09829	.09722.	09615.	09509.	09402.	09295	.09188	.09081	.08974
7	.08868	.08761	.08654	.08547	.08440	.08333	.08226	.08120	.08013	.07906	.07799	.07692
8	.07585	.07479	.07372	.07265	.07158	.07051	.06944	.06838	.06731	.06624	.06517	.06410
9	.06303	.06197	.06090	.05983	.05876	.05769	.05662	.05556	.05449	.05342	.05235	.05128
10	.05621	.04915	.04808	.04701	.04594	.04487	.04380	.04274	.04167	.04060	.03953	.03846
11	.03739	.03632	.03526	.03419	.03312	.03205	.03098	.02991	.02885	.02778	.02671	.02564
12	.02457	.02350	.02244	.02137	.02030	.01923	.01816	.01709	.01603	.01496	.01389	.01283
13	.01175	.01067	.00960	.00855	.00750	.00643	.00535	.00426	.00319	.00213	.00108	

13 YEAR LIFE (Sum of the Years-Digits)

1	.01190	.02381	.03571	.04762	.05952	.07143	.08333	.09524	.10714	.11905	.13095	.14286
2	.14194	.14103	.14011	.13919	.13828	.13736	.13645	.13553	.13462	.13370	.13278	.13187
3	.13095	.13004	.12912	.12821	.12729	.12637	.12546	.12454	.12363	.12271	.12179	.12088
4	.11996	.11905	.11813	.11722	.11630	.11538	.11447	.11355	.11264	.11172	.11081	.10989
5	.10897	.10806	.10714	.10623	.10531	.10440	.10348	.10256	.10165	.10073	.09982	.09890
6	.09799	.09707	.09615	.09524	.09432	.09341	.09249	.09158	.09066	.08974	.08883	.08791
7	.08700	.08608	.08516	.08425	.08333	.08242	.08150	.08059	.07967	.07875	.07784	.07692
8	.07601	.07509	.07418	.07326	.07234	.07143	.07051	.06960	.06868	.06777	.06685	.06593
9	.06502	.06410	.06319	.06227	.06136	.06044	.05952	.05861	.05769	.05678	.05586	.05495
10	.05403	.05311	.05220	.05128	.05037	.04945	.04853	.04762	.04670	.04579	.04487	.04396
11	.04304	.04212	.04121	.04029	.03938	.03846	.03755	.03663	.03571	.03480	.03388	.03297
12	.03205	.03114	.03022	.02930	.02839	.02747	.02656	.02564	.02473	.02381	.02289	.02198
13	.02106	.02015	.01923	.01832	.01740	.01648	.01557	.01465	.01374	.01282	.01190	.01098
14	.01008	.00915	.00825	.00732	.00641	.00550	.00458	.00366	.00274	.00183	.00093	

14 YEAR LIFE (Sum of the Years-Digits)

1	.01111	.02222	.03333	.04444	.05556	.06667	.07778	.08889	.10000	.11111	.12222	.13333
2	.13254	.13175	.13095	.13016	.12937	.12857	.12778	.12698	.12619	.12540	.12460	.12381
3	.12302	.12222	.12143	.12063	.11984	.11905	.11825	.11746	.11667	.11587	.11508	.11429
4	.11349	.11270	.11190	.11111	.11032	.10952	.10873	.10794	.10714	.10635	.10556	.10476
5	.10397	.10317	.10238	.10159	.10079	.10000	.09921	.09841	.09762	.09683	.09603	.09524
6	.09444	.09365	.09286	.09206	.09127	.09048	.08968	.08889	.08810	.08730	.08651	.08571
7	.08492	.08413	.08333	.08254	.08175	.08095	.08016	.07937	.07857	.07778	.07698	.07619
8	.07540	.07460	.07381	.07302	.07222	.07143	.07063	.06984	.06905	.06825	.06746	.06667
9	.06587	.06508	.06429	.06349	.06270	.06190	.06111	.06032	.05952	.05873	.05794	.05714
10	.05635	.05556	.05476	.05397	.05317	.05238	.05159	.05079	.05000	.04921	.04841	.04762
11	.04683	.04603	.04524	.04444	.04365	.04286	.04206	.04127	.04048	.03968	.03889	.03810

14 YEAR LIFE (Sum of the Years-Digits)

12	.03730	.03651	.03571	.03492	.03413	.03333	.03254	.03175	.03095	.03016	.02937	.02857
13	.02778	.02698	.02619	.02540	.02460	.02381	.02302	.02222	.02143	.02063	.01984	.01905
14	.01825	.01746	.01667	.01587	.01508	.01429	.01349	.01270	.01190	.01111	.01032	.00952
15	.00873	.00794	.00715	.00636	.00555	.00476	.00397	.00317	.00238	.00159	.00079	

15 YEAR LIFE (Sum of the Years-Digits)

1	.01042	.02083	.03125	.04167	.05208	.06250	.07292	.08333	.09375	.10417	.11458	.12500
2	.12431	.12361	.12292	.12222	.12153	.12083	.12014	.11944	.11875	.11806	.11736	.11667
3	.11597	.11528	.11458	.11389	.11319	.11250	.11181	.11111	.11042	.10972	.10903	.10833
4	.10764	.10694	.10625	.10556	.10486	.10417	.10347	.10278	.10208	.10139	.10069	.10000
5	.09931	.09861	.09792	.09722	.09653	.09583	.09514	.09444	.09375	.09306	.09236	.09167
6	.09097	.09028	.08958	.08889	.08819	.08750	.08681	.08611	.08542	.08472	.08403	.08333
7	.08264	.08194	.08125	.08056	.07986	.07917	.07847	.07778	.07708	.07639	.07569	.07500
8	.07431	.07361	.07292	.07222	.07153	.07083	.07014	.06944	.06875	.06806	.06736	.06667
9	.06597	.06528	.06458	.06389	.06319	.06250	.06181	.06111	.06042	.05972	.05903	.05833
10	.05764	.05694	.05625	.05556	.05486	.05417	.05347	.05278	.05208	.05139	.05069	.05000
11	.04931	.04861	.04792	.04722	.04653	.04583	.04514	.04444	.04375	.04306	.04236	.04167
12	.04097	.04028	.03958	.03889	.03819	.03750	.03681	.03611	.03542	.03472	.03403	.03333
13	.03264	.03194	.03125	.03056	.02986	.02917	.02847	.02778	.02708	.02639	.02569	.02500
14	.02431	.02361	.02292	.02222	.02153	.02083	.02014	.01944	.01875	.01806	.01736	.01667
15	.01597	.01528	.01458	.01389	.01319	.01250	.01181	.01111	.01042	.00972	.00903	.00833
16	.00762	.00696	.00625	.00554	.00488	.00417	.00345	.00280	.00208	.00137	.00071	

16 YEAR LIFE (Sum of the Years-Digits)

1	.00980	.01961	.02941	.03922	.04902	.05882	.06863	.07843	.08824	.09804	.10784	.11765
2	.11703	.11642	.11581	.11520	.11458	.11397	.11336	.11275	.11213	.11152	.11091	.11029
3	.10968	.10907	.10846	.10784	.10723	.10662	.10600	.10539	.10478	.10417	.10355	.10294

16 YEAR LIFE (Sum of the Years-Digits)

4	.10233	.10172	.10110	.10049	.09988	.09926	.09865	.09804	.09743	.09681	.09620	.09559
5	.09498	.09436	.09375	.09314	.09252	.09191	.09130	.09069	.09007	.08946	.08885	.08824
6	.08762	.08701	.08640	.08578	.08517	.08456	.08395	.08333	.08272	.08211	.08150	.08088
7	.08027	.07966	.07904	.07843	.07782	.07721	.07659	.07598	.07537	.07475	.07414	.07353
8	.07292	.07230	.07169	.07108	.07047	.06985	.06924	.06863	.06801	.06740	.06679	.06618
9	.06556	.06495	.06434	.06373	.06311	.06250	.06189	.06127	.06066	.06005	.05944	.05882
10	.05821	.05760	.05699	.05637	.05576	.05515	.05453	.05392	.05331	.05270	.05208	.05147
11	.05086	.05025	.04963	.04902	.04841	.04779	.04718	.04657	.04596	.04534	.04473	.04412
12	.04350	.04289	.04228	.04167	.04105	.04044	.03983	.03922	.03860	.03799	.03738	.03676
13	.03615	.03554	.03493	.03431	.03370	.03309	.03248	.03186	.03125	.03064	.03002	.02941
14	.02880	.02819	.02757	.02696	.02635	.02574	.02512	.02451	.02390	.02328	.02267	.02206
15	.02145	.02083	.02022	.01961	.01900	.01838	.01777	.01716	.01654	.01593	.01532	.01471
16	.01409	.01348	.01287	.01225	.01164	.01103	.01042	.00980	.00919	.00858	.00797	.00735
17	.00675	.00612	.00551	.00490	.00429	.00368	.00306	.00245	.00184	.00123	.00061	

17 YEAR LIFE (Sum of the Years-Digits)

1	.00926	.01852	.02778	.03704	.04630	.05556	.06481	.07407	.08333	.09259	.10185	.11111
2	.11057	.11002	.10948	.10893	.10839	.10784	.10730	.10675	.10621	.10566	.10512	.10458
3	.10403	.10349	.10294	.10240	.10185	.10131	.10076	.10022	.09967	.09913	.09858	.09804
4	.09749	.09695	.09641	.09586	.09532	.09477	.09423	.09368	.09314	.09259	.09205	.09150
5	.09096	.09041	.08987	.08932	.08878	.08824	.08769	.08715	.08660	.08606	.08551	.08497
6	.08442	.08388	.08333	.08279	.08224	.08170	.08115	.08061	.08007	.07952	.07898	.07843
7	.07789	.07734	.07680	.07625	.07571	.07516	.07462	.07407	.07353	.07298	.07244	.07190
8	.07135	.07081	.07026	.06972	.06917	.06863	.06808	.06754	.06699	.06645	.06590	.06536
9	.06481	.06427	.06373	.06318	.06264	.06209	.06155	.06100	.06046	.05991	.05937	.05882
10	.05828	.05773	.05719	.05664	.05610	.05556	.05501	.05447	.05392	.05338	.05283	.05229
11	.05174	.05120	.05065	.05011	.04956	.04902	.04847	.04793	.04739	.04684	.04630	.04575
12	.04521	.04466	.04412	.04357	.04303	.04248	.04194	.04139	.04085	.04031	.03976	.03922

17 YEAR LIFE (Sum of the Years-Digits)

13	.03867	.03813	.03758	.03704	.03649	.03595	.03540	.03486	.03431	.03377	.03322	.03268
14	.03214	.03159	.03105	.03050	.02996	.02941	.02887	.02832	.02778	.02723	.02669	.02614
15	.02560	.02505	.02451	.02397	.02342	.02288	.02233	.02179	.02124	.02070	.02015	.01961
16	.01906	.01852	.01797	.01743	.01688	.01634	.01580	.01525	.01471	.01416	.01362	.01307
17	.01253	.01198	.01144	.01089	.01035	.00980	.00926	.00871	.00817	.00763	.00708	.00653
18	.00599	.00545	.00489	.00436	.00381	.00326	.00273	.00219	.00163	.00109	.00055	

18 YEAR LIFE (Sum of the Years-Digits)

1	.00877	.01754	.02632	.03509	.04386	.05263	.06140	.07018	.07895	.08772	.09649	.10526
2	.10478	.10429	.10380	.10331	.10283	.10234	.10185	.10136	.10088	.10039	.09990	.09942
3	.09893	.09844	.09795	.09747	.09698	.09649	.09600	.09552	.09503	.09454	.09405	.09357
4	.09308	.09259	.09211	.09162	.09113	.09064	.09016	.08967	.08918	.08869	.08821	.08772
5	.08723	.08674	.08626	.08577	.08528	.08480	.08431	.08382	.08333	.08285	.08236	.08187
6	.08138	.08090	.08041	.07992	.07943	.07895	.07846	.07797	.07749	.07700	.07651	.07602
7	.07554	.07505	.07456	.07407	.07359	.07310	.07261	.07212	.07164	.07115	.07066	.07018
8	.06969	.06920	.06871	.06823	.06774	.06725	.06676	.06628	.06579	.06530	.06481	.06433
9	.06384	.06335	.06287	.06238	.06189	.06140	.06092	.06043	.05994	.05945	.05897	.05848
10	.05799	.05750	.05702	.05653	.05604	.05556	.05507	.05458	.05409	.05361	.05312	.05263
11	.05214	.05166	.05117	.05068	.05019	.04971	.04922	.04873	.04825	.04776	.04727	.04678
12	.04630	.04581	.04532	.04483	.04435	.04386	.04337	.04288	.04240	.04191	.04142	.04094
13	.04045	.03996	.03947	.03899	.03850	.03801	.03752	.03704	.03655	.03606	.03558	.03509
14	.03460	.03411	.03363	.03314	.03265	.03216	.03168	.03119	.03070	.03021	.02973	.02924
15	.02875	.02827	.02778	.02729	.02680	.02632	.02583	.02534	.02485	.02437	.02388	.02339
16	.02290	.02242	.02193	.02144	.02096	.02047	.01998	.01949	.01901	.01852	.01803	.01754
17	.01706	.01657	.01608	.01559	.01511	.01462	.01413	.01365	.01316	.01267	.01218	.01170
18	.01121	.01072	.01023	.00975	.00926	.00877	.00828	.00780	.00731	.00682	.00634	.00584
19	.00536	.00488	.00438	.00390	.00341	.00292	.00245	.00195	.00145	.00098	.00049	

19 YEAR LIFE (Sum of the Years-Digits)

1	.00833	.01667	.02500	.03333	.04167	.05000	.05833	.06667	.07500	.08333	.09167	.10000
2	.09956	.09912	.09868	.09825	.09781	.09737	.09693	.09649	.09605	.09561	.09518	.09474
3	.09430	.09386	.09342	.09298	.09254	.09211	.09167	.09123	.09079	.09035	.08991	.08947
4	.08904	.08860	.08816	.08772	.08728	.08684	.08640	.08596	.08553	.08509	.08465	.08421
5	.08377	.08333	.08289	.08246	.08202	.08158	.08114	.08070	.08026	.07982	.07939	.07895
6	.07851	.07807	.07763	.07719	.07675	.07632	.07588	.07544	.07500	.07456	.07412	.07368
7	.07325	.07281	.07237	.07193	.07149	.07105	.07061	.07018	.06974	.06930	.06886	.06842
8	.06798	.06754	.06711	.06667	.06623	.06579	.06535	.06491	.06447	.06404	.06360	.06316
9	.06272	.06228	.06184	.06140	.06096	.06053	.06009	.05965	.05921	.05877	.05833	.05789
10	.05746	.05702	.05658	.05614	.05570	.05526	.05482	.05439	.05395	.05351	.05307	.05263
11	.05219	.05175	.05132	.05088	.05044	.05000	.04956	.04912	.04868	.04825	.04781	.04737
12	.04693	.04649	.04605	.04561	.04518	.04474	.04430	.04386	.04342	.04298	.04254	.04211
13	.04167	.04123	.04079	.04035	.03991	.03947	.03904	.03860	.03816	.03772	.03728	.03684
14	.03640	.03596	.03553	.03509	.03465	.03421	.03377	.03333	.03289	.03246	.03202	.03158
15	.03114	.03070	.03026	.02982	.02939	.02895	.02851	.02807	.02763	.02719	.02675	.02632
16	.02588	.02544	.02500	.02456	.02412	.02368	.02325	.02281	.02237	.02193	.02149	.02105
17	.02061	.02018	.01974	.01930	.01886	.01842	.01798	.01754	.01711	.01667	.01623	.01579
18	.01535	.01491	.01447	.01404	.01360	.01316	.01272	.01228	.01184	.01140	.01096	.01053
19	.01009	.00965	.00921	.00877	.00833	.00789	.00746	.00702	.00658	.00614	.00570	.00526
20	.00482	.00439	.00395	.00351	.00307	.00263	.00219	.00175	.00132	.00088	.00044	

20 YEAR LIFE (Sum of the Years-Digits)

1	.00794	.01587	.02381	.03175	.03968	.04762	.05556	.06349	.07143	.07937	.08730	.09524
2	.09484	.09444	.09405	.09365	.09325	.09286	.09246	.09206	.09167	.09127	.09087	.09048
3	.09008	.08968	.08929	.08889	.08849	.08810	.08770	.08730	.08690	.08651	.08611	.08571
4	.08532	.08492	.08452	.08413	.08373	.08333	.08294	.08254	.08214	.08175	.08135	.08095
5	.08056	.08016	.07976	.07937	.07897	.07857	.07817	.07778	.07738	.07698	.07659	.07619

20 YEAR LIFE (Sum of the Years-Digits)

6	.07579	.07540	.07500	.07460	.07421	.07381	.07341	.07302	.07262	.07222	.07183	.07143
7	.07103	.07063	.07024	.06984	.06944	.06905	.06865	.06825	.06786	.06746	.06706	.06667
8	.06627	.06587	.06548	.06508	.06468	.06429	.06389	.06349	.06310	.06270	.06230	.06190
9	.06151	.06111	.06071	.06032	.05992	.05952	.05913	.05873	.05833	.05794	.05754	.05714
10	.05675	.05635	.05595	.05556	.05516	.05476	.05437	.05397	.05357	.05317	.05278	.05238
11	.05198	.05159	.05119	.05079	.05040	.05000	.04960	.04921	.04881	.04841	.04802	.04762
12	.04722	.04683	.04643	.04603	.04563	.04524	.04484	.04444	.04405	.04365	.04325	.04286
13	.04246	.04206	.04167	.04127	.04087	.04048	.04008	.03968	.03929	.03889	.03849	.03810
14	.03770	.03730	.03690	.03651	.03611	.03571	.03532	.03492	.03452	.03413	.03373	.03333
15	.03294	.03254	.03214	.03175	.03135	.03095	.03056	.03016	.02976	.02937	.02897	.02857
16	.02817	.02778	.02738	.02698	.02659	.02619	.02579	.02540	.02500	.02460	.02421	.02381
17	.02341	.02302	.02262	.02222	.02183	.02143	.02103	.02063	.02024	.01984	.01944	.01905
18	.01865	.01825	.01786	.01746	.01706	.01667	.01627	.01587	.01548	.01508	.01468	.01429
19	.01389	.01349	.01310	.01270	.01230	.01190	.01151	.01111	.01071	.01032	.00992	.00952
20	.00913	.00873	.00833	.00794	.00754	.00714	.00675	.00635	.00595	.00556	.00516	.00476
21	.00436	.00398	.00357	.00316	.00279	.00238	.00197	.00160	.00119	.00078	.00040	

22 YEAR LIFE (Sum of the Years-Digits)

1	.00725	.01449	.02174	.02899	.03623	.04348	.05072	.05797	.06522	.07246	.07971	.08696
2	.08663	.08630	.08597	.08564	.08531	.08498	.08465	.08432	.08399	.08366	.08333	.08300
3	.08267	.08235	.08202	.08169	.08136	.08103	.08070	.08037	.08004	.07971	.07938	.07905
4	.07872	.07839	.07806	.07773	.07740	.07708	.07675	.07642	.07609	.07576	.07543	.07510
5	.07477	.07444	.07411	.07378	.07345	.07312	.07279	.07246	.07213	.07181	.07148	.07115
6	.07082	.07049	.07016	.06983	.06950	.06917	.06884	.06851	.06818	.06785	.06752	.06719
7	.06686	.06653	.06621	.06588	.06555	.06522	.06489	.06456	.06423	.06390	.06357	.06324
8	.06291	.06258	.06225	.06192	.06159	.06126	.06094	.06061	.06028	.05995	.05962	.05929
9	.05896	.05863	.05830	.05797	.05764	.05731	.05698	.05665	.05632	.05599	.05567	.05534
10	.05501	.05468	.05435	.05402	.05369	.05336	.05303	.05270	.05237	.05204	.05171	.05138

22 YEAR LIFE (Sum of the Years-Digits)

11	.05105	.05072	.05040	.05007	.04974	.04941	.04908	.04875	.04842	.04809	.04776	.04743
12	.04710	.04677	.04644	.04611	.04578	.04545	.04513	.04480	.04447	.04414	.04381	.04348
13	.04315	.04282	.04249	.04216	.04183	.04150	.04117	.04084	.04051	.04018	.03986	.03953
14	.03920	.03887	.03854	.03821	.03788	.03755	.03722	.03689	.03656	.03623	.03590	.03557
15	.03524	.03491	.03458	.03426	.03393	.03360	.03327	.03294	.03261	.03228	.03195	.03162
16	.03129	.03096	.03063	.03030	.02997	.02964	.02931	.02899	.02866	.02833	.02800	.02767
17	.02734	.02701	.02668	.02635	.02602	.02569	.02536	.02503	.02470	.02437	.02404	.02372
18	.02339	.02306	.02273	.02240	.02207	.02174	.02141	.02108	.02075	.02042	.02009	.01976
19	.01943	.01910	.01877	.01845	.01812	.01779	.01746	.01713	.01680	.01647	.01614	.01581
20	.01548	.01515	.01482	.01449	.01416	.01383	.01350	.01318	.01285	.01252	.01219	.01186
21	.01153	.01120	.01087	.01054	.01021	.00988	.00955	.00922	.00889	.00856	.00823	.00791
22	.00758	.00725	.00692	.00659	.00626	.00593	.00560	.00527	.00494	.00461	.00428	.00395
23	.00362	.00330	.00296	.00262	.00231	.00198	.00165	.00131	.00099	.00067	.00033	

25 YEAR LIFE (Sum of the Years-Digits)

1	.00641	.01282	.01923	.02564	.03205	.03846	.04487	.05128	.05769	.06410	.07051	.07692
2	.07667	.07641	.07615	.07590	.07564	.07538	.07513	.07487	.07462	.07436	.07410	.07385
3	.07359	.07333	.07308	.07282	.07256	.07231	.07205	.07179	.07154	.07128	.07103	.07077
4	.07051	.07026	.07000	.06974	.06949	.06923	.06897	.06872	.06846	.06821	.06795	.06769
5	.06744	.06718	.06692	.06667	.06641	.06615	.06590	.06564	.06538	.06513	.06487	.06462
6	.06436	.06410	.06385	.06359	.06333	.06308	.06282	.06256	.06231	.06205	.06179	.06154
7	.06128	.06103	.06077	.06051	.06026	.06000	.05974	.05949	.05923	.05897	.05872	.05846
8	.05821	.05795	.05769	.05744	.05718	.05692	.05667	.05641	.05615	.05590	.05564	.05538
9	.05513	.05487	.05462	.05436	.05410	.05385	.05359	.05333	.05308	.05282	.05256	.05231
10	.05205	.05179	.05154	.05128	.05103	.05077	.05051	.05026	.05000	.04974	.04949	.04923
11	.04897	.04872	.04846	.04821	.04795	.04769	.04744	.04718	.04692	.04667	.04641	.04615
12	.04590	.04564	.04538	.04513	.04487	.04462	.04436	.04410	.04385	.04359	.04333	.04308
13	.04282	.04256	.04231	.04205	.04179	.04154	.04128	.04103	.04077	.04051	.04026	.04000

25 YEAR LIFE (Sum of the Years-Digits)

14	.03974	.03949	.03923	.03897	.03872	.03846	.03821	.03795	.03769	.03744	.03718	.03692
15	.03667	.03641	.03615	.03590	.03564	.03538	.03513	.03487	.03462	.03436	.03410	.03385
16	.03359	.03333	.03308	.03282	.03256	.03231	.03205	.03179	.03154	.03128	.03103	.03077
17	.03051	.03026	.03000	.02974	.02949	.02923	.02897	.02872	.02846	.02821	.02795	.02769
18	.02744	.02718	.02692	.02667	.02641	.02615	.02590	.02564	.02538	.02513	.02487	.02462
19	.02436	.02410	.02385	.02359	.02333	.02308	.02282	.02256	.02231	.02205	.02179	.02154
20	.02128	.02103	.02077	.02051	.02026	.02000	.01974	.01949	.01923	.01897	.01872	.01846
21	.01821	.01795	.01769	.01744	.01718	.01692	.01667	.01641	.01615	.01590	.01564	.01538
22	.01513	.01487	.01462	.01436	.01410	.01385	.01359	.01333	.01308	.01282	.01256	.01231
23	.01205	.01179	.01154	.01128	.01103	.01077	.01051	.01026	.01000	.00974	.00949	.00923
24	.00897	.00872	.00846	.00821	.00795	.00769	.00744	.00718	.00692	.00667	.00641	.00615
25	.00590	.00564	.00538	.00513	.00487	.00462	.00436	.00410	.00385	.00359	.00333	.00308
26	.00281	.00257	.00231	.00204	.00180	.00154	.00128	.00104	.00077	.00051	.00027	

28 YEAR LIFE (Sum of the Years-Digits)

1	.00575	.01149	.01724	.02299	.02874	.03448	.04023	.04598	.05172	.05747	.06322	.06897
2	.06876	.06856	.06835	.06814	.06794	.06773	.06753	.06732	.06712	.06691	.06671	.06650
3	.06630	.06609	.06589	.06568	.06548	.06527	.06507	.06486	.06466	.06445	.06424	.06404
4	.06383	.06363	.06342	.06322	.06301	.06281	.06260	.06240	.06219	.06199	.06178	.06158
5	.06137	.06117	.06096	.06076	.06055	.06034	.06014	.05993	.05973	.05952	.05932	.05911
6	.05891	.05870	.05850	.05829	.05809	.05788	.05768	.05747	.05727	.05706	.05686	.05665
7	.05645	.05624	.05603	.05583	.05562	.05542	.05521	.05501	.05480	.05460	.05439	.05419
8	.05398	.05378	.05357	.05337	.05316	.05296	.05275	.05255	.05234	.05213	.05193	.05172
9	.05152	.05131	.05111	.05090	.05070	.05049	.05029	.05008	.04988	.04967	.04947	.04926
10	.04906	.04885	.04865	.04844	.04823	.04803	.04782	.04762	.04741	.04721	.04700	.04680
11	.04659	.04639	.04618	.04598	.04577	.04557	.04536	.04516	.04495	.04475	.04454	.04433
12	.04413	.04392	.04372	.04351	.04331	.04310	.04290	.04269	.04249	.04228	.04208	.04187
13	.04167	.04146	.04126	.04105	.04085	.04064	.04044	.04023	.04002	.03982	.03961	.03941

28 YEAR LIFE (Sum of the Years-Digits)

14	.03920	.03900	.03879	.03859	.03838	.03818	.03797	.03777	.03756	.03736	.03715	.03695
15	.03674	.03654	.03633	.03612	.03592	.03571	.03551	.03530	.03510	.03489	.03469	.03448
16	.03428	.03407	.03387	.03366	.03346	.03325	.03305	.03284	.03264	.03243	.03222	.03202
17	.03181	.03161	.03140	.03120	.03099	.03079	.03058	.03038	.03017	.02997	.02976	.02956
18	.02935	.02915	.02894	.02874	.02853	.02833	.02812	.02791	.02771	.02750	.02730	.02709
19	.02689	.02668	.02648	.02627	.02607	.02586	.02566	.02545	.02525	.02504	.02484	.02463
20	.02443	.02422	.02401	.02381	.02360	.02340	.02319	.02299	.02278	.02258	.02237	.02217
21	.02196	.02176	.02155	.02135	.02114	.02094	.02073	.02053	.02032	.02011	.01991	.01970
22	.01950	.01929	.01909	.01888	.01868	.01847	.01827	.01806	.01786	.01765	.01745	.01724
23	.01704	.01683	.01663	.01642	.01622	.01601	.01580	.01560	.01539	.01519	.01498	.01478
24	.01457	.01437	.01416	.01396	.01375	.01355	.01334	.01314	.01293	.01273	.01252	.01232
25	.01211	.01190	.01170	.01149	.01129	.01108	.01088	.01067	.01047	.01026	.01006	.00985
26	.00965	.00944	.00924	.00903	.00883	.00862	.00842	.00821	.00800	.00780	.00759	.00739
27	.00718	.00698	.00677	.00657	.00636	.00616	.00595	.00575	.00554	.00534	.00513	.00493
28	.00472	.00452	.00431	.00411	.00390	.00369	.00349	.00328	.00308	.00287	.00267	.00246
29	.00225	.00205	.00185	.00164	.00143	.00124	.00102	.00082	.00062	.00042	.00021	

30 YEAR LIFE (Sum of the Years-Digits)

1	.00538	.01075	.01613	.02151	.02688	.03226	.03763	.04301	.04839	.05376	.05914	.06452
2	.06434	.06416	.06398	.06380	.06362	.06344	.06326	.06308	.06290	.06272	.06254	.06237
3	.06219	.06201	.06183	.06165	.06147	.06129	.06111	.06093	.06075	.06057	.06039	.06022
4	.06004	.05986	.05968	.05950	.05932	.05914	.05896	.05878	.05860	.05842	.05824	.05806
5	.05789	.05771	.05753	.05735	.05717	.05699	.05681	.05663	.05645	.05627	.05609	.05591
6	.05573	.05556	.05538	.05520	.05502	.05484	.05466	.05448	.05430	.05412	.05394	.05376
7	.05358	.05341	.05323	.05305	.05287	.05269	.05251	.05233	.05215	.05197	.05179	.05161
8	.05143	.05125	.05108	.05090	.05072	.05054	.05036	.05018	.05000	.04982	.04964	.04946
9	.04928	.04910	.04892	.04875	.04857	.04839	.04821	.04803	.04785	.04767	.04749	.04731
10	.04713	.04695	.04677	.04659	.04642	.04624	.04606	.04588	.04570	.04552	.04534	.04516

30 YEAR LIFE (Sum of the Years-Digits)

11	.04498	.04480	.04462	.04444	.04427	.04409	.04391	.04373	.04355	.04337	.04319	.04301
12	.04283	.04265	.04247	.04229	.04211	.04194	.04176	.04158	.04140	.04122	.04104	.04086
13	.04068	.04050	.04032	.04014	.03996	.03978	.03961	.03943	.03925	.03907	.03889	.03871
14	.03853	.03835	.03817	.03799	.03781	.03763	.03746	.03728	.03710	.03692	.03674	.03656
15	.03638	.03620	.03602	.03584	.03566	.03548	.03530	.03513	.03495	.03477	.03459	.03441
16	.03423	.03405	.03387	.03369	.03351	.03333	.03315	.03297	.03280	.03262	.03244	.03226
17	.03208	.03190	.03172	.03154	.03136	.03118	.03100	.03082	.03065	.03047	.03029	.03011
18	.02993	.02975	.02957	.02939	.02921	.02903	.02885	.02867	.02849	.02832	.02814	.02796
19	.02778	.02760	.02742	.02724	.02706	.02688	.02670	.02652	.02634	.02616	.02599	.02581
20	.02563	.02545	.02527	.02509	.02491	.02473	.02455	.02437	.02419	.02401	.02384	.02366
21	.02348	.02330	.02312	.02294	.02276	.02258	.02240	.02222	.02204	.02186	.02168	.02151
22	.02133	.02115	.02097	.02079	.02061	.02043	.02025	.02007	.01989	.01971	.01953	.01935
23	.01918	.01900	.01882	.01864	.01846	.01828	.01810	.01792	.01774	.01756	.01738	.01720
24	.01703	.01685	.01667	.01649	.01631	.01613	.01595	.01577	.01559	.01541	.01523	.01505
25	.01487	.01470	.01452	.01434	.01416	.01398	.01380	.01362	.01344	.01326	.01308	.01290
26	.01272	.01254	.01237	.01219	.01201	.01183	.01165	.01147	.01129	.01111	.01093	.01075
27	.01057	.01039	.01022	.01004	.00986	.00968	.00950	.00932	.00914	.00896	.00878	.00860
28	.00842	.00824	.00806	.00789	.00771	.00753	.00735	.00717	.00699	.00681	.00663	.00645
29	.00627	.00609	.00591	.00573	.00556	.00538	.00520	.00502	.00484	.00466	.00448	.00430
30	.00412	.00394	.00376	.00358	.00341	.00323	.00305	.00287	.00269	.00251	.00233	.00215
31	.00197	.00179	.00160	.00142	.00123	.00106	.00089	.00072	.00054	.00038	.00020	

33 YEAR LIFE (Sum of the Years-Digits)

1	.00490	.00980	.01471	.01961	.02451	.02941	.03431	.03922	.04412	.04902	.05392	.05882
2	.05867	.05853	.05838	.05823	.05808	.05793	.05778	.05764	.05749	.05734	.05719	.05704
3	.05689	.05674	.05660	.05645	.05630	.05615	.05600	.05585	.05570	.05556	.05541	.05526
4	.05511	.05496	.05481	.05466	.05452	.05437	.05422	.05407	.05392	.05377	.05362	.05348
5	.05333	.05318	.05303	.05288	.05273	.05258	.05244	.05229	.05214	.05199	.05184	.05169
6	.05154	.05140	.05125	.05110	.05095	.05080	.05065	.05051	.05036	.05021	.05006	.04991

33 YEAR LIFE (Sum of the Years-Digits)

7	.04976	.04961	.04947	.04932	.04917	.04902	.04887	.04872	.04857	.04843	.04828	.04813
8	.04798	.04783	.04768	.04753	.04739	.04724	.04709	.04694	.04679	.04664	.04649	.04635
9	.04620	.04605	.04590	.04575	.04560	.04545	.04531	.04516	.04501	.04486	.04471	.04456
10	.04441	.04427	.04412	.04397	.04382	.04367	.04352	.04337	.04323	.04308	.04293	.04278
11	.04263	.04248	.04234	.04219	.04204	.04189	.04174	.04159	.04144	.04130	.04115	.04100
12	.04085	.04070	.04055	.04040	.04026	.04011	.03996	.03981	.03966	.03951	.03936	.03922
13	.03907	.03892	.03877	.03862	.03847	.03832	.03818	.03803	.03788	.03773	.03758	.03743
14	.03728	.03714	.03699	.03684	.03669	.03654	.03639	.03624	.03610	.03595	.03580	.03565
15	.03550	.03535	.03520	.03506	.03491	.03476	.03461	.03446	.03431	.03417	.03402	.03387
16	.03372	.03357	.03342	.03327	.03313	.03298	.03283	.03268	.03253	.03238	.03223	.03209
17	.03194	.03179	.03164	.03149	.03134	.03119	.03105	.03090	.03075	.03060	.03045	.03030
18	.03015	.03001	.02986	.02971	.02956	.02941	.02926	.02911	.02897	.02882	.02867	.02852
19	.02837	.02822	.02807	.02793	.02778	.02763	.02748	.02733	.02718	.02704	.02689	.02674
20	.02659	.02644	.02629	.02614	.02600	.02585	.02570	.02555	.02540	.02525	.02510	.02496
21	.02481	.02466	.02451	.02436	.02421	.02406	.02392	.02377	.02362	.02347	.02332	.02317
22	.02302	.02288	.02273	.02258	.02243	.02228	.02213	.02198	.02184	.02169	.02154	.02139
23	.02124	.02109	.02094	.02080	.02065	.02050	.02035	.02020	.02005	.01990	.01976	.01961
24	.01946	.01931	.01916	.01901	.01887	.01872	.01857	.01842	.01827	.01812	.01797	.01783
25	.01768	.01753	.01738	.01723	.01708	.01693	.01679	.01664	.01649	.01634	.01619	.01604
26	.01589	.01575	.01560	.01545	.01530	.01515	.01500	.01485	.01471	.01456	.01441	.01426
27	.01411	.01396	.01381	.01367	.01352	.01337	.01322	.01307	.01292	.01277	.01263	.01248
28	.01233	.01218	.01203	.01188	.01173	.01159	.01144	.01129	.01114	.01099	.01084	.01070
29	.01055	.01040	.01025	.01010	.00995	.00980	.00966	.00951	.00936	.00921	.00906	.00891
30	.00876	.00862	.00847	.00832	.00817	.00802	.00787	.00772	.00758	.00743	.00728	.00713
31	.00698	.00683	.00668	.00654	.00639	.00624	.00609	.00594	.00579	.00564	.00550	.00535
32	.00520	.00505	.00490	.00475	.00460	.00446	.00431	.00416	.00401	.00386	.00371	.00357
33	.00342	.00327	.00312	.00297	.00282	.00267	.00253	.00238	.00223	.00208	.00193	.00178
34	.00166	.00148	.00134	.00119	.00103	.00091	.00073	.00060	.00044	.00029	.00016	

35 YEAR LIFE (Sum of the Years-Digits)

1	.00463	.00926	.01389	.01852	.02315	.02778	.03241	.03704	.04167	.04630	.05093	.05556
2	.05542	.05529	.05516	.05503	.05489	.05476	.05463	.05450	.05437	.05423	.05410	.05397
3	.05384	.05370	.05357	.05344	.05331	.05317	.05304	.05291	.05278	.05265	.05251	.05238
4	.05225	.05212	.05198	.05185	.05172	.05159	.05146	.05132	.05119	.05106	.05093	.05079
5	.05066	.05053	.05040	.05026	.05013	.05000	.04987	.04974	.04960	.04947	.04934	.04921
6	.04907	.04894	.04881	.04868	.04854	.04841	.04828	.04815	.04802	.04788	.04775	.04762
7	.04749	.04735	.04722	.04709	.04696	.04683	.04669	.04656	.04643	.04630	.04616	.04603
8	.04590	.04577	.04563	.04550	.04537	.04524	.04511	.04497	.04484	.04471	.04458	.04444
9	.04431	.04418	.04465	.04392	.04378	.04365	.04352	.04339	.04325	.04312	.04299	.04286
10	.04272	.04259	.04246	.04233	.04220	.04206	.04193	.04180	.04167	.04153	.04140	.04127
11	.04114	.04101	.04087	.04074	.04061	.04048	.04034	.04021	,04008	.03995	.03981	.03968
12	.03955	.03942	.03929	.03915	.03902	.03889	.03876	.03862	.03849	.03836	.03823	.03810
13	.03796	.03783	.03770	.03757	.03743	.03730	.03717	.03764	.03690	.03677	.03664	.03651
14	.03638	.03624	.03611	.03598	.03585	.03571	.03558	.03545	.03532	.03519	.03505	.03492
15	.03479	.03466	.03452	.03439	.03426	.03413	.03399	.03386	.03373	.03360	.03347	.03333
16	.03320	.03307	.03294	.03280	.03267	.03254	.03241	.03228	.03214	.03201	.03188	.03175
17	.03161	.03148	.03135	.03122	.03108	.03095	.03082	.03069	.03056	.03042	.03029	.03016
18	.03003	.02989	.02976	.02963	.02950	.02937	.02923	.02910	.02897	.02884	.02870	.02857
19	.02844	.02831	.02817	.02804	.02791	.02778	.02765	.02751	.02738	.02725	.02712	.02698
20	.02685	.02672	.02659	.02646	.02632	.02619	.02606	.02593	.02579	.02566	.02553	.02540
21	.02526	.02513	.02500	.02487	.02474	.02460	.02447	.02434	.02421	.02407	.02394	.02381
22	.02368	.02354	.02341	.02328	.02315	.02302	.02288	.02275	.02262	.02249	.02235	.02222
23	.02209	.02196	.02183	.02169	.02156	.02143	.02130	.02116	.02103	.02090	.02077	.02063
24	.02050	.02037	.02024	.02011	.01997	.01984	.01971	.01958	.01944	.01931	.01918	.01905
25	.01892	.01878	.01865	.01852	.01839	.01825	.01812	.01799	.01786	.01772	.01759	.01746
26	.01733	.01720	.01706	.01693	.01680	.01667	.01653	.01640	.01627	.01614	.01601	.01587
27	.01574	.01561	.01548	.01534	.01521	.01508	.01495	.01481	.01468	.01455	.01442	.01429
28	.01413	.01402	.01389	.01376	.01362	.01349	.01336	.01323	.01310	.01296	.01283	.01270

35 YEAR LIFE (Sum of the Years-Digits)

29	.01257	.01243	.01230	.01217	.01204	.01190	.01177	.01164	.01151	.01138	.01124	.01111
30	.01098	.01085	.01071	.01085	.01045	.01032	.01019	.01065	.00992	.00979	.00966	.00952
31	.00939	.00926	.00913	.00899	.00886	.00873	.00860	.00847	.00833	.00820	.00807	.00794
32	.00780	.00767	.00754	.00741	.00728	.00714	.00701	.00688	.00675	.00661	.00648	.00635
33	.00622	.00608	.00595	.00582	.00569	.00556	.00542	.00529	.00516	.00503	.00489	.00476
34	.00463	.00450	.00437	.00423	.00410	.00397	.00384	.00370	.00357	.00344	.00331	.00317
35	.00304	.00291	.00278	.00265	.00251	.00238	.00225	.00212	.00198	.00185	.00172	.00159
36	.00146	.00133	.00119	.00105	.00093	.00079	.00065	.00052	.00039	.00026	.00013	

40 YEAR LIFE (Sum of the Years-Digits)

1	.00407	.00813	.01220	.01626	.02033	.02439	.02846	.03252	.03659	.04065	.04472	.04878
2	.04868	.04858	.04848	.04837	.04827	.04817	.04807	.04797	.04787	.04776	.04766	.04756
3	.04746	.04736	.04726	.04715	.04705	.04695	.04685	.04675	.04665	.04654	.04644	.04634
4	.04624	.04614	.04604	.04593	.04583	.04573	.04563	.04553	.04543	.04533	.04522	.04512
5	.04502	.04492	.04482	.04472	.04461	.04451	.04441	.04431	.04421	.04411	.04400	.04390
6	.04380	.04370	.04360	.04350	.04339	.04329	.04319	.04309	.04299	.04289	.04278	.04268
7	.04258	.04248	.04238	.04228	.04217	.04207	.04197	.04187	.04177	.04167	.04157	.04146
8	.04136	.04126	.04116	.04106	.04096	.04085	.04075	.04065	.04055	.04045	.04035	.04024
9	.04014	.04004	.03994	.03984	.03974	.03963	.03953	.03943	.03933	.03923	.03913	.03902
10	.03892	.03882	.03872	.03862	.03852	.03841	.03831	.03821	.03811	.03801	.03791	.03780
11	.03770	.03766	.03750	.03740	.03730	.03720	.03709	.03699	.03689	.03679	.03669	.03659
12	.03648	.03638	.03628	.03618	.03608	.03598	.03587	.03577	.03567	.03557	.03547	.03537
13	.03526	.03516	.03506	.03496	.03486	.03476	.03465	.03455	.03445	.03435	.03425	.03415
14	.03404	.03394	.03384	.03374	.03364	.03354	.03343	.03333	.03323	.03313	.03303	.03293
15	.03283	.03272	.03262	.03252	.03242	.03232	.03222	.03211	.03201	.03191	.03181	.03171
16	.03161	.03150	.03140	.03130	.03120	.03110	.03100	.03089	.03079	.03069	.03059	.03049
17	.03039	.03028	.03018	.03008	.02998	.02988	.02978	.02967	.02957	.02947	.02937	.02927
18	.02917	.02907	.02996	.02886	.02876	.02866	.02856	.02846	.02835	.02825	.02815	.02805

40 YEAR LIFE (Sum of the Years-Digits)

19	.02795	.02785	.02774	.02764	.02754	.02744	.02734	.02724	.02713	.02703	.02693	.02683
20	.02673	.02663	.02652	.02642	.02632	.02622	.02612	.02602	.02591	.02581	.02571	.02561
21	.02551	.02541	.02530	.02520	.02510	.02500	.02490	.02480	.02470	.02459	.02449	.02439
22	.02429	.02419	.02409	.02398	.02388	.02378	.02368	.02358	.02348	.02337	.02327	.02317
23	.02307	.02297	.02287	.02276	.02266	.02256	.02246	.02236	.02226	.02215	.02205	.02195
24	.02185	.02175	.02165	.02154	.02144	.02134	.02124	.02114	.02104	.02093	.02083	.02073
25	.02063	.02053	.02043	.02033	.02022	.02012	.02002	.01992	.01982	.01972	.01961	.01951
26	.01941	.01931	.01921	.01911	.01900	.01890	.01880	.01870	.01860	.01850	.01839	.01829
27	.01819	.01809	.01799	.01789	.01778	.01768	.01758	.01748	.01738	.01728	.01717	.01707
28	.01697	.01687	.01677	.01667	.01657	.01646	.01636	.01626	.01616	.01606	.01596	.01585
29	.01575	.01565	.01555	.01545	.01535	.01524	.01514	.01504	.01494	.01484	.01474	.01463
30	.01453	.01443	.01433	.01423	.01413	.01402	.01392	.01382	.01372	.01362	.01352	.01341
31	.01331	.01321	.01311	.01301	.01291	.01280	.01270	.01260	.01250	.01240	.01230	.01220
32	.01209	.01199	.01189	.01179	.01169	.01159	.01148	.01138	.01128	.01118	.01108	.01098
33	.01087	.01077	.01067	.01057	.01047	.01037	.01026	.01016	.01006	.00996	.00986	.00976
34	.00965	.00955	.00945	.00935	.00925	.00915	.00904	.00894	.00884	.00874	.00864	.00854
35	.00843	.00833	.00823	.00813	.00803	.00793	.00783	.00772	.00762	.00752	.00742	.00732
36	.00722	.00711	.00701	.00691	.00681	.00671	.00661	.00650	.00640	.00630	.00620	.00610
37	.00600	.00589	.00579	.00569	.00559	.00549	.00539	.00528	.00518	.00508	.00498	.00488
38	.00478	.00467	.00457	.00447	.00437	.00427	.00417	.00407	.00396	.00386	.00376	.00366
39	.00356	.00346	.00335	.00325	.00315	.00305	.00295	.00285	.00274	.00264	.00254	.00244
40	.00234	.00224	.00213	.00203	.00193	.00183	.00173	.00163	.00152	.00142	.00132	.00122
41	.00112	.00102	.00091	.00081	.00070	.00061	.00051	.00041	.00030	.00020	.00009	

45 YEAR LIFE (Sum of the Years-Digits)

1	.00362	.00725	.01087	.01449	.01812	.02174	.02536	.02899	.03261	.03623	.03986	.04348
2	.04340	.04332	.04324	.04316	.04308	.04300	.04291	.04283	.04275	.04267	.04259	.04251
3	.04243	.04235	.04227	.04219	.04211	.04203	.04195	.04187	.04179	.04171	.04163	.04155

45 YEAR LIFE (Sum of the Years-Digits)

4	.04147	.04138	.04130	.04122	.04114	.04106	.04098	.04090	.04082	.04074	.04066	.04058
5	.04050	.04042	.04034	.04026	.04018	.04010	.04002	.03994	.03986	.03977	.03969	.03961
6	.03953	.03945	.03937	.03929	.03921	.03913	.03905	.03897	.03889	.03881	.03873	.03865
7	.03857	.03849	.03841	.03833	.03824	.03816	.03808	.03800	.03792	.03784	.03776	.03768
8	.03760	.03752	.03744	.03736	.03728	.03720	.03712	.03704	.03696	.03688	.03680	.03671
9	.03663	.03655	.03647	.03639	.03631	.03623	.03615	.03607	.03599	.03591	.03583	.03575
10	.03567	.03559	.03551	.03543	.03535	.03527	.03519	.03510	.03502	.03494	.03486	.03478
11	.03470	.03462	.03454	.03446	.03438	.03430	.03422	.03414	.03406	.03398	.03390	.03382
12	.03374	.03366	.03357	.03349	.03341	.03333	.03325	.03317	.03309	.03301	.03293	.03285
13	.03277	.03269	.03261	.03253	.03245	.03237	.03229	.03221	.03213	.03205	.03196	.03188
14	.03180	.03172	.03164	.03156	.03148	.03140	.03132	.03124	.03116	.03108	.03100	.03092
15	.03084	.03076	.03068	.03060	.03052	.03043	.03035	.03027	.03019	.03011	.03003	.02995
16	.02987	.02979	.02971	.02963	.02955	.02947	.02939	.02931	.02923	.02915	.02907	.02899
17	.02890	.02882	.02874	.02866	.02858	.02850	.02842	.02834	.02826	.02818	.02810	.02802
18	.02794	.02786	.02778	.02770	.02762	.02754	.02746	.02738	.02729	.02721	.02713	.02705
19	.02697	.02689	.02681	.02673	.02665	.02657	.02649	.02641	.02633	.02625	.02617	.02609
20	.02601	.02593	.02585	.02576	.02568	.02560	.02552	.02544	.02536	.02528	.02520	.02512
21	.02504	.02496	.02488	.02480	.02472	.02464	.02456	.02448	.02440	.02432	.02424	.02415
22	.02407	.02399	.02391	.02383	.02375	.02367	.02359	.02351	.02343	.02335	.02327	.02319
23	.02311	.02303	.02295	.02287	.02279	.02271	.02262	.02254	.02246	.02238	.02230	.02222
24	.02214	.02206	.02198	.62190	.02182	.02174	.02166	.02158	.02150	.02142	.02134	.02126
25	.02118	.02110	.02101	.02093	.02085	.02077	.02069	.02061	.02053	.02045	.02037	.02029
26	.02021	.02013	.02005	.01997	.01989	.01981	.01973	.01965	.01957	.01948	.01940	.01932
27	.01924	.01916	.01908	.01900	.01892	.01884	.01876	.01868	.01860	.01852	.01844	.01836
28	.01828	.01820	.01812	.01804	.01795	.01787	.01779	.01771	.01763	.01755	.01747	.01739
29	.01731	.01723	.01715	.01707	.01699	.01691	.01683	.01675	.01667	.01659	.01651	.01643
30	.01634	.01626	.01618	.01610	.01602	.01594	.01586	.01578	.01570	.01562	.01554	.01546
31	.01538	.01530	.01522	.01514	.01506	.01498	.01490	.01481	.01473	.01465	.01457	.01449
32	.01441	.01433	.01425	.01417	.01409	.01401	.01393	.01385	.01377	.01369	.01361	.01353

45 YEAR LIFE (Sum of the Years-Digits)

33	.01345	.01337	.01329	.01320	.01312	.01304	.01296	.01288	.01280	.01272	.01264	.01256
34	.01248	.01240	.01232	.01224	.01216	.01208	.01200	.01192	.01184	.01176	.01167	.01159
35	.01151	.01143	.01135	.01127	.01119	.01111	.01103	.01095	.01087	.01079	.01071	.01063
36	.01055	.01047	.01039	.01031	.01023	.01014	.01006	.00998	.00990	.00982	.00974	.00966
37	.00958	.00950	.00942	.00934	.00926	.00918	.00910	.00902	.00894	.00886	.00878	.00870
38	.00862	.00853	.00845	.00837	.00829	.00821	.00813	.00805	.00797	.00789	.00781	.00773
39	.00765	.00757	.00749	.00741	.00733	.00725	.00717	.00709	.00700	.00692	.00684	.00676
40	.00668	.00660	.00652	.00644	.00636	.00628	.00620	.00612	.00604	.00596	.00684	.00580
41	.00572	.00564	.00556	.00548	.00539	.00531	.00523	.00515	.00507	.00499	.00491	.00483
42	.00475	.00467	.00459	.00451	.00443	.00435	.00427	.00419	.00411	.00403	.00395	.00386
43	.00378	.00370	.00362	.00354	.00346	.00338	.00330	.00322	.00314	.00306	.00298	.00290
44	.00282	.00274	.00266	.00258	.00250	.00242	.00233	.00225	.00217	.00209	.00201	.00193
45	.06185	.00177	.00169	.00161	.00153	.00145	.00137	.00129	.00121	.00113	.00105	.00097
46	.00089	.00080	.00072	.00064	.00056	.00048	.00041	.00032	.00024	.00016	.00007	

50 YEAR LIFE (Sum of the Years-Digits)

1	.00327	.00654	.00980	.01307	.01634	.01961	.02288	.02614	.02941	.03268	.03595	.03922
2	.03915	.03908	.03902	.03895	.03889	.03882	.03876	.03869	.03863	.03856	.03850	.03843
3	.03837	.03830	.03824	.03817	.03810	.03804	.03797	.03791	.03784	.03778	.03771	.03765
4	.03758	.03752	.03745	.03739	.03732	.03725	.03719	.03712	.03706	.03699	.03693	.03686
5	.03680	.03673	.03667	.03660	.03654	.03647	.03641	.03634	.03627	.03621	.03614	.03608
6	.03601	.03595	.03588	.03582	.03575	.03569	.03562	.03556	.03549	.03542	.03536	.03529
7	.03523	.03516	.03510	.03503	.03497	.03490	.03484	.03477	.03471	.03464	.03458	.03451
8	.03444	.03438	.03431	.03425	.03418	.03412	.03405	.03399	.03392	.03386	.03379	.03373
9	.03366	.03359	.03353	.03346	.03340	.03333	.03327	.03320	.03314	.03307	.03301	.03294
10	.03288	.03281	.03275	.03268	.03261	.03255	.03248	.03242	.03235	.03229	.03222	.03216
11	.03209	.03203	.03196	.03190	.03183	.03176	.03170	.03163	.03157	.03150	.03144	.03137
12	.03131	.03124	.03118	.03111	.03105	.03098	.03092	.03085	.03078	.03672	.03065	.03059

50 YEAR LIFE (Sum of the Years-Digits)

13	.03052	.03046	.03039	.03033	.03026	.03020	.03013	.03007	.03000	.02993	.02987	.02980
14	.02974	.02967	.02961	.02954	.02948	.02941	.02935	.02928	.02922	.02915	.02908	.02902
15	.02895	.02889	.02882	.02876	.02869	.02863	.02856	.02850	.02843	.02837	.02830	.02824
16	.02817	.02810	.02804	.02797	.02791	.02784	.02778	.02771	.02765	.02758	.02752	.02745
17	.02739	.02732	.02725	.02719	.02712	.02706	.02699	.02693	.02686	.02680	.02673	.02667
18	.02660	.02654	.02647	.02641	.02634	.02627	.02621	.02614	.02608	.02601	.02595	.02388
19	.02582	.02575	.02569	.02562	.02556	.02549	.02542	.02536	.02529	.02523	.02516	.02510
20	.02503	.02497	.02490	.02484	.02477	.02471	.02464	.02458	.02451	.02444	.02438	.02431
21	.02425	.02418	.02412	.02405	.02399	.02392	.02386	.02379	.02373	.02366	.02359	.02353
22	.02346	.02340	.02333	.02327	.02320	.02314	.02307	.02301	.02294	.02288	.02281	.02275
23	.02268	.02261	.02255	.02248	.02242	.02235	.02229	.02222	.02216	.02209	.02203	.02196
24	.02190	.02183	.02176	.02170	.02163	.02157	.02150	.02144	.02137	.02131	.02124	.02118
25	.02111	.02105	.02098	.02092	.02085	.02078	.02072	.02065	.02059	.02052	.02046	.02039
26	.02033	.02026	.02020	.02013	.02007	.02000	.01993	.01987	.01980	.01974	.01967	.01961
27	.01954	.01948	.01941	.01935	.01928	.01922	.01915	.01908	.01902	.01895	.01889	.01882
28	.01876	.01869	.01863	.01856	.01850	.01843	.01837	.01830	.01824	.01817	.01810	.01804
29	.01797	.01791	.01784	.01778	.01771	.01765	.01758	.01752	.01745	.01739	.01732	.01725
30	.01719	.01712	.01706	.01699	.01693	.01686	.01680	.01673	.01667	.01660	.01654	.01647
31	.01641	.01634	.01627	.01621	.01614	.01608	.01601	.01595	.01588	.01582	.01575	.01569
32	.01562	.01556	.01549	.01542	.01536	.01529	.01523	.01516	.01510	.01503	.01497	.01490
33	.01484	.01477	.01471	.01464	.01458	.01451	.01444	.01438	.01431	.01425	.01418	.01412
34	.01405	.01399	.01392	.01386	.01379	.01373	.01366	.01359	.01353	.01346	.01340	.01333
35	.01327	.01320	.01314	.01307	.01301	.01294	.01288	.01281	.01275	.01268	.01261	.01255
36	.01248	.01242	.01235	.01229	.01222	.01216	.01209	.01203	.01196	.01190	.01183	.01176
37	.01170	.01163	.01157	.01150	.01144	.01137	.01131	.01124	.01118	.01111	.01105	.01098
38	.01092	.01085	.01078	.01072	.01065	.01059	.01052	.01046	.01039	.01033	.01026	.01020
39	.01013	.01007	.01000	.00993	.00987	.00980	.00974	.00967	.00961	.00954	.00948	.00941
40	.00935	.00928	.00922	.00915	.00908	.00902	.00895	.00889	.00882	.00876	.00869	.00863
41	.00856	.00850	.00843	.00837	.00830	.00824	.00817	.00810	.00804	.00797	.00791	.00784

50 YEAR LIFE (Sum of the Years-Digits)

42	.00778	.00771	.00765	.00758	.00752	.00745	.00739	.00732	.00725	.00719	.00712	.00706
43	.00699	.00693	.00686	.00680	.00673	.00667	.00660	.00654	.00647	.00641	.00634	.00627
44	.00621	.00614	.00608	.00601	.00595	.00588	.00582	.00575	.00569	.00562	.00556	.00549
45	.00542	.00536	.00529	.00523	.00516	.00510	.00503	.00497	.00490	.00484	.00477	.00471
46	.00464	.00458	.00451	.00444	.00438	.00431	.00425	.00418	.00412	.00405	.00399	.00392
47	.00386	.00379	.00373	.00366	.00359	.00353	.00346	.00340	.00333	.00327	.00320	.00314
48	.00307	.00301	.00294	.00288	.00281	.00275	.00268	.00261	.00255	.00248	.00242	.00235
49	.00229	.00222	.00216	.00209	.00203	.00196	.00190	.00183	.00176	.00170	.00163	.00157
50	.00150	.00144	.00137	.00131	.00124	.00118	.00111	.00105	.00098	.00092	.00085	.00078
51	.00071	.00065	.00059	.00052	.00046	.00039	.00032	.00027	.00020	.00013	.00007	

60 YEAR LIFE (Sum of the Years-Digits)

1	.00273	.00546	.00820	.01093	.01366	.01639	.01913	.02186	.02459	.02732	.03005	.03279
2	.03274	.03270	.03265	.03260	.03256	.03251	.03247	.03242	.03238	.03233	.03229	.03224
3	.03219	.03215	.03210	.03206	.03201	.03197	.03192	.03188	.03183	.03179	.03174	.03169
4	.03165	.03160	.03156	.03151	.03147	.03142	.03138	.03128	.03133	.03124	.03119	.03115
5	.03110	.03106	.03101	.03097	.03092	.03087	.03083	.03133	.03074	.03069	.03065	.03060
6	.03056	.03051	.03046	.03042	.03037	.03033	.03028	.03024	.03019	.03015	.03010	.03005
7	.03001	.02996	.02992	.02987	.02983	.02978	.02974	.02969	.02964	.02960	.02955	.02951
8	.02946	.02942	.02937	.02933	.02928	.02923	.02919	.02914	.02910	.02905	.02901	.02896
9	.02892	.02887	.02883	.02878	.02873	.02869	.02864	.02860	.02855	.02851	.02846	.02842
10	.02837	.02832	.02828	.02823	.02819	.02814	.02810	.02805	.02801	.02796	.02791	.02787
11	.02782	.02778	.02773	.02769	.02764	.02760	.02755	.02750	.02746	.02741	.02737	.02732
12	.02728	.02723	.02719	.02714	.02709	.02705	.02700	.02696	.02691	.02687	.02682	.02678
13	.02673	.02668	.02664	.02659	.02655	.02650	.02646	.02641	.02637	.02632	.02628	.02623
14	.02618	.02614	.02609	.02605	.02600	.02596	.02591	.02587	.02637	.02577	.02573	.02568
15	.02564	.02559	.02555	.02550	.02546	.02541	.02536	.02532	.02582	.02523	.02518	.02514
16	.02509	.02505	.02500	.02495	.02491	.02486	.02482	.02477	.02473	.02468	.02464	.02459

60 YEAR LIFE (Sum of the Years-Digits)

17	.02454	.02450	.02445	.02441	.02436	.02432	.02427	.02423	.02418	.02413	.02409	.02404
18	.02400	.02395	.02391	.02386	.02382	.02377	.02372	.02368	.02363	.02359	.02354	.02350
19	.02345	.02341	.02336	.02332	.02327	.02322	.02318	.02313	.02309	.02304	.02300	.02295
20	.02291	.02286	.02281	.02277	.02272	.02268	.02263	.02259	.02254	.02250	.02245	.02240
21	.02236	.02231	.02227	.02222	.02218	.02213	.02209	.02204	.02199	.02195	.02190	.02186
22	.02181	.02177	.02172	.02168	.02163	.02158	.02154	.02149	.02145	.02140	.02136	.02131
23	.02127	.02122	.02117	.02113	.02108	.02104	.02045	.02095	.02090	.02086	.02081	.02077
24	.02072	.02067	.02063	.02058	.02054	.02049	.02099	.02040	.02036	.02031	.02026	.02622
25	.02017	.02013	.02008	.02004	.01999	.01995	.01990	.01985	.01981	.01976	.01972	.01967
26	.01963	.01958	.01954	.01949	.01944	.01940	.01935	.01931	.01926	.01922	.01917	.01913
27	.01908	.01903	.01899	.01894	.01890	.01885	.01881	.01876	.01872	.01867	.01862	.01858
28	.01853	.01849	.01844	.01840	.01835	.01831	.01826	.01821	.01817	.01812	.01808	.01803
29	.01799	.01794	.01790	.01785	.01781	.01776	.01771	.01767	.01762	.01758	.01753	.01749
30	.01744	.01740	.01735	.01730	.01726	.01721	.01717	.01712	.01708	.01703	.01699	.01694
31	.01689	.01685	.01680	.01676	.01671	.01667	.01662	.01658	.01653	.01648	.01644	.01639
32	.01635	.01630	.01626	.01621	.01617	.01612	.01607	.01603	.01598	.01594	.01589	.01585
33	.01580	.01576	.01571	.01566	.01562	.01557	.01553	.01548	.01544	.01539	.01535	.01530
34	.01526	.01521	.01516	.01512	.01507	.01503	.01498	.01494	.01489	.01485	.01480	.01475
35	.01471	.01466	.01462	.01457	.01453	.01448	.01444	.01439	.01434	.91430	.01425	.01421
36	.01416	.01412	.01407	.01403	.01398	.01393	.01389	.01384	.01380	.01375	.01371	.01366
37	.01362	.01357	.01352	.01348	.01343	.01339	.01334	.01330	.01325	.01321	.01316	.01311
38	.01307	.01302	.01298	.01293	.01289	.01284	.01280	.01275	.01270	.01266	.01261	.01257
39	.01252	.01248	.01243	.01239	.01234	.01230	.01225	.01220	.01216	.01211	.01207	.01202
40	.01198	.01193	.01189	.01184	.01179	.01175	.01170	.01166	.01161	.01157	.01152	.01148
41	.01143	.01138	.01134	.01129	.01125	.01120	.01116	.01111	.01107	.01102	.01097	.01093
42	.01088	.01084	.01079	.01075	.01070	.01066	.01061	.01056	.01052	.01047	.01043	.01038
43	.01034	.01029	.01025	.01020	.01015	.01011	.01006	.01002	.00997	.00993	.00988	.00984
44	.00979	.00974	.00970	.00965	.00961	.00956	.00952	.00947	.00943	.00938	.00934	.00929
45	.00924	.00920	.00915	.00911	.00906	.00902	.00897	.00893	.00888	.00883	.00879	.00874

60 YEAR LIFE (Sum of the Years-Digits)

46	.00870	.00865	.00861	.00856	.00852	.00847	.00842	.00838	.00833	.00829	.00824	.00820
47	.00815	.00811	.00806	.00801	.00797	.00792	.00788	.00783	.00779	.00774	.00770	.00765
48	.00760	.00756	.00751	.00747	.00742	.00738	.00733	.00729	.00724	.00719	.00715	.00710
49	.00706	.00701	.00697	.00692	.00688	.00683	.00679	.00674	.00669	.00665	.00660	.00656
50	.00651	.00647	.00642	.00638	.00633	.00628	.00624	.00619	.00615	.00610	.00606	.00601
51	.00597	.00592	.00587	.00583	.00578	.00574	.00569	.00565	.00560	.00556	.00551	.00546
52	.00542	.00537	.00533	.00528	.00524	.00519	.00515	.00510	.00505	.00501	.00496	.00492
53	.00487	.00483	.00478	.00474	.00469	.00464	.00460	.00455	.00451	.00446	.00442	.00437
54	.00433	.00428	.00423	.00419	.00414	.00410	.00405	.00401	.00396	.00392	.00387	.00383
55	.00378	.00373	.00369	.00364	.00360	.00355	.00351	.00346	.00342	.00337	.00332	.00328
56	.00323	.00319	.00314	.00310	.00305	.00301	.00296	.00291	.00287	.00282	.00278	.00273
57	.00269	.00264	.00260	.00255	.00250	.00246	.00241	.00237	.00232	.00228	.00223	.00219
58	.00214	.00209	.00205	.00200	.00196	.00191	.00187	.00182	.00178	.00173	.00168	.00164
59	.00159	.00155	.00150	.00146	.00141	.00137	.00132	.00128	.00123	.00118	.00114	.00109
60	.00105	.00100	.00096	.00091	.00087	.00082	.00077	.00073	.00068	.00064	.00059	.00055
61	.00050	.00047	.00041	.00036	.00032	.00028	.00022	.00018	.00014	.00009	.00005	

¶ 630

150-Percent Declining-Balance Decimals with Change to Straight-Line

The tables beginning on the next page give the 150-percent declining-balance decimals and change to straight-line decimals at the point where this method gives a higher rate. Note that these tables are not used to compute MACRS depreciation.

The point of changeover in the tables is determined on the assumption that the salvage value is not more than 10 percent of cost and the taxpayer elects to ignore it (see ¶ 338).

These tables are to be used by applying the declining-balance and straight-line decimals to the original depreciable basis of the asset (generally, cost less any other first-year basis adjustments for credits or deductions claimed with respect to the property). The decimals to be used for an asset are to be located in the column headed by the number of months the asset is held in the first year. (As to the number of months an asset is held, see ¶ 358.)

Example: An asset with an eight-year life is held for 11 months in the first tax year. The 150% declining-balance and straight-line decimals for this asset are listed in the eight-year life table on page 996 in the 11-months column. The decimals are: 1st year, .17188; 2nd year, .15527; 3rd year, .12616; 4th through 8th year, .10755; 9th year, .00894. The decimals are 150% declining-balance for the first three years and straight-line for the last six.

If the asset has an original depreciable basis of $10,000, depreciation without rounding would be as follows:

1st year	$1,718.80
2nd year	1,552.70
3rd year	1,261.60
4th year	1,075.50
5th year	1,075.50
6th year	1,075.50
7th year	1,075.50
8th year	1,075.50
9th year	89.40
Total depreciation	$10,000.00

If depreciation were computed by rounding to the nearest dollar, total depreciation would be $10,003 and an adjustment would have to be made so as not to claim too much depreciation.

150% DECLINING-BALANCE DECIMALS WITH CHANGE TO STRAIGHT-LINE

Months Held in First Year

Years	1	2	3	4	5	6	7	8	9	10	11	12
3 YEAR LIFE (150% Declining-Balance, Change to Straight-Line)												
1	.04167	.08333	.12500	.16667	.20833	.25000	.29167	.33333	.37500	.41667	.45833	.50000
2	.47917	.45833	.43750	.41667	.39583	.37500	.35417	.33333	.31250	.29167	.27083	.25000
Change to Straight-Line												
3	.25000	.25000	.25000	.25000	.25000	.25000	.25000	.25001	.25000	.24999	.25001	.25000
4	.22916	.20834	.18750	.16666	.14584	.12500	.10416	.08333	.06250	.04167	.02083	
4 YEAR LIFE (150% Declining-Balance, Change to Straight-Line)												
1	.03125	.06250	.09375	.12500	.15625	.18750	.21875	.25000	.28125	.31250	.34375	.37500
2	.36328	.35156	.33985	.32813	.31641	.30469	.29297	.28125	.26954	.25782	.24610	.23438
3	.22706	.21973	.21241	.20508								
Change to Straight-Line												
3					.20413	.20312	.20205	.20089	.19965	.19831	.19687	.19531
4	.19743	.19975	.20228	.20507	.20413	.20312	.20205	.20089	.19965	.19831	.19687	.19531
5	.18098	.16646	.15171	.13672	.11908	.10157	.08418	.06697	.04991	.03306	.01641	
5 YEAR LIFE (150% Declining-Balance, Change to Straight-Line)												
1	.02500	.05000	.07500	.10000	.12500	.15000	.17500	.20000	.22500	.25000	.27500	.30000

					5 YEAR LIFE (150% Declining-Balance, Change to Straight-Line)							
2	.29250	.28500	.27750	.27000	.26250	.25500	.24750	.24000	.23250	.22500	.21750	.21000
3	.20475	.19950	.19425	.18900	.18375	.17850	.17325	.16800				
					Change to Straight-Line							
3									.16692	.16579	.16459	.16333
4	.16380	.16429	.16482	.16538	.16597	.16660	.16728	.16800	.16692	.16579	.16459	.16333
5	.16380	.16429	.16482	.16538	.16597	.16660	.16728	.16800	.16692	.16579	.16459	.16334
6	.15015	.13692	.12361	.11024	.09681	.08330	.06969	.05600	.04174	.02763	.01373	
					6 YEAR LIFE (150% Declining-Balance, Change to Straight-Line)							
1	.02083	.04167	.06250	.08333	.10417	.12500	.14583	.16667	.18750	.20833	.22917	.25000
2	.24479	.23958	.23438	.22917	.22396	.21875	.21354	.20833	.20313	.19792	.19271	.18750
3	.18359	.17969	.17578	.17188	.16797	.16407	.16016	.15625	.15235	.14844	.14454	.14063
					Change to Straight-Line							
4–5	.14063	.14062	.14062	.14062	.14062	.14062	.14063	.14063	.14062	.14062	.14062	.14062
6	.14063	.14062	.14062	.14062	.14062	.14062	.14063	.14063	.14062	.14062	.14062	.14063
7	.12890	.11720	.10548	.09376	.08204	.07032	.05858	.04686	.03516	.02345	.01172	
					7 YEAR LIFE (150% Declining-Balance, Change to Straight-Line)							
1	.01786	.03572	.05357	.07143	.08929	.10715	.12500	.14286	.16072	.17858	.19643	.21429
2	.21046	.20664	.20281	.19898	.19516	.19133	.18750	.18368	.17985	.17602	.17220	.16837
3	.16536	.16236	.15935	.15634	.15334	.15033	.14732	.14432	.14131	.13830	.13530	.13229
4	.12993	.12757	.12520	.12284								

Change to Straight-Line

4					.12266	.12249	.12230	.12211	.12191	.12170	.12149	.12126
5–6	.12163	.12201	.12242	.12284	.12266	.12249	.12230	.12211	.12191	.12170	.12149	.12126
7	.12163	.12201	.12242	.12284	.12266	.12249	.12230	.12211	.12191	.12170	.12149	.12127
8	.11150	.10168	.09181	.08189	.07157	.06123	.05098	.04070	.03048	.02030	.01011	

8 YEAR LIFE (150% Declining-Balance, Change to Straight-Line)

1	.01563	.03125	.04688	.06250	.07813	.09375	.10938	.12500	.14063	.15625	.17188	.18750
2	.18457	.18164	.17871	.17578	.17285	.16992	.16699	.16406	.16113	.15820	.15527	.15234
3	.14996	.14758	.14520	.14282	.14044	.13806	.13568	.13330	.13092	.12854	.12616	.12378
4	.12185	.11991	.11798	.11604	.11411	.11218	.11024	.10831				

Change to Straight-Line

4									.10806	.10781	.10755	.10728
5–7	.10739	.10751	.10763	.10776	.10788	.10802	.10816	.10831	.10806	.10781	.10755	.10728
8	.10739	.10751	.10763	.10776	.10788	.10802	.10816	.10831	.10806	.10781	.10755	.10726
9	.09843	.08958	.08071	.07182	.06295	.05401	.04507	.03609	.02702	.01796	.00894	

9 YEAR LIFE (150% Declining-Balance, Change to Straight-Line)

1	.01389	.02778	.04167	.05556	.06945	.08334	.09722	.11111	.12500	.13889	.15278	.16667
2	.16436	.16204	.15973	.15741	.15510	.15278	.15047	.14815	.14584	.14352	.14121	.13889
3	.13696	.13503	.13310	.13117	.12924	.12732	.12539	.12346	.12153	.11960	.11767	.11574
4	.11413	.11253	.11092	.10931	.10770	.10610	.10449	.10288	.10127	.09967	.09806	.09645

Change to Straight-Line

5–8	.09645	.09645	.09645	.09645	.09645	.09645	.09645	.09645	.09645	.09645	.09645	.09645
9	.09645	.09645	.09645	.09645	.09645	.09645	.09645	.09645	.09645	.09645	.09645	.09645
10	.08841	.08037	.07233	.06430	.05626	.04821	.04018	.03215	.02411	.01607	.00803	

10 YEAR LIFE (150% Declining-Balance, Change to Straight-Line)

1	.01250	.02500	.03750	.05000	.06250	.07500	.08750	.10000	.11250	.12500	.13750	.15000
2	.14813	.14625	.14438	.14250	.14063	.13875	.13688	.13500	.13313	.13125	.12938	.12750
3	.12591	.12431	.12272	.12113	.11953	.11794	.11635	.11475	.11316	.11157	.10997	.10838
4	.10703	.10567	.10432	.10296	.10161	.10025	.09890	.09754	.09619	.09483	.09348	.09212
5	.09097	.08982	.08867	.08751								

Change to Straight-Line

5					.08745	.08739	.08733	.08727	.08720	.08714	.08707	.08700
6–9	.08712	.08725	.08738	.08751	.08745	.08739	.08733	.08727	.08720	.08714	.08707	.08700
10	.08712	.08725	.08738	.08751	.08745	.08739	.08733	.08727	.08720	.08714	.08707	.08700
11	.07986	.07270	.06551	.05835	.05103	.04372	.03639	.02909	.02182	.01451	.00725	

11 YEAR LIFE (150% Declining-Balance, Change to Straight-Line)

1	.01136	.02273	.03409	.04545	.05682	.06818	.07954	.09091	.10227	.11363	.12500	.13636
2	.13481	.13326	.13171	.13016	.12861	.12707	.12552	.12397	.12242	.12087	.11932	.11777
3	.11643	.11509	.11376	.11242	.11108	.10974	.10840	.10706	.10573	.10439	.10305	.10171
4	.10055	.09940	.09824	.09709	.09593	.09478	.09362	.09246	.09131	.09015	.08900	.08784
5	.08684	.08584	.08485	.08385	.08285	.08185	.08085	.07985				

Change to Straight-Line

5	.07976	.07967	.07957	.07947								
6–10	.07952	.07956	.07961	.07965	.07970	.07975	.07980	.07986	.07976	.07967	.07957	.07947
11	.07952	.07956	.07961	.07965	.07970	.07975	.07980	.07986	.07976	.07967	.07957	.07950
12	.07289	.06632	.05969	.05313	.04651	.03988	.03327	.02659	.01995	.01327	.00664	

12 YEAR LIFE (150% Declining-Balance, Change to Straight-Line)

1	.01042	.02083	.03125	.04167	.05208	.06250	.07292	.08333	.09375	.10417	.11458	.12500
2	.12370	.12240	.12110	.11979	.11849	.11719	.11589	.11459	.11329	.11198	.11068	.10938
3	.10824	.10710	.10596	.10482	.10368	.10255	.10141	.10027	.09913	.09799	.09685	.09571
4	.09471	.09372	.09272	.09172	.09073	.08973	.08873	.08774	.08674	.08574	.08475	.08375
5	.08288	.08201	.08113	.08026	.07939	.07852	.07764	.07677	.07590	.07503	.07415	.07328

Change to Straight-Line

6–11	.07327	.07327	.07327	.07327	.07327	.07327	.07327	.07327	.07327	.07327	.07327	.07327
12	.07327	.07327	.07327	.07327	.07327	.07327	.07327	.07327	.07327	.07327	.07327	.07326
13	.06716	.06105	.05495	.04885	.04274	.03662	.03052	.02441	.01830	.01220	.00610	

13 YEAR LIFE (150% Declining-Balance, Change to Straight-Line)

1	.00962	.01923	.02885	.03846	.04808	.05769	.06731	.07692	.08654	.09615	.10577	.11538
2	.11427	.11316	.11205	.11094	.10983	.10873	.10762	.10651	.10540	.10429	.10318	.10207
3	.10109	.10011	.09913	.09814	.09716	.09618	.09520	.09422	.09324	.09225	.09127	.09029
4	.08942	.08855	.08769	.08682	.08595	.08508	.08421	.08334	.08248	.08161	.08074	.07987
5	.07910	.07833	.07757	.07680	.07603	.07526	.07449	.07372	.07296	.07219	.07142	.07065
6	.06997	.06929	.06861	.06793								

Change to Straight-Line

6					.06792	.06789	.06786	.06783	.06780	.06778	.06775	.06772
7–12	.06777	.06783	.06788	.06794	.06792	.06789	.06786	.06783	.06780	.06778	.06775	.06772
13	.06777	.06783	.06788	.06794	.06792	.06789	.06786	.06783	.06780	.06778	.06775	.06770
14	.06214	.05652	.05094	.04533	.03959	.03394	.02829	.02265	.01698	.01127	.00562	

14 YEAR LIFE (150% Declining-Balance, Change to Straight-Line)

1	.00893	.01786	.02679	.03571	.04464	.05357	.06250	.07143	.08036	.08928	.09821	.10714
2	.10618	.10523	.10427	.10331	.10236	.10140	.10044	.09949	.09853	.09757	.09662	.09566
3	.09481	.09395	.09310	.09224	.09139	.09054	.08968	.08883	.08797	.08712	.08626	.08541
4	.08465	.08389	.08312	.08236	.08160	.08084	.08007	.07931	.07855	.07779	.07702	.07626
5	.07558	.07490	.07422	.07354	.07286	.07218	.07149	.07081	.07013	.06945	.06877	.06809
6	.06748	.06687	.06627	.06566	.06505	.06444	.06383	.06322				

Change to Straight-Line

6									.06318	.06314	.06310	.06305
7–13	.06307	.06309	.06311	.06314	.06316	.06318	.06321	.06323	.06318	.06314	.06310	.06305
14	.06307	.06309	.06311	.06314	.06316	.06318	.06321	.06323	.06318	.06314	.06310	.06304
15	.05781	.05258	.04735	.04206	.03682	.03159	.02631	.02107	.01584	.01053	.00522	

15 YEAR LIFE (150% Declining-Balance, Change to Straight-Line)

1	.00833	.01667	.02500	.03333	.04167	.05000	.05833	.06667	.07500	.08333	.09167	.10000
2	.09917	.09833	.09750	.09667	.09583	.09500	.09417	.09333	.09250	.09167	.09083	.09000
3	.08925	.08850	.08775	.08700	.08625	.08550	.08475	.08400	.08325	.08250	.08175	.08100
4	.08033	.07965	.07898	.07830	.07763	.07695	.07628	.07560	.07493	.07425	.07358	.07290
5	.07229	.07169	.07108	.07047	.06986	.06926	.06865	.06804	.06743	.06683	.06622	.06561

15 YEAR LIFE (150% Declining-Balance, Change to Straight-Line)

6	.06506	.06452	.06397	.06342	.06288	.06233	.06178	.06124	.06069	.06014	.05960	.05905

Change to Straight-Line

7–14	.05905	.05905	.05905	.05905	.05905	.05905	.05905	.05905	.05905	.05905	.05905	.05905
15	.05905	.05905	.05905	.05905	.05905	.05905	.05905	.05905	.05905	.05905	.05905	.05904
16	.05412	.04919	.04427	.03936	.03443	.02951	.02459	.01967	.01475	.00983	.00490	

16 YEAR LIFE (150% Declining-Balance, Change to Straight-Line)

1	.00781	.01563	.02344	.03125	.03906	.04688	.05469	.06250	.07031	.07813	.08594	.09375
2	.09302	.09229	.09155	.09082	.09009	.08936	.08862	.08789	.08716	.08643	.08569	.08496
3	.08430	.08363	.08297	.08231	.08164	.08098	.08032	.07965	.07899	.07833	.07766	.07700
4	.07640	.07580	.07520	.07459	.07399	.07339	.07279	.07219	.07159	.07098	.07038	.06978
5	.06924	.06869	.06815	.06760	.06706	.06651	.06597	.06542	.06488	.06433	.06379	.06324
6	.06275	.06225	.06176	.06126	.06077	.06028	.05978	.05929	.05879	.05830	.05780	.05731
7	.05686	.05642	.05597	.05552								

Change to Straight-Line

7					.05550	.05549	.05547	.05546	.05544	.05543	.05541	.05540
8–15	.05542	.05545	.05548	.05552	.05550	.05549	.05547	.05546	.05544	.05543	.05541	.05540
16	.05542	.05545	.05548	.05552	.05550	.05549	.05547	.05546	.05544	.05543	.05541	.05536
17	.05084	.04624	.04164	.03697	.03239	.02770	.02313	.01846	.01388	.00920	.00464	

17 YEAR LIFE (150% Declining-Balance, Change to Straight-Line)

1	.00735	.01471	.02206	.02941	.03677	.04412	.05147	.05883	.06618	.07353	.08089	.08824
2	.08759	.08694	.08629	.08564	.08499	.08435	.08370	.08305	.08240	.08175	.08110	.08045

17 YEAR LIFE (150% Declining-Balance, Change to Straight-Line)

3	.07986	.07927	.07868	.07808	.07749	.07690	.07631	.07572	.07513	.07453	.07394	.07335
4	.07281	.07227	.07173	.07119	.07065	.07012	.06958	.06904	.06850	.06796	.06742	.06688
5	.06639	.06590	.06541	.06491	.06442	.06393	.06344	.06295	.06246	.06196	.06147	.06098
6	.06053	.06008	.05964	.05919	.05874	.05829	.05784	.05739	.05695	.05650	.05603	.05560
7	.05519	.05478	.05437	.05396	.05355	.05315	.05274	.05233				

Change to Straight-Line

7									.05230	.05228	.05225	.05223
8–16	.05224	.05225	.05226	.05228	.05229	.05230	.05231	.05232	.05230	.05228	.05225	.05223
17	.05224	.05225	.05226	.05228	.05229	.05230	.05231	.05232	.05230	.05228	.05225	.05220
18	.04788	.04355	.03922	.03482	.03049	.02614	.02182	.01749	.01308	.00869	.00438	

18 YEAR LIFE (150% Declining-Balance, Change to Straight-Line)

1	.00694	.01389	.02083	.02778	.03472	.04167	.04861	.05555	.06250	.06944	.07639	.08333
2	.08275	.08217	.08160	.08102	.08044	.07986	.07928	.07870	.07813	.07755	.07697	.07639
3	.07586	.07533	.07480	.07427	.07374	.07321	.07267	.07214	.07161	.07108	.07055	.07002
4	.06953	.06905	.06856	.06808	.06759	.06711	.06662	.06613	.06565	.06516	.06468	.06419
5	.06374	.06330	.06285	.06241	.06196	.06152	.06107	.06062	.06018	.05973	.05929	.05884
6	.05843	.05802	.05762	.05721	.05680	.05639	.05598	.05557	.05517	.05476	.05435	.05394
7	.05357	.05319	.05282	.05244	.05207	.05170	.05132	.05095	.05057	.05020	.04982	.04945

Change to Straight-Line

8–17	.04944	.04944	.04944	.04944	.04944	.04944	.04944	.04944	.04944	.04944	.04944	.04944
18	.04944	.04944	.04944	.04944	.04944	.04944	.04944	.04944	.04944	.04944	.04944	.04944
19	.04534	.04121	.03708	.03295	.02884	.02470	.02061	.01650	.01235	.00824	.00411	

19 YEAR LIFE (150% Declining-Balance, Change to Straight-Line)

1	.00658	.01316	.01974	.02632	.03290	.03948	.04605	.05263	.05921	.06579	.07237	.07895
2	.07843	.07791	.07739	.07687	.07635	.07584	.07532	.07480	.07428	.07376	.07324	.07272
3	.07224	.07176	.07129	.07081	.07033	.06985	.06937	.06889	.06842	.06794	.06746	.06698
4	.06654	.06610	.06566	.06522	.06478	.06434	.06389	.06345	.06301	.06257	.06213	.06169
5	.06128	.06088	.06047	.06007	.05966	.05926	.05885	.05844	.05804	.05763	.05723	.05682
6	.05645	.05607	.05570	.05532	.05495	.05458	.05420	.05383	.05345	.05308	.05270	.05233
7	.05199	.05164	.05130	.05095	.05061	.05027	.04992	.04958	.04923	.04889	.04854	.04820
8	.04788	.04757	.04725	.04693								

Change to Straight-Line

8	.04692	.04691	.04690	.04690	.04689	.04688	.04687	.04686				
9–18	.04688	.04689	.04691	.04693	.04692	.04691	.04690	.04690	.04689	.04688	.04687	.04686
19	.04688	.04689	.04691	.04693	.04692	.04691	.04690	.04690	.04689	.04688	.04687	.04685
20	.04293	.03912	.03519	.03128	.02738	.02346	.01960	.01558	.01168	.00778	.00389	

20 YEAR LIFE (150% Declining-Balance, Change to Straight-Line)

1	.00625	.01250	.01875	.02500	.03125	.03750	.04375	.05000	.05625	.06250	.06875	.07500
2	.07453	.07406	.07360	.07313	.07266	.07219	.07172	.07125	.07079	.07032	.06985	.06938
3	.06895	.06851	.06808	.06765	.06721	.06678	.06635	.06591	.06548	.06505	.06461	.06418
4	.06378	.06338	.06298	.06258	.06218	.06178	.06137	.06097	.06057	.06017	.05977	.05937
5	.05900	.05863	.05826	.05789	.05752	.05715	.05677	.05640	.05603	.05566	.05529	.05492
6	.05458	.05423	.05389	.05355	.05320	.05286	.05252	.05217	.05183	.05149	.05114	.05080
7	.05048	.05017	.04985	.04953	.04921	.04890	.04858	.04826	.04794	.04763	.04731	.04699
8	.04670	.04640	.04611	.04582	.04552	.04523	.04494	.04464				

Change to Straight-Line

8									.04461	.04460	.04458	.04457
9–19	.04457	.04458	.04459	.04459	.04460	.04461	.04462	.04463	.04461	.04460	.04458	.04457
20	.04457	.04458	.04459	.04459	.04460	.04461	.04462	.04463	.04461	.04460	.04458	.04452
21	.04089	.03716	.03340	.02977	.02605	.02229	.01856	.01484	.01118	.00738	.00374	

22 YEAR LIFE (150% Declining-Balance, Change to Straight-Line)

1	.00568	.01136	.01705	.02273	.02841	.03409	.03977	.04545	.05114	.05682	.06250	.06818
2	.06779	.06741	.06702	.06663	.06624	.06586	.06547	.06508	.06469	.06431	.06392	.06353
3	.06317	.06281	.06245	.06209	.06173	.06137	.06100	.06064	.06028	.05992	.05956	.05920
4	.05886	.05853	.05819	.05785	.05752	.05718	.05684	.05651	.05617	.05583	.05550	.05516
5	.05485	.05453	.05422	.05391	.05359	.05328	.05297	.05265	.05234	.05203	.05171	.05140
6	.05111	.05082	.05053	.05023	.04994	.04965	.04936	.04907	.04878	.04848	.04819	.04790
7	.04763	.04736	.04708	.04681	.04654	.04627	.04599	.04572	.04545	.04518	.04490	.04463
8	.04438	.04412	.04387	.04362	.04336	.04311	.04286	.04260	.04235	.04210	.04184	.04159
9	.04135	.04112	.04088	.04064								

Change to Straight-Line

9					.04064	.04063	.04063	.04062	.04062	.04061	.04061	.04060
10–21	.04061	.04062	.04063	.04065	.04064	.04063	.04063	.04062	.04062	.04061	.04061	.04060
22	.04061	.04062	.04063	.04065	.04064	.04063	.04063	.04062	.04062	.04061	.04061	.04061
23	.03725	.03388	.03052	.02704	.02371	.02037	.01692	.01360	.01012	.00679	.00334	

25 YEAR LIFE (150% Declining-Balance, Change to Straight-Line)

1	.00500	.01000	.01500	.02000	.02500	.03000	.03500	.04000	.04500	.05000	.05500	.06000
2	.05970	.05940	.05910	.05880	.05850	.05820	.05790	.05760	.05730	.05700	.05670	.05640

25 YEAR LIFE (150% Declining-Balance, Change to Straight-Line)

3	.05612	.05584	.05556	.05527	.05499	.05471	.05443	.05415	.05387	.05358	.05330	.05302
4	.05276	.05249	.05223	.05196	.05170	.05143	.05117	.05090	.05064	.05037	.05011	.04984
5	.04959	.04934	.04909	.04884	.04859	.04835	.04810	.04785	.04760	.04735	.04710	.04685
6	.04662	.04638	.04615	.04591	.04568	.04545	.04521	.04498	.04474	.04451	.04427	.04404
7	.04382	.04360	.04338	.04316	.04294	.04272	.04250	.04228	.04206	.04184	.04162	.04140
8	.04119	.04099	.04078	.04057	.04037	.04016	.03995	.03975	.03954	.03933	.03913	.03892
9	.03873	.03853	.03834	.03814	.03795	.03775	.03756	.03736	.03717	.03697	.03678	.03658
10	.03640	.03622	.03603	.03585								

Change to Straight-Line

10	.03584	.03583	.03583	.03582	.03582	.03582	.03581	.03581				
11–24	.03582	.03582	.03583	.03584	.03584	.03583	.03583	.03582	.03582	.03582	.03581	.03581
25	.03582	.03582	.03583	.03584	.03584	.03583	.03583	.03582	.03582	.03582	.03581	.03580
26	.03277	.02991	.02689	.02390	.02084	.01795	.01490	.01201	.00896	.00593	.00303	

28 YEAR LIFE (150% Declining-Balance, Change to Straight-Line)

1	.00446	.00893	.01339	.01786	.02232	.02679	.03125	.03571	.04018	.04464	.04911	.05357
2	.05333	.05309	.05285	.05261	.05237	.05214	.05190	.05166	.05142	.05118	.05094	.05070
3	.05047	.05025	.05002	.04979	.04957	.04934	.04911	.04889	.04866	.04843	.04821	.04798
4	.04777	.04755	.04734	.04712	.04691	.04670	.04648	.04627	.04605	.04584	.04562	.04541
5	.04521	.04501	.04480	.04460	.04440	.04420	.04399	.04379	.04359	.04339	.04318	.04298
6	.04279	.04260	.04241	.04221	.04202	.04183	.04164	.04145	.04126	.04106	.04087	.04068
7	.04050	.04032	.04014	.63995	.03977	.03959	.03941	.03923	.03905	.03886	.03868	.03850
8	.03833	.03816	.03799	.03781	.03764	.03747	.03730	.03713	.03696	.03678	.03661	.03644
9	.03628	.03612	.03595	.03579	.03563	.03547	.03530	.03514	.03498	.03482	.03465	.03449
10	.03434	.03418	.03403	.03387	.03372	.03357	.03341	.03326	.03310	.03295	.03279	.03264
11	.03249	.03235	.03220	.03206								

28 YEAR LIFE (150% Declining-Balance, Change to Straight-Line)

Change to Straight-Line

11					.03205	.03205	.03205	.03204	.03204	.03204	.03204	.03203
12–27	.03204	.03204	.03205	.03206	.03205	.03205	.03205	.03204	.03204	.03204	.03204	.03203
28	.03204	.03204	.03205	.03206	.03205	.03205	.03205	.93204	.03204	.03204	.03204	.03210
29	.02935	.02676	.02403	.02131	.01875	.01600	.01331	.01075	.00803	.00533	.00262	

30 YEAR LIFE (150% Declining-Balance, Change to Straight-Line)

1	.00417	.00833	.01250	.01667	.02083	.02500	.02917	.03333	.03750	.04167	.04583	.05000
2	.04979	.04958	.04938	.04917	.04896	.04875	.04854	.04833	.04813	.04792	.04771	.04750
3	.04730	.04711	.04691	.04671	.04651	.04632	.04612	.04592	.04572	.04553	.04533	.04513
4	.04494	.04475	.04457	.04438	.04419	.04400	.04381	.04362	.04344	.04325	.04306	.04287
5	.04269	.04251	.04234	.04216	.04198	.04180	.04162	.04144	.04127	.04109	.04091	.04073
6	.04056	.04039	.04022	.04005	.03988	.03971	.03954	.03937	.03920	.03903	.03886	.03869
7	.03853	.03837	.03821	.03805	.03789	.03773	.03256	.03740	.03724	.03708	.03692	.03676
8	.03661	.03645	.03630	.03615	.03599	.03584	.03569	.03553	.03538	.03523	.03507	.03492
9	.03477	.03463	.03448	.03434	.03419	.03405	.03390	.03375	.03361	.03346	.03332	.03317
10	.03303	.03289	.03276	.03262	.03248	.03234	.03220	.03206	.03193	.03179	.03165	.03151
11	.03138	.03125	.03112	.03098	03085	.03072	.03059	.03046	.03033	.03019	.03006	.02993

Change to Straight-Line

12–29	.02994	.02994	.02993	.02993	.02994	.02994	.02994	.02994	.02994	.02994	.02994	.02994
30	.02994	.02994	.02993	.02993	.02994	.02994	.02994	.02994	.02994	.02994	.02994	.02987
31	.02737	.02488	.02254	.02005	.01739	.01488	.01240	.0993	.00739	.00490	.00242	

33 YEAR LIFE (150% Declining-Balance, Change to Straight-Line)

1	.00379	.00758	.01136	.01515	.01894	.02273	.02651	.03030	.03409	.03788	.04166	.04545
2	.04528	.04511	.04493	.04476	.04459	.04442	.04424	.04407	.04390	.04373	.04355	.04338
3	.04322	.04305	.04289	.04272	.04256	.04240	.04223	.04207	.04190	.04174	.04157	.04141
4	.04125	.04110	.04094	.04078	.04663	.04047	.04031	.04016	.04000	.03984	.03969	.03953
5	.03938	.03923	.03908	.03893	.03878	.03863	.03848	.03833	.03818	.03803	.03788	.03773
6	.03759	.03745	.03730	.03716	.03702	.03688	.03673	.03659	.03645	.03631	.03616	.03602
7	.03588	.03575	.03561	.03547	.03534	.03520	.03506	.03493	.03479	.03465	.03452	.03438
8	.03425	.03412	.03399	.03386	.03373	.03360	.03347	.03334	.03321	.03308	.03295	.03282
9	.03270	.03257	.03245	.03232	.03220	.03208	.03195	.03183	.03170	.03158	.03145	.03133
10	.03121	.03109	.03098	.03086	.03074	.03062	.03050	.03038	.03027	.03015	.03003	.02991
11	.02980	.02968	.02957	.02946	.02934	.02923	.02912	.02900	.02889	.02878	.02866	.02855
12	.02844	.02833	.02823	.02812	.02801	.02790	.02779	.02768	.62758	.02747	.02736	.02725

Change to Straight-Line

13–32	.02725	.02725	.02725	.02725	02725	.02725	.02725	02725	.02725	.02725	.02725	.02725
33	.02725	.02725	.02725	.02725	.02725	.02725	.02725	.02725	.02725	.02725	.02725	.02724
34	.02496	.02269	.02042	.01816	.01587	.01359	.01136	.00907	.00679	.00451	.00227	

35 YEAR LIFE (150% Declining-Balance, Change to Straight-Line)

1	.00357	.00714	.01072	.01429	.01786	.02143	.02500	.02857	.03215	.03572	.03929	.04286
2	.04271	.04255	.04240	.04225	.04209	.04194	.04179	.04163	.04148	.04133	.04117	.04102
3	.04087	.04073	.04058	.04043	.04029	.04014	.03999	.03985	.03970	.03955	.03941	.03926
4	.03912	.03898	.03884	.03870	.03856	.03842	.03828	.03814	.03800	.03786	.03772	.03758
5	.03745	.03731	.03718	.03704	.03691	.03678	.03664	.03651	.03637	.03624	.03610	.03597
6	.03584	.03571	.03559	.03546	.03533	.03520	.03507	.03494	.03482	.03469	.03456	.03443
7	.03431	.03418	.03406	.03394	.03381	.03369	.03357	.03344	.03332	.03320	.03307	.03293

35 YEAR LIFE (150% Declining-Balance, Change to Straight-Line)

8	.03283	.03272	.03260	.03248	.03236	.03225	.03213	.03201	.03189	.03178	.03166	.03154
9	.03143	.03132	.03120	.03109	.03098	.03087	.03075	.03064	.03053	.03042	.03030	.03019
10	.03008	.02998	.02987	.02976	.02965	.02955	.02944	.02933	.02922	.02912	.02901	.02890
11	.02880	.02869	.02859	.02849	.02838	.02828	.02818	.02807	.02797	.02787	.02776	.02766
12	.02756	.02746	.02736	.02726	.02716	.02707	.02697	.02687	.02677	.02667	.02657	.02647
13	.02638	.02628	.02619	.02609	.02600	.02591	.02581	.02572				

Change to Straight-Line

13									.02571	.02571	.02571	.02570
14–34	.02570	.02571	.02571	.02571	.02571	.02571	.02571	.02571	.62571	.02571	.02571	.02576
35	.02570	.02571	.02571	.02571	.02571	.02571	.02571	.02571	.02571	.02571	.02571	.02577
36	.02365	.02133	.01920	.01710	.01500	.01285	.01076	.00866	.00645	.00422	.00205	

40 YEAR LIFE (150% Declining-Balance, Change to Straight-Line)

1	.00313	.00625	.00938	.01250	.01563	.01875	.02188	.02500	.02813	.03125	.03438	.03750
2	.03738	.03727	.03715	.03703	.03691	.03680	.03668	.03656	.03644	.03633	.03621	.03609
3	.03598	.03587	.03575	.03564	.03553	.03542	.03530	.03519	.03508	.03497	.03485	.03474
4	.03463	.03452	.03442	.03431	.03420	.03409	.03398	.03387	.03377	.03366	.63355	.03344
5	.03334	.03323	.03313	.03302	.03292	.03282	.03271	.03261	.03250	.03240	.03229	.03219
6	.03209	.03199	.03189	.03179	.03169	.03159	.03148	.03138	.03128	.03118	.03108	.03098
7	.03088	.03079	.03069	.03059	.03630	.03040	.03030	.03021	.03011	.03001	.02992	.02982
8	.02973	.02663	.02954	.02945	.02935	.02926	.02917	.02907	.02898	.02889	.02879	.02870
9	.02861	.02852	.02843	.02834	.02825	.02816	.02807	.02798	.02789	.02780	.02771	.02762
10	.02753	.02745	.02736	.02727	.02719	.02710	.02701	.02693	.02684	.02675	.02667	.02658
11	.02650	.02641	.02633	.02625	.02616	.02608	.02600	.02591	.02583	.02575	.02566	.02558
12	.02550	.02542	.02534	.02526	.02518	.02510	.02502	.02494	.02486	.02478	.02470	.02462
13	.02454	.02447	.02439	.02431	.02424	.02416	.02408	.02401	.02393	.02385	.02378	.02370

40 YEAR LIFE (150% Declining-Balance, Change to Straight-Line)

14	.02363	.02355	.02348	.02340	.02333	.02326	.02318	.02311	.02303	.02296	.02288	.02281
15	.02274	.02267	.02260	.02252								
Change to Straight-Line												
15					.02253	.02253	.02253	.02253	.02253	.02253	.02253	.02252
16–39	.02253	.02253	.02253	.02253	.02253	.02253	.02253	.02253	.02253	.02253	.02253	.02252
40	.02253	.02253	.02253	.02253	.02253	.02253	.02253	.02253	.02253	.02253	.02253	.02263
41	.02054	.01871	.01687	.01507	.01314	.01123	.00936	.00745	.00555	.00364	.00175	

45 YEAR LIFE (150% Declining-Balance, Change to Straight-Line)

1	.00278	.00556	.00833	.01111	.01389	.01667	.01944	.02222	.02500	.02778	.03055	.03333
2	.03324	.03315	.03305	.03296	.03287	.03278	.03268	.03259	.03250	.03241	.03231	.03222
3	.03213	.03204	.03195	.03186	.03177	.03169	.03160	.03151	.03142	.03133	.03124	.03115
4	.03106	.03098	.03089	.03080	.03072	.03063	.03054	.03046	.03037	.03028	.03020	.03011
5	.03003	.02994	.02986	.02978	.02969	.02961	.02953	.02944	.02936	.02928	.02919	.02911
6	.02903	.02895	.02887	.02879	.02871	.02863	.02854	.02846	.02838	.02830	.02822	.02814
7	.02806	.02798	.02791	.02783	.02775	.02767	.02759	.02751	.02744	.02736	.02728	.02720
8	.02712	.02705	.02697	.02690	.02682	.02675	.02667	.02659	.02652	.02644	.02637	.02629
9	.02622	.02614	.02607	.02600	.02592	.02585	.02578	.02570	.02563	.02556	.02548	.02541
10	.02534	.02527	.02520	.02513	.02506	.02499	.02491	.02484	.02477	.02470	.02463	.02456
11	.02449	.02442	.02436	.02429	.02422	.02415	.02408	.02401	.02395	.02388	.02381	.02374
12	.02367	.02361	.02354	.02348	.02341	.02335	.02328	.02321	.02315	.02308	.02302	.02295
13	.02289	.02282	.02276	.02270	.02263	.02257	.02251	.02244	.02238	.02232	.02225	.02219
14	.02213	.02207	.02201	.02194	.02188	.02182	.02176	.02170	.02164	.02157	.02151	.02145
15	.02139	.02133	.02127	.02121	.02115	.02110	.02104	.02098	.02092	.02086	.02080	.02074
16	.02068	.02063	.02057	.02051	.02045	.02040	.02034	.02028	.02022	.02017	.02011	.02005

Change to Straight-Line

17–44	.02005	.02005	.02005	.02005	.02005	.02005	.02005	.02005	.02005	.02005	.02005	.02005
45	.02005	.02005	.02005	.02005	.02005	.02005	.02005	.02005	.02005	.02005	.02005	.01996
46	.01829	.01661	.01494	.01326	.01161	.00989	.00826	.00661	.00490	.00323	.00158	

50 YEAR LIFE (150% Declining-Balance, Change to Straight-Line)

1	.00250	.00500	.00750	.01000	.01250	.01500	.01750	.02000	.02250	.02500	.02750	.03000
2	.02993	.02985	.02978	.02970	.02963	.02955	.02948	.02940	.02933	.02925	.02918	.02910
3	.02903	.02896	.02888	.02881	.02874	.02867	.02859	.02852	.02845	.02838	.02830	.02823
4	.02816	.02809	.02802	.02795	.02788	.02781	.02773	.02766	.02759	.02752	.02745	.02738
5	.02731	.02724	.02718	.02711	.02704	.02697	.02690	.02683	.02677	.02670	.02663	.02656
6	.02649	.02643	.02636	.02629	.02623	.02616	.02609	.02603	.02596	.02589	.02583	.02576
7	.02570	.02563	.02557	.02550	.02544	.02538	.02531	.02525	.02518	.02512	.02505	.02499
8	.02493	.02487	.02480	.02474	.02468	.02462	.02455	.02449	.02443	.02437	.02430	.02424
9	.02418	.02412	.02406	.02400	.02394	.02388	.02381	.02375	.02369	.02363	.02357	.02351
10	.02345	.02339	.02333	.02327	.02321	.02316	.02310	.02304	.02298	.02292	.02286	.02280
11	.02274	.02269	.02263	.02257	.02252	.02246	.02240	.02235	.02229	.02223	.02218	.02212
12	.02207	.02201	.02196	.02190	.02185	.02179	.02174	.02168	.02163	.02157	.02152	.02146
13	.02141	.02135	.02130	.02125	.02119	.02114	.02109	.02103	.02098	.02093	.02087	.02082
14	.02077	.02072	.02067	.02061	.02056	.02051	.02046	.02041	.02036	.02030	.02025	.02020
15	.02015	.02010	.02005	.02000	.01995	.01990	.01984	.01979	.01974	.01969	.01964	.01959
16	.01954	.01949	.01944	.01939	.01934	.01930	.01925	.01920	.01915	.01910	.01905	.01900
17	.01895	.01891	.01886	.01881	.01876	.01872	.01867	.01862	.01857	.01853	.01848	.01843
18	.01838	.01834	.01829	.01825	.01820	.01816	.01811	.01806				

Change to Straight-Line

18									.01806	.01806	.01806	.01805
19–49	.01805	.01806	.01806	.01806	.01806	.01806	.01806	.01806	.01806	.01806	.01806	.01805
50	.01805	.01806	.01806	.01806	.01806	.01806	.01806	.01806	.01806	.01806	.01806	.01821
51	.01671	.01489	.01340	.01193	.01042	.00890	.00746	.00597	.00442	.00289	.00136	

60 YEAR LIFE (150% Declining-Balance, Change to Straight-Line)

1	.00208	.00417	.00625	.00833	.01042	.01250	.01458	.01667	.01875	.02083	.02292	.02500
2	.02495	.02490	.02485	.02479	.02474	.02469	.02464	.02459	.02454	.02448	.02443	.02438
3	.02433	.02428	.02423	.02418	.02413	.02408	.02402	.02397	.02392	.02387	.02382	.02377
4	.02372	.02367	.02362	.02357	.02352	.02348	.02343	.02338	.02333	.02328	.02323	.02315
5	.02313	.02308	.02304	.02299	.02294	.02289	.02284	.02279	.02275	.02270	.02265	.02260
6	.02255	.02251	.02246	.02241	.02237	.02232	.02227	.02223	.02218	.02213	.02209	.02204
7	.02199	.02195	.02190	.02186	.02181	.02177	.02172	.02167	.02163	.02158	.02154	.02149
8	.02145	.02140	.02136	.02131	.02127	.02122	.02118	.02113	.02109	.02104	.02100	.02095
9	.02091	.02086	.02082	.02078	.02073	.02069	.02065	.02060	.02056	.02052	.02047	.02043
10	.02039	.02035	.02030	.02026	.02022	.02018	.02013	.02009	.02005	.02001	.01996	.01992
11	.01985	.01984	.01980	.01975	.01971	.01967	.01963	.01959	.01955	.01950	.01946	.01942
12	.01938	.01934	.01930	.01926	.01922	.01918	.01913	.01909	.01905	.01901	.01897	.01893
13	.01889	.01885	.01881	.01877	.01873	.01870	.01866	.01862	.01858	.01854	.01850	.01846
14	.01842	.01838	.01835	.01831	.01827	.01823	.01819	.01815	.01812	.01808	.01804	.01800
15	.01796	.01793	.01789	.01785	.01781	.01778	.01774	.01770	.01766	.01763	.01759	.01755
16	.01751	.01748	.01744	.01740	.01737	.01733	.01729	.01726	.01722	.01718	.01715	.01711
17	.01707	.01704	.01700	.01697	.01693	.01690	.01686	.01682	.01679	.01675	.01672	.01668
18	.01665	.01661	.01658	.01654	.01651	.01647	.01644	.01640	.01637	.01633	.01630	.01626
19	.01623	.01619	.01616	.01612	.01609	.01606	.01602	.01599	.01595	.01592	.01588	.01585
20	.01582	.01578	.01575	.01572	.01568	.01565	.01562	.01558	.01555	.01552	.01548	.01545
21	.01542	.01539	.01535	.01532	.01529	.01526	.01522	.01519	.01516	.01513	.01509	.01506

60 YEAR LIFE (150% Declining-Balance, Change to Straight-Line)

Change to Straight-Line

22–59	.01506	.01506	.01506	.01506	.01506	.01506	.01506	.01506	.01506	.01506	.01506	.01506
60	.01506	.01506	.01506	.01506	.01506	.01506	.01506	.01506	.01506	.01506	.01506	.01519
61	.01393	.01266	.01140	.01017	.00890	.00761	.00640	.00515	.00386	.00263	.00137	

¶ 640

200-Percent Declining-Balance Decimals with Change to Straight-Line

It is a common practice to deduct declining-balance depreciation on item and year's acquisition accounts until it is more advantageous to use the straight-line method. The tables beginning on the next page are set up this way. They give the 200-percent declining-balance decimals and change to straight-line decimals at the point where this method gives the same or a higher rate. Note that these tables are not used to compute MACRS depreciation.

The point of changeover in the tables is determined on the assumption that the salvage value is not more than 10 percent of cost and the taxpayer elects to ignore it (see ¶ 338).

These tables are used by applying the declining-balance and straight-line decimals to the original cost reduced by any first-year basis adjustment for deductions or credits claimed with respect to the property. The decimals for an asset are to be located in the column headed by the number of months the asset is held in the first year. (As to the number of months an asset is held, see ¶ 358.)

Example: An asset with a nine-year useful life is held eight months in the first tax year. The 200% declining-balance and straight-line decimals for this asset are shown in the nine-year life table on page 1015 in the eight-months column. The decimals are: 1st year, .14815; 2nd year, .18930; 3rd year, .14723; 4th year, .11452; 5th year, .08907; 6th through 9th years, .07194; and 10th year, .02397. The decimals are 200% declining-balance for the first five years and straight-line for the last five.

If the asset has a depreciable basis (original cost reduced by any bonus depreciation claimed) of $10,000, depreciation without rounding would be as follows:

1st year	$1,481.50
2nd year	1,893.00
3rd year	1,472.30
4th year	1,145.20
5th year	890.70
6th year	719.40
7th year	719.40
8th year	719.40
9th year	719.40
10th year	239.70
Total depreciation	$10,000.00

If depreciation were computed by rounding to the nearest dollar, total depreciation would be $9,999 and an adjustment would have to be made so as to claim the full amount of depreciation.

Under modified ACRS (MACRS), 3-year property, 5-year property, 7-year property, and 10-year property are generally depreciated under the 200-percent declining-balance method (with a timely switch to the straight-line method). Thus, if, as is generally the case with regard to such MACRS property, the half-year convention applies, decimals from the column for property held six months in the first year (to reflect the half-year convention) from the charts on the following pages for property with a 3-year, 5-year, 7-year, or 10-year life are substantially equivalent to the corresponding percentages set forth in the IRS tables at ¶ 180.

200% DECLINING-BALANCE DECIMALS WITH CHANGE TO STRAIGHT-LINE

Months Held in First Year

Years	1	2	3	4	5	6	7	8	9	10	11	12
3 YEAR LIFE (200% Declining-Balance, Change to Straight-Line)												
1	.05556	.11111	.16667	.22222	.27778	.33334	.38889	.44445	.50000	.55556	.61111	.66667
2	.62963	.59260	.55556	.51852	.48148	.44445	.40741	.37037	.33333	.29630	.25926	.22222
3	.20987	.19753	.18518	.17284	.16049							
Change to Straight-Line												
3						.14814	.14379	.13889	.13334	.12698	.11966	.11111
4	.10494	.09876	.09259	.08642	.08025	.07407	.05991	.04629	.03333	.02115	.00997	
4 YEAR LIFE (200% Declining-Balance, Change to Straight-Line)												
1	.04167	.08333	.12500	.16667	.20833	.25000	.29167	.33333	.37500	.41667	.45833	.50000
2	.47917	.45833	.43750	.41667	.39583	.37500	.35417	.33333	.31250	.29167	.27083	.25000
3	.23958	.22917	.21875	.20833	.19792	.18750	.17708	.16667	.15625	.14583	.13542	.12500
Change to Straight-Line												
4	.12500	.12500	.12500	.12500	.12500	.12500	.12500	.12500	.12500	.12500	.12500	.12500
5	.11458	.10417	.09375	.08333	.07292	.06250	.05208	.04167	.03125	.02083	.01042	
5 YEAR LIFE (200% Declining-Balance, Change to Straight-Line)												
1	.03333	.06667	.10000	.13333	.16667	.20000	.23333	.26667	.30000	.33333	.36667	.40000

					5 YEAR LIFE (200% Declining-Balance, Change to Straight-Line)							
2	.38667	.37333	.36000	.34667	.33333	.32000	.30667	.29333	.28000	.26667	.25333	.24000
3	.23200	.22400	.21600	.20800	.20000	.19200	.18400	.17600	.16800	.16000	.15200	.14400
4	.13920	.13440	.12960	.12480	.12000							
						Change to Straight-Line						
4						.11520	.11421	.11314	.11200	.11077	.10944	.10800
5	.10894	.10996	.11109	.11232	.11368	.11520	.11421	.11314	.11200	.11077	.10944	.10800
6	.09986	.09164	.08331	.07488	.06632	.05760	.04758	.03772	.02800	.01846	.00912	
					6 YEAR LIFE (200% Declining-Balance, Change to Straight-Line)							
1	.02778	.05556	.08333	.11111	.13889	.16667	.19444	.22222	.25000	.27778	.30555	.33333
2	.32407	.31481	.30555	.29629	.28703	.27778	.26852	.25926	.25000	.24074	.23148	.22222
3	.21605	.20988	.20370	.19753	.19136	.18519	.17901	.17284	.16667	.16050	.15432	.14815
4	.14404	.13992	.13581	.13169	.12758	.12346	.11935	.11523	.11112	.10700	.10289	.09877
						Change to Straight-Line						
5	.09876	.09876	.09877	.09877	.09876	.09876	.09876	.09876	.09876	.09876	.09876	.09877
6	.09876	.09876	.09877	.09877	.09876	.09876	.09876	.09876	.09876	.09876	.09876	.09876
7	.09054	.08231	.07407	.06584	.05762	.04938	.04116	.03293	.02469	.01646	.00824	
					7 YEAR LIFE (200% Declining-Balance, Change to Straight-Line)							
1	.02381	.04762	.07143	.09524	.11905	.14286	.16666	.19047	.21428	.23809	.26190	.28571
2	.27891	.27211	.26530	.25850	.25170	.24490	.23809	.23129	.22449	.21769	.21088	.20408
3	.19922	.19436	.18950	.18464	.17978	.17493	.17007	.16521	.16035	.15549	.15063	.14577
4	.14230	.13883	.13536	.13189	.12842	.12495	.12147	.11800	.11453	.11106	.10759	.10412

7 YEAR LIFE (200% Declining-Balance, Change to Straight-Line)												
5	.10164	.09916	.09668	.09420	.09172							
Change to Straight-Line												
5						.08925	.08889	.08851	.08811	.08769	.08724	.08677
6	.08713	.08750	.08790	.08832	.08877	.08925	.08889	.08851	.08811	.08769	.08724	.08677
7	.08713	.08750	.08790	.08832	.08877	.08925	.08889	.08851	.08811	.08769	.08724	.08678
8	.07986	.07292	.06593	.05889	.05179	.04461	.03704	.02950	.02202	.01460	.00728	
8 YEAR LIFE (200% Declining-Balance, Change to Straight-Line)												
1	.02083	.04167	.06250	.08333	.10417	.12500	.14583	.16667	.18750	.20833	.22917	.25000
2	.24479	.23958	.23438	.22917	.22396	.21875	.21354	.20833	.20313	.19792	.19271	.18750
3	.18359	.17969	.17578	.17188	.16797	.16407	.16016	.15625	.15235	.14844	.14454	.14063
4	.13770	.13477	.13184	.12891	.12598	.12305	.12012	.11719	.11426	.11133	.10840	.10547
5	.10327	.10108	.09888	.09668	.09448	.09229	.09009	.08789	.08569	.08350	.08130	.07910
Change to Straight-Line												
6–7	.07910	.07910	.07910	.07910	.07910	.07910	.07910	.07910	.07910	.07910	.07910	.07910
8	.07910	.07910	.07910	.07910	.07910	.07910	.07910	.07910	.07910	.07910	.07910	.07910
9	.07252	.06591	.05932	.05273	.04614	.03954	.03296	.02637	.01977	.01318	.00658	
9 YEAR LIFE (200% Declining-Balance, Change to Straight-Line)												
1	.01852	.03704	.05556	.07407	.09259	.11111	.12963	.14815	.16667	.18518	.20370	.22222
2	.21811	.21399	.20988	.20576	.20165	.19753	.19342	.18930	.18519	.18107	.17696	.17284
3	.16964	.16644	.16324	.16004	.15684	.15364	.15043	.14723	.14403	.14083	.13763	.13443
4	.13194	.12945	.12696	.12447	.12198	.11950	.11701	.11452	.11203	.10954	.10705	.10456

9 YEAR LIFE (200% Declining-Balance, Change to Straight-Line)

5	.10262	.10069	.09875	.09681	.09488	.09294	.09100	.08907	.08713	.08519	.08326	.08132
6	.07981	.07831	.07680	.07530	.07379							
						Change to Straight-Line						
6	.07228	.07212	.07194	.07175	.07157	.07136	.07116					
7–8	.07133	.07150	.07168	.07188	.07208	.07228	.07212	.07194	.07175	.07157	.07136	.07116
9	.07133	.07150	.07168	.07188	.07208	.07228	.07212	.07194	.07175	.07157	.07136	.07115
10	.06537	.05958	.05377	.04791	.04203	.03616	.03003	.02397	.01795	.01191	.00596	

10 YEAR LIFE (200% Declining-Balance, Change to Straight-Line)

1	.01667	.03333	.05000	.06667	.08333	.10000	.11667	.13333	.15000	.16667	.18333	.20000
2	.19667	.19333	.19000	.18667	.18333	.18000	.17667	.17333	.17000	.16667	.16333	.16000
3	.15733	.15467	.15200	.14933	.14667	.14400	.14133	.13867	.13600	.13333	.13067	.12800
4	.12587	.12373	.12160	.11947	.11733	.11520	.11307	.11093	.10880	.10667	.10453	.10240
5	.10069	.09899	.09728	.09557	.09387	.09216	.09045	.08875	.08704	.08533	.08363	.08192
6	.08056	.07919	.07783	.07646	.07510	.07373	.07237	.07100	.06964	.06827	.06691	.06554
						Change to Straight-Line						
7–9	.06553	.06554	.06553	.06554	.06554	.06554	.06553	.06554	.06553	.06553	.06553	.06554
10	.06553	.06554	.06553	.06554	.06554	.06554	.06553	.06554	.06553	.06553	.06553	.06552
11	.06009	.05460	.04917	.04367	.03821	.03275	.02732	.02183	.01640	.01094	.00548	

11 YEAR LIFE (200% Declining-Balance, Change to Straight-Line)

1	.01515	.03030	.04546	.06061	.07576	.09091	.10606	.12121	.13637	.15152	.16667	.18182
2	.17907	.17631	.17356	.17080	.16805	.16529	.16254	.15978	.15703	.15427	.15152	.14876

11 YEAR LIFE (200% Declining-Balance, Change to Straight-Line)

3	.14651	.14425	.14200	.13974	.13749	.13524	.13298	.13073	.12847	.12622	.12396	.12171
4	.11987	.11802	.11618	.11433	.11249	.11065	.10880	.10696	.10511	.10327	.10142	.09958
5	.09807	.09656	.09505	.09354	.09203	.09053	.08902	.08751	.08600	.08449	.08298	.08147
6	.08024	.07900	.07777	.07653	.07530	.07407	.07283	.07160	.07036	.06913	.06789	.06666
7	.06565	.06464	.06363	.06262	.06161							

Change to Straight-Line

7	.06060	.06051	.06041	.06032	.06021	.06011	.06000					
8–10	.06009	.06019	.06028	.06039	.06050	.06060	.06051	.06041	.06032	.06021	.06011	.06000
11	.06009	.06019	.06028	.06039	.06050	.06060	.06051	.06041	.06032	.06021	.06011	.06000
12	.05508	.05016	.04523	.04027	.03527	.03031	.02522	.02016	.01506	.01005	.00501	

12 YEAR LIFE (200% Declining-Balance, Change to Straight-Line)

1	.01389	.02778	.04167	.05556	.06945	08334	09722	.11111	.12500	.13889	.15278	.16667
2	.16436	.16204	.15973	.15741	.15510	.15278	.15047	.14815	.14584	.14352	.14121	.13889
3	.13696	.13503	.13310	.13117	.12924	.12732	.12539	.12346	.12153	.11960	.11767	.11574
4	.11413	.11253	.11092	.10931	.10770	.10610	.10449	.10288	.10127	.09967	.09806	.09645
5	.09511	.09377	.09243	.09109	.08975	.08841	.08707	.08573	.08439	.08305	.08171	.08037
6	.07925	.07814	.07702	.07590	.07479	.07367	.07255	.07144	.07032	.06920	.06809	.06697
7	.06604	.06511	.06418	.06325	.06232	.06139	.06046	.05953	.05860	.05767	.05674	.05581

Change to Straight-Line

8–11	.05582	.05582	.05582	.05582	.05582	.05582	.05582	.05582	.05582	.05582	.05582	.05582
12	.05582	.05582	.05582	.05582	.05582	.05582	.05582	.05582	.05582	.05582	.05582	.05582
13	.05116	.04650	.04185	.03721	.03255	.02789	.02325	.01860	.01395	.00930	.00464	

13 YEAR LIFE (200% Declining-Balance, Change to Straight-Line)

1	.01282	.02564	.03846	.05128	.06410	.07693	.08975	.10257	.11539	.12821	.14103	.15385
2	.15188	.14991	.14793	.14596	.14399	.14202	.14004	.13807	.13610	.13413	.13215	.13018
3	.12851	.12684	.12517	.12350	.12183	.12017	.11850	.11683	.11516	.11349	.11182	.11015
4	.10874	.10733	.10591	.10450	.10309	.10168	.10026	.09885	.09744	.09603	.09461	.09320
5	.09201	.09081	.08962	.08842	.08723	.08603	.08484	.08364	.08245	.08125	.08006	.07886
6	.07785	.07684	.07583	.07482	.07381	.07280	.07178	.07077	.06976	.06875	.06774	.06673
7	.06587	.06502	.06416	.06331	.06245	.06160	.06074	.05988	.05903	.05817	.05732	.05646
8	.05574	.05501	.05429	.05356	.05284							

Change to Straight-Line

8						.05212	.05207	.05201	.05195	.05189	.05183	.05176
9–12	.05182	.05187	.05194	.05200	.05206	.05212	.05207	.05201	.05195	.05189	.05183	.05176
13	.05182	.05187	.05194	.05200	.05206	.05212	.05207	.05201	.05195	.05189	.05183	.05177
14	.04748	.04325	.03893	.03465	.03036	.02605	.02167	.01733	.01297	.00863	.00429	

14 YEAR LIFE (200% Declining-Balance, Change to Straight-Line)

1	.01191	.02381	.03572	.04762	.05953	.07143	.08334	.09524	.10715	.11905	.13096	.14286
2	.14116	.13946	.13776	.13606	.13436	.13266	.13095	.12925	.12755	.12585	.12415	.12245
3	.12099	.11954	.11808	.11662	.11516	.11371	.11225	.11079	.10933	.10788	.10642	.10496
4	.10371	.10246	.10121	.09996	.09871	.09747	.09622	.09497	.09372	.09247	.09122	.08997
5	.08890	.08783	.08676	.08569	.08462	.08355	.08247	.08140	.08033	.07926	.07819	.07712
6	.07620	.07528	.07437	.07345	.07253	.07161	.07069	.06977	.06886	.06794	.06702	.06610
7	.06531	.06453	.06374	.06295	.06217	.06138	.06059	.05981	.05902	.05823	.05745	.05666
8	.05599	.05531	.05464	.05396	.05329	.05262	.05194	.05127	.05059	.04992	.04924	.04857

Change to Straight-Line

9–13	.04855	.04855	.04855	.04855	.04855	.04855	.04855	.04855	.04855	.04855	.04855	.04855
14	.04855	.04855	.04855	.04855	.04855	.04855	.04855	.04855	.04855	.04855	.04855	.04856
15	.04453	.04048	.03642	.03239	.02833	.02427	.02025	.01620	.01215	.00810	.00405	

15 YEAR LIFE (200% Declining-Balance, Change to Straight-Line)

1	.01111	.02222	.03333	.04444	.05555	.06667	.07778	.08889	.10000	.11111	.12222	.13333
2	.13185	.13037	.12889	.12740	.12592	.12444	.12296	.12148	.12000	.11851	.11703	.11555
3	.11427	.11298	.11170	.11041	.10913	.10785	.10656	.10528	.10399	.10271	.10142	.10014
4	.09903	.09792	.09680	.09569	.09458	.09347	.09235	.09124	.09013	.08902	.08790	.08679
5	.08583	.08486	.08390	.08293	.08197	.08101	.08004	.07908	.07811	.07715	.07618	.07522
6	.07438	.07355	.07271	.07188	.07104	.07021	.06937	.06853	.06770	.06686	.06603	.06519
7	.06447	.06374	.06302	.06229	.06157	.06085	.06012	.05940	.05867	.05795	.05722	.05650
8	.05587	.05525	.05462	.05399	.05336	.05274	.05211	.05148	.05085	.05023	.04960	.04897
9	.04843	.04788	.04734	.04679	.04625							

Change to Straight-Line

9						.04570	.04567	.04563	.04559	.04555	.04552	.04547
10–14	.04551	.04555	.04558	.04563	.04567	04570	.04567	.04563	.04559	.04555	.04552	.04547
15	.04551	.04555	.04558	.04563	.04567	.04570	.04567	.04563	.04559	.04555	.04552	.04549
16	.04170	.03793	.03421	.03040	.02661	.02286	.01902	.01521	.01142	.00761	.00376	

16 YEAR LIFE (200% Declining-Balance, Change to Straight-Line)

1	.01042	.02083	.03125	.04167	.05208	.06250	.07292	.08333	.09375	.10417	.11458	.12500
2	.12370	.12240	.12110	.11979	.11849	.11719	.11589	.11459	.11329	.11198	.11068	.10938
3	.10824	.10710	.10596	.10482	.10368	.10255	.10141	.10027	.09913	.09799	.09685	.09571

16 YEAR LIFE (200% Declining-Balance, Change to Straight-Line)

4	.09471	.09372	.09272	.09172	.09073	.08973	.08873	.08774	.08674	.08574	.08475	.08375
5	.08288	.08201	.08113	.08026	.07939	.07852	.07764	.07677	.07590	.07503	.07415	.07328
6	.07252	.07175	.07099	.07023	.06946	.06870	.06794	.06717	.06641	.06565	.06488	.06412
7	.06345	.06279	.06212	.06145	.06078	.06012	.05945	.05878	.05811	.05745	.05678	.05611
8	.05553	.05494	.05436	.05377	.05319	.05261	.05202	.05144	.05085	.05027	.04968	.04910
9	.04859	.04808	.04757	.04705	.04654	.04603	.04552	.04501	.04450	.04398	.04347	.04296

Change to Straight-Line

10–15	.04294	.04294	.04294	.04294	.04294	.04294	.04294	.04294	.04294	.04294	.04294	.04294
16	.04294	.04294	.04294	.04294	.04294	.04294	.04294	.04294	.04294	.04294	.04294	.04295
17	.03938	.03580	.03222	.02666	.02508	.02147	.01790	.01432	.01074	.00716	.00360	

17 YEAR LIFE (200% Declining-Balance, Change to Straight-Line)

1	.00980	.01961	.02941	.03922	.04902	.05883	.06863	.07843	.08824	.09804	.10785	.11765
2	.11650	.11534	.11419	.11304	.11188	.11073	.10958	.10842	.10727	.10612	.10496	.10381
3	.10279	.10178	.10076	.09974	.09872	.09771	.09669	.09567	.09465	.09364	.09262	.09160
4	.09070	.08980	.08891	.08801	.08711	.08621	.08531	.08441	.08352	.08262	.08172	.08082
5	.08003	.07924	.07844	.07765	.07686	.07607	.07527	.07448	.07369	.07290	.07210	.07131
6	.07061	.06991	.06921	.06851	.06781	.06712	.06642	.06572	.06502	.06432	.06362	.06292
7	.06230	.06169	.06107	.06045	.05984	.05922	.05860	.05799	.05737	.05675	.05614	.05552
8	.05498	.05443	.05389	.05334	.05280	.05226	.05171	.05117	.05062	.05008	.04953	.04899
9	.04851	.04803	.04755	.04707	.04659	.04611	.04563	.04515	.04467	.04419	.04371	.04323
10	.04281	.04238	.04196	.04153	.04111							

Change to Straight-Line

10						.04068	.04065	.04063	.04060	.04057	.04055	.04052
11–16	.04054	.04057	.04059	.04062	.04065	.04068	.04065	.04063	.04060	.04057	.04055	.04052
17	.04054	.04057	.04059	.04062	.04065	.04068	.04065	.04063	.04060	.04057	.04055	.04051
18	.03719	.03380	.03048	.02710	.02371	.02030	.01696	.01352	.01015	.00678	.00335	

18 YEAR LIFE (200% Declining-Balance, Change to Straight-Line)

1	.00926	.01852	.02778	.03704	.04630	.05556	.06481	.07407	.08333	.09259	.10185	.11111
2	.11008	.10905	.10802	.10699	.10596	.10494	.10391	.10288	.10185	.10082	.09979	.09876
3	.09785	.09693	.09602	.09510	.09419	.09328	.09236	.09145	.09053	.08962	.08870	.08779
4	.08698	.08617	.08535	.08454	.08373	.08292	.08210	.08129	.08048	.07967	.07885	.07804
5	.07732	.07660	.07587	.07515	.07443	.07371	.07298	.07226	.07154	.07082	.07009	.06937
6	.06873	.06809	.06744	.06680	.06616	.06552	.06487	.06423	.06359	.06295	.06230	.06166
7	.06109	.06052	.05995	.05938	.05881	.05824	.05766	.05709	.05652	.05595	.05538	.05481
8	.05430	.05380	.05329	.05278	.05227	.05177	.05126	.05075	.05024	.04974	.04923	.04872
9	.04827	.04782	.04737	.04692	.04647	.04602	.04556	.04511	.04466	.04421	.04376	.04331
10	.04291	.04251	.04211	.04171	.04131	.04091	.04050	.04010	.03970	.03930	.03890	.03850

Change to Straight-Line

11–17	.03849	.03849	.03849	.03849	.03849	.03849	.03849	.03849	.03849	.03849	.03849	.03849
18	.03849	.03849	.03849	.03849	.03849	.03849	.03849	.03849	.03849	.03849	.03849	.03850
19	.03529	.03207	.02888	.02567	.02245	.01921	.01607	.01285	.00964	.00641	.00323	

19 YEAR LIFE (200% Declining-Balance, Change to Straight-Line)

1	.00877	.01754	.02632	.03509	.04386	.05263	.06140	.07017	.07895	.08772	.09649	.10526
2	.10434	.10341	.10249	.10157	.10064	.09972	.09880	.09787	.09695	.09603	.09510	.09418

19 YEAR LIFE (200% Declining-Balance, Change to Straight-Line)

3	.09335	.09253	.09170	.09088	.09005	.08923	.08840	.08757	.08675	.08592	.08510	.08427
4	.08353	.08279	.08205	.08131	.08057	.07984	.07910	.07836	.07762	.07688	.07614	.07540
5	.07474	.07408	.07342	.07275	.07209	.07143	.07077	.07011	.06945	.06878	.06812	.06746
6	.06687	.06628	.06569	.06509	.06450	.06391	.06332	.06273	.06214	.06154	.06095	.06036
7	.05983	.05930	.05877	.05824	.05771	.05719	.05666	.05613	.05560	.05507	.05454	.05401
8	.05354	.05306	.05259	.05211	.05164	.05117	.05069	.05022	.04974	.04927	.04879	.04332
9	.04790	.04747	.04705	.04662	.04620	.04578	.04535	.04493	.04450	.04408	.04365	.04323
10	.04285	.04247	.04209	.04171	.04133	.04096	.04058	.04020	.03982	.03944	.03906	.03868
11	.03834	.03800	.03766	.03732	.03698							

Change to Straight-Line

11						.03665	.03663	.03661	.03659	.03657	.03656	.03654
12–18	.03655	.03657	.03659	.03661	.03663	.03665	.03663	.03661	.03659	.03657	.03656	.03654
19	.03655	.03657	.03659	.03661	.03663	.03665	.03663	.03661	.03659	.03657	.03656	.03651
20	.03354	.03051	.02745	.02443	.02139	.01829	.01526	.01222	.00917	.00614	.00302	

20 YEAR LIFE (200% Declining-Balance, Change to Straight-Line)

1	.00833	.01667	.02500	.03333	.04167	.05000	.05833	.06667	.07500	.08333	.09167	.10000
2	.09917	.09833	.09750	.09667	.09583	.09500	.09417	.09333	.09250	.09167	.09083	.09000
3	.08925	.08850	.08775	.08700	.08625	.08550	.08475	.08400	.08325	.08250	.08175	.08100
4	.08033	.07965	.07898	.07830	.07763	.07695	.07628	.07560	.07493	.07425	.07358	.07290
5	.07229	.07169	.07108	.07047	.06986	.06926	.06865	.06804	.06743	.06683	.06622	.06561
6	.06506	.06452	.06397	.06342	.06288	.06233	.06178	.06124	.06069	.06014	.05960	.05905
7	.05856	.05807	.05758	.05708	.05659	.05610	.05561	.05512	.05463	.05413	.05364	.05315
8	.05271	.05227	.05182	.05138	.05094	.05050	.05005	.04961	.04917	.04873	.04828	.04784
9	.04744	.04704	.04665	.04625	.04585	.04545	.04505	.04465	.04426	.04386	.04346	.04306
10	.04270	.04234	.04198	.04162	.04126	.04091	.04055	.04019	.03983	.03947	.03911	.03875

20 YEAR LIFE (200% Declining-Balance, Change to Straight-Line)

11	.03843	.03811	.03778	.03746	.03714	.03682	.03649	.03617	.03585	.03553	.03520	.03488
Change to Straight-Line												
12–19	.03486	.03486	.03486	.03486	.03486	.03486	.03486	.03486	.03486	.03486	.03486	.03486
20	.03486	.03486	.03486	.03486	.03486	.03486	.03486	.03486	.03486	.03486	.03486	.03488
21	.03199	.02907	.02617	.02328	.02036	.01744	.01455	.01164	.00872	.00582	.00292	

22 YEAR LIFE (200% Declining-Balance, Change to Straight-Line)

1	.00758	.01515	.02273	.03030	.03788	.04546	05303	.06061	.06818	.07576	.08333	.09091
2	.09022	.08953	.08885	.08816	.08747	.08678	.08609	.08540	.08472	.08403	.08334	.08265
3	.08202	.08140	.08077	.08015	.07952	.07890	.07827	.07764	.07702	.07639	.07577	.07514
4	.07457	.07400	.07343	.07286	.07229	.07173	.07116	.07059	.07002	.06945	.06888	.06831
5	.06779	.06728	.06676	.06624	.06572	.06521	.06469	.06417	.06365	.06314	.06262	.06210
6	.06163	.06116	.06069	.06022	.05975	.05928	.05880	.05833	.05786	.05739	.05692	.05645
7	.05602	.05560	.05517	.05474	.05431	.05389	.05346	.05303	.05260	.05218	.05175	.05132
8	.05093	.05054	.05015	.04976	.04937	.04899	.04860	.04821	.04782	.04743	.04704	.04665
9	.04630	.04594	.04559	.04524	.04488	.04453	.04418	.04382	.04347	.04312	.04276	.04241
10	.04209	.04177	.04145	.04112	.04080	.04048	.04016	.03984	.03952	.03919	.03887	.03855
11	.03826	.03797	.03768	.03738	.03709	.03680	.03651	.03622	.03593	.03563	.03534	.03505
12	.03478	.03452	.03425	.03399	.03372	.03346	.03319	.03292	.03266	.03239	.03213	.03186
Change to Straight-Line												
13–21	.03186	.03186	.03186	.03186	.03186	.03186	.03186	.03186	.03186	.03186	.03186	.03186
22	.03186	.03186	.03186	.03186	.03186	.03186	.03186	.03186	.03186	.03186	.03186	.03186
23	.02921	.02654	.02388	.02124	.01860	.01589	.01326	.01062	.00795	.00530	.00265	

25 YEAR LIFE (200% Declining-Balance, Change to Straight-Line)

1	.00667	.01333	.02000	.02667	.03333	.04000	.04667	.05333	.06000	.06667	.07333	.08000
2	.07947	.07893	.07840	.07787	.07733	.07680	.07627	.07573	.07520	.07467	.07413	.07360
3	.07311	.07262	.07213	.07164	.07115	.07066	.07016	.06967	.06918	.06869	.06820	.06771
4	.06726	.06681	.06636	.06590	.0645	.06500	.06455	.06410	.06365	.06319	.06274	.06229
5	.06188	.06146	.06105	.06063	.06022	.05980	.05939	.05897	.65856	.05814	.05773	.05731
6	.05693	.05655	.05617	.95578	.05540	.05502	.05464	.05426	.05388	.05349	.05311	.05273
7	.05238	.05203	.05168	.05132	.05097	.05062	.05027	.04992	.04957	.04921	.04886	.04851
8	.04819	.04786	.04754	.04722	.04689	.04657	.04625	.04592	.04560	.04528	.04495	.04463
9	.04433	.04404	.04374	.04344	.04314	.04285	.04255	.04225	.04195	.04166	.04136	.04106
10	.04079	.04051	.04024	.03997	.03969	.03942	.03915	.03887	.03860	.03833	.03805	.03778
11	.03753	.03728	.03703	.03677	.03652	.03627	.03602	.03577	.03552	.03526	.03501	.03476
12	.03453	.03430	.03407	.03383	.03360	.03337	.03314	.03291	.63268	.03244	.03221	.03198
13	.03177	.03155	.03134	.03113	.03091	.03070	.03049	03027	.03006	.02985	.02963	.02942
14	.02922	.02903	.02883	.02864	.02844							

Change to Straight-Line

14						.02823	.02822	.02822	.02821	.02820	.02820	.02819
15–24	.02819	.02820	.02821	.02822	.02823	.02823	.02822	.02822	.02821	.02820	.02820	.02819
25	.02819	.02820	.02821	.02822	.02823	.02823	.02822	.02822	.02821	.02820	.02820	.02813
26	.02585	.02350	.02111	.01877	.01643	.01416	.01181	.00939	.00703	.00472	.00229	

28 YEAR LIFE (200% Declining-Balance, Change to Straight-Line)

1	.00595	.01191	.01786	.02381	.02976	.03572	.04167	.04762	.05357	.05953	.06548	.07143
2	.07101	.07058	.07016	.06973	.06931	.06888	.06846	.06803	.06761	.06718	.06676	.06633
3	.06594	.06554	.06515	.06475	.06436	.06396	06357	.06317	.06278	.06238	.06199	.06159
4	.06122	.06086	.06049	.06012	.05976	.05939	.05902	.05866	.05829	.05792	.05756	.05719

28 YEAR LIFE (200% Declining-Balance, Change to Straight-Line)

5	.05685	.05651	.05617	.05583	.05549	.05515	.05480	.05446	.05412	.05378	.05344	.05310
6	.05278	.05247	.05215	.05184	.05152	.05121	.05089	.05057	.05026	.04994	.04963	.04931
7	.04902	.04872	.04843	.04814	.04784	.04755	.04726	.04696	.04667	.04638	.04608	.04579
8	.04552	.04525	.04497	.04470	.04443	.04416	.04388	.04361	.04334	.04307	.04279	.04252
9	.04227	.04201	.04176	.04151	.04125	.04100	.04075	.04049	.04024	.03999	.03973	.03948
10	.03925	.03901	.03878	.03854	.03831	.03807	.03784	.03760	.03737	.03713	.03690	.03666
11	.03644	.03622	.03601	.03579	.03557	.03535	.03513	.03491	.03470	.03448	.03426	.03404
12	.03384	.03364	.03343	.03323	.03303	.03283	.03262	.03242	.03222	.03202	.03181	.03161
13	.03142	.03123	.03105	.03086	.03067	.03048	.03029	.03010	.02992	.02973	.02954	.02935
14	.02918	.02900	.02883	.02865	.02848	.02830	.02813	.02795	.02778	.02760	.02743	.02725
15	.02709	.02693	.02676	.02660	.02644	.02628	.02611	.02595	.02579	.02563	.02546	.02530

Change to Straight-Line

16–27	.02531	.02531	.02531	.02531	.02531	.02531	.02531	.02531	.02531	.02531	.02531	.02531
28	.02531	.02531	.02531	.02531	.02531	.02531	.02531	.02531	.02531	.02531	.02531	.02533
29	.02319	.02109	.01897	.01687	.01475	.01264	.01055	.00847	.00631	.00421	.00211	

30 YEAR LIFE (200% Declining-Balance, Change to Straight-Line)

1	.00556	.01111	.01667	.02222	.02778	.03334	.03889	.04445	.05000	.05556	.06111	.06667
2	.06630	.06593	.06556	.06519	.06482	.06445	.06408	.06371	.06334	.06297	.06260	.06223
3	.06188	.06154	.06119	.06085	.06050	.06016	.05981	.05946	.05912	.05877	.05843	.05808
4	.05776	.05744	.05711	.05679	.05647	.05615	.05582	.05550	.05518	.05486	.05453	.05421
5	.05391	.05361	.05331	.05301	.05271	.05241	.05210	.05180	.05150	.05120	.05090	.05060
6	.05032	.05004	.04976	.04948	.04920	.04892	.04863	.04835	.04807	.04779	.04751	.04723
7	.04697	.04671	.04644	.04618	.04592	.04566	.04539	.04513	.04487	.04461	.04434	.04408
8	.04384	.04359	.04335	.04310	.04286	.04261	.04237	.04212	.04188	.04163	.04139	.04114
9	.04091	.04068	.04046	.04023	.04000	.03977	.03954	.03931	.03909	.03886	.03863	.03840

30 YEAR LIFE (200% Declining-Balance, Change to Straight-Line)

10	.03819	.03797	.03776	.03755	.03733	.03712	.03691	.03669	.03648	.03627	.03605	.03584
11	.03564	.03544	.03524	.03504	.03484	.03465	.03445	.03425	.03405	.03385	.03365	.03345
12	.03326	.03308	.03289	.03271	.03252	.03234	.03215	.03196	.03178	.03159	.03141	.03122
13	.03105	.03087	.03070	.03053	.03035	.03018	.03001	.02983	.02966	.02949	.02931	.02914
14	.02898	.02882	.02866	.02849	.02833	.02817	.02801	.02785	.02769	.02752	.02736	.02720
15	.02705	.02690	.02675	.02660	.02645	.02630	.02614	.02599	.02584	.02569	.02554	.02539
16	.02525	.02511	.02497	.02483	.02469	.02455	.02440	.02426	.02412	.02398	.02384	.02370

Change to Straight-Line

17–29	.02367	.02367	.02367	.02367	.02367	.02367	.02367	.02367	.02367	.02367	.02367	.02367
30	.02367	.02367	.02367	.02367	.02367	.02367	.02367	.02367	.02367	.02367	.02367	.02371
31	.02175	.01978	.01780	.01582	.01385	.01184	.00992	.00796	.00595	.00398	.00202	

33 YEAR LIFE (200% Declining-Balance, Change to Straight-Line)

1	.00505	01010	.01515	.02020	.02525	.03031	.03536	.04041	.04546	.05051	.05556	.06061
2	.06030	.06000	.05969	.05939	.05908	.05878	.05847	.05816	.05786	.05755	.05725	.05694
3	.05665	.05637	.05969	.05579	.05550	.05522	.05493	.05464	.05435	.05407	.05378	.05349
4	.05322	.05295	.05268	.05241	.05214	.05187	.05160	.05133	.05106	.05079	.05052	.05025
5	.05000	.04974	.04949	.04923	.04898	.04873	.04847	.04822	.04796	.04771	.04745	.04720
6	.04696	.04672	.04649	.04625	.04601	.04577	.04553	.04529	.04506	.04482	.04458	.04434
7	.04412	.04389	.04367	.04344	.04322	.04300	.04277	.04255	.04232	.04210	.04187	.04165
8	.04144	.04123	.04102	.04081	.04060	.04039	.04018	.03997	.03976	.03955	.03934	.03913
9	.03893	.03874	.03854	.03834	.03814	.03795	.03775	.03755	.03735	.03716	.03696	.03676
10	.03657	.03639	.03620	.03602	.03583	.03565	.03546	.03527	.03509	.03490	.03472	.03453
11	.03436	.03418	.03401	.03383	.03366	.03349	.03331	.03314	.03296	.03279	.03261	.03244
12	.03228	.03211	.03195	.03178	.03162	.03146	.03129	.03113	.03096	.03080	.03063	.03047
13	.03032	.03016	.03001	.02985	.02970	.02955	.02939	.02924	.02908	.02893	.02877	.02862

33 YEAR LIFE (200% Declining-Balance, Change to Straight-Line)

14	.02848	.02833	.02819	.02804	.02790	.02776	.02761	.02747	.02732	.02718	.02703	.02689
15	.02675	.02662	.02648	.02635	.02621	.02608	.02594	.02580	.02567	.02553	.02540	.02526
16	.02513	.02501	.02488	.02475	.02462	.02450	.02437	.02424	.02411	.02399	.02386	.02373
17	.02361	.02349	.02337	.02325	.02313	.02301	.02289	.02277	02265	.02253	.02241	.02229
18	.02218	.02207	.02195	.02184	.02173							

Change to Straight-Line

18						.02160	.02160	.02160	.02160	.02159	.02159	.02159
19–32	.02159	.02159	.02160	.02160	.02161	.02160	.02160	.02160	.02160	.02159	.02159	.02159
33	.02159	.02159	.02160	.02160	.02161	.02160	.02160	.02160	.02160	.02159	.02159	.02155
34	.01980	.01805	.01615	.01443	.01253	.01088	.00908	.00722	.00538	.00365	.00182	

35 YEAR LIFE (200% Declining-Balance, Change to Straight-Line)

1	.00476	.00952	.01429	.01905	.02381	.02857	.03333	.3809	.04286	04762	.05238	.05714
2	.05687	.05660	.05633	.05605	.05578	.05551	.05524	.05497	.05470	.05442	.05415	.05388
3	.05362	.05337	.05311	.05285	.05260	.05234	.05208	.05183	.05157	.05131	.05106	.05080
4	.05056	.05032	.05008	.04983	.04959	.04935	.04911	.04887	.04863	.04838	.04814	.04790
5	.04767	.04744	.04722	.04699	.04676	.04653	.04630	.04607	.04585	.04562	.04539	.04516
6	.04495	.04473	.04452	.04430	.04409	.04387	.04366	.04344	.04323	.04301	.04280	.04258
7	.04238	.04218	.04197	.04177	.04157	.04137	.04116	.04096	.04076	.04056	.04035	.04015
8	.03996	.03977	.03958	.03939	.03920	.03901	.03881	.03862	.03843	.03824	.03805	.03786
9	.03768	.03750	.03732	.03714	.03696	.03678	.03660	.03642	.03624	.03606	.03588	.03570
10	.03553	.03536	.03519	.03502	.03485	.03468	.03451	.03434	.03417	.03400	.03383	.03366
11	.03350	.03334	.03318	.03302	.03286	.03270	.03254	.03238	.03222	.03206	.03190	.03174
12	.03159	.03144	.03129	.03114	.03099	.03084	.03068	.03053	.03038	.03623	.03008	.02993
13	.02979	.02965	.02950	.02936	.02922	.02908	.02893	.02879	.02865	.02851	.02836	.02822
14	.02809	.02795	.02782	.02768	.02755	.02742	.02728	.02715	.02701	.02688	.02674	.02661

35 YEAR LIFE (200% Declining-Balance, Change to Straight-Line)

15	.02648	.02636	.02623	.02610	.02598	.02585	.02572	.02560	.02547	.02534	.02522	.02509
16	.02497	.02485	.02473	.02461	.02449	.02438	.02426	.02414	.02402	.02390	.02378	.02366
17	.02355	.02344	.02332	.02321	.02310	.02299	.02287	.02276	.02265	.02254	.02242	.02231
18	.02220	.02210	.02199	.02189	.02178	.02168	.02157	.02146	.02136	.02125	.02115	.02104
19	.02094	.02084	.02074	.02064	.02054							

Change to Straight-Line

19						.02040	.02040	.02040	.02039	.02039	.02039	.02039
20–34	.02039	.02039	.02039	.02040	.02040	.02040	.02040	.02040	.02039	.02039	.02039	.02039
35	.02039	.02039	.02039	.02040	.02040	.02040	.02040	.02040	.02039	.02039	.02039	.02033
36	.01867	.01700	.01535	.01356	.01188	.01025	.00855	.00678	.00517	.00344	.00169	

40 YEAR LIFE (200% Declining-Balance, Change to Straight-Line)

1	.00417	.00833	.01250	.01667	.02083	.02500	.02917	.03333	.03750	.04167	.04583	.05000
2	.04979	.04958	.04938	.04917	.04896	.04875	.04854	.04833	.04813	.04792	.04771	.04750
3	.04730	.04711	.04691	.04671	.04651	04632	.04612	.04592	.04572	.04553	.04533	.04513
4	.04494	.04475	.04457	.04438	.04419	.04400	.04381	.04362	.04344	.04325	.04306	.04287
5	.04269	.04251	.04234	.04216	.04198	.04180	04162	04144	.04127	.04109	.04091	.04073
6	.04056	.04039	.04022	.04005	.03988	.03971	.03954	.03937	.03920	.03903	.03886	.03869
7	.03853	.03837	.03821	.03805	.03789	.03773	.03756	.03740	.03724	.03708	.03692	.03676
8	.03661	.03645	.03630	.03615	.03599	.03584	.03569	.03553	.03538	.03523	.03507	.03492
9	.03477	.03463	.03448	.03434	.03419	.03405	.03390	.03375	.03361	.03346	.03332	.03317
10	.03303	.03289	.03276	.03262	.03248	.03234	.03220	.03206	.03193	.03179	.03165	.03151
11	.03138	.03125	.03112	.03098	.03085	.03072	.03059	.03046	.03033	.03019	.03006	.02993
12	.02981	.02968	.02956	.02943	.02931	.02918	.02906	.02893	.02881	.02868	.02856	.02843
13	.02831	.02819	.02808	.02796	.02784	.02772	.02760	.02748	.02737	.02725	.02713	.02701
14	.02690	.02679	.02667	.02656	.02645	.02634	.02622	.02611	.02600	.02589	.02577	.02566

40 YEAR LIFE (200% Declining-Balance, Change to Straight-Line)

15	.02555	.02545	.02534	.02523	.02513	.02502	.02491	02481	.02470	.02459	.02449	.02438
16	.02428	.02418	.02408	.02397	.02387	.02377	.02367	.02357	.02347	.02336	.02326	.02316
17	.02306	.02297	.02287	.02277	.02268	.02258	.02248	.02239	.02229	.02219	.02210	.02200
18	.02191	.02182	.02173	.02163	.02154	.02145	.02136	.02127	.02118	.02108	.02099	.02090
19	.02081	.02073	.02064	.02055	.02047	.02038	.02029	.02021	.02012	.02003	.01995	.01986
20	.01978	.01970	.01961	.01953	.01945	.01937	.01928	.01920	.01912	.01904	.01895	.01887
21	.01879	.01871	.01864	.01856	.01848	.01840	.01832	.01824	.01817	.01809	.01801	.01793
Change to Straight-Line												
22–39	.01793	.01793	.01792	.01793	.01792	.01792	.01793	.01793	.01792	.01792	.01793	.01793
40	.01793	.01793	.01792	.01793	.01792	.01792	.01793	.01793	.01792	.01792	.01793	.01785
41	.01636	.01485	.01351	.01186	.01055	.00905	.00740	.00591	.00454	.00308	.00140	

45 YEAR LIFE (200% Declining-Balance, Change to Straight-Line)

1	.00370	.00741	.01111	.01481	.01852	.02222	.02592	.02963	.03333	.03703	.04074	.04444
2	.04428	.04411	.04395	.04378	.04362	.04346	.04329	.04313	.04296	.04280	.04263	.04247
3	.04231	.04216	.04200	.04184	.04168	.04153	.04137	.04121	.04105	.04090	.04074	.04058
4	.04043	.04028	.04013	.03998	.03983	.03968	.03953	.03938	.03923	.03908	.03893	.03878
5	.03864	.03849	.03835	.03821	.03806	.03792	.03778	.03763	.03749	.03735	.03720	.03706
6	.03692	.03679	.03665	.03651	.03637	.03624	.03610	.03596	.03582	.03569	.03555	.03541
7	.03528	.03515	.03502	.03489	.03476	.03463	.03449	.03436	.03423	.03410	.03397	.03384
8	.03372	.03359	.03347	.03334	.03322	.03309	.03297	.03284	.03272	.03259	.03247	.03234
9	.03222	.03210	.03198	.03186	.03174	.03162	.03150	.03138	.03126	.03114	.03102	.03090
10	.03079	.03067	.03056	.03044	.03033	.03022	.03010	.02999	.02987	.02976	.02964	.02953
11	.02942	.02931	.02920	.02909	.02898	.02888	.02877	.02866	.02855	.02844	.02833	.02822
12	.02812	.02801	.02791	.02780	.02770	.02760	.02749	.02739	.02728	.02718	.02707	.02697
13	.02687	.02677	.02667	.02657	.02647	.02637	.02627	.02617	.02607	.02597	.02587	.02577

45 YEAR LIFE (200% Declining-Balance, Change to Straight-Line)

14	.02567	.02558	.02548	.02539	.02529	.02520	.02510	.02500	.02491	.02481	.02472	.02462
15	.02453	.02444	.02435	.02426	.02417	.02408	.02398	.02389	.02380	.02371	.02362	.02353
16	.02344	.02336	.02327	.02318	.02309	.02301	.02292	.02283	.02274	.02266	.02257	.02248
17	.02240	.02231	.02223	.02215	.02206	.02198	.02190	.02181	.02173	.02165	.02156	.02148
18	.02140	.02132	.02124	.02116	.02108	.02101	.02093	.02085	.02077	.02069	.02061	.02053
19	.02045	.02038	.02030	.02023	.02015	.02008	.02000	.01992	.01985	.01977	.01970	.01962
20	.01955	.01948	.01940	.01933	.01926	.01919	.01911	.01904	.01897	.01890	.01882	.01875
21	.01868	.01861	.01854	.01847	.01840	.01834	.01827	.01820	.01813	.01806	.01799	.01792
22	.01785	.01779	.01772	.01765	.01759	.01752	.01745	.01739	.01732	.01725	.01719	.01712
23	.01706	.01699	.01693	.01687	.01680	.01674	.01668	.01661	.01655	.01649	.01642	.01636
24	.01630	.01624	.01618	.01612	.01606							

Change to Straight-Line

24	.01597	.01597	.01597	.01597	.01597	.01597	.01597					
25–44	.01597	.01597	.01597	.01597	.01597	.01597	.01597	.01597	.01597	.01597	.01597	.01597
45	.01597	.01597	.01597	.01597	.01597	.01597	.01597	.01597	.01597	.01597	.01597	.01591
46	.01460	.01329	.01199	.01070	.00940	.00805	.00674	.00539	.00403	.00264	.00130	

50 YEAR LIFE (200% Declining-Balance, Change to Straight-Line)

1	.00333	.00667	.01000	.01333	.01667	.02000	.02333	.02667	.03000	.03333	.03667	.04000
2	.03987	.03973	.03960	.03947	.03933	.03920	.03907	.03893	.03880	.03867	.03853	.03840
3	.03827	.03814	.03802	.03789	.03776	.03763	.03750	.03737	.03725	.03712	.03699	.03686
4	.03674	.03662	.03649	.03637	.03625	.03613	.03600	.03588	.03576	.03564	.03551	.03539
5	.03527	.03515	.03504	.03492	.03480	.03468	.03456	.03444	.03433	.03421	.03409	.03397
6	.03386	.03374	.03363	.03352	.03340	.03329	.03318	.03306	.03295	.03284	.03272	.03261
7	.03250	.03239	.03229	.03218	.03207	.03196	.03185	.03174	.03164	.03153	.03142	.03131
8	.03121	.03110	.03100	.03089	.03079	.03069	.03058	.03048	.03037	.03027	.03016	.03006

50 YEAR LIFE (200% Declining-Balance, Change to Straight-Line)

9	.02996	.02986	.02976	.02966	.02956	.02946	.02936	.02926	.02916	.02906	.02896	.02886
10	.02876	.02867	.02857	.02848	.02838	.02829	.02819	.02809	.02800	.02790	.02781	.02771
11	.02762	.02753	.02743	.02734	.02725	.02716	.02706	.02697	.02688	.02679	.02669	.02660
12	.02651	.02642	.02634	.02625	.02616	.02607	.02598	.02589	.02581	.02572	.02563	.02554
13	.02546	.02537	.02529	.02520	.02512	.02503	.02495	.02486	.02478	.02469	.02461	.02452
14	.02444	.02436	.02428	.02419	.02411	.02403	.02395	.02387	.02379	.02370	.02362	.02354
15	.02346	.02338	.02331	.02323	.02315	.02307	.02299	.02291	.02284	.02276	.02268	.02260
16	.02253	.02245	.02238	.02230	.02223	.02215	.02208	.02200	.02193	.02185	.02178	.02170
17	.02163	.02156	.02148	.02141	.02134	.02127	.02119	.02112	.02105	.02098	.02090	.02083
18	.02076	.02069	.02062	.02055	.02048	.02042	.02035	.02028	.02021	.02014	.02007	.02000
19	.01993	.01987	.01980	.01973	.01967	.01960	.01953	.01947	.01940	.01933	.01927	.01920
20	.01914	.01907	.01901	.01894	.01888	.01882	.01875	.01869	.01862	.01856	.01849	.01843
21	.01837	.01831	.01825	.01818	.01812	.01806	.01800	.01794	.01788	.01781	.01775	.01769
22	.01763	.01757	.01751	.01745	.01739	.01734	.01728	.01722	.01716	.01710	.01704	.01698
23	.01692	.01687	.01681	.01675	.01670	.01664	.01658	.01653	.01647	.01641	.01636	.01630
24	.01625	.01619	.01614	.01608	.01603	.01598	.01592	.01587	.01581	.01576	.01570	.01565
25	.01560	.01555	.01549	.01544	.01539	.01534	.01528	.01523	.01518	.01513	.01507	.01502
26	.01497	.01492	.01487	.01482	.01477	.01472	.01467	.01462	.01457	.01452	.01447	.01442

Change to Straight-Line

27–49	.01441	.01441	.01441	.01441	.01441	.01441	.01441	.01441	.01441	.01441	.01441	.01441
50	.01441	.01441	.01441	.01441	.01441	.01441	.01441	.01441	.01441	.01441	.01441	.01438
51	.01317	.01198	.01075	.00959	.00836	.00713	.00598	.00477	.00352	.00234	.00117	

60 YEAR LIFE (200% Declining-Balance, Change to Straight-Line)

1	.00278	.00556	.00833	.01111	.01389	.01667	.01944	.02222	.02500	.02778	.03055	.03333
2	.03324	.03315	.03305	.03296	.03287	.03278	.03268	.03259	.03250	.03241	.03231	.03222

60 YEAR LIFE (200% Declining-Balance, Change to Straight-Line)

3	.03213	.03204	.03195	.03186	.03177	.03169	.03160	.03151	.03142	.03133	.03124	.03115
4	.03106	.03098	.03089	.03080	.03072	.03063	.03054	.03046	.03037	.03028	.03020	.03011
5	.03003	.02994	.02986	.02978	.02969	.02961	.02953	.02944	.02936	.02928	.02919	.02911
6	.02903	.02895	.02887	.02879	.02871	.02863	.02854	.02846	.02838	.02830	.02822	.02814
7	.02806	.02798	.02791	.02783	.02775	.02767	.02759	.02751	.02744	.02736	.02728	.02720
8	.02712	.02705	.02697	.02690	.02682	.02675	.02667	.02659	.02652	.02644	.02637	.02629
9	.02622	.02614	.02607	.02600	.02592	.02585	.02578	.02570	.02563	.02556	.02548	.02541
10	.02534	.02527	.02520	.02513	.02506	.02499	.02491	.02484	.02477	.02470	.02463	.02456
11	.02449	.02442	.02436	.02429	.02422	.02415	.02408	.02401	.02395	.02388	.02381	.02374
12	.02367	.02361	.02354	.02348	.02341	.02335	.02328	.02321	.02315	.02308	.02302	.02295
13	.02289	.02282	.02276	.02270	.02263	.02257	.02251	.02244	.02238	.02232	.02225	.02219
14	.02213	.02207	.02201	.02194	.02188	.02182	.02176	.02170	.02164	.02157	.02151	.02145
15	.02139	.02133	.02127	.02121	.02115	.02110	.02104	.02098	.02092	.02086	.02080	.02074
16	.02068	.02063	.02057	.02051	.02045	.02040	.02034	.02028	.02022	.02017	.02011	.02005
17	.01999	.01994	.01988	.01983	.01977	.01972	.01966	.01960	.01955	.01949	.01944	.01938
18	.01933	.01927	.01922	.01916	.01911	.01906	.01900	.01895	.01889	.01884	.01878	.01873
19	.01868	.01863	.01858	.01852	.01847	.01842	.01837	.01832	.01827	.01821	.01816	.01811
20	.01806	.01801	.01796	.01791	.01786	.01781	.01776	.01771	.01766	.01761	.01756	.01751
21	.01746	.01741	.01737	.01732	.01727	.01722	.01717	.01712	.01708	.01703	.01698	.01693
22	.01688	.01684	.01679	.01674	.01670	.01665	.01660	.01656	.01651	.01646	.01642	.01637
23	.01632	.01628	.01623	.01619	.01614	.01610	.01605	.01600	.01596	.01591	.01587	.01582
24	.01578	.01573	.01569	.01564	.01560	.01556	.01551	.01547	.01542	.01538	.01533	.01529
25	.01525	.01521	.01516	.01512	.01508	.01504	.01499	.01495	.01491	.01487	.01482	.01478
26	.01474	.01470	.01466	.01462	.01458	.01454	.01449	.01445	.01441	.01437	.01433	.01429
27	.01425	.01421	.01417	.01413	.01409	.01405	.01401	.01397	.01393	.01389	.01385	.01381
28	.01377	.01373	.01370	.01366	.01362	.01358	.01354	.01350	.01347	.01343	.01339	.01335
29	.01331	.01328	.01324	.01320	.01317	.01313	.01309	.01306	.01302	.01298	.01295	.01291
30	.01287	.01284	.01280	.01277	.01273	.01270	.01266	.01262	.01259	.01255	.01252	.01248
31	.01245	.01241	.01238	.01234	.01231	.01227	.01224	.01220	.01217	.01213	.01210	.01206

60 YEAR LIFE (200% Declining-Balance, Change to Straight-Line)

Change to Straight-Line

32–59	.01205	.01205	.01205	.01205	.01205	.01205	.01205	.01205	.01205	.01205	.01205	.01205
60	.01205	.01205	.01205	.01205	.01205	.01205	.01205	.01205	.01205	.01205	.01205	.01214
61	.01115	.01012	.00911	.00811	.00711	.00604	.00512	.00413	.00306	.00208	.00108	

Case Table

A

ABC Rentals of San Antonio, Inc., 68 TCM 1362, TC Memo. 1994-601, CCH Dec. 50,278(M), aff'd *per curiam*, CA-5 (unpublished opinion), 97-1 USTC ¶50,140, rev'd and rem'd, CA-10, 98-1 USTC ¶50,340 . . . 364

ABCO Oil Corp., 58 TCM 1280, TC Memo. 1990-40, CCH Dec. 46,343(M) . . . 34

A.C. Monk & Company, Inc., CA-4, 82-2 USTC ¶9551 . . . 127A

Abramson, E.D., 86 TC 360, CCH Dec. 42,919 . . . 364

Alabama Coca-Cola Bottling Co., 28 TCM 635, TC Memo. 1969-123, CCH Dec. 29,626(M) . . . 125

Alacare Home Health Services Inc., 81 TCM 1794, TC Memo. 2001-149, CCH Dec. 54,378(M) . . . 307

Arevalo, E.R., 124 TC 244, CCH Dec. 56,026 . . . 74

Atlanta Athletic Club, 61 TCM 2011, TC Memo. 1991-83, CCH Dec. 47,195(M) . . . 5

B

Badger Pipeline Company, 74 TCM 856, TC Memo. 1997-457, CCH Dec. 52,292(M) . . . 125

Bank of Vermont, DC Vt., 88-1 USTC ¶9169 . . . 48

Boddie-Noel Enterprises, Inc., CA-FC, 96-2 USTC ¶50,627 . . . 127; 127A

Brookshire Brothers Holding, Inc., 81 TCM 1799, TC Memo. 2001-150, CCH Dec. 54,379(M) . . . 75

Brown & Williamson Tobacco Corp., DC Ky., 73-1 USTC ¶9317, aff'd *per curiam*, CA-6, 74-1 USTC ¶9271 . . . 127C

Browning Ferris Industries, Inc., 53 TCM 397, TC Memo. 1987-147, CCH Dec. 43,781(M) . . . 360

Brunswick Corporation and Subsidiaries, DC N.D. IL, 2009-1 USTC ¶51,131 . . . 132

Butt, H.E., DC Texas, 2000-2 USTC ¶50,649, 108 FSupp2d 709 . . . 75

C

Campbell, N., TC Summary Opinion 2002-117 . . . 125

Catron, R.E., 50 TC 306, CCH Dec. 28,960 (Acq. 1972-2 CB 1) . . . 127C

Central Citrus Company, 58 TC 365, CCH Dec. 31,403 . . . 127A; 127C

Cincinnati, New Orleans & Tex. Pac. Ry. Co., CtCls, 70-1 USTC ¶9344, 424 F2d 563 . . . 307

Circle K Corporation, 43 TCM 1524, TC Memo. 1982-298, CCH Dec. 39,058(M) . . . 127A

Citizens & Southern Corp., 91 TC 463, CCH Dec. 45,036, aff'd *per curiam*, CA-11, 91-1 USTC ¶50,043 . . . 10; 28

Clajon Gas Co., L.P., 2004-1 USTC ¶50,123 . . . 106

Clinger, W.C., 60 TCM 598, TC Memo. 1990-459, CCH Dec. 46,832(M) . . . 3

Colorado National Bankshares, Inc., 60 TCM 771, TC Memo. 1990-495, CCH Dec. 46,875(M), aff'd, CA-10, 93-1 USTC ¶50,077 . . . 28

Computing & Software, Inc., 64 TC 223, CCH Dec. 33,197 (Acq. 1976-2 CB 1) . . . 10

Comshare, Inc., CA-6, 94-2 USTC ¶50,318 . . . 48

Connecticut Yankee Atomic Power Company, 97-2 USTC ¶50,693, 38 FedCl 721 . . . 3

Consolidated Freightways, CA-9, 83-1 USTC ¶9420, 708 F2d 1385 . . . 127A

Consumers Power, 89 TC 710, CCH Dec. 44,250 . . . 3

Coors Porcelain Co., 52 TC 682, CCH Dec. 29,680, aff'd, CA-10, 70-2 USTC ¶9539 . . . 162

Crane, B.B., SCt, 47-1 USTC ¶9217 . . . 70

D

Daley, D.M., 62 TCM 1197, TC Memo. 1991-555, CCH Dec. 47,732(M) . . . 3

De Cou, 103 TC 80, CCH Dec. 49,998 . . . 162

Dixie Manor, Inc., DC, 79-2 USTC ¶9469, aff'd *per curiam*, 81-1 USTC 9332 . . . 127A

Dougherty Co., P., CA-4, 47-1 USTC ¶9117 . . . 3

Drake II, J.H., DC Ill., 86-2 USTC ¶9746 . . . 266

Drozda, C.E., TC Memo. 1984-19, CCH Dec. 40,926(M) . . . 125

Duaine, L.A., 49 TCM 588, TC Memo. 1985-39, CCH Dec. 41,845(M) . . . 127A

Duke Energy Natural Gas Corporation, CA-10, 99-1 USTC ¶50,449, rev'g, 109 TC 416, CCH Dec. 52,395 . . . 106; 190

E

Eastwood Mall Inc., DC Oh., 95-1 USTC ¶50,236, aff'd, CA-6 (unpublished opinion), 59 F3d 170 (1995) . . . 5

Edinboro Company, DC Pa., 63-2 USTC ¶9759 . . . 5

El Charo TV Rentals, CA-5, 97-1 USTC ¶50,140 . . . 364

Everhardt, C.C., 61 TC 328, CCH Dec. 32,241 . . . 127A

Everson, G., CA-9, 97-1 USTC ¶50,258 . . . 5

F

FedEx Corporation, DC Tenn., 2003-2 USTC ¶50,697, aff'd CA-6 (unpublished opinion), 2005-1 USTC ¶50,186 . . . 125

Film N' Photos, 37 TCM 709, TC Memo. 1978-162, CCH Dec. 35,125(M) . . . 127C

Fox Photo Inc., 60 TCM 85, TC Memo. 1990-348, CCH Dec. 46,709(M) . . . 127C

G

Galazin, R.G., 38 TCM 851, TC Memo. 1979-206, CCH Dec. 36,094(M) . . . 307

Gates, L., DC Pa., 98-1 USTC ¶50,353, aff'd, CA-3 (unpublished opinion), 98-2 USTC ¶50,814 . . . 162

Gladding Dry Goods Co., 2 BTA 336, CCH Dec. 642 . . . 74

Green Forest Manufacturing Inc., TC Memo. 2003-75, CCH Dec. 55,083(M) . . . 75

Greenbaum, L.D., 53 TCM 708, TC Memo. 1987-222, CCH Dec. 43,884(M) . . . 426

Greene, L., 81 TC 132, CCH Dec. 40,390 . . . 364

Grodt and McKay Realty Inc., 77 TC 1221, CCH Dec. 38,472 . . . 74; 126

H

Hable, G.H., 48 TCM 1079, TC Memo. 1984-485, CCH Dec. 41,481(M) . . . 125

Hahn, T., 110 TC 140, CCH Dec. 52,606 (Acq., I.R.B. 2001-42) . . . 488

Hamby, D.L., 56 TCM 783, CCH Dec. 45,204(M) . . . 3

Hamilton Industries, Inc., 97 TC 120, CCH Dec. 47,501 . . . 132

Harrah's Club, CtCls, 81-1 USTC ¶9677 . . . 3

Hart, G.G., 78 TCM 114, TC Memo. 1999-236, CCH Dec. 53,462(M) . . . 127C

Hauptli, Jr., A.J., CA-10, 90-1 USTC ¶50,259 . . . 190

Hawaiian Independent Refinery Inc., CA-FC, 83-1 ustc ¶9141, 697 F2d 1063 . . . 3

Helfand, J.A., 47 TCM 1203, TC Memo. 1984-102, CCH Dec. 41,030(M) . . . 3

Hewlett-Packard, CA-FC, 96-1 USTC ¶50,046 . . . 125

Hillcone Steamship Company, 22 TCM 1096, TC Memo. 1963-220, CCH Dec. 26,265(M) . . . 162

Honeywell Inc. and Subsidiaries, 64 TCM 437, CCH Dec. 48,412(M), aff'd, CA-8 (unpublished opinion), 27 F3d 577 . . . 125

Hospital Corp. of America and Subsidiaries, 109 TC 21, CCH Dec. 52,163 . . . 127; 127A

Hunter, R.L., 46 TC 477, CCH Dec. 28,025 . . . 74

I

Idaho Power Co., SCt, 74-2 USTC ¶9521, 418 US 1 . . . 307

Illinois Cereal Mills, Inc., 46 TCM 1001, TC Memo. 1983-469, CCH Dec. 40,342(M), aff'd, CA-7, 86-1 USTC ¶9371 . . . 127A; 127C

Ingram Industries Inc., 80 TCM 532, TC Memo. 2000-323, CCH Dec. 54,088(M) . . . 125

Iowa 80 Group, Inc. & Subsidiaries, CA-8, 2003-2 USTC ¶50,703, aff'g DC Iowa, 2002-2 USTC ¶50,474 . . . 110

Iowa 80 Group, Inc. & Subsidiaries, CA-8, 2005-1 USTC ¶50,343, aff'g DC Iowa, 2005-1 USTC ¶50,342 . . . 110

IT&S of Iowa, Inc., 97 TC 496, CCH Dec. 47,735 . . . 10; 28

Ithaca Industries, Inc., 97 TC 253, CCH Dec. 47,356, aff'd on another issue, CA-4, 94-1 USTC ¶50,100 . . . 20; 22; 30

J

Jack Kent Cooke, Inc., DC-Va., 96-2 USTC ¶50,483, aff'd per curiam, CA-4 (unpublished opinion), 97-2 USTC ¶ 50,511 . . . 132

JMF, Inc., 67 TCM 3020, TC Memo. 1994-239, CCH Dec. 49,871(M) . . . 125; 190

K

Keller Street Development Company, CA-9, 63-2 USTC ¶9734 . . . 162

King, B.B., 60 TCM 1048, CCH Dec. 46,938(M) . . . 304

King Radio Corporation, Inc., CA-10, 73-2 USTC ¶9766, 486 F2d 1091 . . . 127A

Kiro, Inc., 51 TC 155, CCH Dec. 29,205 (Acq. 1974-2 CB 3) . . . 10

Kittredge, B.R., CA-2, 37-1 USTC ¶9165 . . . 162

Klutz, G.O., 38 TCM 724, TC Memo. 1979-169, CCH Dec. 36,043(M) . . . 300

Kurzet, S.M., 2000-2 USTC ¶50,671 . . . 75

L

La Petite Academy, DC, 95-1 USTC ¶50,193, aff'd, CA-8 (unpublished opinion), 96-1 USTC ¶50,020 . . . 127A

Lane Bryant, Inc., CA-FC, 94-2 USTC ¶50,481 . . . 34

Latimer-Looney Chevrolet, Inc., 19 TC 120, CCH Dec. 19,280 (Acq. 1953-1 CB 5) . . . 5

Lazarus & Co., F. & R., SCt. 39-2 USTC ¶9793 . . . 74

Lemmen, G.B., 77 TC 1326, CCH Dec. 38,510 (Acq. 1983-2 CB 1) . . . 70

Lenington, M.R., 25 TCM 1350, TC Memo. 1966-264, CCH Dec. 28,201(M) . . . 3

Liddle, B.P., 103 TC 285, CCH Dec. 50,060, aff'd, CA-3, 95-2 USTC ¶50,488 . . . 3

L.L. Bean, CA-1, 98-1 USTC ¶50,454 . . . 127C

Lomas Sante Fe, Inc., 74 TC 662, CCH Dec. 37,052, aff'd, CA-9, 82-2 USTC ¶9658 . . . 74

M

Magee-Hale Park-O-Meter Co., 15 TCM 254, TC Memo. 1956-57, CCH Dec. 21,616(M) . . . 26

Maguire/Thomas Partners Fifth and Grand, 89 TCM 799, TC Memo. 2005-34, CCH Dec. 55,939(M) . . . 125

McGrath, M.A., T.C. Memo. 2002-231, CCH Dec. 54,873(M) . . . 126, 304

McManus, J., CA-7, 88-2 USTC ¶9623, 863 F2d 491 . . . 127A

McManus, J., DC, 87-2 USTC ¶9618 . . . 127C

Merchants Refrigerating Co., 60 TC 856, CCH Dec. 32,120 (Acq. 1974-2 CB 3) . . . 127C

Metro National Corporation, 52 TCM 1440, TC Memo. 1987-38, CCH Dec. 43,649(M) . . . 127A

Miller, J., 56 TCM 1242, TC Memo. 1989-66, CCH Dec. 45,485(M) . . . 127A

Minot Federal Savings & Loan Assn., CA-8, 71-1 USTC ¶9131, 435 F2d 1368 . . . 127A

Moore, J.H., 58 TC 1045, CCH Dec. 31,544, aff'd *per curiam*, CA-5, 74-1 USTC ¶9146 . . . 127C

Morris Nachman et al., CA-5, 51-2 USTC ¶9483 . . . 32

Morrison Inc., 51 TCM 748, TC Memo. 1986-29, CCH Dec. 42,963(M) . . . 127A

Munford Inc., CA-11, 88-2 USTC ¶9432 . . . 127C

N

New Gaming Systems, Inc., 82 TCM 794, TC Memo. 2001-277, CCH Dec. 54,520(M) . . . 140

Newark Morning Ledger Co., SCt, 93-1 USTC ¶50,228 . . . 28

Newton Insert Co., 61 TC 570, CCH Dec. 32,439, aff'd *per curiam*, CA-9, 77-1 USTC ¶9132 . . . 26

Norfolk Southern Corp., CA-4, 98-1 USTC ¶50,273, 140 F3d 240 . . . 152

Northen Jr., T.J., T.C. Summary Opinion 2003-113 . . . 125

Northern States Power, CA-8, 98-2 USTC ¶50,671 . . . 3

Norwest Corporation and Subsidiaries, 70 TCM 416, TC Memo. 1995-390, CCH Dec. 50,834(M) . . . 104; 190

Norwest Corporation and Subsidiaries, 111 TC 105, CCH Dec. 52,830 . . . 104; 190

O

O'Shaughnessy, R., CA-8, 2003-1 USTC ¶50,522 . . . 3, 75

Oberman Manufacturing Co., 47 TC 471, CCH Dec. 28,334 . . . 125

1220 Realty Corp., CA-6, 63-2 USTC ¶9703 . . . 74

P

Patton, S.H., 116 TC 206, CCH Dec. 54,307 . . . 304

Penn, M., CA-8, 52-2 USTC ¶9504, cert. denied, 344 US 927 . . . 74

Pierce Estates, 16 TC 1020, CCH Dec. 18,270 . . . 125

Piggly Wiggly Southern Inc., 84 TC 739, CCH Dec. 42,039, aff'd, CA-11, 86-2 USTC ¶9789 . . . 3; 127A

Pontel, G.W., 42 TCM 113, TC Memo. 1981-303, CCH Dec. 37,988(M) . . . 125

Prudential Overall Supply, TC Memo. 2002-103, CCH Dec. 54,723(M) . . . 3

R

Richard S. Miller & Sons, Inc., CtCls, 76-2 USTC ¶9481 . . . 28

RJR Nabisco Inc., 76 TCM 71, TC Memo. 1998-252, CCH Dec. 52,786(M) (Nonacq. I.R.B. 1999-40) . . . 26; 125

Roberts, B.R., 60 TC 861, CCH Dec. 32,121 . . . 127C

Rudolph Investment Corp., 31 TCM 573, TC Memo. 1972-129, CCH Dec. 31,421(M) . . . 5

S

Saginaw Bay Pipeline Co., et al., CA-6, 2003-2 USTC 50,592 . . . 106

Samis, J.M., 76 TC 609, CCH Dec. 37,833 . . . 127A

Sanders, H.K., 75 TC 157, CCH Dec. 37,348 . . . 360

Schrader, E.M. CA-6, 78-2 ustc ¶9824 . . . 3

Scott Paper, 74 TC 137, CCH Dec. 36,920 . . . 127A

Sears Oil Co., Inc., CA-2, 66-1 USTC ¶9384 . . . 3

Selig, B., 70 TCM 1125, TC Memo. 1995-519, CCH Dec. 50,975(M) . . . 3

Simon, R.L., 103 TC 247, CCH Dec. 50,059, aff'd, CA-2, 1995-2 USTC ¶50,552 (Nonacq. I.R.B. 1996-29, 4) . . . 3; 5; 220

Siskiyou Communications 60 TCM 475, TC Memo. 1990-429, CCH Dec. 46,797(M) . . . 3

SMC Corp., CA-6, 82-1 USTC ¶9309 . . . 3

Standard Oil Company (Indiana), 77 TC 349, CCH Dec. 38,141 (1981) . . . 127A

Stark, D.W., 77 TCM 1181, CCH Dec. 53,202(M) . . . 125

Steffens, F.W., CA-11, 83-1 USTC ¶9425 . . . 35

T

Texas Instruments, Inc., CA-5, 77-1 USTC ¶9384 . . . 48

Transamerica Corp., CA-9, 93-2 USTC ¶50,388 . . . 364

Trailmont Park Inc., 30 TCM 871, TC Memo. 1971-212, CCH Dec. 30,950(M) . . . 5

Trentadue, L. 128 TC 91, CCH Dec. 56,886 . . . 118

True, J.D., DC Wyo., 97-2 USTC ¶50,946 . . . 106

Trustmark Corp., 67 TCM 2764, TC Memo. 1994-184, CCH Dec. 49,813(M) . . . 10

Tunnel, R.W., DC Del., 74-1 USTC ¶9122 . . . 5

2554-58 Creston Corp., 40 TC 932, CCH Dec. 26,294 . . . 70

U

Union Pacific Corporation, 91 TC 771, CCH Dec. 44,886 . . . 302

Union Pacific Railroad Co., Inc., CtCls, 75-2 USTC ¶9800, rehearing denied 76-1 USTC ¶9308, 524 F2d 1343, cert. denied 429 US 827 . . . 307

University Country Club, Inc., 64 TC 460, CCH Dec. 33,277 . . . 5

V

Vanalco, Inc., 78 TCM 251, TC Memo. 1999-265, CCH Dec. 53,493(M) . . . 125

W

Waddell, W.R., 86 TC 848, CCH Dec. 43,023, aff'd *per curiam*, CA-9, 88-1 USTC ¶9192 . . . 3; 70

Walgreen Co., 72 TCM 382, TC Memo. 1996-374, CCH Dec. 51,503(M) . . . 75

Warsaw Photographic Associates, Inc., 84 TC 21, CCH Dec. 41,822 . . . 34

W.C. & A.N. Miller Development Co., 81 TC 619, CCH Dec. 40,486 . . . 110

Weirick, 62 TC 446, CCH Dec. 32,668 . . . 127C

Whiteco Indus., Inc., 65 TC 664, CCH Dec. 33,594 . . . 127; 127A; 127C

Wilson, A.M., 41 TCM 381, TC Memo. 1980-514, CCH Dec. 37,407(M) . . . 5

W.K. Co., 56 TC 434, CCH Dec. 30,798, aff'd, CA-7 (unpublished order 5/21/73) . . . 32

Wood, M.H., 61 TCM 2571, TC Memo. 1991-205, CCH Dec. 47,334(M) . . . 3

Finding Lists

Announcements

Announcement	Par. (¶)
99-82, 1999-2 CB 244	104; 191
99-116, I.R.B. 1999-2 CB 763	127
2006-29, 2006-1 CB 879	127D
2008-63, I.R.B. 2008-28	217

General Counsel Memoranda

GCM	Par. (¶)
35693, February 26, 1974	5
36728, May 14, 1976	125
37070, March 30, 1977	127
39443, November 12, 1985	302

IRS Letter Rulings and Technical Advice Memorandums

Ruling No.	Par. (¶)
6606309980A, June 30, 1966	127A
6612301720A, December 30, 1966	127A
7939004, May 30, 1979	5
8102012, September 29, 1980	127A
8248003, September 28, 1981	127C
8424009, March 19, 1984	132
8501006, September 24, 1984	364
8501009, September 28, 1984	127A
8546005, August 20, 1985	302
8630022, April 25, 1986	104
8641006, July 1, 1986	228
8646008, August 5, 1986	162
8711110, December 18, 1986	106
8836002, May 26, 1988	127A
8848039, September 2, 1988	5; 110; 127A
8929047, April 25, 1989	167
9045001, May 3, 1990	152
9101001, September 11, 1990	70
9101003, September 25, 1990	104; 190; 191
9110001, August 2, 1990	70
9126014, March 29, 1991	92; 300
9235004, May 20, 1992	3; 132
9235005, May 20, 1992	125
9323007, March 8, 1993	364
9411002, November 19, 1993	5
9502001, June 30, 1994	106; 190
9502002, June 30, 1994	106; 190
9502003, June 30, 1994	106; 190
9548003, July 31, 1995	190
9708003, October 30, 1996	75
9811004, November 18, 1997	3; 5
9825003, January 30, 1998	125
199305043, May 4, 1993	132
199916040, date not given	3
199921045, April 1, 1999	127
199922033, March 3, 1999	108
199924044, March 24, 1999	127A
199930016, September 27, 1999	125
199937022, June 17, 1999	162
199944006, July 20, 1999	132
199947026, September 29, 1999	124
199950004, August 30, 1999	108
199952010, September 29, 1999	307
200001005, September 10, 1999	126; 162
200012082, December 22, 1999	110
200013038, December 27, 1999	110
200017046, September 10, 1999	110

Ruling No. *Par. (¶)*

200021013, February 17, 2000 5
200022007, February 15, 2000 106
200033002, April 17, 2000 . . . . . . 127A
200041027, July 19, 2000 . . . . 127A
200043016, July 14, 2000 . . . . 5; 125
200046020, August 17, 2000 217
200110001, September 13, 2000 . . . . 127A
200116043, February 13, 2001 5
200122002, January 30, 2001 104
200137026, June 14, 2001 . . . 104; 125; 190
200141026, July 11, 2001 162
200142008, July 5, 2001 150
200147035, August 15, 2001 26
200203009, October 3, 2001 . . . . 127A; 190
200221016, February 13, 2002 190
200227009, March 11, 2002 125
200229021, April 12, 2002 104
200232012, April 26, 2002 190
200236028, June 4, 2002 48
200243002, July 16, 2002 112
200246006, August 15, 2002 125
200252091, October 31, 2002 125
200307087, February 19, 2003 125
200508015, February 25, 2005 106
200526002, May 9, 2005 . . . . . 115; 116
200526019, March 10, 2005 106
200626038, March 3, 2006 . . . . . 127D
200852013, September 24, 2008 74
200912004, December 2, 2008 214
9999-9999-273 152

IRS News Releases

News Release No. *Par. (¶)*

IR-2002-89, July 10, 2002IR-2008-22, February 21, 2008 125
IR-2008-22, February 21, 2008 125

Miscellaneous IRS Documents

Document Type & No. *Par. (¶)*

Chief Counsel Notice 2004-007 . . . . 75, 127

Notices

Notice *Par. (¶)*

87-76, 1987-2 CB 384 150
90-21, 1990-1 CB 332 162
98-45, 1998-2 CB 257 124
2000-4, 2000-1 CB 313 . . . . . . 167; 214
2001-23, 2001-1 CB 911 125
2001-70, 2001-2 CB 437 . . . . 92; 487
2001-74, 2001-2 CB 551 . . . . 92; 487
2003-45, 2003-2 CB 86 92
2004-6, 2004-1 CB 308 307
2006-47, 2006-1 CB 892 . . . . . 106; 364
2006-77, 2006-2 CB 590 . . . . 127G, 127F, 127H, 127I
2007-36, 2007-1 CB 1000 . . . . 127G, 127F, 306
2008-25, I.R.B. 2008-9 . . . . 127G, 127F
2008-67, I.R.B. 2008-32 . . . . 127D; 127G; 306A

Revenue Procedures

Rev. Proc.	Par. (¶)
62-21, 1962-2 CB 418	1, 190; 400; 426
65-13,1965-1 CB 795	1; 402
66-18, 1966-1 CB 646	402
66-39, 1966-2 CB 1244	402
68-27, 1968-2 CB 911	402
68-35, 1968-2 CB 921	402
69-21, 1969-2 CB 303	48; 125
71-25, 1971-2 CB 553	190
72-10, 1972-1 CB 721	190; 406; 485
77-3, 1977-1 CB 535	1
77-10, 1977-1 CB 548	104; 190; 406
81-71, 1981-2 CB 731	74
83-35, 1983-1 CB 745	100; 190; 230; 406; 418; 422
86-14, 1986-1 CB 542	252
87-56, 1987-2 CB 674	1; 100; 104; 190; 191
87-57, 1987-2 CB 687	1; 70; 80; 180
87-58, 1987-2 CB 764	179
88-22, 1988-1 CB 785	190
89-15, 1989-1 CB 816	1; 132; 134; 180
90-10, 1990-1 CB 467	152
90-63, 1990-2 CB 664	26
92-91, 1992-2 CB 503	50
93-51, 1993-2 CB 593	268
94-53, 1994-2 CB 712	200
95-38, 1995-2 CB 397	103
97-10, 1997-1 CB 628	75; 110
97-20, 1997-1 CB 647	200; 204
97-27, 1997-1 CB 680	75
97-30, 1997-1 CB 702	128
97-35, 1997-2 CB 448	26
97-50, 1997-2 CB 525	48
97-58, 1997-2 CB 587	217
98-24, 1998-1 CB 663	200; 204
98-30, 1998-1 CB 930	200; 204
98-39, 1998-1 CB 1320	26
98-47, 1998-2 CB 319	5
98-63, 1998-2 CB 818	217
99-14, 1999-1 CB 413	200; 204
99-38, 1999-2 CB 525	217
2000-18, 2000-1 CB 722	200; 204
2000-48, 2000-2 CB 570	217
2000-50, 2000-2 CB 601	48; 125
2001-19, 2001-1 CB 732	200; 204
2001-28, 2001-1 CB 1156	74
2001-29, 2001-1 CB 1160	74
2001-46, 2001-2 CB 263	106
2001-54, 2001-2 CB 530	217
2002-9, 2002-1 CB 327	75
2002-12, 2002-1 CB 374	125
2002-14, I.R.B. 2002-5	200; 201; 204
2002-17, 2002-1 CB 676	125
2002-19, 2002-1 CB 696	75
2002-27, 2002-1 CB 802	125
2002-33, 2002-1 CB 963	127D
2002-54, 2002-2 C 432	75
2002-61, 2002-2 CB 616	217
2002-65, 2002-2 CB 700	106
2004-11, 2001-1 CB 311	75
2004-20, 2004-1 CB 642	200, 204
2004-23, 2004-1 CB 785	66
2004-36, 2004-1 CB 1063	67
2004-57, 2004-2 CB 498	66
2005-9, 2005-1 CB 303	66
2005-13, 2005-1 CB 759	200; 204
2005-17, 2005-1 CB 797	66
2005-43, 2005-2 CB 107	124A
2005-64, 2005-22 CB 492	217
2005-78, 2005-2 CB 1177	217
2006-12, 2006-1 CB 310	66
2006-16, 2006-1 CB 539	300
2006-18, 2006-1 CB 645	200; 204
2006-37, 2006-2 CB 499	66
2006-43, 2006-2 CB 849	127D; 127E
2006-49, 2006-2 CB 936	217
2007-16, I.R.B. 2007-4	75; 488
2007-30, I.R.B. 2007-18	200; 204
2007-48, 2007-1 CB 1104	125
2007-70, I.R.B. 2007-50	217
2008-22, I.R.B. 2008-12	200
2008-52, I.R.B. 2008-36	26; 75; 110; 344
2008-54, I.R.B. 2008-54	127D; 127E; 127F
2008-65,.R.B. 2008-44	127D
2008-72, I.R.B. 2008-50	217

Rev. Proc.	*Par. (¶)*
2009-16, I.R.B. 2009-6	127D
2009-24, I.R.B. 2009-17	200; 204
2009-33, I.R.B. 2009-29	127D
2009-35, I.R.B. 2009-35	75; 162
2009-50, I.R.B. 2009-45	300; 487

Revenue Rulings

Rev. Rul.	*Par. (¶)*
55-290, 1955-1 CB 320	5
55-540, 1955-2 CB 39	74
60-358, 1960-2 CB 68	10; 364
63-223, 1963-2 CB 100	74
64-273, 1964-2 CB 62	10; 364
65-79, 1965-1 CB 26	127; 127C
65-265, 1965-2 CB 52	5
66-299, 1966-2 CB 14	127A
67-349, 1967-2 CB 48	127A
67-359, 1967-2 CB 9	127A
67-417, 1967-2 CB 49	127A
68-36, 1968-1 CB 357	167
68-193, 1968-1 CB 79	5
68-232, 1968-1 CB 79	3; 228
69-14, 1969-1 CB 26	127A
69-170, 1969-1 CB 28	127
69-487, 1969-2 CB 165	168
69-560, 1969-2 CB 25	104
69-588, 1969-2 CB 137	127A
70-160, 1970-1 CB 7	127A
72-403, 1972-2 CB 102	5
73-357, 1973-2 CB 40	104
74-265, 1974-1 CB 56	5
74-391, 1974-2 CB 9	127A
74-530, 1974-2 CB 188	74
75-34, 1995-1 CB 271	5
75-77, 1975-1 CB 7	127A
75-78, 1975-1 CB 8	127A
75-178, 1975-1 CB 9	127A
77-8, 1977-1 CB 3	127C
77-270, 1977-2 CB 79	5
77-362, 1977-2 CB 8	127A
77-476, 1977-2 CB 5	106; 190; 191
78-28, 1978-1 CB 61	364
79-183, 1979-1 CB 44	127A; 127C
79-285, 1979-2 CB 91	3; 26; 364
80-93, 1980-1 CB 50	5
80-127, 1980-1 CB 53	190
80-151, 1980-1 CB 7	127A
80-311, 1980-2 CB 5	162
81-66, 1981-1 CB 19	104
81-133, 1981-1 CB 21	302
82-22, 1982-1 CB 33	483
83-146, 1983-2 CB 17	127A
86-129, 1986-2 CB 48	208
88-99, 1988-2 CB 33	5
89-7, 1989-1 CB 178	300
89-23, 1989-1 CB 85	26; 125
89-62, 1989-1 CB 78	140; 364
90-9, 1990-1 CB 46	152
91-46, 1991-2 CB 358	58
92-80, 1992-2 CB 57	125
94-38, 1994-1 CB 35	5
95-52, 1995-2 CB 27	102; 104; 364
97-29, 1997-2 CB 22	110
98-25, 1998-1 CB 998	5
2000-4, 2000-1 CB 331	125
2000-7, 2000-1 CB 712	162
2001-4, 2001-1 CB 295	125
2001-20, 2001-1 CB 1143	126
2001-60, 2001-2 CB 587	5
2002-9, 2002-1 614	125
2003-37, 2003-1 CB 717	125
2003-54, 2003-1 CB 982	125
2003-81, 2003-2 CB 126	5; 140; 190
2004-18, 2004-1 CB 509	5
2004-58, 2004-1 CB 1043	67

Quick Reference Tables—Vehicles With GVWR Exceeding 6,000 Pounds and Trucks With Bed Length Less Than 6 Feet

Trucks (including SUVs that are considered trucks) and vans with a gross vehicle weight rating (GVWR) greater than 6,000 pounds are not subject to the annual depreciation limitations applicable to passenger automobiles. See ¶ 200.

Effective for vehicles placed in service after October 22, 2004 and that are not subject to the caps, the Code Sec. 179 expensing allowance is limited to $25,000 in the case of (1) an SUV, (2) a van that does not seat more than 9 persons behind the passenger seat, and (3) a truck with an interior cargo bed length less than 6 feet. Most cargo vans are exempt from the $25,000 limit. See, below.

Table I below lists trucks in excess of 6,000 GVWR.

Table II below lists SUVs in excess of 6,000 GVWR.

Table III below lists vans in excess of 6,000 GVWR.

Table IV below lists trucks in excess of 6,000 GVWR with an interior bed length under 6 feet.

These tables were compiled by CCH Law Editors primarily from information obtained at carsdirect.com and do not necessarily include all qualifying vehicles. Tables I, II, and III only list model years 2002-2010. Table IV only lists model years 2004-2010. Information for earlier years may be obtained at carsdirect.com by clicking on the research tab.

Taxpayers should always independently verify the GVWR, chassis construction, and bed length of a truck before making any purchase or claiming exemption from the depreciation limitations.

Requirement that SUVs must be built on truck chassis to be considered truck has changed. In Rev. Proc. 2003-75, the IRS announced a separate set of depreciation limitations for trucks or vans which do not weigh more than 6,000 pounds. Within this Revenue Procedure, the IRS defined a vehicle as a truck or van only if it is built on a "truck chassis." SUVs and vans that are built on a car chassis, therefore, did not fall within this definition.

Although Rev. Proc. 2003-75 (Section 2.01) states that the definition applies "for purposes of this revenue procedure," the IRS used the same definition in the instructions to Form 4562 and in IRS Publication 463 in the context of determining whether an SUV with a GVWR in excess of 6000 pounds is a truck or a van. By extending the definition in this manner, the IRS seemed to imply that SUVs and vans built on a car chassis (i.e., unibody) were not eligible for the exemption from the annual depreciation caps under the luxury car rules.

In its update of the depreciation caps for 2008 (Rev. Proc. 2008-22) the language defining an SUV built on a truck chassis as a truck was dropped. CCH contacted the IRS and was told informally that this definition was intended as a safe harbor and not to exclude unibody vehicles from truck classification. IRS Publications and Form instructions have now been revised to eliminate any implication that an SUV categorization as a truck is based solely on its platform type. According to the IRS, the determination of whether an SUV is a truck should be based on the manufacturer's classification of the vehicle in accordance with applicable Department of Transportation Standards.

Unfortunately, the Department of Transportation appears to provide several definitions of a truck for various purposes. The question then arises: Which definition should apply for purposes of the Code Sec. 280F depreciation caps?

The best answer may be to use the definition of a truck that applies for purposes of the gas guzzler tax under Code Sec. 4064. First, consistent definitions of the same term should be used within the Internal Revenue Code whenever possible. More importantly, however, Code Sec. 4064(b)(1); and Code Sec. 280F(d)(5) share an essentially common definition of the term passenger automobiles, which is also included in the regulations at Reg. § 1.280F-6(c) and Reg. § 48.4064-1(b)(3). The gas guzzler tax does not apply to nonpassenger automobiles, which includes light trucks. Reg. § 48.4064-1(b)(3)(iv) states that the definition of a light truck for gas guzzler tax purposes is contained at 49 CFR 523.5 (1978).

Those regulations, which are issued by the National Highway Traffic Safety Administration (an agency of the DOT) in connection with CAFÉ (Corporate Average Fuel Economy) standards define a light truck as a four-wheel vehicle that is designed for off-road operation (has four-wheel drive or is more than 6,000 lbs. GVWR and has physical features consistent with those of a truck); or that is designed to perform at least one of the following functions: (1) transport more than 10 people; (2) provide temporary living quarters; (3) transport property in an open bed; (4) permit greater cargo-carrying capacity than passenger-carrying volume; or (5) can be converted to an open bed vehicle by removal of rear seats to form a flat continuous floor with the use of simple tools.

Applying this definition, virtually every, if not all, heavy SUVs qualify as light trucks exempt from the gas guzzler tax. Annual lists of vehicles subject to the gas guzzler tax are located on the Environmental Protection Agency's website at http://www.epa.gov/fueleconomy/guzzler/index.htm

Given the absence of any specific IRS definition of a truck for purposes of Code Sec. 280F (despite the specific regulatory authority granted in Code Sec. 280F(d)(5)(B)(iii)), it seems unlikely that the IRS would retroactively apply any definition that it may ultimately adopt. Thus, it appears reasonable to claim exemption from the depreciation caps if the manufacturer has or is entitled to categorize an SUV in excess of 6,000 GVWR as a light truck for purposes of the gas guzzler tax.

$25,000 Code Section 179 limitation on heavy SUVs, heavy trucks with a cargo bed under 6 feet in length, and certain heavy vans placed in service after October 22, 2004. Effective for vehicles placed in service after October 22, 2004, the maximum Code Sec. 179 expense allowance that may be claimed on a "sport utility vehicle" that is exempt from the luxury car depreciation caps is limited to $25,000 (Code Sec. 179(b)(6), as added by the American Jobs Creation Act of 2004).

The term sport utility vehicle is defined as any 4-wheeled vehicle that is primarily designed or which can be used to carry passengers over public streets, roads, or highways, which is not subject to the depreciation limitations, and which is rated at not more than 14,000 pounds gross vehicle weight. Because this definition is broad enough to encompass most trucks, an exception is made for vehicles which have an open cargo area of at least 6 feet in interior length or a capped cargo area of that length if the cargo area was designed for use as an open area and is not readily accessible directly from the passenger compartment.

The definition of a sport utility vehicle also encompasses vans. Exceptions, however, are made for a vehicle (1) designed to have a seating capacity of more than 9 passengers behind the driver's seat (i.e., certain large commuter vans) or (2) which has an integral enclosure, fully enclosing the driver compartment, does not have seating behind the driver's seat and has no body section protruding more than

30 inches ahead of the leading edge of the windshield (i.e. certain cargo vans). See ¶ 201 for additional details.

GVWR defined. Gross Vehicle Weight Rating is the maximum allowable weight of a fully loaded vehicle (i.e., weight of vehicle, including vehicle options, passengers, cargo, gas, oil, coolant etc.). Generally, the GVWR is equal to the sum of the vehicle's curb weight and payload capacity. The gross vehicle weight rating is located on the vehicle's Safety Compliance Certification Label, which is generally located on the left front door lock facing or the door latch post pillar.

TABLE I — TRUCKS WITH GVWR IN EXCESS of 6,000 LBS.

Cadillac trucks in excess of 6,000 pounds

Escalade EXT (2002 - 2010) (beds under 6', see Table IV)

Chevrolet trucks in excess of 6,000 pounds

Avalanche (2002 - 2010) (beds under 6', see Table IV)

Silverado (2002 - 2010) (certain beds under 6', see Table IV)

SSR (2003 - 2006) (beds under 6', see Table IV) (discontinued in 2007)

Dodge trucks in excess of 6,000 pounds

Dakota (certain models) (certain beds under 6', see Table IV)

2002 - All quad cabs

2003 — All quad cabs and all club cabs (4x2 and 4x4)

2004 — All quad cabs and all 4 x 4 club cabs

2005 - 2008 — All quad cabs and all club cabs

2009 - 2010 — All models

Ram (2002 - 2010) (certain beds under 6', see Table IV)

Ford trucks in excess of 6,000 pounds

F-150 (2002 - 2010) (certain beds under 6', see Table IV)

F-250 (2002 - 2010)

F-350 (2002 - 2010)

F-450 (2008 - 2010)

GMC trucks in excess of 6,000 pounds

Sierra 1500, 2500, 3500 (2002 - 2010) (certain Sierra 1500 beds under 6', see Table IV)

Honda trucks in excess of 6,000 pounds

Ridgeline (2006 - 2010) (bed under 6')

Hummer trucks in excess of 6,000 pounds

H2 SUT (2005 - 2010) (bed under 6')

H3T (2009 - 2010) (bed under 6')

Lincoln trucks in excess of 6,000 pounds

Blackwood Pickup (2002)

Mark LT (2006 - 2008) (bed under 6') (discontinued)

Mitsubishi trucks in excess of 6,000 pounds

Raider (2006 - 2009) (discontinued) (certain beds under 6', see Table IV)

Nissan trucks in excess of 6,000 pounds

Titan (2004 - 2010) (certain beds under 6', see Table IV)

Toyota trucks in excess of 6,000 pounds

Tundra

2007 - 2010 (all models exceed 6,000 lbs GVWR)

2005 and 2006 —All models qualify except (1) Base V-6 2 dr. 4x2 Regular Cab and (2) SR5 V-6 4 dr. 4x2 Access Cab

2004—All models qualify except (1) models with Access Cab Stepside (however, some websites now report a GVWR of 6010), (2) Base 2dr 4x2 regular cab, (3) SR5 V-6 4dr 4x2 Access Cab (V-8 version qualifies), and (4) SR5 V-6 4dr 4x4 Access Cab* (GVW is exactly 6,000 pounds (V-8 version qualifies))

2003—All models qualify except (1) Base 2dr 4x2 Regular Cab, (2) SR5 V-6 4dr 4x2 Access Cab (V-8 version qualifies), and (3) SR5 V-6 4dr 4x4 Access Cab* (GVW is exactly 6,000 pounds (V-8 version qualifies))

2002—All models qualify except (1) Base 2dr 4x2 Regular Cab, (2) SR5 V-6 4dr 4x2 Access Cab (V-8 version qualifies), and (3) SR5 V-6 4dr 4x4 Access Cab* (GVW is exactly 6,000 pounds (V-8 version qualifies))

TABLE II— SUVS AND CROSSOVERS IN EXCESS OF 6,000 LBS. GVWR

Audi suvs in excess of 6,000 pounds

Q7 (2007 - 2010)

BMW suvs in excess of 6,000 pounds

X5 (2002 - 2010)

Cadillac suvs in excess of 6,000 pounds

Escalade, Escalade ESV, Escalade Hybrid (2002 - 2010)

SRX (2004 - 2009) (2010 model no longer exceeds 6,000 pounds)

Chevrolet suvs in excess of 6,000 pounds

Suburban 1500, 2500 (2002 - 2010)

Tahoe, Tahoe Hybrid (2002 - 2010)

TrailBlazer Ext (2002 - 2006)

TrailBlazer SS (2007 - 2009) (discontinued)

Traverse (2009 - 2010)

Chrysler suvs in excess of 6,000 pounds

Aspen (2008 - 2009)

Dodge suvs in excess of 6,000 pounds

Durango, Durango Hybrid (2002 - 2009)

Ford suvs in excess of 6,000 pounds

Excursion (2002 - 2005 (discontinued in 2006))

Expedition (2002 - 2010)

Explorer (2006 - 2010)

---

* A vehicle must have a GVWR in excess of 6,000 pounds to qualify for exemption from caps.

Explorer Sport Trac (2007 - 2010)

Flex AWD (2009 - 2010)

GMC suvs in excess of 6,000 pounds

Acadia (2007 - 2010)

Envoy XL (2002 - 2006)

Envoy XUV (2004, 2005, discontinued in 2006)

Envoy Denali (2005 - 2009) (discontinued in 2010)

Yukon I (2002 - 2010)

Honda suvs in excess of 6,000 pounds

Pilot 4x4 (2009 - 2010)

Hummer suvs in excess of 6,000 pounds

Hummer H1 (2003 - 2006) (discontinued in 2007)

Hummer H2 (2003 - 2010)

Hummer H3 (2008 - 2010; 6001 lbs) (note: 2006 and 2007 models are less than 6,000 pounds)

Infiniti

QX56 (2005 - 2010)

Isuzu suvs in excess of 6,000 pounds

Ascender (2003 all models, 2004 - 2006 (7-passenger models), no 2007/2008 models qualify)

Jeep suvs in excess of 6,000 pounds

Grand Cherokee (2009 - 2010) (all models other than Limited & Laredo)

Grand Cherokee (2005 - 2008) (all models other than Laredo)

Commander (2006 - 2010)

Kia suvs in excess of 6,000 pounds

Borrego (certain EX V6 and EX V8 models) (2009) (2010 data not available)

Land Rover suvs in excess of 6,000 pounds

Discovery (2002 - 2004, discontinued in 2005)

LR3 (2005 - 2009) (discontinued in 2010)

LR4 (2010)

Range Rover (2002 - 2010)

Range Rover Sport (2006 - 2010)

Lexus suvs in excess of 6,000 pounds

GX470 (2004 - 2009)

2003 GX470 does not qualify per manufacturer's recall

LX470 (2002 - 2007)

LX570 (2008 - 2010)

Lincoln suvs in excess of 6,000 pounds

Aviator (2003 - 2005)

MKT (2010)

Navigator (2002 - 2010)

Mazda suvs in excess of 6,000 pounds

CX-9 (certain models below))

Touring AWD (2007 - 2010)

Grand Touring AWD (2007 - 2010)

Sport AWD (2007 - 2010)

Mercedes-Benz suvs in excess of 6,000 pounds

G55 (2004 - 2005, 2007 - 2010)

G500 (2002 - 2008)

G550 (2009)

GL 320 (2007 - 2010)

GL 350 (2010)

GL 450 (2007 - 2010)

GL 550 (2008 - 2010)

ML55 (2002, 2003)

ML63 (2007 - 2010)

ML320 (2007 - 2010)

ML320 (2002, 2003)

ML350 (2006 - 2010)

ML350 (2003, 2004, 2005)

ML 500 (2006 - 2007)

ML500 (2002-2005)

ML 550 (2008 - 2010)

R63 (2007)

R320 (2007 - 2010)

R350 (2006 - 2010)

R500 (2006 - 2007)

Mercury suvs in excess of 6,000 pounds

Mountaineer (2006 - 2010)

Mitsubishi suvs in excess of 6,000 pounds

Montero (2003, 2004, 2005) (2002 and 2006 models have GVWR less than 6,000)

Montero Sport does not qualify

Nissan suvs in excess of 6,000 pounds

Armada (2005 - 2010)

Pathfinder (2008)

Pathfinder Armada (2004)

Porsche suvs in excess of 6,000 pounds

Cayenne (2003 - 2006; 2008 - 2010)

Saab suvs in excess of 6,000 pounds

9-7x (2005 - 2009) (discontinued)

Saturn

Outlook (2007 - 2009) (discontinued)

Toyota suvs in excess of 6,000 pounds

4Runner

2010 all models

2005 - 2009—SR5 Sport V8 4x4; SR5 V8 4x4; Limited V8 4x4

Land Cruiser (2002 - 2010)

Sequoia (2002 - 2010)

Volkswagen suvs in excess of 6,000 pounds

Touareg (2004 - 2010)

Volvo suvs in excess of 6,000 pounds

XC90 (certain models below)

2003—T6 A SR AWD

2004—2.5 T A AWD and T6 A AWD

2005—V8 AWD SR 4dr

2006 - 2010—V8 4dr AWD

TABLE III— VANS IN EXCESS OF 6,000 LBS GVWR

Chevrolet vans in excess of 6,000 pounds

Astro (certain passenger models listed below)

2002—LS all-wheel drive passenger van

2002, 2003, 2004, 2005—LT with 1SE all wheel drive passenger van

2003, 2004, 2005—Base all-wheel drive passenger van

2003, 2004, 2005—LS with 1SC all wheel drive passenger van

Express (2002-2010)

Express LT (2002)

Dodge vans in excess of 6,000 pounds

Ram Van (1500, 2500, 3500) (2002, 2003)

Ram Wagon Van (1500, 2500, 3500) (2002)

Sprinter Van (2500, 3500) (2003 - 2009) (discontinued in 2010)

Ford vans in excess of 6,000 pounds

Econoline

E-150 (2002 - 2010)

E-250 (2002 - 2010)

E-350 (2002 - 2010)

GMC vans in excess of 6,000 pounds

Safari (certain models)

2002—SLE all-wheel drive passenger van

2002—SLT with 1SE all-wheel drive passenger van

2003, 2004, 2005—Base all-wheel drive passenger van

2003, 2004, 2005—SLE with 1SC all-wheel drive passenger van

2003, 2004, 2005—SLT with 1SE all-wheel drive passenger van

Savanna (2002 - 2009)

TABLE IV— TRUCKS IN EXCESS OF 6,000 LBS GVWR WITH BED LENGTH UNDER 6 FT. ($25,000 Expensing Limit Applies)

Cadillac trucks with short bed

Escalade EXT (2004 - 2010)

Chevrolet trucks with short bed

Avalance (2004 - 2010)

SSR (2004-2006) (discontinued in 2007)

Silverado 1500 certain crew cabs and certain extended cabs (2006 - 2010)

Silverado 1500 crew cabs (2004 - 2005)

Dodge trucks with short bed

Dakota quad cabs (2004-2008)

Dakota crew cabs (2009 - 2010)

Ram 1500 crew cabs (2010)

Ram 1500 (certain models) (2004-2009)

Ford trucks with short bed

Explorer Sport Trac (2007 - 2010)

F-150 Super Cab Styleside with 5.5 foot box (2004 - 2010)*

F-150 SuperCrew Cab Styleside with 5.5 foot box (2004 - 2010)

*Super Cab and Super Crew Cab Stylesides are available in 5.5, 6.5, and 8.5 boxes

GMC trucks with short bed

Sierra 1500 Crew Cabs (2004 - 2010)

Sierra 1500 Hybrid Crew Cabs (2009 - 2010)

Sierra Classic 1500 Crew Cabs (2007)

Sierra 1500 Extended Cabs with 5.75 box (2006 - 2009)

Sierra Classic 1500 Extended Cabs with 5.75 box (2007)

Sierra Denali (2005 - 2010)

Honda trucks with short bed

Ridgeline (2006 - 2010)

Hummer trucks with short bed

H2 SUT (2005 - 2010)

H3T (2009 - 2010)

Lincoln trucks with short bed

Mark LT (2006 - 2008) (discontinued)

Mitsubishi trucks with short bed

Raider Double Cabs (2006-2009)

Nissan trucks with short bed

Titan Crew Cabs with "standard beds" (2008 - 2010)

Titan Crew Cabs (all models) (2004-2007)

Primary sources of information: http://www.carsdirect.com, http://www.autos.yahoo.com, and http://autos.aol.com.

Quick Reference Table—State Bonus Depreciation Conformity

IRC § 167 allows a deduction from federal taxable income for the exhaustion, wear and tear of property used in a trade or business, or of property held for the production of income. Under the Modified Accelerated Cost Recovery System (MACRS) and the Accelerated Cost Recovery System (ACRS) of IRC § 168, the cost or other basis of an asset is generally recovered over a specific recovery period. MACRS applies to tangible property generally placed in service after 1986 and the Accelerated Cost Recovery System (ACRS) applies to property placed in service after 1980 and before 1987.

The federal Job Creation and Worker Assistance Act of 2002 (JCWAA) (P.L. 107-147) allowed taxpayers an additional first-year depreciation deduction under IRC § 168(k) equal to 30% of the adjusted basis of qualified property acquired after September 10, 2001 and placed in service before May 6, 2003. The federal Jobs and Growth Tax Relief Reconciliation Act of 2003 (JGTRRA) (P.L. 108-27) increased the additional first-year depreciation allowance to 50% for qualified property acquired after May 5, 2003 and placed in service before January 1, 2005. The American Jobs Creation Act of 2004 (AJCA) (P.L. 108-357) extended the placed in service date to January 1, 2006, for certain property subject to the uniform capitalization rules and a long production period. The AJCA also extended bonus depreciation to noncommercial aircraft and shortened recovery periods for qualified leasehold improvements and restaurant property. The Economic Stimulus Act of 2008 (P.L. 110-185) provides qualifying taxpayers 50% first-year bonus depreciation of the adjusted basis of qualifying property placed in service after December 31, 2007, and before January 1, 2009. The American Recovery and Reinvestment Tax Act of 2009 (P.L. 111-5) extends the 50% first-year bonus depreciation allowance to qualifying property acquired and placed in service before January 1, 2010.

This chart shows the tax treatment by each state and the District of Columbia of federal depreciation under IRC § 167, and IRC § 168, including bonus deprecation under IRC § 168(k). Many states follow federal depreciation rules, but require adjustments to taxable income for bonus depreciation.

States that do not impose a corporate income tax are not included in this chart.

State	Answer	Comments
Alabama ¶ 10-515, ¶ 10-670	Addition required for federal bonus depreciation claimed in tax year 2008. No adjustments to federal deduction required for prior tax years.	
Alaska ¶ 10-515, ¶ 10-525, ¶ 10-600	Addition by oil and gas producers and pipelines required for federal deduction. Subtraction by oil and gas producers and pipelines allowed for depreciation based on federal provisions in effect on June 30, 1981, or financial statement depreciation. No other adjustments to federal deduction, including bonus depreciation, required.	Conformity with 2009 American Recovery Act bonus depreciation has not yet been addressed by the legislature.

State	Answer	Comments
Arizona ¶ 10-670, ¶ 10-900	Addition required for federal deduction, including bonus depreciation. Subtraction allowed for depreciation computed as if bonus depreciation had not been elected for federal purposes.	
Arkansas ¶ 10-670, ¶ 10-900	Subtraction allowed for depreciation computed using federal provisions in effect on January 1, 2009, without regard to bonus depreciation, for property purchased in tax years beginning after 2008. Subtraction allowed for depreciation computed using federal provisions in effect on January 1, 1999, without regard to bonus depreciation, for property purchased in tax years beginning prior to 2008.	
California ¶ 10-670, ¶ 10-900	Addition required if federal deduction exceeds allowable state deduction due to state differences, including: federal bonus depreciation and accelerated depreciation under ACRS and MACRS recovery systems. Subtraction allowed if state deduction exceeds federal deduction due to state differences, including depreciation computed using pre-1981 federal provisions and additional first-year depreciation under state provisions.	Adjustments computed on Form 3885.
Colorado ¶ 10-515, ¶ 10-600	No adjustments to federal deduction, including bonus depreciation, required.	
Connecticut ¶ 10-670, ¶ 10-900	Addition required for federal bonus depreciation. Subtraction allowed for depreciation computed without regard to federal bonus depreciation.	Subtraction adjustment computed on Form CT-1120 ATT.
Delaware ¶ 10-515, ¶ 10-600	No adjustments to federal deduction, including bonus depreciation, required.	Conformity with 2009 American Recovery Act bonus depreciation has not yet been addressed by the legislature.
District of Columbia ¶ 10-900	Subtraction allowed for depreciation computed without regard to federal bonus depreciation.	Federal depreciation form and statement showing computation must be attached to state return.

State	Answer	Comments
Florida ¶ 10-670, ¶ 10-900	Addition required for federal bonus depreciation on property acquired after December 31, 2007, and before January 1, 2010. Subtraction allowed equal to 1/7 of addback amount in first and succeeding six tax years. No adjustments to federal deduction, including bonus depreciation, required for tax years prior to 2008.	
Georgia ¶ 10-670, ¶ 10-900	Addition required for amount of federal deduction, including bonus depreciation and special depreciation provisions relating to: New York Liberty Zone, Gulf Opportunity Zone and Kansas Disaster Area property; qualified reuse and recycling property; federal disaster area property after 2007 and before 2010; and certain retail space improvements, qualified restaurant property and new farm machinery. Subtraction allowed for depreciation computed on a separate basis using Form 4562 to account for state and federal depreciation differences.	Federal and state depreciation forms must be attached to state return. Conformity with 2009 American Recovery Act enhanced deduction limits has not yet been addressed by the legislature.
Hawaii ¶ 10-670, ¶ 10-900	Addition required for federal deduction relating to federal bonus depreciation and depreciation of property on Native American Indian reservations. Subtraction allowed using federal guidelines in effect before federal bonus depreciation provisions.	Adjustment computed by completing federal depreciation form. Federal form and any worksheet showing computation of adjustments must be attached to state return.
Idaho ¶ 10-670, ¶ 10-900	No adjustments to federal deduction, including 2008 federal Economic Stimulus Act bonus depreciation, required for tax years after 2007. Addition and subtraction adjustments required for federal bonus depreciation claimed on property acquired after September 10, 2001, and before December 31, 2007.	Adjustments in tax years prior to 2008 computed by completing and attaching federal depreciation form or detailed computation.

State	Answer	Comments
Illinois ¶ 10-670, ¶ 10-900	Addition required for federal bonus depreciation. Subtraction allowed for tax years after 2000 and before 2006 equal to 42.9% of regular depreciation until bonus depreciation disallowance has been claimed. For tax years after 2005, subtraction allowed equal to 42.9% of regular depreciation on property for which 30% bonus depreciation was taken and 100% of regular depreciation on property for which 50% bonus depreciation deduction was taken.	Adjustments computed on Form IL-4562, which must be attached to state return.
Indiana ¶ 10-670, ¶ 10-900	Addition required for federal bonus depreciation. Subtraction allowed for depreciation computed without regard to bonus depreciation.	
Iowa ¶ 10-670, ¶ 10-900	Addition required for federal deduction relating to: 50% bonus depreciation for assets acquired after December 31, 2007, but before January 1, 2009; 30% federal bonus depreciation for assets acquired after September 10, 2001, but before May 6, 2003; depreciation of safe harbor lease property; and depreciation of speculative shell buildings. No other adjustments to federal deduction, including 50% bonus depreciation for assets acquired after May 5, 2003, but before January 1, 2005, required.	Adjustment computed on Schedule IA 4562A. 2009 American Recovery Act bonus depreciation provision has not been adopted under current IRC conformity or depreciation provision.
Kansas ¶ 10-515	Addition required for federal deduction relating to depreciation of buildings for which disabled access credit was claimed, and depreciation of carbon dioxide capture, sequestration, or utilization machinery and equipment effective for tax years beginning after 2007 if state election was made to claim first-year accelerated depreciation. No other adjustments to federal deduction, including bonus depreciation, required.	
Kentucky ¶ 10-670, ¶ 10-900	Addition required for federal deduction relating to federal bonus depreciation and depreciation by purchaser-lessors on safe harbor lease property. Subtraction allowed relating to depreciation using federal provisions in effect on December 31, 2001 and depreciation by seller-lessees on safe harbor lease property.	Adjustment computed by converting federal form and attaching to state return.

State	Answer	Comments
Louisiana ¶ 10-515, ¶ 10-600	No adjustments to federal deduction, including bonus depreciation, required.	Conformity with 2009 American Recovery Act bonus depreciation has not yet been addressed by the legislature.
Maine ¶ 10-670, ¶ 10-900	Addition required for federal bonus depreciation. Subtraction allowed relating to: depreciation for taxable years beginning after 2008 computed as though bonus depreciation had not been claimed on property placed in service after 2007; 5% of addition modification for property placed in service in 2003, 2004, and 2005 beginning in tax year following year property was placed in service, with remaining 95% of modification recovered evenly over remainder of asset's life beginning in year 3; and equal amounts of addition modification for property placed in service in 2002 over remainder of asset's life beginning in 2004 tax year.	
Maryland ¶ 10-670, ¶ 10-900	Addition required if federal deduction exceeds allowable state deduction due to decoupling from federal bonus depreciation provisions and higher depreciation deduction for certain heavy duty SUV's. Subtraction allowed if state deduction exceeds federal deduction.	Adjustments computed on Form 500 DM.
Massachusetts ¶ 10-670, ¶ 10-900	Addition required for federal bonus depreciation.	
Michigan ¶ 10-515, ¶ 10-670	Addition of federal bonus depreciation required for Michigan Business Tax (MBT) returns due after 2007 tax year. Addition of federal deduction, including bonus depreciation, required for Single Business Tax (SBT) returns due prior to 2008 tax year.	MBT credit is available for portion of denied federal bonus depreciation deduction.
Minnesota ¶ 10-670, ¶ 10-900	Addition required for 80% of federal bonus depreciation. Subtraction allowed for amount of addition adjustment over five following tax years.	
Mississippi ¶ 10-670, ¶ 10-900	Addition required for federal bonus depreciation. Subtraction allowed by computing depreciation without regard to bonus depreciation.	Adjustments computed by converting federal depreciation form.

State	Answer	Comments
Missouri ¶ 10-670, ¶ 10-900	Addition required for 30% federal bonus depreciation on property purchased between July 1, 2002 and June 30, 2003. Subtraction allowed for depreciation on property purchased between July 1, 2002 and June 30, 2003 computed without regard to 30% bonus depreciation. No other adjustments to federal deduction, including 50% bonus depreciation, required.	Conformity with 2009 American Recovery Act bonus depreciation has not yet been addressed by the legislature.
Montana ¶ 10-515, ¶ 10-670	No adjustments to federal deduction, including federal bonus depreciation, required.	
Nebraska ¶ 10-670, ¶ 10-900	Addition required for 85% of federal bonus depreciation in tax years prior to 2006. Subtraction allowed for 20% of addition adjustment over 5 subsequent taxable years. No addition required for federal bonus depreciation, required in tax years after 2005.	Adjustment computed on separate schedule that must be attached to state return.
New Hampshire ¶ 10-670	Addition required for federal bonus depreciation.	
New Jersey ¶ 10-670, ¶ 10-900	Subtraction allowed after recomputing depreciation without regard to federal deduction relating to federal bonus depreciation, accelerated depreciation on property placed in service on or after 1981 and prior to July 7, 1993, and depreciation of safe harbor lease property.	Adjustment computed on Form CBT-100, Schedule S.
New Mexico ¶ 10-515, ¶ 10-600, ¶ 10-800	No adjustments to federal deduction, including bonus depreciation, required.	Conformity with 2009 American Recovery Act bonus depreciation has not yet been addressed by the legislature.

State	Answer	Comments
New York ¶ 10-670, ¶ 10-900	Addition required for federal deduction relating to: federal bonus depreciation on property, except qualified resurgence zone and New York Liberty Zone property, placed in service on or after June 1, 2003 in tax periods beginning after 2002; depreciation of safe harbor lease property; accelerated depreciation on property placed in service either in or outside the state after 1980 in tax periods beginning before 1985; and accelerated depreciation on property placed in service outside the state in tax periods beginning after 1984 and before 1994, if an election was made to continue using depreciation under IRC § 167.	Adjustment computed on Form CT-399.
North Carolina ¶ 10-670, ¶ 10-900	Addition required equal to: 100% of federal bonus depreciation for 2002 taxable year; 70% of federal bonus depreciation for 2003 taxable year; 70% of federal bonus depreciation for 2004 taxable year; and 85% of federal bonus depreciation on property placed in service in 2007 through 2009, including reuse and recycling property, and qualified disaster assistance property. Subtraction allowed in equal installments over five years, beginning: after 2009 taxable year for adjustment made on 2009 tax return; after 2008 taxable year for adjustment made on 2008 tax return; and after 2004 taxable year for adjustment made on 2002, 2003, and 2004 tax returns.	Addition also required for depreciation on a utility plant acquired by a natural gas local distribution company.
North Dakota ¶ 10-670, ¶ 10-900	Addition required for federal deduction relating to accelerated depreciation on property placed in service in 1981 and 1982, and depreciation of safe harbor lease property. No other adjustments to federal deduction, including bonus depreciation, required.	
Ohio ¶ 10-670, ¶ 10-900	Addition required for 5/6 of federal bonus depreciation. Subtraction allowed equal to 1/5 of addition adjustment over following five tax years.	Adjustment computed on Schedule B-4 of Form FT-1120.

State	Answer	Comments
Oklahoma ¶ 10-670, ¶ 10-900	Addition required for federal deduction relating to 80% of amount of 2002 Job Creation and Worker Assistance Act bonus depreciation for assets placed in service after September 10, 2001, and before September 11, 2004; 80% of amount of 2008 Economic Stimulus Act and 2009 American Recovery and Reinvestment Act bonus depreciation for assets placed in service after December 31, 2007, and before January 1, 2010; and depreciation of refinery property located in the state if an election was made to expense 100% of cost. Subtraction allowed for 25% of bonus depreciation addition adjustment over following four tax years.	
Oregon ¶ 10-670, ¶ 10-900	Addition required for federal deduction relating to: federal bonus depreciation after 2008; accelerated depreciation in tax years prior to 2009 on property placed into service on or after January 1, 1981 and before January 1, 1985; and depreciation of safe harbor lease property in tax years prior to 2009. Subtraction of bonus depreciation addback amount allowed in the tax year for which the amount would have been allowed as a federal deduction under IRC as amended and in effect on December 31, 2008, and as applicable to the 2008 tax year.	Adjustments computed on Form 20 depreciation schedule.
Pennsylvania ¶ 10-670, ¶ 10-900	Addition required for federal bonus depreciation. Subtraction allowed in current and subsequent tax years equal to 3/7 of bonus depreciation addition adjustment.	Adjustments computed on Schedule C-3 of corporate tax report.
Rhode Island ¶ 10-670, ¶ 10-900	Addition required for federal bonus depreciation.	
South Carolina ¶ 10-670, ¶ 10-900	Addition required if federal deduction exceeds allowable state deduction due to decoupling from federal bonus depreciation provisions. Subtraction allowed if state deduction exceeds federal deduction.	Schedule showing computation of differences must be attached to state return.
Tennessee ¶ 10-670, ¶ 10-900	Addition required for federal deduction relating to federal bonus depreciation, and depreciation of safe harbor lease property.	Adjustment schedule must be attached to state return.

State	Answer	Comments
Texas ¶ 10-515, ¶ 10-670, ¶ 10-900	Subtraction from total revenue or gross receipts in computing cost of goods sold for revised franchise tax reports, otherwise known as margin tax, includes depreciation. Addition required for federal bonus depreciation in computing franchise tax for reports due prior to 2008 tax year, except for corporations that use FIT (federal income tax) method of reporting taxable capital, including S corporations, close corporations with not more than 35 shareholders, and corporations with taxable capital of less than $1 million.	Conformity with 2009 American Recovery Act bonus depreciation has not yet been addressed by the legislature.
Utah ¶ 10-670, ¶ 10-900	Addition required for depreciation by purchaser-lessors of safe harbor lease property. Subtraction allowed for depreciation by seller-lessees of safe harbor lease property. No other adjustments to federal deduction, including federal bonus depreciation, required.	Conformity with 2009 American Recovery Act bonus depreciation has not yet been addressed by the legislature.
Vermont ¶ 10-670	Addition required for federal bonus depreciation.	Pro-forma federal return or a detailed schedule/spreadsheet must be provided showing recomputed federal taxable income without bonus depreciation. Calculation is required as separate attribute for each affiliate in unitary group. Box on front of return must be checked.
Virginia ¶ 10-670, ¶ 10-900	Addition required if federal deduction exceeds allowable state deduction due to decoupling from federal bonus depreciation provisions. Subtraction allowed if state deduction exceeds federal deduction.	Special depreciation under IRC Secs. 168(k), 168(l), 168(m), 1400L, and 1400N not allowed; however, special depreciation under IRC Sec. 168(n) is allowed.
West Virginia ¶ 10-670	Addition required for federal depreciation of certain water and air pollution control facilities if election was made to expense costs. No other adjustments to federal deduction, including bonus depreciation, required.	

State	Answer	Comments
Wisconsin ¶ 10-670, ¶ 10-900	Addition required if federal deduction exceeds allowable state deduction due to state differences, including federal bonus depreciation, depreciation of safe harbor lease property, and accelerated depreciation of property placed in service from January 1, 1983 through December 31, 1986. Subtraction allowed if state deduction exceeds federal deduction using federal depreciation provisions in effect on December 31, 2000.	

Quick Reference Table—Cost Segregation

[Full Text IRS Document.—CCH.]

December 27, 2004

MEMORANDUM FOR INDUSTRY DIRECTORS, LMSB DIRECTORS, FIELD OPERATIONS DIRECTOR, FIELD SPECIALISTS DIRECTOR, PREFILING AND TECHNICAL GUIDANCE AREA DIRECTORS, SBSE

FROM: Henry V. Singleton Industry Director Retailers, Food, Pharmaceuticals & Healthcare Industry

Steve Burgess Director, Examination, SBSE

SUBJECT: Field Directive on the Planning and Examination of Cost Segregation Issues in the Restaurant Industry

Introduction

This memorandum is intended to provide direction to effectively utilize resources in the classification and examination of a taxpayer who is recovering costs through depreciation of tangible property used in the operation of a restaurant business. This LMSB Directive is not an official pronouncement of the law or the position of the Service and cannot be used, cited or relied upon as such.

The American Jobs Creation Act of 2004, enacted October 22, 2004, modifies I.R.C. § 168. This development has been incorporated into the guidelines through the note to Exhibit A. In addition, this directive has been modified in content and format to conform to the Field Directive issued for the retail industry on December 16, 2004.

Background

The crux of cost segregation is determining whether an asset is I.R.C. Section 1245 property (shorter cost recovery period property, 5 or 7 years) or Section 1250 property (longer cost recovery period property, 39, 31.5 or 15 years). The most common example of section 1245 property is depreciable personal property, such as equipment. The most common examples of section 1250 property are buildings and building components, which generally are not section 1245 property.[1]

The difference in recovery periods has placed the Internal Revenue Service and taxpayers in adversarial positions in determining whether an asset is section 1245 or 1250 property. Frequently, this causes the excessive expenditure of examination resources. The Director for the Retailers, Food, Pharmaceuticals and Healthcare Industry chartered a working group to address the most efficient way to approach cost segregation issues specific to the restaurant industry. The group produced the attached matrix and related definitions as a tool to reduce unnecessary disputes and foster consistent audit treatment.

Planning and Examination Guidance

Attached Exhibit A is a matrix recommending the categorization and general depreciation system recovery period of various restaurant assets. (For recovery periods under IRC section 168(g) alternative depreciation system see Revenue Procedure 87-56, 1987-2 CB 674.) If the taxpayer's tax return position for these assets is consistent with the recommendations in Exhibit A, examiners should not make adjustments to categorization and lives. If the taxpayer reports assets differ-

---

[1] I.R.C. Section 1245 can apply to certain qualified recovery nonresidential real estate placed in service after 1980 and before 1987. *See* I.R.C. Section 1245(a)(5).

ently, then adjustments should be considered. The Industry intends to update Exhibit A regularly.

See the Cost Segregation Audit Techniques Guide for additional guidance. See also Revenue Procedure 2002-12, I.R.B. 2002-3, 374 (Jan. 07, 2002), for the proper treatment of smallwares.

If you have any questions, please contact Philip J. Hofmann Technical Advisor, Food at (316) 352-7434, or Ardell Mueller, Senior Program Analyst, Retailers Food, Pharmaceuticals and Healthcare Industry at (630) 493-5946.

Note: In the case of certain leasehold improvements and restaurant property, the classifications in this directive are superseded to the extent that the American Jobs Creation Act of 2004 modifies IRC Section 168. Thus, a 15-year straight line recovery period should replace the recovery period shown in the following matrix if the asset is "qualified leasehold improvement property" (as defined in IRC Section 168(e)(6)) or "qualified restaurant property" (as defined in IRC Section 168(e)(7)) placed in service by the taxpayer after October 22, 2004 and before January 1, 2006 [before January 1, 2010–CCH].

LMSB DIRECTIVE ON COST SEGREGATION IN THE RESTAURANT INDUSTRY
EXHIBIT A

Asset	*Description*	*Property Type*	*Recovery Period*
Beverage Equipment	Equipment for storage and preparation of beverages and beverage delivery systems. Beverage equipment includes the refrigerators, coolers, dispensing systems, and the dedicated electrical, tubing or piping for beverage equipment. The dispensing system may be gravity, pump or gas driven.	1245	57.0 Distributive Trades and Services—5 Years
Canopies and Awnings	Readily removable equipment or apparatus used for providing shade or cover. Includes canopies that are largely decorative. Does not include canopies that are an integral part of a building's structural shell, such as in the casino industry.	1245	57.0 Distributive Trades and Services—5 Years
Ceiling	Includes all interior ceilings regardless of finish or décor, e.g. drywall or plaster ceilings, acoustic ceilings, suspended ceilings (including all hangers, frames, grids and tiles or panels), decorative metal or tin finishes, kitchen plastic panels, decorative panels, etc.	1250	Building or Building Component—39 Years

Asset	*Description*	*Property Type*	*Recovery Period*
Computers	Desktop and laptop computers, monitors, printers, and other peripheral equipment. Excludes Point of Sale (POS) systems and computers that are an integral part of other equipment (e.g., fire detection systems, heating or cooling systems, etc.).	1245	00.12 Information Systems—5 Years
Concrete Foundations and Footings	Includes formwork, reinforcement, concrete block, and precast or cast-in-place work related to foundations and footings necessary for the proper setting of the building.	1250	Building or Building Component—39 Years
	Foundations or footings for signs, light poles, canopies and other land improvements.	1250	00.3 Land Improvements—15 Years
Data Handling Equipment	Includes adding and accounting machines, calculators, copiers and duplicating machines. Excludes computers and computer peripheral equipment, see *Computers*.	1245	00.13 Data Handling Equipment, except Computers—5 Years
Doors	Interior and exterior doors, regardless of decoration, including but not limited to, double opening doors, overhead doors, revolving doors, mall entrance security gates, roll-up or sliding wire mesh or steel grills and gates. and door hardware (such as doorknobs, closers, kick plates, hinges, locks, automatic openers, etc.).	1250	Building or Building Component—39 Years
	Special lightweight, double action doors installed to prevent accidents in a heavily trafficked area. For example, Elison doors providing easy access between the kitchen and dining areas.	1245	57.0 Distributive Trades and Services—5 Years

Asset	*Description*	*Property Type*	*Recovery Period*
Doors-Air Curtains	Air doors or curtains are air systems located above doors and windows that circulate air to stabilize environments and save energy by minimizing the heated/air conditioned air loss through open doorways and windows. They also effectively repel flying insects, dust, and pollutants.	1250	Building or Building Component—39 Years
Drive-Through Equipment	Drive-through equipment includes the order taking, food delivery and payment processing systems whether mechanical or electronic. Excludes building elements such as doors, bays, or windows; see also **Walls—Exterior**, and **Windows** for drive-through bays and windows.	1245	57.0 Distributive Trades and Services—5 Years
Electrical	Includes all components of the building electrical system used in operation or maintance of the building or necessary to provide general building services such as electrical outlets of general applicability and accessibility, lighting, heating, ventilation, air conditioning and electrical wiring. See also **Kitchen Equipment Hook-up.**	1250	Building or Building Component—39 Years

Asset	*Description*	*Property Type*	*Recovery Period*
	Special electrical connections which are necessary to and used directly with a specific item of machinery or equipment or connections between specific items of individual machinery or equipment; such as dedicated electrical outlets, wiring, conduit, and circuit breakers by which machinery and equipment is connected to the electrical distribution system. Does not include electrical outlets of general applicability and accessibility. See Chapter 5 of the Cost Segregation Audit Techniques Guide for allocation examples.	1245	57.0 Distributive Trades and Services—5 Years
Elevators and Escalators	Elevators and escalators, which include handrails and smoke baffles, are permanently affixed to the building and intended to remain in place. They relate to the operation or maintenance of the building and are structural components.	1250	Building or Building Component—39 Years
Equipment Installation	Expenses incurred in the installation of furnishings and restaurant equipment. Some examples include booths, tables, counters and interior theme décor.	1245	57.0 Distributive Trades and Services—5 Years
Exit Signs	Signs posted along exit routes that indicate the direction of travel to the nearest exit. These signs typically read "EXIT" and may have distinctive colors, illumination, or arrows indicating the direction to the exit.	1250	Building or Building Component—39 years

Asset	*Description*	*Property Type*	*Recovery Period*
Fire Protection & Alarm Systems	Includes sensing devices, computer controls, sprinkler heads, piping or plumbing, pumps, visual and audible alarms, alarm control panels, heat and smoke detection devices, fire escapes, fire doors, emergency exit lighting and signage, and wall mounted fire extinguishers necessary for the protection of the building.	1250	Building or Building Component—39 years
Fire Protection Equipment	Includes special fire detection or suppression systems located in equipment hoods or directly associated with a piece of equipment. For example, a fire extinguisher designed and used for protection against a particular hazard created by the business activity.	1245	57.0 Distributive Trades and Services—5 Years
Fireplaces	Includes masonry and gas fireplaces, flues, chimneys and other components of *built-in* fireplaces.	1250	Building or Building Component—39 Years
Floor Coverings	Floor covering affixed with permanent adhesive, nailed, or screwed in place. Examples include ceramic or quarry tile, marble, paving brick, and other coverings cemented, mudded, or grouted to the floor; epoxy or sealers; and wood flooring.	1250	Building or Building Component—39 Years
	Floor covering that is installed by means of strippable adhesives. For the restaurant industry, all carpeting will be treated as not permanently attached and not intended to be permanent. Excludes rugs or tapestries that are considered artwork and do not suffer wear and tear (e.g. Persian rugs that may appreciate are considered artwork).	1245	57.0 Distributive Trades and Services — 5 Years

Asset	*Description*	*Property Type*	*Recovery Period*
Floors	Includes concrete slabs, and other floor systems. Floors include special treatments applied to or otherwise a permanent part of the floor. For example "superflat" finish, sloped drainage basins or raised perimeter and serving line curb or cooler, freezer and garbage room floors.	1250	Building or Building Component—39 Years
Food Storage and Preparation Equipment	Food storage, cleaning, preparation, and delivery systems including all machinery, equipment, furniture and fixtures used to process food items from storage through delivery to the customer.	1245	57.0 Distributive Trades and Services—5 Years
Food Storage & Preparation Equipment	Food storage, cleaning, preparation, and delivery systems including all machinery, equipment, furniture and fixtures used to process food items from storage through delivery to the customer.	1245	57.0 Distributive Trades and Services — 5 Years
Heating Ventilating & Air Conditioning (HVAC)	Includes all components of a central heating, ventilating and air conditioning system not specifically identified elsewhere. HVAC systems that are installed not only to meet the temperature and humidity requirements of machinery, but are also installed for additional significant purposes, such as customer comfort and ventilation, are building components.	1250	Building or Building Component — 39 Years

Asset	*Description*	*Property Type*	*Recovery Period*
	Only separate kitchen HVAC units that meet the sole justification test are included (i.e., machinery the sole justification for the installation of which is the fact that such machinery is required to meet temperature or humidity requirements which are essential for the operation of other machinery or the processing of materials or foodstuffs.) Kitchen HVAC may meet the sole justification test even though it incidentally provides for the comfort of employees, or serves, to an insubstantial degree, areas where such temperature or humidity requirements are not essential. Includes refrigeration units, condensers, compressors, accumulators, coolers, pumps, connecting pipes, and wiring for the mechanical equipment for climate controlled rooms such as walk-in freezers and coolers. Allocation of HVAC is not appropriate.	1245	57.0 Distributive Trades and Services — 5 Years

Asset	*Description*	*Property Type*	*Recovery Period*
Kitchen Equipment Hook-ups	Includes separate water lines from the incoming water main to equipment (such as steam trays, cooking vessels, or ice machines), gas lines from the building's main gas line to equipment (such as fryers or ovens), and special drain lines from equipment (such as refrigerator or dishwasher) to the drain. Also includes ventilation system or kitchen air makeup unit solely to maintain specific ventilation requirements essential for operation of kitchen equipment, equipment exhaust hoods, and electric outlets and conduit extending back to the circuit box to provide a localized power source for specialized equipment. For example, a dishwasher requires electric and plumbing hook-ups, electrical from the dishwasher to the source of electricity (such as an outlet or junction box), and plumbing to connect the dishwasher to the water line and the drain. Excludes outlets of general applicability and accessibility or kitchen hand sink plumbing; see also ***Electrical, HVAC,*** and ***Plumbing***.	1245	57.0 Distributive Trades and Services — 5 Years
Light Fixtures - Interior	Includes lighting such as recessed and lay-in lighting, night lighting, and exit lighting, as well as decorative lighting fixtures that provide substantially all the artificial illumination in the building or along building walkways. For emergency and exit lighting, see ***Fire Protection & Alarm Systems***.	1250	Building or Building Component — 39 Years

Asset	*Description*	*Property Type*	*Recovery Period*
	Decorative light fixtures are light fixtures, such as neon lights or track lighting, which are decorative in nature and not necessary for the operation of the building. In other words, if the decorative lighting were turned off, the other sources of lighting would provide sufficient light for operation of the building. If the decorative lighting is the primary source of lighting, then it is section 1250 property.	1245	57.0 Distributive Trades and Services — 5 Years
Light Fixtures - Exterior	Exterior lighting whether decorative or not is considered section 1250 property to the extent that the lighting relates to the maintenance or operation of the building. Includes building mounted lighting to illuminate walkways, entrances, parking, etc.	1250	Building or Building Component — 39 Years
	Pole mounted or freestanding outdoor lighting system to illuminate sidewalks, parking or recreation areas. See also ***Poles & Pylons***. Note* asset class 00.3 Land improvements includes both section 1245 and 1250 property per Rev. Proc. 87-56.	See Note*	00.3 Land Improvements — 15 Years
	Plant grow lights or lighting that highlights *only* the landscaping or building exterior (but not parking areas or walkways) does not relate to the maintenance or operation of the building.	1245	57.0 Distributive Trades and Services — 5 Years

Asset	Description	Property Type	Recovery Period
Millwork - Decorative	Decorative millwork is the decorative finish carpentry in the restaurant. Examples include detailed crown moldings, lattice work placed over finished walls or ceilings, cabinets and counters. The decorative millwork serves to enhance the overall theme of the restaurant and is not related to the operation of the building. Excludes cabinets and counters in a restroom; see ***Restroom Accessories***.	1245	57.0 Distributive Trades and Services — 5 Years
Millwork - General Building or Structural	General millwork is all building materials made of finished wood (e.g., doors and frames, window frames, sashes, porch work, mantels, panel work, stairways, and special woodwork). Includes pre-built wooden items brought to the site for installation and items constructed on site such as restroom cabinets, door jambs, moldings, trim, etc.	1250	Building or Building Component — 39 Years
Office Furnishings	Includes desk, chair, credenza, file cabinet, table, or other furniture such as workstations. Also includes telephone equipment, fax machines, and other communications equipment. Does not include communications equipment included in other asset classes in Rev. Proc. 87-56.	1245	00.11 Office Furniture, Fixtures, and Equipment — 7 Years
Parking Lots	Grade level surface parking area usually constructed of asphalt, brick, concrete, stone or similar material. Category includes bumper blocks, curb cuts, curb work, striping, landscape islands, perimeter fences, and sidewalks.	1250	00.3 Land Improvements —15 Years

Asset	*Description*	*Property Type*	*Recovery Period*
Plumbing	All piping, drains, sprinkler mains, valves, sprinkler heads, water flow switches, restroom plumbing fixtures (e.g. toilets) and piping, kitchen hand sinks, electric water coolers, and all other components of a building plumbing system (water or gas) not specifically identified elsewhere. Excludes water or gas connections directly to appliances or kitchen drainage and kitchen hot water heater; see ***Kitchen Equipment Hook-ups***.	1250	Building or Building Component — 39 Years
	Includes water, gas, or refrigerant hook-ups directly connected to appliances or equipment, eyewash stations, kitchen drainage, and kitchen hot water heater. For example, a dishwasher would require special water hook-up.	1245	57.0 Distributive Trades and Services — 5 Years
Point of Sale (POS) Systems	A register or terminal based data collection system used to control and record all sales. Includes cash registers, computerized sales systems, and related peripheral equipment. See also ***Electrical*** for hook-ups.	1245	57.0 Distributive Trades and Services — 5 Years
Poles & Pylons	Light poles for parking areas and other poles poured in concrete footings or bolt-mounted for signage, flags, etc. Note* asset class 00.3 Land Improvements includes both section 1245 and 1250 property per Rev. Proc. 87-56.	See Note*	00.3 Land Improvements — 15 Years

Asset	Description	Property Type	Recovery Period
Restaurant Décor Accessories	Decorative mobile props such as playground equipment, potted plants, hanging mirrors, ceiling fans, and theme related props (such as coat of arms, sporting equipment or memorabilia, artifacts, pictures, plaques, etc., excluding non-depreciable artwork, antiques or collectibles).	1245	57.0 Distributive Trades and Services — 5 Years
Restaurant Furniture	Includes furniture unique to restaurants and distinguishable from office furniture. For example, a high stool in a bar, dining room table and chairs, booths, lockers, or benches. See also ***Office Furnishings***.	1245	57.0 Distributive Trades and Services — 5 Years
Restaurant Non-structural Theme Elements	Interior non-load bearing decorative structures. These are items that do not function as part of the building and are not integrated with building elements such as wiring, plumbing or ventilation. For example a model castle constructed of gypsum board or plaster and wood studs would be considered a non-structural theme element that functions merely as ornamentation. Excludes a half wall whose function is to provide traffic control or space subdivision, see ***Walls - Interior Partitions***. Excludes decorative ceilings, see ***Ceilings***.	1245	57.0 Distributive Trades and Services — 5 Years

Asset	*Description*	*Property Type*	*Recovery Period*
Restroom Accessories	Includes paper towel dispensers, electric hand dryers, towel racks or holders, cup dispensers, purse shelves, toilet paper holders, soap dispensers or holders, lotion dispensers, sanitary napkin dispensers and waste receptacles, coat hooks, grab bars, mirrors, shelves, vanity cabinets, counters, ashtrays, baby changing stations, and other items generally found in public restrooms that are built into or mounted on walls or partitions.	1250	Building or Building Component — 39 Years
Restroom Partitions	Includes shop made and standard manufacture toilet partitions, typically metal, but may be plastic or other materials.	1250	Building or Building Component — 39 Years
Roof	All elements of the roof including but not limited to joists, rafters, deck, shingles, vapor barrier, skylights, trusses, girders and gutters. Determination of whether decorative elements of a roof (e.g. false dormers, mansard) constitute structural building components depends on their integration with the overall roof not their load bearing capacity. If removal of the decorative element results in the direct exposure of building components to water, snow, wind, or moisture damage, or if the decorative element houses lighting fixtures, wiring, or other structural components, then the decorative elements are part of the overall roof system and are structural components of the building.	1250	Building or Building Component — 39 Years

Asset	*Description*	*Property Type*	*Recovery Period*
Security Systems	Includes security equipment for the protection of the building (and its contents) from burglary or vandalism and protection of employees from assault. Examples include window and door locks; card key access systems; keyless entry systems; security cameras, recorders, monitors and related equipment; perimeter and interior building motion detectors; security lighting; alarm systems; and security system wiring and conduit.	1250	Building or Building Component — 39 Years
Signs	Exit signs, restroom identifiers and other signs relating to the operation or maintenance of a building.	1250	Building or Building Component — 39 Years
	Interior and Exterior Signs used for menu display or theme identity. For pylon signs, includes only sign face. See also ***Poles & Pylons***.	1245	57.0 Distributive Trades and Services — 5 Years
Site Preparation, Grading, & Excavation	In general, land preparation costs include one time cost of clearing and grubbing, site stripping, fill or excavation, and grading to allow development of land. Clearing and grubbing is the removal of debris, brush, trees, etc. from the site. Stripping is the removal of the topsoil to provide a stable surface for site and building improvements. The grading of land involves moving soil to produce a more level surface to allow development of the land.		Land
	Clearing, grading, excavating and removal costs directly associated with the construction of buildings and building components are part of the cost of construction of the building.	1250	Building or Building Component — 39 Years

Asset	Description	Property Type	Recovery Period
	Clearing, grading, excavating and removal costs directly associated with the construction of sidewalks, parking areas, roadways and other depreciable land improvements are part of the cost of construction of the improvements.	1250	00.3 Land Improvements — 15 Years
Site Utilities	Site utilities are the systems that are used to distribute utility services from the property line to the restaurant building. Includes water, sanitary sewer, gas, and electrical services.	1250	Building or Building Component — 39 Years
Site Work	Site work includes curbing, paving, general site improvements, fencing, landscaping, roads, sewers, sidewalks, site drainage and all other site improvements not directly related to the building. For sanitary sewers, see ***Site Utilities***.	1250	00.3 Land Improvements — 15 Years
Sound Systems	Equipment and apparatus, including wiring, used to provide amplified music or sound. For example, public address by way of paging a customer or background music. Excludes applications linked to fire protection and alarm systems.	1245	57.0 Distributive Trades and Services — 5 Years
Stonework	Exterior decorative stonework embedded in half walls, such as patio half walls, that are an integral part of a building's structural shell. Such half walls relate to the operation or maintenance of the building.	1250	Building or Building Component — 39 Years
	Includes patio stonework imbedded in the ground or applied to exterior half walls that are not an integral part of the building's structural shell.	1250	00.3 Land Improvements — 15 Years

Asset	*Description*	*Property Type*	*Recovery Period*
Trash Enclosures	Enclosures for waste receptacles that are attached to the building. Typically constructed of the same materials as the building shell with either interior or exterior access. These trash enclosures are an integral part of the building shell and cannot be moved without damage to the underlying building.	1250	Building or Building Component — 39 Years
	Freestanding enclosures for waste receptacles, typically constructed on a concrete pad with its posts set in the concrete. Serves both safety and decorative functions.	1250	00.3 Land Improvements — 15 Years
Upholstery	Any material used in the coverage and protection of furnishings.	1245	57.0 Distributive Trades and Services — 5 Years
Wall Coverings	Includes interior and exterior paint; ceramic or quarry tile, marble, stone, brick and other finishes affixed with mortar, cement or grout; paneling, wainscoting and other wood finishes affixed with nails, screws or permanent adhesives; and sanitary kitchen wall panels such as Fiberglass Reinforced Plastic (FRP), stainless steel or plastic wall panels.	1250	Building or Building Component — 39 Years
	Strippable wallpaper that causes no damage to the underlying wall or wall surface.	1245	57.0 Distributive Trades and Services — 5 Years
Walls - Exterior	Includes all exterior walls and building support regardless of construction materials. Exterior walls may include columns, posts, beams, girders, curtain walls, tilt up panels, studs, framing, sheetrock, insulation, windows, doors, exterior façade, brick, masonry, etc. Also includes drive-through bay, windows, and doors.	1250	Building or Building Component — 39 Years

Asset	*Description*	*Property Type*	*Recovery Period*
Walls - Interior Partitions	Includes all load bearing interior partitions regardless of construction. Also includes non-load bearing partitions regardless of height (typically constructed of studs and sheetrock or other materials) that divide or create rooms or provide traffic control. Includes rough carpentry and plaster, dry wall or gypsum board, and other finishes.	1250	Building or Building Component — 39 Years
	Interior walls where the partition can be 1) readily removed and remain in substantially the same condition after removal as before, or 2) moved and reused, stored or sold in its entirety.	1245	57.0 Distributive Trades and Services — 5 Years
Windows	Exterior windows, including store front windows, drive-through service and carousel windows, and vestibule.	1250	Building or Building Component — 39 Years
Window Treatments	Window treatments such as drapes, curtains, louvers, blinds, post construction tinting or interior decorative theme décor that are readily removable.	1245	57.0 Distributive Trades and Services — 5 Years

Quick Reference Table—Recovery Periods

The table below, although not exhaustive, lists the recovery periods for many depreciable assets under MACRS. Cross references are provided to the applicable CCH discussion in this guide.

How to determine the depreciation period. The principals involved in determining the depreciation period of an asset are described in detail at ¶ 190.

See also ¶ 191 for a comprehensive list of asset classes and recovery periods provided by the IRS in Rev. Proc. 87-56.

Building components. See (1) ¶ 127A for lists of components of buildings that may be depreciated under the cost segregation rules as over shortened recovery periods that usually depend upon the business activity that the building is used in and (2) the cost segregation table that immediately precedes this quick reference table.

Land improvements. Land improvements are generally depreciated over 15 years unless otherwise provided in Rev. Proc. 87-56. See ¶ 5, ¶ 110, ¶ 127C, and the immediately preceding quick reference cost segregation table for building components.

Farm assets. An additional rapid finder table showing the recovery period of farm assets is at ¶ 118.

Assets used in retail or wholesale trade or business and by personal and professional service providers. If an asset is used in the provision of personal or professional services or in a wholesale or retail trade or business that asset is classified as five-year property (Asset Class 57.0) unless it is a specifically described asset in Table B-1 of Rev. Proc. 87-56 (Asset Classes 00.11 through 00.4 at ¶ 191). See ¶ 104 for a detailed discussion, including the types of businesses and professions that are covered by this rule.

Type of Asset/Activity	*Recovery Period* *MACRS*	*Alt. MACRS*
Accountant	See ¶ 104	
Adding machine (¶ 104)	5	6
Aerospace products, assets used in manufacture and assembly of	7	10
Additions and improvements	See ¶ 126	
Agricultural structures, single purpose, post-1988 property (¶ 106)	10	15
Agricultural structures, single purpose, pre-1989 property (¶ 106)	7	15
Agriculture, assets used in (¶ 106, ¶ 118)	7	10
. equipment		
. fences		
. grain bins		
. machinery		
Air conditioning	See ¶ 127A	
Air filtration systems	See ¶ 127A	
Airplanes, used in commercial or contract carrying of passengers (¶ 106)	7	12
Airplane hanger	See ¶ 127C	
Airplanes, not used in commercial or contract carrying of passengers (¶ 104)	5	6
Apparel, assets used in production of (¶ 191)	5	9
Appliances, apartment	See ¶ 104	
Architect	See ¶ 104	

Type of Asset/Activity	*Recovery Period* *MACRS*	*Alt. MACRS*
Art supplies, assets used in production of (¶ 191)	7	12
Artwork	See ¶ 3	
Barber shop	See ¶ 104	
Barges, not used in marine construction (¶ 108)	10	18
Beauty shop	See ¶ 104	
Bed and breakfasts	See ¶ 125	
Bee keeping	See ¶ 106	
Billboards, signs	See ¶ 110, ¶ 127A	
Boats or vessels	See ¶ 108	
Bobcats	See ¶ 125	
Bowling alleys, assets used in (¶ 106)	7	10
Breast implants	See ¶ 125	
Brooms, assets used in production of (¶ 191)	7	12
Buildings	See ¶ 127, ¶ 127C	
Buses (¶ 104)	5	9
Calculators (¶ 104) . . .	5	6
Carpets	See ¶ 127A	
Car wash buildings (¶ 110)	15	20
Carpeting	See ¶ 104, ¶ 127A	
Carpets, assets used in manufacture of (¶ 191)	5	9
Cars (¶ 104)	5	5
Cars, show cars, antiques, exotics	See ¶ 3	
Cash register	See ¶ 191	
Casinos	See ¶ 106	
Cattle, breeding or dairy (¶ 104, ¶ 118)	5	7
Ceilings	See ¶ 127A	
Cement, assets used in producing (¶ 110) . . .	15	20
Cell phone (¶ 106)	7	10
Cellular phone companies	See ¶ 125	
Chemicals, assets used in manufacture of (¶ 191)	5	9.5

Type of Asset/Activity	*Recovery Period* *MACRS*	*Alt. MACRS*
Clay products, assets used in manufacture of (¶ 191)	7	15
Coin operated dispensing machines (¶ 104) . . .	5	9
Communications equipment not in other classes (¶ 106)	7	10
Computer peripheral equipment (¶ 105) . .	5	5
. card punches		
. card readers		
. card sorters		
. data entry devices		
. disc drives, packs, files		
. keypunches		
. magnetic tape feeds		
. mass storage units		
. optical character readers		
. paper tape equipment		
. printers, high speed		
. tape cassettes		
. teleprinters		
. terminals		
Computer software	See ¶ 48, ¶ 102	
Computers (¶ 104)	5	5
Concert halls, assets used in (¶ 106)	7	10
Concrete trucks (¶ 104)	5	6
Construction, assets used in (¶ 104)	5	6
Containers	See ¶ 5	
Convenience store	See ¶ 110	
Copiers (¶ 104)	5	6
Cotton ginning, assets used in (¶ 191)	7	12
Dam	See ¶ 110	
Dental supplies, assets used in manufacture of (¶ 191)	5	9
Dentist	See ¶ 104	
Desks (¶ 106)	7	10
Distribution center	See ¶ 104	
Doctor	See ¶ 104	

Type of Asset/Activity	Recovery Period MACRS	Recovery Period Alt. MACRS
Doors	See ¶ 127A	
Dry cleaning	See ¶ 104	
Dump truck (¶ 104)	5	6
Duplicating equipment (¶ 104)	5	6
Electric utility steam production plants (¶ 191)	20	28
Electrical and non-electrical machinery, assets used to manufacture or rebuild (¶ 191)	3	3
Electrical distribution system	See ¶ 127	
Electronic components, assets used in manufacture of electronic communication, computation, instrumentation and control systems (¶ 191)	7	10
Electronic systems, assets used in manufacture of electronic communication, computation, instrumentation and control systems (¶ 191)	5	6
Elevators and escalators	See ¶ 114, ¶ 116	
Energy maintenance system	See ¶ 127A	
Energy property (¶ 104)	5	
. geothermal		
. ocean thermal		
. solar		
. wind		
Engineer	See ¶ 104	
Environmental cleanup costs	See ¶ 5	
Exterior building ornamentation, facades, balconies	See ¶ 127A	

Type of Asset/Activity	Recovery Period MACRS	Recovery Period Alt. MACRS
Fabric, woven, assets used in production of (¶ 191)	7	11
Farm buildings and property	See ¶ 118	
Fax machines (¶ 106)	7	10
Fences (nonagricultural) (¶ 110)	15	20
Fences (agricultural) (¶ 118)	7	10
Files, office (¶ 106)	7	10
Fire and burglary protection	See ¶ 104 and ¶ 127A	
Fishing vessels (¶ 106)	7	12
Fixtures, office (¶ 106)	7	10
Floor coverings	See ¶ 127A	
Floors, raised floors and concrete floors	See ¶ 127A	
Food and kindred products, manufacturing not otherwise specified (¶ 191)	7	12
Food and beverage manufacturing, special handling devices (¶ 191)	3	4
. fish processing equipment		
.. baskets		
.. boxes		
.. carts		
.. flaking trays		
. palletized containers		
. returnable pallets		
Fork lifts	See ¶ 125	
Furniture, apartment (¶ 104)	5	9
Furniture, assets used in production of	7	10
Furniture, office (¶ 106)	7	10
Furniture rental	See ¶ 104	
Gaming equipment, slots etc. (¶ 106)	7	10
Gasoline station	See ¶ 110, ¶ 125	

Type of Asset/Activity	Recovery Period MACRS	Recovery Period Alt. MACRS
Gas production plants of gas utilities (¶ 191) . .	20	30
Gathering systems, oil and gas	See ¶ 106	
Generators, emergency	See ¶ 127A	
Geothermal energy property (¶ 104)	5	
Glass products, assets used in production of (¶ 191)	7	14
Glass products, manufacture of, special tools (¶ 191)	3	2.5
. molds		
. pallets		
. patterns		
. specialty transfer and shipping devices		
. steel racks		
Goats, breeding (¶ 118)	5	5
Golf course	See ¶ 5	
Grading	See ¶ 5	
Grain and grain mill products, assets used in production of (¶ 191)	10	17
Greenhouses (¶ 108, ¶ 118)	10	15
Gym equipment	See ¶ 125	
Handrails	See ¶ 127A	
Helicopters (¶ 104) . . .	5	6
Hogs, breeding (¶ 102, ¶ 118)	3	3
Home office	See ¶ 116	
Horses	See ¶ 102, ¶ 106, ¶ 118	
Hotels	See ¶ 104	
HVAC	See ¶ 127A	
Horticultural structures, single purpose (¶ 118)	10	15
Indian reservation property	See ¶ 124	
Irrigation system	See ¶ 118	
Jewelry, assets used in production of (¶ 191)	7	12

Type of Asset/Activity	Recovery Period MACRS	Recovery Period Alt. MACRS
Keycard locking system	See ¶ 127A	
Knitted goods, laces, assets used in manufacture of (¶ 191)	5	7.5
Land improvements (¶ 5, ¶ 110, ¶ 127C)	15	20
. bridges		
. canals		
. drainage facilities		
. fences		
. landscaping		
. parking lots		
. radio and television towers		
. roads		
. sewers (non-municipal)		
. sidewalks		
. shrubbery, trees		
. waterways		
. wells (water)		
. wharves and docks		
Land preparation costs .	See ¶ 5, ¶ 110	
Landscaping (¶ 5, ¶ 110)	15	20
Laundry	See ¶ 104	
Lawyer	See ¶ 104	
Leather and leather products, assets used in manufacture of (¶ 191)	7	11
Leasehold improvements	See ¶ 126	
Library	See ¶ 104	
Lighting, interior and exterior	See ¶ 127A	
Limousine (¶ 104)	5	6
Livestock	See ¶ 118	
Logging machinery and equipment (¶ 104) . .	5	6
Lottery terminals (¶ 106)	7	10
Low-income housing (¶ 114)	27.5	40

Type of Asset/Activity	Recovery Period MACRS	Recovery Period Alt. MACRS
Manufactured homes, residential (¶ 114) . .	27.5	40
Manufacturing equipment, semi-conductor (¶ 104) . . .	5	5
Medical supplies, assets used in manufacture of (¶ 191)	5	9
Miniature golf course, assets used in (¶ 106)	7	10
Mining, assets used in mining and quarrying of minerals and milling and other primary preparation of such materials (¶ 191) . . .	7	10
Mobile homes parks . . .	See ¶ 5	
Mobile homes, residential (¶ 114)	27.5	40
Molding, millwork, trim, finish carpentry, paneling	See ¶ 127A	
Mortuary	See ¶ 104	
Motels	See ¶ 104	
Motor homes	See ¶ 104, ¶ 302	
Motion picture films and tapes, assets used in production of (¶ 191)	7	12
Motor transport (freight and passengers) (¶ 104)	5	8
Motor vehicles, assets used in manufacture and assembly of (¶ 191)	7	12
Motor vehicles, manufacture of—special tools (¶ 191) .	3	3
. dies		
. fixtures		
. gauges		
. jigs		
. molds		
. patterns		
Musical instruments, assets used in production of	7	12
Musical instruments (¶ 3, ¶ 104))	5	9
Nonresidential real property (¶ 116)	39	40
Nurseries	See ¶ 118	
Nursing home	See ¶ 114	
Ocean thermal energy property (¶ 104)	5	
Office equipment (¶ 106)	7	10
Office furniture, fixtures (¶ 106)	7	10
Office supplies, assets used in production of (¶ 191)	7	12
Ore trucks (¶ 104)	5	6
Parking buildings (open air) (¶ 127C	39	40
Parking lots (¶ 5, ¶ 110)	15	20
Partitions and walls . . .	See ¶ 127A	
Picnic table (¶ 110) . . .	15	20
Pens, assets used in production of (¶ 191)	7	12
Photographic studio . . .	See ¶ 104	
Pipeline transportation assets (¶ 106)	15	22
Plastic products, finished, assets used in manufacture of (¶ 191)	7	11
Plastic products, finished, manufacture of—special tools (¶ 191) .	3	3.5
. dies		
. fixtures		
. gauges		
. jigs		
. molds		
. patterns		
. specialty transfer and shipping devices		
Playground equipment .	See ¶ 5	
Plumbing and wiring . .	See ¶ 127A	
Pool halls, assets used in (¶ 106)	7	10
Printing, assets used in (¶ 191)	7	11
Professional service provider, assets used in	see ¶ 104	

	Recovery Period	
Type of Asset/Activity	*MACRS*	*Alt. MACRS*
Projector (overhead) (¶ 106)	7	10
Public utility property		
. electric utility steam production plants (¶ 191)	5	5
. gas utility manufactured gas production plants (¶ 191)	20	30
. telephone distribution plants (¶ 110)	15	24
Publishing, assets used in (¶ 191)	7	11
Race cars (¶ 104)	7	10
Race tracks (¶ 110)	15	20
Railroad assets	See ¶ 106	
Recreation, assets used in	See ¶ 106	
Recreational vehicles (RV)		
. actual unloaded weights of less than 13,000 pounds (¶ 104, ¶ 302)	5	5
. actual unloaded weights of 13,000 pounds or more (¶ 104, ¶ 302)	5	6
Rent-to-own property (¶ 102)	3	4
Research and experimentation property (¶ 104)	5	
Residential rental property (¶ 114)	27.5	40
Restaurant buildings and improvements	See ¶ 110	
Restrooms	See ¶ 127A	
Retail improvement property	See ¶ 126	
Roads	See ¶ 5, ¶ 110	
Roofs	See ¶ 125	
Rotable spare parts	See ¶ 125	
Rubber products, assets used in production of (¶ 191)	7	14
Rubber products, manufacture of special tools (¶ 191)	3	4
. jigs and dies		
.. lasts, mandrels, molds, patterns		
. specialty containers		
.. pallets, shells, tire molds		
Safes, office (¶ 106)	7	10
Sawmills	See ¶ 104	
Security systems	See ¶ 127A	
Septic system	See ¶ 127A	
Service station	See ¶ 110	
Sewer tap fees	See ¶ 70	
Sewers, municipal (¶ 113)	25	50
Shed	See ¶ 127C	
Sheep, breeding (¶ 118)	5	5
Ship- and boat-building machinery, assets used in manufacture and repair of ships (¶ 191)	7	12
Ships, not used in marine construction (¶ 108)	10	18
Shop equipment	See ¶ 125	
Signs, billboards, scoreboards	See ¶ 127A	
Site utilities	See ¶ 127A	
Slot machines (¶ 106)	7	10
Small power production facilities, biomass properties (¶ 104)	5	
Smallwares of restaurants and taverns	See ¶ 125	
Sod	See ¶ 5	
Software	See ¶ 48, ¶ 102	
Solar energy property, including solar panels (¶ 104)	5	
Sporting goods, assets used in production of (¶ 191)	7	12

Type of Asset/Activity	Recovery Period MACRS	Alt. MACRS
Storage sheds	See ¶ 127C	
Structural components of buildings	See ¶ 127	
Sugar and sugar products, assets used in production of (¶ 191)	10	18
Taxis (¶ 104)	5	5
Technological equipment (¶ 104)	5	5
. computers & peripheral equipment		
. high technology medical equipment		
. high technology telephone station equipment installed on customer's premises		
Telephone, central office switching equipment (¶ 110)	15	18
Telephone, central office switching equipment, computer based (¶ 104)	5	9.5
Telephone distribution plants (¶ 110)	15	24
Television films and tapes, assets used in production of (¶ 191)	7	12
Textile products, dyeing, finishing & packaging (¶ 191)	5	9
Theaters, assets used in (¶ 106)	7	10
Theme park structures (¶ 106)	7	12.5
Thread, assets used in production of (¶ 191)	7	11
Timber cutting, equipment used in (¶ 191)	5	6
Tires and tubes	See ¶ 125	
Tobacco and tobacco products, assets used in production of cigarettes, cigars, etc.(¶ 191)	7	15
Tobacco barns	See ¶ 127C	
Tools	See ¶ 125	
Toys, assets used in production of (¶ 191)	7	12
Tractor units, over-the-road use (¶ 102)	3	4
Trailer-mounted containers (¶ 104)	5	6
Trailers (¶ 104)	5	6
Transportation equipment		
. air, passenger (¶ 106)	7	12
. motor transport, freight (¶ 191)	5	8
. motor transport, passengers (¶ 191)	5	8
. water, passenger and freight (¶ 110)	15	20
Trees and vines (orchards and vineyards)	See ¶ 108	
Trees, fruit or nut bearing, post-1988 (¶ 108)	10	20
Trellis	See ¶ 118	
Trucks		
. heavy general purpose (¶ 102, ¶ 104)	5	6
.. concrete ready-mix trucks		
.. ore trucks		
.. over-the-road trucks, actual unloaded weight 13,000		
. light general purpose, actual unloaded weight less than 13,000 pounds (¶ 102, ¶ 104)	5	5
Tugs, not used in marine construction (¶ 108)	10	18
Tuxedo rental (¶ 104)	5	9
Typewriters (¶ 104)	5	6
Vegetable oils and products, assets used in manufacture of (¶ 191)	10	18
Vessels, not used in marine construction or primarily for fishing (¶ 108)	10	18
Veterinarians	See ¶ 104	

Type of Asset/Activity	Recovery Period: MACRS	Recovery Period: Alt. MACRS
Video cassettes	See ¶ 140	
Vines, fruit or nut bearing, post-1988 (¶ 108)	10	20
Wall paper and wall coverings	See ¶ 127A	
Walls and partitions	See ¶ 127A	
Warehouse (¶ 127C)	10	20
Wastewater treatment plant, municipal (¶ 110)	15	24
Water heaters and water softners	See ¶ 127A	
Water utility property (¶ 113)	25	50
Web site	See ¶ 125	
Wells (water) (¶ 118)	15	20
Wind energy property (¶ 104)	5	
Wiring and plumbing	See ¶ 127A	
Wood products, assets used in production of (¶ 191)	7	10
Yachts (¶ 108)	10	18
Yarn, assets used in production of (¶ 191)	7	11
Zoning variation	See ¶ 125	

The table above generally does not list structural components of buildings or items affixed or attached to the interior or exterior of a building which are considered personal property, separately depreciable from the building. The classification of property as personal or real (i.e., a structural component) is often unclear and remains the subject of much controversy. See ¶ 127 and ¶ 127A for a detailed discussion.

Structural components (if related to operation and maintenance of building) (¶ 127 and ¶ 127A):

- Acoustical ceilings
- Bathtubs
- Boilers
- Ceilings
- Central air conditioning and heating (including motors, compressors, pipes, and ducts)
- Chimneys
- Doors
- Electrical systems
- Elevators
- Escalators
- Fire escapes
- Floors
- Hot water heaters
- HVAC units
- Keycard door locking system
- Lighting fixtures
- Mechanical service systems
- Paneling
- Partitions (not movable)
- Plumbing
- Plumbing fixtures
- Raised floor
- Roofs
- Siding
- Sinks
- Sprinkler system
- Stairs
- Tiling
- Walls
- Windows
- Wiring

Personal property:

- Carpeting (removable)
- Display racks and shelves
- Electrical and wiring allocable to machinery and equipment
- Partitions (movable)
- Plumbing connections for equipment
- Plumbing for x-ray machines

- Eliason doors
- Folding wall partitions
- Gasoline pumps
- Grocery counters
- Hydraulic car lifts
- Kitchen hoods and exhaust systems
- Kitchen steam lines
- Kitchen water piping
- Neon and other signs
- Printing presses
- Production machinery
- Refrigerators
- Telephone and communications wiring and equipment
- Testing equipment
- Transportation and office equipment
- Vending machines
- Vinyl wall and floor coverings (removable)

Topical Index

Also refer to the quick reference guide immediately preceding this index for depreciation periods of particular assets or assets used in particular business activities. The quick reference guide also includes cross references to related explanations.

All references are to paragraph (¶) numbers.

A

D

K

L

M

N

O

T

U

V

W

Z